Special Edition
Using

Microsoft®
Access
2000

Roger Jennings

201 West 103rd Street
Indianapolis, Indiana 46290

CONTENTS AT A GLANCE

Introduction   1

I   Learning Access Fundamentals
1   Access 2000 for Access 95 and 97 Users—What's New   19
2   Building Your First Access 2000 Application   55
3   Navigating within Access   81
4   Working with Access Databases and Tables   127
5   Entering, Editing, and Validating Data in Tables   185
6   Sorting, Finding, and Filtering Data in Tables   205
7   Linking, Importing, and Exporting Tables   231

II   Getting the Most Out of Queries
8   Designing Access Queries   293
9   Understanding Query Operators and Expressions   319
10   Creating Multitable and Crosstab Queries   353
11   Modifying Data with Action Queries   409

III   Designing Forms and Reports
12   Creating and Using Forms   433
13   Designing Custom Multitable Forms   479
14   Printing Basic Reports and Mailing Labels   533
15   Preparing Advanced Reports   569

IV   Publishing Data on Intranets and the Internet
16   Working with Hyperlinks and HTML   597
17   Generating Web Pages from Tables and Queries   627
18   Designing Data Access Pages   657

V   Integrating Access with Other Office 2000 Applications
19   Adding Charts and Graphics to Forms and Reports   709
20   Using Access with Microsoft Excel   745
21   Using Access with Microsoft Word and Mail Merge   781

VI   Using Advanced Access Techniques
22   Exploring Relational Database Design and Implementation   811
23   Working with Structured Query Language   851
24   Securing Mutiuser Network Applications   885
25   Creating Access Data Projects   943

VII   Programming and Converting Access Applications
26   Writing Visual Basic for Applications Code   991
27   Understanding Universal Data Access, OLE DB, and ADO   1031
28   Responding to Events with VBA 6.0   1083
29   Programming Combo and List Boxes   1127
30   Working with ADO Recordsets, Forms, and Controls   1155
31   Migrating Access 95 and 97 Applications to Access 2000   1181

VIII   Appendix
A   Glossary   1197

Index   1239

SPECIAL EDITION USING MICROSOFT® ACCESS 2000

International Standard Book Number: 0-7897-1606-2

Library of Congress Catalog Card Number: 98-84938

Printed in the United States of America

First Printing: May 1999

05 04 03   12 11 10

TRADEMARKS

WARNING AND DISCLAIMER

Associate Publisher
Dean Miller

Executive Editor
Rosemarie Graham

Acquisitions Editor
Rosemarie Graham

Development Editor
Marla Reece-Hall

Managing Editor
Jodi Jensen

Senior Editor
Susan Ross Moore

Copy Editors
Lisa Lord
June Waldman

Indexer
Bruce Clingaman

Proofreaders
Mary Lagu
Eddie Lushbaugh
Dawn Pearson
Rhonda Tinch-Mize

Technical Editor
Jim Ferguson

Software Development Specialist
Andrea Duvall

Interior Design
Louisa Klucznik

Cover Design
Maureen McCarty

Layout Technicians
Brian Borders
Susan Geiselman
Mark Walchle

Table of Contents

Introduction   1

Who Should Read this Book   4

How this Book Is Organized   5
Part I: Learning Access
Fundamentals   5
Part II: Getting the Most Out of
Queries   6
Part III: Designing Forms and
Reports   7
Part IV: Publishing Data on Intranets
and the Internet   7
Part V: Integrating Access with Other
Office 2000 Applications   8
Part VI: Using Advanced Access
Techniques   8
Part VII: Programming and Converting
Access Applications   9
Glossary   9
The Accompanying CD-ROM   9

How this Book Is Designed   10

Typographic Conventions Used in this
Book   11
Key Combinations and Menu
Choices   11
SQL Statements and Keywords in
Other Languages   12
Typographic Conventions Used for
VBA   12

System Requirements for Access 2000   13

Other Sources of Information for
Access   13
Books   13
Periodicals   15
Internet   15

I Learning Access Fundamentals

**1 Access 2000 for Access 95 and 97 Users:
What's New   19**

Putting Access 2000 in Perspective   20

Deploying Data Access Pages with Office
Web Components   21
The Office Web Components   22
Test Drive a DAP   23
DAP Design Mode   25

Creating Access Data Projects for the
Microsoft Data Engine   26
New ADP Tools and Objects   26
Explore the NorthwindCS Project and
da Vinci Toolset   27

Integrating the Office VBA Editor with
Access   32

Working with the HTML Source Editor
for DAP and DHTML   33

Viewing and Editing Related Records in
Subdatasheets   34

Conforming Jet and SQL Server
7.0/MSDE Databases   35

Giving Access a Year 2000 Facelift   36
Four-Digit Year Option Settings   36
The Database Window   37
Forms and Reports   38
Name AutoCorrect   39
Office 2000-Related Enhancements or
Impediments   40

Installing Access 2000   42
Making an Initial Installation of Access
2000   42
Customizing Access 2000   46

Installing and Configuring the Microsoft
Data Engine   47

In the Real World—Why Upgrade?   51

2 Building Your First Access 2000 Application 55

Understanding Access's Approach to Application Design 56

Creating an Access Application from a Template File 57

Touring the Contact Management Application 62
Table Objects in the Database Window 62
The Switchboard Form 66
Access Forms 67
Access Reports 72
Access Modules 73

Using the Switchboard Manager 75

Exploring Form Design View and VBA Class Modules 77

The Real World—Putting What You've Learned in Perspective 79

3 Navigating Within Access 81

Understanding Access Functions and Modes 82
Defining Access Functions 82
Defining Access Operating Modes 84

Understanding Access's Table Display 85
Maximized Document Windows 87
Document Windows Minimized to Icons 88
The Toolbars in Table Datasheet View 89
Toolbar Customization 93
Right-Click Shortcut Menus 96

Using the Function Keys 97
Global Function Keys 97
Function-Key Assignments for Fields, Grids, and Text Boxes 97

Setting Default Options 98
System Defaults 100
Defaults for Datasheet View 105

Using Access Help 107
Context-Sensitive Help 107
The Help Menu 108
The Microsoft Access Help Window 109
The Office Assistant 114

Using the Database Utilities 118
Compacting and Repairing Databases 118
Converting Databases to Access 2000 Format 120
Converting Databases to Access 97 Format 121
Adding a Switchboard Form 121
Creating .mde Files 123

Troubleshooting 123

In the Real World—HTML Help or Hindrance 124

4 Working with Access Databases and Tables 127

Defining the Elements of Access Databases 128

Understanding Relational Databases 130

Using Access Database Files and Tables 132
The Access System Database 132
Access Library Databases 132

Creating a New Database 133

Understanding the Properties of Tables and Fields 135

Choosing Field Data Types, Sizes, and Formats 140
Choosing Field Sizes for Numeric and Text Data 141
Selecting a Display Format 144
Using Input Masks 150

Using the Northwind Traders Sample
Database 151
    Using the Table Wizard to Create
    New Tables 151

Adding a New Table to an Existing
Database 156
    Designing the Personnel Actions
    Table 158
    Creating the Personnel Actions
    Table 160
    Creating a Table Directly in Datasheet
    View 164

Setting Default Values of Fields 165

Working with Relations, Key Fields, and
Indexes 166
    Establishing Relationships Between
    Tables 166
    Enforcing Referential Integrity 171
    Selecting a Primary Key 172
    Adding Indexes to Tables 174

Altering Fields and Relationships 176
    Rearranging the Sequence of Fields in
    a Table 176
    Changing Field Data Types and
    Sizes 178
    Changing Relationships Between
    Tables 179

Copying and Pasting Tables 180

Troubleshooting 182

In the Real World—Database Strategy
and Table Tactics 182
    Why Table Design Comes Before
    Database Design in This Book 182
    Naming Conventions for Tables and
    Fields 183

**5 Entering, Editing, and Validating Data in
Tables 185**

Entering Test Data in Access Tables 186

Using Keyboard Operations for Entering
and Editing Data 186
    Creating an Experimental Copy of
    Northwind.mdb 187
    Using Data-Entry and Editing
    Keys 188
    Using Key Combinations for Windows
    Clipboard Operations 190
    Using Shortcut Keys for Fields and
    Text Boxes 191
    Setting Data-Entry Options 192

Adding Records to a Table 193

Selecting, Appending, Replacing, and
Deleting Table Records 194

Validating Data Entry 194
    Adding Field-Level Validation
    Rules 195
    Adding Table-Level Validation Rules
    and Using the Expression
    Builder 197

Adding Records to the Personnel Actions
Table 199

Entering Personnel Actions Table Data
and Testing Validation Rules 201

Troubleshooting 202

In the Real World—Heads-Down Data
Entry 203
    Comparing Heads-Down Keypunch
    Data Entry with Access's Datasheet
    View 203
    Replacing the Punched Card Verifying
    Step 204
    Where *Not* to Use Datasheet
    Entry 204

**6 Sorting, Finding, and Filtering Data in
Tables 205**

Understanding the Role of Sorting and
Filtering 206

Sorting Table Data **206**
Freezing Display of a Table Field **207**
Sorting Data on a Single Field **208**
Sorting Data on Multiple Fields **208**
Removing a Table Sort Order and Thawing Columns **209**

Finding Matching Records in a Table **209**

Replacing Matched Field Values Automatically **212**

Filtering Table Data **212**
Filtering by Selection **213**
Filtering by Form **215**
Advanced Filters and Sorts **218**
Adding a Multifield Sort and Compound Filter Criteria **219**
Using Composite Criteria **221**
Saving Your Filter as a Query and Loading a Filter **223**

Customizing Datasheet View **225**

Copying, Exporting, and Mailing Sorted and Filtered Data **227**

Troubleshooting **228**

In the Real World—Computer-Based Sorting and Searching **228**
The Influence of Computer Power on Knuth's Approach **228**
Knuth and Indexes **229**

7 Linking, Importing, and Exporting Tables 231

Moving Data from and to Other Applications **232**

Understanding How Access Handles Tables in Other Database File Formats **233**
Identifying PC Database File Formats **234**

Linking and Importing External ISAM Tables **235**
Linking Visual FoxPro Tables with ODBC **238**
Dealing with Images in External Files **243**
Converting Field Data Types to Access Data Types **244**
Using the Linked Table Manager Add-in to Relink Tables **245**
Importing Versus Linking Database Files as Tables **246**

Importing and Linking Spreadsheet Files **247**
Creating a Table by Importing an Excel Worksheet **248**
Linking Excel Worksheets **256**

Working with Microsoft Outlook and Exchange Folders **258**

Exporting and Importing Jet 4.0 Tables with Outlook **258**
Linking with the Exchange/Outlook Wizard **262**

Importing Text Files **264**
Using the Import Text Wizard **266**
The Import Text Wizard's Advanced Options **271**
Using Delimited Text Files **273**
Handling Fixed-Width Text Files **276**
Appending Text Data to an Existing Table **277**

Using the Clipboard to Import Data **277**
Pasting New Records to a Table **278**
Replacing Records by Pasting from the Clipboard **282**

Exporting Data from Access Tables **283**
Exporting Data Through the Windows Clipboard **283**
Exporting Data as a Text File **284**
Exporting Data in Other File Formats **286**

Troubleshooting 287

In the Real World—Microsoft Giveth and
Microsoft Taketh Away 288

II Getting the Most Out of Queries

8 Designing Access Queries 293

Introducing Queries 294

Trying the Simple Query Wizard 294

Using the Query Design Window 298
  Selecting Fields for Your Query 299
  Selecting Records by Criteria and
  Sorting the Display 302
  Creating More Complex
  Queries 303
  Changing the Names of Query
  Column Headers 305
  Printing Your Query as a Report 307
  Using the Data from Your
  Query 309

Creating Other Types of Queries 311
  Creating and Using a Simple Make-
  Table Action Query 311
  Adding a Parameter to Your Make-
  Table Query 313

Troubleshooting 315

In the Real World—Query Design
Optimization 315
  The Art of Query Design 315
  The Scientific Side of Query
  Design 316

9 Understanding Query Operators and Expressions 319

Writing Expressions for Query Criteria
and Data Validation 320

Understanding the Elements in
Expressions 321
  Operators 322
  Literals 327
  Identifiers 328
  Functions 328
  Intrinsic and Named Constants 339

Creating Access Expressions 340
  Expressions for Creating Default
  Values 340
  Expressions for Validating Data 340
  Expressions for Query Criteria 341
  Expressions for Calculating Query
  Field Values 347
  Other Uses for Expressions 349

Troubleshooting 349

In the Real World—The Algebra of Access
Expressions 350

10 Creating Multitable and Crosstab Queries 353

Introducing Joins on Tables 354

Joining Tables to Create Multitable
Queries 355
  Creating Conventional Single-Column
  Equi-Joins 357
  Specifying a Sort Order for the Query
  Result Set 358
  Creating Queries from Tables with
  Indirect Relationships 360
  Creating Multicolumn Equi-Joins and
  Selecting Unique Values 362

Using Lookup Fields in Tables 365
  Adding a Foreign-Key Dropdown List
  with the Lookup Wizard 366
  Adding a Fixed-Value Lookup List to a
  Table 370

Adding Subdatasheets to a Table or
Query 373
  Table Subdatasheets 374
  Query Subdatasheets 376

Outer, Self, and Theta Joins   378
  Creating Outer Joins   378
  Creating Self-Joins   380
  Creating Not-Equal Theta Joins with
  Criteria   382

Updating Table Data with Queries   383
  Characteristics That Determine
  Whether You Can Update a
  Query   383
  Formatting Data with the Query Field
  Properties Window   384

Making All Fields of Tables
Accessible   386

Making Calculations on Multiple
Records   387
  Using the SQL Aggregate
  Functions   387
  Making Calculations Based on All
  Records of a Table   388
  Making Calculations Based on Selected
  Records of a Table   391

Designing Parameter Queries   393
  Adding a Parameter to the Monthly
  Sales Query   393
  Specifying the Parameter's Data
  Type   394

Creating Crosstab Queries   396
  Using the Wizard to Generate a
  Quarterly Product Sales Crosstab
  Query   396
  Designing a Monthly Product Sales
  Crosstab Query   400
  Using Fixed Column Headings with
  Crosstab Queries   402

Creating Queries from Tables in Other
Databases   403

Troubleshooting   405

In the Real World—Optimizing
Multitable Queries   406
  Subdatasheets   406
  Aggregate Queries   407
  Crosstab Queries   407

**11 Modifying Data with Action
Queries   409**

Getting Acquainted with Action Queries
410

Creating New Tables with Make-Table
Queries   411
  Designing and Testing the Select
  Query   411
  Converting the Select Query to a
  Make-Table Query   413
  Establishing Relationships for the New
  Table   414
  Using the New tblShipAddresses
  Table   416

Creating Action Queries to Append
Records to a Table   416

Deleting Records from a Table with an
Action Query   418

Updating Values of Multiple Records in a
Table   421

Testing Cascading Deletion and
Updating   424
  Creating the Test Tables and
  Establishing Relationships   425
  Testing Cascading Deletion   425
  Testing Cascading Updates   426

Troubleshooting   427

In the Real World—Alternatives to Action
Queries   428
  Browse-Mode Updating   428
  Form-Based Updating   429
  Updating with SQL Statements   429
  Updating with SQL Server Stored
  Procedures   430

III Designing Forms and Reports

12 Creating and Using Forms 433

Understanding the Role of Access Forms and Controls 434

Creating a Transaction-Processing Form with the Form Wizard 435
Choosing Data Sources for the Form 435
Creating the Basic Form with the Form Wizard 436

Using the Form Design Window 442
Elements of the Form Design Window 443
Form Design Toolbar Buttons and Menu Choices 444
The Formatting Toolbar 446
Default Values for Forms 447
Using AutoFormat 448
Changing an Object's Colors 451

Selecting, Editing, and Moving Form Elements and Controls 457
Changing the Size of the Form Header and Form Footer 458
Selecting, Moving, and Sizing a Single Control 458
Aligning Controls to the Grid 459
Selecting and Moving Multiple Control 460
Aligning a Group of Controls 461
Using the Windows Clipboard and Deleting Controls 462
Changing the Color and Border Style of a Control 462
Changing the Content of Text Controls 463
Using the Format Painter 463

Rearranging the Personnel Actions Form 464
Setting Properties of the Main Form 465

Setting the Properties of a Subform 466

Using Transaction-Processing Forms 468
Toolbar Buttons in Form View 468
Using the Personnel Actions Form 469
Appending New Records to the Personnel Actions Table 470
Editing Existing Data 472
Committing and Rolling Back Changes to Tables 473

Modifying the Properties of a Form or Control After Testing 473
Changing the Order of Fields for Data Entry 473
Removing Fields from the Tab Order 474

In the Real World—The Art of Form Design 474
Understand the Audience 475
Design in Client Monitor Resolution 475
Strive for Consistency and Simplicity 475

13 Designing Custom Multitable Forms 479

Expanding Your Form Design Repertoire 480

Understanding the Access Toolbox 480
Control Categories 480
The Toolbox 481
Access's Control Wizards, Builders, and Toolbars 483

Using the Toolbox To Add Controls 487
Creating the Query on Which to Base the Main Form 487
Creating a Blank Form with a Header and Footer 488
Adding a Label to the Form Header 490

Formatting Text and Adjusting Text Control Sizes **491**

Creating Bound, Multiline, and Calculated Text Boxes **493**

Changing the Default View and Obtaining Help for Properties **496**

Adding Option Groups with the Wizard **497**

Using the Clipboard to Copy Controls to Another Form **501**

Using Combo and List Boxes **502**

Creating a Combo Box to Find Specific Records **512**

Creating a Tab Control **516**

Changing One Control Type to Another **520**

Completing the Main Personnel Actions Entry Form **521**

Creating a Subform Using the Subform/Subreport Wizard **523**

Modifying the Design of Continuous Forms **527**

Overriding the Field Properties of Tables **528**

Adding Page Headers and Footers for Printing Forms **529**

Troubleshooting **530**

In the Real World—Access Wizardry **531**

14 **Printing Basic Reports and Mailing Labels 533**

Understanding the Relationship Between Forms and Reports **534**

Categorizing Types of Access Reports **535**

Creating a Grouping Report with the Report Wizard **536**

Using Access's Report Windows **543**

Using AutoFormat and Customizing Report Styles **545**

Modifying a Basic Wizard Report **546**
Deleting, Relocating, and Editing Existing Controls **546**
Adding Calculated Controls to a Report **551**
Aligning and Formatting Controls and Adjusting Line Spacing **554**

Adjusting Margins and Printing Conventional Reports **558**

Preventing Widowed Records with the Group Keep Together Property **561**

Printing Multicolumn Reports as Mailing Labels **562**

Troubleshooting **565**

In the Real World—The Apocryphal Paperless Office **566**

15 **Preparing Advanced Reports 569**

Creating Reports from Scratch **570**

Grouping and Sorting Report Data **570**
Grouping Data **571**
Sorting Data Groups **574**

Working from a Blank Report **575**
Using a Report as a Subreport **576**
Creating the Monthly Sales by Category Report **578**

Incorporating Subreports **581**
Adding a Linked Subreport to a Bound Report **581**
Using Unlinked Subreports and Unbound Reports **584**

Customizing *De Novo* Reports **585**
Adding and Deleting Sections of Your Report **585**
Controlling Page Breaks and Printing Page Headers and Footers **587**

Reducing the Length of Reports 587

Adding Other Controls to Reports 588

Mailing Report Snapshots 588
Viewing and Printing the Report Snapshot 589

Troubleshooting 591

In the Real World—The Art of Report Design 591

IV Publishing Data on Intranets and the Internet

16 Working with Hyperlinks and HTML 597

Data-Enabling Web Pages 598

Putting Microsoft's Internet Program in Perspective 599
The Digital Nervous System and Windows DNA 600
Microsoft's Internet-Related Client Products 602
Microsoft's Server-Side Components 604
Microsoft Technologies Supporting Internet-Related Products 605

Navigating the Web and Intranets with Hyperlinks 606

Understanding Access 2000's Hyperlink Field Data Type 611
Testing Hyperlinks in the Northwind Orders Table 611
Editing and Inserting Conventional Hyperlinks 613
Linking to Bookmarks in a Word Document 614
Specifying Hyperlinks to Pages on an Intranet Server or the Web 617
Adding a ScreenTip to the Hyperlink 618

Using Table Hyperlinks to Open an Access Object 619

Using Hyperlinks with Access Controls 621

Specifying Other Internet Uniform Resource Locators 622

Troubleshooting 623

In the Real World—To Internet or Not 624
Microsoft Gets a Clue and the Virus 624
Innoculation Against Internet Fever 624

17 Generating Web Pages from Tables and Queries 627

Easing the Way to Web-Based Decision Support 628

Exporting Table and Query Datasheets to HTML 628
Creating an Unformatted Web Page 631
Creating a Web Page from a Query 634
Using HTML Templates 637
Using the Access HTML Templates Included with Office 2000 637
Exporting a Query Datasheet with a Template 638
Exporting Reports to HTML 639

Importing Data from HTML Tables 643

Creating Dynamic Web Pages 648
Understanding ASP 649
Creating an ODBC Data Source for ASP 650
Exporting an Access Query to ASP 651

Troubleshooting 654

In the Real World—ASP versus DAP 654

18 Designing Data Access Pages 657

Moving to a New Access Form Model 658

Understanding Access's Dynamic HTML Implementation 659
  Technologies Supporting DHTML and DAP 659
  DOM HTML and DHTML 661

Getting Acquainted with DAP 663
  The Review Products Page 663
  The Review Orders Page 667
  The HTML Source Editor 668
  The Analyze Sales PivotTable Page 669
  The Sales Page 671
  Read-Write Pages 673

Using the Page Wizard to Create Simple DAP 674

Using AutoPage to Create Columnar DAP 679
  Using the Record Navigation Control's Filter and Sort Features 681

Modifying the Design of AutoPage DAP 682
  Altering Record Navigation Control Properties 685

Starting a DAP from Scratch 687
  Adding a PivotTable with the Page Field List 687
  Working with the PivotTable List Control in IE 5.0 689
  Altering Pivot Control Properties in IE 5.0 690

Adding Charts to DAP with a PivotTable List 691
  Designing the Query for the PivotTable List 692
  Adding and Formatting the PivotTable List 693
  Using the Chart Wizard to Bind an Office Chart to the PivotTable List 695
  Generating a Grouped Page 698
  Creating a Three-Level Hierarchical Grouped Page Structure 699
  Filling in the Details 701
  Adding Fields of Related Tables and Captions 701

Troubleshooting 704

In the Real World—Are DAP Ready for Prime Time? 704
  Internet Economics 101 705
  Sweet Spot(s) on the Software Elasticity Curve 705

V Integrating Access with Other Office 2000 Applications

19 Adding Charts and Graphics to Forms and Reports 709

Enlivening Forms and Reports with Graphics 710

Creating Graphs and Charts with Microsoft Graph 2000 710
  Creating the Query on Which to Base the Graph 710
  Using the Chart Wizard to Create an Unlinked Graph 712
  Modifying the Design Features of Your Graph 717
  Creating a Graph from a Crosstab Query 723
  Linking the Graph to a Single Record of a Table or Query 725

Using the Chart Web Control in Pages 728
  Designing Queries for the Chart Web Control 729
  Adding an Office Chart Based on the Single-Column Series 730
  Altering the Properties of the Office Chart 733

Adding a Bound Object Control to a
Form or Report 734
　Including Photos in the Personnel
　Actions Query 735
　Displaying the Employee's Picture in
　the Personnel Actions Form 735
　Scaling Graphic Objects 737
　Examining Bitmap Image File
　Formats 740

Using the Image Control 741

Troubleshooting 743

In the Real World—Visualizing
Data 743
　Meaning, Significance, and
　Visualization 744
　Management by Trend
　Exception 744

20 Using Access with Microsoft Excel 745

Slicing and Dicing Data with
PivotTables 746

Using the Access PivotTable
Wizard 746
　Creating the Query for the
　PivotTable 747
　Generating a PivotTable Form with
　the Wizard 747

Manipulating PivotTables in Excel 754
　Improving PivotTable
　Formatting 754
　Slicing PivotTable Data 757
　Slicing by Filtering 759
　Collapsing or Expanding the Display
　of Detail Data 760
　Changing a Dimension's Axis 762

Formatting PivotTable Reports 763

Creating a PivotChart from a
PivotTable 764

Using Excel as an OLE Server 767
　Embedding a Conventional Excel
　Worksheet in a Form 767
　Extracting Values from an OLE
　Object 771
　Linking to a Range of Cells in an Excel
　Worksheet 772

Troubleshooting 774

In the Real World—OLAP and
PivotTables 775
　Measures and Dimensions 776
　So What's OLAP Have to Do with
　Access 2000? 778

**21 Using Access with Microsoft Word and
Mail Merge 781**

Integrating Access 2000 with
Word 2000 782

Using the Access Mail Merge
Wizard 782
　Using an Existing Main Merge
　Document with a New Data
　Source 786

Using Word 2000's Mail Merge Feature
with Access Databases 789
　Creating a New Mail Merge Data
　Source with Microsoft Query and an
　ODBC Data Source 789
　Creating Form Letters from an
　Existing Query 797

Embedding or Linking Word Documents
in Access Tables 798
　Embedding or Linking a Word 2000
　Document in a Table 800
　Creating a Form to Display the
　Embedded Document 802

Troubleshooting 804

In the Real World—Microsoft Query and
OLE DB 805

VI Using Advanced Access Techniques

22 Exploring Relational Database Design and Implementation 811

Reviewing Access 2000's New Database Design Features 812

Integrating Objects and Relational Databases 813

Understanding Database Systems 813
The Objectives of Database Design 814
The Process of Database Design 815
The Object-Oriented Approach to Database Design 816
Database Terminology 819
Types of Tables and Keys in Relational Databases 820

Data Modeling 821
Application Databases 822
Subject Databases 823
Diagrammatic Data Models 823
Database Schema 824

Normalizing Data to the Relational Model 825
Normalization Rules 825
Types of Relationships 831

Using Access 2000's Table Analyzer Wizard 836

Generating a Data Dictionary with the Database Documenter 841

Using Access Indexes 844

Enforcing Database Integrity 844
Ensuring Entity Integrity and Auditability 845
Maintaining Referential Integrity 848

Troubleshooting 849

In the Real World—Why Learn Relational Theory? 849

23 Working with Structured Query Language 851

Understanding the Role of SQL in Access 2000 852

Using Access to Learn SQL 853

Understanding SQL Grammar 854

Writing SELECT Queries in SQL 855
Using SQL Punctuation and Symbols 857
Using SQL Statements to Create Access Queries 858
Using the SQL Aggregate Functions 861
Creating Joins with SQL 863
Using UNION Queries 865
Implementing Subqueries 867

Writing Action and Crosstab Queries 868

Adding IN to Use Tables in Another Database 869
Working with Another Access Database 870
Using the IN Clause with Other Types of Databases 871
Creating Tables with Jet DDL 872
Comparing ANSI and Jet SQL 873
SQL Reserved Words in Access 873
Jet SQL Reserved Words Corresponding to ANSI SQL Keywords 874
Access Functions and Operators Used in Place of ANSI SQL Keywords 875
Jet SQL Reserved Words, Operators, and Functions Not in ANSI SQL 875
Jet's DISTINCTROW and SQL's DISTINCT Keywords 877
Common ANSI SQL Keywords and Features Not Supported by Jet SQL Reserved Words 880

Using SQL Statements in Forms, Reports, and Macros 880

Troubleshooting 881

In the Real World—SQL As a Second
Language 881
    Making Custom Queries Easy for
    Users 882
    Microsoft English Query 882

**24 Securing Multiuser Network
Applications 885**

Networking Access 2000
Applications 886

Installing Access in a Networked
Environment 886

Sharing Your Access Database Files with
Other Users 887
    Creating a Folder and System File for
    File Sharing 887
    Preparing to Share Your Database
    Files 891
    Splitting Databases for File
    Sharing 893
    Fixing Links, Data Sources, and
    Hyperlinks of DAP 895
    Choosing Workgroups with the
    Workgroup Administrator 898

Using Command-Line Options to Open a
Shared Database 899

Maintaining Database Security 902
    Specifying the Principles of Database
    Security on a LAN 902
    Password-Protecting a Single
    Database 904
    Managing Groups and Users 906

Understanding Database Object
Ownership 914
    Owner Permissions for Objects 915
    Changing the Ownership of Database
    Objects 915

Granting and Revoking Permissions for
Database Objects 917
    Using the Security Wizard to Change
    Permissions 918
    Altering Group Permissions
    Manually 925
    Granting Additional Permissions to
    Specific Users 927
    Granting Permissions for a Database in
    Another Workgroup 928

Sharing Databases on the Network 929
    Sharing Database Files on a Windows
    9x Network 929
    Sharing Files with User-Level
    Security 932
    Sharing Database Files from a Network
    Server 934

Accessing the Shared Workgroup and
Data Files 935
    Attaching the Shared Workgroup
    System File 935
    Refreshing the Links to the Shared
    Data File 936

Administering Databases and
Applications 937
    Backing Up and Restoring
    Databases 938
    Compacting and Repairing Database
    Files 938
    Encrypting and Decrypting Database
    Files 939

Troubleshooting 940

In the Real World—Shared-File versus
Client/Server Back Ends 940

25 Creating Access Data Projects 943

Moving Access to the Client/Server
Model 944

Understanding the Role of MSDE 945
    SQL Server Versions and
    Features 945
    MSDE Benefits 946

Installing and Starting MSDE   947

Getting Acquainted with ADP   953
Accommodating MSDE and SQL
Server 7.0 Features   953
Running the NorthwindCS Sample
Project   954

Using the Project Designer   956
Working with MSDE Tables   957
Exploring MSDE Views   960
Diagramming Table
Relationships   965
Writing Stored Procedures   966
Adding Triggers to a Table   968

Using the Upsizing Wizard to Create
ADP   969
Running the Access Upsizing
Wizard   970
Checking the Wizard's Successes and
Failures   974

Downsizing Databases with the DTS
Wizard   975

Connecting to Remote MSDE
Databases   980
Using the SQL Server Client Network
Utility   981
Testing and Using Remote
Databases   982

Establishing MSDE Security   983

Troubleshooting   986

In the Real World—ADP on Trial   986
ADP Drawbacks   987
SQL Server Advantages—ADP,
MSDE, and SQL Server 7.0   988

VII Programming and Converting Access
Applications

26 Writing Visual Basic for Applications
Code   991

Understanding the Role of VBA in
Access   992

Introducing VBA 6.0   993
Where You Use VBA Code   993
Typographic and Naming Conventions
Used for VBA   994
Modules, Functions, and
Subprocedures   995
Elements of Modules   997
References to VBA and Access
Modules   998
Data Types and Database Objects in
VBA   1000
Variables and Naming
Conventions   1002
Symbolic Constants   1008
VBA Named and Optional
Arguments   1009

Controlling Program Flow   1010
Branching and Labels   1010
Conditional Statements   1011
Repetitive Operations: Looping   1014

Handling Runtime Errors   1016
Detecting the Type of Error with the
Err Object   1017
Using the Error Event in Form and
Report Modules   1018

Exploring the VBA Editor   1018
The Toolbar of the Module
Window   1019
Module Shortcut Keys   1021
The VBA Help System   1021

Examining the Utility Functions
Module **1022**
Adding a Breakpoint to the
IsLoaded() Function **1023**
Printing to the Immediate Window
with the Debug Object **1025**
Using Text Comparison
Options **1027**

In the Real World—Macro
Schizophrenia **1027**

**27 Understanding Universal Data Access,
OLE DB, and ADO 1031**

Gaining a Perspective on Microsoft's New
Data Access Components **1032**

Interfacing with a Wide Range of Data
Sources **1033**
Redesigning from the Bottom up with
OLE DB **1034**
Mapping OLE DB Interfaces to
ADO **1035**
Comparing ADO and DAO
Objects **1037**

Creating ADODB.Recordsets **1038**
Designing a Form Bound to an
ADODB.Recordset Object **1039**

Binding Controls to a Recordset with
Code **1041**

Making the Form Updatable **1043**

Exploring Top-Level ADO Properties,
Methods, and Events **1045**
Object Browser and ADO **1046**

Working with the ADODB.Connection
Object **1048**
Connection Properties **1048**
Errors Collection and Error
Objects **1051**
Connection Methods **1054**
Connection Events **1056**

Using the ADODB.Command
Object **1057**
Command Properties **1057**
Parameters Collection **1059**
Parameter Object **1060**
Command Methods **1062**

Understanding the ADODB.Recordset
Object **1066**
Recordset Properties **1066**
Recordset Methods **1074**
Disconnected Recordsets **1079**
Recordset Events **1080**

Troubleshooting **1080**

In the Real World—Struggling with
ADO **1081**
Why Learn ADO? **1081**
Where's ADOX? **1082**
What's the Upshot? **1082**

**28 Responding to Events with
VBA 6.0 1083**

Introducing Event-Driven
Programming **1084**

Understanding the Role of Class
Modules **1084**
The Main Switchboard Class
Module **1085**
Event-Handling Code in the Main
Switchboard Form **1088**

Examining Project Class Module Members
in the Object Browser and Project
Explorer **1089**

Adding Event-Handling Code with the
Command Button Wizard **1092**

Using Functions to Respond to
Events **1096**

Understanding Access 2000's Event
Repertoire **1098**

Working with Access 2000's DoCmd
Methods   1105
    Arguments of DoCmd Methods   1107

Customizing Applications with
CommandBar Objects   1113

Specifying a Custom CommandBar and
Setting Other Startup Properties   1117

Referring to Access Objects with
VBA   1118
    Referring to Open Forms or Reports
    and Their Properties   1118
    Referring to Controls and Their
    Properties   1119
    Referring to Controls on a Subform or
    the Main Form   1120

Using Alternative Collection
Syntax   1121

Responding to Data Events Triggered by
Forms and Controls   1122

Troubleshooting   1123

In the Real World—Dealing with Event-
Driven Programming   1124

29 **Programming Combo and List
    Boxes   1127**

Streamlining Decision Support Front
Ends   1128

Constraining Query Choices with Combo
Boxes   1128
    Designing the Decision-Support
    Query   1129
    Creating the Form and Adding a List
    Box   1130
    Adding the Query Combo Boxes to the
    Form   1131

Adding Code to Create the Query's SQL
Statement   1135

Converting Your Combo Box Form to an
Access Data Project   1138
    Importing and Testing the Combo Box
    Form   1139
    Conforming Row Source SQL
    Statements to Transact-SQL
    Syntax   1140

Drilling Down from a List Box
Selection   1142
    Creating the Drill-Down Query and
    Adding the List Box   1142
    Programming the Drill-Down List
    Box   1143

Adding New Features to List and Combo
Boxes   1145
    Iterating List Box Items and Selecting
    an Item   1145
    Adding an Option to Select All
    Countries or Products   1146

Dealing with Jet-Specific Functions in
Migrating to ADP   1150

Troubleshooting   1152

In the Real World—Access Combo and
List Boxes   1153

30 **Working with ADO Recordsets, Forms,
    and Controls   1155**

Navigating Recordsets with VBA   1156
    Generating the Temporary
    Recordset   1156
    Applying Move... Methods   1158
    Using the EOF and BOF Properties in
    Loops   1159
    Using the AbsolutePosition
    Property   1161

Using the Find Method and
Bookmarks   1162

Modifying Rows of Recordsets   1164
    Editing and Adding Rows   1164
    Deleting Rows   1165

Populating a Combo Box from a
Recordset **1165**
    Creating frmCombo2 and Altering the
    Combo Box Design **1166**
    Populating the Combo Boxes with
    Code **1168**

Altering the Sequence of Combo Box
Lists **1169**

Filling List Boxes from Recordset
Objects **1171**

Formatting Value List Combo Box
Columns **1174**

Porting frmComboVBA to an Access Data
Project **1178**

Troubleshooting **1178**

In the Real World—Adapting to
ADO **1179**

**31 Migrating Access 9x Applications to
Access 2000 1181**

Understanding the .mdb File Upgrade
Process **1182**

Converting Unsecured Files from Access
9x to Access 2000 **1182**
    Upgrading on First Opening the File
    in Access 2000 **1182**

Upgrading After Opening the File in
Access 2000 **1185**

Converting Secure Access 9x Files **1186**
    Upgrading in a Mixed Access 9x and
    2000 Environment **1187**
    Upgrading the Back-End Database and
    Workgroup File **1187**

Upgrading Access 2.0 Application .mdb
Files to Access 2000 **1188**
    Converting from Win16 to Win32
    Function Calls **1189**
    Accommodating the 32-Index Limit on
    Tables **1191**
    Converting 16-Bit OLE Controls to
    32-Bit ActiveX Controls **1191**

Troubleshooting **1191**

In the Real World—The Upgrade Blues
1191

VIII Appendix

A Glossary 1197

Index 1239

About the Author

Roger Jennings is a consultant specializing in Windows client/server database systems. He was a member of the Microsoft technical beta testing team for all versions of Microsoft Access; every release of Visual Basic since version 2.0; Windows 3.1; Windows for Workgroups 3.1 and 3.11; Windows 95 and 98; Windows NT 3.5, 3.51, 4.0, and 2000 Server; Microsoft Exchange Server, the Microsoft ODBC 2.0 and 2.5 drivers; Microsoft ActiveX Data Objects (ADO); Microsoft SQL Server 6.0, 6.5, and 7.0; and Microsoft OLAP Services for SQL Server. Roger was one of the founding members of Microsoft's Access Insiders group.

Roger is the author of Que Publishing's *Special Edition Using Microsoft Access* titles for Access versions 1.0, 1.1, 2.0, 95, and 97 (first and second editions), and *Platinum Edition Using Access 97*. He also wrote Que's *Special Edition Using Windows NT Server 4*, *Unveiling Windows 95*, *Access Hot Tips*, and *Discover Windows 3.1 Multimedia*. For Macmillan Computer Publishing's Sams imprint, he's written two editions of *Access Developer's Guide*, three editions of *Database Developers Guide with Visual Basic* (for versions 3.0, 4.0, and 6.0), and is series editor for the *Roger Jennings' Database Workshop* titles. Roger is a contributing editor for Fawcette Technical Publication's *Visual Basic Programmer's Journal* (http://www.devx.com/); his "Database Design" columns and feature articles appear regularly in *VBPJ*. Roger co-authored with Microsoft's Greg Nelson "A Client/Server Application: From Concept to Reality" presentation and white paper on Access 2.0, which appeared on the *Microsoft Developer's Network* CD-ROM and in the *Microsoft Developer Network News*.

Roger has more than 25 years of computer-related experience, beginning with his work on the Wang 700 desktop calculator/computer. His full biography is at http://www.mcp.com/publishers/que/authors/roger_jennings/. He's a principal of OakLeaf Systems, a Northern California software consulting firm and is the Webmaster for OakLeaf Music, http://www.oakmusic.com/. You can contact Roger at Roger_Jennings@compuserve.com.

DEDICATION

This book is dedicated to my wife, Alexandra.

ACKNOWLEDGMENTS

Jon Price updated chapters 3 through 7, 14, 15, and 21 of this book. Jon is a San Antonio, Texas programming consultant who began developing Access databases in version 2.0. He's developed an Access sales force automation database for a communications company; a customer courtesy desk database for a grocery chain; an ordering and cataloguing database for a computer firm; a project and clientele tracking database for an engineering company; a loan history and forecasting database for a major bank; a production reporting database for a large insurance company; and an insurance policy generator and growth forecasting database for a major insurance company.

Outside the realm of Access development, Jon spent five years writing AutoLisp programs for AutoCad versions 10 through 14, when he was involved a major design application that's used by several Florida engineering offices. He also developed Paradox 4.x applications using ObjectPal and Approach projects with versions 3.0 and 96. Jon has written many database utilities in Visual Basic 5.0, and has designed front-ends to databases with Visual Basic 3.0 and 5.0. You can contact Jon at `jonprice@stic.net`.

Thanks to **Dave Gainer, Kevin Mineweaser, Richard Dickenson, Charles Allard, Michael Kaplan, Loan Dang, Marc La Pierre, Rob Beene**, all the other **Microsoft Access product support and product management staff**, and members of the **Access Insiders** group. Their collective contributions to the Access Insiders Roundtable and beta newsgroups were of invaluable assistance in the writing of this book.

Rosemarie Graham, executive editor, made sure I didn't fall too far behind the manuscript submission and author review schedule. **Marla Reece-Hall**, development editor, made many contributions to the content and organization of this new edition. Copy editors **Lisa Lord** and **June Waldman** corrected my grammatical and spelling errors. **Susan Moore**, project editor, worked hard to make sure all of the components of this edition flowed through the copy editing process and got to their final destinations on time. **Jim Ferguson** of FMS, Inc., the foremost publisher of Access add-ins, handled the technical editing chores. Jim's also a member of the Access Insiders group. **Mark J. Duvall, Bruce Handley**, and **Dave Juth** gave all of the chapters final technical scrutiny for last-minute changes. The responsibility for any errors or omissions, however, rests solely on my shoulders.

Steven Gray and **Rick Lievano**, authors of *Roger Jennings' Database Workshop: Microsoft Transaction Server 2.0*, created the original version of the Beckwith.mdb database as a Microsoft SQL Server 6.5 database.

TELL US WHAT YOU THINK!

As the reader of this book, *you* are our most important critic and commentator. We value your opinion and want to know what we're doing right, what we could do better, what areas you'd like to see us publish in, and any other words of wisdom you're willing to pass our way.

As an Associate Publisher for Que, I welcome your comments. You can fax, email, or write me directly to let me know what you did or didn't like about this book—as well as what we can do to make our books stronger.

Please note that I cannot help you with technical problems related to the topic of this book, and that due to the high volume of mail I receive, I might not be able to reply to every message.

When you write, please be sure to include this book's title and author as well as your name and phone or fax number. I will carefully review your comments and share them with the author and editors who worked on the book.

Fax: 317.581.4666

Email: feedback@quepublishing.com

Mail: Dean Miller
Associate Publisher
Que Corporation
201 West 103rd Street
Indianapolis, IN 46290 USA

INTRODUCTION

Microsoft Access 2000, Version 9.0 (called Access 2000 in this book), is a powerful and robust 32-bit relational database management system (RDBMS) for creating desktop and client/server database applications that run under Windows 9x and Windows NT 4+. As a component of the Professional and Developer editions of the Microsoft Office 2000 suite, Access 2000 has an upgraded user interface that's consistent with Microsoft Excel 2000 and Word 2000, as well as with Windows 9x common controls, such as an Outlook-style Database window and common file open and save dialogs.

The most significant change from Access 97 is Access 2000's adoption of OLE DB, and ActiveX Data Object Extensions (ADOX) 2.1, ActiveX Data Objects (ADO) 2.1, which replace the venerable Data Access Object (DAO) for new Access applications and Access Data Projects (ADP). OLE DB and ADO are the foundation of Microsoft's Universal Data Access strategy. Chapter 27, "Understanding Universal Data Access, OLE DB, and ADO," provides detailed coverage of Access 2000's new data object model. Fortunately for current users of Access 2.0 through 97, Access 2000 continues to support DAO-based applications with updated DAO 3.6. The future of data, not just database, connectivity for Office and Internet/intranet applications, however, lies with ADO. Don't expect Microsoft to deliver significant updates to DAO beyond version 3.6.

> **Note**
>
> Contrary to the "Jet is dead" rumors that appeared during mid-1998 in the computer trade press, Jet is very much alive and well. Microsoft uses Jet 3.5+ in more than 25 products, including Money, Greetings Workshop, Internet Information Server, Index Server, Project, and SQL Server 7.0. Access 2000 introduces version 4.0 of the Jet database engine, which offers a variety of new and useful features. Jet SQL (often called Access SQL) becomes increasingly compliant with ANSI (standard) SQL with each upgrade. Chapters 22, "Exploring Relational Database Design and Implementation," and 23, "Working with Structured Query Language," cover Jet 4.0's new features.

Like all members of Office 2000, Access 2000 offers a variety of new Internet-related features for creating HTML documents for use on intranets and the Internet; the most important of these for intranets is Data Access Pages (DAP). Microsoft's rallying cry for the retail release of Office 2000 is Total Cost of Ownership (TCO). Ease of use is one of the primary requisites for reducing TCO; Access 2000 includes many new or improved wizards and other aids designed for first-time database users.

A primary reason for Access's success is that it duplicates on the PC desktop many of the features of client/server relational database systems, also called *SQL databases*. Client/server RDBMSs are leading the way in transferring database applications from minicomputers and mainframes to networked PCs—a process called *downsizing*. Despite Access's power, this desktop RDBMS is easy for non-programmers to use. Buttons on upgraded multiple toolbars, which are almost identical across the Office 2000 members, offer shortcuts for menu commands. Office 2000 adaptive menus display only the most common choices; fortunately, you can turn adaptive menus off. An extensive collection of wizards and add-ins handle most of the mundane chores involved in creating and modifying tables, queries, forms, graphs, and reports. Builders aid you in creating complex controls on forms and reports, as well as in writing expressions. Last—and, in this case, least—an animated Office Assistant attempts to anticipate users' questions about Access 2000.

Microsoft Access 1.0 introduced a new approach to writing macros that automate repetitive database operations. The 40+ macro instructions of Access 95 and 97 were remarkably powerful; you could create quite sophisticated database applications by using only Access macros. Access 2000 relegates macros to the "for backward compatibility only" category. Office 2000 brings a common version 6.0 of 32-bit Visual Basic for Applications (VBA) to Access, Excel, Word, and even PowerPoint. Access now uses the same VBA Editor as the other members of Access 2000. Visual Basic 6.0 shares the same VBA engine with members of Office 2000, but doesn't share the Office VBA Editor. VBA's syntax is easy to learn, yet it provides a vocabulary rich enough to satisfy veteran xBase and Paradox application developers. Making the transition from Access macros to VBA is important, because there's no guarantee that future versions of Access will continue to support macro programming.

Access 2000 and Visual Basic 6.0 share the capability to take advantage of ActiveX controls (formerly OLE Controls) that Microsoft, third-party add-in software publishers, and you create. ActiveX controls provide Access 2000 with the extensibility that VBX custom controls brought to Visual Basic. Access 2000 can accommodate almost every 32-bit OLE Control included with the Professional and Enterprise editions of Visual Basic 6.0, but you must license the Office 2000 Developer Edition (ODE) to include Visual Basic's databound controls in your Access applications and projects. The new, lightweight ActiveX controls for Internet and intranet applications, called Office Web Components, enable you to embed charts, spreadsheets, and PivotTables in browser-based applications.

Access is specifically designed for creating multiuser applications where database files are shared on networks, and Access incorporates a sophisticated security system to prevent unauthorized persons from viewing or modifying the databases you create. Access's security system is modeled on that of Microsoft SQL Server. No substantial changes have been made to the Access security system in Access 2000, but the User-Level Security Wizard introduced with Access 95 makes secure applications easier to implement and administer.

Access has a unique database structure that can combine all related data tables and their indexes, forms, reports, and VBA code within a single .mdb database file. It's now a generally accepted database design practice (GADBDP) to use separate .mdb files to contain data and application objects; your application .mdb links tables contained in the data .mdb. (The term *link* replaced *attach* beginning with Access 95.) Access 2000 also offers a secure file format, .mde, so that you can distribute Access applications without exposing your original VBA source code. Data Access Pages (.htm) and Access Data Projects (.adp) are the new file formats of Access 2000.

Access can import data from and export data to the more popular PC database and spreadsheet files, as well as text files. Access also can attach dBASE, FoxPro, and Paradox table files to databases and manipulate these files in their native formats, but support for attached files of these formats is very limited in Access 2000. You also can use Access on workstations that act as clients of networked file and database servers in client/server database systems. Access, therefore, fulfills all the requirements of a professional relational database management system, as well as a front-end development tool for use with client/server databases. Microsoft has made many improvements to these features in Access 2000. The most important new features of Access 2000 are discussed in Chapter 1, "Access 2000 for Access 95 and 97 Users: What's New."

WHO SHOULD READ THIS BOOK

Special Edition Using Access 2000 takes an approach that's different from most books about database management applications. This book doesn't begin with the creation of a database for Widgets, Inc., nor does it require you to type a list of fictional customers for the company's new Widget 2000 product line to learn the basics of Access. Instead, this book makes the following basic assumptions about your interest in Microsoft's relational database management system:

- You can navigate Microsoft Windows 9x or NT 4.0+ with the mouse and keyboard.

- You aren't starting from "ground zero." You now have or will have access via your PC to data that you want to process with a Windows database manager. You have acquired Access and want to learn to use it more quickly and effectively. Or you may be considering using Access as the database manager for yourself, your department or division, or your entire organization.

- Your existing data is in the form of one or more database, spreadsheet, or even plain text files that you want to manipulate with a relational database management system. Access can process the most common varieties of these file types, as well as HTML tables, Exchange messages, and other tabular data sources.

- If you're planning to use Access 2000 as a front end to a client/server RDBMS, you'll use the Microsoft Data Engine (MSDE) that's an integral part of Access 2000. Alternatively, you have SQL Server 6.5 or, preferably, SQL Server 7.0, installed or have an OLE DB data provider or ODBC driver, and the required client license for your SQL database.

- If your data is on a mini- or mainframe computer, you're connected to that computer by a local area network and a database gateway or through terminal emulation software and an adapter card.

If some or all of your data is in the form of ASCII or ANSI text files, or files from a spreadsheet application, you need to know how to create an Access database from the beginning and import the data into Access's own .mdb file structure. If your data is in the form of dBASE, FoxPro, or Paradox files, you can link the files as tables and continue to use them in the format native to your prior database manager. Access 2000 also lets you link Excel and text files to Access databases. The capability to link files in their native format is an important advantage to have during conversion from one database management system to another. Each subject receives thorough coverage in this book.

HOW THIS BOOK IS ORGANIZED

Special Edition Using Access 2000 is divided into seven parts arranged in increasing levels of detail and complexity. Each division after Part I draws on the knowledge and experience you've gained in the prior parts, so use of the book in a linear, front-to-back manner through Part IV, "Publishing Data on Intranets and the Internet," is recommended during the initial learning process. After you absorb the basics, *Special Edition Using Access 2000* becomes a valuable reference tool for the advanced topics.

As you progress through the chapters in this book, you create a model of an Access application called *Personnel Actions*. In Chapter 4, "Working with Access Databases and Tables," you create the Personnel Actions table. In the following chapters, you add new features to the Personnel Actions application. Be sure to perform the example exercises for the Personnel Actions application each time you encounter them, because succeeding examples build on your prior work.

The seven parts of *Special Edition Using Access 2000* and the topics they cover are described in the following sections.

PART I: LEARNING ACCESS FUNDAMENTALS

The chapters in Part I introduce you to Access and many of the unique features that make Access the easiest to use of all database managers. The chapters in Part I deal almost exclusively with tables, the basic elements of Access databases.

- Chapter 1, "Access 2000 for Access 95 and 97 Users: What's New," provides a summary of the most important new features of Access 2000 and a detailed description of each addition and improvement. Much of the content of this chapter is of interest primarily to readers who now use Access 2.0, because most of the changes from Access 95 to 97 to Access 2000 are incremental in nature. Readers new to Access, however, benefit from the explanations of why many of these new features are significant in everyday use of Access 2000, and how they fit into Microsoft's Total Cost of Ownership (TCO) vision.

- In Chapter 2, "Building Your First Access 2000 Application," you use the Database Wizard, introduced by Access 95, to create a database from the standard database templates included with Access 2000. You gain a basic understanding of the standard data-related objects of Access, including tables, forms, reports, and VBA modules. Chapter 2 introduces you to automating Access operations with VBA Class Modules, the replacement for Access macros, and the new Office VBA Editor.

- Chapter 3, "Navigating Within Access," shows you how to navigate Access by explaining its toolbar and menu choices and how they relate to the structure of Access.

- Chapter 4, "Working with Access Databases and Tables," delves into the details of Access tables, shows you how to create tables, and explains how to choose the optimum data types from the many new types Access offers. Chapter 4 introduces Access 2000's new subdatasheet feature for displaying and editing records related to those in the main table datasheet.

- Chapter 5, "Entering, Editing, and Validating Data in Tables," shows you how to arrange the data in tables to suit your needs and limit the data displayed to only that information you want. Using Find and Replace to alter data in the fields of tables also is covered.

- Chapter 6, "Sorting, Finding, and Filtering Data in Tables," describes how to add new records to tables, enter data in the new records, and edit data in existing records. Chapter 6 describes how to make best use of the Filter by Form and Filter by Selection features of Access 2000.

- Chapter 7, "Linking, Importing, and Exporting Tables," explains how to import and export files of other database managers, spreadsheet applications, and even ASCII and HTML files you download from the Internet. Chapter 7 explains the Table Analyzer Wizard that aids in creating a relational database structure from "flat files" in ASCII and spreadsheet formats.

Part II: Getting the Most Out of Queries

The chapters in Part II explain how to create Access queries to select the way you view data contained in tables and how to take advantage of Access's relational database structure to link multiple tables with joins.

- Chapter 8, "Designing Access Queries," starts with simple queries created with Access's graphical Query Design window. You learn how to choose the fields of the tables included in your query and return query result sets from these tables. Chapter 8 shows you how to use the Simple Query Wizard to simplify the design process.

- Chapter 9, "Understanding Query Operators and Expressions," introduces you to the operators and expressions that you need to create queries that provide a meaningful result. You use the improved Immediate window of the Office 2000 VBA Editor to evaluate the expressions you write.

- In Chapter 10, "Creating Multitable and Crosstab Queries," you create relations between tables, called *joins*, and learn how to add criteria to queries so that the query result set includes only those records you want. Chapter 10 also takes you through the process of designing powerful crosstab queries to summarize data and to present information in a format similar to that of worksheets.

- Chapter 11, "Modifying Data with Action Queries," shows you how to develop action queries that update the tables underlying append, delete, update, and make-table queries. Chapter 11 also covers Access 2000's advanced referential integrity features, including cascading updates and cascading deletions.

PART III: DESIGNING FORMS AND REPORTS

The chapters in Part III introduce you to the primary application objects of Access. (Tables and queries are considered database objects.) Forms make your Access applications come alive with the control objects you add by using Access 2000's toolbox. Access's full-featured report generator lets you print fully formatted reports or save reports to files that you can process in Excel 2000 or Word 2000.

- Chapter 12, "Creating and Using Forms," shows you how to use Access's Form Wizards to create simple forms and subforms that you can modify to suit your particular needs. Chapter 12 introduces you to the Subform Builder Wizard that uses drag-and-drop techniques to automatically create subforms for you.

- Chapter 13, "Designing Custom Multitable Forms," shows you how to design custom forms for viewing and entering your own data with Access's advanced form design tools.

- Chapter 14, "Printing Basic Reports and Mailing Labels," describes how to design and print simple reports with Access's Report Wizard and how to print preformatted mailing labels by using the Mailing Label Wizard.

- Chapter 15, "Preparing Advanced Reports," describes how to use more sophisticated sorting and grouping techniques, as well as subreports, to obtain a result that exactly meets your detail and summary data reporting requirements. Chapter 15 also covers the new Access Snapshot Technology that lets you distribute Access reports as Outlook e-mail attachments and the Snapshot Viewer for users without Access to display the attached reports.

PART IV: PUBLISHING DATA ON INTRANETS AND THE INTERNET

The chapters in Part V describe how to take advantage of Access's Internet and intranet features and the new Data Access Pages technology introduced by Access 2000.

- Chapter 16, "Working with Hyperlinks and HTML," describes Microsoft's Internet strategy and introduces you to Access 2000's new Hyperlink field data type. The chapter shows you how to use hyperlinks to connect to Word documents and Excel worksheets, as well as how hyperlinks can open Access form and report objects.

- Chapter 17, "Generating Web Pages from Tables and Queries," describes how to export formatted static Web pages from table and query datasheets. You also learn how to use the Internet Data Connector and Active Server Pages to create browser-independent dynamic Web pages for the Internet.

- Chapter 18, "Designing Data Access Pages," shows you how to generate dynamic Web pages to display and update data on your organization's intranet. The chapter describes how to add PivotTables and charts for data analysis and incorporate the Web-enabled version of subdatasheets for entering and editing database records.

PART V: INTEGRATING ACCESS WITH OTHER OFFICE 2000 APPLICATIONS

The chapters of Part V show you how to use the 32-bit Object Linking and Embedding (OLE) 2.1 features of Access 2000 with the new Microsoft Office Chart 9.0, plus OfficeLinks to Excel 2000 and Word 2000.

- Chapter 19, "Adding Charts and Graphics to Forms and Reports," describes how to use the new Chart Wizard to create databound graphs and charts and shows you how to take advantage of Access OLE Object field data type and bound object frames to display images stored in your Access tables. Adding static graphics to forms and reports with unbound object frames also is covered.

- Chapter 20, "Using Access with Microsoft Excel," gives you detailed examples for using the Access PivotTable Wizard to embed Excel PivotTables in forms. Excel PivotTables let you "slice and dice" data without rewriting queries. Chapter 20 also covers exchanging data between Access and Excel 2000 workbooks by using Access as an OLE 2.1 client and server, without the need to write VBA code.

- Chapter 21, "Using Access with Microsoft Word and Mail Merge," shows you how to store documents in OLE Object fields, explains the OfficeLink Publish It with MS Word option for database publishing, and shows how to use Access 2000's Merge It OfficeLink feature to interactively create form letters and envelopes addressed with data from your Access applications.

PART VI: USING ADVANCED ACCESS TECHNIQUES

The chapters of Part VI cover the theoretical and practical aspects of relational database design and Structured Query Language (SQL), and then go on to describe how to set up and use secure Access applications on a local area network.

- Chapter 22, "Exploring Relational Database Design and Implementation," describes the process you use to create relational database tables from real-world data—a technique called *normalizing the database structure*. This chapter explains how to use the Database Documentor tool included with Access 2000 to create a data dictionary that fully identifies each object in your database.

- Chapter 23, "Working with Structured Query Language," explains how Access uses the Jet dialect of SQL to create queries and how to write your own SQL statements. Special emphasis is given to the newer Jet SQL extensions, such as UNION queries and subqueries, as well as Jet 4.0's implementation of SQL's Data Definition Language (DDL).

- Chapter 24, "Securing Multiuser Network Applications," explains how to set up Access to share database files on a network and how to use the security features of Access to prevent unauthorized viewing of or tampering with your database files.

- Chapter 25, "Creating Access Data Projects," introduces you to the Microsoft Data Engine (MSDE) and its management and shows you how to design Access Data Projects (ADP) that take full advantage of this new embedded version of SQL Server 7.0 that runs on Windows 9x, Windows NT 4.0, and Windows 2000.

PART VII: PROGRAMMING AND CONVERTING ACCESS APPLICATIONS

The chapters in Part VII assume that you have no programming experience in any language. These chapters explain the principles of writing programming code in VBA. They also show you how to apply these principles to automate Access applications and work directly with ADO Recordset objects. Part VII also supplies tips for converting Access 2.0, 95, and 97 applications to Access 2000.

- Chapter 26, "Writing Visual Basic for Applications Code," describes how to use VBA to create user-defined functions stored in modules and to write simple procedures that you activate directly from events. Access's class modules, which let you store event-handling code in Form and Report objects, also are described.

- Chapter 27, "Understanding Universal Data Access, OLE DB, and ADO," explains Microsoft's new approach to data connectivity and describes how to migrate from DAO to ADO and why this direction is important for your new Access applications.

- Chapter 28, "Responding to Events with VBA 6.0," describes how to use VBA event-handling subprocedures in class modules to replace the macros used by earlier versions of Access. This chapter explains the events triggered by Access form, report, and control objects, and how to use methods of the DoCmd object to respond to events, such as clicking a command button.

- Chapter 29, "Programming Combo and List Boxes," shows you how to take maximum advantage of Access 2000's unique combo and list boxes in decision-support applications. This chapter explains the VBA coding techniques for loading combo box lists and populating list boxes based on your combo box selections.

- Chapter 30, "Working with ADO Recordsets, Forms, and Controls," explains VBA coding to manipulate ADODB.Recordset objects, including INSERT, UPDATE, and DELETE operations. The chapter also describes how to take advantage of ADO's explicit transactions and how to populate combo and list boxes directly from Recordsets.

- Chapter 31, "Migrating Access 9x Applications to Access 2000," tells you what changes you need to make when you convert your current 32-bit Access database applications to Access 2000.

GLOSSARY

The "Glossary" presents a descriptive list of the terms, abbreviations, and acronyms used in this book that might not be familiar to you and can't be found in commonly used dictionaries.

THE ACCOMPANYING CD-ROM

The CD-ROM that accompanies this book includes Access 2000 database files containing tables, forms, reports, VBA code, and special files to complement design examples and shows you the expected result. An icon identifies sections that point to chapter files included on the accompanying CD-ROM. A very large (20MB) database, Beckwith.mdb, is included for optional use with some of the examples in this book. Beckwith is a mythical college in Texas with 30,000 students and 2,300 employees. Databases with a large number of records in tables are useful when designing applications to optimize performance.

Because you're likely to use Access as a member of the Microsoft Office 2000 suite of products, this book's CD-ROM also contains selected chapters from Que's *Special Edition Using* series of books on each Office 2000 product. The chapters offer helpful information on such topics as using FrontPage 2000 with Jet and MSDE databases and retrieving data from OLAP servers with Excel 2000.

How this Book Is Designed

The following special features are included in this book to assist readers.

 If you've never used a database management application, you're provided with quick-start examples to gain confidence and experience while using Access with the Northwind Traders sample database. Like Access, this book uses the *tabula rasa* approach: each major topic begins with the assumption that you have no prior experience with the subject. Therefore, when a button from the toolbar or control object toolbox is used, its icon is displayed in the margin.

Tip #0 from 	Tips describe shortcuts and alternative approaches to gaining an objective. These tips are based on the experience the author gained during more than seven years of testing successive alpha and beta versions of Access and Microsoft Office 2000 Developer (MOD).

Note	Notes offer advice to help you use Access, describe differences between various versions of Access, and explain the few remaining anomalies you find in Access 2000.

Caution	Cautions are provided when an action can lead to an unexpected or unpredictable result, including loss of data; the text provides an explanation of how you can avoid such a result.

 NEW 2000 Features that are new or have been modified in Access 2000 are indicated by the 2000 icon in the margin, unless the change is only cosmetic. Where the changes are extensive and apply to an entire section of a chapter, the icon appears to the left or right of the section head.

 Y2K The Year 2000 (Y2K) icon identifies new Access 2000 features that Microsoft designed to solve Y2K issues and specific steps you must take to assure reliable operation of your Access applications during the next century.

Cross-references to specific sections in other chapters follow the material they pertain to, such as in the following sample reference:

→ **See** *"A Section in Another Chapter,"* **p. xxx**.

Most chapters include a "Troubleshooting" section at the end of the tutorial and reference contents. The elements of this section help you solve specific problems—common and uncommon—that you might run into when creating applications that use specific Access features or techniques.

At the end of each chapter is an "In the Real World" section that discusses the relevance of the chapter's content to the realm of production databases, the Internet, and other current computer-related topics that affect Access users and developers. The opinion-editorial (op-ed) style of many of the "In the Real World" sections reflects the author's view of the benefits—or drawbacks—of new Access features and related Microsoft technologies, based on the author's experience with production Access applications installed by several world-wide corporations.

TYPOGRAPHIC CONVENTIONS USED IN THIS BOOK

This book uses various typesetting styles to distinguish between explanatory and instructional text, text you enter in dialogs (set in **bold face**), and text you enter in code-editing windows (set in `monospace` type).

KEY COMBINATIONS AND MENU CHOICES

Key combinations that you use to perform Windows operations are indicated by joining the keys with a plus sign: Alt+F4, for example, indicates that you press and hold the Alt key while pressing the function key F4. In the rare cases when you must press and release a key, and then press another key, the keys are separated by a comma without an intervening space: Alt,F4, for example.

Key combinations that perform menu operations requiring more than one keystroke are called *shortcut keys*. An example of such a shortcut is the Windows 9x key combination Ctrl+C, which substitutes for the Edit menu's Copy command in almost all Windows applications.

Sequences of individual menu items are separated by a comma: Edit, Cut, for example. The Alt key required to activate a choice from the main menu with an accelerator key is assumed and not shown.

Successive entries in dialogs follow the tab order of the dialog. *Tab order* is the sequence in which the caret moves when you press the Tab key to move from one entry or control option to another, a process known as *changing the focus*. The entry or control option with the focus is the one that receives keystrokes or mouse clicks. Command buttons, option buttons, and check box choices are treated similarly to menu choices, but their accelerator key letters in the text aren't underlined.

File and folder names are initial-letter-capitalized in the text and headings of this book to conform with Windows 9x and Windows NT 4.0 file-naming conventions and the appearance of file names in Windows Explorer.

SQL STATEMENTS AND KEYWORDS IN OTHER LANGUAGES

SQL statements and code examples are set in a special monospace font. Keywords of SQL statements, such as SELECT, are set in all uppercase. Ellipses (...) indicate intervening programming code that isn't shown in the text or examples.

Square brackets in **monospace boldface** type (**[]**) that appear within Jet SQL statements don't indicate optional items, as they do in syntax descriptions. In this case, the square brackets are used instead of quotation marks to frame a literal string or to allow use of a table and field names, such as [Personnel Actions], that include embedded spaces or special punctuation, or field names that are identical to reserved words in VBA.

TYPOGRAPHIC CONVENTIONS USED FOR VBA

This book uses a special set of typographic conventions for references to Visual Basic for Applications keywords in the presentation of VBA examples:

- Monospace type is used for all examples of VBA code, as in the following statement:
  ```
  Dim NewArray ( ) As Long
  ReDim NewArray (9, 9, 9)
  ```

- Monospace type also is used when referring to names of properties of Access database objects, such as FormName.Width. The captions for text boxes and drop-down lists in which you enter values of properties, such as Source Connect String, are set in this book's regular textual font.

- **Bold monospace** type is used for all VBA reserved words and type-declaration symbols (which aren't used in the code examples in this book), as shown in the preceding example. Standard function names in VBA also are set in **bold monospace** type so that reserved words, standard function names, and reserved symbols stand out from variable and function names and values you assign to variables.

- *Italic monospace* type indicates a replaceable item, as in
  ```
  Dim DataItem As String
  ```

- ***Bold italic monospace*** type indicates a replaceable reserved word, such as a data type, as in
  ```
  Dim DataItem As DataType
  ```
  DataItem is replaced by a keyword corresponding to the desired VBA data type, such as **String** or **Variant**.

- An ellipsis (...) substitutes for code not shown in syntax and code examples, as in
  ```
  If...Then...Else...End If
  ```

- Braces ({}) enclosing two or more identifiers separated by the pipe symbol (¦) indicate that you must choose one of these identifiers, as in

  `Do {While¦Until}...Loop`

  In this case, you must use the `While` or `Until` reserved word in your statement, but not the braces or the pipe character.

- Square brackets ([ ], not in bold type) enclosing an identifier indicate that the identifier is optional, as in

  `Set tblName = dbName.OpenTable(strTableName[, fExclusive])`

  Here, the `fExclusive` flag, if set `True`, opens the table specified by strTableName for exclusive use. `fExclusive` is an optional argument. Don't include the brackets in any code you type.

SYSTEM REQUIREMENTS FOR ACCESS 2000

Access 2000 is a very resource-intensive application, as are all other Office 2000 members. You'll find execution of Access applications on Pentium PCs slower than 166 MHz to be impaired, at best. Access 2000 requires 16MB of RAM for barely adequate performance with Windows 9x. If you plan to use Access 2000 to handle large databases or run it often with other applications, you should have a minimum of 32MB of RAM under Windows 9x and 64MB of RAM or more for Windows NT 4.0. You also should have a minimum of 300MB of free disk space before installing Office 2000.

OTHER SOURCES OF INFORMATION FOR ACCESS

SQL and relational database design, discussed in Chapters 23 and 24, are the subject of myriad guides and texts covering one or both of these topics. Articles in database-related periodicals and files you read on the Internet or download from online information utilities, such as CompuServe, provide up-to-date assistance in using Access 2000. The following sections provide a bibliography of database-related books and periodicals, as well as a brief description of Web sites and CompuServe forums of interest to Access users.

BOOKS

The following books complement the content of this book by providing detailed coverage of Access and VBA programming techniques, application design, Structured Query Language, client/server databases, and the Windows 9x and Windows NT operating systems:

- *Platinum Edition Using Microsoft Access 2000* by Roger Jennings (Que, to be published in 1999) offers coverage of the advanced Access topics that aren't included in this book, which is intended for beginning through intermediate Access 2000 users. The *Platinum Edition* emphasizes client/server applications with Access Data Projects and OLE DB/ADO, SQL Server stored procedures, advanced VBA programming, the Office 2000 PivotTable service, replicating Access and SQL Server 7.0 databases, and the Office 2000 Developer Edition (ODE).

- *F. Scott Barker's Microsoft Access 2000 Power Programming* by F. Scott Barker (Sams, ISBN 0-672-31506-8) shows you how to get the most out of the Access flavor of VBA 5.0 and complements the VBA programming chapters of Part VII of this book.

- *Understanding the New SQL: A Complete Guide* by Jim Melton and Alan R. Simpson (Morgan Kaufmann Publishers, ISBN 1-55860-245-3) describes the history and implementation of the American National Standards Institute's X3.135.1-1992 standard for the latest official version of Structured Query Language, SQL-92, on which Jet SQL is based. Melton was the editor of the ANSI SQL-92 standard, which consists of more than 500 pages of fine print.

- *Database Developer's Guide with Visual Basic 6* by Roger Jennings (Sams Publishing, ISBN 0-672-31063-5) covers advanced VBA programming with ADO, Remote Data Service (RDS), hierarchical Recordsets, the PivotTable service, DataCubes, and other developer topics. If you have Microsoft Office 2000 Developer, (MOD), this book explains how to take maximum advantage of MOD's Visual Basic 6.0 databound controls and other high-end components for developers.

- *Sams Teach Yourself Microsoft SQL Server 7.0 in 21 Days* by Richard Waymire and Rick Sawtell (Sams, ISBN 0-672-31290-5) is designed to bring system and database administrators, as well as developers, up-to-date on the latest and greatest version of Microsoft SQL Server. Having a tutorial and reference for SQL Server 7.0 is important when working with MSDE, because the embedded version of SQL Server 7.0 that comes with Access 2000 doesn't include SQL Server documentation or administrative tools.

- *Special Edition Using Microsoft Internet Information Server 4* by Nelson Howell, et al. (Que, ISBN 0-7897-1263-6), supplies detailed instructions for setting up an Internet or intranet Web site by using IIS 4.0. *Special Edition Using Microsoft Internet Information Server 4* extends the coverage of this book's Part IV, "Publishing Data on Intranets and the Internet."

- *Special Edition Using Windows NT Server 4*, Second Edition, by Roger Jennings (Que, ISBN 0-7897-1388-8) provides all the information you need to set up Windows NT Server 4.0 for sharing Access databases, install and run Microsoft SQL Server, and create your own intranet Web site with Internet Information Server.

- *Special Edition Using Windows NT Workstation 4.0, Second Edition* by Paul Sanna, et al. (Que, ISBN 0-7897-1384-5), provides coverage of the client-side features of Windows NT 4.0 that are beyond the scope of this book.

- *Platinum Edition Using Windows 98*, by Ron Person, et al. (Que, ISBN 0-7897-1489-2), is a 1,400-page book that covers all aspects of Windows 98 in detail and is especially useful as a reference for Windows 98 client networking and user/policy management.

PERIODICALS

The following are a few magazines and newsletters that cover Access exclusively or in which articles on Microsoft Access appear on a regular basis:

- *Access-Office-VB Advisor*, published by Advisor Communications International, Inc., is a full-color, bimonthly magazine intended to serve Access users and developers. You can supplement your subscription with an accompanying disk that includes sample databases, utilities, and other software tools for Access.

- *Inside Microsoft Access* is a monthly newsletter of Access tips and techniques of the Cobb Group, which publishes various newsletters on products such as Visual Basic and Paradox.

- *Web Builder*, a Web-based publication of Fawcette Technical Publications, Inc., covers Internet- and intranet-related topics, with emphasis on Internet Information Server and Visual Basic, Scripting Edition (VBScript) and ECMAScript (JavaScript or JScript). Fawcette's Web site is at `http://www.devx.com`.

- *Smart Access* is a monthly newsletter of Pinnacle Publishing, Inc., which publishes several other database-related newsletters. *Smart Access* is directed primarily to developers and Access power users. This newsletter tends toward advanced topics, such as creating libraries and using the Windows API with VBA. A disk is included with each issue. Like other publications directed to Access users, much of the content of *Smart Access* is of equal interest to Visual Basic database developers.

- *Visual Basic Programmer's Journal* is a monthly magazine from Fawcette Technical Publications that covers all dialects of VBA. *Visual Basic Programmer's Journal* has a monthly column and many feature articles devoted to database topics of interest to Access and Visual Basic developers.

INTERNET

Microsoft's Web site now is the primary source of new and updated information for Access users and developers. Following are the primary Web sites and newsgroups for Access 2000 users and developers:

- Microsoft's Access home page, `http://www.microsoft.com/access/`, is the jumping-off point for Access users and includes links to all related home pages on the Microsoft Web site.

- Microsoft's Access Developer home page, `http://www.microsoft.com/accessdev/`, provides various links to information of particular interest to the Access developer community. This home page provides a link for downloading the Access 2000 Upsizing Wizard for automating the migration of Access multiuser applications to SQL Server 6.5 databases.

- Microsoft's online support home page, `http://support.microsoft.com/support/`, provides links to Microsoft Knowledgebase pages for all its products. For other support options, go to `http://www.microsoft.com/Support/`.

- *DevX*, Fawcette Technical Publications' new Web site for Windows developers at `http://www.devx.com/`, offers a wide range of database topics, plus news, features, and product reviews of ActiveX controls.

- Microsoft's `msnews.microsoft.com` news server offers various Access-related newsgroups at `microsoft.public.access.`*`subject`*. When this book was written, there were more than 20 Access subject areas.

- The Microsoft Access World Wide Developer Network site at `www.wji.com/access/homepage.html` provides a forum for Access developers with tips and source code, Access User Group meeting announcements, and links to other sites with Access content.

- The Usenet `comp.databases.ms-access` newsgroup is an active community of Access users and developers.

LEARNING ACCESS FUNDAMENTALS

1 Access 2000 for Access 95 and 97 Users: What's New 19

2 Building Your First Access 2000 Application 55

3 Navigating within Access 81

4 Working with Access Databases and Tables 127

5 Entering, Editing, and Validating Data in Tables 185

6 Sorting, Finding, and Filtering Data in Tables 205

7 Linking, Importing, and Exporting Tables 231

CHAPTER 1

ACCESS 2000 FOR ACCESS 95 AND 97 USERS: WHAT'S NEW

In this chapter

Putting Access 2000 in Perspective   20

Deploying Data Access Pages with Office Web Components   21

Creating Access Data Projects for the Microsoft Data Engine   26

Integrating the Office VBA Editor with Access   32

Working with the HTML Source Editor for DAP and DHTML   33

Viewing and Editing Related Records in Subdatasheets   34

Conforming Jet and SQL Server 7.0/MSDE Databases   35

Giving Access a Year 2000 Facelift   36

Installing Access 2000   42

Installing and Configuring the Microsoft Data Engine   47

In the Real World—Why Upgrade?   51

PUTTING ACCESS 2000 IN PERSPECTIVE

Access 2000 is the sixth iteration of Microsoft's formidable desktop database platform and third in the line of 32-bit Access versions. Microsoft Access and its Jet database engine dominate the desktop database market. Jesse Berst, ZDNet columnist and former editor of the "Windows Watcher" newsletter, wrote in early 1998: "Corel's Paradox is dead. Nobody writes in dBASE anymore. Microsoft's Access has this market all tied up." Berst failed to mention Microsoft's own FoxPro database that, despite many loyal developers and users, has become a low-volume niche product. Tens of millions of copies of Access are in use throughout the world for applications ranging from cataloging recipes and CD collections to conducting electronic commerce (*e-commerce*) on the Internet.

Note

Employing the term "users" for consumers of database applications infers that database developers are "pushers." In this book, you are an "Access user" until you create and deploy Access applications for use by colleagues or clients. At that point, you become an "Access developer." The extent to which you promote use by others of your Access applications determines your "pusher" qualification.

Much of Access's success is attributable to its inclusion in Microsoft Office Professional editions. Each version of Access has become more closely integrated with other members of Office. All members of Office 2000 and Visual Basic 6.0 now share a common Visual Basic for Applications (*VBA*) version 6.0. Access 2000 finally has adopted the Office 2000 *VBA Editor* (also called the *Integrated Development Environment* or *IDE*) for writing VBA code to automate Access applications. Writing VBA code is the subject of this book's Part VII, "Programming and Converting Access Applications." Access 2000 also shares, for better or worse, the new Hypertext Markup Language (*HTML*) help system of Office 2000.

Note

Other Office members use the term *macro* for VBA code used to automate common operations or create self-contained applications. Access has its own macro language, which is very different from—and less powerful than—VBA. Access macros are obsolete; Access 2000 retains macro capability only for backward compatibility with prior versions. There is no guarantee that future versions of Access will support macros.

Many of Microsoft's additions and changes to Access 2000 are cosmetic or "ease of use" enhancements that aren't likely to have a major impact on Access users or developers. The sections that follow briefly describe, in approximate order of importance, the new features Microsoft added to Access 2000.

> **Note**
>
> **NEW 2000** This chapter assumes that you're familiar with earlier versions of Access. If you're a new Access user, consider skipping to the section "Installing Access 2000" near the end of this chapter. After you work your way through the first four parts of this book (Chapters 2 through 18), you're likely to find most of the "What's New" information presented here to be more meaningful.
>
> Virtually all the information in this chapter is new, so the New in Access 2000 icon isn't used elsewhere in the chapter.

DEPLOYING DATA ACCESS PAGES WITH OFFICE WEB COMPONENTS

Microsoft's determination to "embrace and extend the Internet" has made Internet publishing a must-have feature for the Office suite, whether or not the term is appropriate for particular members. It's very uncommon to "publish" databases, especially large ones, in conventional HTML tables. Instead, Access 2000 now has the capability to deploy database applications as Data Access Pages (*DAP*), which offer convenient data searching, display, and analysis capabilities. DAP are the subject of Chapter 18, "Designing Data Access Pages."

> **Note**
>
> Microsoft has abandoned the attempt made in Access 97 to generate Active Server Pages (*ASP*) that emulate Access forms. If you export an Access 2000 form to .asp format, you get an HTML table containing the entire content of the form's underlying table or query result set. ASP have the advantage of browser independence, but automatically creating workable ASP lookalikes of complex Access forms is a project of enormous proportions. Access 2000 users must settle for DAP. Unfortunately, there's no Export to DAP or Save as DAP feature for Access 2000 forms.

DAP represent an entirely new approach to moving Access applications to the Internet or, more likely, private intranets. DAP take advantage of two relatively new Internet standards, eXtensible Markup Language (*XML*) and Cascading Style Sheets (*CSS*), to manage the content and appearance of Web pages. XML lets you define your own tags for data fields, such as <CustomerName> or <OrderNumber>. CSS define reusable styles, which Microsoft calls *themes*, to define backgrounds and format blocks of text or other objects on a Web page.

> **Note**
>
> XML and CSS are Internet standards promulgated by the World Wide Web Consortium (*W3C*), but implementation of XML and CSS varies in current versions of Netscape Navigator/Communicator and Microsoft Internet Explorer (IE). Users must have the IE 5.0 browser, which is installed by the Office 2000 setup program, to render Access 2000 DAP. Applications deployed for public consumption on the Internet must support both Netscape and Microsoft browsers. (*Extranets*, which provide controlled, secure Web site access by business partners, are exempt from this rule.) This book calls applications that aren't Netscape-compliant *intranet-only*, meaning that the application is suited for deployment on an organizationwide local area network (*LAN*) or wide area network (*WAN*).

THE OFFICE WEB COMPONENTS

DAP's XML implementation enables the addition of data-bound Office Web Components (*OWC*) to DAP. OWC comprise the following six ActiveX controls designed specifically for Web-based database front ends:

- *PivotTable* is a lightweight version of the Excel PivotTable feature that gives you an expandable, hierarchical view of related tables. You can exchange (pivot) data columns and rows by drag-and-drop methods. Using PivotTables is one of the subjects of Chapter 18, "Designing Data Access Pages." Chapter 20, "Using Access with Microsoft Excel," describes how to use Excel PivotTables in conventional Access forms.

- *Spreadsheet* is a simplified edition of an Excel worksheet with built-in data binding.

- *Chart* is a scaled-down version of the Microsoft Graph 9.0 control described in Chapter 19, "Adding Charts and Graphics to Forms and Reports."

- *Record Navigation* emulates on DAP the record navigation buttons of a conventional data-bound Access form.

- *Expand* enables PivotTables and other hierarchical data controls to selectively display information from related tables. You sometimes see references to the Expand control as the *Expando tool*.

- *Data Source* is an invisible object that provides the connection from an Access or client/server database to visible data-bound objects—text box, PivotTable, chart, spreadsheet, and Record Navigation controls—on DAP.

Tip #1 from

R J

If you're involved with data warehouses or marts and online analytical processing (*OLAP*), become a PivotTable expert. PivotTables are Microsoft's preferred method for displaying and manipulating DataCubes created by Microsoft OLAP Services for SQL Server, a component of Microsoft SQL Server 7.0. *DataCubes* are multidimensional views of aggregate (summarized) data in a nonrelational (hierarchical) format. In 1999 and beyond, you'll see the term *hierarchical* increasingly replace *relational* as data warehouse and their smaller siblings, data marts, gain ground among medium-size and even small enterprises.

You don't need a copy of Access to display DAP; Access 2000 saves DAP in .htm—not .mdb—files. Access displays DAP in Page view for convenience, but IE 5.0 is the primary DAP viewer.

Note

Users of DAP must have Office 2000 installed or have a license for Office 2000 to display DAP with OWC. If licensed users don't have Office 2000 installed, the cabinet (.cab) file containing the OWC must be available on the intranet site. A .cab file contains one or more compressed files, which automatically decompress upon installation on your PC. The first time the user opens a DAP, the `<CodeBase>` tag's content checks to see whether the OWC are installed locally. If not, IE 5.0 automatically downloads and installs the required files.

Test Drive a DAP

Office 2000 Custom Setup, described in the "Making the Initial Installation of Access 2000" section near the end of the chapter, installs a collection of sample DAP in your \Program Files\Microsoft Office\Office\Samples folder. To open the sample Analyze Sales page in IE 5.0, do the following:

1. Launch IE 5.0, and click Work Offline in the Dial-Up Connection dialog if you use a modem to connect to the Internet.

2. Choose File, Open and click Browse in the Open dialog. Navigate in the Microsoft Internet Explorer dialog to the \Program Files\Microsoft Office\Samples folder.

3. Double-click the Analyze Sales.htm item to return to the Open dialog and then click OK to close the Open dialog.

After a second or two needed to connect to the Northwind.mdb sample database and calculate the PivotTable values, the Analyze Sales page appears. The PivotTable's primary data source is the Orders table, which supplies the ShipCountry, ShipName, and OrderID values. The related Employees table supplies the LastName value for salespersons, and the Order Details table provides a calculated value for order subtotals.

To expand the display to show individual orders for customers by salesperson, the next lower level of the Orders hierarchy, click the boxed + symbol to the left of the customer's ShipName value (see Figure 1.1). You can collapse the Salesperson hierarchy by clicking the boxed – symbols to the left of the LastName value. Scrolling to the bottom of the page reveals the Grand Total row; PivotTables let you easily add subtotals and grand totals.

Figure 1.2 shows the sample Sales.htm page in Access Page view, the DAP equivalent of Form View for conventional access forms. Sales.htm is based on Northwind.mdb's Category table and calculates sales by product and category from the Products and Order Details tables. Access employs IE 5.0's XML parser, CSS, the Document Object Model (DOM), and the HTML rendering (layout) engine to display DAP. When you create your own DAP in Page Design mode, Access writes all the XML and HTML for you.

Figure 1.1
IE 5.0 displaying the sample Analyze Sales Data Access Page.

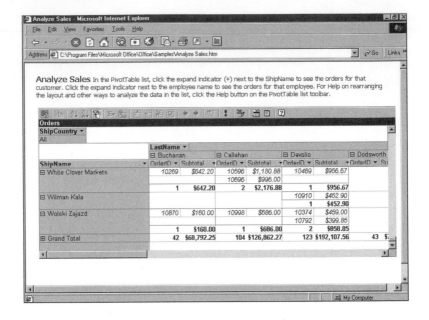

Figure 1.2
Access 2000 displaying the Sales.htm sample XML file in Page view.

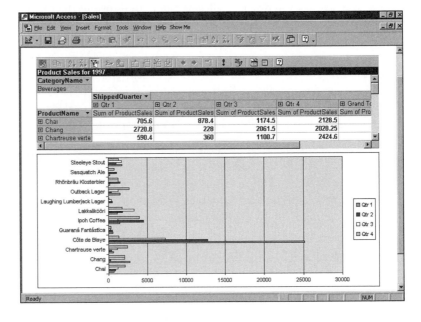

Note

Graphs and charts are the most effective method of summarizing data for management. This book distinguishes graphs, which use lines to represent values of dependent variables, from charts, which offer two- and three-dimensional representation of values. Most business-related graphs and charts have time as one of the axes; if time is on the x (horizontal) axis, the graph is called a *time series*.

Tip #2 from

Create simple DAP and analyze the resulting .htm files in a text editor, such as Notepad (called "Visual Notepad" by HTML authors) to learn XML structure and syntax. XML is one of the most important recent developments in Web technology and is particularly useful for displaying and manipulating complex query result sets. DAP also demonstrate Microsoft's CSS implementation of standard themes for Web pages that you generate with all Office 2000 members.

DAP DESIGN MODE

DAP Design mode differs considerably from conventional Access form design mode. The DAP toolbox contains a set of HTML controls that correspond to native Access controls—less the Bound and Unbound Object Frame, Subform/Subreport, and Tab controls—and adds Bound HTML, Scrolling Text, Bound Hyperlink, Hyperlink, and Hotspot Image controls. Positioning and sizing methods for DAP differ considerably from conventional form design procedures, and there's no Edit, Undo command in this first version of DAP. Creating sophisticated data-bound Web pages with Access 2000, however, is far faster and easier than with alternative platforms, such as FrontPage 2000, Visual Basic 6.0, or Visual InterDev 6.0.

CREATING ACCESS DATA PROJECTS FOR THE MICROSOFT DATA ENGINE

Microsoft wants a larger share of the client/server relational database management system (*RDBMS*) market. Thus Access 2000 includes the Microsoft Data Engine (*MSDE*), the embedded version of Microsoft SQL Server 7.0. MSDE runs under Windows 9x, as well as under Windows NT 4.0 and 2000 Workstation and Server. The differences between MSDE and SQL Server 7.0 for Windows NT Server are as follows:

- MSDE database files are limited to a maximum size of 2GB. SQL Server database files are limited by the amount of physical disk storage available.

- MSDE is fix-tuned for about six simultaneous users. SQL Server 7.0's auto-tuning feature optimizes performance for hundreds or, with the Enterprise Edition, thousands of connections.

- MSDE doesn't include SQL Server 7.0's Enterprise Manager database management tools, which run under Windows NT 4.0+ as a Microsoft Management Console snap-in. You create and modify databases with a subset of Enterprise Manager included with Access 2000. MSDE does include SQL Server's Data Transformation Service (DTS) for importing and exporting SQL Server data.

Tip #3 from	Microsoft says MSDE is suitable for small workgroups (five members or fewer) and that performance deteriorates as you add more simultaneous users. The actual number of simultaneous users MSDE supports primarily is a function of the PC resources (primarily RAM) available. A 233+MHz Pentium II with 128MB of RAM running Windows NT Workstation as a peer server is likely to provide more than adequate performance for 25 or more users running decision support applications.

Access Data Projects (*ADP*) let you connect conventional Access 2000 forms and reports directly to SQL Server 7.0/MSDE, substituting *OLE DB* and ActiveX Data Objects (*ADO*) for the Jet 4.0 database engine. OLE DB, which provides Common Object Model (*COM*) connectivity to Jet, client/server, and a variety of other data source types, is the primary element of Microsoft's new Universal Data Access (*UDA*) architecture. ADO 2.1, an Automation "wrapper" for OLE DB, lets Access forms, reports, pages, projects, and modules act as OLE DB data consumers. Like DAP, ADP have their own file structure and don't store objects in Access .mdb files; ADP use the Microsoft compound document file (DocFile) format with an .adp extension.

→ To learn how UDA, OLE DB, and ADO fit into Microsoft's picture of data access, **see** "Gaining a Perspective on Microsoft's New Data Access Components" **p. 1032**.

Note	Microsoft refers to ADP simply as *projects*. The term *project* is ambiguous in a database application development context; even creating a simple Jet database and a few application objects qualifies as a project. Thus this book uses *ADP*, the extension for project files, when referring to Access 2000 projects.

New ADP Tools and Objects

ADP introduce the following new tools and objects to Access users and developers:

- *Client Server Visual Design Tools* replace Access's Table Design view and Query Design view. These tools, often called by their code name, *da Vinci toolset*, are identical to those used by Visual Studio 6.0.

- *Views* replace Access select queries. Views are precompiled select queries with an important limitation—you can't use ORDER BY to sort a view. You can, however, sort the view within ADP.

- *Stored procedures* replace Access action and parameter queries. Stored procedures are precompiled queries, which may also include sorted select queries, similar to Jet QueryDef objects. For MSDE and SQL Server 6.5+, you write stored procedures in *Transact-SQL*, Microsoft's flavor of ANSI SQL.

- *Database diagrams* replace the Access Relationships window. Database diagrams are a special type of SQL Server object. You can use database diagrams to create and edit relationships between database tables, as well as to add, modify, or delete tables.

- *Data Links* specify the properties of the OLE DB/ADO connection between current Access application objects (forms, reports, pages, and modules).

- *Triggers* are stored procedures that fire when you append, delete, or update one or more tables. You write triggers in Transact-SQL.

EXPLORE THE NORTHWINDCS PROJECT AND DA VINCI TOOLSET

The NorthwindCS.adp sample project and the NorthwindCS.sql *script* (an SQL batch file) is included in your ...\Office\Samples folder.

Tip #4 from

Open the NorthwindCS.sql script in WordPad to gain insight into SQL scripts for creating tables and appending new records to the tables with Transact SQL. (The script is much too large for Notepad.) Image data for the Photo field of the Employees table and the Picture field of the Categories table appears as strings of hexadecimal (0x) byte values. SQL Server doesn't support Access's OLE Object field data type, so images are stored in their native binary (.bmp/.dib bitmap) format. Don't save any accidental changes you make to the script when exiting WordPad.

To give ADP and the da Vinci toolset a trial run, do the following:

1. Install and start MSDE, as described in the "Installing and Configuring the Microsoft Data Engine" section near the end of this chapter.

2. In Access, choose File, Open and double-click NorthwindCS.adp. The Open dialog closes, and a message box asks whether you want to install the sample database.

3. Click Yes to create the NorthwindCS database on your local MSDE server from the NorthwindCS.sql script. Creating the database takes about a minute on a fast PC.

4. Click OK to close the Northwind Traders splash screen.

5. In the Database window, open an existing table or view. Datasheet view is almost identical to that of Access. ADP add two record navigation buttons, an "x" button that turns red while the data sheet is loading, and a maximum records button that opens a slider to set the maximum number of records returned to the datasheet (see Figure 1.3). The default Max Records value is 10,000.

 6. Open the Orders table in Design view. The da Vinci table design view differs greatly from Access's version for Jet databases or tables attached to Jet, as is evident in Figure 1.4.

Figure 1.3
The Orders table of the MSDE NorthwindCS sample database in Datasheet view.

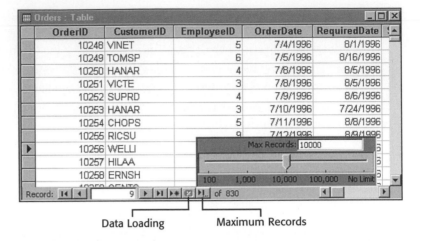

Figure 1.4
The Client Server Visual Design (da Vinci) Tool for tables.

The `identity` attribute of an MSDE/SQL Server primary key field (OrderID in this case) replaces Jet's AutoNumber (formerly Counter) field data type. You can easily set the first value (`seed`, 1 by default) and incremental value (`increment` attribute, also 1 by default.) Only `identity` fields accept `seed` and `increment` values. The `IsRowGUID` attribute indicates that the field contains an automatically generated Globally Unique Identifier (*GUID*, pronounced "goo-id"), which is used primarily to identify rows for replication. The Allow Nulls constraint is the inverse of Jet's Required field property.

7. Open the Order Details Extended view in Design mode and make sure the three view buttons—Diagram, Grid, and SQL—of the toolbar are on (depressed). The da Vinci view designer, which emulates a combination of Access's Query Design and SQL views, appears as shown in Figure 1.5

Passing the mouse over the join symbol displays INNER JOIN: Products.ProductID = [Order Details].ProductID. Right-clicking the join symbol and selecting Properties opens the Properties sheet for the join, which lets you specify RIGHT or LEFT OUTER JOINs.

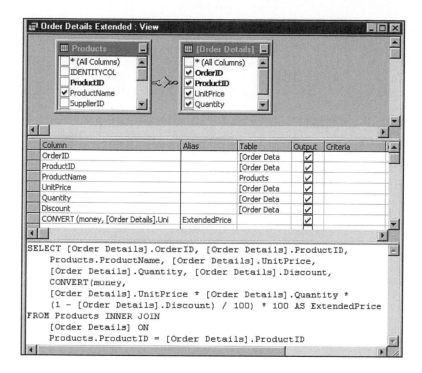

Figure 1.5
The da Vinci view design tool displaying the field lists, join line, column properties, and SQL statement for the Order Details Extended view.

8. Click the Database Diagram shortcut in the Database window and double-click the Relationships shortcut to open the da Vinci Relationships: Diagram window, which offers Design mode only (see Figure 1.6).

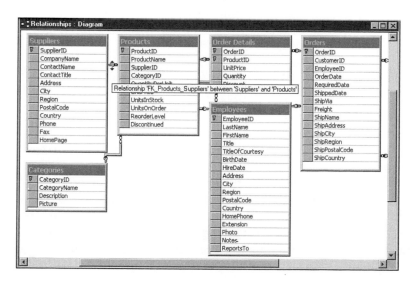

Figure 1.6
The da Vinci database diagram tool displaying the Relationships diagram for the NorthwindCS database.

Tip #5 from

Database diagrams express joins as foreign key (FK) and primary key (PK) CHECK (CK) constraints because the default method of maintaining referential integrity (*RI*) of SQL Server databases is declarative referential integrity (*DRI*). SQL Server 7.0/MSDE doesn't support Jet cascading deletions and updates with DRI. Triggers, which maintain RI of MSDE tables with cascading deletions or updates, are the alternative to DRI.

9. Right-click a join symbol and choose Properties to open the much more complete Properties sheet. Figure 1.7 shows the tabbed dialog of the database diagram for join and table constraints.

Figure 1.7
The Tables page of the Properties sheet for a constraint on the UnitPrice field of the Products table.

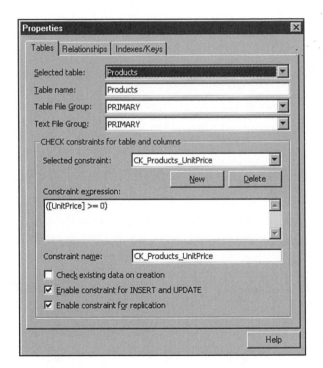

10. Select the Database window's Stored Procedures shortcut and open the Sales by Year parameterized procedure in Design mode. Figure 1.8 shows the da Vinci stored procedure editing window with the Transact-SQL statement for the procedure reformatted for legibility. Like the VBA Editor, the da Vinci editor uses blue for Transact-SQL reserved words. Data types (datetime) appear in green; keywords in WHERE clause constraints (Not Null, And, and Between) in olive; and alias names (Year) in red. These values are defaults; you can change the colors in the Editor Format page of the VBA Editor's Options dialog. The VBA Editor is the subject of the next section, "Integrating the Office VBA Editor with Access."

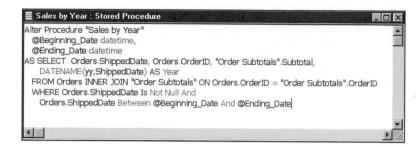

Figure 1.8
The Sales by Year parameterized stored procedure in the da Vinci editing window.

The ALTER PROCEDURE command is new in SQL Server 7.0/MSDE Transact SQL, as are ALTER VIEW and ALTER TABLE. When you create a new stored procedure, the da Vinci editor supplies a CREATE PROCEDURE stub of dubious usefulness.

11. Return to the Database window and click the Tables shortcut of the Object bar. Right-click a table, such as Order Details, and choose Triggers from the context menu to open the Triggers for Table: Order Details dialog. Click New to open the da Vinci Orders_Trigger1 : Trigger editing window. The window opens with a trigger stub that's a bit more useful than that for a new stored procedure (see Figure 1.9).

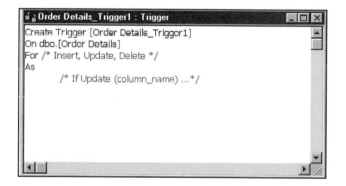

Figure 1.9
The da Vinci Editor window for writing a new trigger on the Order Details table.

You must have a working knowledge of Transact SQL to write INSERT, DELETE, or UPDATE triggers to maintain referential integrity or perform other actions when modifying a table's data.

Fortunately, the new Access Upsizing Wizard (*AUW*) handles with aplomb conversion of tables and most simple queries from Jet to SQL Server. During the upsizing process, the Wizard lets you choose to move your Access 2000 application objects to ADP or retain them in an .mdb file. Unfortunately, the Access 2000 AUW doesn't support prior releases of Access. Even more unfortunately, the current Access 97 and earlier Upsizing Wizards don't support SQL Server 7.0/MSDE.

→ For information on the limitations of the AUW, **see** "Using the Upsizing Wizard to Create ADP," **p. 969**.

Note

ADP introduce an additional .ade file type to prevent others from opening your objects in Design view, reading your VBA source code, and importing or exporting forms. The .ade file type is the ADP analog of .mde files. Microsoft states that Access 2000 .ade files won't run in future versions. You can save your project in .ade format by choosing Tools, Database Utilities, Make ADE File.

INTEGRATING THE OFFICE VBA EDITOR WITH ACCESS

Access is the last VBA-supporting member of Office to gain the questionable benefits of the VBA IDE, as mentioned at the beginning of this chapter. (Visual Basic 6.0 still hasn't adopted the VBA IDE). Unlike the VBA and Access Basic editors of prior versions with their integrated Editor window, the VBA Editor is a separate application whose window opens when you open a module. Figure 1.10 shows the VBA Editor with all windows except the Object Browser open and docked. By default, the VBA Editor docks all windows except the Object Browser. The Immediate window takes the place of the Debug window of Access 97 and earlier.

Figure 1.10
The VBA Editor window displaying the first few lines of code in the Declarations section of NorthwindCS's Startup module.

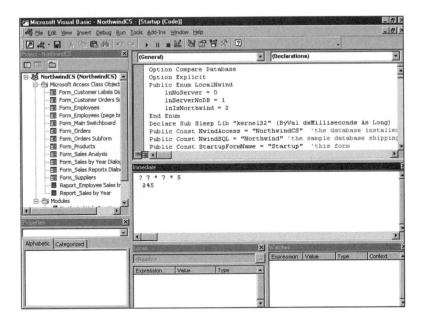

To check out the new VBA Editor, do the following:

1. Click the Modules shortcut of the Objects list and double-click a module, such as the Startup module of NorthwindCS.adp, to open the VBA Editor.

2. Choose Tools, Options to open the tabbed Options dialog, which lets you customize the VBA Editor. The Docking page has check boxes that you can clear if you don't like docked windows.

3. Press Alt+Q or choose File, Close and Return to Microsoft Access to get out of the VBA Editor.

→ To learn about the new features of the VBA Editor, **see** "Exploring the VBA Editor," **p. 1018**.

Tip #6 from	Check out the VBA code of NorthwindCS.adp's Startup module. It's a good example of VBA power programming. Access developers will find the code useful when providing clients with applications that require creation of new databases upon initial installation.

WORKING WITH THE HTML SOURCE EDITOR FOR DAP AND DHTML

Dynamic HTML (DHTML) combines CSS, the DOM, and a browser-compliant scripting language. DHTML lets you minimize round trips to the server to make simple Web page modifications, such as changing the color of a block of text when the reader passes the mouse pointer over the region. You don't need to write scripts to create DAP, but adding JavaScript (JScript in Microsoft parlance) or VBScript to DAP offer increased versatility for your DAP designs.

Note

Netscape's JavaScript, which has only a tenuous relationship to the Java programming language, runs in both Navigator/Communicator and IE browsers. Only IE supports VBScript, a scaled-down version of VBA. DAP is an intranet-only technology because of the IE 5.0 requirement, so you can safely use VBScript with DAP. VBScript lets you leverage your VBA skills in DHTML page development.

Like the VBA Editor, the new HTML Source Editor, part of the Microsoft Development Environment, is a separate application that you open from Page Design view with the View, HTML Source command. Figure 1.11 shows the first few lines of XML code of the View Products page of the Northwind sample database in the color-enhanced HTML Source Editor window.

Note

Installation of the HTML Source Editor isn't an Access setup option, so you're likely to encounter the Windows Installer's message that you must set up the HTML Source Editor from the Office 2000 distribution CD-ROM or a network share.

Figure 1.11
The HTML Source Editor displaying namespace and CSS definitions for Northwind.mdb's View Products page.

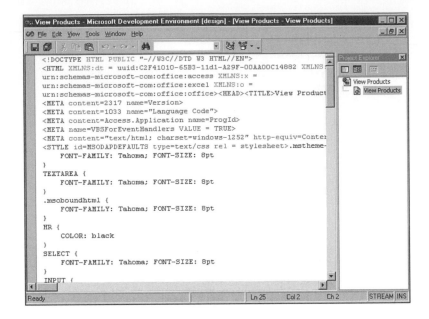

VIEWING AND EDITING RELATED RECORDS IN SUBDATASHEETS

Subdatasheets are a new Access 2000 feature that let you view and edit related records of Jet tables or queries within a single datasheet. For tables, the subdatasheet uses Relationships window data to determine the subordinate records to display; a subdatasheet based on a query uses join information. Clicking the boxed + symbol opens the first-tier subdatasheet; if more tiers of data exist, you can open nested subdatasheets. Figure 1.12 shows Northwind.mdb's Customers tables with related Order Details records nested within the Orders subdatasheet.

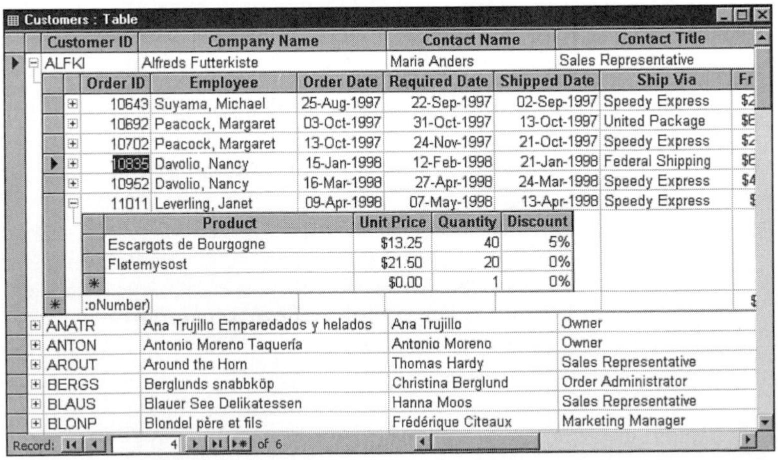

Figure 1.12
Northwind's Customers table displaying related Orders and Order Details records in nested sub-datasheets.

Datasheet view defaults to automatic subdatasheets for related tables. You can disable sub-datasheets by right-clicking the Table Design window, choosing Properties, and setting in the Properties sheet the Subdatasheet Name property value to [None].

CONFORMING JET AND SQL SERVER 7.0/MSDE DATABASES

The Jet .mdb file structure has changed for the fifth time. Access 2000's Jet 4.0 .mdb file structure isn't backward-compatible with Access 97, 95, or 2.0 .mdb files. The requirement that Jet be easily interchangeable with SQL Server 7.0 databases, as well as accommodate new ADP objects in DocFiles, made changes to the Jet 4.0 database structure inevitable.

You can open a database created with a prior version in Access 2000, but you can't open an Access 2000 database in an earlier version. You can't change in Access 2000 the properties of database objects created with prior versions of Access; you must convert the file to Jet 4.0 format to make Design mode changes.

Fortunately, you can *link* (a newer term for *attach*) Access 1.x, 2.0, 95, or 97 tables to Access 2000 applications. You can accommodate simultaneous links to tables in all prior-version .mdb files by database front-end applications created with Access 2000. Unlike most prior versions of Access, Access 2000 can save .mdb files in a prior (Access 97) format.

Additional new Jet and SQL Server 7.0/MSDE features are

- *Record-level (row-level) locking* eliminates the page locks that occur when you update tables. Both Access and SQL Server 7.0 now have 4KB pages (up from 2KB). SQL Server 6.5 offered row-level locking for INSERT operations. Both RDBMSs now provide row-level locking on INSERT, UPDATE, and DELETE.

- *Unicode* support for character and text fields eliminates the need to specify code pages for Eastern European and the *double-byte character sets (DBCS)* used for Asian languages. Dual-font support lets you specify an alternative set of characters that aren't included in the primary font. You select a Substitution Font in the General Page of Access's Options dialog. Unicode requires two bytes for characters in any font, so Jet 4.0 includes Unicode compression to minimize the increase in file size.

- *Decimal* is a new Jet 4.0 data type that emulates the decimal datatype of SQL Server 7.0/MSDE. You specify the Precision property, which determines the total number of digits of the field, and the Scale property, which sets the number of digits to the right of the decimal point. Jet 4.0's default values are Precision = 18 and Scale = 0.

- *Auto-Compact on Close* is an optional Jet 4.0 feature that automatically compacts—and repairs, if necessary—the .mdb file when you close the database. You specify auto-compact in the General page of the Access Options dialog. This feature attempts to emulate the auto-contract feature of SQL Server 7.0/MSDE databases. SQL Server 7.0's new file-system databases automatically grow or shrink as you add or delete records and other objects.

One of the primary incentives for moving to row-level locking in Jet and SQL Server 7.0/MSDE databases is the doubled page size required to maintain performance with Unicode text equivalent to that for prior versions' single-byte character fields. Vendors of enterprise client/server software, such as SAP and PeopleSoft, need row-level locking to minimize update contention in heavily used online transaction processing (*OLTP*) systems. Row-level locking is the default for Jet and MSDE. You can turn off Jet's record-level locking in the Advanced page of the Access Options dialog.

GIVING ACCESS A YEAR 2000 FACELIFT

Many of the new features of Access 2000 are cosmetic and have little, if any, affect on the everyday lives of Access users and developers. Some features appear to be intended solely to expand the "new features list" that accompanies every upgrade of every publishers' productivity software. The following sections describe new Access 2000 features that are of lesser significance.

FOUR-DIGIT YEAR OPTION SETTINGS

NEW 2000 Microsoft has added Year 2000 (Y2K) compliance features to all Office 2000 applications. The General Page of Access 2000's Options dialog, which you open by choosing Tools, Options, has a new Use Four-Digit Year Formatting frame with two check boxes—This Database and All Databases (see Figure 1.13). Marking either check box changes Date/Time field formatting as shown in Table 1.1. Long Date and Time formats don't change; the formatting shown in the Access 2000 Default column is based on the standard Windows Short Date format, m/d/yy.

Figure 1.13
Access 2000's new General Page of the Options dialog with added Four-Digit Year Formatting options.

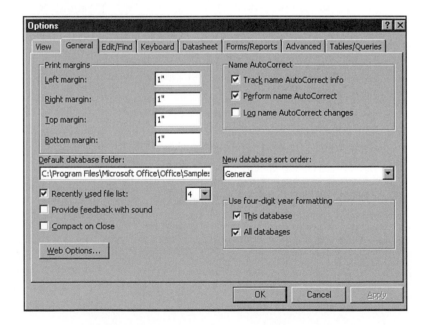

TABLE 1.1   A COMPARISON OF ACCESS 2000 DEFAULT AND FOUR-DIGIT YEAR FORMATTING

Date/Time Format	Access 2000 Default	With Four-Digit Year
General Date (default)	1/15/99 10:10 AM	1/15/1999 10:10 AM
Short Date	1/15/99	1/15/1999
Long Date	Friday January 15, 1999	Friday January 15, 1999
Medium Date	15-Jan-99	15-Jan-1999
Medium Time	10:10 AM	10:10 AM
mm/dd/yy	01/15/99	01/15/1999

Marking the This Database check box sets a flag in the current database, so the formatting changes apply only to the current database. Marking the All Databases check box adds a Registry entry to `HKEY_CURRENT_USER\Software\Microsoft\Office\9.0\Access\Settings`, so opening any database forces four-digit year formatting. In VBA code, you use the `Application.SetOption` method with `Four-Digit Year Formatting` for the database-level option and/or `Four-Digit Year Formatting All Databases` argument for the user-level option. Values are **True** and **False** to set or clear the option(s).

Tip #7 from

Access's Short Date (m/d/yy and mm/dd/yy) formats for the English (United States) locale default to two-digit years unless you change the default date format of Windows or set the Four-Digit Year Formatting option(s). Two-digit year presentation isn't Y2K compliant. To make the Windows short date format Y2K compliant for most applications, open Control Panel's Regional Settings tool, click the Date tab, and change the Short Date style from M/d/yy to M/d/yyyy. The new version of the Northwind sample database has fixed-format (dd-mmm-yyyy) dates in all Date/Time fields. Prior versions of Northwind.mdb use the default Medium Date format (dd-mmm-yy) for Date/Time fields.

THE DATABASE WINDOW

The Database window sports the following added features:

- *Objects bar* emulates Microsoft Outlook's left pane with a collection of shortcuts to display lists of Access objects appropriate to the type of file you open (.mdb or .adp).

- *Object shortcuts* offer you the opportunity to create new objects in Design view, by using a wizard (if available) or by entering data (tables only). You can remove object shortcuts from the list by clearing the New Object Shortcuts check box in the Views page of the Options dialog.

- *Database window toolbar* lets you open objects in normal or Design view, create a new object of the selected type, delete an object, and change how icons display in the object list.

■ *Groups* let you add shortcuts to provide quick access to commonly used objects in your database. Right-click the Database window's title bar and choose New Group to add a group with a name of your choosing. Drag items from the object list to the group shortcut to create a collection. Unfortunately, you can't delete the Favorites group.

Tip #8 from	A group lets you collect all objects for an Access application into a single group, which
	eliminates the need to select objects by type in the Objects bar.

■ *Keyboard object selection* lets you type the first few letters of an object in the list to select it and then press Enter to open the object. If you prefer typing to mousing and you have a large number of objects in the list, you'll like this new feature.

Figure 1.14 shows the Access 2000 Database window with callouts for newly added elements.

Figure 1.14
New features of the Access 2000 Database window.

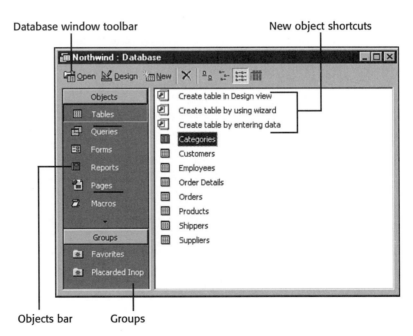

FORMS AND REPORTS

Forms and reports get comparatively short shrift from Microsoft in the new features department. Here's a list of the new form and report features:

■ *Object Grouping* with the Format menu's Group command lets you combine selected controls into a group. The Group and Ungroup commands behave similarly to the grouping operations of diagramming applications such as Visio.

- *Conditional Formatting*, another Format menu choice, opens a dialog that lets you change the font attributes of labels, text boxes, and other controls based on the control's Value property.

- *Subdatasheets in subforms* let you display lower levels of one-to-many relationships in datasheet-style subforms.

- *In-situ subform* editing enables simultaneous Design mode editing of forms and subforms. The Design view of the subform appears within the region you assign to the Subform view in Run mode.

- *Control grouping* lets you define groups of controls that you can relocate as a single element.

- *Properties window in run mode* lets you alter many form and report property values without changing to design view. This feature is a time-saver for Access developers.

- *Justified and Vertical Alignment options* for labels improve the appearance of forms and reports.

 - *Movie tool* lets you add the Windows Media Player to forms and play .asf (ActiveX Streaming Format) and .avi (Audio-Video Interleaved) files to entertain users of your applications. Apparently, Microsoft's idea is to provide easy access to training videos for Access applications.

- *Added graphics formats* accept Web-standard .gif and .jpg files, plus additional graphics file formats, as background images for forms.

- *Read-write access to the* Recordset *property* of a form or report with VBA code is a feature Access developers have requested since version 1.0. You can assign a Recordset you create in a module to a form or report, and manipulate the Recordset of a form or report with code.

Note

Microsoft claims that Report Snapshots are a new Access 2000 feature, but Microsoft released Report Snapshots as a 1997 add-on to Access 97. Report Snapshots (.snp files) let users without Access open reports in their copy of Snapshot Viewer. You save Reports in .snp format by right-clicking the report in the Database window, choosing Export, and selecting Snapshot Format (.snp) in the Save as Type list. The ability to print the Relationships window now is a built-in feature of Access 2000, instead of an add-in.

NAME AUTOCORRECT

Changing the name of an Access object in an application of only moderate complexity leads to a cascade of unresolved references and error messages. Third-party add-ins (notably SpeedFerret) have given much-needed aid to Access developers who decide to change object names midway through a database project. Microsoft now includes Name AutoCorrect as a standard feature of Access 2000. Name AutoCorrect is enabled by default.

Name AutoCorrect doesn't fix the following:

- SQL statements with incorrect references
- Any name changes in ADP or replicated databases
- Linked table name changes in the back-end database
- Menu and toolbar macros referring to renamed objects
- References in VBA code, other than changes to the name of the containing form

If you want to cancel your insurance on object name changes, clear the check boxes in the Name AutoCorrect frame of the Option dialog's General page.

OFFICE 2000-RELATED ENHANCEMENTS OR IMPEDIMENTS

The following sections describe new features common to the major members of the Office 2000 Professional and Premium versions. There is considerable controversy concerning the value of these elements to Access users and developers.

SYNTHETIC SINGLE-DOCUMENT INTERFACE

Access's new single-document interface (*SDI*) emulation fills your taskbar with icons for open access objects. Access is a classic Windows multiple-document interface (*MDI*) application. MDI applications have a single *parent window* (the main Access window) with menus and toolbars. All other MDI windows are called *child windows*; child windows can be maximized, minimized, tiled, and cascaded. Child windows don't have menus but can have their own toolbars.

SDI applications, which Microsoft made the "standard" in Windows 95 and later, open as a single conventional Window. SDI emulation is quite useful when you're working with multiple Word documents and Excel workbooks because you can change quickly from one to the other with Alt+Tab. Most users, however, find Access's SDI emulation to be a pain. Fortunately, you can turn off this impediment by clearing the Windows in Taskbar check box of the Option dialog's View page.

INTELLIMENUS

The Intellimenu feature is one of the most dubious additions to Office 2000. The idea behind Intellimenus appears to be displaying only those menu choices that the least intelligent Office users require for their daily chores. To view all available menu choices, you must expand the drop-down menu by clicking the inverted corporal's stripes (chevrons) at the bottom of the menu.

Access is purported to remember your menu-choice history and prominently display your most frequently used selections. All Office members appear to have a well-developed case of the menu-choice variant of Alzheimer's disease.

HTML HELP

HTML help uses compressed HTML files with the .chm extension that replace conventional Windows .hlp files. The primary beneficiary of HTML help is Microsoft, who now can publish the Help files for applications on the www.microsoft.com site without translating from the conventional Windows Help format. Secondary beneficiaries are book publishers and authors whose sales are aided by the arcane organization and searching features of the Access 2000 implementation of HTML help.

The Access Answer Wizard often appears to use a random-walk approach to selecting topics in response to your entries in the What Do You Want to Do? text box. Typing **I want to go back to .hlp files** and clicking Search elicits the set of Wizard answers shown in Figure 1.15. You must convert your Access 2000 application to Access 97 to fulfill your wish.

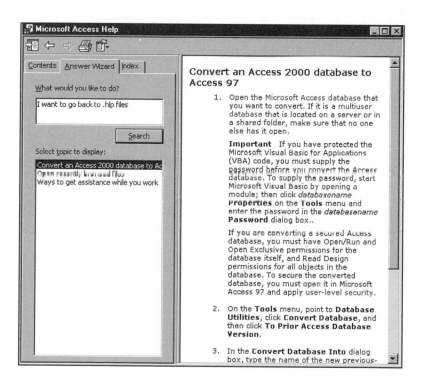

Figure 1.15
The Answer Wizard's response to a request to return to old-style Windows online help.

ONLINE COLLABORATION

"Collaborative computing" is another buzzword of the late 1990s, derived from the work-group collaboration theory of corporate reengineering gurus. Online collaboration, in the form of threaded "Web Discussions" requires installing the Office Web Server to create a "discussion server" that uses SQL Server 7.0/MSDE to maintain order. Both Word 2000 and Excel 2000 offer Web Discussions as a Tools, Online Collaboration menu choice.

Access 2000 doesn't offer Web Discussions, but the Tools, Online Collaboration, Meet Now choice opens a Microsoft NetMeeting dialog that you fill in to set up a new meeting. If you start a NetMeeting session from Design view of an object, other participants can manipulate objects from a remote location. You can learn more about the NetMeeting process by typing **Online Collaboration** in the What Do You Want to Do? text box and double-clicking the About Online Meetings topic.

Tip #9 from	Make sure you back up your database before letting other NetMeeting participants remotely hack your object designs or VBA code. When you permit others to modify your designs, your local mouse pointer becomes inoperative.

INSTALLING ACCESS 2000

Office 2000 Professional Edition includes a redesigned Setup program for installing the individual members of Office 2000, as well as common files used by all member applications. If you select the Typical setup option, many files that you need to take full advantage of Access 2000's features aren't installed. The following sections describe the setup process and how to use the Custom installation to copy the additional files required to gain maximum benefit from this book.

Each version of Office increases fixed disk storage requirements. You should have at least 300MB of free disk space before making a new installation of Office 2000 Professional Edition. The program files occupy about 130MB to 150MB, depending on the installation options you select. If you're updating an Office 97 installation, Office 2000 program files consume an additional 30MB to 50MB, depending on the Office 97 options you installed. You should have at least 50MB of free disk space remaining for data files and documents.

Tip #10 from _R J_	Use the Installer to customize a standard Office 2000 installation. If you've already installed Office 2000 with the default setup options, use Control Panel's Add/Remove Programs tool to rerun your local copy of Office 2000's Setup.exe in Custom setup mode. You need the Office 2000 distribution CD-ROMs or a connection to a networked Office 2000 installation folder to add required files to your local drive.

MAKING AN INITIAL INSTALLATION OF ACCESS 2000

The following steps describe how to install to Windows 9x the Access 2000 components from the Office 2000 distribution CD-ROM, either as a new installation or as an upgrade to a prior version of Office, by using the Custom Setup option:

1. Close all running applications and insert the Office CD1 CD-ROM into your CD-ROM drive. Autoplay starts the installation process, and—after a brief interval—the Welcome to Microsoft Office 2000 dialog appears.

2. Complete the form, including the CD Key (see Figure 1.16). Click Next.

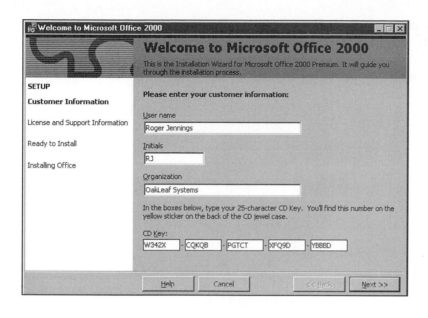

Figure 1.16
Filling in the fields of
the Welcome to
Microsoft Office 2000
dialog.

3. Read the End-User License Agreement (EULA), select the I Accept the Terms of This License Agreement option, and click Next.

4. In the Ready to Install dialog (see Figure 1.17), click the Customize button, which lets you select from a wide range of installation options.

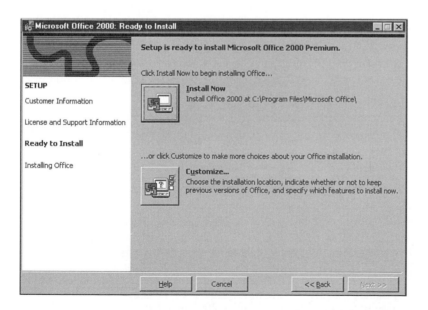

Figure 1.17
The Ready to Install
dialog for choosing
the type of Office
installation.

5. Accept the default C:\Program Files\Microsoft Office folder for installation in the Installation Location dialog (see Figure 1.18) unless you have a good reason to do otherwise, such as preserving your current Office 97 installation. Standard installation requires about 300MB of available disk space. Click Next.

Figure 1.18
Accepting the default location for Office 2000 in the Installation Location dialog.

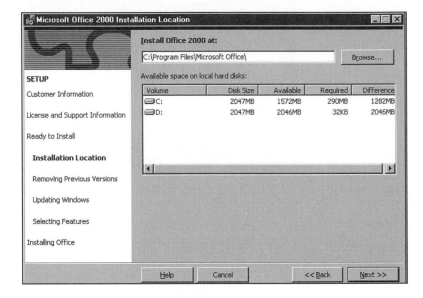

6. Select installation options for Microsoft Word, Excel, PowerPoint, and Outlook by clicking the Disk icon and selecting the installation method from the context menu.

7. In the Select Features dialog, click the + box to expand the Microsoft Access for Windows node. Figure 1.19 shows the standard installation options for Access 2000. Many Access features default to Install on First Use (yellow numeral 1) or don't install (red X).

8. To minimize the inconvenience of inserting distribution CD1 to upgrade your Office installation as you progress through this book, click the Microsoft Access for Windows node and select Run All from My Computer from the context menu. Your Select Features dialog appears as shown in Figure 1.20. Installing all the optional components consumes an additional 25MB of disk space.

Tip #11 from

R J

If you selectively add Access options, you must Select the Northwind SQL Project item and choose Run from My Computer to obtain the files necessary for the examples in Chapter 25, "Creating Access Data Projects." Otherwise, setup doesn't install the two NorthwindCS files.

9. Choose installation options for the other Office 2000 members and then click Install Now to begin the setup process.

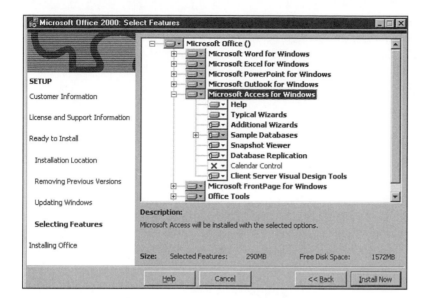

Figure 1.19
Default installation options for Access 2000.

Figure 1.20
The result of specifying that all Access-related components be installed to run from your PC.

10. After a few minutes of frenzied disk activity, a message box appears requesting you to restart your computer. Click Yes.

After restarting, an "Updating system setting" message appears for a minute or two, followed by a "Finishing Microsoft Office 2000 setup" message. The progress indicator cycles several times and then you receive a "Setup succeeded" message. If you have a sound card, the Windows Sound .wav file plays. At this point you're ready to use Access 2000 and the other Office 2000 members. The setup process also installs IE 5.0, which is required for creating DAP and ADP.

Note

There are no material differences in the initial installation of Access 2000 to a PC running Windows NT 4.0 or 2000.

CUSTOMIZING ACCESS 2000

Earlier sections of this chapter contain many references to the Options dialog that let you set global properties for your Access 2000 installation and some database-specific properties. To open the tabbed Option dialog, choose Tools, Options. You must have a database or project open to enable the Options choice. There are many Access 2000 changes to the Options dialog of Access 97 and prior versions.

Following is a brief description of the function of each Option dialog page that changes significantly in Access 2000:

- *View*, shown in Figure 1.21, lets you specify which objects appear in the Database window, taskbar, and Macro Design view. You also can specify single-click opening of objects in the Database window's list and specify a Unicode Substitution Font.

Figure 1.21
The View page of the new Options dialog.

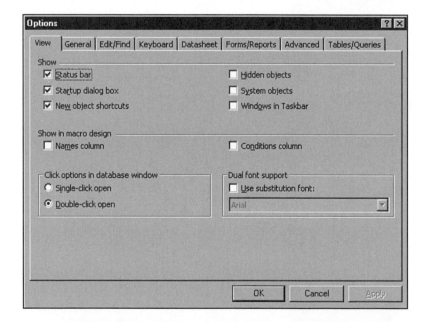

- *General* sets the default print margins, database folder, and sort order. You also can specify automatic Compact on Close and, Name AutoCorrect off or on, and set the Four-Digit Year Formatting options discussed earlier in the chapter. Clicking Web Options opens a simple dialog to select the color and style of hyperlinks.

Tip #12 from

RJ

Set your default database folder to C:\Program Files\Microsoft Office\Office\Samples to minimize the time it takes to navigate from C:\My Documents to the folder containing the Northwind.mdb sample database. Most of the sample projects in this book use the Northwind.mdb database.

Note

The HTML options of Access 97's Hyperlink/HTML Options page are missing in Access 2000. The omission of HTML Template, Data Source Information, and Active Server Pages Output frames reflects Microsoft's insistence that you move to DAP for Web-based Access 2000 applications. This issue is discussed in the "Deploying Data Access Pages with Office Web Components" section earlier in the chapter. Microsoft chose not to fix the security problems with ASP created from Access 97 forms using ControlPad, which made these .asp files of very limited usefulness with IE 4+ browsers.

- *Edit/Find* sets global find/replace and warning behavior, plus database-specific Filter by Form settings.

- *Advanced* sets global DDE, ODBC, database opening mode, and default record-locking options. ODBC options don't apply to OLE DB connections; you set connections to data providers in the Data Link Properties dialog. The new addition is the Open Databases Using Record-Level Locking check box. Access 97's Current Database Only and Error Trapping frames are missing because conditional compilation and error trapping now are elements of the Options dialog of the VBA Editor.

INSTALLING AND CONFIGURING THE MICROSOFT DATA ENGINE

Installation of MSDE isn't integrated with the Office 2000 Setup application, because MSDE uses the SQL Server 7.0 installer. Installing MSDE requires a minimum of about 55MB of free disk space, and you should have at least 100MB of free space to provide 45MB or more for the SQL Server data and log files you add.

1. With the Office 2000 distribution CD1 installed, navigate to the \Sql\X86\Setup folder and double-click the Setupsql.exe item to launch the MSDE Welcome dialog.

   If you're installing MSDE on Windows NT Workstation, you have the option of remote or local installation of MSDE prior to opening of the Welcome dialog.

2. Click Next to open the User Information dialog. Accept the default Name and Company entries from your prior Office 2000 installation unless you have a reason to make changes.

3. Click Next to display the Setup Type dialog (see Figure 1.22). You can install the SQL Server operating files (about 25MB) and data files (about 20MB) on any local logical drive you choose; click the Browse button(s) to select a different drive, folder, or both. If you have sufficient space on your C:\ drive, accept the defaults.

Figure 1.22
Specifying the location of MSDE operating and data files.

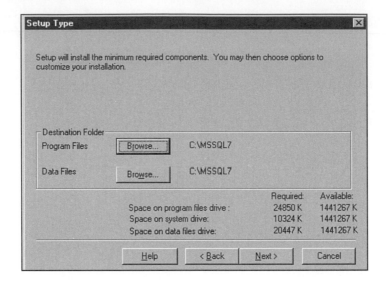

4. Click Next to open the Character Set/Sort Order/Unicode Collation dialog (see Figure 1.23). The 1252/ISO Character Set is the standard for the Americas and Western European countries, dictionary order (case-insensitive) is the most common non-Unicode sort order, and General Unicode is the appropriate locale for US English and many other languages (click Help for a General Unicode language list.) UK English, French, Spanish Modern, and Portuguese locales are available for Canada, Mexico, and the South American countries. Accept the default Unicode collation selection Case-insensitive, Width-insensitive, and Kana-insensitive.

Figure 1.23
Setting sort order for non-Unicode and collation order for Unicode text fields.

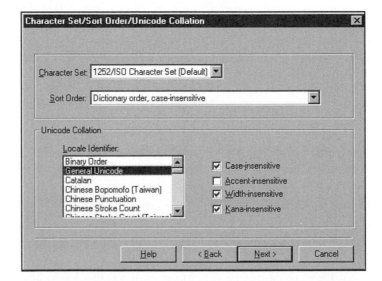

5. Click Next to show the Network Libraries dialog (see Figure 1.24). TCP/IP Sockets is the standard communication protocol, and Port 1433 is the default port for SQL Server 7.0.

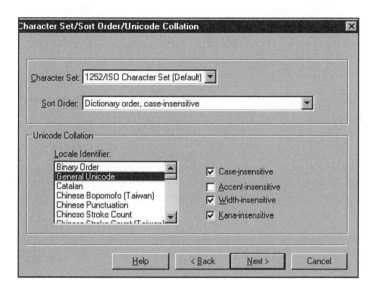

Figure 1.24
Specifying in Windows 9x the Network Libraries used to connect to remote MSDE and SQL Server installations.

Note

Windows 9x doesn't support Named Pipes; if you're installing on Windows NT 4+ Workstation, you can add the Named Protocol if necessary. If you plan to share your MSDE databases with other members of a workgroup connected by NetWare, mark the NWLink IPX/SPX check box and enter the name of the server providing the Novell Bindery service.

6. Click Next to open the Start Copying Files dialog; then click Next again to begin the MSDE installation process. After a couple of minutes, the Setup Complete dialog appears. Click Finish to complete the setup process.

When installing under Windows NT Workstation or Server if the Services Accounts dialog opens prior to the Start Copying Files dialog, accept the defaults, and click Next.

Note

Unlike other versions of SQL Server 7.0, MSDE setup doesn't provide sample files, such as `pubs` or `Northwind`. Setup installs system databases (`master`, `model`, `msdbdata`, and `Tempdb`) and their logs in the \Sql\Data folder.

Installing MSDE adds an Msde item to the Start, Programs menu with the following choices:

- *Client Configuration* lets you change the default network library and server aliases for your PC only.

- *Import and Export* starts the Data Transformation Services Wizard for importing and exporting data. You can use the Wizard to copy data from your Jet .mdb files to MSDE databases or export tables to .mdb files.

- *Server Network Utility* lets you add or remove network libraries (protocols) for your local MSDE installation. You also can check the version and date of each SQL Server protocol stack on your PC.

- *Service Manager* starts and stops MSDE. Stopping MSDE saves PC resources when you aren't using MSDE.

- *Uninstall MSDE* removes your local copy of SQL Server 7.0 operating files from your PC, but doesn't delete any database or log files you've added to the \Sql\Data folder.

Tip #13 from

To uninstall MSDE from a PC running Windows 9x, you must first delete the SQL Server shortcut from the \Windows\Start Menu\Programs\Startup folder and then reboot to remove the SQL Server Service Manager icon from the taskbar.

By default, the MSDE service doesn't start automatically under Windows 9x. If you're a regular user of MSDE or are sharing your MSDE databases on a network, it's a good practice to start MSDE during the startup process. To start MSDE and set it to start when Windows 9x starts, do the following:

1. Choose Start, Programs, Msde, Service Manager to open SQL Server Service Manager's window (see Figure 1.25, left).

Figure 1.25
SQL Server Service Manager's status for a stopped (left) and started (right) MSDE server.

2. Click Start/Continue to start MSDE. After a few seconds of disk activity, the SQL Server icon status symbol changes from a red square to a green arrow, and the Pause and Stop buttons are enabled.

3. Mark the Auto-start Service When OS Starts check box to start MSDE during the Windows 9x startup process (refer to Figure 1.25, right).

4. Close SQL Server Service Manager and then restart your computer to verify that MSDE starts automatically.

Tip #14 from

In the unlikely event you need to auto-start the Microsoft Distributed Transaction Coordinator (MSDTC), the SQL Server Agent (SQLServerAgent), or both, open the Services list in SQL Server Service Manager, select the service you want to auto-start, and mark the Auto-start Service When OS Starts check box. Be sure to select MSSQLServer in the Service list before exiting SQL Server Service Manager.

After you start MSDE, a miniature version of SQL Server Service Manager icon appears to the extreme right of your taskbar tray. If you've specified MSDE auto-start, the icon displays a small green arrow. If you don't auto-start MSDE, you must double-click the taskbar icon to open SQL Server Service Manager and then click Start.

IN THE REAL WORLD—WHY UPGRADE?

Note

At the end of each chapter of this book is an "In the Real World" section. The objective of these sections is to provide insight on how the material in the chapter relates to the real world of production database design and implementation with Access 2000. Like this chapter's "In the Real World," many of these sections include "op-ed" (opinion-editorial) style comments on the significance (or lack of significance) of new Access features, as well as advice based on first-hand experience with production Access applications installed by Fortune 100 firms.

Several years ago, Bill Gates described Microsoft's "subscription model" for productivity and other software products. The idea was to stabilize Microsoft's revenue stream by charging a fixed annual fee, based on the original software license price, for application and operating system upgrades. The obvious problem with such an approach is that many Microsoft products experience major-scale release date slippage. Unlike a monthly magazine subscription, which results in 12 issues arriving per year, you might not receive a full version upgrade in a year's software subscription. The most obvious current example is Windows 2000 (neé Windows NT 5.0), which Microsoft originally scheduled for retail release in 1998. Industry pundits currently predict that Windows 2000 will find its way to retailers' shelves during its eponymous year.

Internet distribution by Microsoft of free Windows add-ons and updates—such as Service and Option Packs for Windows NT, NetShow 3.0 Server, and Windows Media Player—also makes paid subscription services a hard sell. Thus most Access users probably obtain Access 2000 through a standard upgrade license from a prior Access version, usually the last retail release. Microsoft's estimated retail price (ERP) for upgrading from Office 97 or earlier to Office 2000 Professional is $309, but large-volume purchasers receive substantial discounts. The major cost isn't the software license; it's your—or your company's—investment in the time to adapt to and effectively use the new features of the Office suite (or how to disable them). Another cost is the time and effort required to upgrade existing Access databases and front-end applications to a new version.

Access 97 is a remarkably stable product; Jet 3.51 is, with a few minor exceptions in multi-user environments, a superior database engine; ODBC 3.5 works as advertised; and Data Access Objects (DAO) 3.51 offer simple but versatile database access to many programming languages. The overall performance of Access 97, about on a par with 16-bit Access 2.0, was a dramatic improvement over the sluggish responsiveness of Access 95. Execution speed of most well-designed Access 2000 applications is about the same as Access 97's. Upgraded databases take more disk space, but the cost per GB of disk space has dropped to the point that virtually no one (other than a user of an aging laptop PC) considers file size to be an upgrade cost factor. Witness the ever-increasing disk space consumption of Office releases.

So why upgrade to Office 2000 and Access 2000, in particular? Corporate information technology (IT) managers, chief financial officers, and computer journalists ask this rhetorical question every 18 months or so. The real reason, to paraphrase the World War I recruiting poster, is: "Microsoft Wants YOU to Upgrade." This is especially true for Microsoft Office, which provides a substantial part of Microsoft's ever-increasing revenue and earnings. Microsoft program and product managers have spent the majority of their cubicle time for the past two or three years plotting a strategy to entice Office licensees to upgrade from Office version 8.0, even during its development cycle, to Office 2000.

Microsoft commonly uses "freebies" to stimulate the upgrade rate. The MSDE license included with Access 2000 is the biggest Microsoft freebie to date. MSDE lets small firms take advantage of SQL Server 7.0 client/server architecture in a peer-to-peer network without paying a $1,399 server license—which includes five client licenses— or purchasing additional client licenses at about $60 each. Giving away MSDE with Access upgrades created heated controversy between the Office and SQL Server product teams. If you're planning to move to a client/server RDBMS in a workgroup-sized (25 users or fewer) environment, upgrading to Access 2000 is a no-brainer.

DAP is better classified as a new feature than a freebie. Software purchasers are justifiably wary of version 1.0 of any product, and Access 2000 has DAP 1.0. Hopefully, DAP 1.5 or 2.0 will include undo capability. DAP, along with OWC (also version 1.0) show considerable promise and appear to be well suited for quickly deploying custom decision-support applications on intranets. Using the present version of DAP for heads-down OLTP operations (such as telephone order or reservation entry) takes more courage than most IT managers are willing or able to muster.

Both ADP and DAP rely on ADO, which has matured to version 2.1. (Many developers consider ADO 1.0 and 1.5 to have been beta releases, with ADO 2.0 the first production-grade release.) Version 2.5 currently is under development in Redmond. OLE DB and ADO are strategic to Microsoft's database future. The elegant architecture of OLE DB is besmudged by uninspired integration of ADO 2.1 with Access 2000. The two most glaring integration failures are the lack of updatability of form or report Recordsets with ADO, and the inability of Access subforms and reports to take advantage of chaptered (hierarchical) Recordsets created with the Microsoft DataShape OLE DB provider and its SHAPE syntax additions to SQL. OLE DB and ADO, however, are the new wave of Windows database connectivity and threaten the hegemony of ODBC. If your goal is to keep your database skills up to date, taking advantage of Access 2000 to learn OLE DB, ADO, XML, and even CSS techniques is well worth your cash expenditure for an upgrade and the time you spend climbing its learning curve.

Many organizations are reluctant to devote time and energy to an Office 2000 upgrade while the specter of Y2K hovers over the IT department. Microsoft faces the same problem with Windows 2000 due to its untimely projected release date. Regardless of temporary tactical problems, Microsoft's marketing prowess is legend. You're seldom a winner when you bet against Microsoft and the ultimate success of its products, especially Microsoft Office.

--rj

BUILDING YOUR FIRST ACCESS 2000 APPLICATION

In this chapter

Understanding Access's Approach to Application Design   56

Creating an Access Application from a Template File   57

Touring the Contact Management Application   62

Navigating Table Objects in the Database Window   62

Using the Switchboard Form and Other Access Forms   66

Previewing and Printing Access Reports   72

Using the Switchboard Manager   75

Exploring Form Design View and VBA Class Modules   77

The Real World—Putting What You've Learned in Perspective   79

UNDERSTANDING ACCESS'S APPROACH TO APPLICATION DESIGN

Unlike other members of Microsoft Office 2000, Access 2000 requires that you build an application to take advantage of the product's power as a database development platform. Word 2000 and Excel 2000 let you automate simple repetitive operations by recording Visual Basic for Applications (VBA) macros. Access 2000 supports a set of macro commands for compatibility with previous versions, but Access macros don't use VBA. Access doesn't capture your mouse clicks and keystrokes and turn them into a series of macro commands or VBA code. Thus, it's up to you to design and implement the Access applications you need for your database projects.

A full-scale Access application involves at least the following three basic Access object types:

- *Tables* that store the data you or others add to the database
- *Forms* for displaying and entering data, controlling the opening and closing of other forms, and printing reports
- *Reports* to print detail information, summary information, or both in tables

Most Access applications also use *Query objects* to filter, sort, and combine your data, and *Module objects* to store VBA code. Access 2000 forms can (and usually do) contain VBA code in a special type of Module object, called a *Class Module*. All objects that make up your application are stored in a container called a *Database* object, which is a single file with an .mdb extension, such as Northwind.mdb. Access is unique in that it stores an entire database application in a single file. Other desktop databases, such as Microsoft FoxPro, require multiple files to store their objects.

New Access users often find it difficult to "get a grip" on how to start developing a self-contained database application. Dealing with an unfamiliar set of objects tends to intimidate first-time database developers. Fortunately, Microsoft includes with Access 2000 various wizards that guide you, step by step, through complex tasks. One of the most accomplished of the Access wizards is the Database Wizard that creates a typical Access 2000 application from a set of prefabricated database templates. In this chapter, you use the Database Wizard to create a relatively simple but potentially useful Contact Manager application. Then you explore the objects generated by the Wizard to gain perspective on the relationship of Access objects and learn how they're integrated within a typical Access database application.

NEW 2000

Following are the new features of Access 2000 discussed in this chapter:

- *Subdatasheets*, which open when you click a plus sign to the left of the first field in Table Datasheet view. Subdatasheets automatically display records of another table that's related to the current table.
- *Visual Basic for Applications code editor*, which Access 2000 shares with other Office applications. Prior versions of Access used its own VBA editing window for code modules.

> **Note**
>
> This chapter assumes that you've already installed Access 2000. If you haven't, see the "Installing Access 2000" section of Chapter 1, "Access 2000 for Access 95 and 97 Users: What's New."

CREATING AN ACCESS APPLICATION FROM A TEMPLATE FILE

When you launch Access 2000, the Microsoft Access dialog offers you the option of creating a new database or opening an existing database, such as Northwind.mdb, the Northwind Traders sample database located in \Program Files\Microsoft Office\Office\Samples. If you choose to create a new database, you can open a do-it-yourself empty (blank) database or use the Database Wizard to create a database from one of the 10 database templates included with Access 2000. Template files contain the definitions of Table, Form, and Report objects, plus the VBA code required to automate interaction of these objects. Template files also include a relatively small amount of optional sample data, which is useful for learning how to navigate a set of records.

To use the Database Wizard to create a sample application from an Access 2000 template, follow these steps:

1. Choose Programs, Microsoft Access from the Start menu to launch Access 2000 and open the Microsoft Access dialog. (If Access is open, you must close and relaunch it to display this dialog.)

2. Select the Access Database Wizards, Pages, and Projects option (see Figure 2.1). Click OK to open the New dialog.

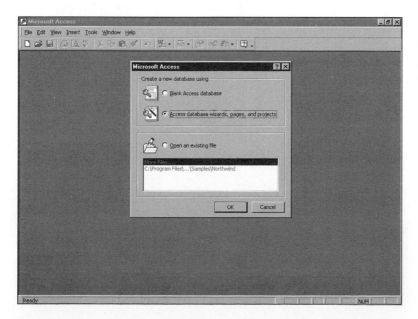

Figure 2.1
Selecting the Access Database Wizards, Pages, and Projects option in the Microsoft Access dialog.

3. Select one of the 10 database templates (*.mdz files) from which to build your new application (see Figure 2.2). Access stores its templates in the \Program Files\ Microsoft Office\Templates\1033 folder. This example uses the Contact Management.mdz template. Click OK to open the File New Database dialog.

Figure 2.2
Selecting the Contact Management template in the Databases page of the New dialog.

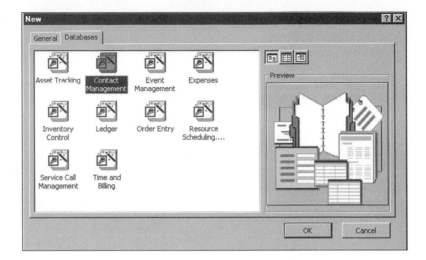

4. The Wizard proposes a default database with the name of the template plus a 1 suffix. The default location of the database file is the \My Documents folder. Accept the default name or shorten it to Contacts.mdb (see Figure 2.3). Click Create to generate an empty Jet 4.0 database file (Contacts.mdb) and start the Database Wizard.

Figure 2.3
Shortening the default database filename, Contact Management1.mdb, to Contacts.mdb.

5. The first dialog of the Database Wizard describes the tables that store user-entered and optional sample information in the new database (see Figure 2.4). Click Next to continue.

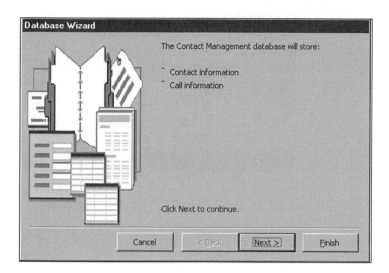

Figure 2.4
The first Database Wizard dialog.

6. The second Wizard dialog lets you add or remove optional fields to one of the three tables. Optional fields appear in italic type in the list. To add or remove an optional field of the Contact Information table, mark or clear the check box (see Figure 2.5).

Note

You can remove only the optional fields you add. You can't remove the standard set of fields that appear in Roman type.

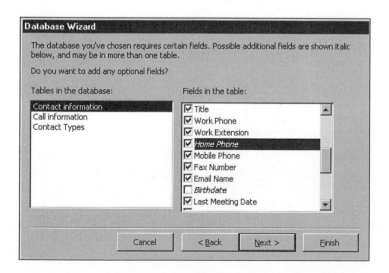

Figure 2.5
Adding the optional Home Phone field to the Contact Information table of Contact.mdb.

7. The third Wizard dialog offers a selection of text colors and background colors or images for the data forms that the Wizard creates. As you select an item in the list, a sample of the style appears in the dialog (see Figure 2.6). Select a form style and click Next to continue.

Figure 2.6
Selecting text color and background color or images for data-entry forms.

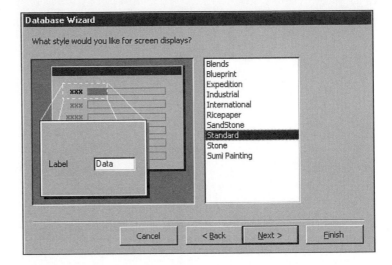

8. The fourth dialog lets you choose a style for printed reports (see Figure 2.7). Pick a report style, such as the conservative Soft Gray and click Next to continue.

Figure 2.7
Selecting the header and type styles for reports in the fourth Wizard dialog.

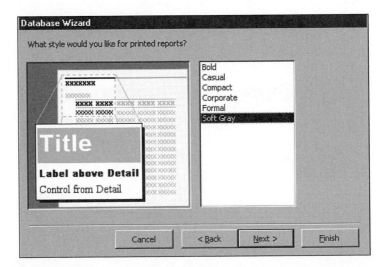

9. You enter the title to appear on your forms and reports in the fifth Wizard dialog (see Figure 2.8). The default title is the name of the template file. Accept or edit the title.

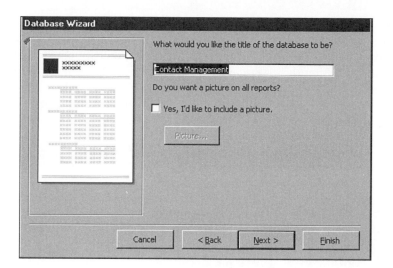

Figure 2.8
Accepting the default title, which appears on forms and reports.

10. If you have a bitmap (.bmp or .dib, device-independent bitmap) or vector (.wmf, Windows metafile, or .emf, cnhanced metafile) image of a logo that's of a size suited to the header of your reports, mark the Yes, I'd Like to Include a Picture check box. (The logo should be about 80 by 80 pixels or less.) Click the Picture button to open the Insert Picture dialog. Sclcct the image file and then click OK to insert the image and close the Insert Picture dialog.

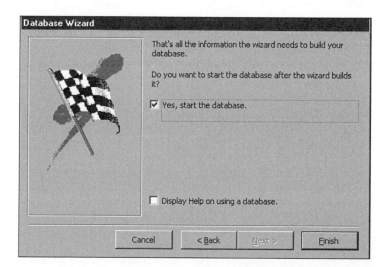

Figure 2.9
The final Database Wizard dialog.

11. Click Next to open the final Wizard dialog (see Figure 2.9). With the Yes, Start the Database check box marked, click Finish to add the objects whose properties you've specified to the database file you named in step 4.

A set of progress bars displays the Wizard's actions. The time required to complete the generation of database objects depends on your CPU's and disk drive's speed; it takes less than 30 seconds to finish the Contact Management database with a 266MHz Pentium II PC and a high-speed fixed-disk drive. After the Wizard completes its work, the Main Switchboard form for the completed Contact Management application appears as shown in Figure 2.10. The Database window, which lets you manually open any of the objects in the Contacts database, is minimized at the bottom left of the display.

Figure 2.10
The Main Switchboard form of the Contact Management application created by the Database Wizard.

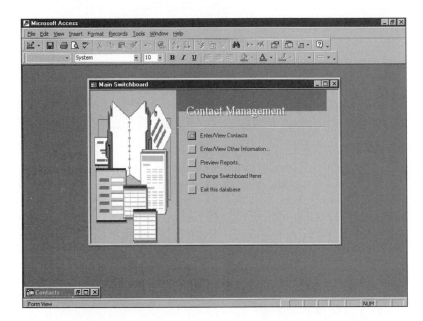

TOURING THE CONTACT MANAGEMENT APPLICATION

The Contact Management application appears quite complex to most first-time Access users. The Database Wizard generates multiple Table, Form, Report, and Module objects in the new database. The following sections explain the purpose of each object in the context of your new Contact Management application.

TABLE OBJECTS IN THE DATABASE WINDOW

Tables are the foundation of Access databases. To examine some Table objects generated from the Contact Management template by the Database Wizard, do the following:

NEW 2000

1. Click the Database window Restore button to open the Database window in Normal mode. An Outlook-style shortcut bar appears at the left of the list.

2. Click the Tables shortcut, if necessary, to display a list of the of three Create Table... options and the four Table objects in the Contacts database (see Figure 2.11).

Figure 2.11
The Tables page of the
Database window display-
ing the Table objects of
Contacts.mdb.

3. Double-click the Contacts item to open the Contacts table in Datasheet view. The fields of the Contacts table correspond to the items in the list of the second Wizard dialog (refer to step 6 in the preceding section). The first field is an Autonumber field that sequentially numbers the records you add; you can't change the value of an Autonumber field.

4. Type a test contact entry in the initially visible fields of the Contacts table. When you type in the First Name cell, a pencil symbol appears to the left of the Contact ID cell, indicating an edit in process, and a new row—called the *tentative append record* in this book—appears below the test contact record (see Figure 2.12). Click in any cell of the tentative append record to save your entry; you must move to another row in the datasheet to assure that entries add to the Contacts table.

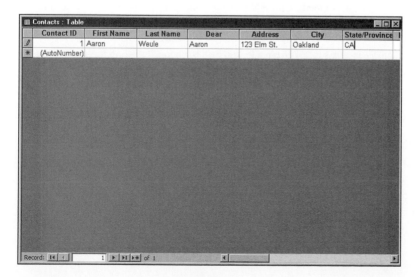

Figure 2.12
The Contacts table
opened in Datasheet view
with a test entry added.

5. Return to the Database window, and double-click to open the Contact Types table. In the Contact Type field, type a typical title, such as **Executive**. Add records with **Director, Manager**, and **Supervisor** as Contact Types. Click in a cell of the first record to save your last entry, and then close the Contact Types window.

6. Use the scrollbar to display the rightmost fields of the Contacts table. Click the Contact Type ID cell of the first record of the table to display a drop-down list button in the grid. Click the button to open a list with items you added to the Contact Types table (see Figure 2.13).

→ If you're not comfortable navigating the interface yet, **see** "Understanding Access's Table Display," **p. 85**.

Figure 2.13
Using the drop-down Lookup list of the Contact table's Contact Type ID field.

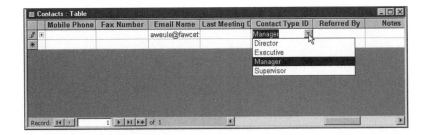

Tip #15 from

The Contact Type ID field of the Contacts table is related to the Contact Type ID field of the Contact Types table, which contains the numeric values 1 (Executive), 2 (Director), 3 (Manager), and any additional records you added in preceding step 4. Relations between tables are the foundation of relational database management systems (RDBMSs). The relation between the Contacts and Contact Types tables is called a *many-to-one* relationship because many records in the Contacts table can relate to a single record in the Contact Types table. The Contact Type ID field of the Contacts table, which actually contains numeric value 1 or 2, is called a *lookup field* because it looks up data in the Contact Types table based on the numeric value and substitutes the corresponding text value for the number. You can change the Contact Type ID from Seller to Buyer by selecting Buyer from the drop-down list.

Additionally, inserting entries from a lookup field is a popular method for avoiding spelling errors and reducing the number of keystrokes for repeated selections.

→ For other examples for using this method of data entry, **see** "Using Lookup Fields in Tables," **p. 365**.

NEW 2000

7. Scroll to the first field (ContactID) of the table and click the plus (+) sign at the left of the ContactID field to open a subdatasheet that displays an empty Calls datasheet for your test contact entry. Subdatasheets, which display records of other tables related to the currently open table, are a new feature of Access 2000. Type entries typical of a phone call in the subdatasheet fields (see Figure 2.14). The Calls table has a many-to-one relationship to the Contacts table.

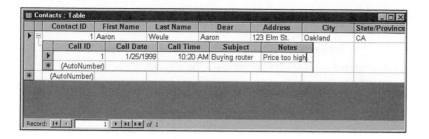

Figure 2.14
The Subdatasheet display based on the Calls table Contact ID field.

8. From the Tools menu, choose Relationships to display graphically in Access's Relationships window the relations between the Contact Types, Contacts, and Calls tables. Drag down the bottom of the Contacts list to expose the ContactTypeID field (see Figure 2.15).

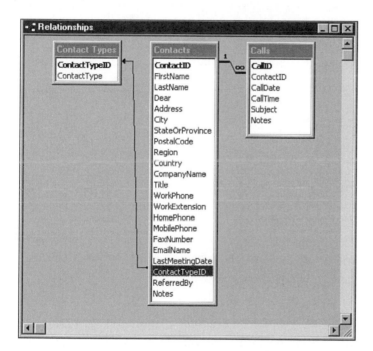

Figure 2.15
Access's graphical Relationships window displaying the relations between the Contact Types, Contacts, and Calls tables of the Contacts.mdb database.

The line between the ContactTypeID fields of the Contact Types and Contacts tables illustrates a many-to-one relation. (The arrowhead identifies the "one" table in the relation.) The line between the ContactID fields of the Contacts and Calls tables also indicates a many-to-one relationship. (The infinity symbol, [inf], identifies the "many" side and the 1 represents the "one" side of the relation.) The ContactID line indicates that Access enforces the *referential integrity* of the relation. Referential integrity is an advanced topic, which is discussed in several chapters later in the book.

→ For more details on how relationships help protect your data, **see** "Enforcing Database Integrity,"
p. 844.

Tip #16 from 	The field names in the Relationships window and the field names that appear in the Datasheet views of the corresponding tables aren't the same. The field names in the Datasheet views are captions, which include spaces for readability. The actual field names, which don't include spaces, appear in the field lists of the Relationships window.

9. Close the Relationships and Contacts: Table windows, saving your layout changes.

THE SWITCHBOARD FORM

The Main Switchboard is the controlling form of the Contact Management application (refer to Figure 2.10). Switchboard forms take the place of the conventional menu choices of Windows applications, which commonly are found in commercial Access applications. The five buttons on the Main Switchboard perform the following functions:

- *Enter/View Contacts* opens the Contacts form, the equivalent of choosing <u>C</u>ontacts from the <u>V</u>iew menu.

- *Enter/View Other Information* replaces the Main Switchboard with the Forms Switchboard page. The Forms Switchboard has two buttons: one to open a small form for adding additional records to the Contact Types table and one to return to the Main Switchboard.

- *Preview Reports* opens the Reports Switchboard page, which lets you preview and print an Alphabetical Contact Listing Report or a Weekly Call Summary Report or return to the Main Switchboard. Preview Reports is equivalent to choosing Print Pre<u>v</u>iew from the <u>F</u>ile menu.

- *Change Switchboard Items* opens the Switchboard Manager form, which lets you customize the Switchboard pages, add a new Switchboard page, or delete a page.

- *Exit This Database* closes the Contacts database but doesn't shut down Access.

Figure 2.16 shows the relationship between the buttons on the three versions of the Switchboard and the forms and reports that make up the Contact Management application. For clarity this diagram omits the Call Details Subform, Call Listing Subform, and Report Date Range form. A *subform* is a form that's contained within another form; subforms are unique to Access. Lines between forms and tables with arrows on each end indicate the capability to display and edit table data. Lines between reports and tables have only a single arrow, because reports involve only reading table data.

→ For help building a new subform, **see** "Creating a Transaction-Processing Form with the Form Wizard,"
p. 435.

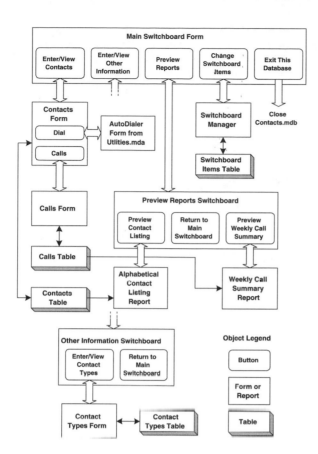

Figure 2.16
A diagram of the relationship of Switchboard buttons to forms, reports, and tables of the Contact Manager application.

PART

I

CH

2

> **Note**
>
> Figure 2.16 shows three individual Switchboard forms. Contact Manager uses records in the Switchboard Items table to customize a single Switchboard form to perform the three functions shown in the diagram.

Compared to menu commands, switchboards offer more control over the sequence of user interaction with data display and entry forms. The Main Switchboard acts as a home base that you return to on completion of one or more specific tasks. Simplified navigation of multiple layers of forms is the reason that many Access developers use switchboards for complex applications.

ACCESS FORMS

The following steps introduce you to Access forms and form-based data entry:

1. Close all open Access windows except the Switchboard form and the Database window.

Note

If you accidentally closed the Switchboard form, open the Database window, click the Forms shortcut, and double-click the Switchboard item in the list to open the Main Switchboard.

2. Click the Enter/View Contacts button to open the Contacts form, which displays in text boxes most of the data you entered in the first record of the Contacts table (see Figure 2.17). The record displayed in the form is called the *current record* of the table.

Figure 2.17
The upper part of the Contacts form displaying most of the information for the first record of the Contacts table.

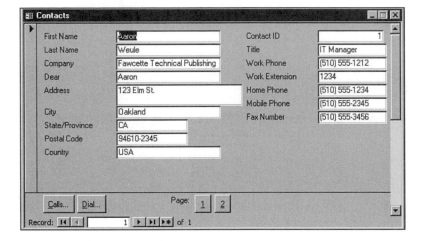

3. Click the Next Record button (with the right-pointing triangle) at the bottom left of the form to display successive records of the Contacts table. If you added only a single Contacts record, the text boxes empty in preparation for adding a new record.

4. Click the First Record button (with the left-pointing triangle and bar) to return to to the first record you typed.

5. Click the 2 button to display the bottom part of the form, which displays the data for the remaining fields of the Contacts table. You also can navigate to the bottom of the display with the form's scrollbar. Clicking inside the Notes text box adds a scrollbar to that box (see Figure 2.18). Click the 1 button to return to the top of the form.

6. Press the Tab key 10 times to move the focus to the Work Phone field. (The Tab key is the primary method of navigating through a form's fields.) Click the Dial button to open the AutoDialer form of the Utility.mda library (see Figure 2.19). Clicking the Setup button opens the Windows 9x or Windows NT Modem Properties sheet. Close the Modem Properties sheet, if you opened it, and then click Cancel to close the AutoDialer form.

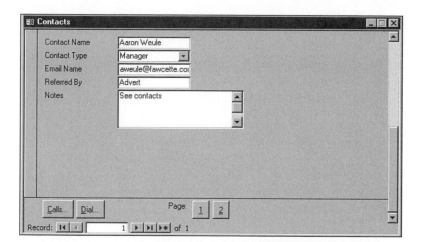

Figure 2.18
The lower part of the Contacts form displayed by clicking the 2 button.

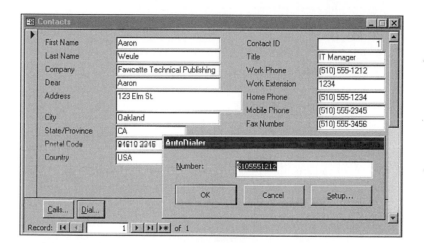

Figure 2.19
The AutoDialer form opened from the Utility.mda library database that's attached when you launch Access.

Note

> AutoDialer uses the Windows 9x or Windows NT built-in Phone Dialer accessory. AutoDialer detects whether the call is within your local dialing area (set by the Dialing Properties sheet that you open from the Modem Properties sheet). The Phone Dialer prepends the required 1 digit to the area code and telephone number when dialing long distance.

---

7. Click the Calls button to open the Calls form, which superimposes over the Contacts form. The Calls form displays only the records in the Calls table for the contact selected in the Contacts form, a process called *synchronizing* forms (see Figure 2.20). The Calls form must display multiple records, so the Calls form uses a Datasheet view of the Calls table.

Figure 2.20
The Calls form synchronized to the current record of the Contacts form.

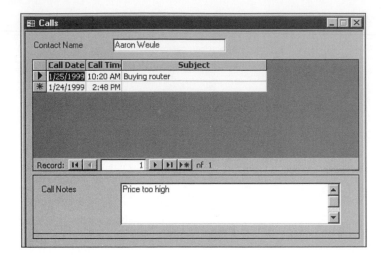

8. Add a new contact record for the Contacts record you entered by clicking the Subject field of the tentative append record and adding some text. When you start typing text, a new tentative append record appears.

9. Click inside the Call Notes text box and type a short transcript of the call (see Figure 2.21). The Call Notes caption and text box are contained in the Call Details Subform.

Figure 2.21
Adding a new record to the Calls form.

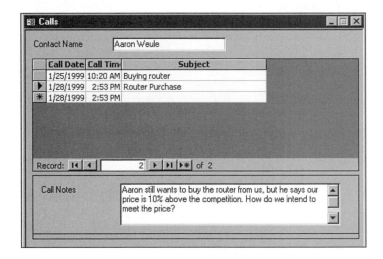

10. To delete the record you just added, click the gray record selector button to the left of the Call Date field and press Delete. You receive the warning message shown in Figure 2.22.

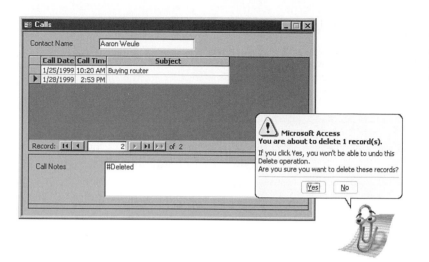

Figure 2.22
Paperclip offering last chance to change your mind before permanently deleting a record.

11. Close the Calls form to return to the Contacts form.

12. If you want to add a new contact record to the Contacts form, click the tentative append record navigation button to open a form in which only the Contact ID field is filled in (see Figure 2.23).

13. Close the Contacts form to return to the Main Switchboard.

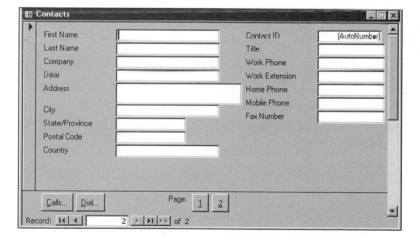

Figure 2.23
The empty record for adding a new contact to the Contacts database.

Note

The Contact ID field uses the AutoNumber field data type, which automatically assigns the next number in sequence to an added record. If you don't enter text in any field and then move the record pointer with the navigation buttons to an active record, the empty record isn't appended.

> To delete a record, click the record selector bar at the left of the form and press the Delete key. If you delete a record of the Contacts table that has related records in the Calls table, the related Calls records are deleted simultaneously, a process called *cascading deletions*. The related Calls records are deleted because referential integrity is enforced between the Calls and Contacts tables, and cascading deletions are specified in the properties of the relation in the Relationships window.

Clicking the Enter/View Other Information button regenerates the Forms Switchboard. To add a new contact type, click the Enter/View Contact Types button to open the simple Contact Types form. Like Contact ID, Contact Type ID is an AutoNumber field. Close the Contact Types form and then click the Return to Main Switchboard button to return the Switchboard form to its original status.

ACCESS REPORTS

Reports are one of Access's strongest selling points. The capability to program the generation of complex, fully formatted reports is what sets Access apart from its competitors, including Microsoft's own Visual Basic. To preview and optionally print the two reports of the Contact Management application, follow these steps:

1. Click the Preview Reports button to generate the Reports Switchboard, and then click the Preview the Alphabetical Contact Listing Report to open the Print Preview window in Normal mode at 100 percent size.

2. Click the Maximize button and type **85** percent in the Zoom list to view almost all the report (see Figure 2.24).

Figure 2.24
The Print Preview window for the Alphabetical Contact Listing report in Maximized mode at 85 percent scale.

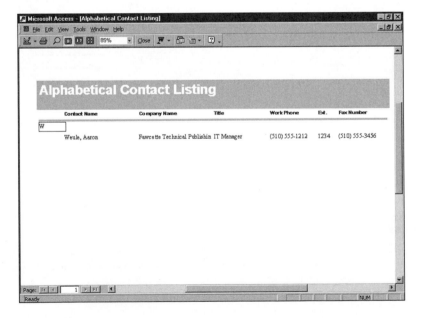

3. To print the report, click the toolbar's Print button.

4. Close the Print Preview window, click the Restore button of the Switchboard form, and click the Preview the Weekly Call Summary Report button to open the Weekly Call Summary form. The default beginning and ending report dates are for the current system date and the preceding six days.

5. Edit the date in the Begin(ning) Call Date text box to a date for which data is available.

6. Click the Preview button to open the report in Print Preview mode. Change the Zoom value to 75% (see Figure 2.25).

7. Print a copy of the report, if you want, and then close the Print Preview window and click the Return to Main Switchboard button.

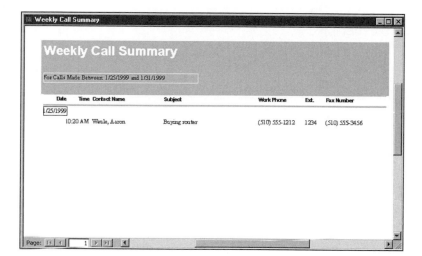

Figure 2.25
The Weekly Call Summary report in Print Preview mode.

ACCESS MODULES

Access modules contain VBA subprocedures and functions that are accessible to VBA code contained in the class module of any form or report. You also can call VBA functions in modules by using the RunCode action of an Access macro. Access 2000 is the first version of Access to take advantage of the shared VBA editor used by other Office applications. Writing VBA subprocedures and functions to automate your Access application is the subject of the chapters in Part VII, "Programming and Converting Access Applications." To see and test a simple example of VBA code for a function, follow these steps:

1. From the Window menu, choose 1 Contacts: Database to open the Database window.

2. Click the Modules tab and then double-click the Global Code item in the list to open the Global Code module in the VBA code editor. The Global Code module contains a single function, IsLoaded (see Figure 2.26), which returns **True** if a specified form is open (loaded) or **False** if not.

Figure 2.26
The single IsLoaded function of the Global Code module created by the Database Wizard.

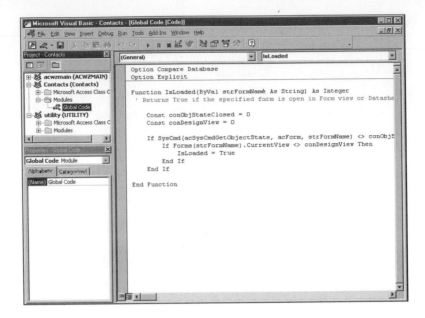

3. To test the IsLoaded function, press Ctrl+G to open the Immediate window. Type **?**
IsLoaded("Switchboard") in the bottom pane of the Immediate window. The VBA
debugger returns –1 (the numeric value of the VBA True intrinsic constant), indicating
that the Switchboard form is open (see Figure 2.27).

4. Close the Immediate, Alt+Tab to Access, and minimize the Database window to return
to the Main Switchboard.

Figure 2.27
Testing the IsLoaded function of the Global Code module in the VBA editor's Immediate window.

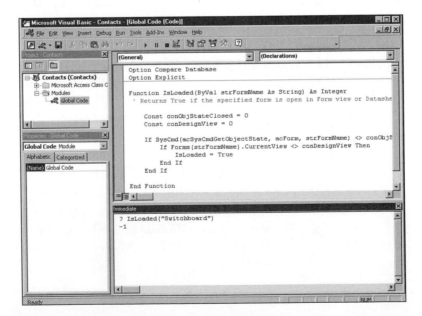

USING THE SWITCHBOARD MANAGER

The Switchboard Manager lets you modify the navigation process for your application. The following steps delete the Forms Switchboard and substitute a button that opens the Contact Types form directly:

1. Click the Change Switchboard Items button of the Main Switchboard to open the Switchboard Manager dialog.

2. Select the Forms Switchboard item in the Switchboard Pages list (see Figure 2.28) and click the Delete button. When the "Are you sure?" message appears, click Yes.

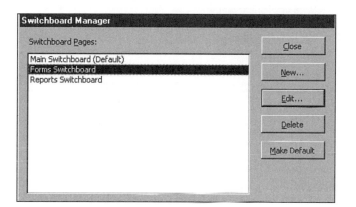

Figure 2.28
Selecting the Forms Switchboard for deletion in the Switchboard Manager dialog.

3. With the Main Switchboard (Default) item selected, click the Edit button to open the Edit Switchboard Page dialog.

4. Select the Enter/View Other Information item in the Items on This Switchboard list (see Figure 2.29) and click Edit to open the Edit Switchboard Item dialog (see Figure 2.30). The Switchboard text box is empty because you deleted the associated switchboard in step 2.

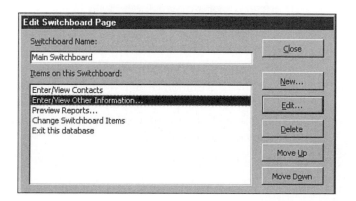

Figure 2.29
Selecting the switchboard item to edit.

Figure 2.30
The Edit Switchboard Item dialog with default entries.

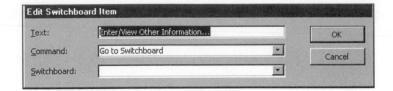

5. Replace the existing content of the Text text box with **Enter/View Contact Types** and select Open Form in Edit Mode from the Command drop-down list (see Figure 2.31).

Figure 2.31
Changing the entries for the Main Switchboard button to open a form directly.

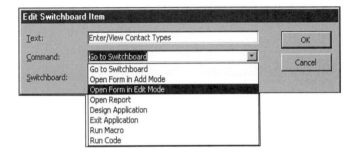

6. Open the Form drop-down list (which replaces the Switchboard list) and select Contact Types (see Figure 2.32). Click OK to accept the changes and return to the Edit Switchboard Page dialog.

Figure 2.32
Selecting the form to open in Edit mode.

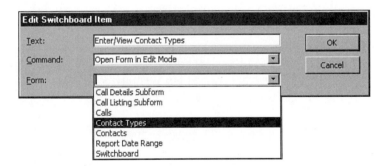

7. The Edit Switchboard Page dialog shows the caption change you made in step 5. Click Close to return to the Switchboard Manager dialog and then click Close again to return to the Main Switchboard form. The second button reflects the caption change. Click the Edit/View Contact Types button to test your work.

8. Close the Contact Types form to return to the Main Switchboard.

You can import a Switchboard form and Switchboard Items table created by the Database Wizard into Access applications you create from scratch and then use the Switchboard

Manager to modify the original design to suit your navigational needs. Starting with a pre-built switchboard saves a substantial amount of design work and VBA code writing.

→ To import a Switchboard form or other database objects, **see** "Linking and Importing External ISAM Tables," **p. 235**.

Exploring Form Design View and VBA Class Modules

PART

I

CH

2

Designing forms and writing VBA code are advanced Access topics, but you can preview the topics covered by later chapters with the following steps:

1. With the Main Switchboard active, click the Design View button at the extreme left of the toolbar to open the Main Switchboard in Design view (see Figure 2.33). The Toolbox, which you use to add controls (text boxes, buttons, and the like) to forms, appears to the left of the Form Design window.

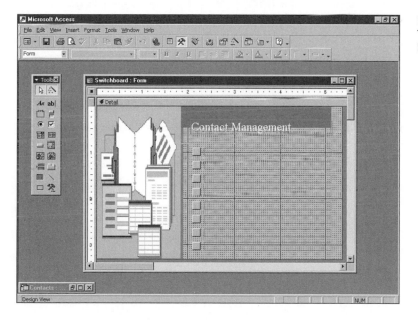

Figure 2.33
The Switchboard form in Design view.

2. Press Ctrl+R to select the entire form and then click the toolbar's Properties button to open the Properties window. By default, the Properties window displays all the properties of the selected object—in this case, the form.

3. Click the Data tab to display only the data-related properties of the form (see Figure 2.34). The most important property is the Record Source, which specifies the Switchboard Items table as the table bound to the form. The Filter property specifies that the form obtains its data from the first record of the Switchboard Items table.

Figure 2.34
Data-related properties of the Switchboard form.

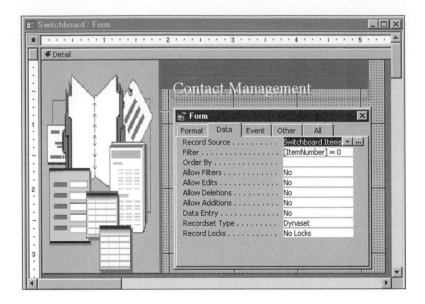

4. Click to select the top button (under the C of Contact Management in the Design view of the form). The Properties window displays the properties of Command Button: Option1.

5. Click the Event tab to display the Event properties of Option1 (see Figure 2.35). The =HandleButtonClick(1) value of the On Click event executes the HandleButtonClick VBA function when you click the button.

Figure 2.35
Event properties of the Option1 command button.

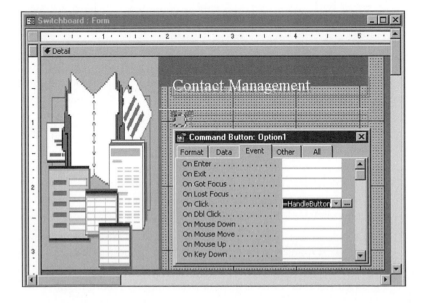

6. Click the Code button to display the Contacts - Form_Switchboard (Code) window of the VBA editor. Page down until you see **Private Function** HandleButtonClick(intBtn **As Integer**), as shown in Figure 2.36. The Option1 button calls this function to handle the On Click event. The (1) suffix of the event value is passed to the function as the value of the intBtn argument. Scroll through the code until you reach the **End Function** statement, which terminates the HandleButtonClick function.

7. Alt+Tab to return to the Switchboard form and then click the Form View button to return the Switchboard form to its original state.

PART

I

CH

2

THE REAL WORLD—PUTTING WHAT YOU'VE LEARNED IN PERSPECTIVE

If you're new to Access, many terms used in this chapter may sound like ancient Aramaic. The objective was to give you an overview of some of the most important objects that make up an Access application, the relationships between these objects, and how you assemble the objects you create into self-contained, easily navigable applications. Using the Database Wizard helps you quickly understand the components and comprehend the behavior of a completed Access application. If you're interested in designing an Access inventory management application, for example, use the Inventory Control template to create a simple sample application. You're likely to find that one of the Database Wizard templates bears some resemblance to your intended application.

If you didn't perform the step-by-step tutorial to create the sample application of this chapter, not to worry. There's a copy of the Contacts.mdb database in the \Seua2k\Chaptr02 folder of the accompanying CD-ROM. Sample databases for most of the chapters from this point forward are included in corresponding \Seua2k\Chaptr## folders.

The remainder of this book covers each category of Access objects in detail, beginning with Table and Query objects and then progressing to Form and Report objects. By the time you get about halfway through this book, you gain the experience necessary to design your own versions of these objects. The last half of this book deals with advanced topics, such as exporting Access forms and reports to World Wide Web pages, creating Data Access Pages, designing relational databases, and writing professional-quality VBA code. The "Real World" sections at the end of each chapter attempt to relate what you've learned to the design and implementation of production Access databases and applications.

--rj

CHAPTER 3

NAVIGATING WITHIN ACCESS

In this chapter

Understanding Access Functions and Modes   82

Defining Access Functions   82

Defining Access Operating Modes   84

Understanding Access's Table Display   85

Using the Function Keys   97

Setting Default Options   98

Using Access Help   107

Understanding the Help Window   109

Using the Database Utilities   118

Converting Databases to Access 2000 Format   120

Creating .mde Files   123

Troubleshooting   123

In the Real World—HTML Help or Hindrance   124

UNDERSTANDING ACCESS FUNCTIONS AND MODES

Access, unlike word processing and spreadsheet applications, is a truly multifunctional program. Although word processing applications, for example, have many sophisticated capabilities, their basic purpose is to support text entry, page layout, and formatted printing. The primary functions and supporting features of all word processing applications are directed to these ends. You perform all word processing operations with views that represent a sheet of paper—usually 8 1/2×11 inches. Most spreadsheet applications use the row-column metaphor for all their functions. In contrast, Access consists of a multitude of related tools for generating, organizing, segregating, displaying, printing, and publishing data. The following sections describe Access's basic functions and operating modes.

DEFINING ACCESS FUNCTIONS

To qualify as a full-fledged relational database management system (RDBMS), an application must perform the following four basic but distinct functions, each with its own presentation (or view) to the user:

- *Data organization* involves creating and manipulating tables that contain data in conventional tabular (row-column or spreadsheet) format, called *Datasheet view* by Access.

- *Table linking and data extraction* link multiple tables by data relationships to create temporary tables, stored in your computer's memory or temporary disk files, that contain the data you choose. Access uses *queries* to link tables and to choose the data to be stored in a temporary table called a Recordset object. A Recordset object consists of the data that results from running the query; Recordset objects are called *virtual tables* because they are stored in your computer's memory rather than in database files. The capability to link tables by relations distinguishes relational database systems from simple list-processing applications, called *flat-file* managers. Data extraction limits the presentation of Recordsets to specific groups of data that meet criteria that you establish. *Expressions* are used to calculate values from data (for example, you can calculate an extended amount by multiplying unit price and quantity) and to display the calculated values as though they were a field in one of the tables.

- *Data entry and editing* require design and implementation of data viewing, entry, and editing forms as an alternative to tabular presentation. A form enables you, rather than the application, to control how the data is presented. Most users find forms much easier to use for data entry than Recordsets in tabular format, especially when many fields are involved. Data entry in forms is a requirement for intranet- and Internet-based applications. The capability to print forms, such as sales orders and invoices, is definitely a benefit to users.

- *Data presentation* requires the creation of reports that can summarize the information in Recordsets that you can view, print, or publish on the Internet or an intranet (the last step in the process). The capability to provide meaningful reports is the ultimate purpose of any database management application. Also, the management of an enterprise usually lends more credence to attractively formatted reports that contain charts or graphs. Charts and graphs summarize the data for those officials who take the "broad brush" approach.

The four basic functions of Access that are implemented as views are organized into the application structure shown in Figure 3.1. If you are creating a new database, you use the basic functions of Access in the top-down sequence shown in Figure 3.1. You choose a function by clicking a button in the Datasheet window (except for security and printing operations, which are menu choices). In most views, you can display the Print Preview window that leads to printing operations by clicking the toolbar's Print Preview button.

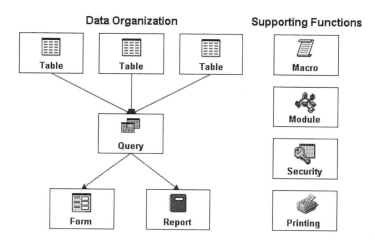

Figure 3.1
The basic and supporting functions of Access.

Five supporting functions apply to all the basic functions of Access:

 ■ *Macros* are sequences of actions that automate repetitive database operations. You create a macro in Access by choosing from a list of available actions in the order in which you want Access to perform them. You can use a macro, for example, to open a report, print the report, and then close the report. (Later this section defines *open* and *close* as they are used in Access terminology.) In prior versions of Access, macros were the primary means of automating database operations. In Access 2000, macros are supported primarily for purposes of compatibility with databases created in earlier Access versions. For Access 2000 databases, you use Visual Basic for Applications *(VBA)* to automate database actions.

 ■ *Modules* are functions and procedures written in the VBA programming language. You use VBA functions to make calculations that are more complex than those that can be expressed easily by a series of conventional mathematical symbols or to make calculations that require decisions to be made. VBA subprocedures are written to perform operations that exceed the capabilities of standard macro actions—one reason macro support is being dropped from Access. You run VBA subprocedures by attaching the subprocedure to particular events, such as clicking a command button with the mouse, that occur when a form or report is the active object. In Access 2000, you can also execute VBA procedures directly from their module.

- *Security* consists of functions available as menu choices and through VBA subprocedures. With security functions in a multiuser environment, you can let other people use your database. You can grant access to user groups and individuals, and you can restrict their ability to view or modify all or a portion of the tables in the database.

- *Printing* lets you print virtually anything you can view in Access's run mode. From the toolbar, you can print your VBA code, but not the macros that you write. (You can use the Documenter to print the content of your macros.)

NEW 2000

- *Publishing* features facilitate distribution of information over corporate intranets and the public Intranet as World Wide Web pages. Access 2000 adds Data Access Pages (DAP) that let you build applications for displaying and updating data in pages that take advantage of Dynamic HTML (DHTML) and Extensible Markup Language (XML).

The terms *open* and *close* have the same basic usage in Access as in other Windows applications but usually involve more than one basic function:

- Opening a database makes its content available to the application through the Database window. You can open only one database at a time during ordinary use of Access. Writing VBA code enables you to work with tables from more than one database. You can achieve the equivalent of multiple open Access databases by *linking* (Access 2000's term for *attaching*) tables from other databases.

- Opening a table displays a Datasheet view of its contents.

- Opening a query opens the tables involved but does not display them. Access then runs the query on these tables to create a tabular Recordset. Changes made to data in the Recordset cause corresponding changes to be made to the data in the tables associated with the query if the Recordset is updatable.

- Opening a form or report automatically opens the table or query that's associated with it. Forms and reports usually are associated with queries, but a query also can employ a single table.

- Closing a query closes the associated tables.

- Closing a form or report closes the associated query and its tables.

DEFINING ACCESS OPERATING MODES

Access has three basic operating modes:

- *Startup mode* enables you to compress, convert, encrypt, decrypt, and repair a database by choosing commands from the Tools menu's Database Utilities and Security submenus before opening a database. These commands, some of which are discussed at the end of this chapter, are available only when you *don't* have a database open.

- *Design mode* enables you to create and modify the structure of tables and queries, develop forms to display and edit your data, and format reports for printing. Access calls design mode *Design view*.

- *Run mode* displays your table, form, and report designs in individual document windows (the default mode). You execute macros by choosing one and then selecting run mode. Run mode does not apply to VBA modules, because functions are executed when encountered as elements of queries, forms, and reports. Procedures in modules are run by macro commands or directly from events of forms and reports. Run mode is called *Datasheet view* for tables and queries, *Form view* for forms, *Page view* for Data Access Pages (DAP), and *Print Preview* for reports.

You can select design or run mode by choosing command buttons in the Datasheet window, buttons on the toolbar, or commands from the <u>V</u>iew menu.

Tip #17 from

To change the default conditions under which Access displays and prints your tables, queries, forms, and reports, choose <u>O</u>ptions from the <u>T</u>ools menu. The section "Setting Default Options" later in this chapter describes options that apply to Access as a whole and those that apply only to tables.

PART

I

CH

3

UNDERSTANDING ACCESS'S TABLE DISPLAY

You're probably familiar with the terms for many of the components that comprise the basic window in which all conventional Windows 9x applications run. The presentation of Access windows varies with each basic function that Access performs. Because Part I, "Learning Access Fundamentals," of this book deals almost exclusively with tables, the examples that follow use Table Datasheet view. Figure 3.2 shows Access 2000's basic display for operations with tables; Table 3.1 describes the window's Access-related components.

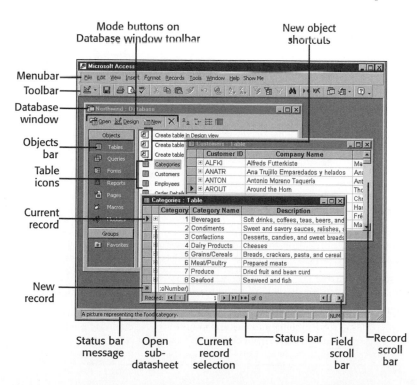

Figure 3.2
Access 2000's basic display for tables.

TABLE 3.1   COMPONENTS OF THE ACCESS DISPLAY FOR TABLES

Term	Description
Current Record button	A button that indicates a single selected record in the table. When you are editing the current record, the button icon displays a pencil rather than a triangular arrow. The Current Record button also is called the *record pointer*.
Current Record selection	Buttons that position the record pointer to the first, next, preceding, and last record number in the table and show the number of the currently selected record. If the table has a key field, the record number reflects the sequence of records in the primary key's sorting order; if there is no primary key in the table, the record number corresponds to the order in which records were physically added to the table.
Database window	The window that controls the operating mode of Access and selects the active document window's current function. From the database components displayed in the Database window, you select the component (such as a particular table) to display in the document window.
Database window toolbar	The toolbar that enables you to open or design the currently selected database object, create a new object, delete an object, and control how icons display in the Database window.
Field scroll bar	The scroll bar that enables you to view table fields that are outside the bounds of the document window. Record scroll bars provide access to records located outside the document window.
Menubar	A bar containing Access main menu choices. The specific menubar choices and the commands in the menus themselves change depending on Access's status. Menubars and toolbars collectively are called *command bars*.
Mode buttons	Three buttons that determine the operating mode of Access. *Open* places Access in run mode. *New* or *Design* puts Access in design mode, where you can create or edit tables.
New object shortcuts	A list of shortcuts to create a new database object.
New record	A button with an asterisk that indicates the location of the next record to be added to a table. Typing data in the new record appends the record to the table and creates another new record.
Objects bar	An Outlook-styled bar with shortcuts to lists of database objects.
Open subdatasheet	A click on the plus sign in the square box opens subdatasheet(s) for each record if the table has subdatasheets.
Status bar	A bar, located at the bottom of the application window, that displays prompts and indicators, such as the status of the Num Lock key.
Toolbar	A bar containing command buttons that duplicate the more commonly used menu choices. The actual number and type of toolbar buttons depend on which basic function of Access you are using.

MAXIMIZED DOCUMENT WINDOWS

Access uses a windowing technique that you should know about; otherwise, you might accidentally minimize or close Access when you intended to minimize or close a maximized document, such as a table. After you click a document window's Maximize button, the document window takes the place of the application window and occupies the entire display, except for the menubar and toolbar (see Figure 3.3). Most other Windows applications that display multiple documents, such as Word and Excel, have a similar capability to expand a document to occupy the entire window.

Note

Access is—and always has been—a multiple document interface (MDI) application. MDI applications have a main (parent) window, which contains multiple document (child) windows. Access 2000 windowing differs from Word 2000 and Excel 2000, both of which have migrated from their prior versions' MDI to the single document interface (SDI). SDI applications display each document in its own main window, which is represented by a document icon in the taskbar, and don't support child windows. Access 2000, by default, emulates SDI by displaying a document icon in the taskbar for each of its child windows.

If your first introduction to the components of Microsoft Office is Office 2000, you might not understand the difference between SDI and MDI components. Thus this and the following section offer a detailed explanation of MDI windowing. If you're familiar with MDI, skip these two sections.

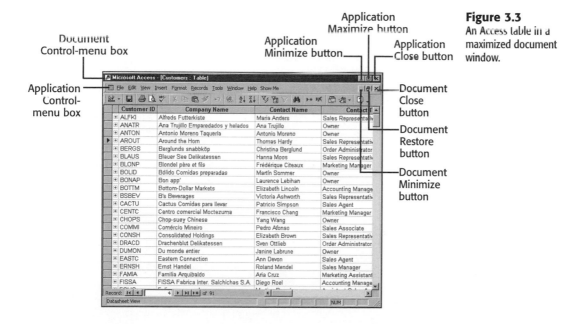

Figure 3.3
An Access table in a maximized document window.

Application Maximize button

Application Minimize button

Application Close button

Document Control-menu box

Application Control-menu box

Document Close button

Document Restore button

Document Minimize button

The document Control-menu box and the document Minimize, Restore, and Close buttons move to the menubar's extreme left and right, respectively. The document's title is added to the application title bar at the top of the display. To return the document window to its original size (established when the application window was first active), click the document Restore button; alternatively, click the document Control-menu box and then choose Restore from the document Control menu. You can close the document window by clicking the document Close button or by double-clicking the document Control-menu box. If you accidentally click the application Close button (or double-click the application Control-menu box just above the document Control-menu box), however, you close Access 2000. You receive no warning that you are about to exit Access unless you've changed the design of an object without saving those changes.

DOCUMENT WINDOWS MINIMIZED TO ICONS

Working with several overlapping windows limits each to a size that enables you to select another by clicking its surface. This overlapping might overly restrict your view of the data that the windows contain. You can minimize Access document windows and the Database window to icons that remain within the application window, as shown at the bottom of Figure 3.4. If you minimize a document window to an icon rather than close it, you can quickly return the window to its original size by double-clicking the icon. If you single-click the icon, you can choose how the window reappears by using the document Control menu, as shown for the Northwind Database window in Figure 3.4. You can also restore, maximize, or close a minimized icon by clicking the corresponding button within the icon.

Figure 3.4
Tables, a query, a form, and the Database window minimized to icons within the application window.

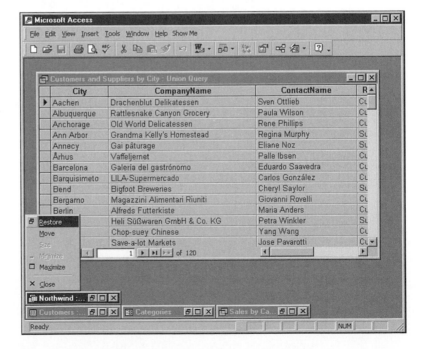

If you choose to display your document window in maximized form by choosing Maximize from the document Control menu that appears when you click the icon, the document hides the icons at the bottom of the application window. In this case, choose the document that you want from the Window menu. If you size your document windows (like the window in Figure 3.4) by dragging their borders, you can avoid the substantial mouse movement and two-step menu-selection process to select the active document.

THE TOOLBARS IN TABLE DATASHEET VIEW

The buttons that appear in Access's toolbar, and the number of toolbars displayed, change according to the function that Access is currently performing. When you are working with tables in run mode, Access 2000 displays the Table Datasheet and the Datasheet Formatting toolbars (see Figures 3.5 and 3.6). The next two sections describe the toolbars that appear in table run mode (Datasheet view). Click the Tables shortcut of the Database window and double click one of the table shortcuts—such as Customers—to follow the text in the next few sections.

PART
I

CH

3

THE TABLE DATASHEET TOOLBAR

The Table Datasheet toolbar appears whenever you open an Access table in Datasheet view. Figure 3.5 shows the Table Datasheet toolbar, and Table 3.2 describes the buttons that appear on the toolbar.

Note

Toolbar buttons provide shortcuts to traditional selection methods, such as choosing menu commands or selecting command or option buttons in a particular sequence. The Menu Sequence columns of Tables 3.2 and 3.3 list how you can duplicate the effect of clicking a toolbar button by using the menus or the command buttons in the Database window.

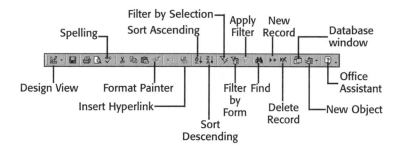

Figure 3.5
Access's Table Datasheet toolbar, displayed when a table is open in Datasheet view.

TABLE 3.2   APPEARANCE AND FUNCTIONS OF BUTTONS AND OTHER ELEMENTS OF THE TABLE DATASHEET TOOLBAR

Icon	Menu Button	Sequence	Function
	Design View**	View, Design View	Changes the table display to design mode, in which you specify the properties of each field of the table.
	Spelling	Tools, Spelling	Starts the spellingchecker
	Format Painter		Copies a control's format to another control. Used only in Design view; it's enabled only when you select a control.
	Insert	Insert, Hyperlink	Opens the Insert Hyperlink dialog, Hyperlink which lets you add a URL or UNC address to a Hyperlink field in a table. Chapter 16, "Working with Hyperlinks and HTML," describes Hyperlink fields in more detail.
	Sort Ascending	Records, Sort, Ascending	Sorts the records in ascending order, based on the current field.
	Sort Descending	Records, Sort, Descending	Sorts the records in descending order, based on the current field.
	Filter by Selection	Records, Filter, Filter by Selection	Filters records based on the selected text in a field.
	Filter by Form	Records, Filter, Filter by Form	Enables you to type criteria in a table datasheet to establish how records are filtered.
	Apply/ Remove	Records, Apply Filter/Sort Filter	Applies or removes a filter.
	Find	Edit, Find	Displays the Find dialog that locates records with specific characters in a single field or all fields.
	New Record	Edit, Go To, New	Selects the tentative append record.
	Delete Record	Edit, Delete Record	Deletes the active record.
	Database	Window, 1 Window	Displays the Database window.
	New Object		Displays a drop-down list from which you choose the type of new object that you want to create: tables, forms, reports, pages, queries, macros, modules or class modules. The first object type in the list is your most recent selection.

Icon	Menu Button	Sequence	Function
[?]	Office Assistant	F1	Activates the Microsoft Office Assistant, described later in the "The Office Assistant" section.
	More Buttons	View, Toolbars Customize	Displays a drop-down list from which you can add or remove buttons from the toolbar.

** You only see this icon if you click the drop down arrow next to the Design view icon or if you change to Design mode. This icon varies by object and mode and the View drop down contains other mode possibilities for different objects.

Note

In Access 2000 and other applications in Microsoft Office 2000, the toolbar buttons appear as flat icons on the toolbar. The toolbar buttons have a raised buttonlike appearance only when the mouse pointer is over them. The exception to this rule is "toggle" buttons—that is, buttons that represent the on/off status of a feature such as the Gridlines button (refer to Table 3.3 and Figure 3.6). When a toggle button is "up," it appears as a flat icon on the toolbar until you move the mouse pointer over it; the button's "up" appearance indicates that the feature controlled by that button is off. Toggle buttons in the "down" positions are shaded so that they look as though they are below the surface of the toolbar; the "down" appearance indicates that the feature controlled by that button is on.

THE DATASHEET FORMATTING TOOLBAR

In addition to the Table Datasheet toolbar, you can display the Datasheet Formatting toolbar whenever you view a table in Datasheet view. From the View menu, choose Toolbars, Formatting (Datasheet) to add the toolbar. The buttons in the Datasheet Formatting toolbar provide shortcuts to various text-formatting commands. In Datasheet view, the text-formatting commands apply to the entire table; you can't format individual cells in Datasheet view. Figure 3.6 shows the Datasheet Formatting toolbar, and Table 3.3 summarizes the action of each button on the toolbar.

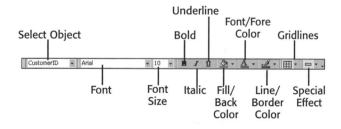

Figure 3.6
The Datasheet Formatting toolbar in Datasheet view.

TABLE 3.3 APPEARANCE AND FUNCTIONS OF BUTTONS AND OTHER ELEMENTS OF THE DATASHEET FORMATTING TOOLBAR

Icon	Menu Button	Sequence	Function
	Go To Field		Displays a drop-down list from which you can jump quickly to any field in the table.
Arial	Font	Format, Font	Lets you select the font (typeface) for text in a table.
10	Font Size	Format, Font	Lets you select the size of the text in a table.
B	Bold	Format, Font	Turns bold text formatting on and off for the text in a table.
I	Italic	Format, Font	Turns italic text formatting on and off for text in a table.
U	Underline	Format, Font	Turns underlining on and off for text in a table.
	Fill/Back Color	Format, Cells	Displays a palette of colors from which to choose the background color for the table's data cells.
A	Font/Fore Color	Format, Font	Displays a palette of colors from which to choose the color of the texte in the table.
	Line/Border Color	Format, Cells	Displays a color palette from which to choose the color of the gridlines that indicate rows and columns in the table.
	Gridlines	Format, Cells	Displays four buttons that enable you to choose which gridlines are shown: horizontal and vertical, vertical only, horizontal only, or none.
	Special Effect	Format, Cells	Displays three buttons that let you choose the cell display style: flat, raised, or sunken.

Note

This chapter concentrates on toolbars for Table and Query Datasheet and Table Design views. Chapter 12, "Creating and Using Forms," describes the toolbars for Form and Form Design views. Chapter 14, "Printing Basic Reports and Mailing Labels," explains the elements of the Report Design and Print Preview toolbars.

TOOLBAR CUSTOMIZATION

Access 2000 uses the resizable, customizable, floating toolbars that have become standard in Microsoft applications such as Excel and Microsoft Word. In Microsoft Office 2000, menubars and toolbars have been combined into a single object, called a *command bar*, and share many features. The primary characteristic that distinguishes a menubar from a toolbar in Access 2000 (and other Office 2000 applications) is that every application has at least one menubar, and the menubar may not be hidden. In all other respects, menubars and toolbars are the same.

The View menu's Toolbars command lets you select which toolbars are currently visible. The Toolbars submenu lists those toolbars pertinent to Access's current operating mode. Figure 3.7 shows the Toolbars submenu for Table Datasheet view. A mark at the left of a menu choice indicates that that specific toolbar is now displayed. To display or hide a toolbar, click its name in the submenu.

Figure 3.7
Displaying or hiding toolbars with the View menu's Toolbars choice.

Note

In Figure 3.7 and other figures throughout this book, you might notice a menu that isn't discussed in the text—Show Me. This menu appears on the menubar only when the Northwind.mdb database is open. The Show Me menu isn't part of Access 2000; instead, it's displayed by Northwind.mdb. If you're interested in viewing help topics relating to the VBA code that is part of the Northwind.mdb sample database, open the Show Me menu.

The Customize choice on the Toolbars submenu opens the Customize dialog (see Figure 3.8), which lets you display as many toolbars at once as will fit in your display or hide toolbars that Access would otherwise display automatically. To display a toolbar, click the Toolbars tab to display the Toolbars page (if necessary) and then click the box to the left of the toolbar name so that the check box is marked. To hide a toolbar, click the box again to clear it.

Tip #18 from

R J

For help in using the Customize dialog, click the Office Assistant button at the lower-left area of the Customize dialog to activate the Office Assistant if it isn't already active (see "Using the Office Assistant" later in this chapter).

Figure 3.8
Selecting the toolbars
to be displayed in the
Customize dialog.

Tip #19 from

When an Access toolbar is in its docked position, it has a fixed width, anchored at its left edge. If you reduce the width of Access's application window by dragging either vertical border inward, the buttons at the docked toolbar's extreme right begin to disappear beyond the application window's right edge. Operating Access in a maximized window with docked toolbars is usually best because you can then easily access all the toolbar buttons when you use the default inline horizontal toolbar.

You also can use the Customize dialog to change the viewing options for toolbars. The Options page enables you to select various toolbar viewing options (see Figure 3.9). If you're using XGA 1,024×768 screen resolution, you might want to mark the Large Icons check box to cause the toolbar button icons to approximately double in size, making them easier to discern and easier to click. The Show ScreenTips on Toolbars check box governs whether Access displays ScreenTips (formerly known as ToolTips), that is, hints on the mouse pointer for toolbar buttons. The Show Shortcut Keys in ScreenTips check box determines whether Access displays the keyboard shortcut (if there is one) as part of the ScreenTip text.

NEW 2000 The List Font Names in Their Font check box, if checked, displays each font name as a sample of the font in lists of fonts. If you mark the check box, font lists use the standard font and display faster. The Show Recently Used Commands First check box, if marked, displays only the menu choices that you use on a regular basis, a feature Microsoft calls Intellimenus. The Show Full Menus After a Short Delay check box governs whether the full Access menu is displayed after you hover your mouse on the menu. The Reset My Usage Data button resets menu and menu usage and toolbar settings.

Finally, the Menu Animations drop-down list lets you select how Access draws menus onscreen. You may select None (for no special effects when drawing menus), Random

(Access randomly chooses an animation effect each time you open a menu), Unfold (the menu unfolds like a fan), or Slide (the menu opens like a roller-shade) as the technique for displaying Access's menus.

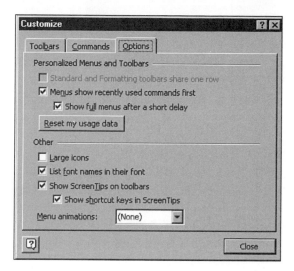

Figure 3.9
Selecting viewing options for toolbars and menus in the Options page of the Customize dialog.

PART

I

CH

3

In addition to displaying multiple toolbars, you can reshape or reposition the toolbars to suit your own taste. Click a blank area of the toolbar and hold down the left mouse button to drag the toolbar to a new location. The toolbar turns into a pop-up floating toolbar, similar to the toolbox that you use to add control objects to forms and reports. Pop-up toolbars always appear on top of any other windows open in your application.

Figure 3.10 shows three floating command bars: the Table Datasheet toolbar, the Formatting Datasheet toolbar, and the Menu Bar. (These are the toolbars discussed in the preceding section that Access displays in Datasheet View mode. The Menu Bar—Access's main menubar—was moved from its position at the top of the Access application window to demonstrate that it's a command bar.) Command bars in their fixed position are called *docked* command bars, whereas command bars in their pop-up window are referred to as *floating* command bars. Floating command bars display the More Buttons button as part of the title bar. After you change a command bar to a floating command bar (or dock it), Access always displays the command bar in that location until you reposition it.

Tip #20 from

You can also dock command bars (menubars and toolbars) at the bottom of the Access application window or at the left or right edge of the application window.

Figure 3.10
Access's Table Datasheet toolbar, Datasheet Formatting toolbar, and main menubar dragged from their default positions at the top of the application window.

RIGHT-CLICK SHORTCUT MENUS

Another feature that Access 2000 shares with other Microsoft applications, as well as with Windows 9.x and Windows NT 4.0, is the shortcut menu that appears when you right-click an Access database object. Shortcut menus (also called *pop-up* or *context* menus) present choices that vary depending on the type of object that you click. Figure 3.11 shows the shortcut menu for a field of a table selected by clicking the field name header.

Figure 3.11
The shortcut menu for a selected column of a table.

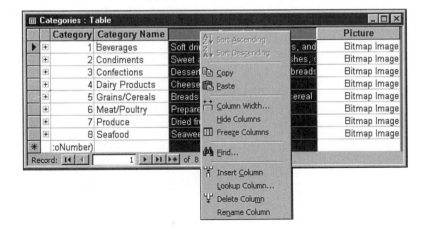

Tip #21 from

R J

Shortcut menus are quite useful and provide shortcuts to many common tasks. If you're not sure what you can do with an object onscreen, try right-clicking it to see what shortcut menu commands are available.

USING THE FUNCTION KEYS

Access assigns specific purposes to all 12 function keys of the 101-key extended keyboard. Some keys, such as Shift+F4 (which you press to find the next occurrence of a match with the Find dialog), derive from other Microsoft applications—in this case, Word. You combine function keys with the Shift, Alt, and Ctrl keys to enable users to perform as many as 96 functions.

GLOBAL FUNCTION KEYS

Windows, rather than Access, uses global function-key assignments, except for F11 and Alt+F1, to perform identical functions in all Windows applications. Table 3.4 lists the global function-key assignments.

TABLE 3.4   GLOBAL FUNCTION-KEY ASSIGNMENTS

Key	Function
F1	Displays context-sensitive help related to the present basic function and status of Access. If a context-sensitive help topic isn't available, F1 starts the Office Assistant (described later in this chapter).
Shift+F1	Adds a question mark to the mouse pointer. Place the mouse pointer with the question mark over an object onscreen for which you want help and then click.
Ctrl+F4	Closes the active window.
Alt+F4	Exits Access or closes a dialog it one is open.
Ctrl+F6	Selects each open window in sequence as the active window.
F11 or Alt+F1	Selects the Database window as the active window.
F12 or Alt+F2	Opens the File Save As dialog.
Shift+F12 or Alt+Shift+F2	Saves your open database; the equivalent of the File menu's Save command.

PART

I

CH

3

FUNCTION-KEY ASSIGNMENTS FOR FIELDS, GRIDS, AND TEXT BOXES

Access assigns function-key combinations that aren't reserved for global operations to actions specific to the basic function that you are performing at the moment. Table 3.5 lists the function-key combinations that apply to fields, grids, and text boxes. (To present complete information, this table repeats some information that appears in the previous tables.)

→ For an extensive list of Access shortcut key assignments, **see** "Using Keyboard Operations for Entering and Editing Data," **p. 186**.

TABLE 3.5 FUNCTION KEYS FOR FIELDS, GRIDS, AND TEXT BOXES

Key	Function
F2	Toggles between displaying the caret for editing and selecting the entire field.
Shift+F2	Opens the Zoom box to make typing expressions and other text easier.
F4	Opens a drop-down combo list or list box.
Shift+F4	Finds the next occurrence of a match of the text typed in the Find or Replace dialog, if the dialog is closed.
F5	Moves the caret to the record-number box. Type the number of the record that you want to display.
F6	In Table Design view, cycles between upper and lower parts of the window. In Form Design view, cycles through the header, body (detail section), and footer.
Shift+F6	In Form Design view, cycles through the footer, body (detail section), and header, moving backward.
F7	Starts the spelling checker.
F8	Turns on extend mode. Press F8 again to extend the selection to a word, the entire field, the whole record, and then all records.
Shift+F8	Reverses the F8 selection process.
Ctrl+F	Opens the Find dialog.
Ctrl+H	Opens the Replace dialog.
Ctrl++ (plus sign)	Adds a new record to the database.
Ctrl+− (minus sign)	Deletes the current record.
Shift+Enter	Saves changes to the active record in the database.
Esc	Undoes changes in the current record or field. By pressing Esc twice, you can undo changes in the current field and record. Also cancels extend mode.

SETTING DEFAULT OPTIONS

You can set about 100 options that establish the default settings for Access. (But you aren't likely to change default options until you are more familiar with Access.) This book is a reference as well as a tutorial guide, and options are a basic element of Access's overall structure, so this section explains how to change these settings.

Note

> The Options dialog discussed in this chapter corresponds to the options available using standard Access (Jet 4.0) databases and not the Microsoft Data Engine (MSDE) used by Access Data Projects (ADP). See Chapter 25, "Creating Access Data Projects," for more information on ADP.

You set defaults by choosing <u>O</u>ptions from the <u>T</u>ools menu. The Options property sheet appears as shown in Figure 3.12. The View, General, Keyboard, and Edit/Find options apply to the system as a whole. The Datasheet, Tables/Queries, and Forms/Reports options apply to table views in Datasheet view, forms, and queries. Advanced options apply mainly to multiuser database performance.

Note

NEW 2000

> If you're familiar with previous Access versions, you might notice the absence of the Module options page. Access 2000 uses the VBA Integrated Design Environment (IDE), so the Module options are found in the IDE by choosing <u>O</u>ptions from the <u>T</u>ools menu. Using the IDE is the subject of Chapter 26, "Writing Visual Basic for Applications Code."

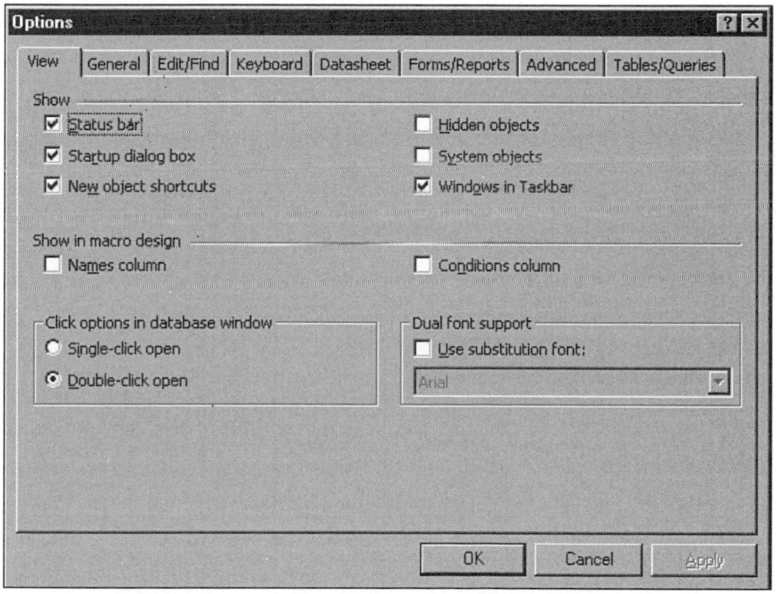

PART

I

CH

3

Figure 3.12
The Options property sheet displaying the View options page.

You select a category by clicking the tab near the top of the Options property sheet. When you change a category, the property sheet displays the options page for that category. Most settings are option buttons and check boxes, although many other items require multiple-choice entries that you select from drop-down lists. In some cases, you must type a specific value from the keyboard. After you complete your changes, click OK to close the property sheet. If you decide not to implement your changes, click Cancel to exit the property sheet without making any changes. The next few sections and their tables summarize options that affect Access as a whole and those options that affect viewing and printing data in Datasheet view.

SYSTEM DEFAULTS

NEW 2000 Access 2000 uses the Windows Registry to store all default properties for displaying and printing the contents of tables, queries, forms, reports, and modules for each user of Access. In prior Access versions, the user default properties resided in the System.mdw workgroup file. The .mdw extension for workgroup system files was new with Access 95, replacing the .MDA extension shared by libraries, wizards, and SYSTEM.MDA in Access 1.x and 2.0. System.mdw also stores usernames and passwords when you secure your Access database or use Access in a multiuser (workgroup) environment. If you use the Security Wizard to secure your database, you should follow the recommendation to create a new workgroup file.

→ **See** "Sharing Your Access Database Files with Other Users," **p. 887**.

> **Note**
>
> Your workgroup file—System.mdw by default—is vital to the proper operation of Access. You should keep a backup copy of it on a floppy disk. After you change any options or implement Access's security features, you should always create an updated backup.

VIEW OPTIONS

The View options, as described in Table 3.6, enable you to customize the appearance of Access's application window.

TABLE 3.6   VIEW OPTIONS FOR THE ACCESS SYSTEM

Option	Function
Show Group	
Status Bar	If marked, displays the status bar at the bottom of the Access application window.
Startup Dialog	If marked, displays the startup dialog whenever you start Access. This dialog prompts you to open an existing database or to create a new one.
New Object Shortcuts	If marked, displays shortcuts for the creation of new objects in the Database window.
Hidden Objects	If marked, displays hidden objects in the Database window.

Option	Function
System Objects	If marked, displays system objects in the Database window.
Windows in Taskbar	If marked, causes the Database window and each open window to display as an icon in the Windows Taskbar; available only if Microsoft Internet Explorer Active Desktop is installed.
Macro Design Group	
Names Column	If marked, displays the Names column in new macros.
Conditions Column	If marked, displays the Conditions column in new macros.
Click Options in Database Window Group	
Single-click Open	If selected, lets you open a database object with a single click instead of the conventional double-click.
Double-click Open	If selected, requires a double-click to open a database object (the default).
Dual Font Support Group	
Use Substitution Font	If marked, enables you to select from the list a default font to use when Access can't display multilingual characters with the default font.

GENERAL OPTIONS

General options apply to Access as a whole (see Table 3.7). The settings that you make on the General options page apply to any new objects that you create (tables, forms, and reports) but don't retroactively affect existing objects. For example, changing the print margins on the General page affects reports that you create subsequently, but not any existing reports. To change the print margins of existing objects, you must change each object's individual printing settings in Design view.

TABLE 3.7   GENERAL OPTIONS FOR THE ACCESS SYSTEM

Option	Function
Default Database Folder	Changes the default folder for the Open Database dialog. The default folder is the Access working folder, indicated by a period.
New Database Sort Order	Sets the alphabetical sort order used for new databases. You can change the sort order for an existing database by selecting a different sort-order setting and then compacting the database by choosing Database Utilities, Compact and Repair Database... from the Tools menu.
Recently Used File List	If marked, Access maintains a list on the File menu of recently opened databases. The default number of files tracked is four, but this setting can be changed by selecting a number from the list.
Provide Feedback with Sound	If marked, Access generates sound—through .WAV files to accompany various tasks.
Compact on Close	If marked, Access automatically compacts and repairs your database, if needed, when you close Access.

continues

TABLE 3.7   CONTINUED

Option	Function
Print Margins Group	
Left Margin	Establishes the default left margin.
Top Margin	Establishes the default top margin.
Right Margin	Establishes the default right margin.
Bottom Margin	Establishes the default bottom margin.
Use Four-Digit Year Formatting Group	
This Database	Applies four-digit year formatting to all Date/Time fields in the current database.
All Databases	Applies four-digit year formatting to all Date/Time fields in every database you open.
Web Options Appearance Group	
Hyperlink Color	Selects the color for hyperlink text that has not been viewed since you opened the database.
Followed Hyperlink Color	Selects the color for hyperlink text that has been viewed since you opened the database.
Underline Hyperlinks	If selected, Access displays hyperlink text with an underline.
Name AutoCorrect Group	
Track Name AutoCorrect	If marked, Access stores information it needs to correct errors caused by renaming database objects. Access only tracks, but does not correct immediately unless the Perform Name AutoCorrect is marked.
Perform Name AutoCorrect	If marked, Access repairs naming errors immediately as the name changes occur.
Log Name AutoCorrect Changes	If marked, Access records in the AutoCorrectLog table the changes made to the database to repair naming errors.

NEW 2000 icons appear beside the *Use Four-Digit Year Formatting Group* and *Name AutoCorrect Group* rows.

Margins usually are expressed in inches. If you're using an international version of Access, margin settings are in centimeters. You also can specify margin settings in twips, the default measurement of Windows and Visual Basic for Applications. A *twip* is 1/20 of a printer's point. A *point* is 1/72 inch, so a twip is 1/1,440 inch.

The 1-inch default margins are arbitrary; you might want to reset them to your preference before creating any forms or reports of your own. If you are using a laser printer, refer to its manual to determine the maximum printable area. The printable area determines the minimum margins that you can use.

Apart from the printing margins, the General option you're most likely to want to change is the default database directory. When you create your own databases, you should store them in a folder dedicated to databases to simplify backup operations. A dedicated database folder also is a good place to keep a backup copy of System.mdw.

→ For more information on Four-Digit Year Formatting options and Year 2000 Compliance issues, **see** "Standard Formats for Number, Date/Time, and Yes/No Data Types," **p. 144**, and "Four-Digit Year Option Settings," **p. 36**.

EDIT/FIND OPTIONS

The Edit/Find options affect the behavior of Access's Find feature for tables in either Form or Datasheet view and when working with VBA code in a module. Table 3.8 summarizes the Edit/Find options and their effects. The options in the Default Find/Replace Behavior group determine the default searching method for the Edit menu's Find and Replace commands. The options in the Confirm group determine which actions Access asks the user to confirm. The final option group in the Edit/Find options page is the Filter by Form Defaults for the current database. These options don't actually affect Access itself, but affect the defaults for the open database.

PART

I

CH

3

TABLE 3.8   EDIT/FIND OPTIONS FOR THE ACCESS SYSTEM

Option	Function
Don't Display Lists More Than This Number of Records Read	Prohibits the display of filter values whenever the number of items in the list exceeds the specified number.
Default Find/Replace Behavior Group	
Fast Search	Sets the default search method to search in the current field and to match the whole field.
General Search	Sets the default search method to search in all fields, matching any part of a field.
Start of Field Search	Causes the default search method to search the current field, matching only the beginning of the field.
Confirm Group	
Record Changes	Causes Access to confirm any changes that you make to a record.
Document Deletions	Causes Access to confirm document (table, form, or report) deletions.
Action Queries	Causes Access to confirm an action query (such as adding or deleting records) before carrying out the query.
Filter by Form Defaults Group	
Local Indexed Fields	Includes local indexed fields in the list of values that you can use when setting filter criteria.
Local Non-Indexed Fields	Includes nonindexed fields in the list of values that you can use when setting filter criteria.
ODBC Fields	Includes fields from remote ODBC tables in the lists of values that you can use when setting filter criteria.

KEYBOARD OPTIONS

Keyboard options are especially important if you are accustomed to a particular type of arrow-key behavior. You probably will want to change keyboard options more than you will change any other options. You alter Keyboard options primarily to expedite keyboard entry of data in Table Datasheet view, so Keyboard options are one of the subjects of Chapter 5, "Entering, Editing, and Validating Data in Tables."

→ **See** "Using Data Entry and Editing Keys," **p. 188**.

ADVANCED OPTIONS

Access has several advanced system options that affect multiuser operations, OLE updates, DDE linking and updating, and tables attached by the ODBC feature of the Jet 4.0 database engine. Table 3.9 describes the Advanced options that you can set. Options in the Default Record Locking group affect how Access locks records in a multiuser environment, and the Default Open Mode option group controls whether Access shares opened databases. The DDE Operations options group controls how Access handles DDE requests from other applications; other options control OLE updating and query updating. The Current Database Only group contains options that relate to any VBA code that may be stored in your database. Usually you don't need to change the Advanced options much unless you're working in a multiuser environment with several users sharing the same database, or the database contains VBA code that uses command arguments and conditional compiler directives.

TABLE 3.9 ADVANCED OPTIONS FOR THE ACCESS SYSTEM

Option	Function
Number of Update Retries	Specifies how many times Access tries to update a query, OLE object, or DDE link before giving up. The default number of tries is 2.
ODBC Refresh Interval (sec)	Specifies how many seconds Access waits before refreshing records that you view through an ODBC connection. The default interval is 1,500 seconds.
Open Databases Using Record-level Locking	If marked, Access only locks the row that is being updated or edited. Versions prior to Access 2000 used page locking, which locked whole pages of data.
Refresh Interval (sec)	Specifies how many seconds Access waits before refreshing remote data. The default Refresh Interval is 60 seconds.
Update Retry Interval (msec)	Specifies how many milliseconds (thousandths of a second) Access waits between attempts at updating an OLE, DDE, ODBC, or other link. The default is 25 ms.
Default Record Locking Group	
No Locks	When selected, leaves all records unlocked in the open database tables so that other networked users can update the records.
All Records	When selected, locks all records in the open database tables. No other networked users can update the records.

Option	Function
E_dited Records	When selected, locks only edited records. When changes to the record are saved, Access unlocks the record.

DDE Operations Group

Option	Function
I_gnore DDE Requests	If enabled, ignores all Dynamic Data Exchange (DDE) requests from other Windows applications.
Enable DDE Ref_resh (default)	If enabled, lets Access dynamically update linked DDE data.DDE data.
OLE/DDE Ti_meout (sec)	Specifies how long Access waits for a response from a DDE or OLE server. If the specified interval passes without a response, Access reports an error. Access's default value for this option is 30 seconds.

Default Open Mode Group

Option	Function
S_hared	When selected, enables other networked users to use the open database simultaneously.
E_xclusive	When selected, opens the database in an exclusive mode so that other network users can't open the database.

DEFAULTS FOR DATASHEET VIEW

You use Datasheet view options to customize the display of all query datasheets and new table and form datasheets (see Table 3.10). As with printing options, to change the display format of existing table and form datasheets, you must edit the appropriate properties of the table or form in Design view. The Datasheet view options that you set don't apply to forms and reports created with Access wizards. Each wizard has its own set of default values. The options in the Default Colors group set the background and foreground colors for text displayed in Datasheet view, whereas the Default Font group's options determine the typeface and text size. The Default Gridlines Showing options determine which gridlines (if any) Access displays in Datasheet view. Finally, the Default Cell Effect options enable you to select a default style for datasheet cells.

TABLE 3.10   OPTIONS FOR DATASHEET VIEWS

Option	Function
D_efault Column Width	Specifies the default column width in inches. Access's default value for this text box setting is 1 inch.
Sho_w Animations	If selected, displays animated cursors and other animation effects. If you have a slow computer, you'll probably want to turn off this option to improve Access's operating speed slightly.

Default Colors Group

Option	Function
Fo_nt	Displays a drop-down list from which you can select the color of the text in new tables, queries, and forms. Access's default font color is black.

continues

TABLE 3.10   CONTINUED

Option	Function
Background	Lets you select the background color of cells in Datasheet view. Access's default background color is white.
Gridlines	Lets you select the color of the gridlines displayed in Datasheet view. Access's default gridline color is silver.
Default Font Group	
Font	Displays a drop-down list from which you can select the typeface that Access uses to display text in Datasheet view. Access's default font is Arial.
Weight	Displays a drop-down list from which you can select the weight of the text characters displayed in Datasheet view. You can select Normal (the default), Thin, Extra Light, Medium, Semi-bold, Bold, Extra Bold, or Heavy.
Size	Enables you to select the default font size, in points. Access's default font size is 10 points.
Italic	If selected, displays all datasheet text in italic.
Underline	If selected, displays all datasheet text with a single underline.
Default Gridlines Showing Group	
Horizontal	If selected, displays horizontal gridlines (that is, gridlines between rows) in Datasheet view. By default, this option and the Vertical Gridlines option are turned on.
Vertical	If selected, displays vertical gridlines (that is, gridlines between columns) in Datasheet view. You can display vertical and horizontal gridlines by combining the Vertical Gridlines option with the Horizontal Gridlines option.
Default cell effect group	
Flat	When selected, displays a data cell as a "flat" cell—that is, the cell has no special shading.
Raised	When selected, adds shadow effects to each data cell so that the cell appears to be raised above the surface of the screen, like a command button.
Sunken	When selected, adds shadow effects to each data cell so that the cell appears to be sunken below the surface of the screen.

Note

The remaining two option categories–Tables/Queries and Forms/Reports–are discussed in the chapters that cover the subject of the particular option category. Also, options related to multiuser, DDE, and ODBC features are described in more detail in the chapters devoted to those special topics.

USING ACCESS HELP

NEW 2000 The Access Help system uses HTML help—the new Microsoft online help standard. HTML help uses compressed HTML documents (.chm) files to replace traditional Windows help files (.htm) and the familiar Help windows. Microsoft's motive for changing the Help system appears to be aimed at eliminating costly conversion of .hlp files on the Microsoft Web site to HTML. Version 1.0 of HTML help in Office 2000, like version 1.0 of most Microsoft products, isn't ready for prime time. You're likely to find Office 2000 to be a hindrance—not an aid—to learning Access 2000.

CONTEXT-SENSITIVE HELP

Context-sensitive help tries to anticipate your need for information by displaying Help windows related to the operating mode, function, and operation in which you are involved or attempting to perform. You can get context-sensitive help in any of the following ways:

PART
I
CH
3

- *By using the help mouse pointer that appears after you click the What's This? button* (located near the top-right corner of the dialog window) in the active dialog. Move the help mouse pointer over the dialog option for which you want help and click again to display a pop-up Help window with information about that dialog option.

- *By using the help mouse pointer that appears after you press Shift+F1* or choose What's This? from the Help menu. Move the help mouse pointer over the item for which you want help and click again to display a pop-up Help window.

- *By pressing the F1 key.* Access displays a Help window with information about the active area (dialog control, window, menu command, and so on) or displays the Office Assistant, described later in this chapter.

- *By clicking the Help button in a dialog.* Use this method, or press the F1 key, for dialogs that don't have a What's This? button.

To get context-sensitive help in an open dialog, click the What's This? button; the mouse pointer changes to a question mark. Move the help mouse pointer over the dialog control that you want help with and click. You can also get context-sensitive help on the active dialog control by pressing F1 or clicking the control with the right mouse button. For example, you might want more information about the effects of the Find and Replace dialog's Match Case option. To find such information, click the What's This? button and then click the Find and Replace dialog's Match Case option. Figure 3.13 shows the resulting pop-up Help window explaining the Match Case option.

Figure 3.13
The context-sensitive help for the Find dialog's Match Case option.

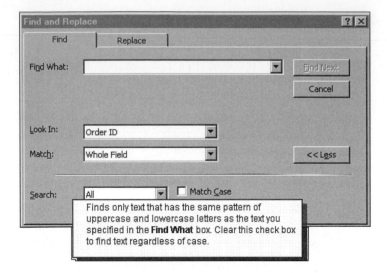

Another method for getting context-sensitive help is to press Shift+F1 (or choose What's This? from the Help menu) and then click the item that you want help with to display the related help topic. Figure 3.14 shows an example that explains the purpose of the Table Datasheet toolbar's Find button.

Figure 3.14
The pop-up Help window explaining the purpose of the toolbar's Find button.

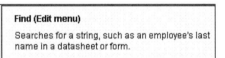

THE HELP MENU

Access's Help menu provides an alternative to using context-sensitive help. Table 3.11 lists the Help menu options.

TABLE 3.11   ACCESS'S HELP MENU OPTIONS

Option	Function
Microsoft Access Help	Activates the Office Assistant, described later in this chapter. If the Office Assistant is turned off, opens the Microsoft Access Help window.
What's This?	Changes the mouse pointer to the Help pointer for obtaining context-sensitive help. Move the Help pointer over the object or menu choice for which you want help and click to display a pop-up Help window.
Office on the Web	Displays a submenu list of Web sites related to Microsoft, Microsoft Access, frequently asked questions, free software, and other topics.

Option	Function
Detect and Repair	Opens the Detect and Repair dialog that attempts to repair a damaged database. If your database exhibits unexpected behavior, such as objects suddenly disappearing, try a Detect and Repair operation.
About Microsoft Access	Displays the copyright notice for Microsoft Access, and the name and organization that you entered during setup. The About dialog also contains two command buttons: one that displays sources of technical support for Access in North America and throughout the world, and another that displays information about your computer system, such as how much memory you've installed, whether you have a math coprocessor, and the amount of remaining disk space.

Tip #22 from

If you have a very serious problem with Access 2000 or other Office 2000 applications, a Microsoft Technical Support representative may request that you send a System Info (MSInfo, .nfo) file for inspection. You can create a .nfo file by choosing File, Save, and providing a file name. The .nfo file contains a substantial amount of information about your PC and the programs you've installed, which is needed to troubleshoot major problems, but .nfo files don't included confidential personal or corporate information, such as passwords. Beta testers routinely provide .nfo files to Microsoft to aid in diagnosing problems.

THE MICROSOFT ACCESS HELP WINDOW

The Office Assistant must be turned off to gain access to the Access Help window. To permanently get rid of the Office Assistant and use the Access Help window, open the Office Assistant, click Options, and clear the Use the Office Assistant check box of the Office Assistant dialog.

The Microsoft Access Help window contains three tabbed pages: Contents, Answer Wizard, and Index. Each page is described in the following sections.

THE CONTENTS PAGE

Figure 3.15 shows the Contents page (you might have to click the Contents tab to bring the table of contents to the front of the window). The Contents page is like the table of contents in a book; it shows the structure of the topics in the Help system based on the topic's title.

Each table of contents entry that has subheadings is indicated by a book icon to its left. To see subheadings for a topic, double-click the closed book icon. The Help system expands the topic list and changes the icon to an open book. (Click the open book icon to hide the expanded subheading branch and change the icon back to a closed book.)

Table of contents headings that lack subheadings have to their left an icon resembling a sheet of paper with a question mark on it. Figure 3.15 shows the Finding and Sorting Data heading expanded to show its subheadings; the Sorting Data in Tables, Queries, Forms, and Pages subheading, in turn, has been expanded, revealing a list of three help topics. To display a topic, click it.

Figure 3.15
The Contents tab of the Microsoft Access Help window, showing expanded headings and subheadings in the left pane and the selected topic in the right pane.

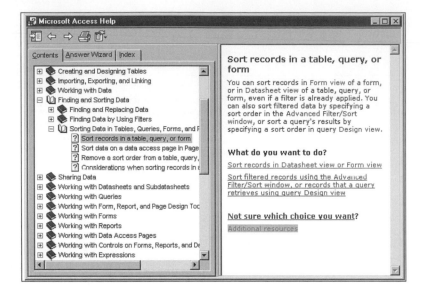

UNDERSTANDING THE HELP WINDOW

You can reposition and resize the Help window by dragging its borders with your mouse. To reposition the Help window, click and drag the help title bar. If the help file on the topic that you selected has more information than can fit in the window, a scroll bar appears at the right of the window. Scroll down to display additional text.

Tip #23 from

To copy text from any Help window, drag the mouse pointer over the text that you want to copy to select it; then press Ctrl+C, or right-click and choose Copy from the context menu. You can then paste the copied help text into any Windows application from the Clipboard.

Most Access Help windows include hyperlinks that provide additional information about a topic. Hyperlinks with solid underlines, such as Form View and Datasheet View in Figure 3.15, display a definition of the term or contain more detailed information about that topic. Figure 3.16 shows the display window that opens when you click the Datasheet View hyperlink.

Some hyperlinks lead to additional help topics. You click the hyperlink that represents the subject about which you want to learn. This action causes a jump to the subject's first help page, which often provides several additional choices for more detailed help on a specific topic.

Most help pages, in addition to providing information about a particular topic, also have step-by-step instructions for the task you are inquiring about. In Figure 3.15, notice that the help topic has a What Do You Want to Do? section. This section lists a variety of tasks that you might be trying to accomplish if you're looking for help on sorting records Each item in the list is a hyperlink. After you click this hyperlink, Access displays a help screen with step-by-step instructions for accomplishing the indicated task.

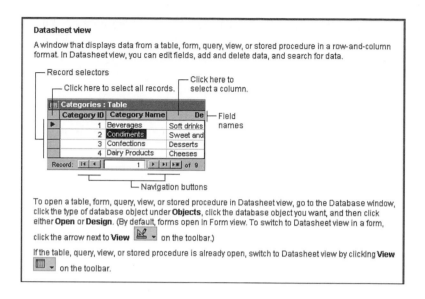

Figure 3.16
The pop-up window displayed by the Datasheet View hyperlink.

PART

I

CH

3

For example, Figure 3.17 shows the tutorial Help window that Access displays if you click Sort Records in Datasheet View or Form View at the bottom of the dialog in Figure 3.16.

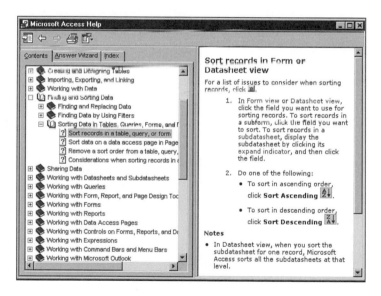

Figure 3.17
A step-by-step help page opened by clicking the first button in the What Do You Want to Do? list from the Sort Records help topic shown in Figure 3.15.

Tip #24 from

To quickly navigate (browse) to previously displayed help pages, use the Back button and Forward buttons. These buttons are similar to those of your Web browser.

Notice the icon in the middle of the step-by-step help page shown in Figure 3.17. This icon, which depicts the Sort Ascending toolbar button described earlier, also is a hyperlink. Clicking this hyperlink displays a pop-up window describing the action of the Sort Ascending toolbar button. Many help topics throughout the Access Help system contain graphic hyperlinks like this one.

Tip #25 from	Whenever you place the mouse pointer over a hyperlink, the pointer turns into a pointing-hand shape.

THE ANSWER WIZARD PAGE

NEW 2000 You can look up help topics by using the Answer Wizard. By attempting to decipher what you type in the What Would You Like to Do? text box, the Answer Wizard provides topics you could be interested in. The list of topics the Answer Wizard provides is similar to the list that the Office Assistant returns (see the "The Office Assistant" section later in this chapter). Figure 3.18 shows topics returned as the results of the search. The first topic in the list automatically opens in the right pane. Click another topic in the Select Topic to Display list to display the related help pages.

Figure 3.18
The Answer Wizard page of the Microsoft Access help dialog.

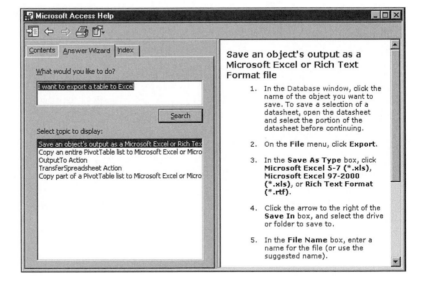

THE INDEX PAGE

You also can look up help topics in an index much like the index at the end of this book. Click the Index tab in the Microsoft Access Help dialog to bring the Index page to the front of the dialog. Figure 3.19 shows the Index page as it appears after you type the topic **help** in the text box, double-click the keyword help in the Or Choose a Keyword list to open the Choose a Topic list, and then double-click the first item in the Choose a Topic list.

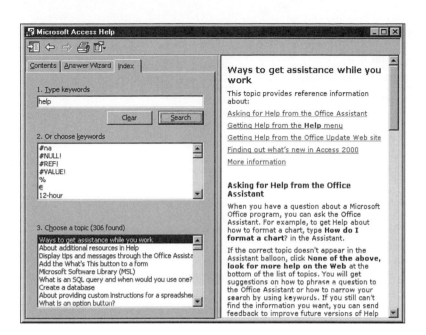

Figure 3.19
The Index page of the Microsoft Access help dialog.

PART

I

CH

3

Using the Index is simple: just type in the text box—labeled 1. Type Keywords—at the top of the page the name of the keyword on which you want help. As you type, the Help system adjusts the keywords list—labeled 2. Or Choose Keywords—to show the keyword that most closely matches the text that you've typed so far. To search for topics related to the keyword in the keyword list, click the Search button. The topics list—labeled 3. Choose a Topic—shows the topics found as a result of the search. Click the topic in the topics list to display the help page for that topic. If you want, you can also use the scroll bar to view the list of available help topics.

THE HELP WINDOW OPTIONS

The Help system lets you print, copy, or change the Help window's style or appearance. To display a menu of options, click the Help window's Options button. Table 3.12 summarizes each menu choice and its effect.

TABLE 3.12   HELP WINDOW OPTIONS

Option	Function
Hide Tabs	Turns off—if on—the display of the Contents, Answer Wizard, and Index tabs.
Show Tabs	Turns on—if off—the display of the Contents, Answer Wizard, and Index tabs.
Back	Displays—in reverse chronological order—a previously displayed help page.
Forward	Displays—in chronological order—a previously displayed help page. The Forward button is available only after clicking the Back button.

continues

TABLE 3.12   CONTINUED

Option	Function
Home	Displays the help page for using the Microsoft Access Help dialog.
Print...	Prints the currently visible help topic on your printer.
Internet Options...	Displays the Internet Options dialog of the Internet Explorer browser.

THE OFFICE ASSISTANT

When the Office Assistant is on, it displays tips related to activities that you are currently performing and provides a means for you to search for help on specific tasks.

The Office Assistant appears as an animated character in its own borderless floating dialog and displays its messages in a "speech" balloon. You can choose one of eight available Office Assistant characters. Figure 3.20 shows Clippit, the default Office Assistant character (an animated paper clip) as it appears while asking whether the user wants to save changes to a table's layout. In this case, the Office Assistant takes the place of Windows' standard message box.

Figure 3.20
The Office Assistant's version of a conventional message box.

Note

All cautions, warnings, requests for confirmation, and other Access messages are displayed in a balloon by the Office Assistant, whenever the Display Alerts option is turned on. Figure 3.21 shows the same message displayed by the Office Assistant in Figure 3.20—generated under the exact same circumstances—as it appears when the Display Alerts option is off.

By default, the Office Assistant is activated. You might find the Office Assistant distracting or prefer to use the Office Assistant only when you specifically want help. You can turn off the Office Assistant by right-clicking the Office Assistant and then choosing Hide from the pop-up menu.

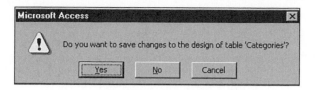

If you hide the Office Assistant, it remains hidden until you turn it on again or until you use a wizard or some other feature of Access that automatically invokes the Office Assistant. Access "remembers" the status of the Office Assistant whenever you close Access; if the Office Assistant was hidden at the time you last exited Access, the Office Assistant remains hidden the next time you start Access.

You can activate the Office Assistant by choosing Show the Office Assistant from the Help menu. Access also starts the Office Assistant if you press F1 for context-sensitive help but can't determine the precise context in which you're working.

To use the Office Assistant to search for help on any topic, click anywhere on the Office Assistant; the Office Assistant displays the balloon shown in Figure 3.22. In the text box, type a question about what you want to do and then click Search. Figure 3.23 shows the Office Assistant's balloon after searching for help topics that answer the question, How Do I Find Text in a Field? The Office Assistant displays a list of topics that answer your question and lead to step-by-step instructions on carrying out various tasks. To initiate a new search, type another question in the text box and click Search again.

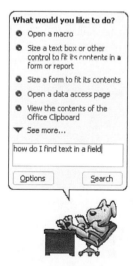

Figure 3.22
Requesting help from
the Office Assistant.

Figure 3.23
Another Office
Assistant, Rocky the
dog, after searching for
help related to finding
text in a field.

> **What would you like to do?**
>
> ● Find specific occurrences of a value in a field
> ● About working with blank fields in queries
> ● Extract part of existing text values using a calculated field
> ● Filter records by selecting values in a form or datasheet
> ● Replace specific occurrences of a value in a field
> ▼ See more...
>
> how do I find text in a field
>
> [Options]   [Search]

Tip #26 from

R J

If you can't find help any other way, use the Office Assistant's Search feature.

As mentioned previously, you can select one of several Office Assistant "characters." You can also modify the Office Assistant's behavior. To change the Office Assistant character or the Office Assistant's behavior, click the Options button in the Office Assistant's balloon, or right-click the Office Assistant window and then select Options from the pop-up menu to open the Office Assistant dialog's default Options page (see Figure 3.24).

Figure 3.24
The Options page of
the Office Assistant
Dialog.

Office Assistant   [?][X]

| Gallery | Options |

☑ Use the Office Assistant

☑ Respond to F1 key   ☑ Move when in the way
☑ Help with wizards   ☑ Guess Help topics
☐ Display alerts   ☑ Make sounds
☐ Search for both product and programming help when programming

Show tips about
☑ Using features more effectively   ☐ Only show high priority tips
☑ Using the mouse more effectively   ☐ Show the Tip of the Day at startup
☑ Keyboard shortcuts   [Reset my tips]

[OK]   [Cancel]

The options in the Assistant Capabilities group affect how much help the Office Assistant provides when it's active. The Show Tips About options group contains settings that affect what kinds of tips the Office Assistant shows you. Table 3.13 lists the available Office Assistant option settings and summarizes their effect.

TABLE 3.13   OFFICE ASSISTANT OPTIONS

Option	Function
Assistant Capabilities Group	
Respond to F1 Key	When selected, causes the Office Assistant to respond to the F1 key. If this check box is cleared, the Microsoft Access Help dialog appears when you press F1.
Help with Wizards	When selected, causes the Access wizards to provide help through the Office Assistant.
Display Alerts	When selected, causes all Access alert messages to be displayed by the Office Assistant; if cleared, Access alert messages appear in a standard dialog, whether or not the Office Assistant is active.
Search for Both Product and Programming Help When Programming	If selected, causes Access to search for help topics in the VBA programming reference and in the Access application help when you are programming in VBA.
Move When in the Way	If selected, causes the Office Assistant window to move out of the way if it would otherwise obscure a dialog, table view, or other onscreen object. Also causes the Office Assistant window to shrink to a smaller size if the Office Assistant isn't used in 5 minutes.
Guess Help Topics	If this option is selected, the Office Assistant offers help based on your current activities.
Make Sounds	If this option is selected, the Office Assistant plays various sound effects as you use it. You must have a sound card and speakers installed in your computer to hear sounds; this option may be selected even if your computer can't play sounds.
Show Tips About Group	
Using Features More Effectively	When selected, this option causes the Office Assistant to display tips to help you learn about Access features you don't know and more effectively use features you do know.
Using the Mouse More Effectively	When this option is selected, the Office Assistant also shows tips related to using the mouse more efficiently in Access.
Keyboard Shortcuts	When this option is selected, the Office Assistant shows tips related to using keyboard shortcuts.

continues

PART

I

CH

3

TABLE 3.13   CONTINUED

Option	Function
Other Tip Options Group	
Only Show High Priority Tips	If selected, limits the tips displayed by the Office with a high priority, such as time-saving alternatives.
Show the Tip of the Day at Startup	When this option is selected, the Office Assistant starts each time you start an Office program and displays a tip of the day.
Reset My Tips	Clicking this command button resets the Office Assistant's internal record of tips you've already seen. Click this button if you want the Office Assistant to display tips you've seen previously.

USING THE DATABASE UTILITIES

NEW 2000 Access 2000 offers five utility functions, which you access by choosing Database Utilities from the Tools menu. You can perform four of these functions (Convert Database, To Prior Access Version; Compact and Repair Database; Switchboard Manager; and Make MDE File) with or without a database open; the fifth utility function (Convert Database, To Current Access Database Version) can be performed only when no database is open. If you have a large database, convert and compact operations take a considerable amount of time. If you select one of the utility operations described in the following sections when you don't already have a database open, the operation involves two dialogs. In the first dialog, you select the database in which Access is to perform the operation; in the second dialog, you type the name of the file that the operation is to create. Default file names for new files are Db#.mdb, where # is a sequential number, beginning with 1, assigned by Access. For the three utility operations you can perform with an open database, only the Make MDE File option displays a dialog. When compacting or repairing an open database, Access assumes that you want to operate on the open database and want the resulting compacted or repaired database to replace the currently open database.

COMPACTING AND REPAIRING DATABASES

After you make numerous additions and changes to objects within a database file—especially additions and deletions of data in tables—the database file can become disorganized. When you delete a record, you don't automatically regain the space in the file that the deleted data occupied. You must compact the database to optimize its file size and the organization of data within the tables that the file contains. When you pack an Access file, you regain space only in 32K increments.

To compact a database, perform the following steps:

1. Open the database you want to compact.
2. From the Tools menu, choose Database Utilities, Compact and Repair Database. Access immediately begins compacting the open database. When Access finishes compacting the database, it returns you to the Database window. Your compacted database is stored with the same name it had before you compacted it.

If you want, you also can compact a database and save the compacted database in a different database file by following these steps:

1. Close any open database.

2. From the Tools menu, choose Database Utilities, Compact and Repair Database. The Database to Compact From dialog appears, as shown in Figure 3.25.

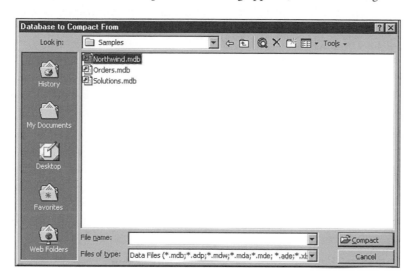

Figure 3.25
The Database to Compact From dialog.

PART

I

CH

3

3. Double-click the name of the database file that you want to compact or click the name and then click Compact. The Compact Database Into dialog appears, as shown in Figure 3.26.

4. In the File Name text box, type the name of the new file that is to result from the compaction process. If you choose to replace the existing file with the compacted version, you see a message box requesting that you confirm your choice. Click Save.

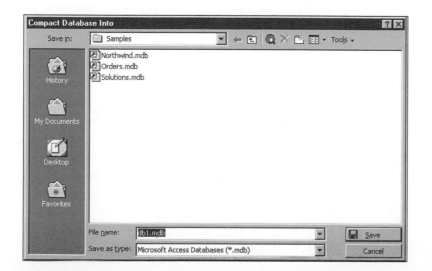

Figure 3.26
The Compact Database Into dialog.

> **Caution**
>
> If the compaction process fails, your database might be damaged. Databases damaged in the compaction process are unlikely to be repairable. Thus you should not compact the database into a new database with the same name. Do so only after backing up your database with a different name, in a different folder, or on a floppy disk.

Access then creates a compacted and repaired version of the file. The progress of the compaction is shown in a blue bar in the status bar. If you decide to use the same file name, the new file replaces the preceding file after compaction.

A database can become corrupted as the result of the following problems:

- Hardware problems that occur when writing to your database file, either locally or on a network server.
- Accidentally restarting the computer while Access databases are open.
- A power failure that occurs after you make modifications to an Access object but before you save the object.

Occasionally, a file might become corrupted without Access detecting the problem. This lack of detection occurs most frequently with corrupted indexes. If Access or your application behaves strangely when you open an existing database and display its contents, try compacting and repairing the database.

Periodically compacting and repairing files usually is the duty of the database administrator in a multiuser environment, typically in relation to backup operations. You should back up your existing file on disk or tape before creating a compacted version. When you're developing an Access 2000 database, you should compact and repair the database frequently. Access 2000 databases that are not compacted grow in size much more rapidly during modification than with Access 95 and earlier versions.

> **Tip #27 from**
>
> **NEW 2000**
>
> To compact the current database automatically each time you close it, choose Tools, Options, click the General tab of the Options dialog, and mark the Compact on Close check box of the General page. Optional automatic compaction is a new feature of Access 2000.

CONVERTING DATABASES TO ACCESS 2000 FORMAT

To convert prior Access version .mdb database files, .MDA library files created with Access 1.x or Access 2.0, and .mda library files created with Access 95 or 97 to the new database format of Access 2000, close any open database. Choose Tools, Database Utilities, Convert Database, To Current Access Database Version. The process of converting database files from earlier versions of Access database formats to that of Access 2000 is almost identical to the second file-compaction process described in the preceding section. The only difference that you'll notice is that the names of the dialogs are Database to Convert From and Database to Convert Into. (Chapter 31, "Migrating Access 9x Applications to Access 2000," covers this conversion process in detail.)

Caution

Although you can convert databases created with earlier versions of Access into Access 2000 format, Access 2000 does not let convert the databases from Access 2000 format to an Access version prior to the Access 97 database format. You only can convert Access 2000 .mdb, .mda, .mdw, and .mde files to their Access 97 counterparts. If you attempt to open an Access 2000 database or library file with the Convert Database menu choice, you receive the following message: "The database you tried to convert was either created in or was already converted to the current version of Microsoft Access." Thus if you want to support users of Access database applications who don't have Access 2000, you must maintain two separate sets of database files. Therefore, you must have the retail versions of any earlier Access versions and Access 2000 available to maintain your application.

If you encounter error messages when converting your .mdb file to Jet 4.0 format, see the "Compile Errors in the Convert Database Process" topic of the "Troubleshooting" section near the end of the chapter.

CONVERTING DATABASES TO ACCESS 97 FORMAT

NEW 2000 To convert Access 2000 databases to Access 97, open the Access 2000 database that you want to convert and then choose Database Utilities, Convert Database, To Prior Access Database Version from the Tools menu. Access displays the Convert Database Into dialog box. In the File Name text box, type the file name to convert into and then click the Save button.

ADDING A SWITCHBOARD FORM

You can add a switchboard form to a database that doesn't have one—such as Northwind.mdb—or modify an existing switchboard form. To add a switchboard to Northwind.mdb, follow these steps:

1. Choose Tools, Database Utilities, Switchboard Manager.

2. If your database doesn't have a switchboard, a message box asks if you would like to create one. Click OK to open the Switchboard Manager dialog with the Main Switchboard (default) selected (see Figure 3.27).

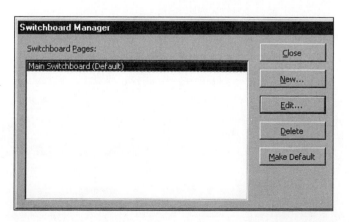

Figure 3.27
The main Switchboard Manager dialog for a database without a switchboard form.

3. Click the Edit button to open the Edit Switchboard Page dialog, then click New to open the Edit Switchboard Item dialog.

4. Select Open Form in Edit Mode from the Command list, select the form to open in the Form list, and type an appropriate caption for the command button in the Text text box (see Figure 3.28).

Figure 3.28
Adding an open form command button to the Northwind Switchboard form.

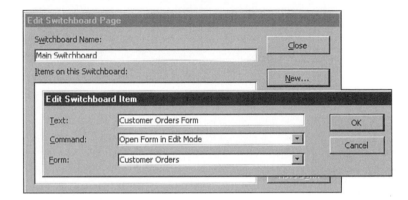

5. Click OK to add the new command to the Main Switchboard form.

6. Click Close twice to close the two Switchboard dialogs, click the Forms shortcut in the Database window, and double-click the Switchboard shortcut to open your new Switchboard form.

7. Click the single command button you added in steps 4 and 5 to open the form you selected (see Figure 3.29).

Figure 3.29
The Customer Orders form opened from the Northwind Switchboard form.

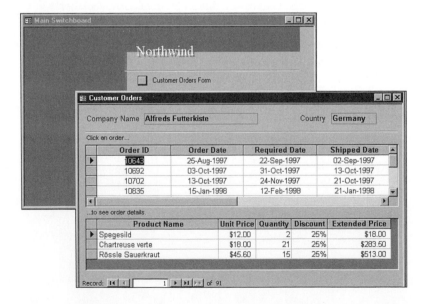

8. Close the two forms, and repeat steps 1, 3, 4, and 5 for each form you want to open with Switchboard form buttons.

9. Add a button named Exit Northwind, and select Exit Application as the command.

Clicking the Exit Northwind button closes the Northwind.mdb database, but doesn't close Access.

CREATING .MDE FILES

An .mde file is a special version of an Access .mdb file. In an .mde file, all VBA code is stored only in compiled format, and the program source code for that database is unavailable. Also, users can no longer modify forms, reports, queries, or tables stored in that database, although those objects can be exported to other databases. Typically, .mde databases are used to create libraries of add-in wizards; create custom database applications intended for commercial or in-house distribution; and provide templates for forms, reports, queries, and other objects for use in other databases.

You can convert any .mdb database to an .mde file by choosing Database Utilities, Make MDE File from the Tools menu. If you have a database open at the time you select this command, Access assumes that you want to save the current open database as an .mde file and immediately displays a Save MDE As dialog. This dialog is essentially the same as any Save As dialog. If you choose Database Utilities, Make MDE File from the Tools menu when no database is open, Access first displays a Database to Save as MDE dialog. Use this dialog to select the .mdb database file that you want to convert to an .mde file.

TROUBLESHOOTING

COMPILE ERRORS IN THE CONVERT DATABASE PROCESS

Error messages appear when converting to Access 2000 from early Access versions.

Access 2.0 and earlier were 16-bit applications. The first error message you might receive is "There are calls to 16-bit dynamic-link libraries (.dll) in this application." In this case, you must alter the code of **Declare** statements to call the current 32-bit equivalents of the 16-bit DLLs. For example, you must change calls to functions in USER.DLL, KERNEL.DLL, and GDI.DLL to User32.dll, Kernel32.dll, and Gdi32.dll, respectively.

A more common error message when converting Access 2.0, 95, and 97 applications is "There were compilation errors during the enabling or conversion of this database." If you're converting from Access 2.0 many of these errors are likely to arise from Access Basic reserved words and symbol usage that VBA 6.0 doesn't support. Similar problems occur with applications that originated in Access 2.0 or earlier and were converted to Access 9x. In some cases, conversion of earlier application versions to Access 97, then to Access 2000 is easier than attempting direct conversion. See Chapter 31 for additional information on conversion issues.

PART

I

CH

3

IN THE REAL WORLD—HTML HELP OR HINDRANCE

The new feature of Access 2000 that users of prior Access versions probably will find most traumatic is the move from the traditional Windows help system (WinHelp32) to HTML Help. Changing to HTML Help violates one of the primary tenets of software development—"If it ain't broke, don't fix it." WinHelp32 is a mature, stable help system that's part of the Windows 9x and Windows NT operating system. Many excellent third-party authoring tools are available for WinHelp32. Microsoft's Office 2000 implementation of HTML Help version 1.2 has the hallmarks of a work in progress.

"If it's meant to be read, convert it to HTML" is today's variation on the navy's "If it doesn't move, paint it" rule. It's a reasonably safe bet that the number of HTML pages on the World Wide Web exceeds the number of pages of books in the average public library. Leading publishers are converting popular books to the special HTML format required by the electronic books typified by NuvoMedia's Rocket eBook (http://www.nuvomedia.com/).

The move to HTML Help was inevitable for the following reasons:

■ There are many more Web page designers than help authors. Whether competency in Web page design aids the writing of meaningful help files remains to be seen.

■ Hyperlinked, forward and back, Web-style navigation is native to the help system. Windows 3.x's 16-bit WinHelp anticipated many of the navigation features employed by HTML. Some early multimedia CD-ROMs used the 16-bit WinHelp engine as a content navigation tool.

■ HTML Help files in their native .htm format can be deployed from a central intranet server or published on the public Web as a software marketing aid.

■ New Internet standards—such as Cascading Style Sheets (CSS) and the Document Object Model (DOM)—combined with Dynamic HTML (DHTML) contribute the capability of customizing the look and feel, respectively, of HTML Help pages.

■ Scripting with JScript or VBScript enables dynamic HTML Help. An DHTML event model and scripting eliminates the need to write custom help DLLs to add new types of action to help files.

■ HTML Help leverages installation of the latest version of Microsoft's Internet Explorer. You must use IE 4+ to open Office 2000's compressed help (.chm) files, which are required for full-text searching.

■ Microsoft saves the time and effort—and thus expense—of converting WinHelp32 .hlp files to HTML for publication on the www.microsoft.com web site.

Microsoft's first attempt to create a multimedia authoring system, Multimedia Viewer, was an extended version of WinHelp. Viewer never achieved a sizable developer base, primarily because its graphics design tools were rudimentary, at best. HTML Help, with DHTML and scripting, makes authoring graphically-intensive, interactive help files a reality. You can expect future versions of Access and the other Office members to take increasing advantage of the standards-based features of HTML Help. Hopefully, Microsoft's future HTML Help implementations won't be as intrusive as the Office 2000 version.

If you're an Access developer and need to move from WinHelp to HTML Help for new applications, the Microsoft Web site has an extensive HTML Help authoring workshop at `http://www.microsoft.com/workshop/author/htmlhelp/default.asp`. You can download version 1.2 of the HTML Help Workshop (4 MB) from `http://www.microsoft.com/workshop/author/htmlhelp/download.asp`.

--rj

CHAPTER **4**

WORKING WITH ACCESS DATABASES AND TABLES

In this chapter

Defining the Elements of Access Databases   128

Understanding Relational Databases   130

Using Access Database Files and Tables   132

Creating a New Database   133

Understanding the Properties of Tables and Fields   135

Choosing Field Data Types, Sizes, and Formats   140

Understanding the Northwind Traders Sample Database   151

Adding a New Table to an Existing Database   156

Setting Default Values of Fields   165

Working with Relations, Key Fields, and Indexes   166

Altering Fields and Relationships   176

Copying and Pasting Tables   180

Troubleshooting   182

In the Real World—Database Strategy and Table Tactics   182

DEFINING THE ELEMENTS OF ACCESS DATABASES

The traditional definition of a *database* is a collection of related data items stored in an organized manner. Access is unique among desktop database development applications because of its all-encompassing database file structure. A single Access .mdb file can contain data objects—tables, indexes, and queries—as well as application objects—forms, reports, macros, and Visual Basic for Applications (VBA) code modules. Thus, you can create a complete Access database application stored in a single .mdb file. Access's all-in-one .mdb file structure makes creating and distributing database applications simpler.

Access databases can include the following elements in a single .mdb database file:

NEW 2000

- *Tables* store data items in a row-column format similar to that used by spreadsheet applications. An Access database can include as many as 32,768 objects (the combination of tables, forms, reports, queries, and so on), and as many as 1,024 tables can be open at one time if you have sufficient resources available. You can import tables from other database applications (such as dBASE, FoxPro, and Paradox), client/server databases (such as Microsoft SQL Server and the new Microsoft Data Engine, MSDE, included with Access 2000), and spreadsheet applications (such as Microsoft Excel and Lotus 1-2-3). You can also link to Access databases other types of database tables, formatted files (Excel worksheet and ASCII text), and other Access databases. Chapter 7, "Linking, Importing, and Exporting Tables," shows you how to use Access 2000 with other data sources.

- *Queries* display selected data contained in as many as 16 tables. With queries, you can specify how to present data by selecting the tables that compose the query and up to 255 specific fields (columns) of the selected tables. You determine the records (rows) to display by specifying the criteria that the data items in the query data must meet to be included in the display. Part II, "Getting the Most Out of Queries," explains how to design Access queries.

- *Forms* display data contained in tables or queries and let you add new data and update or delete existing data. You can incorporate pictures and graphs in your forms, and, if you have a sound card, include narration, music, and even live video in your form. *Subforms* are forms contained within a main form. You learn how to design forms in Chapter 12, "Creating and Using Forms," and Chapter 13, "Designing Custom Multitable Forms," and you learn how to use graphics with forms in Chapter 19, "Adding Charts and Graphics to Forms and Reports."

  Access 2000 forms can also incorporate VBA code in class modules to provide event-handling subprocedures for forms and the controls that appear on forms.

- *Reports* print data from tables or queries in virtually any format you want. Access lets you add graphics to your reports so that you can print a complete, illustrated catalog of products from an Access database. Access's report capabilities are much more flexible than those of most other relational database management applications, including those designed for mini-computers and mainframe computers. Like forms, you can include VBA event-handling subprocedures in Access 2000 reports. Chapter 14, "Printing Basic

Reports and Mailing Labels," and Chapter 15, "Preparing Advanced Reports," cover creating reports. Chapter 28, "Responding to Events with VBA 6.0," describes the specifics of writing event-handling VBA code stored behind forms and reports.

- *Macros* automate Access operations. In previous versions of Access, macros took the place of the programming code required by other database applications, such as xBase, to perform specific actions in response to user-initiated events, such as clicking a command button. Macros now are obsolete; Access 2000 supports macros for compatibility with database applications created with earlier versions of Access. Microsoft recommends that you use VBA program code for event handling in Access 2000 databases; future versions of Access are likely to phase out macro support in favor of VBA-only programming.

- *Modules* contain VBA code that you write to create customized functions for use in forms, reports, and queries, and to supplycommon subprocedures that all your class modules can use. By adding VBA code to your database, you can create complete database applications with customized menus, toolbars, and other features.

→ **See** Chapter 26, "Writing Visual Basic for Applications Code," for a description of how to write VBA code in general.

- *Relationships* define how tables within a database are related to one another. Relationships don't appear in the Database window's Object bar; you choose Tools, Relationships to open the Relationships window for the current database.

- *Pages* are Data Access Pages (DAP) that let you display and edit Access data in Web pages delivered by an intranet server. Chapter 18, "Designing Data Access Pages," has detailed information on DAP.

→ **See** "Deploying Data Access Pages with Office Web Components," **p. 21** for a brief introduction to DAP.

PART

I

CH

4

Note

NEW 2000 Access Data Projects (ADP) introduce three new object classes—Views (similar to Queries), Stored Procedures (also related to Queries), and Database Diagrams (similar to Relationships). ADP connect only to MSDE or SQL Server 6.5+ databases using OLE DB and ActiveX Data Objects (ADO), both of which are new with Access 2000. The details are in Chapter 25, "Creating Access Data Projects." Chapter 27, "Understanding Universal Data Access, OLE DB, and ADO," introduces you to these new Access 2000 features.

→ **See** "Creating Access Data Projects for the Microsoft Data Engine" **p. 26** for an introduction to ADP.

A better definition of an Access *database* is a collection of related data items and, optionally, the methods necessary to select, display, update, and report the data. This definition emphasizes an important distinction between Access and other database management applications. Even client/server database systems such as Microsoft SQL Server, which include all related tables within a single database, don't include the equivalent of forms and reports within the database. You must use another application, called a *front end*, to display, edit, and report data stored in client/server databases. You can use Access to create front ends for client/server databases by linking tables from the client/server database to your Access database. Creating front ends for client/server databases is one of the major applications for Access in medium to large firms.

Tip #28 from

It's good database application development practice to maintain tables that store your application's data in one Access database (.mdb) file and the remainder of your application's objects, such as forms and reports, in a separate .mdb file. For simplicity, this chapter uses the Northwind Traders sample database, which is a self-contained application with a single .mdb file. Chapters 7 and 24, "Securing Multiuser Network Applications," describe how to use or create separate .mdb files to store data and application objects.

This chapter introduces you to Access databases and tables—the fundamental elements of an Access application. There are many references in this book to the term *Access application*, which is an Access database with the following characteristics:

- It contains the queries, forms, reports, and macros necessary to display the data in a meaningful way and to update the data as necessary. This book calls these elements *application objects*.

- It doesn't require the database's users to know how to design any of its elements. All elements of the database are fully predefined during the application's design stage. In most cases, you want to restrict other users from intentionally or unintentionally changing the application's design.

- It's automated by VBA code so that users make choices from command buttons or custom-designed menus rather than from the lists in the Database window.

The easiest way to learn how to create Access applications is to modify the Northwind Traders sample database that's provided with Access. In the following chapters, you add new features to the Personnel Actions application until you have a complete, automated method of adding and editing Personnel Actions data. Therefore, you should read this book sequentially, at least to Chapter 15. Because succeeding examples build on your previous work, perform the sample exercises for the Personnel Actions application each time you encounter them.

UNDERSTANDING RELATIONAL DATABASES

All desktop database managers enable you to enter, edit, view, and print information contained in one or more tables divided into rows and columns. At this point, the definition of a database manager doesn't vary from that of a spreadsheet application—most spreadsheets can emulate simple database functions. Three principal characteristics distinguish relational database management systems (RDBMSs) from spreadsheet applications:

- All RDBMSs are designed to deal efficiently with very large amounts of data—much more than spreadsheets can handle conveniently.

- RDBMSs easily link two or more tables so that they appear to users as though they are one table. This process is difficult or impossible to accomplish with spreadsheets.

- RDBMSs minimize information duplication by requiring repetition of only those data items, such as product or customer codes, by which multiple tables are linked.

Figure 4.1 shows a typical relational database that a manufacturing or distributing firm might use. This database structure is similar to that of the Northwind Traders sample database provided with Access.

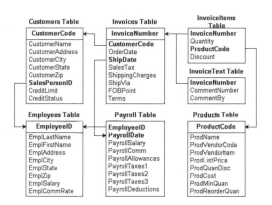

Figure 4.1
A part of a typical database for a manufacturing or distributing firm.

→ For an introduction to relational database principles, **see** "The Process of Database Design," **p. 815.**

If your job is to create an invoice-entry database, you don't need to enter a customer's name and address more than once. Just assign each customer a unique number or code and add to the Customers table a record containing this information. Similarly, you don't need to enter the names and prices of the standard products for each invoice. You assign unique codes to products, and then add records for them to the Products table. When you want to create a new invoice for an existing customer, you enter the customer code and type the codes and quantities for the products ordered. This process adds one record (identified by an automatically assigned sequential numeric code) to the Invoices table and one record for each different item purchased to the InvoiceItems table.

→ To learn how to connect related tables, **see** the section "Joining Tables to Create Multitable Queries," **p. 355**.

Each table is related to the other by the customer, invoice, and product codes and numbers, shown by the connecting lines between the tables in Figure 4.1. The codes and numbers shown in boxes are unique; only one customer corresponds to a particular code, and one invoice or product corresponds to a given number. When you display or print an invoice, the Invoices table is linked (called a *join*) with the Customers and InvoiceItems tables by their codes. In turn, the InvoiceItems table is joined with the Products table by the common value of a ProductCode in the InvoiceItems table and a ProductNumber in the Products table. The links or joins are called *relationships* between tables. Your query (view)

PART

I

CH

4

of the desired sales orders displays the appropriate customer, invoice, items, and product information from the linked records. (The following section explains queries.) You can calculate quantity-price extensions, including discounts, by multiplying the appropriate values stored in the tables. You can add the extended items, sales taxes, and freight charges; you can also calculate the total invoice amount. These calculated values need not be included (and in a properly designed database never are included) in the database tables.

USING ACCESS DATABASE FILES AND TABLES

Access has its own database file structure, similar to that used by client/server RDBMSs, and uses the .mdb extension. As discussed in this chapter's introduction, Access varies from traditional PC databases in that a single file contains all the related tables, indexes, forms, and report definitions. The .mdb file even includes the programming code that you write in VBA. You don't need to be concerned with .mdb file structure because Access handles all the details of file management for you.

Records commonly are called *rows*, and fields often are called *columns*. This book uses the terms *records* and *fields* when referring to database tables, and *rows* and *columns* for sets of records returned by queries.

THE ACCESS SYSTEM DATABASE

In addition to including database files with the .mdb extension, Access includes a master database file, called a *workgroup file*, named System.mdw. This file contains information about the following:

- Names of users and groups of users who can open Access
- User passwords and a unique binary code, called a System ID (SID), that identifies the current user to Access
- Operating preferences that you establish by choosing <u>T</u>ools, <u>O</u>ptions from the menu
- Definitions of customized Access 2000 toolbars that each user creates

→ For more information on user preferences, **see** "Setting Default Options," **p. 98**.

Chapter 24 covers sharing database files and granting permission for others to use the files.

ACCESS LIBRARY DATABASES

Another category of Access database files is *add-ins*, also called *libraries*. Add-ins are Access library databases, usually with an .mde or .mda extension to distinguish them from user databases, that you can link to Access by choosing Re<u>f</u>erences from the Module window's <u>T</u>ools menu, or through the Add-In Manager (which you can access by choosing <u>T</u>ools, Add-<u>I</u>ns).

When you link an Access library, all the elements of the library database are available to you after you open Access. The Access 2000 wizards—which you use to create forms, reports, and graphs—are stored in a series of Access library database files: Acwzlib.mde, Acwztool.mde, and Acwzmain.mde. Another wizard lets you create data dictionaries for Access databases. A *data dictionary* is a detailed written description of each of a database's elements. Add-in library databases are an important and unique feature of Access. Microsoft and other third-party firms provide a wide range of Access libraries to add new features and capabilities to Access.

CREATING A NEW DATABASE

If you have experience with relational database management systems, you might want to start building your own database as you progress through this book. In this case, you need to create a new database file at this point. If database management systems are new to you, however, you should instead explore the sample databases supplied with Access as you progress through the chapters of this book and design your first database by using the principles outlined in Chapter 22, "Exploring Relational Database Design and Implementation." Then return to this section and create your new database file.

To create a new database, follow these steps:

1. If you aren't already running Access, launch it and skip to step 3.

2. If Access is running and the Database window is visible, click its title bar to make it active. If the Database window isn't visible, click the Show Database Window button of the toolbar, choose <u>W</u>indow, <u>1</u> Database from the menu, or press the F11 key.

3. Click the New Database button of the toolbar, or choose <u>F</u>ile, <u>N</u>ew Database from the menu. For the Database toolbar to be visible and the New Database and other database file options to be present when you open the <u>F</u>ile menu, the Access application window must be empty or the Database window must be active. The New dialog appears as shown in Figure 4.2.

   The General page of the New dialog lets you create a blank database, and the Database page lets you use any one of 10 database templates. Access 2000 comes with database templates for asset tracking, contact and event management, and several other typical business database uses. You pick a template that most closely suits the purpose of your new database.

4. For this example, click the General tab, select Database, and then click OK to display the File New Database dialog shown in Figure 4.3.

   Access supplies the default file name, db1.mdb, for new databases. (If you've previously saved a database file as db1.mdb in the current folder, Access proposes db2.mdb as the default.)

Figure 4.2
The New dialog, in which you select the type of database to create.

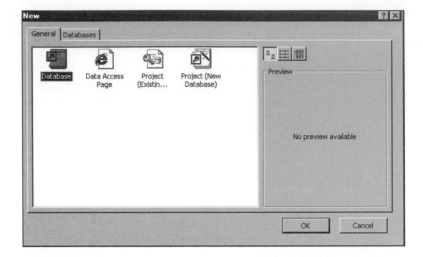

Figure 4.3
The File New Database dialog, in which you enter the new database's name.

5. In the File Name text box, type a file name for the new database. Use conventional Windows 9x file-naming rules; you can use spaces and punctuation in the name. Don't include an extension in the file name; Access automatically supplies the .mdb extension.

6. Click Create or press Enter to create the new database.

   If a database was open when you created the new database, Access closes any windows associated with the database and the Database window. During the process of creating the database, the following message appears in the status bar:

   `Verifying system objects`

Whenever you open a new or existing database, Access checks whether all the database's elements are intact. Access's main window and the Database window for the new database (named db2.mdb for this example) appear as shown in Figure 4.4.

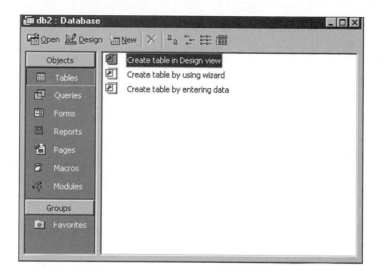

Figure 4.4
The Database window for a newly created database.

PART

I

CH

4

Each new Access 2000 database occupies approximately 96KB of disk space when you create it. Most of the 96KB is space consumed by hidden system tables for adding the information necessary to specify the names and locations of other database elements that the database file contains.

UNDERSTANDING THE PROPERTIES OF TABLES AND FIELDS

Before you add a table to a database that you have created or to one of the sample databases supplied with Access, you need to know the terms and conventions that Access uses to describe the structure of a table and the fields that contain the table's data items. With Access, you specify properties of tables and fields.

 Properties of Access tables apply to the table as a whole. Entering table properties is optional. You enter properties of tables in text boxes of the Table Properties window (see Figure 4.5), which you display by clicking the toolbar's Properties button in Table Design view. Brief descriptions of the ten basic properties of Access tables, all of which are optional, follow:

- *Description*. An optional text explanation of the table's purpose. If you choose View, Details from the menu, the Database window displays this description. This description also is useful with a data dictionary, which you use to document databases and database applications.

- *Validation Rule*. An optional expression (formula) used to establish domain integrity rules for more than one field of the table. The Validation Rule that you enter here applies to the table as a whole, instead of to a single field. Validation Rules and domain integrity are two of the subjects of Chapter 5, "Entering, Editing, and Validating Data in Tables."

- *Validation Text*. An optional property that specifies the text of the message box that opens if you violate a table's Validation Rule expression.

- *Filter*. An optional property value that specifies a constraint to apply to the table whenever it is opened. Filters restrict the number of records that appear, based on selection criteria you supply. Chapter 6, "Sorting, Finding, and Filtering Data in Tables," discusses filters.

- *Order By*. An optional property value that specifies a sort(ing) order to apply to the table whenever it's opened. Chapter 6 also explains sort orders. If you don't specify a sort order, records are displayed in the order of the primary key, if a primary key exists. The "Working with Relations, Key Fields, and Indexes" section, later in the chapter, discusses primary key fields.

NEW 2000 *Subdatasheets* are a new feature of Access 2000 and are briefly described in Chapter 1's "Viewing and Editing Related Records in Subdatasheets" section. Subdatasheets display sets of records of related tables in nested datasheets. You can use subdatasheets in the Datasheet view of tables and queries, and also in subforms. The following table properties apply to subdatasheets:

- *Subdatasheet Name*. An optional value that determines whether and how subdatasheets display data in related records. The default value is [Auto], which automatically adds subdatasheets for records linked from related tables. A value of [None] turns off subdatasheets.

- *Link Child Fields*. If a Subdatasheet Name value is supplied, Link Child Fields specifies the name of the linked field of the related (subordinate) table whose records appear in the subdatasheet. You don't need to specify a value if the Subdatasheet Name property value is [Auto].

- *Link Master Fields*. If a Subdatasheet Name value is supplied, Link Master Fields specifies the name of linking field of the table for the superior datasheet or subdatasheet.

- *Subdatasheet Height*. If a Subdatasheet Name value is supplied, Subdatasheet Height specifies the maximum height of the subdatasheet. A value of 0 (the default) allows the subdatasheet to display all related records, limited only by the size of the superior datasheet or subdatasheet.

- *Subdatasheet Expanded*. If a Subdatasheet Name value is supplied, Subdatasheet Expanded controls the initial display of the subdatasheet. Setting the value to Yes causes the datasheet to open with all subdatasheets expanded (open).

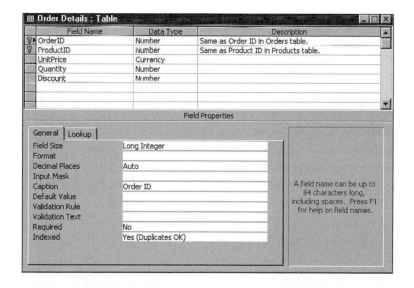

Figure 4.5
The Table Properties window for the Northwind Traders sample database's Order Details table.

Access 2000 provides an Indexes window to specify the primary key and all table indexes. Later in this chapter, the section "Adding Indexes to Tables" describes how to use the Indexes window.

 You assign each field of an Access table a set of properties. The first three field properties are assigned within the Table Design grid, the upper pane of the Table Design window shown in Figure 4.6. To assign the Primary Key property, select the field and click the Primary Key button on the toolbar (the Order Details table shown in Figure 4.6 has a primary key on two fields, called a *composite primary key*). You set the remaining property values in the Table Design window's lower pane, Field Properties.

PART

I

CH

4

Figure 4.6
The Table Design window for the Northwind Traders sample database's Order Details table.

The following list summarizes the properties you set in the Table Design grid:

- *Field Name.* You type the name of the field in the Table Design grid's first column. Field names can be as long as 64 characters and can include embedded (but not leading) spaces and punctuation—except periods (.), exclamation marks (!), and square brackets ([]). Field names are mandatory, and you cannot assign the same field name to more than one field. It's good database programming practice not to include spaces in field names. (Substitute an underscore (_) for spaces or use uppercase and lowercase letters to improve the readability of field names.) Minimizing the length of field names conserves resources.

- *Data Type.* You select data types from a drop-down list in the Table Design grid's second column. Data types include Text, Memo, Number, Date/Time, Currency, AutoNumber, Yes/No, OLE Object, Hyperlink, and Lookup Wizard. Choosing a data type is the subject of the next section.

- *Description.* You can enter an optional description of the field in the text box in the Table Design grid's third column. If you add a description, it appears in the status bar at the lower left of Access's window when you select the field for data entry or editing.

- *Primary Key.* To choose a field as the primary-key field, select the field by clicking the field-selection button to the left of the Field Name column, and then click the Primary Key button on the toolbar. The Order Details table has a composite primary key consisting of the OrderID and ProductID fields. (See "Selecting a Primary Key" later in this chapter for instructions on how to create a composite primary key.)

Depending on the specific data type that you choose for a field, you can set additional properties for a table field. You set these additional properties on the General page of the Table Design window's Field Properties pane by selecting from drop-down or combo lists or by typing values in text boxes. (You use the Field Properties pane's Lookup page to set the control type for lookup fields on forms—list box, combo list, and so on. Chapter 13, "Designing Custom Multitable Forms," describes how to use lookup fields.) The following list summarizes the General field properties:

- *Field Size.* You enter the field size for the Text data type in this text box. (See the "Fixed-Width Text Fields" section later in this chapter to learn how to select a text field size.) For most Numeric data types, you determine the field size by selecting from a drop-down list. The new Decimal data type requires that you type values for Precision and Scale. Field size doesn't apply to the Date/Time, Yes/No, Currency, Memo, Hyperlink, or OLE Object data type.

- *Format.* You can select a standard, predefined format in which to display the values in the field from the drop-down combo list that's applicable to the data type that you selected (except Text). Alternatively, you can enter a custom format in the text box (see "Custom Display Formats" later in this chapter). The Format property does not affect the data values; it affects only how these values are displayed. The Format property doesn't apply to OLE Object fields.

NEW 2000 ■ *Precision*. This property appears only when you select the Decimal data type. Precision defines the total number of digits to represent a numeric value. The default is 18, and the maximum value is 28 for Jet .mdb files and 38 for MSDE databases.

NEW 2000 ■ *Scale*. Like Precision, this property appears only for the Decimal data type. Scale determines the number of decimal digits to the right of the decimal point. The value of Scale must be less than or equal to the Precision value.

■ *Decimal Places*. You can select Auto or a specific number of decimal places from the drop-down combo list, or you can enter a number in the text box. The Decimal Places property applies only to Number and Currency fields. Like the Format property, the Decimal Places property affects only the display, not the data values, of the field.

■ *Input Mask*. Input masks are character strings, similar to the character strings used for the Format property, that determine how to display data during data entry and editing. If you click the builder ... button for a field of the Text, Currency, Number, or Date/Time field data type, Access starts the Input Mask Wizard to provide you with a predetermined selection of standard input masks, such as telephone numbers with optional area codes.

■ *Caption*. If you want a name (other than the field name) to appear in the field name header button in Table Datasheet view, you can enter in the Caption list box an alias for the field name. The restrictions on punctuation symbols do not apply to the Caption property. (You can use periods, exclamation points, and square brackets.)

■ *Default Value*. By entering a value in the Default Value text box, you specify a default value that Access automatically enters in the field when a new record is added to the table. The current date is a common default value for a Date/Time field. (See "Setting Default Values of Fields" later in this chapter for more information.) Default values don't apply to fields with AutoNumber or OLE Object field data types.

■ *Validation Rule*. Validation rules test the value entered in a field against criteria that you supply in the form of an Access expression. Chapter 9, "Understanding Query Operators and Expressions," explains expressions. The Validation Rule property is not available for fields with AutoNumber, Memo, or OLE Object field data types. Adding validation rules to table fields is one of the subjects in Chapter 5.

■ *Validation Text*. You enter the text that is to appear in the status bar if the value entered does not meet the Validation Rule criteria.

■ *Required*. If you set the value of the Required property to Yes, you must enter a value in the field. Setting the Required property to Yes is the equivalent of typing Is Not Null as a field validation rule. (You do not need to set the value of the Required property to Yes for fields included in the primary key because Access does not permit **Null** values in primary-key fields.)

■ *Allow Zero Length*. If you set the value of the Allow Zero Length property to Yes and the Required property is also Yes, the field must contain at least one character. The Allow Zero Length property applies to the Text, Memo, and Hyperlink field data types only. A zero-length string ("") and the **Null** value are not the same.

PART

I

CH

4

- *Indexed*. From the drop-down list, you can select between an index that allows duplicate values or one that requires each value of the field to be unique. You remove an existing index (except from a field that is a single primary-key field) by selecting No. The Indexed property is not available for Memo, OLE Object, or Hyperlink fields. (See "Adding Indexes to Tables" later in this chapter for more information on indexes.)

- *New Values*. This property applies only to AutoNumber fields. You select either Increment or Random from a drop-down list. If you set the New Values property to Increment, Access generates new values for the AutoNumber field by adding 1 to the highest existing AutoNumber field value. If you set the property to Random, Access generates new values for the AutoNumber field by producing a pseudo-random long integer. The "Gaps in AutoNumber Field Values" element of the "Troubleshooting" section near the end of the chapter discusses issues when you delete records from a table with an AutoNumber field.

To add your first table, Personnel Actions, to the Northwind Traders database, you must choose appropriate data types, sizes, and formats for your table's fields.

CHOOSING FIELD DATA TYPES, SIZES, AND FORMATS

You must assign a field data type to each field of a table, unless you want to use the Text data type that Access assigns by default. One principle of relational database design is that all the data in a single field consists of one data type. Access provides a much wider variety of data types and formats from which to choose than most PC database managers. In addition to setting the data type, you can set other field properties that determine the format, size, and other characteristics of the data that affect its appearance and the accuracy with which numerical values are stored. Table 4.1 lists the field data types that you can select for data contained in Access tables.

TABLE 4.1   FIELD DATA TYPES AVAILABLE IN ACCESS

Information	Data Type	Description of Data Type
Characters	Text	Text fields are most common, so Access assigns Text as the default data type. A Text field can contain as many as 255 characters, and you can designate a maximum length less than or equal to 255. Access assigns a default length of 50 characters.
NEW 2000	Memo	Memo fields ordinarily can contain as many as 65,535 characters. You use them to provide descriptive comments. Access displays the contents of Memo fields in Datasheet view. A Memo field cannot be a key field.
Numeric Values	Number	Various numeric data subtypes are available. You choose the appropriate data subtype by selecting one of the Field Size property settings listed in Table 4.2. You specify how to display the number by setting its Format property to one of the formats listed in Table 4.3.

Information	Data Type	Description of Data Type
	AutoNumber	An AutoNumber field is a numeric (Long Integer) value that Access automatically fills in for each new record you add to a table. Access can increment the AutoNumber field by 1 for each new record, or fill in the field with a randomly generated number, depending on the New Values property setting that you choose. The maximum number of records in a table that can use the AutoNumber field is slightly more than 2 billion.
	Yes/No	Logical (Boolean) fields in Access use (Logicalnumeric values: –1 for Yes (True) and fields) 0 for No (False). You use the Format property to display Yes/No fields as Yes or No, True or False, On or Off, or –1 or 0. (You can also use any non-zero number to represent True.) Logical fields cannot be key fields but can be indexed.
	Currency	Currency is a special fixed format with four decimal places designed to prevent rounding errors that would affect accounting operations where the value must match to the penny.
Dates and Times	Date/Time	Dates and times are stored in a special fixed format. The date is represented by the whole number portion of the Date/Time value, and the time is represented by its decimal fraction. You control how Access displays dates by selecting one of the Date/Time Format properties listed in Table 4.3.
Large Objects	OLE Object	Includes bitmapped graphics, vector-type (BLOBs, drawings, waveform audio files, and other binary data types that can be created by an large ActiveX component application objects). You cannot assign an OLE Object as a key field, nor can you include an OLE Object field in an index.
Web and other	Hyperlink	Hyperlink fields store Web page HTML document addresses. A Web address stored in addresses the Hyperlink field may refer to a Web page on the Internet or one stored locally on your computer or network. Clicking a Hyperlink field causes Access to start your Web browser and display the referenced Web page; choose Insert, Hyperlink to add a new hyperlink address.

Regardless of the length you set for Text fields in Access, the database file stores them in variable-length records. All trailing spaces are removed. Fixed-length character fields in conventional PC RDBMSs waste the bytes used to pad short text entries in long fields.

CHOOSING FIELD SIZES FOR NUMERIC AND TEXT DATA

The Field Size property of a field determines which data type a Number field uses or how many characters fixed-length text fields can accept. Field Size properties are called *subtypes* to distinguish them from the *data types* listed in Table 4.1. For numbers, you select a Field Size property value from the Field Size drop-down list in the Table Design window's Field Properties pane (see Figure 4.7).

PART

I

CH

4

SUBTYPES FOR NUMERIC DATA

The Number data type of Table 4.1 isn't a fully specified data type. You must select one of the subtypes from those listed in Table 4.2 for the Field Size property to define the numeric data type properly. To select a data subtype for a Number field, follow these steps:

1. Select the Data Type cell of the Number field for which you want to select the subtype.

2. Click the Field Size text box in the Field Properties window. You also can press F6 to switch windows, and then use the arrow keys to position the caret within the Field Size text box.

3. Click the drop-down arrow to open the list of choices shown in Figure 4.7. You can also press the F4 key to open the list.

Figure 4.7
Selecting a subtype for the Number data type from the Field Size list.

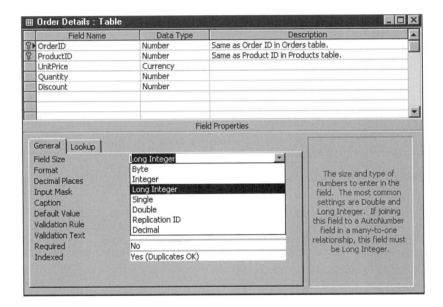

4. Select the data subtype. Table 4.2 describes data subtypes. When you make a selection, the list closes.

After you select a Field Size property, you select a Format property from those listed in Table 4.3 to determine how to display the data. Table 4.2 includes the Currency data type because it also can be considered a subtype of the Number data type.

Regardless of how you format your data for display, the number of decimal digits, the range, and the storage requirement remains that specified by the Field Size property. These data types are available in Visual Basic for Applications 6.0. VBA includes all the data types listed in Table 4.2 as reserved words. You can't use a reserved data type word for any purpose in VBA functions and procedures other than to specify a data type.

TABLE 4.2   SUBTYPES OF THE NUMBER DATA TYPE DETERMINED BY THE FIELD SIZE PROPERTY

Field Size	Decimals	Range of Values	Bytes
Y2K Decimal	28 places	$-10^{\wedge}28$ to $10^{\wedge}28 - 1$	14
Double	15 places	$-1.797 * 10^{\wedge}308$ to $+1.797 * 10^{\wedge}308$	8
Single	7 places	$-3.4 * 10^{\wedge}38$ to $+3.4 * 10^{\wedge}38$	4
Long Integer	None	$-2,147,483,648$ to $+2,147,483,647$	4
Integer	None	$-32,768$ to $32,767$	2
Byte	None	0 to 255	1
Currency (a data type, not a subtype)	4 places	-922337203685477.5808 to $+922337203685477.5808$	8

As a rule, you select the Field Size property that results in the smallest number of bytes that encompasses the range of values you expect and that expresses the value in sufficient precision for your needs. Mathematical operations with Integer and Long Integer proceed more quickly than those with Single and Double data types (called *floating-point* numbers) or the Currency and Date/Time data types (*fixed-point* numbers). Microsoft added the Decimal data subtype for conformance with the SQL Server 7.0/MSDE `decimal` data type.

FIXED-WIDTH TEXT FIELDS

You can create a fixed-width Text field by setting the value of the Field Size property. By default, Access creates a 50-character-wide Text field. Enter the number, from 1 to 255, in the Field Size cell corresponding to the fixed length that you want. If the data you import to the field is longer than the selected field size, Access truncates the data; thus, you lose the far right characters that exceed your specified limit. You therefore enter a field length value that accommodates the maximum number of characters that you expect to enter in the field.

Tip #29 from

The terms *fixed-width* and *fixed-length* have two different meanings in Access. Even if you specify a fixed-width for a field of the Text field data type, Access stores the data in the field in variable-length format.

NEW 2000 Access 2000 Text, Hyperlink, and Memo fields store characters in the *Unicode* format introduced by Windows NT 4.0. As mentioned briefly in Chapter 1, Unicode uses two bytes to store each character; this makes Unicode compatible with Asian languages that formerly required double-byte character sets (DBCS) to provide for the larger number of pictographic characters. Unicode storage ordinarily doubles the size of conventional (ANSI) text and memo fields. Access 2000 provides a new feature called *Unicode compression*, which stores characters whose value begins with 0—the entire Latin alphabet—as a single byte. When you retrieve character data, Access expands each character value to two bytes.

Note

Despite Unicode compression, Jet databases containing tables with large amounts of text are substantially larger than their non-Unicode predecessors. When updating a large Jet database, make sure to reserve disk space for at least a 50 percent increase in size.

SUBTYPES FOR THE OLE OBJECT DATA TYPE

Fields that have data types other than characters and numbers must use the OLE (object linking and embedding) Object data type. Chapter 19 explains the OLE Object field data type. The data subtype is determined by the OLE server used to create the data, instead of by an entry in a text box or a selection from a list box.

SELECTING A DISPLAY FORMAT

You establish the Format property for the data types that you select so that Access displays them appropriately for your application. You select a format by selecting the field and then clicking the Format text box in the Field Properties window. Figure 4.8 shows the choices that Access offers for formatting the Long Integer data type. You format Number, Date/Time, and Yes/No data types by selecting a standard format or creating your own custom format. The following sections describe these two methods.

Figure 4.8
Assigning a standard format to a Long Integer field.

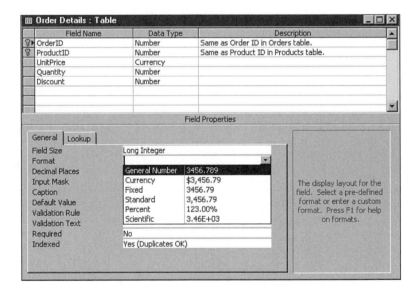

STANDARD FORMATS FOR NUMBER, DATE/TIME, AND YES/NO DATA TYPES

Access provides 17 standard formats that apply to the numeric values in fields of the Number, Date/Time, and Yes/No data types. The standard formats shown in Table 4.3 should meet most of your needs.

TABLE 4.3   STANDARD DISPLAY FORMATS FOR ACCESS'S NUMBER, DATE/TIME, AND YES/NO DATA TYPES

Data Type	Format	Appearance
Number	General Number	1234.5
	Currency	$1,234.50
	Fixed	12345
	Standard	1,234.50
	Percent	0.1234 = 12.34%
	Scientific	1.23E+03
Date/Time	General Date	3/1/99 4:00:00 PM
	Long Date	Thursday, March 1, 1999
	Medium Date	1-Mar-1999
	Short Date	3/1/1999
	Long Time	4:00:00 PM
	Medium Time	04:00 PM
	Short Time	16:00
Yes/No	Yes/No	Yes or No
	True/False	True or False
	On/Off	On or Off
	None	−1 or 0

NEW 2000 Microsoft's Year 2000 (Y2K) compliance features include a new addition to the General Page for Access 2000's Options dialog. The Use Four-Digit Year Formatting frame has two check boxes—This Database and All Databases. Marking either check box changes Date/Time field formatting as shown in table 4.4. Long Date and Time formats don't change; the formatting shown in the Access 2000 Default column is based on the standard Windows Short Date format, m/d/yy.

TABLE 4.4   A COMPARISON OF ACCESS 2000 DEFAULT AND FOUR-DIGIT YEAR FORMATTING

Date/Time Format	Access 2000 Default	With Four-Digit Year
General Date (default)	1/15/99 10:10 AM	1/15/1999 10:10 AM
Short Date	1/15/99	1/15/1999
Long Date	Friday January 15, 1999	Friday January 15, 1999
Medium Date	15-Jan-99	15-Jan-1999
Medium Time	10:10 AM	10:10 AM
mm/dd/yy	01/15/99	01/15/1999

Marking the This Database check box sets a flag in the current database, so the formatting changes apply only to the current database. Marking the All Databases check box adds a Registry entry to your PC, so opening any database forces four-digit year formatting.

Tip #30 from

Access's Short Date (m/d/yy and mm/dd/yy) formats for the English (United States) locale default to two-digit years unless you change the default date format of Windows or set the Four-Digit Year Formatting option(s). Two-digit year presentation isn't Y2K compliant. To make the Windows short date format Y2K compliant for most applications, open Control Panel's Regional Settings tool, click the Date tab, and change the Short Date style from M/d/yy to M/d/yyyy. The new version of the Northwind sample database has fixed-format (dd-mmm-yyyy) dates in all Date/Time fields. Prior versions of Northwind.mdb use the default Medium Date format (dd-mmm-yy) for Date/Time fields.

Note

NEW 2000

The new version of the Northwind sample database has fixed-format (dd-mmm-yyyy) dates in all Date/Time fields. Previous versions of Northwind.mdb use the Medium Date format for Date/Time fields.

THE Null VALUE IN ACCESS TABLES

Fields in Access tables can have a special value, **Null**, which is a new term for most users of PC-based database management systems. The **Null** value indicates that the field contains no data at all. **Null** isn't the same as a numeric value of zero, nor is it equivalent to blank text that consists of one or more spaces. **Null** is similar but not equivalent to an empty string (a string of zero length, often called a *null string*). For now, the best synonym for **Null** is *no entry*. (**Null** is set in monospace boldface type because it is a reserved word in VBA.)

The **Null** value is useful for determining whether a value has been entered in a field, especially a numeric field in which zero values are valid. Until the advent of Access, the capability to use **Null** values in database managers running on PCs was limited to fields in the tables of client/server database systems, such as Microsoft SQL Server. Later, the sections "Custom Display Formats" and "Setting Default Values of Fields" use the **Null** value.

CUSTOM DISPLAY FORMATS

To display a format that's not a standard format in Access, you must create a custom format. You can set a custom display format for any field type, except OLE Object, by creating an image of the format with combinations of a special set of characters called *placeholders* (see Table 4.5). Figure 4.9 shows an example of a custom format for date and time. If you type **mmmm dd", "yyyy - hh:nn** as the format, the date 03/01/99 displays as March 1, 1999 - 00:00.

Except as noted, the sample numeric value that Table 4.4 uses is 1234.5. *Italic* type distinguishes the placeholders that you type from the surrounding text. The resulting display is shown in monospace type.

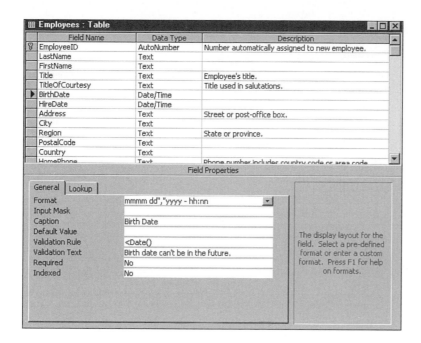

Figure 4.9
A custom date and
time format entry in
the Format text box.

PART

I

CH

4

TABLE 4.5   PLACEHOLDERS FOR CREATING CUSTOM DISPLAY FORMATS

Placeholder	Function
Empty string	Displays the number with no formatting. Enter an empty string by deleting the value in the Format field of the Field Properties pane.
0	Displays a digit if one exists in the position, or a zero if not. You can use the 0 placeholder to display leading zeros for whole numbers and trailing zeros in decimal fractions. *00000.000* displays 01234.500.
#	Displays a digit, if one exists in the position; otherwise, displays zeros. The # placeholder is similar to 0, except that leading and trailing zeros aren't displayed. *#####.###* displays 1234.5.
$	Displays a dollar sign in the position. *$###,###.00* displays $1,234.50.
.	Displays a decimal point at the indicated position in a string of 0 and # placeholders. *##.##* displays 1234.5.
%	Multiplies the value by 100 and adds a percent sign in the position shown with 0 and # placeholders. *#0.00%* displays 0.12345 as 12.35% (12.345 is rounded to 12.35).
,	Adds commas as thousands separators in strings of 0 and # placeholders. *###,###,###*.00 displays 1,234.50.
E- e-	Displays values in scientific format with the sign of exponent for negative values only. *#.####E-00* displays 1.2345E03. 0.12345 is displayed as 1.2345E-01.

continues

TABLE 4.5	CONTINUED
Placeholder	**Function**
E+ e+	Displays values in scientific format with the sign of exponent for positive and negative values. *#.####E+00* displays 1.2345E+03.
/	Separates the day, month, and year to format date values. Typing **mm/dd/yyyy** displays 03/06/1999. (You can substitute hyphens to display 06-06-1999.)
m	Specifies how to display months for dates. *m* displays 1, *mm* displays 01, *mmm* displays Jan, and *mmmm* displays January.
d	Specifies how to display days for dates. *d* displays 1, *dd* displays 01, *ddd* displays Mon, and *dddd* displays Monday.
y	Specifies how to display years for dates. *yy* displays 99; *yyyy* displays 1999.
:	Separates hours, minutes, and seconds in format time values. *hh:mm:ss* displays 02:02:02.
h	Specifies how to display hours for time. *h* displays 2; *hh* displays 02. If you use an AM/PM placeholder, *h* or *hh* displays 4 PM for 16:00 hours.
n	Minutes placeholder for time. *n* displays 1; *nn* displays 01. *hhnn* "hours" displays 1600 hours.
s	Seconds placeholder for time. *s* displays 1; *ss* displays 01.
AM/PM	Displays time in 12-hour time with AM or PM appended. *h:nn* AM/PM displays 4:00 PM. Alternative formats include am/pm, A/P, and a/p.
@	Indicates that a character is required in the position in a Text or Memo field. You can use @ to format telephone numbers in a Text field, as in @@@-@@@-@@@@ or (@@@) @@@-@@@@.
&	Indicates that a character in a Text or Memo field is optional.
>	Changes all text characters in the field to uppercase.
<	Changes all text characters in the field to lowercase.
*	Displays the character following the asterisk as a fill character for empty spaces in a field. *"ABCD"*x in an eight-character field appears as ABCDxxxx.

The Format property is one of the few examples in Access where you can select from a list of options or type your own entry. Format uses a true drop-down combo list; lists that enable you to select only from the listed options are *drop-down lists*. You don't need to enter the quotation marks shown in Figure 4.9 surrounding the comma and space in the Format text box (**mmmm dd", "yyyy - hh:nn**) because Access does this for you. The comma is a non-standard formatting symbol for dates (but is standard for number fields). When you create non-standard formatting characters in the Field Properties window, Access automatically encloses them in double quotation marks.

When you change Format or any other property field, and then change to Datasheet view in run mode to view the result of your work, you must first save the updated table design. The confirmation dialog shown in Figure 4.10 asks you to confirm any design changes.

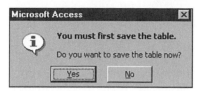

Figure 4.10
The confirmation dialog for changes to a field's format.

If you apply the custom format string *mmmm dd"*, *"yyyy – hh:nn* (refer to Figure 4.9) to the Birth Date field of the Employees table, the Birth Date field entries appear as shown in Figure 4.11. For example, Nancy Davolio's birth date appears as December 08, 1948 - 00:00. The original format of the Birth Date field was Medium Date, the format also used for the Hire Date field.

You need to expand the width of the Birth Date field to accommodate the additional characters in the Long Date format. You increase the field's width by dragging the field name header's right vertical bar to the right to display the entire field. Access displays the time of birth as 00:00 because the decimal fraction that determines time is 0 for all entries in the Birth Date field.

		Last Name	First Name	Title	Birth Date
▶	⊞	Davolio	Nancy	Sales Representative	December 08,1968 - 0:00
	⊞	Fuller	Andrew	Vice President, Sales	February 19,1952 - 0:00
	⊞	Leverling	Janet	Sales Representative	August 30,1963 - 0:00
	⊞	Peacock	Margaret	Sales Representative	September 19,1958 - 0:00
	⊞	Buchanan	Steven	Sales Manager	March 04,1955 - 0:00
	⊞	Suyama	Michael	Sales Representative	July 02,1963 - 0:00
	⊞	King	Robert	Sales Representative	May 29,1980 - 0:00
	⊞	Callahan	Laura	Inside Sales Coordinator	January 09,1958 - 0:00
	⊞	Dodsworth	Anne	Sales Representative	July 02,1969 - 0:00

Record: ◀◀ ◀ 1 ▶ ▶◀ ▶* of 9

Figure 4.11
Comparing date formats.

PART

I

CH

4

The following is an example that formats negative numbers enclosed in parentheses and replaces a Null entry with text:

```
$###,###,##0.00;$(###,###,##0.00);0.00;"No Entry Here"
```

The entries 1234567.89, –1234567.89, 0, and a Null default value appear as follows:

```
$1,234,567.89
$(1,234,567.89)
0.00
No Entry Here
```

USING INPUT MASKS

Access 2000 lets you restrict entries in Text fields to numbers or to otherwise control the formatting of entered data. Access 2000's Input Mask property is used to format telephone numbers, Social Security numbers, ZIP codes, and similar data. Table 4.6 lists the placeholders that you can use in character strings for input masks in fields of the Text field data type.

TABLE 4.6 PLACEHOLDERS FOR CREATING INPUT MASKS

Placeholder	Function
Empty string	No input mask.
0	Number (0–9) or sign (+/–) required.
9	Number (0–9) optional (a space if nothing is entered).
#	Number (0–9) or space optional (a space if nothing is entered).
L	Letter (A–z) required.
?	Letter (A–z) not required (a space if nothing is entered).
A	Letter (A–z) or number (0–9) required.
a	Letter (A–z) or number (0–9) optional.
&	Any character or a space required.
C	Any character or a space optional.
. , : ; / ( )	Literal decimal, thousands, date, time, and special separators.
>	All characters to the right are converted to uppercase.
<	All characters to the right are converted to lowercase.
!	Fills the mask from right to left.
\	Precedes the other placeholders to include the literal character in a format string.

For example, typing **\(000") "000\-0000** as the value of the Input Mask property results in the appearance of (___) ___-____ for a blank telephone number cell of a table. Typing **000\-00\-0000** creates a mask for Social Security numbers, ___-__-____. When you type the telephone number or Social Security number, the digits that you type replace the underscores.

Note

The \ characters (often called *escape characters*) that precede parentheses and hyphens specify that the character that follows is a literal, not a formatting character. If the format includes spaces, enclose the spaces and adjacent literal characters in double quotation marks.

Access 2000 includes an Input Mask Wizard that opens when you move to the Input Mask field for the Text or Date/Time field data type and click the builder (...) button at the extreme right of the text box. Figure 4.12 shows the opening dialog of the Input Mask Wizard, which provides 10 common input mask formats from which you can pick.

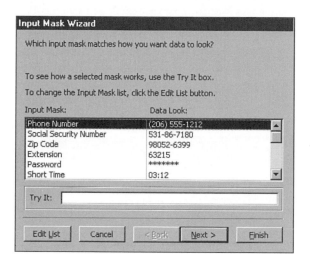

Figure 4.12
The Input Mask Wizard for Text and Date/Time field data types.

USING THE NORTHWIND TRADERS SAMPLE DATABASE

One fundamental problem with books about database management applications is the usual method of demonstrating how to create a "typical" database. You are asked to type fictitious names, addresses, and telephone numbers into a Customers table. Next, you must create additional tables that relate these fictitious customers to their purchases of various widgets in assorted sizes and quantities. This process is unrewarding for readers and authors, and few readers ever complete the exercises.

Therefore, this book takes a different track. Access includes a comprehensive and interesting sample database, Northwind Traders. Rather than create a new database at this point, you create a new table as an addition to the Northwind Traders database. Adding a new table minimizes the amount of typing required and requires just a few entries to make the table functional. The new Personnel Actions table demonstrates many elements of relational database design. Before you proceed to create the Personnel Actions table, try the quick example of adding a new table to the Northwind Traders sample database in the following section.

USING THE TABLE WIZARD TO CREATE NEW TABLES

Access includes various wizards that simplify the creation of new database objects. (*Wizards* lead you through a predetermined set of steps that determine the characteristics of the object you want to create). Access 2000 includes a Table Wizard that you can use to create new tables based on prefabricated designs for 25 business-oriented and 20 personal-type tables. Many of the business-oriented table designs are based on tables contained in Northwind.mdb.

The Table Wizard serves as an excellent introduction to the use of Access wizards in general. Follow these steps to create a new Access table that catalogs a video collection:

1. If the Employees table is open, close it by clicking the Close Window button to make the Database window active. Alternatively, click the Database Window button of the toolbar.

2. Click the Table button of the Database window, if it isn't selected, and then click the New button to display the New Table dialog shown in Figure 4.13.

Figure 4.13
The New Table dialog.

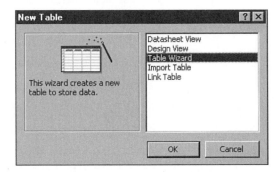

3. Select Table Wizard in the list, and click OK to display the opening dialog of the Table Wizard. (If you select Datasheet view, Access creates a blank table with default fields; Design view creates a blank table and displays it in design mode, ready for you to add fields. The Import Table and Link Table wizards import databases and link external tables to a database, respectively.)

4. Click the Personal option to display a list of tables for personal use in the Sample Tables list, and then use the vertical scroll bar to display the Video Collection entry in the list.

5. In the Sample Tables list, click the Video Collection entry to display the predetermined set of field names for the new table in the Sample Fields list.

6. Click the >> button to add all the fields from the Sample Fields list to the Fields in My New Table list. (The > button adds a single selected field from the Sample Fields list, the < button removes a single selected field from the My New Table list, and the << button deletes all the fields in the My New Table list.) The Table Wizard's dialog now appears as shown in Figure 4.14.

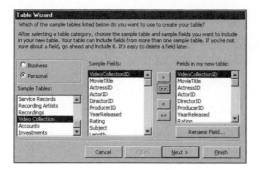

Figure 4.14
Adding fields to the new Video Collection table.

7. Click Next to display the second Table Wizard dialog in which you select the name for your new table, and select how to determine the table's primary-key field. Accept the default table name or enter a name of your choice, and then select the "No, I'll Set the Primary Key" option. The Table Wizard's second dialog appears as shown in Figure 4.15.

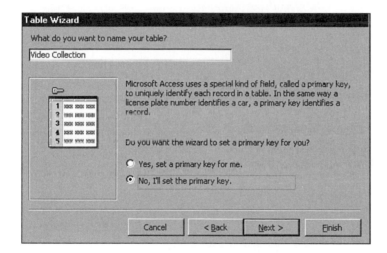

Figure 4.15
Selecting a table name and determining the table's primary key.

8. Click Next to display the dialog shown in Figure 4.16, in which you select the primary-key field and its data type. The VideoCollectionID field is the logical choice for a primary key, and the AutoNumber field data type, which automatically creates a sequential number for the VideoCollectionID, is appropriate in this case. (The Table Wizard's Consecutive Numbers Microsoft Access Assigns Automatically to New Records option creates an AutoNumber type field.) Thus, you can accept the default values determined by the Table Wizard.

Figure 4.16
The Table Wizard's
primary-key dialog.

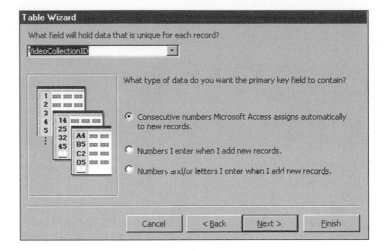

9. Click Next to continue with the next stage of the table design definition process. The Table Wizard's relationships dialog (see Figure 4.17) opens only if other tables already exist in the database in which you're creating the new table. Because almost every database consists of two or more related tables, the Table Wizard gives you an opportunity to define the relationships between tables. By default, the new table has no relationships to other tables in the database. In this exercise, you don't add any table relationships to the new Video Collection table.

Figure 4.17
Specifying relation-
ships between fields
in the new table and
other tables.

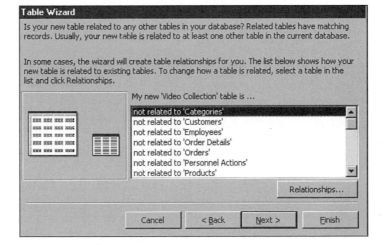

10. Click Next to finish designing the table. Access displays the final step of the Table Wizard (see Figure 4.18).

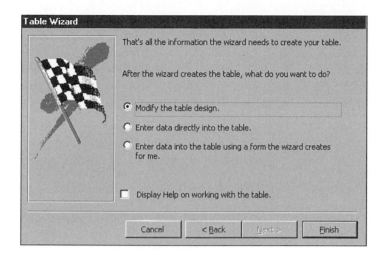

Figure 4.18
The final Table Wizard dialog.

11. Select the Modify the Table Design option, and then click the Finish button to display your new table in design mode (see Figure 4.19).

12. After you finish reviewing the design of your new table, click the Close Window button to close the table.

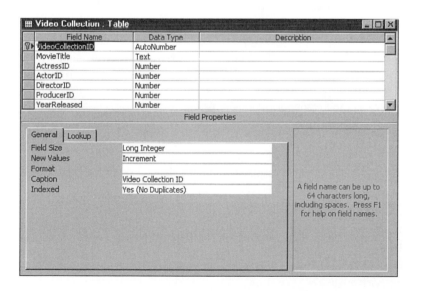

Figure 4.19
The new Video Collection table in design mode.

Tip #31 from

In any wizard, you can always redo a step by clicking the Back button until you return to the step that you want to redo.

 If you want to delete the Video Collection table from Northwind.mdb, click the Database Window button of the toolbar, click the Table button if the Tables list is not open, and then click the Video Collection entry in the Table list to select (highlight) it. Press Delete, and then click OK when the message box asks you to confirm the deletion. (You must close a table before you can delete it.)

Tip #32 from

Creating tables based on the sample tables provided by the Table Wizard has limited usefulness in real-life business applications. In most cases, you import data from another database or spreadsheet application to create your Access tables. If you can't import the data, you probably need to define the tables' fields to suit particular business needs. Thus, in the remainder of this chapter, you design a new database table by using the traditional method of manually adding fields to a blank table design and then specifying the properties of each field.

ADDING A NEW TABLE TO AN EXISTING DATABASE

The Northwind Traders database includes an Employees table that provides most of the information about the firm's employees that is typical of personnel tables. The following sections explain how to add a table called Personnel Actions to the database. The Personnel Actions table is a record of hire date, salary, commission rate, bonuses, performance reviews, and other compensation-related events for employees. Because Personnel Actions is based on information in the Employees table, the first step is to review the Employees table's structure to see how you can use it with your new table. Table structure is displayed in design mode. In the next chapter, "Entering, Editing, and Validating Data in Tables," you add validation rules to the Personnel Actions table and enter records in the table.

To open the Employees table in design mode, follow these steps:

 1. Close any Access document windows that you have open, and then click the Table shortcut in the Database window to display the list of tables in the Northwind.mdb database.

2. Click Employees in the Database window, and then click the Design button. You also can open the Employees table by double-clicking the Database window entry and then clicking the Tables toolbar's Design View button.

3. The Design grid for the Employees table opens. Maximize the document window to the size of your Access window.

4. Close the Properties window, if it opens. Alternatively, you can choose View, Properties.

The menu command toggles the visibility of the Table Properties window. The Properties icon to the left of the Properties command has a sunken appearance to indicate that the Properties window is always visible in Table Design view.

At this point, your display resembles that shown in Figure 4.20.

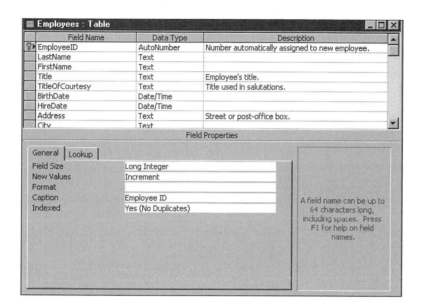

Figure 4.20
The Table Design view of the Employees table.

The Table Design window displays the field names and data types and provides a third column for an optional description of each field in the table. This display is called a *grid* rather than a *datasheet* because the display doesn't contain data from a table. A scroll bar is provided, whether or not more fields exist in the table than the window can display. The Field Properties pane lets you set additional properties of individual fields and briefly describes the purpose of each grid column and of the Field Properties entries as you select them. You cannot resize this pane.

One field is conspicuous by its absence: the Social Security number that most firms use in databases to identify their personnel. The EmployeeID field is an adequate substitute for the Social Security number for a sample table because a unique sequential number (the AutoNumber field data type) is assigned to each employee. Click the Datasheet View button to display the data in the EmployeeID field, and then return to design mode by clicking the Design View button.

PART

I

CH

4

DESIGNING THE PERSONNEL ACTIONS TABLE

Rather than add fields for entries (such as salary, commission rate, and bonuses) to the Employees table, you should place employee remuneration data in a table of its own, for the following reasons:

- Multiple personnel actions are taken for individual employees over time. If you add these actions to records in the Employees table, you have to create many additional fields to hold an arbitrary number of personnel actions. If, for example, quarterly performance reviews are entered, you have to add a new field for every quarter to hold the review information. In this situation, flat-file managers encounter difficulties.

- You can categorize personnel actions by type so that any action taken can use a common set of field names and field data types. This feature makes the design of the Personnel Actions table simple.

- You can identify employees uniquely by their EmployeeID numbers. Therefore, records for entries of personnel actions can be related to the Employees table by an EmployeeID field. This feature eliminates the necessity of adding employee names and other information to the records in the Personnel Action table. You link the Employees table to the Personnel table by the EmployeeID field, and the two tables are joined; they act as though they are a single table. Minimizing information duplication to only what is required to link the tables is your reward for choosing a relational, rather than a flat-file, database management system. (In an actual business's employee database, you would probably use the employee's Social Security number as the unique identifier for each employee and as the link to the Personnel Actions table.)

- Personnel actions usually are considered confidential information and are made accessible only to a limited number of people. Although Access lets you grant permission for others to view specific fields, restricting permission to view an entire table is simpler.

The next step is to design the Personnel Actions table. Chapter 22 discusses the theory of database design and the tables that make up databases. Because the Personnel Actions table has an easily discernible relationship to the Employees table, the theoretical background isn't necessary for this example.

DETERMINING WHAT INFORMATION THE TABLE SHOULD INCLUDE

Designing a table requires that you identify the type of information the table should contain. Information associated with typical personnel actions might consist of the following items:

- *Important dates.* The date of hire and termination, if applicable, are important dates, but so are the dates when the employer adjusts salaries, changes commission rates, and grants bonuses. You should accompany each action with the date when it was scheduled to occur and the date when it actually occurred.

- *Types of actions.* Less typing is required if personnel actions are identified by a code character rather than a full-text description of the action. This feature saves valuable disk space, too. First-letter abbreviations used as codes, such as H for *hired*, T for *terminated*, and Q for *quarterly review*, are easy to remember.

- *Initiation and approval of actions.* As a rule, the employee's supervisor initiates a personnel action, and the supervisor's manager approves it. Therefore, the table should include the supervisor's and manager's EmployeeID number.

- *Amounts involved.* Salaries are assumed to be paid bimonthly based on a monthly amount, bonuses are paid quarterly with quarterly performance reviews, and commissions are paid on a percentage of sales made by the employee.

- *Performance rating.* Rating employee performance by a numerical value is a universal, but somewhat arbitrary, practice. Scales of 1 to 9 are common, with exceptional performance ranked as 9 and candidacy for termination as 1.

- *Summaries and comments.* The table should provide for a summary of performance, an explanation of exceptionally high or low ratings, and reasons for adjusting salaries or bonuses.

If you are involved in personnel management, you probably can think of additional information that the table might include, such as accruable sick leave and vacation hours per pay period. The Personnel Actions table is just an example; it isn't meant to add full-scale human resources development capabilities to the database. The limited amount of data described serves to demonstrate several uses of the new table in this and subsequent chapters.

PART

I

CH

4

ASSIGNING INFORMATION TO FIELDS

After you determine the types of information—called *data entities* or just *entities*—to include in the table, you must assign each data entity to a field of the table. This process involves picking a field name that must be unique within the table. Table 4.7 lists the candidate fields for the Personnel Actions table. *Candidate fields* are written descriptions of the fields proposed for the table. Data types have been assigned from those listed in Table 4.8 in the following section.

Tip #33 from

R J

Although the table name contains a space, the field names of the Personnel Actions table don't contain spaces (as shown in Table 4.8). As mentioned earlier in this book, including spaces in table names or field names is not good database design practice. In this case, the table names include a space to demonstrate the special rule (enclosing the name within square brackets) that you must observe when referring to object names that include spaces. The Northwind Traders sample database includes spaces in many of its table names, so the use of spaces here is consistent with the other tables in the database.

TABLE 4.7 CANDIDATE FIELDS FOR THE PERSONNEL ACTIONS TABLE		
Field Name	**Data Type**	**Description**
paID	Number	The employee to whom the action applies. paID numbers are assigned based on the EmployeeID field of the Employee table (to which the Personnel Actions table is linked).
paType	Text	Code for the type of action taken: H is for hired; C, commission rate adjustment; Q, quarterly review; Y, yearly review; S, salary adjustment; B, bonus adjustment; and T, terminated.
paInitiatedBy	Number	The EmployeeID number of the supervisor who initiates or is responsible for recommending the action.
paScheduledDate	Date/Time	The date when the action is scheduled to occur.
paApprovedBy	Number	The EmployeeID number of the manager who approves the action proposed by the supervisor.
paEffectiveDate	Date/Time	The date when the action occurred. The effective date remains blank if the action has not occurred.
paRating	Number	Performance on a scale of 1–9, with higher numbers indicating better performance. A blank indicates no rating; 0 is reserved for terminated employees.
paAmount	Currency	The salary per month, the bonus per quarter, or commission rate as a percent of the amount of the order, expressed as a decimal fraction.
paComments	Memo	Abstracts of performance reviews and comments on actions proposed or taken. The comments can be of unlimited length. The supervisor and manager can contribute to the comments.

Tip #34 from

Use distinctive names for each field. This example precedes each field name with the abbreviation *pa* to identify the field with the Personnel Actions table. A common practice is to use similar names for fields that contain identical data but are located in different tables. Because of the way that Access uses field names in expressions for validating data entry and calculating field values (discussed later in this chapter and in Chapter 9), the best practice is to assign related, but distinctive, names to such fields.

CREATING THE PERSONNEL ACTIONS TABLE

Now you can put to work what you have learned about field names, data types, and formats by adding the Personnel Actions table to the Northwind Traders database. Table 4.8 shows the field names, taken from Table 4.7, and the set of properties that you assign to the fields. The text in the Caption column substitutes for the Field Name property that is otherwise displayed in the field header buttons.

TABLE 4.8   FIELD PROPERTIES FOR THE PERSONNEL ACTIONS TABLE

Field Name	Caption	Data Type	Field Size	Format
paID	ID	Number	Long Integer	General Number
paType	Type	Text	1	>@ (all uppercase)
paInitiatedBy	Initiated By	Number	Long Integer	General Number
paScheduledDate	Scheduled	Date/Time	N/A	Short Date
paApprovedBy	Approved By	Number	Long Integer	General Number
paEffectiveDate	Effective	Date/Time	N/A	Short Date
paRating	Rating	Number	Integer	General Number
paAmount	Amount	Currency	N/A	#,##0.00#
paComments	Comments	Memo	N/A	(None)

You must set the paID field's Field Size property to the Long Integer data type, although you might not expect Northwind Traders to have more than the 32,767 employees that an integer allows. You must use the Long Integer data type because the AutoNumber field data type of the Employees table's EmployeeID field is a Long Integer. Later in this chapter, the section "Enforcing Referential Integrity" explains why paID's data type must match that of the Employees table's EmployeeID number field.

To add the new Personnel Actions table to the Northwind Traders database, complete the following steps:

1. Close the Employees table, if it is open, by clicking the Close Window button to make the Database window active.

2. Click the Tables shortcut of the Database window, if it isn't selected, and then click the New button. Select Design View in the New Table dialog and click OK. Access enters design mode and opens a blank grid where you enter field names, data types, and optional comments. By default, Access selects the grid's first cell.

3. Type **paID** as the first field name. Press Enter to accept the field name; Access adds the default field type, Text.

4. Press F4 to open the Data Type list. (You use the function keys rather than the mouse because your entries are from the keyboard.)

5. Use the arrow keys to select the Number data type and press Enter to accept your selection (see Figure 4.21).

Figure 4.21
Entering the paID
field's data type.

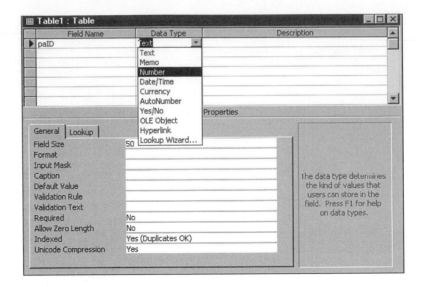

6. Press F6 to move to the Field Properties window's Field Size text box. Access has already entered Long Integer as the value of the default Field Size property. To learn more about the Field Size property, press F1 for help.

   Whenever you create a new Number type field, Access enters Long Integer in the Field Size property as the default. Because the paID field should be a Long Integer, you don't need to set the Field Size property for this field and can skip to step 8; continue with step 7 when you enter the other fields from Table 4.8.

7. For Number data types, press F4 to open the Field Size list. Select from the list the appropriate field size value for the field, and press Enter.

8. Press the down arrow to select the Format text box. You can press F1 for context-sensitive help on the Format property.

9. Press F4 to open the Format list, select General Number from the list, and press Enter (see Figure 4.22).

10. Press the down-arrow key three times, bypassing the Decimal Places and Input Mask properties, and select the Caption text box. You skip the Decimal Places property; Long Integers cannot have decimal fractions, so Decimal Places can remain set to Auto. You skip the Input Mask property because this field doesn't need an input mask.

11. Type **ID** as the caption and press Enter. ID is used as the Caption property to minimize the column width necessary to display the paID number.

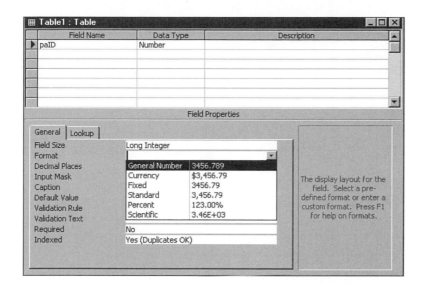

Figure 4.22
Assigning the General Number format to the paID field.

12. Press F6 to return to the Table Design grid. You complete the remaining properties for each field after entering the basic properties shown in Table 4.8.

Tip #35 from

You use descriptions to create prompts that appear in the status bar when you are adding or editing records in run mode's Datasheet view. Although descriptions are optional, it's good database design practice to enter the field's purpose if its use isn't obvious from its Field Name or Caption property. You can skip the Caption property entries for now. After completing the basic steps described here, refer to Table 4.8 and enter the captions as a group.

13. Press Enter to move the caret to the first cell of the next row of the grid.

14. Repeat steps 3 through 12, entering the values shown in Table 4.8 for each of the eight remaining fields of the Personnel Action table. N/A (not applicable) means that the entry in Table 4.8 doesn't apply to the field's data type.

Your Table Design grid should now look similar to the one shown in Figure 4.23. You can double-check your properties entries by selecting each field name with the arrow keys and reading the values shown in the property text boxes of the Field Properties window.

Click the Datasheet toolbar button to return to Datasheet view in Run mode to view the results of your work. You see the "Do you want to save the table now?" message. Click OK; a Save As dialog opens, requesting that you give your table a name and suggesting the default table name, Table1. Type **Personnel Actions**, as shown in Figure 4.24, and press Enter or click OK.

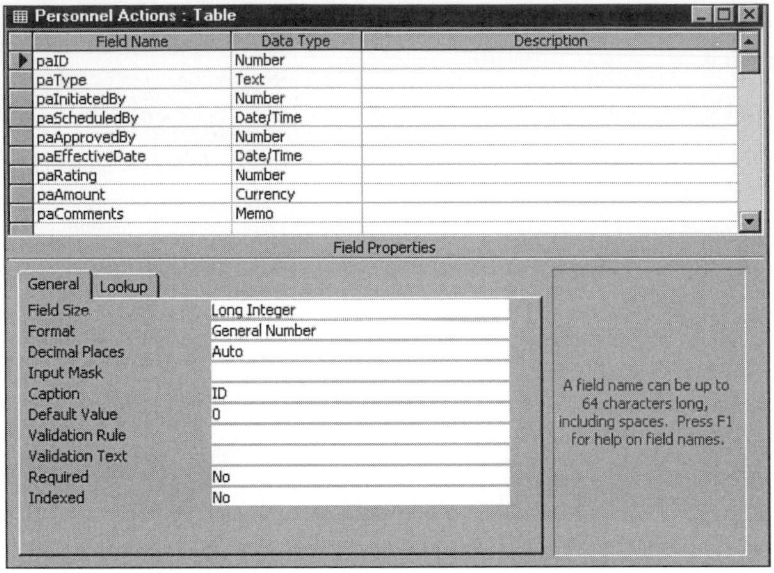

Figure 4.23
The initial design of the Personnel Actions table.

Figure 4.24
The Save As dialog for naming the Personnel Actions table.

At this point, Access displays a dialog informing you that the new table does not have a primary key. You add primary keys to the Personnel Actions table later in this chapter, so click No in this dialog.

Your table opens in Datasheet view, with its first default record. To view all the fields of your new table, narrow the field name header buttons by dragging to the left the right vertical bar that separates each header. When you finish adjusting your fields' display widths, the Personnel Actions table appears in Datasheet view (see Figure 4.25). Only the empty tentative append record (a new record that Access adds to your table if you enter values in the cells) is present. You have more property values to add to your Personnel Actions table, so don't enter data in the tentative append record at this point.

CREATING A TABLE DIRECTLY IN DATASHEET VIEW

If you're a complete database novice and under pressure to create database tables immediately, Access lets you create tables directly in Datasheet view. When you create a table in Datasheet view, Access displays an empty table with a default structure of 20 fields and 30 empty records. You then enter data directly into the table. When you save the table, Access analyzes the data you have entered and selects a field type for each field that best matches the data you have entered.

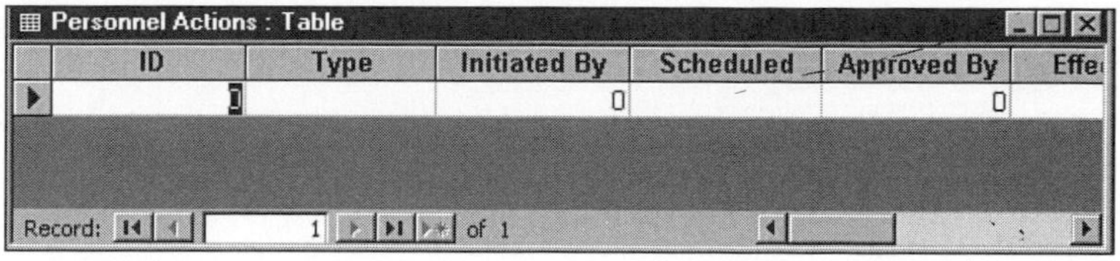

Figure 4.25
The tentative append record of the Personnel Actions table.

SETTING DEFAULT VALUES OF FIELDS

Access 2000 assigns Number and Currency fields a default value of 0; all other field types are empty by default. (Notice that the tentative append record in Figure 4.25 has zeros entered in all the Number and Currency fields.) In all versions of Access, Text, Memo, and Date fields are empty by default. You can save data-entry time by establishing your own default values for fields; in some cases, Access 2000's default values for Number and Currency fields may be inappropriate, and you'll need to change them. Table 4.9 lists the default values for the Personnel Actions table's fields.

TABLE 4.9   DEFAULT FIELD VALUES FOR THE PERSONNEL ACTIONS TABLE

Field Name	Default Value	Comments
paID	No entry	0 is not a valid Employee ID number, so you should remove Access's default.
paType	Q	Quarterly performance reviews are the most common personnel action.
paInitiatedBy	No entry	0 is not a valid Employee ID number.
paScheduledDate	=Date()	This expression enters today's date from the computer system's clock.
paApprovedBy	No entry	0 is not a valid Employee ID.
paEffectiveDate	=Date()+28	This expression enters today's date plus 28 days.
paRating	No entry	In many cases, a rating does not apply. A 0 rating is reserved for terminated employees.
paAmount	No entry	If a salary, bonus, or commission has no change, no entry should appear. 0 would indicate no salary, for example.
paComments	No change	For now, Access's default is adequate.

If you don't enter anything in the Default Value text box, you create a **Null** default value. You can use **Null** values for testing whether a value has been entered into a field. Such a test can ensure that users have entered required data. The Date()+28 default is an *expression* that returns the date (according to your computer's clock) plus four weeks. You use expressions to enter values in fields, make calculations, and perform other useful duties, such as validating data entries. Expressions are discussed briefly in the next section and in greater detail in Chapter 9. Expressions that establish default values are always preceded by an equal sign.

To assign the new default values from those of Table 4.9 to the fields of the Personnel Actions table, complete these steps:

1. Change to design mode by choosing View, Design View. Select the paID field.

2. Press F6 to switch to the Field Properties window, and then move the caret to the Default Value text box. Press Delete to clear the text box.

3. Press F6 to switch back to the Table Design grid. Move to the next field and press F6 again.

4. Press Create the default values for the eight remaining fields from the entries shown in Table 4.9, repeating steps 1 through 3. For example, after selecting the Default Value text box for the paType field, type **Q** to set the default value; Access automatically surrounds Q with double quotes. Enter **=Date()** for the paScheduledDate field and then **=Date()+28** for the paEffectiveDate Date field. Delete any default values that might appear in the other fields that call for no entry in Table 4.9.

5. After completing your default entries, choose View, Datasheet View to return to Run mode. A dialog opens, requesting that you confirm your changes. Click OK. The Personnel Actions table now appears in Datasheet view with the new default entries you have assigned (see Figure 4.26).

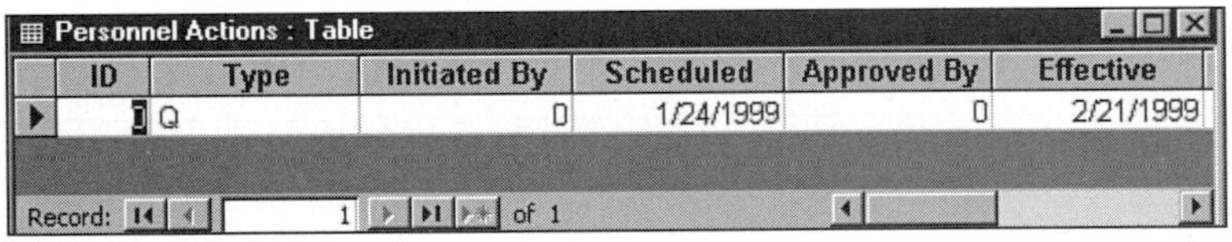

Figure 4.26
The first record of the Personnel Actions table with the new default values.

ID	Type	Initiated By	Scheduled	Approved By	Effective
1	Q	0	1/24/1999	0	2/21/1999

Record: 1 of 1

WORKING WITH RELATIONS, KEY FIELDS, AND INDEXES

Your final tasks before adding records to the Personnel Actions table are to determine the relationship between Personnel Actions and an existing table in the database, assign a primary-key field, and add indexes to your table.

ESTABLISHING RELATIONSHIPS BETWEEN TABLES

Relationships between existing tables and your new table determine the field used as the new table's primary key.

The following four possibilities exist for relationships between tables:

■ *One-to-one* relationships require that the key field's value in only one record in your new table matches a single corresponding value of the related field in the existing table.

- *Many-to-one* relationships allow your new table to have more than one value in the key field corresponding to a single value in the related field of the existing table.

- *One-to-many* relationships require that your new table's primary-key field be unique, but the values in the foreign-key field of the new table can match many entries in the related field of the existing database. In this type, the related field of the existing database has a many-to-one relationship with the primary-key field of the new database.

- *Many-to-many* relationships are free-for-alls in which no unique relationship exists between the key fields in the existing table or the new table, and both of the tables' foreign-key fields contain duplicate values.

Keep in mind that the many-to-one relationship and one-to-many relationship are the same thing depending on the table's vantage point. When viewed from the existing table's standpoint, the relationship to your new table is one-to-many. Chapter 22 explains the four types of relationships more comprehensively

➔ For the list of these four types, **see** the section "Types of Relationships," **p. 831**.

Many entries in the Personnel Actions table may apply to a single employee whose record appears in the Employees table. A record is created in Personnel Actions when the employee is hired, and a record is created for each quarterly and yearly performance review. Also, any changes made to bonuses or commissions other than as the result of a performance review are entered, and employees may be terminated. Over time, the number of records in the Personnel Actions table is likely to be greater by a factor of 10 or more than the number of records in the Employees table. Thus, the records in the new Personnel table have a many-to-one relationship with the records in the Employees table. Establishing the relationships between the new and existing tables when you create the new table enables Access to re-establish the relationship automatically when you use the tables in queries, forms, and reports.

Access requires that the two fields participating in the relationship have exactly the same data type. In the case of the Number field data type, the Field Size property of the two fields must be identical. You cannot, for example, create a relationship between an AutoNumber type field (which uses a Long Integer data type) and a field containing Byte, Integer, Single, Double, or Currency data. On the other hand, Access lets you relate two tables by text fields of different lengths. Such a relationship, if created, can lead to strange behavior when you create queries, which is the subject of Part II, "Getting the Most Out of Queries." As a rule, the relationships between text fields should use fields of the same length.

Access 2000 uses a graphical Relationships window to display and create the relationships among tables in a database. To establish the relationships between two tables with Access's Relationships window, follow these steps:

1. Close the Personnel Actions table by clicking the Close Window button. If the Employees table is open, close it. You cannot create or modify relationships between open tables.

PART

I

CH

4

2. Before you can establish relationships, the Database window must be active. If it isn't, click it, and then click the Show Database Window toolbar button or choose Window, 1 Northwind : Database. As many as nine of the windows for database objects that you have opened appear as numbered choices in the Window menu. (The Database window is always number 1.)

3. Click the Relationships button of the toolbar or choose Tools, Relationships. The Relationships window for the Northwind Traders database opens (see Figure 4.27).

4. Click the Show Table button of the toolbar or choose Relationships, Show Table. The Show Table dialog opens (see Figure 4.28).

Figure 4.27
The Relationships window.

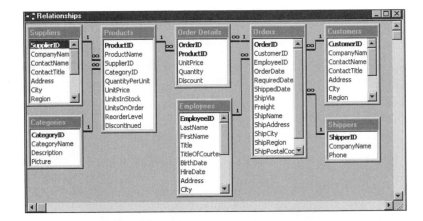

Figure 4.28
The Show Table dialog, used to add tables to the Relationships window.

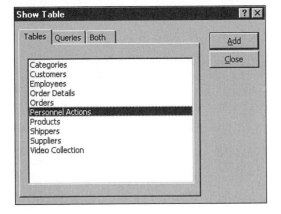

5. Add the Personnel Actions table to the Relationships window by double-clicking the Personnel Actions entry in the Tables list, or by clicking the entry to select it and then clicking the Add button. Click the Close button to close the Show Table dialog.

6. The relationship of the Personnel Actions table to the Employees table is based on the Personnel Actions table's paID field and the Employees table's EmployeeID field. Click the Employees table's EmployeeID field and, holding the left mouse button down, drag it to the Personnel Actions table's paID field. Release the mouse button to drop the field symbol on the paID field. The Edit Relationships dialog opens (see Figure 4.29).

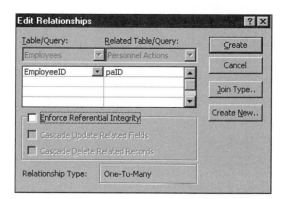

Figure 4.29
Defining a relationship with the Edit Relationships dialog.

Note

The sequence of the drag-and-drop operation to create a new relationship is important. Drag the field from the *one* side of a one-to-many relationship and drop it on the *many* side. This sequence ensures that the primary (or base) table for the *one* side of the relationship appears in the Table/Query list and that the table for the *many* side appears in the Related Table/Query list. If you reverse the relationships (creating a many-to-one relationship) and attempt to enforce referential integrity, you receive an error message in the final step of the process when you attempt to create the relationship.

7. Click the Join Type button to display the Join Properties dialog shown in Figure 4.30. You want to create a one-to-many join between the Employees table's EmployeeID field (the *one* side) and the Personnel Actions table's paID field (the *many* side). You want to display all Employee records, even if one or more records doesn't have corresponding record(s) in Personnel Actions. To do so, select option 2 in the Join Properties dialog. Click OK to close the dialog and return to the Relationships dialog.

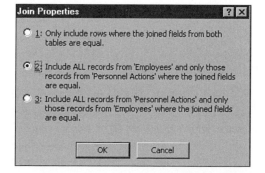

Figure 4.30
Choosing the type of join for the Personnel Actions and Employees tables.

8. The Relationships dialog offers the Enforce Referential Integrity check box so that you can specify that Access perform validation testing and accept entries in the paID field that correspond to values for the Employees table's EmployeeID field. This process is called *enforcing* (or maintaining) referential integrity. The following section discusses referential integrity. The relationship between these two tables requires enforced referential integrity, so make sure you select this check box. The Relationships dialog now looks like the one shown in Figure 4.31.

Figure 4.31
The Relationships dialog entries for a one-to-many relationship with referential integrity enforced.

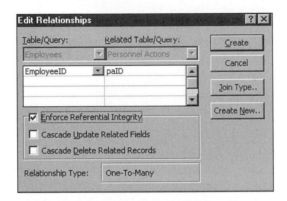

Note

Access 2000 automatically maintains referential integrity of tables by providing check boxes you can mark to cause cascading updates to, and cascade deletions of, related records when the primary table changes. The following section discusses cascading updates and deletions. Access enables the cascade check boxes only if you elect to enforce referential integrity.

9. Click the Create button to accept the new relationship and display it in the Relationships window (see Figure 4.32).

10. Click the Close Window button to close the Relationships window and return to the Database window. Click Yes when asked to confirm that you want to save the layout changes to the Relationships diagram.

NEW 2000

Access uses the relationship that you have created when you create queries and design forms and reports that require data in the Personnel Actions table. Access does not require that the related table be indexed. New in Access 2000 is the Print Relationships menu command, which gives you a convenient means of printing the relationships. In Access 97, the Print Relationships command was provided as an add-in.

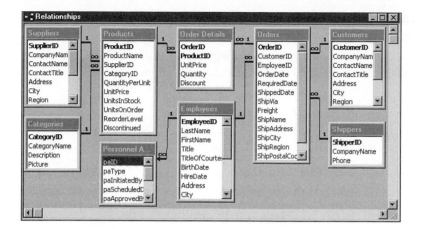

Figure 4.32
The Relationships window with the new Personnel Actions relationship added.

ENFORCING REFERENTIAL INTEGRITY

The capability to enforce referential integrity automatically is an important feature of Access; few other PC relational database managers include this feature. Referential integrity prevents the creation of *orphan records* with no connection to a primary table. An example of an orphan record is a record for a personnel action for paID 10 when you have records in the Employees file for employees numbered only 1 through 9. You could not know who employee 10 is until you enter the next employee hired. Then the orphan record, intended for some other employee, is linked, improperly, to the new employee's record.

UNDERSTANDING HOW REFERENTIAL INTEGRITY IS ENFORCED

Referential integrity enforcement prevents you from deleting or modifying values of a primary table's record on which related records depend. If you terminate an employee and then try to delete the employee's record from the Employees table, Access prevents you from doing so. Access displays a message box informing you that you must delete all records related to the primary table's record before you can delete the primary record. You can't change a value in the Employees table's EmployeeID field because the field data type is AutoNumber. If the data types are such that you can change the value of an EmployeeID on which related records depend, however, Access also displays a warning message.

Similarly, if you attempt to change an employee ID value in the paID field of the Personnel Actions table to a value that does not exist in the Employees table's EmployeeID field, you incur an error message again. Thus, enforcing referential integrity eliminates the need to validate entries in the paID field with the Validation Rule property. With referential integrity enforced, Access automatically ensures that the value you enter corresponds to a valid EmployeeID value when you save the new or edited record.

PART

I

CH

4

CASCADING UPDATES AND DELETIONS

Access 2000's cascading deletion and cascading update options for tables with enforced referential integrity makes maintaining referential integrity easy: Just mark the Cascade Update Related Fields and Cascade Delete Related Records check boxes. Access 2000 does all the work for you.

> **Note**
>
> Automatically enforcing referential integrity is usually, but not always, good database design practice. An example of where you would *not* want to employ cascade deletions is between the EmployeeID fields of the Orders and Employee tables. If you terminate an employee and then attempt to delete the employee's record, you might accidentally choose to delete the dependent records in the Orders table. Deleting records in the Orders table could have serious consequences from a marketing and accounting standpoint. (In practice, however, you probably would not delete a terminated employee's record.)

SELECTING A PRIMARY KEY

You do not need to designate a primary-key field for a table that is never used as a primary table. A *primary table* contains information representing an object, such as a person or an invoice, and only one record uniquely associated with that object. The Personnel Actions table can qualify as a primary table because it identifies an object—in this case, the equivalent of a paper form representing the outcome of two actions: initiation and approval. Personnel Actions, however, probably would not be used as a primary table in a relationship with another table.

Using a key field is a simple method of preventing the duplication of records in a table. Access requires that you specify a primary key if you want to create a one-to-one relationship or to update two or more tables at the same time. Chapter 10 covers this subject.

The primary table participating in relations that you set with the Relationships window must have a primary key. Access considers a table without a primary-key field to be an oddity; therefore, when you make changes to the table and return to Design view, you might see a message stating that you haven't created a key field. (Access 2000 asks only once whether you want to add a primary-key field.) Related tables can have primary-key fields and often do. A primary-key field is useful for preventing the accidental addition of duplicate records.

You can create primary keys on more than one field. In the case of the Personnel Actions table, a primary key that prevents duplicate records must consist of more than one field because more than one personnel action for an employee can be scheduled or approved on the same date. If you establish the rule that no more than one type of personnel action for an employee can be scheduled for the same date, you can create a primary key that consists of the paID, paType, and paScheduledDate fields. When you create a primary key, Access creates an index based on the primary key. The next section and Chapter 22 discuss indexes in detail.

To create a multiple-field primary key and index for the Personnel Actions table, follow these steps:

1. Open the Personnel Actions table from the Database window in Design view.

2. Click the selection button for the paID field.

3. Ctrl+click the selection button for the paType field. In most instances, when you Ctrl+click a selection button, you can make multiple selections.

4. Ctrl+click the selection button for the paScheduledDate field.

   If you accidentally select one of the other fields, click the field's selection button again to deselect it.

5. Click the Primary Key toolbar button. Symbols of keys appear in each selected field, indicating their inclusion in the primary key (see Figure 4.33).

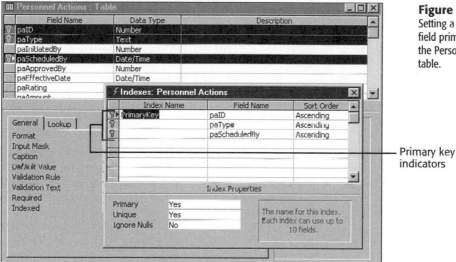

Figure 4.33
Setting a multiple-field primary key for the Personnel Actions table.

Primary key indicators

PART

I

CH

4

6. To determine the sequence of the fields in the primary key, click the toolbar's Index button to display the Indexes window as shown in Figure 4.33.

   In Access, you can create multiple-field primary keys and indexes with fields of different data types. The capability to concatenate different data types to form an index instruction or a string is the result of Access's Variant data type.

→ For information on the Variant data type and concatenating strings, **see** "The Variant Data Type in Access and VBA," **p. 331.**

→ **See** "Data Types and Database Objects in VBA," **p. 1000,** for details on using the Variant data type with objects.

You now have a multiple-field primary key and a corresponding index to the Personnel Actions table that precludes the addition of records that duplicate records with the same primary key.

ADDING INDEXES TO TABLES

Although Access creates an index on the primary key, you might want to create an index on some other field or fields in the table. Indexes speed searches for records that contain specific types of data. You might want to find all personnel actions that occurred in a given period and all quarterly reviews for all employees in paScheduledDate sequence, for example. If you have many records in the table, an index speeds up the searching process. A disadvantage of multiple indexes is that data-entry operations are slowed by the time it takes to update the additional indexes. You can create as many as 32 indexes for each Access table, and five of those can be of the multiple-field type. Each multiple-field index can include as many as 10 fields.

Tip #36 from	Add only indexes you need to improve search performance. Each index you add slows addition of new records, because adding a new record requires an additon to each index. Similarly, editing indexed fields is slower, because the edit updates the record and the index. When you create relationships between tables, Access automatically creates a hidden index on the related fields, if the index doesn't already exist. Hidden indexes count against the 32-index limit of each table. If an extra index appears in the Indexes dialog, see the "Extra Indexes Added by Access" item in the "Troubleshooting" section near the end of this chapter.

To create a single-field index for the Personnel Actions table based on the paEffectiveDate field, and a multiple-field index based on the paType and the paScheduledDate fields, follow these steps:

1. Select the paEffectiveDate field by clicking its selection button.

2. Select the Indexed text box in the Field Properties window.

3. Open the Indexed drop-down list by clicking the arrow button or pressing F4. The list appears, as shown in Figure 4.34.

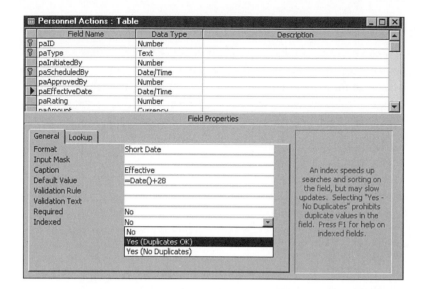

Figure 4.34
Creating a single-field
index on the
paEffectiveDate field.

4. In this case, duplicate entries are acceptable, so click Yes (Duplicates OK) and close the list. You can create only a single-field index with this method.

5. Click the Indexes button if the Indexes window is not open. The Primary Key and paEffectiveDate indexes already created appear in the list boxes. Enter **paType/Date** as the name of the composite index, and then select paType in the Field Name drop-down list; move the caret to the next row of the Field Name column and select paScheduledDate to create a multiple-field index on these two fields (see Figure 4.35).

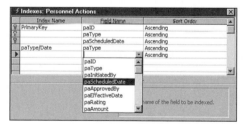

Figure 4.35
Creating a multiple-
field index.

6. Click the Datasheet View button to return to Run mode. Click OK when the message box asks whether you want to save your design changes. A message in the status bar indicates that Access is creating the new indexes as you leave design mode.

You now have three indexes for the Primary Key table: the index automatically created for the primary key, the single-key index on paEffectiveDate, and the multiple-key index on paType and paScheduledDate.

PART

I

CH

4

ALTERING FIELDS AND RELATIONSHIPS

When you are designing your own database, you often discover that you must alter the original choices you made for the sequence of fields in a table, data types, or relationships between tables. One reason for adding substantial numbers of records to tables during the testing process is to discover any necessary changes before putting the database into daily use.

You can change formats, validation rules and text, lengths of Text fields, and other minor items in the table by changing to design mode, selecting the field to modify, and making the changes in the property boxes. Changing data types can cause a loss of data, however, so be sure to read the later section "Changing Field Data Types and Sizes" before you attempt to make such changes. Changing relationships between tables is considered a drastic action if you have entered a substantial amount of data, so this subject is also covered later in "Changing Relationships Between Tables."

REARRANGING THE SEQUENCE OF FIELDS IN A TABLE

If you're typing historical data in Datasheet view, you might find that the sequence of entries isn't optimum. You might, for example, be entering data from a printed form with a top-to-bottom, left-to-right sequence that doesn't correspond to the left-to-right sequence of the corresponding fields in your table. Access makes rearranging the order of fields in tables a matter of dragging and dropping fields where you want them. You can decide whether to make the revised layout temporary or permanent when you close the table.

To rearrange the fields of the Personnel Actions table, follow these steps:

1. Click the Datasheet View button. Rearranging the sequence of fields is the only table design change you can implement in Access's Datasheet view.

2. Click the field name button of the field you want to move. This action selects the field name button and all the field's data cells.

3. Hold down the left mouse button while over the field name button. The mouse pointer turns into the drag-and-drop symbol, and a heavy vertical bar marks the field's far-left position. Figure 4.36 shows the paScheduledDate field being moved to a position immediately to the left of the paEffectiveDate field.

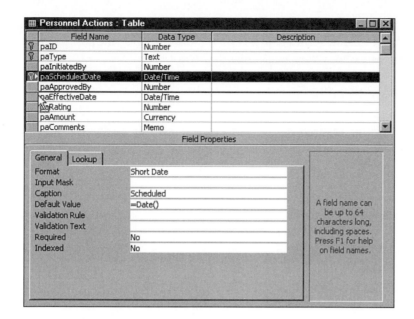

Figure 4.36
Dragging a field to a new position in Datasheet view.

4. Move the vertical bar to the new position for the selected field and release the mouse button. The field assumes the new position shown in Figure 4.37.

5. When you close the Personnel Actions table, you see the familiar Save Changes message box. To make the modification permanent, click OK; otherwise, click No.

Figure 4.37
The paScheduledDate field dropped into a new position.

	ID	Type	Initiated By	Approved By	Scheduled	Effective	Rating	Am
►	1	H		1		5/1/1992	5/1/1992		2
	2	H		1		8/14/1992	8/14/1992		3
	3	H		1		4/1/1992	4/1/1992		2
	4	H		2	2	5/3/1993	5/3/1993		2
	5	H		2	2	10/17/1993	10/17/1993		2
	5	Q		2	2	1/1/1997	2/11/1997	8	2
	5	Q		2	2	3/31/1997	5/12/1997	7	3
	5	Q		2	2	6/30/1997	8/11/1997	8	3
	5	Q		2	2	9/30/1997	11/11/1997	8	4
	5	Y		7	7	1/1/1998	2/11/1998	9	4
	6	H		5	2	10/17/1993	10/17/1993	8	4
	7	H		5	2	1/2/1994	1/2/1994		3
	8	H		2	2	3/5/1994	3/5/1994		2
	9	H		5	2	11/15/1994	11/15/1994		3
*		Q				1/24/1999	2/21/1999		

Record: 14 ◄ | 1 | ► ►I ►* of 14

To reposition fields in Design view, click the select button of the row of the field you want to move and then drag the row vertically to a new location. Changing the position of a table's field doesn't change any of the field's other properties.

CHANGING FIELD DATA TYPES AND SIZES

You might have to change a field data type as the design of your database develops or if you import tables from another database, a spreadsheet, or a text file. If you import tables, the data type automatically chosen by Access during the importation process probably won't be what you want, especially with Number fields. Chapter 7 discusses importing and exporting tables and data from other applications. Another example of altering field properties is changing the number of characters in fixed-length Text fields to accommodate entries that are longer than expected, or converting variable-length Text fields to fixed-length fields.

> **Caution**
>
> Before making changes to the field data types of a table that contains substantial amounts of data, back up the table by copying or exporting it to a backup Access database. If you accidentally lose parts of the data contained in the table (such as decimal fractions) while changing the field data type, you can import the backup table to your current database. Chapter 7 covers the simple and quick process of exporting Access tables. After creating a backup database file, you can copy a table to Windows Clipboard and then paste the table to the backup database. The later section "Copying and Pasting Tables" discusses copying and pasting tables to and from the Clipboard.

NUMERIC FIELDS

Changing a data type to one that requires more bytes of storage is, in almost all circumstances, safe. You do not sacrifice your data's accuracy. Changing a numeric data type from Byte to Integer to Long Integer to Single and, finally, to Double does not affect your data's value because each change, except for Long Integer to Single, requires more bytes of storage for a data value. Changing from Long Integer to Single and Single to Currency involves the same number of bytes and decreases the accuracy of the data only in exceptional circumstances. The exceptions can occur when you are using very high numbers or extremely small decimal fractions, such as in some scientific and engineering calculations.

On the other hand, if you change to a data type with fewer data bytes required to store it, Access might truncate your data. If you change from a fixed-point format (Currency) or floating-point format (Single or Double) to Byte, Integer, or Long Integer, any decimal fractions in your data are truncated. *Truncation* means reducing the number of digits in a number to fit the new Field Size property that you choose. If you change a numeric data type from Single to Currency, for example, you might lose your Single data in the fifth, sixth, and seventh decimal places (if any exists) because Single provides as many as seven decimal places and Currency provides only four.

You can't convert any field type to an AutoNumber-type field. You can use the AutoNumber field only as a record counter; the only way you can enter a new value in an AutoNumber field is by appending new records. You can't edit an AutoNumber field. When you delete a record in Access, the AutoNumber values of the higher-numbered records are *not* reduced by 1. Sequential Access AutoNumber field values are assigned to records in the order in which the records were entered, not in the order of the primary key.

TEXT FIELDS

You can convert Text fields to Memo fields without Access truncating your text. Converting a Memo field to a Text field, however, truncates characters beyond the 255-character limit of Text fields. Similarly, if you convert a variable-length Text field to a fixed-length field, and some records contain character strings that exceed the length you chose, Access truncates these strings.

CONVERSION BETWEEN NUMBER, DATE, AND TEXT FIELD DATA TYPES

Access makes many conversions between Number, Date, and Text field data types for you. Conversion from Number or Date to Text field data types does not follow the Format property that you assigned to the original data type. Numbers are converted with the General Number format, and dates use the Short Date format. Access is quite intelligent in the methods it uses to convert suitable Text fields to Number data types. For example, it accepts dollar signs, commas, and decimals during the conversion, but ignores trailing spaces. Access converts dates and times in the following Text formats to internal Date/Time values that you then can format the way you want.

```
1/4/1999 10:00 AM
04-Jan-99
January 4
10:00
10:00:00
```

CHANGING RELATIONSHIPS BETWEEN TABLES

Adding new relationships between tables is a straightforward process, but changing relationships might require you to change data types so that the related fields have the same data type. To change a relationship between two tables, complete the following steps:

1. Close the tables involved in the relationship.

2. If the Database window is not active, click the Show Database Window button, or choose <u>W</u>indow, <u>1</u> Database.

3. Display the Relationships window by clicking the Relationships button of the toolbar or by choosing <u>T</u>ools, <u>R</u>elationships.

4. Click the join line that connects to the field whose data type you want to change. When you select the join line, the line becomes darker (wider), as shown in Figure 4.38.

PART

I

CH

4

Figure 4.38
Selecting a relationship to delete or modify.

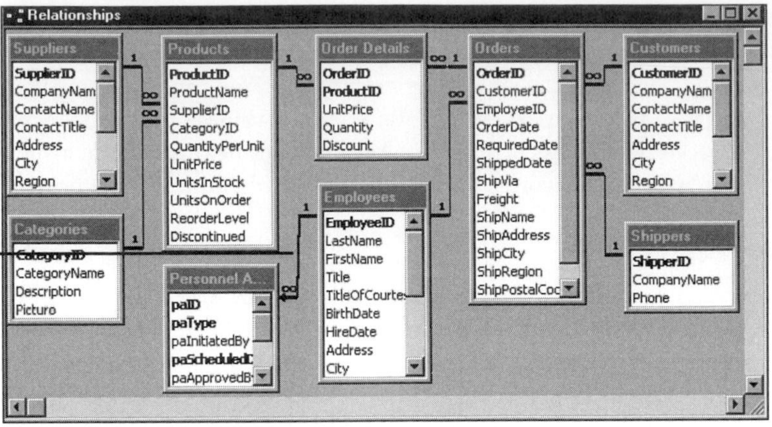

Join line selected for deletion

5. Press Delete to clear the existing relationship. Click Yes when the message box asks you to confirm your deletion.

6. If you are changing the data type of a field that constitutes or is a member field of the primary table's primary key, delete all other relationships that exist between the primary table and every other table to which it is related.

7. Change the data types of the fields in the tables so that the data types match in the new relationships.

8. Re-create the relationships by using the procedure described earlier in the section "Establishing Relationships Between Tables."

COPYING AND PASTING TABLES

To copy a complete table or records of a table to the Windows Clipboard, use the same methods that apply to most other Windows applications. (Using the Clipboard to paste individual records or sets of records into a table is one of the subjects of the next chapter.) You can copy tables into other databases, such as a general-purpose backup database, by using the Clipboard; however, exporting a table to a temporary database file, described in Chapter 7 is a more expeditious method.

To copy a table to another Access database, a destination database must exist. To create a backup database and copy the contents of the Personnel Actions table to the database, follow these steps:

1. Make the Database window active by clicking it, if it is accessible, or by choosing Window, 1 Database.

2. Click the Tables tab, if necessary, to display the list of tables.

3. Select the table that you want to copy to the new database.

4. Click the Copy button on the toolbar, press Ctrl+C, or choose Edit, Copy.

   If you plan to copy the table to your current database, skip to step 7.

5. If you've created a destination backup database, choose File, Open Database to open the database; then skip to step 7.

6. To create a backup database, choose File, New Database; then choose a blank database and name it backup.mdb or another appropriate file name. Access creates your Backup.mdb database, which occupies approximately 96KB without any tables (this is called *overhead*). Your new database is now active.

7. Click the Paste button on the toolbar, press Ctrl+V, or choose Edit, Paste. The Paste Table As dialog appears (see Figure 4.39).

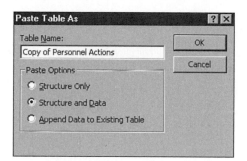

Figure 4.39
The Paste Table As dialog.

8. You have three options for pasting the backup table to the destination database. The most common choice is Structure and Data, with which you can create a new table or replace the data in a table with the name you enter in the Table Name text box. You can also paste only the structure and then append data to the table later by selecting Structure Only, or append the records to an existing table of the name that you enter. For this example, accept the default: Structure and Data.

9. Your current or backup database now has a copy of the table that you selected, and the name you entered appears in the backup's Database window. You can save multiple copies of the same table under different names if you are making a series of changes to the table that might affect the integrity of the data that it contains.

To delete a table from a database, select the table name in the Database window and then press Delete. A confirmation message box appears. Click Yes to delete the table forever. You can't choose Edit, Undo after deleting a table.

PART

I

CH

4

TROUBLESHOOTING

GAPS IN AUTONUMBER FIELD VALUES

When I accidentally add a new record to a table with an AutoNumber field and then delete it, the next record I add has the wrong AutoNumber value—increment of 2 instead of 1.

That's the major drawback of AutoNumber fields, especially when the AutoNumber field value corresponds to a physical record, such as an invoice or check number. The AutoNumber feature offers no simple method of replacing an incorrect record that you delete from the table. The best approach, which insures that your table is auditable, is to never delete a record from a table with an AutoNumber field. Instead, type **VOID** in an appropriate field, and add an explanation (if there's a field available to do so).

EXTRA INDEXES ADDED BY ACCESS

After you specify a primary key on a field containing the characters "ID", an additional index appears for the field.

In many cases, Access automatically specifies a primary key and index on fields whose names contain the characters "ID", "key", "code", and "num" when you create or import tables. This behavior is controlled by the contents of the AutoIndex on Import/Create text box of the Tables/Queries page of the Options dialog. When you change the primary key field(s), the old index remains. You can safely delete the automatically added index.

IN THE REAL WORLD—DATABASE STRATEGY AND TABLE TACTICS

In warfare, strategy defines the objective; tactics specify the battlefield methods to achieve the strategic objective. Carl von Clauswitz' *On War* is the seminal 19th century study of strategy and tactics of modern warfare. Niccolo Machiavelli's *The Art of War* and Che Guevera's *On Guerilla Warfare* provide earlier and later takes, respectively, on the subject. Designing strategic databases and laying out the tables that comprise the database shouldn't—but often does—involve open or guerilla hostilities between the participants. As a database and table designer, try to remain on the side of your product's consumers; you might win a battle or two, but the consumers (users) ultimately will win the war. This is especially true when the consumers control your database implementation budget.

WHY TABLE DESIGN COMES BEFORE DATABASE DESIGN IN THIS BOOK

Production database design requires strategic planning, including business process analysis, determination of workflow paths, identifying physical and temporal relationships between data entities, and other considerations that are well beyond the scope of this introductory chapter on Access table design. Designing tables constitutes the tactics of database implementation. In warfare and database design, it's essential to possess a well-defined strategy before you decide on the tactics. Failure to do so creates situations analogous to the early-1999 confrontations between NATO and the Serbs over the fate of Kosovo and the ethnic Albanians living in political subdivisions of former Yugoslavia.

Adding new tables to a database on an *ad hoc* basis is a necessary element of the Access learning curve. Conversance with table terminology is necessary to comprehend relational database design. You must understand table properties—field names, data types, primary keys, indexes, relationships, default values, validation rules, and the like—just to proceed to the next major topic of this book, the design of Access queries. Starting this book with a chapter on the theory of relational database design would be the equivalent of beginning flight training in a Boeing 757 instead of a Cessna 150 or 172.

Another reason for putting the cart (tables) before the horse (database design) is that the majority of new Access users have existing tabular data sources to import or link to a new Access database. If someone's already entered the data you need into another desktop database manager or a spreadsheet, don't go through the agony of retyping data into a table. Chapter 7 shows you how to get external data into an Access table. Once you have the data in a Jet table, you can change field names and sequence, assign primary keys, add default values and validation rules, and specify relationships with other tables.

NAMING CONVENTIONS FOR TABLES AND FIELDS

There are several schools of thought on naming tables and fields, but most Access developers agree on one rule: Don't add spaces to table or field names. The Personnel Actions table violates this rule to demonstrate in later chapters issues that arise with spaces in Access object names, especially when upsizing to MSDE/SQL Server tables. Northwind.mdb contains only one table, Order Details, with a space in its name, and none of the current Northwind.mdb tables have spaces in field names.

Many developers use "tbl" as a table name prefix for consistency with other Access object type identification prefixes, such as "frm" for forms and "rpt" for reports. Using a table object identifier prefix is uncommon in real-world production databases, but using table names that identify the source document or object of the table, such as "Orders", "Invoices", "Products", and the like is a good database design practice. Use plural nouns when naming tables, because tables contain multiple representative instances of objects.

Many database administrators (DBAs) require a short prefix to field names that identify the table that contains the fields. A field name prefix indicates to developers the source of the field without the necessity of having to refer to a database diagram or a table field list. Another benefit of adding a prefix based on a table name is avoidance of duplicate names in primary-key and foreign-key pairs. The field names of Personnel Actions begin with "pa"; this distinguishes the paID field (foreign key) from the EmployeeID (primary key) field of the Employees table when you create a relationship between the tables, and when you join the Personnel Actions and Employees tables to create multitable queries, the subject of Chapter 10.

Some developers add to field names a prefix—such as "dat" (for Date/Time) or "txt" (for Text)—that specifies the Jet data type, following the generally-accepted convention for adding a data type prefix to VBA variable and constant names. This practice is becoming less common as more developers work interchangeably with Jet and MSDE/SQL Server databases. Some corresponding Jet and SQL Server data type names aren't the same; conflicts between Jet-based and SQL Server prefixes can cause confusion when upsizing Jet databases to MSDE or SQL Server 7.0.

--rj

CHAPTER 5

ENTERING, EDITING, AND VALIDATING DATA IN TABLES

In this chapter

Entering Test Data in Access Tables   186

Using Keyboard Operations for Entering and Editing Data   186

Adding Records to a Table   193

Selecting, Appending, Replacing, and Deleting Table Records   194

Validating Data Entry   194

Adding Records to the Personnel Actions Table   199

Entering Personnel Actions Table Data and Testing Validation Rules   201

Troubleshooting   202

In the Real World—Heads-Down Data Entry   203

Entering Test Data in Access Tables

Ease of data entry is a primary criterion for an effective database development environment. Most of your Access database applications probably use forms for data entry. However, in many instances, entering data in Table Datasheet view is more expeditious than using a form, especially during the database development cycle. For example, it's a good idea to test your proposed database structure before you commit to designing the forms and reports. Although the new Name AutoCorrect feature in Access 2000 reduces discrepancies, changing table and field names or altering relationships between tables after you create a collection of forms and reports can involve a substantial amount of work.

To test the database design, you often need to enter test data. In this instance, using Table Datasheet view to enter data makes more sense than using a form. Even if you import data from another database type or from a worksheet, you likely need to edit the data to make it compatible with your new application. The first part of this chapter concentrates on data entry and editing methods.

Another important factor in a database development environment is the capability to maintain the domain integrity of your data. *Domain integrity rules* limit the values you enter in fields to a range or set.

Like Access 97, Access 2000 lets you enforce domain integrity rules (often called *business rules*) at the field and table levels. You enforce domain integrity by entering expressions as the value of the Validation Rule property of fields and tables. This chapter teaches you how to use simple expressions for domain integrity validation rules. After you master Access operators and expressions (the subject of Chapter 9, "Understanding Query Operators and Expressions"), you can write complex validation rules that minimize the possibility of erroneous data in your tables.

Using Keyboard Operations for Entering and Editing Data

Although Access is mouse-oriented, keyboard equivalents are available for the most common actions. One reason for providing keyboard commands is that constantly shifting the hand from a keyboard to a mouse and back can reduce data-entry rates by more than half. Shifting between a keyboard and mouse can also lead to or aggravate repetitive stress injury (RSI), of which the most common type is carpal tunnel syndrome (CTS).

Keyboard operations are as important in a data-entry environment as they are in word processing applications. Consequently, the information concerning key combinations for data entry appears here instead of being relegated to fine print in an appendix. The data-entry procedures you learn in the following sections prove quite useful when you come to the "Entering Personnel Actions Table Data and Testing Validation Rules" section near the end of the chapter.

CREATING AN EXPERIMENTAL COPY OF NORTHWIND.MDB

If you want to experiment with the keyboard operations described in the following sections, you're wise to work with a copy of the Northwind.mdb database. By using a copy, you don't need to worry about making changes that affect the sample database. Experimenting also gives you the opportunity to try the Access database-compacting operation described in Chapter 3, "Navigating Within Access."

Tip #37 from	If you're short on fixed-disk space, open a new database and copy just the Northwind.mdb Customers and Orders tables to your new database as described in the "Copying and Pasting Tables" section of Chapter 4, "Working with Access Databases and Tables."

To compact Northwind.mdb to a new copy of Northwind.mdb, follow these steps:

1. Close all open Access document windows, then close the Database window.

2. Choose Tools, Database Utilities, Compact and Repair Database to open the Database to Compact From dialog. In this case, the file is compacted to make a copy of the Northwind.mdb file.

3. Double-click the Northwind.mdb item in the Database to Compact From dialog's list box. The Compact Into dialog appears.

4. You can accept the default file name (db1.mdb) in the Filename text box, or you can enter a more creative name, such as **Illwind.mdb**, in the Filename text box, and then click Save. Compacting a database file with a new name creates a new, compacted database that you can use for testing.

5. Choose File, Open Database. Double-click db1.mdb or the name of your file from step 4.

6. Open the Customers table by double-clicking its entry in the Database window.

> **Note**
>
> Most keyboard operations described in the following sections apply to tables and updatable queries in Datasheet view, text boxes on forms, and text boxes used for entering property values in Properties windows and in the Field Properties grid of Table Design view. In the examples, the Arrow Key Behavior property is set to Next Character rather than the default Next Field value. (See the later section "Setting Data-Entry Options" for instructions on how to change the value of the Arrow Key Behavior property.) When the Arrow Key Behavior property is set to Next Field, the arrow keys move the caret from field to field. Data-entry operators accustomed to DOS or mainframe database applications might prefer to use the Next Character setting.

USING DATA-ENTRY AND EDITING KEYS

Arrow keys and key combinations in Access are, for the most part, identical to those used in other Windows applications. The F2 key, used for editing cell contents in Excel, has a different function in Access, however—it toggles between editing and select mode. *Toggle* means to alternate between two states. In the editing state, the caret indicates the insertion point in the field; the key combinations shown in Table 5.1 are active. If the field is selected (indicated by a black background with white type), the editing keys behave as indicated in Table 5.2.

Note

In the following tables, the term *field* is used in place of the more specific description *data cell* or *cell* to maintain consistency with Access documentation and Help windows.

TABLE 5.1   KEYS FOR EDITING FIELDS, GRIDS, AND TEXT BOXES

Key	Function
F2	Toggles between displaying the caret for editing and selecting the entire field. The field must be deselected (black text on a white background) and the caret must be visible for the keys in this table to operate as described.
End	Moves the caret to the end of the field in a single-line field or the end of the line in a mutiple-line field.
Ctrl+End	Moves the caret to the end of a multiple-line field.
←	Moves the caret one character to the left until you reach the first character in the line.
Ctrl+←	Moves the caret one word to the left until you reach the first word in the line.
Home	Moves the caret to the beginning of the line.
Ctrl+Home	Moves the caret to the beginning of the field in multiple-line fields.
Backspace	Deletes the entire selection or the character to the left of the caret.
Delete	Deletes the entire selection or the character to the right of the caret.
Ctrl+Z or Alt+Backspace	Undoes typing, a replace operation, or any other change to the record since the last time it was saved. An edited record is saved to the database when you move to a new record or close the editing window.
Esc	Undoes changes to the current field. Press Esc twice to undo changes to the current field and to the entire current record, if you edited other fields.

TABLE 5.2 KEYS FOR SELECTING TEXT IN FIELDS, GRIDS, AND TEXT BOXES

Key	Function
Text Within a Field	
F2	Toggles between displaying the caret for editing and selecting the entire field. The field must be selected (white type on a black background) for the keys in this table to operate as described.
Shift+→	Selects or deselects one character to the right.
Ctrl+Shift+→	Selects or deselects one word to the right. Includes trailing spaces.
Shift+←	Selects or deselects one character to the left.
Ctrl+Shift+←	Selects or deselects one word to the left.
Next Field	
Tab or Enter	Selects the next field. The "Setting Data-Entry Options" section later in this chapter tells you how to change the effect of the Enter key.
Record	
Shift+spacebar	Selects or deselects the entire current record.
↑	Selects the preceding record when a record is selected.
↓	Selects the next record when a record is selected.
Column	
Ctrl+spacebar	Toggles selection of the current column.
←	Selects the column to the left (if a column is selected and a column is to the left).
Fields and Records	
F8	Turns on Extend mode. You see "EXT" in the status bar. In Extend mode, pressing F8 extends the selection to the word, then the field, then the record, and then all the records.
Shift+F8	Reverses the last F8.
Esc	Cancels Extend mode.

PART

I

CH

5

Operations that select the entire field or a portion of the field, as listed in Table 5.2, generally are used with Windows Clipboard operations. Selecting an entire field and then pressing Delete or typing a character is a quick way of ridding the field of its original contents.

USING KEY COMBINATIONS FOR WINDOWS CLIPBOARD OPERATIONS

In Table Datasheet view, the Clipboard is used primarily for transferring Access data between applications. However, you can also use the Clipboard for repetitive data entry. Access 2000 lets you select a rectangular block of data cells in a table and copy the block to the Clipboard. To select a block of cells, follow these steps:

1. Position the mouse pointer at the left edge of the top-left cell of the block you want to select. The mouse pointer (shaped like an I-beam until this point) turns into a cross similar to the mouse pointer for Excel worksheets.

2. Drag the mouse pointer to the right edge of the bottom-right cell of the desired block.

3. The selected block appears in reverse type (white on black, also called *reverse video*). Release the mouse button when the selection meets your requirement.

Figure 5.1 shows a selected block of data in the Customers table. You can copy data blocks but can't cut them.

Figure 5.1
Selecting a rectangular data block in Table Datasheet view.

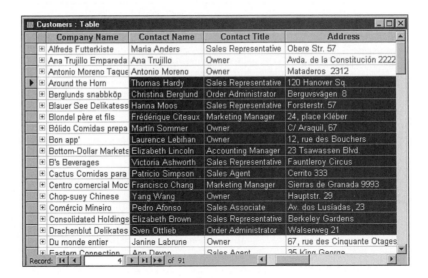

Table 5.3 lists the key combinations for copying or cutting data to and pasting data from the Clipboard. When you paste data from the Clipboard, all of it is pasted to a single cell if the data is of the correct data type and fits within the field size.

TABLE 5.3   KEY COMBINATIONS FOR WINDOWS CLIPBOARD OPERATIONS

Key	Function
Ctrl+C or Ctrl+Insert	Copies the selection to the Clipboard.
Ctrl+V or Shift+Insert	Pastes the Clipboard's contents at the caret's location.

Key	Function
Ctrl+X or Shift+Delete	Copies the selection to the Clipboard and then deletes it. This operation also is called a *cut*. You can cut only the content of a single cell you select with the caret.
Ctrl+Z or Alt+Backspace	Undoes your last Cut, Delete, or Paste operation.

Tip #38 from

If you attempt to paste a rectangular block into a cell, you receive a "Data too long for field" error message. Access then creates a Paste Errors table that contains the contents of the rectangular block, which is a quick way to create a new table. If you create a table this way, rename it immediately; otherwise, Access overwrites the table with a new Paste Errors table the next time a paste error occurs. If you encounter other problems with pasting data to a table, see the "Field Property Values Cause Paste Failures" and "Multiple Record Selection Causes Silent Paste Failures" topics of the Troubleshooting section near the end of the chapter.

USING SHORTCUT KEYS FOR FIELDS AND TEXT BOXES

Shortcut keys minimize the number of keystrokes required to accomplish common data-entry tasks. Most shortcut key combinations use the Ctrl key with other keys. Ctrl+C, Ctrl+V, and Ctrl+X for Clipboard operations are examples of global shortcut keys in Windows 9x. Table 5.4 lists shortcut keys for field and text box entries.

TABLE 5.4   SHORTCUT KEYS FOR TEXT BOXES AND FIELDS IN TABLES

Key	Function
Ctrl+; (semicolon)	Inserts the current date.
Ctrl+: (colon)	Inserts the current time.
Ctrl+' (apostrophe) or Ctrl+" (quote)	Inserts the value from the same field in the preceding record.
Ctrl+Enter	Inserts a newline character (carriage return plus line feed) in a text box.
Ctrl++ (plus)	Adds a new record to the table.
Ctrl+− (minus)	Deletes the current record from the table.
Shift+Enter	Saves all changes to the current record.

PART

I

CH

5

Tip #39 from

Emulating the data-entry key behavior of DOS or mainframe RDBMSs can make a major difference in the acceptance of your database applications by data-entry operators with years of experience with DOS or mainframe database applications.

SETTING DATA-ENTRY OPTIONS

To modify the behavior of the arrow keys and the Tab and Enter keys, choose Tools, Options and click the Keyboard tab to display the keyboard options settings. Table 5.5 lists the available options with the default values. These keyboard options let you make the behavior of the data-entry keys similar to that of DOS database managers.

TABLE 5.5   KEYBOARD OPTIONS FOR THE ACCESS SYSTEM

Option	Function
Cursor Stops at First/Last Field	Selecting this option keeps the caret from moving to another record when the left or right arrow keys are pressed and the caret is in the first or last field of the record.
Move After Enter Group	
Don't Move	When this option is selected, the caret remains in the current field when you press Enter.
Next Field (default)	When this option is selected, the caret moves to the next the next field when you press Enter. Use this setting to duplicate xBase behavior.
Next Record	When this option is selected, the caret moves down the column to the next record when you press Enter.
Arrow Key Behavior Group	
Next Field (default)	If this option is selected, pressing the right or left arrow keys moves the caret to the next field.
Next Character	If this option is selected, pressing the right or left arrow keys moves the caret to the previous or next character in the same field. Use this setting if you want to duplicate the behavior of xBase or mainframe databases.
Behavior Entering Field Group	
Select Entire Field (default)	When this option is selected, the entire field's contents are selected when you use the arrow keys to move the caret into the field.
Go to Start of Field	Selecting this option causes the caret to move to the beginning of the field when you use the arrow keys to move the caret into the field.
Go to End of Field	Selecting this option causes the caret to move to the end of the field when you use the arrow keys to move the caret into the field. Use this setting to duplicate xBase and mainframe database behavior.

ADDING RECORDS TO A TABLE

When you open an updatable table in Datasheet view, the last row is an empty placeholder for a new record, called the *tentative append record* in this book. (An *updatable table* is one whose data you can add to or edit.) An asterisk in the last record selection button in the datasheet indicates the tentative append record. Record selection buttons are the gray buttons in the leftmost column of Table Datasheet view. If you open a database for read-only access, the tentative append record doesn't appear. Tables attached from other databases can also be read-only the updatability of attached tables is discussed in Chapter 7, "Linking, Importing, and Exporting Tables."

Tip #40 from

To go to the tentative append record quickly, click the New Record navigation or toolbar button.

When you place the caret in a field of the tentative append record, the record selection button's asterisk symbol turns into the selected record symbol. When you add data to a field of the selected tentative append record, the selected record symbol changes to the edit symbol (a pencil), and a new tentative append record appears in the row after your addition. Figure 5.2 shows a new record in the process of being added to the Customers table. The CustomerID field has an input mask that requires you to enter five letters, which are capitalized automatically as you enter them. The input mask changes the caret from an I-beam to a reverse-video block.

→ To review how inputs masks work, **see** "Using Input Masks," **p. 150**.

Customers : Table			
Company Name	**Contact Name**	**Contact Title**	**Address**
⊞ Tradição Hipermercad	Anabela Domingues	Sales Representative	Av. Inês de Castro, 414
⊞ Trail's Head Gourmet F	Helvetius Nagy	Sales Associate	722 DaVinci Blvd.
⊞ Vaffeljernet	Palle Ibsen	Sales Manager	Smagsløget 45
⊞ Victuailles en stock	Mary Saveley	Sales Agent	2, rue du Commerce
⊞ Vins et alcools Cheval	Paul Henriot	Accounting Manager	59 rue de l'Abbaye
⊞ Die Wandernde Kuh	Rita Müller	Sales Representative	Adenauerallee 900
⊞ Wartian Herkku	Pirkko Koskitalo	Accounting Manager	Torikatu 38
⊞ Wellington Importador	Paula Parente	Sales Manager	Rua do Mercado, 12
⊞ White Clover Markets	Karl Jablonski	Owner	305 - 14th Ave. S.
⊞ Wilman Kala	Matti Karttunen	Owner/Marketing Assi	Keskuskatu 45
⊞ Wolski Zajazd	Zbyszek Piestrzeni	Owner	ul. Filtrowa 68
⊞ YYZ			

Record: I◄ ◄ 92 ► ►I ►* of 92

Figure 5.2
Adding a new record to the Customer table.

To cancel the addition of a new record, press the Esc(ape) key twice. Pressing Esc once cancels the changes you made to the current field. If you only start to edit in one field and then press Esc, you also cancel addition of the new record.

SELECTING, APPENDING, REPLACING, AND DELETING TABLE RECORDS

You can select a single record or a group of records to copy or cut to the Clipboard, or to delete from the table, by the following methods:

- To select a single record, click its record selection button.
- To select a contiguous group of records, click the first record's selection button and then drag the mouse pointer along the record selection buttons to the last record of the group.
- Alternatively, to select a group of records, click the first record's selection button and then Shift+click the last record to include in the group. You can also press Shift+↓ to select a group of records.

Note

You can cut groups of records to the Clipboard, deleting them from the table, but you can't cut data blocks. A *group of records* includes all fields of one or more selected records. A *data block* consists of a selection in a table datasheet that doesn't include all fields of the selected rows. The Edit, Cut command is enabled for groups of records and disabled for data blocks.

You can cut or copy and append duplicate records to the same table (if appending the duplicate records doesn't cause a primary-key violation) or to another table. You can't cut records from a primary table that has dependent records in a related table if you enforce referential integrity. The following methods apply to appending or replacing the content of records with records stored in the Clipboard:

- To append records from the Clipboard to a table, choose Edit, Paste Append. (No shortcut key exists for Paste Append.)
- To replace the content of a record(s) with data from the Clipboard, select the record(s) whose content you want to replace and then press Ctrl+V. Only the number of records you select or the number of records stored in the Clipboard (whichever is fewer) is replaced.

To delete one or more records, select the records you want to delete and press Delete. If deletion is allowed, a message box asks you to confirm your deletion. You can't undo deletions of records.

VALIDATING DATA ENTRY

The data entered in tables must be accurate if the database is to be valuable to you or your organization. Even the most experienced data-entry operators occasionally enter incorrect information. To add simple tests for the reasonableness of entries, add short expressions as a

Validation Rule in the General page of Table Design view's Field Properties pane. If the entered data fails to pass your validation rule, a message box informs the operator that a violation occurred. Validating data maintains the domain integrity of your tables.

Expressions are the core element of computer programming. Access lets you create expressions without requiring that you be a programmer, although some familiarity with a programming language is helpful. Expressions use the familiar arithmetic symbols +, –, * (multiply), and / (divide). These symbols are called *operators* because they operate on (use) the values that precede and follow them. These operators are reserved symbols in VBA. The values operated on by operators are called *operands*.

You can also use operators to compare two values; the < (less than) and > (greater than) symbols are examples of *comparison operators*. And, Or, Is, Not, Between, and Like are called *logical operators*. Comparison and logical operators return only True, False, and unknown (the Null value). The & operator combines two text entries (*character strings* or just *strings*) into a single string. (You can use + in Access to concatenate strings, but & is the preferred symbol because it leaves no doubt as to the intended operation. Using the + operator with numbers and strings may be ambiguous to both Access and users as to whether string concatenation or arithmetic addition is intended.) To qualify as an expression, at least one operator must be included. You can construct complex expressions by combining the different operators according to rules that apply to each operator involved. The collection of these rules is called *operator syntax*.

→ To learn more about Access operators, **see** "Understanding the Elements in Expressions," **p. 321**

Data validation rules use expressions that result in one of two values: True or False. Entries in a data cell are accepted if the result of the validation is true and rejected if it's false. If the data is rejected by the validation rule, the text you enter as the Validation Text property value appears in a message box. Chapter 9, "Understanding Query Operators and Expressions," explains the syntax of Access validation expressions.

ADDING FIELD-LEVEL VALIDATION RULES

Validation rules that restrict the values entered in a field and are based on only one field are called *field-level validation rules*. Table 5.6 lists the simple field-level validation rules used for some fields in the Personnel Actions table you created in Chapter 4.

TABLE 5.6   VALIDATION CRITERIA FOR THE FIELDS OF THE PERSONNEL ACTIONS TABLE

Field Name	Validation Rule	Validation Text
paID	>0	Please enter a valid employee ID number.
paType	"H" Or "S" Or "Q" Or "Y" Or "B" Or "C"	Only H, S, Q, Y, B, and C codes can be entered.
paInitiated By	>0	Please enter a valid supervisor ID number.

continues

PART

I

CH

5

TABLE 5.6 CONTINUED

Field Name	Validation Rule	Validation Text
paScheduledDate	Between **Date**() -3650 **And** **Date**() + 365	Scheduled dates can't be more than 10 years ago or more than one year from now.
paApprovedBy	>0 **Or** **Is** **Null**	Enter a valid manager ID number or leave blank if not approved.
paRating	Between 0 **And** 9 **Or** **Is** **Null**	Rating range is 0 for terminated employees, 1 to 9, or blank.
paAmount	None	None
paComments	None	None

Tip #41 from

Use the In operator to simplify expressions with multiple Or operators. For example, you can replace the Validation Rule property value for the paType field with In("H", "S", "Q", "Y", "B", "C"), which has a few less characters.

In their present form, the validation rules for fields that require employee ID numbers can't ensure that a valid ID number is entered. You could enter a number greater than the total number of employees in the firm. The validation rule for the paID field tests the EmployeeID number field of the Employees table to determine whether the paID number is present. You don't need to create this test because the rules of referential integrity perform this validation for you. Validation rules for paInitiatedBy and paApprovedBy require tests based on entries in the Employees table.

→ To review relational reference rules, **see** "Enforcing Referential Integrity," **p. 171**.

To add the validation rules to the Personnel Actions table, follow these steps:

1. Open the Personnel Actions table, if it isn't already open, by double-clicking its name in the Database window.

 2. Return to Design mode by clicking the Design View button. The paID field is selected.

3. Press F6 to switch to the Field Properties window, and then move to the Validation Rule text box.

4. Enter **>0** and move to the Validation Text text box.

5. Type **Please enter a valid employee ID number**. The text scrolls to the left when it becomes longer than can be displayed in the text box. To display the beginning of the text, press Home. Press End to position the caret at the last character. Press Enter to complete the operation.

6. Enter **Yes** in the Required text box, or select Yes from the drop-down list. Figure 5.3 shows your entries in the Field Properties text boxes.

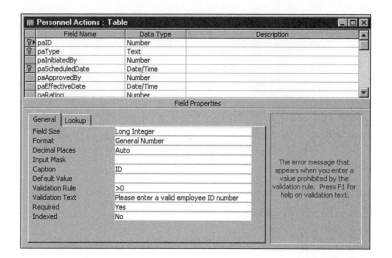

Figure 5.3
The Field Properties text boxes, showing your first validation entries.

7. Press F6 to switch back to the Table Design grid. Move to the next field and press F6.

8. Enter the validation rule and validation text for the six remaining fields listed in Table 5.6 that use data-entry validation, repeating steps 2 through 5. Square brackets ([ ]) enclose field names that include punctuation or spaces. Enter **Yes** in the Required text box for the paType, paInitiatedBy, and paScheduledDate fields.

You test your validation rule entries later in the "Entering Personnel Actions Table Data and Testing Validation Rules" section.

ADDING TABLE-LEVEL VALIDATION RULES AND USING THE EXPRESSION BUILDER

One field, paEffectiveDate, requires a validation rule that depends on paScheduledDate's value. The effective date of the personnel department's action shouldn't be before the scheduled date for the review that results in the action. You can't refer to other field names in a validation rule expression in Access 2000; instead, you add such validation rules in the Table Properties window. Validation rules in which the value of one field depends on a previously entered value in another field of the current record are called *table-level validation rules*.

The following steps create a table-level validation rule for the paEffectiveDate field:

1. Click the Properties toolbar button to display the Table Properties window (see Figure 5.4).

2. Enter **Personnel Department Actions** in the Description text box (see Figure 5.4).

3. In the Validation Rule text box, click the Ellipsis button to display the Expression Builder dialog (see Figure 5.5). The current table, Personnel Actions, is selected in the lefthand list, and the fields of the table appear in the center list.

4. Double-click paEffectiveDate in the center list to place [paEffectiveDate] in the Expression Builder's text box at the top of the dialog.

Figure 5.4
Adding a table
description in the
Table Properties
window.

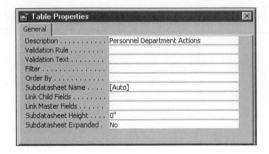

5. Enter **>=** in the text box and double-click paScheduledDate in the center list to add [paScheduledDate] to the expression.

6. To accept a blank entry if the effective date of the personnel action isn't scheduled, add **Or [paEffectiveDate] Is Null** to the expression. Your expression appears as shown in Figure 5.5.

Figure 5.5
Creating a validation
rule with the
Expression Builder.

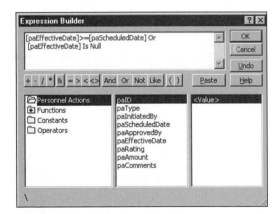

7. Click OK to add the table-level validation rule and close the Expression Builder dialog.

8. In the Validation Text textbox, enter **Effective date must be on or after scheduled date**. Your Table Properties window appears as shown in Figure 5.6.

9. Click the Close Window button of the Table Properties window or click the Properties button on the toolbar to close the window.

Table Properties

General

Description	Personnel Department Actions
Validation Rule	[paEffectiveDate]>=[paScheduledDate] Or [paEffec
Validation Text	Effective date must be on or after scheduled date
Filter	
Order By	
Subdatasheet Name	[Auto]
Link Child Fields	
Link Master Fields	
Subdatasheet Height	0"
Subdatasheet Expanded .	No

Figure 5.6
Adding validation text
to a table-level valida-
tion rule.

ADDING RECORDS TO THE PERSONNEL ACTIONS TABLE

Now you can test your work in creating the Personnel Actions table and check whether
Access is enforcing domain integrity. Table 5.7 shows the initial entries for each employee
of Northwind Traders. No Rating entries appear in Table 5.7 because ratings don't apply to
newly hired employees.

TABLE 5.7 FIRST NINE ENTRIES FOR THE PERSONNEL ACTIONS TABLE

ID	Type	Initiated By	Scheduled	Approved By	Effective Date	New Amount	Comments
1	H	1	01-May-1992		01-May-1992	2,000	Hired
2	H	1	14-Aug-1992		14-Aug-1992	3,500	Hired
3	H	1	01-Apr-1992		01-Apr-1992	2,250	Hired
4	H	2	03-May-1993	2	03-May-1993	2,250	Hired
5	H	2	17-Oct-1993	2	17-Oct-1993	2,500	Hired
6	H	5	17-Oct-1993	2	17-Oct-1993	4,000	Hired
7	H	5	02-Jan-1994	2	02-Jan-1994	3,000	Hired
8	H	2	05-Mar-1994	2	05-Mar-1994	2,500	Hired
9	H	5	15-Nov-1994	2	15-Nov-1994	3,000	Hired

Entering historical information in a table in Datasheet view is a relatively fast process for
experienced data-entry operators. This process also gives you a chance to test your default
entries and Format properties for each field. You can enter bogus values that don't comply
with your validation rules to verify that your rules are operational. To add the first nine historical records to the Personnel Actions table with the data from Table 5.7, follow these
steps:

1. Click the toolbar's Datasheet button to return to Datasheet view in Run mode, if necessary. The caret is positioned in the paID field of the default first record.

2. Enter the paID of the employee. Press Enter, Tab, or the right-arrow key to move to the next field and to add a new default blank record to the view but not to the table's content. A new record is added to the table only when a value is entered in one of the fields of the default blank record.

3. Type **H** in the Type field, and move to the next field.

4. Type the numeric value for the paInitiatedBy field. (You need a value in this field for each employee because of the field's validation rule.) Move to the next field.

5. Type the paScheduledDate entry. You don't need to delete the default date value; typing a new date replaces the default value. Then press Enter, Tab, or the right-arrow key.

6. If a value is in the table for paApprovedBy, type the value. Then press Enter, Tab, or the right-arrow key.

7. Type the paEffectiveDate entry. Press Enter, Tab, or the right-arrow key twice to skip the Rating field, which is inapplicable to newly hired employees.

8. Enter the paAmount of the monthly salary at the time of hiring. Press Enter, Tab, or the right-arrow key.

9. Type **Hired** or any other comment you care to make in the paComments field. Move to the paID field of the next default blank record.

10. Repeat steps 2 through 9 for eight more employees in Table 5.7. (You can add similar records for employees 10 through 15, if you want.)

When you complete your entries, the Personnel Actions table appears as shown in Figure 5.7.

Figure 5.7
The first nine records of the Personnel Actions table.

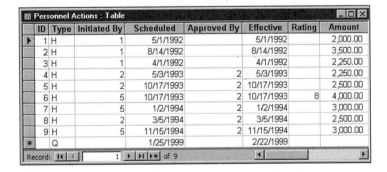

ID	Type	Initiated By	Scheduled	Approved By	Effective	Rating	Amount
1	H	1	5/1/1992		5/1/1992		2,000.00
2	H	1	8/14/1992		8/14/1992		3,500.00
3	H	1	4/1/1992		4/1/1992		2,250.00
4	H	2	5/3/1993	2	5/3/1993		2,250.00
5	H	2	10/17/1993	2	10/17/1993		2,500.00
6	H	5	10/17/1993	2	10/17/1993	8	4,000.00
7	H	5	1/2/1994	2	1/2/1994		3,000.00
8	H	2	3/5/1994	2	3/5/1994		2,500.00
9	H	5	11/15/1994	2	11/15/1994		3,000.00
*	Q		1/25/1999		2/22/1999		

Record: I◀ ◀ [1] ▶ ▶I ▶* of 9

If you're not sure how to respond to data input error messages on validated fields, see "Error Messages from Validation Enforcement" in "Troubleshooting" at the end of the chapter.

ENTERING PERSONNEL ACTIONS TABLE DATA AND TESTING VALIDATION RULES

You can experiment with entering table data and testing your validation rules at the same time. Testing database applications often requires much more time and effort than creating them. The following basic tests are required to confirm your validation rules:

- *Referential integrity.* Type **25** in the paID field and **2** in the paInitiatedBy field of the default blank record (number 10) and then press the up-arrow key. Pressing the up-arrow key tells Access that you're finished with the current record and to move up to the preceding record with the caret in the same field. Access then tests the primary-key integrity before enabling you to leave the current record. If you've turned off the Office Assistant, the message box shown in Figure 5.8 appears; otherwise the Assistant delivers the message. Click OK or press Enter.

Figure 5.8
The message box indicating an entry that violates referential integrity rules.

- *No duplicates restriction for primary key.* In the record just added, attempt to duplicate exactly the entries for record 9, and then press the up-arrow key. You see the message box shown in Figure 5.9, if you've turned off the Assistant. Click OK or press Enter.

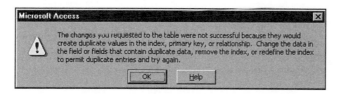

Figure 5.9
The message box alerting you that a record has a duplicate key.

PART

I

CH

5

- *paType validation.* Type **x** and press the right-arrow key to display the message box with the validation text you entered for the paType field (see Figure 5.10). Click OK or press Enter.

Figure 5.10
The message box displayed when an entry violates a validation rule.

Type **q** and move to the paInitiatedBy field. When the caret leaves the paType field, the q changes to Q because of the > format character used. Type **0** (an invalid employee ID number), and press the right-arrow key to display the message box shown in Figure 5.11. Click OK or press Enter.

Figure 5.11
The message box that appears in response to an invalid employee ID number entry.

Continue with the testing. Type a date, such as **1/31/1999**, for the paScheduledDate, and type a date one day earlier (such as **1/30/1999**) for the paEffectiveDate to display the error message boxes with the validation text you entered. (You must move the caret to a different record to cause the table-level validation rule to be applied.) Enter a valid date after the test. To edit a field, rather than retype it, press F2 to deselect the entire field and display the caret for editing. F2 toggles selection and editing operations.

When you finish your testing, click the selection button of the last record you added, and then press Delete. The confirmation message shown in Figure 5.12 appears.

Figure 5.12
The confirmation message when deleting one or more records.

TROUBLESHOOTING

FIELD PROPERTY VALUES CAUSE PASTE FAILURES

Access beeps when attempting to paste data into a cell.

The paste operation would violate a domain or referential integrity rule, usually the Field Size property value. For instance, if you attempt to paste more than five characters into the CustomerID field of the Customers table, the paste operation fails silently. Make sure that the cells or blocks of cells you paste conform to Field Size and other data validation rules.

MULTIPLE RECORD SELECTION CAUSES SILENT PASTE FAILURES

Nothing happens when attempting to paste data into a cell.

Selecting multiple records, then attempting to paste the records into a single cell, even the first cell of the tentative append record, results in a silent paste failure. Access limits multiple-record insert operations to the Edit, Paste Append command.

ERROR MESSAGES FROM VALIDATION ENFORCEMENT

Error messages appear when entering data in fields with validation rules.

Edit or re-enter the data to conform to the data types and validation rules for the field. Error messages that appear when you enter the data correctly indicate that something is amiss with your validation rules. In this case, change to design mode and review your validation rules for the offending fields against those listed in Table 5.6. You may want to remove the validation rule temporarily by selecting the entire expression and cutting it to the Clipboard. (You can paste the expression back into the text box later.) Return to Run mode to continue with your entries.

IN THE REAL WORLD—HEADS-DOWN DATA ENTRY

This chapter's tables that list shortcut key combinations to expedite data entry make dull reading, at best. *Special Edition Using Access 2000* serves as both a tutorial and a reference, and references must be comprehensive. Thus detailed lists of Access 2000 features and their functions, no matter how tedious the list or the features and functions, are unavoidable.

You probably won't appreciate the benefits of Access's data entry shortcut keys until you must type a large amount of table data in a Datasheet view. Clearly, it's preferable to import existing data, taking advantage of Access's flexible data import features described in Chapter 7, "Linking, Importing, and Exporting Tables." Almost everyone, however, faces the inevitable chore of typing table data, such as testing entries for a new database.

COMPARING HEADS-DOWN KEYPUNCH DATA ENTRY WITH ACCESS'S DATASHEET VIEW

In the days of mainframe computers, most of which were less powerful than today's PCs, IBM 026 or 029 keypunch operators generated decks of 80-column punched cards from stacks of source documents. Keypunch operators often received piecework wages, based on the number of cards they produced; salaried operators usually had to fill a daily quota. Thus the eyes of keypunch operators were focused eight hours per day on the top document of a stack, giving rise to the term "heads-down data entry."

Note

If you've never seen a punched card machine, there's a picture of an IBM 029 keypunch at `http://info.ox.ac.uk/ctitext/history/keypnch.html`. Dr. Tim Bergen of the American University teaches a History of Computing course and has posted much of the course material on Punched Card Computing at `http://www.csis.american.edu/~tbergin/history/punch/`.

Datasheet view of a table or updatable query is the simplest and quickest means for heads-down addition of large numbers of records to tables. The need to scroll horizontally to expose more than the first few columns of a wide table, such as that for a customer name and address list, makes Datasheet entry a bit more cumbersome. If you're a good typist, using shortcut keys for column navigation quickly becomes second nature.

Datasheet view for adding related records was cumbersome in previous versions of Access, so most developers are accustomed to creating data entry form-subform pairs, described in Chapter 13, "Designing Custom Multitable Forms." Access 2000, however, offers subdatasheets that let you add multiple related records almost as effortlessly as adding single records to base tables. The major shortcoming of subdatasheets is that expanding the subdatasheet requires a mouse click on the + symbol. Moving between heads-down keyboard data entry and mouse operations greatly reduces data entry operator productivity.

REPLACING THE PUNCHED CARD VERIFYING STEP

Verifying data to preserve domain integrity was a critical step in the keypunch process. The most common method of data verification, sometimes called validation, was retyping the original data to determine if the second typing pass matched the first. Clearly, this approach isn't practical in Datasheet view, although you could implement punched-card verification with a simple form and some VBA code to compare the two sets of entries.

Data verification and validation aren't quite synonymous. Verification attempts to eliminate typographic errors by duplication, while validation primarily tests data entry conformance to a fixed set of rules. The more clever you become in writing well-defined Access Validation Rules, the better the overall accuracy of the input data. Although form-level validation is more flexible, field- and table-level validation applies to data you enter with any form that's bound to the table. Thus you avoid having to recreate validation operations in each of the multiple forms that permit table data entry. The most vexing annoyance with field- and table-level validation is having to repeatedly close Validation Text message boxes that describe data entry errors.

WHERE *NOT* TO USE DATASHEET ENTRY

Datasheet entry works well for "punching" standard documents on a routine basis. Datasheet entry isn't suited to *ad hoc* situations, such as taking telephone orders or reservations, or other activities that involve lookup operations on related tables. The "In the Real World—The Art of Form Design" section of Chapter 12, "Creating and Using Forms," describes some of the features of a typical Access data entry form designed for heads-down telephone order taking. A single form with list and text boxes, and a subform that appear and disappear in concert with the current operating mode lets the operator quickly find an existing customer's record, list the customer's past and current orders, and add a new order with multiple line items. The form is designed expressly for keyboard-only operations to eliminate the transition to and from a mouse or trackball.

--rj

CHAPTER 6

SORTING, FINDING, AND FILTERING DATA IN TABLES

In this chapter

Understanding the Role of Sorting and Filtering Records   206

Sorting Table Data   206

Finding Matching Records in a Table   209

Replacing Matched Field Values Automatically   212

Customizing Datasheet View   225

Troubleshooting   228

In the Real World—Computer-Based Sorting and Searching   228

UNDERSTANDING THE ROLE OF SORTING AND FILTERING

Microsoft Access provides a variety of sorting and filtering features that make customizing the display data in Table Datasheet view a quick and simple process. Sorting and filtering records in tables is quite useful when you use data in a table to create a mailing list or print a particular set of records.

Access also includes versatile search and replace facilities that let you locate every record that matches a value you specify and then, optionally, change that value. Using the Search features, you can quickly locate values even in large tables. Search and replace often is needed when you import data from another database or a worksheet, which is the subject of the next chapter.

Access's sorting, filtering, searching, and replacing features actually are implemented by behind-the-scenes queries that Access creates for you. When you reach Part II, "Getting the Most out of Queries," of this book, which deals exclusively with queries, you'll probably choose to implement these features in Access's graphical Query Design window. Learning the fundamentals of these operations with tables, however, makes queries easier to understand. You also can apply filters to query result sets, use the find feature with queries in Datasheet view, and use search and replace on the result sets of updatable queries.

SORTING TABLE DATA

A fundamental requirement of a database development environment is the capability to sort records quickly so that they appear in the desired sequence. Early desktop database managers required you to create a new copy of a table if you physically wanted to sort the table's records in a new order. Creating and specifying an index on a field let you display or print the table in the desired order. If you wanted to sort the data by two or more fields, however, you had to create a composite index on the fields, or presort the data in the order of one or more fields and then apply the single-field index.

Modern desktop database development systems, such as Access, never require you to physically sort the table. Instead, the physical location of the records in the file is the order in which the records were entered. By default, Access displays records in the order of the primary key. If your table doesn't have a primary key, the records display in the order in which you enter them. Unlike dBASE and its clones, you cannot choose a specific Access index to alter the order in which the records display in Table Datasheet view of the user interface (UI). You can, however, specify an index to speed retrieval of records of tables you manipulate with VBA code. Access uses sorting methods to display records in the desired order. If an index exists on the field in which you sort the records, the sorting process is much quicker. Access automatically uses indexes, if indexes exist, to speed the sort in a process called *query optimization*. Access's indexes and query optimization methods are discussed in Chapter 22, "Exploring Relational Database Design and Implementation."

The following sections show how to use Access's sorting methods to display records in the sequence you want. The Customers table of Northwind.mdb is used for most examples in this chapter because it's typical of a table whose data you can use for various purposes.

FREEZING DISPLAY OF A TABLE FIELD

If the table you're sorting contains more fields than you can display in Access's Table Datasheet view, you can freeze one or more fields to make viewing the sorted data easier. *Freezing* a field makes the field visible at all times, regardless of which other fields you display by manipulating the horizontal scroll bar. To freeze the Customer ID and Company Name fields of the Customers table, follow these steps:

1. Open the Customers table in Datasheet view.
2. Click the field header button of the Customer ID field to select the first field.
3. Shift+click the Company Name field header button. Alternatively, you can drag the mouse from the Customer ID field to the Company Name field to select the first and second fields.
4. From the Format menu, choose Freeze Columns.

When you scroll to fields to the right of the frozen columns, your Datasheet view of the Customers table appears as shown in Figure 6.1. A solid vertical line replaces the half-tone gridline between the frozen and *thawed* (selectable) field columns.

Figure 6.1
The Northwind.mdb Customers table with the CustomerID and CompanyName columns frozen.

Customer ID	Company Name	Region	Postal Code	Country
ALFKI	Alfreds Futterkiste		12209	Germany
ANATR	Ana Trujillo Emparedados y helado		05021	Mexico
ANTON	Antonio Moreno Taquería		05023	Mexico
AROUT	Around the Horn		WA1 1DP	UK
BERGS	Berglunds snabbköp		S-958 22	Sweden
BLAUS	Blauer See Delikatessen		68306	Germany
BLONP	Blondel père et fils		67000	France
BOLID	Bólido Comidas preparadas		28023	Spain
BONAP	Bon app'		13008	France
BOTTM	Bottom-Dollar Markets	BC	T2F 8M4	Canada
BSBEV	B's Beverages		EC2 5NT	UK
CACTU	Cactus Comidas para llevar		1010	Argentina
CENTC	Centro comercial Moctezuma		05022	Mexico
CHOPS	Chop-suey Chinese		3012	Switzerland
COMMI	Comércio Mineiro	SP	05432-043	Brazil

Record: 1 of 91

PART

I

CH

6

Tip #42 from

R J

If you frequently freeze columns, you can add the Freeze Columns button from the Datasheet collection to your Datasheet toolbar.

→ **See** "Customizable Toolbars," **p. 484**, to learn how to customize your toolbars.

SORTING DATA ON A SINGLE FIELD

Access provides an easy way to sort data in the Datasheet view, called a Quick Sort. Simply click the top of the field you want to use to sort the table's data and click either the sort ascending or the sort descending icon on the toolbar. In mailing lists, a standard practice in the United States is to sort the records in ascending zip code order. This practice often is also observed in other countries that use postal codes. To Quick Sort the Customers table in the order of the Postal Code field, follow these steps:

1. Select the Postal Code field by clicking its field header button.

2. Click the Sort Ascending (A-Z) button of the toolbar or choose Sort and then Ascending from the Records menu.

   Your Customers table quickly is sorted into the order shown in Figure 6.2.

Figure 6.2
Applying an ascending sort order to the Postal Code field.

	Customer ID	Company Name	Region	Postal Code	Country	
⊞	HUNGO	Hungry Owl All-Night Grocers	Co. Cork		Ireland	
⊞	WOLZA	Wolski Zajazd		01-012	Poland	
⊞	QUICK	QUICK-Stop		01307	Germany	
⊞	QUEDE	Que Delícia	RJ	02389-673	Brazil	
⊞	RICAR	Ricardo Adocicados	RJ	02389-890	Brazil	
⊞	MORGK	Morgenstern Gesundkost		04179	Germany	
⊞	GOURL	Gourmet Lanchonetes	SP	04876-786	Brazil	
⊞	ANATR	Ana Trujillo Emparedados y helado		05021	Mexico	
⊞	CENTC	Centro comercial Moctezuma		05022	Mexico	
⊞	ANTON	Antonio Moreno Taquería		05023	Mexico	
⊞	PERIC	Pericles Comidas clásicas		05033	Mexico	
⊞	TORTU	Tortuga Restaurante		05033	Mexico	
⊞	COMMI	Comércio Mineiro	SP	05432-043	Brazil	
⊞	FAMIA	Familia Arquibaldo	SP	05442-030	Brazil	
⊞	HANAR	Hanari Carnes	RJ	05454-876	Brazil	

Record: 1 of 91

SORTING DATA ON MULTIPLE FIELDS

Although the sort operation in the preceding section accomplishes exactly what you specify, the result is less than useful because of the variants of postal-code formats used in different countries. What's needed here is a multiple-field sort: first on the Country field and then on the Postal Code field. Thus you might select the Country and the Postal Code fields to perform the multicolumn sort. The Quick Sort technique, however, automatically applies the sorting priority to the leftmost field you select, Postal Code. Access offers two methods of handling this problem: reorder the field display or specify the sort order in a Filter window. Filters are discussed later the "Filtering Table Data" section, so follow these steps to use the reordering process:

1. Select the Country field by clicking its field header button.

2. Hold down the left mouse button and drag the Country field to the left of the Postal Code field. Release the left mouse button to drop the field in its new location.

3. Shift+click the header button of the Postal Code field to select the Country and Postal Code columns.

4. Click the Sort Ascending button of the toolbar or choose <u>S</u>ort and then <u>A</u>scending from the <u>R</u>ecords menu.

The sorted table, shown in Figure 6.3, now makes much more sense. A multiple-field sort on a table sometimes is called a *composite sort*.

Customer ID	Company Name	Region	Country	Postal Code
⊞ RANCH	Rancho grande		Argentina	1010
⊞ OCEAN	Océano Atlántico Ltda.		Argentina	1010
⊞ CACTU	Cactus Comidas para llevar		Argentina	1010
⊞ PICCO	Piccolo und mehr		Austria	5020
⊞ ERNSH	Ernst Handel		Austria	8010
⊞ MAISD	Maison Dewey		Belgium	B-1180
⊞ SUPRD	Suprêmes délices		Belgium	B-6000
⊞ QUEDE	Que Delícia	RJ	Brazil	02389-673
⊞ RICAR	Ricardo Adocicados	RJ	Brazil	02389-890
⊞ GOURL	Gourmet Lanchonetes	SP	Brazil	04876-786
⊞ COMMI	Comércio Mineiro	SP	Brazil	05432-043
⊞ FAMIA	Família Arquibaldo	SP	Brazil	05442-030
⊞ HANAR	Hanari Carnes	RJ	Brazil	05454 876
⊞ QUEEN	Queen Cozinha	SP	Brazil	05487-020
⊞ TRADH	Tradição Hipermercados	SP	Brazil	05634-030

Record: ⏮ ◀ 1 ▶ ⏭ ▶* of 91

Figure 6.3
The effect of a multiple-field sort on the Country and Postal Code fields of the Customers table.

REMOVING A TABLE SORT ORDER AND THAWING COLUMNS

After you freeze columns and apply sort orders to a table, you might want to return the table to its original condition. To do so, Access offers you the following choices:

- To return the Datasheet view of an Access table with a primary key to its original sort order, select the field(s) that comprise the primary key (in the order of the primary key fields).

- To return to the original order when the table has no primary key field, close the table *without* saving the changes and then reopen the table.

- To thaw your frozen columns, choose Unfreeze All Columns from the F<u>o</u>rmat menu.

- To return the sequence of fields to its original state, drag the fields you moved back to their prior position or close the table *without* saving your changes.

If you make substantial changes to the layout of the table and apply a sort order, it is usually quicker to close and reopen the table. (*Don't* save your changes to the table layout.)

FINDING MATCHING RECORDS IN A TABLE

To search for and select records with field values that match (or partially match) a particular value, use Access's Find feature. To find Lulå (a relatively large city in northern Sweden close to the Arctic Circle) in the City field, follow these steps:

PART

I

CH

6

1. In the Customers table, select the field (City) you want to search by clicking its header button or by placing the caret in the field.

 2. Click the toolbar's Find button or choose <u>F</u>ind from the <u>E</u>dit menu to display the Find and Replace dialog (see Figure 6.4). You can also display this dialog by pressing Ctrl+F. The dialog opens with the Find page active by default.

Figure 6.4
The opened Find in Field dialog with the City field selected.

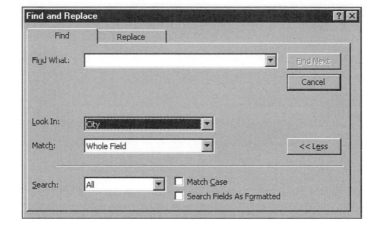

3. Type the name of the city (**Lulea**) in the Find What text box (see Figure 6.5). Making an entry in the Find What text box enables the Find Next command button.

4. Select Whole Field from the Match drop-down list. (The other choices, Start of Field and Any Part of Field, are just as effective in this case.)

   The default value of the Search option button is satisfactory, and matching case or format is not important here.

5. Click the Find Next button. If you don't have a Scandinavian keyboard, Access displays the message box shown in Figure 6.6.

Figure 6.5
Attempting to find Lulå in the City field.

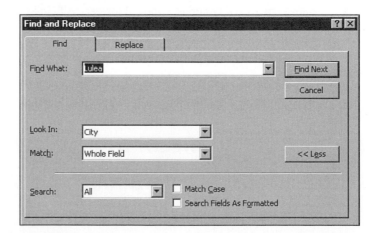

Figure 6.6
The message box that appears when Access can't find a match to the content of the Find What text box.

The "finished searching" message indicates that the Find feature didn't locate a match between the present position of the record pointer and the last record of the table. Access missed your entry because the Scandinavian diacritical ° is missing over the *a* in *Lulea*. In the ANSI character set, *a* has a value of 97, and *å* has a value of 229.

Tip #43 from

RJ

> To enter international (extended) characters in the Find What text box, type the English letters and then use the Windows 9x or Windows NT 4.0+ Character Map (Charmap.exe) applet to find and copy the extended character to the Clipboard. (Don't worry about choosing the correct font.) Paste the character into the Find What text box at the appropriate location.

If the letters preceding an extended character are sufficient to define your search parameter, follow these steps to find Lulå:

1. Type **Lule**, omitting the *a*, in the Find What text box.
2. Select Start of Field from the Match drop-down list.
3. Click the Find Next button. Access finds and highlights Lulå in the City field (see Figure 6.7).

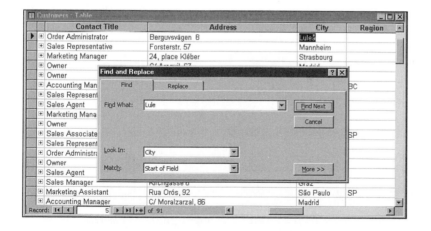

Figure 6.7
Finding a record that contains a special character.

PART

I

CH

6

You also can find entries in any part of the field. If you type **ule** in the Find What text box and choose Any Part of Field from the Match drop-down list, you get a match on Lulå. However, you could also match Thule, the location of the Bluie West One airfield (also known as Thule Air Force Base) in Greenland. (There's no actual entry for Thule in the Customers table.)

Searching all fields for an entry is usually much slower than searching a single field, especially if you have an index on the field being searched. Unless you specify the Any Part of Field Match option, Access uses the index to speed the searching operation.

Following is a list of the options available in the Find dialog when you expand it by clicking the More button:

- To specify a case-sensitive search, mark the Match Case check box.

- To search by using the field's format, mark the Search Fields as Formatted check box. This way you can enter a search term that matches the formatted appearance of the field, rather than the native (unformatted) value, if you applied a Format property value to the field. Using the Search Fields as Formatted option slows the search operation; indexes are not used.

- To find additional matches, if any, click the Find Next button. If the Search option is set to Down, clicking the Find Next button starts the search at the current position of the record pointer and searches to the end of the table.

- To start the search at the last record of the table, select Up in the Search drop-down list.

REPLACING MATCHED FIELD VALUES AUTOMATICALLY

The Find and Replace dialog's Replace page lets you replace values selectively in fields that match the entry in the Find What text box. To open the dialog with the Replace page active, choose Edit, Replace or press Ctrl+H. The derivation of the shortcut key combination for the Edit menu's Replace command—Ctrl+H—is a mystery.

The entries to search for *Lulå* and replace with *Lulea* appear in Figure 6.8. To replace entries selectively, click the Find Next button and then click the Replace button for those records in which you want to replace the value. You can do a bulk replace in all matching records by clicking the Replace All button.

→ **See** "Updating Values of Multiple Records in a Table," **p. 421**.

FILTERING TABLE DATA

Access lets you apply a filter to specify the records that appear in the Datasheet view of a table or a query result set. For example, if you want to view only those customers located in Germany, you use a filter to limit the displayed records to only those whose Country field contains the text *Germany*. Access gives you three different ways to apply filters to the data in a table:

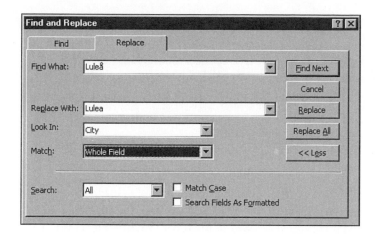

Figure 6.8
The Replace dialog.

- *Filter by selection* is the fastest and simplest way to apply a filter. You establish the filter criteria by selecting all or part of the data in one of the table's fields; Access displays only records that match the selected sample. With a filter by selection, you can filter records based only on criteria in a single field of the table.

- *Filter by form* is the second fastest way to apply a filter. You enter the filter criteria into a blank datasheet form of the table; Access displays records that match the combined criteria in each field. Use a filter by form to quickly filter records based on criteria in more than one field.

- *Advanced filter/sort* is the most powerful type of filter to use. With an advanced filter/sort, you can make an Access filter do double duty because you also can add a sort order on one or more fields.

FILTERING BY SELECTION

Creating a filter by selection is as easy as selecting text in a field. When you apply the filter, Access uses the selected text to determine which records to display. Table 6.1 summarizes which records are displayed, depending on how you select text in the field. In all cases, Access applies the filter criteria only to the field in which you have selected text. Filter by selection allows you to establish filter criteria for only a single field at one time.

PART
I

CH
6

TABLE 6.1 HOW SELECTED TEXT AFFECTS FILTER BY SELECTION

Selected Text	Filter Effect
Entire field	Displays only records whose fields contain exactly matching values
Beginning of field	Displays records where the text at the beginning of the field matches the selected text
End of field	Displays records where the text at the end of the field matches the selected text
Characters anywhere	Displays records in which any part of the field in field, except matches anywhere in the selected text beginning or end

To create a Filter by Selection on the Customers table (displaying only those customers located in Germany), follow these steps:

1. If necessary, open the Customers table in Datasheet view and use the scroll bars to make the Country field visible in the Table window.

2. Click the First Record button to make the first record in the table the active record.

3. Select all the text in the Country field of the first record in the Customers table. (This entry should be Germany.)

4. Click the Filter by Selection toolbar button or from the Records menu choose Filter, Filter by Selection. Access applies the filter as shown in Figure 6.9.

Notice that the Apply Filter toolbar button is now displayed in a "down" position, indicating that a filter is being applied to the table, and the ToolTip changes to *Remove Filter*. The legend (Filtered) is also added to the record selection and status bar at the bottom of the Table window.

Figure 6.9
A filter by selection applied to the Customers Table to display only those customers in Germany.

	Customer ID	Company Name	Region	Country	Postal Code	Phone
⊞	QUICK	QUICK-Stop		Germany	01307	0372-035188
⊞	MORGK	Morgenstern Gesundkost		Germany	04179	0342-023176
⊞	ALFKI	Alfreds Futterkiste		Germany	12209	030-0074321
⊞	KOENE	Königlich Essen		Germany	14776	0555-09876
⊞	TOMSP	Toms Spezialitäten		Germany	44087	0251-031259
⊞	OTTIK	Ottilies Käseladen		Germany	50739	0221-0644327
⊞	DRACD	Drachenblut Delikatessen		Germany	52066	0241-039123
⊞	LEHMS	Lehmanns Marktstand		Germany	60528	069-0245984
⊞	BLAUS	Blauer See Delikatessen		Germany	68306	0621-08460
⊞	WANDK	Die Wandernde Kuh		Germany	70563	0711-020361
⊞	FRANK	Frankenversand		Germany	80805	089-0877310

Record: 1 of 11 (Filtered)

Tip #44 from

 Use the Find and Replace dialog to quickly locate the first record of a group you're interested in filtering and then apply a filter by selection.

As mentioned previously, you can also apply a filter by selection based on partially selected text in a field. Figure 6.10 shows the Customers table with a different filter by selection applied—this time, only the letters *er* in the Country field were selected.

Tip #45 from

You can apply a filter by selection to more than one field at a time. For example, after applying a filter by selection to display only those customers in Germany, you could then move to the City field and apply a second filter by selection for Berlin. The resulting table display will then include only those customers in Berlin, Germany. An easier way to apply filters based on more than one field value is to use a filter by form, described in the next section.

Customers : Table						
Customer ID	**Company Name**	**Region**	**Country**	**Postal Code**	**Phone**	
⊞ WANDK	Die Wandernde Kuh		Germany	70563	0711-020361	
⊞ TOMSP	Toms Spezialitäten		Germany	44087	0251-031259	
⊞ RICSU	Richter Supermarkt		Switzerland	1203	0897-034214	
⊞ QUICK	QUICK-Stop		Germany	01307	0372-035188	
⊞ OTTIK	Ottilies Käseladen		Germany	50739	0221-0644327	
⊞ MORGK	Morgenstern Gesundkost		Germany	04179	0342-023176	
⊞ LEHMS	Lehmanns Marktstand		Germany	60528	069-0245984	
⊞ KOENE	Königlich Essen		Germany	14776	0555-09876	
⊞ FRANK	Frankenversand		Germany	80805	089-0877310	
⊞ DRACD	Drachenblut Delikatessen		Germany	52066	0241-039123	
⊞ CHOPS	Chop-suey Chinese		Switzerland	3012	0452-076545	
⊞ BLAUS	Blauer See Delikatessen		Germany	68306	0621-08460	
⊞ ALFKI	Alfreds Futterkiste		Germany	12209	030-0074321	

Record: 1 of 13 (Filtered)

Figure 6.10
The Customers table, this time filtered by selecting the letters *er* in the Country field.

Note

To remove a filter, click the Remove Filter toolbar button. This button is really the same as the Apply Filter button—the button is "down" whenever a filter is in effect and "up" otherwise.

FILTERING BY FORM

Filtering by form is slightly more complex than filtering by selection but allows you to filter records based on criteria in more than one field at a time. For example, you saw in the preceding section how to use a filter by selection to view only those customers in Germany. To further limit the displayed records to those customers located in Berlin, Germany, use a filter by form.

In a filter by form, Access displays a blank form for the table (see Figure 6.11). This window is called a *form* to distinguish it from the Table Datasheet window, although it's not the same as the data-entry forms discussed later in this book. You can combine criteria in a filter by form with a logical **Or** condition or a logical **And** condition. For example, you can filter the Customers table to display only those customers in the United States or Canada. As another example, you could filter the Customers table to display only those customers in the United States and in zip codes beginning with the digit 9 (such as 94609 or 90807).

→ To learn more about using query expressions in the fields of the Filter by Form window, **see** "Understanding the Elements in Expressions," **p. 321**.

→ **See** "Creating Access Expressions," **p. 340**.

→ **See** "Expressions for Query Criteria," **p. 341**.

To create a filter by form on the Customers table (displaying only those customers in the United States or Canada), follow these steps:

1. If necessary, open the Customers table in Datasheet view and make the Country field column visible in the Table window.

2. Click the Filter by Form toolbar button or from the <u>R</u>ecords menu choose <u>F</u>ilter, <u>F</u>ilter by Form to display the Filter by Form window (see Figure 6.11).

Figure 6.11
An empty Filter by Form window for the Customers table.

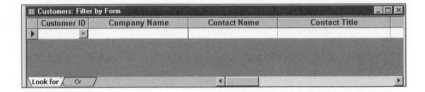

3. Make the Country field visible in the Filter by Form window if necessary. (The Customer ID and Company Name columns in the figures have been frozen, as described previously in this chapter.)

4. Click inside the Country field and open the Country list box, or press F4. The drop-down list contains a list of all the unique values in the Country field (see Figure 6.12).

Figure 6.12
Selecting the first country to filter for in the Customers table.

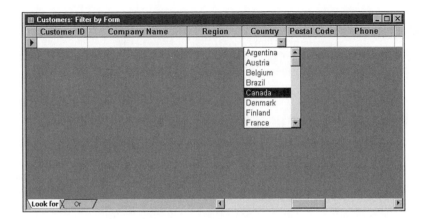

5. Select Canada in the list box, as shown in Figure 6.12. Access automatically adds the quotation marks around the value you select and enters it into the Country field form box.

6. Click the Or tab at the bottom of the Filter by Form window. Access combines criteria that you enter on separate tabs in the Filter by Form window with a logical **Or** condition. When you add an **Or** condition, a tab for another **Or** condition appears.

7. Click the arrow to open the Country list box or press F4. Select USA from the drop-down list (see Figure 6.13).

8. Click the Apply Filter button. Access applies the new filter to the table, displaying the records shown in Figure 6.14.

You can also combine filter criteria in a logical **And** condition by entering criteria in more than one field on the same tab of the Form window. For example, you want to filter the Orders table to find all orders handled by Nancy Davolio and shipped to France. You easily can use a Filter by Form to do so, as the following example shows:

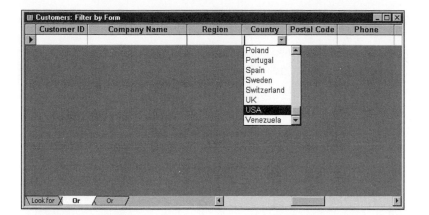

Figure 6.13
Selecting the Or condition for the Filter by Form in the Customers table.

Figure 6.14
The result of the Filter by Form displaying only those records for customers in Canada or the USA.

1. Open the Orders table, if necessary, and freeze the Order ID, Customer, and Employee columns. Then position the Ship Country column so that it's visible (see Figure 6.15). Freezing the columns isn't an essential step, but it makes setting up the filter and viewing the filtered data easier.

 2. Click the Filter by Form toolbar button to display the Filter by Form window.

 3. Click the Clear Grid toolbar button or choose Clear Filter from the Edit menu to clear any previous filter criteria from the Filter by Form grid.

4. Use the drop-down list in the Employee field to select Davolio, Nancy, and then use the drop-down list in the Ship Country column to select France. You must add quotes around text criterion that includes a comma (see Figure 6.16).

 5. Click the Apply Filter button. Access applies the new filter to the table, displaying the records shown in Figure 6.17. This filter shows only those records for orders that were handled by Nancy Davolio *and* shipped to France.

Order ID	Customer	Employee	Ship Country
10248	Vins et alcools Chevalier	Buchanan, Steven	France
10249	Toms Spezialitäten	Suyama, Michael	Germany
10250	Hanari Carnes	Peacock, Margaret	Brazil
10251	Victuailles en stock	Leverling, Janet	France
10252	Suprêmes délices	Peacock, Margaret	Belgium
10253	Hanari Carnes	Leverling, Janet	Brazil
10254	Chop-suey Chinese	Buchanan, Steven	Switzerland
10255	Richter Supermarkt	Dodsworth, Anne	Switzerland
10256	Wellington Importadora	Leverling, Janet	Brazil
10257	HILARIÓN-Abastos	Peacock, Margaret	Venezuela
10258	Ernst Handel	Davolio, Nancy	Austria
10259	Centro comercial Moctezuma	Peacock, Margaret	Mexico
10260	Ottilies Käseladen	Peacock, Margaret	Germany
10261	Que Delícia	Peacock, Margaret	Brazil
10262	Rattlesnake Canyon Grocery	Callahan, Laura	USA
10263	Ernst Handel	Dodsworth, Anne	Austria
10264	Folk och fä HB	Suyama, Michael	Sweden

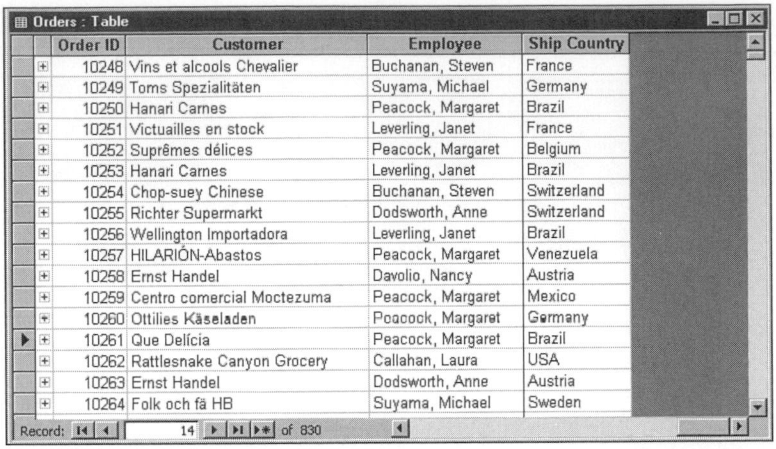

Figure 6.15
The Orders table with the Order ID, Customer, and Employee columns frozen, and the Ship Country column scrolled to be visible.

Order ID	Customer	Employee	Ship Postal Code	Ship Country
		"Davolio, Nancy"		"France"

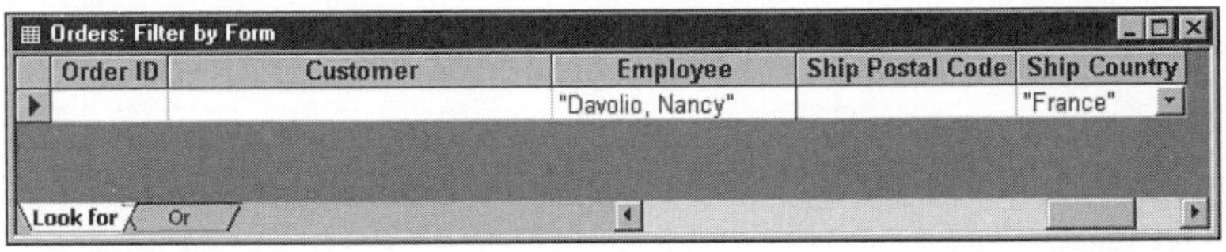

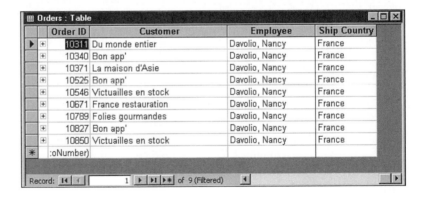

Figure 6.16
Combining criteria in two fields in a logical ***And*** condition.

Order ID	Customer	Employee	Ship Country
10311	Du monde entier	Davolio, Nancy	France
10340	Bon app'	Davolio, Nancy	France
10371	La maison d'Asie	Davolio, Nancy	France
10525	Bon app'	Davolio, Nancy	France
10546	Victuailles en stock	Davolio, Nancy	France
10671	France restauration	Davolio, Nancy	France
10789	Folies gourmandes	Davolio, Nancy	France
10827	Bon app'	Davolio, Nancy	France
10850	Victuailles en stock	Davolio, Nancy	France
:oNumber)			

Figure 6.17
The Orders table records displayed by the filter by form shown in Figure 6.16.

If Access doesn't return the records you expected, try the solution in the "Troubleshooting" section at the end of the chapter.

Advanced Filters and Sorts

Filters in Access, as mentioned previously, are queries in disguise, and provide a useful introduction to Access queries, the subject of Part II of this book, "Getting the Most Out of Queries." Creating an advanced filter/sort is very much like creating a query, with some basic differences, as follows:

- The Show Table dialog doesn't appear.
- The SQL button is missing from the toolbar, so you can't display the underlying SQL statement.
- The Show row is missing from the Filter Design grid.

Filters are limited to using one table or query that Access automatically specifies when you enter filter design mode. You can save a filter you create as a query or load a filter from a query, but Access has no provision for saving a filter as a filter. The following sections describe how to add criteria to filter records and to add a sort order in the Filter Design window.

ADDING A MULTIFIELD SORT AND COMPOUND FILTER CRITERIA

In its default configuration, the Datasheet toolbar doesn't have an Advanced Filter/Sort button. Instead, you start the advanced filter/sort operation from the Records menu by choosing Filter, Advanced Filter/Sort. To create a filter on the Orders table (which provides more records to filter than the Customers table), follow these steps:

1. Close and reopen the Orders table in Datasheet view to clear filter or sort criteria you applied previously.

2. From the Records menu, choose Filter, Advanced Filter/Sort to display the Filter window (see Figure 6.18). The default filter name, Filter1, is concatenated with the table name to create the default name of the first filter, OrdersFilter1. The Field List window for the Orders table appears in the upper pane of the Filter window.

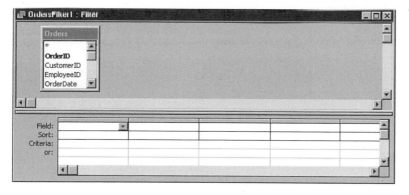

Figure 6.18
The Filter Design window opened by choosing Filter, Advanced Filter/Sort from the Records menu.

PART

I

CH

6

Tip #46 from

RJ

Although the Datasheet toolbar doesn't have an Advanced Filter/Sort command button in its default configuration, you can customize the Datasheet toolbar to add an Advanced Filter/Sort button.

3. One field that you might want to use to sort or limit displayed records is OrderID. Click it in the field list in the upper pane and drag it to the first column of the Field row of the Filter Design grid in the lower pane. (When your mouse pointer reaches the lower pane, the pointer turns into a field symbol.)

4. Repeat step 3 for other fields on which you want to sort or establish criteria. Candidates are CustomerID, ShipName, ShipCountry, ShipPostalCode, OrderDate, and ShippedDate.

5. Add an ascending sort to the ShipCountry and ShipPostalCode fields to check the sorting capabilities of your first advanced filter. Your Filter Design window appears as shown in Figure 6.19.

Figure 6.19
Adding fields and sort orders to the Filter Design window.

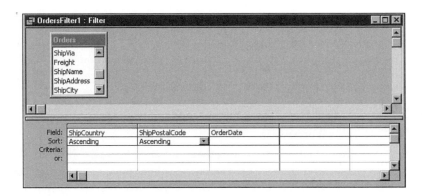

6. Click the Apply Filter toolbar button or choose Apply Filter/Sort from the Filter menu.

7. Use the horizontal scroll bar of the datasheet to reveal the ShipCountry and ShipPostalCode fields. Your sorted table appears as shown in Figure 6.20.

Figure 6.20
The Orders table, ordered by the ShipCountry and ShipPostalCode fields.

Order ID	Customer	Employee	Ship Postal Code	Ship Country
10898	Océano Atlántico Ltda.	Peacock, Margaret	1010	Argentina
11019	Rancho grande	Suyama, Michael	1010	Argentina
10986	Océano Atlántico Ltda.	Callahan, Laura	1010	Argentina
10958	Océano Atlántico Ltda.	King, Robert	1010	Argentina
10937	Cactus Comidas para llevar	King, Robert	1010	Argentina
10716	Rancho grande	Peacock, Margaret	1010	Argentina
10409	Océano Atlántico Ltda.	Leverling, Janet	1010	Argentina
10916	Rancho grande	Davolio, Nancy	1010	Argentina
11054	Cactus Comidas para llevar	Callahan, Laura	1010	Argentina
10881	Cactus Comidas para llevar	Peacock, Margaret	1010	Argentina
10448	Rancho grande	Peacock, Margaret	1010	Argentina
10828	Rancho grande	Dodsworth, Anne	1010	Argentina
10782	Cactus Comidas para llevar	Dodsworth, Anne	1010	Argentina
10819	Cactus Comidas para llevar	Fuller, Andrew	1010	Argentina
10521	Cactus Comidas para llevar	Callahan, Laura	1010	Argentina
10531	Océano Atlántico Ltda.	King, Robert	1010	Argentina
10686	Piccolo und mehr	Fuller, Andrew	5020	Austria

Record: 11 of 830

8. From the Records menu, choose Filter, Advanced Filter/Sort to display the Filter Design window so that you can edit the filter criteria. Access displays the Filter Design window with all the criteria from the preceding filter already entered.

9. Type **USA** in the Criteria row of the Ship Country column to limit records to those orders shipped to an address in the United States. Access automatically adds double quotes (") around "USA", indicating that the entry is text, not a number.

10. Click the Apply Filter button of the toolbar or choose Apply Filter/Sort from the Filter menu and scroll to display the sorted fields. Only records with destinations in the United States appear, as shown in Figure 6.21. (The first three columns of the table have been frozen, and the Ship Country and Ship Postal Code columns have been scrolled into visibility to achieve the table appearance in Figure 6.21.)

Order ID	Customer	Employee	Ship Postal Code	Ship Country
10624	The Cracker Box	Peacock, Margaret	59801	USA
10775	The Cracker Box	King, Robert	59801	USA
11003	The Cracker Box	Leverling, Janet	59801	USA
10271	Split Rail Beer & Ale	Suyama, Michael	82520	USA
10385	Split Rail Beer & Ale	Davolio, Nancy	82520	USA
10369	Split Rail Beer & Ale	Callahan, Laura	82520	USA
10349	Split Rail Beer & Ale	King, Robert	82520	USA
10821	Split Rail Beer & Ale	Davolio, Nancy	82520	USA
10432	Split Rail Beer & Ale	Leverling, Janet	82520	USA
10974	Split Rail Beer & Ale	Leverling, Janet	82520	USA
10329	Split Rail Beer & Ale	Peacock, Margaret	82520	USA
10756	Split Rail Beer & Ale	Callahan, Laura	02520	USA
10678	Save-a-lot Markets	King, Robert	83720	USA
10748	Save-a-lot Markets	Leverling, Janet	83720	USA
10757	Save-a-lot Markets	Suyama, Michael	83720	USA
10815	Save-a-lot Markets	Fuller, Andrew	83720	USA
10607	Save-a-lot Markets	Buchanan, Steven	83720	USA

Record: 1 of 122 (Filtered)

Figure 6.21
The result of applying a "USA" criterion to the Ship Country column.

USING COMPOSITE CRITERIA

You can apply composite criteria to expand or further limit the records that Access displays. Composite criteria are applied to more than one field. To display all orders received on or after 1/1/1997 with destinations in North America, try the following:

1. From the Records menu, choose Filter, Advanced Filter/Sort to display the Filter Design window.

2. Type **Canada** in the second criteria row of the ShipCountry column and **Mexico** in the third row; then move the caret to a different cell. When you add criteria under one another, the effect is to make the criteria alternative—that is, combined in a logical **Or** condition.

3. Type **>=#1/1/1997#** in the first criteria line of the OrderDate field. When you add criteria on the same line as another criterion, the criteria is additive (a logical **And** condition)—that is, orders for placed on or after 1/1/1997. The # symbols indicate to Access that the enclosed value is of the Date/Time data type.

PART
I
CH
6

4. Press F2 to select the date entry you made in step 3 and then press Ctrl+C to copy the expression to the Clipboard. Position the caret in the second row of the Order Date column and press Ctrl+V to add the same expression for Canada. Repeat this process to add the date criterion for Mexican orders. Your Filter Design grid now appears as shown in Figure 6.22. You must repeat the date criterion for each country criterion because of a limitation in constructing SQL statements from Access query grids, which is discussed shortly.

5. Click the Apply Filter button to display your newly filtered datasheet (see Figure 6.23, which is scrolled to show the three countries).

Figure 6.22
The Filter grid with composite criteria added.

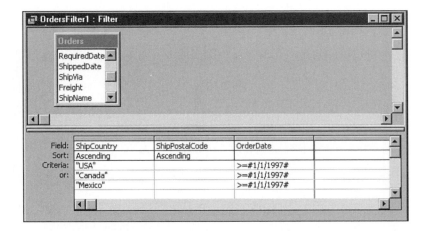

Figure 6.23
The result of the filter of Figure 6.22 applied to the Orders datasheet.

	Order ID	Customer	Employee	Ship Postal Code	Ship Country
+	10495	Laughing Bacchus Wine Cellars	Leverling, Janet	V3F 2K1	Canada
+	10620	Laughing Bacchus Wine Cellars	Fuller, Andrew	V3F 2K1	Canada
+	10759	Ana Trujillo Emparedados y hela	Leverling, Janet	05021	Mexico
+	10926	Ana Trujillo Emparedados y hela	Peacock, Margaret	05021	Mexico
+	10625	Ana Trujillo Emparedados y hela	Leverling, Janet	05021	Mexico
+	10573	Antonio Moreno Taquería	King, Robert	05023	Mexico
+	10535	Antonio Moreno Taquería	Peacock, Margaret	05023	Mexico
+	10507	Antonio Moreno Taquería	King, Robert	05023	Mexico
+	10856	Antonio Moreno Taquería	Leverling, Janet	05023	Mexico
+	10682	Antonio Moreno Taquería	Leverling, Janet	05023	Mexico
+	10677	Antonio Moreno Taquería	Davolio, Nancy	05023	Mexico
+	11069	Tortuga Restaurante	Davolio, Nancy	05033	Mexico
+	11073	Pericles Comidas clásicas	Fuller, Andrew	05033	Mexico
+	10502	Pericles Comidas clásicas	Fuller, Andrew	05033	Mexico
+	10995	Pericles Comidas clásicas	Davolio, Nancy	05033	Mexico
+	10915	Tortuga Restaurante	Fuller, Andrew	05033	Mexico
+	10676	Tortuga Restaurante	Fuller, Andrew	05033	Mexico
+	10576	Tortuga Restaurante	Leverling, Janet	05033	Mexico
+	10842	Tortuga Restaurante	Davolio, Nancy	05033	Mexico
+	10518	Tortuga Restaurante	Peacock, Margaret	05033	Mexico
+	10474	Pericles Comidas clásicas	Buchanan, Steven	05033	Mexico
+	10624	The Cracker Box	Peacock, Margaret	59801	USA
+	11003	The Cracker Box	Leverling, Janet	59801	USA

Record: 1 of 144 (Filtered)

→ To become more familiar with the power of selecting data with criteria, **see** "Using the Query Design Window," **p. 298**.

SAVING YOUR FILTER AS A QUERY AND LOADING A FILTER

Access doesn't have a persistent Filter object. A *persistent* database object is one you create that's stored as a component of your database's .mdb file. All persistent database objects appear as items in one of the list boxes of the Database window. A filter is equivalent to a single-table query, so Access lets you save your filter as a QueryDef object. Access saves the names of the filters associated with each table in the system tables of your database when you save a filter as a query. This feature is the principal advantage of using a filter rather than a query when only a single table is involved.

To save your filter and remove the filter from the Orders table, follow these steps:

1. From the Records menu, choose Filter, Advanced Filter/Sort to display the Filter Design window if it isn't already displayed.

2. From the File menu, choose Save As Query to display the Save as Query dialog or click the Save as Query toolbar button.

3. Enter a descriptive name—such as **fltOrdersNorthAmerica**— for your filter in the Query Name text box. Using the **flt** prefix distinguishes the filters you save from conventional queries (see Figure 6.24).

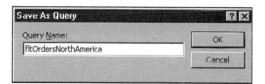

Figure 6.24
Naming the QueryDef object that contains a filter.

4. Click OK to save the filter and close the Filter window.

5. Click the Remove Filter toolbar button to remove the filter from the Orders datasheet.

6. A filter remains in memory while the table to which it applies is open. To close the filter, close the Orders table.

Re-creating a filter from the filter you saved as a query requires the following steps:

1. Reopen the Orders table in Datasheet view.

2. From the Records menu, choose Filter, Advanced Filter/Sort to open the Filters window with an empty filter.

3. Click the Load from Query toolbar button or choose Load from Query from the File menu to display the Applicable Filter dialog (see Figure 6.25).

4. Double-click the **fltOrdersNorthAmerica** filter to load the saved query into the Filter window.

PART

I

CH

6

Figure 6.25
A saved filter listed in the
Applicable Filter dialog.

5. Click the Apply Filter toolbar button to display the resulting filter set in the Orders datasheet.

You can save the preceding steps by simply executing the saved query. You execute a query the same way you open a table:

1. Close the Orders table.

2. Click the Database window's Queries shortcut to list the saved queries.

3. Double-click the fltOrdersNorthAmerica item. The datasheet of the fltOrdersNorthAmerica: Select Query window that appears is identical to the datasheet you created in step 5 of the preceding operation.

4. Click the Design View toolbar button to display the query design (see Figure 6.26). If you added more than the three columns to the filter, columns in which no selection criteria or sort order were entered don't appear in the query's grid.

Figure 6.26
The Query Design view of
a saved filter.

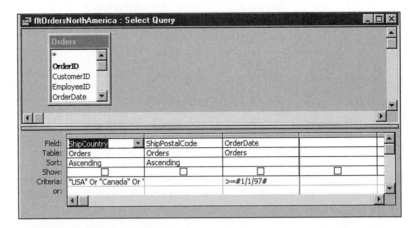

Access adds a multitude of parentheses, as well as table name qualifiers, to the field names of the statements created from QBE grids. Most of the parentheses are superfluous; they're present to help the Jet database engine's query parser execute queries that are more complex. Table name qualifiers aren't necessary in an SQL statement when only one table is included in the FROM clause.

CUSTOMIZING DATASHEET VIEW

To customize the appearance of the Datasheet view, you can hide the fields you don't want to appear in your datasheet, change the height of the record rows, eliminate the gridlines, and select a different font for your display. The following list describes each option for customizing Table and Query Datasheet views:

- To hide a field, select it by clicking its header or placing the caret in the column for the field. Then choose Hide Columns from the Format menu.

- To show a hidden field, choose Unhide Columns from the Format menu to display the Unhide Columns dialog (see Figure 6.27). A mark next to the field name in the Column list indicates columns appearing in Datasheet view. Click the box to the left of the field name to toggle between hiding and showing the column.

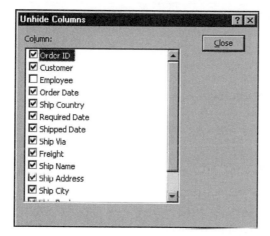

Figure 6.27
The Unhide Columns dialog, which allows you to show and hide datasheet fields.

- To change the font used to display and print the datasheet, use the Font drop-down list on the Formatting toolbar (if it's displayed) or choose Font from the Format menu to display the Font dialog. (The Font dialog is one of the common dialogs of Windows 95 and Windows NT 4.0. Other common dialogs include the Open and Save dialogs.)

- To remove gridlines from the display and printed versions of the datasheet, use the Gridlines Shown drop-down list on the Formatting toolbar or choose Datasheet from the Format menu. If you use the Gridlines Shown drop-down list, Access displays a palette of four gridline display choices: Both, Horizontal, Vertical, and None; click the button corresponding to the gridline display you want. If you use the Format menu, Access displays the Datasheet Formatting dialog, shown in Fig 6.28, which contains check boxes for the horizontal and vertical gridlines. Select or clear the check boxes for the desired gridline display.

PART

I

CH

6

Figure 6.28
Formatting the datasheet.

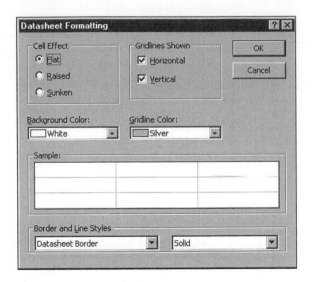

- To change the height of the rows as displayed and printed, position the mouse pointer at the bottom edge of one of the record selector buttons. The pointer turns into a double-headed arrow (see Figure 6.29). Drag the bottom edge of the button to adjust the height of all the rows. Alternatively, choose Row Height from the Format menu and set the height in points in the Row Height dialog. (Multiply the size of your font by about 1.25 to obtain normal row spacing; printers call 10-point type with 12-point spacing 10 on 12.)

- To change the width of the columns to accommodate a larger font, choose Column Width from the Format menu and then click the Best Fit button to let Access determine the size of your columns. Double-clicking the divider You might need to adjust individual column widths by dragging the right edge of the field header with the mouse.

Figure 6.29 shows the Orders datasheet with several columns hidden, gridlines off, 9-point Garamond TrueType font, and the height of the rows adjusted to accommodate the smaller font.

Tip #47 from

R J

For the greatest printing speed, choose a typeface family native to your printer, such as Helvetica for PostScript or Swiss for LaserJet printers. (Native fonts are indicated by a printer and page symbol next to the typeface family name in the Font list.) Alternatively, choose a TrueType face, such as the default Arial, for display and printing.

Orders : Table

Order ID	Customer	Employee	Order Date	Required Date
10248	Vins et alcools Chevalier	Buchanan, Steven	04-Jul-1996	01-Aug-1996
10249	Toms Spezialitäten	Suyama, Michael	05-Jul-1996	16-Aug-1996
10250	Hanari Carnes	Peacock, Margaret	08-Jul-1996	05-Aug-1996
10251	Victuailles en stock	Leverling, Janet	08-Jul-1996	05-Aug-1996
10252	Suprêmes délices	Peacock, Margaret	08-Jul-1996	06-Aug-1996
10253	Hanari Carnes	Leverling, Janet	10-Jul-1996	24-Jul-1996
10254	Chop-suey Chinese	Buchanan, Steven	11-Jul-1996	08-Aug-1996
10255	Richter Supermarkt	Dodsworth, Anne	12-Jul-1996	09-Aug-1996
10256	Wellington Importadora	Leverling, Janet	15-Jul-1996	12-Aug-1996
10257	HILARIÓN-Abastos	Peacock, Margaret	16-Jul-1996	13-Aug-1996
10258	Ernst Handel	Davolio, Nancy	17-Jul-1996	14-Aug-1996
10259	Centro comercial Moctezuma	Peacock, Margaret	18-Jul-1996	15-Aug-1996
10260	Ottilies Käseladen	Peacock, Margaret	19-Jul-1996	16-Aug-1996
10261	Que Delícia	Peacock, Margaret	19-Jul-1996	16-Aug-1996
10262	Rattlesnake Canyon Grocery	Callahan, Laura	22-Jul-1996	19-Aug-1996
10263	Ernst Handel	Dodsworth, Anne	23-Jul-1996	20-Aug-1996
10264	Folk och fä HB	Suyama, Michael	24-Jul-1996	21-Aug-1996
10265	Blondel père et fils	Fuller, Andrew	25-Jul-1996	22-Aug-1996
10266	Wartian Herkku	Leverling, Janet	26-Jul-1996	06-Sep-1996
10267	Frankenversand	Peacock, Margaret	29-Jul-1996	26-Aug-1996
10268	GROSELLA-Restaurante	Callahan, Laura	30-Jul-1996	27-Aug-1996
10269	White Clover Markets	Buchanan, Steven	31-Jul-1996	14-Aug-1996

Record: 1 of 831

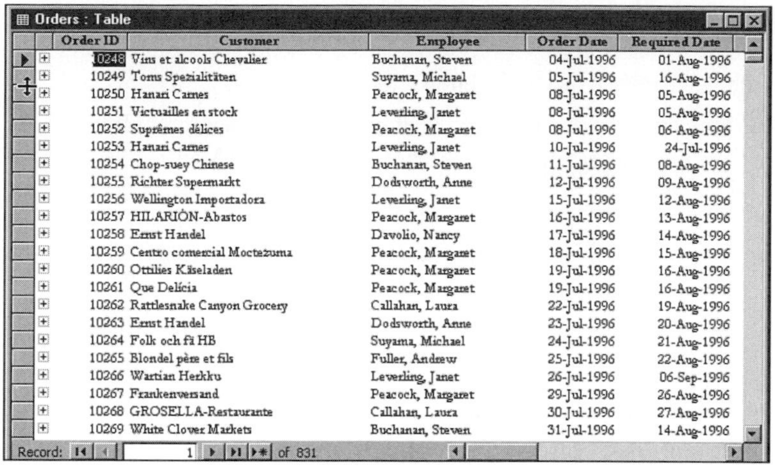

Figure 6.29
The Orders datasheet in a customized view.

COPYING, EXPORTING, AND MAILING SORTED AND FILTERED DATA

A primary use for filters and customized datasheets is for exporting the filtered records to another application, such as Microsoft Excel or Word. Various methods for exporting filtered and custom-formatted records are available:

→ For more information on exporting sets of records for use by other applications, **see** "Exporting Data from Access Tables," **p. 203**.

- Copy the entire datasheet to the Clipboard and then paste the datasheet into the other application. Hidden columns don't appear, but formatting (font, font attributes, and row height) is preserved.
- Use the Save As/Export feature to export the datasheet to an Excel worksheet (.xls) or a Rich Text Format (.rtf) file for Word or other Windows word processing applications. (From the File menu, choose Save As/Export, select To an External File or Database in the Save As dialog, and then select the file type you want in the Save as Type drop-down list of the Save Table In dialog.) Save As/Export preserves the attributes you use to customize the filtered and sorted data when you choose Excel format. Hidden columns, however, appear when you open the resulting file in any version of Excel.

- Choose Tool, Office Links, Analyze It with MS Excel to save the filtered or sorted data in an Excel worksheet; choose Tool, Office Links, Publish It with MS Word to save the data as an RTF document. Whether you choose to Analyze It or Publish It, Access starts Excel or Word with the exported document displayed.

- Choose <u>T</u>ool, Office <u>L</u>inks, <u>M</u>erge It with MS Word to create form letters with Microsoft Word. Using Mail Merge with Microsoft Word is discussed in Chapter 21, "Using Access with Microsoft Word and Mail Merge."

- Send the file as an attachment to a Microsoft Mail or Exchange message. Hidden columns don't appear, but formatting isn't preserved in Microsoft Mail messages. (The attached file is in Excel BIFF format.)

If you make the Database window the active window and choose <u>F</u>ile, Save <u>A</u>s/Export, the entire content of the table is exported regardless of the filter you added.

TROUBLESHOOTING

FILTER BY FORM DOESN'T FIND THE EXPECTED RECORDS

Either too few records or records extraneous to the filter appear when using Filter by Form.

Access keeps your last filter settings for a table until you close the table. If you've applied a different filter—whether through filter by selection or filter by form earlier in your current work session—Access may be applying additional filter criteria that you're not expecting. Choose <u>R</u>emove Filter/Sort from the <u>R</u>ecords menu to clear all previous filter criteria and ensure that the new filter criteria you enter are the only ones in effect.

IN THE REAL WORLD—COMPUTER-BASED SORTING AND SEARCHING

Donald E. Knuth's *Sorting and Searching*, volume 3 of his *The Art of Computer Programming* series, is the seminal work on computer algorithms (programs) to perform sorts and searches. Dr. Knuth is Professor Emeritus of The Art of Computer Programming at Stanford University, and is equally well known in the computer-based publishing industry for his TeX and METAFONT type design and typesetting programs. Addison-Wesley published the first edition of *Sorting and Searching* in 1973. There's a good probability that every student who was granted a computer science degree during and after the mid-1970s has a well worn copy of Knuth's classic text. Knuth updated *Sorting and Searching* with a second edition in mid-1998; the book remains required reading for assembly-language programmers, but you need a good foundation in combinatorial mathematics and set theory to fully understand the contents.

THE INFLUENCE OF COMPUTER POWER ON KNUTH'S APPROACH

As Knuth points out in the first page of the chapter on sorting, a better term to describe the process is "ordering." (The 724-page book has only two chapters—Chapter 6, "Sorting," and Chapter 7, "Searching"). Structured Query Language (SQL) takes Knuth's advice and uses ORDER BY clauses to define sort sequences. One of the dictionary definitions of the verb "to sort" is "to arrange according to characteristics," and the definition of "order" includes "arrange" as a synonym. Both sort and order infer that the process physically moves records; this was the case in the 1970s, a period when punched cards were the dominant means of computer data entry and storage. The advent of magnetic tape drives eliminated the need for punched card sorting and collating machines, but sorting still required individual records be rewritten to tape in the chosen order. Decks of punched cards and magnetic tape use sequential access, so sorting by merging expedites searching—assuming that records matching your search criteria appear early in the deck or tape. Thus the "Sorting" chapter precedes "Searching."

Today's PCs are far more powerful than the largest mainframe computers of the 1970s. Multi-gigabyte fixed disk drives in PC clients dwarf the storage capabilities of tape and multi-spindle disk drives of the 1970s and early 1980s. When you apply a sort order to a Jet table or query, records don't change position; Access simply displays the table records in the desired sequence. If you have plenty of RAM, all the record resequencing occurs in memory because Jet picks those records needed to populate the visible rows of the datasheet, plus some additional records to make page down operations go faster. When Jet runs out of RAM, temporary disk files store the overflow. It's no longer necessary to optimize searching by prior sorting; the brute force approach (searching a random-order file) usually is fast enough for files of moderate (10,000 records) to even large size (100,000+ records).

KNUTH AND INDEXES

One of Knuth's other contributions to computer science is his analysis of binary tree searching on ordered tables. An ordered table is one in which the records are physically or logically organized in alphabetic or numeric order by the key field being searched. Binary tree searches optimize the searching process by minimizing the number of comparisons required to zero-in on the record(s) with the desired value. Knuth went into great detail on "hashing" algorithms that create a set of unique values to identify each record. Hashing greatly speeds searching on the key field of tables when the key field comprises more than a few characters. The "hash tables" of early databases are called indexes today. Access 2000's Microsoft Data Engine (MSDE) and SQL Server 7.0 still generate temporary hash tables when needed to speed query processing.

Two Russian mathematicians, G. M. Adelson-Velski and E. M. Landis, proposed a balanced binary tree indexing structure in 1963. In a balanced binary tree structure, the length of the search path to any ordered record is never more than 45 percent longer than the optimum. Jet, like most other desktop RDBMSs, has a balanced binary tree (B-tree) structure; a Jet primary key index orders the records.

When you search on a field that isn't ordered, called a secondary key, search efficiency drops rapidly. The early 1970s approaches, including a process called *combinatorial hashing*, have given way to secondary indexes on unordered keys, such as postal codes in a table where the primary key is a customer name or code. Each secondary key you add decreases the speed at which you can insert new records because of the need to rebalance the trees of

PART

I

CH

6

the indexes. Despite the performance of today's PC clients and servers, it's still a good idea to minimize the number of secondary indexes on tables used for online transaction processing (OLTP).

It isn't necessary to understand the underlying details of hashing and balanced B-tree indexes to take full advantage of Access's searching and sorting features. Familiarity with the surprisingly efficient methodology employed in the early days of computing, however, offers a useful perspective on the dramatic improvements in database design and implementation that's occurred in the 27 years since Knuth published the first edition *Searching and Sorting*.

--rj

LINKING, IMPORTING, AND EXPORTING TABLES

In this chapter

Moving Data from and to Other Applications   232

Understanding How Access Handles Tables in Other Database File Formats   233

Linking and Importing External ISAM Tables   235

Dealing with Images in External Files   243

Converting Field Data Types to Access Data Types   244

Using the Linked Table Manager Add-in to Relink Tables   245

Importing and Linking Spreadsheet Files   247

Working with Microsoft Outlook and Exchange Folders   258

Importing Text Files   264

Using the Clipboard to Import Data   277

Exporting Data from Access Tables   283

Troubleshooting   287

In the Real World—Microsoft Giveth and Microsoft Taketh Away   288

MOVING DATA FROM AND TO OTHER APPLICATIONS

Undoubtedly, more than 90 percent of personal computer users have data that can be processed through database management techniques. Any data that a computer can arrange in tabular form—even tables in word processing files—can be converted to database tables. The strength of a relational database management system (RDBMS) lies in its capability to handle large numbers of individual pieces of data stored in tables and to relate the pieces of data in a meaningful way.

PC users acquire RDBMSs when the amount of data created exceeds a standard productivity application's capability to manipulate the data effectively. A common example is a large mailing list created in Microsoft Word. As the number of names in the list increases, using Word to make selective mailings and maintain histories of responses to mailings becomes increasingly difficult. A PC RDBMS is the most effective type of application for manipulating large lists.

One strong point of Access is its capability to transform existing database tables, spreadsheets, and text files created by other DOS and Windows applications into the Access .mdb format—a process known as *importing* a file. Access can *export* (create) table files in any format in which it can import the files. Most client/server RDBMSs can import and export only text-type files.

Access can link a database table file created by Access or another RDBMS to your current Access database; Access then acts as a database front end. Because Access has a linking capability, it can use a file created by another RDBMS in its native form. This capability is far less common in other PC and client/server RDBMSs. When you link a database table from a different RDBMS, you can display and update the linked table as though it were an Access table contained in your .mdb file. If the file containing the table is shared on a network, others can use the file with their applications while it is linked to your database. This capability to link files is important for two reasons: you can have only one Access database open at a time, and you can create new applications in Access that can coexist with applications created by other database managers. Access 2000 also can link Outlook and Microsoft Exchange mail, contacts, tasks, and calendar folders, and Outlook Express mail. Outlook 2000 also lets you import and export folders to Jet 4.0 tables.

This chapter deals primarily with what are known as *desktop database-development applications*—a term that distinguishes them from client/server RDBMSs, such as Microsoft SQL Server, Sybase, Oracle, and Informix databases. Client/server RDBMSs are designed specifically for use with networked PCs and—except for the Microsoft Data Engine (MSDE)—require you to set aside a PC for use as a database application server to run the RDBMS and store the database files. Desktop RDBMSs, such as dBASE, Visual FoxPro, and Paradox, are more widely used than client/server systems. Most desktop RDBMSs can share files on a network, but several publishers of desktop RDBMSs require that you purchase a special multiuser version of the RDBMS to do so. Multiuser desktop RDBMSs— while accommodating the workstation-server configuration required by conventional networks such as Novell NetWare, Windows NT Server, or IBM Warp Server—are especially well suited to the peer-to-peer networks discussed in Chapter 24, "Securing Multiuser Network Applications." Chapter 24 explains how to use Access with shared database files.

UNDERSTANDING HOW ACCESS HANDLES TABLES IN OTHER DATABASE FILE FORMATS

Conventional desktop database development applications maintain each table in an individual file. Each file contains a header followed by the data. A *header* is a group of bytes that provide information on the file's structure, such as the names and types of fields, number of records in the table, and file length. When you create a table file in dBASE, Visual FoxPro, or Paradox, for example, the file contains only a header. As you add records to the file, the file size increases by the number of bytes required for one record, and the header is updated to reflect the new file size and record count.

Desktop RDBMSs create a variety of supplemental files, some of which are required to import, link, or export RDBMSs:

- dBASE and Visual FoxPro store memo-type data in a separate .dbt file. If a dBASE table file contains a memo field, the .dbt file must be available. If the .dbt file is missing, you can't import or link dBASE or Visual FoxPro tables that contain a memo field.

- Use of .ndx (dBASE III), .mdx (dBASE IV), or .idx or .cdx (FoxPro) index files is optional. You always should use index files when you have them. If you don't link the index files when you link an indexed .dbf table file, modifications you make to the linked tables aren't reflected in the index, which causes errors to occur when you try to use the indexed tables with dBASE or Visual FoxPro.

- Paradox stores information about the primary-key index file (.px) in the associated table (.db) file; the .px file for the .db file must be available for Access to open a Paradox .db file for updating. Access links the .px file automatically if it exists. Like dBASE, Paradox stores memo-type data in a separate file with a .mb extension.

Note

NEW 2000

Microsoft has dramatically reduced native support for dBASE and Paradox tables in Access 2000. Linked dBASE and Paradox files are read-only and you can't export or attach dBASE or Paradox indexes unless you have the Borland Database Engine (BDE) from Inprise Corporation installed on your computer. You can obtain more information on the BDE, which is included with the Delphi 4.0 development platform, at http://www.borland.com/bde/. If you have a BDE version earlier than 5.01, you can obtain a no-charge upgrade to version 5.01 at http://www.borland.com/devsupport/bde/bdeupdate.html.

PART

I

CH

7

All supplemental files must be in the same folder as the related database file to be used by Access.

Note

The default folder for exporting and importing files is C:\My Documents in Windows9x and C:\Winnt\Profiles*UserName*\Personal in Windows NT, unless you've changed the Default Database Folder entry in the General page of the Options dialog.

The header of an Access 2000 .mdb file varies from conventional PC RDBMS files in that an .mdb header consists of a collection of system tables that contain information on all the tables, indexes, macros, and VBA functions and procedures stored in a single Access file. The Access system tables also contain information on the location and characteristics of other PC RDBMS files that you linked to your Access database. Access's system tables are similar to the tables used in client/server databases that maintain information on the content of database devices (files), the databases, and the tables contained in the devices.

Note

You can view the Access 2000 system tables by choosing Tools, Options. Select the View tab and, in the Show group, select System Objects.

Never modify anything in these tables (most of them are read-only). Some database developers have used the data and values in these tables to aid in referencing items in the database. This isn't a good practice because the design of these tables isn't guaranteed to remain consistent from version to version and could result in substantial rework to convert a database application to a new version of Access.

IDENTIFYING PC DATABASE FILE FORMATS

Access can import and export the following types of database table files used by the most common PC database managers:

- *dBASE .dbf table and .dbt memo files as well as dBASE III .ndx and dBASE IV, 5.0, and 7.0 .mdx index files*. dBASE III+ files are a common denominator of the PC RDBMS industry. Most PC RDBMSs and all common spreadsheet applications can import and export .dbf files; the most popular formats are dBASE III and IV. Some of these RDBMSs can update existing .ndx and .mdx index files, and a few RDBMSs can create these index files. Access 2000 links and exports .ndx and .mdx indexes only if you have the BDE installed. You must have version 5.01+ of the BDE to import, export, or link dBASE 7.0 tables.

- *Visual FoxPro .dbf table and .dbc database files*. You can import Visual FoxPro files, but you can't export them. Access 2000 uses the Microsoft Visual FoxPro ODBC driver for import and linking operations. Prior to OLE DB and ActiveX Data Objects (ADO), Open Database Connectivity (ODBC) was Microsoft's preferred technology for connecting to client/server databases and other data sources.

> **Note**
>
>
> **NEW 2000**
>
> The direct (ISAM) export, import, and link capabilities of Access 9x for Microsoft FoxPro 2.0, 2.5, 2.6, and 3.0 files are missing in Access 2000. Like dBASE and Paradox, Access 2000 has reduced support for Visual FoxPro files. Unlike dBASE and Paradox, however, Microsoft provides support for linking Visual FoxPro files with Office 2000.

- *Paradox 3.x, 4.x, 5.x, 7.x, and 8.x .db table, and .px primary-key files.* Access 2000 supports importing and exporting Paradox 3.x, 4.x, and 5.x .db and .mb files. You can link Paradox files with .px indexes only if you have the BDE installed.

> **Note**
>
> If you work in a multiuser environment, you must have exclusive access to the file you intend to import. No one else can have this file open when you initiate the importing process, and everyone else is denied access to the file until you close the Import dialog. You also must have exclusive access to linked dBASE and Paradox files if you don't have a copy of the BDE.

> **Caution**
>
> Make sure that you work on a backup, not on the original copy of the linked file, until you're certain that your updates to the data in the linked table are valid for the existing database application.

LINKING AND IMPORTING EXTERNAL ISAM TABLES

ISAM is an acronym for *indexed sequential access method*, the architecture used for all desktop RDBMS tables. To link or import an xBase or Paradox file as a table in an Access 2000 database, follow these steps:

> **Note**
>
> *Linking* an external file to an Access database was referred to as *attaching* a table in versions of Access before Access 95. Don't confuse linking an external file to an Access database with OLE links; when you link an external file, you just give access information about the external file necessary to open, read, and modify the data in that file.

1. Click the Show Database Window toolbar button or choose <u>W</u>indow, <u>1</u> Database. Access doesn't require all open tables to be closed before you link or import a table.

2. If you have a test database that you can use for this procedure, click the Open Database toolbar button or choose <u>F</u>ile, <u>O</u>pen Database; then select the test database, open it, and skip to step 5.

3. If you don't have a test database, create a sample to use throughout this chapter. Click the New Database toolbar button or choose <u>F</u>ile, <u>N</u>ew Database to display the New dialog.

PART

I

CH

7

4. Double-click the Database icon in the New dialog; Access displays the File New Database dialog. Type a name, such as **MDB Test.mdb**, in the File Name text box and click Create. You must wait while Access creates and tests the new database.

5. In this example, you link an external table to the database. Choose File, Get External Data, Link Tables. The Link dialog appears (see Figure 7.1); the Link dialog is a variation of the common Windows 95 and Windows NT 4.0 Open dialog. If you choose File, Get External Data, Import, the Import dialog appears.

6. Use the Files of Type drop-down list to select the file type you want to link. (If you have a suitable Paradox table to link, select Paradox. Otherwise, select dBASE III, dBASE IV, or another database type as appropriate to the format of your table file.)

7. Double-click the name of the table you want to link or import (or click the name to select it and then click the Link button). Access supplies the standard extensions for dBASE and Paradox table files.

Figure 7.1
The Link dialog in which you select external files for linking to an Access database.

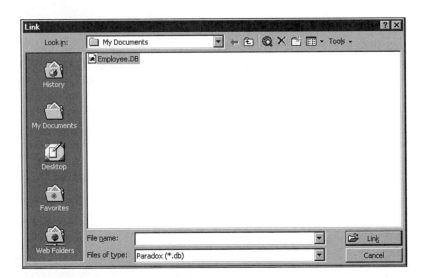

Tip #48 from

> You can link prior versions of Access tables to an Access 2000 database. Linking prior versions solves the problem of sharing data of mixed version databases, which is another reason to always use one .mdb file for tables and another .mdb file for your application database objects. If you need to share data .mdb files you create in Access 2000 with client PCs running Access 97, you can save the data .mdb file in Access 97 format.
>
> → To review the Jet 4.0 to 3.51 conversion process, **see** "Converting Databases to Access 97 Format," **p. 121**.

8. If the file you choose is encrypted and requires a password to decrypt it, the Password Required dialog appears. Type the password and press Enter.

9. After you successfully link or import the file, a dialog confirms this operation (see Figure 7.2). If you link more than one table with the same name, Access automatically appends a sequential digit to the table name.

Figure 7.2
The success message that appears after you link an external table to a database.

The Link (or Import) dialog remains open; if you want to link or import additional external tables to this database (most Paradox and xBase databases consist of several separate table files), repeat steps 6 through 9 for all the files you want to link or import. If you're linking external Access tables, you may select at once all the tables you want to link by simply clicking each one.

10. In the Link dialog, click Close. The table(s) you linked or imported now are listed in the Database window. If you linked a file, Access adds an icon that indicates the type of database table and an arrow that indicates that the table is linked (see Figure 7.3).

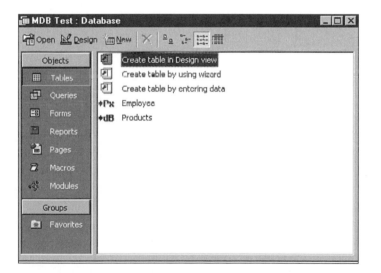

Figure 7.3
The special icons displayed in the Database window indicating linked dBASE and Paradox tables.

11. Select the table you linked and then click the Open button to display the records in Table Datasheet view (see Figure 7.4). Alternatively, you can double-click the table name.

After you link an external file as a table, you can use it almost as though it were a table in your own database. If you don't have the BDE installed, linked dBASE and Paradox tables are read-only. A general limitation is that you can't change the structure of a linked table: field names, field data types, or the Field Size properties.

Figure 7.4
The Datasheet view of a
linked Paradox file.

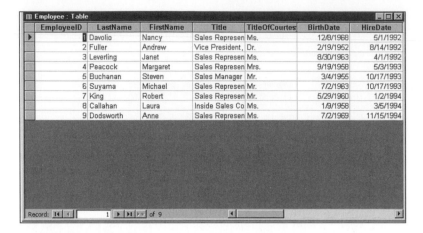

EmployeeID	LastName	FirstName	Title	TitleOfCourtes	BirthDate	HireDate
1	Davolio	Nancy	Sales Represen	Ms.	12/8/1968	5/1/1992
2	Fuller	Andrew	Vice President,	Dr.	2/19/1952	8/14/1992
3	Leverling	Janet	Sales Represen	Ms.	8/30/1963	4/1/1992
4	Peacock	Margaret	Sales Represen	Mrs.	9/19/1958	5/3/1993
5	Buchanan	Steven	Sales Manager	Mr.	3/4/1955	10/17/1993
6	Suyama	Michael	Sales Represen	Mr.	7/2/1963	10/17/1993
7	King	Robert	Sales Represen	Mr.	5/29/1960	1/2/1994
8	Callahan	Laura	Inside Sales Co	Ms.	1/9/1958	3/5/1994
9	Dodsworth	Anne	Sales Represen	Ms.	7/2/1969	11/15/1994

Record: 1 of 9

Tip #49 from

Although you can't change field properties for linked tables, you can change the name of the attached table within this database only. Choose Edit, Rename and type the new name for the table. The name for the table (called an *alias*) is changed only in the current Access database and not in the native database.

LINKING VISUAL FOXPRO TABLES WITH ODBC

You can use the ODBC drivers provided with Office 2000 to link Visual FoxPro databases or tables to your Access databases. You must use the 32-bit ODBC Manager application supplied with Access 2000 (and installed into the Windows 9x, Windows NT 4.0, and Windows 2000 Control Panel) to create an ODBC data source for your FoxPro tables or databases. *Data source* is a synonym for *database* when you use the ODBC Application Programming Interface (API) to link tables. (In Windows NT and Windows 2000, the ODBC Manager is referred to as the *ODBC Administrator*.)

Tip #50 from

Office 2000 installs 32-bit Excel, FoxPro, Paradox, Access, dBASE, and Text file ODBC drivers, plus the SQL Server driver. ODBC and the ODBC drivers are installed if you choose a Complete Microsoft Office 2000 or Access 2000 setup, but you must explicitly specify installation of the SQL Server ODBC driver during the setup process. If you don't have the ODBC drivers on your system, you can rerun Setup to install them. Additional ODBC drivers are available from various third-party vendors.

Note

Microsoft is in the process of replacing ODBC with OLE DB, but hasn't yet created OLE DB data providers for FoxPro files. (OLE DB data providers correspond to ODBC drivers.) OLE DB is one of the subjects of Chapter 27, "Understanding Universal Data Access, OLE DB, and ADO."

Assuming that you installed the ODBC Manager and ODBC drivers, follow these steps to link Visual FoxPro table(s) to an Access database via ODBC:

1. With an Access database open, choose <u>F</u>ile, Get External <u>D</u>ata, <u>L</u>ink Table to display the Link dialog (refer to Figure 7.1).

2. Select ODBC Databases in the Files of Type drop-down list. Access closes the Link dialog and displays the Select Data Source dialog. If you want to create a file to define a data source that you can share with others, accept the default File Data Source page. This example uses a data source entry in the local PC's Registry, so click the Machine Data Sources tab (see Figure 7.5).

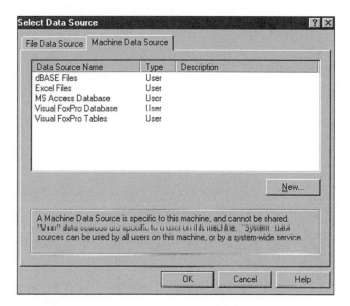

Figure 7.5
Select Data Source dialog displaying the default set of ODBC Machine Data Sources installed by Office 2000.

3. Click New to open the first Create New Data Source Wizard dialog (see Figure 7.6).

Figure 7.6
The opening dialog of the Create New Data Source Wizard.

4. Select the User Data Source option if you want the new data source to be available only to you, the data source type used for this example. If you want anyone who logs on to your computer to be able to use your new data source, select the System Data Source option. Click Next to continue with the Create New Data Source Wizard.

5. Select the database driver appropriate for the database you want to link. Select the Microsoft Visual FoxPro Driver (see Figure 7.7). Click Finish to display this Wizard's final dialog.

Figure 7.7
Selecting the Visual FoxPro ODBC driver.

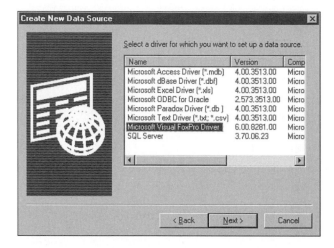

6. The final dialog displays summary information about the type of data source you've created (system or user) and the name of the database driver you selected (see Figure 7.8). Click Finish to complete the creation of your new data source.

Figure 7.8
The Create New Data Source Wizard's final dialog for a Visual FoxPro ODBC data source.

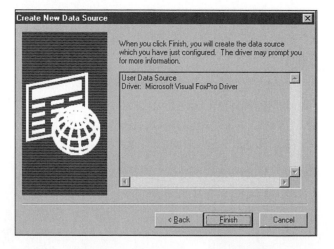

7. After creating a new data source, you must configure it. Access now displays the ODBC Microsoft Visual FoxPro Setup dialog. Type a name for your data source in the Data Source Name text box and type a description of the data source in the Description text

box. If a .dbc file contains your Visual FoxPro tables, select the Visual FoxPro Database option; if the files are in .dbf format, select the Free Table Directory option (see Figure 7.9).

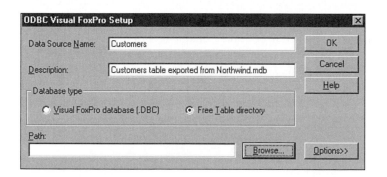

Figure 7.9
Configuring a new Visual FoxPro ODBC data source to use independent .dbf files.

8. Click Browse to display the Select Directory Containing Free Tables dialog. The Select Directory... dialog is a Windows 3.x-style file-opening dialog. If needed, use the Drives and Directories lists to navigate to the correct folder in which your FoxPro files are stored and select its name in the Folders list (see Figure 7.10).

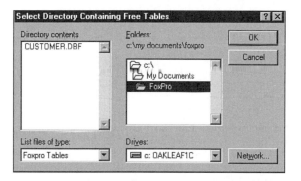

Figure 7.10
Selecting the folder containing the Visual FoxPro .dbf files.

9. Click OK twice to return to the Select Data Source dialog, select your new data source in the Data Source Name list (refer to Figure 7.5), and then click OK. Access opens the Link Tables dialog (see Figure 7.11).

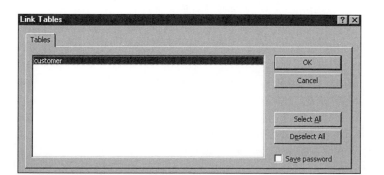

Figure 7.11
Selecting the FoxPro table(s) to link to your database.

PART

I

CH

7

10. The Link Tables dialog lists the FoxPro tables in the folder you selected in step 8. Click each table name to select it. (This example has only one FoxPro table, customers.) After you select all the tables that you want to link, click OK. Access closes the Link Tables dialog and displays the Select Unique Record Identifier dialog.

11. If you want to be able to update the data in the ODBC-linked table, you must select a field (or combination of fields) that creates a unique record identification for each row in the table—essentially, you create a surrogate primary key for the linked table. To select a field, click it, and then click OK. In this case the primary key field is customerid (see Figure 7.12).

Figure 7.12
Selecting a field in the linked table to create a surrogate primary key.

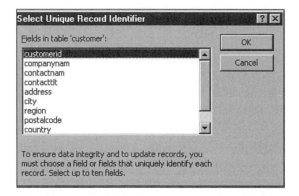

Your linked Visual FoxPro table appears in the Database window (with the ODBC globe turned to display Africa), as shown in Figure 7.13. All tables linked by ODBC display the globe icon. Double-click the table icon to display your newly-linked Visual FoxPro table. By default, Visual FoxPro field names appear in lower case.

 Access detects problems with linked or imported tables that may cause errors when you try to use the tables with Access. Importing and linking errors are the subject of the "Troubleshooting" section near the end of this chapter.

Figure 7.13
Identifying Visual FoxPro tables linked with ODBC drivers by the globe icon.

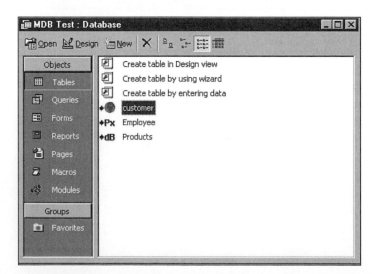

DEALING WITH IMAGES IN EXTERNAL FILES

Most database managers designed for Windows include some form of graphics field data type. Paradox for Windows, for example, provides a special field data type for graphics. Although early version of dBASE lack a field data type for graphics, third-party software firms publish applications that let you store images in dBASE memo fields. Various add-on applications for desktop RDBMSs let programmers display and edit graphic images. The images usually are in individual files, but a few third-party applications continue to place images in memo files.

When you try to import or link Paradox or dBASE .dbt files containing images or other binary data, you might receive an error message that the memo file is corrupted or that you can't import the .db or .dbf file that contains the offending memo or graphics field. In rare cases—usually involving tiny images—you can import the .dbf and .dbt files, but you see random characters in the Access memo field. With Paradox tables, the graphics or binary fields simply disappear from the table.

If a dialog appears that reports a problem during importing or linking a file, the linking or importing process is canceled.

The following recommendations can help you deal with graphic images processed with other RDBMSs and add-on applications:

- Use add-on applications for xBase clones and compilers that operate with the original graphics files in their native format, such as .tif, .pcx, .gif, or .tga. In nearly all cases, the original graphics file is on your computer's fixed disk or on a file server. You can link or embed the graphics file in an Access OLE Object field by using the techniques described in Chapter 19, "Adding Charts and Graphics to Forms, and Reports."

- Don't use add-on applications that incorporate graphics in .dbt files. If you're committed to this approach, use the following steps to place the offending memo file in a new file.

- If you use Paradox 4.x or Paradox for Windows with application development in Access, maintain files with graphics fields (as well as any OLE fields in Paradox for Windows tables) separate from files containing conventional data types.

- Use an OLE server that can process the graphics file type of the original image. Windows Paint is limited to Windows bitmap files (.bmp and .dib) and can only read—not save—.pcx files. To display the image in a form or report, you can create a reduced-size, 16-color or 256-color, Windows bitmap file to be displayed as a bound object. Chapter 19 discusses methods of handling images in this way.

To link or import an xBase file containing a memo field or a Paradox file containing graphics fields, you must be familiar with file-restructuring methods for dBASE or Paradox. To restructure an xBase file with a memo file containing graphic images, follow these steps:

1. Make a copy of the file and give it a new name.

2. Modify the structure of the original file by deleting all but the related fields and the memo or graphics field of the original file. Modifying the new file with Modify Structure creates a backup of the original file with a .bak extension.

3. Modify the structure of the new file by deleting the memo or graphics field.

4. Add a field for the path and file name of the original graphics file if it isn't already included. Access then can use the location of the original graphics file to pass the file name to an OLE server. You must write some VBA code, however, to handle this process. See Chapter 26, "Writing Visual Basic for Applications Code," and Chapter 28, "Responding to Events with VBA 6.0," for examples of writing VBA code.

5. Modify the source code of your original application, establishing a one-to-one relationship between the new files.

CONVERTING FIELD DATA TYPES TO ACCESS DATA TYPES

When you import or link a file, Access reads the header of the file and converts the field data types to Access data types. Access usually is quite successful in this conversion because Access offers a greater variety of data types than most of the other widely used PC RDBMSs. Table 7.1 shows the correspondence of field data types between dBASE, Paradox, and Access files.

TABLE 7.1 FIELD DATA TYPE CONVERSION BETWEEN ACCESS AND OTHER RDBMSS

dBASE III/IV/5	Paradox 3.x, 4.x, 5.0	Access
Character	Alphanumeric	Text (Specify Size property)
Numeric, Float*	Number, Money, BCD*	Number (Double) Number (Single) Number (Byte)
	Short Number	Number (Integer)
	Long Number	Number (Long)
	AutoIncrement	AutoNumber
Logical	Logical	Yes/No
Date	Date, Time, Timestamp*	Date/Time
Memo	Memo, Formatted Memo, Binary*	Memo
	OLE	OLE

*Sometimes two types of field data, separated by commas, are shown within a single column in Table 7.1. When Access exports a table that contains a data type that corresponds with one of the two field data types, the first data type is assigned to the field in the exported table. The Float data type is available only in dBASE IV and 5.

Tip #51 from

If you're importing tables, you can change the field data type and the Field Size property to make them more suitable to the type of information contained in the field. When you change a data type or Field Size, however, follow the precautions noted in Chapter 4, "Working with Access Databases and Tables." Remember that you can't change the field data type or Field Size property of linked tables. You can, however, use the Format property with imported or linked tables to display the data in any format compatible with the field data type of imported or linked files. You can change any remaining properties applicable to the field data type, such as validation rules and text. By using the Caption property, you can give the field a new and more descriptive name.

→ **See** "Choosing Field Data Types, Sizes, and Formats," **p. 140**.

→ **See** "Adding Indexes to Tables," **p. 174**.

USING THE LINKED TABLE MANAGER ADD-IN TO RELINK TABLES

Moving linked files to another folder or logical drive causes the existing links to break. Access 2000 provides an add-in assistant known as the Linked Table Manager to simplify relinking tables. (The Linked Table Manager was known as the Attachment Manager in Access 2.0.)

If you move an Access, dBASE, FoxPro, or Paradox file that provides a table linked to an Access 2000 database, choose Tools, Add-Ins, Linked Table Manager. The Linked Table Manager's window lists all the linked tables except linked ODBC tables. Access also displays the path to the database containing the linked table(s) at the time the link was created. (You also can view the path to the database containing a linked table by opening the linked table in Design view and opening the Table Properties window.) Click the check box of the file(s) whose location(s) changed (see Figure 7.14).

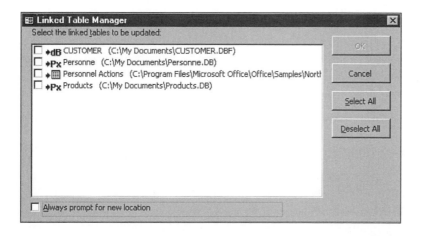

Figure 7.14
The Linked Table Manager add-in, which lets you update the path to linked tables.

PART

I

CH

7

Click OK to display the Select New Location of *TableName* dialog shown in Figure 7.15. Select the folder and file where the table is located; then click Open to change the link reference and close the dialog. If Access successfully refreshes the table links, it displays a dialog saying so; click OK to close the success message dialog. Click the Close button of the Linked Table Manager to close the add-in.

Figure 7.15
Changing the location of a table with the Linked Table Manager add-in.

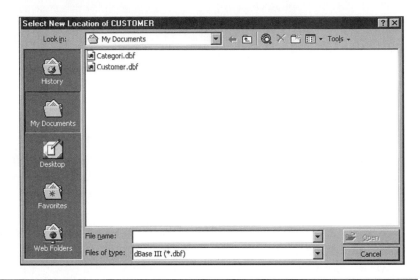

Note

The Linked Table Manager can refresh links only for tables that have been moved to another disk or folder—the table must have the same name. If the linked table's file was renamed, you must delete the table link from your Access database and relink the table under its new name.

IMPORTING VERSUS LINKING DATABASE FILES AS TABLES

The preceding examples demonstrate the differences between the behavior of Access with linked and imported database files. You should link tables contained in another database file if any of the following conditions exist:

- You share the file with others who are allowed to update the file, or you make updates of the file available to others.
- You use another RDBMS to modify the file in any way.
- The file is resident on another computer, such as a server, and its size is larger than fits comfortably on your fixed disk.
- You observe the recommended database application development practice of maintaining separate .mdb files for tables and your application's objects.

You should import a table when one of the following conditions exists:

- You're developing an application and want to use data types or Field Size properties different from those Access has chosen for you.

- You or the users of your application don't have online access to the required database files and can't link them.

- You want to use a key field different from the field specified in a Paradox or client/server table. This situation can occur when the structure of one or more of the files you plan to use seriously violates one or more of the normalization rules described in Chapter 22, "Exploring Relational Database Design and Implementation."

- You need Access to allow duplicate values in your table when a primary-key field precludes duplicate values.

If you decide to use a temporarily imported table in an application that, when completed, also will use a linked table, make sure that you don't change any field names, field data types, or Field Size properties after you import the table. If you change Field Name properties, you may have to make many changes to forms, reports, macros, and VBA code when you change to a linked table. If your application involves Paradox and client/server database tables, don't change the primary-key fields of these tables. With dBASE tables, make sure that the indexes you create correspond to the indexes of the associated .ndx or .mdx files.

IMPORTING AND LINKING SPREADSHEET FILES

Access can import files created by spreadsheet and related applications, such as project management systems, in the following formats:

- Excel 2.x, 3.0, 4.0, 5.0, 95, 97, and 2000 .xls files as well as task and resource files created by Microsoft Project in .xls format.

- Lotus 1-2-3 .wks (Release 1 and Symphony), .wk1 (Release 2), and .wk3 (Release 3 and later) files. Most spreadsheet applications can export files to at least one of these Lotus formats.

You can use OLE to embed or link charts created by Microsoft Excel and stored in files with an .xlc extension. Copy the contents of the file to the Windows Clipboard from Excel. Choose Edit, Paste to embed or link (via OLE) the chart in fields of the OLE Object type; then display the chart on a form or print it on a report as an unbound object. Similarly, you can embed or link most views displayed in Microsoft Project, which also uses the Microsoft Chart applet; the exceptions are task and resource forms and the Task PERT chart. Chapters 19 through 21 describe OLE linking and embedding techniques.

Creating a Table by Importing an Excel Worksheet

Figure 7.16 illustrates the preferred format for exporting data from Excel and other spreadsheet applications to Access tables. Most spreadsheet applications refer to the format as a *database*. The names of the fields are typed in the first row and the remainder of the database range consists of data. The type of data in each column must be consistent within the database range you select.

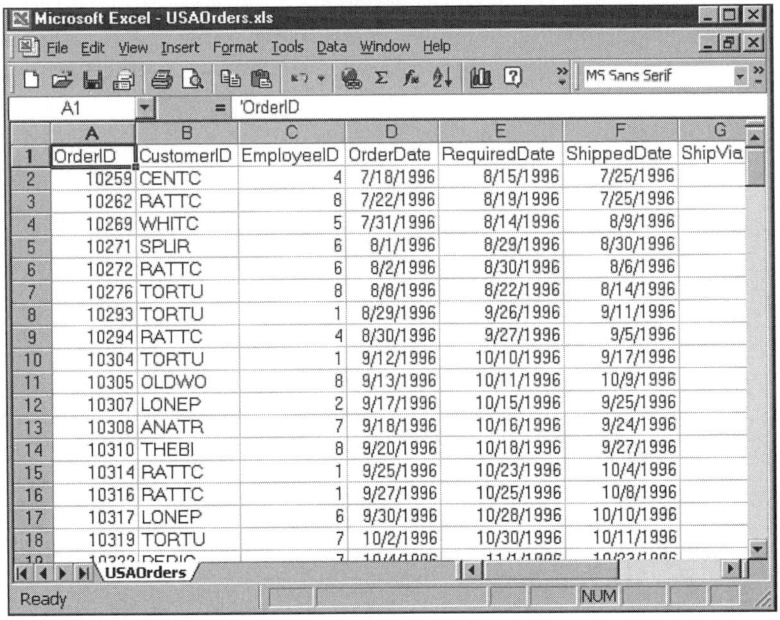

	A	B	C	D	E	F	G
1	OrderID	CustomerID	EmployeeID	OrderDate	RequiredDate	ShippedDate	ShipVia
2	10259	CENTC	4	7/18/1996	8/15/1996	7/25/1996	
3	10262	RATTC	8	7/22/1996	8/19/1996	7/25/1996	
4	10269	WHITC	5	7/31/1996	8/14/1996	8/9/1996	
5	10271	SPLIR	6	8/1/1996	8/29/1996	8/30/1996	
6	10272	RATTC	6	8/2/1996	8/30/1996	8/6/1996	
7	10276	TORTU	8	8/8/1996	8/22/1996	8/14/1996	
8	10293	TORTU	1	8/29/1996	9/26/1996	9/11/1996	
9	10294	RATTC	4	8/30/1996	9/27/1996	9/5/1996	
10	10304	TORTU	1	9/12/1996	10/10/1996	9/17/1996	
11	10305	OLDWO	8	9/13/1996	10/11/1996	10/9/1996	
12	10307	LONEP	2	9/17/1996	10/15/1996	9/25/1996	
13	10308	ANATR	7	9/18/1996	10/16/1996	9/24/1996	
14	10310	THEBI	8	9/20/1996	10/18/1996	9/27/1996	
15	10314	RATTC	1	9/25/1996	10/23/1996	10/4/1996	
16	10316	RATTC	1	9/27/1996	10/25/1996	10/8/1996	
17	10317	LONEP	6	9/30/1996	10/28/1996	10/10/1996	
18	10319	TORTU	7	10/2/1996	10/30/1996	10/11/1996	

Figure 7.16
Data from a subset of the Orders table in a Microsoft Excel 2000 worksheet.

Caution

All cells that comprise the worksheet range to be imported into an Access table must have frozen values. *Frozen values* substitute numeric results for the Excel expressions used to create the values. When cells include formulas, Access imports the cells as blank data cells. Freezing the values causes Access to overwrite the formulas in the spreadsheet that has the frozen values. If the range to import includes formulas, save a copy of your .xls file with a new name. Open the new workbook, select the worksheet and range to import, and freeze the values by pressing Ctrl+C. Choose Paste Special from the Edit menu, select the Values option, and click OK. Save the new spreadsheet by its new name and use this file to import the data. The section "Using the Clipboard to Import Data" later in this chapter presents an alternative to this procedure.

Tip #52 from RJ

You get an opportunity to assign field names to the columns in the worksheet during the importation process, although the process is easier if you add field names as column headings first.

To prepare the data in an Excel spreadsheet for importation into an Access table, follow these steps:

1. Launch Excel and then open the .xls file that contains the data you want to import.

2. Add field names above the first row of the data you plan to export (if you haven't done so). Field names can't include periods (.), exclamation points (!), or square brackets ([]). You can't have duplicate field names. If you include improper characters in field names or use duplicate field names, you see an error message when you attempt to import the worksheet.

3. If your worksheet contains cells with data you don't want to include in the imported table, select the range that contains the field names row and all the rows of data needed for the table. From Excel's Insert menu, choose Name, Define and name the range.

4. If the worksheet cells include expressions, freeze the values as described in the caution preceding these steps.

5. Save the Excel file (use a different file name if you froze values) and exit Excel to conserve Windows resources for Access if your computer has less than 16MB of memory.

Now you're ready to import worksheets from the Excel workbook file. To import the prepared data from an Excel spreadsheet into an Access table, follow these steps:

1. Launch Access, if it's not running, and open the database to which you want to add the new table. The Database window must be active before you can import a file.

2. Choose File, Get External Data, Import in Access to open the Import dialog (see Figure 7.17). The Files of Type drop-down list provides several more formats for importing tables than it provides for linking files.

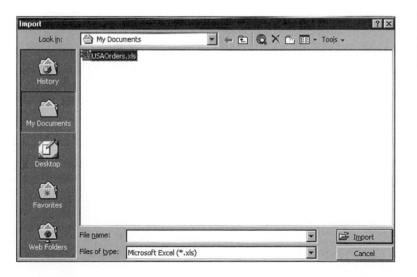

Figure 7.17
Choosing Excel spreadsheet formats in the Import dialog.

3. Select Microsoft Excel (*.xls) in the Files of Type drop-down list and then double-click the name of the Excel workbook that contains the spreadsheet you want to import (you also can click the file name to select it and then click Import). Access invokes the Import Spreadsheet Wizard (see Figure 7.18).

Figure 7.18
The opening dialog of the Import Spreadsheet Wizard.

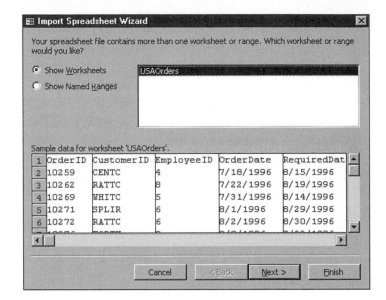

4. If you're importing an entire worksheet, select the Show Worksheets option; if you're importing a named range, select the Show Named Ranges option. The Import Spreadsheet Wizard lists the worksheets or named data ranges, depending on the option you select in the list box in the upper-right corner of the Wizard's opening dialog.

5. Select the worksheet or the named data range that you want to import in the list box. The Import Spreadsheet Wizard shows a sample view of the data in the worksheet or named range at the bottom of the dialog.

6. Click Next to move to the next dialog of the Spreadsheet Import Wizard, shown in Figure 7.19.

7. If the first row of your spreadsheet data contains the field names for the imported table, select the First Row Contains Column Headings check box. Click Next to continue with the third step; the Import Spreadsheet Wizard displays the dialog shown in Figure 7.20.

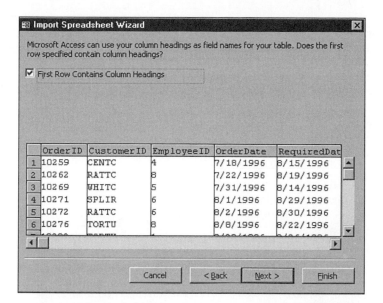

Figure 7.19
Selecting whether the first row of imported data contains field names.

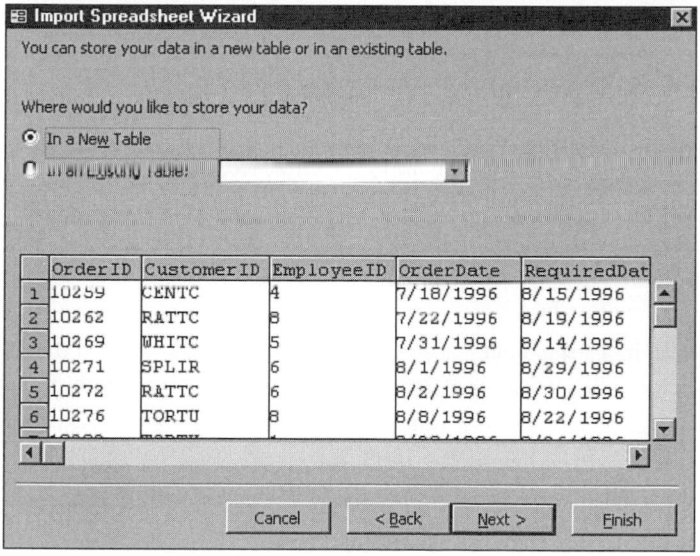

Figure 7.20
Choosing whether to create a new table from the imported data or to add it to an existing table.

8. If you want to create a new table to hold the imported spreadsheet data, select the In a New Table option. To add the imported data to an existing table, select the In an Existing Table option and select the table you want to add the imported data to in the drop-down list. Click Next to continue with the fourth step; the Import Spreadsheet Wizard displays the dialog shown in Figure 7.21.

PART

I

CH

7

Note

If you elect to add the imported data to an existing table, the Import Spreadsheet Wizard skips over all intervening steps and goes immediately to its final dialog, described in step 16.

Figure 7.21
Selecting field names, indexes, and the field's data type.

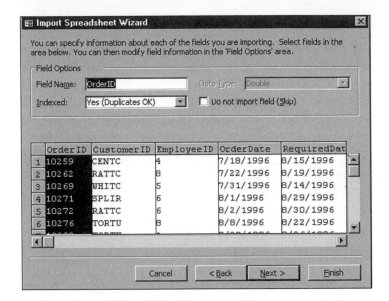

9. If you want to exclude a column from the imported database, select the column by clicking it, select the Do Not Import Field (Skip) check box, and skip to step 12.

10. The Import Spreadsheet Wizard lets you edit or add the field names for the spreadsheet columns; click the column whose name you want to edit or add and then type the name in the Field Name text box.

11. If you want Access to index this field, choose the appropriate index type in the Indexed list box; you may choose No index, Yes (Duplicates OK), or Yes (No Duplicates).

12. If the data in the spreadsheet column is unformatted or is formatted as text, Access lets you select the data type for the field in the Data Type drop-down list. The Data Type control is disabled in Figure 7.21 because the cells in the selected column of the Excel worksheet have a Double number format; Access recognizes the Double format and automatically selects a Double data type for this field.

13. Repeat steps 9 through 12 for each column in the worksheet or data range that you import. When you are satisfied with your options for each column, click Next to move to the next dialog in the Import Spreadsheet Wizard (see Figure 7.22).

Tip #53 from

Use an existing field column in the worksheet for a primary-key field if the column contains only unique values. In Figure 7.22, the OrderID field is known to contain unique values.

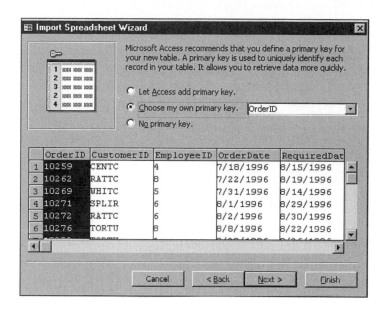

Figure 7.22
Selecting a primary key for the new table.

14. Select the Let Access Add Primary Key option to have Access add an AutoNumber field to the imported table; Access fills in a unique number for each existing row in the worksheet that you're importing. Select the Choose My Own Primary Key option and select the primary-key field in the drop-down list if you know you can use a column in the worksheet or data range as a primary key for the imported table. If this imported table doesn't need a primary key, select the No Primary Key option.

15. Click Next to move to the final dialog of the Import Spreadsheet Wizard (see Figure 7.23). Type the name of the new table in the Import to Table text box; Access uses the name of the worksheet or data range as the default table name. If you want to use the Table Analyzer Wizard to split the imported table into two or more related tables, select the check box labeled I Would Like a Wizard to Analyze My Table After Importing the Data. (You can use the Table Analyzer Wizard at any time on any table by choosing Tools, Analyze, Table.)

16. Click Finish to complete the importing process. Access closes the Import Spreadsheet Wizard and imports the data. When Access completes the import process without errors, it displays the dialog shown in Figure 7.24.

PART

I

CH

7

Access analyzes approximately the first 20 rows of the spreadsheet you are importing and assigns data types to the imported fields based on this analysis. If every cell in a column has a numeric or date value, the columns convert to Number and Date/Time field data types, respectively. If a column contains mixed text and numbers, Access converts the column as a text field. If, however, a column contains numeric data in the first 20 rows (the rows that Access analyzes) and then has one or more text entries, Access doesn't convert these rows.

Figure 7.23
Giving the new table a name in the Import Spreadsheet Wizard's final dialog.

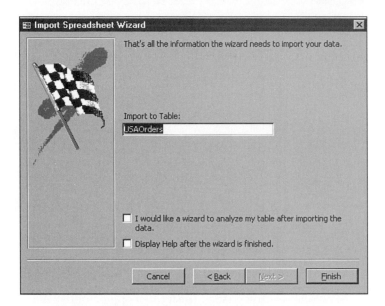

Figure 7.24
The message displayed by the Import Spreadsheet Wizard after successfully importing a spreadsheet.

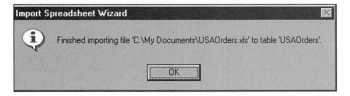

If Access encounters cell values that it can't convert to the data type that it assigned to the imported field, Access creates an Import Errors table with one record for each error. You can review this table, select the records in which the errors are reported, and fix them. A better approach, however, is to correct the cells in the spreadsheet, resave the file, and import the corrected data.

Tip #54 from

R J

The Import Spreadsheet Wizard doesn't display an error message when it encounters inconsistent field data types; it just creates the Import Errors table. You must look in the Database window to see whether the Import Errors table is present. After you resolve the import errors, make sure that you delete the Import Errors table so that you can more easily detect errors the next time you import a spreadsheet or other external file.

The Database window now contains a new table with the name you typed in the final step of the Import Spreadsheet Wizard. If you import another file with the same name as your spreadsheet file name, Access asks if you want to overwrite the existing table.

To verify that you obtained the desired result, double-click the name of the imported table in the Database window to display the new table in Datasheet view. Figure 7.25 illustrates a portion of the Access table created from the USAOrders worksheet in the USAOrders.xls spreadsheet file shown in Figure 7.16.

USAOrders : Table

OrderID	CustomerID	EmployeeID	OrderDate	RequiredDate	ShippedDate
10259	CENTC	4	7/18/1996	8/15/1996	7/25/1996
10262	RATTC	8	7/22/1996	8/19/1996	7/25/1996
10269	WHITC	5	7/31/1996	8/14/1996	8/9/1996
10271	SPLIR	6	8/1/1996	8/29/1996	8/30/1996
10272	RATTC	6	8/2/1996	8/30/1996	8/6/1996
10276	TORTU	8	8/8/1996	8/22/1996	8/14/1996
10293	TORTU	1	8/29/1996	9/26/1996	9/11/1996
10294	RATTC	4	8/30/1996	9/27/1996	9/5/1996
10304	TORTU	1	9/12/1996	10/10/1996	9/17/1996
10305	OLDWO	8	9/13/1996	10/11/1996	10/9/1996
10307	LONEP	2	9/17/1996	10/15/1996	9/25/1996
10308	ANATR	7	9/18/1996	10/16/1996	9/24/1996
10310	THEBI	8	9/20/1996	10/18/1996	9/27/1996
10314	RATTC	1	9/25/1996	10/23/1996	10/4/1996
10316	RATTC	1	9/27/1996	10/25/1996	10/8/1996
10317	LONEP	6	9/30/1996	10/28/1996	10/10/1996
10319	TORTU	7	10/2/1996	10/30/1996	10/11/1996
10322	PERIC	7	10/4/1996	11/1/1996	10/23/1996
10324	SAVEA	9	10/8/1996	11/5/1996	10/10/1996

Record: 1 of 180

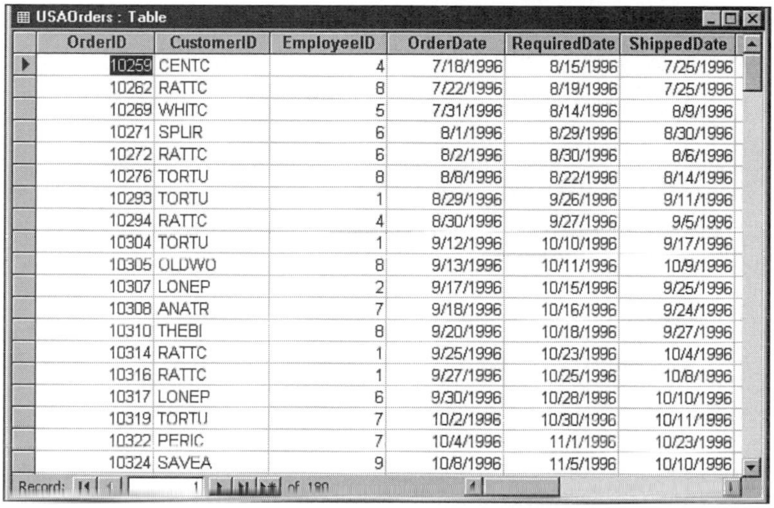

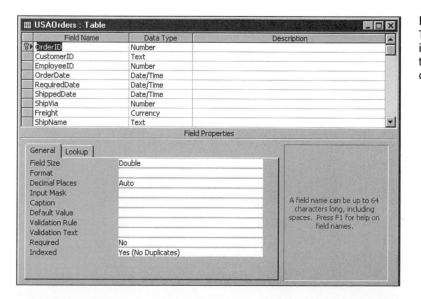

Figure 7.25
The imported Excel worksheet data in an Access table.

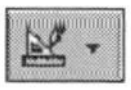

To display the .xls file data types that Access chose, click the Design View toolbar button. Figure 7.26 shows the structure of the new USAOrders table.

USAOrders : Table

Field Name	Data Type	Description
OrderID	Number	
CustomerID	Text	
EmployeeID	Number	
OrderDate	Date/Time	
RequiredDate	Date/Time	
ShippedDate	Date/Time	
ShipVia	Number	
Freight	Currency	
ShipName	Text	

Field Properties

General | Lookup

Field Size	Double
Format	
Decimal Places	Auto
Input Mask	
Caption	
Default Value	
Validation Rule	
Validation Text	
Required	No
Indexed	Yes (No Duplicates)

A field name can be up to 64 characters long, including spaces. Press F1 for help on field names.

Figure 7.26
The structure of the imported USAOrders table based on Excel data types.

After you successfully import the table, you may want to change the properties of the fields. Unlike the procedure with linked files, Access places no restrictions on altering the field properties of imported files.

LINKING EXCEL WORKSHEETS

NEW 2000

Prior to Access 2000, you could link Excel worksheets with the ISAM and ODBC drivers; Access 2000 no longer permits use of the ODBC driver to link Excel worksheets. Like RDBMS tables, the advantages of linking an Excel worksheet are that you always work with the latest version of the worksheet, and you can alter worksheet cell values from within Access.

To link an Excel 2000 worksheet to a Jet 4.0 table, do the following:

1. Open the database to which you want to link the worksheet, if necessary, and choose File, Get External Data, Link Tables to open the Link dialog. Select Microsoft Excel (*.xls) from the Files of Type list.

2. Navigate to the folder containing the worksheet you want to link, select the folder, and click Link to open the Link Spreadsheet Wizard (see Figure 7.27).

Figure 7.27
The first dialog of the Link Spreadsheet Wizard.

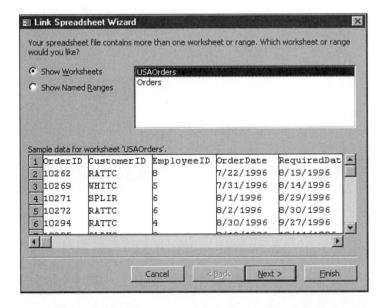

> **Note**
>
> The first Wizard dialog shown in Figure 7.27 appears only if you have more than one worksheet in the Excel workbook, or if a workbook with a single worksheet has at least one name range.

3. Select the worksheet or named range to which you want to link, and then click the Next button.

4. The Wizard automatically detects that the first row contains column headings (see Figure 7.28). If the Wizard guesses incorrectly, mark or clear the First Row Contains Column Headings check box. Click Next to continue.

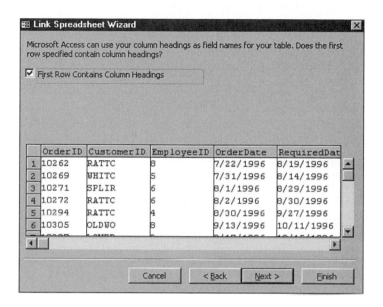

Figure 7.28
The second dialog of the Link Spreadsheet Wizard.

5. The Wizard proposes the name of the worksheet as the table name. Change the table name if you want; then click Finish to link the table. The linked table is identified in your Database window by an Excel icon and an arrow (see Figure 7.29).

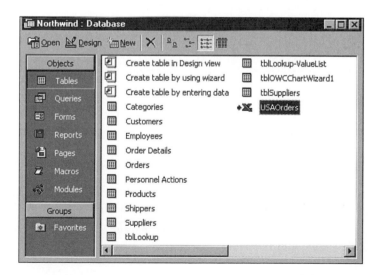

Figure 7.29
The link to an Excel worksheet in the Tables page of the Database window.

PART

I

CH

7

6. Open the linked table in Design view, clicking OK to acknowledge that you can't change the design of a linked table. The Wizard makes the correct choices of data types, with the minor exception that integer values in the OrderID and EmployeeID columns appear as the Double numeric field data type.

WORKING WITH MICROSOFT OUTLOOK AND EXCHANGE FOLDERS

Microsoft Outlook 2000 lets you import from and export data to a wide range of file types, including Jet 4.0 databases. For example, you can export data to the Timex Datalink Watch and import Internet-standard VCARD, iCalendar, or vCalendar files. Outlook's import capability is far more eclectic than that of Access; you can import from the ACT! and ECCO personal information manager (PIM) applications, Lotus Organizer, Sidekick 2.0 and 95, and Schedule+ files.

Tip #55 from

RJ

If you want to put data from ACT!, ECCO, Organizer, or Sidekick into Access 2000, importing to Outlook and exporting to Access is the best alternative until you update these applications to versions that accommodate Jet 4.0.

NEW 2000 Access 2000 adds the Exchange/Outlook Wizard for linking to the contents of Outlook's private and Exchange's public folders. The following two sections show you how to export, import, and link Contacts folders. The Contacts folder is most commonly used with databases; working with other folders follows a similar course.

Note

You must have the Outlook Import/Export engine installed to try the examples in the following two sections. If you haven't installed the engine, you receive a "Would you like to install it now?" message after you specify the action you want to take.

EXPORTING AND IMPORTING JET 4.0 TABLES WITH OUTLOOK

To import an Access table to an Outlook 2000 contacts folder, do the following:

1. Open Outlook and select the folder to which you want to import. (Create a new empty Contacts subfolder when you are testing import and export operations.)

2. Choose File, Import and Export to open the Import and Export Wizard. Select Import from Another File or Program in the Choose an Action to Perform list (see Figure 7.30), and click Next.

3. Select Microsoft Access in the Import a File dialog (see Figure 7.31), and click Next.

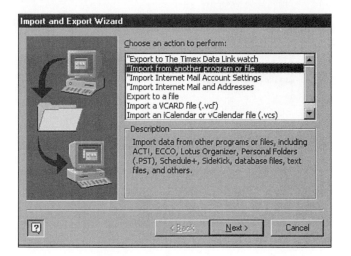

Figure 7.30
Selecting the file option operation in the first Outlook Import and Export Wizard dialog.

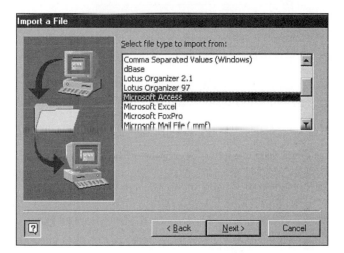

Figure 7.31
Specifying Microsoft Access as the import file type.

4. Click Browse to open the Browse dialog, and then navigate to and select the .mdb file that contains the table you want to import. This example uses Northwind.mdb's Customers table. Select an option for handling duplicates, and then click Next (see Figure 7.32).

PART

I

CH

7

Figure 7.32
Specifying the .mdb file
and handling of duplicate
records.

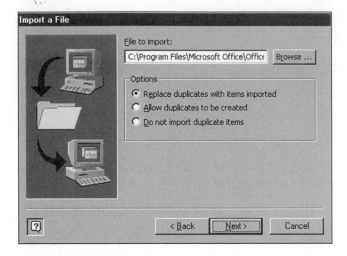

Tip #56 from

Make sure the .mdb file from which you intend to import the data is closed at this point. If
the .mdb file is open, you receive an error message when you attempt to complete the
next step.

5. The destination folder you specified or added in step 1 is selected in the Import a File
dialog (see Figure 7.33). If you didn't select a folder, you must do so at this point. Click
Next.

Figure 7.33
Confirming the destina-
tion folder for the
imported records.

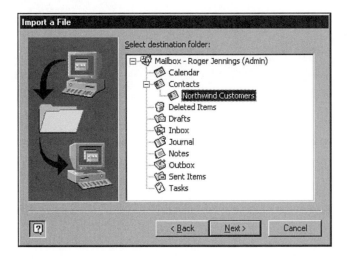

6. Mark the Import *TableName* into the *FolderName* option for the table to import, Customers for this example.

7. Click Map Custom Fields to open the Map Custom Fields dialog, and drag from the left list the fields you want to include in the Contacts list to the appropriate Outlook field name in the right list (see Figure 7.34). Fields that you don't drag to the right list aren't included in the new Contacts folder.

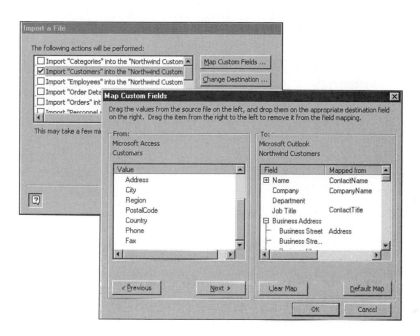

Figure 7.34
Mapping table fields to the Outlook standard Contacts fields.

8. Click OK to close the Map Custom Fields dialog; then click Finish to close the Import File dialog and complete the import process. When the records are imported, Outlook automatically displays them (see Figure 7.35).

Exporting Contacts or other Outlook records to an Access table with the Import and Export Wizard follows the pattern of the preceding steps. Select the folder to export, choose File, Import and Export, select Export to a File, Microsoft Access, confirm the folder selection, specify the destination .mdb file, and export the records to a table with the name of the folder or a name you specify.

Figure 7.35
Outlook 2000 displaying
newly-imported Contacts
records.

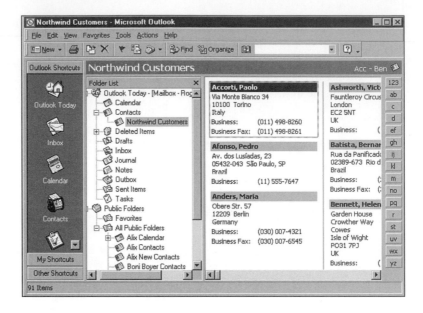

LINKING WITH THE EXCHANGE/OUTLOOK WIZARD

**NEW
2000**

Access's new Exchange/Outlook Wizard provides the capability of linking records in Outlook or Exchange folders to Jet 4.0 table(s). Linking is a better option than importing because your Access table always is up to date with information entered in Outlook, and vice-versa.

Tip #57 from

> Outlook 2000 must be configured as your default email client to enable linking to the Contacts and other folders. To change the default from Outlook Express or another email application to Outlook, launch Internet Explorer (IE) 5.0, choose Tools, Internet Options, click the Programs tab, Select Microsoft Outlook in the E-Mail list, and click OK to close the Internet Options dialog.

To link a Contacts folder to an Access 2000 table, follow these steps:

1. Open the database to which you want to link the Outlook folder and choose File, Get External Data, Link Tables to open the Link dialog.

2. Select Outlook() or Exchange() in the Files of Type list to open the Link Exchange/Outlook Wizard.

3. Expand the nodes as necessary to open the folder to link. This example uses the Northwind Contacts Exchange Public Folder created by copying the personal folder in the preceding section (see Figure 7.36.)

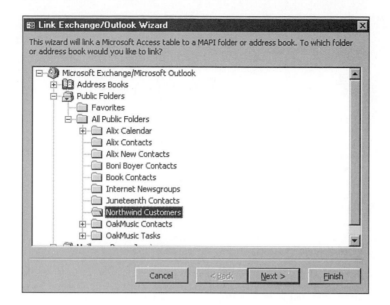

Figure 7.36
Selecting an Exchange
Public Folder to link.

4. Click Next to open the second (and last) Wizard dialog, in which you accept the folder
   name as the table name, or change it to your liking.

5. Click Finish to link the table. Your linked table appears in the Database window, identified by an envelope icon with an adjacent arrow (see Figure 7.37).

Figure 7.37
The linked Exchange
Public Folder item in the
Tables page of the
Database window.

6. Open the linked table in Datasheet view. The rows appear in random order.

7. Select the Company column and apply an ascending sort. The Datasheet view of your
   table appears as shown in figure 7.38.

PART

I

CH

7

Figure 7.38
The linked Outlook folder sorted on the Company field.

The response of linked Exchange public folders to changes, sorting, and other operations is slower than linked database tables due to a combination of Mail API (MAPI) translator and network delays.

IMPORTING TEXT FILES

If the data you want to import into an Access table was developed in a word processor, database, or other application that can't export the data as a .dbf, .wk?, or .xls file, you need to create a text file in one of the text formats supported by Access. (A *text file* is a file with data consisting of characters that you can read with a text editor, such as Windows Notepad or the DOS EDIT.COM text editor.) Most DOS- and Windows-compatible data files created from data in mainframe computers and files converted from nine-track magnetic tapes are text files, and Access imports these files in various formats.

Access refers to the characters that separate fields as *delimiters* or *separators*. In this book, the term *delimiter* refers to characters that identify the end of a field; the term *text identifiers* refers to the single and double quotation marks that you can use to distinguish text from numeric data.

Note

Extended Binary-Coded-Decimal Interchange Code (EBCDIC) is a proprietary format used by IBM to encode data stored on nine-track tape and other data interchange media. EBCDIC is similar to the American National Standards Institute (ANSI) and American Standard Code for Information Interchange (ASCII) codes. You need to convert EBCDIC-encoded data to ANSI or ASCII code before you can import the data into an Access table. Nine-track tape drives designed for PC applications and service bureaus that provide tape-to-disk conversion services handle the EBCDIC-ASCII conversion. The printable (text) characters with values 32 through 127 are the same in ANSI and ASCII, so conversion from ASCII to ANSI (the character set used by Windows and Access) seldom is necessary.

Table 7.2 details the formats that Access supports.

TABLE 7.2   TEXT FILE FORMATS SUPPORTED BY ACCESS 2000

Format	Description
Comma-delimited text files (also called CSV or Comma-Separated Value files)	Commas separate (delimit) fields. The newline pair, carriage return (ASCII character 13), and line feed (ASCII character 10) separate records. Some applications enclose all values within double quotation marks, a format often called *mail-merge* format. Other applications enclose only text (strings) in quotation marks to differentiate between text and numeric values, the standard format for files created by the xBase command COPY TO FILENAME DELIMITED.
Tab-delimited text files (also called ASCII files)	These files treat all values as text and separate fields with tabs. Records are separated by newline pairs. Most word processing applications use this format to export tabular text.
Space-delimited files	Access can use spaces to separate fields in a line of text. The use of spaces as delimiter characters is uncommon because it can cause what should be single fields, such as names and addresses, to be divided inconsistently into different fields.
Fixed-width text files	Access separates (parses) the individual records into fields based on the position of the data items in a line of text. Newline pairs separate records; every record must have exactly the same length. Spaces pad the fields to a specified fixed width. Using spaces to specify field width is the most common format for data exported by mainframes and minicomputers on nine-track tape.

PART

I

CH

7

USING THE IMPORT TEXT WIZARD

To import any of the text file types listed in Table 7.2, you follow a procedure similar to the procedure for importing any external data into Access. To import a text file, follow these steps:

1. Open the database into which you want to import the text file and make the Database window active if necessary.

2. Choose File, Get External Data, Import to open the Import dialog.

3. Select Text Files (*.txt, *.csv, *.tab, or *.asc) in the Files of Type drop-down list. Use the Look In drop-down list to select the folder that contains the text file you want to import and double-click the text file's name. Access now starts the Import Text Wizard (see Figure 7.39).

Figure 7.39
Choosing whether the text file you're importing is delimited or fixed-width text.

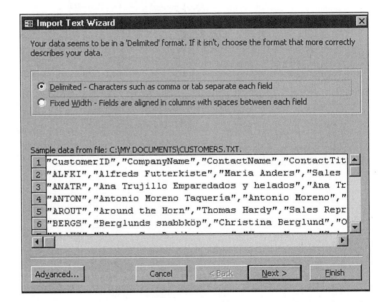

4. Select the Delimited option to import a delimited text file or select Fixed Width to import a fixed-width text file. The Import Text Wizard displays a sample of the text file's contents in the lower portion of the dialog to help you determine the correct file type. Figure 7.39 shows a comma-delimited text file being imported. Click Next to proceed to the next step in the Import Text Wizard. If you selected Delimited as the file type, the Import Text Wizard displays the dialog shown in Figure 7.40; if you selected the Fixed Width option, the Wizard displays the dialog in Figure 7.41.

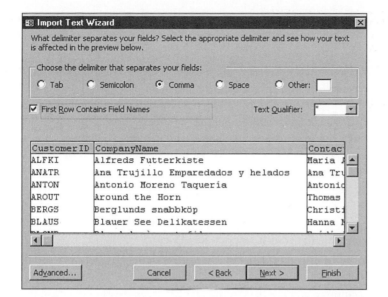

Figure 7.40
The second step of the Import Text Wizard for delimited text files.

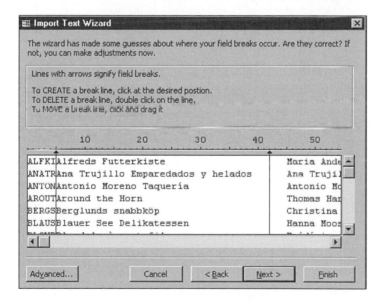

Figure 7.41
The second step of the Import Text Wizard for fixed-width text files.

Tip #58 from

In almost every case, you will select the Delimited option. Use the Delimited option for comma-delimited, tab-delimited, and all other types of delimited text files. Use fixed-width for space-delimited text files and for text files actually formatted as fixed width.

5. If you're importing a delimited text file, select the delimiter character that separates fields in the table (most delimited files use the default comma separator). If the text file you're importing uses a text qualifier other than double quotation marks, type it in the Text Qualifier text box. If the first line in the text file contains field names (such as the column headings in a spreadsheet file), select the First Row Contains Field Names check box. Click Next to move to the next step of the Import Text Wizard.

If you're importing a fixed-width text file, the Import Text Wizard analyzes the columns and makes an approximation about where the field breaks lie. Scan through the sample data at the bottom of the dialog; if the field breaks aren't in the right place, there are too many field breaks, or there aren't enough field breaks, you can add, delete, or move the field breaks that the Import Text Wizard suggests. To move a field break, drag it with the mouse. To remove a field break, double-click it. To add a field break, click at the desired location. When you're satisfied with the field break arrangement, click Next to continue with the Import Text Wizard.

6. The Import Text Wizard displays the dialog shown in Figure 7.42. Choose the In a New Table option to create a new Access table for the imported text file. Choose the In an Existing Table option to add the data in the text file to an existing database table; then select the table to which you want to add the data in the accompanying drop-down list. Click Next to continue with the Import Text Wizard. (If you selected the In an Existing Table option, the Import Text Wizard skips directly to its final step, step 9 of this procedure.)

Figure 7.42
Choosing whether to create a new table or to add the imported text data to an existing table.

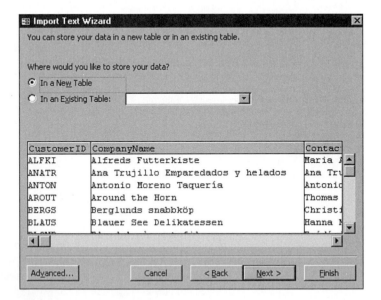

Access matches fields from left to right when you import a text file into an existing table. You must make sure that the data types of the fields in the imported text file match those in the Access table; otherwise, the added data values aren't inserted into the correct fields. In most cases, you end up with many import errors in the Import Errors table. If you're not certain that the format of your input data exactly matches the format of the desired table, you can choose the In a New Table option and then place your data in the existing table with an Append query, as discussed in Chapter 11, "Modifying Data with Action Queries."

7. The Import Text Wizard displays the dialog shown in Figure 7.43. The Wizard lets you edit field names, choose whether to use index and what kind to use for each field, and adjust each field's data type. To set the options for a field, click the field column at the bottom of the dialog to select it; you then can edit the field name, select an index method in the Indexed drop-down list, and select the data type for the field in the Data Type drop-down list. Select the Do Not Import Field (Skip) check box if you don't want to import the select field column. When you're satisfied with your field settings, click Next.

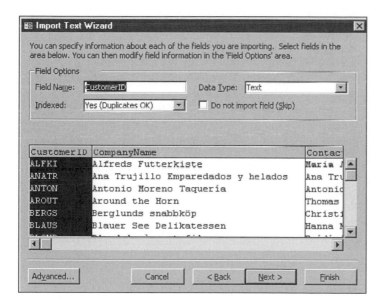

Figure 7.43
Editing field names and selecting the index type and the data types for fields.

8. The Import Text Wizard displays the dialog in Figure 7.44. Choose the appropriate option for the primary key: allow Access to add a new field with an automatically generated primary key, select an existing field to use as a primary key yourself, or import the table without a primary key. Click Next.

PART

I

CH

7

Figure 7.44
Selecting a primary key
for the imported text
data.

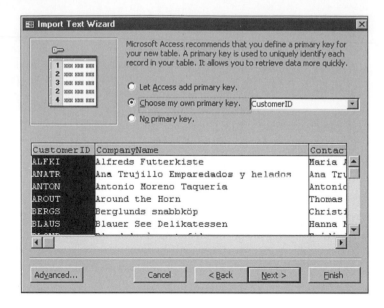

9. The Import Text Wizard displays its final dialog, shown in Figure 7.45. You must type the name for the new imported table. The Import Text Wizard displays this dialog even if you chose to import the text file into an existing table. Access enters either a default table name that's the same as the original name of the text file or the table name you selected for importing the data into. Edit the table name, or type a different table name, if you want. Click Finish to import the text file.

Figure 7.45
Giving the new table a
name in the Import Text
Wizard's final dialog.

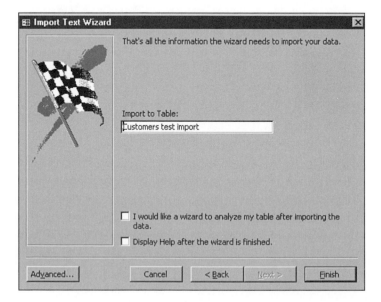

The Import Text Wizard imports the text file and displays a success message. As with other import operations, Access creates an Import Errors table to document any errors that occurred during the import process and displays a message informing you that errors occurred.

The specific values you should select for field delimiters and text qualifiers are described in following sections, along with some tips on importing fixed-width text files.

THE IMPORT TEXT WIZARD'S ADVANCED OPTIONS

Occasionally, you may find that you import text data from the same text file more than once or that you have several text files with the same format. A typical situation in many corporations is that data from the company's mainframe computer system is provided to desktop computer users in the form of a text file report. Frequently, reports are delivered over the network in a text file, using the same name for the text file each time. You can use the Import Text Wizard's advanced options to configure Access to import a text file and save these options so that you don't have to go through every step in the Wizard every time you import the text file.

Every dialog of the Import Text Wizard has an Advanced button. Clicking this button displays a special dialog that shows all the Import Text Wizard settings in a single dialog and allows you to select a few options, such as date formatting, that don't appear in the regular Import Text Wizard dialogs. If you select the Delimited option, the Customers Import Specification dialog has the options and field grid shown in Figure 7.46. If you select the Fixed-Width option, the dialog has the options and field grid shown in Figure 7.47

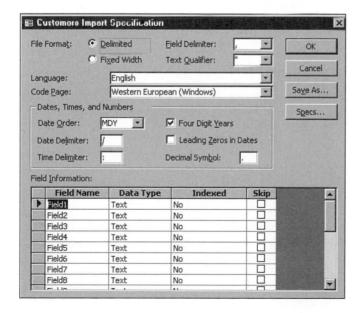

Figure 7.46
Setting import specifications for delimited text files.

Figure 7.47
Specifying import specifications for fixed-width
text files.

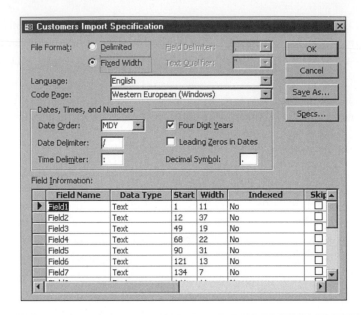

Tip #59 from

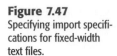

For text files you intend to import only once, it's much easier to import the file by stepping
through the Import Text Wizard.

You can select the following options in the Advanced dialog:

- *File Format.* Use these option buttons to choose which type of text file format you're
  importing: delimited or fixed width. The file format you select determines which specific options are available.

- *Field Delimiter.* Use this drop-down list to select the symbol that delimits fields in the
  text file. This option is disabled for fixed-width text files.

- *Text Qualifier.* Use this drop-down list to select the symbol that marks the beginning
  and end of text strings in the text file. This option is disabled for fixed-width text files.

- *Language* and *Code Page.* Use these lists to handle localized text files.

- *Date Order.* If the data in the text file uses a European or other date format that varies
  from the month-day-year format typical in the United States, select the appropriate
  date order in the Date Order drop-down list.

- *Date Delimiter and Time Delimiter.* Type the symbol used to separate the month, day,
  and year in a date in the Date Delimiter text box; type the symbol used to separate
  hours, minutes, and seconds in the Time Delimiter text box. For example, in the
  United States the date delimiter is the slash (/) character, and the time delimiter is the
  colon (:).

- *Four Digit Years.* Mark this check box if the dates in the text file use four digits for the
  year, such as 8/28/1999.

- *Leading Zeros in Dates.* Mark this check box if the dates in the text file have leading zeros, such as 08/09/1999.

- *Decimal Symbol.* Type the symbol used for the decimal separator in numeric values in the text box. In the United States, the decimal symbol is the period (.), but many European nations use a comma (,).

- *Field Information.* The appearance of this grid depends on the file format you select. For a delimited text file, the Field Information grid lets you edit field names, select the field's data type and indexing, and specify whether to skip the field in importing (refer to Figure 7.46). For a fixed-width text file, the Field Information grid lets you perform the same operations but adds specifications for the starting column and width of each field (refer to Figure 7.47).

- *Save As.* Click this button to display the Save Import/Export Specification dialog. By typing a name for the specification and clicking OK, you can save the file import settings for later use.

- *Specs.* Click this button to display the Load Import/Export Specification dialog. Select a previously saved specification and click OK to use import settings that you defined previously.

The following sections on using delimited and fixed-width text files discuss the application of some of these advanced options in greater detail.

Using Delimited Text Files

Delimited files can accept a wide variety of field- and record-delimiting characters. The native format of WordPerfect secondary merge files, for example, uses control characters to separate fields and records. Access provides commas, tabs, and spaces as standard field delimiters. You can type any printable character, such as an asterisk or a dollar sign, in the text box as a delimiter (refer to Figure 7.41). Because spaces and other special-character delimiting are seldom used, this chapter discusses only comma-delimited (.csv) and tab-delimited files.

Word processing applications use both commas and tabs as delimiters in the mail-merge files that they or other applications create for personalized documents. The newline pair is universally used to indicate the end of a record in mail-merge files; a record always consists of a single line of text.

Comma-Delimited Text Files Without Text-Identifier Characters

Comma-delimited files come with or without quotation marks surrounding text fields. The quotation marks, usually the standard double quotation marks ("), identify the fields within them as having the Text data type. Fields without quotation marks are processed as numeric values if they contain only numbers. Not all applications offer this capability; .csv files, for example, exported by Excel don't enclose text within quotation marks. Figure 7.48 shows a typical Excel .csv file opened in Windows Notepad.

Figure 7.48
A .csv text file exported by Excel and displayed in Windows Notepad.

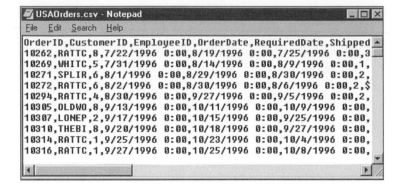

Tip #60 from

Using Notepad to view files that fit within its 60KB file-size limitation is a quick way to determine the type of text file with which you are dealing. If the file is longer than 60KB, you can use Windows WordPad to view the file. Make sure, however, that you don't save the file as a .doc file after you view or edit it. If you used WordPad to edit the file, choose File, Save As and specify a text (.txt) file.

Caution

If you export the Orders table from Northwind.mdb to Excel, and then use Excel to create an Orders.csv file and import the file into an Access table, you may receive an extraordinary number of errors. Most of these errors are due to a mixture of numeric values for United States ZIP codes and alphanumeric values used for Canadian and European postal codes.

The first data cell in the Postal Code column is a number, so the Access import procedure determines that the field should have the Number field data type. Therefore, mixed-value fields (letters and numbers) cause import errors. When you are working with Access tables, a wise policy is to not import delimited text files without text-identification characters.

COMMA-DELIMITED TEXT FILES WITH TEXT-IDENTIFIER CHARACTERS

The default delimited text file type of dBASE, named .sdf for Standard Data Format and created by the COPY TO FILENAME DELIMITED command, creates comma-delimited files with text fields enclosed in double quotation marks. (Date and Numeric field types don't have quotation marks.) This type of delimited file is standard in many other database systems, as well as project and personal information management applications. Figure 7.49 shows an example of a delimited text file containing text qualifiers.

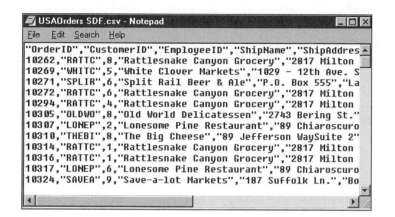

Figure 7.49
A dBASE .sdf file displayed in Windows Notepad.

> **Note**
>
> When you create a DOS dBASE III+ file from an Access file, Access translates characters with ANSI values 128 through 255 to the PC-8 character set used by character-based DOS and OS/2 applications. Letters with diacritical marks and special characters of Scandinavian and romanized Slavic languages don't have the same values in PC-8. These letters and characters appear onscreen as black rectangles because the PC-8 values don't correspond to printable ANSI values. For text files that don't use the Windows ANSI character set, use the Import Text Wizard's advanced options to select the appropriate character set.

TAB-DELIMITED TEXT FILES

Word processing applications often use tab characters to separate fields in mail-merge files. These characters usually define table fields when you convert conventional text to tabular format (and vice versa) in word processors such as Word 2000. Tab-delimited text files rarely use text-qualifier characters. When exporting tab-delimited text files (described later in this chapter), Access adds double quotation marks as text-identifier characters so that Word doesn't interpret embedded newline pairs (carriage return and line feed, or CR/LF) in text fields as the end of the record. (Allowing embedded newline pairs in text fields isn't a recommended database design practice.)

Many organizations acquire RDBMSs because the data becomes too large for their word processing application to maintain mailing lists for direct-mail advertising and other promotional and fund-raising purposes. RDBMSs also let you create specialized merge data files for specific types of customers, ranges of ZIP codes, and other parameters you select.

Fortunately, Access has a simple process for converting the merge data files that most word processors use to text files that an Access database application can import and maintain. In Word 2000, for example, you open the merge data file in whatever format you use (usually the native .doc) and save the document in Text Only (.txt) format under a different file name. WordPerfect 5+ (using CONVERT.EXE) and WordPerfect for Windows offer a variety of export formats for their secondary merge files. Unless you have a specific file type in mind, select the tab-delimited format for these files.

HANDLING FIXED-WIDTH TEXT FILES

If you have a choice of text file formats for the data you plan to import into Access, avoid using fixed-width text files by choosing a delimited file format. If you are importing data created by a mainframe or minicomputer, however, the data probably is in fixed-width format, in which case you must name the fields rather than rely on the first line of the text file to provide names for you. Fixed-width text files seldom come with a field name header in the first line.

A fixed-width text file resembles the file in Figure 7.50. Fixed-width text files often contain more spaces than data characters. In a tab-delimited file, the spaces between fields aren't included in the file itself, but are added by the text editor when tab characters (ASCII or ANSI character 9) are encountered. In a fixed-width file, an ASCII or ANSI character 32 represents each space.

Figure 7.50
Padding fixed-width records to the same length with spaces.

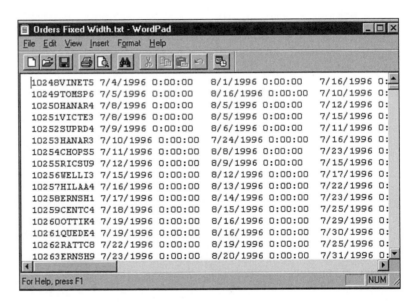

<table>
<tr><td>10248VINET5</td><td>7/4/1996 0:00:00</td><td>8/1/1996 0:00:00</td><td>7/16/1996 0:</td></tr>
<tr><td>10249TOMSP6</td><td>7/5/1996 0:00:00</td><td>8/16/1996 0:00:00</td><td>7/10/1996 0:</td></tr>
<tr><td>10250HANAR4</td><td>7/8/1996 0:00:00</td><td>8/5/1996 0:00:00</td><td>7/12/1996 0:</td></tr>
<tr><td>10251VICTE3</td><td>7/8/1996 0:00:00</td><td>8/5/1996 0:00:00</td><td>7/15/1996 0:</td></tr>
<tr><td>10252SUPRD4</td><td>7/9/1996 0:00:00</td><td>8/6/1996 0:00:00</td><td>7/11/1996 0:</td></tr>
<tr><td>10253HANAR3</td><td>7/10/1996 0:00:00</td><td>7/24/1996 0:00:00</td><td>7/16/1996 0:</td></tr>
<tr><td>10254CHOPS5</td><td>7/11/1996 0:00:00</td><td>8/8/1996 0:00:00</td><td>7/23/1996 0:</td></tr>
<tr><td>10255RICSU9</td><td>7/12/1996 0:00:00</td><td>8/9/1996 0:00:00</td><td>7/15/1996 0:</td></tr>
<tr><td>10256WELLI3</td><td>7/15/1996 0:00:00</td><td>8/12/1996 0:00:00</td><td>7/17/1996 0:</td></tr>
<tr><td>10257HILAA4</td><td>7/16/1996 0:00:00</td><td>8/13/1996 0:00:00</td><td>7/22/1996 0:</td></tr>
<tr><td>10258ERNSH1</td><td>7/17/1996 0:00:00</td><td>8/14/1996 0:00:00</td><td>7/23/1996 0:</td></tr>
<tr><td>10259CENTC4</td><td>7/18/1996 0:00:00</td><td>8/15/1996 0:00:00</td><td>7/25/1996 0:</td></tr>
<tr><td>10260OTTIK4</td><td>7/19/1996 0:00:00</td><td>8/16/1996 0:00:00</td><td>7/29/1996 0:</td></tr>
<tr><td>10261QUEDE4</td><td>7/19/1996 0:00:00</td><td>8/16/1996 0:00:00</td><td>7/30/1996 0:</td></tr>
<tr><td>10262RATTC8</td><td>7/22/1996 0:00:00</td><td>8/19/1996 0:00:00</td><td>7/25/1996 0:</td></tr>
<tr><td>10263ERNSH9</td><td>7/23/1996 0:00:00</td><td>8/20/1996 0:00:00</td><td>7/31/1996 0:</td></tr>
</table>

Note

The fields of fixed-width text files often run together; the first four fields of the Orders Fixed Width.txt file shown in Figure 7.50 are Order ID (five digits), Customer ID (four letters), Employee ID (one digit), and Order Date (16 characters). The Order Date field is padded with spaces to a width of 16 characters. The appearance of the data in Figure 7.50 is typical of COBOL "text dumps" from mainframe and minicomputer tables. If you have the COBOL file description for the fixed-width table, it's far easier to complete the import specification.

 If you encounter errors during importing, see "Importing Fixed-Width Text Files" in the "Troubleshooting" section at the end of this chapter.

APPENDING TEXT DATA TO AN EXISTING TABLE

Access lets you append data from text files to an existing table. You can update an imported file with new text data by appending it directly from the source text file—rather than by creating a new Access table—and then appending the new table to the existing one.

You can append a text file to an existing table by following these steps:

1. Make a backup copy of your table in the same database or another database, in case an error occurs during the importing operation.

2. Choose File, Get External Data, Import and then select a text file as though you're going to import it to a new table.

3. Make sure that you select the In an Existing Table option and specify a table name in step 3 of the Import Text Wizard (refer to Figure 7.42).

4. If you used the Advanced button to create and save an import specification, click Advanced to display the one of advanced options dialogs, and then click Specs to load the previously saved import specification.

5. Proceed with the importation process as you would for any other text file.

At the end of the appending process, a message box appears. The Import Errors table displays any errors.

Note

Maintaining a backup copy of the table to which you are appending files is important. If you have a problem with field delimiters or field lengths, or if you accidentally select the wrong import specification for the file, you can end up with one error for each appended record. Then if you don't have a backup file, you must delete the appended records and start over. To use a backup table file, close and delete the damaged table. Then choose Edit, Rename to change the name of the backup table to the name of the damaged table.

USING THE CLIPBOARD TO IMPORT DATA

If another Windows application generates the data you want to import, you can use the Windows Clipboard to transfer the data without creating a file. This technique is useful for making corrections to a single record with many fields or for appending new records to a table. This process requires a table with the proper field structure so that you can paste the data copied to the Clipboard into the other application. Pasting rows from an Excel spreadsheet, for example, requires a table with fields containing data types that correspond to those of each column that you copy to the Clipboard. Other Windows applications that can copy tabular data to the Clipboard use similar techniques.

NEW 2000 In addition to the standard Windows Clipboard, Office 2000 has its own enhanced Office Clipboard. The Office Clipboard can collect up to 12 items to paste into your Office 2000 application. The Office Clipboard isn't evident until you do two Clipboard collect operations—cut or copy—in a row. Figure 7.51 shows the Office Clipboard toolbar with several collection items from different Windows applications.

Figure 7.51
The Office Clipboard toolbar with several items available to all Office 2000 members.

Although the Office Clipboard can be used to paste only into another Office 2000 application, the items can be collected from other non-Office Windows applications.

PASTING NEW RECORDS TO A TABLE

To import data from the Clipboard and then append the data to an existing table or table structure, use the following procedure:

1. Open the application you are using—in this case, Microsoft Excel—to copy the data to the Clipboard. Then open the file containing the data.

2. Select the range to be appended to the table (see Figure 7.52). The Excel columns you select must start with the column that corresponds to the first field of your Access table. You don't, however, need to copy all the columns that correspond to fields in your table. Access supplies blank values in the columns of your appended records that aren't included in your Excel range. Remember that if any of the columns you select contain formulas, the values must be frozen.

Figure 7.52
Selecting cells in Excel to be appended to an Access table by copying to the Clipboard.

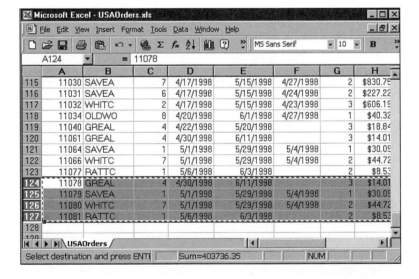

3. To copy the selected cells to the Clipboard, press Ctrl+C or choose Edit, Copy.

4. Launch Access if necessary; then in Datasheet view, open the table to which you're appending the records.

5. Choose Paste Append from Access's Edit menu or click the item in the Office Clipboard. If no errors occur during the pasting process, a message box reports how many new records you are about to add (see Figure 7.53). Click Yes. The records are appended to the bottom of your Access table (see Figure 7.54). Choose Records, Remove Filter/Sort to place the appended records in the correct order.

Figure 7.53
The message that appears when Access successfully appends records pasted from the Clipboard.

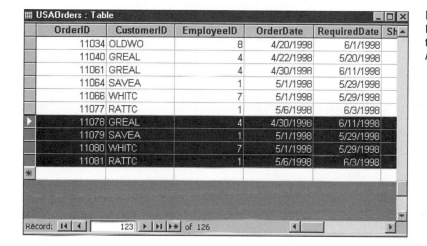

Figure 7.54
Records appended from the Clipboard to an Access table.

Note

The fields you add to a table by using Paste Append must correspond (from left to right) to the fields in the table you are pasting the data into (the target). You can't, therefore, paste append records into a table with an AutoNumber field unless the records you're appending have already been assigned unique numeric values greater than the highest AutoNumber value now existing in the target table. Otherwise, the fields of the pasted data don't match the left-to-right order of the fields in the target table, and all the pasted records will end up in the Paste Errors table.

 If you encounter paste errors, see "Importing Spreadsheets" in the "Troubleshooting" section at the end of this chapter.

PART

I

CH

7

Errors caused by duplicate primary-key violations result in the following series of cascading message boxes:

1. Figure 7.55 shows the first message you receive that indicates a primary-key violation. Click OK.

Figure 7.55
The message informing you that a pasted record duplicates a primary-key value.

2. A message box enables you to suppress further error messages (see Figure 7.56). To cancel the append operation, click Cancel. Otherwise, click Yes to try to paste the remaining records without reporting further errors. If you want to see which errors occur as they are encountered, click No.

Figure 7.56
Choosing whether to view error messages for each pasted record.

3. A message box reports where the records that couldn't be pasted were placed (see Figure 7.57). Click OK.

Figure 7.57
The message reporting that some records couldn't be pasted.

Figure 7.58 illustrates the result of this Pandora's box of messages. The set of four records copied to the Clipboard from Excel had all been previously pasted into the Access table; all four records duplicated key field values in the existing table. Access pasted records without problems into the table and inserted the four records with duplicate key values into a Paste Errors table.

Paste Errors : Table				
Field0	Field1	Field2	Field3	Fi(
11078	GREAL	4	4/30/1998	6/11/19
11079	SAVEA	1	5/1/1998	5/29/19
11080	WHITC	7	5/1/1998	5/29/19
11081	RATTC	1	5/6/1998	6/3/199

Record: 14 4 [1] ▶ ▶I ▶* of 4

Figure 7.58
The Paste Errors table showing records that Access couldn't paste from the Clipboard.

If you specified one or more primary-key fields for your table, records that duplicate key field values aren't appended. Tables without primary-key fields don't preclude adding duplicate records.

The capability to index a non-key field with the condition "no duplicates allowed" is useful when you make new entries into a spreadsheet or word processing document and want to append the new entries as records to a table. You preserve the uniqueness of the records by preventing the addition of records that duplicate records already in your table.

Note

When pasting or importing large numbers of records to a table, you must specify primary-key fields or a no-duplicates-allowed index for fields that later may become the primary key before you import any data. If you import the data before you create the primary-key fields index, you may find many duplicate records in the table. Then when Access tries to create a no-duplicates index on the key fields, you see the message "Can't have duplicate key." You must manually review all the added records for duplicates because Access doesn't create an Errors table in this case.

If, however, the data you are importing contains redundant information that you ultimately will remove to one or more secondary tables, you must import every record. Don't assign key fields or no-duplicates indexes in this case.

Tip #61 from

If you encounter the "Can't have duplicate key" error message when trying to establish a primary key, you can quickly find the duplicates by opening a new query and selecting the Find Duplicates Query Wizard. This Wizard creates a query that locates the duplicates without your having to search through each record.

REPLACING RECORDS BY PASTING FROM THE CLIPBOARD

You can replace existing records in an Access table by pasting data in the Clipboard over the records. This process is useful when you're updating records with data from another Windows application. The data you paste must have a one-to-one column-to-field correspondence and must begin with the first field of the table. You don't need to paste new data in all the fields, however. If no data is pasted in a field that's outside the copied data's range, that field retains its original values.

To use data in the Clipboard to replace existing records in a table, follow this procedure:

1. Select and copy the data from the other application that you want to paste to the Clipboard, using the method previously described for appending records from Clipboard data.

   If you choose more than one row of data in Excel, for example, the rows must have a one-to-one correspondence with the records to be replaced in the Access table. The one-to-one correspondence is likely to occur only if the table is indexed and the source data you are copying is sorted in the same order as the index. You can paste only contiguous rows from Excel.

2. Open your Access table. To select the records to be replaced by the Clipboard data, click the selection button for a single record or drag the mouse across the buttons for multiple records.

   If you're replacing multiple records, the number of records you select must be equal to or exceed the number of rows you copied to the Clipboard. If the number of records selected is less than the number of rows, the remaining rows are ignored.

   If you're replacing records in a table with key fields or a no-duplicates index, the columns of the replacement data corresponding to the key or indexed fields of the table must match exactly the key fields of the selected records. Otherwise, you see the key duplication error message sequence.

3. Choose Paste from Access's Edit menu. In this case, the contents of the existing records are overwritten rather than appended, and you see a dialog that tells you how many records will be replaced.

When you use Paste for a replacement record rather than Paste Append for a new record with an identical key field value, Access suppresses the key violation error messages.

Note

If you don't select one or more records to be replaced by the Pasting operation, and the caret is located within a data cell of one of your records or a data cell is selected, Access attempts to paste all the data in the Clipboard to this one cell, rather than to the records. If the data doesn't create a mismatch type error or exceed 255 characters (if the caret is in a Text field), you don't receive a warning message. If you notice unexpected data values in the cell, Access pasted all the data to a single cell. Press Esc before selecting another record; Access restores the original value of the data cell.

EXPORTING DATA FROM ACCESS TABLES

You can export data contained in Access tables in any format you can use to import data, with the exception of Visual FoxPro files. The most common export operation with PC RDBMSs is the creation of mail-merge files, used with word processing applications and spreadsheet files. In most cases, you may want to export the result of a query, enabling you to select specific records to export rather than the entire contents of a file. Exporting tables created from action queries is discussed in Chapter 11.

EXPORTING DATA THROUGH THE WINDOWS CLIPBOARD

If a Windows application is to use your exported data, the simplest method to export data is to copy the records you want to export to the Windows Clipboard and then paste the data into the other application. You can copy specific groups of contiguous records to the Clipboard by using the techniques described in Chapter 5, "Entering, Editing, and Validating Data in Tables."

To create a merge data file from the Customers table of the Northwind sample database for use with Word, follow these steps:

1. Open the Northwind.mdb database.
2. Open the Customers table.
3. Select the records to copy by selecting the upper-left corner of the block with the F2 key, holding down the Shift key, and using the arrow keys to define the records you want to copy to the Clipboard. Alternatively, you can select the area to copy by placing the cursor at the upper-left corner of the block you want to copy; the cursor turns into a big plus symbol. Hold down the left mouse button and drag to the lower-right corner of the block. Datasheet view should look like the window in Figure 7.59. (If you want to select all fields of all records in the table, choose Edit, Select All Records.)

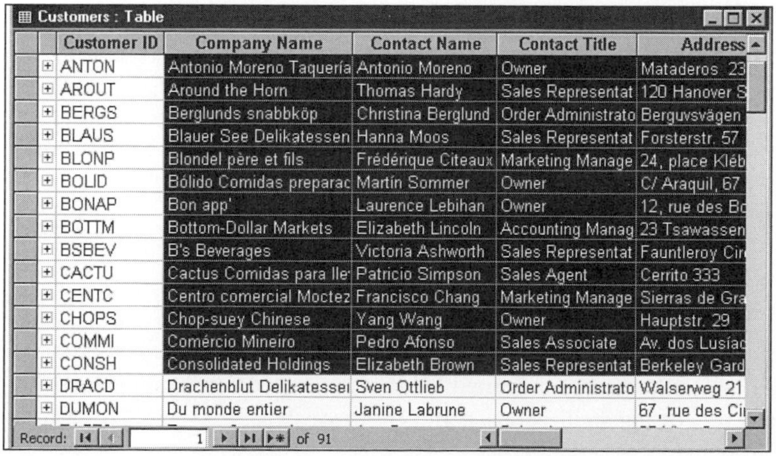

Customer ID	Company Name	Contact Name	Contact Title	Address
ANTON	Antonio Moreno Taquería	Antonio Moreno	Owner	Mataderos 23
AROUT	Around the Horn	Thomas Hardy	Sales Representat	120 Hanover S
BERGS	Berglunds snabbköp	Christina Berglund	Order Administrato	Berguvsvägen
BLAUS	Blauer See Delikatessen	Hanna Moos	Sales Representat	Forsterstr. 57
BLONP	Blondel père et fils	Frédérique Citeaux	Marketing Manage	24, place Kléb
BOLID	Bólido Comidas preparac	Martín Sommer	Owner	C/ Araquil, 67
BONAP	Bon app'	Laurence Lebihan	Owner	12, rue des Bo
BOTTM	Bottom-Dollar Markets	Elizabeth Lincoln	Accounting Manag	23 Tsawassen
BSBEV	B's Beverages	Victoria Ashworth	Sales Representat	Fauntleroy Cir
CACTU	Cactus Comidas para lle	Patricio Simpson	Sales Agent	Cerrito 333
CENTC	Centro comercial Moctez	Francisco Chang	Marketing Manage	Sierras de Gra
CHOPS	Chop-suey Chinese	Yang Wang	Owner	Hauptstr. 29
COMMI	Comércio Mineiro	Pedro Afonso	Sales Associate	Av. dos Lusíac
CONSH	Consolidated Holdings	Elizabeth Brown	Sales Representat	Berkeley Gard
DRACD	Drachenblut Delikatesse	Sven Ottlieb	Order Administrato	Walserweg 21
DUMON	Du monde entier	Janine Labrune	Owner	67, rue des Ci

Figure 7.59
Selecting records in an Access table to copy to the Clipboard.

4. Press Ctrl+C or choose <u>E</u>dit, <u>C</u>opy to copy the selected records to the Clipboard.

5. Open Word and choose <u>F</u>ile, <u>N</u>ew to create a new document for your merge data file.

6. Press Ctrl+V or choose <u>E</u>dit, <u>P</u>aste to paste the records from the Clipboard into your new document. Access 2000 pastes the records as a fully formatted table in Word (see Figure 7.60). The column widths you select in Access are used to define the column widths of the Word table.

Figure 7.60
Access data pasted into a Word document as a fully formatted table.

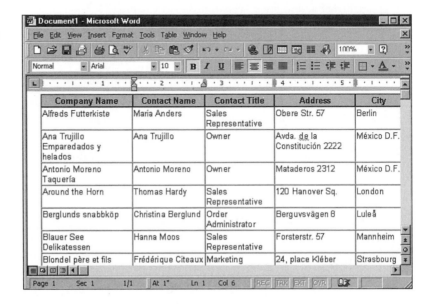

When you copy Access records to the Clipboard, the first line contains field names, no matter what group of records you select. If you append individual records or groups of records to those already pasted to a document in another application, you must manually remove the duplicated field names.

Tip #62 from

The field names pasted into Word documents contain spaces. Spaces, however, aren't allowed in the first row (field names) for merge data documents. Delete the spaces or replace them with underscores so that Word accepts the names. If you don't remove the spaces, you receive an error message when you try to use the document during the merge operation.

EXPORTING DATA AS A TEXT FILE

Exporting a table involves a sequence of operations similar to importing a file with the same format. To export a table as a comma-delimited file that you can use as a merge file with a wide variety of word processing applications, complete these steps:

1. Activate the Database window, display the Tables shortcut, and select the table you want to export.

2. Choose File, Export.

3. Access displays the Export Table *Tablename To* dialog. Select Text Files in the Save as Type drop-down list (the title of the dialog changes to Export Table *Tablename As*, as shown in Figure 7.61). Use the Save In drop-down list to select the drive and folder in which you want to store the exported file, type a name for the exported file in the File Name text box, and then click Save.

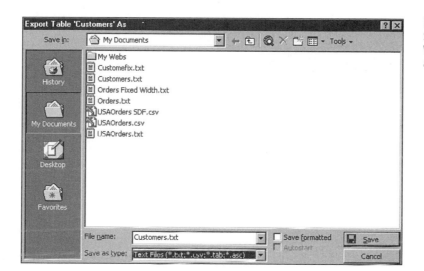

Figure 7.61
Starting the Text Export Wizard by saving a table as a text file.

4. Access starts the Text Export Wizard. Using the Text Export Wizard, including its advanced options, is the same as using the Import Text Wizard described previously, except that the result is an external file instead of an Access table. (When exporting a text file, the Text Export Wizard doesn't have a step to edit field names or select field data types; these options aren't relevant when exporting data.)

To finish exporting the text file, follow the procedures as though you were importing a text file. Figure 7.62 shows the exported Customers table from the Northwind.mdb database displayed by Windows Notepad.

Note

The two highlighted lines in Figure 7.62 are a single record from the Access table that was split into two text records during the export process. A newline pair is included in the Address field of the record for Consolidated Holdings. The purpose of the newline pair is to separate a single field into two lines—Berkeley Gardens and 12 Brewery. Use of newline pairs within fields causes many problems with exported files. As mentioned earlier, use of embedded newline pairs in text fields isn't good database design practice. Use two address fields if you need secondary address lines.

PART

I

CH

7

Figure 7.62
A comma-delimited text file exported from the Customers table.

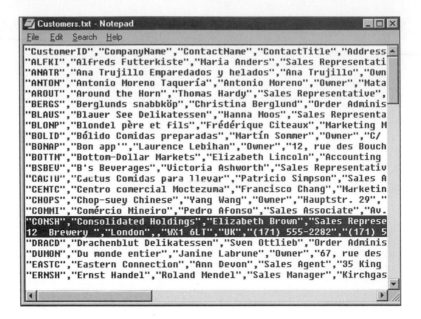

The records in files created by Access are exported in the order of the primary key. Any other order you may have created is ignored. If you don't assign primary-key fields, the records are exported in the sequence in which you entered them into the table.

EXPORTING DATA IN OTHER FILE FORMATS

In addition to text files, you can export data to any other file format that Access can import. Access supports exports to the following file formats:

- Excel .xls files (versions 3.0 through 2000)
- Lotus 1-2-3 .wk? files
- Rich Text Format (.rtf) files for Microsoft Word and other Windows word processing applications
- Hypertext Markup Language (.htm) for static display of data in pages delivered from any Web server
- Active Server Pages (.asp) for static display of data in browser-independent Web pages delivered from Internet Information Server 3+

- Paradox for DOS 3.x, 4.x, 5.0, 7.x, and 8.x; versions 7.x and 8.x require the BDE
- dBASE III/III+, IV, 5.0, and 7.0; version 7.0 requires the BDE.
- Any format supported by an installed ODBC driver, except export of Visual FoxPro files

TROUBLESHOOTING

THE INCORRECT PASSWORD DIALOG

You receive a "Can't decrypt file" message, even though the file isn't encrypted.

If you type a wrong password or just press Enter, Access informs you that it can't decrypt the file. You do, however, get another opportunity to type the password or click Cancel to terminate the attempt (see Figure 7.63).

Figure 7.63
The message indicating an incorrect password entry to a Paradox 5 table.

THE NULL VALUE IN INDEX DIALOG

You encounter a "Can't have Null value in index" message.

Occasionally, older Paradox .px index files don't have an index value for a record; when this situation occurs, you see a warning dialog with the message "Can't have Null value in index." Usually, you can disregard the message and continue linking or importing the file. The offending record, however, may not appear in the table; fixing the file in Paradox and starting over is better than ignoring the message.

THE MISSING MEMO FILE DIALOG

A "Cannot locate the requested Xbase memo file" message appears.

Both dBASE and Paradox use additional memo files to store the data from memo fields in a particular table. dBASE memo files have the .dbt file type, and Paradox memo files have the .mb file type. Access correctly decides that it can't import or link an external table if it can't open the table's associated memo file—either because the memo file doesn't exist, isn't in the same folder as the table with which it is associated, or contains nontext data.

If the table you're trying to link or import is a dBASE table, Access displays the error dialog shown in Figure 7.64. If the table you're trying to link is a Paradox table, however, you receive the less informative error message shown in Figure 7.65. For assistance in solving the problem, click the Help button. To close the error dialog, click OK; Access then cancels the linking or importation.

PART

I

CH

7

Figure 7.64
The error message when Access can't open a required dBASE or FoxPro memo file.

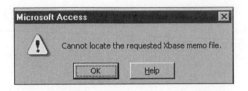

Figure 7.65
The error message when Access can't open a required Paradox memo file.

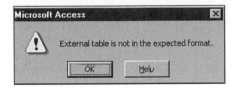

IMPORTING FIXED-WIDTH TEXT FILES

When importing tables created from fixed-width text files, many errors occur.

You probably miscalculated one or more of the starting positions of a field. Locate the first field name with a problem; the names following it usually have problems, too. Close all open tables. From the Database window, select the table you imported and press Delete. If you have an Import Errors table, delete it, too. You can't delete an open table. Perform the importation process again and reposition the field breaks in the Import Text Wizard. Remember that Access analyzes only the first 20 lines of the text file, so the guesses it makes about where to position the field breaks might be incorrect and might not allow enough room for the actual width of a field.

IMPORTING SPREADSHEETS

Paste errors occur when I paste spreadsheet cells into a table.

Errors usually occur during the Paste/Append process for one of two reasons—the data types in the Excel cells don't match those in the corresponding fields of your Access table, or you attempted to paste records with data that duplicates information in key fields of the table. Both error types cause Access to create a Paste Errors table that contains information on the records with the errors. The Paste Errors table for field-type mismatches is similar in purpose and appearance to the Import Errors table described in the "Creating a Table by Importing an Excel Worksheet" section of this chapter.

IN THE REAL WORLD—MICROSOFT GIVETH AND MICROSOFT TAKETH AWAY

Despite issues with Microsoft bundling no-additional-charge features in Windows 98, Windows NT 4.0, and Windows 2000, there's still no such thing as a free lunch when you upgrade to Access 2000. Long-standing dBASE and Paradox import, export, and linking features have disappeared in Access 2000, and even Microsoft's Visual FoxPro gets slighted by losing its ISAM driver and .dbf export capability. If you need to work with linked dBASE or Paradox tables and don't want to spring for a BDE license, you're stuck with using earlier versions of Access.

A plausible explanation for disappearing desktop database file compatibility is that Access dominates the market, and virtually everyone who needed to migrate from xBase and Paradox tables already has done so in an earlier version of Access. There's no question that dBASE and its clones, Paradox, and other competing desktop database platforms (with the significant exception of FileMaker Pro) linger in a state of semi-suspended animation. Developers with a substantial investment in xBase or Paradox Application Language (PAL) are loathe to climb the VBA, Java, or C++ learning curve; thus xBase and PAL programmers constitute a continuing, if shrinking, upgrade market for Inprise/Borland and Microsoft. It's probably safe to say that few, if any, newcomers choose the current version of dBASE, Visual FoxPro, or Paradox as their introductory database design and development learning tool.

Note

The preceding observations aren't intended to denigrate other desktop RDBMS development platforms. dBASE and Visual FoxPro have a devoted following of accomplished developers. However, it's a reasonably safe bet that most of dBASE and Visual FoxPro programmers' income derives from maintenance of and extensions to existing applications, not from entirely new database projects. Visual FoxPro is a member of the Visual Studio development suite, which carries a substantially higher estimated retail price than Office 2000.

Microsoft taketh away xBase and Paradox connectivity, but giveth links to Outlook and Exchange folders. Fair bargain? Probably, because it's an equally reasonable bet that more Access users are interested in Outlook/Exchange than xBase/Paradox connectivity. However, it's even more reasonable to expect better than tit-for-tat when shelling out substantial cash—even your employer's cash—for an Office upgrade.

The most significant giveth in Access 2000 for business purchasers—especially small businesses—is the Microsoft Data Engine, a euphemism for the embedded version of SQL Server 7.0. MSDE enables Access Data Projects (ADP), which are the subject of Chapter 25, "Creating Access Data Projects." Developers can learn client/server front-end design techniques without spending substantial sums for SQL Server 7.0 server- and client-side licenses. It's now feasible for the most cash-starved businesses to replace workgroup-size multiuser Access applications with ADPs and far more robust and, surprisingly, easier-to-administer MSDE databases.

It's probably too early to tell whether the other major new Access 2000 element, Data Access Pages (DAP), is an upgrade gimme or gotcha. Version 1.0 of DAP, the subject of Chapter 18, "Designing Data Access Pages," has the vagaries of version 1.0 of any software product. DAP have a tenuous connection to Access, being equally at home with Jet and SQL Server databases. DAP just as well could have made its debut as a Visual Basic or Visual InterDev add-on. For better or worse, it's an Access 2000 feature, much to the probable consternation of the vast majority of Access users.

PART

I

CH

7

Last on the giveth list is ADO. ADO is a freebie, because you can download the entire current set of Microsoft Data Access Components (MDAC) from http://www.microsoft.com/data and use them with any database front-end platform that supports 32-bit Windows and a COM-complaint scripting language. Chapter 27 contains more than you're likely to want to know about ADO, especially if you're new to VBA programming. ADO 2.1 doesn't offer parity with DAO, but it's required to implement ADP, DAP, and most other Microsoft Web-related database connectivity technologies. ADO doesn't qualify as a free lunch, however, because you'll pay a haute cuisine price in time and effort to climb the ADO learning curve.

--rj

PART II

GETTING THE MOST OUT OF QUERIES

8 Designing Access Queries 293

9 Understanding Query Operators and Expressions 319

10 Creating Multitable and Crosstab Queries 353

11 Modifying Data with Action Queries 409

CHAPTER 8

DESIGNING ACCESS QUERIES

In this chapter

Introducing Queries   294

Trying the Simple Query Wizard   294

Using the Query Design Window   298

Selecting Fields for Your Query   299

Selecting Records by Criteria and Sorting the Display   302

Creating More Complex Queries   303

Changing the Names of Query Column Headers   305

Printing Your Query as a Report   307

Using the Data from Your Query   309

Creating and Using a Simple Make-Table Action Query   311

Adding a Parameter to Your Make-Table Query   313

Troubleshooting   315

In the Real World—Query Design Optimization   315

INTRODUCING QUERIES

Queries are an essential tool in any database management system. You use queries to select records, update tables, and add new records to tables. Most often you use queries to select specific groups of records that meet criteria you specify. You can also use queries to combine information from different tables, providing a unified view of related data items. In this chapter, you learn the basics of creating your own select queries, including specifying selection criteria and using the results of your queries to generate reports and create new tables. You create queries using more than one table in Chapter 10, "Creating Multitable and Crosstab Queries," after you learn the details of how to use operators and create expressions in Chapter 9, "Understanding Query Operators and Expressions."

TRYING THE SIMPLE QUERY WIZARD

The Simple Query Wizard is aptly named; it's capable of generating only trivial select queries. If you don't have a numeric field in the table on which you base the query, the Wizard has only two dialogs   one to select the table(s) and fields to include and the other to name the query. Following are the characteristics of the Simple Query Wizard:

- You can't add selection criteria or specify the sort order of the query.

- You can't change the order of the fields in the query; fields always appear in the sequence in which you add them in the first Wizard dialog.

- If one or more of your selected fields is numeric, the Wizard lets you produce a summary query that shows the total, average, minimum, or maximum value of the numeric field(s). You also can include a count of the number of records in the query result set.

- If one or more of your selected fields is of the Date/Time data type, you can specify summary query grouping by date range—day, month, quarter, or year.

Tip #63 from	Use Crosstab queries for grouping records with numeric values, especially when you're interested in returning a time series, such as monthly, quarterly, or yearly totals or averages. Crosstab queries deliver greatly enhanced grouping capability and show the query result set in a much more readable format compared to that delivered by the Simple Query Wizard. Chapter 10 shows you how to take maximum advantage of crosstab queries.

To give the Simple Query Wizard a test drive, do the following:

1. Open the Northwind database, if necessary, to display the Database window and click the Queries shortcut.

2. Double-click the Create Query by Using Wizard shortcut to open the Simple Query Wizard's first dialog.

3. Select Table: Orders in the Tables/Queries list to use a table with both numeric

(Freight) and Date/Time (OrderDate, RequiredDate, and ShippedDate) fields. All the fields of the Orders table appear in the Available Fields list.

4. Select the OrderID field in the Available Fields list and click the right-arrow (>) button to add OrderID to the Selected Fields list and remove it from the Available Fields list. Alternatively, you can double-click the field to add to the query.

5. Repeat step 4 for the CustomerID, OrderDate and Freight fields. The first Wizard dialog appears as shown in Figure 8.1.

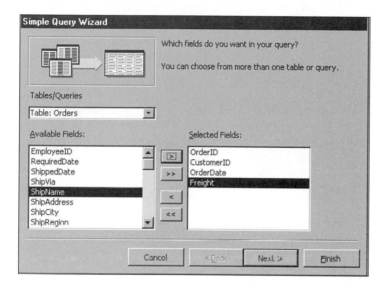

Figure 8.1
The first dialog of the Simple Query Wizard with four fields of the Orders table selected.

6. Click Next to open the second Wizard dialog that lets you select between detail and summary queries. Accept the Detail option (see Figure 8.2).

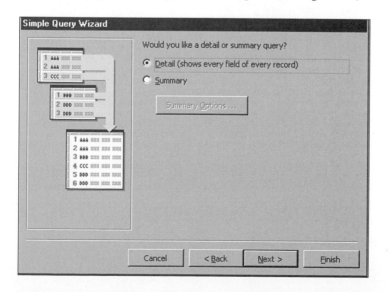

Figure 8.2
The Wizard's second dialog in which you select the type of query to generate.

7. Click Next to open the final dialog (see Figure 8.3). Accept the default query name, Orders Query, and click Finish to display the query result set in Datasheet view (see Figure 8.4).

Figure 8.3
The final Wizard dialog for naming the query and determining the display mode.

Figure 8.4
The Wizard's Orders Query in Datasheet view.

Order ID	Customer	Order Date	Freight
10248	Vins et alcools Chevalier	04-Jul-1996	$32.38
10249	Toms Spezialitäten	05-Jul-1996	$11.61
10250	Hanari Carnes	08-Jul-1996	$65.83
10251	Victuailles en stock	08-Jul-1996	$41.34
10252	Suprêmes délices	09-Jul-1996	$51.30
10253	Hanari Carnes	10-Jul-1996	$58.17
10254	Chop-suey Chinese	11-Jul-1996	$22.98
10255	Richter Supermarkt	12-Jul-1996	$148.33
10256	Wellington Importadora	15-Jul-1996	$13.97
10257	HILARIÓN-Abastos	16-Jul-1996	$81.91
10258	Ernst Handel	17-Jul-1996	$140.51
10259	Centro comercial Moctezuma	18-Jul-1996	$3.25
10260	Ottilies Käseladen	19-Jul-1996	$55.09

Record: 1 of 830

If you want to test the Simple Query Wizard's capability to base a query on another query and check the Wizard's summary query capabilities, do the following:

1. Return to the Database window and double-click the Create Query by Using Wizard shortcut to open the Simple Query Wizard's first dialog. Select Query: Orders Query in the Tables/Queries list.

Access calls a query whose source is a query, rather than a table, a *subquery*.

2. Add only the OrderDate and Freight fields to the Selected Fields list.

   Summary queries must include only the field(s) by which the data is grouped (OrderDate) and the numeric value(s) to be summarized. If you add other fields, such as OrderID, every record appears in the summary query, and you don't obtain the summary you're seeking.

3. Click Next to open the second Wizard dialog (refer to Figure 8.2). Select the Summary option and then click Summary Options to open the identically named dialog. Mark the Avg check box to calculate the average freight cost and mark the Count Records in Query check box to add a column with the record count for the group (see Figure 8.5).

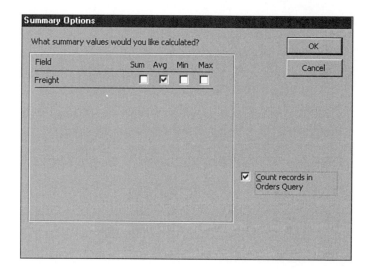

Figure 8.5
Specifying the type of summary calculation and adding a column with the number of records for each group.

4. Click OK to return to the second Wizard dialog and then click Next to move to the third Wizard dialog. The Wizard has detected the OrderDate Date/Time field and offers you the choice of date grouping; select Quarter (see Figure 8.6).

5. Click Next to open the last Wizard dialog and accept the default query name, Orders Query Query, or pick another.

6. Click Finish to execute the summary query. The query result set appears as shown in Figure 8.7.

Summary queries are a common element of *decision-support* applications that deliver time-based trend data to management. Summary queries also are the foundation for graphical data analysis, which is the primary subject of Chapter 19, "Adding Charts and Graphics to Forms and Reports."

Figure 8.6
Choosing the date grouping criterion.

Orders Query Query : Select Query

OrderDate By Quarter	Avg Of Freight	Count Of Orders Query
Q3 1996	$54.41	70
Q4 1996	$78.92	82
Q1 1997	$62.27	92
Q2 1997	$88.74	93
Q3 1997	$85.18	103
Q4 1997	$80.94	120
Q1 1998	$83.05	182
Q2 1998	$80.44	88

Record: 1 of 8

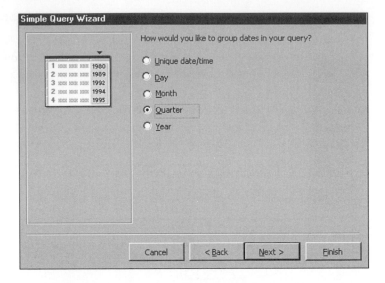

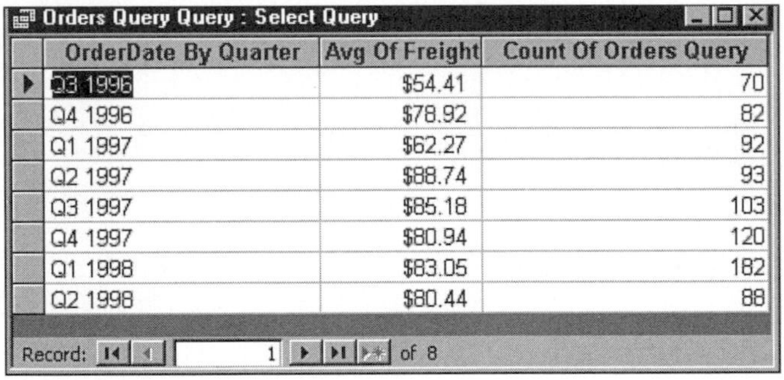

Figure 8.7
Datasheet view of a simple summary query.

USING THE QUERY DESIGN WINDOW

The Simple Query Wizard has limited usefulness, so the better approach is to design your queries from scratch in Access's graphical Query Design window. The Query Design window is one of Access's most powerful features.

To devise a simple query that lets you customize mailing lists for selected customers of Northwind Traders, for example, follow these steps:

1. Open the Northwind database, if necessary, to display the Database window and click the Queries shortcut.

NEW 2000

2. Double-click the Create Query in Design View shortcut to open the Query Design window.

The Show Table dialog is superimposed on the Query Design window, as shown in Figure 8.8. The tabbed lists in the Show Table dialog let you select from all existing tables, all queries, or a combination of all tables and queries. You can base a new query on one or more previously entered tables or queries.

Query window —

Show Table dialog

Figure 8.8
Starting the design of a new query with the Show Table dialog.

Note

If you select a table in the Tables page of the Database window and then click the New Object Access toolbar button and select Query from the dropdown menu, Access 2000 automatically places the selected table in the Query Design window, without displaying the Show Tables dialog described in step 2.

3. This example uses only tables in the query, so accept the default selection of Tables. Click (or use the down-arrow key to select) Customers in the Show Table list to select the Customers table and then click the Add button. Alternatively, double-click Customers to add the table to the query. You can use more than one table in a query by choosing another related table from the list and choosing Add again. This example, however, uses only one table. After selecting the tables that you want to use, click Close.

The Fields list for the Customers table appears at the left in the upper pane of the Query Design window, and a blank Query Design grid appears in the lower pane. The Fields list displays all the names of the fields of the Customers table, but you must scroll to display more than five entries with the default Fields list size. The asterisk (*) item at the top of the list is a shortcut symbol for adding all table fields to the query.

SELECTING FIELDS FOR YOUR QUERY

After you add a table from the Show Table dialog, the next step is to decide which of the table's fields to include in your query. Because you plan to use this query to create a customer mailing list, you must include the fields that make up a personalized mailing address.

To select the fields to include in the Query Design grid, follow these steps:

 1. When you open the Query Design window, the caret is located in the Field row of the first column. Click the List Box button that appears in the right corner of the first column or press F4 to open the Field Names list (see Figure 8.9).

Figure 8.9
Adding a field to the Query Design grid with the Field Names list.

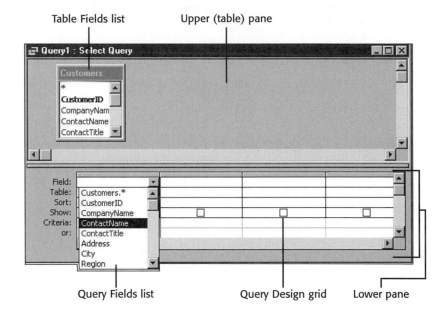

Table Fields list   Upper (table) pane

Query Fields list   Query Design grid   Lower pane

2. Select the ContactName field as the first field header of the query or use the down-arrow key to highlight the name and press Enter. The Field list in the lower pane closes.

3. Move the caret to the second column by using the right arrow or Tab key. (Notice that the List Box button moves to the second column along with the caret.) Double-click CompanyName in the Customers Field list in the upper pane to add CompanyName as the second field of your query. Double-clicking entries in the upper pane's list is the second method that Access provides to add fields to a query.

4. Access offers a third method of adding fields to your query: the drag-and-drop method. To use the drag-and-drop method to add the Address, City, Region, PostalCode, and Country fields to columns 3 through 7, first select the fields. In the Customers Field list of the upper pane's Query Design window, click Address, and then Shift+click Country. Alternatively, select Address with the down-arrow key, hold the Shift or Ctrl key, and press the down-arrow key four more times. You've selected the Address, City, and Region fields, as shown in Figure 8.10.

Multiple-field drag-
and-drop cursor

International Do
Not Enter cursor

Figure 8.10
Selecting multiple
fields and using the
drag-and-drop
method to add fields
to the Query Design
grid.

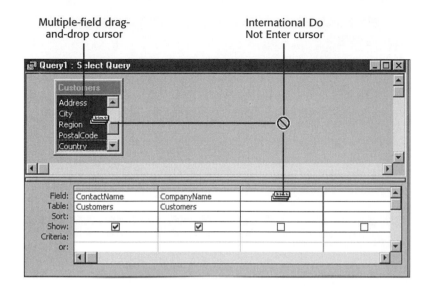

5. Position the mouse pointer over the selected fields and click the left mouse button. Your mouse pointer turns into a symbol representing the three selected field names. Drag the symbol for the three fields to the third column of your query's Field row, as shown in Figure 8.11, and release the left mouse button.

   Access adds the five fields to your query, in sequence, starting with the column in which you drop the symbol. When the mouse pointer is in an area where you can't drop the fields, it becomes the international Do Not Enter symbol shown in the upper pane of the Query Design window of Figure 8.10.

6. The Query Design grid in the lower pane displays four columns (in the default width) in a normal Query Design window. This query uses seven fields, so you need to drag the edges of the Query Design window to increase the width of the grid's display to expose two additional empty fields. To reduce the columns' width, drag the divider of the grid's header bars to the left. Click the scroll-right button (on the horizontal scroll-bar at the bottom of the window) or drag the scrollbar slider button to the right to expose the remaining fields (see Figure 8.11).

7. Click the Datasheet View toolbar button to enter Run mode. Expect a brief waiting period while Access processes your query on the Customers table. Alternatively, click the Run toolbar button to run your query against the Customers table.

Because you haven't yet entered any selection criteria in the Criteria row of the Query Design grid, your query result set in the Customers table displays all records. These records appear in the order of the primary key index on the CustomerID field because you haven't specified a sorting order in the Sort row of the Query Design grid. (The values in the CustomerID field are alphabetic codes derived from the Company Name field.) Figure 8.12 shows the result of your first query after adjusting the width of the fields.

Figure 8.11
The seven field names included in the new query.

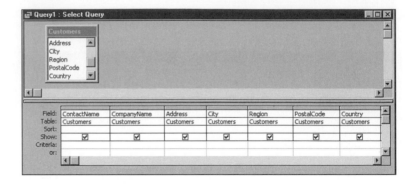

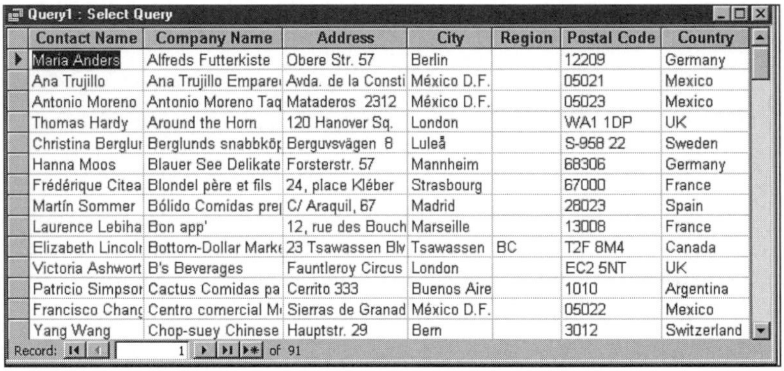

Figure 8.12
The query result set containing all records of the Customers table.

SELECTING RECORDS BY CRITERIA AND SORTING THE DISPLAY

The mailing for which you're creating a list with your sample query is to be sent to U.S. customers only, so you want to include in your query only those records that have USA in the Country field. Selecting records based on the values of fields—that is, establishing the criteria for the records to be returned (displayed) by the query—is the heart of the query process.

Take the following steps to establish criteria for selecting the records to make up your mailing list:

1. Click the Design View toolbar button to return to Design mode. The partially filled Query Design grid replaces the mailing list onscreen.

2. To restrict the result of your query to firms in the United States, type **USA** in the Criteria row of the Country column. Entering a criterion's value without preceding the value with an operator indicates that the value of the field must match the value of the expression USA. You don't need to add quotation marks to the expression; Access adds them for you (see the Country column in Figure 8.13).

3. Click the Show check box in the Country column to clear the check mark that appeared when you added the column. After you deactivate the Show check box, the Country field doesn't appear when you run your query. If you don't deactivate a Show check box, that field in the query appears in the query's result by default.

4. Move the caret to the Postal Code column's Sort row and press F4 to display the sorting options for that field: Ascending, Descending, and (Not Sorted). Select the Ascending option to sort the query by Postal Code from low codes to high.

At this point, the Query Design grid appears as shown in Figure 8.13.

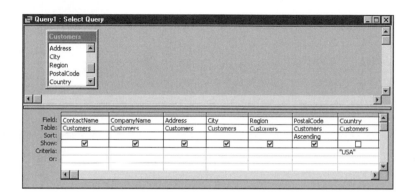

Figure 8.13
Adding a selection criterion to the Country field and an Ascending sort order to the PostalCode field.

5. Click the Datasheet View or Run button on the toolbar to display the result of your criterion and sorting order.

Figure 8.14 displays the query result table (also called a *query result set*) that Access refers to as an updatable `Recordset`, which is indicated by the tentative append (*) in the last (empty) row of the query result set. A `Recordset` object is a temporary table stored in your computer's memory; it's not a permanent component of the database file. You can edit the data in any visible fields of the underlying table(s) in Query Datasheet view if your `Recordset` is updatable.

After you save the query, the Northwind.mdb file saves only the design specifications of the query, not the values that the query contains. The query design specification is called a `QueryDef` object.

CREATING MORE COMPLEX QUERIES

To limit your mailing to customers in a particular state or group of states, you can add a Criteria expression to the Region or PostalCode field. To restrict the mailing to customers in California, Oregon, and Washington, for example, you can specify that the value of the PostalCode field must be equal to or greater than 90000. Alternatively, you can specify that Region values must be CA, OR, and WA.

Figure 8.14
The query result set, sorted in ascending order by Postal Code.

Follow these steps to restrict your mailing to customers in California, Oregon, and Washington:

1. Click the Design View toolbar button to return to Design mode.

2. Move to the Region column and type **CA** in the first criterion row of the Region column. Access adds the quotation marks around CA (as it did when you restricted your mailing to U.S. locations with the USA criterion).

3. Press the down-arrow key to move to the next criterion row in the Region column. Type **OR** and then move to the third criterion row and type **WA**. Your query design now appears as shown in Figure 8.15. Access adds the required quotation marks to these criteria also.

4. Click the Datasheet View or Run toolbar button to return to Run mode. The query result set appears as shown in Figure 8.16.

Figure 8.15
Adding criteria to the Region field of the Query Design grid.

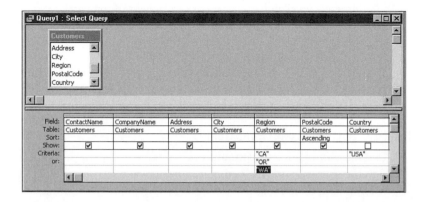

Figure 8.16
The query result set for customers in California, Oregon, and Washington.

Note

After you type a criterion on the same line as a previously entered criterion in another field, only those records that meet both criteria are selected for display. In the preceding example, therefore, only those records with Region values equal to CA and Country values equal to USA are displayed.

To be displayed, records for Region values OR and WA need not have Country values equal to USA, because the USA criterion is missing from the OR and WA rows. This omission doesn't really affect the selection of records in this case, because all OR and WA records are also USA records. To eliminate possible ambiguity, however, USA should appear in each criterion row that contains a state code.

CHANGING THE NAMES OF QUERY COLUMN HEADERS

You can substitute a query's field header names with column header names of your choice—a process called *aliasing*—but only if the header name hasn't been changed by an entry in the field Caption property of the table. If yours is a U.S. firm, for example, you might want to change Region to State and PostalCode to ZIP. (Canadian firms might want to change only Region to Province.)

As demonstrated in the following example, you can't change the PostalCode field for queries based on the Customers table because the PostalCode field previously has been changed (aliased) to Postal Code by the Caption property for the field. You can, however, make the change to the Region field because this field isn't aliased at the table level.

Tip #64 from

RJ

If you already have a main document for mail merge operation, substitute the main merge document's merge field names for the table's field header names in your query.

Note

Field names in queries that have been altered by use of the Caption property in the source table can't be aliased, so don't use the Caption property of table fields. If you want to display different field headers, use a query for this purpose. In a client/server RDBMS, such a query is called a SQL VIEW. Aliasing field names in tables rather than in queries isn't considered a generally accepted database design practice.

To change the query column header names, perform the following steps:

1. Switch to Design mode by clicking the toolbar's Design View button. Then move to the Field column containing the field header name that you want to change—in this case, the Region column.

2. Press F2 to deselect the field; then press Home to move the caret to the first character position.

3. Type the new name for the column and follow the name with a colon (with no spaces):

   State:

   The colon separates the new column name that you type from the existing table field name, which shifts to the right to make room for your addition. The result, in this example, is State: Region (see Figure 8.17).

Figure 8.17
Changing the names of the Region and Postal Code column headers.

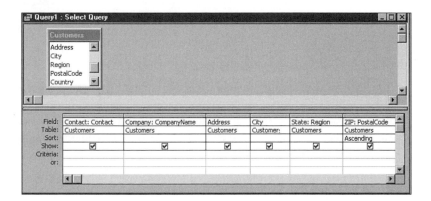

4. Use the arrow key to move to the PostalCode field and repeat steps 2 and 3, typing **ZIP:** as that header's new name. The result is ZIP:PostalCode (see Figure 8.17).

5. Change the column header for the ContactName field to Contact; change the column header for the CompanyName field to Company (refer to steps 2, 3, and 4).

6. Delete the CA, OR, and WA criteria from the State:Region column so that all records for the U.S. appear.

7. Click the toolbar's Query Datasheet View or Run button to execute the query. Observe that only the Region column header is changed to State; the other columns are unaffected by the alias entry (see Figure 8.18).

Contact Name	Company Name	Address	City	State	Postal Code
Liu Wong	The Cracker Box	55 Grizzly Peak R	Butte	MT	59801
Art Braunschwei	Split Rail Beer & Ale	P.O. Box 555	Lander	WY	82520
Jose Pavarotti	Save-a-lot Markets	187 Suffolk Ln.	Boise	ID	83720
Paula Wilson	Rattlesnake Canyon	2817 Milton Dr.	Albuquerque	NM	87110
Jaime Yorres	Let's Stop N Shop	87 Polk St.	San Francis	CA	94117
Liz Nixon	The Big Cheese	89 Jefferson Way	Portland	OR	97201
Fran Wilson	Lonesome Pine Res	89 Chiaroscuro Rd	Portland	OR	97219
Howard Snyder	Great Lakes Food N	2732 Baker Blvd.	Eugene	OR	97403
Yoshi Latimer	Hungry Coyote Impc	City Center Plaza	Elgin	OR	97827
Helvetius Nagy	Trail's Head Gourme	722 DaVinci Blvd.	Kirkland	WA	98034
Karl Jablonski	White Clover Market	305 - 14th Ave. S.	Seattle	WA	98128
John Steel	Lazy K Kountry Sto	12 Orchestra Terra	Walla Walla	WA	99362
Rene Phillips	Old World Delicates	2743 Bering St.	Anchorage	AK	99508

Record: 14 | ◄ | 1 ► | ►I | ►* | of 13

Figure 8.18
The query result set, with only one new column header.

8. Choose File, Save or press Ctrl+S, and save your query with the name **qryUSMailList**.

> **Note**
>
> To make field aliasing in queries operable, in Table Design view delete the entry in the Caption field for each aliased field of the table. In the following sections, the entries in the Caption property of the ContactName, CompanyName, and PostalCode fields of the Customers table have been deleted. Deleting these entries makes the aliases you entered in the preceding example work as expected.

PRINTING YOUR QUERY AS A REPORT

Queries are often used to print quick, ad hoc reports. Access 2000 lets you print your report to a printer, a Word for Windows .rtf (rich-text format) file, an Excel worksheet .xls file, or a DOS .txt (text) file or as an attachment to an Exchange message. You also can publish a query to a Web server.

→ **See** "Exporting Table and Query Datasheets to HTML," **p. 628**.

Previewing your query table's appearance to see how the table will appear when printed is usually a good idea. After you determine from the preview that everything in the table is correct, you can print the finished query result set in various formats.

To preview a query result set before printing it, follow these steps:

1. In Query Datasheet view, click the Print Preview toolbar button. A miniature version of the query table appears in Report Preview mode.

2. Position the Zoom pointer (the magnifying glass cursor) at the upper-left corner of the miniature table and click the left mouse button or the Zoom button above the window to view the report at approximately the scale at which it will print.

3. Use the vertical and horizontal scrollbar buttons to position the preview in the window (see Figure 8.19).

Figure 8.19
Previewing the
Mailing List query
table at zoomed
scale.

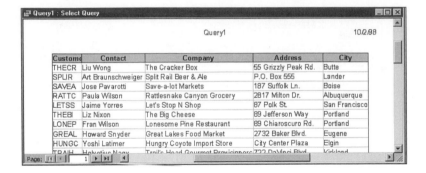

Note

Field width in the query table is based on the column width that you last established in Run mode. You might have to drag the right edge of the field header buttons to the right to increase the columns' width so that the printed report doesn't truncate the data. If the query data's width exceeds the available printing width (the paper width minus the width of the left and right margins), Access prints two or more sheets for each page of the report.

4. Right-click the Print Preview window and choose Page Setup to open the Page Setup dialog shown in Figure 8.20. If necessary, click the Margins tab to display the Margins page.

Figure 8.20
The Margins page of
the Page Setup dialog.

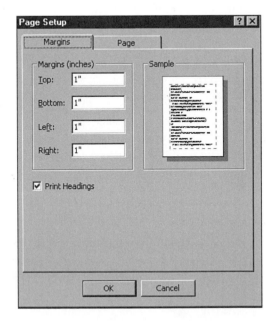

5. Enter any changes that you want to make to the margins; mark the Print Headings check box if you want to print the field header names. Click the Page tab to change the print orientation, paper size or source, or printer. Then click OK to return to Print Preview.

6. Click the Print toolbar button to print your query data.

USING THE DATA FROM YOUR QUERY

Occasionally, you might want to use data from your query as part of a different Windows application without printing the data in a report. The simplest technique for transferring data in your query to another Windows application is to use the Clipboard. Clipboard operations for data in query tables are identical to those operations for tables described in Chapter 7, "Linking, Importing, and Exporting Tables."

→ **See** "Using the Clipboard to Import Data," **p. 285**.

Access 2000 includes a Merge It with MS Word choice when you click the arrow next to the Office Links toolbar button. Merge It automatically creates a Word mail merge document. Performing automated operations manually, however, gives you insight into how Access 2000 implements Office Links.

→ **See** "Using the Access Mail Merge Wizard," **p. 782**.

To manually generate a merge data file for Word directly from a query, for example, follow these steps:

1. In Query Datasheet view, choose Edit, Select All Records.

Tip #65 from

R J

For a partial mailing, such as to firms in California only, you can select the individual records by dragging the mouse over the records' selection buttons.

---

2. Press Ctrl+C or choose Edit, Copy to copy the selected records to the Clipboard.

3. Run Word and, if necessary, choose File, New to open a new document.

4. Press Ctrl+V or choose Edit, Paste. Your Access mailing records are added as a table to the Word document (see Figure 8.21).

5. Convert the table to the tab-delimited format necessary for Word merge data files. Place the caret in one of the cells of the table and choose Table, Select Table to select all the rows and columns of the table.

6. Choose Table, Convert Table to Text to display the dialog that lets you pick the field-delimiter character. Accept the default Tab selection in the Convert Table to Text dialog and click OK. Your merge data file appears as shown in Figure 8.22.

Figure 8.21
The query result set copied to a Word for Windows document.

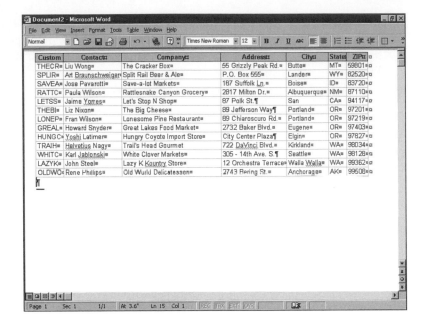

Figure 8.22
A Microsoft Word merge data file with extra newline pairs embedded.

<table>
<tr><td>Note</td></tr>
</table>

Some records of this query also contain *newline pairs* (paragraph marks) embedded in fields that result in premature ends of these records. An example of a spurious newline pair in the Address field is highlighted for the Let's Stop 'N Shop record in Figure 8.22. Replace the extra newline pairs with commas and spaces and delete the quotation marks that enclose fields containing extra headline pairs before using the document in a merge operation.

CREATING OTHER TYPES OF QUERIES

Access lets you create the following four basic types of queries to achieve different objectives:

- *Select* queries extract data from one or more tables and display the data in tabular form.

- *Crosstab* queries summarize data from one or more tables in the form of a spreadsheet. Such queries are useful for analyzing data and creating graphs or charts based on the sum of the numeric field values of many records.

- *Action* queries create new database tables from query tables or make major alterations to a table. Such queries let you add or delete records from a table or to make changes to records based on expressions that you enter in a query design.

- *Parameter* queries repeatedly use a query and make only simple changes to its criteria. The mailing list query that you created earlier is an excellent candidate for a parameter query because you can change the criterion of the Region field for mailings to different groups of customers. When you run a parameter query, Access displays a dialog to prompt you for the new criterion. Parameter queries aren't actually a separate query type because you can add the parameter function to select, crosstab, and action queries.

Chapter 10 and Chapter 11, "Modifying Data with Action Queries," explain how to create each of the four query types. Creating a table from the mailing list query to export to a mail merge file is an example of an action query. (In fact, this is the simplest example of an action query and also the safest because make-table queries don't modify data in existing tables. A *make-table query* creates a new table from your query result set.)

CREATING AND USING A SIMPLE MAKE-TABLE ACTION QUERY

To create a table from your mailing list query, you first must convert the query from a select to an action query. Follow these steps to make this change:

1. Open your mailing list query in Query Design view and choose Query, Make-Table Query. (You can access the Query menu only in Query Design view.) Alternatively, click the Query Type toolbar button and select Make-Table Query to open the Make Table dialog.

2. In the Table Name text box, type a descriptive table name for your query table, such as **tblUSMailList** (see Figure 8.23).

   The Make Table dialog lets you define your query table's properties further in several ways. You can add the table to the Northwind database by choosing the Current Database option (the default). You also can pick the Another Database option to add the table to a different database that you specify in the File Name text box.

Figure 8.23
The Make Table dialog, in which you enter a name for the table the query creates and specify the new table's location.

3. Click OK. Access converts your select query to the make-table type of action query.

4. Close your query by clicking the Close Window button. Access displays a message dialog asking whether you want to save changes to your query; click Yes. Your query name in the Database window now is prefixed by an exclamation point, which indicates that the query is an action query (see Figure 8.24).

Figure 8.24
A highlighted action query in the list of queries.

Now that you've converted your query from a select query to an action query, you can create a new U.S. mailing list table. To create the table, follow these steps:

1. Run the newly converted action query table to create your mailing list by double-clicking its name in the Queries page of the Database window (refer to Figure 8.24).

When you open an action query table, it performs the desired action—in this case, creating the tblUSMailList table—rather than simply displaying a select query result set. Before Access carries out the action, however, a message appears (see Figure 8.25) to warn you that the query will modify the data in the tblUSMailList table (even though you haven't yet created the table). If you're using the Office Assistant, the Assistant you chose delivers the message.

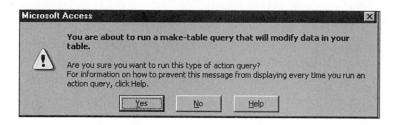

Figure 8.25
The message box that appears after you open an action query.

2. Click Yes to dismiss the message box and continue the operation. A second message appears to tell you the number of records (13 in this case) that are added to the table.

3. Click Yes. Because you haven't run this action query before, running it now creates the new tblUSMailList table.

 4. Click the Tables Object shortcut in the Database window. Access adds the new tblUSMailList table to the list of tables in the Northwind database.

5. Double-click the tblUSMailList item to open the table. Its contents are identical to the contents of the Datasheet view of the make-table query.

After you create the new table, you can export its data to any of the other file formats supported by Access. To do so, use the methods described in Chapter 7.

ADDING A PARAMETER TO YOUR MAKE-TABLE QUERY

A simple modification to your mailing list query lets you enter a selection criterion, called a *parameter*, from a prompt created by Access. Follow these steps:

 1. Close the tblUSMailList table and then click the Queries Object shortcut in the Database window.

 2. Select the qryUSMailList query that you created earlier in the chapter and then click the Design button to display your make-table action query in Design mode.

3. Type **[Enter the state code:]** in the first criterion row of the State: Region column, as shown in Figure 8.26. The enclosing square brackets indicate that the entry is a prompt for a parameter when you run the action query.

4. Close and save changes to the action query, right-click the qryUSMailList query, and choose Rename.

5. Rename your query by entering **qryStateMailList** in the text box.

6. Double-click the qryStateMailList item. You see the message indicating that data will be modified (refer to Figure 8.23).

7. Click Yes. Another message appears, warning that you are about to overwrite the data in the table created by the last execution of your query.

Figure 8.26
Entering a parameter prompt as a criterion in Query Design view.

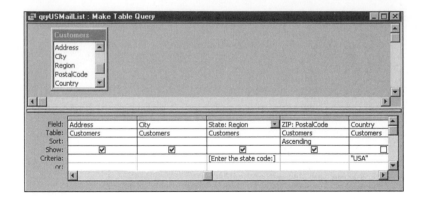

Field:	Address	City	State: Region	ZIP: PostalCode	Country
Table:	Customers	Customers	Customers	Customers	Customers
Sort:				Ascending	
Show:	☑	☑	☑	☑	☐
Criteria:			[Enter the state code:]		"USA"
or:					

Note

Each time a make-table query is executed, it creates a new table with whatever name you've specified in the Make Table dialog. If a table with that name already exists, its contents are lost and replaced by the result set of the make-table query. If you want a make-table query to create a table with a different name, you must choose the Query menu's Make-table Query command and enter a new name in the Make Table dialog.

8. Click Yes. Access displays the Enter Parameter Value dialog, which contains a prompt for you to enter the state criterion (see Figure 8.27).

9. Type **WA** and then press Enter or click OK. (You don't need to type an equal sign before the state code because Access enters the equal sign for you.)

   Another message indicates the number of records in the new version of the tblUSMailList table that have a value in the Regions field that matches your state parameter entry.

10. Click Yes to close the message box and execute the make-table query.

 11. Click the Tables Object shortcut in the Database window and select tblUSMailList. Click the Open button. Records only for customers in Washington appear in the table.

Figure 8.27
The text box for entering a parameter to be used as a select criterion.

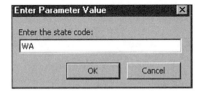

You can delete the new table from the Northwind database by closing the table, selecting the tblUSMailList table in the Database window, and then pressing Delete. Access requests that you confirm your deletion. Click OK to remove the table from the database.

Troubleshooting

Missing Required Fields

I created a query that shows the tentative append record, but when I try to add a new record, I receive a `The field 'FieldName' can't contain a Null value because the Required property is set to True` *error message. I don't want FieldName in the query.*

You must include in your query result set all columns whose Required property value is set to Yes. This means, of course, that each of these fields must have a value typed in it. A unique primary key value is required to add a new record to any table with a primary key. For example, attempting to add a new record to a query on the Customers table that doesn't include CustomerID and CustomerName columns fails, because CustomerID is the primary key and CustomerName is a required field of the table.

Non-Updatable Summary Queries

I can't update data in my summary query.

Summary queries aggregate data, so there's no direct relationship between the content of a query row and records in the underlying table(s). This means that there's no way for changes to aggregated values (dates, totals, averages, and the like) to propagate back to the table records. If you want to fudge the figures, change your select summary query to a make-table summary query, then alter the data in the new table.

In the Real World—Query Design Optimization

The objective of select query design is to convert raw data to useful information. The design of decision-support queries in production database applications is a combination of art and science.

The Art of Query Design

An artful query design returns the result set in the format that's most meaningful to the recipient. For example, a query that displays orders sorted by customer and uses the customer code for identification might be understandable by a salesperson, but not management. Salespeople are likely to know the codes for their particular customers. Few sales or marketing managers, however, are capable of memorizing hundreds or thousands of codes. This is especially true if the codes are numeric, rather than based on the first few letters of customers' names, as is the case for the Northwind Customers table. Fortunately, Access's table lookup feature propagates to queries; when you specify CustomerID as a query column, table lookup in the Customers table automatically substitutes CompanyName for CustomerID in the query result set.

Another aspect of the art of query design is appropriate left-to-right and top-to-bottom ordering of query columns. If your summary query is a time series—such as the Orders Query Query you created in the "Trying the Simple Query Wizard" section at the beginning of the chapter—the Order Date column is the most important, so it appears in the leftmost column. If you're writing Access applications for others, make sure to interview prospective users to determine their column presentation priorities. Use drag-and-drop to optimize the relative position of columns in Datasheet view.

Try not to require users to scroll a datasheet view to the right to display important columns. Consider using a smaller datasheet font size (8.5 or 9 points) to reduce column width. In query Datasheet view, choose Format, Font to open the Font dialog. If users must scroll the data, freeze the field(s) by which users identify the row—usually the primary key field. Right-click the field-name header of the rightmost query column to freeze, and choose Freeze Columns from the context menu. You unfreeze columns by choosing Format, Unfreeze All Columns. You can't drag-and-drop frozen columns.

Most recent data probably is what users want, so applying a descending sort on the Order Date column aids information usability. You can quickly apply a descending sort on a date column in Datasheet view by right-clicking the field-name header, and choosing Sort Descending from the context menu. You can save all design modifications you make in Query Design view.

Apply intuition and inductive reasoning when designing decision-support queries. Access makes it easy to alter presentation of your queries in Datasheet view. As in music, painting, dance, and the other performing and pictorial arts, practice and experimentation are the keys to query artistry.

THE SCIENTIFIC SIDE OF QUERY DESIGN

The scientific part of query design is optimizing query performance. All production database applications deliver query result sets over some type of network, usually a Local Area Network (LAN) but often a Wide Area Network (WAN). The Internet is an example of the widest-area network ever devised. The performance of queries executed over LANs and, especially, WANs is dependent on a multitude of factors, the most important of which is network traffic, followed by the type of network connection. Even if you're writing queries for execution on a single PC, plan ahead for networking, even at home. Home networking is today's hot topic for PC hardware vendors. Current home networks, many of which operate at speeds of 1 Mbps or less, are at least 10 times slower than the now-obsolescent 10BaseT LANs in most offices.

 The tables of the Northwind.mdb sample database contains far fewer records than you find in typical production databases. The 10-person Northwind Traders sales force produced only 1077 orders over a span of almost two years, indicating a serious lack of sales productivity (or that Northwind Traders is a coverup for smuggling or other nefarious activities). If you have 15 MB of disk space to spare, install the Beckwith.mdb database from the \Seua2k\Beckwith folder of the accompanying CD-ROM and run test queries against its tables. To better emulate network performance, install Beckwith.mdb on a file-sharing server and link the tables to a new .mdb file on your client PC. The Students table has about 30,000 rows, which is more typical of a production customer table. The Enrollments table has 50,000 records.

With networked data, smaller definitely is better. Limit the data returned by your query to only that required by your application's immediate need. It's especially necessary to restrict the amount of data you send to modem-connected mobile users, whether they dial into your LAN or get their data over the Internet. You minimize the amount of data sent "over the wire" to database users' PCs in two ways—setting precise criteria and limiting the number of columns.

Setting precise criteria minimizes the number of rows sent to the client PC. For example, restrict initial queries against large tables—such as orders or invoices— to provide only the current month's orders. Create separate "last month," "this quarter," and "last quarter" queries for users who need historical data. Access's query expression service lets you write queries that automatically roll over when the month or quarter changes.

→ **See** "Functions," **p. 328**.

There's seldom a reason to include all fields (by using *) in a query. Include in the initial query only those fields necessary to provide the basics. For example, you might want to include the ShipName column in a query on the Orders table in order to identify the customer, but don't include the ShipAddress, ShipCity, ShipRegion, ShipPostalCode, and ShipCountry columns in management reports. Only salespeople and shipping departments need detailed destination data. Salespeople only need shipping information for their particular accounts, so you can use EmployeeID as a criterion to limit the number of records that have large text fields.

Don't include OLE Object (usually images) or Memo fields in initial queries unless they're absolutely essential. Access doesn't automatically retrieve these data types unless the user double-clicks an OLE Object cell or moves the caret to a Memo field, but data in OLE Object and Memo fields often is very large. A modem-connected user who accidentally double-clicks a 1-MB high-resolution image won't be happy when his or her computer is tied up for several minutes downloading unwanted data. If some users require either of these field data types, create a special query for them.

The science of query design requires detailed analysis and deductive reasoning. Keep these basic query design rules in mind as you progress through the remaining chapters of the "Getting the Most Out of Queries" part of this book.

CHAPTER 9

UNDERSTANDING QUERY OPERATORS AND EXPRESSIONS

In this chapter

Understanding the Elements in Expressions   321

Operators   322

Arithmetic Operators   322

Assignment and Comparison Operators   323

Logical Operators   324

Identifiers   328

Functions   328

Numeric, Logical, Date/Time, and **string** Data-Type Conversion Functions   338

Intrinsic and Named Constants   339

Expressions for Creating Default Values   340

Expressions for Validating Data   340

Expressions for Query Criteria   341

In the Real World—The Algebra of Access Expressions   350

WRITING EXPRESSIONS FOR QUERY CRITERIA AND DATA VALIDATION

Chapter 5, "Entering, Editing, and Validating Data in Tables," briefly introduced you to operators and the expressions that use them when you added validation rules to table fields. Chapter 8, "Designing Access Queries," touched on expressions again when you devised selection criteria for the query that you created. You must use expressions with the forms (Chapter 12, "Creating and Using Forms," and Chapter 13, "Designing Custom Multitable Forms"); reports (Chapter 14, "Printing Basic Reports and Mailing Labels," and Chapter 15, "Preparing Advanced Reports"); and queries (Chapter 8 and Chapter 10, "Creating Multitable and Crosstab Queries") that you combine when creating custom Access applications. Furthermore, you use expressions extensively when programming with Access VBA (Chapters 26 through 30). To work effectively with Access, therefore, you must know how to create simple expressions that use Access's group of functions and operators.

If you use Microsoft Excel, you might be familiar with employing operators to create expressions. In spreadsheet applications, expressions are called *formulas*. As discussed in Chapter 4, "Working with Access Databases and Tables," the syntax for expressions that create default values, such as **=Date + 28**, is similar to formula entries in Excel. Conditional expressions that use the **=IIF** function in Excel use the **IIf** function in Access.

Much of this chapter is devoted to describing the functions available in Access for dealing with data of the Numeric, Date/Time and Text field data type. Functions play important roles in every element of Access, from validation rules for tables and fields of tables to the control of program flow with VBA. You use functions when creating queries, forms, reports, and even more extensively when writing VBA code. To use Access 2000 effectively, you must know what functions are available to you.

NEW 2000 Following are the new functions and features in Access 2000 that are germane to this chapter:

- MonthName and WeekdayName functions return a **String** containing the localized (language- or locale-dependent) name of a month and day, respectively.

- Filter, InstrRev, Join, Replace, Split, and StrReverse are new string manipulation functions.

- Round returns a numeric value rounded to the specified number of decimal places.

- VBA 6.0 adds four specialized Format... functions: FormatCurrency, FormatDateTime, FormatNumber, and FormatPercent that you can substitute for the generic Format function in VBA code, but not in queries.

- The VBA Editor, common to all VBA-enabled Office 2000 members, replaces the Module window of Access 97 and earlier.

- The Debug window of prior versions of Access now is called the *Immediate window*. You use the VBA Editor's Immediate window in this chapter to experiment with expressions and functions.

UNDERSTANDING THE ELEMENTS IN EXPRESSIONS

An *expression* is a statement of intent. If you want an action to occur after meeting a specific condition, your expression must specify that condition. To select records in a query that contains ZIP field values of `90000` or higher, for example, you use the expression

```
ZIP>=90000
```

You can use expressions in arithmetic calculations also. If you need an ExtendedAmount field in a query, for example, you use

```
ExtendedAmount: Quantity * UnitPrice
```

as the expression to create calculated values in the data cells of the ExtendedAmount column.

To qualify as an expression, a statement must have at least one operator and at least one literal, identifier, or function. The following list describes these elements:

- *Operators* include the familiar arithmetic symbols +, −, * (multiply), and / (divide), as well as many other symbols and abbreviations. Some operators are specific to Access or SQL, such as the `Between`, `In`, `Is`, and `Like` operators.

- *Literals* consist of values that you type, such as **12345** or **ABCDE**. Literals are used most often to create default values and, in combination with field identifiers, to compare values in table fields and query columns.

- *Identifiers* are the names of objects in Access (such as fields in tables) that return distinct numeric or text values. The term *return*, when used with expressions, means that the present value of the identifier is substituted for its name in the expression. For example, the field name identifier `CompanyName` in an expression returns the value (a firm name) of the CompanyName field for the currently selected record. Access has five predefined named constants that also serve as identifiers: **True**, **False**, Yes, No, and **Null**. Named constants and variables that you create in Access VBA also are identifiers.

- *Functions* return a value in place of the function name in the expression, such as the **Date** and **Format** functions, which are used in the examples in Chapter 5. Unlike identifiers, most functions require that you supply with parentheses an identifier or value as an argument. Later in this chapter, the section "Functions" explains functions and their arguments.

When literals, identifiers, or functions are used with operators, these combinations are called *operands*. The following sections explain these four elements of expressions more thoroughly.

Note

Expressions in this book appear in monospace type to distinguish expressions from the explanatory text. Operators, including symbolic operators, built-in functions, and other reserved words and symbols of VBA, are set in **monospace bold** type. (VBA reserved words appear in blue color in the Code-Editing window of modules.) SQL operators and names of Access objects are set in monospace type.

OPERATORS

Access and VBA provide six categories of operators that you can use to create expressions:

- *Arithmetic* operators perform addition, subtraction, multiplication, and division.
- *Assignment* and *comparison* operators set values and compare values.
- *Logical* operators deal with values that can only be true or false.
- *Concatenation* operators combine strings of characters.
- *Identifier* operators create unambiguous names for database objects so that you can assign the same field name, for example, in several tables and queries.
- Other operators, such as the Like, Is, and Between operators, simplify the creation of expressions for selecting records with queries.

Operators in the first four categories are available in almost all programming languages. Identifier operators are specific to Access; the other operators of the last category are provided only in relational database management systems (RDBMSs) that create queries based on Structured Query Language (SQL) or a proprietary query language. SQL is the subject of Chapter 23, "Working with Structured Query Language." The following sections explain how to use each of the operators in these categories.

ARITHMETIC OPERATORS

Arithmetic operators operate only on numeric values and must have two numeric operands, with the following exceptions:

- When the minus sign (-) changes the sign (negates the value) of an operand. In this case, the minus sign is called the *unary minus*.
- When the equal sign (=) assigns a value to an Access object or an Access VBA variable identifier.

Table 9.1 lists the arithmetic operators that you can use in Access expressions.

TABLE 9.1 ARITHMETIC OPERATORS

Operator	Description	Example
+	Adds two operands	`Subtotal + Tax`
-	Subtracts two operands	`Date - 30`
- (unary)	Changes the sign of an operand	`-12345`
*	Multiplies two operands	`Units * UnitPrice`
/	Divides one operand by another	`Quantity / 12.55`
\	Divides one integer operand by another	`Units \ 2`
Mod	Returns the remainder of division by an integer	`Units` **Mod** `12`
^	Raises an operand to a power (exponent)	`Value ^ Exponent`

PART

II

CH

9

Access operators are identical to operators used all versions of BASIC, including VBA. If you aren't familiar with BASIC programming, the following operators need further explanation.

Operator	Description
\	The integer division symbol is the equivalent of "goes into," as used in the litany of elementary school arithmetic: Three goes into 13 four times, with one left over. When you use integer division, operators with decimal fractions are rounded to integers, but any decimal fraction in the result is truncated.
Mod	An abbreviation for modulus, this operator returns the left over value of integer division. Therefore, 13 **Mod** 4, for example, returns 1.
^	The exponentiation operator raises the first operand to the power of the second. For example, 2 ^ 4, or two to the fourth power, returns 16 (2*2*2*2).

These three operators seldom are used in business applications but often are used in Access VBA program code.

ASSIGNMENT AND COMPARISON OPERATORS

Table 9.1 omits the equal sign associated with arithmetic expressions because in Access you use it in two ways—neither of which falls under the arithmetic category. The most common use of the equal sign is as an assignment operator; = assigns the value of a single operand to an Access object or to a variable or constant. When you use the expression = "Q" to assign a default value to a field, the equal sign acts as an assignment value. Otherwise, = is a comparison operator that determines whether one of two operands is equal to the other.

Comparison operators compare the values of two operands and return logical values (**True** or **False**) depending on the relationship between the two operands and the operator. An exception is when one of the operands has the **Null** value. In this case, any comparison returns a value of **Null**. Because **Null** represents an unknown value, you cannot compare an unknown value with a known value and come to a valid **True** or **False** conclusion.

Table 9.2 lists the comparison operators available in Access.

TABLE 9.2 COMPARISON OPERATORS

Operator	Description	Example	Result
<	Less than	123 < 1000	True
<=	Less than or equal to	15 <= 15	True
=	Equal to	2 = 4	False
>=	Greater than or equal to	1234 >= 456	True
>	Greater than	123 > 123	False
<>	Not equal	123 <> 456	True

The principal uses of comparison operators are to create validation rules, to establish criteria for selecting records in queries, to determine actions taken by macros, to create joins using the SQL WHERE clause, and to control program flow in Access VBA.

LOGICAL OPERATORS

Logical operators (also called *Boolean operators*) are used most often to combine the results of two or more comparison expressions into a single result. Logical operators can combine only expressions that return the logical values **True**, **False**, or **Null**. With the exception of **Not**, which is the logical equivalent of the unary minus, logical operators always require two operands.

Table 9.3 lists the Access logical operators.

TABLE 9.3   LOGICAL OPERATORS

Operator	Description	Example 1 Example 2	Result 1 Result 2
And	Logical and	True And True True And False	True False
Or	Inclusive or	True Or False False Or False	True False
Not	Logical not	Not True Not False	False True
Xor	Exclusive or	True Xor False True Xor True	True False

The logical operators **And, Or**, and **Not** are used extensively in Access expressions and SQL statements; in SQL statements these operators are uppercase, as in AND, OR, and NOT. **Xor** is seldom used in Access. **Eqv** (equivalent) and **Imp** (implication) are rarely seen, even in programming code, so Table 9.3 omits these two operators.

CONCATENATION OPERATORS

Concatenation operators combine two text values into a single string of characters. If you concatenate ABC with DEF, for example, the result is ABCDEF. The ampersand (**&**) is the preferred concatenation operator in Access. Concatenation is one of the subjects of "The *Variant* Data Type in Access" section later in the chapter.

Tip #66 from

Don't use the + symbol to concatenate strings in queries or Jet SQL. In Jet SQL and VBA, + is reserved for addition of numbers; & concatenates literals and variables of any field data type. The & operator performs implicit type conversion from numbers to text; the & operator treats all variables as character strings. Thus 1234 & 5678 returns 12345678, not 6912.

Note

Transact-SQL, the SQL dialect for the Microsoft Data Engine (MSDE), uses the + symbol for string concatenation. The SQL-92 specification, however, designates two vertical bars (pipe symbols) as the official concatenation operator, as in 'String1' ¦¦ 'String2'. The string concatenation symbol is one of the least consistent elements of common flavors of SQL.

IDENTIFIER OPERATORS

The *identifier operators*, **!** (the exclamation point, often called the *bang operator*) and **.** (the period, called the *dot operator* in Access), are separators and perform the following operations:

- Combine the names of object classes and object names to select a specific object or property of an object. For example, the following expression identifies the Personnel Actions form:

`Forms!PersonnelActions`

This identification is necessary because you might also have a table called PersonnelActions.

- Distinguish object names from property names. Consider the following expression:

`TextBox1.FontSize = 8`

`TextBox1` is a control object, and `FontSize` is a property.

- Identify specific fields in tables, as in the following expression, which specifies the Company Name field of the Customers table:

`Customers!CompanyName`

You use the `!` character to separate object references; the general syntax is `ObjectClass!ObjectName`. The `.` character separates objects and their properties or methods, as in `ObjectClass!Object.Property` or `ObjectClass!ObjectName.Method`.

OTHER OPERATORS

The remaining Access operators are related to the comparison operators. These operators return **True** or **False**, depending on whether the value in a field meets the chosen operator's specification. A **True** value causes a record to be included in a query; a **False** value rejects the record. When you use these operators in validation rules, entries are accepted or rejected based on the logical value returned by the expression.

Table 9.4 lists the four other operators used in Access queries and validation rules.

TABLE 9.4   OTHER OPERATORS

Operator	Description	Example
Is	Used with Null to determine whether a value is **Null** or **Not Null**	`Is Null` `Is Not Null`
Like	Determines whether a string value begins with one or more characters (for Like to work properly, you must add a wild card, *, or one or more ?s)	`Like "Jon*"` `Like "FILE????"`
In	Determines whether a string value is a member of a list of values	`In("CA", "OR", "WA")`
Between	Determines whether a numeric or date value lies within a specified range of values	`Between 1 And 5`

You use the wildcard characters * and ? with the Like operator the same way that you use them in DOS. The * (often called *star* or *splat*) takes the place of any number of characters. The ? takes the place of a single character. For example, Like "Jon*" returns **True** for values such as *Jones* or *Jonathan*. Like "*on*" returns **True** for any value that contains *on*. Like "FILE????" returns **True** for *FILENAME*, but not for *FILE000* or *FILENUMBER*. Wildcard characters can precede the characters that you want to match, as in Like "*son" or Like "????NAME".

Except for Is, the operators in this other category are equivalent to the SQL reserved words LIKE, IN, and BETWEEN. Access includes these operators to promote compatibility with SQL. You can create each of these operators by combining other Access operators or functions. Like "Jon*" is the equivalent of Access VBA's **InStr**(**Left**(*FieldName*, 3), "Jon"); In("CA", "OR", "WA") is similar to **InStr**("CAORWA", *FieldName*), except that no matches occur for the ambiguous A0 and RW. Between 1 And 5 is the equivalent of >= 1 **And** <= 5.

Part

II

Ch

9

Tip #67 from 	Always use Between...And, not the >= and <= comparison operators, to specify a range of dates. You must repeat the field name when using the comparison operators, as in *DateValue* >= #1/1/1999# **And** *DateValue* <= #12/31/1999#. Between syntax is shorter and easier to understand, as demonstrated by *DateValue* Between #1/1/1999# And #12/31/1999#

LITERALS

Access provides three types of literals that you can combine with operators to create expressions. The following list describes these types of literals:

- *Numeric* literals are typed as a series of digits, including the arithmetic sign and decimal point if applicable. You don't have to prefix positive numbers with the plus sign; Access assumes positive values unless the minus sign is present. Numeric literals can include E or e and the sign of the exponent to indicate an exponent in scientific notation—for example, -1.23E-02.

- *Text* (or *string*) literals can include any printable character, plus unprintable characters returned by the **Chr** function. The **Chr** function returns the characters specified by a numeric value from the ANSI character table (similar to the ASCII character table) that Windows uses. For example, **Chr**(9) returns the Tab character. Printable characters include the letters A through Z, numbers 0 through 9, punctuation symbols, and other special keyboard symbols such as the tilde (~). Access expressions require that you enclose string literals within double quotation marks (""). Combinations of printable and unprintable characters are concatenated with the ampersand. For example, the following expression separates two strings with a newline pair.

  "First line" **&** **Chr**(13) **&** **Chr**(10) **&** "Second line"

  Chr(13) is the carriage return (CR), and **Chr**(10) is the line-feed (LF) character; together they form the newline pair.

When you enter string literals in the cells of tables and Query Design grids, Access adds the quotation marks for you. In other places, you must enter the quotation marks yourself.

■ *Date/time* literals are enclosed within number or pound signs (#), as in the expressions #1-Jan-80# or #10:20:30#. Access adds the enclosing pound signs if the program detects that you are typing into a Design grid a date or time in one of the standard Access Date/Time formats.

IDENTIFIERS

An *identifier* usually is the name of an object; databases, tables, fields, queries, forms, and reports are objects in Access. Each object has a name that uniquely identifies that object. Sometimes, to identify a subobject, an identifier name consists of a *family name* (object class) separated from a *given name* (object name) by a bang symbol or a period (an identifier operator). The family name of the identifier comes first, followed by the separator and then the given name. SQL uses the period as an object separator. An example of an identifier in an SQL statement is as follows:

```
Customers.Address
```

In this example, the identifier for the Address field object is contained in the Customers table object. *Customers* is the family name of the object (the table), and *Address* is the given name of the subobject (the field). In Access, however, you use the ! symbol to separate table names and field names. (The period separates objects and their properties.) If an identifier contains a space or other punctuation, enclose the identifier within square brackets, as in this example:

```
[Order Details]!Quantity
```

You cannot include periods or exclamation points within the names of identifiers; [Unit!Price], for example, is not allowed.

In simple queries that use only one table, you can omit the TableName. prefix. You use identifiers to return the values of fields in form and report objects. Chapters 12 through 15 cover the specific method of identifying objects within forms and reports.

FUNCTIONS

Functions return values to their names; functions can take the place of identifiers in expressions. One of the most common functions used in Access expressions is **Now**, which returns to its name the date and time from your computer's internal clock. If you type **Now** as the DefaultValue property of a table's Date/Time field, for example, 3/15/99 9:00 appears in the field when you change to Datasheet view (at 9:00 A.M. on March 15, 1999).

→ **See** "Modules, Functions, and Subprocedures," **p. 995**.

Access and VBA define about 150 individual functions. The following list groups functions by purpose:

- *Date and time* functions manipulate date/time values in fields or Date/Time values that you enter as literals. You can extract parts of dates (such as the year or day of the month) and parts of times (such as hours and minutes) with date and time functions.

- *Text-manipulation* functions are used for working with strings of characters.

- *Data-type conversion* functions enable you to specify the data type of values in numeric fields instead of depending on Access to pick the most appropriate data type.

- *Mathematic* and *trigonometric* functions perform on numeric values operations that are beyond the capability of the standard Access arithmetic operators. You can use simple trigonometric functions, for example, to calculate the length of the sides of a right triangle (if you know the length of one side and the included angle).

- *Financial* functions are similar to functions provided by Lotus 1-2-3 and Microsoft Excel. They calculate depreciation, values of annuities, and rates of return on investments. To determine the present value of a lottery prize paid out in 25 equal yearly installments, for example, you can use the PV function.

- *General-purpose* functions don't fit any of the preceding classifications; you use these functions to create Access queries, forms, and reports.

- *Other functions* include those that perform dynamic data exchange (DDE) with other Windows applications, domain aggregate functions, SQL aggregate functions, and functions used primarily in Access VBA programming.

Only the first three groups of functions commonly are used in Access queries; Chapters 28 through 30 offer examples of the use of some of members of the last four function groups.

USING THE IMMEDIATE WINDOW

When you write VBA programming code in a module, the Immediate window is available to assist you in debugging your code. You also can use the module's Immediate window to demonstrate the use and syntax of functions.

To experiment with some of the functions described in the following sections, open the Northwind database and perform these steps:

1. Click the Modules shortcut in the Database window.

2. Double-click the Utility Functions module to open it in the VBA Editor. If you haven't changed the docking options for the VBA Editor, the Immediate window appears at the bottom of the Editor's window.

3. Type **?Now** in the bottom portion of the Immediate window (see Figure 9.1) and press Enter. The date and time from your computer's clock appear on the next line. The **?** is shorthand for the VBA **Print** statement (which displays the value of a function or variable) and must be added to the **Now** function to display the function's value.

   If you neglected to precede the function entry with **?** or **Print**, an error message appears, indicating that Access expected you to type a statement or an equal sign. Click OK and type **?** before the function name in the Immediate window. Press End to return the caret to the end of the line and then press Enter to retry the test.

Figure 9.1
Using the Immediate window of a temporary module to experiment with functions.

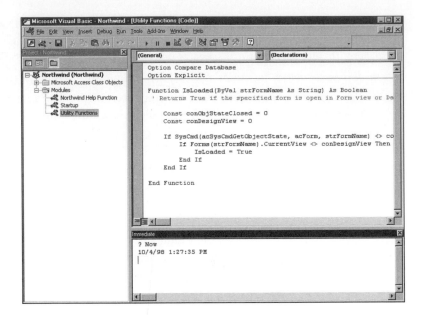

4. To reposition the Immediate window more easily, click its title bar and drag the window to a central area of your display where it remains undocked.

As you type in your functions in the Immediate window, Access displays an Autocompletion ToolTip, showing the function's name and its complete argument list. You must type a space or opening parenthesis after the function name to make open the popup Autocompletion window. An *argument list* is the list of information that you specify for the function to work on—for example, if you use the **Sqr** function to compute the square root of a number, you must supply a number inside the function's parentheses. Figure 9.2 shows the popup Help window for the **Sqr** function. You can turn this feature on and off by choosing Tools, Options and marking or clearing the Auto Quick Info option on the Editor page.

Figure 9.2
A popup statement Autocompletion ToolTip appears as you type functions in the Immediate window.

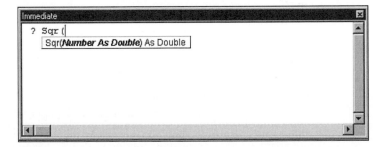

Tip #68 from

Obtain online help for a function by placing the caret within the function name and pressing F1 to display the Visual Basic Reference topic for the function (see Figure 9.3).

Note

If you specified Install on First Use, rather than Run from My Computer, for Access and VBA help files, you receive a `This Feature Is Not Installed` message. In this case, you must have the distribution CD-ROM available or have access to a networked Office 2000 installation share to install the required HTML help files.

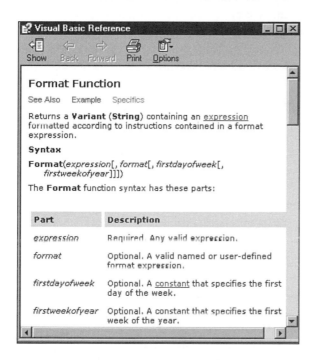

Figure 9.3
The `Format` function Help window.

If you click an enabled Example link in any function Help window, the window displays an example of the function used in Access VBA code. These examples show the syntax of the functions and appropriate arguments. The examples, however, usually aren't applicable to the function's use in an Access query or validation rule.

THE `Variant` DATA TYPE IN ACCESS AND VBA

Variant is a special data type unique to Microsoft Visual Basic dialects. The **Variant** data type enables you to concatenate values that ordinarily have different data types, such as an integer and a character string. The capability to concatenate different data types is called *turning off data-type checking*. **Variant** values are related to the **As Any** data type that Access VBA uses to turn off data-type checking when declaring external functions contained in Windows Dynamic Link Libraries (DLLs).

The **Variant** data type enables you to concatenate field values of tables and queries that have dissimilar data types without using VBA's data-type conversion functions such as **Str**. (**Str** converts numeric values to the **String** data type) The **Variant** data type also simplifies expressions that combine field values to create concatenated indexes. The **Variant** data type also enables you to use the **&** symbol to concatenate values of different data types. SQL requires you to use the ampersand for such concatenation.

→ **See** "Access Intrinsic Constants," **p. 1008**.

Table 9.5 lists the 16 common subtypes of the **Variant** data type of Access VBA, along with the names of the intrinsic Visual Basic constants, vbConstant, corresponding to the **Variant** subtype value. In addition to the Access intrinsic constants, VBA provides its own set of intrinsic constants, which are prefixed with vb. Access intrinsic constants are prefixed with ac. Intrinsic constants, which you use primarily when writing Access VBA code, are one of the subjects of Chapter 27, "Understanding Universal Data Access, OLE DB, and ADO."

TABLE 9.5   SUBTYPES OF THE *Variant* DATA TYPE

Subtype	Constant	Corresponds To	Stored As
0	(None)	**Empty** (uninitialized)	Not applicable
1	vbNull	**Null** (no valid data)	Not applicable
2	vbInteger	**Integer**	2-byte integer
3	vbLong	**Long**	4-byte long integer
4	vbSingle	**Single**	4-byte single-precision floating point
5	vbDouble	**Double**	8-byte double-precision floating point
6	vbCurrency	**Currency**	4-byte fixed point
7	vbDate	Date/Time	8-byte double-precision floating point
8	vbString	**String**	Conventional string variable
9	vbObject	**Object**	Automation object
10	vbError	**Error**	**Error** data type (error number)
11	vbBoolean	**Boolean**	**True** or **False** values only
12	vbVariant	**Variant**	Used with **Variant** arrays
13	vbDataObject	Special	Non-Automation object
17	vbByte	**Byte**	Numeric value from 0–255
8192	vbArray	**Array**	Used with **Variant** arrays

You can concatenate **Variant** values with **Variant** subtypes 1–8 listed in Table 9.5. You can concatenate a subtype 8 **Variant** (**String**) with a subtype 5 **Variant** (**Double**), for example, without receiving from Access the Type Mismatch error message displayed when you attempt this concatenation with conventional **String** (text) and **Double** data types. Access returns a value with the **Variant** subtype corresponding to the highest subtype number of the concatenated values. This example, therefore, returns a subtype 8 (**String**) **Variant** because 8 is greater than 5, the subtype number for the **Double** value. If you concatenate a subtype 2 (**Integer**) value with a subtype 3 (**Long**) value, Access returns subtype 3 **Variant** data.

Distinguishing between the **Empty** and **Null Variant** subtypes is important. **Empty** indicates that a variable that you created with VBA code has a name but doesn't have an initial value. **Empty** applies only to Access VBA variables (see Chapter 26, "Writing Visual Basic for Applications Code"). **Null** indicates that a data cell doesn't contain an entry. You can assign the **Null** value to a variable, in which case the variable is initialized to the **Null** value, **Variant** subtype 1.

→ **See** "Variables and Naming Conventions," **p. 1002**.

FUNCTIONS FOR DATE AND TIME

NEW 2000

Access offers a variety of functions for dealing with dates and times. If you've used Visual Basic, you probably recognize most of the functions applicable to the Date/Time field data types shown in Table 9.6. VBA has several Date/Time functions, such as **DateAdd** and **DateDiff**, to simplify the calculation of date values. **MonthName** and **WeekdayName** functions are new to VBA 6.0. The following examples use the year 1998 because 1998 is the latest year for which data is available in the tables of Northwind.mdb.

TABLE 9.6	ACCESS FUNCTIONS FOR DATE AND TIME		
Function	**Description**	**Example**	**Returns**
Date	Returns the current system date and time as a subtype 7 date **Variant** or a standard date **String** subtype 8.	Date	7/15/98 07-15-98
DateAdd	Returns a subtype 7 date with a specified number of days ("d"), weeks ("ww"), months ("m"), or years ("y") added to the date.	DateAdd("d",31, #7/15/98#)	8/15/98
DateDiff Date	Returns an **Integer** representing the difference between two dates using the d/w/m/y specification.	DateDiff("d",Date, #4/15/98#)	-91 (assuming = 7/15/98)
DatePart	Returns the specified part of a date such as day, month, year, day of week ("w"), and so on, as an **Integer**.	DatePart ("w", #7/15/98)	7 (Saturday)

continues

TABLE 9.6 CONTINUED

Function	Description	Example	Returns
DateSerial	Returns a subtype 7 **Variant** from year, month, and day arguments.	DateSerial (98,7,15)	7/15/98
DateValue	Returns a subtype 7 **Variant** that corresponds to a date argument in a character format.	DateValue ("15-Jul-98")	7/15/98
Day	Returns an **Integer** between 1 and 31 [inclusive] that represents a day of the month from a Date/Time value.	Day(Date)	15 (assuming that the date is the 15th of the month)
Hour	Returns an **Integer** between 0 and 23 (inclusive) that represents the hour of the Date/Time value.	Hour (#2:30 PM#)	14
Minute	Returns an **Integer** between 0 and 59 (inclusive) that represents the minute of a Date/Time value.	Minute (#2:30 PM#)	30
Month	Returns an **Integer** between 1 and 12 (inclusive) that represents the month of a Date/Time value.	Month(#15-Jul-98#)	7
MonthName	Returns the full or abbreviated name of a month from the month number (1 to 12). If you omit the second argument, the function returns the full name.	MonthName (10, **False**) MonthName (10, **True**)	October Oct
Now	Returns the date and time of a computer's system clock as a **Variant** of subtype 7.	Now	7/15/98 11:57:28 AM
Second	Returns an **Integer** between 0 and 59 (inclusive) that represents the second of a Date/Time value.	Second (Now)	28
Time,	Returns the Time portion of a Date/Time value from the system clock.	Time	11:57:20 AM
TimeSerial	Returns the time serial value of the time expressed in integer hours, minutes, and seconds.	TimeSerial (11,57,20)	11:57:20 AM

Function	Description	Example	Returns
TimeValue	Returns the time serial value of the time (entered as the **String** value) as a subtype 7 **Variant**.	TimeValue ("11:57")	11:57
Weekday	Returns day of the week (Sunday = 1) corresponding to the date as an **Integer**.	Weekday (#7/15/98#)	7
WeekdayName	Returns the full or abbreviated name of the day from the day number (0 to 7). Setting the second argument to **True** abbreviates the name. A third optional argument lets you specify the first day of the week.	WeekdayName (4, **False**) WeekdayName (4, **True**)	Wednesday Wed
Year	Returns the year of a Date/Time value as an **Integer**.	Year (#7/15/1998#)	1998

TEXT-MANIPULATION FUNCTIONS

Table 9.7 lists the functions that deal with the Text field data type, corresponding to the **String** VBA data type. Most of these functions are modeled on BASIC string functions.

TABLE 9.7   FUNCTIONS FOR THE *String* DATA TYPE

Function	Description	Example	Returns
Asc	Returns ANSI numeric value of character as an **Integer**.	Asc("C")	67
Chr	Returns character corresponding to the numeric ANSI value as a **String**.	Chr(67) Chr(10)	C (line feed)
Format	Formats an expression in accordance with appropriate format strings.	Format (Date, "dd-mmm-yy")	15-Jul-98
InStr	Returns the position of one string within another.	InStr ("ABCD","C")	3
LCase	Returns the lowercase version of a string.	LCase ("ABCD")	abcd
Left	Returns the leftmost characters of a string ("ABCDEF",3).	Left	ABC
Len	Returns the number of characters in a string as a **Long**.	Len("ABCDE")	5

continues

TABLE 9.7   CONTINUED

Function	Description	Example	Returns
LTrim	Removes leading spaces from string.	LTrim (" ABC")	ABC
Mid	Returns a portion of a string.	Mid ("ABCDE",2,3)	BCD
Right	Returns the rightmost characters of a string.	Right ("ABCDEF",3)	DEF
RTrim	Removes trailing spaces from a string.	RTrim ("ABC ")	ABC
Space	Returns a string consisting of a specified number of spaces.	Space(5)	
Str	Converts the numeric value of any data type to a string.	Str(123.45)	123.45
StrComp	Compares two strings for equivalence and returns the integer result of the comparison.	StrComp ("ABC", "abc")	0
String	Returns a string consisting of specified repeated characters.	String (5, "A")	AAAAA
Trim	Removes leading and trailing spaces from a string.	Trim (" ABC ")	ABC
UCase	Returns the uppercase version of a string.	UCase ("abc")	ABC
Val	Returns the numeric value of a string in a data type appropriate to the argument's format.	Val ("123.45")	123.45

Note

VBA includes two versions of many functions that return **String** variables—one with and one without the BASIC-language **$ String** type identification character. This book doesn't use type identification characters, so the second form of the function is omitted from the tables in this chapter.

Figure 9.4 shows Immediate window examples of common string-manipulation functions. The Immediate window is particular valuable for learning exactly how these functions behave with different types of literal values.

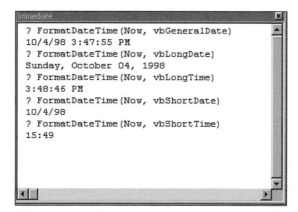

```
Immediate                              ×
? Asc("C")
  67
? Chr(67)
C
? Format(Date, "dd-mmm-yyyy")
04-Oct-1998
? Instr("ABCD", "C")
  3
? Left("ABCDEF", 3)
ABC
? Mid("ABCDEF", 3, 2)
CD
```

Figure 9.4
Testing string-manipulation functions in the Immediate window.

NEW 2000 Chapter 4 explains the syntax of the **Format** function, which you can use with Jet queries and in VBA code. The following list shows you how to use the new localized **Format...** functions of VBA 6.0, which you *can't* use in Jet queries:

- **FormatCurrency**(*NumericValue*[, *DigitsAfterDecimal* [, *IncludeLeadingDigit* [, *ParensForNegativeNumbers* [, *GroupDigits*]]]]) returns a value formatted with the localized currency symbol, including the Euro. With the exception of *NumericValue*, the arguments are optional. If *IncludeLeadingDigit* is **True**, fractional values are pre-fixed with $0 in North America. Setting GroupDigits to **True** applies the group delim-iter, comma (as in $1,000) for North America.

- **FormatDateTime**(*DateValue*[, *NamedFormat*]) returns a date string whose format depends on the value of *NamedFormat*. Valid values of *NamedFormat* are vbGeneralDate, vbLongDate, vbShortDate, vbLongTime, or vbShortTime. Figure 9.5 illustrates the use of the **FormatDateTime** function.

```
Immediate                              ×
? FormatDateTime(Now, vbGeneralDate)
10/4/98 3:47:55 PM
? FormatDateTime(Now, vbLongDate)
Sunday, October 04, 1998
? FormatDateTime(Now, vbLongTime)
3:48:46 PM
? FormatDateTime(Now, vbShortDate)
10/4/98
? FormatDateTime(Now, vbShortTime)
15:49
```

Figure 9.5
Experimenting with VBA 6.0's new **FormatDateTime** function.

- **FormatNumber**(*NumericValue*[, *DigitsAfterDecimal* [, *IncludeLeadingDigit* [, *ParensForNegativeNumbers* [, *GroupDigits*]]]]) returns the same values as FormatCurrency, but without the currency symbol.

- **FormatPercent**(*NumericValue*[, *DigitsAfterDecimal* [, *IncludeLeadingDigit* [, *ParensForNegativeNumbers* [, *GroupDigits*]]]]) returns the same values as **FormatNumber**, but multiplies *NumericValue* by 100 and adds a trailing % symbol.

Note

If you attempt to use any of the VBA 6.0 Format... functions in a Jet query, you receive an "Undefined function 'Format*Type*' in expression" error when you execute the query.

→ To find techniques for formatting you can safely use with Jet, **see** "Custom Display Formats," **p. 146**.

NUMERIC, LOGICAL, DATE/TIME, AND String DATA-TYPE CONVERSION FUNCTIONS

You can assign a particular data type to a numeric value with any of the data-type conversion functions. After you *freeze* (or *coerce*) a data type with one of the numeric data-type conversion functions, you cannot concatenate that data type with the **String** data type.

Table 9.8 lists the 11 numeric data-type conversion functions of Access 2000. The *NumValue* argument in the Syntax column can be any numeric or **String** value. However, if you use a **String** value as the argument of a numeric-type conversion function, the first character of the argument's value must be a digit, a dollar sign, a plus symbol, or a minus symbol. The most commonly used conversion function in queries is **CCur**.

TABLE 9.8 DATA-TYPE CONVERSION FUNCTIONS FOR NUMERIC, TIME/DATE, AND STRING VALUES

Function	Description	Syntax
CBool	Converts a numeric value to a **Boolean** (**True** or **False**) data type.	**CBool**(*NumValue*)
Cbyte	Converts a numeric value to a **Byte** (0–255) data type.	**CByte**(*NumValue*)
CCur	Converts a numeric value to a **Currency** data type.	**CCur**(*NumValue*)
CDate	Converts a numeric value to a **Date** value (**CDate** replaces **CVDate**, which is obsolete).	**CDate**(*NumValue*)
CDbl	Converts a numeric value to a **Double** data type.	**CDbl**(*NumValue*)
CInt	Converts a numeric value to an **Integer** data type.	**CInt**(*NumValue*)
CLng	Converts a numeric value to a **Long** integer data type.	**CLng**(*NumValue*)

Function	Description	Syntax
CSng	Converts a numeric value to a **Single** data type.	CSng(*NumValue*)
CStr	Converts a numeric value to a **String** data type.	CStr(*NumValue*)
CVar	Converts a numeric value to a **Variant** data type.	CVar(*NumValue*)
CVErr	Converts a valid error number to create user-defined errors.	CVErr(*NumValue*)
Nz	Converts a **Null** Value to 0 or a zero-length string, depending on the context of use.	Nz(*FieldValue*[, *ReturnValue*])

NEW 2000

The Nz (**Null**-to-zero) function accepts only a **Variant** *FieldValue* argument. Nz returns non-**Null** **Variant** argument values unchanged. When used in a Jet query, Nz returns an empty string (" ") for **Null** argument values, unless you specify 0 or another literal, such as "Null" as the value of the optional *ReturnValue* argument. The Jet Expression Service supplies the Nz function; it's not a VBA reserved word.

Tip #69 from

> Use Nz to format the result sets of your crosstab queries, replacing **Null** values with 0. When you execute a crosstab query—such as quarterly product sales by region—cells for products with no sales in a region for the quarter are empty. Empty cells might mislead management into believing information is missing. Applying the Nz function puts a 0 in empty cells, eliminating the ambiguity.

INTRINSIC AND NAMED CONSTANTS

As noted earlier in this chapter, VBA and Access have many predefined intrinsic constants. The names of these constants are considered *keywords* because you cannot use these names for any purpose other than returning the value represented by the names, such as -1 for **True** and Yes, 0 for **False** and No. (**True** and Yes are Access synonyms, as are **False** and No, so you can use these pairs of values interchangeably in Access, but not in VBA.) As mentioned earlier in the chapter, **Null** indicates a field with no valid entry. **True**, **False**, and **Null** are the most commonly used VBA intrinsic constants.

Symbolic constants, which you define, return a single, predetermined value for the entire Access session. You can create named constants for use with forms and reports by defining them in the declarations section of an Access VBA module. Chapter 26, "Writing Visual Basic for Applications Code," describes how to create and use symbolic (named) constants.

→ To find which constants are built into Access, **see** "Symbolic Constants," **p. 1008**.

CREATING ACCESS EXPRESSIONS

Chapter 5 uses several functions to validate data entry for most fields in the Personnel Actions table. Chapter 8 uses an expression to select the states to be included in a mailing-list query. These examples provide the foundation on which to build more complex expressions that can define more precisely the validation rules and query criteria for real-life database applications.

→ **See** "Validating Data Entry," **p. 194** for examples using functions to help restrict data entry.

→ For information on how to enter expressions in a query, **see** " Selecting Records by Criteria and Sorting the Display," **p. 302**.

The topics that follow provide a few examples of typical expressions for creating default values for fields, validating data entry, creating query criteria, and calculating field values. The examples demonstrate the similarity of syntax for expressions with different purposes. Part III of this book, "Designing Forms and Reports," provides additional examples of expressions designed for use in forms and reports; Part VII, "Programming and Converting Access Applications," explains the use of expressions with Access VBA code.

EXPRESSIONS FOR CREATING DEFAULT VALUES

Expressions that create default field values can speed the entry of new records. Assigning values ordinarily requires you to use the assignment operator (=). When entering a default value in the properties pane for a table in Design mode, however, you can enter a simple literal. An example is the Q default value assigned to the paType field in Chapter 4. In this case, Access infers the = assignment operator and the quotation marks surrounding the Q. To adhere to the rules of creating expressions, the default value entry must be = "Q". You often can use shorthand techniques when typing expressions because Access infers the missing characters. If you type **= "Q"**, you achieve the same result; Access doesn't infer the extra characters.

You can use complex expressions for default values if the result of the expression conforms to or can be converted by Access to the proper field data type. You can type **= 1** as the default value for the paType field, for example, although 1 is a Numeric field data type and paType is a Text type field.

EXPRESSIONS FOR VALIDATING DATA

The Personnel Actions table uses several expressions to validate data entry. The validation rule for the paID field is > 0; the rule for the paType field is "S" **Or** "Q" **Or** "Y" **Or** "B" **Or** "C"; the rule for the paApprovedBy field is > 0 **Or Is Null**. The validation rule for the paID field is equivalent to the following imaginary in-line VBA **IIf** function:

```
IIf(DataEntry > 0, paID = DataEntry,
    MsgBox("Please enter a valid employee ID number."))
```

Access tests *DataEntry* in the validation rule expression. If the validation expression returns **True**, the value of *DataEntry* replaces the value in the current record's field. If the expression returns **False**, a message box displays the validation text that you typed. **MsgBox** is a function used in VBA programming to display a message box onscreen. You cannot type the imaginary validation rule just described; Access infers the equivalent of the imaginary **IIf** expression after you add the `ValidationRule` and `ValidationText` properties with entries in the two text boxes for the paID field.

You might change the expression `"S" Or "Q" Or "Y" Or "B" Or "C"`, which you use to test the paType field, to a function. The **In** function provides a simpler expression that accomplishes the same objective:

```
In("S", "Q", "Y", "B", "C")
```

Alternatively, you can use the following table-level validation expression:

```
InStr("SQYBC",[paID]) > 0
```

Both expressions give the same result, but you can use **InStr** only for table-level validation because one of its arguments refers to a field name. Thus, the **In** function provides the better solution.

EXPRESSIONS FOR QUERY CRITERIA

When creating Chapter 8's qryUSMailingList query to select records from the states of California, Oregon, and Washington, you type **CA**, **OR**, and **WA** on separate lines; Access adds the equal sign and double quotes around the literals for you. A better expression is **In**(`"CA"`, `"OR"`, `"WA"`), entered on the same line as the `="USA"` criterion for the Country field. This expression corrects the failure to test the Country field for a value equal to USA for the OR and WA entries.

→ **See** "Creating More Complex Queries," **p. 303**, if you're not sure how multiple criteria should look in the grid.

You can use a wide range of other functions to select specific records to be returned to a query table. Table 9.9 shows some typical functions used as query criteria applicable to the Northwind Traders tables. Table 9.9 uses 1997 as the year value, because 1997 has a full calendar year of data in the Northwind.mdb tables.

TABLE 9.9   TYPICAL EXPRESSIONS USED AS QUERY CRITERIA

Field	Expression	Records Returned
Customers Table		
Country	**Not** `"USA"` **And** **Not** `"Canada"`	Firms other than those in the U.S. and Canada.
Country	**Not** (`"USA"` **Or** `"Canada"`)	Firms other than those in the U.S. and Canada; the parentheses apply the condition to both literals.
CompanyName	`Like "[N-Z]*"`	Firms with names beginning with N through Z, outside the U.S.

continues

TABLE 9.9   CONTINUED

Field	Expression	Records Returned
CompanyName	Like S* Or Like V*	Firms with names beginning with S or V (Access adds Like and quotation marks).
CompanyName	Like "*shop*"	Firms with *shop*, *Shop*, *Shoppe*, or *SHOPPING* in the firm name.
PostalCode	>=90000	Firms with postal codes greater than or equal to 90000.
Orders Table		
OrderDate	Year([OrderDate]) = 1997	Orders received to date, beginning with 1/1/1997.
OrderDate	Like "*/*/97"	Orders received to date, beginning with 1/1/1997; using wild cards simplifies expressions.
OrderDate	Like "1/*/97"	Orders received in the month of January 1997.
OrderDate	Like "1/?/97"	Orders received from the 1st to the 9th of January 1997.
OrderDate	Year([OrderDate] = 1997 And DatePart("q", [OrderDate]) = 1	Orders received in the first quarter of 1997.
OrderDate	Between #1/1/97# And #3/31/97#	Orders received in the first quarter of 1997.
OrderDate	Year([OrderDate] = 1997 And DatePart("ww", [OrderDate]) = 10	Orders received in the 10th week of 1997.
OrderDate	>= DateValue ("1/15/97")	Orders received on or after 1/15/97.
Shipped Date	Is Null	Orders not yet shipped.
Order Amount	>= 5000	Orders with values greater than or equal to $5,000.
Order Amount	Between 5000 And 10000	Orders with values greater than or equal to $5,000 and less than or equal to $10,000.
Order Amount	< 1000	Orders less than $1,000.

The wildcard characters used in Like expressions simplify the creation of criteria for selecting names and dates. As in DOS, the asterisk (*) substitutes for any legal number of characters, and the question mark (?) substitutes for a single character. When a wildcard character prefixes or appends a string, the matching process loses its default case sensitivity. If you want to match a string without regard to case, use the following expression:

UCase(*FieldName*) = "*MATCH STRING*"

ENTERING A QUERY CRITERION

To experiment with query criteria expressions, follow these steps:

PART

II

CH

9

1. Click the Queries shortcut of the Database window and then double-click the Create Query in the Design View shortcut to open the Query Design window and the Add Tables dialog.

2. Select the Customers table from the Tables list of the Show Table dialog, hold Ctrl and click Order Details and Orders, click Add, and then click Close. The CustomerID fields of the Customers and Orders tables and the OrderID fields of the Orders and Order Details tables are joined; *joins* are indicated by a line between the fields of the two tables. (Chapter 10 covers joining multiple tables.)

3. Add the CompanyName, PostalCode, and Country fields of the Customers table to the query. You can add fields by selecting them from the Field drop-down list in the Query Design grid, by clicking a field in the Customers field list above the grid and dragging the field to the desired Field cell in the grid, or by double-clicking a field in the Customers field list above the grid.

4. Add to the query the OrderID, OrderDate, ShippedDate, and Freight fields of the Orders table. Use the horizontal scrollbar slider under the Query Design grid to expose additional field columns as necessary. Choose View, Table Names to display the table names in the Tables row of the Query Design grid if necessary. Place the caret in the Sort row of the OrderID field, press F4 to open the Sort list box, and select Ascending Sort.

5. Click the Totals button of the toolbar or choose View, Totals to add the Total row to the Query Design grid. The default value, Group By, is added to the Total cell for each field of your query.

6. Scroll the grid so that the Freight column appears. Click the selection bar above the Field row to select the Freight column, and press the Insert key to add a new column.

7. Type **Amount: CCur([UnitPrice]*[Quantity]*(1–[Discount]))** in the new column's Field cell (see Figure 9.6). This expression calculates the net amount of each line item in the Order Details table and formats the column as if the field data type were Currency. The next section discusses how to use expressions to create calculated fields.

Figure 9.6
The query design for testing the use of expressions to select records with values that meet criteria.

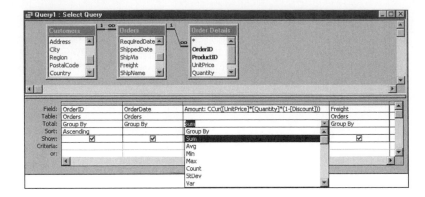

8. Move the caret to the Total row of the new column and press F4 to open the drop-down list. Select Sum from the list (refer to Figure 9.6). The Sum option totals the net amount for all the line items of each order in the Orders table. In the next chapter, you learn the details of how to create queries that group data.

→ For other ways you can manipulate results from queries, **see** "Making Calculations Based on Selected Records of a Table," **p. 391**.

The Total row for all the other columns of the query shows Group By. Make sure that you mark the Show check box so that your new query column appears when you run the query. (Don't make an entry in the Table row of your new query column; if you do, you receive an error message when you run the query.)

9. Click the Run or Datasheet View button of the toolbar to run your new query. Your query appears as shown in Figure 9.7. The Amount column contains the total amount of the order, net of any discounts.

Figure 9.7
The query result set for the query design shown in Figure 9.6.

Company Name	Postal Code	Country	Order ID	Order Date	Shipped Date	Amount	Freight
Alfreds Futterkiste	12209	Germany	10643	25-Aug-1997	02-Sep-1997	$814.50	$29.46
Alfreds Futterkiste	12209	Germany	10692	03-Oct-1997	13-Oct-1997	$878.00	$61.02
Alfreds Futterkiste	12209	Germany	10702	13-Oct-1997	21-Oct-1997	$330.00	$23.94
Alfreds Futterkiste	12209	Germany	10835	15-Jan-1998	21-Jan-1998	$845.80	$69.53
Alfreds Futterkiste	12209	Germany	10952	16-Mar-1998	24-Mar-1998	$471.20	$40.42
Alfreds Futterkiste	12209	Germany	11011	09-Apr-1998	13-Apr-1998	$933.50	$1.21
Ana Trujillo Emparedados y	05021	Mexico	10308	18-Sep-1996	24-Sep-1996	$88.80	$1.61
Ana Trujillo Emparedados y	05021	Mexico	10625	08-Aug-1997	14-Aug-1997	$479.75	$43.90
Ana Trujillo Emparedados y	05021	Mexico	10759	28-Nov-1997	12-Dec-1997	$320.00	$11.99
Ana Trujillo Emparedados y	05021	Mexico	10926	04-Mar-1998	11-Mar-1998	$514.40	$39.92
Antonio Moreno Taquería	05023	Mexico	10365	27-Nov-1996	02-Dec-1996	$403.20	$22.00
Antonio Moreno Taquería	05023	Mexico	10507	15-Apr-1997	22-Apr-1997	$749.06	$47.45
Antonio Moreno Taquería	05023	Mexico	10535	13-May-1997	21-May-1997	$1,940.85	$15.64
Antonio Moreno Taquería	05023	Mexico	10573	19-Jun-1997	20-Jun-1997	$2,082.00	$84.84

Record: 1 of 830

USING THE EXPRESSION BUILDER TO ADD QUERY CRITERIA

After creating and testing your query, you can apply criteria to limit the number of records that the query returns. You can use Access's Expression Builder to simplify the process of adding record-selection criteria to your query. To test some of the expressions listed in Table 9.9, follow these steps:

1. Click the Design View button of the toolbar to change to Query Design mode.

2. Place the caret in the Criteria row of the field for which you want to establish a record-selection criterion.

3. Click the Build button of the toolbar to display the Expression Builder's window. Alternatively, you can right-click the Criteria row and then choose Build from the popup menu.

4. In the Expression text box at the top of Expression Builder's window, type one of the expressions from Table 9.9. Figure 9.8 shows the sample expression Like "*shop*" that applies to the Criteria row of the Company Name column. You can use the Like button under the expression text box as a shortcut for entering Like.

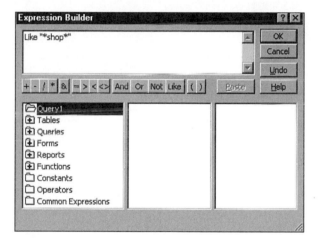

Figure 9.8
Entering a criterion in the Expression Builder to create a criterion to match *shop*.

5. Click OK to return to the Query Design grid. In the field where the caret is located, the Expression Builder places the expression that you built (see Figure 9.9).

6. Click the Run button of the toolbar to test the expression. The query result for the example in Figure 9.9 appears as shown in Figure 9.10.

Figure 9.9
The Query Design grid with the expression that you created in the Expression Builder.

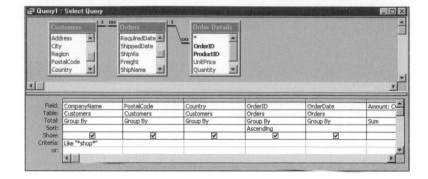

Figure 9.10
The query result set resulting from adding the `Like "*shop*"` criteria to the Company Name field.

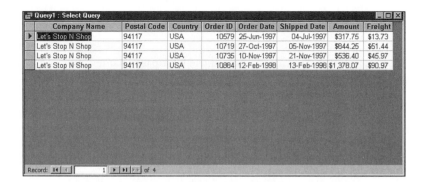

7. Return to Query Design mode; then select and delete the expression by pressing the Delete key.

8. Repeat steps 2 through 7 for each expression that you want to test. When you test expressions using Date/Time functions, sort the OrderDate field in ascending order. Similarly, sort on the Amount field when queries are based on amount criteria. You can alter the expressions and try combinations with the implied And condition by entering criteria for other fields in the same row. Access warns you with an error message if you make a mistake in an expression's syntax.

9. After you finish experimenting, save your query with a descriptive name, such as **qryOrderAmount**.

The preceding query is included in Express.mdb sample file, located in the \Seua2k\Chaptr09 folder of the accompanying CD-ROM. If you bypassed the preceding steps, you can run qryOrderAmount from tables linked to C:\Program Files\Microsoft Office\Office\Samples\Northwind.mdb or import the query into Northwind.mdb, and then compare the result set with Figure 9.10.

EXPRESSIONS FOR CALCULATING QUERY FIELD VALUES

The preceding section demonstrates that you can use expressions to create new, calculated fields in query tables. Calculated fields display data computed based on the values of other fields in the same row of the query table. Table 9.10 shows some representative expressions that you can use to create calculated query fields. Notice that field names must be enclosed with square brackets when typed in the Query Design window.

TABLE 9.10   TYPICAL EXPRESSIONS TO CREATE CALCULATED QUERY FIELDS

Column Name	Expression	Values Calculated
TotalAmount	`[Amount] + [Freight]`	Sum of the OrderAmount and Freight fields.
FreightPercent	`100 * [Freight]/[Amount]`	Freight charges as a percentage of the order amount.
FreightPct	`Format([Freight]/[Amount], "Percent")`	Freight charges as a percentage of the order amount, but with formatting applied.
SalesTax	`Format([Amount] * 0.05, "$#,###.00")`	Sales tax of 5 percent of the amount of the order added with a display similar to the Currency data type.

To create a query containing calculated fields, follow these steps:

1. In Query Design view, move to the first blank column of the query that you created in the preceding section. Type the column name shown in Table 9.10, followed by a colon and then the expression. (Click the Build button of the toolbar to use the Expression Builder to enter the following expression:

   `FreightPct: Format([Freight]/[Amount],"Percent")`

   If you don't type the field name and colon, Access provides the default Expr1 as the calculated field name.

2. Place the caret in the Total cell of the calculated field and select Expression from the drop-down list, as shown in Figure 9.11. If you don't select Expression, your query opens a Parameters dialog or returns an error message when you attempt to execute it.

To avoid this error, see the "Query Expressions Fail to Execute" element of the "Troubleshooting" section at the end of the chapter.

3. Remove the `Like "*shop*"` criterion from the CustomerName column.

4. Run the query. The result set for the query with the calculated field appears as shown in Figure 9.12.

5. Repeat steps 1, 2, and 3 for each of the four examples in Table 9.9.

Figure 9.11
The query design for two of the calculated fields of Table 9.9.

qryFreightPct : Select Query

Company Name	Postal Code	Country	Order ID	Order Date	Shipped Date	Amount	Freight	FreightPct
Alfreds Futterkiste	12209	Germany	10643	25-Aug-1997	02-Sep-1997	$814.50	$29.46	3.62%
Alfreds Futterkiste	12209	Germany	10692	03-Oct-1997	13-Oct-1997	$878.00	$61.02	6.95%
Alfreds Futterkiste	12209	Germany	10702	13-Oct-1997	21-Oct-1997	$330.00	$23.94	7.25%
Alfreds Futterkiste	12209	Germany	10835	15-Jan-1998	21-Jan-1998	$845.80	$69.53	8.22%
Alfreds Futterkiste	12209	Germany	10952	16-Mar-1998	24-Mar-1998	$471.20	$40.42	8.58%
Alfreds Futterkiste	12209	Germany	11011	09-Apr-1998	13-Apr-1998	$933.50	$1.21	0.13%
Ana Trujillo Empar	05021	Mexico	10308	18-Sep-1996	24-Sep-1996	$88.80	$1.61	1.81%
Ana Trujillo Empar	05021	Mexico	10625	08-Aug-1997	14-Aug-1997	$479.75	$43.90	9.15%
Ana Trujillo Empar	05021	Mexico	10759	28-Nov-1997	12-Dec-1997	$320.00	$11.99	3.75%
Ana Trujillo Empar	05021	Mexico	10926	04-Mar-1998	11-Mar-1998	$514.40	$39.92	7.76%
Antonio Moreno Ta	05023	Mexico	10365	27-Nov-1996	02-Dec-1996	$403.20	$22.00	5.46%
Antonio Moreno Ta	05023	Mexico	10507	15-Apr-1997	22-Apr-1997	$749.06	$47.45	6.33%
Antonio Moreno Ta	05023	Mexico	10535	13-May-1997	21-May-1997	1,940.85	$15.64	0.81%
Antonio Moreno Ta	05023	Mexico	10573	19-Jun-1997	20-Jun-1997	2,082.00	$84.84	4.07%

Record: 1 of 830

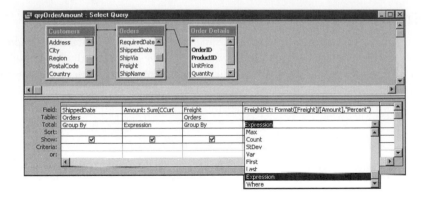

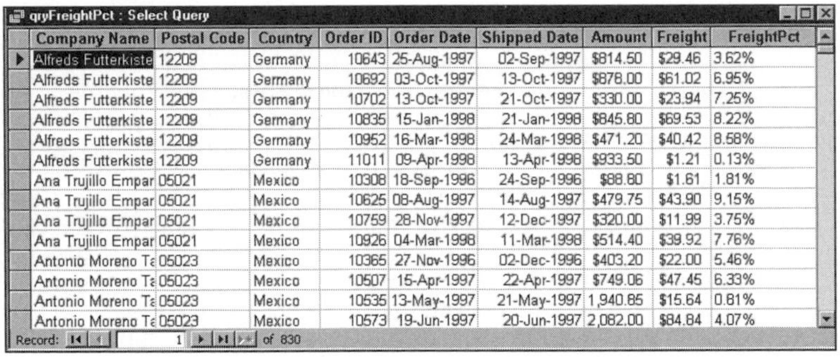

Figure 9.12
The query result set displaying the order total and freight charges as a percent of the order amount.

NEW 2000 You use the `Format` function with your expression as its first argument to display the calculated values in a more readable form. When you add the percent symbol (`%`) to a format expression or specify `"Percent"` as the format, the value of the expression argument multiplies by 100 and the percent symbol preceded by a space appends to the displayed value.

If you run into a "Can't evaluate expression" or "Wrong data type" error, check the "Troubleshooting" section near the end of this chapter.

Power Tools: The preceding query also is included as qryFreightPct in the Express.mdb file on the accompanying CD-ROM.

Tip #70 from RJ

Use the `Format` function with custom percent formatting if you want fewer or more decimal places. For example, if you only want one digit to the right of the decimal separator, substitute `FreightPct: Format([Freight]/[Amount],"#0.0%")` for the standard formatting in the preceding example. Adding the `%` symbol to the format string automatically multiplies the value argument by 100.

OTHER USES FOR EXPRESSIONS

You can use expressions with update queries, to calculate fields in forms and reports, as conditions for the execution of a VBA procedure, or as an argument for an action you program in VBA. SQL SELECT statements use expressions as in the following query criterion:

```
WHERE [Birth Date] >= #1/1/60#
```

See Chapter 23, "Working with Structured Query Language," for more information on SQL criteria for selecting sets of records. Access VBA code also takes advantage of expressions extensively to control program flow. The chapters focusing on SQL and Access VBA programming (Part VI, "Using Advanced Access Techniques," and Part VII, "Programming and Converting Access Applications") show you how to use such expressions.

PART

II

CH

9

TROUBLESHOOTING

QUERY EXPRESSIONS FAIL TO EXECUTE

When attempting to execute a query that contains an expression, a "Can't evaluate expression" or "Wrong data type" message box appears.

The "Can't evaluate expression" message usually indicates a typographic error in naming a function or an object. Depending on the use of the function, an Enter Parameter Value dialog might appear if the named object does not exist. The "Wrong data type" message is most likely to occur as a result of attempting to use mathematic or trigonometric operators with values of the Text or Date/Time field data types. If your expression refers to a control contained in a Form or Report object, the form or report must be open when you execute the function.

FOUR-DIGIT YEARS TURN INTO TWO DIGITS IN QUERY CRITERIA

NEW 2000

*When I type **Between #1/1/1997# and #12/31/1997#** in the Criteria cell of Query Design view, Access changes my entry to **Between #1/1/97# and #12/31/97#**, which isn't Y2K-compliant.*

By default, Access 2000 drops the century digits when creating Jet SQL statements to execute queries, regardless of the formatting applied to the underlying table—mm-ddd-yyyy for all date fields in Northwind.mdb. You solve this Y2K compliance problem by choosing Tools, Options, clicking the General tab, and marking the This Database check box in the Use Four-Digit Year Formatting frame. If you want to make all of your databases Y2K-compliant, mark the All Databases check box, too.

IN THE REAL WORLD—THE ALGEBRA OF ACCESS EXPRESSIONS

A junior high school algebra class provides most students their first introduction to abstract mathematics. Expressions (algebraic formulas) are crucial to the majority of decision-support queries you design, as well as presentation of calculated data in form and report text boxes and other text-based controls. The colon following the column name of a calculated expression is equivalent of an equal sign; in mathematic terms, `Amount:` **`CCur`**`([UnitPrice]` `*[Quantity]*(1-[Discount]))` is the equivalent of `curAmount = ` **`CCur`**`(sngUnitPrice*int` `Quantity*(1-sngDiscount))` in VBA.

Similarly, functions that convert data types and format query columns also are important to forms and reports. The classic definition of a function is this: If when X is given, Y is determined, then Y is a function of X. For example, in `Price:` **`Format`**`([UnitPrice],` `"#,##0.00")`, the value of the UnitPrice field (X) uniquely determines the value of the calculated Price (Y) column. The fact that queries can have calculated and specially formatted columns is one of the reasons that this book uses the term *column* with queries and *field* for tables.

In most cases, it's a good design practice to base forms and reports on queries with pre-calculated and pre-formatted columns, rather than calculating and formatting values for individual text boxes. It's quicker and easier to check your expressions in the query result set, and you don't need to add expressions or formatting (or both) to every text box, subform, and other control that displays the data.

The only drawback of this approach is that calculating and formatting columns of queries with a large number of rows slows performance, but usually only slightly. For instance, formatting the StudentID column of the 45,000-record StudentTransactions table of the Beckwith.mdb database with the `ID:` **`Left`**`([StudentID],3) &` `"-" &` **`Mid`**`([StudentID],4,3)` `&` `"-" &` **`Right`**`([StudentID],3)` expression causes an imperceptible effect on query execution speed. Bear in mind, however, that adding calculated columns to queries against networked databases increases the amount of data sent "over the wire." Calculated columns slow networked query execution by the proportion of characters added per row, as does applying formatting that increases the number of characters per column.

Expressions and, to a lesser extent, functions play a major role in query criteria. When you type a criterion—such as `CA`—in the query design grid, Access converts the criterion to a valid Jet SQL expression, in this case `WHERE` *`FieldName`* `= "CA"`. In this case the equal sign is the identity operator. Another use for the identity operator is in creating joins using SQL `WHERE` clauses, as in `WHERE` *`Table2.PrimaryKey`* `=` *`Table1.ForeignKey`*.

You can perform logical operations on query result sets with the **`IIf`** (inline **`If`**) function, whose arguments can contain other functions. For instance, the equivalent of the `Province:` `Nz([Region], "None")` expression is `Province:` **`IIf`**`(`**`IsNull`**`([Region]),"None",[Region])`. You must use the **`IIf`** function in Data Access Pages (DAP), the subject of Chapter 18, "Designing Data Access Pages," because the execution environment of DAP, Internet

Explorer (IE) 5+, doesn't support the Access Expression Service. The lack of the Access Expression Service is one of the reasons that there's no "Data Access Page Wizard" to convert conventional Access forms to DAP.

You encounter a more vexing issue when you upgrade Jet select queries to SQL Server views with MSDE, one of the subjects of Chapter 25, "Creating Access Data Projects." Transact-SQL, like IE, doesn't support the Jet Expression Service. Transact-SQL has its own set of data type conversion and other formatting functions, many of which vary greatly from their Jet counterparts. The Upsizing Wizard converts simple Jet queries to SQL Server views, but you can expect to spend a substantial amount of time with SQL Server Books Online when you attempt to upsize more complex Jet queries to MSDE views.

--rj

PART

II

CH

9

CHAPTER 10

CREATING MULTITABLE AND CROSSTAB QUERIES

In this chapter

Introducing Joins on Tables   354

Joining Tables to Create Multitable Queries   355

Using Lookup Fields in Tables   365

Adding Subdatasheets to a Table or Query   373

Outer, Self, and Theta Joins   378

Updating Table Data with Queries   383

Making All Fields of Tables Accessible   386

Making Calculations on Multiple Records   387

Designing Parameter Queries   393

Creating Crosstab Queries   396

Creating Queries from Tables in Other Databases   403

Troubleshooting   405

In the Real World—Optimizing Multiple Queries   406

INTRODUCING JOINS ON TABLES

Your purpose in acquiring Access is undoubtedly to take advantage of its relational database management capabilities. To do so, you must be able to link related tables based on key fields that have values in common—a process known as a *join* in database terms. Chapter 8, "Designing Access Queries," and Chapter 9, "Understanding Query Operators and Expressions," showed you how to create simple queries based on a single table. If you tried the examples in Chapter 9, you saw a glimpse of a multiple-table query when you joined the Order Details table to the Orders table that you then joined to the Customers table to create the query for testing expressions. The first part of this chapter deals exclusively with queries created from multiple tables that are related through joins.

This chapter provides examples of queries that use each of the four basic types of joins that you can create in Access's Query Design view: *equi-joins*, *outer joins*, *self-joins*, and *theta joins*. Note, however, the two types of queries that you can't create in Access's Query Design window: UNION queries and subqueries based on tables. To create these types of queries, you must write SQL statements—the subject of Chapter 23, "Working with Structured Query Language."

Some of the sample queries in this chapter use the Personnel Actions table that you created in Chapter 4, "Working with Access Databases and Tables." If you didn't create the Personnel Actions table, refer to the "Creating the Personnel Actions Table" section of Chapter 4 for instructions on how to build or import this table.

Other sample queries build on queries that you create in preceding sections. You will find, therefore, that reading this chapter and creating the sample queries sequentially, as the queries appear in text, is more efficient than taking the random approach.

This chapter also includes descriptions and examples of four of the five categories of queries that you can create with Access: select, summary, parameter, and crosstab queries. Four types of queries in the action category let you create or modify data in tables: *make-table*, *append*, *delete*, and *update*. Chapter 11, "Modifying Data with Action Queries," presents typical applications for and examples of each type of action query.

NEW 2000 The following new Access 2000 features apply to the subject matter of this chapter:

- New Query Properties—Subdatasheet Name, Link Child Fields, Link Master Fields, Subdatasheet Height, and Subdatasheet Expanded—accommodate subdatasheets in query result sets.

- You now can print the contents of the Relationships window. When the Relationships window has the focus, choosing File, Print Relationships creates a report from the contents of the Relationships window and then displays the report in Print Preview mode for subsequent printing.

- You can send a Relationships diagram as an email attachment in Report Snapshot format. The recipient must have Access 2000 or the Report Snapshot viewer installed.

JOINING TABLES TO CREATE MULTITABLE QUERIES

Before you can create joins between tables, you must know which fields are related by common values. As mentioned in Chapter 4, assigning identical names to primary- and foreign-key fields in different tables that contain related data is a common practice. This approach, used by Microsoft when creating the Northwind sample database, makes determining relationships and creating joins among tables easier. The CustomerID field in the Customers table and the CustomerID field in the Orders table, for example, are used to join orders with customers.

Figure 10.1 shows the structure of the Northwind database with a graphical display of the joins between the tables. Access query designs indicate joins with lines between field names of different tables. Bold type indicates primary-key fields. Each join usually involves at least one primary-key field.

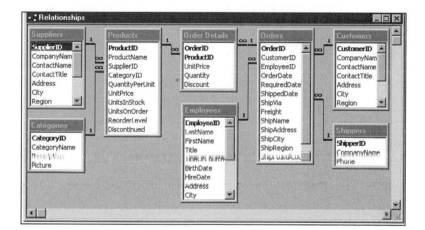

Figure 10.1
The joins between the tables of the Northwind sample database.

You can display the structure of the joins between the tables in Access 2000's Northwind database by giving the Database window the focus (press F11) and then clicking the Relationship button of the toolbar or by choosing Tools, Relationships. The 1 above the line that shows the join between two tables in Figure 10.1 indicates the "one" side of a *one-to-many relationship*; the infinity symbol (∞) indicates the "many" side.

Access 2000 lets you choose between displaying only the direct relationships for a single table (the Show Direct Relationships button on the toolbar) or all relationships for all tables in a database (the Show All Relationships button). All tables of Northwind.mdb appear by default when you open the Relationships window of the Northwind sample database. In this case, clicking the Show Direct Relationships button has no effect.

Tip #71 from

> To show relationships for only one table, click the toolbar's Clear Layout button, click the Show Table button to display the Show Table dialog, select the table to display in the Tables list, and then click Add and Close. Click the Show Direct Relationships button to display the relationships for the selected table. Clearing the layout of the Relationships windows doesn't affect the underlying relationships between the tables. The Show Direct Relationships feature is useful primarily with databases that contain many related tables.

Access supports four types of joins in the Query Design window:

■ *Equi-joins* (also called *inner joins*) are the most common join for creating select queries. Equi-joins display in one table all the records with corresponding records in another table. The correspondence between records is determined by identical values (WHERE *field1* = *field2* in SQL) in the fields that join the tables. In most cases, joins are based on a unique primary-key field in one table and a foreign-key field in the other table in a one-to-many relationship. If none of the table's records that act as the *many* side of the relationship has a field value that corresponds to a record in the table of the *one* side, the corresponding records in the *one* side don't appear in the query result.

Access automatically creates the joins between tables if the tables share a common field name that is a primary key of one of the tables. These joins are also automatically created if you previously specified the relationships between the tables in the Relationships window.

■ *Outer joins* are used in database maintenance to remove orphan records and duplicate data from tables by creating new tables that contain records with unique values. Outer joins display records in one member of the join, regardless of whether corresponding records exist on the other side of the join.

■ *Self-joins* relate data within a single table. You create a self-join in Access by adding to the query a duplicate of the table (Access provides an alias for the duplicate) and then creating joins between the fields of the copies.

■ *Theta joins* relate data by using comparison operators other than =. Theta joins include *not-equal joins* (<>) used in queries designed to return records that lack a particular relationship. You implement theta joins by WHERE criteria rather than by the SQL JOIN reserved word. The Query Design window doesn't indicate theta joins by drawing lines between field names, and theta joins do not appear in the Relationships window.

The Beckwith.mdb database, in the \Beckwith folder of the accompanying CD-ROM, has a circular set of relationships. Open Beckwith.mdb, either from the CD-ROM or from a copy on your fixed disk, and then click the Relationships button to open the Relationships window (see Figure 10.2). Sections are many-to-one related to Courses, Departments are one-to-many related to Courses, and Employees are many-to-one related to Departments and one-to-many related to Sections. You also can see a circular relationship between Courses, Enrollments, Students, Grades, and Courses. Beckwith.mdb is useful when you want to test the relative performance of queries with large numbers of records. The mythical Beckwith College in Navasota, Texas, has 30,000 students, 2,320 employees, and offers 1,770 sections of 590 courses in 14 departments.

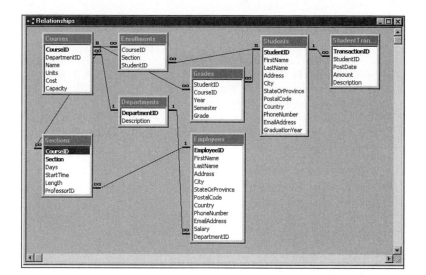

Figure 10.2
The relationships between tables in the Beckwith sample database.

Note

There is a minor relational defect in the design of the Beckwith database. It's quite possible that a professor could be assigned to more than one department, which isn't permissible with the design shown in Figure 10.2. Assigning professors to more than one department requires a *many-to-many relationship* and an Employee-Departments relation table.

CREATING CONVENTIONAL SINGLE-COLUMN EQUI-JOINS

Joins based on one column in each table are known as *single-column equi-joins*. The following list details the basic rules for creating a database that lets you use simple single-column equi-joins for all queries:

- Each table on the *one* side of the relationship must have a primary key with a No Duplicates index to maintain referential integrity. Access automatically creates a No Duplicates index on the primary-key field(s) of a table.

- Many-to-many relationships, such as the relationship of Orders to Products, are implemented by an intermediary table (in this case, Order Details) having a one-to-many relationship (Orders to Order Details) with one table and a many-to-one relationship (Order Details to Products) with another.

- Duplicated data in tables, where applicable, is extracted to a new table that has a primary-key, no-duplicates, one-to-many relationship with the table from which the duplicate data is extracted. Using a multicolumn primary key to identify extracted data uniquely often is necessary because individual key fields might contain duplicate data. The combination (also known as *concatenation)* of the values of the key fields, however, must be unique. Access 2000's Table Analyzer Wizard locates and extracts most duplicate data automatically. Chapter 11 describes how to extract duplicate data manually from tables.

→ If you need help using the Make-Table query, **see** "Creating New Tables with Make-Table Queries," **p. 411**.

→ If you're not sure how to create relationships, **see** "Establishing Relationships Between Tables," **p. 166**.

All the joins in the Northwind database, shown by the lines that connect field names of adjacent tables in Figure 10.1, are single-column equi-joins between tables with one-to-many relationships. Access uses the ANSI SQL-92 reserved words INNER JOIN to identify conventional equi-joins, and LEFT JOIN or RIGHT JOIN to specify outer joins.

→ To learn more about SQL join terminology, **see** "Creating Joins with SQL," **p. 863**.

Among the most common uses for queries based on equi-joins is matching customer names and addresses with orders received. You might want to create a simple report, for example, that lists the customer name, order number, order date, and amount. To create a conventional one-to-many, single-column equi-join query that relates Northwind's customers to their orders, sorted by company and order date, follow these steps:

1. If Northwind.mdb is open, close all windows except the Database window; otherwise open Northwind.mdb.

2. Click the Queries shortcut of the Database window and then double-click the Create Query in Design View shortcut. Access displays the Show Table dialog superimposed on an empty Query Design window.

3. Select the Customers table from the Show Table list and click the Add button. Alternatively, you can double-click the Customers table name to add the table to the query. Access adds to the Query Design window the Field Names list for Customers.

4. Double-click the Orders table in the Show Table list and then click the Close button. Access adds to the window the Field Names list for Orders, plus a line that indicates a join between the CustomerID fields of the two tables. Access creates the join automatically because CustomerID is the primary key field of the Customers table, and Access found a field with the same field name (a foreign key) in the Orders table.

5. To identify each order with the customer's name, select the CompanyName field of the Customers table and drag the field symbol to the Field row of the Query Design grid's first column.

6. Select the OrderID field of the Orders table and drag the field symbol to the second column's Field row. Drag the OrderDate field to the third column. Your query design appears as shown in Figure 10.3.

7. Click the Run or Query View button to display the result of the query, the Recordset shown in Figure 10.4. Notice that the field headers of the query result set show the captions for the table fields, which include spaces, rather than the actual field names, which don't have spaces.

SPECIFYING A SORT ORDER FOR THE QUERY RESULT SET

Access displays query result sets in the order of the index on the primary-key field. If more than one column represents a primary-key field, Access sorts simple query result sets in left-to-right key-field column precedence. Because CompanyName is the leftmost primary-key field, the query result set displays all orders for a single company in order-number sequence. You can override the primary-key display order by adding a sort order to the query. For example, if you want to see the most recent orders first, you can specify a descending sort by the order date. To add this sort sequence to your query, follow these steps:

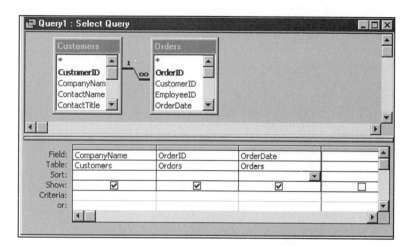

Figure 10.3
A query to display orders placed by customers, sorted by company name and order date.

PART

II

Cн

10

Figure 10.4
The result of the query design of Figure 10.3 that joins the Customers and Orders tables.

→ For more information on primary-key indexes, **see** "Adding Indexes to Tables," **p. 174**.

1. Click the Design View button to return to Query Design mode.

2. Place the caret in the Sort row of the Order Date column of the Query Design grid and press F4 to open the dropdown list.

3. Select Descending from the dropdown list to specify a descending sort on date—latest orders first (see Figure 10.5).

Figure 10.5
Adding a special sort order to the query.

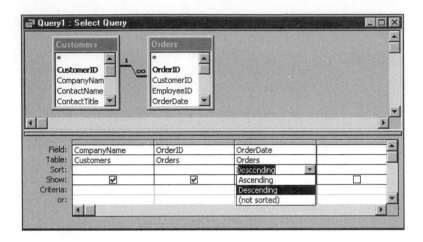

4. Click the Run button or the Datasheet View button to display the query result set with the new sort order (see Figure 10.6).

Figure 10.6
The result of adding a descending sort on Order Date to the query.

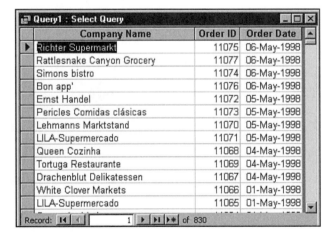

CREATING QUERIES FROM TABLES WITH INDIRECT RELATIONSHIPS

You can create queries that return indirectly related records, such as the categories of products purchased by each customer. You must include in the queries each table that serves as a link in the chain of joins. If you are creating queries to display the categories of products purchased by each customer, for example, include each of the tables that link the chain of joins between the Customers and Categories tables. This chain includes the Customers, Orders, Order Details, Products, and Categories tables. You don't need to add any fields, however, from the intermediate tables to the Query Design grid; the CompanyName and the CategoryName fields suffice.

To modify your customers and orders query so that you create a query that displays fields of indirectly related records, follow these steps:

1. In Query Design view, delete the OrderID column of the query by clicking the thin bar above the Field row to select (highlight) the entire column and then press the Delete key. Perform the same action for the OrderDate columns so that only the CompanyName column appears in the query.

2. Click the Show Table button of the toolbar or choose Query, Show Table and add the Order Details, Products, and Categories tables to the query, in sequence; then click the Close button of the Add Table dialog. The upper pane of Figure 10.7 shows the chain of joins that Access automatically creates between Customers and Categories based on the primary-key field of each intervening table and the identically named foreign-key field in the adjacent table.

PART

II

CH

10

Tip #72 from

As you add tables to the Query Design window, the table field lists might not appear in the upper pane. Use the upper pane's vertical scrollbar to display the "hidden" tables. You can drag the table field lists to the top of the upper pane and then rearrange the field lists to match the appearance of Figure 10.7.

3. Drag the CategoryName from the Categories field list to the Field row of the grid's second column. Alternatively, you can double-click the field name to add it to the next empty column of the grid (see Figure 10.7).

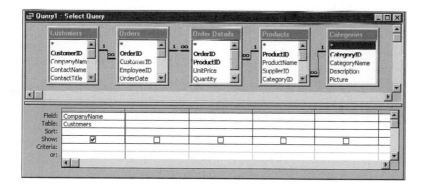

Figure 10.7
The chain of joins required to create queries from tables that have an indirect relationship.

4. Click the Run button. The query result set shown in Figure 10.8 appears.

5. Close the query by clicking the window close box. This query is only an example, so you don't need to save it.

Figure 10.8
The Customers-
Categories
Recordset, resulting
from the query of
Figure 10.7.

Tip #73 from

The query result set of Figure 10.8 has more than 2,100 rows, most of which are duplicates. To eliminate the duplication, right-click an empty area of the Query Design view's upper pane, and choose Properties to open the Query Properties sheet. Double-click the Unique Values text box to set Unique Values to Yes. Run the query again to verify the duplicate rows are gone. The "Creating Multicolumn Equi-Joins and Selecting Unique Values" section later in the chapter gives you other examples of use of the Unique Values query property.

Queries made on indirectly related tables are common, especially when you want to analyze the data with SQL aggregate functions or Access's crosstab queries. For more information, see the sections "Using the SQL Aggregate Functions" and "Creating Crosstab Queries" later in this chapter.

CREATING MULTICOLUMN EQUI-JOINS AND SELECTING UNIQUE VALUES

You can have more than one join between a pair of tables. You might, for example, want to create a query that returns the names of customers for which the billing and shipping addresses are the same. The billing address is the Address field of the Customers table, and the shipping address is the ShipAddress field of the Orders table. Therefore, you need to match the CustomerID fields in the two tables and Customers.Address with Orders.ShipAddress. This task requires a *multicolumn equi-join*.

To create this example of an address-matching multicolumn equi-join, follow these steps:

1. Open a new query in Design view.
2. Add the Customers and Orders tables to the query and close the Add Tables dialog.
3. Click and drag the Address field of the Customers table's Field List box to the ShipAddress field of the Orders table's Field List box. This creates another join, indicated by the new line between Address and ShipAddress (see the top pane of Figure 10.9). The new line between Address and ShipAddress has dots at both ends, indicating that the join is between a pair of fields that don't have a specified relationship, the same field name, or a primary-key index.

4. Drag the Customers table's CompanyName and Address fields to the Field row of the first and second query columns and then drop the fields. Drag the Orders table's ShipAddress field to the query's third column and drop the field in the Field row (see the lower pane of Figure 10.9).

Manually added join

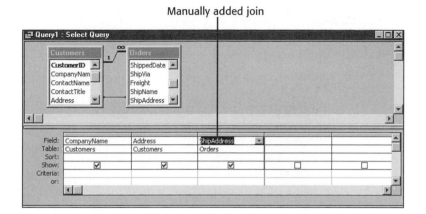

Figure 10.9
Creating a multicolumn equi-join by dragging one field name to a field in another table.

 5. Click the Run button. Figure 10.10 shows the query's result.

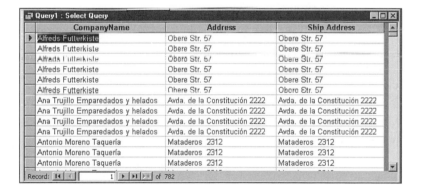

Figure 10.10
A query result set of orders for customers who have the same billing and shipping addresses.

6. To eliminate the duplicate rows, you must use the Unique Values option of the Query Properties window. To display the Query Properties window, which is shown in Figure 10.11, click the Design View button, and then click the toolbar's Properties button or double-click an empty area in the Query Design window's upper pane. If the title bar of the Properties window displays Field Properties or Field List, click an empty area in the Query Design window's upper pane so that the title bar displays Query Properties. Alternatively, right-click an empty region of the upper pane and select Properties from the popup menu.

7. By default, both the Unique Records query property and the Unique Values property are set to No. Place the caret in the Unique Values text box and press F4 to open the

dropdown list. Select Yes and close the list. Setting the Unique Values property to Yes adds the ANSI SQL reserved word DISTINCT to the query. Click the Properties button again to close the Properties window.

→ For more information on removing duplicate records, **see** "Jet's DISTINCTROW and SQL's DISTINCT Keywords," **p. 877**.

Tip #74 from

Alternatively, you can change the property settings for the Unique Records and Unique Values properties by double-clicking their text boxes in the Properties window. All properties with Yes/No values let you toggle their value by double-clicking.

Figure 10.11
Using the Query Properties window to display only rows with unique values.

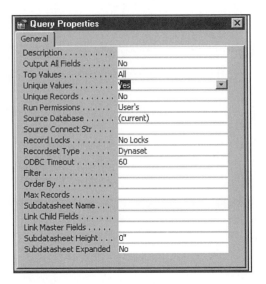

8. Click the Run button of the toolbar. The result set no longer contains duplicate rows, as shown in Figure 10.12.

Figure 10.12
The query result set after you remove duplicate rows.

CompanyName	Address	Ship Address
Alfreds Futterkiste	Obere Str. 57	Obere Str. 57
Ana Trujillo Emparedados y helados	Avda. de la Constitución 2222	Avda. de la Constitución 2222
Antonio Moreno Taquería	Mataderos 2312	Mataderos 2312
Berglunds snabbköp	Berguvsvägen 8	Berguvsvägen 8
Blauer See Delikatessen	Forsterstr. 57	Forsterstr. 57
Blondel père et fils	24, place Kléber	24, place Kléber
Bólido Comidas preparadas	C/ Araquil, 67	C/ Araquil, 67
Bon app'	12, rue des Bouchers	12, rue des Bouchers
Bottom-Dollar Markets	23 Tsawassen Blvd.	23 Tsawassen Blvd.
B's Beverages	Fauntleroy Circus	Fauntleroy Circus
Cactus Comidas para llevar	Cerrito 333	Cerrito 333
Centro comercial Moctezuma	Sierras de Granada 9993	Sierras de Granada 9993
Comércio Mineiro	Av. dos Lusíadas, 23	Av. dos Lusíadas, 23

Record: 1 of 84

9. Click the Close Window button to close the query without saving it. You then avoid cluttering the Database window's Queries list with obsolete query examples.

Because most of the orders have the same billing and shipping addresses, a more useful query is to find the orders for which the customer's billing and shipping addresses differ. You can't create this query with a multicolumn equi-join, however, because the INNER JOIN reserved word in Access SQL doesn't accept the <> operator. Adding a not-equal join uses a criterion rather than a multicolumn join, as explained in the section "Creating Not-Equal Theta Joins with Criteria" later in this chapter.

 If you encounter the Enter Parameter dialog when attempting to execute the preceding query, see the "Missing Objects in Queries" member of the "Troubleshooting" section near the end of this chapter.

Using Lookup Fields in Tables

PART
II
Ch
10

Access 2000's lookup feature for table fields lets you substitute dropdown list boxes or list boxes for conventional field text boxes. The lookup feature is a one-to-many query that Access automatically creates for you. The lookup feature lets you provide a list of acceptable values for a particular field. When you select the value from the list, the value automatically is entered in the field of the current record. You can specify either of the following two types of lookup field:

- In a field that contains foreign-key values, a list of values from one or more fields of a related base table. The purpose of this type of lookup field is to add or alter foreign-key values, preserving relational integrity by assuring that foreign-key values match a primary-key value. A relationship must preexist in the Relationships window between the tables to define a field as containing a foreign key. As an example, the Orders table of Northwind.mdb has two foreign-key fields: CustomerID and EmployeeID. The lookup feature of the CustomerID field displays in a dropdown list the CompanyName field value from the Customers table. The EmployeeID field displays the LastName and FirstName fields of the Employees table, separated by a comma and space (see Figure 10.13).

	Order ID	Customer	Employee	Order Date	Required Date
	10248	Vins et alcools Chevalier	Buchanan, Steven	04-Jul-96	01-Aug-96
	10249	Vaffeljernet	Suyama, Michael	05-Jul-96	16-Aug-96
	10250	Victuailles en stock	Peacock, Margaret	08-Jul-96	05-Aug-96
	10251	Vins et alcools Chevalier	Leverling, Janet	08-Jul-96	05-Aug-96
	10252	Wartian Herkku	Peacock, Margaret	09-Jul-96	06-Aug-96
	10253	Wellington Importadora	Leverling, Janet	10-Jul-96	24-Jul-96
	10254	White Clover Markets	Buchanan, Steven	11-Jul-96	08-Aug-96
	10255	Wilman Kala	Dodsworth, Anne	12-Jul-96	09-Aug-96
	10256	Wolski Zajazd	Leverling, Janet	15-Jul-96	12-Aug-96
	10257	HILARIÓN-Abastos	Peacock, Margaret	16-Jul-96	13-Aug-96
	10258	Ernst Handel	Davolio, Nancy	17-Jul-96	14-Aug-96
	10259	Centro comercial Moctezuma	Peacock, Margaret	18-Jul-96	15-Aug-96
	10260	Ottilies Käseladen	Peacock, Margaret	19-Jul-96	16-Aug-96
	10261	Que Delícia	Peacock, Margaret	19-Jul-96	16-Aug-96
	10262	Rattlesnake Canyon Grocery	Callahan, Laura	22-Jul-96	19-Aug-96

Record: 1 of 830

Figure 10.13
A lookup field's dropdown value list.

■ In any field except a single primary-key field, a list of fixed values from which to select. Field lists preserve referential integrity by restricting to primary-key values choices of foreign-key field values.

You can add a new lookup field in either Design view or Table Datasheet view; however, in Design view you can add the lookup feature only to an existing field. In Datasheet view, only the combo box control is displayed, even if you specify a list box control. You can display a combo box or a list box on a form that is bound to a table with lookup fields. In practice, the dropdown list (a combo box with the Limit to List property set to Yes) is the most common type of lookup field control. The following sections describe how to add foreign-key and fixed-list lookup features to table fields.

ADDING A FOREIGN-KEY DROPDOWN LIST WITH THE LOOKUP WIZARD

The Personnel Actions table you created in earlier chapters of this book is a candidate for a lookup field that uses a foreign-key dropdown list. Follow these steps to use the Lookup Wizard to change the paID field of the Personnel Actions table to a lookup field:

1. In the Database window, select the Personnel Actions table and press Ctrl+C to copy the table to the Clipboard.

2. Press Ctrl+V to display the Paste Table As dialog. Enter a name for the copy, such as **tblLookup**, and click the OK button to create the copy with the structure and data.

3. Open the table copy in Design view and select the paInitiatedBy field. Click the Lookup tab to display the current lookup properties; a text box control has no lookup properties. Open the Data Type dropdown list and select Lookup Wizard (see Figure 10.14). The first dialog of the Lookup Wizard appears.

Figure 10.14
Selecting the Lookup Wizard to add the lookup feature to a field.

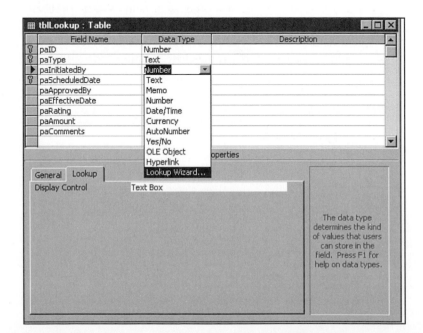

4. You want the field to look up values in another table (Employees), so accept the first (default) option (see Figure 10.15). Click the Next button to display the Lookup Wizard's second dialog.

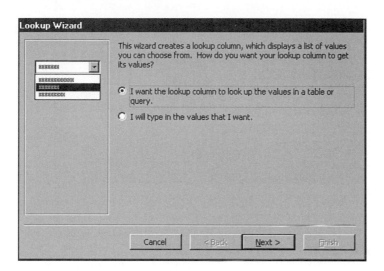

Figure 10.15
Selecting between a foreign-key of a table and a fixed-list lookup in the first dialog of the Lookup Wizard.

5. With the View Tables option enabled, select the Employees base table to which the paInitiatedBy field is related (see Figure 10.16). Click the Next button to display the third dialog.

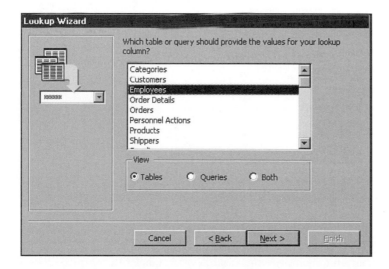

Figure 10.16
Choosing the base table or query for a foreign-key lookup field.

6. Click the > button three times to add the EmployeeID, LastName, and FirstName fields to your lookup list (see Figure 10.17). You must include the base table key field that is related to your foreign-key field. Click the Next button for the fourth dialog.

Figure 10.17
Selecting the fields to include in your lookup list.

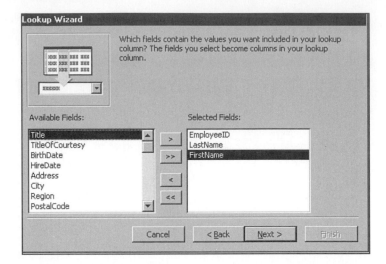

7. Adjust the widths of the columns to display the first and last names without excessive trailing white space. The Wizard determines that EmployeeID is the key column and recommends hiding the key column (see Figure 10.18). Click Next to display the fifth and final dialog.

Figure 10.18
Adjusting column widths of the lookup list and hiding the key column.

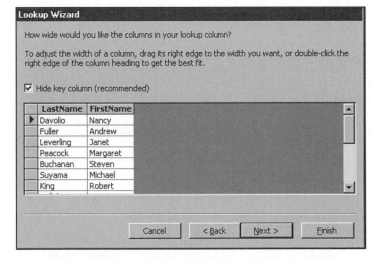

8. Type **Initiated By** as the label for the lookup field in the text box.

9. Click the Finish button to complete the wizard's work. Click OK when the wizard asks whether you'd like to save the table design. Your new lookup field properties appear as shown in Figure 10.19. The Jet SQL query statement created by the Wizard as the Row Source property is SELECT DISTINCTROW [Employees].[EmployeeID], [Employees].[LastName], [Employees].[FirstName] FROM [Employees];.

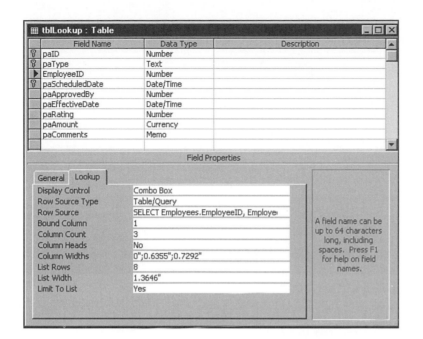

Figure 10.19
Lookup properties
added to the
paInitiatedBy field.

Tip #75 from

Preceding step 6 adds fields in their table order, but you can add fields with the Lookup
Wizard in any order you prefer. Alternatively, you can rearrange columns by editing the
Row Source property's SQL statement after you create the lookup list.

---

10. The Wizard has renamed the paInitiatedBy field to EmployeeID, so change the Field
    Name Property back to paInitiatedBy. Changing the field name doesn't affect the
    lookup operation.

 11. Click the Table View button and save your changes to display the table datasheet. Only
    the first visible column of the list appears in the Initiated By column. Adjust the width
    of the Initiated By column to the width of the dropdown list, about 1.5 inches. With
    the caret in the Initiated By column, open the dropdown list to display the Wizard's
    work (see Figure 10.20).

12. Return to Design view, select the Row Source property of the paInitiatedBy field, and
    click the Build button to display the Row Source SQL statement in Query Design view
    (see Figure 10.21); then close the Query Design window.

Tip #76 from

Make sure to correct the lookup field's name to the orginal value if the Lookup Wizard
changes it. The Wizard changes the field name if it isn't the same as that of the base table's
field. Although Name AutoCorrect can handle field name changes, it's a much better database design practice to freeze the names of tables and fields. Change table and field
names during the development process only if absolutely necessary.

Figure 10.20
The dropdown lookup list created by the Lookup Wizard.

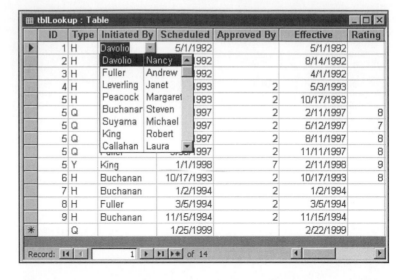

Figure 10.21
The Row Source property's SQL statement in Query Design view.

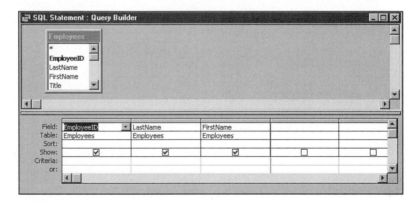

→ If you need a list of the properties of the combo box control created by the Wizard, **see** "Using Combo and List Boxes" **p 502**.

Tip #77 from

If a relationship exists between the lookup field and the field of the base table, Access recreates the relationship. In this case, extra tables with a _1 or _2 suffix appear in the Relationships window. This problem appeared in Access 95 and isn't fixed in Access 2000. You can delete the spurious tables from the Relationships window without affecting operation of your lookup field.

ADDING A FIXED-VALUE LOOKUP LIST TO A TABLE

You add the alternative lookup feature—a fixed list of values—using the Lookup Wizard in much the same way as you created the foreign-key lookup list in the preceding section. To add a fixed-list lookup feature to the paType field of your copy of the Personnel Actions table, follow these steps:

1. Select the paType field, open the Data Type list, and select Lookup Wizard to launch the Wizard.

2. In the first Lookup Wizard dialog, select the I Will Type in the Values That I Want option and click the Next button.

3. In the second Lookup Wizard dialog, type **2** in the Number of Columns text box and press the Tab key to create the second list column.

4. Type **H**, **Hired**; **Q**, **Quarterly Review**; **Y**, **Yearly Review**; and **S**, **Salary Adjustment** in the Col1 and Col2 columns of four rows. Adjust the width of the columns to suit the entries (see Figure 10.22). Click the Next button to display the Wizard's third dialog.

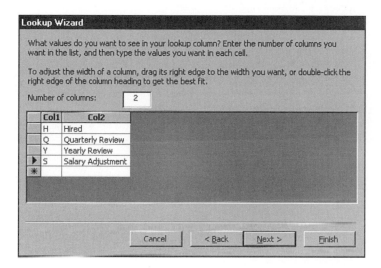

Figure 10.22
Adding the lookup list values in the Lookup Wizard's second dialog.

5. The paType field uses single-character abbreviations for the type of personnel actions, so select Col1 as the "field that uniquely identifies the row." (The paType field doesn't uniquely identify the row; Col1 contains the single-character value that you want to insert into the field.) Click the Next button to display the fourth and final Wizard dialog.

6. Type **Type** as the label for your column and click the Finish button. The lookup properties for the paType field appear as shown in Figure 10.23. The Row Source Type is Value List. The Row Source contains the following values:
```
"H";"Hired";"Q";"Quarterly Review";"Y";"Yearly Review";"S";"Salary
Adjustment".
```

7. The Wizard again changes the field name, this time to the name of the label, so change the value of the Field Name property to **paType**.

8. Click the Table View button and save the changes to your table. Increase the width of the Type column to about 1.5 inches, place the caret in the Type column, and open the fixed value list to check the Wizard's work (see Figure 10.24).

Figure 10.23
Lookup field properties created with a value list.

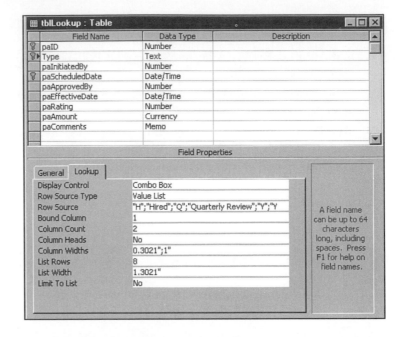

Figure 10.24
The fixed value list created by the Lookup Wizard.

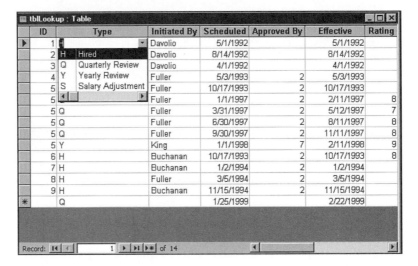

9. If you don't want the abbreviation to appear in the dropdown list, change the first entry of the Column Widths property value to **0**.

10. If you want to remove the lookup feature from a field, select the field, click the Lookup tab, and choose Text Box from the dropdown Display Control list.

Tip #78 from 	Set the List Width property of a lookup field to a value that displays enough characters of the descriptive column to offer an unambiguous selection. The List Width property determines the minimum width of the list, so you don't need to expand the width of the field in datasheet view.

Note	The lookup feature has generated controversy among seasoned database developers. Relational database purists object to embedding queries as table properties. Another objection to the use of foreign-key, dropdown lists is that it is easy for uninitiated users to inadvertently change data in a table after opening the list. Access 2000's lookup feature, however, is a useful tool, especially for new database users.

ADDING SUBDATASHEETS TO A TABLE OR QUERY

Subdatasheets are closely related to lookup fields, but serve a different purpose. Subdatasheets display related table values in an embedded datasheet, whereas lookup fields display base table values in a combo box or list box. Both of these Access features depend on the equivalent of one-to-many queries; the difference between the queries is that the many side of a subdatasheet is a related table, whereas a lookup field uses a query against a base table to supply the many side values. You also can cascade subdatasheets to display related data of multiply joined tables, a feature not applicable to lookup fields, but a table or query can't have more than one subdatasheet. Figure 10.25 illustrates the Customers table displaying the Orders subdatasheet for Alfreds Futterkiste with embedded sub-subdatasheets that display Order Details records for the first three orders.

Figure 10.25
The Customers table with the Orders subdatasheet and Order Details sub-subdatasheets expanded.

Customer ID	Company Name	Contact Name	Contact Title
ALFKI	Alfreds Futterkiste	Maria Anders	Sales Representative

Order ID	Employee	Order Date	Required Date	Shipped Date	Ship Via
10643	Suyama, Michael	25-Aug-1997	22-Sep-1997	02-Sep-1997	Speedy Express

Product	Unit Price	Quantity	Discount
Rössle Sauerkraut	$45.60	15	25%
Chartreuse verte	$18.00	21	25%
Spegesild	$12.00	2	25%
*	$0.00	0	0%

Order ID	Employee	Order Date	Required Date	Shipped Date	Ship Via
10692	Peacock, Margaret	03-Oct-1997	31-Oct-1997	13-Oct-1997	United Package

Product	Unit Price	Quantity	Discount
Vegie-spread	$43.90	20	0%
*	$0.00	0	0%

Order ID	Employee	Order Date	Required Date	Shipped Date	Ship Via
10702	Peacock, Margaret	13-Oct-1997	24-Nov-1997	21-Oct-1997	Speedy Express

Product	Unit Price	Quantity	Discount
Aniseed Syrup	$10.00	6	0%
Lakkalikööri	$18.00	15	0%
*	$0.00	0	0%

Order ID	Employee	Order Date	Required Date	Shipped Date	Ship Via
10835	Davolio, Nancy	15-Jan-1998	12-Feb-1998	21-Jan-1998	Federal Shipping
10952	Davolio, Nancy	16-Mar-1998	27-Apr-1998	24-Mar-1998	Speedy Express
11011	Leverling, Janet	09-Apr-1998	07-May-1998	13-Apr-1998	Speedy Express
*	:oNumber)				

Customer ID	Company Name	Contact Name	Contact Title
ANATR	Ana Trujillo Emparedados y helados	Ana Trujillo	Owner

Record: 1 of 3

→ For more information on subdatasheet, **see** "Understanding the Properties of Tables and Fields," **p. 135**.

> **Note**
>
> Subdatasheets resemble the format of Visual Basic 6.0's Hierarchical FlexGrid (MSHFlexGrid) control, which displays related values in an expandable grid. Unlike subdatasheets, the MSHFlexGrid control is read-only and uses a non-standard SHAPE query syntax to populate the grid.

TABLE SUBDATASHEETS

Most of the tables of Northwind.mdb already have subdatasheets; Employees doesn't. To add a Personnel Actions subdatasheet to the Employees table, follow these steps:

1. If you haven't done so already, add a relationship between the paID field of the Personnel Actions table and the EmployeeID field of the Employees table.

   Choose <u>T</u>ools, <u>R</u>elationships to open the Relationships window, click the toolbar's Show Table button, and add the Personnel Actions table. Drag the EmployeeID field of the Employees table to the paID field of the Personnel Actions table, mark the Enforce Referential Integrity check box of the Edit Relationships table, click Create to establish the relationship, and then close the Relationships window, saving your changes.

→ If you need a review of planning and creating relationships, **see** "Working with Relations, Key Fields, and Indexes" **p. 166**.

2. Open the Employees table in Datasheet view.

3. Click one of the + symbols in the first column of the Employees datasheet to open the Insert Subdatasheet dialog.

4. Select the Personnel Actions table in the list. The paID foreign-key field appears in the Link Child Fields drop-down list and the EmployeeID field appears in the Link Master Fields list (see Figure 10.26). The Relationships table supplies the default values for the two drop-down lists.

Figure 10.26
Adding the Personnel Actions table as a subdatasheet of the Employees table.

The Link Master Fields and Link Child Fields values create a one-to-many join on the specified fields.

5. Click OK to add the subdatasheet and close the dialog.

6. Click one or two of the + symbols in the Employees datasheet to display the newly added subdatasheets (see Figure 10.27).

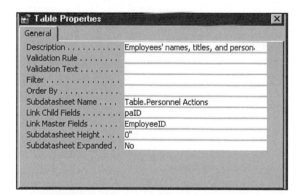

Employees : Table

		Employee ID	Last Name	First Name	Title	Title Of	Birth Date	Hire Date
▶	⊟	1	Davolio	Nancy	Sales Representative	Ms.	08-Dec-68	01-May-1992	507 -

	Type	Initiated By	Approved By	Scheduled	Effective	Rating	Amount	Comments
▶	I	1		5/1/1992	5/1/1992		2,000.00	Hired
✱	Q			1/26/1999	2/23/1999			

⊞		2	Fuller	Andrew	Vice President, Sales	Dr.	19-Feb-52	14-Aug-1992	908 W
⊞		3	Leverling	Janet	Sales Representative	Ms.	30-Aug-63	01-Apr-1992	722 M
⊞		4	Peacock	Margaret	Sales Representative	Mrs.	19-Sep-58	03-May-1993	4110 (
⊟		5	Buchanan	Steven	Sales Manager	Mr.	04-Mar-55	17-Oct-1993	14 Ga

	Type	Initiated By	Approved By	Scheduled	Effective	Rating	Amount	Comments
	H	2	2	10/17/1993	10/17/1993		2,500.00	Hired
	Q	2	2	1/1/1997	2/11/1997	8	2,750.00	First quarterly re
	Q	2	2	3/31/1997	5/12/1997	7	3,000.00	Steve could imp
	Q	2	2	6/30/1997	8/11/1997	8	3,500.00	Steve's sales ar
	Q	2	2	9/30/1997	11/11/1997	8	4,000.00	Steve continues
	Y	7	7	1/1/1990	2/11/1998	9	4,250.00	Despite Steve b
✱	Q			1/26/1999	2/23/1999			

⊞		6	Suyama	Michael	Sales Representative	Mr.	02-Jul-63	17-Oct-1993	Coven
⊞		7	King	Robert	Sales Representative	Mr.	29-May-60	02-Jan-1994	Edgeh
⊞		8	Callahan	Laura	Inside Sales Coordinator	Ms.	09-Jan-58	05-Mar-1994	4726 —
⊞		9	Dodsworth	Anne	Sales Representative	Ms.	02-Jul-69	15-Nov-1994	7 Hou
✱		(AutoNumber)						

Record: |◄| ◄ | 1 | ► | ►| | ►✱ | of 1

Figure 10.27
Two expanded Personnel Actions table subdatasheets.

7. Change to Table Design view and click the Properties button to display the Table Properties window. The selections you make in the Insert Subdatasheet dialog appear in the subdatasheet-related properties of the table (see Figure 10.28).

Table Properties

General

Description	Employees' names, titles, and person.
Validation Rule	
Validation Text	
Filter	
Order By	
Subdatasheet Name	Table.Personnel Actions
Link Child Fields	paID
Link Master Fields	EmployeeID
Subdatasheet Height	0"
Subdatasheet Expanded .	No

Figure 10.28
The Employees Table Properties window showing values added to the Subdatasheet Name, Link Child Fields, Link Master Fields, and Subdatasheet Height and Expanded properties.

Note

The child (foreign-key) field, paID, doesn't appear as a column of the subdatasheet. When you add a new record in the subdatasheet, Access automatically inserts into the related record the primary-key value of the selected record of the base table.

Tip #79 from

> The default value of the Subdatasheet Name property for new tables you create is [Auto], which doesn't add the column of boxed + symbols to a new table datasheet. To open the Add Subdatasheet dialog for a new table, choose Insert, Subdatasheet. Alternatively, you can set the subdatasheet properties directly in the Table Properties window. To remove a subdatasheet, set the Subdatasheet Name property value to [None]. If you remove a subdatasheet from a table, setting Subdatasheet Name to [Auto] displays the boxed + symbols and lets you add a new subdatasheet in Design view.

QUERY SUBDATASHEETS

If you don't want your subdatasheet to display all of the related table's columns, you must design a simple select query with only the desired fields and then use the query to populate the subdatasheet. As an example, you can minimize the width of the Orders subdatasheet of the Customers table by doing the following:

1. Create a simple select query, qryShortOrders, that includes only the OrderID, CustomerID (required to for the master-child join), OrderDate, ShippedDate, and ShippedVia fields of the Orders table.

2. Open the Customers table in Design view, open the Table Properties window, and select Query.qryShortOrders from the Subdatasheet Name list to replace the Orders table. CustomerID remains the value of the linked fields.

3. Return to Datasheet view, saving your changes. The expanded subdatasheet appears as shown in Figure 10.29, without the + sign column for the Order Details sub-sub-datasheet.

Figure 10.29
The Customers table with a subdatasheet based on a query.

Customer ID	Company Name	Contact Name
⊟ ALFKI	Alfreds Futterkiste	Maria Anders

	Order ID	Order Date	Shipped Date	Ship Via
▶	10643	25-Aug-1997	02-Sep-1997	Speedy Express
	10692	03-Oct-1997	13-Oct-1997	United Package
	10702	13-Oct-1997	21-Oct-1997	Speedy Express
	10835	15-Jan-1998	21-Jan-1998	Federal Shipping
	10952	16-Mar-1998	24-Mar-1998	Speedy Express
	11011	09-Apr-1998	13-Apr-1998	Speedy Express
✱	:oNumber)			

Customer ID	Company Name	Contact Name
⊞ ANATR	Ana Trujillo Emparedados y helados	Ana Trujillo
⊞ ANTON	Antonio Moreno Taquería	Antonio Moreno
⊞ AROUT	Around the Horn	Thomas Hardy
⊞ BERGS	Berglunds snabbköp	Christina Berglund
⊞ BLAUS	Blauer See Delikatessen	Hanna Moos
⊞ BLONP	Blondel père et fils	Frédérique Citeaux

Record: ◄◄ ◄ 1 ► ►► ►✱ of 6

4. Close the Customers table, open qryShortOrders in Design view, right-click an empty area of the upper pane, and choose Properties to open the Query Properties window.

5. Select Table.Order Details in the Subdatasheet Name field and then type **OrderID** in the two Link...Fields text boxes (see Figure 10.30).

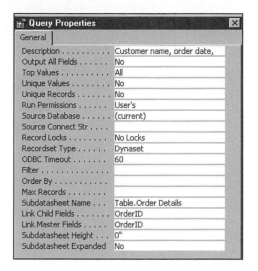

PART

II

CH

10

Figure 10.30
Adding a subdatasheet to a query by entries in the Query Properties sheet.

6. Run the query and then expand one or more of the subdatasheets to test your work (see Figure 10.31).

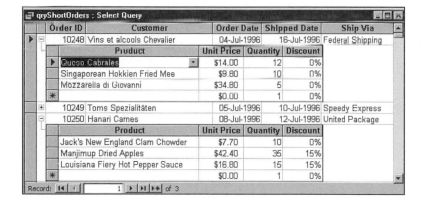

Figure 10.31
The Order Details sub-datasheet added to the qryShortOrders query.

7. Close qryShortOrders, save your changes, open the Customers table, and display the subdatasheets. The new version of the Customers table appears as shown in Figure 10.32.

Tip #80 from

RJ

Include all fields with required values in your query if you want to update or add new records in a query-based datasheet. If you don't include all required fields, you receive an error message when you attempt to add a new record.

Figure 10.32
The Customers table with the query-based Orders subdatasheet and the Order Details sub-subdatasheet.

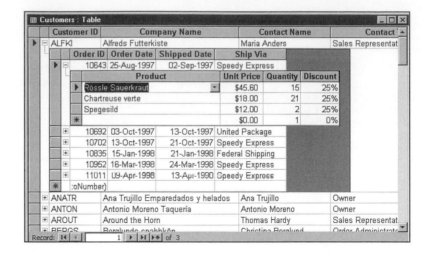

OUTER, SELF, AND THETA JOINS

The preceding sections of this chapter described the equi-join or, in the parlance of SQL-92, an inner join. Inner joins are the most common type of join in database applications. Access also lets you create three other joins: outer, self, and theta. The following sections describe these three less-common types of joins.

CREATING OUTER JOINS

Outer joins let you display the fields of all records in a table participating in a query, regardless of whether corresponding records exist in the joined table. With Access, you can choose between left and right outer joins.

A left outer join query in Access displays all the records in the table with the unique primary key, regardless of whether matching records exist in the *many* table. Conversely, a right outer join query displays all the records in the *many* table, regardless of a record's existence in the primary table. Records in the *many* table without corresponding records in the *one* table usually, but not necessarily, are orphan records; these kinds of records may have a many-to-one relationship to another table.

To practice creating a left outer join to detect whether records are missing for an employee in the Personnel Actions table, follow these steps:

1. Open a new query and add the Employees and Personnel Actions tables.

2. Drag the EmployeeID field symbol to the paID field of Personnel Actions to create an equi-join between these fields if Access didn't create the join. (Access automatically creates the join if you established a relationship between these two fields when you created the Personnel Actions table or earlier in this chapter.)

3. Select and drag the LastName and FirstName fields of the Employees table to columns 1 and 2 of the Query Design grid. Select and drag the paType and paScheduledDate fields of the Personnel Actions table to columns 3 and 4.

4. Click the line joining EmployeeID with paID to select it, as shown in Figure 10.33. The thickness of the center part of the line increases to indicate the selection. (In Figure 10.33, the two Field List boxes are separated so that the thin section of the join line is apparent.)

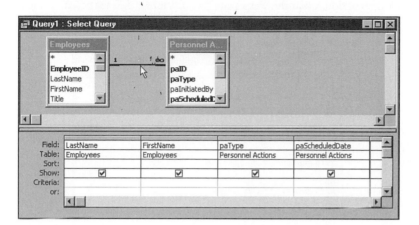

PART

II

CH

10

Figure 10.33
Selecting a join to change its property from an inner to a left or right outer join.

 NEW 2000

5. Double-click the thin section of the join line. (Double-clicking either of the line's thick sections displays the Query Properties window.) Access 2000's enhanced Join Properties dialog in Figure 10.34 appears. Type 1 is a conventional inner join, type 2 is a left join, and type 3 is a right join.

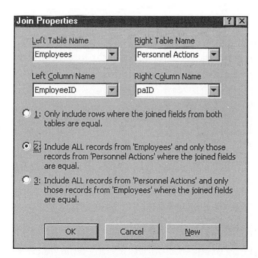

Figure 10.34
The Join Properties dialog for choosing inner, left, or right joins.

6. Select a type 2 join—a left join—by selecting option 2. Click OK to close the dialog.

Access adds an arrowhead to the line that joins EmployeeID and paID. The direction of the arrow, left to right, indicates that you have created a left join between the tables.

7. Click the Run button of the toolbar to display the result of the left join query. In Figure 10.35, three employees without a record in the Personnel Actions table appear in the result table's last rows. Your query result set may differ, depending on the number of entries that you made when creating the Personnel Actions table. (If all employees show a personnel action, open the Personnel Actions table, delete the entries for a few employees, and then rerun the query.)

Figure 10.35
The result of creating a left join between the ID fields of the Employees and Personnel Actions tables.

Last Name	Title	Type	Scheduled
Davolio	Sales Representative	H	5/1/1992
Fuller	Vice President, Sales	H	8/14/1992
Leverling	Sales Representative	H	4/1/1992
Peacock	Sales Representative	H	5/3/1993
Buchanan	Sales Manager	H	10/17/1993
Buchanan	Sales Manager	Q	1/1/1997
Buchanan	Sales Manager	Q	3/31/1997
Buchanan	Sales Manager	Q	6/30/1997
Buchanan	Sales Manager	Q	9/30/1997
Buchanan	Sales Manager	Y	1/1/1998
Suyama	Sales Representative	H	10/17/1993
King	Sales Representative	H	1/2/1994
Callahan	Inside Sales Coordinator	H	3/5/1994
Dodsworth	Sales Representative	H	11/15/1994

Record: 1 of 14

8. Close, but don't save, the query.

If you could add a personnel action for a nonexistent EmployeeID (the validation rule that you added in Chapter 9 prevents you from doing so), a right join would show the invalid entry with blank employee name fields.

CREATING SELF-JOINS

Self-joins relate values in a single table. Creating a self-join requires that you add to the query a copy of the table and then add a join between the related fields. An example of self-join use is to determine whether supervisors have approved personnel actions that they initiated, which is prohibited by the imaginary personnel manual for Northwind Traders.

To create this kind of self-join for the Personnel Actions table, follow these steps:

1. Open a new query and add the Personnel Actions table.

2. Add to the query another copy of the Personnel Actions table by clicking the Add button again. Access names the copy Personnel Actions_1. Close the Show Tables dialog.

3. Drag the original table's paInitiatedBy field to the copied table's paApprovedBy field. The join appears as shown in the upper pane of Figure 10.36.

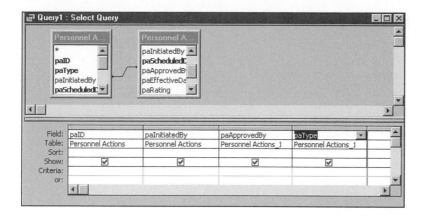

Figure 10.36
Designing the query for a self-join on the Personnel Actions table.

4. Drag the paID and paInitiatedBy fields of the original table, and the paApprovedBy and paType fields of the copy of the Personnel Actions table, to the Field row of columns 1–4, respectively, of the Query Design grid.

 5. With self-joins, you must specify that only unique values are included. Click the Properties button on the toolbar or double-click an empty area in the Query Design window's upper pane, and set the value of the Query Properties window's Unique Values property to Yes. Click the Properties button again to close the Query Properties window.

 6. Click the Run button of the toolbar to display the records in which the same employee initiated and approved a personnel action, as shown in Figure 10.37. In this case, EmployeeID 2 (Mr. Fuller) is a vice president and can override personnel policy. (Your results may differ, depending on the number of entries you made in the Personnel Actions table.)

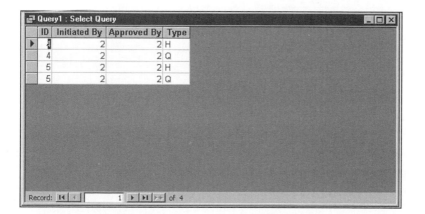

Figure 10.37
The result of a self-join that tests for supervisors approving personnel actions that they initiated.

CREATING NOT-EQUAL THETA JOINS WITH CRITERIA

Most joins are based on fields with equal values, but sometimes you need to create a join on unequal fields. Joins that you create graphically in Access are restricted to conventional equi-joins and outer joins. You can create the equivalent of a not-equal theta join by applying a criterion to one of the two fields you want to test for not-equal values.

Finding customers that have different billing and shipping addresses, as mentioned previously, is an example in which a not-equal theta join is useful. To create the equivalent of this join, follow these steps:

1. Create a new query and add the Customers and Orders tables.

2. Select the Customers table's CompanyName and Address fields and the Orders table's ShipAddress field. Drag them to the Query Design grid's first three columns.

3. Type **<> Customers.Address** in the Criteria row of the ShipAddress column. (Access automatically adds square brackets surrounding table and field names, regardless of whether the names include spaces or other punctuation.) The Query Design window appears as shown in Figure 10.38.

   Typing **<> Orders.ShipAddress** in the Address column gives an equivalent result.

Figure 10.38
Designing the query for a not-equal theta join.

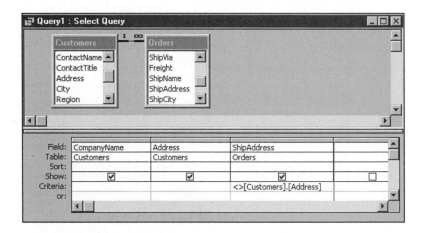

4. Click the toolbar's Properties button or double-click an empty area in the Query Design window's upper pane to open the Query Properties window and set the value of the Unique Values property to Yes.

5. Run the query. Only the records for customers that placed orders with different billing and shipping addresses appear, as shown in Figure 10.39.

6. Click the Close Window button and save your query if desired.

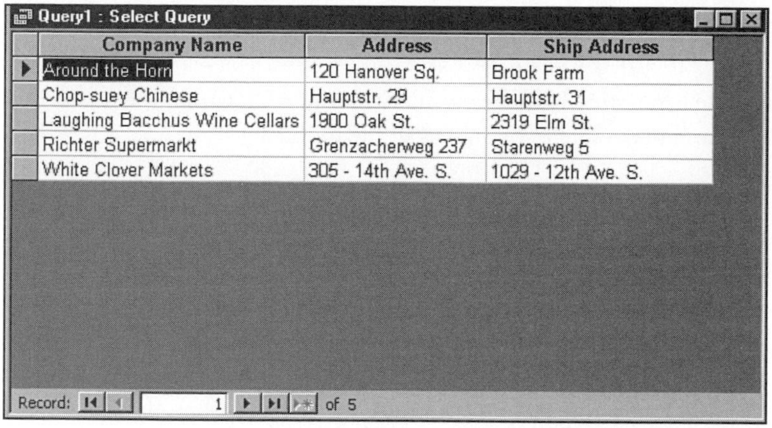

Figure 10.39
The result of a not-equal theta join designed to identify different billing and shipping addresses.

UPDATING TABLE DATA WITH QUERIES

Many of the queries that you create with the Unique Records property set to Yes are updatable because you use Access SQL's DISTINCTROW modifier to create them. These queries create Recordset objects of the updatable Dynaset type. You can't update table data with a query unless you see the tentative (blank) append record (with the asterisk in the select button) at the end of the query result table. Queries that you create with the Unique Values property set to Yes aren't updatable. The next few sections describe the conditions under which you can update a record of a table included in a query. The following sections also discuss how to use the Output Field Properties window to format query data display and editing.

Note

> You can't set both the Unique Values and Unique Records properties to Yes—these choices are mutually exclusive. In Access 2000, the default setting of both the Unique Values and Unique Records properties is No.

CHARACTERISTICS THAT DETERMINE WHETHER YOU CAN UPDATE A QUERY

Adding new records to tables or updating existing data in tables included in a query is a definite advantage in some circumstances. Correcting data errors that appear when you run the query is especially tempting. Unfortunately, you can't append or update records in most of the queries that you create. The following properties of a query prevent you from appending and updating records:

- The Unique Values property is set to Yes in the Query Properties window.
- Self-joins are used in the query.
- Access SQL aggregate functions, such as Sum( ), are employed in the query. Crosstab queries, for example, use SQL aggregate functions.
- No primary-key fields with a unique (No Duplicates) index exist for the *one* table in a one-to-many relationship.

When designing a query to use as the basis of a form for data entry or editing, make sure that none of the preceding properties apply to the query.

If none of the preceding properties apply to the query or any table within the query, you can append records to and update fields of queries in the following:

- A single-table query
- Both tables in a one-to-one relationship
- The *many* table in a one-to-many relationship
- The *one* table in a one-to-many relationship if none of the fields of the *many* table appear in the query

Updating the *one* table in a one-to-many query is a special case in Access. To enable updates to this table, follow these steps:

1. Add to the query, the primary-key field or fields of the *one* table and additional fields to update.
2. Add the field or fields of the *many* table that correspond to the key field or fields of the *one* table; this step is required to select the appropriate records for updating.
3. Add the criteria to select the records for updating to the fields chosen in step 2.
4. Click the Show box so that the *many* table field(s) does not appear in the query.

After following these steps, you can edit the non-key fields of the *one* table. You can't, however, alter the values of key fields that have relationships with records in the *many* table. Such a modification violates referential integrity. You also can't update a calculated column of a query; tables can't include calculated values.

Tip #81 from 	By adding lookup fields to tables, you often can avoid writing one-to-many queries and precisely following the preceding rules to make such queries updatable. For example, the Orders table, which includes three lookup fields (CustomerID, EmployeeID, and ShipVia), is updatable. If you want to allow updates in Datasheet view (called *browse updating*), using lookup fields is a better approach than creating an updatable query. Most database developers consider simple browse updating to be a poor practice because of the potential for inadvertent data-entry errors.

FORMATTING DATA WITH THE QUERY FIELD PROPERTIES WINDOW

The display format of data in queries is inherited from the format of the data in the tables that underlie the query. You can override the table format by using the **Format**(*ColumnName*, *FormatString*) function.

→ For more information, **see** "Understanding Query Operators and Expressions" to create a calculated field **p. 319**.

 Access 2000 provides an easier method: the Field Properties window that you can use to format the display of query data. You also can create an input mask to aid in updating the query data. To open the Field Properties window, place the caret in the Field cell of the query column that you want to format, and then click the Properties button of the toolbar or double-click an empty area in the upper pane of the Query Design window. Figure 10.40 shows the Field Properties window for a simple query based on the Personnel Actions Query. By default, Access's General Date, Medium Date, and Short Date formats don't display four-digit years, which is required by Year 2000 (Y2K) display standards. Typing **m/d/yyyy** or **mm/dd/yyyy** in the Short Date Style text box of the Date/Time page of Control Panel's Regional Settings tool solves the General Date and Short Date format, but doesn't affect the Medium Date style. To obtain a four-digit year display with Medium Date format, you must type the Format descriptor string—**dd-mmm-yyyy**—in the Format text box. All sample tables in Northwind.mdb have the custom dd-mm-yyyy format applied, but Personnel Actions doesn't.

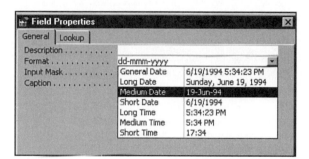

Figure 10.40
Changing the Medium Date display format for a query column of the Date/Time field data type to conform to Y2K standards.

Tip #82 from

Don't depend on users changing the Short Date Format with Control Panel's Regional Settings tool to make your application Y2K compliant. Marking the All Databases check box of the Use Four-Digit Year Formatting option (on the General page of the Options dialog) solves most Y2K issues. To be safe, however, take the Microsoft approach and use fixed four-digit year formats for all your date fields.

The Field Properties window displays the following subset of the properties that apply to a table's fields:

- *Description*. Lets you enter the text to appear in the status bar when the user selects the field in Datasheet view.

- *Format*. Lets you control the appearance of the data in Datasheet view, such as Short Date.

- *Input Mask*. Lets you specify the format for entering data, such as `90/90/0000`. (To create an input mask that is appropriate for the field data type, click the ellipsis button to open the Input Mask Wizard.)

- *Caption*. Lets you change the query column heading, such as Received, for the Order Date column.

Each of the preceding query properties follows the rules described in Chapter 4 for setting table field properties. Adding a value (Received) for the Caption property of a query against the Orders table is the equivalent of adding a column alias by typing **Received:** as a prefix in the Order Date column's Field cell. The value of the Input Mask property need not correspond exactly to the value of the Format property, but input mask characters don't appear if you try to use a Short Date mask with a Medium Date format you apply in the query. For example, the Received (OrderDate) field in Figure 10.41, which shows the effect of setting the property values shown in the preceding list, has a single-digit (no leading zero) month and day for the Short Date display format and an input mask for updating in with two-digit months and days. Most typists prefer to enter a consistent number of digits in a field when possible.

 If your query has tables linked to dBASE, FoxPro, or other non-Access tables and you can't update records in or add records to the query result set, see "Queries with Linked Tables Aren't Updatable" in the "Troubleshooting" section near the end of this chapter.

Figure 10.41
Editing an order record with an Order Date input mask.

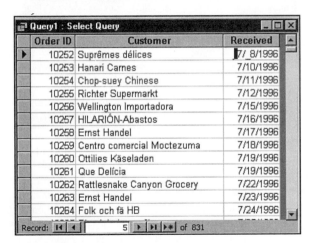

MAKING ALL FIELDS OF TABLES ACCESSIBLE

Most queries that you create include only the fields you specifically choose. To choose these fields, you either select them from or type them into the dropdown combo list in the Query Design grid's Field row, or you drag the field names from the field lists to the appropriate cells in the Field row. You can, however, include all fields of a table in a query. Access provides the following three methods for including all fields of a table in a query:

- Double-click the field list title bar of the table to selects all of the fields in the field list and then drag the field list to the Query Design grid. Each field appears in a column of the grid.

- Drag the asterisk (*) to a single Query Design grid column. To sort on or apply selection criteria to a field, drag the field to the Query Design grid and clear the Show check box for the field.

- Set the Output All Fields property value in the Query Properties sheet to Yes to add with asterisks all fields of all tables to the grid.

MAKING CALCULATIONS ON MULTIPLE RECORDS

One of SQL's most powerful capabilities is that of obtaining summary information almost instantly from specified sets of records in tables. Summarized information from databases is the basis for virtually all management information systems (MIS). These systems usually answer questions such as, What are our sales to date for this month? or How did last month's sales compare with the same month last year? To answer these questions, you must create queries that make calculations on field values from all or selected sets of records in a table. To make calculations on table values, you must create a query that uses the table and employ Access's SQL aggregate functions to perform the calculations.

USING THE SQL AGGREGATE FUNCTIONS

Summary calculations on fields of tables included in query result tables use the SQL aggregate functions listed in Table 10.1. These are called *aggregate functions* because they apply to groups (aggregations) of data cells. The SQL aggregate functions satisfy the requirements of most queries needed for business applications. You can write special user-defined functions with Access VBA code to apply more sophisticated statistical, scientific, or engineering aggregate functions to your data.

PART

II

CH

10

TABLE 10.1   SQL AGGREGATE FUNCTIONS

Function	Description	Field Types
Avg()	Average of values in a field	All types except Text, Memo, and OLE Object
Count()	Number of **Not Null** values in a field	All field types
First()	Value of a field of the first record	All field types
Last()	Value of a field of the last record	All field types
Max()	Greatest value in a field	All types except Memo and OLE Object
Min()	Least value in a field	All types except Memo and OLE Object
StDev(), StDevP()	Statistical standard deviation of values in a field	All types except Text, Memo, and OLE Object
Sum()	Total of values in a field	All types except Text, Memo, and OLE Object
Var(), VarP()	Statistical variation of values in a field	All types except Text, Memo, and OLE Object

StDev() and Var() evaluate population samples. You can choose these functions from the dropdown list in the Query Design grid's Total row. (The Total row appears when you click the Totals button of the toolbar or choose View, Totals.) StDevP() and VarP() evaluate populations and must be entered as expressions. If you're familiar with statistical principles, you recognize the difference in the calculation methods of standard deviation and variance for populations and samples of populations. The following section explains the method of choosing the SQL aggregate function for the column of a query.

Note

ANSI SQL and most SQL (client/server) databases support the equivalent of Access SQL's Avg(), Count(), First(), Last(), Max(), Min(), and Sum() aggregate functions as AVG(), COUNT(), FIRST(), LAST(), MAX(), MIN(), and SUM(), respectively. ANSI SQL and few, if any, SQL databases provide equivalents of the StdDev(), StdDevP(), Var(), and VarP() functions.

MAKING CALCULATIONS BASED ON ALL RECORDS OF A TABLE

Managers, especially sales and marketing managers, are most often concerned with information about orders received and shipments made during specific periods of time. Financial managers are interested in calculated values, such as the total amount of unpaid invoices and the average number of days between the invoice and payment dates. Occasionally, you might want to make calculations on all records of a table, such as finding the historical average value of all invoices issued by a firm. Usually, however, you apply criteria to the query to select specific records that you want to total.

 Access considers all SQL aggregate functions to be members of the Totals class of functions. You create queries that return any or all SQL aggregate functions by clicking the Totals button (with the Greek sigma, Σ, which represents summation) on the toolbar.

The Orders table of Access 2000's Northwind.mdb sample database doesn't include an OrderAmount field that represents the total amount of the order, less freight. (The "Entering a Query Criterion" section of Chapter 9 used a simplified version of this example to demonstrate the use of functions to calculate field values.) To create a sample query that uses the SQL aggregate functions to display the total number of orders; total sales; and the average, minimum, and maximum order values, you need a field that contains the total amount of each order. Follow these steps to create a new table that includes an additional field with a computed Order Amount:

 1. Create a new query and add the Orders and Order Details tables to it.

2. Drag the OrderID field of the Orders table to the first column of the Query Design grid and then drag the OrderDate field to the second column.

 3. Type **Order Amount: Sum([Quantity]*[UnitPrice]*(1-[Discount]))** in the Field row of the third (empty) column. This expression sums the net amount of all line items for each order. With the caret in the Order Amount column, click the Properties button of the toolbar to open the Field Properties window, and then select Currency from the Format list.

4. Click the Totals button on the toolbar. A new row, Total, is added to the Query Design grid. Access adds Group By, the default action, to each cell in the Total row. The following section discusses the use of Group By.

5. Move to the third column's Total row and press F4 to display the dropdown list of SQL aggregate functions. Select Expression from the list. Your Query Design grid appears as shown in Figure 10.42.

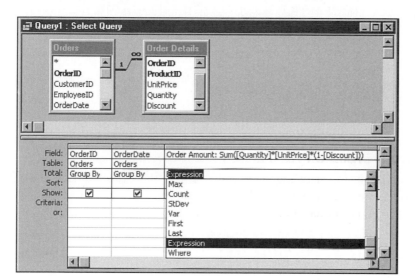

Figure 10.42
Creating a calculated field with the Sum() function.

6. Click the Run button to test your initial entries. Your query in Datasheet view appears as in Figure 10.43.

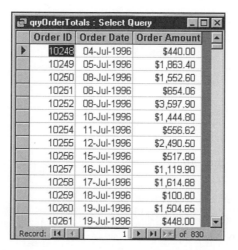

Figure 10.43
Running the query design shown in Figure 10.42.

7. Close and save your query with the name **qryOrderTotals**.

Tip #83 from

When you apply the Format property to the Order Amount column by selecting Currency in the Field Properties window, successive queries that you create don't inherit the value of the Format property (instead, the default Format value, Double, is applied). If you type `Order Amount: CCur(Sum([Quantity]*[UnitPrice]*(1-[Discount])))` in the Order Amount column's Field row, however, the Format property of successive queries containing the Order Amount field is set to VBA's `Currency` data type. The `CCur()` VBA function coerces the field's data type to `Currency`.

Follow these steps to apply the SQL aggregate functions to the Order Amounts field of the query result set of the qryOrderTotals query:

1. Open a new query and add the qryOrderTotals query. (To base a query on a previously saved query, click the Queries tab of the Show Table dialog and add the query as you would a table. A query based on another query is called a *nested* query.)

2. Drag the OrderID field to the first column and then drag the Order Amount column four times to the adjacent column to create four Order Amount columns.

3. Choose <u>V</u>iew, <u>T</u>otals to add the Total row to your Query Design grid. Alternatively, right-click in the grid region and choose Totals from the popup menu.

4. Move to the Total row of the OrderID column and press F4 to display the dropdown list of SQL aggregate functions. Choose Count as the function for the OrderID, as shown in Figure 10.44.

Figure 10.44
Choosing the SQL aggregate function for calculations based on multiple records in a table.

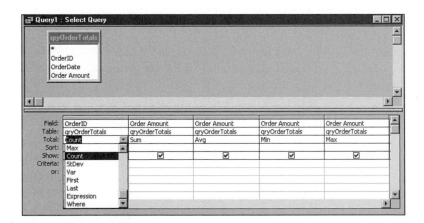

5. Move to the first Order Amount column, open the list, and choose Sum from the Total dropdown list. Repeat the process, choosing Avg for the second Order Amount column, Min for the third, and Max for the fourth.

6. Place the caret in the Count field and click the Properties button of the toolbar (or right-click in the Count field and then click Properties in the popup menu) to display the Field Properties window. Type **Count** as the value of the Caption property.

7. Repeat step 6 for the four Order Amount columns, typing **Currency** for the Format property and typing **Sum**, **Average**, **Minimum**, and **Maximum** as the values of the Caption property for the four columns, respectively. (You don't need to set the Format property if you used the `CCur()` function in the Order Totals query.)

8. Click the Run button to display the query's result. You haven't specified criteria for the fields, so the result shown in Figure 10.45 is for the whole table.

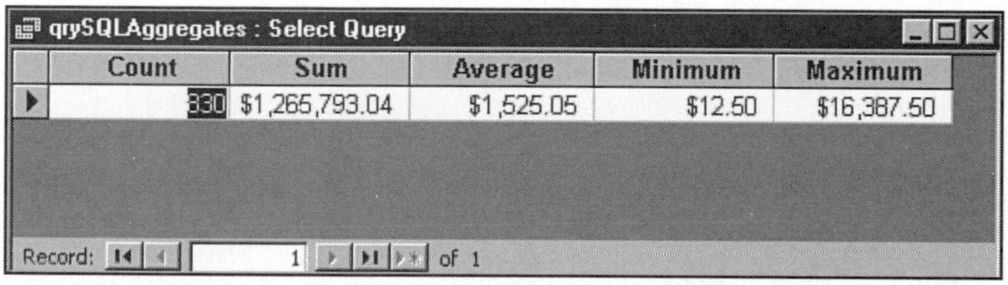

Count	Sum	Average	Minimum	Maximum
880	$1,265,793.04	$1,525.05	$12.50	$16,387.50

Figure 10.45
The result of the all-records query shown in Figure 10.44.

PART
II

CH
10

9. Save your query with a descriptive name, such as **qrySQLAggregates**, because you use this query in the two sections that follow.

MAKING CALCULATIONS BASED ON SELECTED RECORDS OF A TABLE

The preceding sample query performed calculations on all orders received by Northwind Traders that were entered in the Orders table. Usually, you are interested in a specific set of records—a range of dates, for example—from which to calculate aggregate values. To restrict the calculation to orders that Northwind received in March 1998, follow these steps:

1. Return to design mode so that you can add criteria to select a specific group of records based on the date of the order.

2. Drag the OrderDate field onto the OrderID column to add OrderDate as the first column of the query. You need the OrderDate field to restrict the data to a range of dates.

3. Open the Total dropdown list in the Order Date column and choose Where to replace the default Group By. Access deselects the Show box of the OrderDate column.

4. In the Order Date column's Criteria row, type **Like "3/*/1998"** to restrict the totals to orders received in the month of March 1998 (see Figure 10.46). When you use the `Like` criterion, Access adds the quotation marks if you forget to type them.

5. Click the Run button on the toolbar to display the result: the count, total, and average value of orders received during the month of March 1998 (see Figure 10.47).

You can create a more useful grouping of records by replacing the field name with an expression. For example, you can group aggregates by the year and month (or year and

Figure 10.46
Adding a Where criterion to restrict the totals to a range of records.

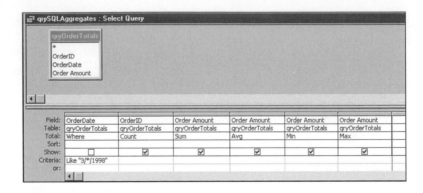

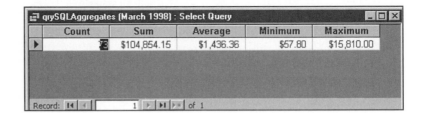

Figure 10.47
The result of adding the Where criterion to the OrderDate field of the query.

quarter) by grouping on the value of an expression created with the Format function. The following steps produce a sales summary record for each month of 1997, the latest year for which 12 months of data are available in the Orders table:

1. Return to Query design view, and then click the header bar of the query's OrderDate column to select the first column. Press the Insert key to add a new, empty column to the query.

2. Type **Month: Format([OrderDate],"yyyy-mm")** in the first (empty) column's Field row. (You use the "yyyy-mm" format so that the records sort in date order. For a single year, you also can use "m" or "mm", but not "mmm", because "mmm" sorts in alphabetic sequence starting with Apr.)

3. Change the Where criterion of the Order Date column to **Like "*/*/1997"** to return a full year of data. Your query design appears as shown in Figure 10.48. (The Order Date column in Figure 10.48 is moved from its rightmost position to the second column of the query design grid.)

4. Click the toolbar's Run button to display the result of your query (see Figure 10.49). The query creates sales summary data for each month of 1997.

5. Choose File, Save As and save the query under a different name, such as **qryMonthlySales**, because you modify the query in the next section.

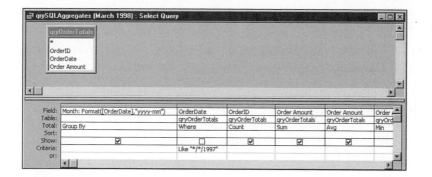

Figure 10.48
Designing a query for a yearly sales summary by month.

Figure 10.49
The result set of the query design shown in Figure 10.48.

Month	Count	Sum	Average	Minimum	Maximum
1997-01	33	$61,258.07	$1,856.31	$49.80	$11,188.40
1997-02	29	$38,483.63	$1,327.02	$174.90	$4,924.13
1997-03	30	$38,547.22	$1,284.91	$147.00	$10,495.60
1997-04	31	$53,032.95	$1,710.74	$136.80	$9,921.30
1997-05	32	$53,781.29	$1,680.67	$110.00	$10,191.70
1997-06	30	$36,362.80	$1,212.09	$155.00	$2,944.40
1997-07	33	$51,020.86	$1,546.09	$23.80	$6,475.40
1997-08	33	$47,287.67	$1,432.96	$55.80	$5,510.59
1997-09	37	$55,629.24	$1,503.49	$45.00	$5,256.50
1997-10	38	$66,749.23	$1,756.56	$93.50	$10,164.80
1997-11	34	$43,533.81	$1,280.41	$52.35	$4,529.80
1997-12	48	$71,398.43	$1,487.47	$12.50	$6,635.27

Record: 1 of 12

PART
II

CH

10

DESIGNING PARAMETER QUERIES

If you expect to run a summary or another type of query repeatedly with changes to the criteria, you can convert the query to a parameter query. Parameter queries—which Chapter 8, "Designing Access Queries," explained briefly—enable you to enter criteria with the Enter Parameter Value dialog. Access prompts you for each parameter. For the qryMonthlySales query that you created previously in this chapter, the only parameter likely to change is the range of dates for which you want to generate the product sales data. The two sections that follow show you how to add a parameter to a query and specify the data type of the para-meter.

ADDING A PARAMETER TO THE MONTHLY SALES QUERY

To convert the qryMonthlySales summary query to a parameter query, you first create prompts for the Enter Parameter Value dialog that appears when the query runs. You create parameter queries by substituting the text with which to prompt, enclosed within square brackets, for actual values. Follow these steps:

1. In Design mode, open the qryMonthlySales query that you created in the preceding section.

2. With the caret in the Month column's Field row, press F2 to select the expression in the Field cell. Then press Ctrl+C to copy the expression to the Clipboard.

3. Move the caret to the OrderDate column's Field row and press F2 to select OrderDate. Then press Ctrl+V to replace OrderDate with the expression used for the first column.

4. Move to the OrderDate column's Criteria cell and replace Like "*/*/1997" with **[Enter the year and month in YYYY-MM format:]** (see Figure 10.50).

Figure 10.50
The expression to create the Enter Parameter Value dialog with boxes for the year and month.

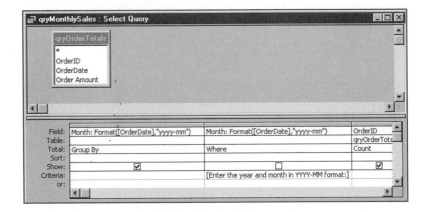

Figure 10.51
The Enter Parameter Value dialog for entering the year and month.

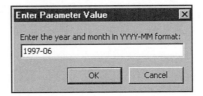

5. Click the Run button. The Enter Parameter Value dialog opens with the label that you assigned as the value of the criterion in step 4.

6. Type **1997-06** in the text box to display the data for June 1997, as shown in Figure 10.51.

7. Click OK to run the query. The result appears as shown in Figure 10.52.

Figure 10.52
The query result for the 1997-06 parameter.

Month	Count	Sum	Average	Minimum	Maximum
1997-06	30	$36,362.80	$1,212.09	$155.00	$2,944.40

Record: ◄◄ ◄ 1 ► ►◄ ►* of 1

SPECIFYING THE PARAMETER'S DATA TYPE

The default field data type for parameters of Access queries is Text. If the parameter creates a criterion for a query column of the Date/Time or Number field data type, you must assign a data type to each entry that is made through an Enter Parameter Value dialog. Data types for values entered as parameters are established in the Query Parameters dialog. Follow these steps to add an optional data type specification to your parameter:

1. Use the mouse to select Enter the Year and Month in YY-MM Format in the Month column's Criteria cell (omit the square brackets) and copy the text of the prompt to the Clipboard by pressing Ctrl+C.

2. Choose Query, Parameters to display the Query Parameters dialog.

3. To insert the prompt in the Parameter column of the dialog, place the caret in the column and press Ctrl+V. The prompt entry in the Parameter column must match the prompt entry in the Criteria field exactly; copying and pasting the prompt text ensures an exact match. Do not include the square brackets in the Parameter column.

4. Press Tab to move to the Data Type column, press F4 to open the Data Type drop-down list, and select Date/Time (see Figure 10.53). Click OK to close the dialog.

Figure 10.53
The Query Parameters dialog for assigning data types to user-entered parameters.

Tip #84 from

Complete your query design and testing before you convert any type of query to a parameter query. Using fixed criteria with the query maintains consistency during the testing process. Furthermore, you can make repeated changes between Design and Run mode more quickly if you don't have to enter one or more parameters in the process. After you finish testing the query, edit the criteria to add the Enter Parameter Value dialog.

The parameter-conversion process described in this section applies to all types of queries that you create if one or more of the query columns includes a criterion expression. The advantage of the parameter query is that you or a user of the database can run a query for any range of values—in this case, dates—such as the current month to date, a particular fiscal quarter, or an entire fiscal year.

CREATING CROSSTAB QUERIES

Crosstab queries are summary queries that let you determine exactly how the summary data appears onscreen. Crosstab queries display summarized data in the traditional row-column form of spreadsheets and are closely related to Excel PivotTables.

➔ For more information on PivotTables, **see** "Adding a PivotTable with the Page Field List," **p. 687** and "Slicing and Dicing Data with PivotTables," **p. 746**.

With crosstab queries, you can perform the following processes:

- Specify the field that creates labels (headings) for rows by using the Group By instruction.
- Determine the field(s) that create(s) column headers and the criteria that determine the values appearing under the headers.
- Assign calculated data values to the cells of the resulting row-column grid.

The following list details the advantages of using crosstab queries:

- You can display a substantial amount of summary data in a compact format familiar to anyone who uses a spreadsheet application or columnar accounting form.
- The summary data is presented in a format that is ideally suited for creating graphs and charts automatically with the Access Chart Wizard.
- Designing queries to create multiple levels of detail is quick and easy. Queries with identical columns but fewer rows can represent increasingly summarized data. Highly summarized queries are ideal to begin a drill-down procedure by instructing the user, for example, to click the Details button to display sales by product.

Using crosstab queries imposes only one restriction: You can't sort your result table on calculated values in columns. You can't, therefore, create a query that ranks products by sales volume. Columns are likely to have values that cause conflicts in the sorting order of the row. You can choose an ascending sort, a descending sort, or no sort on the row label values in the first column.

USING THE WIZARD TO GENERATE A QUARTERLY PRODUCT SALES CROSSTAB QUERY

Access 2000's Crosstab Query Wizard can generate a crosstab query from a single table. If you must include more than one table to get the result you want from the Wizard, you must design your own crosstab query. Follow these steps to create a query and then use the Crosstab Query Wizard to generate a result set that shows quarterly sales by product for the year 1997:

1. Create a new query in Design view and add the Orders table and Order Details Extended query. Drag the OrderDate field of the Orders table and the ProductID, ProductName, and ExtendedPrice fields of the Order Details Extended query to the grid. Add **Like "*/*/1997"** as the criterion of the OrderDate field to restrict the data to a single year (see Figure 10.54).

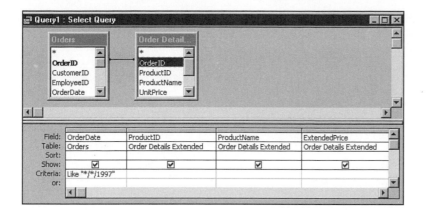

Figure 10.54
Designing the source query for the Wizard's crosstab query.

2. With the ProductID field selected, click the Properties button, click the Lookup tab, and select Text Box in the Display Control to revert from the ProductName lookup to the numeric ProductID value. Click Run to verify your design (see Figure 10.55).

Figure 10.55
The result set of the query design of Figure 10.54.

Order Date	Product	Product Name	Extended Price
01-Jan-1997	29	Thüringer Rostbratwurst	$2,079.00
01-Jan-1997	35	Steeleye Stout	$504.00
01-Jan-1997	49	Maxilaku	$480.00
01-Jan-1997	30	Nord-Ost Matjeshering	$372.60
01-Jan-1997	56	Gnocchi di nonna Alice	$2,128.00
01-Jan-1997	66	Louisiana Fiery Hot Pepper Sauce	$336.00
01-Jan-1997	71	Flötemysost	$1,032.00
02-Jan-1997	23	Tunnbröd	$432.00
02-Jan-1997	63	Vegie-spread	$2,281.50
03-Jan-1997	16	Pavlova	$248.11
03-Jan-1997	48	Chocolade	$606.90
03-Jan-1997	26	Gumbär Gummibärchen	$709.65
03-Jan-1997	42	Singaporean Hokkien Fried Mee	$425.60
03-Jan-1997	49	Maxilaku	$456.00

Record: 1 of 1059

3. Close and save the query as **qryCTWizSource**.

4. Click the New button to open the New Query dialog and double-click the Crosstab Query Wizard to open the Wizard's first dialog.

5. Select the Queries option and then select qryCTWizSource from the list (see Figure 10.56). Click Next.

6. Double-click the ProductID field to move ProductID from the Available Fields to the Selected Fields list. Do the same for the ProductName field. The second Wizard dialog appears as shown in Figure 10.57. Click Next.

Figure 10.56
Selecting
qryCTWizSource as
the source for the
Wizard's crosstab
query.

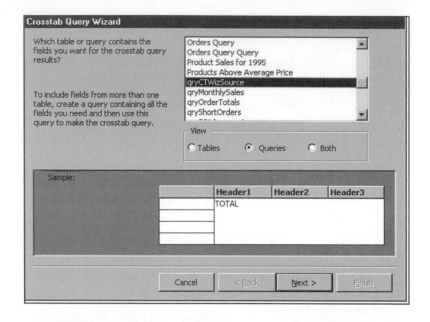

Figure 10.57
Specifying ProductID
and ProductName as
the row headers for
the crosstab query.

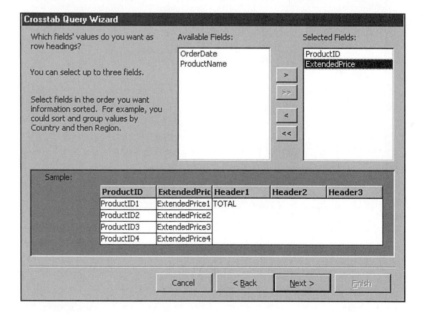

7. Accept the default OrderDate field for the column headings (see Figure 10.58). Click Next.

8. Select Quarter as the date interval for the columns (see Figure 10.59). Click Next.

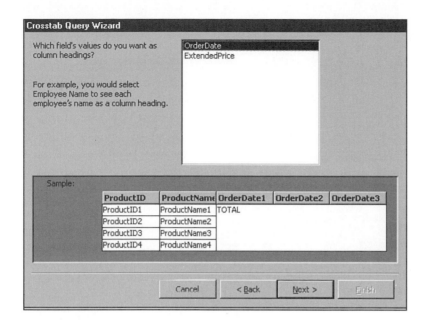

Figure 10.58
Specifying OrderDate to supply the column headers for the crosstab query.

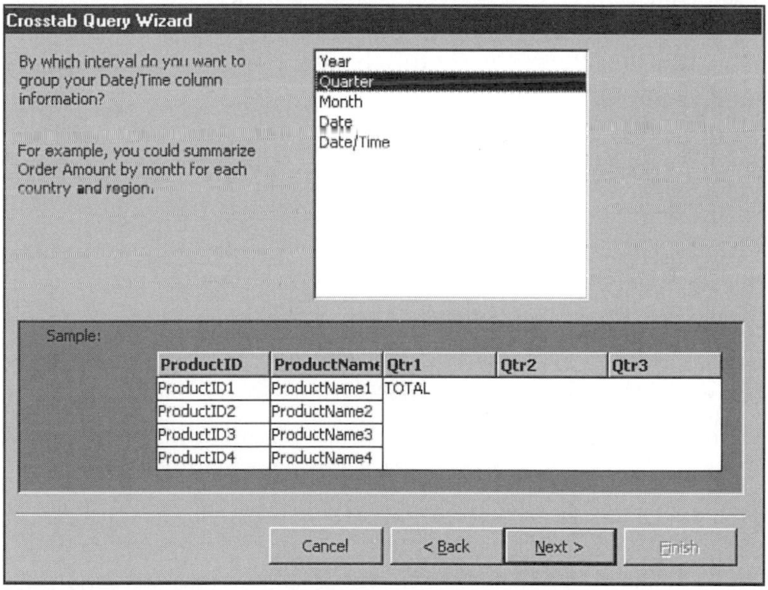

Figure 10.59
Specifying quarterly sales data.

9. Select Sum as the aggregate function to total sales for each quarter. Leave the Yes, Include Row Sums check box marked to include a column that shows the total sales for the four quarters (see Figure 10.60). Click Next.

10. In the final Wizard dialog, type **qry1997QuarterlyProductSales** as the name of the query and click Finish to display the crosstab query result set (see Figure 10.61).

Figure 10.60
Choosing the Sum SQL aggregate function and adding row totals for the year 1997.

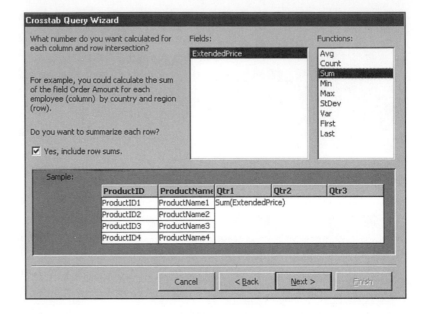

Figure 10.61
The quarterly product sales crosstab query generated by the Crosstab Query Wizard.

Product Name	Total Of ExtendedPrice	Qtr 1	Qtr 2	Qtr 3	Qtr 4
Chai	$4,887.00	$705.60	$878.40	$1,174.50	$2,128.50
Chang	$7,038.55	$2,435.80	$228.00	$2,061.50	$2,313.25
Aniseed Syrup	$1,724.00	$544.00	$600.00	$140.00	$440.00
Chef Anton's Cajun Seasoning	$5,214.88	$225.28	$2,970.00	$1,337.60	$682.00
Chef Anton's Gumbo Mix	$373.62			$288.22	$85.40
Grandma's Boysenberry Spread	$2,500.00			$1,750.00	$750.00
Uncle Bob's Organic Dried Pears	$9,186.30	$1,084.80	$1,575.00	$2,700.00	$3,826.50
Northwoods Cranberry Sauce	$4,260.00		$1,300.00		$2,960.00
Mishi Kobe Niku	$6,935.50	$1,396.80	$1,319.20	$3,637.50	$582.00
Ikura	$9,935.50	$1,215.20	$688.20	$4,212.90	$3,819.20
Queso Cabrales	$6,911.94	$1,630.44	$2,756.25	$504.00	$2,021.25
Queso Manchego La Pastora	$8,335.30	$456.00	$1,396.50	$4,962.80	$1,520.00
Konbu	$812.94	$13.44	$168.00	$469.50	$162.00
Tofu	$6,234.48	$1,432.20	$2,734.20	$1,318.27	$749.81

Record: 14 | 1 | of 77

DESIGNING A MONTHLY PRODUCT SALES CROSSTAB QUERY

You can bypass the source query step required by the Query Wizard by manually designing your crosstab query. To create in Query Design view a typical crosstab query that displays products in rows and the monthly sales volume for each product in the corresponding columns, follow these steps:

1. Open a new query and add the Products, Order Details, and Orders tables to the query.

2. Drag the ProductID and ProductName fields from the Products table to the query's first two columns and then drag the OrderDate field of the Orders table to the third column.

3. Choose Query, Crosstab Query. The title bar of the query changes from Query1: Select Query to Query1: Crosstab Query. Another row, Crosstab, is added to the Query Design grid.

4. Open the dropdown list of the ProductID column's Crosstab row and select Row Heading. Repeat this process for the ProductName column. These two columns provide the required row headings for your crosstab.

5. Open the Total dropdown list of the OrderDate column and select Where. Type **Like "*/*/1997"** in this column's Criteria row.

6. Move to the next (empty) column's Field row and type the following:

```
Sales: Sum([Order Details].[Quantity]*[Order Details].[UnitPrice])
```

Move to the Total row, choose Expression from the dropdown list, and then choose Value from the Crosstab row. The expression calculates the gross amount of the orders received for each product that populates your crosstab query's data cells. (You need to specify the Orders Detail table name; if you don't, you receive an "Ambiguous field reference" error message.)

7. In the next (empty) column's Field row, type **Format([OrderDate], "mmm")**. Access adds a default field name, Expr1:. Accept the default because the **Format** function that you added creates the column names, the three-letter abbreviation for the months of the year ("mmm" format), when you run the query. The months of the year (Jan through Dec) are your column headings, so move to the Crosstab row and choose Column Heading from the dropdown list. The design of your crosstab query appears as shown in Figure 10.62.

PART
II

CH
10

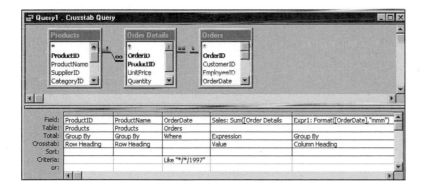

Figure 10.62
The design of a crosstab query for monthly sales of products.

8. Click the Run button to execute the query. A period of disk activity occurs, followed by a display of the crosstab query's result, shown in Figure 10.63.

Notice that the crosstab query result contains a major defect: The columns are arranged alphabetically by month name rather than in calendar order. You can solve this problem by using fixed column headings, which you learn about in the following section, "Using Fixed Column Headings with Crosstab Queries."

Figure 10.63
The first result set from the crosstab query design shown in Figure 10.62.

Product ID	Product Name	Apr	Aug	Dec	Feb
1	Chai	$720.00	$720.00		
2	Chang	$228.00	$1,900.00	$1,615.00	$83
3	Aniseed Syrup			$200.00	
4	Chef Anton's Cajun Seasoning	$1,100.00	$770.00		
5	Chef Anton's Gumbo Mix		$320.25		
6	Grandma's Boysenberry Spread		$1,750.00		
7	Uncle Bob's Organic Dried Pears	$1,500.00	$1,050.00	$1,140.00	$38
8	Northwoods Cranberry Sauce	$1,360.00		$1,200.00	
9	Mishi Kobe Niku	$1,552.00			
10	Ikura	$496.00	$558.00	$1,612.00	$84
11	Queso Cabrales		$210.00	$1,785.00	$70
12	Queso Manchego La Pastora		$1,368.00		$45
13	Konbu	$60.00	$78.00	$120.00	

Record: ◄◄ ◄ 1 ► ►► ►* of 77

USING FIXED COLUMN HEADINGS WITH CROSSTAB QUERIES

Access uses an alphabetical or numerical sort on row and column headings to establish the sequence of appearance in the crosstab query result table. For this reason, if you use short or full names for months, the sequence is in alphabetic rather than calendar order. You can correct this problem by assigning fixed column headings to the crosstab query. Follow these steps to modify and rerun the query:

→ To review the ways Access lets you manipulate dates and time, **see** "Functions for Date and Time," **p. 333**.

1. Return to Query Design mode and click the Properties button of the toolbar, or double-click an empty area in the Query Design window's upper pane. The Query Properties window contains an option that appears only for crosstab queries: Column Headings.

2. In the Column Headings text box, type the three-letter abbreviations of all 12 months of the year (see Figure 10.64). You must spell the abbreviations of the months correctly; data for months with spelling mistakes doesn't appear. You can separate entries with commas or semicolons, and you don't need to type quotation marks, because Access adds them. Spaces are unnecessary and undesirable between the Column Headings values. After you complete all 12 entries, close the Query Properties window.

Figure 10.64
Entering fixed column headings in the crosstab Query Properties window.

Query Properties	
General	
Description	
Column Headings	"Jan","Feb","Mar","Apr","May","Jun","Jul","Aug","Sep","Oct","Nov","Dec"
Run Permissions	User's
Source Database	(current)
Source Connect Str	
Record Locks	No Locks
Recordset Type	Dynaset
ODBC Timeout	60
Subdatasheet Name . . .	
Link Child Fields	
Link Master Fields	
Subdatasheet Height . . .	0"
Subdatasheet Expanded	No

3. Click the Run button of the toolbar. Now the result table, shown in Figure 10.65, includes columns for all 12 months, although you can see only January through April in Figure 10.65. (Scroll to the right to see the remaining months.) If the crosstab appears differently, check whether you properly entered the fixed column headings in the Query Properties window. A misspelled month causes Access to omit the month from the query result set; if you specified "mmmm" instead of "mmm", most of your month columns will be blank.

Product ID	Product Name	Jan	Feb	Mar	Apr	May
1	Chai	$489.60		$216.00	$720.00	$144.00
2	Chang	$912.00	$836.00	$912.00	$228.00	
3	Aniseed Syrup	$400.00		$160.00		$600.00
4	Chef Anton's Cajun Seasoning			$281.60	1,100.00	$2,200.00
5	Chef Anton's Gumbo Mix					
6	Grandma's Boysenberry Spread					
7	Uncle Bob's Organic Dried Pears		$384.00	$720.00	1,500.00	$300.00
8	Northwoods Cranberry Sauce				1,360.00	
9	Mishi Kobe Niku	$1,552.00			1,552.00	
10	Ikura		$843.20	$496.00	$496.00	$62.00
11	Queso Cabrales	$504.00	$705.60	$504.00		$1,953.00
12	Queso Manchego La Pastora		$456.00			$1,710.00
13	Konbu	$9.60		$4.80	$60.00	$108.00
14	Tofu	$1,246.20		$223.20	1,627.50	

Record: 1 of 77

Figure 10.65
The result table from the crosstab query design with fixed column headings and a date-limiting criterion.

4. Choose File, Save As and save the query with an appropriate name, such as **qry1997MonthlyProductSales**.

You can produce a printed report quickly from the query by clicking the Print Preview button on the toolbar and then clicking the Print button.

Tip #85 from

You might want to use fixed column headings if you use the Group By instruction with country names. Users in the United States will probably place USA first, and Canadian firms will undoubtedly choose Canada as the first entry. If you add a record with a new country, you must remember to update the list of fixed column headings with the new country value. Fixed column headings have another hidden benefit: they usually make crosstab queries operate more quickly.

CREATING QUERIES FROM TABLES IN OTHER DATABASES

Access's Query Properties window includes two properties that let you create a query based on tables contained in a database other than the current database. Access calls the database that you open after you launch Access the *current database*. Databases other than the current database commonly are called *external* databases. The use of these two properties is as follows:

- The value of the Source Database property for desktop databases is the path to the external database and, for Jet databases, the name of the database file. To run a query against tables contained in the Beckwith.mdb sample database from the accompanying CD-ROM, replace (current) in the Source Database text box with the following, as shown in Figure 10.66:

  C:\Seua2k\Beckwith\Beckwith.mdb.

  You must have installed the sample files from the CD-ROM in the default C:\Seua2k folder for this connection string to work.

Figure 10.66

Setting the Source Database property for a query against an external database.

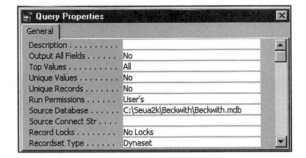

- The value of the Source Connect Str property also depends on the type of external database being used. If your external Access database is not secure, leave the Source Connect Str text box empty; otherwise, type **UID=*UserID*;PWD=*Password*** to specify the user ID and password needed to open the external database. For other desktop databases, you type the product name, such as **Paradox 3.5** or **dBASE IV**. ODBC data sources require the complete ODBC connect string.

Running a query against an external database is related to running a query against linked tables. When you link tables, the data in the tables is available at any time that your application is running. When you run a query against an external database, the connection to the external database is open only while your query is open in Design or Run mode. A slight performance penalty exists for running queries against an external database—each time that you run the query, Access must make a connection to open the database. The connection is closed when you close the query.

Figure 10.67 shows a query design based on tables attached from the Beckwith.mdb sample database. Figure 10.68 shows the result of executing the query design of Figure 10.67.

Note

The Joins.mdb database in the \Seua2k\Chaptr10 folder of the accompanying CD-ROM includes all of the sample queries of this chapter.

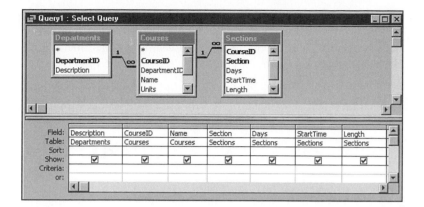

Figure 10.67
A query design based on tables in an external Jet database.

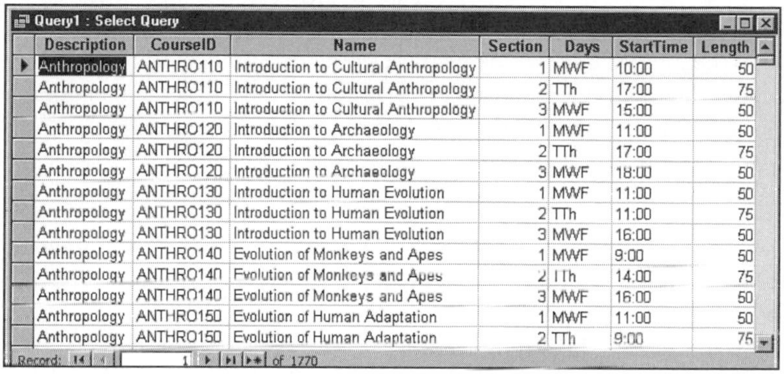

Figure 10.68
The query result set of the query design shown in Figure 10.67.

TROUBLESHOOTING

MISSING OBJECTS IN QUERIES

When I run my query, an Enter Parameter Value dialog appears that asks me to enter a value. I didn't specify a parameter for the query.

The Enter Parameter Value dialog appears when the Jet engine's query parser can't identify an object specified in the query or evaluate an expression. Usually, the Enter Parameter Value dialog appears because of a typographic error. Intentionally creating parameter queries is the subject of this chapter's "Designing Parameter Queries" section.

QUERIES WITH LINKED TABLES AREN'T UPDATABLE

I can't create an updatable one-to-many query with my linked dBASE or FoxPro tables despite the fact that my query displays only fields from the many side of the relationship.

You must specify (or create) primary-key indexes for each dBASE or FoxPro table that participates in the query. The field or fields that you choose must uniquely identify a record;

the index doesn't allow duplicate values. Delete the attachment to the dBASE or FoxPro tables and then reattach the table with the primary-key indexes. Make sure that you specify which index is the primary-key index in the Select Unique Record Identifier dialog that appears after you attach each table.

Also, make sure that you don't include the field of the *many*-side table on which the join is created in the query. If you add the joined field to the field list, your query isn't updatable.

IN THE REAL WORLD—OPTIMIZING MULTITABLE QUERIES

Chapter 8's "In the Real World—Query Design Optimization" section discusses the art and science of query design to optimize the presentation of information and query performance. The single-table query design recommendations apply equally to multitable queries.

This chapter is one of the longest in the book because of the importance of multitable select and aggregate queries in production database applications. Joins are fundamental to relational databases, as Chapter 22, "Exploring Relational Database Design and Implementation," demonstrates. You're likely to find that more than 75% of the queries you create require at least one join, and a substantial percentage need two or more joins.

Tip #86 from

> Use the base table's primary-key field name as the foreign-key field name for related tables. The Personnel Actions table' paID foreign-key field, which joins to the Employees table's EmployeeID field violates this recommendation. Using paID instead of EmployeeID is intended only to demonstrate how to create joins between dissimilar field names, not as a recommended field naming convention. (Including a reference—usually abbreviated—to the table name in field names is common primarily in non-relational databases.)

SUBDATASHEETS

NEW 2000 Access 2000's new subdatasheet feature is useful for *browse-mode editing* of related tables, but not much else. Browse-mode is a term for editing table data in a datasheet. It's easy for inexperienced users to make errors when editing datasheets, so minimize use of updatable datasheets and subdatasheets in production Access applications. Instead, use multitable forms—the subject of Chapter 13, "Designing Custom Multitable Forms"—that display a single record of the base table in the main form and show related records in a subform.

Tip #87 from

> Browse-mode editing operations in multiuser and client/server environments are the bane of database administrators (DBAs) because they require multiple database connections and create a substantial amount of network traffic.

If you need a hierarchical display of data from related tables, Visual Basic 6.0's Hierarchical DataGrid, an ActiveX control, is a much better choice than a subdatasheet. The

Hierarchical DataGrid control is read-only, so it's well suited to decision-support applications. You must have a license for the Office 2000 Developer Edition (ODE) to use Visual Basic 6.0 ActiveX controls in Access 2000 forms. Alternatively, you can license an enhanced version of the Hierarchical DataGrid control, VSFlexGrid, from Videosoft (http://www.videosoft.com). Using data-bound Visual Basic 6.0 or third-party ActiveX controls with Access 2000 requires VBA programming.

AGGREGATE QUERIES

Aggregate queries generate summary data that's critical for decision-support analysis. Aggregate queries offer quick and easy totaling of orders, sales, and other financial data for one or more time periods. Aggregation methods create large-scale data warehouses and smaller data marts, which are used in on-line analytical processing (OLAP) applications. Experience with SQL aggregation techniques is a necessity for understanding OLAP methodology.

PART
II
CH
10

Tip #88 from

RJ

Apply "reasonableness" tests against every summary query you design. Testing becomes increasingly important as the significance of data to others grows. It's very embarrassing to find that you provided data for 1998 when your manager needed 1999 information. Become familiar with trends in the summary data generated by your queries, and compare new query result sets with previous values. If the comparison shows unexpected changes (good or bad), run a simple summary query for one or two periods to verify your data. If the summary data still fails the reasonableness test, you must review the underlying detail data (called drilling down.) Familiarity with the detail data you summarize is job insurance when your manager says the "numbers don't look right to me."

CROSSTAB QUERIES

Access crosstab queries are summary queries with result sets conveniently organized in row-column format. Most executives prefer the crosstab formats for time series and other comparative financial analyses. Access's Crosstab Query Wizard does a respectable job of generating simple crosstab queries for you. Designing crosstab queries that are more complex than the Wizard can handle requires that you first gain experience writing conventional summary queries.

One of the primary issues with Jet crosstab queries is that the Jet SQL reserved words, PIVOT and TRANSFORM, both of which you need to generate crosstab queries, aren't available in SQL Server's Transact-SQL or any other client/server SQL dialect. Thus you can't automatically upsize Access 2000 Jet applications that include crosstab queries to Access Data Projects (ADP). (You can't automatically upsize UNION queries, either). ADP substitute SQL Server views for select queries; you create views by writing Transact-SQL SELECT queries. (ADP are the subject of Chapter 25, "Creating Access Data Projects.") You're likely to find you must write VBA code to reformat summary views to the crosstab format.

Tip #89 from

If your data source is a client/server RDBMS, generate the summary query on the server with an Access passthrough query, then use the Access query result set as the data source for the crosstab query. This is a much more efficient method than attaching client/server tables to your Access database and executing the query locally. Passthrough queries are beyond the scope of this book, but you can find out more about them by searching online help for "passthrough."

One of the first (version 1.1) large-scale Access client/server applications used this approach to query a multi-GB IBM DB2 database running under VMS on a Hitachi mainframe. A description of this application, which was the subject of a presentation at Microsoft Tech*Ed, is available at `http://premium.microsoft.com/msdn/library/conf/html/sa060.htm`. This approach doesn't work with ADP, because ADP connect to the Microsoft Data Engine (MSDE) or SQL Server and don't permit use of Jet database objects.

--rj

CHAPTER 11

MODIFYING DATA WITH ACTION QUERIES

In this chapter

Getting Acquainted with Action Queries   410

Creating New Tables with Make-Table Queries   411

Designing and Testing the Select Query   411

Converting the Select Query to a Make-Table Query   411

Establishing Relationships for the New Table   414

Creating Action Queries to Append Records to a Table   416

Deleting Records from a Table with an Action Query   418

Updating Values of Multiple Records in a Table   421

Testing Cascading Deletion and Updating   424

Troubleshooting   427

In the Real World—Alternatives to Action Queries   428

GETTING ACQUAINTED WITH ACTION QUERIES

Action queries create new tables or modify the data in existing tables. Access offers the following four types of action queries:

- *Make-table* queries create new tables from the data contained in query result sets. One of the most common applications for make-table queries is to create tables that you can export to other applications or that summarize data from other tables. A make-table query provides a convenient way to copy a table to another database. In some cases, you can use make-table queries to speed the generation of multiple forms and reports based on a single, complex query.

- *Append* queries add new records to tables from the query's result set.

- *Delete* queries delete records from tables that correspond to the rows of the query result set.

- *Update* queries change the values of existing fields of table records corresponding to rows of the query result set.

This chapter shows you how to create each of the four types of action queries and how to use Access's cascading deletions and cascading updates of related records. This chapter covers cascading deletions and cascading updates because these referential integrity features are related to delete and update action queries, respectively.

NEW 2000 The following new Access 2000 features apply to action queries:

- You can maintain referential integrity without creating foreign-key indexes. Multiple foreign-key indexes slow the addition and deletion of records. Unfortunately, you must use the Jet SQL Data Definition Language (DDL) statements with the NO INDEX qualifier to take advantage of this feature. Chapter 23, "Working with Structured Query Language," shows you how to write Jet SQL statements.

- Row-level locking minimizes concurrency problems when multiple users attempt to execute action queries on the same 4KB page. Row-level locking, however, isn't implemented for memo field edits and on updates to indexed columns. Chapter 24, "Securing Multiuser Network Applications," describes the benefits of row-level locking for shared Jet databases.

- When an excessive number of row locks would be required for a large update query operation, Jet 4.0 attempts to place a temporary exclusive lock on the entire table.

Unless you're developing multiuser Access applications that share Jet databases, you won't find these features very interesting.

CREATING NEW TABLES WITH MAKE-TABLE QUERIES

In the following sections, you learn how to use a make-table query to create a new table, Shipping Address, for customers that have different shipping and billing addresses. This process enables the deletion of the shipping address data that, in most of the records in the Orders table, duplicates the address data in the Customers table. Removing duplicated data to new tables is an important step when you're converting data contained in a flat (nonrelational) database to a relational database structure. You can use the Table Analyzer Wizard, described in Chapter 22, "Exploring Relational Database Design and Implementation," to perform an operation similar to that described in the following sections. Removing duplicated data manually, however, is one of the best methods of demonstrating how to design make-table queries.

Caution

Always make a backup copy of a table that you intend to modify with an action query. Changes made to table data with action queries are permanent; an error can render a table useless. Invalid changes made to a table with an action query containing a design error often are difficult to detect.

→ To use a wizard to remove duplicate data, **see** "Using Access 2000's Table Analyzer Wizard," **p. 836**.

→ To use a wizard to remove duplicate data, **see** "Using Access 2000's Table Analyzer Wizard," **p. 836**.

The example that you create in the following sections extracts data from the Orders table based on data in the Customers table and creates a new table, tblShipAddresses. A modification of the query that you created in the "Creating Not-Equal Theta Joins with Criteria" section of Chapter 10, "Creating Multitable and Crosstab Queries," generates the data for the new table. Make-table queries are useful in converting flat-file tables that contain duplicated data, including tables created by spreadsheet applications, to relational form.

DESIGNING AND TESTING THE SELECT QUERY

To create the new shipping addresses table from the data in the Orders table, you first must build a select query. To build a select query, follow these steps:

1. Create a new query and add the Customers and Orders tables to it.

2. Drag the CustomerID field from the Customers table and drop it in the query's first column. The CustomerID field links the Shipping Address table to the Orders table.

3. Drag the ShipName, ShipAddress, ShipCity, ShipRegion, ShipPostalCode, and ShipCountry fields and drop them in columns 2–7, respectively. You use these fields, in addition to CustomerID, to create the new Shipping Address table.

   Next, you add criteria to select only those records of the Orders table for which the ShipName doesn't match the CompanyName or the ShipAddress doesn't match the Customers table's address.

4. In the ShipName column's first Criteria row, type the following:

   <>[Customers].[CompanyName]

5. In the next row of the ShipAddress column, type the following:

<>[*Customers*].[*Address*]

This entry and the CompanyName criterion must be in different Criteria rows so that the **Or** operator is applied to the two criteria. The Query Design grid appears as shown in Figure 11.1.

Figure 11.1
Creating the select query for the new Shipping Address table.

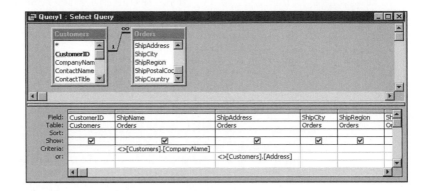

> **Note**
>
> A more precise approach is to add additional **Or** criteria to test for not-equal cities, regions, postal codes, and countries. A customer having exactly the same address in two different cities, however, is highly improbable.

6. Double-click an empty area in the Query Design window's upper pane to open the Query Properties window. Open the Unique Values drop-down list and select Yes.

7. Click the toolbar's Run button to run the select query. Data for customers that placed orders with different billing and shipping addresses appears, as shown in Figure 11.2.

Figure 11.2
The data to be added to the new shipping address table.

Customer ID	Ship Name	Ship Address	Ship City	Ship Regio
ALFKI	Alfred's Futterkiste	Obere Str. 57	Berlin	
AROUT	Around the Horn	Brook Farm	Colchester	Essex
CHOPS	Chop-suey Chinese	Hauptstr. 31	Bern	
GALED	Galería del gastrónomo	Rambla de Cataluña, 23	Barcelona	
LAUGB	Laughing Bacchus Wine Cellars	2319 Elm St.	Vancouver	BC
RICSU	Richter Supermarkt	Starenweg 5	Genève	
WHITC	White Clover Markets	1029 - 12th Ave. S.	Seattle	WA
WOLZA	Wolski Zajazd	ul. Filtrowa 68	Warszawa	

Record: 1 of 8

CONVERTING THE SELECT QUERY TO A MAKE-TABLE QUERY

Now that you've tested the select query to make sure that it creates the necessary data, you can create the table from the query. To create the table, follow these steps:

1. Return to Design view and choose Query, Make-Table Query. The Make Table dialog appears. Type the name of the table, **tblShipAddresses**, in the Table Name text box (see Figure 11.3). Click OK.

Figure 11.3
The Make Table dialog for make-table queries.

2. Click the Run button on the toolbar. A message confirms the number of records that you are adding to the new table. Click Yes to create the new tblShipAddresses table.

3. Press F11 to activate the Database window, click the Table shortcut, and open the new tblShipAddresses table. The entries appear as shown in Figure 11.4.

PART

II

CH

11

CustomerID	ShipName	ShipAddress	ShipCity	ShipRegion	ShipPostalCod	ShipCountry
ALFKI	Alfred's Futterki	Obere Str. 57	Berlin		12209	Germany
AROUT	Around the Horr	Brook Farm	Colchester	Essex	CO7 6JX	UK
CHOPS	Chop-suey Chin	Hauptstr. 31	Bern		3012	Switzerland
GALED	Galería del gast	Rambla de Cata	Barcelona		8022	Spain
LAUGB	Laughing Bacch	2319 Elm St.	Vancouver	BC	V3F 2K1	Canada
RICSU	Richter Superm	Starenweg 5	Genève		1204	Switzerland
WHITC	White Clover M	1029 - 12th Ave	Seattle	WA	98124	USA
WOLZA	Wolski Zajazd	ul. Filtrowa 68	Warszawa		01-012	Poland

Record: 1 of 8

Figure 11.4
The tblShipAddresses table created by the make-table query.

Now complete the design of the new tblShipAddresses table by following these steps:

1. Click the Design View button of the toolbar. The table's basic design is inherited from the properties of the fields of the tables used to create the new table. The tblShipAddresses table does not, however, inherit the primary-key assignment from the Customers table's CustomerID field.

2. Choose the CustomerID field, open the Indexed property drop-down list, and choose the Yes (Duplicates OK) value. Indexing improves the performance of queries when you have multiple shipping addresses for customers.

3. The CustomerID, ShipName, ShipAddress, ShipCity, and ShipCountry fields are required, so set the value for each of these fields' Required property to Yes.

4. Many countries don't have values for the ShipRegion field, and a few countries don't use postal codes, so set the Allow Zero Length property to Yes for the ShipRegion and ShipPostalCode fields.

ESTABLISHING RELATIONSHIPS FOR THE NEW TABLE

Now you must complete the process of adding the new table to your database by establishing default relationships and enforcing referential integrity so that all records in the tblShipAddress table have a corresponding record in the Customers table. Access 2000's graphical Relationships window makes this process simple and intuitive. To establish the relationship of tblShipAddress and the Customers table, follow these steps:

1. Close the tblShipAddress table. Answer Yes when asked whether you want to save changes to the table's design and answer Yes again when asked whether you want to apply the new data integrity rules to the table. Press F11 to make the Database window active.

2. Click the Relationships button of the toolbar or choose Tools, Relationships to open the Relationships window that establishes the default relationships between tables. Click the toolbar's Show Table button and double-click the tblShipAddresses table to add the table to the Relationships window; then click the Close button. Move the tblShipAddresses field list to the position shown in Figure 11.5.

Figure 11.5
Adding the tblShipAddresses table to the Relationships window.

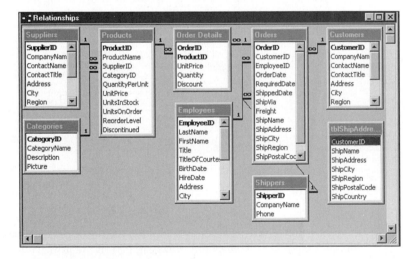

3. Click the Customers table's CustomerID field, drag the field symbol to the tblShipAddresses table's CustomerID field, and drop the symbol. (The direction in which you drag the field is important). The Edit Relationships dialog opens (see Figure 11.6).

The field that you select to drag appears in the Table/Query list (the *one* side of the relationship), and the field on which you drop the dragged field appears in the Related Table/Query list (the *many* side of the relationship).

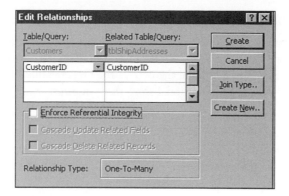

Figure 11.6
The Edit Relationships dialog for the new shipping addresses table.

4. Mark the Enforce Referential Integrity check box. Access sets the default relation type, One-To-Many, which is the correct choice for this relation. Access also establishes a conventional equi-join as the default join type, so in this case you don't need to click the Join Type button to display the Join Properties window. Select the Cascade Update Related Fields and the Cascade Delete Related Records check boxes to maintain referential integrity automatically.

5. Click the Create button of the Edit Relationships dialog to close it. Your Relationships window appears as shown in Figure 11.7.

The 1 and ∞ symbols indicate a one-to-many relationship

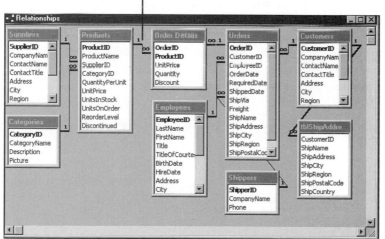

Figure 11.7
The Relationships window showing a one-to-many relationship established for the new table.

PART

II

CH

11

6. Close the Relationships window and click Yes to save your changes. Save your make-table query with an appropriate name, such as **qryMakeShipAddressesTable**.

USING THE NEW tblShipAddresses TABLE

After creating a new table from a make-table query, you must take care of several house-keeping chores before you can take advantage of your new table. The purpose of creating the new shipping addresses table is to eliminate the data in the Orders table that duplicates information in the Customers table. The additional steps that you must take to use the new table include the following:

- You need a new Number (Long Integer) field, ShipID, for the tblShipAddresses and Orders tables. In the Orders table's ShipID field, you can have a 0 value to indicate that the shipping and billing addresses are the same. You then assign a sequential number to each shipping address for each customer. (In this case, the value of the ShipID field is 1 for all records in tblShipAddresses.) By adding the ShipID field to the tblShipAddresses table, you can create a composite primary key on the CustomerID and ShipID fields.

- Don't delete fields that contain duplicated data extracted to a new table until you confirm that the extracted data is correct and modify all the queries, forms, and reports that use the table. You use the update query described later in this chapter to assign the correct ShipID field value for each record in the Orders table. After you verify that you've assigned the correct value of the ShipID field, you can delete the duplicate fields.

- Add the new table to any queries, forms, reports, macros, and modules that require the extracted information.

- Change references to fields in the original table in all database objects that refer to fields in the new table.

During this process, you have the opportunity to test the modification before deleting the duplicated fields from the original table. Making a backup copy of the table before you delete the fields also is a low-cost insurance policy.

CREATING ACTION QUERIES TO APPEND RECORDS TO A TABLE

A make-table query creates the new table structure from the structure of the records that underlie the query. Only the fields of the records that appear in the query are added to the new table's structure. If you design and save a Shipping Address table before extracting the duplicated data from the Orders table, you can use an append query to add the extracted data to the new table.

Another situation in which append queries are useful is when removing duplicate data from a table currently in use. In this case, you use make-table queries to create the related tables and then change them to append queries. You change the type of query by opening the Query menu and choosing Select, Crosstab, Make Table, Append, or Delete, or by clicking the Query Type button of the toolbar while in Design mode and choosing the type of query from the menu.

An append query also differs from a make-table query because an append query can have fewer fields than the table to which the query is appending the data. Otherwise, the make-table and append processes are basically identical. To append records to the tblShipAddress table, for example, follow these steps:

 1. Open the tblShipAddresses table in Datasheet view, choose Edit, Select All Records, and then press the Delete key to delete all the records from the table. Click Yes when asked to confirm the deletion and then close the table.

 2. Open your make-table query, qryMakeShipAddressesTable, from the Database window in Design mode.

Take extra care when designing action queries not to execute the query prematurely. If you double-click qryMakeShipAddressesTable or open qryMakeShipAddressesTable in Datasheet view, you run the make-table query.

 3. Choose Query, Append Query or use the Query Type toolbar icon to an append query. The Append dialog appears with tblShipAddresses as the default value in the Table Name drop-down list. Click the OK button to close the Append dialog and add the Append To row to the Query Design grid (see Figure 11.8).

To append data to a table, the field names of the query and of the table to which you are appending the records must be identical, or you must specify the field of the table to which the append query column applies. Access doesn't append data to fields in which the field name differs by even a single space character. The Query Design grid for append queries has an additional row, Append To (shown in Figure 11.8), that Access attempts to match by comparing field names of the query and the table. Default values appear in the Append To row of columns for which a match occurs. If a match doesn't occur, open the Append To row's drop-down list and select the destination table's field.

Figure 11.8
The Append Query
Design grid with the
added Append To
row.

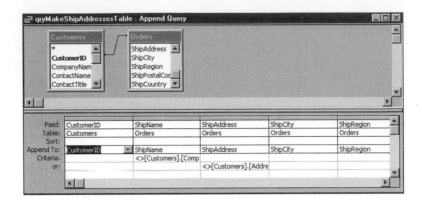

4. Click the toolbar's Run button to execute the append query. A message box displays the number of records that the query will append to the table. Click Yes to append the records.

5. Open the tblShipAddresses table to verify that you've added the records.

 If you can't add a primary key on a table to which you've appended new records, see the "Appending Records Causes Primary Key Problems" topic of the "Troubleshooting" section near the end of the chapter.

Tip #93 from

You can't append records containing values that duplicate those of the key fields in existing records. If you try to do so, a message box indicates the number of records that cause key-field violations. Unlike the paste append operation, however, Access doesn't create a Paste Errors table that contains the unappended records.

→ For a refresher on paste append, **see** "Using Access 2000's Table Analyzer Wizard," **p. 836**.

DELETING RECORDS FROM A TABLE WITH AN ACTION QUERY

Tip #94 from

It's a good practice to run a select query to display the records that you are about to delete and then convert the select query to a delete query.

Often you might have to delete records from a table. For example, you might want to delete records for canceled orders or for customers that have made no purchases for several years. Deleting records from a table with a delete query is the reverse of the append process. You create a select query with all fields (using the * choice from the field list) and then add the individual fields to be used to specify the criteria for deleting specific records. If you don't specify any criteria, Access deletes all the table's records when you convert the select query into a delete query and run it against the table.

To give you some practice at deleting records—you stop short of actual deletion in this case, however—suppose that Northwind Traders' credit manager has advised you that Austrian authorities have declared Ernst Handel (CustomerID ERNSH) insolvent and that you are to cancel and delete any orders from Ernst Handel not yet shipped. To design the query that selects all of Ernst Handel's open orders, follow these steps:

1. Open a new query and add the Orders table to it.

2. Drag the * (all fields) item from the field list to the Field cell of the query's first column.

3. Drag the CustomerID field to the second column's Field cell. You need this field to select a specific customer's record. The fields that make up the query must be exactly those of the Orders table, so clear the Show box to prevent the CustomerID field from appearing in the query's result twice. This field is already included in the first column's * indicator.

4. In the CustomerID field's Criteria cell, type **ERNSH** to represent Ernst Handel's ID.

5. A **Null** value in the ShippedDate field indicates orders that have not shipped. Drag the ShippedDate field from the field list to the third column's Field cell. Click the Show box to prevent the ShippedDate field from appearing in the query's result twice, because the first column also includes that field.

6. In the ShippedDate field's Criteria cell, type **Is Null**. To ensure that you delete only records for Ernst Handel *and* only those that have not been shipped, you must place this criterion on the same line as that for the CustomerID field. The select query design for the delete query appears as shown in Figure 11.9.

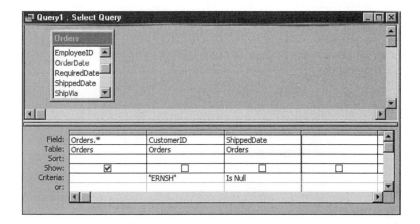

Figure 11.9
The select query design for a delete query.

7. Run the select query to display the records to delete when the delete query runs. Figure 11.10 shows the query result set.

Figure 11.10
The unshipped orders for Ernst Handel to be deleted from the Orders table.

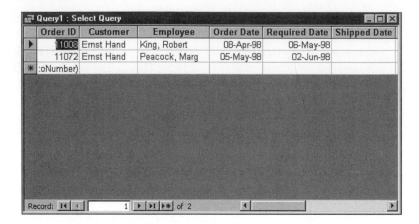

To proceed with the simulated deletion, follow these steps:

1. Click the toolbar's Database Window button to activate the Database window and then click the Tables button to display the table list. Create a copy of the Orders table by clicking the Orders table entry and pressing Ctrl+C to copy the table to the Clipboard. Press Ctrl+V. The Paste Table As dialog appears. Type **tblOrders** as the name of the new table copy and press Enter. Repeat this process for the Order Details table, naming it **tblOrderDetails**. These two tables are backup tables in case you actually delete the two records for Ernst Handel.

2. Open your select query in Design mode and choose Query, Delete Query. Access then replaces the select query grid's Sort and Show rows with the Delete row, as shown in Figure 11.11. The From value in the Delete row's first column, Orders, indicates that Access will delete records that match the Field specification from the Orders table. The Where values in the remaining two cells indicate fields that specify the deletion criteria.

Figure 11.11
The delete query design created from the select query of Figure 11.10.

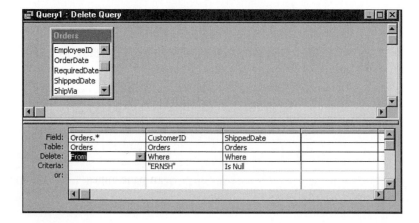

3. Click the Run button. A message box asks you to confirm the deletion of the rows. Click No to prevent the deletion.

4. Close and don't save your query.

Tip #95 from

Deleting records in a *one* table when records corresponding to the deleted records exist in a related *many* table violates the rules of referential integrity; the records in the many table would be made orphans. In this situation, referential integrity is enforced with cascading deletions for the Order Details and Orders table. If you delete the two ERNSH records, Jet deletes the corresponding Order Detail records and then deletes the Orders records.

If you accidentally delete records for Ernst Handel, reverse the process that you used to make the backup tables: copy the backup tables—tblOrders and tblOrderDetails—to Orders and Order Details, respectively. You use the tblOrders table in the following section.

UPDATING VALUES OF MULTIPLE RECORDS IN A TABLE

Update queries change the values of data in a table. Such queries are useful when you must update field values for many records with a common expression. For example, you might need to increase or decrease the unit prices of all products or products within a particular category by a fixed percentage.

To see how an update query works, you perform some of the housekeeping chores discussed earlier in the chapter that are associated with using the tblShipAddress table. To implement this example, you must have created the tblShipAddress table, as described in the "Creating New Tables with Make-Table Queries" section earlier in this chapter. You also must modify the tblOrders and tblShipAddresses tables to include a field for the ShipID code, by following these steps:

1. Click the Tables shortcut in the Database window and open the tblOrders table in Design mode. If you didn't create the tblOrders table as a backup table for the example of the preceding section, do so now.

2. Select the ShipVia field by clicking the selection button and then press Insert to add a new field between ShipDate and ShipVia. (Access inserts fields in tables above the selected field.)

3. Type **ShipID** as the field name, select Number as the field data type, and select Long Integer as the field's Field Size. Set the Required property value to Yes and the Indexed property value to No. The table design pane appears as in Figure 11.12 (which shows the new ShipID field selected).

Figure 11.12
Adding the ShipID field to the tblOrders table.

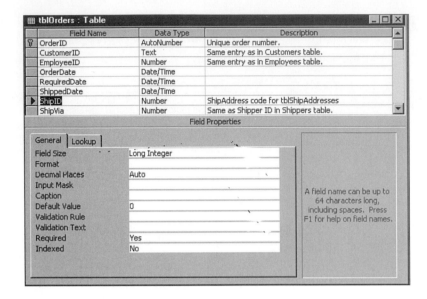

4. Close the tblOrders table and save the changes to your design. You changed the domain integrity rules when you added the Required property, so a message box asks whether you want to test domain integrity. Click No to avoid the test, which would fail because no values have been added to the ShipID field.

5. Open the tblShipAddresses table in Datasheet view.

6. Click the ShipName field header and choose Insert, Column to add a Field1 field between the CustomerID and the ShipName fields.

7. Type **1** in the Field1 cell for each record of the tblShipAddress table.

8. Change to Design mode and change the name of Field1 to **ShipID**. Access 2000 detects from your data entries that the field should be a Number field and assigns Long Integer as the default Field Size property value. Change the value of the Required property to Yes.

9. Select both the CustomerID and the ShipID fields by clicking and dragging the mouse.

10. Click the toolbar's Primary Key button to create a composite primary key on the CustomerID and ShipID fields and then close the tblShipAddress table. This time you test the changes that you made to the table, so click Yes when the Data Integrity Rules message box appears.

Now you must set up a query to select the orders to which you want to add a value of 1 to the ShipID field to indicate the use of data from the tblShipAddresses table. This query is quite similar to that which you used to create the tblShipAddresses table earlier in this chapter. Follow these steps to design your update query:

1. Create a new query and add the Customers and tblOrders tables to it.

2. Drag the tblOrders table's ShipName and ShipAddress fields to the first two columns of the Query Design grid.

3. Type **<>[Customers].[CompanyName]** in the first Criteria row of the ShipName column and **<>[Customers].[Address]** in the second Criteria row of the ShipAddress column. Your query design appears as shown in Figure 11.13.

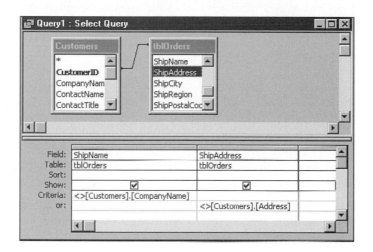

Figure 11.13
The select query to test for orders that require *1* as the value of ShipID.

4. Run the query to verify that you have correctly selected the set of records to be updated. In this case, you don't specify Unique Values, because you must change every tblOrders record that meets the query criteria.

After ensuring that you've selected the appropriate records of the tblOrders table for updating, you're ready to convert the select query to an update query by following these steps:

1. Return to Query Design mode and drag the tblOrders table's ShipID field to the query's first column.

2. Choose Query, Update Query. A new Update To row replaces the Sort and Show rows of the select Query Design grid.

3. In the ShipID column's Update To cell, type **1** to set ShipID's value to 1 for orders that require the use of a record from the tblShipAddresses table. The Update Query Design grid appears as shown in Figure 11.14. The Update To cells of the remaining fields are blank, indicating that Access is not to update values in these fields.

Figure 11.14
The completed
Update Query Design
grid.

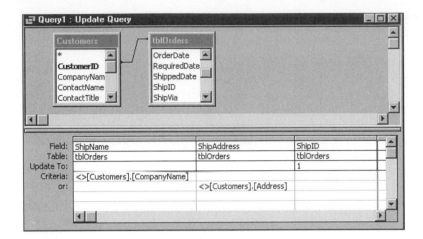

4. Run the update query. A message box indicates the number of records to be updated.

5. Click the Database Window button and open the tblOrders table. Check a few records to see that you correctly added the ShipID value of 1.

6. You must add 0 values to the ShipID cells of records that have the same shipping and billing addresses. Close and don't save the update query, create a new query, and add only the tblOrders table.

7. Drag the ShipID field to the query's first column and choose Query, Update Query.

8. Type **0** in the Update To row and **Is Null** in the Criteria row. Then click the Run Query button to replace **Null** values in the ShipID column with **0**.

After you check the tblOrders table to verify the result of your second update query, you can change to Table Design mode and safely delete the ShipName, ShipAddress, ShipCity, ShipRegion, ShipPostalCode, and ShipCountry fields.

TESTING CASCADING DELETION AND UPDATING

When you delete a record in a primary or base table on which records in a related table depend, *cascading deletion* automatically deletes the dependent records. Similarly, if you modify the value of a table's primary-key field and a related table has records related by the primary-key field's value, *cascading updating* changes the value of the related foreign-key field for the related records to the new primary-key field value.

Cascading deletions and cascading updates are special types of action queries that the Jet engine executes for you. The following three sections show you how to use Access's cascading deletion and cascading updating features with a set of test tables copied from the Orders and Order Details tables of Northwind.mdb.

CREATING THE TEST TABLES AND ESTABLISHING RELATIONSHIPS

When experimenting with database features, you should work with test tables rather than live data. As mentioned in the note at the beginning of this chapter, using copied test tables is particularly advisable when the tables are participants in action queries. The remaining sections of this chapter use the two test tables, tblOrders and tblOrderDetails, that you create in preceding sections:

1. Open the tblOrders table in Table Design view.

2. Change the field data type of the OrderID field from AutoNumber to Number and make sure that the Field Size property is set to Long Integer. (This change is necessary to test cascading updates in the next section.)

Cascading deletions and updates require that you establish a default relationship between the primary and related tables, and enforce referential integrity. To add both cascading deletions and updates to the tblOrderDetails table, follow these steps:

1. Click the toolbar's Relationships button to display the Relationships window.

2. Scroll right to an empty area of the Relationships window.

3. Click the toolbar's Show Table button to display the Add Table dialog. Alternatively, right-click the upper pane of the Query window and choose Show Table.

4. Double-click the tblOrders and tblOrderDetails items in the list and then click the Close button to close the Show Table dialog.

5. Click and drag the OrderID field of tblOrders to the tblOrderDetails table's OrderID field to establish a one-to-many join on the OrderID field. The Relationships window appears.

6. Mark the Enforce Referential Integrity check box to enable the two cascade check boxes.

7. Mark the Cascade Update Related Fields and Cascade Delete Related Records check boxes, as shown in Figure 11.15.

8. Click the Relationships dialog's Create button to make your changes to the join effective and then click the close window box to close the Relationships window. Click Yes when Access asks if you want to save your changes to the window's layout.

> ⚠ *If you receive an error message when you click the Create button, see the "Access Won't Create a Relationship to a New Table" topic of the "Troubleshooting" section near the end of the chapter.*

TESTING CASCADING DELETION

To try cascading deletion with the test tables, follow these steps:

1. Open the tblOrders and tblOrderDetails tables in Datasheet view.

2. Click the surface of the tblOrders datasheet to make it the active window and then click a record-selection button to pick an order in tblOrders to delete.

PART

II

CH

11

3. Press the Delete key to tentatively delete the selected records and the related order's line-item records in tblOrderDetails.

4. A message asks you to confirm the deletion. Click Yes to delete the records.

Figure 11.15
Setting the cascading deletions and updates options.

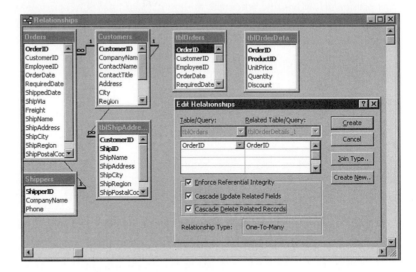

To verify that you have deleted the related records, you can scroll to the related record or records for the order that you deleted in the tblOrderDetails table. If you opened tblOrderDetails in step 1, the data cell values for the deleted related records are replaced with #Deleted.

TESTING CASCADING UPDATES

Cascading updates to the foreign-key field of records that depend on a primary-key value that you want to change in a primary table is a valuable feature of Access. Performing updates of primary-key values while enforcing referential integrity is not a simple process; Chapter 4, "Working with Access Databases and Tables," briefly discusses the problems associated with performing such updates manually. To see how Access takes the complexity out of cascading updates, follow these steps:

1. With the tblOrders and tblOrderDetails windows open, size and position the two datasheets as shown in Figure 11.16. Then click the surface of the tblOrders2 datasheet to make it the active window. Positioning the two table datasheet windows as shown in Figure 11.16 enables you to see the cascading updates in the tblOrderDetails window as they occur.

2. Change the value of the OrderID cell of the first record to the order number that you deleted in the preceding section. Alternatively, change the value of the OrderID cell to a value, such as **20000**, that's outside the range of the values of the test table.

3. Move the caret to another record to cause the cascading update to occur. You immediately see the changes in the OrderID foreign-key field of the related dependent records (see Figure 11.16).

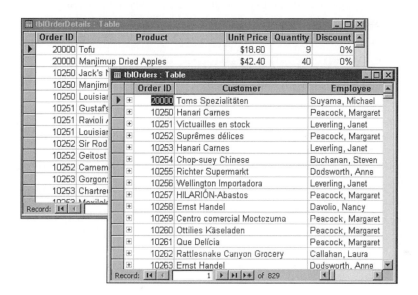

Figure 11.16
An example of a cascading update.

No confirmation message appears when you execute a cascading update, because the effect is reversible. If you make an erroneous entry that causes an undesired cascading update, you can simply change the entry to its original value by reentering the original or the correct value manually.

TROUBLESHOOTING

APPENDING RECORDS CAUSES PRIMARY KEY PROBLEMS

After appending records to an existing table, I can't create a primary key on the table.

The Unique Values Only test that you specify in the Query Properties window applies only to the query, not to the table to which you append the records. If you want to preclude the possibility of appending duplicate records to the tblShipAddress table, you must first create the composite primary key, discussed in the "Using the New tblShipAddresses Table" section, which creates a No Duplicates index on the primary key, and then append the records.

ACCESS WON'T CREATE A RELATIONSHIP TO A NEW TABLE

When I try to enforce referential integrity, I get a "Can't create relationship to enforce referential integrity" message.

You dragged the field symbols in the wrong direction when you created the relationship. The related table is in the Table/Query list and the primary or base table is in the Related Table/Query list. Close the Edit Relationships dialog, click the thin area of the join line to select the join, and then press the Delete key to delete the join. Make sure that you drag the field name that you want from the primary table to the related table.

IN THE REAL WORLD—ALTERNATIVES TO ACTION QUERIES

Microsoft calls any Access query that alters table data an *action query*; the more common name is *update query*, as in updating the database. With Access, however, there's a good reason to distinguish graphical action queries from the update queries used in online transaction processing (OLTP). Access's graphical action queries are intended primarily for bulk operations—adding, altering, or deleting large numbers of records in a single operation. OLTP usually deals with a single record or a few related records per operation. Creating a new Access action query each time you must update a single record clearly is an inefficient process, even if you add a parameter to designate the record you want to update or delete.

Note

The sections that follow deal with advanced Access topics, which are covered in detail by chapters later in this book. In the real world, production databases reside on a file or application server and multiple users connect their client PC's front-end applications to networked shared-file (Jet) or client/server (MSDE or SQL Server) databases. Chapter 24, "Securing Multiuser Network Applications," and Chapter 25, "Creating Access Data Projects," deal with shared-file and client/server-type databases, respectively. The purpose of this In the Real World episode is to demonstrate the many options that Access offers for executing action queries and their equivalents.

BROWSE-MODE UPDATING

Browse-mode table editing in Datasheet view is the obvious alternative to action queries when you need to add, alter, or delete only one or a few records. In the real world of networked multiuser databases, however, database administrators (DBAs) discourage or prohibit browse-mode editing because browsing usually requires multiple database connections for a single client PC and generates a substantial amount of network traffic. Further, multiuser browse-mode editing often results in contention problems when two users attempt to edit the same record. Jet's optimistic record locking approach minimizes such conflicts, but resolving which user's edit of a record is correct often requires manual intervention by the DBA or a supervisor. DBAs, especially, don't like to get involved with table-level contention issues. DBAs suffer perpetual contention with information technology managers and chief financial officers.

FORM-BASED UPDATING

Form-based updates are the most common approach for production Access applications using Jet databases. Designing Access forms for OLTP applications is the subject of the next two chapters. Typically, the main form displays in text boxes field values of a single record, for example an invoice. Data from related tables, such as invoice line items, appear in a multi-row subform. Conventional Access form-based updating, however, is a variation on the browse-mode datasheet updating process. The client PC maintains at least one connection to the database tables while the editing application is open and generates a significant amount of network traffic during the editing process.

The primary advantage of form-based over datasheet updating is that you can add to the form VBA code that resolves contention issues in error handling procedures. An even better approach to contention problems is to write VBA code that takes advantage of the new data-related events of ActiveX Data Objects (ADO). You must be a fluent VBA programmer, however, to write effective event-handling subprocedures for Access 2000's new form Recordsets.

→ For insight into ADO's data-related events, **see** "Recordset Events," **p. 1080**.

UPDATING WITH SQL STATEMENTS

Sending SQL INSERT (append), UPDATE, or DELETE queries over the network to the database server is a much more efficient process than browse-mode editing with datasheets or forms. You send an SQL SELECT query to the database to retrieve only the record(s) you need, disconnect from the database, edit the records, open a connection and send one of the three types of SQL update queries, then close the connection. Following is a typical SQL statement to add a new order with three line items to Northwind.mdb's Orders and Order Details table:

```
INSERT INTO Orders
    VALUES(11093, 'KOENE', 1,
        '5/15/1998', '6/1/1998', NULL, 3, NULL,
        'Königlich Essen',
        'Maubelstr. 90',
        'Brandenburg', '', '14776',
        'Germany';)

INSERT INTO [Order Details]
    VALUES(11093, 24, 4.5, 24, 0);

INSERT INTO [Order Details]
    VALUES(11093, 36, 19, 36, 0);

INSERT INTO [Order Details]
    VALUES(11093, 42, 9.8, 12, 0);
```

The preceding SQL INSERT statement contains a substantial amount of text overhead, but executes very quickly over a network connection. You can quickly convert the statement into a transaction by adding a BEGIN TRANSACTION prefix and a COMMIT [TRANSACTION] suffix. Wrapping the statement in a transaction assures that either all INSERT operations succeed or the entire operation fails and no change occurs to either of the tables. Adding TRANSACTION statements qualifies the operation for OLTP.

→ For an explanation of SQL append update syntax, **see** "Writing Action and Crosstab Queries," **p. 868**.

Note

Another update alternative is to use an ADO 2.1 disconnected Recordset to retrieve and update records. The advantage of disconnected Recordsets is that ADO handles most of the disconnecting and reconnecting chores for you. Disconnected Recordsets also let you edit multiple groups of records, then send only the changes to the database with the UpdateBatch method. Sending only the changes is especially efficient for UPDATE operations.

→ For details on how you can easily disconnect and reconnect Recordsets for batch edits, **see** "Disconnected Recordsets," **p. 1079**.

UPDATING WITH SQL SERVER STORED PROCEDURES

The fastest and by far the most efficient method of updating is by using a parameterized stored procedure with a client/server database, such as MSDE or SQL Server 7.0. A stored procedure is a precompiled query that's similar to a stored Access query (called a QueryDef object). Access 2000's new Access Data Projects (ADP), the subject of Chapter 25, substitute MSDE/SQL Server stored procedures for action QueryDefs. SQL Server 7.0—and thus MSDE—execute stored procedures much faster than prior SQL Server versions; often by a factor of 10 or more.

You send the new values to add or change as stored procedure parameters. It's a common practice to write a separate stored procedure for INSERT, UPDATE, and DELETE operations. DBAs greatly appreciate developers who take full advantage of stored procedures. Well-written stored procedures let DBAs spend more of their time contending with management, instead of putting out fires started by contentious OLTP users.

--rj

PART III

DESIGNING FORMS AND REPORTS

12 Creating and Using Forms 433

13 Designing Custom Multitable Forms 479

14 Printing Basic Reports and Mailing Labels 533

15 Preparing Advanced Reports 569

CHAPTER 12

CREATING AND USING FORMS

In this chapter

Understanding the Role of Access Forms and Controls   434

Creating a Transaction-Processing Form with the Form Wizard   435

Using the Form Design Window   442

Selecting, Editing, and Moving Form Elements and Controls   457

Rearranging the Personnel Actions Form   464

Using Transaction-Processing Forms   468

Modifying the Properties of a Form or Control After Testing   473

In the Real World—The Art of Form Design   474

UNDERSTANDING THE ROLE OF ACCESS FORMS AND CONTROLS

Access *forms* create the user interface to your tables. Although you can use Table view and Query view to perform many of the same functions as forms, forms offer the advantage of presenting data in an organized and attractive manner. You can arrange the location of fields on a form so that data entry or editing operations for a single record follow a left-to-right, top-to-bottom sequence. Forms let you create multiple-choice selections for fields that use shorthand codes to represent a set of allowable values. A properly designed form speeds data entry and minimizes operator keying errors.

Forms are constructed from a collection of individual design elements called *controls* or *control objects*. Controls are the components you see in the windows and dialogs of Access and other Windows applications. You use *text boxes* to enter and edit data, *labels* to hold field names, and *object frames* to display graphics. A form consists of a window in which you place two types of controls: dynamic controls that display the data from your tables and static controls for labels or logos.

This chapter concentrates on creating forms that use dynamic text-based controls and *subforms*. A subform is a datasheet or form contained within a form. Part V, "Integrating Access with Other Office 2000 Applications," shows you how to use Microsoft ActiveX technology to incorporate graphs and other graphical elements in forms and reports.

NEW 2000 Following are the new form-related features of Access 2000:

- *Subdatasheets in subforms* let you display lower levels of one-to-many relationships in datasheet-style subforms.

- *In-situ subform* editing enables simultaneous Design mode editing of forms and subforms. The Design view of the subform appears within the region you assign to the Subform view in Run mode.

- *Name AutoCorrect* automatically updates your forms and underlying queries for changes to object names, such as altering the name of a field in a table. To take advantage of Name Autocorrect, you must mark the Track Name Autocorrect Info check box on the General page of the Options dialog before making changes.

- *Control grouping* lets you define groups of controls that you can relocate as a single element.

- *Form view editing* lets you change many properties of controls without changing to Design mode.

- *Justified and Vertical Alignment options* for labels improve the appearance of forms and reports.

- *Movie tool* lets you add the Windows Media Player to forms and play .asf (ActiveX Streaming Format) and .avi (Audio-Video Interleaved) files to entertain users of your applications. Apparently, Microsoft's idea is to provide easy access to training videos for Access applications.

- *Added graphics formats* accept Web-standard .gif and .jpg files, plus additional graphics file formats, as background images for forms.

CREATING A TRANSACTION-PROCESSING FORM WITH THE FORM WIZARD

The content and appearance of your form depend on its use in your database application. Database applications fall into two basic categories:

- *Transaction processing* applications add new records to tables or edit existing records. Transaction-processing applications require write access to (permissions for) the tables that are linked to the form.

- *Decision-support* applications supply information as graphs, tables, or individual data elements but don't allow the user to add or edit data. Decision-support applications require only read access to the tables that are linked to the form.

The form that you create in this example is typical of transaction-processing forms used to add new *records* to the *many* side of a *one-to-many relationship*. Adding line items to an invoice is an example of when a form of this kind—called a *one-to-many form*—is necessary. The object of the Personnel Actions form is to add new records to the Personnel Actions *table* or to let you edit the existing records.

Note

If you didn't add the Personnel Actions table shown in Figure 12.3 to the Northwind Traders database in Chapter 4, "Working with Access Databases and Tables," or Chapter 5, "Entering, Editing, and Validating Data in Tables," do so before proceeding with this example.

If you didn't add records to the Personnel Actions table when you created it in Chapter 4, "Working with Access Databases and Tables," you can add them with the Personnel Actions form you're going to create now with the assistance of Access's Form Wizard. Alternatively, you can import the personnel actions table from the Persacts.mdb database in the \Chaptr12 folder of the accompanying CD-ROM.

Note

If you import the Personnel Actions table from Persacts.mdb, make sure to establish a one-to-many relationship between the Employees and Personnel Actions table, as described in Chapter 4.

→ If you need information on creating or altering relationships, **see** "Establishing Relationships between Tables," **p. 166**.

CHOOSING DATA SOURCES FOR THE FORM

The Personnel Actions form that you create in this exercise lets you add new entries to the Personnel Actions table. The form also has a subform that displays all previous personnel actions for a given employee. The majority of forms found in common database applications are one-to-many forms, and most one-to-many forms require a subform to display data from the many side of the relationship.

PART

III

CH

12

The Personnel Actions form is intended as both a transaction-processing form and a decision-support form. The Employees table is the source of the data for the main form, and you use a subform to display, add, and edit records to the Personnel Actions table. This method lets you add new employees to the Employees table as well as add new Personnel Actions records for any employee.

CREATING THE BASIC FORM WITH THE FORM WIZARD

The easiest way to create a form and subform is with the Access Form Wizard. The Form Wizard lets you create forms (with or without subforms) that contain fields from one or more tables or queries. The Form Wizard creates the basic design of the form and adds text box controls to display and edit the values of data items.

To create in Northwind.mdb the Personnel Actions form with the Form Wizard, follow these steps:

1. Click the Forms shortcut of the Database window and then click the New button to open the New Form dialog.
2. Select Form Wizard from the list in the New Form dialog. Access 2000's Form Wizard lets you create forms with or without a subform. The Design View choice opens a blank form in Design mode.

> **Note**
>
> The various AutoForm choices automatically create forms with the specified layouts: Columnar, Tabular, and Datasheet. The Chart Wizard choice invokes the Chart Wizard to add a graph or chart to your form, and the PivotTable Wizard choice helps you create a form based on Excel pivot tables.

→ For examples of use of the Chart Wizard and PivotTable Wizard, **see** "Using the Chart Wizard to Create an Unlinked Graph," **p. 712** and "Generating a PivotTable Form with the Wizard," **p. 747**, respectively.

3. The drop-down list at the bottom of the New Form dialog lists the existing tables and queries that can serve as a source of data for a form. Select the Employees table (see Figure 12.1).

Figure 12.1
The New Form dialog with initial selections for the Personnel Actions form.

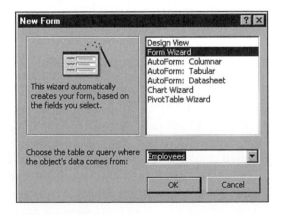

4. Click OK, and Access displays the first dialog of the Form Wizard.

5. Click to select the EmployeeID field in the Available Fields list, then click the > button to move the EmployeeID field from the Available Fields list to the Selected Fields list. Alternatively, you can double-click the field name to move it.

   Repeat this step for the LastName, FirstName, and Title fields of the Employees table so that you can edit data in these fields (see Figure 12.2).

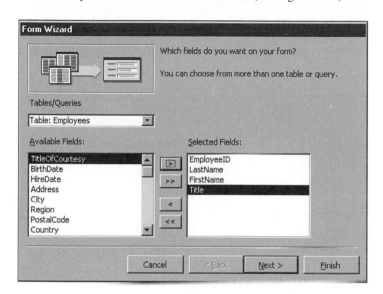

Figure 12.2
Selecting the Employees fields to display in your form.

6. Open the Tables/Queries drop-down list and select the Personnel Actions table. The Available Fields list changes to show the available fields in the Personnel Actions table.

7. Click the >> button to copy all of the fields from the Available Fields list to the Selected Fields list.

PART
III
CH
12

Note

If you haven't established a one-to-many relationship between the Employees and Personnel Actions table, you receive an error message at this point. When you acknowledge the error message, the Relationships window opens. Add the relationship between EmployeeID and paID and close the Relationships window. You must then start over from step 1.

Tip #96 from

RJ

It's easy to change the sequence of location of form fields from the default—the order of fields in the table—proposed by the Wizard. Select the first field and click > to position it at the upper left corner of the form. Select and click > to add the remaining fields in the sequence you want. If you've added many fields to a form, but later decide to change your layout, it's usually faster to delete the newly created form, and then start over with the Wizard.

8. The EmployeeID field from the Employees table is included in the Selected Fields list, so you don't need to include the paID field from the Personnel Actions table on the form. Select the paID field in the list of Selected Fields and then click the < button to move this field out of the Selected Fields list and back to the Available Fields list (see Figure 12.3).

Figure 12.3
Selecting all but one of the Personnel Actions fields.

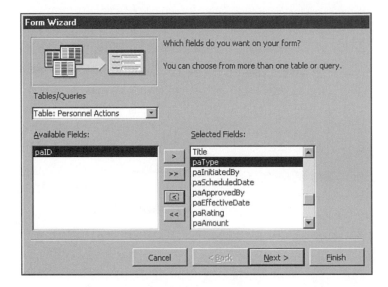

9. Click the Next button to display the Form Wizard's second dialog, shown in Figure 12.4.

Figure 12.4
The Form Wizard's default values for a form-subform relationship.

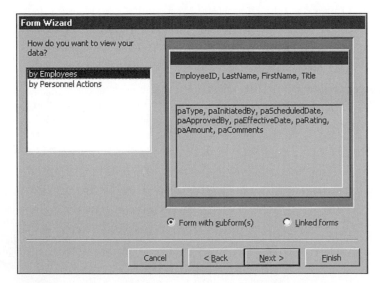

Note

If you realize that you made an error—or if you change your mind about something—and you're on a later step of the Form Wizard, you can click the Back button to return to and modify your previous choices. You can also click Cancel at any time to abort the form creation and get back to the Database window.

10. The fields you've selected to appear on the form come from two different tables, so the Form Wizard asks how you want to view the data. Because you want to view the data by employee, with the employee's personnel action data in a subform, accept By Employees (the default) and make sure that the Form with Subform(s) option is selected (see Figure 12.4). The picture in the upper-right area of the Form Wizard dialog shows the fields of the master form (from the Employees table), with a sunken frame containing the fields of the subform (from the Personnel Actions table).

Note

In one-to-many forms, the subform needs to be linked to the main form so that all records displayed in the subform are related to the current record displayed in the main form. The Access 2000 Form Wizard obtains the information it needs to link the main form and subform from a join in the Relationships window (in this case, between the Employees table and the Personnel Actions table).

11. Click Next to open the third Wizard dialog, which asks you to select the layout style for the subform. Select the Tabular option (see Figure 12.5). This option creates a subform that displays the data from the Personnel Actions table in a tabular format that is similar to Datasheet view but has a structure in which you can change the formatting (colors, column headings, and so on).

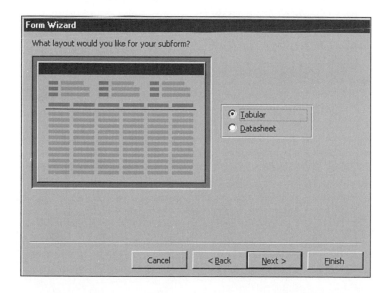

Figure 12.5
Selecting a tabular layout for the Personnel Actions subform.

12. Click Next to move to the fourth Wizard dialog, which asks you to select a style for the new form. The Access Form Wizard has several predefined styles. Because the sample form you're creating is for use by a data-entry operator and doesn't require special effects to highlight or decorate any fields, accept the Standard default (see Figure 12.6).

Figure 12.6
Selecting a predefined form style in the Form Wizard.

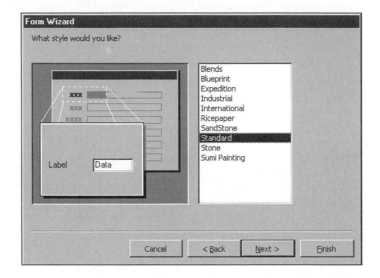

13. Click Next to open the last Form Wizard dialog, which asks you to type a name for the master form and subform. Type **frmPersonnelActions** in the Form text box and **sbfPersonnelActions** in the Subform text box (see Figure 12.7). Accept the default Open the Form to View or Enter Information option and then click Finish to complete your form. (If you want Access to display help for working with your completed form, select the Display Help on Working with the Form check box before you click Finish.)

Figure 12.7
Typing a name for the main form and its subform.

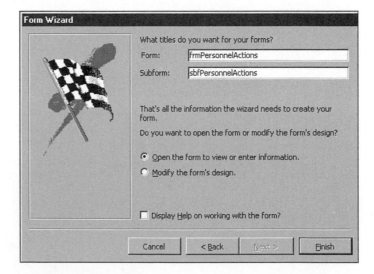

Tip #97 from

Access suggests default names for the form and any subforms; but the default names sel-dom are appropriate to production databases. When naming forms, make sure to specify names that are indicative of what the form really does. Also, make sure that you include the name of the main form (or an abbreviation) in the name of your subform so that the relationship between the form and subform is evident. Using standard Access naming con-ventions—frm and sbf prefixes for forms and subforms, respectively—is the approach used by most Access developers. You later can set the Caption property value of the form to a name meaningful to users.

The Form Wizard creates and automatically saves the form and subform. After creating the form, the Wizard displays the form with the Text Box: Employee ID properties sheet super-imposed. Close the properties sheet to view the entire form (see Figure 12.8).

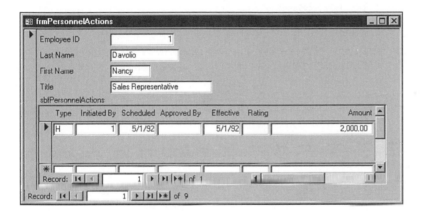

Figure 12.8
The basic Personnel Action form created by the Form Wizard.

On the main form, the Form Wizard creates a single column of text boxes—each with an associated label—for entering or editing data values in each field from the Employees table that you placed on this form. The subform contains all the fields from the Personnel Actions table (except the paID field) arranged in a tabular layout. Access uses the field names as default text box labels and also as column headings for the tabular subform. Access uses the name that you entered for the subform as the label for the subform area.

In Figure 12.8, notice that the paAmount and paComments fields are partially or com-pletely obscured, and scrollbars appear in the subform area. The subform is larger than the area created for it in the main form, so Access automatically adds scrollbars to let you access all data displayed in the subform. The subform's record navigation buttons let you scroll all records related to the current record of the main form.

The basic form as created by the Form Wizard is immediately usable, but could benefit from cosmetic adjustments to the layout of both the main form and subform. The remain-ing discussions and exercises in this chapter show you how to modify forms created with the Form Wizard; you can apply these form-editing skills when you create your own forms from scratch, as described in the next chapter.

PART

III

CH

12

Tip #98 from

No matter how expert you become at designing Access forms, using the Form Wizard to create the basic form design saves you time.

USING THE FORM DESIGN WINDOW

To modify the design of your new form, click the Design View button on the toolbar to open the Form Design window (see Figure 12.9, where the Design window has been maximized and the height of the form has been increased). The floating window that appears in Form Design mode contains an undocked toolbar, called the *toolbox*, that lets you place new control elements on a form. Using the toolbox to add new control elements to the form is covered in the next chapter. For this exercise, hide the toolbox by clicking the Toolbox button on the Forms toolbar or by clicking the Close Window button in the upper-right corner of the toolbox.

Note

Access usually shows the toolbox automatically whenever you enter Form Design mode. If you've manually closed the toolbox, Access does not automatically display it the next time you open the Form Design window. To display the toolbox, click the Toolbox button on the Forms toolbar, or choose View, Toolbox.

The Personnel Action Entry (frmPersonnelActions) form lets you experiment with methods of modifying forms and their contents, which are described in the following sections.

Figure 12.9
The basic
frmPersonnelActions
form in Design view.

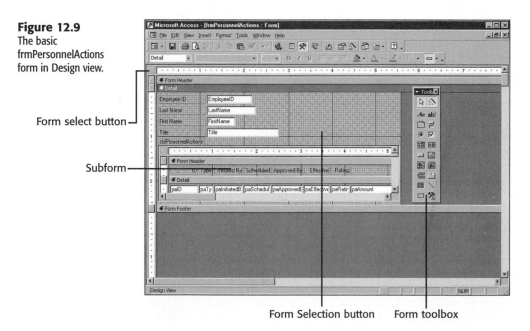

Form select button

Subform

Form Selection button   Form toolbox

PART

III

CH

12

Tip #99 from

> Use the Form Selector button to select the entire form when a section or control is the currently-selected object. Clicking the Form Selector button is much faster than choosing Edit, Select Form. It's even faster, however, to press Ctrl+R.

Caution

> Don't save the form with the changes you make when following the instructions in this section. These changes are for demonstration only. Saving these changes would permanently modify the form you created in the preceding section. If you really want to experiment, you can make a copy of the frmPersonnelActions main form and sbfPersonnelActions subform and then work with the form copies. (Make a backup copy of a form the same way you make a backup copy of a table: choose Edit, Copy to copy the selected form and then choose Edit, Paste to paste a copy of the form.)

ELEMENTS OF THE FORM DESIGN WINDOW

Forms can be divided into five sections: Form Header, Page Header, Detail, Page Footer, and Form Footer. Headers and footers are optional. The Form Design window includes the following basic elements:

- The Form Design toolbar contains buttons that are shortcuts for menu selections in Form Design mode. The functions of the buttons and their equivalent menu choices are listed in tables in the next section, "Form Design Toolbar Buttons and Menu Choices."

- The Formatting toolbar contains buttons that are shortcuts for color, text, border, and various other formatting options. The functions of the formatting buttons and their equivalent menu choices are listed in tables in the next section.

- Vertical and horizontal rulers help you determine the size and placement of objects on the form.

Tip #100 from

> The rulers are calibrated in inches for the United States version of Access and in centimeters for versions of Access that are supplied to countries where the metric system is used.

- A vertical line (shown to the left of the toolbox in Figure 12.9) indicates the position of the right margin of the form. You can move this margin indicator line by clicking and dragging it to the desired location.

- The top of the Form Footer bar represents the bottom margin of the form. You can click and drag this bar to a new location. Margins are important when you are designing a subform to fit within a rectangle of a predetermined size on the main form.

- Vertical and horizontal scroll bars let you view portions of the form outside the boundaries of the form window.

- A Form Header bar defines the height of the form's header section. The bar appears only if you choose to add a header and footer to your form or create the form with the Form Wizard. The Form Header section contains static text, graphic images, and other controls that appear at the top of form. The Form Header appears only on the first page of a multipage form; subsequent printed pages of forms display an optional Page Header. (Page Headers and Footers don't appear on your monitor in Form view.) You add Form and Page Headers by choosing View, Form Header/Footer and View, Page Header/Footer, respectively.

- A Form Detail bar divides the Form Header from the rest of the form. Form controls that display data from your tables and queries, plus static data elements such as labels and logos, are on the Form Detail bar.

- A Form Footer bar defines the height of the form's footer section. The Form Footer section is similar in function to the Form Header section. If you print a multipage form, the Form Footer appears only at the bottom of the last page; optional Page Footers appear at the bottom of preceding printed pages.

Note

Although the form shown in Figure 12.9 has both Form Header and Form Footer sections, neither section takes up any space on the form—that's why the Form Header bar touches the Detail bar, and the Form Footer bar touches the bottom margin of the form. Even though no text or other information is in the header and footer areas, the Form Wizard adds these two elements to the form automatically. When you create a new, blank form without using the Form Wizard, header and footer sections aren't added automatically.

You delete Form Header and Form Footer sections by choosing View, Form Header/Footer to clear the menu check mark. Similarly, you delete Page Headers for printed forms, by choosing View, Page Header/Footer.

Note

If a header or footer section contains any text or other form controls when you try to delete it, Access displays a dialog warning that you are about to lose the contents of the header and footer.

FORM DESIGN TOOLBAR BUTTONS AND MENU CHOICES

The Form Design toolbar of Access 2000 contains several buttons that apply only to the design of forms. You select color and font options from the Format toolbar. Table 12.1 lists the function and equivalent menu choice for each of the Form Design toolbar buttons that are specific to Access 2000. The buttons that relate to text and color formatting are described in the following section, "The Formatting Toolbar."

TABLE 12.1 STANDARD TOOLBAR BUTTONS IN FORM DESIGN MODE

Button	Function	Menu Choice
	Displays the form in Run mode (clicking the arrow at the right of this button displays a drop-down list that lets you select Datasheet view).	View, Form View
	Saves the current form.	File, Save
	Prints all records in the table using the on-screen form to format the printed data and using the current printer settings.	n/a
	Selects Print Preview to display how your form appears if printed. You can print the form from the Print Preview window.	File, Print Preview
	Starts the spelling checker to check the spelling of data (disabled in Form view).	Tools, Spelling
	Copies formatting from selected objects to another object of similar type.	n/a
	Undoes the last change you made to the form.	Edit, Undo
	Inserts a new Hyperlink control or allows you to edit an existing Hyperlink control.	Insert, Hyperlink
	Displays a list of the fields in the query or table that is the data source for the main form.	View, Field List
	Displays or closes the toolbox.	View, Toolbox
	Applies your choice of several predefined form formats, including formatting for the background bitmap of a form, text fonts, and color settings.	Format, AutoFormat
	Opens the VBA Editor for the code behind the active form.	View, Code
	Displays the Properties window for one of the two sections of the form when you click the section bars or displays the properties of a control when you select it.	View, Properties
	Displays the Build Wizard for the selected object or property in the form. This is enabled only if Access has a builder for the selected item.	n/a
	Displays the Database window.	Window, 1 Database
	Creates a new object. Click the arrow at the right of this button to see a drop-down list of the objects you can create. You can't add an AutoForm or AutoReport in Form Design view.	n/a

PART

III

CH

12

Figure 12.10 shows the Form Design window after adding Page Headers and Footers to the form and clicking the Properties button with the EmployeeID text box selected.

Figure 12.10
The Form Design window with the Properties window open.

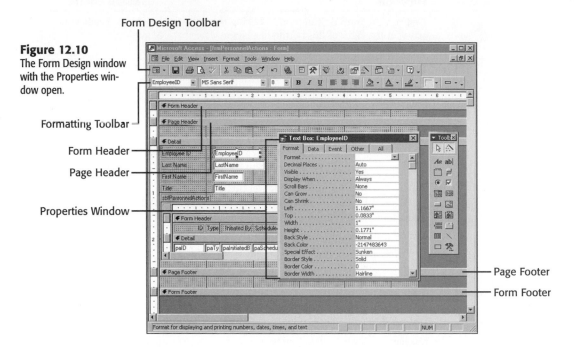

THE FORMATTING TOOLBAR

Access 2000 displays in Form and Report Design view shortcut buttons and drop-down lists for all text formatting, line, color, and cell effects options on a separate toolbar: the Formatting toolbar. The Object list at the extreme left of the Formatting toolbar displays the name of the currently selected object on the form and lets you rapidly select another object on the form by selecting its name in the list. In Figure 12.10, the EmployeeID text box is the currently selected object.

Table 12.2 lists the function of each text-formatting button and its equivalent property setting.

TABLE 12.2	TOOLBAR BUTTONS FOR TEXT CONTROLS IN FORM DESIGN MODE	
Button	**Function**	**Property and Value**
B	Sets text style to bold (the default for titles and labels).	Font Weight = Bold
I	Sets italic text style.	Font Italic = Yes

Button	Function	Property and Value
U	Sets underline text style.	Font Underline = Yes
	Left-justifies text within border.	Text Align = Left
	Centers text horizontally within border.	Text Align = Center
	Right justifies text within border.	Text Align = Right
	Displays a color palette from which you choose the background color for the selected object.	Back Color = *number*
	Displays a color palette from which you choose the color of the text in the selected object.	Fore Color = *number*
	Displays a color palette from which you choose the color for the border of the selected object.	Border Color = *number*
	Displays a drop-down list from which you choose the width of the selected object's borders. You may select a hairline width or widths ranging from 1 to 6 points.	Border Width = *width*
	Displays a drop-down list from which you choose a special effect for how the selected object is displayed. You may choose Flat, Raised, Sunken, Etched, Shadowed, or Chiseled.	Special Effect = *name*

PART

III

CH

12

DEFAULT VALUES FOR FORMS

You can change some of the default values used in the creation of all forms by choosing Tools, Options and clicking the Forms/Reports tab (see Figure 12.11). You can create a form to use as a template and replace the standard template, and you can determine how objects are displayed when chosen. The effects of these options are described in the sections that follow. The options that you or other Access users choose in the Options dialog are saved for each user ID in the MSysOptions table of the current System.mdw workgroup system file. Workgroup files are one of the primary subjects of Chapter 24, "Securing Multiuser Network Applications." Access Data Projects (ADP) store option values in the .adp file.

You can change the default values for the current form, section, or controls by choosing the object and then changing the default values displayed in the Properties window for that object. You can also use the AutoFormat feature to quickly apply a predefined format to all controls in the form. The next section describes using AutoFormat to change a form's appearance, and subsequent sections describe ways to change the format of text or controls manually on a form.

Figure 12.11
The Forms/Reports page
of the Options dialog.

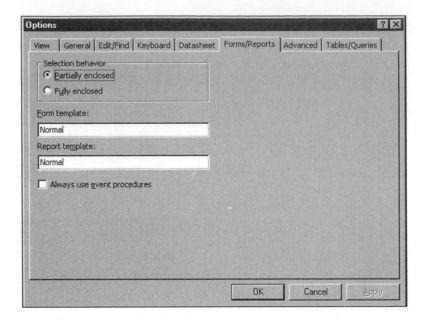

Tip #101 from

R J

Check the title bar of the Properties window before you change property values to make
sure the selected object is the one whose properties you want to change. It's a common
practice to leave the Properties window open as you alter the form design, and the
selected object might not be the object you intend.

USING AUTOFORMAT

AutoFormat lets you apply a predefined format to an entire form with only a few mouse
clicks. Access 2000 comes with several predefined formats, and you also can create your
own formats for use with AutoFormat. The AutoFormat dialog is similar to the third
Form Wizard (form layout) dialog described earlier in the chapter.

APPLYING AN AUTOFORMAT

To apply a format to a form with AutoFormat, follow these steps:

1. Press Ctrl+R to apply your AutoFormat selection to the entire form. If you select a
   control or other object, AutoFormat is applied only to the selected object.

2. Click the AutoFormat button on the toolbar to open the AutoFormat dialog shown in
   Figure 12.12.

3. Click to select the format you want to use in the Form AutoFormats list; a preview of
   the format you select appears in the window in the center of the dialog.

4. Click OK to apply the format to the form. Figure 12.13 shows the frmPersonnelActions form after the International format has been applied.

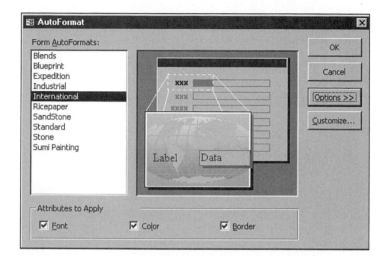

Figure 12.12
Using AutoFormat to apply a predefined format to an entire form.

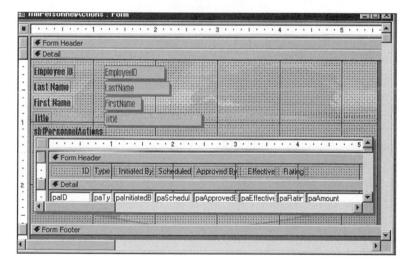

Figure 12.13
The frmPersonnelActions form after applying the International format.

The AutoFormat dialog, expanded by clicking the Options button, lets you omit the application of font, color, or border style information to your form when you apply the AutoFormat. Deselect the check box for the elements of the AutoFormat that you don't want AutoFormat to apply to your form.

CREATING, CUSTOMIZING, AND DELETING AUTOFORMATS

The predefined AutoFormat styles might not suit your tastes, or you might want to create AutoFormat styles specific to your company or application.

To create a new AutoFormat or customize an existing one, follow these steps:

1. Create a form and alter its appearance (using the techniques described in the next five sections of this chapter) so that the form has the font, border, background picture, and other options adjusted exactly the way you want them for your new or customized AutoFormat.

2. Click the AutoFormat button to display the AutoFormat dialog. If you want to modify an existing AutoFormat, select it in the Form AutoFormats list now.

3. Click the Customize button to display the Customize AutoFormat dialog shown in Figure 12.14.

Figure 12.14
The Customize AutoFormat dialog used to create, modify, or delete an AutoFormat.

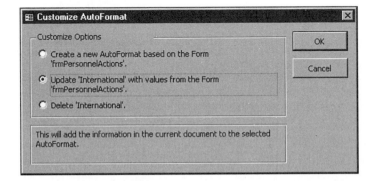

4. Select the Create a new AutoFormat based on the Form *formname* option, or the Update *formatname* with values from the Form *formname* option to create or modify an AutoFormat, respectively. (Deleting AutoFormats is covered later in this section.)

5. Click OK. If you're creating a new AutoFormat, the New Style Name dialog appears. Type an appropriate name for your new AutoFormat and click OK. Access now creates or updates the AutoFormat and returns you to the AutoFormat dialog.

6. Click Close to close the AutoFormat dialog.

If you've created your own AutoFormats, you might want to delete an AutoFormat that you no longer use. To delete an AutoFormat, follow these steps:

1. Open any form in Design view.

2. Click the AutoFormat button to display the AutoFormat dialog.

3. Click to select the AutoFormat you want to delete in the Form AutoFormats list and then click the Customize button. Access displays the Customize AutoFormat dialog.

4. Select the Delete *formname* option and click OK. Access deletes that AutoFormat from the list.

Caution

> Access doesn't ask for confirmation when you delete an AutoFormat; make sure to select the correct AutoFormat for deletion before you click OK.

5. Click Close to close the AutoFormat dialog.

Applying formatting to a form through an AutoFormat style is by far the easiest way to create standardized forms for your database application—especially because the Form Wizard uses the same format style list as the AutoFormat feature. In other words, any AutoFormats you create become available in the Form Wizard dialog, also.

The next few sections of this chapter describe how you can customize the appearance of various objects on a form.

Changing an Object's Colors

You select object colors through the buttons on the Formatting toolbar, as well as through property settings that are accessible through the Properties window of the form and individual objects on the form. The following sections describe how to use the Formatting toolbar controls and the Property dialog to change background and foreground colors of form sections and control objects, as well as border properties of control objects.

Background Colors

The background color (Back Color property) of a form section (Header, Detail, or Footer) applies to all areas of that section except those occupied by control objects. The default background color of all sections of forms created by the Form Wizard depends on the specific form style you choose when you create the form; the Standard format scheme used to create the frmPersonnelActions form, for example, is the Windows system color for 3D Objects (the default is light gray).

The default color choices on the palette displayed by the Fill/Back Color toolbar button are 16 of the standard system colors of Windows 9x and Windows NT. If you're creating a form that you intend to print, a dark or deeply textured background will not only be distracting but will also consume substantial amounts of printer toner. Data-entry operators often prefer a white background rather than a gray, colored, or textured background. Colored backgrounds limit text visibility.

PART
III
CH
12

Note

> If you've selected a picture as the background for a form—or used an AutoFormat style that includes a background picture, such as the International style pictured in Figure 12.15—then any changes you make in the background color of the form are hidden by the overlying picture.

To change the background color of a section of a form, follow these steps:

1. Click an empty area within the section of the form (Header, Detail, or Footer) whose background color you want to change. This step selects the appropriate section.

2. Click the Fill/Back Color button on the toolbar to display the color palette.

3. Click the box that contains the color you want to use.

Because the background color of each form section is independent, you must repeat the process if you want to change the color for other sections of your form. The Transparent button of the Fill/Back Color palette is disabled when a form section is chosen because a transparent background color isn't applicable to forms.

You choose the background color for a control object, such as a label, just as you do for a form. In most cases, the chosen background color of labels is the same as that of the form, so click the Transparent button to allow the background color to appear. The default value of the Back Color property of text boxes is white so that text boxes (and the data they contain) contrast with the form's background color.

CHANGING THE BACKGROUND BITMAP

NEW 2000 You can use a bitmap picture as the background for a form. Unlike background colors, of which you can have several, you select a single bitmap picture for the entire form. Access 2000 comes with a few bitmap pictures that it uses in the AutoFormat formats—International, for example, uses the Globe.wmf graphics file (stored in the Program Files\Microsoft Office\Access\Bitmaps\Styles folder) as the background for the form. You can use any.bmp, .dib, .emf, .gif, .ico, .jpg, .pcx, .png, or .wmf graphics file as a background for a form. The ability to use compressed .gif, .jpg, .pcx, and .png files is new with Access 2000.

Tip #102 from

Forms with bitmap graphics as a background can look dramatic and, therefore, are best suited for public-access information terminals or decision-support forms. These forms, however, tend to be more visually complex than Standard-formatted forms, which might make it difficult for users to read text labels or identify specific fields on the form. For accurate, high-speed data entry, you should keep your transaction-processing forms visually simple so that users can easily distinguish data fields on the form and easily read text labels.

You set or remove a form's background bitmap through the Properties window of the form; you can also specify several viewing and formatting properties for the background picture. Follow these steps to set the background picture properties of a form:

1. Open the form in Design view if necessary.

2. Click the square at the upper-left corner of the Form Design window (where the horizontal and vertical rulers meet) to select the form as a whole. A black square appears when the form is selected (see Figure 12.19).

3. If the Properties window isn't already open, click the Properties button on the toolbar to display this window.

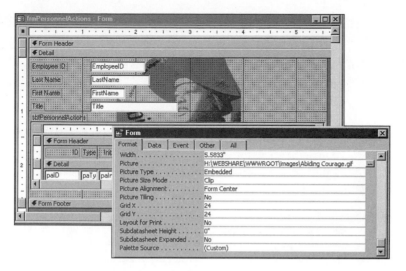

Figure 12.15
Setting the filename and formatting properties for a scanned image of a book front cover used as a form's background picture.

4. Click the Format tab in the Properties window and scroll down to the end of the Format properties list to view the various Picture properties: Picture, Picture Type, Picture Size Mode, Picture Alignment, and Picture Tiling. These properties and their effects are described in the list following these numbered steps.

5. Set the various Picture properties until you are satisfied with the appearance of the form. As you change each property, results of the change become immediately visible on the form.

6. Click the Close window button in the Properties window to close this window.

The following list summarizes form properties related to the background picture, available choices for each property, and the effects of each choice.

- The Picture property contains the folder path and filename of the graphics file that Access uses as the form's background. You may either type the folder path and filename directly in the Picture property text box, or you may use the builder to help you select the background graphics file. To use the builder, click the Picture property field to select that field and then click the Build button that appears next to the text box. Access displays the Insert Picture dialog shown in Figure 12.16. The Insert Picture dialog is a standard Office 2000 dialog for opening files. Click the Preview button (second button from the right), if necessary, to display the background image. When you locate the graphics file you want, click to select its name and then click OK to have Access fill in the Picture property.

Tip #103 from

R J

To remove a background picture, simply delete the entry in the Picture text box and click Yes when asked if you want to remove the picture from the form.

Figure 12.16
The Insert Picture dialog used to select a picture as a form's background.

- The Picture Type property specifies the OLE or ActiveX method that Access uses to attach the background picture to the form. You can select either Embedded or Linked as the picture type. You usually should use the Embedded picture type, especially if you intend to distribute your database application—the resulting form is self-contained and doesn't rely on the presence of external files that might be moved or deleted. If you have many forms that use the same background bitmap graphic, however, linking the background picture can save some disk space.

- The Picture Size Mode property controls how Access sizes the background picture. The available choices are Clip, Stretch, and Zoom. Clip causes Access to display the picture at its full size behind the form; if the picture is larger than the form, the picture is clipped to fit the form. If the picture is smaller than the form, the form's own background color shows in any part of the form background not covered by the picture. Stretch causes Access to stretch the picture vertically and horizontally to match the size of the form; the Stretch option permits distortions in the picture. Zoom causes Access to magnify the picture, without distortion, to fit the size of the form.

- The Picture Alignment property controls where Access positions the background picture. The available choices are Top-left (aligns the upper-left corner of the picture with the upper-left corner of the form window), Top-right (aligns the upper-right corner of the picture with the upper-right corner of the form window), Center (places the picture in the center of the form window), Bottom-left (aligns the lower-left corner of the picture with the lower-left corner of the form), Bottom-right (aligns the lower-right corner of the picture with the lower-right corner of the form), and Form Center (centers the picture on the form).

Tip #104 from

RJ

To ensure that a background picture is displayed relative to the form, rather than the form's window, select Form Center as the value for the Picture Alignment property.

■ The Picture Tiling property has two permissible values: Yes or No. *Tiling* means that the picture is repeatedly displayed to fill the entire form or form window (if the Picture Alignment property is set to Form Center, the tiling fills just the form).

Now that you know how to adjust the background picture and colors of a form, the next section describes how to adjust the foreground colors and border properties of the form and objects on the form.

FOREGROUND COLOR, BORDER COLOR, AND BORDER STYLE

You may set the foreground color, border color, and border width through buttons on the Formatting toolbar or directly in the Properties window for a selected control. To set a border style (solid style or a variety of dashed-line styles), you must set the property directly in the Properties window.

Foreground color (the Fore Color property) is applicable only to control objects. (The Font/Fore Color button on the toolbar is disabled when you select a form section.) Foreground color specifies the color for the text in labels and text boxes. The default value of the Fore Color property is black. You choose border colors for control objects that have borders by using the Line/Border Color toolbar button.

The Special Effects button of the Formatting toolbar allows you to simulate special effects for control objects, such as a raised or sunken appearance. The Line/Border Width button allows you to control the width of the border of controls. The Formatting toolbar buttons were listed earlier in this chapter in Table 12.2. Table 12.3 lists the property name for each border property and the specific values that each may have.

To set a control's foreground color, border width, or border color by using the Formatting toolbar buttons, first click the control whose properties you want to change and then click the arrow to the right of the toolbar button for the property you want to change. Click the color or line width you want for the control.

To set a control's foreground color, border width, border color, or border style in the Properties window, first select the control whose properties you want to change by clicking it. If necessary, open the Properties window by clicking the Properties button on the toolbar. Click the Format tab in the Properties window and then scroll to the text box for the property you want to change. Most of the border properties are selected from drop-down lists; color properties require you to type a number that represents the desired color in Windows 9x or Windows NT color notation. (Windows color notation is too complex to explain here; the easiest way to enter color values is with the toolbar buttons or by using the color builder described in the following section, "Creating Custom Colors with the Color Builder.")

TABLE 12.3 BORDER STYLE PROPERTIES AND VALUES

Property Name	Function	Values
Border Style	Determines the line style of the border.	Transparent, Solid, Dashes, Short Dashes, Dots, Sparse Dots, Dash Dot, Dash Dot Dot
Border Color	Sets the color of the border.	Depends on the color
Border Width	Determines the width of the border.	Hairline, or any whole point size from 1 to 6

CREATING CUSTOM COLORS WITH THE COLOR BUILDER

If you aren't satisfied with one of the 16 Windows system colors for your form sections or control objects, you can specify your own custom colors by following these steps:

1. Place the caret in the Back Color, Fore Color, or Border Color text box of the Properties window for a control.

2. Click the ellipsis button to display the Color dialog. The basic form of this dialog enables you to choose from a set of 48 colors. If one of these colors suits your taste, click the color square and then click OK to assign that color as the value of the property, and close the dialog. If you want a custom color, proceed to step 3.

3. Click the Define Custom Colors button to expand the Color dialog to include the Hue/Saturation and Luminance windows, as shown in Figure 12.17.

4. Click and drag the cursor within the square Hue/Saturation area to choose the color you want.

5. Click and drag the arrow at the right of the rectangular luminance area while observing the Color block; release the mouse button when the Color block has the luminance (brightness) value you want.

6. Click Add to Custom Colors to add your new color to the first of the 16 custom color blocks.

7. Click the new custom color block to select it. Click OK to add this color value to the property, and close the Color dialog.

Many PCs used for data entry and editing applications run in 256-color VGA or SVGA mode because this mode is slightly faster than the standard 24-bit or 32-bit true-color mode used by most of today's PCs. In 256-color VGA mode, any colors you choose or create, other than the standard Windows 256-color palette, are simulated by a dithering process. *Dithering* alternates pixels of differing colors to create the usually imperfect illusion of a solid color.

Tip #105 from

It's a good programming practice to stick with the 16 system colors of Windows because added color depth slightly decreases the speed of opening forms.

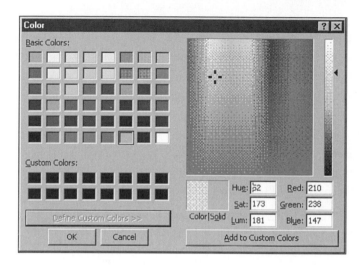

Figure 12.17
Defining a custom color in the expanded Color dialog.

SELECTING, EDITING, AND MOVING FORM ELEMENTS AND CONTROLS

The properties that apply to the entire form, to the five sections of the form, and to each control object on the form are determined by the values shown in the Properties window. To view the Properties window for a control, select the control by clicking anywhere on its surface; then click the Properties button on the toolbar. Alternatively, right-click the control and choose Properties from the popup menu.

The following list describes how to select and display the properties of form sections and control objects:

- *Header section only*. To select the Form Header, click the Form Header or Page Header bar. The set of properties you work with applies only to the Form Header or Page Header section. A Form Header and Footer appear when you choose View, Form Header/Footer. A Page Header and Footer appear when you choose View, Page Header/ Footer. Page Headers and Footers primarily are used in conjunction with printing forms. You delete headers and footers by choosing View, Form Header/Footer or View, Page Header/Footer a second time.

- *Detail section only*. To select the Detail section, click the Detail bar. You get a set of properties similar to those of the Form Header section, but all of these apply to the Detail section.

PART
III

CH
12

- *Footer section only*. To select the Footer section, click the Form Footer or Page Footer bar. A set of properties identical to the header properties is available for the footer sections. A Form Footer appears only if a Form Header has been added. The same applies to Page Headers and Footers.

- *Control object* (or both elements of a control with an associated label). Click the surface of the control to select the control. Each type of control has its own set of properties. Displaying the properties of multiple-control objects is the subject of the section "Selecting, Moving, and Sizing a Single Control" later in this chapter.

CHANGING THE SIZE OF THE FORM HEADER AND FORM FOOTER

You can change the height of a form section by dragging the Form Header, Page Header, Detail, Page Footer, or Form Footer bar vertically with the mouse. When you position the mouse pointer at the top edge of a section divider bar, it turns into a line with two vertical arrows. You drag the pointer with the mouse to adjust the size of the section above the mouse pointer.

The height of the Detail section is determined by the vertical dimension of the window in which the form is displayed, less the combined heights of all the header and footer sections that are fixed in position. When you adjust the vertical scroll bar, only the Detail section scrolls.

SELECTING, MOVING, AND SIZING A SINGLE CONTROL

When you select a control object by clicking its surface, the object is enclosed by a shadow line with an anchor rectangle at its upper-left corner and five smaller, rectangular sizing handles (see Figure 12.18).

Note   Text boxes, combo boxes, check boxes, and option buttons have associated (attached) labels. When you select one of these objects, the label and object are selected as a unit.

The following choices are available for moving or changing the size of a control object (the numbers correspond to the numbers in Figure 12.18):

- *To select a control (and its associated label, if any)*, click anywhere on its surface.

- *To move the control (and its associated label, if any) to a new position*, move the mouse pointer within the outline of the object at any point other than the small resizing handles or the confines of a text box (where the cursor can become an editing caret). The mouse pointer becomes a hand symbol when it's on an area that you can use to move the entire control. Press and hold down the left mouse button while dragging the hand symbol to the new location for the control. An outline of the control indicates its position as you move the mouse. When the control is where you want it to be, release the mouse button to drop the control in its new position.

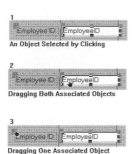

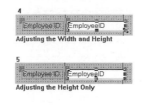

Figure 12.18
The appearance of a control object selected for relocation and resizing.

1 — An Object Selected by Clicking

2 — Dragging Both Associated Objects

3 — Dragging One Associated Object

4 — Adjusting the Width and Height

5 — Adjusting the Height Only

6 — Adjusting the Height of a Label

Tip #106 from
RJ

If the control doesn't have an associated label, you can drag the control's anchor handle at the upper-left corner to move the control.

- *To separately move the elements of a control that has an associated label,* position the mouse pointer on the anchor handle in the upper-left corner of the control that you want to move. The mouse pointer becomes a hand with an extended finger. Click and drag the individual element to its new position and then release the mouse button.

- *To simultaneously adjust the width and height of a control,* click the small sizing handle at any of the three corners of the outline of the control. The mouse pointer becomes a diagonal two-headed arrow. Click and drag this arrow to a new position and then release the mouse button.

- *To adjust only the height of the control,* click the sizing handle on one of the horizontal surfaces of the outline. The mouse pointer becomes a vertical, two-headed arrow. Click and drag this arrow to a new position and then release the mouse button.

Selecting and deselecting controls is a *toggling* process. Toggling means repeating an action with the effect of alternating between On and Off conditions. The Properties, Field List, and Toolbox buttons on the toolbar—as well as their corresponding menu choices—are toggles. The Properties window, for example, appears and disappears if you repeatedly click the Properties button.

ALIGNING CONTROLS TO THE GRID

The Form Design window includes a grid that consists of one-pixel dots with a default spacing of 24 to the inch horizontally and 24 to the inch vertically. When the grid is visible, you can use the grid dots to assist in maintaining the horizontal and vertical alignment of rows and columns of controls. Even if the grid isn't visible, you can cause controls to "snap to the grid" by choosing Format, Snap to Grid. This menu command is a toggle, and when Snap to Grid is active, the menu choice is checked. Whenever you move a control while Snap to Grid is active, the upper-left corner of the object jumps to the closest grid dot.

You can cause the size of control objects to conform to grid spacing by choosing Format, Size, To Grid. You also can make the size of the control fit its content by choosing Format, Size, To Fit.

PART
III

CH
12

Tip #107 from

If Snap to Grid is on and you want to locate or size a control without reference to the grid, press and hold the Ctrl key while you move or resize the control.

Toggling the View, Grid menu command controls the visibility of the grid; by default, the grid is visible for all new forms. If the grid spacing is set to more than 24 per inch or 10 per centimeter, the dots aren't visible. For "non-metrified" users, better values are 10 per inch for Grid X and 12 per inch for Grid Y. This grid dot spacing is optimum for text controls that use the default 8-point MS Sans Serif font. To change the grid spacing for a form, follow these steps:

1. Choose Edit, Select Form.
2. Click the Properties button on the toolbar to make the form properties appear.

3. Click the Format tab in the Properties window to display the formatting properties and then scroll through the list until the Grid X and Grid Y properties are visible.
4. Change the value of Grid X to **10** dots per inch (dpi) and Grid Y to **12** dpi, or change both values to **16** (if you want controls to align with inch ruler ticks). Metrified users are likely to prefer a value of 10 for both Grid X and Grid Y.

SELECTING AND MOVING MULTIPLE CONTROL

You can select and move several objects at a time by using one of the following methods:

- *Enclose the objects with a rectangle.* Begin by clicking the surface of the form outside the outline of a control object. Press and hold down the mouse button while dragging the mouse pointer to create an enclosing rectangle that includes each of the objects you want to select (see Figure 12.19). Release the mouse button. You may now move the group of objects by clicking and dragging the anchor handle of any one of them.

- *Click to select one object; then hold down the Shift key while you click to select the next object.* You can repeat this step as many times as necessary to select all the objects you want.

- *To remove a selected object from a group,* hold down the Shift key and click the object with the mouse to deselect it. To deselect an entire group, click any inactive area of the form. An inactive area is an area outside the outline of a control.

NEW 2000

- *To create a group of the multiselected objects,* choose Format, Group. The selection rectangle permanently encloses the objects, which lose their individual selection rectangles. Choose Format, Ungroup to remove the group attribute from the enclosed objects.

If you select or deselect a control with an associated label, the label is selected or deselected along with the control.

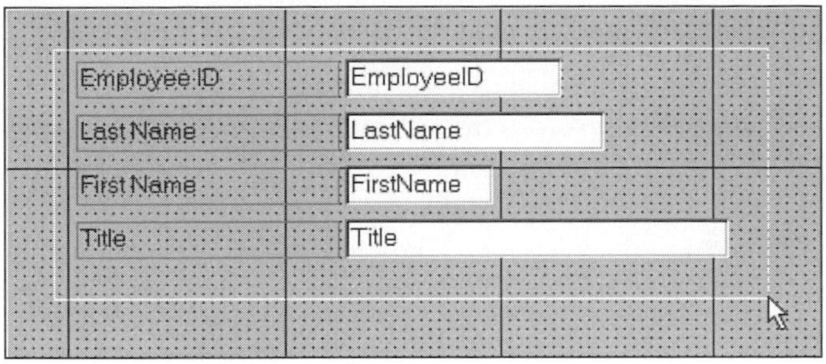

Figure 12.19
Selecting a group of objects by dragging a selection rectangle.

The selection rectangle selects a control if any part of the control is included within the rectangle. This behavior is unlike many drawing applications in which the entire object must be enclosed to be selected. You can change the behavior of Access's selection rectangle to require full enclosure of the object by choosing Tools, Options; selecting the Forms/Reports tab (refer back to Figure 12.11); and changing the value of the Selection Behavior option from Partially Enclosed to Fully Enclosed.

ALIGNING A GROUP OF CONTROLS

You can align selected individual controls, or groups of controls, to the grid or each other by choosing Format, Align and completing the following actions:

- To fine-adjust the position of a control by the width of a single pixel, select the control and press Ctrl+*Arrow*.

- To align a selected control (or group of controls) to the grid, choose To Grid from the submenu.

- To adjust the positions of controls within a selected columnar group so that their left edges fall into vertical alignment with the far-left control, choose Left from the submenu.

- To adjust the positions of controls within a selected columnar group so that their right edges fall into vertical alignment with the right edge of the far-right control, choose Right from the submenu.

- To align rows of controls at their top edges, choose Top from the submenu.

- To align rows of controls at their bottom edges, choose Bottom from the submenu.

Your forms have a more professional appearance if you take the time to align groups of controls vertically and horizontally.

Tip #108 from

RJ

To quickly select a group of controls in a column or row, click the within the horizontal or vertical ruler, respectively. This shortcut selects all controls intersected by the vertical or horizontal projection of the arrow that appears when you move the mouse within the ruler.

USING THE WINDOWS CLIPBOARD AND DELETING CONTROLS

All conventional Windows Clipboard commands apply to control objects. You can cut or copy a selected control or group of controls to the Clipboard. After that, you can paste the control or group to the form using Edit menu commands and then relocate the pasted control or group as desired. Access uses the Windows keyboard shortcut keys: Ctrl+X to cut, Ctrl+C to copy selected controls to the Clipboard, and Ctrl+V to paste the Clipboard contents. The traditional Shift+Delete, Ctrl+Insert, and Shift+Insert commands perform the same operations.

You can delete a control by selecting it and then pressing Delete. If you accidentally delete a label associated with a control, do the following: select another label, copy it to the Clipboard, select the control with which the label needs to be associated, and paste the label to the control.

CHANGING THE COLOR AND BORDER STYLE OF A CONTROL

As mentioned earlier in this chapter, the default color for the text and borders of controls is black. Borders are one pixel wide (called *hairline* width). Some objects, such as text boxes, have default borders. Labels have a gray background color by default, but a better choice for the default label color would have been transparent. *Transparent* means that the background color of the object under the control (the form section, in this case) appears within the control except in areas of the control that are occupied by text or pictures.

You control the color and border widths of a control from the Line/Border Color and Line/Border Width buttons on the Formatting toolbar. You must select a border style directly in the Properties window.

To change the color or border width of a selected control or group of controls, follow these steps:

1. Select the control(s) whose color or border width you want to change.

2. Click the arrow of the Fill/Back Color toolbar button to open the color palette popup window. Click the color square you want or click the Transparent button to make the background transparent.

3. Click the arrow of the Line/Border Color toolbar button to open the color palette popup window, where you change the border color for any selected control with borders.

4. Click the arrow of the Line/Border Width toolbar button to open the border width popup window, where you change the thickness of the border for any selected control whose borders are enabled.

5. Click the arrow of the Font/Fore Color toolbar button to open the color palette popup window, where you change the color of the text of selected controls.

Note	The general practice for Windows database entry forms is to indicate editable elements with borders and clear backgrounds. Still, some popular software uses reverse video as the default to indicate editable text. You can create the effect of reverse video by choosing black or another dark color for the fill of a text box control and a light color for its text. If you decide to implement reverse text, remember that reverse text is more difficult to read than normal text, so consider using a larger font and adding the bold attribute to ensure legibility.

To set the border style, you must select the Border Style property directly in the Properties window, as explained earlier in this chapter.

CHANGING THE CONTENT OF TEXT CONTROLS

You can edit the content of text controls by using conventional Windows text-editing techniques. When you place the mouse pointer within the confines of a text control and click the mouse button, the mouse pointer becomes the Windows text-editing caret that you use to insert or delete text. You can select text by dragging the mouse over it or by holding down Shift and moving the caret with the arrow keys. All Windows Clipboard operations are applicable to text within controls. Keyboard text selection and editing techniques using the arrow keys in combination with Shift are available, also.

If you change the name of a field in a text box and make an error naming the field, you receive a "#Name?" error message in the offending text box when you select Run mode. Following is a better method of changing a text box with an associated label:

1. Delete the existing field control by clicking to select it and then pressing Delete.
2. Click the Field List button in the Properties bar to display the Field List dialog.
3. Scroll through the entries in the list until you find the field name you want.
4. Click the field name to select it; then drag the field name to the location of the deleted control. Release the mouse button to drop the new name.
5. Close the Field List dialog when you're finished.

You can relocate and resize the new field caption and text box (or edit the caption) as necessary.

USING THE FORMAT PAINTER

The Format Painter lets you quickly copy the format of any control on the form to any other control on the form. The Format Painter copies only those formatting properties that are relevant to the control on which you apply the Format Painter. To use the Format Painter, follow these steps:

1. Select the control with the formatting you want to copy.
2. Click or double-click the Format Painter button on the toolbar; the mouse cursor changes to a pointing arrow with a paintbrush icon attached to it. (Double-clicking

PART
III

CH
12

"locks" the Format Painter on. Double-click the Format Painter button only if you want to copy the formatting to more than one control.)

3. Click any control that you want to copy the formatting to; the Format Painter copies all relevant formatting properties to this control. If you didn't double-click the Format Painter button, the Format Painter turns itself off after copying the formatting properties to one control.

4. If you locked the Format Painter on by double-clicking its button, you can repeat step 3 as many times as you want. Click the Format Painter button again to turn off the Format Painter.

Typically, you use the Format Painter to quickly set the formatting properties for field text labels, or in any situation where selecting several controls by dragging a selection rectangle seems undesirable. By locking the Format Painter, it's easy to format several controls one after another.

REARRANGING THE PERSONNEL ACTIONS FORM

The objective of the following procedure is to rearrange the controls on the frmPersonnelActions form so that all of the elements on the form (and its subform) are completely visible in the form window. Another objective is to optimize the position of the fields for data entry. After you complete the following steps, your main form with its embedded subform appears as shown in Figure 12.20, and your subform appears as shown in Figure 12.21.

Figure 12.20
The frmPersonnelActions form after relocating and resizing its control objects.

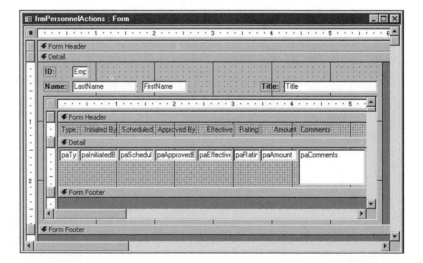

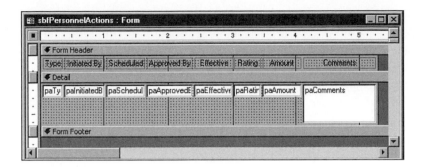

Figure 12.21
The sbfPersonnelActions subform after modifying its appearance.

SETTING PROPERTIES OF THE MAIN FORM

To change the color of form objects and rearrange the controls of the frmPersonnelActions form to correspond with the positions shown in Figure 12.21, follow these steps:

1. Close the frmPersonnelActions form by clicking the Close window button. Don't save any changes you made in the preceding section.

2. Select frmPersonnelActions from the Forms list in the Database window and click the Design button.

3. Click the Maximize window button to maximize the Form Design window if it isn't already maximized.

4. Choose Edit, Select Form, and then click the Properties button on the toolbar.

5. Click the Format tab of the Properties window and then scroll through the properties list until you see Grid X and Grid Y. Change the Grid X property to **10** and the Grid Y property value to **12**. (Metric users may prefer a 5-by-5 grid, providing 2 mm resolution.)

6. Close the Properties window by clicking the Properties button on the toolbar again.

7. Drag the right margin of the form from its present position (5.5 inches) to 6 inches.

8. Click the Title field text box to select the text box and its label.

9. Move the mouse pointer onto the selected Title field until the pointer changes to the shape of a hand. Click and drag the Title field to the right of the EmployeeID text box.

10. Delete the FirstName label (click the label and then press Delete). Next use the technique described in steps 8 and 9 to select the FirstName field and drag it to a position to the right of the LastName field (refer to Figure 12.20).

11. Edit the LastName label to read **Name:**, the EmployeeID label to read **ID:**, and the Title label to read **Title:**.

12. Delete the sbfPersonnelActions field label (the size and content of the subform is sufficient to identify it) and drag the subform control to a position below the FirstName and LastName fields (refer to Figure 12.20).

13. Click and drag the Form Footer bar to approximately 2.75 inches. (Alternatively, you can type the detail section's height directly in the Height property on the Format sheet of the Properties window.) At present, the dimensions of your form are 6×2.7 inches.

14. Resize the sbfPersonnelActions subform control on the form so that its left, right, and bottom edges are one grid mark inside the edges of the form (this makes the sbfPersonnelActions subform control about 5.8×1 7/8 inches).

15. Click the text label of the EmployeeID field to select it and then click the Bold and Align Right buttons on the Formatting toolbar to make the text label bold and right justified.

16. Double-click the Format Painter button on the toolbar (remember that this step locks the Format Painter).

17. In turn, click the text labels for all of the remaining controls on the form to apply the formatting with the Format Painter.

18. Click the Format Painter button on the toolbar again to turn off the Format Painter.

19. Adjust the widths of the labels and text boxes to suit their content (refer to Figure 12.20).

20. Select the form, click the Properties button. and set the Allow Additions and Allow Deletions properties to No. Setting these property values to No prevents you from adding or deleting employee records in this form.

21. Click the Save button on the toolbar (or choose File, Save) to save your changes to the frmPersonnelActions form.

You may need to adjust the sizes of some controls individually to make their appearance consistent with other controls. When you complete your rearrangement, click the Form View button to review your work.

SETTING THE PROPERTIES OF A SUBFORM

You can learn about modifying the properties of a subform by working with the subform used to create the history of prior Personnel Actions for an employee. In this example, editing or deleting entries using the subform is not allowed, but you can add new entries. The subform needs to be modified so that all of its columns are readable without horizontal scrolling.

Tip #109 from	Although you can use Access 2000's new in-situ subform editing feature to alter the design of a subform, in most cases it's easier to use the traditional method of subform design modification. In-situ editing is better suited for changing subform property values than for altering subform dimensions.

To change the properties of the Personnel Actions subform, follow these steps:

1. Close the frmPersonnelActions form. You can't modify the design of a subform while the main form is open.

2. Open the sbfPersonnelActions subform from the Database window in Design view.

3. Select the form and use the Properties window to make sure that the Grid X and Grid Y properties are both set to 24. The finer grid lets you make more precise changes to the size of subform controls. Close the Properties window.

4. Using the same techniques you used when working with the main form, resize the label boxes in the Form Header section of the form so that they match what you saw in Figure 12.21. Use the Format Painter to center the text in every text label in the Form Header section.

5. Adjust the field text boxes in the Detail section of the form, if necessary, to line up with the headings in the Form Header section (refer to Figure 12.21).

6. Drag the right edge of the form to the left until the form is 5 3/8 inches in width and then drag the Form Footer upward so that the Detail section is about 5/8 inches high.

7. Choose Edit, Select Form to select the form; then click the Properties button on the toolbar to display the Properties window for the subform.

8. Click the Data tab in the Properties window so that the Allow Edits, Allow Deletions, and Allow Additions properties are visible.

9. Set the Allow Edits and Allow Deletions property value to **No**; this setting prevents the user from editing or deleting Personnel Action records displayed in this subform.

10. Close the sbfPersonnelActions subform and save your changes.

To see how the new form and subform look, open the frmPersonnelActions form; the adjusted form and subform should appear similar to Figure 12.22. Notice that there's no horizontal scroll bar and that the appearance and visibility of fields and column headings in the subform have improved. By changing the size of the subform control in the main form and resizing the subform to fit completely within the subform control (allowing room for the vertical scrollbar), the subform now fits completely in the main form. Notice also the tentative append record that is visible as the second record in the subform.

PART

III

CH

12

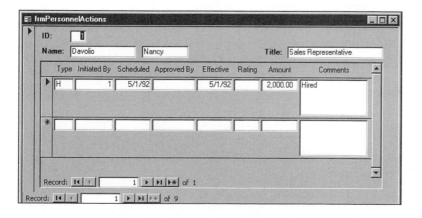

Figure 12.22
The completed frmPersonnelActions and sbfPersonnelActions forms in Form view.

Note

You can set the Data Entry property to Yes to achieve a result that is similar to setting the Allow Edits and Allow Deletions property to No and the Allow Additions property to Yes. When you set the Data Entry property to Yes, however, only the tentative new record appears—no prior entries appear in the subform.

USING TRANSACTION-PROCESSING FORMS

As noted near the beginning of this chapter, the purpose of transaction-processing forms is to add new records to, delete records from, or edit data in one or more tables that underlie the form. This section describes how to add new records to the Personnel Actions table with the frmPersonnelActions form.

TOOLBAR BUTTONS IN FORM VIEW

When you display your form in Run mode (Form view), the toolbar contains the command buttons listed in Table 12.4. This table lists all the buttons that appear on the toolbar, along with each button's function and the equivalent menu choice.

TABLE 12.4   STANDARD TOOLBAR BUTTONS IN FORM RUN MODE

Button	Function	Menu Choice
	Selects Form Design mode.	View, Design View
	Saves the form layout.	File, Save
	Prints the form.	File, Print
	Selects Print Preview to display how your form will appear if printed. You can print the form directly from the Print Preview window.	File, Print Preview
	Starts the spelling checker to check the spelling of the current selection or field.	Tools, Spelling
	Format Painter. This button is always disabled in Form view.	n/a
	Undoes the most recent change to a record.	Edit, Undo
	Inserts a new Hyperlink or allows you to edit an existing Hyperlink.	Insert, Hyperlink
	Sorts records in ascending order based on the current field.	Records, Sort, Ascending
	Sorts records in descending order based on the current field.	Records, Sort, Descending

Button	Function	Menu Choice
	Filters records based on selected text in a field.	Records, Filter, Filter by Selection
	Filters records based on criteria you enter in a form's fields.	Records, Filter, Filter by Form
	Applies a filter. Click this button a second time to show all records.	Records, Apply Filter/Sort or Records, Remove Filter/Sort
	Searches for a value in the selected field or in all fields. Displays the Find dialog.	Edit, Find
	Goes to the tentative append record.	Edit, Go To, New Record
	Deletes the current record.	Edit, Delete Record
	Displays the Properties window for the form and its objects in Form view.	View, Properties
	Gives the Database window the focus.	Window 1 Database
	Displays a drop-down list of new database objects.	n/a

NEW 2000

The Find button serves the same purpose for forms in Run mode as it does for tables and queries. You type characters in the Find dialog using wild cards if needed. When you execute the search, Access displays the first record that matches your entry if a match is found.

The Sort Ascending, Sort Descending, Filter by Selection, and Filter by Form buttons work the same way in Form view as they do in Datasheet view. Using these filter buttons is described in Chapter 6, "Sorting, Finding, and Filtering Data in Tables." Sorting specified in the form overrides the sort criteria of the primary query used as the source of the data (if your form is based on a query, rather than directly on one or more tables). The filter or sort criteria you specify don't take effect until you click the Apply Filter/Sort button or make the equivalent Records, Apply Filter/Sort menu choice.

Note

Some toolbar buttons are disabled as a result of your form design or its property values. For example, the Delete Record button is disabled when the Personnel Actions form is open because you've set the Allow Deletions property value to No for the both form and subform.

USING THE PERSONNEL ACTIONS FORM

Forms you create with the Form Wizard use the standard record-navigation buttons located at the bottom of the form. The record-navigation buttons perform the same functions with forms as they do with tables and queries. You can select the first or last records in the table or query that is the source of data for your main form, or you can select the next or previous record. Subforms always include their own set of record-selection buttons that operate independently of the set for the main form.

Navigation between the text boxes used for entering or editing data in the form is similar to navigation in queries and tables in Datasheet view except that the up-arrow and down-arrow keys cause the caret to move between fields rather than between records. Accept the values you've entered by pressing Enter or Tab.

APPENDING NEW RECORDS TO THE PERSONNEL ACTIONS TABLE

In the Datasheet view of a table or query, the last record in the datasheet is provided as a *tentative append record* (indicated by an asterisk on the record-selection button). If you enter data in this record, the data automatically is appended to the table and Access starts a new tentative append record. Forms also provide a tentative append record, unless you set the Allow Additions property for the form to No.

To append a new record to the Personnel Actions table and enter the required data, follow these steps:

 1. Open the frmPersonnelActions form if it isn't already open or click the Form View button if you're in Design view. Data for the first record of the Employees table—with the matching data from the corresponding record(s) in the Personnel Actions table—appears in the text-box controls of your form.

Because data from the Employees table is included in the main form, the ID number, name, and title of the employee appear in the text boxes on the main form. Your form design lets you edit the LastName, FirstName, and Title data, although these fields are incorporated in the table (Employees) on the one side of a one-to-many relationship. The editing capability of a form is the same as that for the underlying table or query that serves as its source unless you change the form's editing capabilities by setting the form's Allow Editing property and other related properties.

If you added an entry for the chosen employee ID when you created the Personnel Actions table in Chapter 4, the entry appears in the subform's fields. The subform's data display is linked to the data in the main form through the one-to-many relationship between the Employees table and the Personnel Actions table. The subform only displays records from the Personnel Actions table whose paID fields match the value of the EmployeeID field of the record currently displayed by the main form.

 2. Access places the caret in the first text box of the main form, the ID text box. The first example uses Steven Buchanan, whose employee ID is 5, so you should do the following: Click the Find button on the toolbar to open the Find dialog, type **5** in the Find What text box, make sure that the Search Only Current Field option is selected, and click Find First. Access displays the Employees table data for Steven Buchanan in the main form and his Personnel Actions records in the subform. Click Close to close the Find dialog.

3. Click in the Type field of the tentative append record in the subform. If the tentative append record in the subform isn't visible, click in any field in the subform and then click the New Record button on the toolbar to move to the tentative append record at the end of the existing Personnel Actions table entries for Steven Buchanan.

4. Type a valid Personnel Action type (H, S, Q, Y, B, or C, because of the field's validation rule) in the Type text box. Default date values appear in the Scheduled and Effective fields. In this example, you bring Steven Buchanan's Personnel Actions records up-to-date by adding quarterly performance review information. Press Tab or Enter to accept the Type and move the caret to the next data-entry text box, Initiated By.

Note

> The short date values in this version of the subform aren't Year 2000 (Y2K) compliant. Altering display formats for Y2K compliance is one of the subjects of the next chapter.

5. Mr. Buchanan reports to the vice president of sales, Andrew Fuller, whose employee ID is 2. Type **2** in the Initiated By text box and press Enter.

   The pencil symbol, which indicates that you're editing a record, replaces the triangle at the top of the Record Selector bar to the left of the record that you are entering. The Description property you entered for the field in the table underlying this query appears in the status bar and changes as you move the caret to the next field. (To change a previous entry, press Shift+Tab, or use the up- and down-arrow keys to maneuver to whichever text box contains a value you want to change.)

6. Mr. Buchanan was hired on 10/17/93, so his quarterly performance reviews should be about three months apart. Northwind Traders had no human resources (HR) department to maintain HR data until mid-1998, so accept the default scheduled date (today).

7. Because Mr. Fuller is a vice president, he has the authority to approve salary increases. Type Mr. Fuller's employee ID, **2**, in the Approved By text box and then press Enter to move the caret to the next field.

8. The effective date for salary adjustments for Northwind Traders is the 1st or 15th day of the month in which the performance review is scheduled. Type the appropriate date in the Effective text box.

9. You can type any number from **0** (terminated) to **9** (excellent) in the Rating text box, which reflects the employee's performance.

10. You can be as generous as you want with the salary increase that you enter in the New Amount text box. The value of the New Amount is a new monthly salary (or a new commission percentage), not an incremental value.

11. In the Comments multiline text box to the right of the New Amount field, add any comments you care to make concerning how generous or stingy you were with this salary increase. The multiline text box includes a scroll bar that appears when the caret is within the text box.

12. When you complete your entries, Access stores them in a memory buffer but does not add the new record to the Personnel Actions table. You can add the record to the table by doing any of the following: pressing Shift+Enter; choosing Records, Save Record; clicking the New Record button; or changing the position of the record pointer with the Prior or Next record selector button. If you want to cancel the addition of a record, press Esc.

13. Repeat steps 3 through 12 to add a few additional records.

Tip #110 from

If you click the New Record button on the toolbar (or the Next record selector button) and then decide that you don't want to add any more data, simply click the Prior button to make sure this new record is not added to the table. If the table has required fields without default values, however, you must enter a value for each required field, then delete the added record.

When adding a record, your form appears like the one shown in Figure 12.23. Each record for an employee appears in the subform datasheet in the order of the primary key fields of the Personnel Actions table.

Figure 12.23
The Personnel Actions form after appending subform records for a single employee.

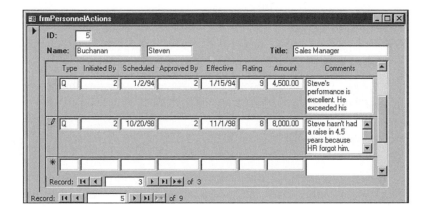

EDITING EXISTING DATA

You can edit existing records the same way you add new records. Use the Next button to find the record you want to edit and then make your changes. You can use the toolbar's Find button to locate records by employee ID, by one of the dates in the record, or by a word or phrase contained in the paComments field. If you prefer to order the records by paEffective date to find all records for which an effective date hasn't been entered, use the Filter by Form button and specify an Ascending Sort on the paEffective field. Click the Apply Filter button to apply the sort to the records.

COMMITTING AND ROLLING BACK CHANGES TO TABLES

As with tentative append records, Access doesn't apply record edits to the underlying table until you move the record pointer with the record-selection buttons (or choose Records, Save Record). Either action is the equivalent of the CommitTrans instruction in transaction-processing terminology.

 Rollback reverses a CommitTrans instruction. You can do the equivalent of rolling back a single transaction by clicking the Undo button on the toolbar immediately after you save the record to the table (or by choosing Edit, Undo Saved Record if that choice is available).

MODIFYING THE PROPERTIES OF A FORM OR CONTROL AFTER TESTING

The entries you added and edited gave you an opportunity to test your form. Testing a form to ensure that it accomplishes the objectives you have in mind usually takes much longer than creating the form and the query that underlies it. During the testing process, you might notice that the order of the fields isn't what you want or that records in the subform aren't displayed in an appropriate sequence. The following two sections deal with modifying the properties of the form and subform control.

CHANGING THE ORDER OF FIELDS FOR DATA ENTRY

The order in which the editing caret moves from one field to the next is determined by the Tab Order property of each control. The Form Wizard established the tab order of the controls when you first created the form. The default Tab Order property of each field is assigned, beginning with the value 0, in the sequence in which you add the fields. Because the Form Wizard created a single-column form, the order of the controls in Personnel Actions is top to bottom. The tab order originally assigned doesn't change when you relocate a control.

To change the sequence of entries—for example, to match the pattern of entries on a paper form—follow these steps:

1. Click the Design View button on the toolbar.
2. Choose View, Tab Order to display the Tab Order dialog shown in Figure 12.24. The order of entry is shown by the sequence of field names in the Custom Order list. (In this example, changing the sequence of the entries is unnecessary because the sequence is logical, even after moving the controls to their present locations on the Personnel Actions form.)
3. Click the Auto Order button if you want to reorder the entry sequence going left to right across each row of fields, then top to bottom.
4. Drag any control to a new location by clicking the button at the left of its name and dropping it wherever you want it to be in the sequence.

5. Click OK to implement the changes you made; click Cancel to retain the original entry sequence.

Using the Auto Order button to change the tab order of fields on a form also changes the left-to-right order of the table fields in Datasheet view to correspond to the Auto Order field sequence.

Figure 12.24
Changing the sequence of data-entry fields in the Tab Order dialog.

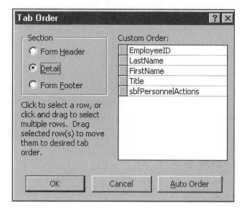

REMOVING FIELDS FROM THE TAB ORDER

Access 2000 lets you set the value of the Tab Stop property to No in order to prevent controls from receiving the focus in the tab order. To remove a control from the tab order, select the control, open the Properties window, select Other Properties, and change the value of Tab Stop property to **No**. You can't edit the EmployeeID field, so set the Tab Stop property to No for this control.

Tip #111 from

Setting the Tab Stop property's value to No doesn't disable a given control, but it removes the control from the tab sequence. As a result, the control can't be selected by pressing the Tab key, but can still be selected by clicking it with the mouse.

IN THE REAL WORLD—THE ART OF FORM DESIGN

Creating an effective form design for data entry requires a unique combination of graphic design and programming skills. Whether your goal is to develop conventional Access frontends for Jet or SQL Server databases, or to design Data Access Pages (DAP) that run over an intranet, the basic methodology of form design is the same. Large database development projects usually begin with a detailed specification for the database, plus a set of descriptions of each data display and entry form. Small- to medium-sized organizations, however, seldom have the resources to develop an all-encompassing specification before embarking on a project. If your objective is to develop from scratch Access forms for decision-support or online transaction processing (OLTP) applications, keep in mind the guidelines of this and the following chapter's "Real World" sections.

Understand the Audience

Your first task is to determine how your Access application fits into the organization's business processes. If the application is for decision support, determine its audience. Most executives want a broad-brush, organization-wide view of the data, which usually entails graphical presentation of the information. Generating graphs is the primary topic of Chapter 19, "Adding Charts and Graphics to Forms and Reports." Managers commonly request graphs or charts for trend analysis, together with tabular summary information for their area of responsibility. PivotTables, described in Chapter 20, "Using Access with Microsoft Excel," let managers "slice and dice" the data to present multiple views of the data. Supervisors need very detailed information to handle day-to-day employee performance and productivity issues. Thus your decision-support application is likely to require several forms, each tailored to the information needs of users at different levels in the organization's hierarchy.

OLTP front-ends differ dramatically from decision-support applications. A single-purpose OLTP form for online order entry differs dramatically from the interrelated multiple forms of a complex accounting system. For heads-down OLTP—typified by telephone order or reservation applications—keyboard-only data entry is the rule. One of the primary objectives of OLTP form design is minimizing operator fatigue; tired operators tend to enter inaccurate data. OLTP forms need to be simple, fast, and easily readable. Easy reading implies larger-than-standard fonts—at least 10 points—and subdued form colors.

Design in Client Monitor Resolution

You might have a 1,280×960 monitor and a 3-D graphics accelerator with 32-bit color depth, but it's not very likely that all of the users of your application are so fortunate. In the Access 2.0 era, designing for 640×480 resolution was the rule; in those days, most laptop and many desktop PCs had standard 256-color VGA displays. Today, most mobile and desktop PCs support at least 800×600 (SVGA) resolution. When designing your forms for SVGA resolution, switch to 800×600 display mode, even if you have a 21-inch monitor. Make sure to test your form designs with the 14- or 15-inch monitors that commonly are assigned to data-entry operators. If your application must support mobile users having a variety of laptop and notebook hardware, make sure to check for adequate contrast and text readability on laptop and notebook PCs with 10-inch or smaller passive- and active-matrix LCD displays. The low contrast of passive-matrix LCDs, especially in a well-lighted environment, presents the greatest challenge to form designers.

Strive for Consistency and Simplicity

Microsoft's goal for the Office suite is visual and operational consistency between members. Design your Access decision support-forms to emulate the "look and feel" of other Office

2000 members, especially Microsoft Excel. It's a likely bet that most decision-support users are familiar with Excel.

Simplicity is the watchword when designing OLTP forms. Provide only the elements—forms and controls—required for data-entry operators to get their work done. Above all, attempt to design a single form that handles all aspects of the OLTP process. Opening a new form for each step in the data entry process causes visual discontinuities that lead to operator fatigue. Substitute visually simple list boxes for read-only datasheets; show and hide the list boxes with VBA code to minimize screen clutter.

Figure 12.25 shows the single form of an Access demonstration OLTP application, A2koltp.mdb, in order lookup mode. A2KOLTP.mdb originated as a Microsoft Tech*Ed presentation for designers of Access 2.0 client/server OLTP front-ends. Typing the first letter or two of a customer name in the Bill To text box and pressing Return opens a list box of customer matches. Selecting the customer in the left list box with the down-arrow key and pressing return opens the right text box from which you select with the down-arrow key an existing order to review. Pressing return again fills the Ship To information text boxes and shows a list box of order line items (see Figure 12.26). Each command button and data field group has a shortcut key to eliminate the need for mouse operations. Many of the "Real World" sections of the remaining chapters of this book use A2koltp.mdb as an example of Access form and application design for production front-ends.

Figure 12.25
Selecting a customer and an open order in the single form of the A2koltp.mdb application.

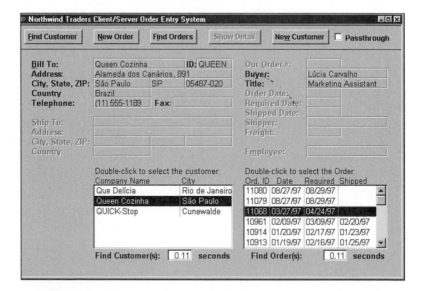

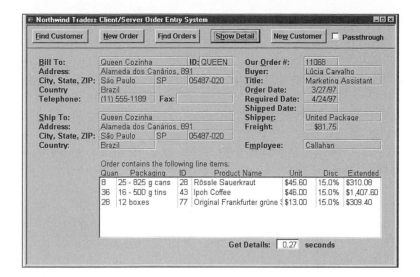

Figure 12.26
Shipping and line item information for the order selected in Figure 12.25.

--rj

CHAPTER **13**

DESIGNING CUSTOM MULTITABLE FORMS

In this chapter

Expanding Your Form Design Repertoire   480

Understanding the Access Toolbox   480

Completing the Main Personnel Actions Entry Form   521

Creating a Subform Using the Subform/Subreport Wizard   523

Modifying the Design of Continuous Forms   527

Overriding the Field Properties of Tables   528

Adding Page Headers and Footers for Printing Forms   529

Troubleshooting   530

In the Real World—Access Wizardry   531

EXPANDING YOUR FORM DESIGN REPERTOIRE

The controls that the Form Wizard adds to the forms it creates are only a sampling of the 17 *native control* objects offered by Access 2000. Native controls are built into Access; you also can add various ActiveX controls to Access forms. Until now, you used the Form Wizard to create the labels, text boxes, and subform controls for displaying and editing data in the Personnel Actions table. These three controls are sufficient for creating a conventional transaction processing form.

The remaining 14 controls described in this chapter let you take full advantage of the Windows graphical user environment. You add controls to the form by using the Access Toolbox. List and combo boxes increase data-entry productivity and accuracy by letting you select from a list of predefined values instead of requiring you to type the value. Option buttons, toggle buttons, and check boxes supply values to Yes/No fields. If you place option buttons, toggle buttons, and check boxes in an option frame, these controls determine the numeric value of the option frame. The Image control supplements the Bound and Unbound Object Frame controls for adding pictures to your forms. Page breaks control how forms print. Access 2000's Tab control lets you create tabbed forms to display related data on forms and subforms in a space-saving and more clearly organized fashion. Command buttons can execute Access VBA procedures.

NEW → The new form-related features of Access 2000 are listed at the beginning of the previous chapter;
2000 see "Creating and Using Forms," **page 433**.

UNDERSTANDING THE ACCESS TOOLBOX

The Access 2000 Toolbox is based on the Toolbox that Microsoft first created for Visual Basic. Essentially, the Access Toolbox is a variety of toolbar. You select one of the 20 buttons that appear in the Toolbox to add a native control, represented by that tool's symbol, to the form, so you can select a control, enable or disable the Control Wizards, or add a Microsoft or third-party ActiveX control to the form. When you create a report, the Toolbox serves the same purpose—although tools that require user input, such as combo boxes, seldom are used in reports.

CONTROL CATEGORIES

Three control object categories exist in Access forms and reports:

- *Bound controls* are associated with a field in the data source for the form or subform. The data source can be a table or query. Bound controls display and update values of the data cell in the associated field of the currently selected record. Text boxes are the most common bound control. You can display the content of graphic objects or play a waveform audio file with a bound OLE object. You can bind toggle buttons and check boxes to Yes/No fields. Option button groups bind to fields with numeric values. All bound controls have associated labels that display the Caption property of the field; you can edit or delete these labels without affecting the bound control.

- *Unbound controls* display data you provide that is independent of the form's or subform's data source. You use the unbound OLE object to add a drawing or bitmapped image to a form. You can use lines and rectangles to divide a form into logical groups or simulate boxes used on the paper form. Unbound text boxes are used to enter data that isn't intended to update a field in the data source but is intended for other purposes, such as establishing a value used in an expression. Some unbound controls, such as unbound text boxes, include labels; others, such as unbound OLE objects, don't have labels. Labels also are unbound controls.

- *Calculated controls* use expressions as their source of data. Usually, the expression includes the value of a field, but you also can use values created by unbound text boxes in calculated control expressions.

THE TOOLBOX

 You use the Access Toolbox to add control objects to forms and reports. The Toolbox appears only in Design mode for forms and reports, and it appears only if you click the Toolbox button on the toolbar or toggle the <u>V</u>iew, T<u>o</u>olbox menu choice. When the Toolbox is visible, the Toolbox menu choice is checked; Figure 13.1 shows the Toolbox in its default mode—a two-column floating toolbar. You can select one of the 17 controls and and three other buttons, whose names and functions are listed in Table 13.1.

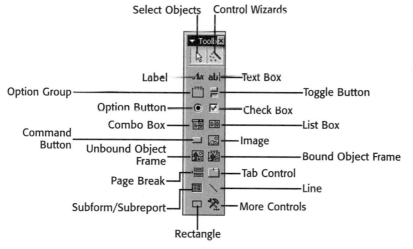

Figure 13.1
The Access 2000 Toolbox opened as a floating window.

PART

III

CH

13

TABLE 13.1 NAMES AND FUNCTIONS OF BUTTONS OF THE ACCESS TOOLBOX

Tool	Name	Function
	Select Objects	Changes mouse pointer to the object selection tool. Deselects a previously selected tool and returns the mouse pointer to normal selection function. Select Objects is the default tool when you open the Toolbox.
	Control Wizards	Turns the Control Wizards on and off. Control Wizards aid you in designing complex controls, such as option groups, list boxes, and combo boxes.
	Label	Creates a box that contains fixed descriptive or instructional text.
	Text Box	Creates a box to display and allow editing of text data.
	Option Group	Creates a frame of adjustable size in which you can place toggle buttons, option buttons, or check boxes. Only one of the objects within an object group frame may be selected. When you select an object within an option group, the previously selected object is deselected.
	Toggle Button	Creates a button that changes from On to Off when clicked. The On state corresponds to Yes (–1), and the Off state corresponds to No (0). When used within an option group, toggling one button On toggles a previously selected button Off. You can use toggle buttons to let the user select one value from a set of values.
	Option Button	Creates a round button (originally called a *radio button*) that behaves identically to a toggle button. Option buttons are most commonly used within option groups to select between values in a set where the choices are mutually exclusive.
	Check Box	Creates a check box that toggles On and Off. Multiple check boxes should be used outside option groups so that you can select more than one check box at a time.
	Combo Box	Creates a combo box with an editable text box where you can enter a value, as well as a list from which you can select a value from a set of choices.
	List Box	Creates a dropdown list box from which you can select a value. A list box is simply the list portion of a combo box.
	Command Button	Creates a command button that, when clicked, triggers an event that can execute an Access VBA event-handling procedure.
	Image	Displays a static graphic on a form or report. This is not an OLE image, so you can't edit it after placing it on the form.
	Unbound Object	Adds an OLE object created by an OLE server application, such as Microsoft Chart or Paint, to a form or report.

Tool	Name	Function
	Bound Object	Displays the content of an OLE field of a record if the field contains a graphic object. If the field contains no graphic object, the icon that represents the object appears, such as the Sound Recorder's icon for a linked or embedded .wav file.
	Page Break	Causes the printer to start a new page at the location of the page break on the form or report. Page breaks don't appear in form or report Run mode.
	Tab Control	Inserts a tab control to create tabbed forms. (The tab control looks like the tabbed pages you've seen in the Properties windows and dialogs throughout this book.) Pages of a tab control can contain other bound or unbound controls, including subform/subreport controls.
	Subform	Adds a subform or subreport to a main form or report, respectively. The subform or subreport you intend to add must exist before you use this control.
	Line	Creates a straight line that you can size and relocate. The color and width of the line can be changed by using the Formatting toolbar buttons or the Properties window.
	Rectangle	Creates a rectangle that you can size and relocate. The border color, width, and fill color of the rectangle are determined by selections from the palette.
	More Controls	Clicking this tool opens a scrolling list of ActiveX controls that you can use in your forms and reports. The ActiveX controls available through the More Controls list aren't part of Access; ActiveX controls are supplied as .ocx files with Office 2000, Visual Basic, and various third-party tool libraries.

Using controls in the design of reports is discussed in the following two chapters, "Printing Basic Reports and Mailing Labels" and "Preparing Advanced Reports." The use of bound and unbound OLE objects is described in Chapter 19, "Adding Charts and Graphics to Forms and Reports." Using command buttons to execute Access VBA code is covered in Part VII of this book, "Programming and Converting Access Applications." You learn how to use the remaining 14 controls on your forms in the following sections.

ACCESS'S CONTROL WIZARDS, BUILDERS, AND TOOLBARS

Access provides a number of features to aid you in designing and using more complex forms. Three of these features—Control Wizards, Builders, and customizable toolbars—are described in the three sections that follow.

ACCESS CONTROL WIZARDS

Much of the success of Access is attributable to the Form Wizard, Report Wizard, and Chart Wizard that simplify the process of creating database objects. The first wizard appeared in Microsoft Publisher, and most of Microsoft's productivity applications now include a variety of wizards. Chapter 12, "Creating and Using Forms," introduced the Form Wizard; the Report Wizard is discussed in Chapter 14 and the Chart Wizard is described in Chapter 19. In this chapter, you are introduced to a Control Wizard each time you add a control for which a wizard is available.

ACCESS BUILDERS

Builders are another feature that makes Access easy to use. You use the Expression Builder, introduced in Chapter 4, "Working with Access Databases and Tables," to create expressions that supply values to calculated controls on a form or report. The Query Builder creates the SQL statements you need when you create list boxes or combo boxes whose Row Source property is an SQL statement that executes a select query. The Query Builder is described in the section "Using the Query Builder to Populate a Combo Box" near the end of this chapter.

CUSTOMIZABLE TOOLBARS

The preceding chapters demonstrated that Access toolbars include many shortcut buttons to expedite designing and using Access database objects. Access 2000, like most other contemporary Microsoft applications, lets you customize the toolbars to your own set of preferences. Access 2000 stores customized toolbars in System.mdw. Toolbars that you create yourself are stored in a hidden system table—MSysCmdbars—in each database.

You can convert conventional floating design tools, such as the Toolbox, to conventional toolbars by the drag-and-drop method. To anchor the Toolbox as a toolbar, also called *docking the toolbar*, follow these steps:

1. Press and hold down the mouse button while the mouse pointer is on the Toolbox's title bar, and drag the Toolbox toward the top of Access's parent window.

   When the Toolbox reaches the toolbar area, the dotted outline changes from a rectangle approximately the size of the Toolbox into a wider rectangle only as high as a toolbar.

2. Release the mouse button to change the Toolbox to an anchored toolbar positioned below the standard Form Design toolbar.

Tip #112 from

R J

You can anchor or dock a toolbar to any edge of Access's parent window. Press and hold down the mouse button on an empty area of the toolbar (not covered by a button), and drag the toolbar until its outline appears along the left, right, or bottom edge of the window. If you drop the toolbar within the confines of Access's main window, it becomes a floating toolbar.

You can add or delete buttons from toolbars with the Customize Toolbars dialog. To add form design utility buttons to the Toolbox toolbar (whether it's docked or floating), do the following:

1. Choose View, Toolbars, Customize to display the Customize dialog. Alternatively, click the down arrow at the top left of the Toolbox, choose Add or Remove Buttons from the context menu, and select Customize from the button list.

Tip #113 from

You can also open the Customize dialog by right-clicking any part of a toolbar and choosing Customize on the resulting context menu.

---

2. Click the Commands tab, and select Form/Report Design from the Categories list. The optional buttons applicable to form design operations appear in the Commands list, as shown in Figure 13.2.

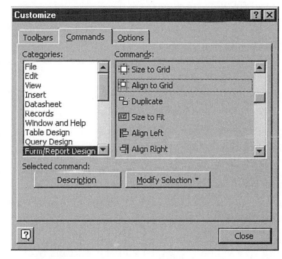

Figure 13.2
The Toolbox with the Align to Grid command added and the open Customize dialog used to add commands.

3. The most useful optional buttons for form design are control alignment and sizing buttons. Press and hold down the mouse button on the Align to Grid command, drag this button to the Toolbox toolbar, and drop it to the right of the Rectangle button. The right margin of the Toolbox toolbar expands to accommodate the new button (if you customize the Toolbox while it's floating, the window expands to accommodate the new button). You can drag the Align to Grid button slightly to the right to create a gap between the new button and the Rectangle button.

4. Repeat step 3 for the Size to Fit, Size to Grid, and Align Left commands, dropping each button to the right of the preceding button. You now have four new and useful design buttons available in your Toolbox.

The Customize dialog for toolbars provides the following additional capabilities:

- To remove buttons from the toolbar, open the Customize dialog; click and drag the buttons you don't want, and drop them anywhere off the toolbar.

- To reset the toolbar to its default design, open the Customize dialog. In the Toolbars list, select the toolbar you want to reset, and click the Reset button. A message box asks you to confirm that you want to abandon any changes you made to the toolbar.

- To create a button that opens or runs a database object, open the Customize dialog, display the Commands page, and scroll the Categories list to display the All *Objects* items. When, for example, you select All Tables, the tables of the current database appear in the Commands list. Select a table name, such as Employees, and drag the selected item to an empty spot on a toolbar. The ScreenTip for the new button displays Open Table 'Employees'. (If you select All Macros and drag a macro object to the toolbar, the button you add runs the macro when clicked.)

- To substitute text or a different image for the picture on the buttons you add to a toolbar, open the Customize dialog. Click the button you want to change with the right mouse button to display the button shortcut menu. Click Choose Button Face to display the Choose Button Face dialog. Click one of the images offered, or click the Text check box and type the text you want to display in the text box. To edit the button's image, click Edit Button Image.

- To create a new empty toolbar that you can customize with any set of the supplied buttons you want, open the Customize dialog and select Utility 1 or Utility 2 on the Toolbars page. If there's space to the right of an existing toolbar, the empty toolbar appears in this space. Otherwise, Access creates a new toolbar row for the empty toolbar. The Utility 1 and Utility 2 toolbars and the changes you make to them are available in any Access database you open.

- To create a custom toolbar that becomes part of your currently open database, open the Customize dialog and click New on the Toolbars page. The New Toolbar dialog appears, requesting a name for the new toolbar (Custom 1 is the default). Access creates a new floating tool window to which you add buttons from the Commands page of the Customize dialog. You can anchor the custom tool window to the toolbar, if you want.

- To delete a custom toolbar, open the Customize dialog, select the custom toolbar on the Toolbars page, and click the Delete button. You are requested to confirm the deletion. The Delete button is disabled when you select one of Access's standard toolbars in the list.

Custom toolbars to which you assign names become part of your database application and are stored in the current database file; they are available only when the database in which they are stored is open. Built-in Access toolbars that you customize are stored in System.mdw and are available in any Access work session.

USING THE TOOLBOX TO ADD CONTROLS

Using the Form Wizard or the AutoForm feature of Access 2000 simplifies the generation of standard forms for displaying and updating data in tables. Creating forms in Form Design view by adding controls from the Toolbox provides much greater design flexibility than automated form generation. The examples in this chapter use the Personnel Actions table that you created in Chapter 4, and a query, qryPersonnelActions, which you create in the next section. If you haven't created the Personnel Actions table, you can import it from the Persacts.mdb database in the \Chaptr12 folder of the accompanying CD-ROM.

→ **See** "Creating the Personnel Actions Table," **p. 160**.

CREATING THE QUERY ON WHICH TO BASE THE MAIN FORM

The Personnel Actions table identifies employees only by their ID numbers, located in the paID field. As before, you need to display the employee's name and title on the form to avoid entering records for the wrong person. The form design example in this chapter uses a one-to-many query to provide a single source of data for the Personnel Actions form.

To create the Personnel Actions query that serves as the data source for your main form, follow these steps:

1. Close any open Northwind forms, click the Table shortcut of the Database window, and select Personnel Actions in the table list. Click the New Query button to open the New Query dialog, and click OK with Design View selected to open Query1 with the Personnel Actions table added.

2. Click the Show Table button on the toolbar to open the Show Table dialog, and add the Employees table to your query.

3. If you defined relationships for the Personnel Action table as described in Chapter 4, the upper pane of the query window appears, as shown in Figure 13.3. The line connecting the two tables indicates that a many-to-one relationship exists between the paID field in the Personnel Action table and the EmployeeID field of the Employees table.

   If you didn't define any relationships, the join line doesn't appear. In this case, you need to drag the paID field from the Personnel Actions field list to the EmployeeID field of the Employees field list to create a join between these two fields.

PART

III

CH

13

Figure 13.3
The upper pane of the Query Design window for the Personnel Actions query.

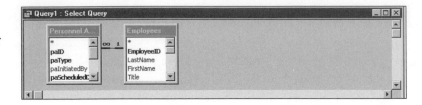

5. Click the * field of the Personnel Actions table, drag it to and drop it in the first column of the Query Design grid. This adds all the fields to the Personnel Actions table to your query.

6. Click the LastName field of the Employees table, drag it to the Query grid, and drop it in the second column.

7. From the Employees table, click and drag the FirstName, Title, HireDate, Extension, ReportsTo, Photo, and Notes fields. Drop them in columns 3, 4, 5, 6, 7, 8, and 9 of the Query grid, respectively, as shown in Figure 13.4.

Figure 13.4
The Query grid for the Personnel Actions query.

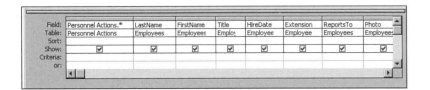

8. To simplify finding an employee, click the Sort row of the LastName column and select an Ascending sort.

 9. Click the Run button of the toolbar to check your work, and then close the new query. Click Yes when the message box asks if you want to save the query.

10. In the Save As dialog, name the query **qryPersonnelActions** and click OK.

Now that you've created the query that provides a unified record source for the main form, you're ready to begin creating your custom multitable form.

CREATING A BLANK FORM WITH A HEADER AND FOOTER

When you create a form without using the Form Wizard, Access opens a default blank form to which you add controls that you select from the Toolbox. To open a blank form to begin duplicating the form you created with the Form Wizard in Chapter 12, do the following:

1. In the Database window, click the Forms shortcut, and click the New button to open the New Form dialog.

2. With the default Design View selected in the upper list of the New Form dialog, select qryPersonnelActions in the lower dropdown list (see Figure 13.5). Click OK.

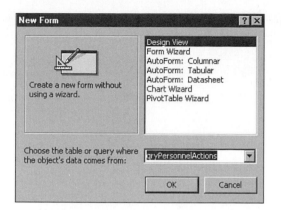

Figure 13.5
Selecting qryPersonnelActions as the data source of the form in the New Form dialog.

3. Access creates a new blank form with the default title Form1 with the Toolbox and the field list for the qryPersonnelActions query. Click the Maximize button of the Form Design window to expand the form to fill the document window and dock the Toolbox at the top of the form.

   If the Toolbox or field list isn't visible, click the appropriate button on the Form Design (top) toolbar.

4. Choose View, Form Header/Footer. If the grid doesn't appear on the form, choose View, Grid.

   The default width of blank forms is 5 inches. The default height of the Form Header and Footer sections is 0.25 inch, and the height of the Detail section is 2 inches.

5. To adjust the height of the form's Detail section, place the mouse pointer on the top line of the Form Footer bar. The mouse pointer becomes a double-headed arrow with a line between the heads. Hold down the left mouse button and drag the bar to create a Detail section height of about 3.0 inches, measured by the left vertical ruler. The active surface of the form, which is gray with the default 24×24 grid dots, expands vertically as you move the Form Footer bar downward, as shown in Figure 13.6.

6. Minimize the Form Footer section by dragging the bottom margin of the form to the bottom of the Form Footer bar.

7. Drag the right margin of the form to 6 inches as measured by the horizontal ruler at the top of the form.

You're using the blank form to create a form similar to the frmPersonnelActions form that you created in Chapter 12.

Figure 13.6
Expanding the Detail
section of the blank form.

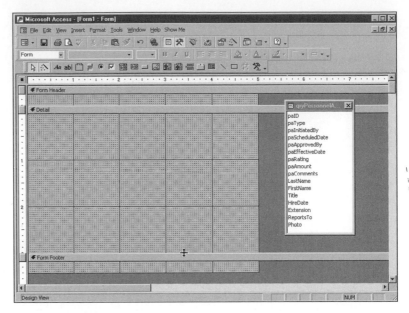

ADDING A LABEL TO THE FORM HEADER

The label is the simplest control in the Toolbox to use. Labels are *unbound* and *static*, and they display only the text you enter. *Static* means that the label retains the value you originally assigned as long as the form is displayed. To add a label to the Form Header section, complete the following steps:

1. Click the Label button in the Toolbox. When you move the mouse pointer to the form's active area, the pointer becomes the symbol for the Label button, combined with a crosshair—the center point of the crosshair defines the position of the control's upper-left corner.

2. Locate the crosshair at the upper-left of the Form Header section. Press and hold down the left mouse button while you drag the crosshair to the position for the lower-right corner of the label (see Figure 13.7).

   As you drag the crosshair, the outline of the container for the label follows your movement. The number of lines and characters that the text box can display in the currently selected font is shown in the status bar.

3. If you move the crosshair beyond the bottom of the Form Header section, the Form Header bar expands to accommodate the size of the label after you release the left mouse button. When the label is the size you want, release the mouse button.

4. The mouse pointer becomes the text editing caret inside the outline of the label. Type **Personnel Action Entry** as the text for the label, and click anywhere outside the label to finish its creation. If you don't type at least one text character in a label after creating it, the box disappears the next time you click the mouse.

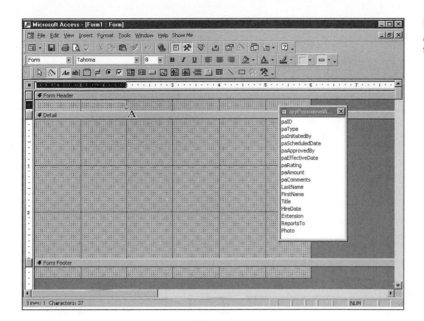

Figure 13.7
Adding a label control to
the Form Header.

→ For tips on manipulating elements of a form, **see** "Selecting, Moving, and Sizing a Single Control,"
p. 458.

You use the basic process described in the preceding steps to add most of the other types of
controls to a form. (Some Toolbox buttons, such as the graph and command buttons,
launch a Control Wizard to help you create the control if the Control Wizards button is
activated.) After you add the control, you use the anchor and sizing handles described in
Chapter 12 to move the control to the desired position and to size the control to accommodate the content. The location of the anchor handle determines the Left (horizontal) and
Top (vertical) properties of the control. The sizing handles establish the control's Width
and Height properties.

FORMATTING TEXT AND ADJUSTING TEXT CONTROL SIZES

When you select a control that accepts text as the value, the typeface and font size combo
boxes appear on the toolbar. To format the text that appears in a label or text box, do the
following:

1. Click the Personnel Action Entry label you created in the preceding section to select
   the label, and click the Properties button of the toolbar to open the Properties window
   for the label. Alternatively, double-click the unselected label.

NEW 2000

2. Open the Font list on the Formatting toolbar and select the typeface family you want.

   Arial   ▼   Tahoma, the default, is Access 2000's new default font.
   (MS Sans Serif was the default typeface in previous
   versions of Access).

   `10 ▼` 3. Open the Font Size list and select 14 points.

4. Click the Bold attribute button on the toolbar.

5. The size of the label you created isn't large enough to display the larger font. To adjust the size of the label to accommodate the content of the label, click the Size to Fit button—if you added it to the Toolbox—or choose F<u>o</u>rmat, <u>S</u>ize, To <u>F</u>it. Access resizes the label's text box to display the entire label; if necessary, Access also increases the size of the Form Header section.

Tip #114 from

The two F<u>o</u>rmat commands—<u>S</u>ize, To <u>G</u>rid and <u>S</u>ize, To <u>F</u>it—work slightly differently, depending on whether one or more controls are selected. If one or more controls are selected when you execute one of the sizing commands, the command is applied to the selected control(s). If no controls are selected, the chosen sizing command applies as the default to all objects you subsequently create, move, or resize.

When you change the properties of a control, the new values are reflected in the Properties window for the control, as shown in Figure 13.8. If you move or resize the label, you see the label's Left, Top, Width, and Height values change in the Properties window. You usually use the Properties window to actually change the characteristics of a control only if a toolbar button or menu choice isn't available.

Figure 13.8
The form title label and its Properties window.

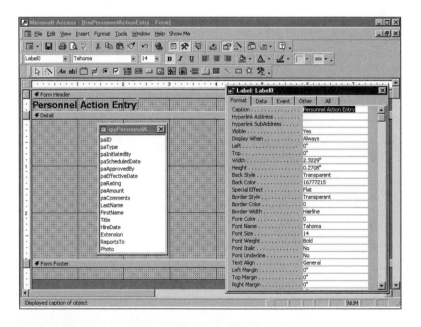

You can select different fonts and the Bold, Italic, and Underline attributes (or a combination) for any label or caption for a control. You can assign the text content of list boxes and combo boxes to a typeface or size other than the default, but this practice is uncommon in Windows applications.

CREATING BOUND, MULTILINE, AND CALCULATED TEXT BOXES

Access uses the following four basic kinds of text boxes:

- *Single-line text boxes* are usually bound to controls on the form or to fields in a table or query.

- *Multiline text boxes* are usually bound to Memo field types and include a vertical scroll bar to allow access to text that doesn't fit within the box's dimensions.

- *Calculated text boxes* obtain values from expressions that begin with = (equal sign) and are usually a single line. If you include a field value, such as [paScheduledDate], in the expression for a calculated text box, the text box is bound to that field. Otherwise, calculated text boxes are unbound. You cannot edit the value of a calculated text box.

- *Unbound text boxes* can be used to supply values—such as limiting dates—to Access VBA procedures. An unbound text box that doesn't contain a calculation expression can be edited.

The following sections show you how to create the first three types of text boxes.

ADDING TEXT BOXES BOUND TO FIELDS

The most common text box used in Access forms is the single-line bound text box that makes up the majority of the controls for the frmPersonnelActions form of Chapter 12. To add a text box that's bound to a field of the form's data source with the field list window, do the following:

1. If necessary, click the Field List button of the toolbar to redisplay the field list.

2. Click and drag the paID field in the field list window to the upper-left corner of the form's Detail section. When you move the mouse pointer to the active area of the form, the pointer becomes a field symbol, but no crosshair appears. The position of the field symbol indicates the upper-left corner of the text box, not the label, so drop the symbol in the approximate position of the text box anchor handle, as shown in Figure 13.9.

3. Drag the text box by the anchor handle closer to the ID label, and decrease the box's width.

4. Small type sizes outside a field text box are more readable when you turn the Bold attribute on. Select the ID label and click the Bold button.

PART
III

CH
13

Note

When Access creates a label for a text box that's associated with a form control, the bound object's name is the value for the text label. If the form control is bound to a table object, such as a field, that has a Caption property (and the Caption property isn't empty), Access uses the value of the Caption property as the default value for the text label of the bound form control. When you created the Personnel Actions table in Chapter 4, you set the Caption property for each field name. The paID field has a Caption property set to ID, so the label for the text box bound to the paID field is also ID.

Figure 13.9
Adding a text box control
bound to the paID field.

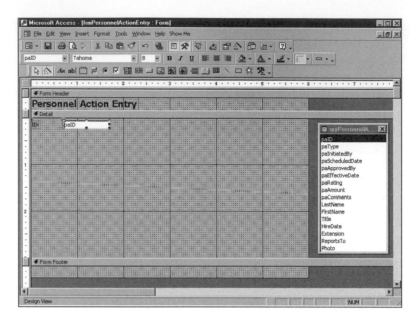

 5. Drag the paComments field from the list box to the form about 0.75 inch below the ID
label, delete the label, and resize the text box to the approximate dimensions shown in
Figure 13.10. When you add a text box bound to a memo field, Access automatically
sets the Scrollbars property to Vertical.

6. Choose File, Save, and type the name **frmPersonnelActionEntry** in the Form Name
text box of the Save As dialog. Click OK.

ADDING A CALCULATED TEXT BOX AND FORMATTING DATE/TIME VALUES

You can display the result of all valid Access expressions in a calculated text box. An expression must begin with = and may use Access functions to return values. As mentioned in the introduction to this section, you can use calculated text boxes to display calculations based on the values of fields. To create a calculated text box that displays the current date and time, do the following:

 1. Close the field list and Properties windows. Click the Text Box tool in the Toolbox, and
add an unbound text box at the right of the Form Header section of the form.

B 2. Edit the label of the new text box to read Date/Time:, and relocate the label so that it
is adjacent to the text box. Apply the Bold attribute to the label.

3. Type **=Now** in the text box to display the current date and time from your computer's
clock; Access adds a trailing parenthesis pair for you. Adjust the width of the label and
the text box to accommodate the approximate length of the text.

4. Click the View button to change to Form view and inspect the default date format,
MM/DD/YY HH:MM:SS AM/PM for North America. The default date format
doesn't comply with Year 2000 (Y2K) standards unless you've selected Four-Digit Year
Y2K Formatting in the General page of the Options dialog.

NEW
2000

5. To assure compliance with Y2K standards and delete the seconds value, open the Properties window for the text box, and click the Format tab. Select the Format property and type **mm/dd/yyyy hh:nn ampm** in the text box.

6. Click the View button to switch to Form view. Your reformatted Date/Time text box appears, as shown in Figure 13.10. Access 2000 lets you alter properties of text boxes and other controls in Form and Form Design views.

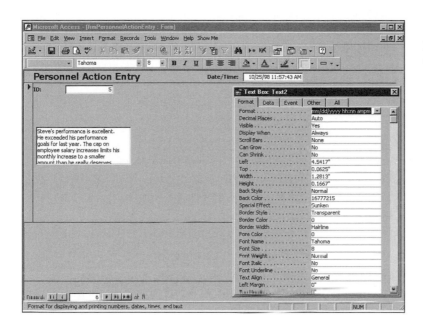

Figure 13.10
An unbound Date/Time text box formatted for Y2K conformance.

USING THE CLIPBOARD WITH CONTROLS

You can use the Windows Clipboard to easily make copies of controls and their properties. As an example, create a copy of one of the Date/Time control using the Clipboard by performing the following steps:

1. Return to Form Design mode and select the unbound Date/Time control and its label by clicking the field text box. Both the label and the text box are selected, as indicated by the selection handles on both controls.

2. Copy the selected control to the Clipboard by pressing Ctrl+C.

3. Click the Detail bar to select the Detail section, and paste the copy of the control below the original version by pressing Ctrl+V.

4. Click the Format property in the Properties window for the copied control, and select Long Date from the dropdown list.

5. To check the appearance of the controls you've created, click the View button on the toolbar.

PART

III

CH

13

6. Return to Design view and delete the added Date/Time text box and label. To do so, enclose both with a selection boundary created by dragging the mouse pointer across the text boxes from the upper-left to the lower-right corner. Press Delete. (You need the Date/Time text box only in the Form Header section for this form.)

CHANGING THE DEFAULT VIEW AND OBTAINING HELP FOR PROPERTIES

A form that fills Access's Design window might not necessarily fill the window in Run mode. Run mode may allow the beginning of a second copy of the form to appear. The second copy is created because the Default View property has a value of Continuous Forms. (In Access 2.0, the default property value for Default view was Continuous Forms; in Access 95 and 2000, the default value of Default view is Single Form—your test form won't show the second form at the bottom of the screen.) Forms have the following three Default View property values from which you can choose:

- *Single Form* displays one record at a time in one form.

- *Continuous Forms* displays multiple records, each record having a copy of the form's Detail section. You can use the vertical scroll bar or the record selection buttons to select which record to display. Continuous Forms view is the default value for subforms created by the Form Wizard.

- *Datasheet* displays the form fields arranged in rows and columns.

To change the form's Default View property, do the following:

1. Click the View button on the toolbar to return to Form Design view.

2. Choose Edit, Select Form.

3. Click the Properties button on the toolbar if the Properties window isn't visible. Click the Format tab in the Properties window.

4. Click the Default View property to open the list.

5. Select the value you want for this property for the current form. For this exercise, select Single Form (the default) from the list.

6. While Default view is selected, press F1. The Help window for the Default View property appears. This Help window also explains how the Default View and Views Allowed properties relate to each another.

   The vertical scroll bar disappears from the form in Run mode if a single form fits within its MDI child window.

You can verify your changes to the Default View property by clicking the View button to review the form's appearance.

ADDING OPTION GROUPS WITH THE WIZARD

Option buttons, toggle buttons, and check boxes can return only Yes/No (–1/0 or True/False) values when used by themselves on a form. Here, their use as bound controls is limited to providing values to Yes/No fields in a table. When you place any of these controls within an option group, the buttons or check boxes can return a number you specify for the control's Option Value property.

The capability of assigning numbers to the Option Value property lets you use one of the preceding three controls inside an option group frame for assigning values to the paRating field of the Personnel Actions table. Option buttons are most commonly used in Windows applications to select one value from a limited number of values.

By default, all controls you add with the Toolbox are unbound controls. You can bind a control to a field by selecting the control you want to use and clicking the field name in the Field List window to which you want the control bound. Another way of binding a control is to create an unbound control with a tool, and type the name of a field in the Control Source property text box (reach the Control Source text box by clicking the Data tab in the Properties window for the control).

The Option Group Wizard is one of three Control Wizards that take you step by step through the creation of complex controls. To create an option group for the paRating field of the Personnel Actions table with the Option Group Wizard, follow these steps:

1. Click the Control Wizards tool to turn on the wizards if the toggle button isn't On (the default value). Toggle buttons indicate the On (True) state with a sunken appearance.

2. Click the Option Group tool, position the pointer where you want the upper-left corner of the option group, and click the mouse button to display the first dialog of the Option Group Wizard.

3. Type five of the nine ratings in the Label Names datasheet: **Excellent**, **Good**, **Acceptable**, **Fair**, and **Poor** (see Figure 13.11). Click the Next button to display the second dialog of the Option Group Wizard, shown in Figure 13.12.

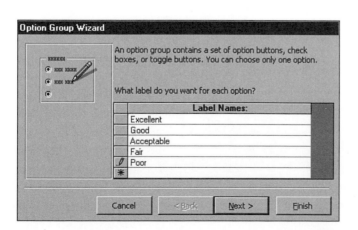

Figure 13.11
Specifying option button captions in the opening dialog of the Option Group Wizard.

Figure 13.12
Choosing a default value
for the options group.

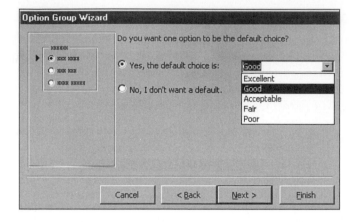

4. The second dialog lets you set an optional default value for the option group. Select
   the option named Yes, the Default Choice Is, and open the dropdown list. Select Good,
   as shown in Figure 13.12, and click Next. If you need to, you can always return to the
   previous step by clicking Back.

5. The third dialog of the Option Group Wizard provides for the assignment of option
   values to each option button of the group. Type **9**, **7**, **5**, **3**, and **1** in the five text boxes,
   as illustrated in Figure 13.13, and click the Next button.

   The domain integrity rule for the paRating field provides for nine different ratings.
   Nine option buttons, however, occupy too much space on a form, so only five of the
   nine ratings are provided here.

Figure 13.13
Assigning the numeric
OptionValue property to
the option buttons.

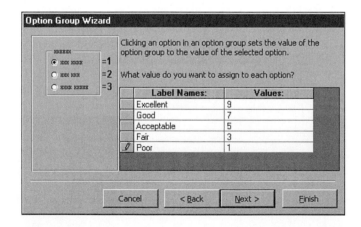

6. The fourth Option Group Wizard dialog lets you bind the option frame to a field of a table or a column of a query that acts as the Record Source of the bound form. Select the paRating column of the qryPersonnelActions query to which your form is bound (see Figure 13.14). Click Next to continue with the next stage of the wizard.

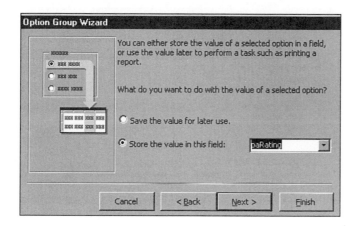

Figure 13.14
Binding the option group to a column of the form's Record Source.

7. The fifth dialog lets you determine the style of the option group, as well as the type of controls (option buttons, check boxes, or toggle buttons) to add to the option group. You can preview the appearance of your option group and button style choices in the Sample pane. For this example, accept the defaults, Option Buttons and Etched (see Figure 13.15).

The sunken and raised styles of option groups, option buttons, and check boxes are applicable only to control objects on forms with a Back Color property other than white.

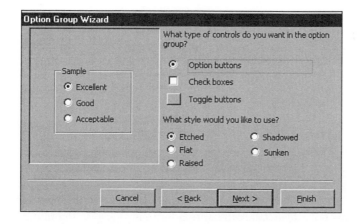

Figure 13.15
Selecting a style for the option group and determining the type of button to add.

PART

III

CH

13

8. The last dialog provides a text box for entering the value of the Caption property of the label for the option group. Type **Rating**, as shown in Figure 13.16, and click Finish to let the wizard complete its work. Your completed Rating option group appears as shown in Figure 13.17.

Figure 13.16
Assigning the value of the Caption property for the option group's label.

Figure 13.17
The option group created by the Option Group Wizard.

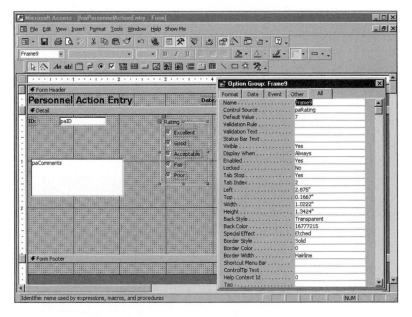

To test your new bound option group, add a text box that is bound to the paRating column of the query underlying the form. Figure 13.18 shows the option group in Form view with the space between the buttons closed up, the Bold attribute applied to the option group label, and the Rating text box added. Click the option buttons to display the rating value in the text box.

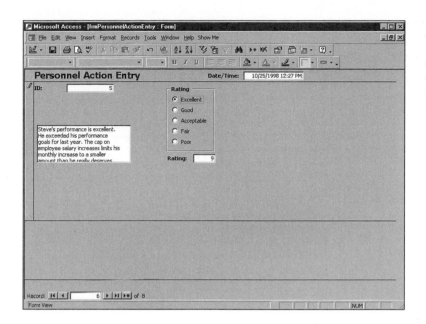

Figure 13.18
The new option group in
Form view with a text box
for the Rating field added
to show the effect of
selecting different
options.

USING THE CLIPBOARD TO COPY CONTROLS TO ANOTHER FORM

Access's capability of copying controls and their properties to the Windows Clipboard
allows you to create controls on one form and copy them to another. If you use a standard
header style, you can copy the controls in the header of a previously designed form to a new
form and edit the content as necessary. The form that contains the controls to be copied
need not be in the same database as the destination form in which the copy is pasted. You
can create a library of standard controls in a dedicated form that is used only for holding
standard controls.

The Time/Date calculated text box is a candidate to add to Chapter 12's
frmPersonnelActions form. You might want to add a Time/Date text box to the Form
Header or Detail section of all your transaction forms. To add the Time/Date control to
the frmPersonnelActions form, do the following:

1. Click the Design View button, and select the Time/Date control and its label by clicking the field text box.

2. Press Ctrl+C to copy the selected control(s) to the Clipboard.

3. Press F11, and open the frmPersonnelActions form from the Database window in
   Design mode.

4. Click the Detail section selection bar, and press Ctrl+V. A copy of the control appears
   at the upper-left corner of the Detail section.

   Controls are pasted to the section of the form that is presently selected. You cannot
   drag controls between sections of a form.

5. Position the mouse pointer over the copied option group so that the pointer becomes a hand symbol.

6. Hold down the mouse button and drag the option group to a position under the Title label and text box.

 7. Click the View button on the toolbar. The Personnel Action Entry form in Run mode appears, as shown in Figure 13.19.

 8. Return to Design mode, click the Save button to save your changes, and close the frmPersonnelActions form.

⚡ *If you receive an error message when the focus moves to controls you've copied to another form, **see** "Error Messages on Copied Controls" in "Troubleshooting" near the end of this chapter.*

Figure 13.19
The added Date/Time text box displayed in Form view.

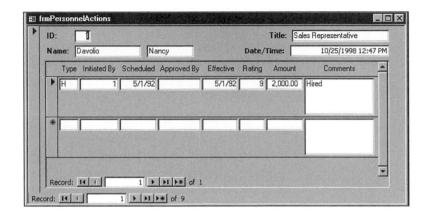

USING COMBO AND LIST BOXES

Combo and list boxes both serve the same basic purpose by letting you pick a value from a list, rather than type the value in a text box. These two kinds of list boxes are especially useful when you need to enter a code that represents the name of a person, firm, or product. You don't need to refer to a paper list of the codes and names to make the entry. The following list describes the differences between combo and list boxes:

■ *Dropdown combo boxes and dropdown lists* consume less space than list boxes in the form, but you must open these controls to select a value. Combo boxes in Access are dropdown lists plus a text box, not traditional combo boxes that display the list at all times. You can allow the user to enter a value in the text box element of the dropdown combo list or limit the selection to just the members in the dropdown list. If you limit the choice to members of the dropdown list (sometimes called a *pick list*), the user can still use the edit box to type the beginning of the list value—Access searches for a matching entry. This feature reduces the time needed to locate a choice in a long list.

■ *List boxes* don't need to be opened to display their content; the portion of the list that fits within the size of the list box you assign is visible at all times. Your choice is limited to values included in the list.

In the majority of cases, you bind the dropdown list or combo box to a field so that the choice updates the value of this field. Two-column controls are most commonly used. The first column contains the code that updates the value of the field to which the control is bound, and the second column contains the name associated with the code. An example of when a limit-to-list, multiple-column, dropdown list is most useful is assigning supervisor and manager employee ID numbers to the paInitiatedBy and paApprovedBy fields in the frmPersonnelActionsEntry form.

USING THE COMBO BOX WIZARD

Designing combo boxes is a more complex process than creating an option group, so you're likely to use the Combo Box Wizard for all the combo boxes you add to forms. Follow these steps to use the Combo Box Wizard to create the paInitiatedBy dropdown list that lets you select from a list of Northwind Traders' employees:

1. Open the frmPersonnelActionsEntry form (that you created and saved earlier in this chapter) from the Database window in Design mode if it is not presently open.

2. Click the Control Wizards button, if necessary, so that the wizards are turned on.

3. Click the Combo Box tool in the Toolbox. The mouse pointer turns into a combo box symbol while on the active surface of the form.

4. Click the Field List button to display the Field List window.

5. Drag the paInitiatedBy field to a position at the top and rightmost edge of the form's Detail section, opposite the paID field (look ahead to Figure 13.26). The first Combo Box Wizard dialog appears.

6. You want the combo box to look up values in the Employees table, so accept the default option button and then click Next (see Figure 13.20). Your selection specifies Table/Query as the value of the Record Source property of the combo box. The second Combo Box Wizard dialog appears.

7. Select Employees from the list of tables in the list (see Figure 13.21). Click Next to reach the third dialog.

8. You need the EmployeeID and LastName fields of the Employees table for your combo box. EmployeeID serves as the bound field, and your combo box displays the LastName field. EmployeeID is selected in the Available Fields list by default, so click the > button to move EmployeeID to the Selected Fields list. LastName is selected automatically, so click the > button again to move LastName to the Selected Fields list. Your Combo Box Wizard dialog appears as shown in Figure 13.22. This selection specifies the SQL SELECT query that serves as the value of the Row Source property and populates the combo box's list. Click Next to reach the fourth dialog.

PART

III

CH

13

Figure 13.20
Selecting the source of list values in the opening dialog of the Combo Box Wizard.

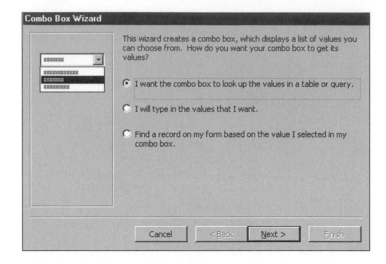

Figure 13.21
Selecting the table in which you want the combo box to look up values.

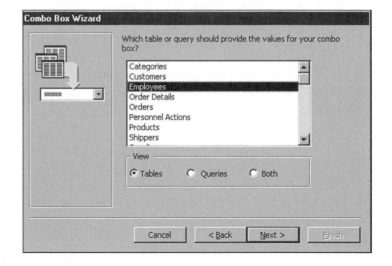

9. The fourth dialog (see Figure 13.23) displays the value list for the combo box. Access has successfully determined that the EmployeeID field is the key field of the Employees table and has assumed (correctly) that the EmployeeID field is the bound field for the combo box. The Hide Key Column check box is selected by default; this option causes Access to hide the bound column of the combo box. The result is that, although you've selected two columns for the combo box, only one column (the LastName field) is displayed in the combo box's list. The EmployeeID column is hidden and used only to supply the data value for the paInitiatedBy field. Resize the LastName column by dragging the right edge of the column leftward—you want the column wide enough to display everyone's last name but not any wider than absolutely necessary. Click Next to continue to the fifth Combo Box Wizard dialog.

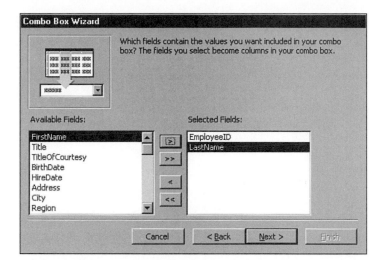

Figure 13.22
Selecting fields of the table with which to populate the combo box.

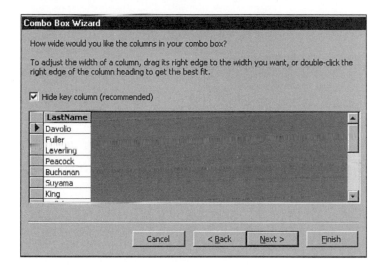

Figure 13.23
Selecting the column width for the combo box and a hidden key field column.

10. Your combo box supplies the EmployeeID value corresponding to the name you select to the paInitiatedBy field. You previously specified that the Control Source property is paInitiatedBy when you dragged the field symbol to the form in step 5. The Combo Box Wizard uses your previous selection as the default value of the Control Source property (see Figure 13.24), so accept the default value by clicking the Next button to display the sixth and final dialog.

11. The last dialog lets you edit the label associated with the combo box (see Figure 13.25). Type **Initiated By:** and click Finish to add the combo box to your form. Your combo box in Design mode appears as shown in Figure 13.26.

PART

III

CH

13

Figure 13.24
Assigning the Control
Source property value.

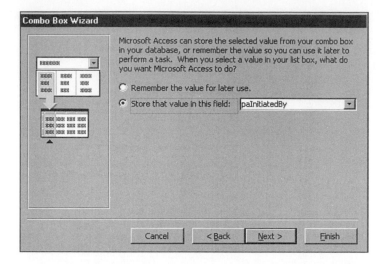

Figure 13.25
The final Combo Box
Wizard dialog lets you
edit the control's label.

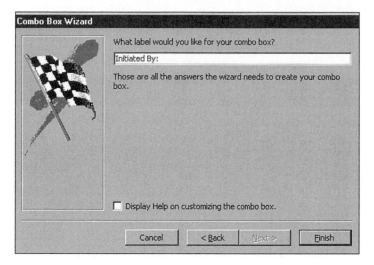

12. Click the Form View button on the toolbar to test your combo box (see Figure 13.27). Change the Initiated By value to another person, such as Mr. Fuller, the Vice President of Sales, and then move the record pointer to make the change permanent. Return to the original record, and open the combo box to verify that the combo box is bound to the paInitiatedBy field.

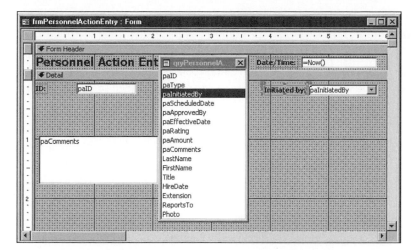

Figure 13.26
The new combo box in Design mode.

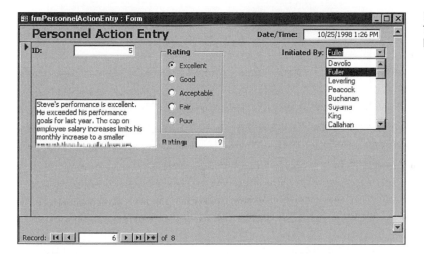

Figure 13.27
The Initiated By combo box in Run mode.

USING THE QUERY BUILDER TO POPULATE A COMBO BOX

If the Row Source Type property for a combo box is Table/Query, you can substitute an *SQL* statement for a named table or query as the value of the Row Source property. In the case of queries, the advantage of the substitution is that this process prevents the list of queries in the Database window from becoming cluttered with named queries used to create a multitude of combo boxes. For either tables or queries, you can choose only the fields or columns you want for the text box, eliminating the need to hide columns. In addition, you can specify a sort order for the list element of your combo box.

To invoke Access 2000's Query Builder to create an SQL statement for populating a manually added Approved By combo box, follow these steps:

PART

III

CH

13

1. Return to or open frmPersonnelActionEntry in Design mode, and click the Control Wizards button of the Toolbox to add the combo box manually. Click the Field List button, if necessary, to display the field list.

2. Click the Combo Box button of the Toolbox, and then drag the paApprovedby field to add a new combo box under the Initiated By combo box you added in the preceding section.

3. Select the Row Source property, and click the Build button to launch the Query Builder. The Query Builder's window is identical in most respects to the Query Design window, but its title and behavior differ.

4. Add the Employees table to the query, and then close the Show Table dialog. Drag the EmployeeID and LastName fields to columns 1 and 2 of the Query Design grid.

5. You want an ascending sort on the LastName field, so select Ascending in the Sort list box. Your query design appears as shown in Figure 13.28.

Figure 13.28
The design of the query to create the SQL statement for the Approved By combo box.

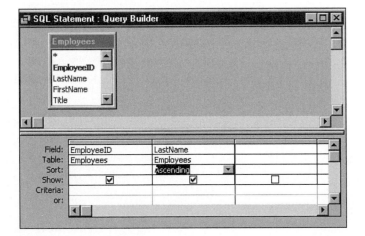

When you use the Query Builder, you can test the results of your query by clicking the Run button on the toolbar. Access executes the query and displays a Datasheet view of the query's results.

6. Click the Close window button to close the Query Builder. The message box shown in Figure 13.29 appears for confirmation of your change to the Row Source property value, instead of asking if you want to save your query. Click Yes and the SQL statement derived from the graphical Query Design grid appears as the value of the Row Source property.

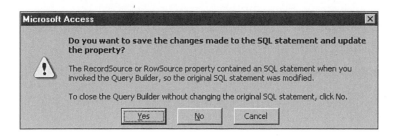

Figure 13.29
Confirming your change to the Row Source property value.

7. Change the Column Count property value to **2** and type **0.2;0.8** in the Column Widths text box. You specify column widths in inches, separated by semicolons. (Metrified users specify column widths in cm).

Tip #116 from

RJ

You can display only the LastName field in the combo box, making the combo box similar in appearance to Initiated By, by setting the first Column Widths value to **0**.

---

8. Switch to Form view to test the effect of adding the sort (the ORDER BY clause) to the query (see Figure 13.30). Writing your own SQL statements to fill combo boxes with values is discussed in Chapter 23, "Working with Structured Query Language."

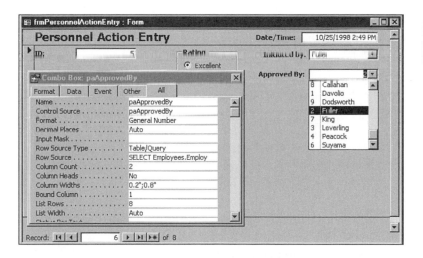

Figure 13.30
Properties of the paApprovedBy combo box in Form view.

PART
III

CH

13

CREATING A COMBO BOX WITH A LIST OF STATIC VALUES

Another application for list boxes and combo boxes is picking values from a static list of options that you create. A dropdown list to choose a Rating value saves space in a form compared with the equivalent control created with option buttons within an option frame. As you design more complex forms, you find that display "real estate" becomes increasingly valuable.

The option frame you added to the frmPersonnelActionEntry form provides a choice of only five of the possible 10 ratings. To add a dropdown list with the Combo Box Wizard to allow entry of all possible values, do the following:

1. Click the Design View button on the toolbar (if the form isn't already in Design view). Click the Control Wizards button in the Toolbox, if necessary, to enable the Combo Box Wizard.

2. Open the Field List window, if necessary, and then click the Combo Box tool in the Toolbox. Drag the paRating field symbol to a position underneath the Approved By combo box you added previously. The first Combo Box Wizard dialog appears.

3. Select the I Will Type In the Values That I Want option, and then click Next to reach the second dialog.

4. The Rating combo box requires two columns: the first column contains the allowable values of paRating, 0 through 9, and the second column contains the corresponding description of each rating code. Enter **2** as the number of columns.

5. Access assigns Row Source property values in column-row sequence; you enter each of the values for the columns in the first row and then do the same for the remaining rows. Type **9 Excellent**, **8 Very Good**, **7 Good**, **6 Average**, **5 Acceptable**, **4 Marginal**, **3 Fair**, **2 Sub-par**, **1 Poor**, **0 Terminated** (don't type the commas).

6. Set the widths of the columns you want by dragging the edge of each column header button to the left, as shown in Figure 13.31. If you don't want the rating number to appear, drag the left edge of column 1 fully to the left to reduce its width to 0. When you've adjusted the column widths, click Next to open the third dialog.

Figure 13.31
Setting the column widths of the combo box.

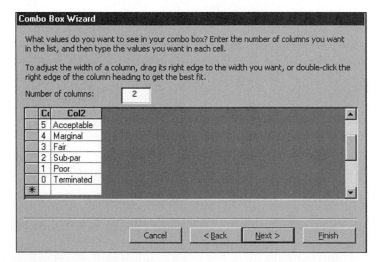

7. Select Col1, the rating number code, as the bound column for your value list—that is, the column containing the value you want to store or use later (see Figure 13.32); this column must contain unique values. Click Next to open the fourth dialog.

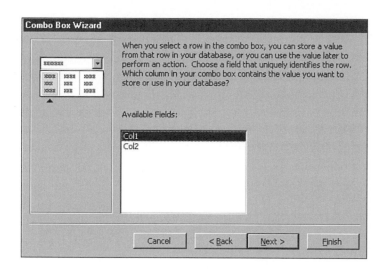

Figure 13.32
Choosing a column to bind to a field of a table or a column of a query.

8. Accept the default value (the paRating field) in this dialog by clicking Next to go to the final dialog of the Combo Box Wizard.

9. Type **Rating:** as the label for the new combo box control, and click Finish to complete the combo box specification and return to Design mode.

10. Open the Properties window for the combo box, and then click the Data tab in the Properties window. Set Limit to List to Yes to convert the dropdown combo to a dropdown list. Notice that Access has added commas after the numbers, semicolons between the row entries, and quotation marks to surround the text values in the Row Source property. You use this format when you enter list values manually.

11. Click the Form View button on the toolbar to display the form. The open Rating static-value combo box and its Properties window appear as shown in Figure 13.33.

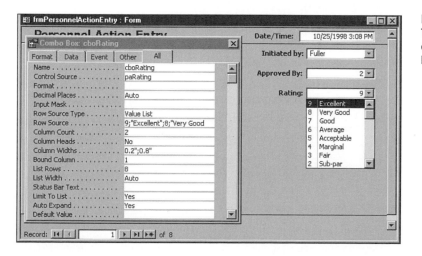

Figure 13.33
The Rating static-value combo box opened in Form view.

Another opportunity to use a static-value combo box is as a substitute for the Type text box. Several kinds of performance reviews exist: Quarterly, Yearly, Bonus, Salary, Commission, and so on, each represented by an initial letter code.

Tip #117 from

You can improve the appearance of columns of labels and associated text, list, and combo boxes by right-aligning the text of the labels and left-aligning the text of the boxes. Select all the labels in a column with the mouse, and click the Align Right button on the toolbar. Then select all the boxes and click the Align Left button.

CREATING A COMBO BOX TO FIND SPECIFIC RECORDS

The Combo Box Wizard in Access 2000 includes a third type of combo list box that you can create—a combo list that locates a record on the form based on a value you select from the list. You can use this type of combo box, for example, to create a Find Last Name box on the frmPersonnelActionEntry form that contains a dropdown list of all last names from the Employees table. Thus, you can quickly find Personnel Actions records for those employees.

To create a combo box that finds records on the form based on a value you select in the combo box, follow these steps:

1. Click the Design View button on the toolbar (if the form isn't already in Design view). Click the Control Wizards button in the Toolbox, if necessary, to enable the Combo Box Wizard.

2. Click the Combo Box tool in the Toolbox, and then click and drag on the surface of the form's Detail section to create the new combo box in a position underneath the Rating dropdown box you created previously. Release the mouse, and the first Combo Box Wizard dialog appears.

3. Click the Find a Record on My Form Based On the Value I Selected in My Combo Box option. Click Next to open the second dialog.

4. Scroll the Available Fields list until the LastName field is visible. Click to select this field, and then click the > button to move it to the Selected Fields list (see Figure 13.34). Click Next to open the third dialog.

Tip #118 from

When creating a combo box to find records, select only one field. The combo box won't work for finding records if you select more than one field for the combo box's lists.

5. The Combo Box Wizard now displays a list of the field values from the column you just selected. Double-click the right edge of the LastName column to get the best column-width fit for the data values in the column, and then click Next to go to the fourth and final step of the wizard.

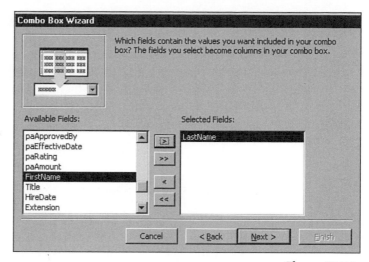

Figure 13.34

6. Type **Zoom to:** as the label for the new combo box, and then click Finish to complete the new combo box control. Your form appear as shown in Figure 13.35.

 7. Click the Form View button on the toolbar to display the form. The open Zoom to: combo box appears as shown in Figure 13.36.

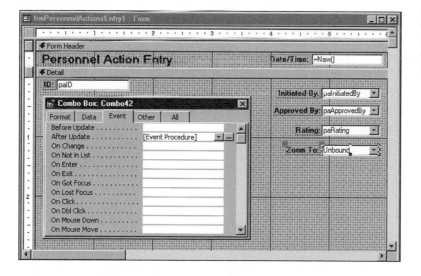

Figure 13.35
The new combo box that finds a record on the form based on a value selected in the control.

PART

III

CH

13

Figure 13.36
The combo box for finding a record on the form in Form view.

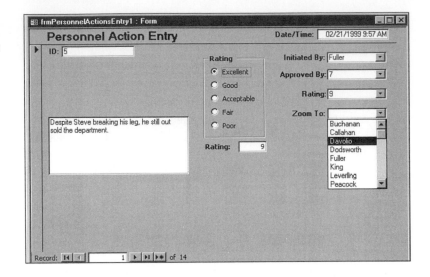

When you create this type of combo box, the Combo Box Wizard automatically creates a *VBA event subprocedure* for the After Update property of the combo box (refer to the Property window in Figure 13.35). An event subprocedure is a VBA procedure that Access executes automatically whenever a particular event occurs—in this case, updating the combo box. Chapter 26, "Writing Visual Basic for Applications Code," describes how to write Access VBA code and Chapter 28, "Responding to Events with VBA 6.0" describes how to write event-handling subprocedures.

To view the event procedure code that the wizard created for your new combo box, open the Properties window for the Zoom to: combo box, click the Events tab in the window, select the After Update property text box, and then click the .... Access opens the VBA Editor window shown in Figure 13.37. After you've looked at the code, close the VBA Editor and return to Design mode.

To use a combo box of this type, select a value from the list. As soon as you select the new value, Access updates the combo box's text box, which then invokes the VBA code for the After Update event procedure. The VBA code in the After Update procedure finds the first record in the form's record set with a matching value and displays it. You can use this type of combo box only to find the first matching record in a `Recordset`.

Tip #119 from

RJ

> Always use unbound combo box controls for record selection. If you bind a record-selection combo box to a field, the combo box updates field values with its value.

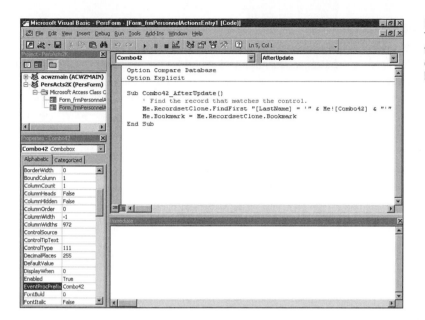

Figure 13.37
The VBA Editor's window for the After Update event procedure of the locating combo box.

Because the field on the form is based on the LastName column of the form's underlying query, you see an entry in the list for each and every last name entry in the record set produced by the qryPersonnelActions query. If, for instance, more than one Personnel Action record exists for Steve Buchanan, then Buchanan appears in the combo list as many times as there are records for him. To display a unique list of last names to be located on the form, change the Row Source property to obtain the LastName field values for the combo box list through an SQL statement based on a query from the Employees table.

To change the Row Source property, follow the procedure you learned in the "Using the Query Builder to Populate a Combo Box" section, earlier in this chapter: Open the Properties window of the Zoom to: combo box, click the Data tab, select the Row Source text box, and then open the Query Builder. Change the query so that it uses the Employees table, as shown in Figure 13.38, and change the Limit to List property value to **Yes**.

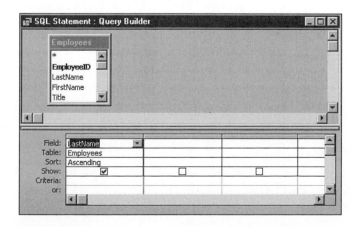

Figure 13.38
The Query Builder window for the new combo box showing the Employees table selected as the new Row Source property value for the combo box.

PART

III

CH

13

CREATING A TAB CONTROL

The Tab control lets you easily create multipage forms in a tabbed dialog, similar to the tabbed pages you've seen in the Properties window, in the Options dialog, and elsewhere in Access. The Tab control is a relatively easy and very efficient alternative to creating multipage forms with the Page Break control. You can use the Tab control to conserve space onscreen and to show information from one or more tables. This section shows you how to add a Tab control to a form. You also learn to set the important properties of the Tab control as a whole, as well as the properties of individual pages of the Tab control.

To add a Tab control to the frmPersonnelActionEntry form, follow these steps:

1. Click the Design View button on the toolbar if the frmPersonnelActionEntry form isn't already in Design view. No wizard for the Tab control exists, so the status of the Control Wizards button doesn't matter.

2. Click the Tab Control tool in the Toolbox; the mouse cursor changes to the Tab Control icon while it is over the active surface of the form.

3. Click and drag on the surface of the form's Detail section to create the new Tab control near the bottom center of the form (see Figure 13.39).

Figure 13.39
A new Tab control showing the default two pages and default page captions.

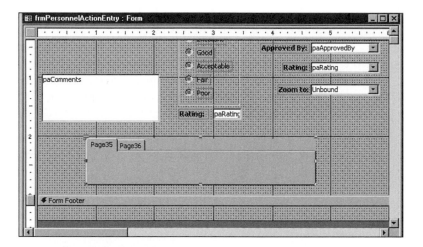

By default, Access creates a Tab control with two pages. Each page's tab displays the name of the page combined with a sequential number corresponding to the number of controls you placed on your form in this work session. The next few sections describe how to change the page tab's caption, add or delete pages in the Tab control, add controls to the pages, and set the page and Tab control properties.

ADDING TAB CONTROL PAGES

Depending on the data you want to display and how you want to organize that data, you might want to include more than two pages in your Tab control. To add a page to a tab control and then delete it, follow these steps:

1. Click the tab of the page you want the new page inserted in front of. Access brings the page you select to the front of the Tab control.

2. Using the right mouse button, click on the edge of the Tab control (the blank space along the top of the tab rows is easiest) to display the context menu.

3. Choose Insert Page; Access inserts a new page in the Tab control after the currently selected page.

CHANGING THE PAGE ORDER

Because Access adds new pages to a Tab control after the currently selected page, it isn't possible to add a new page at the beginning of the existing tab pages. As a result, if you want the new Tab control page to appear as the first page in the Tab control, you must change the order of pages in the Tab control. You might also want to change the order of Tab control pages as you work with and test your forms—in general, you should place the most frequently used (or most important) page at the front of the Tab control.

To change the order of pages in a Tab control, follow these steps:

1. Right-click one of the tabs and choose Page Order to open the Page Order dialog shown in Figure 13.40.

2. In the Page Order list, select the page whose position you want to change.

3. Click the Move Up or Move Down buttons, as appropriate, until the page is in the position you want.

4. Repeat steps 3 and 4 until you have arranged the Tab control pages in the order you want, and then click OK to close the Page Order dialog and apply the new page order to the Tab control.

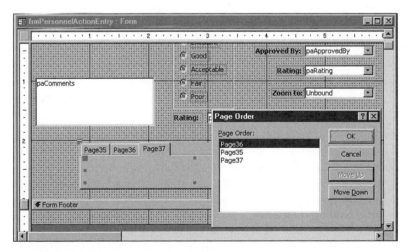

Figure 13.40
Changing the page order of the Tab control in the Page Order dialog.

PART

III

CH

13

DELETING A TAB CONTROL PAGE

At some point, you might decide that you don't want or need a page in a Tab control. The frmPersonnelActionEntry form needs only two pages in its Tab control. If you added a page to the Tab control by following the steps at the beginning of this section, you can delete a page from the Tab control by following this procedure:

1. Click the page tab of the page you want to delete; Access brings that page to the front of the Tab control.
2. Right-click the tab to open the Tab control's context menu.
3. Choose Delete Page; Access deletes the currently selected Tab control page.

SETTING THE TAB CONTROL'S PROPERTIES

Two sets of properties govern the appearance and behavior of a Tab control. A set of properties exists for the entire Tab control, and a separate set of properties exists for each page in the Tab control. The following list summarizes the important properties of the Tab control and its pages; the remaining property settings for the Tab control and its pages are similar to those you've seen for other controls (height, width, color, and so on):

- *Caption* is a text property controls the text that appears on the page's tab and applies to individual Tab control pages only. If this property is empty (the default), then the page's Name property is displayed on the page's tab.

- *MultiRow* is a Yes/No property applies to the Tab control as a whole and controls whether the Tab control can display more than one row of tabs. (The Options dialog, reached by choosing Tools, Options, is an example of a multirow tabbed dialog.) The default setting is No; in this case, if there are more tabs than fit in the width of the Tab control, Access displays a scroll button in the Tab control. If you change this property to Yes and there are more page tabs than will fit in the width of the Tab control, Access displays multiple rows of tabs.

- *Picture* displays an icon in any or all of the page tabs in a Tab control by using this property, which applies to pages only. You can use any of Access's built-in icons or insert any bitmapped (.bmp) graphics file as the page's tab icon.

- *Style* applies to the Tab control as a whole and controls the style in which the Tab control's page tabs are displayed. The default setting, Tabs, produces the standard page tabs you're accustomed to seeing in the Properties window and in various dialogs in Access and Windows. Two other settings are available: Buttons and None. The Buttons setting causes the page tabs to be displayed as command buttons in a row across the top of the Tab control. The None setting causes the Tab control to omit the page tabs altogether. Use the None setting if you want to control which page of the Tab control has the focus with command buttons or option buttons located outside the Tab control. However, using command buttons external to the Tab control to change pages requires writing Access VBA program code. You should use the default Tabs setting unless you have a very specific reason for doing otherwise—using the Tabs setting ensures that the appearance of your Tab controls is consistent with other portions of the Access user interface. Using this setting also saves you the effort of writing VBA program code.

- *TabFixedHeight* and *TabFixedWidth* apply to the Tab control as a whole and govern the height and width of the page tabs in the control, respectively. The default setting for these properties is 0. When these properties are set to 0, the Tab control sizes the page tabs to accommodate the size of the Caption for the page. If you want all the page tabs to have the same height or width, enter a value (in inches or centimeters, depending on your specific version of Access) in the corresponding property text box.

To display the Properties window for the entire Tab control, right-click on the edge of the Tab control, and choose Properties from the resulting context menu (see Figure 13.41). Alternatively, click the edge of the Tab control to select it (clicking the blank area to the right of the page tabs is easiest), and then click the Properties button on the toolbar to display the Properties window.

To display the Properties window for an individual page in the Tab control, click the page's tab to select it, and then click the Properties button on the toolbar to display the page's Properties window.

The Tab control in the frmPersonnelActionEntry form uses one page to display company information about an employee: the employee's job title, supervisor, company telephone extension, hire date, and photo. The second Tab control page displays a history of that employee's personnel actions. Follow these steps to set the Caption property for the frmPersonnelActionEntry form's Tab control:

1. Click the Design View button on the toolbar if the frmPersonnelActionEntry form isn't already in Design view.

2. Click the first page of the Tab control to select it, and then click the Properties button on the toolbar to display that page's Properties window (see Figure 13.41).

3. Click the Format tab, if necessary, to display the Format properties for the Tab control page.

4. Type **Company Info** in the Caption property's text box.

5. Click the second page of the Tab control to select it; the contents of the Property dialog change to show the properties of the second Tab control page.

6. Type **History** in the Caption property text box for the second page of the Tab control, and close the Properties window.

PART
III

CH
13

Figure 13.41 shows the Tab control with both page captions set and the first page of the Tab control selected. Notice that the sizing handles visible in the Tab control are *inside* the control—this position indicates that the page, not the entire control, is currently selected. When the entire Tab control is selected, the sizing handles appear at the edge of the Tab control.

Figure 13.41
Setting the Caption property of a page in a Tab control.

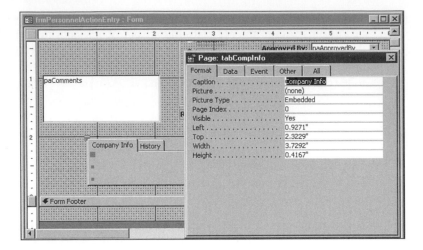

PLACING OTHER CONTROLS ON TAB PAGES

You can place any of Access's 16 other types of controls on the pages of a Tab control—labels, text boxes, list boxes, even subforms. To add a control of any type to a Tab control's page, follow this procedure:

1. In Design view, click the page tab you want to add the control to; Access selects the page and brings it to the front of the Tab control.

2. Add the desired control to the Tab control's page using the techniques presented earlier in this chapter for creating controls on the Detail or Header/Footer sections of a form.

   Alternatively, you can copy controls from the same or another form and paste them into the Tab control's pages by using the same techniques you learned for copying and pasting controls on a form's Detail and Header/Footer sections. You cannot drag controls from the form's Detail or Header/Footer sections onto the Tab control's page.

As you proceed with the examples in this chapter and complete the frmPersonnelActionEntry form, you place various bound and unbound controls on the pages of the Tab control.

CHANGING ONE CONTROL TYPE TO ANOTHER

If you made a mistake in selecting the type of control in earlier versions of Access, you would have to delete the control and start over. Access 2000 lets you "morph" a control of one type to become a control of a compatible type. You can change an option button to a check box, for example, or you can change a toggle button to an option button. You can't, however, change a text box to an object frame or other control with a different field data type. To change a control to a different type, follow these steps:

1. In the form's Design view, select the control whose type you want to change.

2. Choose Format, Change To to see a submenu of form control types. Only the submenu choices for control types that are compatible with the selected control are enabled.

3. Select the control type you want from the submenu. Access changes the control type.

COMPLETING THE MAIN PERSONNEL ACTIONS ENTRY FORM

In the following sections of this chapter, you learn how to use the Control Wizards to help you add a subform to a form. Before you add the subform, however, you should complete the main frmPersonnelActionEntry form. Like the form that you created with the Form Wizard in Chapter 12, the purpose of this form is to display records from the Personnel Actions table so that a user can view the history of an employee's personnel actions. The form also conveniently provides a means of adding new personnel action records.

In the form you created in Chapter 12, you viewed the history of personnel records and also added new records in a tabular subform; information from the Employees table was displayed only on the main form. In this custom form, you place fields from the Personnel Actions table on the main form to make adding new records to the Personnel Actions table easier, and the Tab control is used to contain the subform as well as additional information from the Employees table. The subform on the second page of the Tab control displays only historic personnel action records. The frmPersonnelActionEntry form has fields from the Personnel Actions table on both the main form and the subform, and it uses the qryPersonnelActions query you created at the beginning of this chapter as the form's data source. If you were creating a full-scale human resources database application, you might choose the Employees table as the data source for the form and design a subform for editing the Personnel Actions table. You might then put this subform on a third Tab control page or display the history in a subform of the subform.

To complete the main form, follow these steps (refer to Figure 13.42 for field placement):

1. Click the Design View button on the toolbar (if the frmPersonnelActionEntry form isn't already in Design view). Delete the Rating option frame and text box, if you have done this previously.

2. If necessary, click the Toolbox button to enable the Control Wizards, and then click the Field List button on the toolbar to open the Field List dialog if it isn't already open.

3. Drag the LastName field from the Field List to a position to the right of the ID field text box; when you release the mouse, Access creates a text box for the field. Edit the field's label to read **Name:**.

4. Drag the FirstName field from the Field List to a position to the right of the LastName field; delete the FirstName field's label.

5. Drag the paType field from the Field List to a position at the right of the FirstName field.

6. Repeat step 5 for the paScheduledDate, paEffectiveDate, and paAmount fields (refer to Figure 13.42 for field positioning and sizing). You must move the Approved By, Rating, and Zoom to: fields that you placed on the form earlier in this chapter.

7. Resize the paComments field so that it's underneath the paID and name fields (see Figure 13.42). Next, resize the Tab control so that it fills the width of the form and extends from an area below the paComments field to the bottom of the form. The Tab control needs to be as large as possible in order to display the most data in the subform that you add later to its second page.

8. Click the first tab of the Tab control to bring it to the front, and then drag the Title field from the Field List to a position near the top left corner of the Company Info page.

9. Repeat step 8 for the ReportsTo, Extension, and HireDate fields (refer to Figure 13.42 for field placement).

10. Drag the Photo field onto the right side of the Tab control's first page and delete its label (the fact that this field displays a photo of the employee is enough to identify the field). Size and position the Photo field at the right edge of the Tab control's page; you might need to resize the Tab control and the form after inserting the Photo field.

11. Double-click the Photo field to display its Properties window, click the Format tab, and select the Size Mode property's text box. Select Zoom from the dropdown list to have the employee photo scaled down to fit the photo field's size.

Tip #120 from

Use the Format Painter to format the text labels of the fields. Using the Format Painter is described in preceding Chapter 12. Setting the Size Mode property for images is one of the subjects of Chapter 19.

12. Drag the Notes field onto the bottom left side of the Tab control's first page and delete its label. Refer to Figure 13.42 for placement and sizing.

13. Use the techniques you learned in Chapter 12 to move, rearrange, and change the label formats to match the appearance of Figure 13.42. (All labels are bold and right-aligned.)

14. Change the Format property value of the paScheduledDate and paEffectiveDate text boxes to **mm/dd/yyyy** for Y2K compliance, and change the Format property value of the Amount date from #,##0.00# to **$#,##0.00** to add a dollar sign.

15. To replace number with text in the paApprovedBy, and paRating text boxes, change the Column Widths property value from 0.2";0.8" to **0";0.8"**.

16. Test your new fields by clicking the Form View button on the toolbar. Your form appears as shown in Figure 13.43.

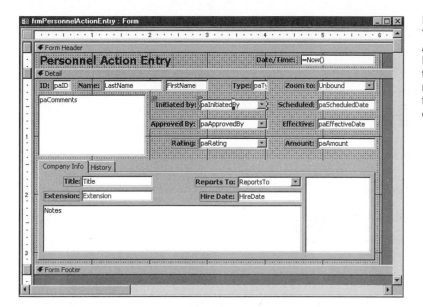

Figure 13.42
The frmPersonnel ActionEntry form in Design view, showing the final placement and formatting of the main form fields and the first page of the Tab control.

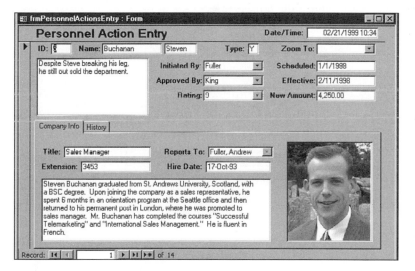

Figure 13.43
The sbfPATest form of Figure 13.42 displayed in Form view.

CREATING A SUBFORM USING THE SUBFORM/SUBREPORT WIZARD

The frmPersonnelActionEntry form needs a subform in which to view the history of personnel actions for the employee displayed in the main part of the form. Access 2000's Subform/Subreport Wizard makes it possible for you to create a new subform at the same time that you add the subform field to the main form or, as in this example, a page in a Tab control. To take advantage of this feature, follow these steps:

1. Click the Design View button on the toolbar if the frmPersonnelActionEntry form isn't already in Design view.

2. Click the Control Wizards button to enable the Control Wizards if the button isn't already down.

3. Click the second tab of the Tab control to bring its second page to the front. Click the Subform button in the Toolbox, and then click the top-left corner of the second Tab control page to open the first dialog of the Subform/Subreport Wizard.

4. You can use this wizard either to create a new subform based on a table or query or to insert an existing subform (see Figure 13.44). (You learn how to insert an existing form as a subform in the section "Modifying the Design of Continuous Forms" later in this chapter.) For this example, select the Use Existing Tables and Queries option, and click Next to open the second dialog.

5. The Subform/Subreport Wizard asks you to indicate which table or query the new subform is based on and which fields appear in the subform (see Figure 13.45). Select Table: Personnnel Actions in the Tables and Queries dropdown list. To expedite field selection, click the >> button to copy all the fields to the Selected Fields list. Select the paComments field in the Selected Fields list, and click the < button to remove this field from the list. Click Next to open the third dialog.

Figure 13.44
Choosing whether to use an existing form as the subform or to use a table or query to create a new subform.

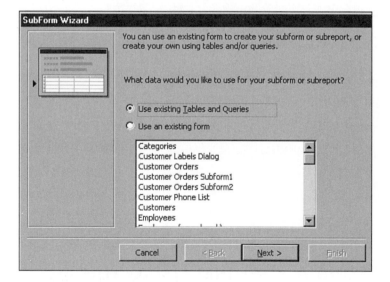

6. The wizard now asks you to specify the link between the main form and the subform. You can select from a list of possible relationships that Access has determined or define your own link. Click the Define My Own option, and the wizard dialog changes to show four dropdown list text boxes

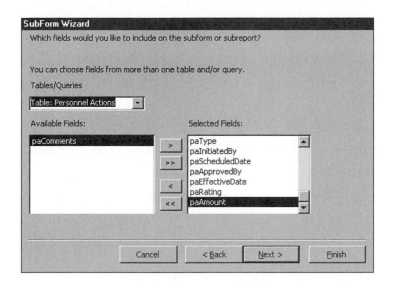

Figure 13.45
Selecting the data source and fields for the new subform.

7. In the upper Form/Report Fields list, select paID as the linking field; in the upper Subform/Subreport Fields list, also select paID as the linking field (see Figure 13.46). Click Next to go to the fourth and final dialog of the wizard.

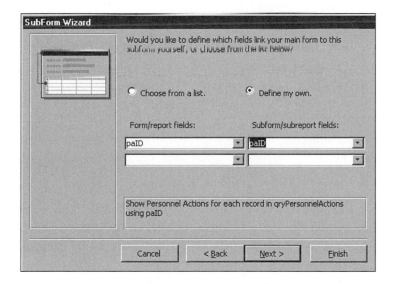

Figure 13.46
Defining the link between the main form (Master) and the subform (Child).

8. Type **sbfPATest** as the name of this new subform, and click Finish to complete the subform's specifications. Access creates and saves the new form; it inserts the completed subform into the History page of the Tab control (see Figure 13.47). Access assigns the text you entered for the subform's name to the label for the subform.

9. To change the subform from Datasheet view to a continuous subform, close the form, save your changes, open sbfPATest in Design view, and open the Form Properties window. In the Format page, change the value of the Default View property to Continuous Forms, then close and save changes to sbfPATest. Reopen frmPersonnelActionsEntry in Design view.

Figure 13.47
The initial subform in Design view.

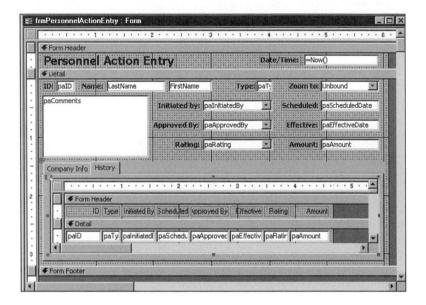

10. To optimize the initial design of the subform, select all subform labels, drag them to the top of the Form Header section, and then click the Bold button. Drag the Detail section header up to the bottom of the labels. Adjust the width of the labels and the text boxes to suit their contents.

11. To minimize the height of the Detail section records, select all the text boxes, drag the text box group to the top of the Detail section, and then drag the Form Footer bar to the bottom of the labels.

12. Select the paScheduledDate text box and apply the mm/dd/yyyy format to assure Y2K compliance. Do the same for the paEffectiveDate text box. Add a dollar sign to the format string for the paAmount text box.

13. Click the Form View button on the toolbar to check the appearance of the new subform. Your form appears as shown in Figure 13.48.

14. Close the frmPersonnelActionEntry form and save your changes.

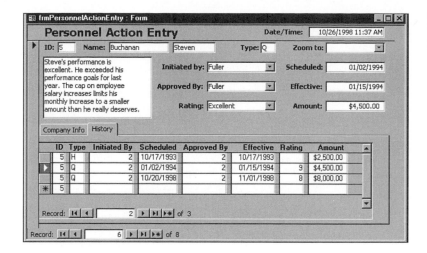

Figure 13.48
The new subform in Form view.

MODIFYING THE DESIGN OF CONTINUOUS FORMS

The default design of the History page's subform as created by the Subform Wizard lets you edit records of the Personnel Actions table. The term *History* implies read-only access to the table in the Tab control. Therefore, you should alter the properties of the subform to make the form read-only and remove unnecessary controls. For example, the vertical scroll bar lets you display any Personnel Actions record for the employee, so you don't need record navigation buttons, nor do you need record selectors.

NEW 2000 Access 2000's new in-situ subform editing feature lets you change many of the properties of subforms with the main form open in Design mode. Unfortunately, you can't change property values, such as Record Selectors and Navigation Buttons, that affect the structure of the subform. Therefore, you must change the design of the subform independently of its main form container. To further optimize the design of the sbfPATest subform, follow these steps:

1. Open sbfPATest in Design view, and then click the Properties button to display the properties of the subform.

2. In the Format page of the Properties window, set the Views Allowed property value to Form, Scroll Bars to Vertical, Record Selectors to No, and Navigation Buttons to No.

3. In the Data page, set the Recordset Type to Snapshot. Doing so has the same effect as setting Allow Edits, Allow Deletions, and Allow Additions to No. Your subform is now read-only because all snapshot-type Recordsets are read-only.

4. In the Other page, set the Tab Stop property to No to prevent the subform from receiving the focus when tabbing through the other controls on the form.

5. Select the paID text box and set its Tab Stop property to No. Do the same for the LastName and FirstName text boxes.

6. Set the tab order by changing to Design view, and choose <u>V</u>iew, Ta<u>b</u> Order to open the Tab Order dialog. Click Auto Order to set the tab order of the controls for which the Tab Order property is Yes. The default control tab order is top-right to bottom-left.

7. Close sbfPATest and save your changes.

8. Open frmPersonnelActionEntry in Run mode to verify your changes to the subform (see Figure 13.49).

Figure 13.49
The read-only version of the History subform.

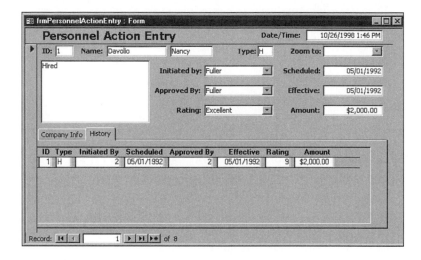

Tip #121 from

Removing from the tab order text boxes and other controls that you seldom or can't edit speeds data entry. To further optimize data entry, set the Tab Stop property of all controls on both pages of the Tab control to No.

Overriding the Field Properties of Tables

Access uses the table's property values assigned to the fields as defaults. The form or subform inherits these properties from the table or query on which the form is based. You can override the inherited properties, except for the Validation Rule property, by assigning a different set of values in the Properties window for the control. Properties of controls bound to fields of tables or queries that are inherited from the table's field properties are shown in the following list:

- Format
- Decimal Places
- Status Bar Text

- Validation Rule
- Validation Text
- Default Value
- Typeface characteristics (such as Font Name, Font Size, Font Bold, Font Italic, and Font Underline)

Values of field properties that you override with properties in a form apply only when the data is displayed and edited with the form. You can establish validation rules for controls bound to fields that differ from properties of the field established by the table, but you can only narrow the rule. The table-level validation rule for the content of the paType field, for example, limits entries to the letters H, S, Q, Y, B, and C. The validation rule you establish in a form cannot broaden the allowable entries; if you add T as a valid choice by editing the validation rule for the paType field to **InStr("HSQYBCT",[PA Type])>0**, you receive an error when you type T.

However, you can narrow the range of allowable entries by substituting **InStr("SQYB",[PA Type])>0**. Notice that you can use expressions that refer to the field name in validation rule expressions in forms; such expressions are not permitted in table validation rule expressions in Access 2000.

ADDING PAGE HEADERS AND FOOTERS FOR PRINTING FORMS

Access lets you add a separate pair of sections, Page Header and Page Footer, that appear only when the form prints. You add both of these sections to the form at once by choosing View, Page Header/Footer. The following list shows the purposes of Page Headers and Footers:

- *Page Header* sections enable you to use a different title for the printed version. The depth of the Page Header can be adjusted to control the location where the Detail section of the form is printed on the page.
- *Page Footer* sections enable you to add dates and page numbers to the printed form.

Page Header and Page Footer sections appear only in the printed form, not when you display the form onscreen in Form view. Figure 13.50 shows the frmPersonnelActionEntry form in Design mode with Page Header and Page Footer sections added.

PART

III

CH

13

Figure 13.50
The frmPersonnel
ActionEntry form with
Page Header and Page
Footer sections added.

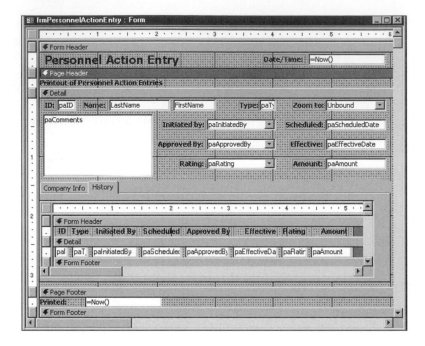

With the Display When (Format) property of the Properties window for the Form Header and Form Footer sections, you can control whether these sections appear in the printed form. In Figure 13.50, the Form Header duplicates the information in the Page Header (except for the Date/Time label and text box), so you don't want to print both. To control when a section of the form prints or is displayed, perform the following steps:

1. Double-click the title bar of whichever section of the form you want to change; this opens the related Properties window. (The Page Header and Page Footer sections don't have a Display When property; these sections appear only when printing.)

2. Click the Format tab if the formatting properties aren't already showing. Click to drop down the Display When list.

3. To display but not print this section in Form view, select Screen Only.

4. To print but not display this section, select Print Only.

TROUBLESHOOTING

ERROR MESSAGES ON COPIED CONTROLS

A control copied to another form throws error messages whenever that control gets the focus.

When you copy a control to a form that uses a data source different from the one used to create the original control, you need to change the Control Source property to correspond with the field to which the new control is to be bound. Changing the Control Source property doesn't change the Status Bar Text, Validation Rule, or Validation Text properties for the new control source. You must enter the appropriate values manually.

In the Real World—Access Wizardry

Access 1.0 had only a few wizards; Access 2000 has 47. Microsoft defines a wizard as "A Microsoft Access tool that asks you questions and creates and object according to your questions." The "Wizards, add-ins, and builders in Microsoft Access 2000" online help topic lists 51 wizards, but four items in the list—Documentor, Macro-To-Module Converter, Subform/Subreport Field Linker, and Switchboard Manager—don't carry the Wizard suffix and are better classified as utilities. It's difficult to obtain an accurate Wizard count in other members of Office 2000, but it's probable that Access 2000 has more wizards than all other Office members combined.

Form-related wizards are the most numerous. The following 10 wizards, listed in alphabetical order, assist you in creating custom forms:

- AutoDialer Wizard determines modem settings for an AutoDialer button.
- AutoForm Wizard automatically generates a form.
- AutoFormat Wizard applies a specific format to a form.
- Chart Wizard adds to a form a graph or chart bound to a table or query.
- Combo Box Wizard generates one of three classes of bound and unbound combo box controls on a form.
- Command Button Wizard adds a command button control.
- Form Wizard generates a new form.
- Option Group Wizard adds a group of option buttons.
- Subform/Subreport Field Linker creates or alters links between a main form and subform.
- Subform/Subreport Wizard adds a new subform.

One of the reasons that Access 2000 has the largest wizard population is that Access is the most complex of the Office 2000 members—from both the user and developer standpoint. Access's complexity, compared with Word, Excel, PowerPoint, and Outlook, undoubtedly is the reason that Microsoft doesn't include Access 2000 in the Standard or Small Business editions of Office 2000. The omission of Access from the Small Business edition is surprising, because establishing and maintaining databases is crucial for almost every enterprise, regardless of size.

Wizards are classified as Access add-ins, which also include builders, menu add-ins, and a new class of Component Object Model (COM) add-ins. The standard set of wizards and builders that come with Access appear in the `HKEY_LOCAL_MACHINE\Software\Microsoft\Office\9.0\Access\Wizards` key of the Registry. Figure 13.51 shows the top-level Registry keys for the Control and Form wizards used in this and the preceding chapter. Microsoft classifies Access builders as `Property Wizards` in the registry.

Figure 13.51

Registry keys for Access 2000's wizards, with the Control Wizards and Form Wizards keys expanded one level.

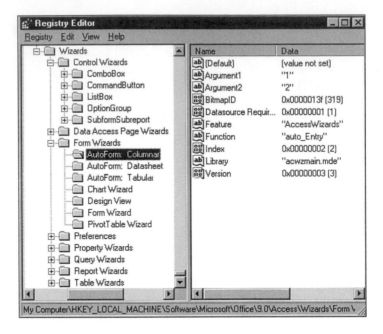

Most of the wizards are contained in the Acwzmain.mde file in your …\Office\1033 folder; the Acwztool.mde Advanced Wizards file includes the Add-In Manager and some builders; and Acwzlib.mde holds the Import/Export Wizards. You can open the Acwz….mde files in Access 2000, but you can't make changes to objects. It's unfortunate that Microsoft uses the .mde format to prevent viewing the wizard VBA code; Access wizards are excellent examples of VBA power programming in action.

The current crop of standard Access wizards are contained in Access libraries because they originated in prior versions of Access. New Microsoft and third-party add-ins probably will arrive in COM Add-In format. COM Add-Ins are wizards and builders in COM .dll files that developers can write with Visual Basic, Visual C++, and other programming environments that support COM. The advantage of COM Add-Ins is that you can use them with any Office 2000 application, not just Access. If you want to learn more about or create COM Add-Ins, you need the Microsoft Office 2000 Developer (MOD). The Microsoft Office Developer Forum has a list of MOD features at http://www.microsoft.com/officedev/ode/ode2kfeat.htm.

--rj

CHAPTER 14

PRINTING BASIC REPORTS AND MAILING LABELS

In this chapter

Understanding the Relationship Between Forms and Reports   534

Categorizing Types of Access Reports   535

Creating a Grouping Report with the Report Wizard   536

Using Access's Reports Windows   543

Using AutoFormat and Customizing Report Styles   545

Modifying a Basic Wizard Report   546

Deleting, Relocating, and Editing Existing Controls   546

Adding Calculated Controls to a Report   551

Aligning and Formatting Controls and Adjusting Line Spacing   554

Adjusting Margins and Printing Conventional Reports   558

Preventing Widowed Records with the Group Keep Together Property   561

Printing Multicolumn Reports as Mailing Labels   562

Troubleshooting   565

In the Real World—The Apocryphal Paperless Office   566

UNDERSTANDING THE RELATIONSHIP BETWEEN FORMS AND REPORTS

The final product of most database applications is a report. Access combines data in tables, queries, and even forms to produce a report that you can print and distribute to people who need or request it. Some reports consist of a single page, such as an order acknowledgment, invoice, graph, or chart. Multipage Access reports— typified by catalogs, general ledgers, and financial statements—are more common than the single-page variety. Most multipage reports are analogous to a continuous form that's been optimized for printing.

Most methods of creating Access forms, which you learn about in Chapter 12, "Creating and Using Forms," and Chapter 13, "Designing Custom Multitable Forms," also apply to reports. The following list details the principal differences between reports and forms:

- Reports are intended for printing only and, unlike forms, aren't designed for display in a window. When you view an 8 ½- × 11-inch report in Print Preview, its content isn't legible. In the zoomed (full-page) view, only a part of the report is visible in the Print Preview window.

- You can't change the value of the underlying data for a report with a control object from the toolbox as you can with forms. With reports, Access disregards user input from combo boxes, option buttons, check boxes, and the like. You can use these controls, however, to display lookup values and to indicate the status of Yes/No option buttons, check boxes, and fields with values derived from multiple-choice lists.

- Reports don't provide a Datasheet view. Only Print Preview and Report Design views are available.

- You can create an unbound report that isn't linked to a source of data. Unbound reports are used as "containers" for individual subreports that bind to unrelated data sources.

- The Printer Setup dialog controls the minimum left, right, top, and bottom printing margins of reports. If a report is less than the printable page width, the report's design determines the right margin. You can increase the left margin over the default setting by positioning the print fields to the right of the display's left margin.

- In multicolumn reports, the number of columns, the column width, and the column spacing are controlled by settings in the Printer Setup dialog, not by controls that you add or properties that you set in Design mode.

Access reports share many characteristics of forms, including the following:

- *Report Wizards* create the three basic kinds of reports: single-column, groups/totals, and mailing labels. You can modify as necessary the reports that the Report Wizard creates. The function of the Report Wizard is similar to that of the Form Wizard discussed in Chapter 12.

- *Sections* include report headers and footers, which appear once at the beginning and at the end of the report, and page headers and footers, which print at the top and bottom of each page. The report footer often is used to print grand totals. Report sections correspond to similarly named form sections.

- *Group sections* of reports, as a whole, comprise the equivalent of the Detail section of forms. Groups often are referred to as *bands*, and the process of grouping records is known as *banding*. You can add Group Headers that include a title for each group, and Group Footers to print group subtotals. You can place static (unbound) graphics in header and footer sections and bound graphics within group sections.

- *Controls* are added to reports from the Access toolbox and then moved and sized with their handles.

- *Subreports* can be incorporated into reports the same way you add subform controls within main forms.

CATEGORIZING TYPES OF ACCESS REPORTS

Reports created by Access fall into six basic types, also called *layouts*, that are detailed in the following list:

- *Single-column reports* list in one long column of text boxes the values of each field in each record of a table or query. A label indicates the name of a field, and a text box to the right of the label provides the values. Access 2000's AutoReport feature creates a single-column report with a single click of the toolbar's AutoReport button. Single-column reports are seldom used because the format wastes paper.

- *Tabular reports* provide a column for each field of the table or query and print the value of each field of the records in rows under the column header. If you have more columns than can fit on one page, additional pages print in sequence until all columns are printed; then the next group of records is printed.

- *Multicolumn reports* are created from single-column reports by using the "newspaper" or "snaking" column approach of desktop publishing and word processing applications. Information that doesn't fit in the first column flows to the top of the second column, and so on. The format of multicolumn tables wastes less paper, but the uses are limited because the column alignment is unlikely to correspond with what you want.

- *Groups/totals reports* are the most common kind of report. Access groups/totals reports summarize data for groups of records and then add grand totals at the end of the report.

- *Mailing labels* are a special kind of multicolumn report that prints names and addresses (or other multifield data) in groups. Each group of fields constitutes a cell in a grid. The design of the stock adhesive label on which you are printing determines how many rows and columns are on a page.

- *Unbound reports* contain subreports based on unrelated data sources, such as tables or queries.

The first five types of reports use a table or query as the data source, as do forms. These kinds of reports are said to be *bound* to the data source. The main report of an unbound report is not linked to a table or query as a data source. The subreports contained by an unbound report, however, must be bound to a data source. *Unbound reports* let you incorporate subreports that are bound to independent tables or queries.

CREATING A GROUPING REPORT WITH THE REPORT WIZARD

This section shows you how to use the Report Wizard to create a grouping report based on data in the Products and Suppliers tables of the Northwind Traders sample database. (Like the Form Wizard, the Report Wizard lets you create reports that contain data from more than one table without first creating a query.) This report displays the quantity of each specialty food product in inventory, grouped by product category.

To create an inventory report, you modify the basic report created by the Report Wizard. The process of creating a basic report with the Report Wizard is similar to the process that you used to create a form in Chapter 12. An advantage of using the Report Wizard to introduce the topic of designing Access reports is that the steps for this process are parallel to the steps you take when you start with a default blank report. Chapter 15, "Preparing Advanced Reports," explains how to start with a blank report and create more complex reports.

To create a Products on Hand by Category report, follow these steps:

1. Click the Reports shortcut in the Database window and then click the New button. Access displays the New Report dialog (see Figure 14.1).

Figure 14.1
The New Report dialog in which you select the report's type and data source.

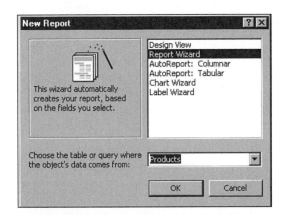

2. Like forms, reports require a data source, which can be a table or query. Select the Products table from the choices offered in the New Report dialog's drop-down list (refer to Figure 14.1). Select Report Wizard from the list in the dialog's right side and click OK. The Report Wizard displays its opening dialog.

3. The fields that you select to display represent rows of the report. You want the report to print the product name and supplier so that users don't have to refer to another report to associate codes with names. The fields from the Products table that you need for this report are CategoryID, ProductID, ProductName, SupplierID, and UnitsInStock. With the > button, select these fields in sequence from the Available Fields list. As you add fields to the Selected Fields list, Access removes the field names from the Available Fields list. Alternatively, you can double-click the field name in the Available Fields list to move the field name to the Selected Fields list. The fields appear from left to right in the report, based on the top-to-bottom sequence in which the fields appear in the Selected Fields list.

4. To demonstrate how the Wizard deals with reports that bind to more than one table, add the CompanyName field from the Suppliers table. Open the Tables/Queries drop-down list and select Table: Suppliers (see Figure 14.2).

Figure 14.2
Selecting the fields of a report from one or more tables or queries in the Report Wizard's opening dialog.

Tip #122 from

R J

You can retrace your steps to correct an error by clicking the Back button whenever it is activated. The Finish button accepts all defaults and jumps to the end of the Wizard, so you shouldn't use this button until you're familiar with the Report Wizard's default selections.

5. Instead of presenting the supplier name as the report's last field, you want the report's CompanyName column to follow the SupplierID report column. Select the SupplierID field in the Selected Fields list. Now select the CompanyName field from the Available Fields list and click the > button. Access moves the CompanyName field from the Available Fields list and inserts the field into the Selected Fields list, after the SupplierID field and before the UnitsInStock field (refer to Figure 14.2). Click Next to continue with the Report Wizard (see Figure 14.3).

Note

The purpose of adding the CompanyName field of the Suppliers table is to demonstrate how the Wizard handles the design of reports based on more than one table. If you don't add the CompanyName field, the Wizard dialog of step 6 doesn't appear. The SupplierID field of the Products table is a lookup field, so CompanyName appears in lieu of the numeric SupplierID value. You remove the duplicate field when you modify the report later in the chapter.

6. The Report Wizard asks how you want to view the data in the report. Notice the Show Me More Information button near the left center of the Wizard dialog. Click this button to display the first of a series of hint dialogs for the Report Wizard. If you click the Show Me Examples option, Access displays additional hint screens. These screens use examples from the Sales Reps, Customers, and Orders tables to show you the different groupings that the Report Wizard can automatically add to the report. Click the Close button repeatedly until you return to the Report Wizard dialog shown in Figure 14.3.

Figure 14.3
Choosing how you want to view your data.

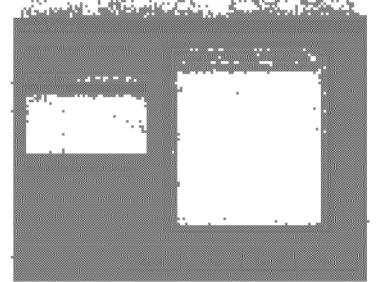

7. For this report, you select your own groupings. Select By Products in the list and click Next to continue with the Report Wizard.

8. The Report Wizard asks whether you want to add any grouping levels to the report. Select the CategoryID field in the list and click the > button to establish the grouping by the Products' category. The Report Wizard dialog now appears, as shown in Figure 14.4.

9. Click the Grouping Options button. The Report Wizard displays the Grouping Intervals dialog shown in Figure 14.5. By changing the grouping interval, you can affect how Access groups data in the report. For numeric fields, you can group items by 10s, 50s, 100s, and so on. For text fields, you can group items based on the first letter, the first three letters, and so on.

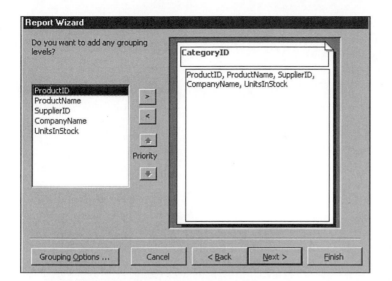

Figure 14.4
Selecting grouping levels
for your report.

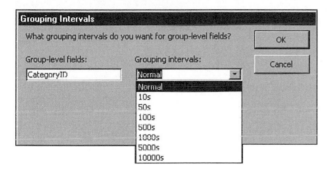

Figure 14.5
Selecting grouping inter-
vals for your report.

Tip #123 from

If your application uses a text-coding scheme, such as BEVA for alcoholic beverages and
BEVN for nonalcoholic beverages, you can combine all beverages in a single group by
selecting 1st 3 Characters from the Grouping Intervals list. Access 2000 provides this option
for numeric fields and for fields of the Text data type.

10. This report doesn't require any special grouping interval, so select Normal in the
Grouping Intervals list and click OK to return to the Report Wizard (refer to Figure
14.4). Click Next to continue with the Report Wizard.

11. You can sort the records within groups by any field that you select (see Figure 14.6),
with up to four different sorted fields. The dialog doesn't offer CategoryID as a choice
because the records already are grouped on this field, and the field on which the grouping is based is sorted automatically by the table's primary key. Select ProductID in the
first drop-down list.

PART
III

Cн

14

By default, the sort order is ascending; if you want a descending sort order, click the button to the right of the drop-down list. (This button is a toggle control; click it again to return to an ascending sort.)

Figure 14.6
Selecting a sort order for fields within groups.

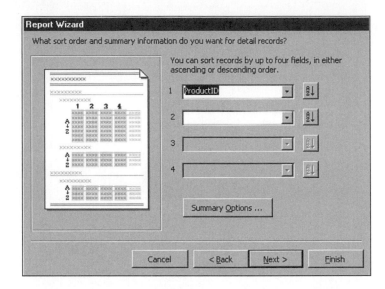

12. Click the Summary Options button to display the Summary Options dialog (see Figure 14.7). If you want to add summary information to a report column, you set the options for that column in this dialog. The Report Wizard lists all of the numeric fields on the report that aren't AutoNumber fields and offers you check boxes to select a Sum, Average, Minimum, and Maximum for that report column. Depending on the check boxes that you select, the Report Wizard adds those summary fields to the end of the report.

Figure 14.7
Choosing the summary data you want to include in your report in the Summary Options dialog of the Report Wizard.

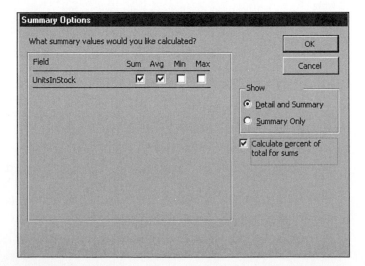

The Show option group lets you select whether the report shows the summary fields only or the full report with the summary fields added at the end of each group and at the end of the report. For this report, select the Sum and Avg check boxes for the UnitsInStock field, the Detail and Summary option, and the Calculate Percent of Total for Sums check box. (The Calculate Percent of Total for Sums check box displays the group's total as a percentage of the grand total for all groups.) Click OK to return to the Report Wizard dialog.

13. Click Next to continue with the Report Wizard. As shown in Figure 14.8, the Wizard asks you to select a layout for your report. The window on the left shows a preview of the layout style that you select. For this report, select Stepped in the Layout option group.

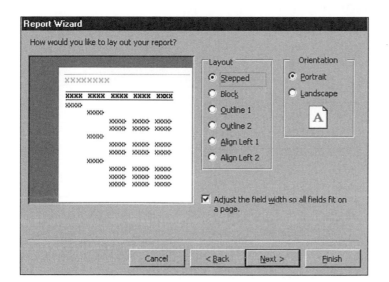

Figure 14.8
Choosing a layout format for a report.

14. By default, the Report Wizard selects the Adjust the Field Width So All Fields Fit on a Page check box. As a rule, you should select this option to save paper and make your report more legible. In the Orientation option group, you select the report's printing orientation. Make sure that you select the default Portrait option. Click Next to continue with the Report Wizard.

Tip #124 from

RJ

When you restrict field widths to fit all fields on a page, fields with long lines of text often are truncated in the final report. You can adjust field widths in Report Design view to accommodate long text lines or change to multiline text boxes.

PART

III

CH

14

15. Select one of the predefined report styles for your report. The window on the left shows a preview of the selected style (see Figure 14.9). (You can customize or create your own styles for the Report Wizard to use. This activity is described in the "Using AutoFormat and Customizing Report Styles" section later in this chapter.) Select the Compact style and then click Next to display the final Report Wizard dialog.

Figure 14.9
Selecting a style for your report.

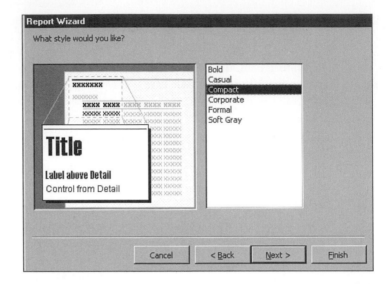

16. Type **Products on Hand by Category** as the title for the new report; the Report Wizard also uses this title as the name of the saved report it creates (see Figure 14.10). Select the Preview the Report option and click Finish to complete your report specification. The Report Wizard creates the report and displays it in Print Preview mode. (To get Help with the report, click the Display Help on Working with the Report? check box.)

Figure 14.10
Giving your report a file name and title and choosing how you want to view the completed report.

Figure 14.11 shows the basic report that the Report Wizard creates. Use the vertical and horizontal scroll bars to position the preview as shown. When you're finished previewing the Products on Hand by Category report, close it.

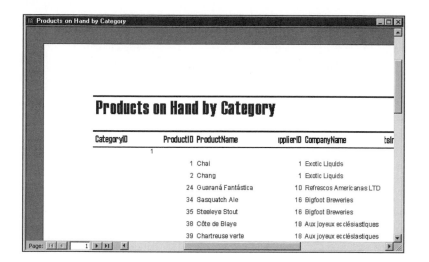

Figure 14.11
The basic report created by the Report Wizard, shown in a maximized window.

Tip #125 from

R J

Unlike Access's record navigation text boxes, Print Preview's Page text box shows only the current report page. To obtain a page count, the Access report engine must paginate the report; pagination can take a considerable period of time for very long reports. To display the total number of report pages in the Pages text box, click the Last Page button (arrow and bar) at the bottom of the Print Preview window.

With a few simple modifications, you can obtain a finished report with the information necessary to analyze Northwind's current inventory. The modifications correct obvious defects in the Wizard-designed report, such as the excess width of the CategoryID column, cut-off names in the Product Names column, duplication of the Supplier and Company Name columns, and the truncated Units in Stock heading. You make these changes in the "Modifying a Basic Report Wizard Report" section later in this chapter.

USING ACCESS'S REPORT WINDOWS

The windows that you use to design and run Access reports are easier to use than the windows that you use for other basic Access functions. To open an existing Access report, such as the Products on Hand by Category report you just created and closed, click the Reports shortcut in the Database window and then select a report name from the Database window. If you click the Design button or the New button to create a new report, the Design Mode toolbar appears with the buttons listed in Table 14.1.

PART

III

CH

14

TABLE 14.1   ACCESS-SPECIFIC TOOLBAR BUTTONS IN REPORT DESIGN MODE

Button	Function	Menu Choice
	Selects Print Preview to display how your report appears when printed. You can print the form from the Print Preview window. (Same as the Print Preview button.)	View, Print Preview
	Prints the report without displaying the Print dialog. Access prints the report using the current printer settings.	Not applicable
	Selects Print Preview to display how your report appears when printed. You can print the form from the Print Preview window.	File, Print Preview
	Starts the spelling checker to check the selected label control's spelling.	Tools, Spelling
	Inserts a new Hyperlink control or allows you to edit an existing Hyperlink control.	Insert, Hyperlink
	Displays a list of fields in the query or table that is the main report's data source.	View, Field List
	Displays or closes the toolbox.	View, Toolbox
	Displays the Sorting and Grouping dialog in which you can establish the structure of reports and the order in which the report presents the data.	View, Sorting and Grouping
	Applies your choice of several predefined report formats, including formatting for the text fonts and color settings.	Format, AutoFormat
	Opens the VBA Editor window in which you can edit event-handling code.	View, Code
	Displays the Properties window for the entire report, the sections of the report when you click the section divider bars, or the properties of a control when a control is selected.	View, Properties
	Displays a Build Wizard for the selected object or property in the report. This button is enabled only if Access has a builder for the selected item.	Not applicable
	Displays the Database window.	Window, 1 Database
	Creates a new object. Click the arrow to the right of this button to see a drop-down list of objects that you can create.	Not applicable
	Displays the Microsoft Office Assistant that, in turn, displays help text related to the actions you are performing.	Help, Microsoft Access Help

Many of the buttons listed in Table 14.1 serve the same purposes for both forms and reports. As is the case for Form Design mode, the Formatting toolbar's buttons for formatting text are enabled only when a control object that can contain text is selected. The Formatting toolbar for reports is identical to the Formatting toolbar for forms.

→ For a list of the formatting icons and their uses, **see** Table 12.2 in section "The Formatting Toolbar," **p. 446**.

If you double-click the name of an existing report or click the Preview button in the Database window, the report displays in Print Preview mode, which is the Run mode for reports. Table 14.2 lists the toolbar's buttons in Print Preview mode.

TABLE 14.2   STANDARD TOOLBAR BUTTONS IN REPORT PRINT PREVIEW MODE

Button	Function	Menu Choice
	Prints the report without displaying the Print dialog. The report is printed using the current printer settings.	Not applicable
	Toggles between full-page and full-size (100%) views of the report. Clicking the mouse when its pointer appears as the magnifying glass symbol produces the same effect.	View, Zoom
	Displays one full page.	View, Pages, 1
	Displays two full pages.	View, Pages, 2
	Displays a palette from which you can select several multiple-page views of the report.	
Fit	Changes the size of the view from 200 percent to 10 percent or fits the report to the window.	View, Zoom
	Displays a drop-down list of shortcut commands for Microsoft Office Links: Merge It, Publish It with MS Word, and Analyze It with MS Excel.	Tools, OfficeLinks
	Opens the Database window.	Window, 1 Database
	Creates a new object. Click the arrow at the right of this button to display a drop-down list of objects that you can create. This icon usually appears as the New Object: Table icon, but it toggles to whatever object you last created using the icon.	Not applicable

Chapter 21, "Using Access with Microsoft Word and Mail Merge," discusses using the Office Links button to print reports as files in Rich Text Format. Chapter 20, "Using Access with Microsoft Excel," discusses printing files in Excel BIFF format.

USING AUTOFORMAT AND CUSTOMIZING REPORT STYLES

The AutoFormat toolbar button works the same way for reports as for forms. Chapter 12 contains a detailed, step-by-step explanation of how to use Access 2000's AutoFormat button and how to customize the predefined AutoFormat styles or create your own AutoFormat styles.

→ **See** the instructions in the "Using AutoFormat" section of Chapter 12, **p. 448**, to apply an AutoFormat style to a report or define or customize a report AutoFormat style.

PART

III

CH

14

Tip #126 from

R J

Access stores styles for reports and forms separately, so you must create separate AutoFormat styles for your reports. As with forms, to create an AutoFormat style for customized reports, first create a report that contains controls that are formatted for your new style. Click the AutoFormat button on the toolbar, and then click the Customize button in the AutoFormat dialog to customize the format. Choose a naming convention for report AutoFormat styles, such as rptSales or rptCustomers.

MODIFYING A BASIC WIZARD REPORT

The Report Wizard tries to create the optimum final report in the first pass. Usually, the Wizard comes close enough to a finished product that you spend far less time modifying a Wizard-created basic report than creating a report from the default blank template.

In the following sections, you use Access's report design features to make the report more attractive and easier to read.

DELETING, RELOCATING, AND EDITING EXISTING CONTROLS

The first step in modifying the Wizard's report is to modify the existing controls on the report. You don't need to align the labels and text boxes precisely during the initial modification; the section "Aligning Controls Horizontally and Vertically" later in this chapter covers control alignment. To create space for additional controls on the report, follow these steps:

 1. Open Products on Hand by Category in Report Design mode, if necessary. The Products on Hand by Category report, as created by the Report Wizard, appears as shown in Figure 14.12.

Figure 14.12
The basic report in Design mode.

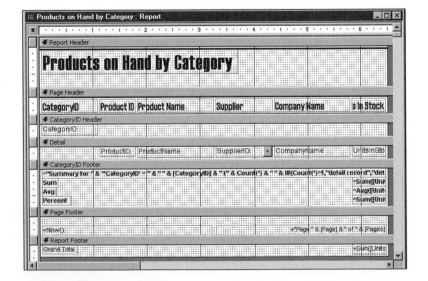

2. The SupplierID and CompanyName fields are redundant in this report because the SupplierID field is a lookup field. Select the Company Name label in the Page Header section, hold down the Shift key, and click the CompanyName field in the Detail section. Press Delete to remove the field and label from the report. (Don't worry about aligning the fields and labels yet.)

3. This report is more useful if you include the dollar value of both the inventory and number of units on hand. To accommodate one or two additional columns, you must compress the fields' widths. CategoryID occupies a column, but you can display this column's content in the CategoryID footer (or header) without using the extra column space. Select and delete the CategoryID label from the Page Header section; do the same for the CategoryID text box from the CategoryID Header section. For this report, you'll put the CategoryID name in the footer section of the group, so drag the Detail section bar upward to eliminate the space occupied by the CategoryID Header. Your report appears as shown in Figure 14.13.

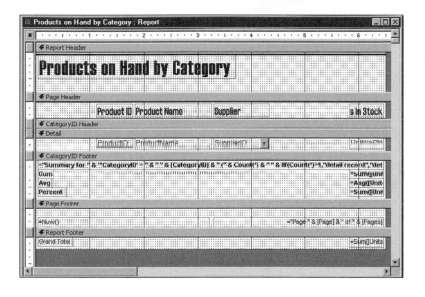

Figure 14.13
The basic report after deleting the CompanyName and CategoryID labels and text boxs, and closing the space for the CategoryID Header.

4. All Page Header labels, Detail text boxes, and Totals text boxes in the CategoryID Footer and Report Footer sections must move to the left as a group. Click the Product ID label to select it and then press and hold down Shift. Click the remaining Page Header labels, each of the Detail text boxes, the three summary field text boxes in the CategoryID Footer section, and the Grand Total text box in the Report Footer section. Now release Shift. (To select all labels and text boxes, scroll the report to the right and left and up and down.)

5. Position the mouse pointer over the Product ID label at a location where the pointer turns into the graphic of a palm of a hand. Hold down the left mouse button and drag the selected fields to the left margin. Your report appears as shown in Figure 14.14.

PART

III

CH

14

Figure 14.14
Moving selected labels and text boxes to the report's left margin.

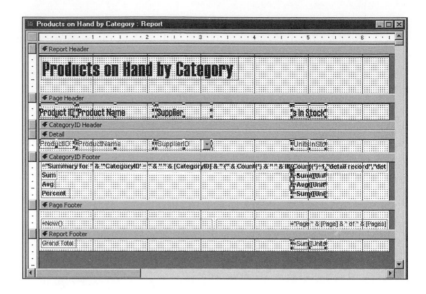

 6. You can more easily edit and position the labels if you left-justify them. Click a blank area of the report to deselect the group, select all of the Page Header labels, and click the Align Left button on the toolbar.

7. Edit the Product ID label to read **ID** and edit the Units In Stock label to read only **Units**. Select all the labels in the Page Header and choose F̲ormat, S̲ize, To F̲it. Resize the widths of the ProductID, SupplierID, and UnitsInStock text boxes in the Detail section to match the width of the labels in the Page Header. Relocate the labels to provide more space for the Product Name and Supplier columns and gain additional space on the right side of the report, as shown in Figure 14.15.

Figure 14.15
The Products on Hand by Category report after you edit, resize, and relocate existing controls.

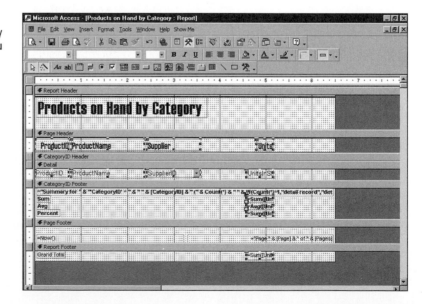

8. By default, the Report Wizard adds to the CategoryID Footer a calculated field (visible in Figure 14.13). The calculated field displays the group's field name (CategoryID) and value to help identify the group footer's summary fields. For example, for CategoryID 1, the calculated field displays in Print Preview mode the following:

```
"Summary for 'CategoryID' = 1 (12 detail records)."
```

For this report, you want a more explicit description of the product category—more than just the CategoryID number. Delete the Category ID Footer's calculated field that starts with ="Summary for" for now; you replace it in the next few steps.

Tip #127 from 	Not every table that you use in your reports will have lookup fields, however, nor is it necessarily desirable to create lookup fields for all numeric code fields (such as CategoryID and SupplierID). If you want to display a looked-up value for a field that isn't defined as a lookup field, you use Access's domain aggregate function, DLookUp(), to find values from another table that correspond to a value in one of the report's fields. For example, to display both the actual CategoryID number and the CategoryName in the CategoryID Footer of the Products on Hand by Category report, you can use the DLookUp() function to display the text of the CategoryName field from the Categories table, and a bound text field to display the CategoryID number from the Products table. The expression you use is: **=DLookUp("[CategoryName]","Categories","[CategoryID] = Report!CategoryID")** **& " Category"** [CategoryName] is the value that you want to return to the text box. Categories is the table that contains the CategoryName field. [CategoryID] = Report!CategoryID is the criterion that selects the record in the Categories table with a CategoryID value that is equal to the value in your report's CategoryID text box. The Report prefix is necessary to distinguish between the CategoryID field of the Categories table and a control object of the same name. (Report is necessary in this example because Access has automatically named the report's CategoryID text box control as CategoryID.)

To add a new calculated field to display the CategoryName field in the CategoryID footer, and complete the redesign of the report, do the following:

1. You now must add a bound text box to identify the subtotal in the CategoryID Footer section. Click the Field List button on the toolbar. Select CategoryID from the list in the Field List window.

2. Click and drag the field symbol mouse pointer to the left margin of the CategoryID Footer in place of the text box you deleted. Because the CategoryID field is a lookup field, it displays with a drop-down list button for the field box. When printed or displayed in Print Preview, this field shows the CategoryID name rather than the numeric code. Click the Field List button on the toolbar to close the Field List window.

3. Select the label of the CategoryID field that you just placed and then use the Font and

Arial

10

B

Size drop-down lists on the Formatting toolbar to set the label's font to Arial and the label's size to 8 points. Next select the CategoryID text box, click the Bold button on the toolbar to add the bold attribute to the CategoryID text box, and select the Arial font at a size of 8 points. Figure 14.16 shows the new bound CategoryID field in place of the calculated field that you deleted in step 8.

Figure 14.16
The Products on Hand by Category report after adding the CategoryID lookup field to the CategoryID Footer section.

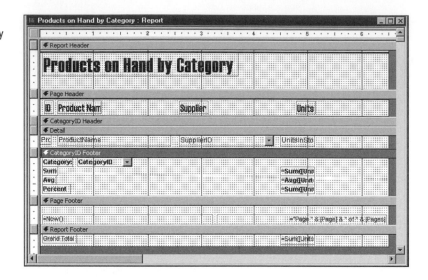

4. Drag the two calculated fields (=Now and ="Page...") in the Page Footer section until they are one grid mark away from the top of the Page Footer section. Drag the Report Footer bar upward to reduce the Page Footer's height.

5. For this report, the Avg field is unnecessary; delete it and its label and then rearrange the remaining fields and labels. Click and drag the =Sum([UnitsInStock])/[UnitsInStock Grand Total Sum] text box from its present location below the =Sum([UnitsInStock]) text box to a position at the top of the CategoryID Footer, near the page's right edge. Drag the =Sum([UnitsInStock]) field to a position at the bottom of the CategoryID Footer bar and near the center of the page. Move up the Page Footer divider bar to reduce the footer's depth.

Tip #128 from

To differentiate between calculated field text boxes that show only the first few characters of the expression, temporarily increase their width. Shift+F2 doesn't open the Zoom window for report text boxes, and there's no Zoom choice in the text boxes' context menu.

---

6. Select the Grand Total label and text box in the Report Footer section and apply the Bold attribute. Your final report design appears as shown in Figure 14.17.

 If you get a blank page after each page when you print or preview a report, see the suggestion in "Eliminating Empty Pages" in the "Troubleshooting" section near the end of this chapter.

 To check the progress of your work, periodically click the toolbar's Print Preview button to display the report prior to printing. Figure 14.18 shows your Products on Hand by Category report in Print Preview mode.

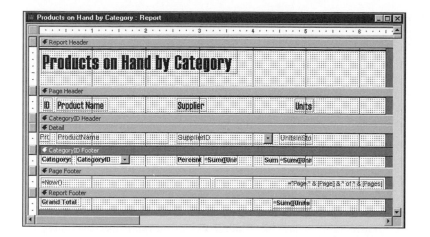

Figure 14.17
The completely modified Products on Hand by Category report in Design mode.

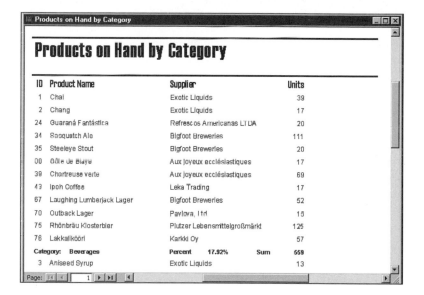

Figure 14.18
Previewing the Products on Hand by Category report.

ADDING CALCULATED CONTROLS TO A REPORT

Calculated controls are quite useful in reports. You use calculated controls to determine extended values, such as quantity times unit price or quantity times cost. Now you have enough space at the right of the report to add two columns: one for the UnitPrice field and one for the extended inventory value, which is UnitPrice multiplied by UnitsInStock. The following subsections explain how to add these controls.

PART

III

CH

14

CHANGING THE REPORT'S RECORD SOURCE

You created the Products on Hand by Category report by selecting fields directly from the Products and Suppliers tables in the Report Wizard. Therefore, the Record Source property for the report as a whole is an SQL statement that selects only the fields that you chose initially in the Report Wizard. Although you can add fields to the report by creating unbound text box controls and using the Expression Builder to create an expression to retrieve the desired value, it's much easier to create a query to select the desired fields and then substitute the new query as the report's data source. You also can specify record selection criteria in a query.

To create a query for use with the Products on Hand by Category report, follow these steps:

1. Create a new query in Design view.

2. Double-click the Products table in the Show Table dialog and then close the dialog.

3. Drag * from the field list to the first column of the query.

4. Drag the Discontinued field to the query grid's second column.

5. Clear the Show check box for the Discontinued field and then type **False** in the Discontinued field's first Criteria row (see Figure 14.19).

Figure 14.19
The query that contains all fields from the Products table and excludes discontinued products.

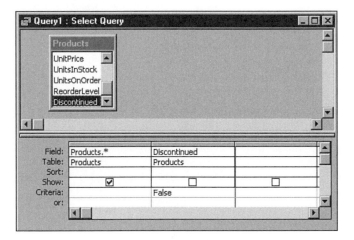

6. Run the query to test your work, close the Query window, and save your changes using the name **qryProductsOnHand**.

The query that you have just created contains all the fields from the Products table and excludes discontinued products from the record set. (In other words, the query includes only those records whose Discontinued field contains the `False` or No value.)

To change the report's Record Source property, follow these steps:

1. Open the Products on Hand by Category report in Design mode. and press Ctrl+R to select the report.

2. Click the toolbar's Properties button to open the report's Properties window. Then click the Data tab to display the report's data properties.

3. Click the Record Source text box and then use the drop-down list to select the qryProductsOnHand query as the report's new Record Source property.

4. Check the report in Print Preview mode, and then save the changes to the report.

ADDING THE CALCULATED FIELDS

Now that you've changed the report's record source, you have easy access to the UnitPrice field that you need for adding the calculated fields to the report. To add the UnitPrice field and the Value calculated fields to the report, follow these steps:

1. Display the Products on Hand by Category report in Design mode if necessary. Then click the toolbar's Toolbox button to display the Access toolbox if it isn't already displayed.

2. Click the Label tool in the toolbox and place the label to the right of the Units label in the Page Header section. Type **Price** as the caption.

3. Add another label to the right of Price and type **Value**.

4. Select both labels, change the Font to Hattenschweiler, and change the Size to 14 points.

5. Click the toolbar's Field List button to display the Field List window. Select UnitPrice and drag the field symbol to a position under the Price label in the Detail section. Drop the text box and then delete the UnitPrice field's label in the report's Detail section.

6. To create the calculated Value text box, click the Text Box button in the toolbox and add the text box to the right of the Unit Price text box.

Tip #129 from

R T

A good way to enter complex expressions is to display the Properties window, enter the expression as the Control Source property, and open the Zoom box with Shift+F2 so you can see the entire expression as you enter it.

---

7. Open the Properties sheet for the new Value text box. Click in the Control Source property and press Shift+F2 to open the Zoom box. Type **=[UnitsInStock]*[UnitPrice]** as the expression. Delete the field label for this text box in the report's Detail section.

8. Drag the Percent label and text box to the left, and change the label caption to **Percent Cat. Units.**

9. Repeat steps 6 and 7 to add a calculated text box in the CategoryID Footer section, but type **=Sum([UnitsInStock]*[UnitPrice])** as the subtotal expression. Click the toolbar's Bold button to set the Font Weight property to Bold. In the Properties window, click the Other tab and then set this text box's Name property as **txtCatValue**. Type Value as the name of the label and change the font to 8 point Arial bold.

PART

III

CH

14

10. Repeat step 9 to create the grand total value box with the
    =Sum([UnitsInStock]*[UnitPrice]) expression in the Report Footer section. In the
    Other page of the Properties window, set this text box's Name property as
    txtTotalValue. Change the label caption to Value.

11. Add another unbound text box to the right of the Percent Units text box in the
    CategoryID Footer section. Type **=[txtCatValue]/[txtTotalValue]** as the value of the
    Control Source property and set the Format property's value to Percent and the Font
    Weight to Bold. Change the label caption to Value and conform the font. The report
    design appears as shown in Figure 14.20.

    *If a Parameters dialog appears when you test your report in Preview mode, see the "Unexpected
    Parameters Dialog" topic of the "Troubleshooting" section near the end of the chapter.*

Figure 14.20
Adding the Price, Value,
Cat(egory) Value,
(Category) Value percent-
age, and Grand Total
Value fields to the report.

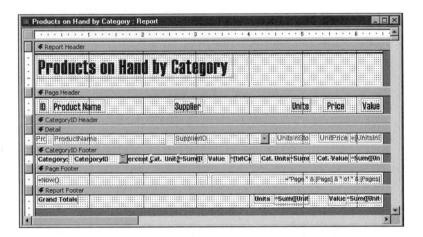

12. Click the toolbar's Report View button to check the result of your additions. Use the
    vertical scroll bar, if necessary, to display the category subtotal. The next section
    describes how you can correct any values that are not aligned properly and the spacing
    of the Detail section's rows.

13. Click the Bottom of Report page selector button to display the grand totals for the
    report (see Figure 14.21). The record selector buttons become page selector buttons
    when you display reports in Print Preview mode.

ALIGNING AND FORMATTING CONTROLS AND ADJUSTING LINE SPACING

The exact alignment of label and text box controls is more important on reports than it is
on forms because in the printed report any misalignment is obvious. Formatting the controls further improves the report's appearance and readability.

The spacing of the report's rows in the Detail section is controlled by the section's depth.
Likewise, you can control the white space above and below the headers and footers by
adjusting the depth of their sections and the vertical position of the controls within the sec-

tions. To create a professional-looking report, you must adjust the controls' alignment and formatting as well as the sections' line spacing.

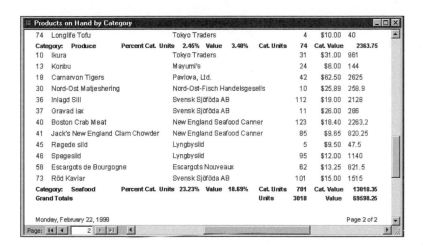

Figure 14.21
The last page of the report, which displays grand totals for Units and Value.

ALIGNING CONTROLS HORIZONTALLY AND VERTICALLY

You align controls by first selecting the rows to align and then aligning the columns. Access provides several control-sizing and alignment options to make the process easier. To size and align the controls that you created, follow these steps:

1. Click the Print Preview toolbar's Close button to return to Design mode.

2. You can simultaneously adjust the height of all text boxes to fit the font used for their contents. Choose Edit, Select All to select all the controls in the report.

3. Choose Format, Size, To Fit to adjust the height of the selected controls. Access adjusts all the controls to the proper height. To deselect all the controls, click a blank area of the report.

4. Select all labels in the Page Header sections. Choose Format, Align, Top. This process aligns the tops of each selected label with the uppermost selected label. Click a blank area of the report to deselect the labels.

5. Select all text boxes in the Detail section and repeat step 4 for the text boxes.

6. Select the labels and text boxes in the CategoryID Footer and Report Footer sections and repeat step 4.

7. Select all controls in the Units column. Choose Format, Align, Right so that Access aligns the column to the right edge of the text farthest to the right of the column. Next click the toolbar's Align Right button to right-align the contents of the labels and text boxes. (The first part of this step aligns the controls themselves to the rightmost control, and the second part right-aligns the text or data displayed by the selected controls.)

8. Select all controls in the Price column and repeat step 7.

9. Select all controls in the Values column (except the Page Footer text box) and repeat step 7.

10. Click the toolbar's Report View button to display the report with the improved alignment of rows and columns.

FORMATTING CONTROLS

As you can see in Figure 14.21, you must revise the formatting of several controls. Although ProductID values are right-aligned, centering or left-justification is more appropriate for values used as codes rather than as numbers to total. The repeated dollar signs in the Unit Price field detract from the report's readability.

To change the Format property of these fields, follow these steps:

1. Click the toolbar's Close button to return to Design mode.

2. Double-click the UnitPrice text box to open its Properties window and then click the Format tab of the Properties window.

3. In the Format text box, select Standard. This format eliminates the dollar sign but preserves the monetary formatting.

4. Repeat steps 2 and 3 for the Values text box. The Detail section doesn't require dollar signs.

Tip #130 from

If you select Currency formatting instead of typing **$#,#00.00** to add a dollar sign to the value, your totals don't align. Currency formatting offsets the number to the left to provide space for the parentheses that accountants use to specify negative monetary values.

---

5. Select the txtCatValue in the CategoryID Footer. Click the Properties window's Format tab and type **$#,##0.00** in the Format field. Accountants use dollar signs to identify subtotals and totals in ledgers.

6. Select the txtTotalValue text box in the Report Footer and type **$#,#00.00** as the Format property for the grand total values.

7. The grand total value in the Report Footer is the report's most important element, so click the toolbar's Line/Border Color button and then click the black box to give this field a black border. Next click the Line/Border Width button and then the 2-point border button. This procedure increases the thickness of the border around the grand total.

8. Click the toolbar's Report View button to check your formatting modifications. Click the Bottom of Report page selector button to display the last page of the report (see Figure 14.22).

Figure 14.22
The last page of the report with the correct Format property assigned to the values.

10	Ikura	Tokyo Traders	31	31.00	961.00
13	Konbu	Mayumi's	24	6.00	144.00
18	Carnarvon Tigers	Pavlova, Ltd.	42	62.50	2,625.00
30	Nord-Ost Matjeshering	Nord-Ost-Fisch Handelsgesells	10	25.89	258.90
36	Inlagd Sill	Svensk Sjöföda AB	112	19.00	2,128.00
37	Gravad lax	Svensk Sjöföda AB	11	26.00	286.00
40	Boston Crab Meat	New England Seafood Canner	123	18.40	2,263.20
41	Jack's New England Clam Chowder	New England Seafood Canner	85	9.65	820.25
45	Røgede sild	Lyngbysild	5	9.50	47.50
46	Spegesild	Lyngbysild	95	12.00	1,140.00
58	Escargots de Bourgogne	Escargots Nouveaux	62	13.25	821.50
73	Röd Kaviar	Svensk Sjöföda AB	101	15.00	1,515.00

Category: Seafood   Percent Cat. Units 23.23% Value 18.69% Cat. Units 701   Cat. Value $13,010.35
Grand Totals   Units   3018 Value $69,598.25

Monday, February 22, 1999   Page 2 of 2

ADJUSTING LINE SPACING

In the Page Header section, the controls are placed further apart than is necessary, and the depth of the controls in the Report Header section is out of proportion with the size of the text. The line spacing of the remainder of the report's sections is satisfactory, but you can also change this spacing. Minimizing line spacing allows you to print a report on fewer sheets of paper.

Tip #131 from

You might have to return to Design mode and adjust the width or position of the Cat(egory) and Grand Totals text boxes to align these values with those for the individual products.

To change the spacing of the report's Page Header and Detail sections, follow these steps:

Tip #132 from

You can adjust the size of controls and the line spacing more precisely if you choose Format, Snap to Grid. This command toggles the Snap to Grid feature on and off.

1. Click the toolbar's Close button to return to Design mode.
2. Select all the labels in the Page Header and move the group as close to the top of the section as possible.
3. Click the bottom line of the Page Header and move the line as close to the bottom of the text boxes as possible. (To select the line, you may have to move the CategoryID Header section downward temporarily.)
4. Click a blank area of the report and then move the CategoryID Header section to the bottom of the labels. You can't reduce a section's depth to less than the Height property of the label that has the maximum height in the section.

5. Select both text boxes in the Page Footer section, and move the boxes as a group to the top of the section. Move the Page footer to the bottom of the text boxes.

6. Move the line and label in the Report Header section upward to minimize the amount of white space in the Report Header.

7. Click the toolbar's Report View button to check the Page Header depth and line spacing of the Detail section. The spacing shown in Figure 14.23 is close to the minimum that you can achieve. You can't reduce a section's line spacing to less than that required by the tallest text box or label by reducing the section's Height property in the Properties box. If you try this approach, Access rejects the entry and substitutes the prior value.

8. Click the toolbar's Zoom button to display the report in full-page view. Clicking the mouse when the pointer is the magnifying glass symbol has the same effect as clicking the Zoom button. Alternate clicks toggle between full-size and full-page views.

9. Choose File, Save to save your changes.

Figure 14.23
The report in Report view after you adjust the depth of the Report Header, Page Header, and Detail sections.

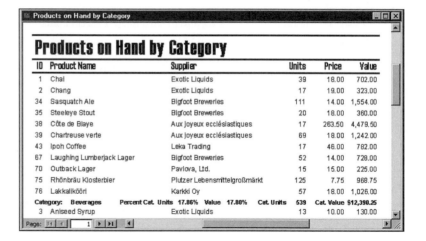

The Products on Hand by Category report is included on the accompanying CD-ROM as Reports.mdb in the \Seua2k\Chaptr14 folder.

ADJUSTING MARGINS AND PRINTING CONVENTIONAL REPORTS

The full-page Report View shows the report as it would print using Access's default printing margins of 1 inch on the top, bottom, and sides of the report (see Figure 14.24). In the Print Setup dialog, you can adjust the printed version of the report. The procedure for printing a report applies to printing the data contained in tables and queries as well as single-record or continuous forms.

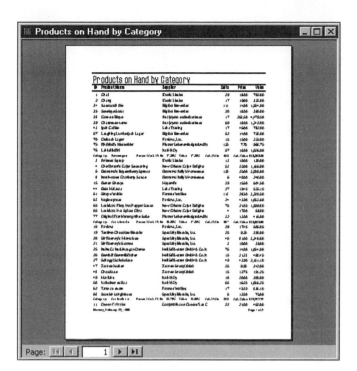

Figure 14.24
The completed report in full-page view.

To change the printing margins for a report, follow these steps:

1. Choose File, Page Setup to open the Page Setup dialog.

2. The Page Setup dialog is similar to the Print and Page Setup dialogs of other Windows applications, with a section for printing margins included. To increase the amount of information on a page, decrease the top and bottom margins. By selecting the Print Data Only check box, you can print only the data in the report; the Report and Page Headers and Footers don't print.

3. In the Left text box, type **2.0** to specify a 2-inch left margin and type **0.5** in the Right text box. In the Top, and Bottom text boxes, type **0.75** inches (see Figure 14.25). Click OK to see a full-page view of the report with the revised margins (see Figure 14.26).

Tip #133 from

RJ

The printing margins that you establish for a report in the Page Setup dialog apply to the active report only; each report has a unique set of margins. When you save the report, Access saves the margin settings.

PART

III

CH

14

Figure 14.25
The Page Setup dialog for printing data sheets, forms, and reports.

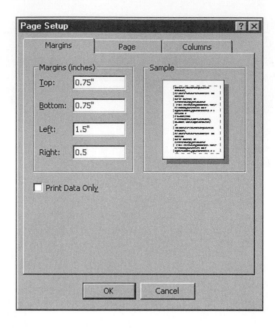

Figure 14.26
The full-page preview of the report with new printing margins applied.

4. To print the report, click the toolbar's Print button. Access immediately prints the report using the current printer options. If you want to change the selected printer, page orientation, graphics quality, or other printer options, choose File, Print. The standard Print dialog appears for the printer specified in Windows as the default printer. Figure 14.27 shows, for example, the Print dialog for a networked HP DeskJet Printer.

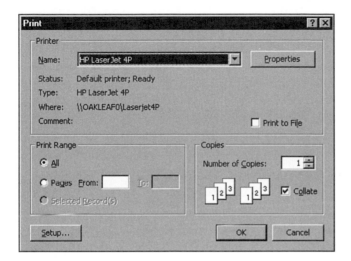

Figure 14.27
The Print dialog controls printing of datasheets, forms, and reports.

5. You can print all or part of a report or print the report to a file for later printing; you can also select the number of copies to print. By choosing the Properties button, you can change the parameters that apply to the printer you are using. Click OK to print the report.

The Page Setup dialog (refer to Figure 14.25) includes a Page tab that lets you select the paper size and orientation. The dialog also includes a Columns page that allows you to establish specifications for printing mailing labels and other multiple-column reports. The next section describes these specifications and how you set them.

PREVENTING WIDOWED RECORDS WITH THE GROUP KEEP TOGETHER PROPERTY

Access includes a Keep Together property for groups that prevents widowed records from appearing at the bottom of the page. Depending on your report section depths, you might find that only a few records of the next group (called *widowed records*) appear at the bottom of the page. You can force a page break when an entire group does not fit on one page by following these steps:

1. With the report in Design view, click the toolbar's Sorting and Grouping button to open the Sorting and Grouping dialog.

2. Select the field with the group symbol in the selection button that corresponds to the group that you want to keep together. In this example, select CategoryID.

3. Open the Keep Together drop-down list and select Whole Group, as shown in Figure 14.28.

Figure 14.28
Setting the report group's Keep Together property.

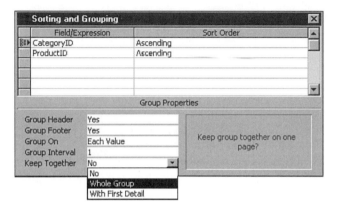

4. Close the Sorting and Grouping dialog and click the Report View button to see the result of applying the group Keep Together property.

Tip #134 from

> If you want to delete or add a Group Header or Footer singly (rather than in pairs), select Yes or No in the appropriate property field of the Sorting and Grouping dialog.

The Report Wizard makes the other entries in the Sorting and Grouping dialog for you. The next chapter describes how to use the Sorting and Grouping dialog to design reports without the aid of the Wizard.

PRINTING MULTICOLUMN REPORTS AS MAILING LABELS

Access lets you print multicolumn reports. You can create a single-column report with the Report Wizard, for example, and then arrange the report to print values from the Detail section in a specified number of columns across the page. The most common application of multicolumn reports is the creation of mailing labels.

You can create mailing lists with the Report Wizard, or you can start with a blank form. The Report Wizard's advantage is that it includes the dimensions of virtually every kind of adhesive label for dot-matrix or laser printers made by the Avery Commercial Products division. You select the product number of the label that you plan to use, and Access determines the number of columns, rows per page, and margins for the report's Detail section. You can also customize the Report Wizard for labels with unusual sizes or that other manufacturers produce.

The Northwind Traders database includes a Customer Labels report that you can modify to suit the design of any mailing label. Figure 14.29 shows the Detail section of the Customer Labels report with the font changed to Courier New in a 10-point font and the size of the label adjusted to 2.5×0.833 inches.

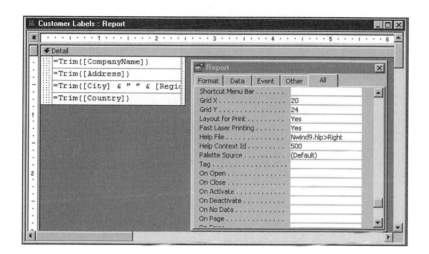

Figure 14.29
The modified Customer Labels report in Design mode.

You specify the number of columns in a row and the number of rows on a page by selecting settings in the Columns page in the Page Setup dialog, as shown in Figure 14.30. This dialog appears when you choose File, Page Setup in either Print Preview or Report Design mode.

The dialog's text boxes, check boxes, and option buttons allow you to perform the following procedures:

- The Number of Columns property sets the number of labels across the page. In this example, this property is set to 3, so the labels print three across.

Note

> The Left and Top margin settings (which you set on the Margins tab of the Page Setup dialog) specify the position at which Access prints the upper-left corner of the first label on the page. For most laser and inkjet printers, these values can't be less than about 0.25 inches. Labels designed for laser and inkjet printers are die cut so that the marginal areas remain on the backing sheet when you remove the individual labels.

- The Width property in the Column Size group overrides the left margin, and the Height property overrides the bottom margin that you establish in Report Design view only if you don't select Same as Detail to use the margins you set in the Detail section.

Figure 14.30
The Columns tab of the
Page Setup dialog

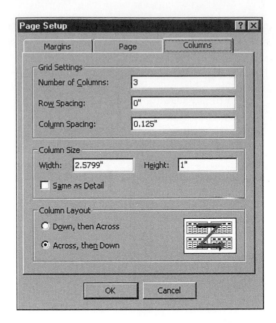

- Column Spacing specifies the position of the left edge of columns to the right of the first column.

- Row Spacing and the Height property determine the number of labels that fit vertically on a page and the vertical distance between successive labels. If you set Row Spacing to 0, the depth of your Detail section determines the vertical spacing of the labels.

- The Across, Then Down option causes the labels to print in columns from left to right and then in rows from the top to the bottom of the page. This setting is preferred for mailing labels because it wastes less label stock for continuous-feed printers.

- The Down, Then Across option causes the labels to print in *snaking* column style. The first column is filled from top to bottom, then the second column is filled from top to bottom, and so on.

After you set the dimensions of the mailing labels and click OK, the full-size view of the labels appears in Print Preview mode, as shown in Figure 14.31.

Click the toolbar's Zoom button to display the full-page layout. To test the label layout properties that you set, print only the labels' first page on standard paper or a xerographic duplicate of the label template supplied with labels designed for laser printing.

Note

You might have to make minor alignment adjustments because the upper-left corner of the printer's image and the upper-left corner of the paper might not correspond exactly.

If you select the Down, Then Across option, the technique for printing successive Detail rows is identical to that which word processing and page-layout applications such as Adobe PageMaker use to create newspaper (snaking) columns. When the first column fills to the page's height, Detail rows fill the next column to the right.

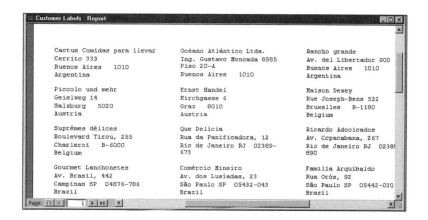

Figure 14.31
Three-across mailing labels shown in Report View's full-size view.

Note

Newspaper columns are suitable for mailing labels but are difficult to format correctly when you convert other kinds of single-column reports to multiple columns. For newspaper columns to operate at all, you must set the Keep Together property of the report's Detail section to No and then set the Detail section's height so that the field data for a single record appears in a single set of rows. If the Detail data includes Memo fields with variable amounts of text in a text box with the Can Grow property set to Yes, formatting newspaper columns properly becomes almost impossible. Instead of having Access attempt to create newspaper columns, an easier approach is to lay out the Detail section with multiple columns in Design mode.

TROUBLESHOOTING

ELIMINATING EMPTY PAGES

When previewing or printing a report, Access displays or prints a blank page after each page with data.

If a report's width becomes greater than the net printable width (the paper width minus the sum of the left and right margins), the number of report pages doubles. Columns of fields that don't fit a page's width print on a second page, similar to the printing method used by spreadsheet applications. If you set your right margin beyond the right printing margin or if the right edge of any control on the report extends past the right printing margin, the added pages often are blank. Change the printing margins or reduce the width of your report so that it conforms to the printable page width. (See the section "Adjusting Margins and Printing Conventional Reports" earlier in this chapter.)

UNEXPECTED PARAMETERS DIALOGS

A Parameters dialog appears when changing to report Preview mode, but the query to which the report is bound doesn't have parameters.

You misspelled one or more objects—usually text box or query field names—in expressions for text boxes or other controls that use calculated values. Click Cancel and verify that the expression in the Record Source property for each text box or other control on the report contains valid object names.

IN THE REAL WORLD—THE APOCRYPHAL PAPERLESS OFFICE

Business magazines of the 1980s and early 1990s touted the forthcoming "paperless office." Articles envisioned scanning incoming documents, storing the images in disk files, and handling all document processing on PC workstations. Document imaging and storage system vendors introduced a wide range of expensive hardware to support the paperless office concept. A new breed of consultants arrived on the scene to develop the workflow systems required to integrate document processing hardware with existing business processes. Document imaging and workflow systems have become a multi-billion dollar industry.

The automotive and other large firms developed electronic document interchange (EDI) to process orders, invoices, and payments electronically. E-mail became a top contender to eliminate ever-growing piles of interoffice memos. Now the Internet and corporate intranets promise to reduce the exchange of paper between business partners engaged in electronic commerce.

Paperless office is an oxymoron—the most popular PC peripheral component continues to be the printer. Sales of printer paper continue to grow at better than 10% per year, and the market for copiers and fax machines shows no signs of a significant slowdown. According to Hewlett-Packard, 90% of information in 1997 was stored on paper and 10% was in digital format; by 2004, H-P estimates that paper-based storage will drop to 30%, with digital files holding 70%. The total amount of stored information doubles every four years or so. H-P projects a continuing increase in the demand for printers and paper.

It's clear that people continue to desire printed information, despite electronic alternatives. The need for printed reports increases with the level of the recipient in the management hierarchy. Few chief executive officers—at least outside of the computer industry—are computer-literate, and only a small minority are PC power users.

Beginning with version 1.0, one of Access's strongest selling points has been its versatile, integrated report printing capabilities. The granular report event model lets you write VBA code to customize report generation. Most other database front-end development platforms have add-on report generators, such as Seagate Software's Crystal Reports. Visual Basic 6.0's Report Designer, which replaces prior versions' Crystal Reports add-on, doesn't even come close to offering the rich feature set of Access 2000 reports.

As this chapter demonstrates, designing and implementing informative, attractive reports can be a tedious process. Exact alignment and proper formatting of labels, text boxes, lines, and other report controls is far more important to reports than forms. Spending the time needed to make reports concise and graphically appealing is worthwhile, especially when you consider that paper reports most likely are destined for management. Cubicle dwellers now fulfill most of their information needs electronically.

There have been surprisingly few changes to Access's report printing engine over the years, and Access 2000 incorporates no major new report features. (Microsoft released Report Snapshots, one of the subjects of the next chapter, as an add-in for Access 97.) Access reports represent one case where Microsoft appears to have taken "If it ain't broke, don't fix it" seriously.

--rj

CHAPTER 15

PREPARING ADVANCED REPORTS

In this chapter

Creating Reports from Scratch   570

Grouping and Sorting Report Data   570

Grouping Data   571

Sorting Data Groups   574

Working from a Blank Report   575

Using a Report as a Subreport   576

Creating the Monthly Sales by Category Report   578

Adding a Linked Subreport to a Bound Report   581

Using Unlinked Subreports and Unbound Reports   584

Adding and Deleting Sections of Your Report   585

Customizing *De Novo* Reports   585

Controlling Page Breaks and Printing Headers and Footers   587

Adding Other Controls to Reports   588

Mailing Report Snapshots   588

Troubleshooting   591

In the Real World—The Art of Report Design   591

CREATING REPORTS FROM SCRATCH

Access 2000's Report Wizard can create reports that you can use "as is" or modify to suit most of your database reporting requirements. In some cases, however, you might have to create reports that are more complex than or different from those offered by the Report Wizard. For example, you might have to apply special grouping and sorting methods to your reports. Including subreports within your reports requires that you start from a blank report form instead of using the Report Wizard.

To understand fully the process of designing advanced Access reports, you must be familiar with Access functions, which is one of the subjects of Chapter 9, "Understanding Query Operators and Expressions." You also must understand the methods that you use to create and design forms, which are covered in Chapters 12, "Creating and Using Forms," and 13, "Designing Custom Multitable Forms." Reports make extensive use of Access functions such as Sum() and expressions like ="Subtotal of" & [*Field Name*] & ":". If you skipped Chapters 9, 12, or 13, you might want to refer to the appropriate sections of those chapters whenever you encounter unfamiliar subjects or terminology in this chapter.

GROUPING AND SORTING REPORT DATA

Most reports you create require that you organize the data into groups and subgroups in a style similar to the outline of a book. The Report Wizard lets you establish the initial grouping and sorting properties for your data, but you might want to rearrange your report's data after reviewing the Report Wizard's first draft.

 The Sorting and Grouping dialog (see Figure 15.1) lets you modify these report properties in Design mode. This section uses the Products on Hand by Category report that you created in the preceding chapter. The sorting and grouping methods described here, however, apply to any report that you create. To display the dialog, open the report in Design view and click the toolbar's Sorting and Grouping button.

Figure 15.1
The Sorting and Grouping dialog lets you create or alter report groups and the sort order within groups.

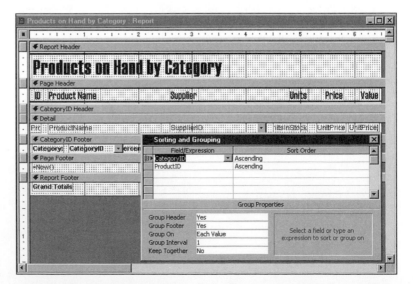

The Sorting and Grouping dialog lets you determine the fields or expressions on which Access is to group the products, up to a maximum of 10 fields or expressions. You can sort the grouped data in ascending or descending order, but you must select one or the other; "unsorted" isn't an option. The Sorting and Grouping symbol in the selection button at the left of the window indicates that Access uses the field or expression in the adjacent column to group the records.

GROUPING DATA

The method that you use to group data depends on the data in the field by which you group. You can group by categories, in which case a unique value must represent each category. You can group data by a range of values, which usually are numeric but also can be alphabetic. You can use the data in a field to group the data, or you can substitute an expression as the basis for the grouping.

Reports demonstrating the grouping examples of the following sections are included in the Reports2.mdb database in the \Seua2k\Chaptr15 folder of the accompanying CD-ROM.

GROUPING BY NUMERIC VALUES

When you told the Report Wizard in the preceding chapter to use CategoryID as the field by which to group, you elected to group by a numeric value. You can alter the grouping sequence easily by using the Sorting and Grouping dialog.

→ To review the Report Wizard process, **see** "Creating a Grouping Report with the Report Wizard," **p. 536**.

To group by SupplierID, for example, do the following:

1. If you don't already have it open, open the Products On Hand by Category report in Design view and click the Sorting and Grouping icon on the toolbar.

2. Select SupplierID as the first group field. When you change the group field, Access automatically renames the Group Header and Footer sections from CategoryID to SupplierID.

3. Delete the CategoryID drop-down list in the SupplierID Footer section; CategoryID isn't appropriate to the new grouping.

4. Open the Field List and drag the SupplierID field to the SupplierID Footer section, and drop it in the position formerly occupied by CategoryID. SupplierID is a lookup field, so the new control for the field is a drop-down list.

5. Delete the label and position the SupplierID list at the top left of the Footer. Shorten the captions of the labels of the other controls in the Footer and move them to make room for the long CompanyName values displayed by the SupplierID list. (You can delete the Units and Value labels for columns four and six of the form, if you want.) Widen the SupplierID list and apply the Bold attribute. Optionally, select all of the controls in the SupplierID Footer section, and change the Font Size to 9 points (see Figure 15.2).

Figure 15.2
Altering the Product on Hand by Category report to grouping by SupplierID.

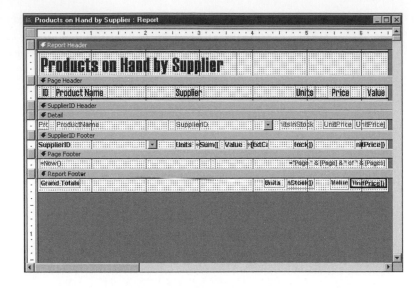

6. Change the title in the report header to **Products On Hand by Supplier**, and then choose File, Save As and save the report under the same name. Figure 15.3 shows the appearance of your report in Print Preview mode.

Figure 15.3
The effect of changing the report grouping so that it displays records by SupplierID.

Products on Hand by Supplier

ID	Product Name	Supplier	Units	Price	Value
1	Chai	Exotic Liquids	39	18.00	702.00
2	Chang	Exotic Liquids	17	19.00	323.00
3	Aniseed Syrup	Exotic Liquids	13	10.00	130.00
Exotic Liquids		**Units 2.29% Value 1.66%**	**69**		**$1,155.00**
4	Chef Anton's Cajun Seasoning	New Orleans Cajun Delights	53	22.00	1,166.00
65	Louisiana Fiery Hot Pepper Sauce	New Orleans Cajun Delights	76	21.05	1,599.80
66	Louisiana Hot Spiced Okra	New Orleans Cajun Delights	4	17.00	68.00
New Orleans Cajun Delights		**Units 4.41% Value 4.07%**	**133**		**$2,833.80**
6	Grandma's Boysenberry Spread	Grandma Kelly's Homestead	120	25.00	3,000.00
7	Uncle Bob's Organic Dried Pears	Grandma Kelly's Homestead	15	30.00	450.00
8	Northwoods Cranberry Sauce	Grandma Kelly's Homestead	6	40.00	240.00
Grandma Kelly's Homestead		**Units 4.67% Value 5.30%**	**141**		**$3,690.00**
10	Ikura	Tokyo Traders	31	31.00	961.00
74	Longlife Tofu	Tokyo Traders	4	10.00	40.00
Tokyo Traders		**Units 1.16% Value 1.44%**	**35**		**$1,001.00**
11	Queso Cabrales	Cooperativa de Quesos 'Las Ca	22	21.00	462.00
12	Queso Manchego La Pastora	Cooperativa de Quesos 'Las Ca	86	38.00	3,268.00
Cooperativa de Quesos 'Las Cabras'		**Units 3.58% Value 5.36%**	**108**		**$3,730.00**

Page: 1

GROUPING BY ALPHABETIC CODE CHARACTERS

If you use a systematic code for grouping, you can group by the first five or fewer characters of the code field. With an expression, you can group by any set of characters within a field. To group by the second and third digits of a code, for example, use the following expression:

`=Mid([FieldName],2,2).`

GROUPING WITH SUBGROUPS

If your table or query contains appropriate data, you can group reports by more than one level by creating subgroups. The Employee Sales by Country report (one of the Northwind Traders sample reports), for example, uses groups (Country) and subgroups (the employee's name—the actual group is an Access expression that combines the FirstName and LastName fields) to organize orders received within a range of dates. Open the Employee Sales by Country report in Design mode to view the additional section created by a subgroup.

USING A FUNCTION TO GROUP BY RANGE

You often must sort reports by ranges of values. (If you opened the Employee Sales by Country report, close it and reopen the Products on Hand by Category report in Design mode.) If you want to divide the Products on Hand by Category report into a maximum of six sections—each beginning with a five-letter group of the alphabet (A through E, F through J, and so on) based on the ProductName field—the entries in the Sorting and Grouping dialog should look like the entries in Figure 15.4.

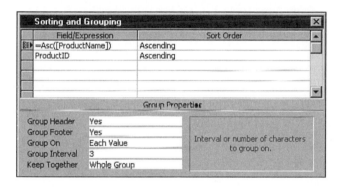

Figure 15.4
Sorting and Grouping criteria to group records in alphabetical intervals.

VBA's =**Asc**([ProductName]) function returns the ASCII (numeric) value of the first character of its string argument, the ProductName field. You set the Group On specification to Interval and then set the Group Interval to 3. This setup groups the data into names beginning with A through C, D through F, and so on. You must add an ascending sort on ProductName to assure alphabetic sorting within the group (see Figure 15.5). You delete all text boxes in the Group Footer because subtotals by alphabetic groups aren't significant. Although of limited value in this report, an alphabetic grouping often is useful for formatting long, alphabetized lists to assist readers in finding a particular record.

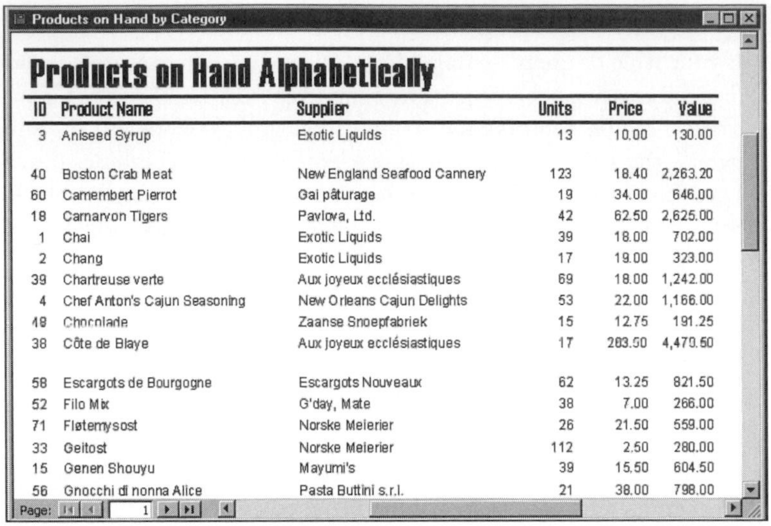

Figure 15.5
A report that categorizes products by three-letter alphabetic intervals.

Products on Hand Alphabetically

ID	Product Name	Supplier	Units	Price	Value
3	Aniseed Syrup	Exotic Liquids	13	10.00	130.00
40	Boston Crab Meat	New England Seafood Cannery	123	18.40	2,263.20
60	Camembert Pierrot	Gai pâturage	19	34.00	646.00
18	Carnarvon Tigers	Pavlova, Ltd.	42	62.50	2,625.00
1	Chai	Exotic Liquids	39	18.00	702.00
2	Chang	Exotic Liquids	17	19.00	323.00
39	Chartreuse verte	Aux joyeux ecclésiastiques	69	18.00	1,242.00
4	Chef Anton's Cajun Seasoning	New Orleans Cajun Delights	53	22.00	1,166.00
48	Chocolade	Zaanse Snoepfabriek	15	12.75	191.25
38	Côte de Blaye	Aux joyeux ecclésiastiques	17	263.50	4,479.50
58	Escargots de Bourgogne	Escargots Nouveaux	62	13.25	821.50
52	Filo Mix	G'day, Mate	38	7.00	266.00
71	Fløtemysost	Norske Meierier	26	21.50	559.00
33	Geitost	Norske Meierier	112	2.50	280.00
15	Genen Shouyu	Mayumi's	39	15.50	604.50
56	Gnocchi di nonna Alice	Pasta Buttini s.r.l.	21	38.00	798.00

Page: 1

GROUPING ON DATE AND TIME

If you group data on a field with a Date/Time data type, Access lets you set the Sorting and Grouping dialog's Group On property to Year, Qtr (quarter), Month, Week, Day, Hour, or Minute. To group records so that values of the same quarter for several years print in sequence, type the following in the Field/Expression column of the Sorting and Grouping dialog:

```
=DatePart("q",[FieldName])
```

→ For a full listing of ways you can sort by date or time, **see** "Functions for Date and Time," **p. 333**.

SORTING DATA GROUPS

Although most data sorting within groups is based on the values contained in a field, you also can sort by expressions. When compiling an inventory valuation list, the products with the highest extended inventory value are the most important. The report's users might want these products listed first in a group. This decision requires sorting the records within groups on the expression =[UnitsInStock]*[UnitPrice], the same expression that Access uses to calculate the report's Value column. A descending sort is necessary to place the highest values at the top of the report. Figure 15.6 shows the required entries in the Sorting and Grouping dialog.

The descending sort on the inventory value expression results in the report shown in Figure 15.7. As expected, the products with the highest inventory value appear first in each category.

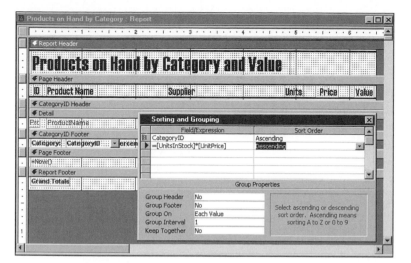

Figure 15.6
Sorting data by each
record on an expression.

Figure 15.7
The Products on Hand by
Category and Value
report, showing records
sorted by inventory value
within groups.

Products on Hand by Category and Value

ID	Product Name	Supplier	Units	Price	Value
38	Côte de Blaye	Aux joyeux ecclésiastiques	17	263.50	4,479.50
34	Sasquatch Ale	Bigfoot Breweries	111	14.00	1,554.00
39	Chartreuse verte	Aux joyeux ecclésiastiques	69	18.00	1,242.00
76	Lakkalikööri	Karkki Oy	57	18.00	1,026.00
75	Rhönbräu Klosterbier	Plutzer Lebensmittelgroßmärkt	125	7.75	968.75
43	Ipoh Coffee	Leka Trading	17	46.00	782.00
67	Laughing Lumberjack Lager	Bigfoot Breweries	52	14.00	728.00
1	Chai	Exotic Liquids	39	10.00	702.00
35	Steeleye Stout	Bigfoot Breweries	20	18.00	360.00
2	Chang	Exotic Liquids	17	19.00	323.00
70	Outback Lager	Pavlova, Ltd.	15	15.00	225.00

Category: Beverages   Percent Cat. Units 17.86%   Value 17.80%   Cat. Units 539   Cat. Value $12,390.25

61	Sirop d'érable	Forêts d'érables	113	28.50	3,220.50
6	Grandma's Boysenberry Spread	Grandma Kelly's Homestead	120	25.00	3,000.00
65	Louisiana Fiery Hot Pepper Sauce	New Orleans Cajun Delights	76	21.05	1,599.80
4	Chef Anton's Cajun Seasoning	New Orleans Cajun Delights	53	22.00	1,166.00

WORKING FROM A BLANK REPORT

Usually, the fastest way to set up a report is to use the Report Wizard to create a basic
report and then modify the basic report as described in Chapter 14, "Printing Basic Reports
and Mailing Labels," and previous sections of this chapter. If you're creating a report style
that the Wizard can't handle or a report containing a subreport, however, modifying a standard report style created by the Report Wizard could take longer than creating a report by
using the default blank report that Access provides.

USING A REPORT AS A SUBREPORT

The report includes information about total monthly sales of products by category. Comparing the monthly sales to the inventory level of a category allows the report's user to estimate inventory turnover rates. This report serves two purposes—a primary report and a subreport within another report. You add the Monthly Sales by Category report as a subreport of the Products on Hand by Category report in the "Incorporating Subreports" section later in this chapter.

To create a report to use as the Monthly Sales by Category subreport (rpt1997MonthlyCategorySales) in the following section of this chapter, "Adding and Deleting Sections of Your Report," you need to base the subreport on a query, qry1997MonthlyProductSales, adapted for this purpose.

 A copy of the qry1997MonthlyProductSales query is included in the Reports2.mdb database in the \Seua2k\Chaptr15 folder of the accompanying CD-ROM.

→ To review how to create this query, **see** "Designing a Monthly Product Sales Crosstab Query," **p. 400**.

To modify the query for this subreport, follow these steps:

1. Close the Products on Hand by Category report and click the Query shortcut in the Database window.

2. Open the qry1997MonthlyProductSales in Design view.

3. In the grid, change the first column's field name from ProductID to CategoryID by opening the Field drop-down list and clicking the CategoryID field name. You need the CategoryID field to link with the CategoryID field in the qryProductOnHand query that the Products on Hand by Category report uses as its data source.

4. Delete the ProductName column. The modified query appears as shown in Figure 15.8.

Figure 15.8
The modified crosstab query for the Monthly Sales by Category subreport.

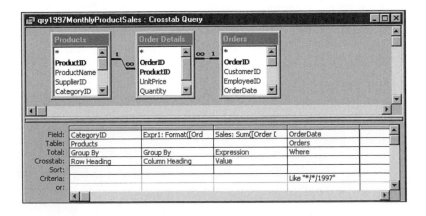

5. Choose File, Save As and name the modified query **qry1997MonthlyCategorySales**. Your query result set appears as shown in Figure 15.9.

Category	Jan	Feb	Mar	Apr	May
Beverages	$24,224.40	$3,090.40	$11,027.20	$7,377.50	$15,654.00
Condiments	$5,698.80	$6,618.40	$1,905.90	$5,903.00	$5,728.80
Confections	$9,582.30	$7,413.50	$3,324.90	$11,714.65	$7,997.50
Dairy Products	$9,872.00	$5,616.00	$9,844.40	$6,647.00	$11,491.50
Grains/Cereals	$4,570.20	$5,043.40	$3,350.00	$6,555.60	$2,551.50
Meat/Poultry	$7,775.80	$8,442.90	$3,271.60	$6,846.24	$3,548.05
Produce	$2,895.00	$2,698.80	$3,676.80	$6,137.10	$3,481.20
Seafood	$2,074.30	$2,283.80	$3,579.10	$4,518.30	$6,371.15

Record: 1 of 8

Figure 15.9
The result set returned by the crosstab query of Figure 15.7.

6. Open the New Object drop-down list on the toolbar and select New Report from the list. The New Report dialog appears.

7. Access automatically selects qry1997MonthlyCategorySales as the query on which to base the report. Select Design View from the list and click OK. Access creates the default blank report shown in Figure 15.10.

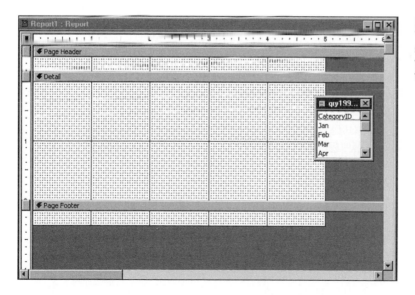

Figure 15.10
The default report presented by Access after you select Design View in the New dialog.

CREATING THE MONTHLY SALES BY CATEGORY REPORT

The crosstab query that acts as the Monthly Sales by Category report's data source is closely related to a report, but the crosstab query doesn't include detail records (see Chapter 10). Each row of the query consists of subtotals of sales for a category for each month of the year. One row appears below the inventory value subtotal when you link the subreport (child) to the main (master) report, so this report needs only a Detail section. Each detail row, however, requires a header label to print the month. The CategoryID field is included so that you can verify that the data is linked correctly.

To create the Monthly Sales by Category report (and later a subreport), follow these steps:

1. Open a new report in Design view, selecting qry1997MonthlyCategorySales as its data source.

2. Delete the default Page Header and Page Footer sections by choosing View, Page Header/Footer to clear the toggle check mark. By default, blank reports have 24×24 grid dots, and Snap to Grid is selected.

3. Drag the right margin of the Detail section to the right so that the report is about 6.4 inches wide.

4. Click the toolbar's Sorting and Grouping button to display the dialog, and select CategoryID as the field to use to sort the data with a standard ascending sort. Close the Sorting and Grouping dialog.

5. Click the toolbar's Field List button, if necessary, select CategoryID, and drag its field symbol to the Detail section.

6. Click the CategoryID label and relocate the label to the upper left of the Detail section directly over the CategoryID combo box. (CategoryID appears as a dummy combo box, not a text box, in Report Design view because CategoryID is a lookup field.) Adjust the depth of the label and text box to 0.2 inches (four grid dots) and the width to 1 inch. Edit the label's text to **Category**.

7. Click and drag the field list's Jan field to the right of the CategoryID field. Move the label to the top of the section, adjacent to the right border of the field to its left. Move the text box under the label. Adjust the label and text box depth to four dots and the width to about 16 dots. Edit the label's text to delete the colon.

8. Repeat step 6 for the month fields of Feb through Jun. The report design now appears as shown in Figure 15.11.

9. Click each label while holding down the Shift key so that you select all labels (but only the labels).

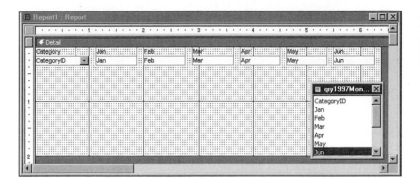

Figure 15.11
The report with labels
and text boxes added for
the first six months of
1997.

10. Click the toolbar's Bold button to add the bold attribute to the labels. Then click the Center button to center the labels above the text boxes.

11. Select the CategoryID text box and click the toolbar's Bold button.

12. Choose Edit, Select All, and drag the labels and text boxes so that the tops of the labels are two dots down from the top of the Detail section. Click a blank area of the report to deselect the controls.

13. If the toolbox is invisible, click the Toolbox button of the toolbar. Click the Line tool and add a line at the top edge of the labels. Drag the line's right-end handle to the right edge of the Jun text box.

14. Click the drop-down list of the Line/Border Width button on the toolbar and click the 1-point line-thickness button.

15. Repeat steps 12 and 13 for another identical line but add the new line under the labels (and above the text boxes).

16. Drag the Detail section's margins to within two dots of the bottom and right edge of the controls. The report's design appears as shown in Figure 15.12.

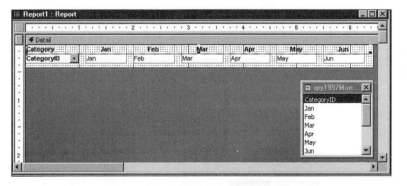

Figure 15.12
The layout of the new
report's Detail section
with the two added lines
selected.

17. Click the toolbar's View button to verify the design (see Figure 15.13).

Figure 15.13
The monthly category sales report in Print Preview mode.

rpt1997MonthlyCategorySales : Report

Category	Jan	Feb	Mar	Apr	May	Jun
Beverages	$24,224.40	$3,090.40	$11,027.20	$7,377.50	$15,654.00	$3,602.00
Category	Jan	Feb	Mar	Apr	May	Jun
Condiments	$5,698.80	$6,618.40	$1,905.90	$5,903.00	$5,728.80	$1,886.85
Category	Jan	Feb	Mar	Apr	May	Jun
Confections	$9,582.30	$7,413.50	$3,324.90	$11,714.65	$7,997.50	$2,494.40
Category	Jan	Feb	Mar	Apr	May	Jun
Dairy Products	$9,872.00	$5,616.00	$9,844.40	$6,647.00	$11,491.50	$9,507.70
Category	Jan	Feb	Mar	Apr	May	Jun
Grains/Cereals	$4,570.20	$5,043.40	$3,350.00	$6,555.60	$2,551.50	$6,882.50
Category	Jan	Feb	Mar	Apr	May	Jun
Meat/Poultry	$7,775.80	$8,442.90	$3,271.60	$6,846.24	$3,548.05	$5,006.30
Category	Jan	Feb	Mar	Apr	May	Jun
Produce	$2,895.00	$2,698.80	$3,676.80	$6,137.10	$3,481.20	$6,231.00
Category	Jan	Feb	Mar	Apr	May	Jun
Seafood	$2,074.30	$2,283.80	$3,579.10	$4,518.30	$6,371.15	$3,477.25

Page: 1

18. Choose File, Save As and type **rpt1997MonthlyCategorySales** as the report's name.

To add to your report the remaining months of the year, follow these steps:

1. To accommodate another row of labels and text boxes, increase the depth of the Detail section by dragging the bottom margin down (about 1 inch).

2. Choose Edit, Select All.

3. Press Ctrl+C to copy the labels and text boxes to the Clipboard.

4. Press Ctrl+V to paste a copy of the labels and text boxes to the Detail section.

5. Move this copy under the original labels and text boxes. Space the copy two grid dots below the originals

6. Click a blank area of the report to deselect the controls; then select the new CategoryID text box. Delete the CategoryID text box. When you delete this text box, you also delete the associated label.

7. Edit both the labels and text boxes to display Jul through Dec. (Access automatically resizes the labels to fit the new text value and automatically sets the text boxes' Control Source property to match the field name you type into the text box.)

8. Drag up the bottom margin to within two dots of the bottom of the text boxes in the second row. The final design appears in Figure 15.14.

10. Click the toolbar's Print Preview button to display the double-row report (see Figure 15.15).

11. Close the rpt1997MonthlyCategorySales report and save the changes.

The technique of copying controls to the Clipboard, pasting copies to reports, and then editing the copies is often faster than creating duplicate controls that differ from one another only in the text of labels and text boxes.

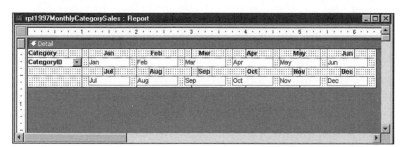

Figure 15.14
The final design of the rpt1997MonthlyCategory Sales report.

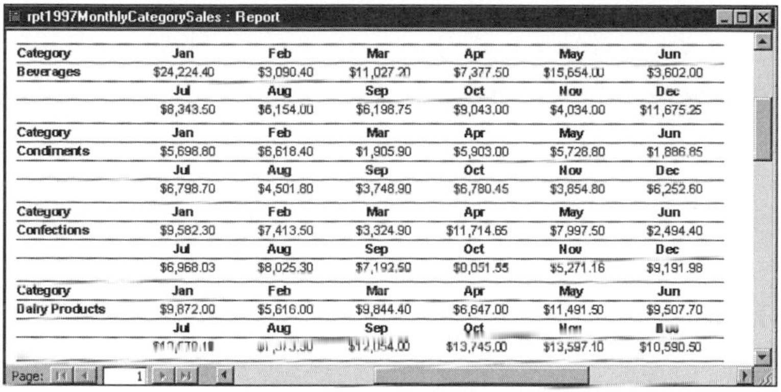

Figure 15.15
The rpt1997Monthly CategorySales report in Print Preview.

INCORPORATING SUBREPORTS

Reports, like forms, can include subreports. Unlike the Form Wizard, however, the Report Wizard offers no option of automatically creating reports that include subreports. You can add subreports to reports that you create with the Report Wizard, or you can create subreports from blank reports, as shown in the preceding section, "Working From a Blank Report."

ADDING A LINKED SUBREPORT TO A BOUND REPORT

If a main report is bound to a table or query as a data source and the subreport's data source can be related to the main report's data source, you can link the subreport's data to the main report's data.

To add and link the rpt1997MonthlyCategorySales report as a subreport to the Products on Hand by Category report, for example, follow these steps:

1. Open the Products on Hand by Category report in Design mode.

2. Drag down the top of the Page Footer border to make room for the subreport in the CategoryID Footer section (about 0.5 inch).

3. Click the toolbar's Database Window button. If the Database window is maximized, click the Restore button.

4. Click and drag the small Report icon from the left of the rpt1997MonthlyCategorySales report to a location inside the CategoryID Footer section. Drop the icon below the CategoryID text box. You must be able to see the location where you want to drop the new subreport in the Report Design window, as shown in Figure 15.18.

5. At the point where you drop the icon, Access creates a subreport box that is similar to a text box. This subreport box has an associated label (see Figure 15.18). Delete the label.

Figure 15.16
Dragging and dropping a report as a subreport within another report.

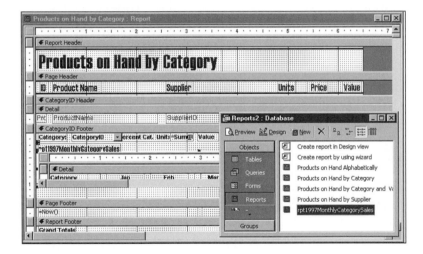

6. Click the Maximize button to restore the Report Design window.

7. Adjust the CategoryID Footer's depth to provide about 0.1-inch margins above and below the section's controls.

NEW 2000

8. You need to link the data in the subreport to the data of the main report so that only the sales data corresponding to a specific group's CategoryID value appears on screen. Select the subreport box and click the Properties button to display the subreport's Properties window. Click the Data tab, and click the builder button to open the new Subreport Field Linker dialog (see Figure 15.17)

Access attempts to create the link. If the main report and subreports are based on tables and a relationship is set between the tables, Access creates the link to the related fields. If the main report is grouped to a key field and the subreport's table or query contains a field of the same name and data type, Access creates the link. Click OK to close the the Subform Field Linker dialog.

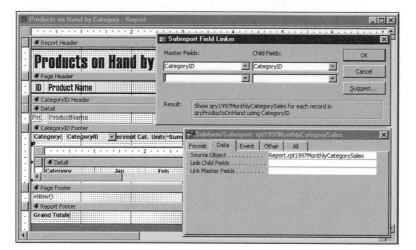

Figure 15.17
Setting the properties to link the subreport to the main report in Access 2000's new Subreport Linker dialog.

9. Click the toolbar's Print Preview button to display the report in the full-size view. The subreport appears as shown at the bottom of Figure 15.18. Click the page selector buttons to view other parts of the subreport to confirm that the linkage is correct.

10. Choose File, Save As, and save the modified report as **rpt1997ProductsOnHandWithSales**.

You can add and link several subreports to the main report if each subreport has a field in common with the main report's data source.

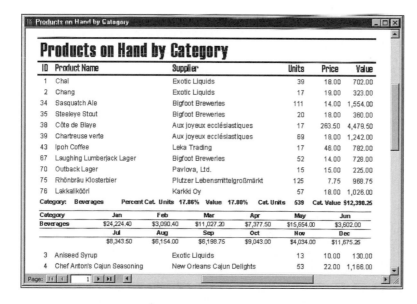

Figure 15.18
The rpt1997Monthly CategorySales subreport linked to the Products on Hand by Category report.

Tip #135 from

You can use calculated values to link main reports and subreports. Calculated values often are based on time—months, quarters, or years. To link main reports and subreports by calculated values, you must create queries for both the main report and subreport that include the calculated value in a field, such as Month or Year. You create the calculated field in each query by using the corresponding Access date function, `Month` or `Year`. To group by quarters, select `Interval` for the Group On property and set the value of the Group Interval property to `3`. You can't use `Qtr` as the Group On property because the calculated value lacks the Date/Time field data type.

 If you receive an error message when you try to create a link between the main report and subreport, turn to "Link Expression Errors," in the "Troubleshooting" section at the end of this chapter.

USING UNLINKED SUBREPORTS AND UNBOUND REPORTS

Most reports that you create use subreports that are linked to the main report's data source. You can, however, insert independent subreports within main reports. In this case, you don't enter values for the Link Child Fields and Link Master Fields properties—in fact, if Access adds values, you delete them. The subreport's data source can be related to or completely independent of the main report's data source. Figure 15.21 shows the effect of including an unlinked subreport in a main report. Figure 15.21 shows a portion of page 2 of the rpt1997MonthlyCategorySales subreport within the rpt1997ProductsOnHandWithSalesSales report after deleting the CategoryID values of the Link Child Fields and Link Master Fields properties. Notice that without the link the subreport displays all records instead of just those records related to the particular category in which the subreport appears. You must set the CategoryID Footer section's Keep Together property to No to display the subform. The Keep Together property is one of the subjects of the "Controlling Page Breaks and Printing Page Headers and Footers" section later in the chapter.

Figure 15.19
The appearance of the rpt1997MonthlyCategory Sales subreport for the beverages category when the linking properties have been deleted.

Products on Hand by Category						
70 Outback Lager		Pavlova, Ltd.		15	15.00	225.00
75 Rhönbräu Klosterbier		Plutzer Lebensmittelgroßmärkt		125	7.75	968.75
76 Lakkalikööri		Karkki Oy		57	18.00	1,026.00
Category: Beverages		Percent Cat. Units 17.86%	Value 17.80%	**Cat. Units 539**	**Cat. Value $12,390.25**	

Category	Jan	Feb	Mar	Apr	May	Jun
Beverages	$24,224.40	$3,090.40	$11,027.20	$7,377.50	$15,654.00	$3,602.00
	Jul	Aug	Sep	Oct	Nov	Dec
	$8,343.50	$6,154.00	$6,198.75	$9,043.00	$4,034.00	$11,675.25
Category	Jan	Feb	Mar	Apr	May	Jun
Condiments	$5,698.80	$6,618.40	$1,905.90	$5,903.00	$5,728.80	$1,886.85
	Jul	Aug	Sep	Oct	Nov	Dec
	$6,798.70	$4,501.80	$3,748.90	$6,780.45	$3,854.80	$6,252.60
Category	Jan	Feb	Mar	Apr	May	Jun
Confections	$9,582.30	$7,413.50	$3,324.90	$11,714.65	$7,997.50	$2,494.40
	Jul	Aug	Sep	Oct	Nov	Dec
	$6,968.03	$8,025.30	$7,192.50	$8,051.55	$5,271.16	$9,191.98
Category	Jan	Feb	Mar	Apr	May	Jun
Dairy Products	$9,872.00	$5,616.00	$9,844.40	$6,647.00	$11,491.50	$9,507.70
	Jul	Aug	Sep	Oct	Nov	Dec
	$13,570.10	$7,375.50	$12,054.00	$13,745.00	$13,597.10	$10,590.50
Category	Jan	Feb	Mar	Apr	May	Jun
Grains/Cereals	$4,570.20	$5,043.40	$3,350.00	$6,555.60	$2,551.50	$6,882.50
	Jul	Aug	Sep	Oct	Nov	Dec

Page: 1

You can add multiple subreports to an unbound report if all the subreports fit on one page of the report or across the page. In the latter case, you can use the landscape-printing orientation to increase the available page width. To create an unbound report with multiple subreports, follow these steps:

1. Click the Report shortcut in the Database window, if necessary, and then click the New button to display the New Report dialog.

2. Keep the text box for the New Report dialog's data source blank, select Design View in the list, and then click OK. This action creates an unbound report.

3 Click the toolbar's Database Window button to display the Database window and then drag the Report icon for the first subreport to the blank form's Detail section.

4. Drag the Report icon for the second subreport to the blank form's Detail section. If the two subreports fit vertically on one page, place the second subreport below the first subreport. If either subreport requires more than a page, place the second subreport to the right of the first. In this case, you must add column labels for the subreports in the main report's Page Header section so that each page identifies the columns.

Tip #136 from

R J

> You can also add subreports to a report by using the Toolbox's subform/subreport tool. Use the procedures for adding subforms that you learned in Chapter 13.

CUSTOMIZING *DE NOVO* REPORTS

Most of the preceding examples in this chapter are based on a standard report structure and template you chose when creating the Products on Hand by Category report in Chapter 14. When you start a report from scratch, you must add sections required by your reports, set up printing parameters, and, if the number of records in the data source is large, consider limiting the number of detail rows to supply only the most significant information.

ADDING AND DELETING SECTIONS OF YOUR REPORT

When you create a report from a blank template or modify a report created by the Report Wizard, add new sections to the report by using the following guidelines:

- To add Report Headers and Footers as a pair, choose <u>V</u>iew, Report <u>H</u>eader/Footer.

- To add Page Headers and Footers as a pair, choose <u>V</u>iew, <u>P</u>age Header/Footer.

- To add a Group Header or Footer, click the toolbar's Sorting and Grouping button and set the Group Header or Group Footer property value to Yes.

Figure 15.20 shows a blank report, with the headers and footers for each section that you can include in a report. (Although Figure 15.20 shows only one group, you may add up to 10 group levels to your report.)

Figure 15.20
A blank report with all sections added.

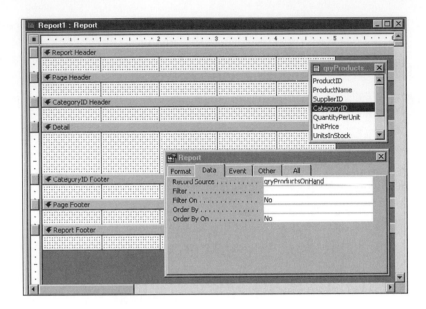

If you group the data in more than one level (group, subgroup, sub-subgroup), you can add a Group Header and Footer for each level of grouping. This action adds to your report another pair of sections for each subgroup level.

You delete sections from reports by using methods similar to those that you use to create the sections. To delete unwanted sections, use the following guidelines:

- To delete the Detail section or an individual Report Header, Report Footer, Page Header, or Page Footer section, delete all controls from the section, and then drag up the divider bar below so that the section has no depth. To delete a Report Footer, drag the report's bottom margin to the Report Footer border. These actions do not actually delete the sections, but sections with no depth do not print or affect the report's layout.

- To delete Report Headers and Footers as a pair, choose View, Report Header/Footer. If the Report Header or Footer includes a control, a message box warns you that you will lose the controls in the deleted sections.

- To delete Page Headers and Footers as a pair, choose View, Page Header/Footer. A warning message box appears if either section contains controls.

 - To delete a Group Header or Footer, click the toolbar's Sorting and Grouping button and set the Group Header or Group Footer property's value to No.

Tip #137 from

Page and Report Headers and Footers that incorporate thin lines at the upper border of the header or footer can be difficult to delete individually. To make these lines visible, choose Edit, Select All to add sizing anchors to the lines. Hold down the Shift key and click the controls that you want to save in order to deselect these controls. Then press the Delete key to delete the remaining selected lines.

CONTROLLING PAGE BREAKS AND PRINTING PAGE HEADERS AND FOOTERS

The Force New Page and Keep Together properties of the report's Group Header, Detail, and Group Footer sections control manual page breaks. To set these properties, double-click the group's section border to display the section's Properties window. Force New Page causes an unconditional page break immediately before printing the section. If you set the Keep Together property to Yes and insufficient room is available on the current page to print the entire section, a page break occurs and the section prints on the next page.

To control whether Page Headers or Footers print on the first or last page of a report, choose Edit, Select Report and then click the toolbar's Properties button. You then select the Page Headers and Page Footers printing option in the Format page of the Properties window (see Figure 15.11).

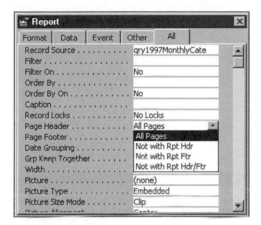

Figure 15.21
The Properties window for a report, displaying page-section printing options.

REDUCING THE LENGTH OF REPORTS

A report's properties or controls don't limit the number of rows of detail data that a report presents. One way of minimizing detail data is to write a TopN or TopNPercent query using Jet SQL. (Search the online help for the TopValues property to learn more about TopN and TopNPercent queries.) All rows of a table or query appear somewhere in the report's Detail section, if the report includes a Detail section with at least one control. To include only a selected range of dates in a report, for example, you must base the report on a query with the criteria necessary to select the Detail records or apply a filter to the report. If the user is to select the range of records to include in the report, use a parameter query as the report's data source.

ADDING OTHER CONTROLS TO REPORTS

Access places no limit on the toolbox controls that you can add to reports. So far, the controls that you have modified or added have been limited to labels, text boxes, lines, and the combo boxes that Access places automatically for fields configured as lookup fields. These four kinds of controls are likely to comprise more than 90 percent of the controls used in the reports you create. Controls that require user interaction, such as lists and combo boxes, can be used in a nonprinting section of the report, but practical use of these controls in reports is limited. The following list describes other controls that you might want to add to reports:

- *Bound object frames* print the contents of the OLE Object field data type. An OLE object can be a still or animated graphic, a video clip, a waveform or CD audio, or even MIDI music. Reports are designed only for printing, so animated graphics, video, and sound are inappropriate for reports.

- *Unbound object frames* display OLE objects created by server applications, such as Microsoft Graph (included with Access), Windows Paint, Excel, or the Microsoft WordArt or Equation Editor OLE applets included with Microsoft Word. Usually, you place unbound objects in the report's Form Header or Form Footer section, but you can add a logo to the top of each page by placing the image object in the Page Header section. A graph or chart created by the Chart Wizard is a special kind of unbound OLE object.

- *Lines* and *rectangles* (also called *shapes*) create decorative elements on reports. Lines of varying widths can separate the sections of the report or emphasize a particular section.

- *Check boxes* and *option buttons* can be used to indicate the values of Yes/No fields or within group frames to indicate multiple-choice selections. Group frames, option buttons, and check boxes used in reports indicate only the value of data cells and do not change the values. Reports seldom use toggle buttons.

Bound and unbound object frames are the subject of Chapter 19, "Adding Charts and Graphics to Forms and Reports."

MAILING REPORT SNAPSHOTS

NEW 2000 Outlook or Outlook Express let you send a report as a Report Snapshot attachment to a message. Microsoft released Report Snapshots (.snp) as an add-in for Access 97; the Report Snapshot feature is built into Access 2000. The advantage of a Report Snapshot is that recipients don't need Access to view the reports. If the recipient doesn't have the Snapshot viewer (Snapview.exe and Snapview.hlp) installed, he or she must obtain it from you or the Microsoft Web Site at http://www.microsoft.com/accessdev/prodinfo/snapshot.htm. :

> **Note**
>
> You can also publish your reports as HTML pages to make them available on the Internet or your company's intranet. Part IV, "Publishing Data on Intranets and the Internet," of this book describes using HTML in Access.

To send a report in Snapshot format, follow these steps:

1. Make sure that your email client (Outlook or Outlook Express) is operational. You must have a functioning email system—typically Microsoft Exchange Server—to export a report Snapshot.

2. In the Database window, select a report. You don't need to open the report to send it.

3. Choose File, Send To, Mail Recipient (As Attachment) to open the Send dialog.

4. Select Snapshot Format from the Select Format list, click OK to close the Send dialog. Access creates the attachment file and opens your email application. The attachment icon appears in the body of the message.

4. Complete the message (see Figure 15.22) and send it to the recipient. To test the Snapshot Viewer, send the message to yourself.

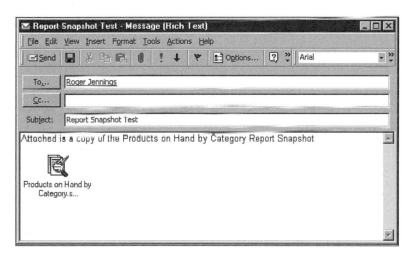

Figure 15.22
Sending an Outlook message with an attached Access Snapshot of the Northwind Traders Catalog report.

VIEWING AND PRINTING THE REPORT SNAPSHOT

To view and print a copy of the report Snapshot attached to an email message, follow these steps:

1. Open the message in an email client, such as Outlook (see Figure 15.23).

Figure 15.23
An inbox message with a report Snapshot attachment.

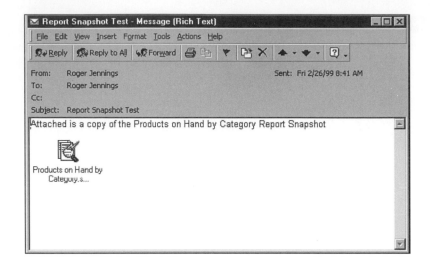

2. Double-click the *ReportName*.snp icon to display the Opening Mail Attachment dialog.

3. Select the Open It option; then click OK to open Snapshot Viewer and display the first page of the report (see Figure 15.24).

Figure 15.24
Snapshot Viewer displaying the full-size first page of the Products on Hand by Category report.

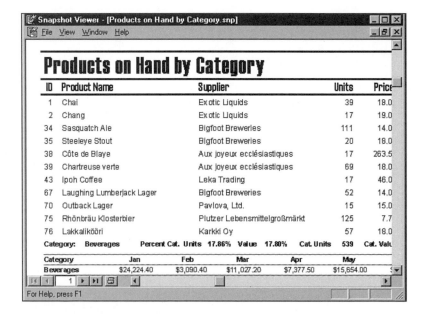

4. To print the report Snapshot, choose <u>P</u>rint from the <u>F</u>ile menu.

TROUBLESHOOTING

LINK EXPRESSION ERRORS

Attempting to create a link between the main report and subreport causes a "Can't evaluate expression" error message.

The most likely cause is that you are trying to create a master-child (or, more properly, parent-child) link with an incompatible data type. Parent-child linkages are similar to joins of queries that use the WHERE *SubreportName.FieldName* = *ReportName.FieldName* criterion. As with joins, the data types of the linked fields of tables or columns of queries must be identical. You can't, for example, link a field of the Text data type with a field of the Integer data type, even if your text field contains only numbers. If you use an expression to create the link, the data type that the expression returns must match the field value. You can use the data type conversion functions described in Chapter 9 to change the data type that the expression returns to that of the linked field. For example, you can link a text field that contains numbers to a field of the Long Integer data type by entering **=CLng**(*TextField*) as the linking value.

REPORT SNAPSHOTS WON'T OPEN

Selecting the Open It option in the Opening Mail Attachment dialog results in a "The Managed Software Installer failed to install the program associated with this file" error message.

The most likely cause of this error is that SnapView.exe is missing from your PC. In this case, open Control Panel, and double-click the Add/Remove Programs icon to open the Add/Remove Programs dialog. Select Office 2000, and click Add/Remove to open the Microsoft Office Maintenance Mode dialog. Click Add or Remove Features to open the Update Features dialog, expand the Microsoft Access for Windows node, set Snapshot Viewer to Run from My Computer, and click Update Now.

If SnapView.exe is present, you have a Registry problem—the association between the .snp file extension and SnapView.exe is missing. In this case, repeat the preceding Add/Remove Programs process to enter Office 2000 Maintenance Mode, but click the Repair Office button instead of the Add or Remove Features button.

IN THE REAL WORLD—THE ART OF REPORT DESIGN

Designing reports that deliver useful information in a graphically appealing format is a challenge. The challenge becomes acute when you're faced with the prospect of designing a very complex report, such as a physician's patient history, that derives its information from multiple related tables. In the case of a patient history, some of the tables contain memo fields with large blocks of formatted text that describe diagnosis and treatment. Specialists often want reports that print from OLE Object fields embedded images generated from digital cameras, scanned photographs, or single-frame captures from a video camera. Most physicians also need billing reports that conform to state and federal government agency standards, as well as health insurers' requirements.

Fortunately, Access 2000's report engine and graphical Report Design mode can handle just about any report format imaginable. Report generation flexibility is one of the primary reasons that database developers haven't abandoned Access for Visual Basic, which offers greater versatility in program structure and form design than Access.

It's impossible for two chapters of reasonable length to cover in detail every feature of the report engine. This chapter and its predecessor provide only an introduction to report design and demonstrate the basic elements of reports and subreports. Complete coverage of Access's reporting capabilities, including the use of VBA to respond to report events and set printer properties, would fill a book of 500 pages or more.

One of the ways to gain a better perspective on designing Access reports is to check out reports generated by commercial Access applications. For example, Database Creations, Inc.'s Yes! I Can Run My Business small-business accounting application offers examples of a multitude of reports in eight categories (see Figure 18.25). Figure 18.26 shows part of the Assets page of balance sheet—from sample data—in Print Preview mode. You can download a working demonstration version of the application from http://www.caryp.com/.

Figure 15.25
The report selection form of Database Creations' small-business accounting system.

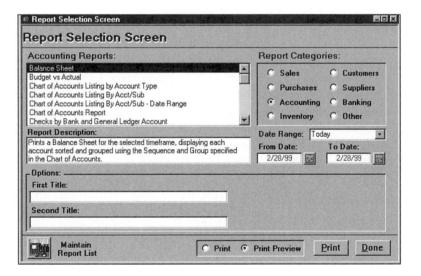

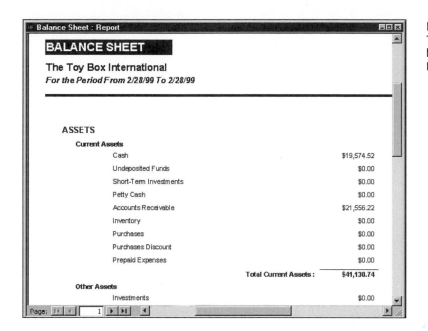

Figure 15.26
The first page of a typical balance sheet in Print Preview mode.

For larger businesses, eTEK International (formerly MTX, Inc.) offers its Access-based Millenium+ accounting application. Millenium+ has examples of more than 100 different accounting reports. You can obtain a demonstration version of Millenium+ at http://www.mtxi.com/. You also can take advantage of demonstration versions of commercial Access applications to learn the basics of Access application design and navigation methodology.

Several independent software vendors (ISVs) make useful add-ins for Access reports. As an example, the SkanData BarCoder (http://www.skandata.com/barcoder.html) lets you print Code 39 bar codes directly from Access reports. SkanData also offers bar-code reader add-ins for inventory tracking and related applications.

--rj

PUBLISHING DATA ON INTRANETS AND THE INTERNET

16   Working with Hyperlinks and HTML   597

17   Generating Web Pages from Tables and Queries   627

18   Designing Data Access Pages   657

CHAPTER 16

WORKING WITH HYPERLINKS AND HTML

In this chapter

Data-Enabling Web Pages   598

Putting Microsoft's Internet Program in Perspective   599

Navigating the Web and Intranets with Hyperlinks   606

Understanding Access 2000's Hyperlink Field Data Type   611

Using Hyperlinks with Access Controls   621

Specifying Other Internet Uniform Resource Locators   622

Troubleshooting   623

In the Real World — To Internet or Not   624

DATA-ENABLING WEB PAGES

The Internet has made the most profound change in the direction of the computer software industry since the introduction of Windows 3.0. Virtually every software product published since early 1996 has some connection with the Internet, even if tenuous, and this trend shows no indication of slackening. All members of Microsoft Office 2000 are "Internet enabled" to a greater extent than their predecessors. Word 2000 lets you convert conventional .doc files to conventional .htm Web pages. PowerPoint 2000 encourages you to create presentations for broadcasting via the World Wide Web. Excel 2000 lets you export worksheets to HTML tables. FrontPage 2000 lets you generate and deploy dynamic, data-driven Web pages connected to Jet or SQL Server databases. Each Office 2000 Internet enhancement relies on *hyperlinks*, which lead from one document to another related document, and *Hypertext Markup Language (HTML)*, a variant of the *Standard Generalized Markup Language (SGML)* designed for text document formatting. Word, Excel, and PowerPoint use *Extensible Markup Language (XML)*, an extension to HTML that preserves formatting and other application-specific data, as an optional native file format.

> **Note**
>
> The XML Document Type Definition (DTD) for Office 2000 documents is exceedingly complex. To gain insight into how Microsoft uses XML to preserve document formatting, save a Word 2000 document to XML by choosing File, Save as Web Page and then open the .htm file in WordPad. Depending on your document content and formatting, the .htm version of your .doc file is 50% to 100% larger than the conventional .doc version because of XML overhead. Access 2000 uses XML to store Data Access Pages (DAP) and ActiveX Data Objects (ADO) Recordsets. XML is destined to play an important role in Web-based database content presentation because of its capability to separate data manipulation from HTML page-formatting functions.
>
> → For more information on the potential of DAP, **see** "Generating a Grouped Page," **p. 698**.

Databases play an important role in Internet publishing and are the backbone of e-commerce. Private intranets, which quickly deliver up-to-date information within an organization, have an even greater potential for exploiting relational database technology. Microsoft has equipped Access 2000 with a variety of enhancements for distributing data via private intranets and the public Internet. Access 2000 also includes features that let your Access applications interact directly with documents located on the World Wide Web.

NEW 2000 Following are the new Internet-related features of Access 2000 that are covered in this and the two succeeding chapters:

- *Enhanced hyperlinks* let you and your users navigate conventional Access applications as if you were in a Web browser. The new Edit Hyperlink dialog, common to all Office 2000 members, lets you open a new database object, such as a form or report, with a hyperlink. You also can add ScreenTips (the equivalent of a ToolTip for an Access control) that appear in IE 4+ browsers when you pass the mouse pointer over the hyperlink.

- *Memo field indexing* speeds searches and the sorting of fields of the Hyperlink data type, which is an Access-specific type of Memo field. The index is limited to the first 255 characters of the Memo field, which accommodates virtually all Web addresses.

- *Data Access Pages* let you distribute data-bound forms as Dynamic HTML (DHTML) pages on an intranet. Grouped Data Access Pages let users drill down into the detail behind summary information. You must have Internet Explorer 5+ installed to design or view Data Access Pages.

→ To try drilling down with DAP, **see** "Generating a Grouped Page," **p. 698**.

- *Office Web Components* (OWC) contained in Data Access Pages provide lightweight spreadsheet, graph, and PivotTable features to other Office 2000 users on your intranet. Clients must have Office 2000 to take advantage of OWC. The Data Source component provides the binding between your Jet .mdb file and the other elements of the Data Access Page.

→ For more information about OWC, **see** "Adding a PivotTable with the Page Field List," **p. 687** and "Adding Charts to DAP with a PivotTable List," **p. 691**.

PUTTING MICROSOFT'S INTERNET PROGRAM IN PERSPECTIVE

The overwhelming majority of Office 2000's new features are Internet related. Microsoft now devotes the bulk of its development efforts to features that enhance Internet and intranet communication and commerce. Microsoft adheres to public Internet standards in many of its software offerings, but most of the new features of Office 2000, and Access 2000 in particular, incorporate or require proprietary Microsoft components.

This book classifies Microsoft technologies in the following two categories:

- *Internet-compliant* technologies fully accommodate current versions of Netscape Navigator *and* Microsoft Internet Explorer browsers running under any supported operating system. Microsoft and Netscape had about an equal share of the browser market when this book was written. Internet-compliant technologies generate *conventional* (also called *vanilla*) *HTML*, as defined by the World Wide Web Consortium (W3C). HTML 4.0 is the current W3C "recommendation," a euphemism for specification. You and users of your Access 2000 applications don't need browser-specific add-ins or other accoutrements to view Internet-compliant documents. Web server components need not comply with public standards if they deliver Internet-compliant HTML to users.

Note

You can download the complete HTML 4.0 specification from W3C at `http://www.w3.org/MarkUp/`. This page explains differences between the three "flavors" of HTML 4.0—Transitional, Strict, and Frameset. The W3C Web site also offers a 10-Minute Guide to HTML for new users of the language and links to related topics, such as XML, *Cascading Style Sheets (CSS)*, and the Document Object Model (DOM).

- *Intranet-only technologies* require a specific browser, special plug-ins, or other proprietary components to display a document properly. Thus intranet-only applications aren't suited to publications destined for the World Wide Web. Many of the new Office 2000 features not only require the Office Server Extensions (OSE) on the Internet server but also require users to run Internet Explorer 5.0 and have an Office 2000 client license. To take advantage of most of the new Microsoft intranet-only features, everone on the network must have the required client software installed. These requirements are a major deterrent to early implementation of several of the new Access 2000 features described in the sections that follow.

Note

> *Extranets* are a special intranet-only category. An extranet is an extension of an organization's private intranet to permit access by other authorized organizations, such as customers or suppliers. Outside organizations use a secure connection to the extranet, usually provided by a virtual private network (VPN) that encrypts transmissions. In most cases, the operator of the extranet is in a position to specify the software required for access.

THE DIGITAL NERVOUS SYSTEM AND WINDOWS DNA

Bill Gates introduced Microsoft's vision of a *Digital Nervous System (DNS)* at the first annual Microsoft CEO Summit Conference held in Seattle on May 8, 1997. The idea behind DNS is that remaining competitive in the "digital age" requires firms to adopt a new information technology mindset. By the second CEO Summit Conference in May 1998, the Digital Nervous System concept had evolved into the following six tenets:

- *PC computing architecture*, implying use of Microsoft Windows as the PC operating system
- *All information in digital form*, meaning the elimination of paper documents in the workflow process
- *Universal email*, handled by Microsoft Outlook or Outlook express
- *Ubiquitous connectivity*, via intranets and Internet sites running Microsoft Internet Information Server
- *Common end-user productivity tools*, specifically Microsoft Office, Internet Explorer, and add-ons such as Microsoft Media Player
- *Integrated business-specific applications*, most of which rely on databases, such as Jet and SQL Server, for information storage and retrieval

Microsoft calls Office 2000 "the Entry Point to the Digital Nervous System" for gathering information, analyzing data to "generate insights," synthesizing information in the "most appropriate form," and publishing insights. Access 2000 enables all four activities.

Tip #138 from

`http://www.microsoft.com/dns/` provides additional background data on Microsoft's vision of the . You can read a transcript of Bill Gates's May 1998 address at `http://www.microsoft.com/billgates/download/docs/5-28ceosummitpc.doc.`

The purported benefits of implementing a Digital Nervous System are the capability of an organization to

- *Act faster* by making information immediately available to those who need it
- *React to anything* by allowing affected decision makers and their subordinates to collaborate, regardless of location and time zone
- *Make informed decisions* by providing access to summarized and detailed data
- *Get closer to customers* with extranets that allow selective external access to private intranet data via a secure network connection
- *Focus on business, not technology,* by using Microsoft's integrated software solutions to gain the preceding benefits

Windows Distributed interNet Applications Architecture (DNA, not WDNAA) is Microsoft's implementation layer for the Digital Nervous System. Microsoft defines Windows DNA as follows:

> "Windows DNA applications use a standard set of Windows-based services that address the requirements of all tiers of modern distributed applications: user interface and navigation, business processes, and storage.

> "The heart of Windows DNA is the integration of Web and client/server application development models through a common object model. Windows DNA uses a common set of services such as components, Dynamic HTML, Web browser and server, scripting, transactions, message queuing, security, directory, database and data access, systems management, and user interface. These services are exposed in a unified way at all tiers for applications to use.

> "In addition, because Windows DNA fully embraces an open approach to Web computing, it builds on the many important standards Efforts approved by bodies such as the World Wide Web Consortium (W3C) and the Internet Engineering Task Force (IETF)."

Note

The preceding quotation is from Microsoft's September 1997 Windows DNA white paper, "Integrating Web and Client/Server Computing," available at `http://www.microsoft.com/dna/overview/dnawp.asp.`

Windows DNA is a synonym for "COM everywhere." The Common Object Model (COM) or Distributed COM (DCOM) is the "unified way" to interconnect the components of Windows DNA. COM and DCOM are two of the subjects of the

"Microsoft Technologies Supporting Internet-Related Products" section, later in the chapter. The ActiveX Data Object (ADO) is Microsoft's preferred implementation of "database and data access," and you can expect that all future Microsoft Internet-related products will depend on COM-based OLE DB and ADO, to the exclusion of traditional database connectivity technologies, such as Access's Data Access Object (DAO) and the Open Database Connectivity (ODBC) API. Chapter 27, "Understanding Universal Data Access, OLE DB, and ADO," covers Access 2000's implementation of ADO 2.1.

MICROSOFT'S INTERNET-RELATED CLIENT PRODUCTS

Following is a list of the current versions of Microsoft's most important client-side products and technologies for the Internet and intranets as of spring 1999:

- *Internet Explorer (IE) 5.0* is Microsoft's latest entry in the Web browser sweepstakes. Office 2000 includes IE 5.0, which is required to take full advantage of the Office 2000 Internet feature set and to design or view Access 2000 Data Access Pages. IE 5.0 supports HTML 4.0, DHTML, CSS, XML, ActiveX, DirectX, most W3C browser standards, and proprietary Microsoft technologies. Figure 16.1 shows Internet Explorer 5.0 displaying a page of the OakLeaf Music Web site, which is used for many of the Internet examples in this book.

Figure 16.1
Internet Explorer 5.0 displaying a page from the OakLeaf Music Web site.

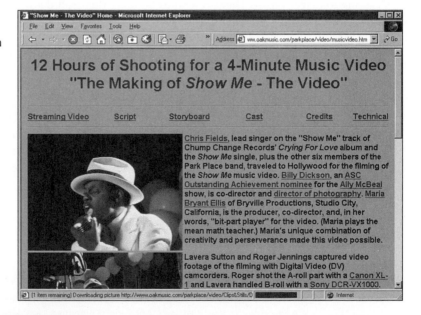

- *NetMeeting 2.1* is an extension to IE 4+ for collaborative computing. NetMeeting includes Internet telephony for voice communication, built-in videoconferencing, multiuser data conferencing for application sharing, an electronic whiteboard for diagramming, chat, and binary file transfer. You can download the current version of NetMeeting from `http://www.microsoft.com/netmeeting/`.

■ *Windows Media* (formerly NetShow, DirectShow, and ActiveMovie) delivers live and on-demand multimedia content over the Internet and intranets with the Windows Media Player for IE 4+. Windows Media replaces Microsoft's aging Video for Windows .avi files with .asf (ActiveX Streaming Format) files. Windows Media enables unicasting (for the Internet) and multicasting (for intranets) of live audio, video, and data, plus storing and streaming of narrated graphics (*illustrated audio*), from Windows NT Server NetShow Services, which are described in the next section. More information on Windows Media is available from http://www.microsoft.com/windows/windowsmedia/. The http://www.oakmusic.com Web site offers weekly live Internet audio broadcasts and on-demand broadcast archives in Windows Media format.

PART

IV

CH

16

■ *FrontPage 2000* is an easy-to-use Web page authoring and Web site management system that supports ActiveX technologies and Java components. FrontPage 2000 includes a Database Connectivity Wizard that simplifies the design of Web pages that offer user-defined queries. Figure 16.2 shows the FrontPage 2000 Explorer's hyperlink map of the first level of the OakLeaf Music Web site imported to the default location. FrontPage 2000 is a member of Office 2000 Premium, but Microsoft also sells it as a separate retail product. Get the latest information on FrontPage, which is Internet compliant if you don't add ActiveX controls to your pages, from http://www.microsoft.com/frontpage/.

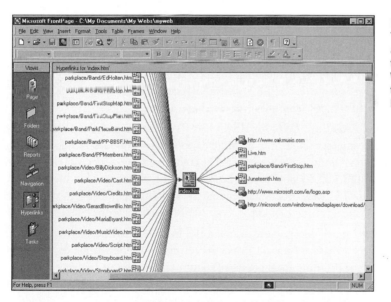

Figure 16.2
The hyperlink map of an imported copy of the OakLeaf Music Web site displayed in the FrontPage 2000 Explorer window.

■ *Office Web Components* are lightweight ActiveX PivotTable, Chart and other data-related controls designed specifically for intranet applications, such as Access 2000's new Data Access Pages. You must have Office 2000 installed on each client that uses Web Components. Alternatively, if an organization has an enterprisewide license for Office 2000, users of earlier versions of Office can download required components from the Microsoft Web site.

- *Personal Web Server* (*PWS*) is a peer Web server for Windows 9x and Windows NT 4.0 Workstation. PWS is classified as a client component because it doesn't qualify as a production-class Web server. FrontPage 2000, a component of Office 2000 Premium, installs PWS during the FrontPage setup operation. You also can install PWS from the Windows 98 distribution CD-ROM or the Windows NT 4.0 Option Pack. The Office Server Extensions, described in the next section, require Windows NT, so you only can install them to PWS if you're running Windows NT 4+ Workstation.

> **Caution**
>
> Installing PWS from the Windows 98 distribution CD-ROM or from the Windows NT 4.0 Option Pack after installing Office 2000 is problematic.
>
> → For consideration of installation sequence issues, **see** "Installing Access 2000," **p. 42**.

MICROSOFT'S SERVER-SIDE COMPONENTS

Microsoft requires that you install Windows NT 4.0 Server with Service Pack (SP) 3+ to take advantage of the new intranet-only features of Access 2000 and the other members of Office 2000 Professional or Premium. Following are Microsoft's Internet-related Windows NT services, most of which are pertinent to Access 2000:

- *Internet Information Server* (*IIS*) *4.0* is a high-performance Internet/intranet delivery system that's closely integrated with Windows NT 4.0's security features. Your intranet server must run IIS 4.0, which is available from the Windows NT 4.0 Option pack, to install the Office Server Extensions. IIS 5.0, part of Windows 2000 Server, was in the beta test stage when this book was written. Get the latest information about IIS 4.0 at http://www.microsoft.com/ntserver/nts/web/default.asp.

- *Office Server Extensions* (*OSE*) for IIS 4+ and PWS running under Windows NT 4+ Workstation support publishing documents to IIS, let you use Windows Explorer to view contents of an intranet server, enable collaboration on HTML documents and exchange of HTML document annotations (Web Discussions), and let you subscribe to email notices of HTML document changes (Web Subscriptions). Installing OSE isn't required to take advantage of any Access 2000 features, except collaboration.

- *Proxy Server 2.0* provides secure access to the Internet via internal local area networks (LANs) with a software firewall. Proxy Server improves performance for networked users by *caching* (holding local copies of) commonly accessed Internet content. You can download a free 30-day evaluation copy of Proxy Server 2.0 from Microsoft's Web site at http://www.backoffice.microsoft.com/downtrial/.

- *Index Server 2.0* performs full-text searches and retrieves information from any Web browser. Index Server is an optionally installable component of IIS 4.0. Index Server 2.0 supports HTML, text, and Microsoft Office document formats, so you don't need to convert documents to HTML for indexing.

- *Site Server 3.0* provides a comprehensive Web site environment for creation, deployment, and advanced management of Web sites. The Commerce Edition of Site Server includes the electronic commerce features of Microsoft's former Merchant Server. A 90-day trial version of both versions of Site Server is available for downloading at http://www.backoffice.microsoft.com/downtrial/.

■ *NetShow Services* are a proprietary extension to Windows NT 4.0 Server that delivers streaming audio and video (.asf) files via the Internet or intranet to Windows Media Player on clients. A technical description of NetShow 3.0 is at http://www.microsoft.com/ntserver/mediaserv/default.asp You can order the NetShow Services JumpStart CD-ROM at http://www.microsoft.com/ntserver/nts/downloads/default.asp or download most of its content from the "Other Downloads" section of http://www.microsoft.com/NTServer/all/downloads.asp. The NetShow Theater Server 3.0, which requires per stream server licenses, delivers DVD-quality MPEG-2 video and audio content over high-bandwidth intranets. You can download a 120-day trial version of Theater Server 3.0 from http://www.microsoft.com/Theater/.

MICROSOFT TECHNOLOGIES SUPPORTING INTERNET-RELATED PRODUCTS

Behind the new products listed in the preceding section are Microsoft technologies that make the products possible. The following list, current as of early 1999, describes the specifications that provide the foundation for current and future Microsoft Internet products:

■ *Common Object Model (COM)* is the foundation for Object Linking and Embedding (OLE) and ActiveX technologies. COM is a specification for creating interactive software components, called *objects*, that become the building blocks of larger applications. The Microsoft COM site at http://www.microsoft.com/com/ offers white papers and presentations that describe the technical and marketing features of COM and related object technologies.

■ *Distributed COM (DCOM)* implements COM over local and wide area networks, including the Internet. Microsoft first implemented the final version of DCOM (formerly *NetworkOLE*) in Windows NT 4.0 and then followed up with a DCOM for Windows 95 add-in; Windows 98 includes DCOM capability. COM+ ("COM plus"), which was in the beta testing stage when this book was written, is DCOM's successor in Windows 2000.

■ *ActiveX* denotes a collection of COM technologies intended by Microsoft to "activate the Internet" by allowing authors and graphics designers to create dynamic Web pages. The most important ActiveX components for Access 2000 users are ActiveX Data Objects (ADO) 2.1, which substitutes for the Data Access Object (DAO) 3.6 and earlier, and ActiveX controls, a replacement for the heavyweight OLE Controls of Access 95.

■ *Internet Services API (ISAPI)* is a set of extensions to Internet Information Server that lets developers write Windows Data Definition Languages (DLLs) to replace slower-performing common gateway interface (CGI) scripts. The most useful ISAPI extension for Access users is the Internet Database Connector (IDC), a simple (but obsolescent) method of binding Access and SQL Server databases to Web pages.

- *Active Server Pages (ASP)* is a feature of IIS 4.0 that lets you include VBScript on the server to automate the creation of custom Web pages based on input from Web browsers. Visual Basic 6.0's Web Classes let you use VBA to program the content and interactive elements of Web pages. ASP is Internet compliant, because it delivers *vanilla HTML* to any Web browser.

- *Visual Basic, Scripting Edition (VBScript or VBS)* is a simplified subset of Visual Basic, Applications Edition (VBA), the programming language of Access 2000 and most other Office 2000 members. You incorporate VBScript code in Web pages to program ActiveX controls. VBScript also is used for server-side scripting in Active Server Pages. After you learn VBA, writing VBScript code embedded in Web pages for server- or client-side execution is relatively easy. The Microsoft Scripting Technologies page at `http://msdn.microsoft.com/scripting/` links to pages that describe VBScript. VBScript is for intranet-only applications.

- *JScript*, Microsoft's implementation of ECMAScript, is the browser-independent scripting language used by FrontPage 2000. ECMAScript is the standards-compliant version of Netscape's JavaScript; ECMA is the acronym for the European Computer Manufacturers Association, which is the custodian of the ECMAScript specification. ECMAScript and JavaScript have only a tenuous association with Sun Microsystems' Java programming language. The Microsoft Scripting Technologies page also provides links to JScript.

- *Dynamic HTML* is a client-side technology that lets you automate various Web page functions with a client-side scripting language. The advantage of DHTML is that you can eliminate multiple round-trips to the server by performing simple operations, such as expanding lists or displaying different sets of data, by running scripts within the client's browser. Unfortunately, the Netscape and Microsoft DHTML implementations differ; thus today's DHTML is an intranet-only technology. You can learn more about Microsoft's version of DHTML at `http://www.microsoft.com/workshop/ author/default.asp`.

This book classifies only two of the members of the preceding Microsoft Internet-related technologies list—ASP and JScript—as Internet compliant. The Java programming language and Microsoft's Windows-centric Visual J++ version isn't included in the preceding list because Java, like Visual Basic and Visual C++, is a general purpose programming language.

NAVIGATING THE WEB AND INTRANETS WITH HYPERLINKS

Hyperlinks can point to the default home page of a Web site, such as `http:// www.oakmusic.com`, or to the default page of an intranet server, as in `http://oakleaf0`, the IIS 4.0 intranet server used to write the Internet-related chapters of this book. (OAKLEAF0 is the NetBIOS name of the server on which IIS 4.0 is installed.)

You don't need to specify the default page, which usually is `default.htm`, as in `http://oakleaf0/default.htm`, `default.asp` (for Active Server Pages) or `index.htm` (most common on UNIX Web servers), to open the home page of the site or the default page of a subsite.

Hyperlinks to Web pages traditionally have used *relative paths* to specify the folders that store HTML pages, graphic images, or scripts that control the customization of pages. For example, the default folder for the OAKLEAF0 server is C:\InetPub\wwwroot; the Park Place band's intranet home page is at `C:\InetPub\wwwroot\parkplace`. The server name (`oakleaf0`) you include in the uniform resource locator (URL) for the site's home page specifies the default part of the path (typically C:\InetPub\wwwroot) for an intranet server. Extended paths in the URL (`...\parkplace`) are relative (added) to the default Web server path. Understanding the difference between fully qualified paths (starting with a logical drive letter or *SERVERNAME*) and relative paths (based on the default Web root folder) is very important to your use of hyperlinks with Access 2000.

IIS 4.0's *virtual directory* feature (also called a *virtual root*) frees you from the need to maintain all files for an intranet or Internet site in a single folder hierarchy on a particular Web server. If you want to test with an IIS 4.0 intranet server the Web pages you create on your networked PC with Access 2000, you or your organization's Webmaster can add a virtual test directory. You must run IIS 4.0 with OSE to intranet enable the Web-based collaboration features of Office 2000.

You use IIS 4.0's snap-in for the Microsoft Management Console (MMC) and the Virtual Directory Wizard to specify the virtual directory name and the location of the folder with your local Web site. For example, if you've created a site with PWS in the default C:\Inetpub\Wwwroot folder of a client PC (in this case OAKLEAF1) networked to the intranet server, you can create a virtual directory in your IIS 4.0 Web server for this subsite by following these steps:

1. If the folder containing your Web files (C:\InetPub\Wwwroot for this example) isn't shared for file operations, open Windows Explorer, right click the folder, choose S̲haring, click the Sharing (not the Web Sharing) tab, and share the folder with read/write access. Specify a descriptive share name, such as **TestWeb**.

2. Choose Start, P̲rograms, Windows NT 4.0 Option Pack, Microsoft Internet Information Server, Internet Service Manager to open MMC with the Internet Service Manager snap-in active.

3. Select the Default Web Server item of the console list. The content of your Default Web Server depends on your IIS 4.0 installation and the structure of your existing intranet site.

4. Click Action and choose New, Virtual Directory from the context menu to open the first dialog of the Virtual Directory Wizard.

5. Type a name for the virtual directory, such as the **TestWeb** share name, in the alias text box (see Figure 16.3). The virtual directory share name becomes the extended URL for the subsite, as in `http://oakleaf0/TestWeb/`.

Figure 16.3
Specifying the name of the new virtual directory in the Wizard's first dialog.

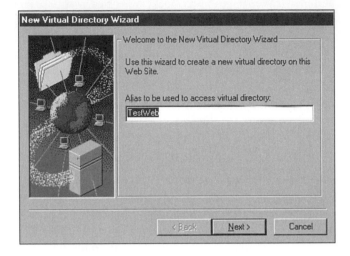

6. Click Next to open the second Wizard dialog and click Browse to open the Browse for Folder dialog. Navigate to and select the share you created in step 1, \\oakleaf1\ TESTWEB for this example. Click OK to return to the Wizard (see Figure 16.4).

Figure 16.4
Adding the path to the share for the new virtual directory.

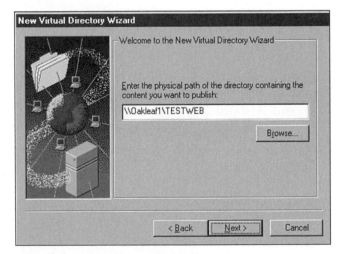

7. Click Next to open the third Wizard dialog and type a user name and password valid for access to the share. Even if you didn't password protect the share, you must enter a valid domain user name and password (see Figure 16.5).

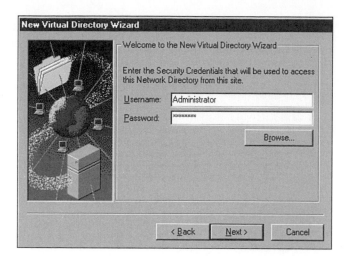

Figure 16.5
Providing the required username and password for the share.

8. Click Next to confirm the password and then click OK. The fourth Wizard dialog lets you specify permissions for users of your subsite. Unless you have specific reasons for doing so, accept the default values (Read and Script Access) as shown in Figure 16.6.

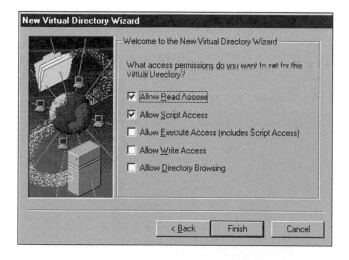

Figure 16.6
Specifying user permissions for your IIS 4.0 subsite

9. Click Finish to close the last Wizard dialog and to add the virtual directory to IIS 4.0's Default Web Site. A special icon (a Microsoft Transaction Server billiard ball inside a box) indicates a virtual directory (see Figure 16.7).

You now can access the site by appending the subsite name to that of the server, `oakleaf0/testweb` for this example. You don't need to add the `http://` prefix or `/` suffix; IE adds them for you.

Figure 16.7
The TestWeb site added as a virtual directory to an IIS 4.0 intranet server.

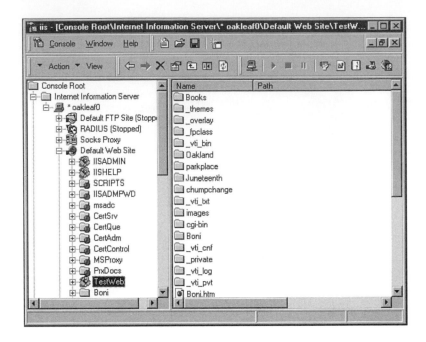

10. To change access or security settings of the subsite, right-click the virtual directory item and choose Properties to open the *Subsitename* Properties sheet (see Figure 16.8). The five property pages let you set the same properties for a subsite as for the default Web site.

Figure 16.8
Setting other subsite properties in the TestWeb Properties sheet.

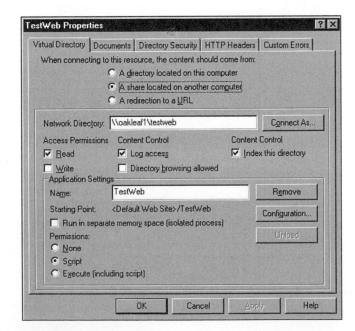

If you have a problem connecting to an IIS 4.0 virtual directory, see the "Intranet Connection Problems" topic of the "Troubleshooting" section near the end of the chapter.

UNDERSTANDING ACCESS 2000'S HYPERLINK FIELD DATA TYPE

Access 97 added a new member, *Hyperlink*, to the repertoire of Access field data types. Hyperlink isn't a Jet 4.0 data type, because Jet 4.0 stores Access Hyperlink values in Memo fields. Access 2000's Hyperlink data type simply interprets the value of the Memo field as a hyperlink and formats the display accordingly.

A Hyperlink field value consists of at least one of the following three components:

- *Display text*, an optional descriptive name for the hyperlink that appears as emphasized text, usually underlined and having a distinctive color.

- *Address*, a required reference to the location of a related document. The reference can be an Internet URL for World Wide Web and File Transfer Protocol (FTP) sites, a relative or fully qualified path and filename, or a file on a network server specified by uniform naming convention (UNC). The "Specifying Other Internet Uniform Resource Locators Additional" section later in the chapter decribes additional protocol identifers.

- *Subaddress*, an optional reference to a named location in a related document, such as a bookmark in a Word or HTML document, or a named range in an Excel worksheet.

Individual components of Hyperlink values are separated by the pound sign , the same delimiter used for Jet date values. Following are examples of typical Hyperlink values:

- `Microsoft Web Site#http://www.microsoft.com` displays *Microsoft Web Site* in the text and jumps to the home page of `www.microsoft.com` when clicked.

- `Yen Conversion#c:\currency\1998dec.xls#Yen` displays *Yen Conversion* and points to the c:\currency\1998dec.xls file's Yen named range.

- `#\\Server1\Documents\Reports\1998sales.doc#Drugs` displays and points to the Drugs bookmark in the 1998sales.doc Word document in the shared \Documents\Reports folder of Server1. If you don't include a display text value, the address and subaddress values are displayed.

- `#frmProducts` points to the frmProducts form in the currently open database.

TESTING HYPERLINKS IN THE NORTHWIND ORDERS TABLE

Northwind.mdb's Suppliers table (see Figure 16.9) includes a Home Page Hyperlink field that includes links to Web pages located in your \Program Files\Microsoft Office\Office\Samples folder and to placeholder pages in the `http://www.microsoft.com/ accessdev/sampleapps` folder. Hyperlinks stored in tables are useful for creating searchable databases that store links to your favorite Web sites and their pages. Hyperlinks in tables also offer automatic navigation assistance within large corporate intranets. For example, you can create a table with document names, keywords, and other identifying information and then use a query to locate and display only those documents meeting criteria you establish.

Postal Code	Country	Phone	Fax	Home Page
EC1 4SD	UK	(171) 555-2222		
70117	USA	(100) 555-4822		CAJUN.HTM
48104	USA	(313) 555-5735	(313) 555-3349	
100	Japan	(03) 3555-5011		
33007	Spain	(98) 598 76 54		
545	Japan	(06) 431-7877		Mayumi's (on the World Wide Web)
3058	Australia	(03) 444-2343	(03) 444-6588	
M14 GSD	UK	(161) 555-4448		
S-345 67	Sweden	031-987 65 43	031 987 65 91	
5442	Brazil	(11) 555 4640		
10785	Germany	(010) 9984510		
60439	Germany	(069) 992755		Plutzer (on the World Wide Web)
27478	Germany	(04721) 8713	(04721) 8714	
48100	Italy	(0544) 60323	(0544) 60603	FORMAGGI.HTM
1320	Norway	(0)2-953010		
97101	USA	(503) 555-9931		
S-123 45	Sweden	08-123 45 67		
75004	France	(1) 03.83.00.68	(1) 03.83.00.62	
02134	USA	(617) 555-3267	(617) 555-3389	
0512	Singapore	555-8787		

Record: 2 of 29

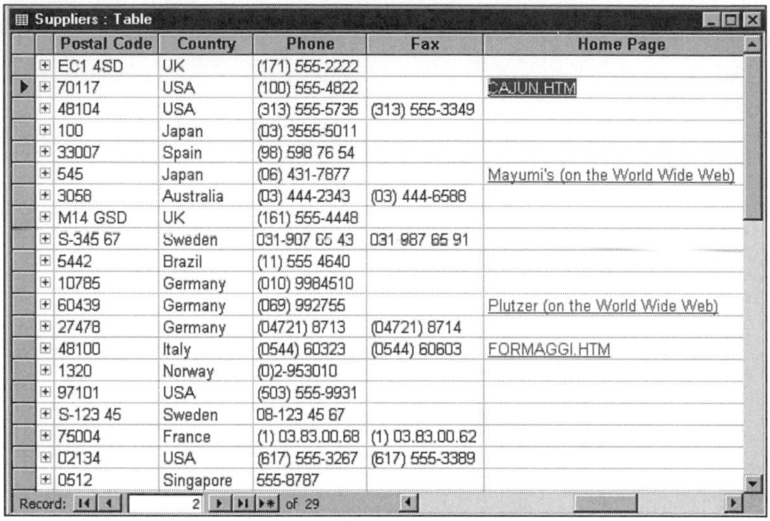

Figure 16.9
The Home Page Hyperlink field of Northwind.mdb's Suppliers table.

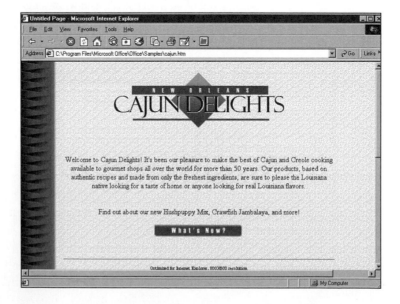

The CAJUN.HTM and FORMAGGI.HTM hyperlinks point to individual Cajun.htm and Formaggi.htm files, respectively, with fully qualified paths. Clicking either hyperlink opens Internet Explorer 5.0 (or another browser that you've specified as your default browser) to display the file. Figure 16.10 shows Cajun.htm open in Internet Explorer 5.0. If you click one of the links with (on the World Wide Web) in the display text in the Home Page field, as shown in 16.9, your browser connects to the Web site and opens the specified page.

Figure 16.10
The home page for the Cajun Delights (Cajun.htm) hyperlink of the Suppliers table opened in Internet Explorer 5.0.

Tip #140 from

When you open IE 5.0 from an Access 2000 hyperlink, Access automatically minimizes. Each hyperlink you click opens another independent instance of IE 5.0 to display the page. Microsoft claims that this behavior is "by design," but hasn't explained why opening multiple instances of IE is an appropriate design.

EDITING AND INSERTING CONVENTIONAL HYPERLINKS

NEW 2000 To edit an existing Hyperlink value or add a new hyperlink to a table, right-click a cell in a Hyperlink field to open the context menu and choose Hyperlink, Edit Hyperlink (see Figure 16.11) to open the new Edit Hyperlink dialog, which the other members of Office 2000 share. Figure 16.12 shows the URL entry for the Plutzer home page located on the Microsoft Web site. If you're creating a new hyperlink, type or paste the Internet URL of the page in the Link to File or URL drop-down combo box. Alternatively, click the Browsed Pages shortcut and select from prior URLs that you've opened in IE 5.0.

Tip #141 from

To link to a file, click the Recent Files shortcut to display a list of last-opened files or click File to open the Link to File dialog and then navigate to select the file for the link.

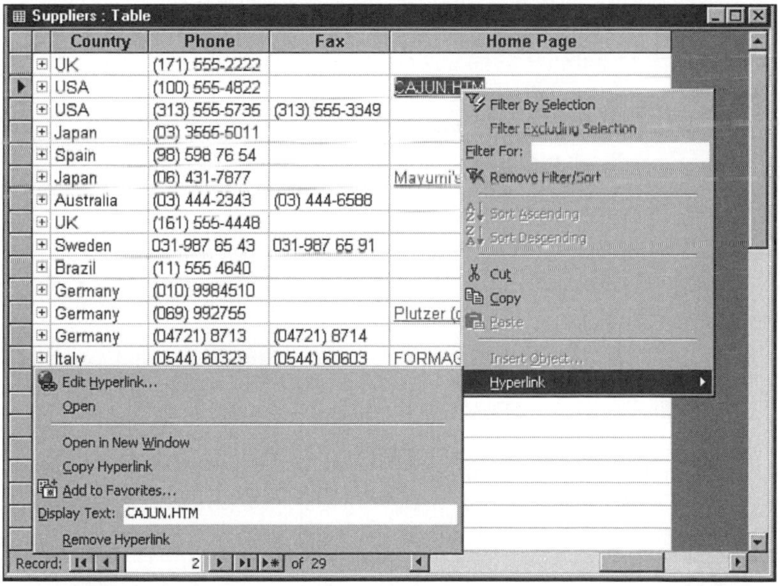

Figure 16.11
The pop-up menu and submenu for editing or creating a Hyperlink value.

Figure 16.12
The Edit Hyperlink dialog with an entry for a hyperlink to a page on the World Wide Web.

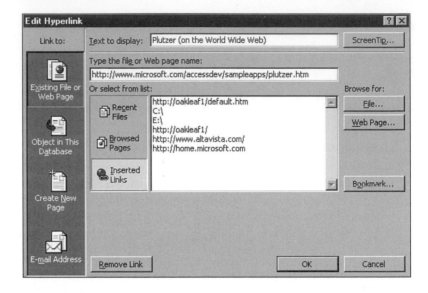

Tip #142 from

RJ

You also can edit the display text element of the Hyperlink value in the text box of the pop-up submenu that opens when you choose Hyperlink from the first pop-up menu (refer to Figure 16.11).

LINKING TO BOOKMARKS IN A WORD DOCUMENT

To create a link that uses a hyperlink subaddress to locate a specific bookmark in an existing Word document, follow these steps:

1. Create a new table with at least one Text field to identify the document and a Hyperlink field to contain the subject links to the bookmarks. Open the new table in Datasheet view.

2. Type the document name in the text field and move to the Hyperlink field, but don't enter display text.

Note

If you type display text in the Hyperlink field, an HTTP: // URL prefix is added to the display text to create a default URL in the Edit Hyperlink dialog's Link to URL or File combo box. This addition isn't helpful when you want to link to a file.

3. Right-click the empty cell in the Hyperlink field and choose Hyperlink, Edit Hyperlink to open the Edit Hyperlink dialog.

4. Click the File button to open the Link to File dialog (see Figure 16.13). Select the .doc file to link and click OK to close the dialog. The fully qualified path to the selected file appears in the Link to URL or File combo box (see Figure 16.14).

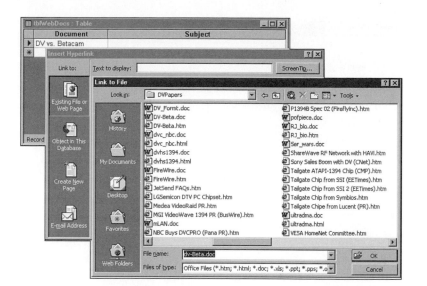

Figure 16.13
Specifying the file for a hyperlink in the Link to File dialog.

Tip #143 from

After you've created the first hyperlink to a file, you can save time by selecting the file-name in the list box if you're adding links to more than one bookmark in the file. Figure 16.14 shows the recently inserted links list after adding the first link.

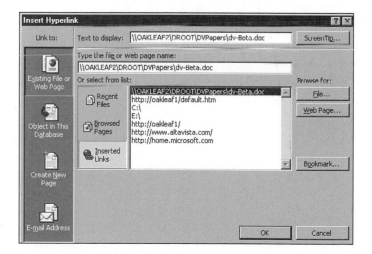

Figure 16.14
The full path to the file displayed in the URL or Link to File combo box.

5. Type **#** followed by the name of the bookmark or a brief description of the bookmarked link in the Type the File or Web Page Name text box (**#silkpurse** for this example). Then replace the file path and bookmark name with the text to appear in the Hyperlink field (**SilkPurse**) in the Text to Display text box (see Figure 16.15). Click OK to close the Edit Hyperlink dialog, and the display text appears in the Hyperlink field (see Figure 16.16).

Figure 16.15
Specifying a bookmark for the hyperlink to the Word .doc file and briefly describing the link.

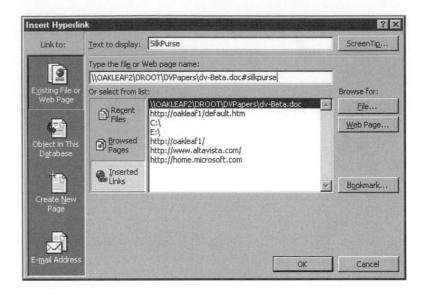

Tip #144 from

NEW 2000

As was the case with Access 97, you can't use the Bookmark button next to the Named Location in Access 2000's File text box to display a list of bookmarks in Word .doc files or named ranges in Excel worksheets. (The Bookmark button replaces Access 97's Browse button.) The Bookmark button displays only objects in the currently open Jet database. Access 97's text box for adding bookmark or range names and the Use Relative Path check box are missing from Access 2000's Edit Hyperlink dialog.

Figure 16.16
The test table with links to several bookmarks in a Word 2000 document (DV-Beta.doc).

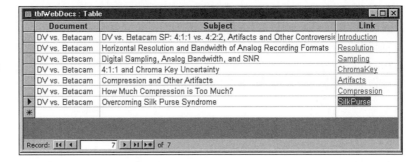

7. When you click the new hyperlink entry, Word 2000 opens the specified .doc file and selects the bookmark name you entered in step 5 (see Figure 16.17).

8. Click the Back button of Word's Web toolbar to return to Access.

9. Click the Forward button of Access's Web toolbar to return to Word and the open document.

10. Close Word when you're finished experimenting.

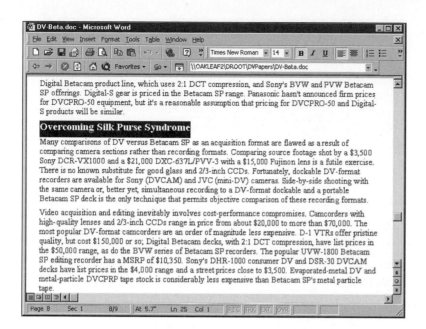

Figure 16.17
The hyperlinked document opened in Word *2000* with the specified bookmark selected.

This procedure also applies to Excel worksheets and PowerPoint presentations. Specify the name of an Excel 2000 range or the number of a PowerPoint slide in the same manner as a Word bookmark name.

SPECIFYING HYPERLINKS TO PAGES ON AN INTRANET SERVER OR THE WEB

You can establish links to pages on an intranet server by using the following generalized URL format:

```
http://servername/folder[/pagename.htm[#bookmarkname]]
```

For example, to specify a link to the default page of the chumpchange virtual directory of the \InetPub\wwwroot folder on OAKLEAF0, discussed earlier in the chapter, type **http://oakleaf0/chumpchange** in the Link to URL or File text box. Alternatively, you can specify a particular page in a subfolder, such as **.../parkplace/band/ppmembers.htm**. To define a jump to an *anchor* (the term for the HTML equivalent of a bookmark) in the Web page, add **#anchorname** (see Figure 16.18).

Tip #145 from

RJ

> You can omit the http:// prefix when you type a server name as an intranet URL into the URL text box of IE. However, you must add the http:// prefix in the URL for a link to a named server. Omitting the prefix indicates a file path, rather than a URL.

Figure 16.18
Specifying a hyperlink jump to a page and bookmark on an intranet server.

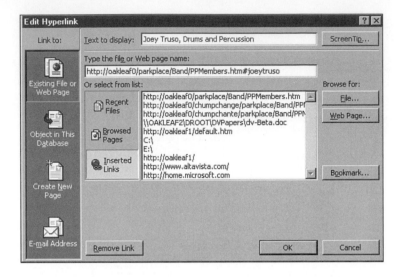

You similarly specify a Web location with an optional page name and anchor:

`http://www.sitename.com/folder[/pagename.htm[#anchorname]]`

Figure 16.19 shows the page of the OakLeaf Music site positioned to the anchor specified by this Web link: `http://www.oakmusic.com/parkplace/Band/PPMembers.htm#JoeyTruso`.

Figure 16.19
A Web page displayed by making the jump to a document and anchor on an Internet site.

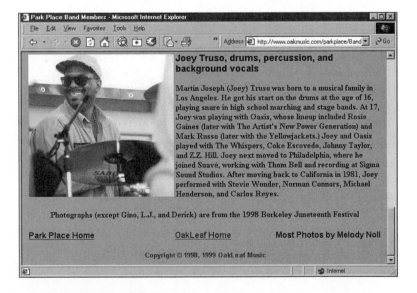

ADDING A SCREENTIP TO THE HYPERLINK

NEW 2000 Clicking the ScreenTip button of the Edit Hyperlink dialog opens the small Set Hyperlink Screen Tip dialog. Type additional information to help users of your table in the text box

(see Figure 16.20) and then click OK to return to the Edit Hyperlink dialog.
When you close the dialog and hover the mouse pointer over the hyperlink, the text you
typed appears in the equivalent to the ToolTip for an Access control.

Figure 16.20
Adding a Screen Tip to
a table hyperlink item.

Using Table Hyperlinks to Open an Access Object

In addition to using hyperlinks in tables to open documents in IE 5.0, Word 2000, Excel
2000, or PowerPoint 2000, you can specify an object to open in another Access 2000 database file. For example, you can open a designated form in the Address List sample Access
application (Address.mdb), which is in the same folder as Northwind.mdb, by following
these steps:

1. Open the Suppliers table of Northwind.mdb and move to an empty cell in the Home
   Page field.

2. Right-click the empty Hyperlink cell and choose Hyperlink, Edit Hyperlink to open
   the Edit Hyperlink dialog.

3. Click the File button, select Address.mdb, and click OK to specify the Address List
   database application as the address of the hyperlink. In this case, you can delete the
   path prefix to create a relative link because Address.mdb and Northwind.mdb are in
   the same folder.

4. Click the Bookmark button to open the Select Place in Document dialog that displays
   the objects in the selected .mdb file.

5. Click to expand the Forms node and select one of the forms in Address.mdb, such
   as Household (see Figure 16.21). Click OK to close the Select Location dialog.

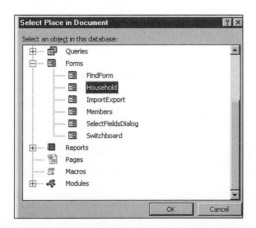

Figure 16.21
Selecting an Access
form to open in a
hyperlinked .mdb file.

6. The type of object (Form in this case) followed by a space and the name of the object appears as #Form Household in the Type the File or Web Page Name text box (see Figure 16.22). Click OK to close the Edit Hyperlink dialog.

Figure 16.22
The link to open the Household form of Address.mdb.

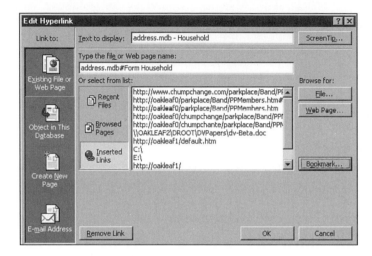

7. Click the new hyperlink. A second instance of Access launches, opens Address.mdb, and then opens the Household form (see Figure 16.23).

Figure 16.23
The Household form opened in another instance of Access by the hyperlink of Figure 16.22.

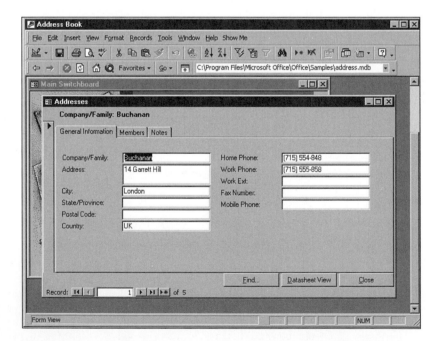

8. Close the second instance of Access and clear the test Hyperlink value you created.

Note

Access 2000 uses Windows *dynamic data exchange (DDE)* to process hyperlinks to applications that reside on your PC. The address component of the Hyperlink value corresponds to DDE's `TopicName` argument of the `DDEInitiate` command; the `ServiceName` argument is derived from the file extension. The subaddress component corresponds to the `ItemName` argument of the `DDERequest` command. Despite Microsoft's promotion of COM-based Automation to manipulate objects in other applications or instances of applications, Office 2000 members still use DDE as the primary means of interapplication communication.

PART

IV

CH

16

USING HYPERLINKS WITH ACCESS CONTROLS

You can use hyperlinks with Access controls such as command buttons, combo boxes, and labels to jump to another document or open an object within the current or another Access database. Control-based hyperlinks can substitute for switchboard forms. To create a form with a command button to open Northwind.mdb's Orders form with a hyperlink, follow these steps:

1. Open Northwind.mdb, if necessary, and create a new form in Design view.

2. Disable the Control Wizards and add a command button to the form.

3. With the command button selected, click the Properties toolbar button to open the Properties window and click the Format tab.

4. In the Caption property text box, type **Open Orders Form** to create the display text component of the hyperlink.

5. Leave the Hyperlink Address property text box empty, specifying that the object you want to open is in the current database.

6. Select the Hyperlink Subaddress property text box and click the Builder button to open the Insert Hyperlink dialog.

7. Click the Object in This Database button, expand the Forms node, select the Orders form, and then click OK. `Form Orders` appears in the Hyperlink Subaddress property text box, and the command button's caption appears underlined in blue type (see Figure 16.24).

8. Change to Form view and click the command button to open the Orders form.

9. Close, but don't save, your test form.

Tip #146 from

R J

Using command buttons with hyperlinks to open forms lets you take advantage of Access 2000's *lightweight forms* (forms without VBA code in class modules). You can open—but not close—a form with a hyperlink. As a result, users of your application might face a large number of simultaneously open forms. Having more than two open forms at a time is likely to confuse users new to Access applications.

Figure 16.24
A command button that uses a hyperlink to open a form in the current database.

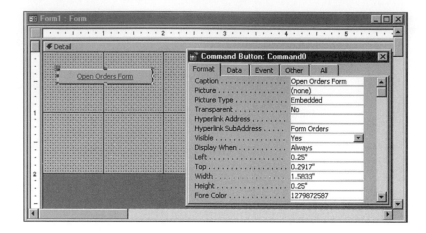

SPECIFYING OTHER INTERNET UNIFORM RESOURCE LOCATORS

Internet URLs consist of an abbreviation for a protocol that defines the type of object (usually a document) and the location (address) of the desired object on the Internet or an intranet. In all cases, the protocol and the address are separated by the standard two virgules (forward slashes) and a colon, as in `http://www.microsoft.com` or `ftp://ftp.microsoft.com`. Access 2000 hyperlinks support the `http` (Hypertext Transport Protocol) and `ftp` URL prefixes with IE and other Web browsers.

Access 2000's Hyperlink fields recognize the URL prefixes listed in Table 16.1. You need the appropriate software installed and registered on your PC to use prefixes other than `http` and `ftp`.

TABLE 16.1   URL PREFIXES RECOGNIZED BY ACCESS 2000 HYPERLINK FIELDS

URL Prefix	Protocol Name	Description of Protocol
cid	CompuServe Information Dialer (CID)	Attempts to create a connection with Point-to-Point Protocol (PPP) to the Internet by using the CompuServe dialer.
file	File	Opens a file specified by a fully qualified path and filename.
ftp	File Transfer	Transfers files stored on an FTP server.
gopher	Gopher	Obtains information from a Gopher server.
http	Hypertext Transfer	Opens a Web page.
https	Hypertext Transfer with Security	Attempts to open a connection to a Web page with Secure Sockets Layer (SSL) encryption.

URL Prefix	Protocol Name	Description of Protocol
mailto	Electronic mail	Sends a message via your preferred email program by using the mailto:*mailbox@domainname* URL format.
mid	Musical Instrument Digital Interface (MIDI)	Uses your audio adapter card to play.mid files.
mms	Microsoft Media Server (MMS)	Plays streaming media files (such as .asf files).
msn	Microsoft Network	Jumps to a location on the Microsoft Network.
news	News protocol	Starts your news reader program (typically Outlook or Outlook Express) for the specified news group by using the news:newsgroupname URL format.
nntp	Network News Transfer	Same as **news**, but uses the conventional **nntp://*newsgroupname*** URL format.
pnm	RealAudio protocol	Uses your audio adapter card to play RealNetworks's Real Audio files.
prospero	Prospero	Accesses the Prospero distributed file system for UNIX hosts.
rlogin	Terminal login	Tries to start a Rlogin terminal emulation program on a UNIX host.
telnet	Terminal emulation	Tries to start a Telnet terminal emulation program with a UNIX host.
tn3270	IBM 3270 terminal emulation	Tries to start an IBM 3270 terminal emulation program.
wais	Wide Area Information Servers	Connects to a WAIS search services database.

TROUBLESHOOTING

INTRANET CONNECTION PROBLEMS

Typing a known-good server name as a URL causes a "The Web page you requested is not available offline" message.

This problem is most common when you ordinarily connect to the Internet via a dialup connection, but use a network connection to an intranet server. The default for IE 5.0 is a dialup connection; when you make the dialup connection, you then can connect to the intranet server. To eliminate the need to establish a dialup connection first, Choose IE 5.0's Tools, Internet Options command, and click the Connections tab. In the Dialup Settings frame of the Connections page, select the Dial Whenever a Network Connection is not

Present option, and click OK to close the Internet Options dialog. When you want a dialup Internet connection, double-click the appropriate connection icon in the Dialup Networking folder of My Computer or Explorer to open the Connect To dialog, and click Connect. You can shortcut the process by adding a desktop shortcut for the dialup connection to your desktop.

IN THE REAL WORLD—TO INTERNET OR NOT

The Center for Disease Control hasn't ranked Internet Fever as a public health menace, but there's no question that it's highly contagious. Microsoft napped during Internet Fever's incubation phase. The Internet's "open standards" approach to worldwide networking and information sharing didn't mesh with Microsoft's proprietary lock on the PC operating system market. The most conspicuous example of Microsoft's then-shortsighted view of the Internet was the Microsoft Network (MSN) online service. Microsoft envisioned MSN as a must-have for Windows 95 users and an AOL-killer. MSN had its own non-standard communication protocols, proprietary content development tools (called Blackbird), and, of course, the look and feel of Windows. The most charitable description of MSN to appear in the trade press at the time was "underwhelming."

MICROSOFT GETS A CLUE AND THE VIRUS

On December 7, 1995, Bill Gates infected the entire Microsoft organization with his new rallying cry: "Embrace and extend the Internet." From that point forward, Microsoft contracted full-blown Internet Fever. To spread the Internet Fever virus in Redmond, Gates initiated a major reorganization that gave Internet-related development programs top priority at Microsoft. The result of diverting a large part of Microsoft's considerable technical and economic resources to the Internet was a flood of new products, technology incentives, and press releases. Just keeping up with Microsoft's product announcements bordered on a full-time occupation.

One of the symptoms of Internet Fever is Internet Dementia. Individual investors and venture capitalists are especially prone to this malady; but software programmers, information technology managers, chief executive and financial officers, and even boards of directors are equally at risk. Internet Dementia causes a narrowing of the victims' world-view, a side-effect called Internet Tunnel Vision (ITV). ITV is analogous to glaucoma's narrowing of one's peripheral vision. All a publicly traded company need do to instantly multiply its per-share price is add .com to its name or announce an intent to enter into Internet e-commerce. Similarly, issuing press releases describing "exciting new Internet features" for Windows productivity applications encourages costly software upgrades. Those with ITV are especially susceptible to such blandishments.

INNOCULATION AGAINST INTERNET FEVER

None of the new Internet-related features of Office 2000 comes even close to making Access 2000 the Holy Grail of computing—the "Internet killer application." Prior versions of Access captured the desktop RDBMS market for Microsoft while offering only marginal

Internet features, such as the Hyperlink fields described in this chapter. Minimizing Access and opening another instance of IE each time you click a Hyperlink value isn't likely to win the "Best New Internet Feature of the Year" award.

As noted in other "In the Real World" sections, conventional Access applications will continue to have their place, even in organizations whose entire staff exhibits signs of ITV. The Internet and intranets serve best when dispensing information, not entering it. Start by adopting Internet or intranet deployment for simple decision-support applications, such as distributing static Access reports as Web pages. You can use Active Server Pages (ASP) to assure that the data in your reports is current. The next chapter covers exporting data as HTML pages and ASP.

PART

IV

CH

16

For interactive Web pages on an intranet where all users have IE 5.0 and Office 2000 licenses, give DAP and OWC a try. Access 2000 incorporates DAP version 1.0; at best, version 1.0 of any software is chancy for production front-ends. If you need interactive connectivity to your databases over the public Internet, consider FrontPage 2000's Database Wizard. The alternative is to learn Visual InterDev 6.0, which is no small chore, or evaluate third-party platforms for database front-end development.

Be wary of requests for intranet-based data-entry front ends. Lightweight Web page controls—text boxes, option groups, check boxes, combo lists, and list boxes—don't offer their Access counterpart's rich set of features. For heads-down data entry, Web-based front ends don't come close to competing with the performance of well-designed Access applications.

Finally, beware the Circus' Song of thin-client computing with a Web browser as the sole user interface. Today's browsers aren't thin. You can prove this premise by downloading the full install of IE 5.0 from the Microsoft Web site. If your only tool is a hammer, everything looks like a nail; similarly, if your only user interface is a Web browser, everything acts like a Web page. Forward and Back button navigation is adequate only for very simple decision-support front ends. Providing Web clients with the interactive features of conventional Access applications requires a combination of superior page design skill and expert script programming ability, both of which involve a major investment of learning time and effort. Bear in mind also that you don't have a thin client when your pages interpret and execute thousands of lines of embedded XML and JScript.

--rj

CHAPTER 17

GENERATING WEB PAGES FROM TABLES AND QUERIES

In this chapter

Easing the Way to Web-Based Decision Support   628

Exporting Table and Query Datasheets to HTML   628

Using HTML Templates   637

Exporting Reports to HTML   639

Importing Data from HTML Tables   643

Creating Dynamic Web Pages   648

Troubleshooting   654

In the Real World—ASP versus DAP   654

EASING THE WAY TO WEB-BASED DECISION SUPPORT

The easiest approach to creating Web pages is to export existing content from applications with which you're familiar. Each member of Office 2000 is capable of exporting documents to formatted HTML files with a File menu choice or a wizard. Access 2000 gives you several options for creating static and dynamic Web pages from data contained in Jet tables. This chapter covers methods for generating Internet-compliant static and dynamic Web pages. *Internet-compliant* content, defined in the "Putting Microsoft's Internet Program in Perspective" section of the preceding chapter, works with any browser on any operating system. *Static* Web pages require you to replace a page when the underlying data changes; *dynamic* pages update automatically when the data changes and let users execute queries against databases. The next chapter, "Designing Data Access Pages," describes how to create intranet-only pages that take advantage of Dynamic HTML (DHTML) data binding.

You don't need to be an HTML expert to export data from Access 2000 objects to static Web pages and to semi-dynamic Web pages that deliver current data but don't offer query capability. In fact, you don't need to have any knowledge of HTML and its formatting tags to do the examples in this chapter. An elementary understanding of using basic HTML tags, however, lets you alter the predetermined format of exported data to improve the appearance or utility of your Web pages. Thus, the HTML source for some of the examples in this chapter is included in the form of code listings or examples in the text.

EXPORTING TABLE AND QUERY DATASHEETS TO HTML

Northwind.mdb's Suppliers table is a good choice for exporting to a Web page because it contains relatively few fields and records. The Suppliers table also includes four hyperlinks, two of which link to sample home pages in your ...\Office\Samples folder. To create a formatted Web page from the Suppliers table, follow these steps:

1. Open Northwind.mdb, if necessary, and select the Suppliers table in the Database window.

2. Choose File, Export to open the Export Table 'Suppliers' As dialog.

3. Navigate in the Save In dropdown list to the ...\Office\Sample folder or in a folder of your Web server, such as ...\Wwwroot.

4. In the Save as Type dropdown list, select HTML Documents (*.html, *.htm), as shown in Figure 17.1. The table name is the default file name. UNIX servers commonly use the .html extension, while .htm is more common for Windows NT 4+ servers. Internet Explorer (IE) 5.0 handles .html (the default) and .htm extensions equally well.

5. Selecting HTML Documents enables the Save Formatted check box, which you must mark to include Access 2000's automatic HTML formatting. When you mark the Save Formatted check box, the Autostart check box is enabled. Mark the Autostart check box to have IE 5.0 or another default browser display the page when exporting finishes (see Figure 17.2).

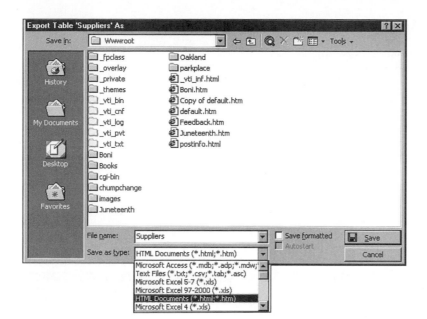

Figure 17.1
Selecting HTML Documents as the format for exporting the content of an Access 2000 table.

Figure 17.2
Specifying HTML formatting with the Save Formatted option and opening the exported .html file in your default browser with the Autostart option.

6. Click the Save button to close the Export Table 'Suppliers' As dialog and begin the export process. Click OK to close the HTML Output Options dialog, leaving the HTML Template text box empty (see Figure 17.3). The section "Using HTML Templates" later in the chapter describes how to base the design of your Web page on an HTML template.

7. When the formatted Suppliers.html Web page automatically appears in your browser (see Figure 17.4), scroll to the right to display the Home Page table column. If you

saved the HTML file to …\Office\Samples, click one of the local hyperlinks (CAJUN.HTM or FORMAGGI.HTM) to test the links to the sample Web pages in your …\Office\Samples folder.

HTML formats hyperlinks with `<A HREF=location>` tags that include the location of the linked document. If you saved the HTML file in folder other than …\Office\Samples, the `CAJUN.HTM` and `FORMAGGI.HTM` links don't work, because these relative links don't include a path prefix.

Figure 17.3
You can initiate a find in a Approach through variety of ways.

Figure 17.4
IE 5.0 displaying the formatted Web page created from the Suppliers table.

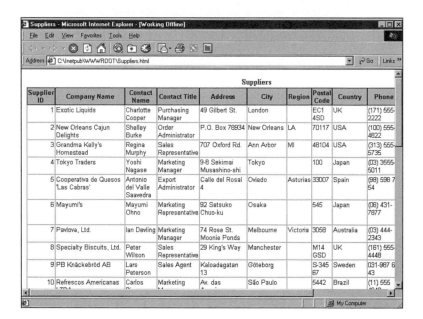

Note

HTML uses *tags* to identify the beginning and end of HTML documents (`<HTML>` and `</HTML>`), titles (`<TITLE>` and `</TITLE>`), and other elements of the page. HTML 4.0, the current version of HTML when Microsoft released Access 2000, has hundreds of tags for formatting, creating control objects on pages, and other uses.

→ Look for *Special Edition Using HTML 4, Fifth Edition* by Molly Holzschlag from Que Publishing, ISBN 0-7897-1851-0 for more information on using these and other tags to create Web pages.

8. Choose <u>V</u>iew, Sour<u>c</u>e from IE 5.0's menu to display the HTML source for the Suppliers.html file in Windows Notepad (see Figure 17.5). If the size of the file is larger than about 50KB, you get a message that the file is too large for Notepad and are given the option to open the file in WordPad.

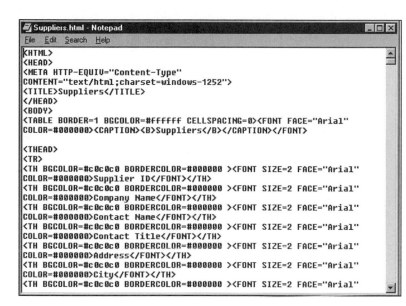

Figure 17.5
The first few lines of the HTML source for the Suppliers.html file.

9. Close Notepad and your browser, and then return to Access.

Note

 NEW 2000 Access 2000 doesn't have Access 97's <u>F</u>ile, Save As HTML menu choice, nor does it offer the prior version's Publish to the Web Wizard. Thus, exporting data in HTML format is a manual process in Access 2000, undoubtedly as a result of Microsoft's preference for Data Access Pages. Data Access Pages rely on users having Microsoft Internet Explorer 4+, and adding Office Web Components to Data Access Pages requires all users to have an Office 2000 license. Thus, Data Access Pages aren't Internet-compliant, but are suited for intranet deployment where all its users have Office 2000 licenses. The examples in this chapter create "vanilla" HTML pages that run in any browser on any operating system.

CREATING AN UNFORMATTED WEB PAGE

The vast majority of the content of the Suppliers.html file is HTML formatting instructions for colors and text fonts. The color and font formatting instructions obscure the HTML text that creates the tabular structure of the Web page. Much of the formatting content is duplicated throughout the source code; duplicate formatting is typical when you use tools that automatically create Web pages for you.

To create a Web page with a simple HTML table that doesn't include extra formatting instructions, modify the process described in the preceding example as follows:

1. Repeat steps 2, 3, and 4 of the preceding example. In step 4, change the name of the file to **Suppliers (Unformatted)**.

2. With the Save Formatted check box cleared, click the Export button to create the unformatted Web page. In this case, the HTML Output Options dialog doesn't appear.

3. Open Explorer, navigate to the folder in which you stored the exported file, and double-click the Suppliers (Unformatted).html item to launch your browser and display the unformatted Web page in IE 5.0 (see Figure 17.6).

Figure 17.6
The Suppliers (Unformatted).html file displayed in IE 5.0.

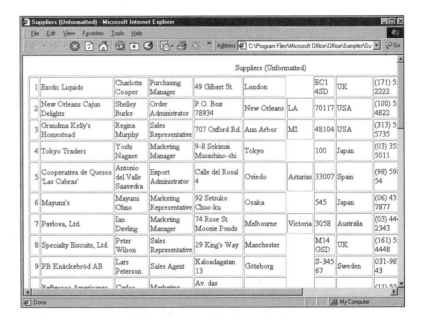

4. Choose <u>V</u>iew, Sour<u>c</u>e from IE 5.0's menu to display in Notepad the simplified HTML source for the page (see Figure 17.7). All the font and color formatting is removed, and the source only includes the most basic HTML tags to create a title for the browser's title bar, caption, and the table containing the data. The unformatted table doesn't include a header for field names and uses the default HTML table borders.

5. After you've reviewed the HTML source code, close Notepad and your browser to return to Access.

Listing 17.1 shows the HTML source for the unformatted page, with only the first two and the last rows of data. (An ellipsis (...) replaces missing table data rows.) <TR>...</TR> tags define the beginning and end of a table row. Individual data cells of the table are defined by <TD>...</TD> pairs. Unless the ALIGN=RIGHT attribute for numeric values is applied to a cell, the default left alignment for text prevails.

Figure 17.7
Simplified HTML source for the unformatted version of the page created from the Suppliers table.

LISTING 17.1   HTML SOURCE FOR THE SUPPLIERS (UNFORMATTED).HTML FILE WITH SOURCE ONLY FOR THE FIRST TWO AND LAST RECORDS

```
<HTML DIR=LTR>
<HEAD>
<META HTTP-EQUIV="Content-Type" CONTENT="text/html; charset=Windows-1252">
<TITLE>Suppliers (Unformatted)</TITLE>
</HEAD>
<BODY>
<TABLE DIR=LTR BORDER>
<CAPTION>Suppliers (Unformatted)</CAPTION>
<TR>
<TD DIR=LTR ALIGN=RIGHT>1</TD>
<TD DIR=LTR ALIGN=LEFT>Exotic Liquids</TD>
<TD DIR=LTR ALIGN=LEFT>Charlotte Cooper</TD>
<TD DIR=LTR ALIGN=LEFT>Purchasing Manager</TD>
<TD DIR=LTR ALIGN=LEFT>49 Gilbert St.</TD>
<TD DIR=LTR ALIGN=LEFT>London</TD>
<TD></TD>
<TD DIR=LTR ALIGN=LEFT>EC1 4SD</TD>
<TD DIR=LTR ALIGN=LEFT>UK</TD>
<TD DIR=LTR ALIGN=LEFT>(171) 555-2222</TD>
<TD></TD>
<TD></TD>
</TR>
...
<TR>
<TD DIR=LTR ALIGN=RIGHT>24</TD>
<TD DIR=LTR ALIGN=LEFT>G'day, Mate</TD>
<TD DIR=LTR ALIGN=LEFT>Wendy Mackenzie</TD>
<TD DIR=LTR ALIGN=LEFT>Sales Representative</TD>
```

continues

PART

IV

CH

17

LISTING 17.1   CONTINUED

```
<TD DIR=LTR ALIGN=LEFT>170 Prince Edward Parade&#13;&#10;<BR>Hunter's Hill</TD>
<TD DIR=LTR ALIGN=LEFT>Sydney</TD>
<TD DIR=LTR ALIGN=LEFT>NSW</TD>
<TD DIR=LTR ALIGN=LEFT>2042</TD>
<TD DIR=LTR ALIGN=LEFT>Australia</TD>
<TD DIR=LTR ALIGN=LEFT>(02) 555-5914</TD>
<TD DIR=LTR ALIGN=LEFT>(02) 555-4873</TD>
<TD DIR=LTR ALIGN=LEFT>
<A HREF="http://www.microsoft.com/accessdev/sampleapps/gdaymate.htm">G'day Mate
(on the World Wide Web)</A></TD>
</TR>
...
<TR>
<TD DIR=LTR ALIGN=RIGHT>29</TD>
<TD DIR=LTR ALIGN=LEFT>Forêts d'érables</TD>
<TD DIR=LTR ALIGN=LEFT>Chantal Goulet</TD>
<TD DIR=LTR ALIGN=LEFT>Accounting Manager</TD>
<TD DIR=LTR ALIGN=LEFT>148 rue Chasseur</TD>
<TD DIR=LTR ALIGN=LEFT>Ste-Hyacinthe</TD>
<TD DIR=LTR ALIGN=LEFT>Québec</TD>
<TD DIR=LTR ALIGN=LEFT>J2S 7S8</TD>
<TD DIR=LTR ALIGN=LEFT>Canada</TD>
<TD DIR=LTR ALIGN=LEFT>(514) 555-2955</TD>
<TD DIR=LTR ALIGN=LEFT>(514) 555-2921</TD>
<TD></TD>
</TR>
</TABLE>
</BODY>
</HTML>
```

HTML uses the `&charname;` format to specify special characters. For example, `&ecirc;` inserts the letter *e* with a circumflex (ê) for `Forêts`, and `&eacute` inserts the letter *e* with an acute (é) in both `d'érables` and `Québec` in the last row of the table in Listing 17.1. `</TABLE>`, `</BODY>`, and `</HTML>` denote the end of the table, body part, and document.

Tip #147 from

> Files containing conventional (unformatted) HTML tables are much smaller than Access 2000's formatted files. As an example, Suppliers.html (34K) is more than twice the size of Suppliers (Unformatted).html (14K). It's uncommon to export tables with large numbers of records to single Web pages because they are slow to load in the user's browser and make finding the desired row a chore. If you must create a static Web page from a table or query with a large number of rows, choose the unformatted version to reduce file size and speed display in the browser.

CREATING A WEB PAGE FROM A QUERY

Tables in Web pages exported from entire Access tables often contain much more than users want to know, so most static Web pages include only a subset of the records and columns of large tables. The objective of reducing the number of columns is to eliminate the need for horizontal scrolling to review the information presented. Queries let you specify the columns that appear in the page. Multiple queries with different criteria let you create a series of Web pages opened by hyperlinks on a home page.

Tip #148 from	If you use a parameterized query, you're prompted to enter the parameter value before Access creates the HTML file. If you use parameterized queries to create multiple pages, remember to save the resulting file with an appropriate file name to prevent overwriting files created with other parameter values. All the Web pages you create from a single parameterized query have the same title and caption, which limits the utility of parameterized queries for creating static Web pages.

The following example uses a query to display only the North American customers of Northwind Traders in a format that doesn't require horizontal scrolling. The resulting Web page almost fills the width of the display area of a browser on PCs using either 640×480 or 800×600 video resolution. Although 800×600 is the most common resolution for today's desktop PCs with 15-inch and larger monitors, you should also make sure your Web page design is suitable for the 640×480 resolution used by the installed base of older laptop computers and hand-held devices running Windows CE.

PART

IV

CH

17

Follow these steps to create the sample query and Web page:

1. Create a new query and add only the Customers table.
2. Add the CustomerID, CompanyName, City, Region, PostalCode, Phone, and Country fields to the query design grid.
3. Add **USA**, **Canada**, and **Mexico** in three Criteria cells of the Country field and save your query with the name **North American Customers** (see Figure 17.8).

Tip #149 from	The export process uses the query object name for the title and caption of the Web page. Thus, using the qry prefix for query names isn't recommended when you design queries for export to Web pages.

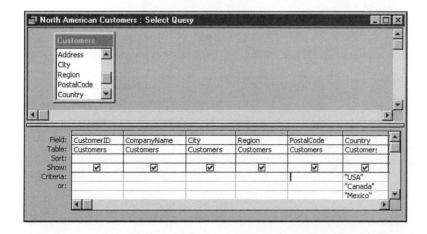

Figure 17.8
Designing a query to display selected records in a Web page without a horizontal scroll bar.

4. Run your query to change to Datasheet view and test the design (see Figure 17.9).

North American Customers : Select Query

Customer ID	Company Name	City	Region	Postal Code	Country
ANATR	Ana Trujillo Emparedados y helados	México D.F.		05021	Mexico
ANTON	Antonio Moreno Taquería	México D.F.		05023	Mexico
BOTTM	Bottom-Dollar Markets	Tsawassen	BC	T2F 8M4	Canada
CENTC	Centro comercial Moctezuma	México D.F.		05022	Mexico
GREAL	Great Lakes Food Market	Eugene	OR	97403	USA
HUNGC	Hungry Coyote Import Store	Elgin	OR	97827	USA
LAUGB	Laughing Bacchus Wine Cellars	Vancouver	BC	V3F 2K1	Canada
LAZYK	Lazy K Kountry Store	Walla Walla	WA	99362	USA
LETSS	Let's Stop N Shop	San Francisco	CA	94117	USA
LONEP	Lonesome Pine Restaurant	Portland	OR	97219	USA
MEREP	Mère Paillarde	Montréal	Québec	H1J 1C3	Canada
OLDWO	Old World Delicatessen	Anchorage	AK	99508	USA
PERIC	Pericles Comidas clásicas	México D.F.		05033	Mexico
RATTC	Rattlesnake Canyon Grocery	Albuquerque	NM	87110	USA

Record: 1 of 21

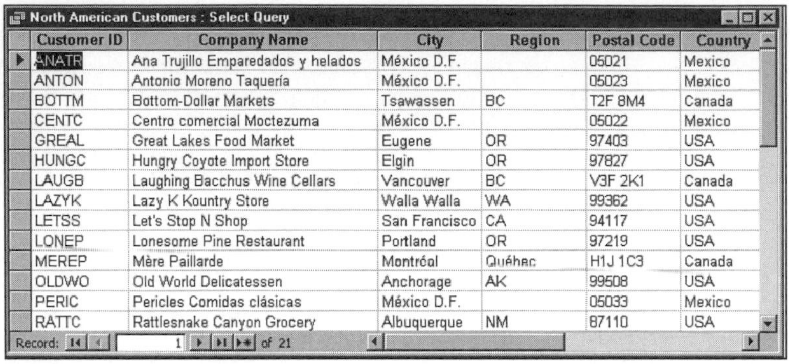

Figure 17.9
The query result set of the query design of Figure 17.8.

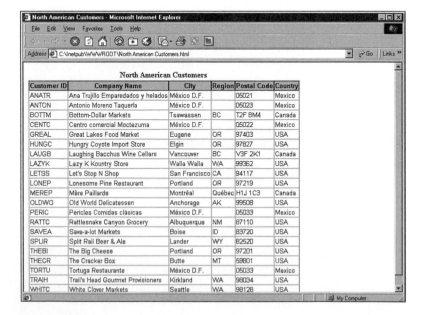

5. Choose File, Export, to open the Export Query dialog, and choose the location for your file.Select HTML Documents (*.html, *.htm) in the Files of Type dropdown list and mark the Save Formatted and Autostart check boxes.
6. Click Save All, and then click OK when the HTML Options dialog appears. After a few seconds, your query result set appears in your default Web browser. Figure 17.10 shows the formatted page in IE 5.0 at 800×600 resolution. The appearance of the table is identical in 640×480 resolution.

North American Customers

Customer ID	Company Name	City	Region	Postal Code	Country
ANATR	Ana Trujillo Emparedados y helados	México D.F.		05021	Mexico
ANTON	Antonio Moreno Taquería	México D.F.		05023	Mexico
BOTTM	Bottom-Dollar Markets	Tsawassen	BC	T2F 8M4	Canada
CENTC	Centro comercial Moctezuma	México D.F.		05022	Mexico
GREAL	Great Lakes Food Market	Eugene	OR	97403	USA
HUNGC	Hungry Coyote Import Store	Elgin	OR	97827	USA
LAUGB	Laughing Bacchus Wine Cellars	Vancouver	BC	V3F 2K1	Canada
LAZYK	Lazy K Kountry Store	Walla Walla	WA	99362	USA
LETSS	Let's Stop N Shop	San Francisco	CA	94117	USA
LONEP	Lonesome Pine Restaurant	Portland	OR	97219	USA
MEREP	Mère Paillarde	Montréal	Québec	H1J 1C3	Canada
OLDWO	Old World Delicatessen	Anchorage	AK	99508	USA
PERIC	Pericles Comidas clásicas	México D.F.		05033	Mexico
RATTC	Rattlesnake Canyon Grocery	Albuquerque	NM	87110	USA
SAVEA	Save-a-lot Markets	Boise	ID	83720	USA
SPLIR	Split Rail Beer & Ale	Lander	WY	82520	USA
THEBI	The Big Cheese	Portland	OR	97201	USA
THECR	The Cracker Box	Butte	MT	59801	USA
TORTU	Tortuga Restaurante	México D.F.		05033	Mexico
TRAIH	Trail's Head Gourmet Provisioners	Kirkland	WA	98034	USA
WHITC	White Clover Markets	Seattle	WA	98128	USA

Figure 17.10
The Web page created from the query datasheet of Figure 17.9.

Using HTML Templates

Most commercial Web sites use HTML templates to provide a consistent corporate or organizational image and to add visual interest to Web pages without writing a lot of HTML source for each page. The majority of Web page authoring applications, such as Microsoft FrontPage 2000, include a variety of templates from which you quickly can create Web pages with a standardized appearance.

Using the Access HTML Templates Included with Office 2000

Microsoft included with Access 97 a variety of HTML templates (.htm files) in the \Program Files\Microsoft Office\Templates\Access folder. These templated included a "Created with Microsoft Access" logo and a different background color and pattern. Access 2000 includes only one Access template file, Nwindtem.htm in the …\Office\Samples folder. Figure 17.11 shows the Nwindtem.htm template displayed in IE 5.0.

PART

IV

CH

17

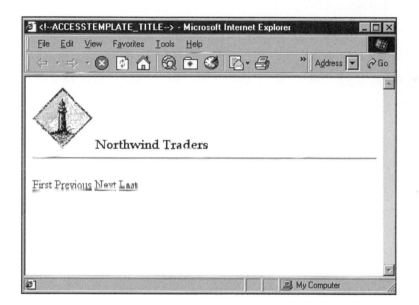

Figure 17.11
The Nwindtem.htm template file displayed in IE 5.0.

When you choose View, Source from IE 5.0's menu to display the HTML source of an Access HTML template file, the content appears similar to that shown for Nwindtem.htm invv Figure 17.12. The `<! Text >` tag normally is used to add invisible comments to a Web page. The Access 2000 export feature interprets comment text in the format `<!-- AccessTemplate_Element-->` to mean "replace this line with the specified *Element*." Microsoft calls these comment lines *Access HTML Template Tags*. Table 17.1 lists the Access HTML Template Tags recognized by Access 2000. The `...Page` anchor tags listed in Table 17.1 are used with multiple-page exports from Access reports, the subject of the section "Exporting Reports to HTML" later in this chapter.

Figure 17.12
The HTML source for
the Nwindtem.htm
template file.

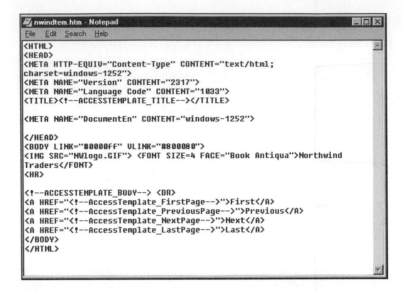

```
<HTML>
<HEAD>
<META HTTP-EQUIV="Content-Type" CONTENT="text/html;
charset=windows-1252">
<META NAME="Version" CONTENT="2317">
<META NAME="Language Code" CONTENT="1033">
<TITLE><!--ACCESSTEMPLATE_TITLE--></TITLE>

<META NAME="DocumentEn" CONTENT="windows-1252">

</HEAD>
<BODY LINK="#0000ff" VLINK="#800080">
<IMG SRC="NWlogo.GIF"> <FONT SIZE=4 FACE="Book Antiqua">Northwind
Traders</FONT>
<HR>

<!--ACCESSTEMPLATE_BODY--> <DR>
<A HREF="<!--AccessTemplate_FirstPage-->">First</A>
<A HREF="<!--AccessTemplate_PreviousPage-->">Previous</A>
<A HREF="<!--AccessTemplate_NextPage-->">Next</A>
<A HREF="<!--AccessTemplate_LastPage-->">Last</A>
</BODY>
</HTML>
```

TABLE 17.1   REPLACEABLE ACCESS HTML TEMPLATE TAGS RECOGNIZED BY ACCESS 2000

Access HTML Template Tag	Purpose
`<!--AccessTemplate_Title-->`	The object name that appears in the browser's title bar.
`<!--AcessTemplate_Body-->`	The table created from the object's output.
`<!--AccessTemplate_FirstPage-->`	Anchor tag to first page.
`<!--AccessTemplate_PreviousPage-->`	Anchor tag to previous page.
`<!--AccessTemplate_NextPage-->`	Anchor tag to next page.
`<!--AccessTemplate_LastPage-->`	Anchor tag to last page.
`<!--AccessTemplate_PageNumber-->`	Displays the current page number.

EXPORTING A QUERY DATASHEET WITH A TEMPLATE

To add a template to a Web page created from a query datasheet, follow these steps:

1. Create the query design, save the query with an appropriate name for the title and caption, and execute the query to open it in Datasheet view. This example uses a modified version (US Customers) of the North American Customers query that displays only customers in the U.S.

2. Copy the graphics files required by the template to the folder in which you intend to save your exported Web page. For the Nwindtem.htm template, copy the Nwlogo.gif file to …\Wwwroot, assuming you're using this folder to store your .html files.

Tip #150 from

It's a better Web design practice to place all graphics files in an ...\Images folder, rather than in the same folder as the page(s) that display them. Using an ...\Images folder lets you reuse standard .gif or .jpg files in multiple pages and provides a central storage point for easier graphics file management.

3. Choose File, Export to open the Export Query '*Query Name*' In dialog and select the folder in which to save the file. Select HTML Documents (*.html, *.htm) in the Save as Type dropdown list and mark the Save Formatted and Autostart check boxes. Change the name of the file in the File Name combo box, if you want to use a non-default file name. Click Save to continue.

4. When the HTML Options dialog appears, click the Browse button to select your template in the HTML Template To Use dialog—...\Office\Samples\Nwindtem.htm for this example (see Figure 17.13).

Figure 17.13
Specifying the Access HTML template for an exported Web page.

Tip #151 from

When you specify a template in the HTML Options dialog, the template becomes the default template for the succeeding Web pages you export.

5. Click OK to export the query datasheet and open the Web page in your browser. The logo appears at the top of the page, and the template adds the First, Previous, Next, and Last hyperlinks below the formatted table (see Figure 17.14).

6. Choose View, Source from IE 5.0's menu to view in Notepad the HTML lines added by the Nwindtem.htm template. Figure 17.15 shows the `<IMG SRC = "NWlogo.gif">` tag for the logo.

EXPORTING REPORTS TO HTML

NEW 2000 You can export an Access report to HTML in a manner similar to that for table or query datasheets. Unlike static datasheets, exporting a multipage report creates multiple Web pages, one for each page of the report. Unlike Access 97, you don't need to specify a template (Nwindtem.htm) for multipage reports.

PART
IV

Ch

17

Figure 17.14
The Web page created with the Nwindtem.htm template that adds a logo at the top and non-functioning hyperlinks at the bottom.

Figure 17.15
The first few lines of the HTML source for a Web page created with the Nwlogo.htm template.

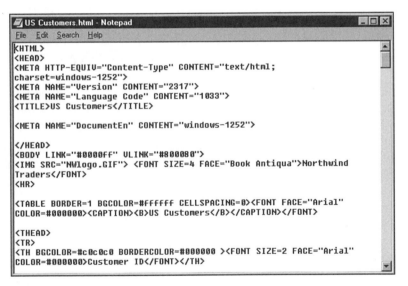

Note

You can export Access Reports to static Web pages only. This limitation is logical because a Web page is the equivalent of a printed report, which must be physically replaced when updated. Unlike Word 2000's File, Save As Web Page menu choice, the exporting process for Access 2000 reports doesn't process graphic images. If you want to add graphics to a report beyond the image(s) added by the template, you must create a .gif, .jpg, or .png file from each graphic image of the report, and then manually add a `<IMG SRC="filename.ext">` tag in the appropriate location of each report page. The graphics files must be located in the same folder as the associated .html file, unless you add a well-formed path to the *filename.ext* element of the tag.

To export the Catalog report of Northwind.mdb to a series of Web pages having hyperlink navigation features, follow these steps:

1. Select the Catalog report in the Database window.

2. Choose File, Export to open the Export Report 'Catalog' As dialog, and select the destination folder in the Save In drop-down list. Select HTML Documents (*.html, *.htm) in the Save As Type drop-down list and mark the Autostart check box. (The Save Formatted check box is marked and disabled; you can't export an unformatted report.) Click Save to continue.

3. When the HTML Options dialog appears, clear the text box entry, if it specifies a template file, and click OK. open the first page of the Catalog report in your browser. As expected, the large Northwind Traders graphic is missing from the first page, Catalog.html.

4. Click the Next hyperlink to proceed to the second page of the Catalog, and then scroll to the bottom of the page and click the Next button to display the third page (see Figure 17.16). When you export a report, the Access export feature appends Page# to the file name of the report for pages 2 and higher.

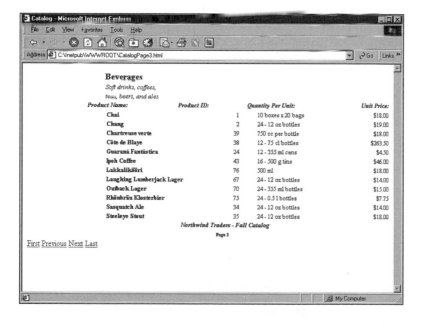

Figure 17.16
The third Web page (CatalogPage3.html) of the Catalog report.

5. Choose View, Source in IE 5.0 to display the HTML source for CatalogPage3.html in Notepad, and then scroll to the bottom of the file (see Figure 17.17). Each page of a report has a different set of HTML Previous and Next anchor lines for navigation. For page 3 of the catalog, the Previous and Next anchor lines are <A HREF="CatalogPage2.html">Previous</A> and <A HREF="CatalogPage4.html">Next</A>, respectively. The First (<A HREF="Catalog.html">First</A>) and Last (<A HREF="CatalogPage9.html">Last</A>) anchors are the same for all pages of the report.

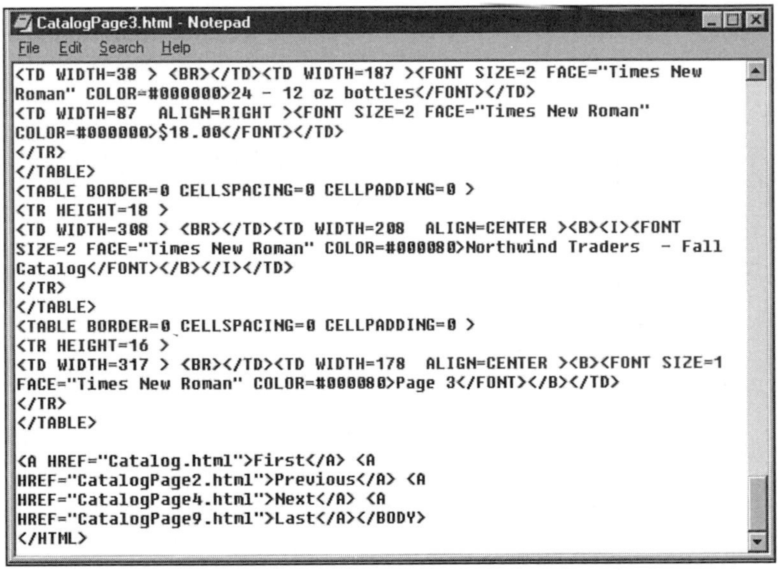

```
<TD WIDTH=38 > <BR></TD><TD WIDTH=187 ><FONT SIZE=2 FACE="Times New
Roman" COLOR=#000000>24 - 12 oz bottles</FONT></TD>
<TD WIDTH=87  ALIGN=RIGHT ><FONT SIZE=2 FACE="Times New Roman"
COLOR=#000000>$18.00</FONT></TD>
</TR>
</TABLE>
<TABLE BORDER=0 CELLSPACING=0 CELLPADDING=0 >
<TR HEIGHT=18 >
<TD WIDTH=308 > <BR></TD><TD WIDTH=208  ALIGN=CENTER ><B><I><FONT
SIZE=2 FACE="Times New Roman" COLOR=#000080>Northwind Traders  - Fall
Catalog</FONT></B></I></TD>
</TR>
</TABLE>
<TABLE BORDER=0 CELLSPACING=0 CELLPADDING=0 >
<TR HEIGHT=16 >
<TD WIDTH=317 > <BR></TD><TD WIDTH=178  ALIGN=CENTER ><B><FONT SIZE=1
FACE="Times New Roman" COLOR=#000080>Page 3</FONT></B></TD>
</TR>
</TABLE>

<A HREF="Catalog.html">First</A> <A
HREF="CatalogPage2.html">Previous</A> <A
HREF="CatalogPage4.html">Next</A> <A
HREF="CatalogPage9.html">Last</A></BODY>
</HTML>
```

Figure 17.17
The anchor tags of the third page (CatalogPage3.html) of the Catalog report.

Reports are formatted as HTML tables without borders (<TABLE BORDER=0>), which emulates on a Web page the appearance of Access 2000's reports in Preview mode and when printed. As a general rule, Access reports are the best choice for exporting large amounts of data to Web pages. You have much more control over the appearance of the Web page with exported reports than when you export a datasheet with the same content. To optimize the appearance of Web pages created from reports, you must design the report specifically for export to HTML.

Note

Report formatting fails for complex reports that contain a combination of graphic elements and text. As an example, compare the last Web page (CatalogPage9.html) of the Catalog series with the last page of the Catalog report in Access' report Preview mode. All the graphic elements in the order form are missing from the last Web page.

IMPORTING DATA FROM HTML TABLES

Access 2000 includes the capability to import or link data from an HTML table to a Jet 4.0 table. This feature appears to have been included in Access 2000 for HTML symmetry; apparently, the theory is that if you can export to HTML, you should also be able to import from HTML. Few Access users are likely to make use of this feature because relatively little useful, public domain (not copyrighted) tabular data is available on the Internet. For completeness, however, following is an example of importing data from an HTML page created in the section "Exporting Table and Query Datasheets to HTML" earlier in this chapter:

1. Choose File, Get External Data, Import to open the Import dialog. Navigate to the folder in which you stored Suppliers.html and select HTML Documents (*.html, *.htm) in the Files of Type dropdown list (see Figure 17.18).

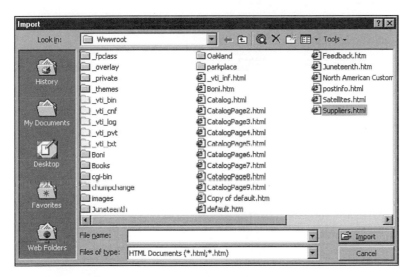

Figure 17.18
Displaying .html and .htm files in the Import dialog.

2. Select the Suppliers.html file you created in the "Exporting Table and Query Datasheets to HTML" section at the beginning of this chapter and click the Import button to close the Import dialog and open the first Import HTML Wizard dialog.

3. The Wizard imports the table header data, if present, together with the table data. The formatted version of Suppliers.html includes headers, so check the First Row Contains Column Headings check box (see Figure 17.19).

4. Click the Advanced button to open the Suppliers Import Specification dialog. This dialog lets you customize import operations on date and time fields and select the decimal symbol. You can change the field names, data types, and indexing for each of the fields, as well as skip the import of specific fields. Change the Data Type of the PostalCode column from Long Integer to Text. The Supplier ID field is the primary key, so specify a No Duplicates index on the field (see Figure 17.20). Data types and indexes for the remaining fields are satisfactory.

Figure 17.19
Specifying column headers in the Import HTML Wizard's first dialog.

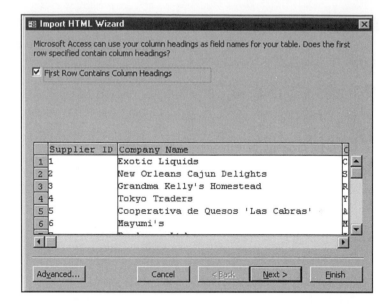

Figure 17.20
Specifying field data types and indexes in the Suppliers Import Specification dialog.

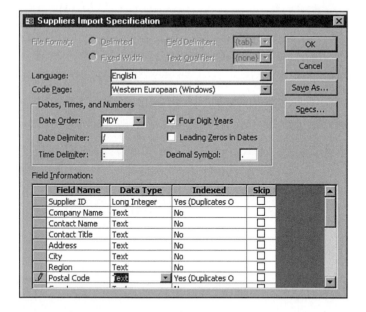

Tip #152 from

RJ

Always set the data type of postal code fields to text. If the first few rows contain U.S. (5-digit numeric) ZIP codes, the Wizard assumes that all postal codes are numeric and assigns the Long Integer data type. You receive Import Errors messages when the Wizard encounters an alphanumeric postal code, such as those used in Canada and the U.K. Other countries sometimes prefix a alphabetic country-code abbreviation, such as S-15151 (Sweden).

Note

> Alternatively, you can specify field data types and indexing in the third Wizard dialog. The Wizard proposes to add Duplicates OK indexes on any field that contains ID or Code in the column name.

If you encounter unexpected import errors see the "HTML Table Import Errors" topic of the "Troubleshooting" section near the end of the chapter.

5. Click the Save As button to save the Import Specification. Edit or type a new name for the specification in the Specification Name text box of the Save Import/Export Specification dialog (see Figure 17.21). Click OK to close the dialog, and then click OK to close the Suppliers Import Specification dialog.

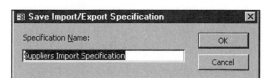

Figure 17.21
Editing the default name for the saved Suppliers Import Specification.

PART
IV

CH

17

6. Click Next to display the second Import HTML Wizard dialog. Select the In a New Table option to store the data in a new table whose name you specify at the end of the import process (see Figure 17.22). Click Next.

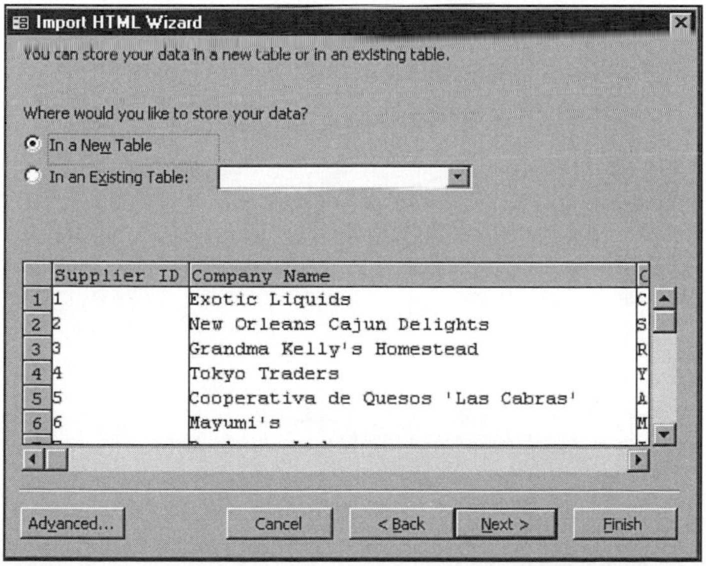

Figure 17.22
Specifying import of the tabular HTML data to a new table.

Note

> If your HTML table includes date fields, added combo and text boxes let you specify date formats. You can select a period or comma as the decimal symbol if the table includes real numbers.

7. You can make last-minute changes to field names, data types, and indexes in the third Wizard dialog (see Figure 17.23). If you made the required changes to the Suppliers Import Specification dialog in step 4, click Next.

Figure 17.23
A second chance to change field names, data types, and indexes offered by the third Wizard dialog.

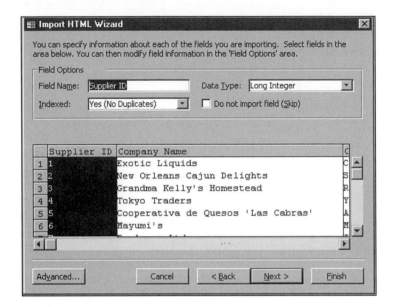

8. By default, the Wizard proposes adding a numeric primary key field to the table. The Supplier ID field qualifies as a primary key, so select the Choose My Own Primary Key option and pick the Supplier ID field in the dropdown list (see Figure 17.24). Click Next.

Figure 17.24
Selecting the Supplier ID field as the primary key for the imported table.

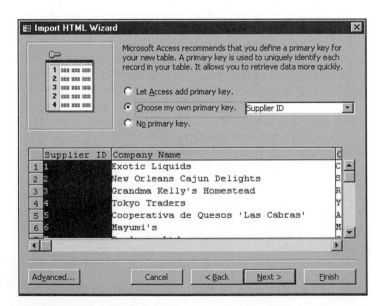

9. There is a Suppliers table in Northwind.mdb, so edit the proposed table name to tblSuppliers (see Figure 17.25). You don't need to analyze the Suppliers table, so don't mark the I Would Like a Wizard to Analyze check box. Click Finish to export the HTML table to tblSuppliers and terminate the Wizard.

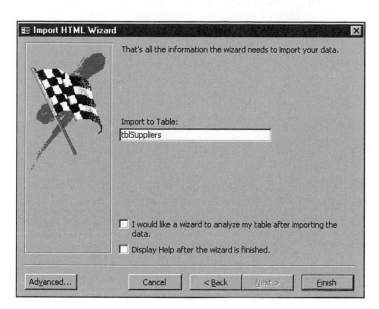

Figure 17.25
Editing the name of the new table in the final Wizard dialog.

PART

IV

CH

17

Note

If data in your source HTML table violates primary key integrity or has rows with data type conflicts, the Wizard generates an import errors table. If an import errors table is present, check its contents to determine the source of the problem(s).

---

10. Open the tblSuppliers table to verify the import wizardry. The table is essentially identical to the original Suppliers table from which the Web page was created (see Figure 17.26). The most significant differences are the field data type of the Supplier ID column (Long Integer, not AutoNumber) and the field names (derived from the Caption property of the original table).

Note

Most of the information available on the Internet is subject to copyright, either explicitly (by a copyright notice on the Web site's home page) or implicitly (by statute). Importing and using copyrighted content from the Internet for most purposes is prohibited by federal copyright statutes, unless you have express permission of the copyright owner to use the content. If you intend to import and use information created by others and published on the Internet, consult an attorney before using the information.

Figure 17.26
The exported
tblSuppliers table in
Datasheet view.

Supplier ID	Company Nam	Contact Name	Contact Title	Address	City
1	Exotic Liquids	Charlotte Coope	Purchasing Mar	49 Gilbert St.	London
2	New Orleans Ca	Shelley Burke	Order Administr	P.O. Box 78934	New Orleans
3	Grandma Kelly's	Regina Murphy	Sales Represen	707 Oxford Rd.	Ann Arbor
4	Tokyo Traders	Yoshi Nagase	Marketing Mana	9-8 Sekimai	Tokyo
5	Cooperativa de	Antonio del Vall	Export Administ	Calle del Rosal	Oviedo
6	Mayumi's	Mayumi Ohno	Marketing Repre	92 Setsuko	Osaka
7	Pavlova, Ltd.	Ian Devling	Marketing Mana	74 Rose St.	Melbourne
8	Specialty Biscu	Peter Wilson	Sales Represen	29 King's Way	Manchester
9	PB Knäckebröd	Lars Peterson	Sales Agent	Kaloadagatan 1:	Göteborg
10	Refrescos Amer	Carlos Diaz	Marketing Mana	Av. das America	São Paulo
11	Heli Süßwaren	Petra Winkler	Sales Manager	Tiergartenstraße	Berlin
12	Plutzer Lebensr	Martin Bein	International Ma	Bogenallee 51	Frankfurt
13	Nord-Ost-Fisch	Sven Petersen	Coordinator For	Frahmredder 11	Cuxhaven
14	Formaggi Fortin	Elio Rossi	Sales Represen	Viale Dante, 75	Ravenna
15	Norske Meierier	Beate Vileid	Marketing Mana	Hatlevegen 5	Sandvika
16	Bigfoot Brewerie	Cheryl Saylor	Regional Accou	3400 - 8th Aven	Bend
17	Svensk Sjöföda	Michael Biörn	Sales Represen	Brovallavägen 3	Stockholm

Record: 1 of 29

CREATING DYNAMIC WEB PAGES

Dynamic Web pages let users create their own select queries to return custom data sets in tabular format or display forms that users can edit or to which they can add data. If you have Office 2000 Premium, it's easier to create and deploy data-enabled, Internet-compliant Web pages with FrontPage 2000 than with Access 2000. If you need the ability to delete or edit data from a browser-independent Web page, Visual InterDev 6.0 is the better choice.

Tip #153 from

To learn how to import or link your Access 2000 database to a FrontPage Web, launch FrontPage, open your Web, type **Access database** in the Answer Wizard's What Would You Like To Do? text box, and select the "Use an Access database in a Web topic." FrontPage includes a Database Results Wizard to automate authoring data display pages. You can also generate a new Jet database and table from your FrontPage 2000 form design.

Access 2000 offers the following three methods for creating dynamic, data-enabled Web pages:

- *Internet Database Connector* (*IDC*) merges an .htx (template) file with an HTML page for data display and uses an .idc file to define the data source and SQL query to execute. IDC uses ODBC and an Internet Information Server (IIS) helper file (Httpodbc.dll) to connect to your Access database. You can execute the equivalent of an Access parameterized query, specify the sort sequence, and design other query custom features. You can export Access tables and queries to .idc/.htx files, but customizing the display of query result sets requires HTML authoring expertise. IDC was Microsoft's first and simplest approach to generating data-enabled Web pages; most Web sites running IIS have abandoned IDC in favor of Active Server Pages.

- *Active Server Pages* (*ASP*) is Microsoft's mainstream technology for designing interactive, Internet-compliant Web pages. ASP use ActiveX Data Objects (ADO) for database connectivity. ADO is one of the subjects of Chapter 27, "Understanding Universal Data Access, OLE DB, and ADO." The majority of the content of Microsoft's Web site (http://www.microsoft.com) uses ASP. You can export Access tables, queries, and forms to ASP, but many of the features of Access 97's File, Save as HTML menu choice are missing in Access 2000. Exporting an Access 2000 form, for instance, results in a page with a tabular display of the underlying data, not an HTML representation of the form.

NEW 2000
- *Data Access Pages* (*DAP*), the subject of the next chapter, use Access 2000's new Data Access Page designer to implement Microsoft's version of DHTML and DHTML data binding with ADO. DAP let you take advantage of Office Web Components to add charts, spreadsheets, and PivotTables to your pages. Microsoft DHTML isn't compatible with Netscape's current version, so DAP are suited only for intranets where all users have IE 4+ installed.

> **Note**   **NEW 2000**   Keep an installation of Access 97 active if you need to use Access to generate .idc/.htx files from tables and queries or .asp files from forms. Fortunately, Access 2000 lets you convert a database to Access 97 format; you then use Access 97's Publish to the Web Wizard to quickly create interactive Web pages from tables, queries, and forms.

PART
IV

CH
17

UNDERSTANDING ASP

Active Server Pages is a mature Microsoft technology that generates browser-independent HTML from directives contained in an .asp file. ASP is a *server side* component of IIS 3+ and PWS; the Web server interprets the .asp file and sends a corresponding .htm file to the client's browser. If the .asp file contains scripts created with VBScript or JScript, the server's script engine executes the code. HTTP is a stateless protocol, so any changes made by the viewer to an interactive page, even the most trivial, must be sent to the server; the server then returns an updated version of the page. This process is called a *server round-trip*.

DAP, on the other hand, is a *client-side* technology. The Web server sends the entire content of the .htm file for the page; script embedded in the file executes on the client. DAP minimizes the number of server round-trips, an important consideration for highly trafficked Web sites.

You can open an .asp file directly in IE, but you're not likely to see any content in your browser. If you have FrontPage 2000 installed with default properties, attempting to open an .asp file in IE automatically launches FrontPage. Earlier versions of FrontPage open the FrontPage Editor. If the .asp file you want to open is on a machine with PWS or IIS, you open it in IE with a conventional domain name URL—
http://www.*domain*.com/*pagename*.asp—or an intranet URL—[http://]*servername*/*pagename*.asp. The Web server executes the .asp file and generates an .htm file for the requester.

CREATING AN ODBC DATA SOURCE FOR ASP

ASP use ADO for database connectivity, but Access 2000's ASP export feature doesn't use the Jet native OLE DB data provider, commonly known as *Jolt*. Therefore, you must have an ODBC system or file data source for your database on the server that hosts the .asp file. System data sources, which are accessible to all database applications running on the server, are more efficient than file data sources.

To create a system data source on the Web server—PWS running under Windows 98, for this example—do the following:

1. Launch Control Panel's ODBC Data Sources (32-bit) tool, which opens the ODBC Data Source Administrator dialog.

2. Click the System tab to display a list of all system data sources, called DSNs (data source names).

3. Click the Add button to open the Create New Data Source dialog, and select Microsoft Access Driver (*.mdb) in the Name list (see Figure 17.27).

Figure 17.27
Selecting the Access
ODBC driver in the
Create New Data
Source dialog.

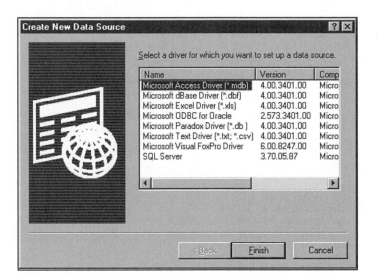

4. Click Finish to open the ODBC Microsoft Access Setup dialog.

5. Type a short DSN in the Data Source Name text box, and add an optional description of the data source in the Description text box.

6. Click Select to open the Select Database dialog, navigate to the …\Office\Samples folder, and double-click Northwind.mdb in the Database Name text box to specify the database and return to the Setup dialog (see Figure 17.28). Northwind.mdb isn't secure, so you don't need to specify a system database.

7. Click OK twice to close the Setup and Administrator dialogs, and then close Control Panel.

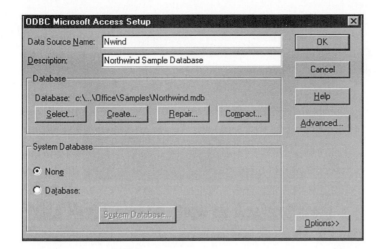

Figure 17.28
Specifying the system DSN for Northwind.mdb.

EXPORTING AN ACCESS QUERY TO ASP

To export the North American Customers query you created earlier in the chapter to an .asp file, do the following:

1. Select North American Customers in the queries list, press F2, and change its name to **North_American_Customers**, substituting underscores for spaces. Spaces aren't permitted in URLs, and Access 2000 doesn't replace spaces in exported object names with underscores or the %32% HTML symbol for a space.

   Alternatively, you can change the file name in following step 3.

2. Choose File, Export to open the Export Query 'North_American_Customers' As dialog.

3. Select the destination folder, \Inetpub\Wwwroot for this example, in the Save In list, and then select Microsoft Active Server Pages (*.asp) in the Save As Type list (see Figure 17.29). Selecting .asp disables the Save Formatted and Autostart check boxes.

4. Click Save to close the Export dialog and open the Microsoft Active Server Pages Output Options dialog.

5. Specify an HTML template for the file, if you like, and type the name of the system DSN you created in the preceding section in the Data Source Name text box.

6. Type **http://*servername*** in the Server URL text box; ***servername*** is the network name of the Web server (oakleaf1 for this example). Type a timeout value in minutes in the Session Timeout text box (see Figure 17.30).

7. Click Save to create North_American_Customers.asp and close the Output Options dialog.

8. Close Access to prevent locking problems with Northwind.mdb, and then launch IE.

Figure 17.29
Specifying the location, file name, and file type for an exported .asp file.

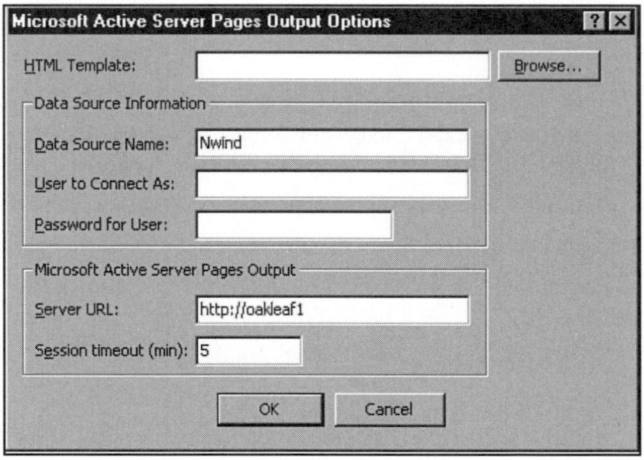

Figure 17.30
Adding the DSN, server URL, and session timeout for the .asp file.

9. Type **http://*servername*/North_American_Customers.asp** in the Address text box and press Enter to execute the .asp file, which returns `North_American_Customers[1].htm` to your browser (see Figure 17.31).

10. Choose View, Source to open North_American_Customers[1].htm in Notepad (see Figure 17.32) or your chosen HTML editor. The HTML source text is almost identical to that of the static North American Query exported to HTML (refer to Figure 17.15). Only the HTML template content is missing.

The advantage of creating ASPs to display tabular data from queries, compared to a simple query export operation, is that the data delivered is current as of the moment IIS generates the .htm page. Like tables and queries exported directly to .html files, the .htm page created by export to an .asp file is read-only.

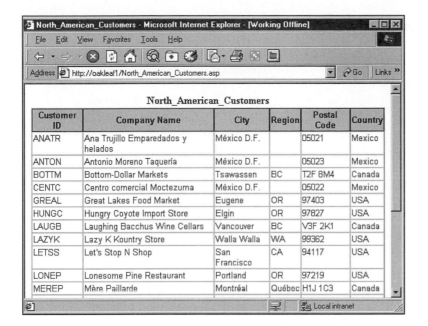

Figure 17.31
The HTML page generated by North_American_Customers.asp.

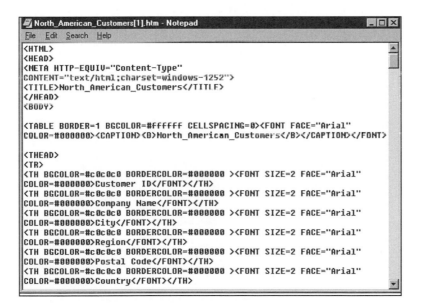

Figure 17.32
The first part of the HTML source text generated by the exported .asp file.

TROUBLESHOOTING

HTML TABLE IMPORT ERRORS

Importing HTML tables generates unexpected "Import Errors" messages

The Import HTML Wizard, like the Text Import Wizard, checks the values of each column for the first few rows of the HTML table. The first test is to determine if the column contains alphabetic characters; if so, the Wizard sets the Jet data type to Text. If the Wizard detects only numeric values, it also tests for a currency symbol and a decimal separator. If the currency symbol is present, the Wizard chooses the Currency data type; if not, the data type becomes Double if a decimal separator is present, otherwise the data type becomes Long Integer. If subsequent rows of a column contain entries that conflict with the selected data type, import errors occur. You can avoid most, if not all, import errors by choosing Text for the data type of all columns, then inspecting the table in Datasheet view to determine the appropriate field data type for each column.

IN THE REAL WORLD—ASP VERSUS DAP

Access 97 offered the capability of exporting an Access form to an .asp file. The resulting forms—created in part by the ActiveX HTML Layout Control—weren't pretty, but simple forms worked as advertised. Figure 17.33 illustrates the Customers.asp file created by Access 97 from the Northwind.mdb Customers table. The Country drop-down list lets you apply a filter to the query to display only records from the specified country. Unlike the ASP generated in this chapter's example, Customers.asp was capable of updating the underlying Customers table.

Figure 17.33
The Customers.asp file generated by Access 97 opened in IE 5.0.

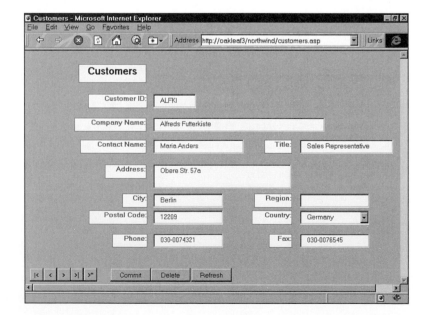

The obvious advantage of ASP is that the technology generates .htm files displaying forms that are compatible with any browser, not just Microsoft's current version of IE. Generic HTML controls placed by the Layout Control behaved the same in all browsers. Access 97's form export to ASP feature let you learn the basics of creating and deploying data-bound ASP without requiring a full understanding of the underlying technology. ASP export in Access 97 also introduced ActiveX Data Objects 1.0 to Access programmers. Access 97-generated ASP had some significant limitations, but most Access developers expected the problems to be overcome in V.next (Access 2000).

ASP is great technology and is the foundation of the commercial success of IIS 3+ as a Web server and Windows NT 4.0 as an operating system for Web servers. Many large publishing and e-commerce sites use ASP; Fawcette Technical Publishing's DevX Web site (http://www.devx.com) is a good example. DevX's target audience is Web, Visual Basic, and Java developers, plus information technology managers who pay a substantial semi-annual fee to subscribe at the site's Premier membership level. DevX must combine up-to-date technical content, stored in SQL Server databases, with top performance to maintain subscriber loyalty. ASP technology is a major contributor to the success of the DevX site.

PART

IV

CH

17

> **Note**
>
> Microsoft's general-interest Slate Web site (http://www.slate.com) abandoned attempts to charge users for most of its content in February, 1999 and moved to an advertising-supported business model. DevX, which offers free Registered and paid Premier membership levels, is one of the few commercial Internet sites that has succeeded in charging for content. DevX also has substantial advertising income.

Now Microsoft wants Access users and developers to move from ASP in favor of DAP. The party line is that the Layout Control, better known as ControlPad, isn't "safe for scripting," so it was necessary to abandon form-to-ASP support in Access 2000. The irony in Microsoft's proposed ASP to DAP transition is that there's no support for form-to-DAP conversion in Access 2000.

Only time will tell if DAP succeeds as a proprietary—and thus intranet-only—technology or suffers the same fate as Access 97's form-to-ADP feature. As you progress through the next chapter, follow the steps carefully and remember to save your DAP frequently. If DAP succeeds, hopefully V.next will offer an Edit, Undo command.

--rj

CHAPTER 18

DESIGNING DATA ACCESS PAGES

In this chapter

Moving to a New Access Form Model   658

Understanding Access's Dynamic HTML Implementation   659

Getting Acquainted with DAP   663

Using the Page Wizard to Create Simple DAP   674

Using AutoPage to Create Columnar DAP   679

Starting a DAP from Scratch   687

Adding Charts to DAP with a PivotTable List   691

Generating a Grouped Page   698

Troubleshooting   704

In the Real World—Are DAP Ready for Prime Time?   704

MOVING TO A NEW ACCESS FORM MODEL

Data Access Pages (DAP) are a radical departure from traditional Access database applications. Unlike other Access objects stored in .mdb files, Access stores DAP in Dynamic HTML (DHTML) files with a standard .htm extension. DAP that appear when you click the Database window's Pages shortcut, such as the sample pages installed by Office 2000's setup program, represent links to the corresponding DHTML files. The Enter Details item, for example, is a link to the Enter Details.htm file in your ...\Office\Sample folder. DAP uses DHTML Data Binding to ActiveX Data Object (ADO) Recordsets generated from Jet 4.0 and earlier databases. Users view DAP in Internet Explorer (IE) 5.0, so they don't need a copy of Access 2000; nor do you need to purchase the Office 2000 Developer Edition to distribute a runtime version of your DAP. However, DAP users must have an Office 2000 license because most DAP rely on the Office Web Components (OWC) for data presentation.

Access 2000 includes a new designer and control toolbox for DAP. A *designer* is a design-mode tool that automatically generates code to re-create in run mode the objects whose properties you set in a graphical user interface (GUI). Access 2000's DAP Designer differs greatly from Access's Form Design mode. DAP Designer has its own Page toolbar and a Page Toolbox of DHTML-compliant controls.

If you're new to authoring dynamic Web pages, you first must grasp the terminology used by DAP. Internet-related terminology is replete with three- to five-letter acronyms (TLA and 5LA, respectively) that belie the complexity of the underlying technology. Therefore, this chapter begins with a brief explanation of DHTML and related Web authoring methodology. If you're an accomplished Internet content creator or are well acquainted with Visual Basic 6.0's DHTML Pages feature, skip to the "Getting Acquainted with DAP" section.

NEW 2000 This chapter covers the following features that are new in Access 2000:

- *Data Access Pages* let you create data-enabled DHTML pages from Access tables and queries. Unfortunately, Access 2000's version of DAP doesn't let you export forms to DHTML pages.

- *Record Navigation* is a lightweight ActiveX control that binds the DHTML page to an Access table or query. The Expand control works with the Record Navigation control to emulate Access 2000's subdatasheets.

- *Bound HTML* and *Bound Hyperlink* controls provide read-only display of values from a table field or query column. Conventional HTML elements, such as text boxes and option buttons, provide update capability.

- *Office Web Components* add Spreadsheet, PivotTable, and Chart elements to your DAP. Users must have an Office 2000 license to view DAP that use Office Web Components.

■ *Movie control* lets you display audio/video content in your DAP, such as a talking head video that teaches others how to get the maximum benefit from your newly deployed DAP. The Movie control also plays audio-only Active Streaming Format (.asf, Windows Media) files.

The preceding list doesn't include new features implemented by the upgrade from IE 4.0 to IE 5.0; you must have IE 5+ installed to design and display DAP in Access 2000. Users must have IE 5+ to use any DAP you create.

UNDERSTANDING ACCESS'S DYNAMIC HTML IMPLEMENTATION

Dynamic HTML doesn't currently have the status of an Internet standard, so DHTML implementations vary between browser suppliers. An *Internet standard*, in this book, is defined as a World Wide Web Consortium (W3C) Recommendation or an Internet Engineering Task Force (IETF) Request for Comment (RFC). A *W3C Recommendation* or *IEFT RFC* is a euphemism for *specification*; the term *specification* doesn't appeal to Internet purists (called anarchists by some) who believe in a consensus-based Internet without the profit motive of commercial software publishers and content providers. W3C and IETF working groups, which create the W3C Recommendations, occupy the full time of many employees of Adobe, Apple, IBM, Macromedia, Microsoft, Netscape, and other major suppliers to the PC industry. Most of today's W3C standards represent consensus among W3C voting members—vendors plus a few governments and universities—not the Internet community as a whole.

PART
IV

CH
18

TECHNOLOGIES SUPPORTING DHTML AND DAP

W3C stated in late 1998: "Dynamic HTML is still in its infancy and current implementations are experimental." In this case, *experimental* is a euphemism for *proprietary*. Following is a brief description of the two Internet standards and four Microsoft (proprietary) technologies that provide the foundation for Microsoft DHTML and its use by DAP:

■ *Document Object Model* (*DOM*) is a World Wide Web Consortium (W3C) Recommendation (a W3C) adopted on October 1, 1998. The complete DOM Level 1, Version 1.0 Recommendation is at http://www.w3.org/TR/REC-DOM-Level-1/. DOM consists of a Core component (DOM Core) that supports Extensible Markup Language and provides the underpinnings for DOM's HTML component (DOM HTML). Microsoft's "An Introduction to the Dynamic HTML Object Model" article at http://www.microsoft.com/workshop/author/om/dynamicom.asp offers a brief introduction to the relationship between DOM and DHTML.

- *Extensible Markup Language* (*XML*) 1.0 became a W3C Recommendation in February 1998. The complete text of the Recommendation is at http://www.w3.org/TR/REC-xml. The fundamental objective of XML was to provide a means for supporting a simplified version of Standard Generalized Markup Language (SGML) on the Web by allowing developer-definable tags. Word 2000 and Excel 2000 documents use XML to preserve formatting and other special features, such as Word revision marks and Excel formulas. DAP use XML for data definitions and HTML for displaying data and other visible elements. The most common application for XML is Web pages that manipulate information from databases. IE 4+ supports XML.

- *Cascading Style Sheets* (*CSS*) let you specify the onscreen presentation and printed format of HTML documents without the need to invent new HTML formatting tags. CSS *rules* let you specify the exact location of elements, such as blocks of text or images, as well as the color, type family, and font of text. W3C adopted the CSS Level 2 (CSS2) Recommendation (this time also called a specification) in May 1998; you can read the complete W3C Recommendation at http://www.w3.org/TR/REC-CSS2/. DHTML lets you change CSS rules on-the-fly to specify the properties of an object in response to events, such as passing the mouse pointer over a headline or clicking a block of text. IE 4.0 introduced support for a subset of the CSS1 specification.

- *DHTML Behaviors* are Microsoft's approach to separating scripting code from HTML content. DHTML Behaviors let you store scripting code in HTML Component (.htc) files. Separating script from HTML content makes the page source code easier to read and lets you reuse standard event-handling procedures, such as highlighting text. Users must have IE 5+ installed to enable DHTML Behaviors on client PCs.

- *Data Binding* in DHTML takes advantage of custom XML tags to define database connections, execute queries, and organize the structure of data returned by queries. You use the DAP Designer's Record Navigation control to connect to your access database and specify the table or query for your page(s). The DAP Designer's toolbox offers a special set of controls that you bind to the Record Navigation control to display and update data.

- *OLE DB* and *ActiveX Data Objects* (*ADO*) provide the underlying database connectivity for DHTML Data Binding and DAP. Chapter 27, "Understanding Universal Data Access, OLE DB, and ADO," explains these two related data access technologies.

Fortunately, you don't need to fully understand the object models and syntax of the preceding technologies to generate DAP with Access 2000. If you want to understand how Microsoft implements DHTML and XML for data manipulation, however, Access 2000's DAP is a very useful learning tool.

Note

There are two other pending W3C standards, in the working draft stage when this book was written, that ultimately will affect the way you implement DAP. Extensible Style Language (XSL) is a W3C Draft Recommendation (`http://www.w3.org/TR/WD-xsl`) for transforming XML documents into formatted HTML. Extensible Query Language (XQL) is an extension to XSL that lets you query the content of XML documents. XQL was in the early experimental stage when this book was written; papers from the December, 1998 W3C Query Languages Workshop are at `http://www.w3.org/TandS/QL/QL98/pp.html`. Microsoft claims that IE 5.0 supports both XSL and XQL, but documentation for its XQL features isn't included in the release version of IE 5.0. A description of IE 5.0's XSL support is at `http://www.microsoft.com/xml/xsl/reference/start.asp`.

DOM HTML AND DHTML

DOM HTML describes elements of conventional HTML Web pages as a collection of predefined hierarchical objects based on W3C-standard HTML tags. Listing 18.1 shows the HTML source for a simple three-column, three-row FrontPage 2000 table with row-column (R*n*C*n*) text in each cell.

LISTING 18.1   HTML SOURCE FOR A THREE-COLUMN, THREE-ROW TABLE

```
<html>
<head>
<meta http-equiv="Content-Language" content="en-us">
<meta name="GENERATOR" content="Microsoft FrontPage 4.0">
<meta name="ProgId" content="FrontPage.Editor.Document">
<title>New Page 1</title>
</head>

<body>
<table border="1" width="100%">
  <tr>
    <td width="33%">R1C1</td>
    <td width="33%">R1C2</td>
    <td width="34%">R1C3</td>
  </tr>
  <tr>
    <td width="33%">R2C1</td>
    <td width="33%">R2C2</td>
    <td width="34%">R2C3</td>
  </tr>
  <tr>
    <td width="33%">R3C1</td>
    <td width="33%">R3C2</td>
    <td width="34%">R3C4</td>
  </tr>
</table>
</body>
</html>
```

Figure 18.1 illustrates the object hierarchy of the HTML elements defined by Listing 18.1. Like the master-child relationships of forms and subforms, DOM defines parent-child(ren) relationships between objects and properties, which can also be collections of objects. The <HTML> tag defines the document parent object; the document object has a child <HEAD> element, which contains <META> and <TITLE> children, and a <BODY> element (body object), which contains all other elements of the page. The <TABLE> element contains a collection of <TR> row elements, each of which contains a <TD> data or column collection. Microsoft's DOM for DHTML is very complex.

Figure 18.1
A simplified object model
for the HTML page of
Listing 18.1.

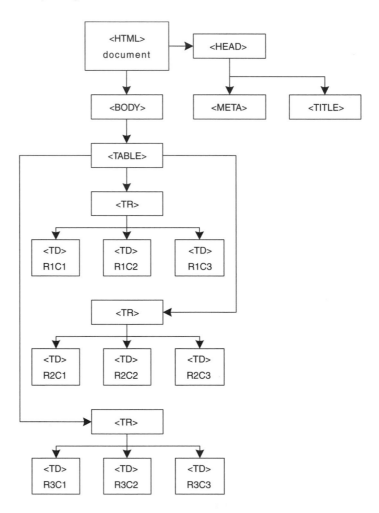

Note

Microsoft's DHTML documentation and this chapter use the terms *element* (HTML tag) and *object* interchangeably.

DOM HTML also defines an event model for objects. The event model lets Web page authors specify what occurs when a page loads in your browser or you click an element. Event-handling code, written in a scripting language, specifies the action taken when an event occurs. An object must have a unique Id property value, similar to the Name property of Access controls, to connect event-handling code to the object.

W3C's DOM Recommendation encompasses browser-independent Java (from Sun Microsystems) and ECMAScript (formerly Netscape's JavaScript) languages, which Microsoft supplies as Visual J++ and JScript, respectively. Microsoft's version of DHTML also accommodates VBScript, which only IE supports. IE 4+ and Netscape Navigator/Communicator 4+ don't support W3C DOM to the same extent, and earlier browser versions don't support DOM at all. Thus Microsoft DHTML is limited to intranets where users have installed IE 4+, and DAP is further restricted by requiring users to install IE 5.0.

GETTING ACQUAINTED WITH DAP

Access 2000 includes sample DAP to introduce Microsoft's new approach to creating data display and editing forms. With Northwind.mdb open, click the Database window's Pages shortcut to display the list of sample pages. Double-click the page name in the Database window's list to open a page in DAP Page view. DAP Page view uses IE 5.0's XML parser and HTML engine to display the page in a window similar to that for displaying conventional Access forms. The Page View menu substitutes for the Form View menu when you open DAP.

THE REVIEW PRODUCTS PAGE

The majority of DAP you design probably will be read-only pages for displaying summary data, detail data, or both. The simplest read-only sample page is Review Products, shown in Figure 18.2, which displays records of the Categories related records from the Products tables in groups of three records from each table.

The Record Navigation control emulates a combination of Access's standard record navigation buttons (First, Prev(ious), Next, and Last record), plus Sort Ascending, Sort Descending, Apply Filter, and Toggle Filter buttons from the Page toolbar. The buttons are disabled or enabled, depending on the position of the record pointer. The Help button opens the "Get Help on Specific Areas in a Data Access Page" online help topic. The Product Information page is read-only, so the Add New Record button for the tentative append record doesn't appear.

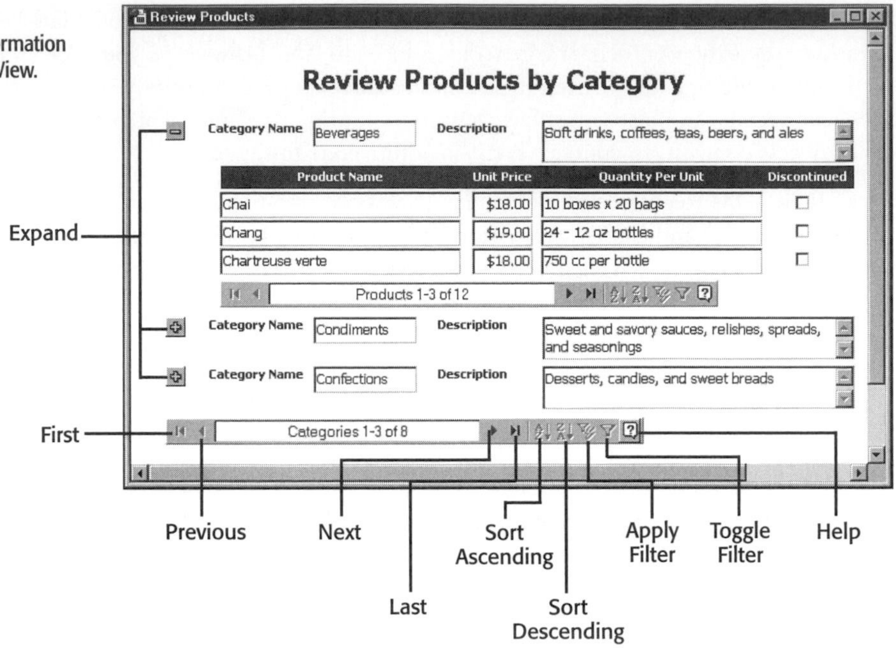

Figure 18.2
The Product Information sample in Page View.

The Review Products page illustrates how DAP displays master-child table relationships in multiple regions separated by headers. The Expand control toggles between expanded (see Beverages category in Figure 18.2), which displays related Product records in groups of three, and contracted (plus, see Condiments and Confections categories in Figure 18.2), which hides the Products group.

DAP are designed for viewing within IE 5+. To duplicate the DAP users' view of the read-only Review Products page, do the following:

1. Launch IE 5.0 and click Work Offline to dismiss the Dial-up Connection dialog, if it appears.

2. Choose File, Open to display the Open dialog.

3. Click Browse to open the Microsoft Internet Explorer dialog.

4. Navigate to the …\Office\Samples folder and double-click the Review Products.htm file to return to the Open dialog.

5. Click OK to close the Open dialog and display the Review Products page in IE 5.0 (see Figure 18.3).

   The page displays a group of three of the eight product categories in HTML text boxes and the three Expand controls default to the contracted state. Grouping more than one set of records causes DAP to be read-only.

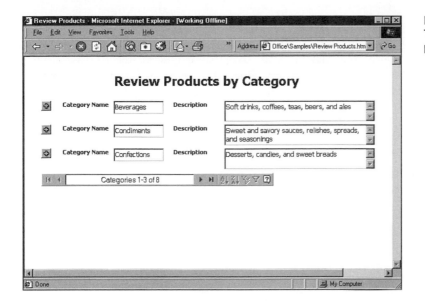

Figure 18.3
The Review Products.htm
page opened in IE 5.0.

 6. Click one of the Expand controls to display members of the corresponding Category
record. A second group of three HTML text boxes and a Record Navigation control
display related records from the Products table below the two Category table fields (see
Figure 18.4).

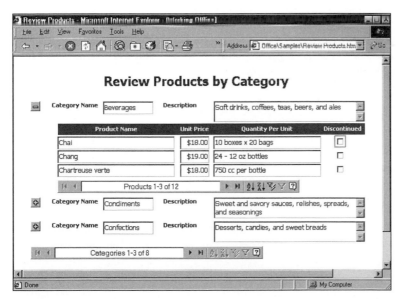

Figure 18.4
The Review Products.htm
page with the Beverages
category expanded.

7. Click the Next Record button of the Categories Record Navigation control, which causes the Categories Expand button to return to its collapsed default state.

8. Choose <u>V</u>iew, Sour<u>c</u>e to display the XML code that defines the Record Navigation control's connection to Northwind.mdb. Figure 18.5 shows Notepad displaying only part of the XML code necessary to support the Record Navigation control.

Figure 18.5
Part of the XML source code to define the native Jet OLE DB data provider and Northwind.mdb as the ADO data source for the Review Orders page.

> **Note**
>
> DAP use the native OLE DB provider for Jet–Microsoft.Jet.OLEDB.4.0–more commonly known as Jolt. Code that begins with the `Jet OLEDB:` prefix sets the properties of the OLE DB data source.

9. Close Notepad, IE 5.0, and the Review Products page.

It's clear from the complexity of the XML source code shown in Figure 18.5 that few, if any, Access users or developers are likely to type their own XML source in Notepad or any other HTML editor. The DAP Designer automatically generates the underlying XML and HTML source code as you add objects to DAP in Page Design mode. When you edit or move an object, the DAP Designer alters the HTML code within the division (<DIV>...</DIV>) that contains the object. DAP use CSS to fix the relative position of each visible object on the page. The position reference point is the upper-left corner of the section in which the object appears.

THE REVIEW ORDERS PAGE

The Review Orders page—titled View Orders by Company—opens with only a dropdown list visible (see Figure 18.6). A query against the Customers table populates the Select a Company list. When you make a company selection, a query against the Order tables displays five-member groups of orders placed by the company. Expanding an order displays related records from the Order Details table (see Figure 18.7).

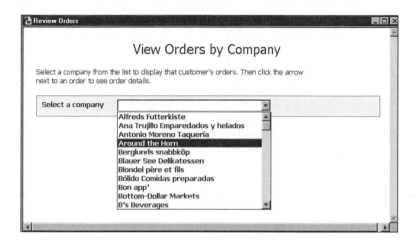

Figure 18.6
The Review Orders page when opened in Access.

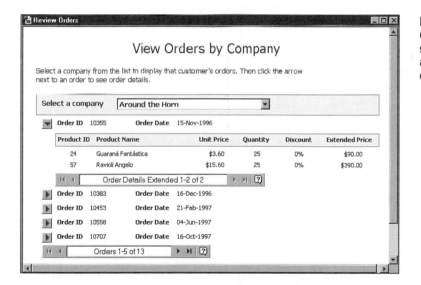

Figure 18.7
Groups of orders for a selected company with an order expanded to display its line items.

Clicking the Design View toolbar button opens the Page Designer. If the toolbox isn't visible, choose View, Toolbox; to display the floating Alignment and Sizing toolbar, choose Format, Alignment and sizing. Figure 18.8 shows the Review Orders page in Design mode with the Select A Company dropdown list selected, plus the DAP toolbox, and Alignment and Sizing toolbar open.

Figure 18.8
The Review Orders page opened in the DAP Designer.

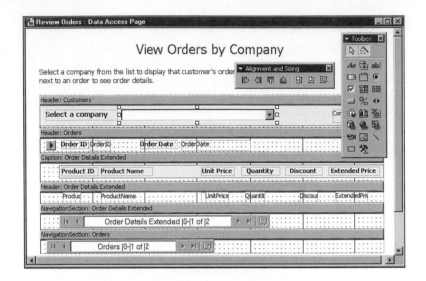

The Review Orders page is divided into the following types of sections:

- *Header* sections contain controls, such as the dropdown company selection list, Expand buttons, labels, and bound text boxes.

- *Caption* sections contain labels for columnar Header sections.

- *Navigation* sections contain a RecordNavigation control that specifies the data source for bound controls in its corresponding Header section. You nest a Header-Navigation section pair for each lower level of the display hierarchy.

Each page section is a DOM object that contains HTML control objects that you add from the toolbar.

THE HTML SOURCE EDITOR

Unlike IE, which uses Notepad to display HTML Source code, the Designer uses a new HTML Source Editor derived from that of Visual Studio 6.0. Choosing View, HTML Source opens the HTML Source Editor, if you installed it during the Office 2000 setup process, or a message box asking if you want to install it. The HTML Source Editor, which carries the Microsoft Development Environment (MDE) title, defaults to a color-coded HTML editing window with a docked Project Explorer window (see Figure 18.9). MDE also offers its own Object Browser, which is empty for this sample page.

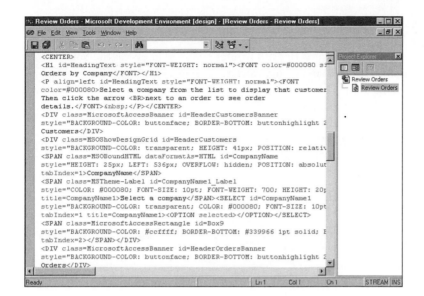

Figure 18.9
The HTML Source Editor
(Microsoft Design
Environment) displaying
part of the HTML source
code for the Review
Orders page.

THE ANALYZE SALES PIVOTTABLE PAGE

The Analyze Sales page contains only an OWC PivotTable list control within an Unbound
Header section. Microsoft adds the *list* suffix to distinguish OWC from Excel PivotTables.
The PivotTable list has its own data binding mechanism, so a RecordNavigation control
isn't needed. In this page, the PivotTable list binds to Northwind.mdb's Orders table.
Figure 18.10 shows the Analyze Sales page opened in IE 5.0. Rows and columns are collapsed by default; collapsing rows and columns displays summary information (counts,
subtotals, and grand totals) only.

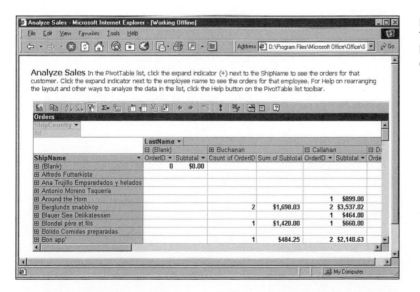

Figure 18.10
The Analyze Sales.htm
PivotTable page file
opened in IE 5.0.

PivotTable lists include the ability to filter rows and columns in the IE 5.0 window or in Access Page view. Filter lists include default (All) and (Blank) selections; the (Blank) filter displays **Null** field values only. Figure 18.11 illustrates applying filters on the ShipCountry (USA) and LastName (Buchanan) fields, and then expanding all rows and the LastName column. The LastName filter list is a double-exposure relocated to the right of the rows; you can't open both filter lists at the same time.

Figure 18.11
Applying a filter to the rows and columns of a PivotTable list.

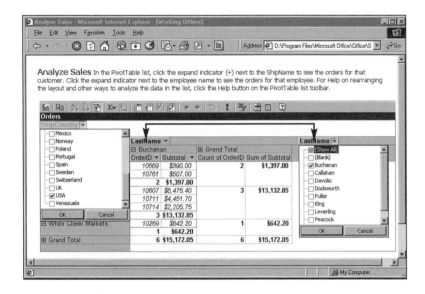

You also can alter the structure of the PivotTable list in Access's Page mode or IE 5.0 to slice and dice data, a process described in greater detail in Chapter 20, "Using Access with Microsoft Excel." As an example, dragging the ShipCountry filter button to the left of the ShipName field creates hierarchical row fields of countries and companies within the countries. Figure 18.12 shows the row field hierarchy with (Blank) and Buchanan removed from the LastName filter list. Clicking the Help button of the PivotTable toolbar opens the "About PivotTable Lists" topic, which links to topics that explain PivotTable terminology.

→ To gain a better understanding of PivotTables, **see** "Slicing and Dicing Data with PivotTables," **p. 746**.

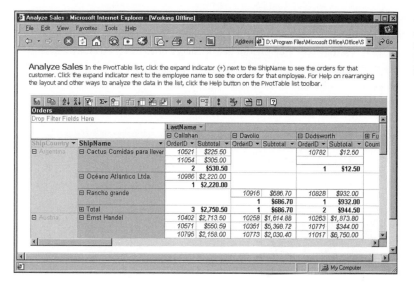

Figure 18.12
Applying a filter to the rows and columns of a PivotTable list displayed in IE 5.0.

THE SALES PAGE

The Sales page incorporates a simple PivotTable list based on the Product Sales for 1997 query, a select query that reports quarterly orders (not sales) for each of Northwind Traders' 77 products. The Sales PivotTable list is analogous to a Jet crosstab query with crossfooting (row and column totals, called Grand Totals) added. The PivotTable list provides the data source for an OWC Graph control that displays quarterly orders for the category of products selected with the CategoryName filter. Figure 18.13 shows the Sales page in Access's Page view; the PivotTable list is scrolled to show the crossfoot order totals.

PART
IV
CH
18

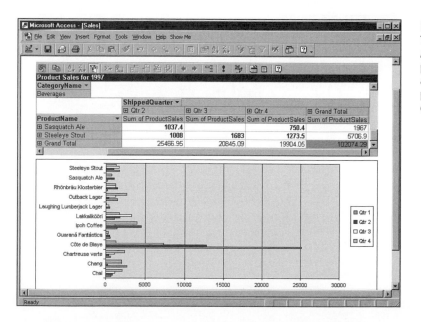

Figure 18.13
The Sales page in Access's Page view displaying 1997 quarterly and yearly orders for products in the Beverages category.

The horizontal bar graph is linked to the PivotTable list's row fields, so dragging the CategoryName filter to the left of the ProductName row field graphs quarterly sales by category (see Figure 18.14). Categories and products appear in bottom-to-top alphabetic order, the reverse of their order in the PivotTable list. Expanding the CategoryName field results in a hierarchical chart of orders for each category and all products in the expanded category (see Figure 18.15).

Figure 18.14
Graphing data from the leftmost row field of a PivotTable list.

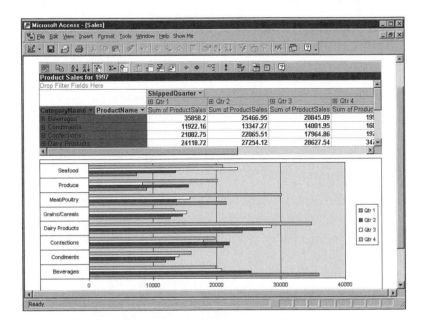

Figure 18.15
A hierarchical categories and products chart generated by expanding the Beverages row field.

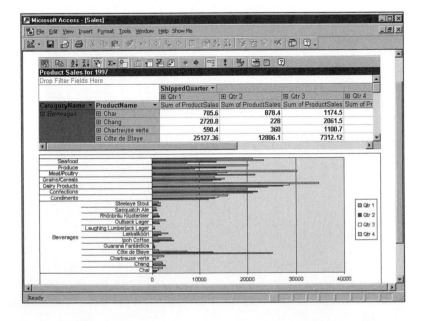

Note

If you select (All) from the CategoryName filter, the graph attempts to display four bars for all 77 products—a total of 308 bars—without increasing the depth of the chart. The result is a jumble of unreadable product names and overlapping bars. Scaling the height of the chart to match the number of chart members requires you to program a DHTML chart behavior with VBScript or Jscript. Writing DAP scripts is a developer topic that's beyond the scope of this book.

READ-WRITE PAGES

Access 2000 comes with an example of a read-write page—View Products.htm —that connects to the Products, Suppliers, and Categories tables. You select the CompanyName of the supplier and the CategoryName for the product from a pair of drop-down lists. The remainder of the fields, with the exception of Discontinued, display in bound text boxes. Enabling read-write access to tables adds four buttons to the Record Navigation control: Add (New), Delete (Record), Save (Edit), and Undo (Edit). Making a change to one of the field values of the record enables the Save and Undo buttons (see Figure 18.16).

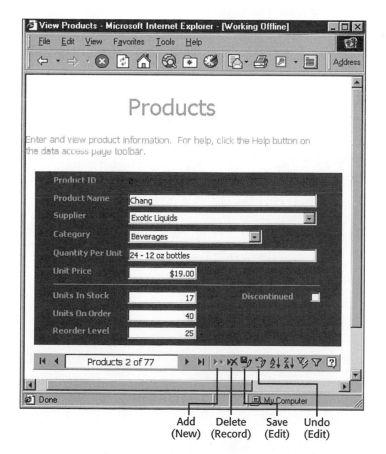

Figure 18.16
The Products page with the record editing buttons enabled.

PART
IV

CH
18

DAP aren't well suited for high-speed (called "heads-down") order entry, but are useful for non-production applications, such as maintaining telephone and mailing lists, adding new products to a database, and the like.

USING THE PAGE WIZARD TO CREATE SIMPLE DAP

The Page Wizard is the quickest route to creating DAP from multiple, related tables. The Page Wizard lets you specify individual table fields for multiple record groupings. To take full advantage of the Wizard, however, you must understand the grouping process, which the "Generating a Grouped Page" section, near the end of the chapter, explains.

To generate a page to display related records from the Categories, Products, and Suppliers tables, do the following:

1. With the Pages shortcut selected in the Database window for Northwind.mdb, double-click the "Create Data Access Page by Using Wizard" shortcut to open the first Page Wizard dialog.

2. In the Tables/Queries list, select Categories, then select CategoryName in the Available Fields list, and click > to add CategoryName to the Selected Fields list.

3. Repeat step 2, adding the ProductID, ProductName, and UnitPrice fields of the Products table, and the CompanyName field of the Suppliers table to the Selected Fields list (see Figure 18.17).

Figure 18.17
Adding fields of the Categories, Products, and Suppliers tables to the page design.

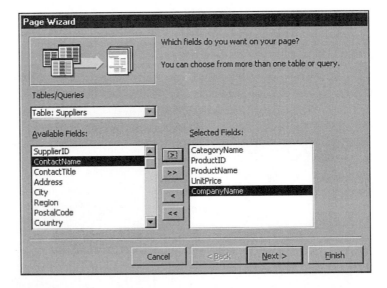

4. Click Next to open the second Wizard dialog for grouping levels (see Figure 18.18). Grouping levels in DAP are similar to those for Access reports. Grouping isn't useful for this example, however, so click Next to open the third Wizard dialog.

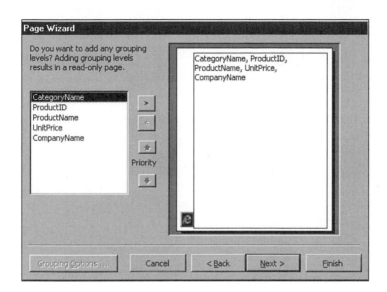

Figure 18.18
The Page Wizard's grouping dialog.

5. Open the first sort order dropdown list and select ProductName for an alphabetic sort on the names of products within the selected category (see Figure 18.19). Click Next to open the last Wizard dialog.

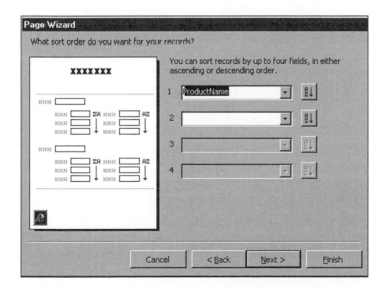

Figure 18.19
Specifying sorting on the ProductName field of the Products table.

6. Type an appropriate title, such as **Products and Suppliers by Category** in the text box, select the Modify the Page's Design option, and mark the Do You Want to Apply a Theme to Your Page check box (see Figure 18.20).

Figure 18.20
Completing the specifications for generating the page.

Caution

If you marked Microsoft Office, Office Tools, Themes as Not Available when installing Office 2000, clear the Do You Want to Apply a Theme to Your Page check box. The Wizard fails if it can't find themes on your fixed disk or load them from the CD-ROM.

7. Click Finish to initiate creation of the page. After a few seconds of disk activity, the Theme dialog appears with the default Straight Edge theme selected (see Figure 18.21).

Straight Edge is one of the more conservative Typical Themes; most of the themes in the Choose a Theme list are Additional Themes that load on first use. You can make Straight Edge the theme for successive pages by clicking Set Default and clicking Yes to close the Set Default Themes message box.

Note

Themes are a set of CSS with predefined fonts and background graphics. Marking the Vivid Colors check box changes the heading color from black to dark blue. Few graphic artists would consider dark blue to be a "vivid color."

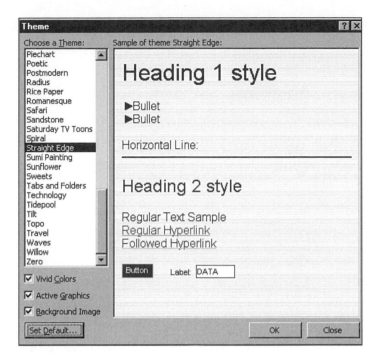

Figure 18.21
Selecting a theme for the page.

8. Click OK to close the Theme dialog and display your new page in Design view (see Figure 18.22).

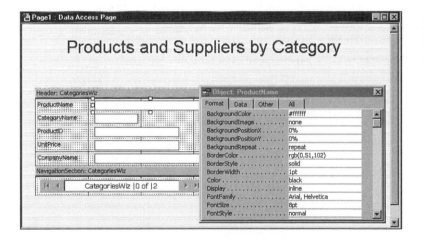

Figure 18.22
The Products and Suppliers by Category page in Design view.

9. Click the Page View button to execute the page's source code and emulate its appearance in IE 5.0 (see Figure 18.23).

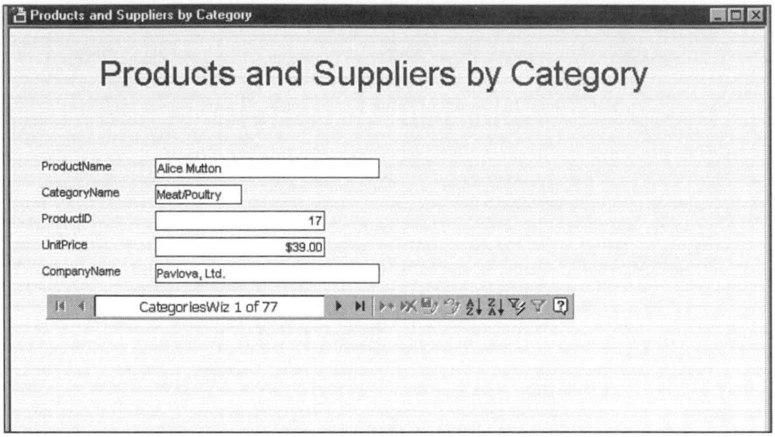

Figure 18.23
The Wizard-generated page in Page view.

10. Save the page with an appropriate name, such as **ProductsAndSuppliersByCategory.htm**, in your working or ...\Office\Samples folder.

Note

If you receive "A link to this Data Access Page could not be created because the database connot be exclusively locked" error, close any other DAP open in IE or Notepad, and then save the page.

When you save DAP, Access creates a subfolder named *PageName*_files—ProductsAndSuppliersByCategory_files for this example—that stores the theme stylesheets (.css files), graphics files (.gif or .jpg files), and a list of the files (filelist.xml) for the page (see Figure 18.24). Double-clicking filelist.xml displays its text in IE 5.0 (see Figure 18.25).

Figure 18.24
Typical contents of the *PageName*_files folder that contains the theme stylesheets, graphics, and filelist files.

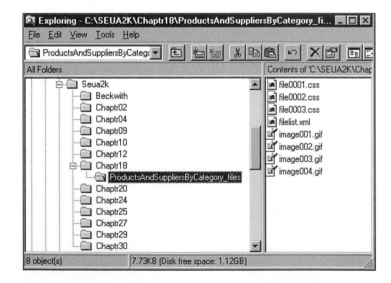

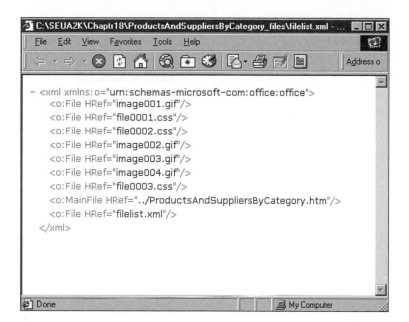

Figure 18.25
IE 5.0 displaying the
filelist.xml file for the
ProductsAndSuppliersBy
Category page.

Tip #154 from

R-J

The link from the `MainFile` to `filelist.xml` is relative. If you relocate *PageName*.htm, you must also relocate the *PageName*_files subfolder and its contents to the folder containing *PageName*.htm. Double-click .css files to open them in FrontPage 2000; .gif files usually open in Microsoft Photo Editor. Installing other Microsoft and third-party software, however, often changes file associations. See the "DAP Lose Their Style" topic in the "Troubleshooting" section near the end of the chapter for the symptoms of lost filelist.xml and .css files.

The ProductsAndSuppliersByCategory.htm page is located in the \Seua2k\Chaptr18 folder of the accompanying CD-ROM.

USING AUTOPAGE TO CREATE COLUMNAR DAP

Access 2000's AutoPage feature generates a simple DAP from tables or queries. If all you need is a simple page that displays one record at a time, AutoPage is the fastest approach. To test the AutoPage feature, do the following:

1. Click the Database window's Pages shortcut, if necessary, and click the New button to open the New Data Access Page dialog.

2. Select AutoPage: Columnar in the list and a table or query in the dropdown list. This example uses the Quarterly Orders by Product query (see Figure 18.26).

Figure 18.26
Selecting the AutoPage option and the query on which to base the page.

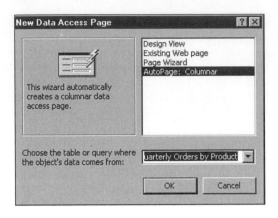

3. Click OK to generate the page. After a second or two, depending on the speed of your PC, the page opens in Page view (see Figure 18.27). If you specified a default theme when testing the Page Wizard, the default theme is applied automatically to your page.

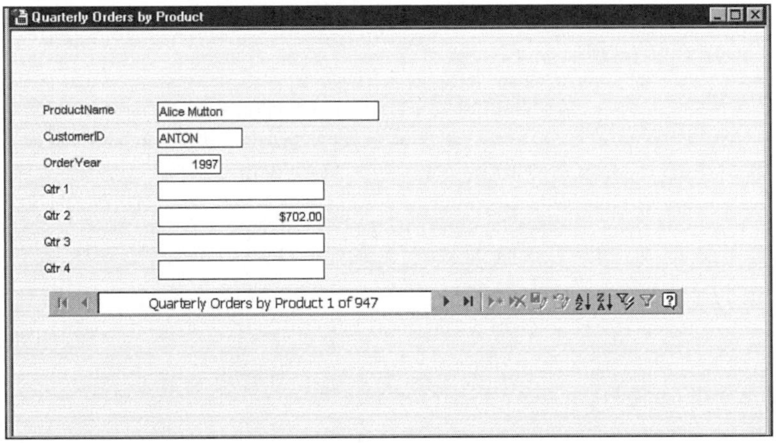

Figure 18.27
The Quarterly Orders by Product page in Page view.

Note

The Quarterly Orders by Product page is read-only because its underlying summary query is read-only. All Jet queries that return aggregate values, such as crosstabs, are read-only.

4. Choose File, Save and save the page as **QuarterlyOrdersByProduct.htm** in your working folder.

Note

Microsoft's sample DAP have filenames that include spaces. Spaces in production Web page filenames are uncommon and can cause problems with some Web servers and browsers. DAP require IE 5.0 for viewing and usually run from a Microsoft Web server, so spaces in file names aren't fatal. It's a good HTML programming practice, however, to remove spaces or other non-standard punctuation (except hyphens) from .htm file names.

Field labels in DAP display the field name of the underlying table, not the caption. For example, the caption of the CustomerID field of the originating query is Customer. Caption is an Access property that doesn't appear in the SQL statement that creates the query in DAP.

The Quarterly Orders by Product query displays the CompanyName field of the Customers table in the Customer column of Datasheet view, but not in the CustomerID field of your page. Customer is a lookup field; lookup fields don't propagate to DAP. To make your DAP more readable, add a join on the foreign key (CustomerID field of the Orders table) to the primary key of the base table (CustomerID field of the Customers table) and add the descriptive field to the query field list.

USING THE RECORD NAVIGATION CONTROL'S FILTER AND SORT FEATURES

Filtering by selection and sorting with the Record Navigation control is similar to using the filter and sort buttons of the toolbar in Datasheet view. The Quarterly Orders by Product query returns 947 rows, so filtering by CustomerID is useful to display a subset of the data by customer. You can also perform an ascending or descending sort on any field, and combine filters and sorting.

Sorting and filtering records in DAP follows a pattern similar to that for conventional Access datasheets, forms, and reports. To experiment the Record Navigation control's filter and sort features with the Quarterly Orders by Product page, do the following:

1. Click the CustomerID field's text box to select the field, and then click the Apply Filter button. When you apply a filter, the Toggle Filter button changes to the depressed state. If you selected the first record for ANTON (Antonio Moreno Taquería), the filter returns 13 records, as illustrated by Figure 18.28.

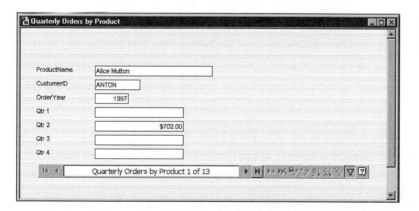

Figure 18.28
Applying a filter on the CustomerID field.

Note There's no visible feedback to indicate that a read-only field is selected in DAP.

2. Click the Toggle Filter button to remove the filter. The caption of the Record Navigation control confirms that the original 947 records are accessible.

3. Click one of the Qtr field text boxes, and then click the Sort Descending button to display the largest dollar value of an order in that quarter of 1997. Click the Last and First record buttons to refresh the underlying Recordset. After you apply a sorting sequence, the sort buttons are disabled until you select another field. Figure 18.29 shows the result of a descending sort on the Qtr 1 field.

Figure 18.29
Sorting for the largest order for any product in 1997Q1.

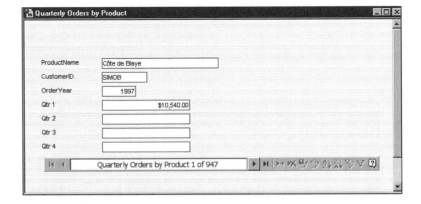

4. Click to select the ProductName field, and then click the Apply Filter button to restrict the active records to a single product, Coâte de Blaye for this example.

5. Click the Qtr 2 field text box, apply a descending sort, and click the Last and First record buttons to display the largest order for the selected product in 1997Q2.

Tip #156 from

RJ

Provide a hyperlinked help page for users of your DAP who don't have experience with Access filtering and sorting techniques. You can write your help pages with any HTML editing tool, such as FrontPage 2000, or edit AutoForm DAP to create text-only pages.

MODIFYING THE DESIGN OF AUTOPAGE DAP

The AutoPage feature seldom formats DAP satisfactorily, so you should optimize the size and location of the fields to conform to the form design standards discussed in the chapters of Section III, "Designing Forms and Reports." The process of resizing and moving controls on DAP, however, differs significantly from that of conventional Access forms and reports.

Caution

Unlike Design mode for Access objects, the DAP Designer doesn't have an undo feature, so you must be very careful when modifying or editing DAP. If you accidentally delete a control, you must re-create the control from scratch.

Following are the basic procedures for resizing, relocating, and editing controls and sections of DAP:

- *Resize an element* by clicking it once to display six sizing handles (see Figure 18.30). When you pass the mouse pointer over a sizing handle, the mouse pointer changes from a pointer or an I-beam to a four-headed arrow. Drag the arrow in the direction of the change you want to make.

- *Move an element* by clicking it once to select it, and then position the mouse pointer adjacent to the element, where the pointer turns into a four-headed arrow but is not positioned on a sizing handle. Drag the element to its new location.

Note

The DAP designer doesn't let you multi-select or group controls. You must alter the position and properties of each control individually.

- *Move a label* independently of its associated (parent) text box by clicking and dragging it. If you click and drag a text box, the (child) label follows the movement of the text box.

Tip #157 from

When moving a text box with a child label, move the parent text box to the desired location, and then move the label independently of the text box.

- *Change the caption* of a label or the default text of a text box by clicking the element twice in succession—once to select it, and then again to edit its content. In edit mode, a diagonally hatched border surrounds the element (see Figure 18.30). Double-clicking an element opens its Object: *ElementName* window.

- *Set the font attributes and alignment* of label captions and text box contents by selecting the element and clicking the appropriate button of the Format (Page) toolbar, which closely resembles the Format toolbar for Access forms and reports.

- *Change the depth or width of a section* by clicking its header to expose the section's sizing rectangles, and then drag the sizing rectangle in the appropriate direction. The minimum size of a section is that required to encompass all its elements.

- *Alter the property values of an element* by double-clicking the element to open its Object: *ElementName* window, which is the DAP equivalent of Access's Properties window (see Figure 18.30).

PART

IV

CH

18

Figure 18.30
The AutoPage: Columnar page in Page Design mode with the ProductName text box selected for editing and the Object: ProductName text box properties window open.

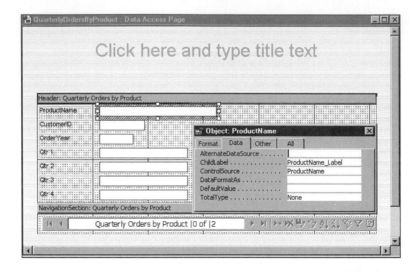

To improve the design of your columnar AutoPage, follow these steps:

1. Click the toobar's Design button to change to the DAP Designer window, if necessary. A previously hidden element appears for the title of your page. The dynamic elements of the page appear in two sections—Header and Navigation. Changing to Page view selects the first active HTML element, the ProductName child label (refer to Figure 18.30).

2. Click the default title and type a title for the page, such as **1997 Quarterly Orders by Product**.

3. Press the down arrow key, if necessary, to move the empty text region below the title, and type a brief description of what the viewer can do with the page.

4. Change the ProductName label caption to **Product Name:**, CustomerID to **Customer Code:**, OrderYear to **Order Year:**, and Qtr 1...Qtr 4 to **Quarter 1...Quarter 4**.

5. Select each label in sequence, setting the alignment to right and applying the bold attribute. Right-align the CustomerID text box.

6. Adjust the size of the text boxes and labels and reposition them as shown in Figure 18.31. An invisible grid helps you align the elements.

7. Select the Header section and drag the height sizing rectangle close to the bottom of the Order Year and Quarter text boxes (see Figure 18.31).

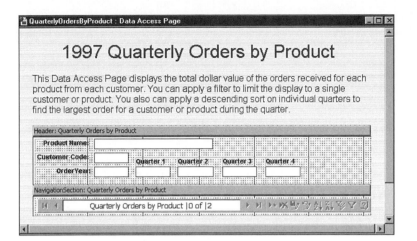

Figure 18.31
The redesigned Quarterly Orders by Product page in the DAP Designer.

 8. Change to Page view to check the result of your work (see Figure 18.32).

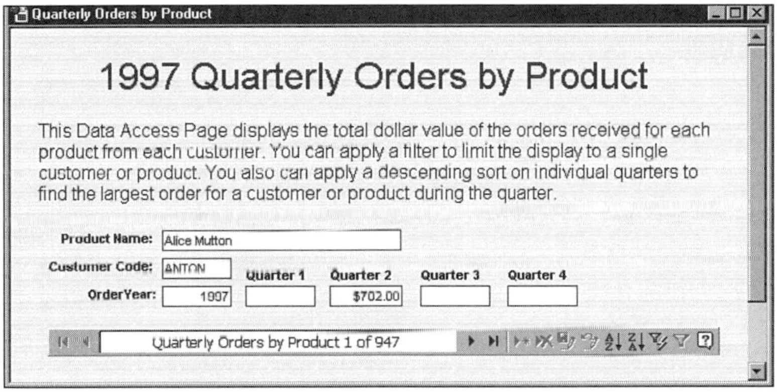

Figure 18.32
The page of Figure 18.31 in Page view.

Tip #158 from

R J

Test in Page view and save your DAP frequently during the modification process because you are working with version 1.0 of Microsoft DAP.

ALTERING RECORD NAVIGATION CONTROL PROPERTIES

The four record editing buttons of the Record Navigation control are disabled because the underlying ADO `Recordset` is read-only. You can delete these superfluous buttons by changing the properties of the Record Navigation control. Each control on the form has its own set of property values that you can alter in the Object: *ObjectName* properties window.

> **Note**
>
> The DAP Designer's properties window is almost identical to Access's Properties window for form and report objects. Most property names are longer than those for Access objects, and property values (other than text strings) are in lowercase. Most property values have dropdown lists to choose alternative values. You can open the help topic for a property by selecting the property value and pressing F1.

To remove the New (Record), Delete (Record), Save (Edits), and Undo (Edits) buttons of the Record Navigation control, do the following:

1. In DAP design mode, double-click the Record Navigation control to open the Orders: QuarterlyOrdersByProduct Navigation properties window.

2. Click the Other tab and scroll to expose the property names beginning with Show....

3. Double-click the text box for the ShowDelButton property to change the value from True to False.

4. Repeat step 3 for the ShowNewButton, ShowSaveButton, and ShowUndoButton properties (see Figure 18.33).

Figure 18.33
Property settings to remove the four record editing buttons.

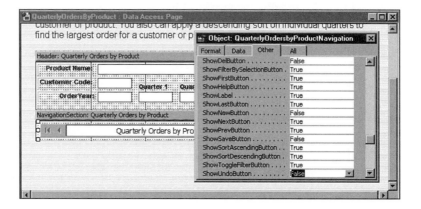

5. Change to Page view to display the modified Record Navigation control (see Figure 18.34).

The QuarterlyOrdersByProduct.htm page is located in the \Seua2k\Chaptr18 folder of the accompanying CD-ROM.

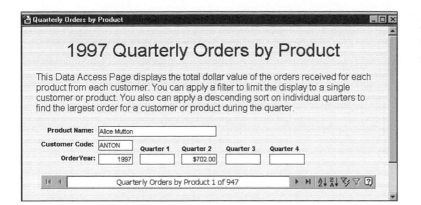

Figure 18.34
The Quarterly Orders by Product page with record editing buttons removed.

STARTING A DAP FROM SCRATCH

The Page Wizard and AutoPage have a limited repertoire of page design features, so creating DAP from scratch or from an existing Web page is an alternative when you want custom page features. For instance, you can create hyperlinked help DAP for your applications by opening a DAP, deleting the Header section, and typing the heading and body text of your help page in the default <H1> and <P> elements provided.

Opening new DAP by double-clicking the Create a Data Access Page in Design View item opens the DAP Designer with a page having the default <TITLE> and <H1> text elements and a single unbound Section. You use the Page Field List to bind the page to a data source through a Record Navigation control and add bound PivotTable or text box controls to the page.

ADDING A PIVOTTABLE WITH THE PAGE FIELD LIST

The Page Field list lets you select a table or query from the current database to serve as the data source for bound text boxes or a PivotTable Office Web Control (OWC) to display data.

1. Double-click the Create a Data Access Page in Design View shortcut of the Database window's Pages list to open a new page.

 2. Click the Page toolbar's Field List button to open the Page Field List for Northwind.mdb.

   The Database page of the Field List window displays tables and queries of Northwind.mdb that can act as data sources for DAP. After you bind a section or control to a data source, the data source appears when you click the Page tab.

3. Expand the Tables or Queries node and drag a table or query item from the Field List to the page's Section: Unbound area. This example uses the Suppliers table. When dragging the source to the page, the mouse pointer turns into a field bar and the destination section of the page gains a blue border (see Figure 18.35).

PART
IV

CH

18

Figure 18.35
Dragging a data source (Suppliers table) from the Page Field List to the Section: Unbound region of a new page.

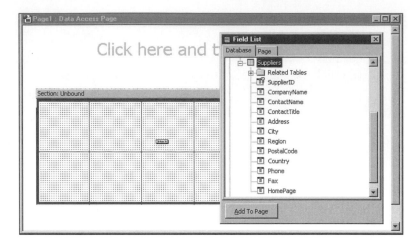

4. Release the mouse to open the so-called "Layout Wizard" dialog, which lets you choose between a column of text boxes for individual fields or a PivotTable to display the field values.

   If you want to create a page for editing and updating a table or an updatable query, choose the Individual Control Option to add a column of text boxes and a Record Navigation control. The PivotTable List option adds a read-only OWC PivotTable control to the form. Using the PivotTable control requires all users of your page to have the Office Web Controls installed.

> **Note**
>
> The Layout Wizard doesn't meet the generally accepted definition of a wizard; it's simply a dialog with two option buttons.

5. Select the PivotTable List option to add a PivotTable control to the Section: Unbound region (see Figure 18.36). Click OK to get rid of the "Wizard."

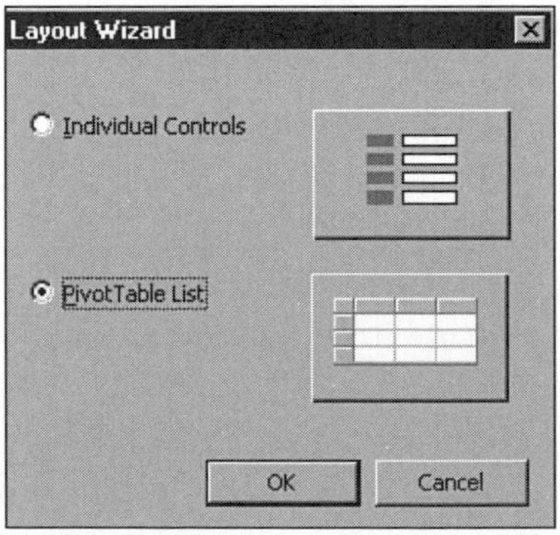

Figure 18.36
The "Layout Wizard" that lets you select between a column of bound text boxes or a PivotTable to display the field values.

6. Add a title and heading to the page.

7. Click to activate the PivotTable list, right-click the list, and choose Property Toolbox to open the PivotTable list's expandable toolbox. Expand the toolbox's Show/Hide section and click the Toolbar icon to add the PivotTable list toolbar (see Figure 18.37).

8. Adjust the width and depth of the PivotTable control to suit your page size, and then adjust the depth of Section: Unbound to the size of the PivotTable (see Figure 18.37).

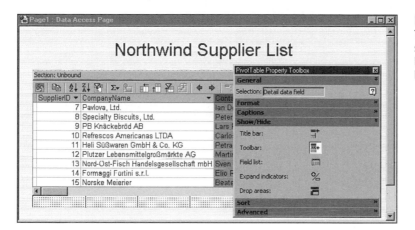

Figure 18.37
The Suppliers PivotTable selected in the DAP Designer with the Property Toolbox open.

9. Click the toolbar's Save button to open the Save As Data Access Page dialog, and save the page in your working or Samples folder as **SuppliersList.htm**.

 The SuppliersList.htm page is located in the \Seua2k\Chaptr18 folder of the accompanying CD-ROM.

WORKING WITH THE PIVOTTABLE LIST CONTROL IN IE 5.0

The PivotTable list OWC control is better suited to analyzing numeric than it is to analyzing text information, but you can test a few PivotTable features with the Suppliers List page by following these steps:

1. Launch IE 5.0, if necessary, and open SuppliersList.htm.

 2. Click the CompanyName column header to enable sorting and filtering, and then click the Sort Ascending button to sort the PivotTable in alphabetic order by company name.

 3. Click the PivotTable toolbar's AutoCalc button and choose Count from the context menu to count the number of suppliers (see Figure 18.38).

Figure 18.38
IE 5.0 displaying the SuppliersList.htm page with a row count.

4. Select the CompanyName column and click the PivotTable's Promote button to move the column to the left of the SupplierID column. The Promote and Demote buttons let you rearrange the column sequence.

ALTERING PIVOT CONTROL PROPERTIES IN IE 5.0

The PivotTable Property Toolbox lets you modify in IE 5.0 and Access Page view many properties of the PivotTable. The PivotTable control saves (persists) the changes you make to its appearance.

To alter a few of the PivotTable control's properties, do the following:

1. Select the SupplierID column and click the PivotTable toolbar's Property Toolbox button to open the PivotTable Property Toolbox window, and then expand the Captions section of the Property Toolbox.

   If you want to show the drop areas for pivoting operations, click the Drop Areas button in the Show/Hide section of the Property Toolbox.

2. Type **ID** in the Caption text box to change the CompanyID caption to ID (see Figure 18.39). You can make the other column captions more readable by selecting the column and changing the caption text with the Property Toolbox.

3. Click the PivotTable toolbar's Field List button to open the PivotTable Field List window (see Figure 18.39).

4. Select the Country field, select Filter Area from the Add To list of the Field List, and click Add To to add the filter.

5. Close the Field List and Property Toolbox, and select a country in the filter list. Figure 18.40 shows the result of selecting Germany.

Figure 18.39
The SuppliersList.htm page in Access's Page view with the PivotTable Field List and Property Toolbox windows open.

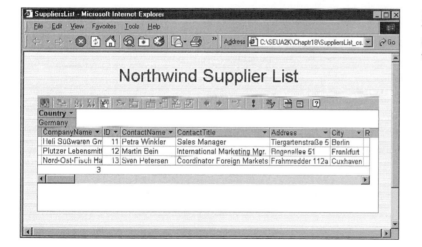

Figure 18.40
The result of applying Germany as the value of the Country filter.

6. Close IE 5.0 and return to Access.

ADDING CHARTS TO DAP WITH A PIVOTTABLE LIST

Combining an expandable PivotTable lists and an OWC Chart provides a combination of detail and summary information in a single page. The Chart Wizard makes it easy to base a chart on totals fields of a PivotTable list.

DESIGNING THE QUERY FOR THE PIVOTTABLE LIST

The PivotTable list of this example displays summary and detail information for 1997 orders organized by employee name in columns and countries in rows. The detail information consists of OrderID, ShippedDate, and Order Amount.

Tip #159 from 	Use detail, not summary select queries or crosstab queries as the foundation of PivotTable lists that serve as Chart data sources. Charts whose data source is a PivotTable list base their data presentation on totals fields (Sum Of *ValueColumnName* subtotals). If you don't include totals fields, your Chart object won't display your data.

To create the orders by employee and country query, do the following:

1. Open a new query in design view and add the Employees table, Orders table, and the Orders Subtotals query to the query.

2. Drag the LastName field of the Employees table to first query column. Change the name of the column to Name by prefixing **Name:** and a space to the column name.

3. Drag the ShipCountry, ShippedDate, and OrderID fields of the Orders table to query colums two, three, and four. Prefix the column names with **Country:** , **Date:** , and **ID:** , respectively, with spaces after the colon.

4. Drag the Subtotal column of the Order Subtotals query to the fifth query column, and prefix **Amount:** and a space to the column name.

5. Add a **Between #1/1/1997# And #12/31/1997#** criterion to the ShippedDate column. Your query design appears as shown in Figure 18.41.

Figure 18.41
The query design for the PivotTable list.

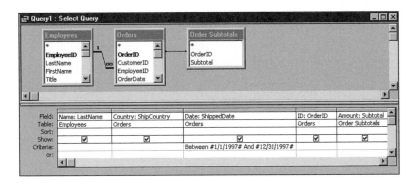

6. Run your query to verify proper execution (see Figure 18.42), save it as **qryEmplOrdersByCountry**, and close it.

SQL Don't be concerned about the query's failure to display all but the Amount column alias. You can verify the proper aliases by changing to SQL View and examining the AS *Alias* modifiers for each field.

Query1 : Select Query

	Last Name	Ship Country	Shipped Date	Order ID	Amount
▶	Callahan	Ireland	16-Jan-1997	10380	$1,313.82
	Fuller	Austria	01-Jan-1997	10392	$1,440.00
	Davolio	USA	03-Jan-1997	10393	$2,556.95
	Davolio	USA	03-Jan-1997	10394	$442.00
	Suyama	Venezuela	03-Jan-1997	10395	$2,122.92
	Davolio	Germany	06-Jan-1997	10396	$1,903.80
	Buchanan	Portugal	02-Jan-1997	10397	$716.72
	Fuller	USA	09-Jan-1997	10398	$2,505.60
	Callahan	Denmark	08-Jan-1997	10399	$1,765.60
	Davolio	UK	16-Jan-1997	10400	$3,063.00
	Davolio	USA	10-Jan-1997	10401	$3,868.60
	Callahan	Austria	10-Jan-1997	10402	$2,713.50
	Peacock	Austria	09-Jan-1997	10403	$855.01
	Fuller	Italy	08-Jan-1997	10404	$1,591.25

Record: 1 of 398

Figure 18.42
The query of Figure 18.41 in Datasheet view.

Note

Only shipped orders appear in the detail cells because ShippedDate is the selection criterion; thus an alternative name for the query would be qryEmplSalesByCountry. The Northwind.mdb sample application doesn't include a table of invoices, nor does it have a means for processing backorders. If you want to include in the detail cells orders not shipped in 1997, substitute the OrderDate field for the ShippedDate field.

PART IV

CH 18

ADDING AND FORMATTING THE PIVOTTABLE LIST

The preceding examples of adding PivotTable lists to DAP haven't delved into the details of formatting lists to expand summary data and show underlying detail information. In this section, you learn how to use the PivotTable's Properties Toolbox to modify the PivotTable presentation.

To add the PivotTable list:

1. Create a new page in Design view.
2. Add a title to the page, such as **1997 Employee Orders by Country** or **1997 Employee Sales by Country**.
3. Click the Field List button, and drag qryEmplOrdersByCountry to Section: Unbound.
4. Select the PivotTable List option in the Layout Wizard dialog and click OK.
5. Close the Field List, click to select Section: Unbound, click to select the PivotTable list, increase the list width to about 75% of your display width, and increase the depth of the list to show at least 9 rows.
6. Right-click an empty area of the list, choose Properties Toolbox, expand the Show/Hide toolbox section, and click Toolbar to add the PivotTable toolbar (see Figure 18.43).

Figure 18.43
The initial design of the PivotTable list.

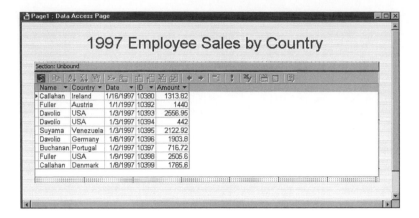

7. Select the Name column, and click the Move To Column Area list toolbar button of the PivotTable to position employee names in columns and establish a column hierarchy and Name filter.

8. Select the Country column, and click the Move To Row Area toolbar button to establish the row hierarchy and Country filter.

9. Select the first Amount column and click the AutoCalc button to create the required total cells for the graph. If a list opens, choose Sum.

10. With the Amount column selected, open the Properties Toolbox, expand the Format section, and select Currency from the Number Format list. Your PivotTable list appears as shown in Figure 18.44.

Figure 18.44
The almost-final design of the PivotTable list.

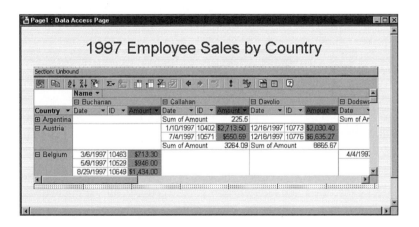

11. You can't format the subtotal (Sum of Amount) or Grand Totals cells with the detail cells expanded, so select the Name filter then click the depressed Expand toggle button to collapse the detail information.

12. Click one of the Sum of Amount header cells and click the Properties Toolbox button. Expand the Format section, if necessary, and select currency in the Number Format list. All but the Grand Totals values now have Currency format applied (see Figure 18.45).

You can't apply numeric formatting to Grand Totals values, because the formatting of the subtotals determines Grand Totals formatting in Page view. You can, however, apply the Bold attribute in the Format section of the Properties Toolbox to emphasize Grand Totals cells.

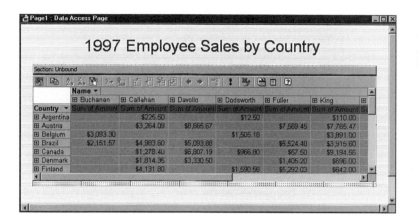

Figure 18.45
Currency formatting applied to the PivotTable list's totals cells.

13. Save your page as **EmplOrdersByCountry.htm** in your working or …\Office\Samples folder.

USING THE CHART WIZARD TO BIND AN OFFICE CHART TO THE PIVOTTABLE LIST

The final step in the process is to add an Office Chart control to the page and bind the chart to the PivotTable list. To generate the Chart, do the following:

1. Increase the height of Section: Unbound to about 600 pixels.

Tip #160 from	Setting the Height property of the SectionUnbound object is easier than dragging the bottom of Section: Unbound in the Page Designer. Select the section, then click the Properties button to open the Object: SectionUnbound properties sheet. In the Format list, scroll to the Height property and type the new value in pixels. All DAP dimensions are in display pixels, not Access's inches or centimeters or VBA's twips (twentieth of a point or 1/120 inch).

2. Click the Toolbox button of the Page Design toolbar and click to select the Office Chart control.

3. Draw a graph that occupies the remaining space of Section: Unbound. When you release the mouse, the first dialog of the Chart Wizard appears.

4. Select Bar in the Chart Type list and accept the default multibar Chart Subtype (see Figure 18.46), and click Next.

Figure 18.46
Selecting the type and subtype of chart in the Chart Wizard's first dialog.

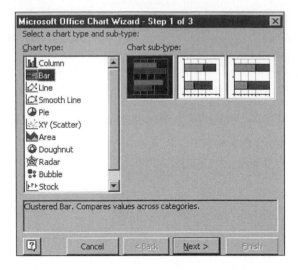

5. Select Microsoft Office PivotTable in the Available Data Sources list (see Figure 18.47), and click Next.

Figure 18.47
Specifying the page's PivotTable list as the data source for the chart.

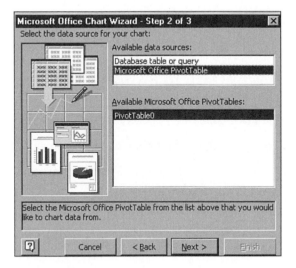

6. The series data for the legend is employee names, so select the Series in Columns option (see Figure 18.48), and click Finish to add the chart.

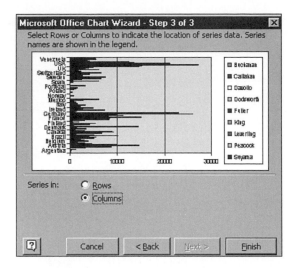

Figure 18.48
Selecting the source of
the legend entries in the
final Chart Wizard dialog.

7. Re-adjust the dimensions of the chart, if necessary, to provide sufficient depth to display the eight color-coded employee bars for each country. Figure 18.49 shows the top two-thirds the chart.

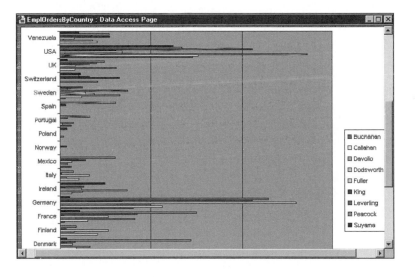

Figure 18.49
Most of the added chart
with no Name or Country
filter applied.

8. Close and save your page in Access, and then open it in IE 5.0.

9. Open the Name filter, clear the (All) item, and select one or two employees for which to graph orders. Expand the Columns to display detail data behind the totals fields. The number of employees you choose determines the thickness and spacing of the bars (see Figure 18.50).

Figure 18.50
IE 5.0 displaying the EmplOrdersByCountry. htm page with a two-employee filter.

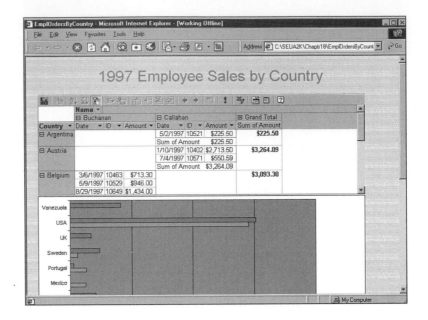

 The EmplOrdersByCountry.htm page is located in the \Seua2k\Chaptr18 folder of the accompanying CD-ROM. If you didn't create the qryEmplOrdersByCountry query, copy it from the DAPQuery.mdb file to your working copy of Northwind.mdb. Double-click the Edit Page That Already Exists shortcut to create a link to the copy of EmpOrdersByCountry.htm page on your fixed disk drive.

The preceding steps apply to most types of charts you bind to PivotTable lists. You also can bind with the Chart Wizard an OWC Chart control directly to a summary query. Chapter 19, "Adding Charts and Graphics to Forms and Reports," covers embedding the Microsoft Graph control in conventional forms and reports. Binding an Office Chart directly to a query uses a process that's quite similar to that for Microsoft Graph.

 If you encounter a problem connecting to the data source for your page when you deploy DAP on a production server, see the "DAP Clients Can't Find the Jet Data Source" topic of the "Troubleshooting" section near the end of the chapter.

→ To learn about binding charts and graphs to queries, **see** "Creating Graphs and Charts with Microsoft Graph 2000," **p. 710**.

GENERATING A GROUPED PAGE

Grouped pages display records of related tables in a set of hierarchical page sections, each of which has its own Record Navigation control. The section hierarchy is based on the relationships between the sections' tables as displayed in the Field List. You use the Field List to add individual text boxes or a PivotTable control to display field values from the base and related tables.

CREATING A THREE-LEVEL HIERARCHICAL GROUPED PAGE STRUCTURE

The first step in designing a grouped page is to create the group structure. Follow these steps to establish a three-level grouped hierarchy from the Customers, Orders, and Order Details table:

1. Open a new page in Design view, open the Field List, and expand the Customers table node.

2. Drag the CustomerID field to the Section: Unbound region. The Section: Unbound caption changes to Header: Customers, and a NavigationSection: Customers appears at the bottom of the page.

3. Adjust the size of the CustomerID text box to accommodate the five-character CustomerID value. Apply the Bold attribute to the label.

4. With the CustomerID text box selected, click the Promote button of the toolbar to add an Expand control to the section and create an additional Header: Customer section. Header: Customers changes to Header: Customers-CustomerID, and the Name label and CompanyName text box moves to the new section.

5. Expand the Field List's Related Tables and Orders nodes, and drag the OrderID field to the Header: Customers section. Select the Individual Controls option in the Layout Wizard dialog and click OK to add an OrderID text box. The section name changes to Header: Orders.

PART
IV
CH
18

> **Note**
>
> Make sure to select tables at the second and lower levels of the hierarchy from the Field List's Related Tables node to preserve in your page the relationships between the tables.

6. Select the OrderID text box and click the Promote button. Header: Orders changes to Header: Orders-OrderID, and a new Header: Orders section is added to the page.

7. Return to the DAP Designer, scroll in the Field List to the Order Details table node, and expand the Order Details and Related Tables nodes.

8. Drag the ProductID field to the Orders-OrderID section. The section name changes to Header: Order Details.

9. Drag the UnitPrice, Quantity, and Discount fields to the Header: Order Details section.

10. Adjust the size and location of the newly added labels and text boxes, then apply bold formatting to the labels (see Figure 18.51).

11. Change to Page view to check your work so far. Click the Expand control of the Customers section to display the first five OrderID values for ALKFI, and expand one or two of the OrderIDs (see Figure 18.52).

Figure 18.51
The three-level
Customers-Orders-Order
Details grouped page
hierarchy

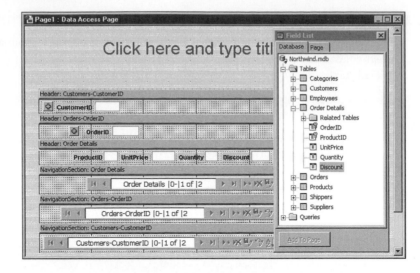

Figure 18.52
The initial design of
Figure 18.51 in Page view.

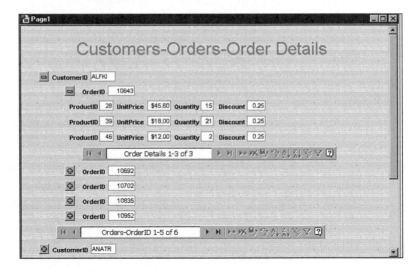

Tip #161 from

Always test your design in Page view before saving your work. When working with DAP, save early and often, but make sure you don't save a version that generates a runtime error. If you save a page with a runtime error, you probably won't be able to fix the error when returning to the DAP Designer, and you must re-create the design from scratch.

12. Add a title and optional descriptive text, and save your page with a short file name, such as **CustsOrdsDtls.htm**.

FILLING IN THE DETAILS

To make the grouped page more readable and informative by adding more fields to the existing headers, do the following:

1. Return to the Page Designer, open the Field List, and expand the Customers table node, if necessary.

B

2. Drag the CompanyName and Country fields to the Customers-CustomerID section; replace the GroupOfFieldName label caption with **Name** and **Country**, respectively. Adjust the size of the labels and text boxes, and apply the Bold attribute to the labels.

3. Move to the Orders node, and expand it, if necessary. Drag the OrderDate and ShippedDate fields to the Orders-OrderID section, and repeat the adjustments of step 2 (see Figure 18.53).

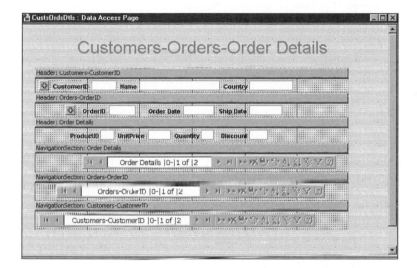

Figure 18.53
Additional grouped fields added to the first two levels of the hierarchy.

4. Test your page in Page view, and save the page.

5. Open the page in IE 5.0 to test your work (see Figure 18.54).

ADDING FIELDS OF RELATED TABLES AND CAPTIONS

Most folks have problems associating names with numeric codes, so adding the ProductName field of the Products table to the Header: Order Details-OrderID section makes your page more useful. The Order Details data is more readable when you add a Caption section. To add the ProductName field and a Caption section to your page, do the following:

1. Return to Access and, if necessary, open the CustOrdsDtls page in the Designer.

2. Open the Field list, expand the Products table node, drag the ProductName field to the Header: Order Details-OrderID section, change the label caption to Product Name, and apply the Bold attribute.

Figure 18.54
The CustOrdsDtls.htm
form opened in IE 5.0.

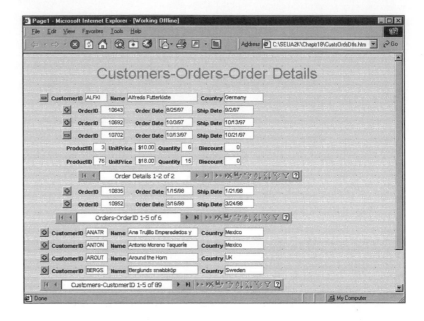

 3. Click the Sorting and Grouping button of the toolbar to open the Sorting and Grouping window.

4. Select Order Details in the Group Record Source list, and change the value of the Caption Section property from No to Yes (see Figure 18.55) to add a Caption: Order Details section to the page.

Figure 18.55
Adding a caption section
to the Order Details-
OrderID section in the
Sorting and Grouping
window.

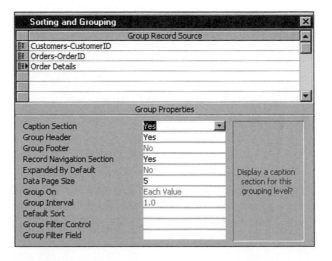

5. Drag the Order Details labels from the Header: Order Details section to the Caption: Order Details section. Adjust the position and size of the labels and text boxes as illustrated by Figure 18.56.

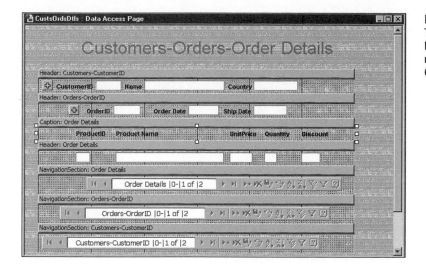

Figure 18.56
The Caption: Order Details section with labels moved from the Header: Order Details section.

6. Improve the appearance of the OrderDate and ShippedDate text boxes by selecting the text books and clicking the Align Right button.

7. Save and check your work in IE 5.0 (see Figure 18.57).

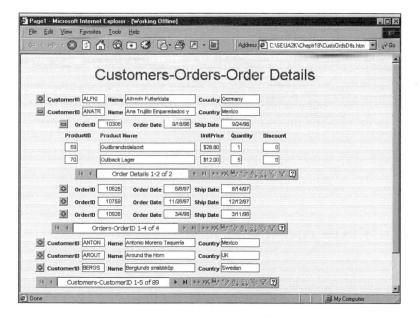

Figure 18.57
IE 5.0 displaying the final CustOrdsDtls.htm form.

Note

You can't display an OLE Object field in DAP. If you add the Categories or Employees table to a page with individual text box controls, the Picture or Photo text box displays characters representing the first few hexadecimal values of the data in the OLE Object field. To display a picture in DAP, add a field with the well-formed path to a .gif or .jpg file and display the image in an Image control. The Page Image control is quite similar functionally to the native Access Image control.

TROUBLESHOOTING

DAP LOSE THEIR STYLE

DAP open with the default font (Times New Roman), default colors (black and white), and no background images.

You moved the page's *PageName*.htm file to another folder, but didn't move the associated *PageName*_files folder to the folder containing the .css files, which define the page's styles. When DHTML pages can't find their .css files, you don't receive an error message. Always move the *PageName*.htm file and the associated *PageName*_files folder as a pair.

DAP CLIENTS CAN'T FIND THE JET DATA SOURCE

An "Unable to initialize the data provider" or "FilePathName is not a valid path" message appears when attempting to run DAP deployed on the network.

The connection string for the Jet data source of your page(s) is incorrect. The connection string includes the well-formed (complete) path to the associated .mdb file. When the client executes the DAP from the file or Web server, the location of the shared .mdb file specified by the XML `<a:ConnectionString>` element is incorrect. You must use Uniform Naming Convention (UNC) paths to specify the path, as in *ServerName**ShareName**FileName*.mdb. The fastest method to correct this problem is to open the offending DAP .htm files in IE 5.0, and choose View, Source to open Notepad. Search for <a:Connect, and substitute *ServerName**ShareName*\ for the C:*FolderName*\ path in the connection string.

IN THE REAL WORLD—ARE DAP READY FOR PRIME TIME?

Data Access Pages are a representation of fledgling technology that's dependent on immature standards. Nonetheless, DAP and related forms-based XML data access architectures have an excellent chance for short-term success in intranet environments and longer-term adoption as an Internet standard or pseudo-standard. The reputed Chinese curse, "May you lead an *interesting* life," is apt; the architecture of DAP and Microsoft's implementation of the DAP Designer qualify as *interesting* technology. The major end-user and developer issues with DAP, other than the vicissitudes of version 1.0 of the DAP Designer, are:

1. DAP are suited only for intranets because they involve Microsoft proprietary technology.

2. DAP require end users (consumers) to have Office 2000 client licenses, regardless of whether the client PCs run members of the Office 2000 suite.

Internet Economics 101

Internet-related software has caught the market by storm and undoubtedly garners the highest unit sales of any software category. The basic business problem with Internet-related software is that consumer expectations are based on the browser model—freely distributable with no license fees. Linux notwithstanding, it's nearly impossible to write a viable business plan that's based on giving away your product(s). It's even less probable that distributing the source code for your software is a yellow brick road to software riches, regardless of the market share you gain. 100% of the freebie market nets zero product revenue.

Conventional economic supply-demand theory doesn't apply to software that's distributed via the Internet. Once you post a freely-downloadable copy of your software on a Web server, the supply is effectively infinite and your marginal cost of another copy is zero, or at least extremely close to nothing. One of the related tenets of economics is the theory of *elasticity of demand*—there's little or no demand for products priced extremely high, but there is an extremely large demand for very low-priced (or free) products. (Conventional economic theory doesn't accommodate free products; economists assume that anything of value has a finite marginal production cost.)

PART

IV

CH

18

Sweet Spot(s) on the Software Elasticity Curve

The end-points of the elasticity curve are fixed; connecting the dots between the end-points is the challenge faced by marketing executives and others seeking to maximize revenue. Some firms use the dartboard approach to spotting the dots; Microsoft doesn't. Microsoft is expert at maximizing revenue; revenue equals the number of licenses sold times the price of the license. The marginal cost of software licenses is close to zero—CD-ROMs (and audio CDs) cost less than 35 cents each when manufactured in large volume. High-volume corporate licenses allow multiple software installations from a single CD-ROM.

Unlike Internet users, managers of corporate intranets don't have an expectation of free software; corporate information technology types are accustomed to shelling out millions of dollars per year for server and client licenses. Many of these folks are suspicious of free software; they believe that, like advice, free software is worth what you pay for it. Reluctance to run the free Apache Web server under the free Linux operating system creates the market for Windows NT Server and Internet Information Server, as well as competing operating systems and Web servers. Sites that use Windows NT Server also are likely to buy Microsoft SQL Server licenses. The combined price of the Windows NT and SQL Server licenses is substantially lower than that of Oracle 8+ running under Sun's Solaris flavor of UNIX. The Web server sweet spot is department- or division-level intranets, plus the large number of Web sites that have low to moderate traffic.

Intranets are the major current and potential source of Internet-related client software licensing revenue. Microsoft maximizes client-side revenue by leveraging its free IE browser to increase productivity software (Office 2000) and Web site authoring (FrontPage 2000) software and development (Visual Studio 6.0) revenue. The sweet spot on the client side is mid-sized to large firms that pay $200 to $400 per client PC for upgrades. Adding intranet-related features to Office 2000 accelerates the upgrade process and, potentially, might increase the total number of Office licenses by 10% or 20%. With an installed base of tens of millions license for Microsoft Office, that's close to a billion dollars of incremental license revenue.

The upshot of this "In the Real World" section is that, in the real world, maximization of revenue determines software licensing policies and pricing. It's not realistic to expect Microsoft, at least in the short term, to freely distribute Office Web Components in order to make DAP into a runtime product, despite the precedent of runtime Access. In the long term, OWCs might become distributable with applications created by future versions of Visual Studio, just as Visual Basic 6.0's ActiveX controls are distributable when you purchase a Microsoft Office 2000 Developer license. As economist John Maynard Keynes observed, however, "In the long term, we are all dead."

--rj

INTEGRATING ACCESS WITH OTHER OFFICE 2000 APPLICATIONS

19   Adding Charts and Graphics to Forms and Reports   709

20   Using Access with Microsoft Excel   745

21   Using Access with Microsoft Word and Mail Merge   781

CHAPTER 19

ADDING CHARTS AND GRAPHICS TO FORMS AND REPORTS

In this chapter

Enlivening Forms and Reports with Graphics   710

Creating Graphs and Charts with Microsoft Graph 2000   710

Modifying the Design Features of Your Graph   717

Creating a Graph from a Crosstab Query   723

Linking the Graph to a Single Record of a Table or Query   725

Using the Chart Web Control in Pages   728

Adding an Office Chart Based on the Single-Column Series   730

Altering the Properties of the Office Chart   733

Adding a Bound Object Control to a Form or Report   734

Using the Image Control   741

Troubleshooting   743

ENLIVENING FORMS AND REPORTS WITH GRAPHICS

One of the most important features of a decision-support database front end is the ability to display graphs and charts based on queries. Visualization of information extracted from databases, as well as from larger data marts and warehouses, is critical. Time-series graphs give management instant insight into trends of bookings (orders), sales (shipments), costs, gross margins, and profits. You also can create graphs to show more complex relationships, such as the effect of increasing or decreasing advertising expenditures on sales to differing age groups in various regions. Because of the importance of graphs to organizations of all sizes, this chapter begins by showing you how to get the most out of the graphing and charting features of Access 2000.

> **Note**
>
> Microsoft uses the terms *graph* and *chart* interchangeably. This book defines a graph (short for graphic formula) as a diagram that shows the direct relationship between one variable (such as time) and one or more other variables (orders, sales, and so on). Charts add other visual features, such as areas (pie, bar, and stacked bar, for instance) to present relationships between variables.

Access 2000 also lets you add static images and audio/video content to forms, pages, and reports. You can choose between storing multimedia content in OLE Object fields of Access tables or linking to the content's source files. The Internet has opened a new multimedia distribution mechanism for images, sound, and streaming video. Access 2000's Bound Object Frame and Image controls now support Internet-standard image file formats—.gif and .jpg—along with traditional .bmp, .ico, .tif, .wmf, and .emf files. The second part of this chapter shows you how to incorporate static images in Access objects.

CREATING GRAPHS AND CHARTS WITH MICROSOFT GRAPH 2000

Microsoft Graph 2000 (called in this book by its file name, Graph9) is a 32-bit OLE mini-server application (Graph9.exe) that's identical to version 8 supplied with Access 97. An OLE miniserver is an application that you can only run from within an OLE container application, such as Access. All Office 2000 members use Graph9, which originated as the charting component of Microsoft Excel. The sections that follow describe how to use Access's Chart Wizard to add graphs and charts to Access 2000 forms and reports. The "Using the Chart Web Control in Pages" section, later in the chapter, explains how you add charts and graphs to Data Access Pages (DAP).

CREATING THE QUERY ON WHICH TO BASE THE GRAPH

Most graphs required by management are the time-series type, as noted at the beginning of this chapter. Time-series graphs track the history of financial performance data, such as orders received, product sales, gross margin, and the like. In smaller firms, this data comes from tables that store entries from the original documents (such as sales orders and invoices) that underlie the summary information.

This type of detail data often is called a *line-item source*. Because a multibillion-dollar firm can accumulate several million line-item records in a single year, larger firms usually store summaries of the line-item source data in tables; this technique improves the performance of queries. Summary data is referred to as *rolled-up* data or, simply, *rollups*. Rollups of data on mainframe computers often are stored in client/server relational database management systems (RDBMSs) running under UNIX or Windows NT to create *data warehouses* or *data marts*. Although rolling up data from relational tables violates two of the guiding principles of relational theory—don't duplicate data in tables and don't store derived data in tables—databases of rolled-up data are very common. As you move into the client/server realm with Access Data Projects (ADP) and SQL Server, you're likely to encounter many rollup tables derived from production databases.

Note

The full version of Microsoft SQL Server 7.0 includes Microsoft OLAP Services, code-named "Plato" during its development. *OLAP* is an acronym for online analytical processing, which manipulates multidimensional data extracted from production databases.

Northwind Traders is a relatively small firm that receives very few orders, so it isn't necessary to roll up line-item data to obtain acceptable query performance on a reasonably fast (Pentium or better) computer. To create a time-series summary query designed specifically for the Chart Wizard, follow these steps:

1. In the Database window, open a new query and add the Categories, Products, Order Details, and Orders table to the query. Joins are created for you between the primary-key and foreign-key fields of each table.

2. Drag the CategoryName field of the Categories table to the first column.

3. Drag the UnitPrice field of the Order Details table to the second column. Edit the Field row of the column to read as follows:

   `Amount: CCur([Order Details].[UnitPrice]*[Order Details].[Quantity]*(1 -[Order Details].[Discount]))`

   The **CCur** function is required to change the field data type to **Currency** when applying a discount calculation.

Tip #162 from

RJ

With the caret in the Field row of the second column, press Shift+F2 to open the Zoom window to make entering the preceding expression easier.

4. Drag the ShippedDate field of the Orders table to the third column. Add an ascending sort on this column.

PART

V

CH

19

5. Add the criterion **Between #1/1/1997# And #12/31/1997#** to the ShippedDate column so as to include only 1997 orders. This example uses the year 1997 instead of 1998 because data is available for all 12 months of 1997.

6. Save your query with the name **qryChartWizard** (see Figure 19.1).

→ To help make your database Y2K compliant, **see** "Four-Digit Year Option Settings," **p. 36**.

Figure 19.1
A query design for creating a graph with Access 2000's Chart Wizard.

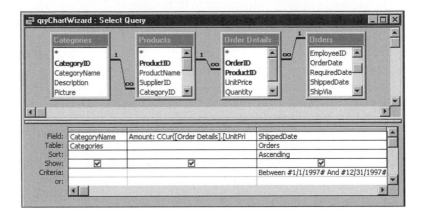

6. Click the Run button to test your query (see Figure 19.2), then close it.

Figure 19.2
The query result set of the query in Figure 19.1.

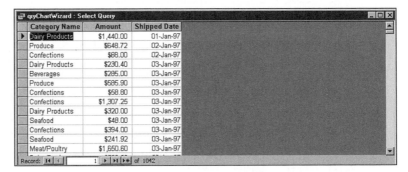

USING THE CHART WIZARD TO CREATE AN UNLINKED GRAPH

Although it's possible to create a graph or chart by using the Insert Object method and selecting the Microsoft Graph 2000 object type, the Chart Wizard makes this process much simpler. You can use the Chart Wizard to create two different classes of graphs and charts:

■ *Unlinked* (also called *nonlinked*) line graphs display a line for each row of the query. You can also create unlinked stacked column charts and multiple-area charts.

■ A *linked* graph or chart is bound to the current record of the form on which it is located and displays only a single set of values from one row of your table or query at a time.

This section shows you how to create an unlinked line graph based on a query. The next section describes how to use Graph9 to display alternative presentations of your data in the form of bar and area charts. In the last section of this chapter, you create a graph that is linked to a specific record of a query result set.

To create an unlinked graph that displays the data from the qryChartWizard query, follow these steps:

1. Click the Database window's Forms shortcut, click New, select Chart Wizard in the list box, and select qryChartWizard in the drop-down list (see Figure 19.3). Click OK to launch the Chart Wizard.

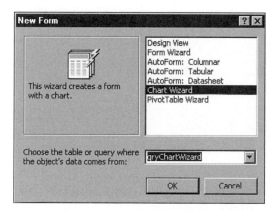

Figure 19.3
Selecting the Chart Wizard and the query on which to base the graph.

→ For tips on how to determine the fields to use for a crosstab query, **see** "Creating Crosstab Queries," **p. 396**.

2. Click the >> button to add all three fields to your graph (see Figure 19.4). Click the Next button to display the Chart Wizard's second dialog.

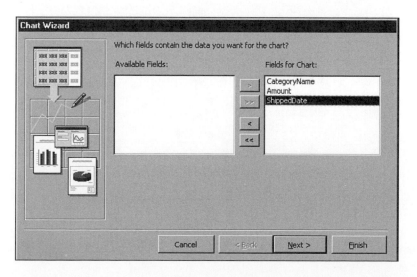

Figure 19.4
Selecting the fields to include in the graph.

PART

V

CH

19

3. Click the Line Chart button (the third from the left in the third row of the buttons that display the available graph styles), as shown in Figure 19.5. Click the Next button to display the third Chart Wizard dialog.

Figure 19.5
Selecting the type of graph or chart.

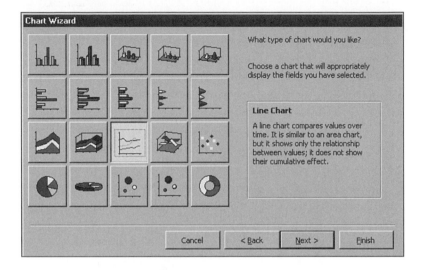

4. The Chart Wizard attempts to design a crosstab query based on the data types of the query result set. In this case, the Chart Wizard makes a mistake by assuming you want months in the legend box and product categories along the graph's horizontal x-axis (see Figure 19.6).

Figure 19.6
The Chart Wizard's first try at guessing the type of crosstab query to create.

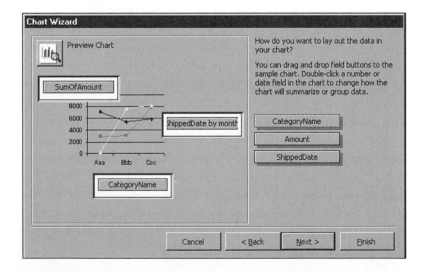

5. You want the categories in the legend and the months of 1997 across the x-axis. Drag the CategoryName button from the right side of the dialog to the drop box under the

legend, and drag the ShippedDate button to the drop box under the x-axis. The button title, partly obscured, is ShippedDate by month (see Figure 19.7).

You can double-click the ShippedDate by month button and select from a variety of GROUP BY date criteria, ranging from Year to Minute, and specify an optional range of dates. Click the Next button to go to the fourth and final Chart Wizard Dialog.

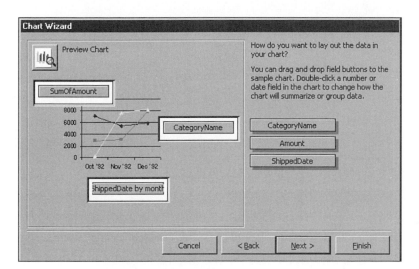

Figure 19.7
Correcting the Chart Wizard's crosstab query guesswork.

Tip #163 from

Click the Chart Preview button to display an expanded—but not full-size—view of your graph. The size relationship between objects in Chart Preview isn't representative of that of your final graph or chart.

6. Type **1997 Monthly Sales by Category** in the text box to add a title to your graph. Click the Yes, Display a Legend option, if necessary, to display the Category legend (see Figure 19.8). Accept the remainder of the defaults.

7. Click the Finish button to display your graph in Form view, along with the Properties window for the OLEUnbound0 object frame.

Tip #164 from **NEW 2000**

Access 2000 lets you set object properties in either Form or Design view.

In the miniature version illustrated by Figure 19.9, some month labels are missing and the legend crowds the graph and label. You fix these problems in the next section of this chapter, "Modifying the Design Features of Your Graph."

  8. Click the Design View button of the toolbar and increase the size of your graph to at least 5.5 inches wide by 2.5 inches high (see Figure 19.10).

PART
V
CH
19

Figure 19.8
Adding a title and legend to your graph.

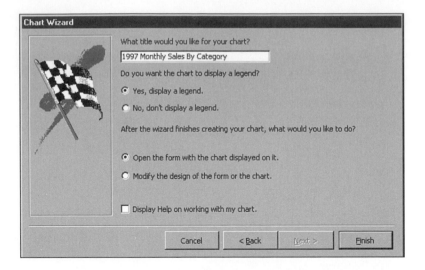

Figure 19.9
The unbound graph in Form view as completed by the Chart Wizard.

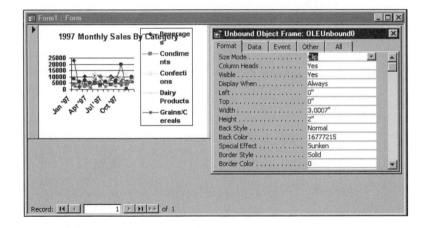

Tip #165 from

Prior MSGraph versions displayed a standard sample graph in Design mode; Graph9 displays the graph based on your design.

9. Make sure that the Enabled property value of the unbound object frame is set to Yes and the Locked Property is set to No (the defaults).

10. The chart is in an unbound object frame, so you don't need form adornments for record manipulation. Select the form and set the Scroll Bars property of the form to Neither, the Record Selectors to No, and the Navigation Buttons to No.

11. Use the sizing handles of the unbound object frame to create a 1/8-inch form border around the frame. Leaving a small form area around the object makes the activation process more evident.

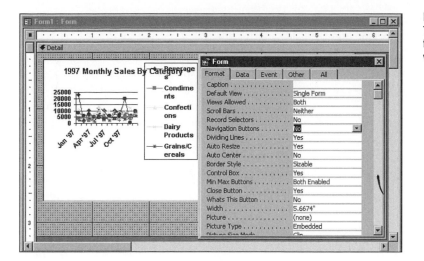

Figure 19.10
The expanded object frame in Form Design view.

12. Save your form with a descriptive name, such as `frmChartWizard`. Return to Form view in preparation for changing the size and type of your graph.

Tip #166 from

When you complete your design, set the value of the Enabled property to No so that users of your application can't activate the graph and alter its design.

MODIFYING THE DESIGN FEATURES OF YOUR GRAPH

PART

V

CH

19

Graph9 is an OLE miniserver, so you can activate Graph9 in place and modify the design of your graph. Graph9 also supports Automation, letting you use VBA code to automate design changes. This section shows you how to use Graph9 to edit the design of the graph manually, as well as how to change the line graph to an area or column chart.

To activate your graph and change its design with Graph9, follow these steps:

1. Display the form in Form view and then double-click the graph to activate Graph9 in place. A diagonally hashed border surrounds the graph; Graph9's menus replace or supplement those of Access 2000. (The activation border is missing from the left and top of the object frame if you didn't create some space on the form around the object frame in step 11 of the preceding section.)

Tip #167 from

Menu commands of an OLE server or miniserver added to those of the container application are called *grafted menus*. The process that adds the menu commands is called *menu negotiation*.

---

2. Drag the middle-right sizing handle to the right border of your enlarged unbound object frame. Drag the middle-bottom sizing handle to the bottom border of the object frame.

3. Choose <u>V</u>iew, <u>D</u>atasheet, if necessary, to inspect the data series that Access has transmitted to Graph9 (see Figure 19.11).

4. You can change the type family and font size of your chart's labels and legend. Double-click the graph title to open the Format Chart Title dialog. Click the Font tab, set the size of the chart title to 12 points (see Figure 19.12), clear the AutoScale check box, and then click OK to close the dialog. Double-click the legend to open the Format Legend dialog, set the size of the legend font to 7 points, and clear the AutoScale check box.

Figure 19.11
The expanded version of the chart displaying part of the datasheet for the graph.

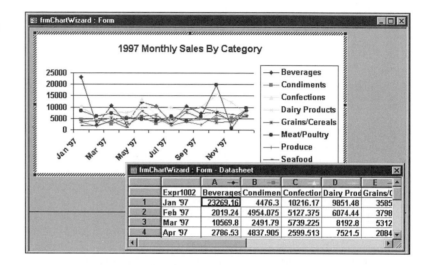

Figure 19.12
Changing the font size of the graph's title.

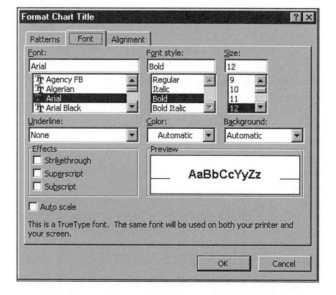

5. The y-axis labels should be formatted as currency, so double-click one of its labels to display the Format Axis dialog, set the font size to 9 points, and clear the AutoScale check box.

6. Click the Number tab, select Currency in the Category list, and enter **0** in the Decimal Places text box (see Figure 19.13). Click OK to close the y-axis Format Axis dialog.

7. The default font size for axis labels at a graph size of 6.5 by 2.5 inches is 9.75 points, which causes Graph9 to label the x-axis diagonally. Double-click the x-axis and change its font size to 9 points, also clearing the AutoScale check box.

8. Click OK to close the dialog and apply the new format. Click the form region outside the graph to deactivate Graph9, then save your changes. Your line graph appears as shown in Figure 19.14.

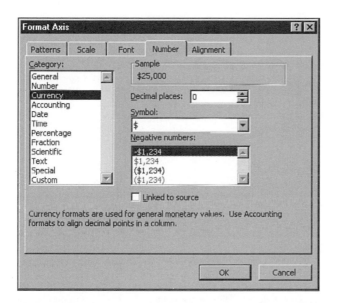

Figure 19.13
Formatting the numeric values of the y-axis.

PART
V

CH
19

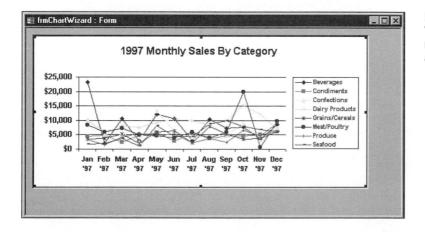

Figure 19.14
The line graph with reformatted y-axis labels and a larger graph title.

You might want to change the line graph to some other type of chart (such as area or stacked column) for a specific purpose. Area charts, for example, are especially effective as a way to display the contribution of individual product categories to total sales. To change the line graph to another type of chart, follow these steps:

1. Double-click the graph to activate it and then choose Chart, Chart Type to open the Chart Type dialog with the Standard type page active.

2. Select Area in the Chart Type list (see Figure 19.15).

Figure 19.15
Changing the line graph to a stacked area chart.

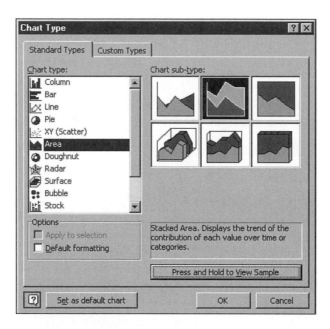

> **Tip #168 from**
> *RJ*
>
> You can preview your chart by clicking and holding down the left mouse button on the Press and Hold to View Sample button.

3. Select the stacked area chart as the Chart Sub-type list (the middle chart in the first row—see Figure 19.15). Click OK to change your line graph into an area chart, as shown in Figure 19.16. The contribution of each category appears as an individually colored area, and the top line segment represents total sales.

> **Tip #169 from**
> *RJ*
>
> To get help with the Chart Type dialog, click the Office Assistant button at the lower left of the dialog.

4. To convert the area chart into a stacked column chart, choose Chart, Chart Type; display the Standard Types page of the Chart Type dialog; select Column in the Chart

Type list; and then select the stacked column chart (the middle button in the first row) as the Chart Sub-type (see Figure 19.17).

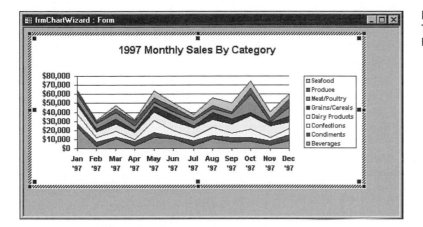

Figure 19.16
The stacked area chart in Form view.

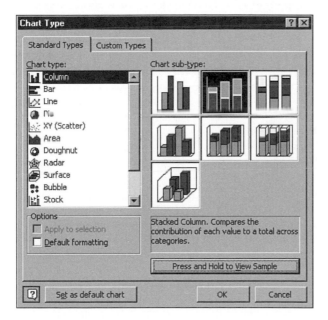

Figure 19.17
Selecting a stacked column chart type.

PART

V

CH

19

5. Click OK to close the Chart Type dialog. Your stacked column chart appears as shown in Figure 19.18.

6. Another subtype of the area chart and stacked column chart is the *percentage distribution* chart. To create the distribution-of-sales graph shown in Figure 19.19, repeat steps 4 and 5 but select the 100% Stacked Column picture (the third thumbnail in the top row) with equal column heights as the Chart Sub-type. Click OK to close the Chart Type dialog.

Figure 19.18
The stacked column chart in Form view.

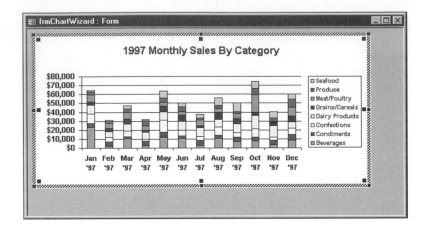

7. Because you previously set the format of the y-axis to eliminate the decimals, you need to change the format of the y-axis manually to Percentage. Double-click the y-axis, select Percentage in the Format Axis dialog's Category list on the Number page, make sure that Decimal Places is set to **0**, and then click OK to apply the format. Your chart appears as shown in Figure 19.19.

Figure 19.19
The percentage distribution column chart.

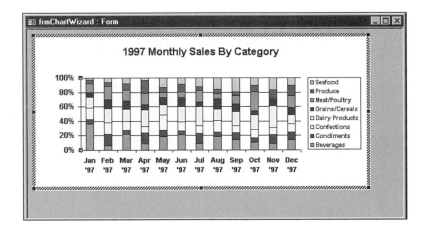

8. Change the Chart Type back to a line graph in preparation for the linked graph example of the next section, "Creating a Graph from a Crosstab Query." Change the y-axis format to Currency, click inside the form region outside the object frame to deactivate the graph, and then save your form. Of the four types of charts demonstrated, most users find the area chart best for displaying time-series data for multiple values that have meaningful total values.

> **Note**
>
> The process of adding an unbound graph to an Access report is identical to that for forms. Unless you have a color printer, you should select a line graph subtype that identifies data points with a different symbol for each category. For area and stacked column charts, select a series of hatched patterns to differentiate the product categories.

> **Tip #170 from**
>
> *RJ*
>
> The Custom Types page of the Chart Types dialog offers a selection of B&W...chart types specifically designed for monochrome printers.

CREATING A GRAPH FROM A CROSSTAB QUERY

NEW 2000 Access 2000's Chart Wizard is quite parochial: It insists on creating a crosstab query for you. After you've created a chart with the Chart Wizard, however, you can change the graph's Row Source property value to specify a previously created crosstab query of your own design. You also need to design your own crosstab query for use in the next section and for adding graphs to DAPs with the Chart Web Component.

> **Note**
>
> You must create the qry1997SalesMonthlyByCategory query and use the query as the Row Source of the unbound object frame to complete the linked graph example in the following section. The linked graph example doesn't work with the crosstab query created by the Chart Wizard in the preceding steps. The Chart Wizard's crosstab query result set has months in rows and categories in columns.

To create the qry1997SalesMonthlyByCategory query from qryChartWizard, follow these steps:

1. Create a new query in Design view, add the qryChartWizard query, and choose Query, Crossta<u>b</u> Query.

2. Drag the CategoryName field to the first column of the query and select RowHeading in the Crosstab row.

3. Alias the CategoryName field by typing **Categories:** at the beginning of the Field text box.

4. Drag the ShippedDate field to the second column of the query grid and select ColumnHeading in the Crosstab row.

5. Change the statement in the Fields row of the ShippedDate column to **Expr1:Format([ShippedDate], "mmm")** to use three-letter month abbreviations.

6. Drag the Amount field to the third column, set the Total cell to Sum, and set the Crosstab cell to Value (see Figure 19.20).

7. Double-click an empty region of the upper query pane to open the Query Properties sheet. In the Column Headings text box, type the 12 month abbreviations, **Jan, …Dec**, separated by commas to arrange the columns in date, not alphabetic, sequence. Access adds the quotes around the month abbreviations for you (see Figure 19.21).

Figure 19.20
The design of a query that displays monthly sales by product category.

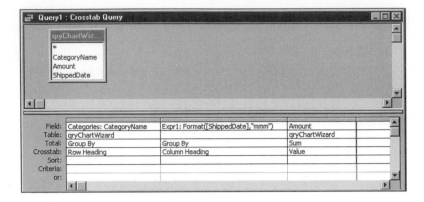

Figure 19.21
Specifying fixed column headers for 12 months.

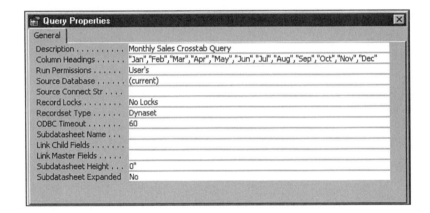

9. Save your query as **qry1997SalesMonthlyByCategory**.

10. Click the Run button of the toolbar to check your query result set (see Figure 19.22).

Figure 19.22
Part of the result set of the qry1997SalesMonthly ByCategory query.

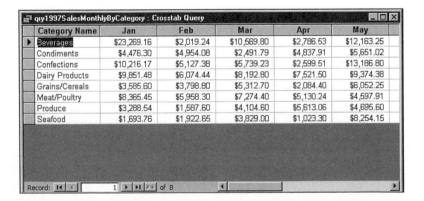

Category Name	Jan	Feb	Mar	Apr	May
Beverages	$23,269.16	$2,019.24	$10,569.80	$2,786.53	$12,163.25
Condiments	$4,476.30	$4,954.08	$2,491.79	$4,837.91	$5,651.02
Confections	$10,216.17	$5,127.38	$5,739.23	$2,599.51	$13,186.80
Dairy Products	$9,851.48	$6,074.44	$8,192.80	$7,521.50	$9,374.38
Grains/Cereals	$3,585.60	$3,798.80	$5,312.70	$2,084.40	$6,052.25
Meat/Poultry	$8,365.45	$5,958.30	$7,274.40	$5,130.24	$4,597.91
Produce	$3,288.54	$1,587.60	$4,104.60	$5,613.06	$4,695.60
Seafood	$1,693.76	$1,922.65	$3,829.00	$1,023.30	$8,254.15

11. Open frmChartWizard, if necessary, select the chart, and open its Properties window.

12. Click the Data tab, open the Row Source list box, and select qry1997SalesMonthlyByCategory as the value of the Row Source property. The graph displays category labels on the x-axis and month labels in the legend.

13. In Form view, double-click to activate the graph and choose Data, Series in Rows from Access's menu. Graph9 grafts the Data menu to Access's menubar. Verify that your line greaph is the same as the graph that the Chart Wizard created in the preceding section (refer to Figure 19.14).

 If you're having trouble getting labels into the correct location, see "Reversing the X-Axis and Legend Labels" in the "Troubleshooting" section at the end of this chapter.

LINKING THE GRAPH TO A SINGLE RECORD OF A TABLE OR QUERY

You create a linked graph or chart by setting the values of the Graph9 object's Link Child Fields and Link Master Fields properties. The link is similar to that between a form and subform. A linked graph displays the data series from the current row of the table or query that serves as the Record Source of the form. As you move the record pointer, the graph is redrawn to reflect the data values in the selected row. The qry1997SalesMonthlyByCategory query, described in the preceding section, is required for this example.

→ *To review the linking process between master and child forms or reports, **see** "Creating a Subform Using the Subform/Subreport Wizard" **p. 523**.*

To change the frmChartWizard form to accommodate a linked graph, follow these steps:

 1. Open frmChartWizard in Design or Form view, click an empty region to select the form, and then click the Properties button of the toolbar to open the Properties window for the form.

2. Click the Data tab, open the Record Source list box, and select qry1997SalesMonthlyByCategory as the value of the Record Source property of the form, which binds the form to the crosstab query.

3. Your form needs record-navigation buttons for a linked query, so click the Format tab and set the value of the Navigation Buttons property to Yes.

4. Select the unbound object frame and then click the Data tab. Verify that qry1997SalesMonthlyByCategory is the Row Source for the chart. Type **Categories** as the value of the Link Child Fields and Link Master Fields properties (see Figure 19.23). Disregard the error messages that appear after typing the Link Child Fields value.

Using this technique, you create the link between the current record of the form and the row of the query that serves as the Row Source property of the graph (through the Categories field of the query).

 5. To test your linked graph, click the Form View button of the toolbar. If (in the preceding section) you saved the line graph version of the form, your graph appears as shown in Figure 19.24.

PART

V

CH

19

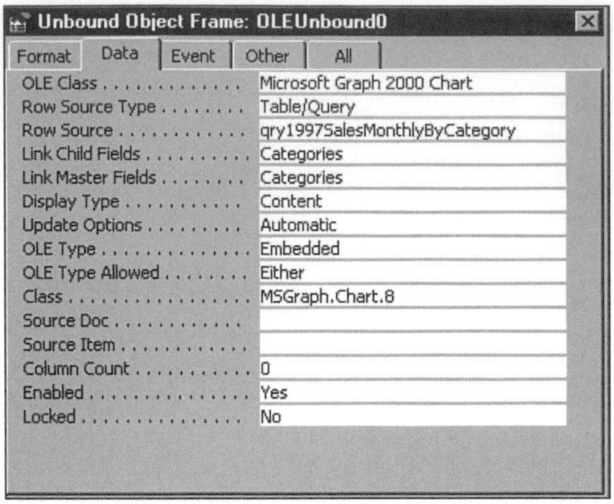

Figure 19.23
Linking the graph's Row
Source property to the
current record of the
form.

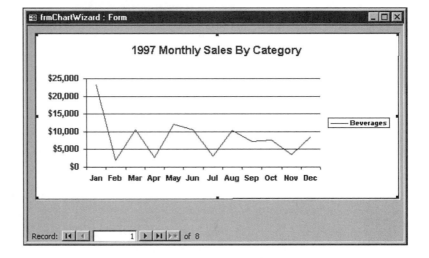

Figure 19.24
The linked version of the
1997 Monthly Sales by
Category graph.

6. The single line appears a bit anemic for a graph of this size, so double-click the graph to activate it in place. Double-click anywhere on the line to display the Format Data Series dialog. Click the Patterns tab to bring that page to the front of the dialog. Open the Weight drop-down list and choose the thickest line it offers. To change the data-point marker, open the Style drop-down list and select the square shape. Use the drop-down lists to set the Foreground and Background colors of the marker to automatic to add solid markers of the color complementary to the line (see Figure 19.25). Click OK to close the dialog and implement your design changes.

7. Double-click the legend box to open the Format Legend dialog. On the Patterns page, click the None option in the Border frame to remove the border from the legend. Click the Font tab, set the Bold attribute on, and change the font size to 11 points. Click OK to close the dialog and apply your modification to the legend.

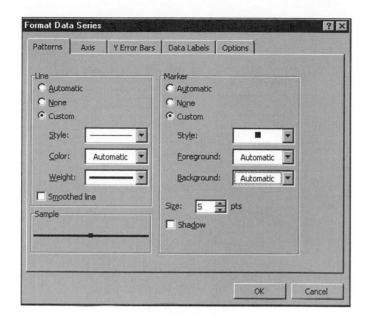

Figure 19.25
Increasing the thickness of and changing the markers for the data series line.

8. To use your enhanced legend as a subtitle for the chart, click and drag the legend to a location under the chart title, as shown in Figure 19.26. Click over the plot area to display the chart's sizing handles; drag the middle sizing handle to the right to increase the size of the plot area.

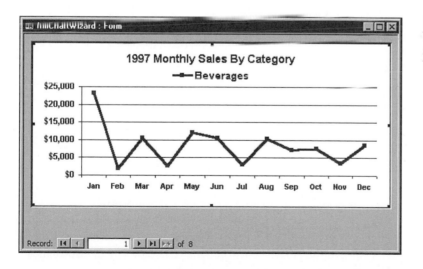

Figure 19.26
The Form view of the graph with added design features.

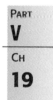

PART

V

CH

19

9. Click anywhere on the form outside of the chart to close Graph9 and return to Access. Click the record selection buttons to display a graph of the sales for each of the eight categories.

10. Graph9 offers a variety of three-dimensional chart formats. Figure 19.27 illustrates a 3D column chart. You can change the perspective of the graph by activating the chart and selecting the Corners part of the chart. Click one of the Corners' selection squares and drag the square to change the perspective.

Tip #171 from

Use the Chart Objects list (at the top left of the Graph9 toolbar) to select objects in the chart, such as the corners, walls, series, and other elements of a bar chart.

Figure 19.27
The line graph converted to a 3D column chart.

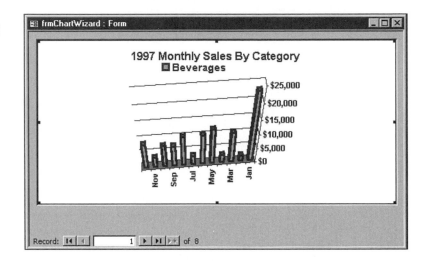

11. Change back to the line graph and deactivate the graph by clicking the form outside the bound object frame. Choose File, Save As; then save your bound form with a new name, such as `frmLinkedGraph`.

USING THE CHART WEB CONTROL IN PAGES

The Chart Office Web Control is a lightweight version of Graph9 with its own lightweight Office Chart Wizard (OCW). Charts you generate with the OCW are very similar to corresponding Graph9 charts. The Chart control is an ActiveX control, not an OLE mini-server, so you don't have the benefit of grafted menus to set chart properties. After you've created a chart with the OCW, you can alter only a few of its properties. If you want to create with Access dynamic charts and graphs for Web pages, the Chart control is your only choice; Graph9 doesn't work in the HTML environment. The only way of displaying a Graph9 object in a Web page is to use a screen capture utility to take a .gif or .jpg shapshot of the graph or chart, and then add a link to the static graphic.

The OCW doesn't accommodate conventional crosstab queries; instead, it wants two-column (for a single series) or three-column (for multiple series) aggregate query result sets. The OCW also accepts data from PivotTable and Spreadsheet controls.

DESIGNING QUERIES FOR THE CHART WEB CONTROL

The OCW accepts queries that contain series identifiers, such as the eight CategoryName values of the Categories table, in a single column or in multiple columns. The structure of the result set of an acceptable single-category-column query, based on the qryChartWizard, appears in Figure 19.28. The Category Name column provides the labels for the series; the Month column supplies the x-axis labels; and the SumOfAmount column provides the plotted values. Compared to multicolumn queries suited to the OCW, queries with single-column categories are easier to design.

Category Name	Month	SumOfAmount
Beverages	Jan	$23,269.16
Condiments	Jan	$4,476.30
Confections	Jan	$10,216.17
Dairy Products	Jan	$9,851.48
Grains/Cereals	Jan	$3,585.60
Meat/Poultry	Jan	$8,365.45
Produce	Jan	$3,288.54
Seafood	Jan	$1,693.76
Beverages	Feb	$2,019.24
Condiments	Feb	$4,954.08
Confections	Feb	$5,127.38
Dairy Products	Feb	$6,074.44
Grains/Cereals	Feb	$3,798.80
Meat/Poultry	Feb	$5,958.30
Produce	Feb	$1,587.60
Seafood	Feb	$1,922.65

Record: 1 of 96

Figure 19.28
An aggregate query result set with categories in a single column (Category Name).

To generate the query result set shown in Figure 19.28 for the OCW, do the following:

1. Open a new query in Design mode and add qryChartWizard.

2. Drag the CategoryName field to the first column, ShippedDate to the second, and Amount to the third.

3. Click the toolbar's Totals button to enable aggregation. Accept the default Group By in the first and second cell and select Sum in the third cell of the Totals row.

4. Edit the Field cell of the second column to `Month: Format([ShippedDate],"mmm")`.

5. Drag the ShippedDate field to the fourth column, edit its Field cell to `Month([ShippedDate])`, and apply an Ascending sort to the column. Sorting on the month number organizes the abbreviated month names in the proper sequence (see Figure 19.29).

6. Run the query and check its result set against that of Figure 19.28.

7. Close and save your query with the name `qryOWCChartWizard1`.

Figure 19.29
The query design to produce the aggregate query result set of Figure 19.28.

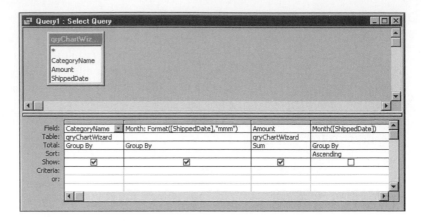

Tip #172 from

R J

Nested queries don't deliver optimal performance because two queries must execute in succession to deliver the result set to the graph. To improve performance, you can change qryChartWizard to an aggregate query that returns a result set identical to that of Figure 19.28.

ADDING AN OFFICE CHART BASED ON THE SINGLE-COLUMN SERIES

After you have a query that meets the OCW's requirements, you can add a multiline graph to a page by doing the following:

1. Open a new unbound page in Design view. (Leaving the data source text box of the New Data Access Page dialog creates an unbound page.) Add a title and brief description to the page.

 2. Choose View, Toolbox if the toolbox isn't visible, make sure the Control Wizards button is active (depressed), and click the Office Chart control.

 3. Drag the mouse in the Section: Unbound region to create a graph about 600 pixels wide and 300 pixels high. When you release the mouse, the first dialog of the Microsoft Office Chart Wizard opens.

4. Select Line in the Chart Type list; choose the default—the line chart in the upper left—for the Chart Sub-type (see Figure 19.30); and click Next to open the second Wizard dialog.

5. Select qryOWCChartWizard1 query in the Available Database Tables list (see Figure 19.31) and click Next to open the third dialog.

6. Your query has only one column for legend labels, so select the Entries for the Legend Are in One Column option (see Figure 19.32) and click Next to proceed to the fourth and final dialog.

7. Select CategoryName for the Series Names, SumOfAmount for the Values, and Month for the Category (x) Axis Labels (see Figure 19.33).

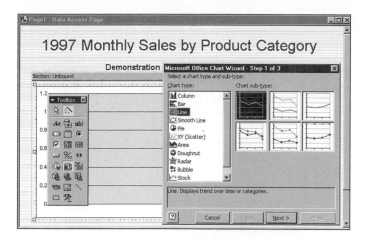

Figure 19.30
Selecting a graph or chart type in the first Office Chart Wizard dialog.

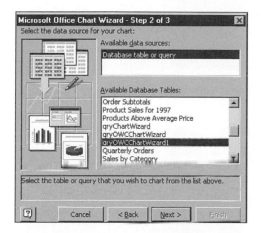

Figure 19.31
Picking the data source for the graph in the second Wizard dialog.

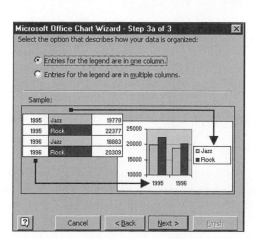

Figure 19.32
Selecting the data source format to generate the graph.

PART

V

CH

19

Figure 19.33
Specifying the query
column names for the
legend labels, plotted
values, and x-axis labels.

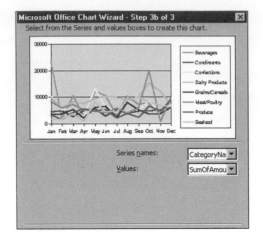

8. Click Finish to dismiss the Wizard and display your graph in the DAP Designer (see Figure 19.34). Save your page as **1997SalesMonthlyByCategory.htm**.

Figure 19.34
The 1997 Monthly Sales
by Product Category
graph in Design view.

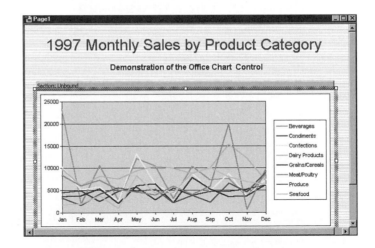

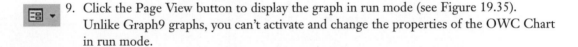

Tip #173 from

R J

As recommended in the preceding chapter on DAP basics, save your pages early and often, but make sure to check pages in Page view before saving. If a change you make doesn't work in Page view, you can close your page without saving changes and then start from the last known good page.

9. Click the Page View button to display the graph in run mode (see Figure 19.35). Unlike Graph9 graphs, you can't activate and change the properties of the OWC Chart in run mode.

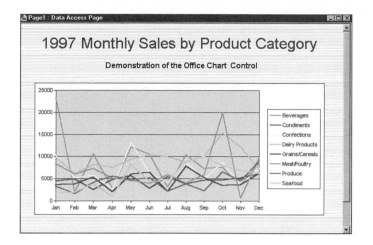

Figure 19.35
The 1997 Sales graph in Page view.

ALTERING THE PROPERTIES OF THE OFFICE CHART

NEW 2000 Office Web Controls substitute a Properties Toolbox for the conventional properties sheets or dialogs of ActiveX controls. To change the chart type and properties of chart objects, do the following:

1. In the Page Designer, click the chart to activate it. (Activation adds a hashed border around the chart.) Right-click the graph and choose Property Toolbox to open the Chart Property Toolbox.

2. Click the Chart Type button in the General section of the Chart Property Toolbox to open the first Office Chart Wizard dialog. Select Area as the Chart Type and then click to select the stacked area chart as the Chart Sub-type (see Figure 19.36). Click OK to apply the change and close the Wizard dialog.

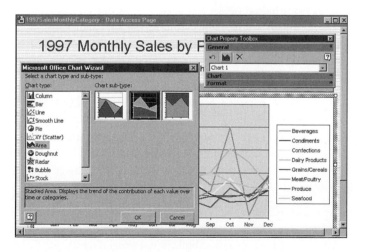

Figure 19.36
Changing the Office chart type with the Chart Property Toolbox.

PART

V

CH

19

3. Click to select the y-axis labels, expand the Font section of the Chart Properties Toolbox, and select Currency as the Number Format to apply currency formatting to the y-axis (see Figure 19.37).

Figure 19.37
Setting the y-axis labels to currency format.

You also can change font size, font attributes, border color, background color, and the like by selecting a Chart object and altering properties exposed in the Format and Font sections of the Chart Properties Toolbox.

ADDING A BOUND OBJECT CONTROL TO A FORM OR REPORT

 Like Graph9 graphs and charts, graphic images and other OLE objects stored in OLE Object fields of Access tables use a bound object frame control to display their presentation. The *bound object frame control* is an OLE container within which a bitmapped or vector-based image can be displayed. Other OLE objects that rely on data stored in OLE Object fields, such as Sound Recorder and Media Player objects, plus data-bound ActiveX controls appear in the bound object frame.

In the case of still graphic images, the presentation within the bound object frame is a copy of the object's data property. Animated images and video objects usually display the first image in the animation sequence or video clip. Sound objects substitute the icon of the OLE server with which their file type is associated in the Registry. Double-clicking the bound object frame launches the OLE server that you used to add the object to a data cell in an OLE Object field of your table.

In Chapter 13, "Designing Custom Multitable Forms," you learned how to add a bound object frame to an Access form. Here you learn the details of displaying and editing a photograph in the Personnel Actions Entry form you built in the preceding chapters. You also learn how to scale the photograph within the bound object frame so that you get exactly the look you want.

INCLUDING PHOTOS IN THE PERSONNEL ACTIONS QUERY

The majority of Access applications use the OLE Object field data type to store only graphic images. The Northwind Traders Employees table includes a photograph for each employee as one such graphic image. You use the OLE Object field data type to add the photograph to your Personnel Actions Entry form. The bound object frame is linked to the Photo field of the qryPersonnelActions query.

→ For the design of the qryPersonnelActions query, **see** "Creating the Query on Which to Base the Main Form," **p. 487**.

To run the qryPersonnelActions query so you can view one of the photographs in Windows 98 Paint, follow these steps:

1. From the Database window, open the qryPersonnelActions query.

2. Drag the horizontal scroll bar button to the right to display the Photo field in the query result set.

3. Double-click one of the Bitmap Image data cells to display the image in Windows 98 Paint. The chosen image appears in the Paint window (see Figure 19.38).

Figure 19.38
Editing the Photo field of the qryPersonnelActions query.

4. Choose E_xit & Return to qryPersonnelActions:Select Query from Paint's _File menu to close the editing window.

5. Choose Close from Access's _File menu to close the query.

If you don't see the image after double-clicking a cell in the OLE Object field, try the suggestion in "Fixing Errors When Opening OLE Objects" in the "Troubleshooting" section at the end of this chapter.

The behavior of Windows Paint is similar to that of other OLE 2+ local server applications used to add or edit the values (contents) of data cells in OLE Object fields.

DISPLAYING THE EMPLOYEE'S PICTURE IN THE PERSONNEL ACTIONS FORM

You can edit OLE objects in Access tables and queries only through the window of the OLE server you used (Paint, in this example) to add the objects to the table. The presentation of OLE objects is, however, stored in the OLE field and displayed automatically in a bound or unbound object frame. You double-click within the object frame to edit the object.

You added a bound object frame to the Personnel Actions Entry form in Chapter 13. For this exercise, you create a temporary form as a way to experiment with bound object frames. To add a bound object frame to your experimental form so that you can display the Photo field of your qryPersonnelActions query, follow these steps:

1. Click the Forms shortcut of the Database window and then click New to display the New Form dialog.

2. Select **qryPersonnelActions** as the data source for the new form, select Design View in the list, and then click OK to display the new form in Design view.

3. Click the Field List button and select Photo from the Field List window.

4. Select the Photo field and drag the Field symbol to the approximate position of the upper-left corner of the new form. Access creates a bound object frame rather than a text box when you create a control directly from a field of the OLE Object type in the Field List dialog.

5. Position and size the new bound object frame, as shown in Figure 19.39.

6. Click the Form View button to display your form with the photograph. The form appears as in Figure 19.40. Notice that the photo doesn't fill the entire frame. You may still need (or want) to scale the image, which is the subject of the next section.

Figure 19.39
Adding a bound object frame to a form.

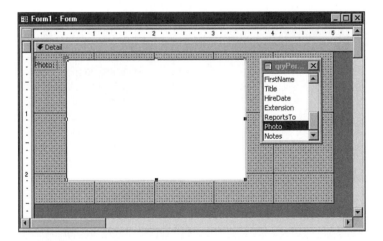

An alternative method for creating a bound object frame is to click the Bound Object Frame tool of the toolbox, click the Photo field, and drag the Field symbol to the form. The extra step here serves no purpose because Access chooses a bound object frame for you when the field you choose in the Field list is of the OLE Object data type.

Figure 19.40
Viewing the form with
the added Photo bound
object frame.

When you use either the Bound Object Frame tool, the value of the Enabled property is
set to Yes and the Locked property is set to No. The effect of these two properties is as
follows:

■ When an object frame is disabled (the Enabled property is set to No), you can't double-click the object to launch the OLE server that created the object's content. The
setting of the Locked property has no effect in this case.

■ When an object is enabled and locked (the Locked property is set to Yes), you can
launch the OLE server, but any edits you make to the content of the object are dis-
carded when you close the server application.

> **Note**
>
> In Form view with the default values of the Enabled and Locked properties—Yes and No,
> respectively—double-click the Photo object frame to launch Windows Paint, which assumes
> the role of the active application through in-place activation. Paint is an OLE 2.1 server, so
> Paint grafts its menu choices to the Access menubar, a process also called *menu negotia-
> tion*. Paint's View, Image, and Options menu choices replace several of Access's menu
> choices (see Figure 19.41). You can edit the bitmap in Paint and then save the changes to
> the OLE data in the Employees table when you close Paint. You click the form outside the
> Photo image to close (deactivate) Paint.

SCALING GRAPHIC OBJECTS

Access provides three methods for scaling graphic objects within the confines of a bound
object frame. You select one of these methods by choosing the value of the Size Mode
property in the Bound Object Frame Properties window, displayed in Figure 19.42.

Figure 19.41
Windows Paint activated in place to edit a bitmap image object.

Figure 19.42
Setting the Size Mode property of an object frame.

The three options offered for the value of the Size Mode property display the image in the following ways:

- *Clip*, the default, displays the image in its original aspect ratio. The aspect ratio is the ratio of the width to the height of an image, measured in pixels or inches. A *pixel* is the smallest element of a bitmap that your computer can display—a single dot. The aspect ratio of the standard VGA display, for example, is 640×480 pixels, which is 1.33:1. If the entire image does not fit within the frame, the bottom or right of the image is cropped. *Cropping* is a graphic arts term that means cutting off the portions of an image outside of a window of a specified size, as shown in the top picture of Figure 19.43.

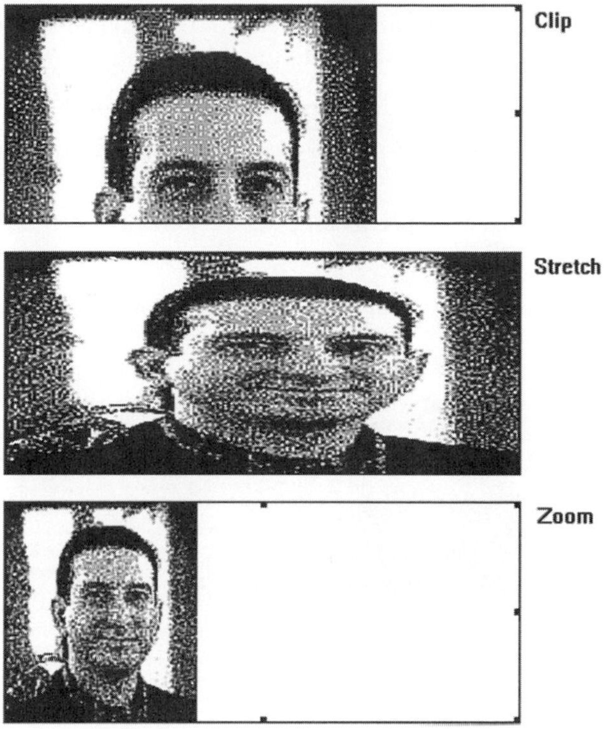

Clip

Stretch

Zoom

Figure 19.43
Comparing the Clip, Stretch, and Zoom values of the Size Mode property.

- *Stretch* independently enlarges or shrinks the horizontal and vertical dimensions of the image to fill the frame. If the aspect ratio of the frame is not identical to that of the image, the image is distorted, as illustrated by the center image of Figure 19.43.

- *Zoom* enlarges or shrinks the horizontal or vertical dimension of the image so that it fits within the frame, and the original aspect ratio is maintained. If your frame has an aspect ratio different from that of the image, a portion of the frame is empty, as shown in the bottom image of Figure 19.43.

The bound object frames in Figure 19.43 have been shortened vertically and expanded horizontally to accent the effects of the Stretch and Zoom property values.

Access can't specify a particular area of the image to be clipped, so zooming to maintain the original aspect ratio is the best choice in this case. When you scale or zoom a bitmapped image, the apparent contrast is likely to increase, as shown in the center and bottom images of Figure 19.43. This increase results from deleting a sufficient number of pixels in the image to make it fit the frame, which increases the graininess. The increase in graininess and contrast is less evident in 256-color (8 bits per pixel) or higher color depth bitmaps; the photos of employees are 16-color (4 bits per pixel) bitmaps.

PART

V

CH

19

To apply the Zoom property to your bound object frame in Design mode, follow these steps:

1. Select the Photo bound object frame and decrease its size to about 1.5 by 1.5 inches.

2. Click the Properties button on the toolbar to open the Bound Object Frame Properties window. Click the Format tab.

3. Click the Size Mode text box and open its list box.

4. Select Zoom.

5. Click the Form View button of the toolbar to display your form, which now appears as shown in Figure 19.44.

Figure 19.44
The bound object frame with Zoom as the value of the Size Mode property.

6. If your frame includes an empty area, as illustrated in Figure 19.44, return to Design mode, adjust the size of the frame, and rerun the form to verify that the frame has the correct dimensions.

7. Choose File, Close and save your changes to the form; you might save this experimental form as **frmPhotoForm**.

The technique described in this section lets you add a bound object frame containing a vector image created with a drawing application, to add a sound clip from a .wav or .mid file, or to add any other OLE object type that you can select from the Insert Object dialog.

EXAMINING BITMAP IMAGE FILE FORMATS

Graphics files are identified by generally accepted file extensions; these serve to define most (or all) of the format's basic characteristics. The following file extensions identify bitmap image files that have achieved the status of "industry standards" for the PC. Most commercial bitmap image editing applications support these formats. The "standard" extensions follow:

■ *.bmp* is for Windows bitmap files in 1-, 2-, 4-, 8-, and 24-bit color depths. .bmp files contain a bitmap information header that defines the size of the image, the number of color planes, the type of compression used (if any), and information on the palette used. A *header* is a block of data in the file that precedes the image data.

- *.dib* is for device-independent bitmap files. The .dib file format is a variant of the .bmp format; to define the RGB values of the colors used, it includes a color table in the header.

- *.pcx* is for files that are compatible with ZSoft Paintbrush applications. Windows Paint can't save files in .pcx format. (Paint refers to .pcx files as PC Paintbrush format.) .pcx files are compressed by a method called *run-length encoding* (*RLE*), which can decrease the size of bitmap files by a factor of three or more, depending on their content.

- *.tif* (an abbreviated form of TIFF) is for tagged image format files. The TIFF format was originally developed by Aldus Corporation and now is managed by Microsoft Corporation. Originally, TIFF files were used primarily for storing scanned images, but now they are used by a substantial number of applications (including those for Windows) as the preferred bitmap format.

- *.jpg* is for files created by applications that offer compression and decompression options for Joint Photographic Experts Group (JPEG) graphics. JPEG has developed a standard methodology to compress and decompress still-color images. Special JPEG adapter cards are available to speed the compression and decompression processes.

- *.gif* is for the graphics interchange file format used to archive bitmapped images on CompuServe and other online services. Shareware and freeware .gif file conversion applications for all popular types of personal computers are available for downloading from CompuServe's Graphic Support forum (GO GRAPHSUP). The .gif format has been the standard bitmap format for background images of the Internet's World Wide Web pages, partially supplanted by the use of JPEG compression.

PART

V

CH

19

Tip #174 from	If you have an OLE server application that supports the .jpg format, store individual bitmap images in .jpg and not the .bmp files used by Windows Paint. The JPEG compression offered by most current Windows image editing applications provides greater compression than .pcx or .gif for color images, especially images with more than 256 colors (16-bit or 24-bit color).
R J	If your use of images is intended primarily for printing (as in desktop publishing) and you don't have a color printer, use shades of gray for vector-based images. The 256-grayscale palette is preferred for printing bitmapped images; change color images to grayscale if your image-editing application supports this conversion.

USING THE IMAGE CONTROL

NEW 2000 Access 2000 offers the Image control—similar to the image control of Visual Basic 6.0—to display .bmp, .dib, .pcx, .gif, or .jpg bitmaps; Windows Metafile Format (.wmf); or enhanced metafile (.emf) vector images in forms and reports. The ability of the Image control to handle .pcx, .gif, and .jpg formats is new in Access 2000.

To add an Image control to your frmPhotoForm form, created in the earlier "Scaling Graphic Objects" section, follow these steps:

1. Open frmPhotoForm in Design view, click the Image control of the toolbox, and draw an image control about 0.75 by 0.75 inches. The Insert Picture dialog appears.

2. Navigate to the ...\Office\Samples folder and double-click the Nwlogo.gif file to insert the picture in the Image control. Your image control appears, as shown in Figure 19.45.

Tip #175 from	Unlike object frames, image controls, by default, center clipped images in their frame. Image frames have a Picture Alignment property that lets you choose how to align the image.
RJ	

Figure 19.45
The clipped Northwind logo in an image frame.

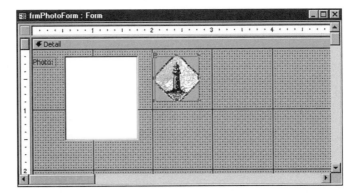

3. Image controls have default Special Effect, Border Style, and Back Color properties that are suitable for adding logos to forms. Thus you need only change the Size Mode property of the image control to Zoom. Figure 19.46 shows the result of the preceding steps in Form view.

Figure 19.46
The Northwind logo zoomed in an image frame.

You use the preceding process to add images to reports and DAP. By default, Image controls imbed the image file within the form and report; images for pages are stored in the associated *PageName*_files folder. If you use the same image in several forms, reports, and pages, change the value of the PictureType property, which is accessible only in Design mode, from Embedded to Linked.

Troubleshooting

Reversing the X-Axis and Legend Labels

After changing the Row Source property of a chart to the qry1997MonthlySalesByCategory query, the product categories appear in the chart as the x-axis labels, and the month abbreviations appear in the legend.

In the example of the "Creating a Graph from a Crosstab Query" section, you didn't change to Series in Rows in step 13. Crosstab queries you design can have the legend values (representing a series of lines) as column headers or row headers. If your x-axis and legend labels are wrong, activate the chart, choose <u>D</u>ata, and then choose either Series in <u>C</u>olumns or Series in <u>R</u>ows to make the change.

Fixing Errors When Opening OLE Objects

An "Insufficient memory" or "Application not properly registered" message appears after double-clicking a data cell in the OLE Object field.

Either of the two messages can occur under low-memory conditions. First, try closing all other running applications and then double-clicking the data cell again. "Insufficient memory" errors commonly result from insufficient free disk space on the drive used for the Windows swap or paging file. If you continue to receive registration error messages, exit and restart Windows. If this procedure doesn't solve the problem, open the Registry Editor (RegEdit); choose <u>E</u>dit, <u>F</u>ind; and search for the `Bitmap Image` value. Expand the CLSID entry for Bitmap Image and select the `LocalServer32` item. Verify that the value for `LocalServer32` is `C:\PROGRA~1\ACCESS~1\MSPAINT.EXE`—or the location of Mspaint.exe on your PC. (The `LocalServer32` entry contains the DOS name of the folder in which Paint is installed: C:\Program Files\Accessories, by default.) If you need to change the entry, double-click the "ab" icon in the right pane to open the Edit String dialog and correct the entry as necessary.

In the Real World—Visualizing Data

Database developers, who deal with tables and query result sets on a daily basis, tend to forget that consumers of their products aren't necessarily fond of tabular data. Having to scan—let alone digest—reams of tabular data, whether on paper or PC monitor, is one of the curses of the cubicle. Management executives primarily are interested in trends and exceptions. Only when trends go the wrong way or exceptions hit the bottom line are suits or pinstripes likely to be interested in detail data. (The term *suits* has come to mean middle management; *pinstripes* distinguish top executives, bankers, and eastern venture capitalists.)

Meaning, Significance, and Visualization

Data becomes information when one grasps the meaning and significance of the data. Well-designed charts and graphs based on summary queries make the data contained in millions of rows of transactional tables meaningful. The significance of information is in the eye of the beholder. If your bonus is based on sales, trends in sales determine much of your income; if you're a profit-sharing participant, it's the bottom line that counts. As noted at the beginning of the chapter, time-series graphs and charts are most common, because spotting trends and taking action based on trends is one of management's primary responsibilities. Trends inherently are historical in nature; regression analysis and other statistical methods enable projecting historical performance to the future with varying degrees of risk. In many cases, the experienced eye of a seasoned executive can better project future trends than the most sophisticated statistical algorithms.

Data visualization, the foundation of graphs based on queries, is more of an art than a science. Edward R. Tufte's self-published 1983 classic, *The Visual Display of Quantitative Information*, is still a best-seller—at least by computer book standards. Tufte's sequel, *Envisioning Information* (1990), deals primarily with cartography. The final volume of the triology, *Visual Explanations: Images and Quantities, Evidence and Narrative* (1997), covers presentation of dynamic data. Tufte describes his three books as "pictures of numbers, pictures of nouns, and pictures of verbs." Anyone designing Access graphs and charts for any purpose other than entertainment should own a copy of *The Visual Display of Quantitative Information*. Once you become acquainted with Tufte's seminal work, you're very likely to acquire his other two books.

Management by Trend Exception

Most managers and executives suffer from information overload. One of the approaches to making information delivered to management more effective is to flag situations where performance falls outside of the expected or budgeted range. Multiline graphs, which present actual versus projected performance, are especially useful for flagging poor or exceptional results at the region, department, division, or corporate level. Regression methods often are more useful in actual-versus-budgeted graphs, because extrapolated trend lines that cross budget lines in the wrong direction are immediately visible to the most harried executive. Adding budgetary data usually requires a nested union query to combine summary results from transaction data and pre-summarized budget data.

You can't generate extrapolated values from queries against historical data, but you can use VBA code and statistical functions to add future data points to a saved copy of the graph's Recordset—which requires you to use ActiveX Data Objects (ADO)—or directly to columns you add to the Datasheet of the graph—which necessitates your understanding Graph9's convoluted object model. These advanced programming topics are beyond the scope of this book, but you should be aware that Access graphs and charts are fully capable of extensive programmatic cutomization.

--rj

CHAPTER 20 ▶

USING ACCESS WITH MICROSOFT EXCEL

In this chapter

Slicing and Dicing Data with PivotTables   746

Creating the Query for the PivotTable   747

Generating a PivotTable Form with the Wizard   747

Manipulating PivotTables in Excel   754

Improving PivotTable Formatting   754

Slicing PivotTable Data   757

Formatting PivotTable Reports   763

Creating a PivotChart from a PivotTable   764

Using Excel as an OLE Server   767

Embedding a Conventional Excel Worksheet in a Form   767

Troubleshooting   774

In the Real World—OLAP and PivotTables   775

SLICING AND DICING DATA WITH PIVOTTABLES

Excel's PivotTable feature, which originated with Excel 5.0, delivers extraordinarily ad hoc data analysis capability, often called "slicing and dicing" the data. Chapter 18, "Designing Data Access Pages," shows you how to use the PivotTable ActiveX control—a lightweight version of the Excel 2000 PivotTable that's designed primarily for intranet applications. This chapter shows you how to take full advantage of Excel 2000 PivotTables embedded in Access 2000 forms. You need a local copy of Excel 2000 to perform this chapter's examples.

Excel PivotTables are Microsoft's preferred method for presentation of OLAP data from Microsoft OLAP Services for SQL Server. To aid developers, Microsoft supplies an OLE DB PivotTable Service provider that works with data cubes. Learning how to create Excel PivotTables from Jet databases is a helpful introduction to the more complex process of presenting data cubes in PivotTables.

Excel PivotTables closely resemble Access crosstab queries, which are one of the main topics of Chapter 10, "Creating Multitable and Crosstab Queries." Both PivotTables and crosstab queries employ aggregate functions—sum, average, count, standard deviation, variance, and the like—to summarize data, but most PivotTables deal only with totals. Crosstab queries are limited to creating row-by-row subtotals; PivotTables not only provide subtotals but also supply grand totals and crossfoot totals. Crossfooting is an accounting term for testing the accuracy of a set of numerical values by comparing grand totals calculated by row and by column. One of the primary advantages of Excel PivotTables is that the user, not the database developer who designed the query, can control data presentation.

PivotTables let you swap axes and apply filters to the underlying data. Like Access filters, PivotTable filters remove extraneous or unneeded data from the current view. You also can apply one of a set of predetermined styles to format Excel PivotTable reports.

Tip #176 from

Substitute Excel PivotTables for crosstab queries when your data presentation needs crossfooting or you want to apply sophisticated report formatting to the presentation. It's much faster to use PivotTable features to generate row totals, subtotals, and grand totals than it is to use crosstab queries. Another advantage of PivotTables is that their users can set the amount of detail information that appears in the report and then generate their own graphs or charts from the presentation.

USING THE ACCESS PIVOTTABLE WIZARD

The Access PivotTable Wizard simplifies adding data-bound PivotTables to Access forms. Data-bound PivotTables maintain up-to-date information as changes occur to the Jet tables that underlie the query on which you base the Excel PivotTable. The sections that follow describe how to create an Excel PivotTable in a bound object frame container within an Access form.

CREATING THE QUERY FOR THE PIVOTTABLE

Queries designed for competent PivotTable users should offer a high degree of flexibility for slicing and dicing the data within a single Access form. For example, sales and marketing managers are likely to want to explore the total value of orders received each quarter by salesperson, customer, product, or country, or any combination of these selection criteria. Thus your query must supply more than the ordinary amount of data to the PivotTable.

To create a simple query that supplies the underlying data for a versatile PivotTable, do the following:

1. Open a new query in Design view.

2. Add the Employees, Orders, and Customers tables, plus the Order Details Extended query.

3. Drag the LastName field of the Employees table to the query grid, followed in order by the CompanyName field of the Customers table, the ProductName field of the Order Details Extended query, the ShipCountry and OrderDate fields of the Orders table, and the Extended Price field of the Order Details Extended query.

4. Add a **Between #1/1/1997# And #12/31/1997#** criterion to the OrderDate column to restrict the data to the last full year for which order data exists in Northwind.mdb. Clear the Show check box for this column.

Tip #177 from

R J **Y2K**

> If Access truncates the century values of the dates to #1/1/97# and #12/31/98#, respectively, you haven't set the Four-Digit Date Format option in the General Page of the Options dialog described in Chapter 1, "Access 2000 for Access 9x Users—What's New." Truncating century digits is a violation of basic Y2K conformance requirements.
>
> → For a description of how to set the Four-Digit Date Format options, **see** "Four-Digit Year Option Settings," **p. 36**

5. Drag the OrderDate field from the Orders table to create a new column to the left of the existing OrderDate field. Replace the content of the Field cell of this column with **Quarter: Format([OrderDate],"q")** to create a calculated column to display the number of the calendar quarter in which the order was received. Save the query as **qryPivotTable**. Your query appears as shown in Figure 20.1.

6. Run the query to check your work (see Figure 20.2).

GENERATING A PIVOTTABLE FORM WITH THE WIZARD

Access's PivotTable Wizard combines an Access add-in and elements of the Excel PivotTable Wizard to generate simple PivotTable forms automatically. To create a PivotTable form based on qryPivotTable, do the following:

1. Click the Database window's Form shortcut and then click the New button to open the New Form dialog.

PART

V

CH

20

Figure 20.1
The PivotTable query design.

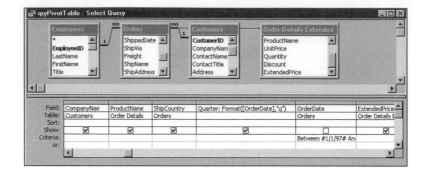

Figure 20.2
The output of the qryPivotTable query.

Last Name	Company Name	Product Name	Ship Country	Quarter	Extended Price
Davolio	Eastern Connection	Thüringer Rostbratwurst	UK	1	$2,079.00
Davolio	Eastern Connection	Steeleye Stout	UK	1	$504.00
Davolio	Eastern Connection	Maxilaku	UK	1	$480.00
Davolio	Rattlesnake Canyon Groce	Nord-Ost Matjeshering	USA	1	$372.60
Davolio	Rattlesnake Canyon Groce	Gnocchi di nonna Alice	USA	1	$2,128.00
Davolio	Rattlesnake Canyon Groce	Louisiana Fiery Hot Pepper	USA	1	$336.00
Davolio	Rattlesnake Canyon Groce	Fløtemysost	USA	1	$1,032.00
Callahan	Ernst Handel	Tunnbröd	Austria	1	$432.00
Callahan	Ernst Handel	Vegie-spread	Austria	1	$2,281.50
Peacock	Ernst Handel	Pavlova	Austria	1	$248.11
Peacock	Ernst Handel	Chocolade	Austria	1	$606.90
Fuller	Magazzini Alimentari Riuni	Gumbär Gummibärchen	Italy	1	$709.65
Fuller	Magazzini Alimentari Riuni	Singaporean Hokkien Fried	Italy	1	$425.60

2. Click to select the Pivot Table Wizard in the list and select qryPivotTable in the drop-down list as the data source for the PivotTable.

Tip #178 from

You can omit selection of the data source from the drop-down list at this point, if you want, because you can select the data source for the PivotTable later in step 4.

---

3. Click OK to open the first PivotTable Wizard dialog, which explains the capabilities of PivotTables (see Figure 20.3).

4. Click Next to open the second dialog in which you select the columns to include in the PivotTable. Click the double right arrow (>>) to add all fields to the PivotTable (see Figure 20.4).

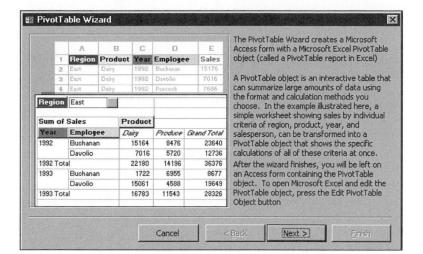

Figure 20.3
The PivotTable Wizard's introductory dialog.

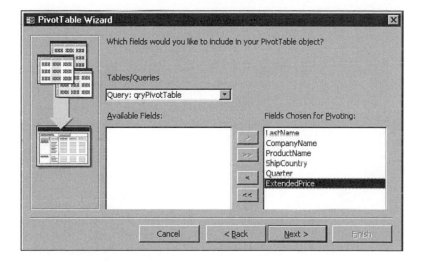

Figure 20.4
Selecting all query columns for inclusion in the PivotTable.

5. Click OK to start an instance of an Excel 2000 workbook named Object and display the last PivotTable Wizard dialog, which is provided by Excel (see Figure 20.5).

6. Click Layout to open the Wizard's Layout dialog. Extended Price is the data to aggregate (a *measure* or *fact* in OLAP terminology), so drag the ExtendedPrice button to the Data region. The Wizard automatically adds Sum of ExtendedPrice to the data region (see Figure 20.6).

Figure 20.5
The last Wizard dialog created by a new instance of Excel 2000.

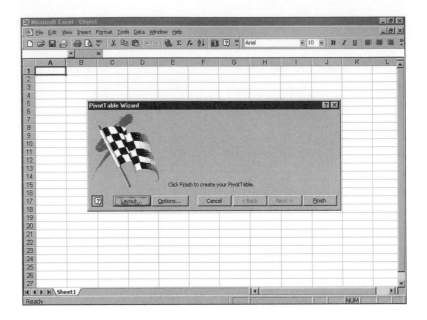

Figure 20.6
Specifying ExtendedPrice as the data for the PivotTable.

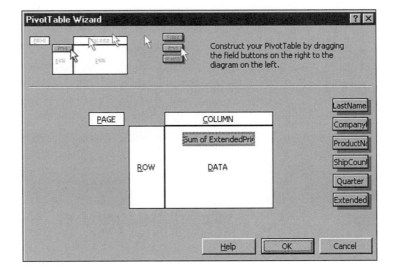

7. To create a simple PivotTable displaying orders by employee and product for each quarter of 1997, drag the LastName and ProductName buttons to the Row region and drag the Quarter button to the Column region (see Figure 20.7). In OLAP terminology, employee, product, and quarter are *dimensions*.

8. Click OK to return to the last Wizard dialog and click Options to display the PivotTable Options dialog, which supplies default values for a variety of PivotTable properties.

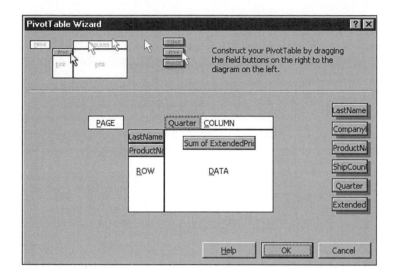

Figure 20.7
Designing a PivotTable to display the value of 1997 orders by employee and product.

9. Accept the default properties and type **0** in the For Empty Cells, Show text box to substitute zeros for **Null** data values (see Figure 20.8).

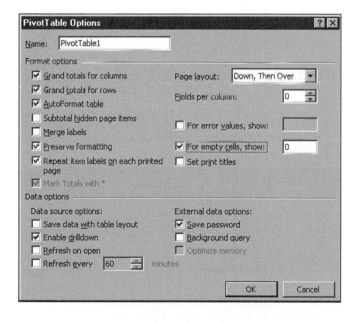

Figure 20.8
Replacing Null values with zeros in the PivotTable Options dialog.

Tip #179 from

R J

You can automatically store a snapshot of the query result set for your PivotTable by marking the Save Data with Table Layout check box in the Data Options frame. This option lets road warriors who aren't connected to a networked data .mdb file open the PivotTable.

> If you save a data snapshot, execute Data, Refresh Data the first time you activate the PivotTable when connected to the network. (Microsoft says Access automatically refreshes the data when you open the PivotTable form, but you're likely to find situations where automatic refresh doesn't work.)

10. Click OK to return to the Wizard dialog and click Finish to open the new Excel PivotTable embedded as an OLE object in an Unbound Object Frame control of a new form (see Figure 20.9). If your PivotTable is empty at this time, don't be concerned.

Figure 20.9
The Excel PivotTable embedded in an Unbound Object Frame.

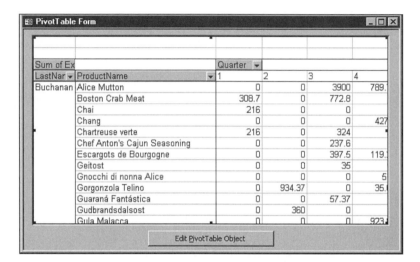

11. Click the Edit Pivot Table Object button to activate Excel 2000 and display the PivotTable in the underlying workbook (see Figure 20.10). You make all changes to the PivotTable in the Excel instance, not in the embedded form object. The PivotTable form serves only as a link to the instance of Excel required to alter the PivotTable presentation.

Note

The unbound Excel Worksheet object embedded in the form is enabled and not locked, but the Excel menu choices grafted to Access's Format menu (Font, Datasheet, Row Height, Column Width, and others) are disabled. The presentation of the Worksheet object in the form also omits its adornments. *Adornment* is an OLE term that refers to application-specific navigation elements, such as scroll bars, row and column headers, custom mouse pointers, and the like. You can't manipulate the PivotTable presentation in the Access form, which makes Form view analogous to Print Preview for a report.

Open Excel 2000's window instead of working with an activated instance of the PivotTable in Form Design mode. You can activate in place an instance of the PivotTable by double-clicking it in Form Design mode. Activation in Design mode makes Excel adornments appear and enables in Access grafted Excel menus. A PivotTable activated in place behaves similarly to an Excel worksheet, but working in the full Excel window is much less constraining.

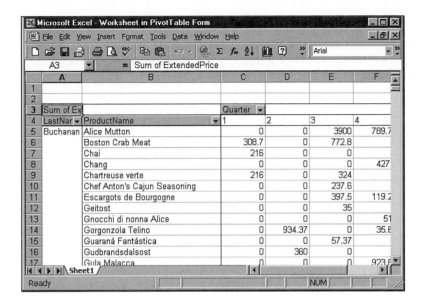

Figure 20.10
An activated instance of Excel displaying the PivotTable in a Workbook object.

12. Widen the Excel window to expose the Grand Total crossfoot values for the full year's sales of each product by employee and then scroll down to row 42, which displays the Buchanan subtotals for each quarter and the entire year (see Figure 20.11). Excel uses its outlining methods to generate subtotals.

Figure 20.11
Excel 1997 quarterly orders and year subtotals for Steve Buchanan.

	A	B	C	D	E	F	G
30		Rhönbräu Klosterbier	62	0	0	139.5	201.5
31		Røgede sild	0	807.5	0	0	807.5
32		Rössle Sauerkraut	655.2	0	912	0	1567.2
33		Scottish Longbreads	0	250	0	0	250
34		Singaporean Hokkien Fried Mee	560	0	0	0	560
35		Sir Rodney's Scones	126	0	0	0	126
36		Teatime Chocolate Biscuits	153.3	0	0	110.4	263.7
37		Tofu	223.2	0	697.5	0	920.7
38		Tourtière	0	0	263.73	0	263.73
39		Uncle Bob's Organic Dried Pears	0	0	1350	0	1350
40		Vegie-spread	0	263.4	0	0	263.4
41		Zaanse koeken	0	0	0	356.25	356.25
42	Buchanan Total		2520.4	7537.67	12085.8	8572.57	30716.44
43	Callahan	Alice Mutton	0	0	0	1803.75	1803.75
44		Boston Crab Meat	0	239.2	0	0	239.2
45		Camembert Pierrot	1088	0	0	0	1088
46		Carnarvon Tigers	0	0	0	1612.5	1612.5

PART

V

CH

20

13. Scroll to the last row (495) of the worksheet to display the grand totals of orders received during each quarter and for the year (see Figure 20.12).

Figure 20.12
Grand total crossfeet for orders: quarterly and for the year.

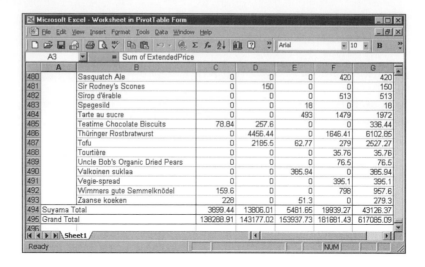

	A	B	C	D	E	F	G
480		Sasquatch Ale	0	0	0	420	420
481		Sir Rodney's Scones	0	150	0	0	150
482		Sirop d'érable	0	0	0	513	513
483		Spegesild	0	0	18	0	18
484		Tarte au sucre	0	0	493	1479	1972
485		Teatime Chocolate Biscuits	78.84	257.6	0	0	336.44
486		Thüringer Rostbratwurst	0	4456.44	0	1646.41	6102.85
487		Tofu	0	2185.5	62.77	279	2527.27
488		Tourtière	0	0	0	35.76	35.76
489		Uncle Bob's Organic Dried Pears	0	0	0	76.5	76.5
490		Valkoinen suklaa	0	0	385.94	0	385.94
491		Vegie-spread	0	0	0	395.1	395.1
492		Wimmers gute Semmelknödel	159.6	0	0	798	957.6
493		Zaanse koeken	228	0	51.3	0	279.3
494	Suyama Total		3899.44	13806.01	5481.65	19939.27	43126.37
495	Grand Total		138288.91	143177.02	153937.73	181681.43	617085.09
496							

14. Close the instance of Excel and save your form as **frmPivotTable**.

MANIPULATING PIVOTTABLES IN EXCEL

Opening the PivotTable worksheet in the Excel window provides access to all the data manipulation and design features of Excel PivotTables. The following sections describe elementary modifications to the PivotTable design. A full discourse on all of the features of Excel PivotTables is beyond the scope of this book.

For a thorough understanding of Excel PivotTables and their features, see Chapter 20 of *Special Edition Using Microsoft Excel 2000*, from Que Publishing, which appears on the accompanying CD-ROM.

Tip #180 from

Don't confuse Excel PivotTables with the Access PivotTable lists you add to Data Access Pages (DAP) with the Office Web Components' PivotTable control. PivotTable lists emulate Excel PivotTables, but don't offer the latter's full feature set. Most of the Access help topics for PivotTables apply to PivotTable lists, not Excel 2000 PivotTables. Open online help from the activated instance of Excel, not from Access, type **pivottable** in the What Would You Like to Do text box, and click Search for assistance with Excel PivotTables and PivotTable reports. Excel 2000's online help for PivotTables includes topics on using PivotTables with OLAP data sources.

IMPROVING PIVOTTABLE FORMATTING

You can change the display names of dimensions and change numeric formatting in the query or the worksheet. Substituting Amount for Sum of ExtendedPrice, and formatting numeric values to remove decimal values and adding thousands separators makes the

PivotTable more readable. As a rule, it's a better practice to make these changes to the PivotTable than in a query because you might use the same query as the data source for many Access forms and reports, some of which require currency formatting with two decimal places.

Note

It's a common accounting practice to use full currency formatting—including the currency symbol for the locale—only for subtotals and grand totals.

To alter the name and format of the measure, follow these steps:

1. Click the Edit PivotTable Object button or double-click the object frame to activate the instance of Excel and then scroll to the top of the worksheet if necessary.

2. Double-click the Sum of ExtendedPrice button (cell A3) to open the PivotTable Field dialog for the ExtendedPrice source field. If Excel throws a "Pivot table saved without underlying data" error, execute the Data, Refresh Data command.

3. Replace the content of the Name text box with **Amount** (see Figure 20.13).

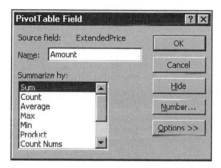

Figure 20.13
Changing the name of the Sum of ExtendedPrice data field to Amount.

4. Click Number to open Excel's Format Cells dialog. Select Number in the Category list, specify 0 Decimal Places, and mark the Use Thousands Separator (,) check box to format the measure (see Figure 20.14).

Note

The thousands separator is either a comma or period, depending on the locale you specify with Control Panel's Regional Setting tool.

5. Click OK twice to return to the worksheet.

6. Select the Grand Total column (G) by clicking its header button and choose Format, Cells to open the fully tabbed version of the Format Cells dialog.

7. Select Currency from the Category list, set Decimal Places to 0, and select the appropriate currency character from the Symbol list. Click OK to apply full currency formatting to the Grand Total column.

Figure 20.14
Changing measure formatting to omit decimal values and add the thousands separator.

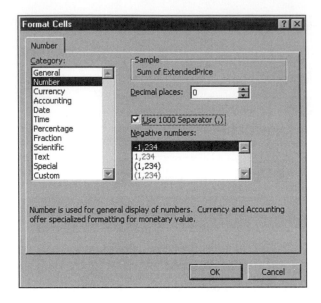

8. Select the Grand Total column header cell and replace Grand Total with **1997 Total**.

9. Add a title, such as **Northwind Traders 1997 Product Sales Analysis**, to the worksheet (see Figure 20.15).

Figure 20.15
The PivotTable in Excel with the measure's name changed and formatting applied to the measure.

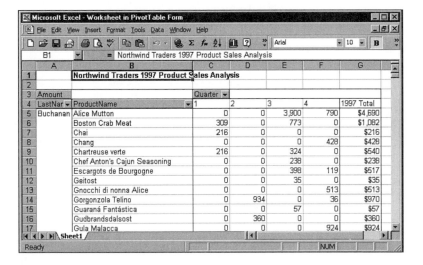

10. Close Excel to return to Access, change to Form Design view, and expand the width of the unbound object frame and form to accommodate the 1997 Total column.

11. Double-click the unbound object frame to in-place activate the worksheet. When you activate the object in Design view, grafted Excel menu choices replace many of Access's menus (see Figure 20.16).

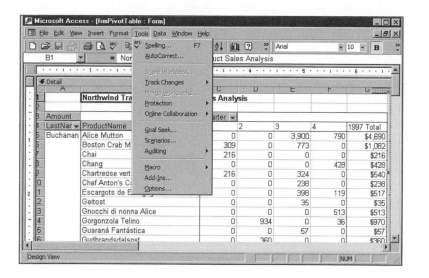

Figure 20.16
The PivotTable's work-sheet activated in place in Form Design view.

12. Click the square button at the upper left of the form (at the intersection of the rulers), and then return to run mode so you can check the PivotTable's presentation (see Figure 20.17).

LastNar ▼	ProductName	1	2	3	4	1997 Total
Buchanan	Alice Mutton	0	0	3,900	790	$4,690
	Boston Crab Meat	309	0	773	0	$1,082
	Chai	216	0	0	0	$216
	Chang	0	0	0	428	$428
	Chartreuse verte	216	0	324	0	$540
	Chef Anton's Cajun Seasoning	0	0	238	0	$238
	Escargots de Bourgogne	0	0	398	119	$517
	Geitost	0	0	35	0	$35
	Gnocchi di nonna Alice	0	0	0	513	$513
	Gorgonzola Telino	0	934	0	36	$970
	Guaraná Fantástica	0	0	57	0	$57
	Gudbrandsdalsost	0	360	0	0	$360
	Gula Malacca	0	0	0	924	$924

Northwind Traders 1997 Product Sales Analysis

Edit PivotTable Object

Figure 20.17
Presentation of the for-matted PivotTable in Access Form view.

SLICING PIVOTTABLE DATA

You can restrict (slice) the PivotTable's presentation to specific members of dimensions, such as a single quarter, salesperson, or product, or to any combination of dimension members. For example, to display data only for Michael Suyama in the first half of 1997, do the following:

1. Double-click the PivotTable in Run mode to open the Excel window.

2. Click the Amount button, and choose <u>D</u>ata, <u>R</u>efresh Data to requery the underlying data source. If you don't refresh the data at the beginning of the slicing process, you receive messages insisting that you do so when attempting to make changes. (A more friendly approach would have been to provide a Refresh button in the message box.)

> *If the <u>D</u>ata, <u>R</u>efresh Data menu choice is disabled when you receive Excel's request to refresh, see the "Disabled Refresh Data Menu Choice" item in the "Troubleshooting" section at the end of the chapter.*

3. Click the LastName field's arrow button to open a list of employees, clear all but the Suyama check boxes, and click OK.

4. Click the Quarter field's arrow button and clear the 3 and 4 check boxes (see Figure 20.18, which is a double-exposure for steps 3 and 4). Click OK to make the changes.

Figure 20.18
Slicing data by excluding dimension members.

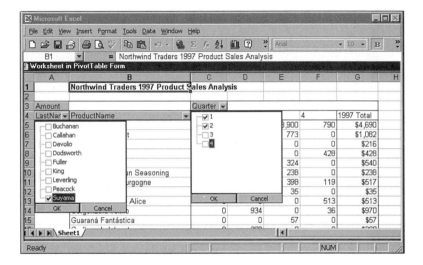

5. Close Excel to return to Access. The sliced PivotTable presentation appears as shown in Figure 20.19.

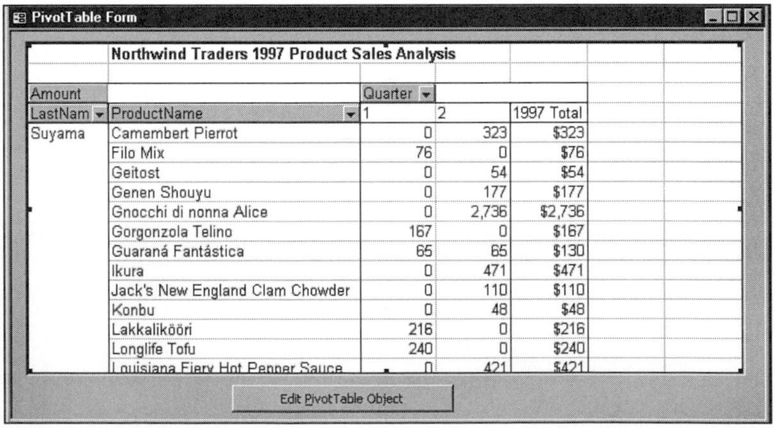

Figure 20.19
Sliced data presentation in the Access form.

6. Reopen the Excel window and mark all LastName and Quarter check boxes to return the PivotTable to its original structure.

SLICING BY FILTERING

For dimensions with many members, such as ProductName, it's much faster to apply a filter to the field. Excel's AutoFilter feature closely resembles Access's Filter by Form feature. To use AutoFilter to show only a single product, do the following:

1. Click the B column heading and then choose Data, Filter, AutoFilter to add a drop-down list to the ProductName column.

2. Open the list and select a product, such as Gorgonzola Telino (see Figure 20.20). When the list closes, your worksheet appears as shown in Figure 20.21.

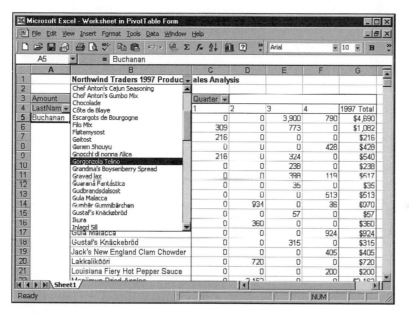

Figure 20.20
Applying Excel's AutoFilter feature to a PivotTable field.

> **Note**
> Unfortunately, AutoFilter doesn't compute the grand total value of the filtered records.

3. Choose Data, Filter, Show All to reveal the hidden records and then choose Data, Filter, AutoFilter to clear its check mark and remove the drop-down list arrow from the ProductName column.

PART
V

CH
20

Figure 20.21
The result of selecting a
single product with
AutoFilter.

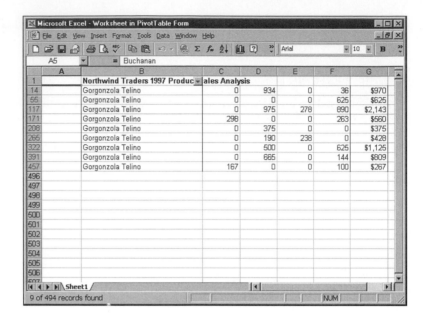

COLLAPSING OR EXPANDING THE DISPLAY OF DETAIL DATA

As noted earlier in the chapter, Excel uses outlining to generate subtotals. You can quickly remove the ProductName detail records at the second level of the outline by hiding the ProductName column or expand the level of detail by adding another dimension. Follow these steps to explore detail management:

1. Right-click the ProductName button to select the field and then choose Group and Outline, Hide Detail from the context menu. Only the subtotals and grand totals appear, as shown in Figure 20.22.

2. Choose Edit, Undo Show/Hide Detail or press Ctrl+Z to reveal the hidden details records.

3. Repeat step 1, but choose Show Detail to open the Show Detail dialog, and select ShipCountry (see Figure 20.23).

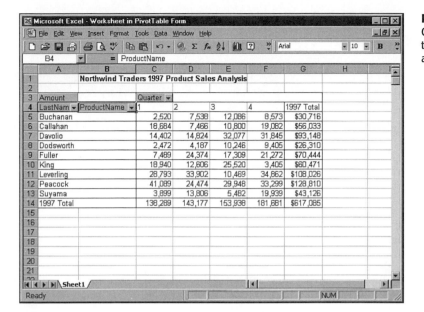

Figure 20.22
Collapsing the PivotTable to display only subtotals and grand totals.

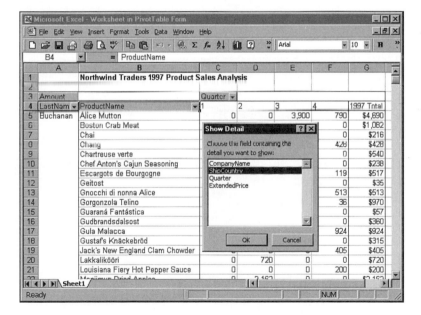

Figure 20.23
Adding another dimension, ShipCountry, to the PivotTable.

PART

V

CH

20

4. Click OK to close the Show Detail dialog and display the expanded PivotTable (see Figure 20.24).

Figure 20.24
The PivotTable with the ShipCountry dimension added.

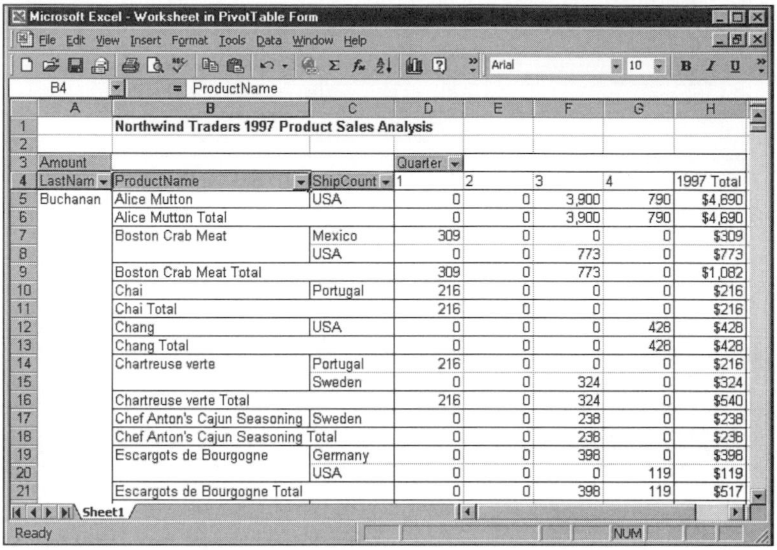

	A	B	C	D	E	F	G	H
1		Northwind Traders 1997 Product Sales Analysis						
2								
3	Amount			Quarter				
4	LastNam	ProductName	ShipCount	1	2	3	4	1997 Total
5	Buchanan	Alice Mutton	USA	0	0	3,900	790	$4,690
6		Alice Mutton Total		0	0	3,900	790	$4,690
7		Boston Crab Meat	Mexico	309	0	0	0	$309
8			USA	0	0	773	0	$773
9		Boston Crab Meat Total		309	0	773	0	$1,082
10		Chai	Portugal	216	0	0	0	$216
11		Chai Total		216	0	0	0	$216
12		Chang	USA	0	0	0	428	$428
13		Chang Total		0	0	0	428	$428
14		Chartreuse verte	Portugal	216	0	0	0	$216
15			Sweden	0	0	324	0	$324
16		Chartreuse verte Total		216	0	324	0	$540
17		Chef Anton's Cajun Seasoning	Sweden	0	0	238	0	$238
18		Chef Anton's Cajun Seasoning Total		0	0	238	0	$238
19		Escargots de Bourgogne	Germany	0	0	398	0	$398
20			USA	0	0	0	119	$119
21		Escargots de Bourgogne Total		0	0	398	119	$517

Changing a Dimension's Axis

You dice data by changing the axis on which the dimension appears; Excel calls changing axes *pivoting*. For example, you can reorder the PivotTable to display sales by ShipCountry, LastName, and ProductName by dragging the ShipCountry field button to the LastName field (see Figure 20.25).

Figure 20.25
Pivoting the ShipCountry dimension.

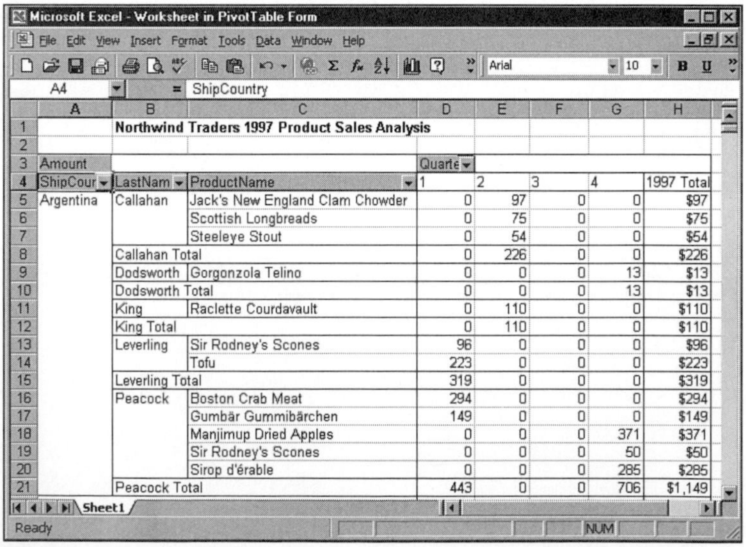

	A	B	C	D	E	F	G	H
1		Northwind Traders 1997 Product Sales Analysis						
2								
3	Amount			Quarte				
4	ShipCour	LastNam	ProductName	1	2	3	4	1997 Total
5	Argentina	Callahan	Jack's New England Clam Chowder	0	97	0	0	$97
6			Scottish Longbreads	0	75	0	0	$75
7			Steeleye Stout	0	54	0	0	$54
8		Callahan Total		0	226	0	0	$226
9		Dodsworth	Gorgonzola Telino	0	0	0	13	$13
10		Dodsworth Total		0	0	0	13	$13
11		King	Raclette Courdavault	0	110	0	0	$110
12		King Total		0	110	0	0	$110
13		Leverling	Sir Rodney's Scones	96	0	0	0	$96
14			Tofu	223	0	0	0	$223
15		Leverling Total		319	0	0	0	$319
16		Peacock	Boston Crab Meat	294	0	0	0	$294
17			Gumbär Gummibärchen	149	0	0	0	$149
18			Manjimup Dried Apples	0	0	0	371	$371
19			Sir Rodney's Scones	0	0	0	50	$50
20			Sirop d'érable	0	0	0	285	$285
21		Peacock Total		443	0	0	706	$1,149

Similarly, dragging the Quarter button to the ShipCountry field adds another level of detail to the dimensions. To return the pivot table to its original form, press Ctrl+Z twice.

> **Note**
>
> You change the relative order of the dimension hierarchy by dragging a dimension button to the left (promotion) or right (demotion).

FORMATTING PIVOTTABLE REPORTS

Excel's AutoFormat feature lets you generate PivotTable reports in a set of predefined, standard formats. To format your PivotTable as a Pivot Table report, do the following:

1. Right-click within the PivotTable area and choose Forma<u>t</u> Report to open the AutoFormat dialog, which offers 12 standard PivotTable report formats, including no formatting (see Figure 20.26).

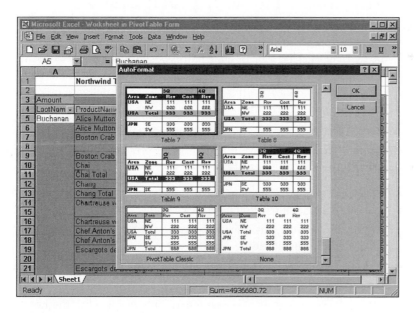

Figure 20.26
The AutoFormat dialog showing 6 of the 12 available PivotTable report formats.

PART

V

CH

20

> **Note**
>
> The bitmap images of the available formats don't show your PivotTable dimensions; the dimensions of the bitmaps are illustrative only.

2. Click your choice of formats and then click OK to close the dialog. Figure 20.27 illustrates the Report 7 format, which automatically includes the entire dimension hierarchy, in Access Run mode.

Figure 20.27
Access displaying the Report 7 AutoFormat applied to original version of the PivotTable.

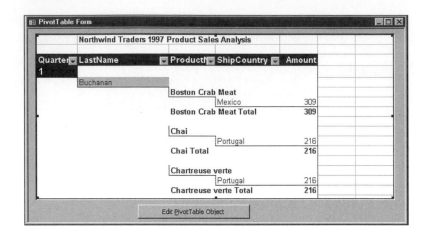

CREATING A PIVOTCHART FROM A PIVOTTABLE

PivotCharts offer an alternative to Access charts you create with the Chart Wizard, as described in the preceding chapter, "Adding Charts and Graphics to Forms and Reports." You create PivotCharts by right-clicking a PivotTable and choosing PivotChart from the context menu. Excel PivotCharts use the Microsoft Graph 2000 (Graph9) engine that's common to all Office members. PivotCharts offer features, such as the ability to quickly alter a chart's design to increase or decrease the level of detail, that enable users to customize their graphical view of the data.

To add a PivotChart to the worksheet and have it appear as the presentation in the Access PivotTable form, follow these steps:

1. Reduce the level of detail in the PivotTable report by applying the Hide Detail choice to the ProductName and ShipCountry dimensions (see Figure 20.28).

   If you don't reduce the detail level, your chart appears similar to a view of audio white noise in a digital audio-editing application.

2. Right-click the PivotTable region and select PivotChart to create the PivotChart in a new sheet.

3. Double-click the Chart Title to open the Format Chart Title dialog, click the Font tab, and set the font to 18-point Arial bold. If the Chart Title doesn't appear on the chart, choose Chart, Chart Options to open the dialog.

4. Replace the Total Chart Title with **Northwind Traders 1997 Quarterly Sales by Employee** (see Figure 20.29).

5. Close Excel to return to Access. Selecting Clip as the value of the Size Mode property causes only a small part of the PivotTable to appear in the form.

6. Change to Form Design view, select the object frame, set the Size Mode property to Stretch, and increase the size of the object frame and form to display the chart with acceptable—if not optimal—resolution.

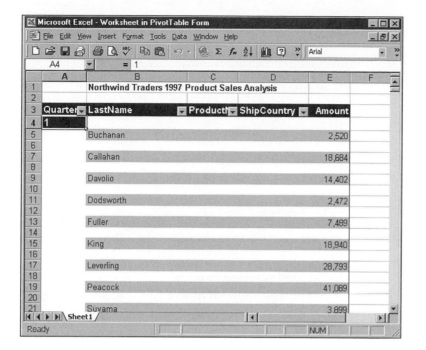

Figure 20.28
The PivotTable report with a reduced detail level suitable for a PivotChart.

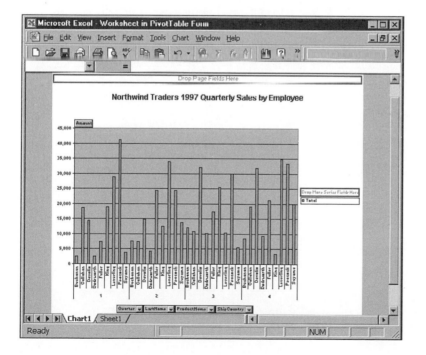

Figure 20.29
The PivotChart in the Excel window

7. Return to Run mode to display the chart (see Figure 20.30).

Figure 20.30
The PivotChart presentation in the Access form.

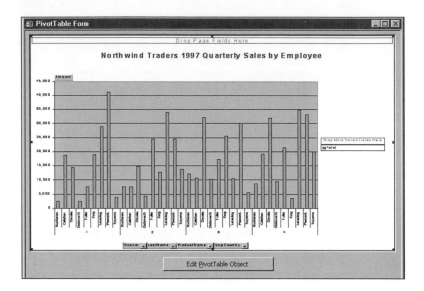

8. Drag the LastName field button to the left of the Quarter button to reduce the level of detail in the PivotChart (see Figure 20.31). Dragging the LastName button to the right of the Quarter button restores the original detail level.

Figure 20.31
The PivotChart with the level of detail reduced.

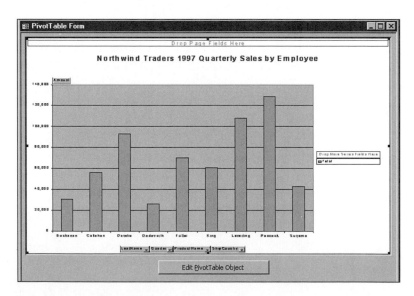

Note

The qryPivotTable query and frmPivotTable form are included in the ExcelOLE.mdb file in the \SEUA97\Chaptr20 folder of the accompanying CD-ROM. Import qryPivotTable and frmPivotTable into your working copy of Northwind.mdb to make the objects operational.

USING EXCEL AS AN OLE SERVER

This section describes methods of creating links between data cells in OLE Object fields and worksheets created with Excel 2000. You can embed or link an Excel worksheet or graph as a bound or unbound OLE object. You can copy data from the OLE worksheet object to the Clipboard and then paste the data into a bound or unbound text box. The following sections provide examples of these techniques. The step-by-step examples in this section assume that you're familiar with the use of Excel 2000 or earlier.

EMBEDDING A CONVENTIONAL EXCEL WORKSHEET IN A FORM

You can embed an entire Excel worksheet in an unbound object frame by using the simple process that follows. In this case, the presentation of an Excel worksheet (or what you can display of the worksheet in a bound object frame) is the entire content of the worksheet. The examples for embedding an Excel worksheet in this and the following section use a sample stock price worksheet that contains several days of high, low, and close prices, plus trading volume data. The data is several years old.

To embed an Excel worksheet in an unbound object frame of a new form, follow these steps:

1. Create a new Stocks.mdb database and add a new blank form in Design view. Initially, size the form to about 3.75 inches high by 6 inches wide.

2. Click the Toolbox button of the toolbar, if necessary, and select the unbound object frame tool. Create a frame with the left corner at about .5 inches from the form's left edge and about 0.375 inches from the top. Drag the lower-right corner frame until it almost fills the form. The Insert Object dialog appears.

Tip #181 from

The dimensions of these margins are important; see the "Excel Adornments Don't Appear in Activated Object Frame" topic of the "Troubleshooting" section at the end of this chapter.

PART

V

CH

20

3. Click the Create from File option and then click the Browse button to open the Browse Dialog and locate the folder containing the Stocks.xls file—\Seua2k\Chaptr20. Select Stocks.xls (or the name of any other Excel 95 or later workbook file you want to embed) in the file list, and then click OK to close the Browse dialog. Then click OK to close the Insert Object dialog (see Figure 20.32).

Figure 20.32
Inserting an unbound object from an Excel 2000 file.

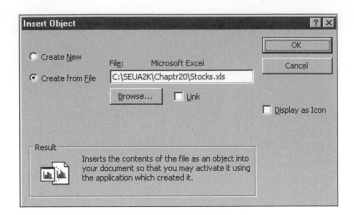

If you receive an error message when you attempt to embed an Excel workbook, see the " Excel Workbook Won't Embed in an Object Frame" topic in the "Troubleshooting" section at the end of the chapter.

4. Select the unbound object frame and drag the right border to about 5.5 inches. Drag the bottom border to about 3.375 inches.

 5. Click the Properties button of the toolbar. Click the Data tab and set the value of the Enabled property to Yes and the Locked property to No. If you don't enable and unlock the object frame, you can't activate the object (see Figure 20.33).

Figure 20.33
Setting the Enabled and Locked properties of the object to allow in-place activation.

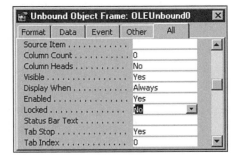

6. Press Ctrl+R to select the form and set the Scroll Bars property value to Neither, Record Selectors to No, and Navigation Buttons to No.

7. Save the form as **frmExcel1**.

 8. Click the Form View button of the toolbar to display the presentation of your worksheet (see Figure 20.34). If only part of a column displays, return to Design view and adjust the width of your object frame so that a full column is displayed with a 0.25-inch border at the right. You also may need to adjust the height of the form to provide a 0.25-inch border at the bottom.

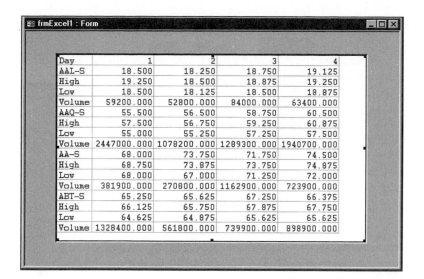

Figure 20.34
The presentation of a worksheet in an unbound object frame.

The worksheet that appears in the object frame is the selected worksheet when you last saved the .xls file.

9. Double-click the object frame to activate the worksheet in place. If you've set the left and top positions of your object frame and provided the proper internal borders, your activated worksheet appears as shown in Figure 20.35. Excel 2000's Edit and View menus replace Access's Edit and View menus, and Excel's Insert, Format, Tools, and Data menus are added to Access's menu. The toolbars that normally appear when you open Excel are added to Access 2000's toolbars. Activated mode is indicated by a hashed border around the object frame.

   When the object is activated, you can perform any operation that's possible in Excel 2000 except operations that require use of Excel's File menu—such as saving the workbook to a file or printing the worksheet.

10. Click outside the unbound object frame to deactivate the object and then return to Presentation mode so that Access's menubar is active.

11. Right-click the object frame Worksheet Object, Open to open Excel 2000's window with the embedded data as the source of Excel's current workbook (see Figure 20.36). When you open Excel, you can print the worksheet or save the embedded workbook to a file.

12. Choose File, Exit to close the instance of Excel and return to Presentation mode.

13. Close your form and save the changes.

If Excel adornments are missing when you activate the object, see the "Excel Adornments Don't Appear in Activated Object Frame" item in the "Troubleshooting" section at the end of the chapter.

PART

V

CH

20

Figure 20.35
The worksheet activated in place.

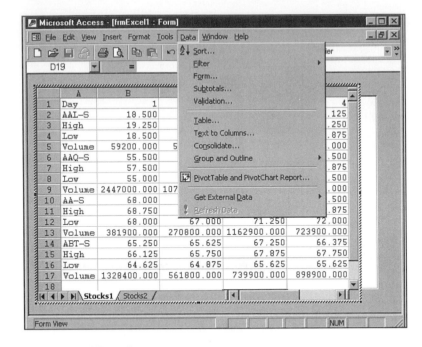

Figure 20.36
Opening Excel 2000 in its own window (from Presentation mode).

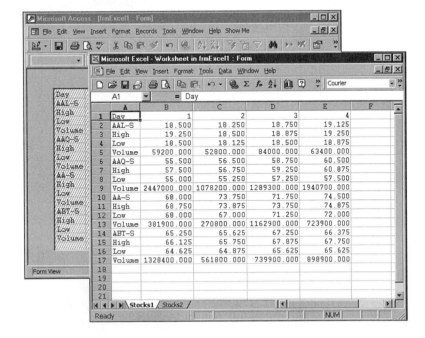

EXTRACTING VALUES FROM AN OLE OBJECT

You can copy individual numeric or text values from a linked or embedded Excel OLE object and place the values in a form text box. Once in a text box, you can manipulate the values by conventional Access methods.

To include the close, high, and low values of the AAL-S stock in a multiline text box added to the form you created in the preceding section, follow these steps:

1. In Design view, increase the depth of the form and move the object frame down to make room for a multiline text box at the top of the form.

2. Add a text box to the form, and set the value of the Scrollbars property to Vertical.

3. In Form view, double-click the unbound object frame to activate the workbook object.

> **Caution**
>
> You must copy and paste the selected values while the form is in Form view; otherwise, the pasted text becomes the text box's Control Source property, resulting in the display of the #Name? error when you display the form in Form view.

4. Select the cell or range of cells you want to import to a text control object. In this case, select A2:E5 to return four days of price data for the AA-S stock.

5. Choose Edit, Copy or press Ctrl+C to copy the A2:E5 range to the Clipboard.

6. Select the text box, which deactivates the object frame, and then choose Edit, Paste Special to display the Paste Special dialog. When you paste data items from an embedded object into a text box, the only option you have is to paste them as text (see Figure 20.37). Click OK to paste the text into the text box.

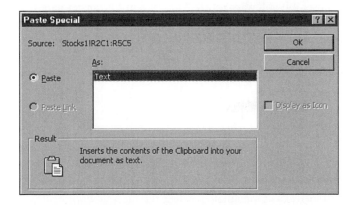

Figure 20.37
Pasting a selection from an embedded Excel worksheet as text.

7. The pasted data items appear as shown in Figure 20.38. The square boxes between the values in the text box represent the tab characters that Excel uses to separate data columns in a row.

If you create one or more bound text boxes with a numeric data type, you can paste a number from a selected single cell to each text box and then use the values to update the fields of the table to which the text box is bound. A more efficient method, however, is to use VBA code and Automation to update values in tables with data from another application. Automation (formerly OLE Automation) is a Microsoft term for controlling an OLE server—Excel in this case—from an OLE-enabled client—Access.

Figure 20.38
A selection from an embedded Excel worksheet pasted into an unbound text box.

frmExcel1 : Form				
High□19.250□18.500□18.875□19.250				
Low□18.500□18.125□18.500□18.875				
Volume□59200.000□52800.000□84000.000□63400.000				

Day	1	2	3	4
AAL-S	18.500	18.250	18.750	19.125
High	19.250	18.500	18.875	19.250
Low	18.500	18.125	18.500	18.875
Volume	59200.000	52800.000	84000.000	63400.000
AAQ-S	55.500	56.500	58.750	60.500
High	57.500	56.750	59.250	60.875
Low	55.000	55.250	57.250	57.500
Volume	2447000.000	1078200.000	1289300.000	1940700.000
AA-S	68.000	73.750	71.750	74.500
High	68.750	73.875	73.750	74.875
Low	68.000	67.000	71.250	72.000
Volume	381900.000	270800.000	1162900.000	723900.000
ABT-S	65.250	65.625	67.250	66.375
High	66.125	65.750	67.875	67.750
Low	64.625	64.875	65.625	65.625
Volume	1328400.000	561800.000	739900.000	898900.000

LINKING TO A RANGE OF CELLS IN AN EXCEL WORKSHEET

Embedding Excel objects is useful if you want to use Automation to transfer data from a Recordset object to embedded worksheet cells. In most cases, however, creating an OLE link to all or a range of cells in a worksheet is a more common practice. Linking allows you to display or edit the most recent version of the worksheet's data from its source file. Any changes you make in Access are reflected when you close Excel if you save the changes.

The conventional process of linking a file in Excel is similar to that for using OLE to link graphics files; in-place activation is not available with linked objects. To create a link with a range of cells in an Excel file, perform the following steps:

1. Open a new, blank Access form.

2. Launch Excel independently of Access.

3. Choose File, Open, and in Excel's Open dialog, select the file and worksheet you want to link. This example uses the Stocks2 worksheet of Stocks.xls.

4. Select the cells of the worksheet to be included in your Access table and then copy the selected cells to the Clipboard with Ctrl+C. Cell range A1:E17 of the Stocks2 worksheet is used in this example.

5. In Access choose <u>E</u>dit, Paste <u>S</u>pecial to display the Paste Special dialog. Click the Paste Link option button. Your only choices for a linked object are the object or text contained in the selected data items. The data source, Stocks2!R1C1:R17C5, appears in the Source label (see Figure 20.39).

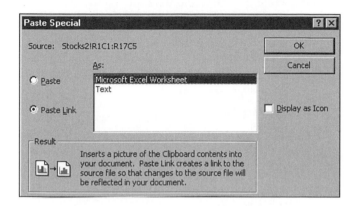

Figure 20.39
The Paste Link dialog for a linked range of cells in an Excel worksheet.

6. Click OK to create the unbound object frame containing the presentation of the selected cells. You don't need to provide for margins in the design because in-place activation is not available with linked objects.

 7. Open the Properties window and set the value of the Enabled property of the object frame to Yes and the Locked property of the frame to No.

 8. Click the Form View button of the toolbar. The presentation of your linked object appears, as shown in Figure 20.40.

Day	1	2	3	4
AAL–S	18.500	18.250	18.750	19.125
High	19.250	18.500	18.875	19.250
Low	18.500	18.125	18.500	18.875
Volume	59200.000	52800.000	84000.000	63400.000
AAQ–S	55.500	56.500	58.750	60.500
High	57.500	56.750	59.250	60.875
Low	55.000	55.250	57.250	57.500
Volume	2447000.000	1078200.000	1289300.000	1940700.000
AA–S	68.000	73.750	71.750	74.500
High	68.750	73.875	73.750	74.875
Low	68.000	67.000	71.250	72.000
Volume	381900.000	270800.000	1162900.000	723900.000
ABT–S	65.250	65.625	67.250	66.375
High	66.125	65.750	67.875	67.750
Low	64.625	64.875	65.625	65.625
Volume	1328400.000	561800.000	739900.000	898900.000

Record: ◄◄ ◄ 1 ► ►► ►* of 1

Figure 20.40
The presentation of a linked range of worksheet cells.

PART

V

CH

20

9. Double-click the presentation of the worksheet to launch Excel in its own window with the linked cells selected (see Figure 20.41). As noted earlier in this section, in-place activation does not apply to linked objects.

Figure 20.41
The instance of Excel launched by double-clicking the linked cells' presentation.

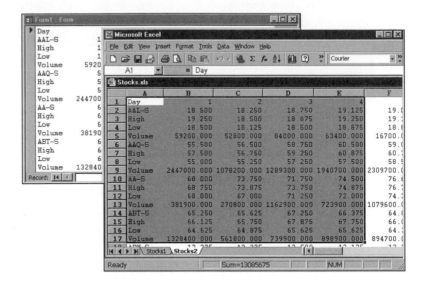

10. In Excel choose File, Exit to return the focus to Access. If you have made changes to the data, you can elect to save the changes at this point. If you receive a warning about a large amount of data saved in the Clipboard, click No to discard it.

 The ExcelOLE.mdb database in the \Seua2k\Chaptr20 folder of the accompanying CD-ROM includes the two forms created in the preceding examples of embedding and linking Excel worksheets.

TROUBLESHOOTING

DISABLED REFRESH DATA MENU CHOICE

I receive a message that I must refresh the data of the PivotTable, but the Data, Refresh Data menu choice is disabled.

This problem appears to be the result of a minor bug in Excel's PivotTable code. To enable the Refresh Data menu choice, type a few characters in any empty cell and then delete the characters.

EXCEL WORKBOOK WON'T EMBED IN AN OBJECT FRAME

A message box appears, indicating that the Excel worksheet is corrupted, that Excel is not properly registered, or that not enough available memory exists to open Excel.

Close other open applications and try again. If the procedure continues to display error messages, exit Windows and start over. (An application has failed to release its global memory blocks when closing.) If you continue to receive error messages that refer to the Registry, you need to verify with RegEdit.exe that the Registry entries for Excel are correct.

EXCEL ADORNMENTS DON'T APPEAR IN ACTIVATED OBJECT FRAME

Excel's column selection buttons, row selection buttons, worksheet tabs, horizontal scroll bar, or the vertical scroll bar don't appear when the object is activated.

Two sets of critical factors determine the visibility of *adornments*, as the preceding objects are called, when you activate an object in place. The top position of the object frame must provide room for the column selector buttons in the form area (0.25 inches), and the left position of the frame must provide space for the row selector buttons (0.5 inches). The visibility of the horizontal and vertical scroll bars is determined by the internal margin of the object, the space between the edge of the worksheet presentation, and the bottom and right edge of the object frame (0.25 inches each).

If, after setting these values, all the adornments shown in Figure 20.35 don't appear, position the mouse pointer on the upper-left corner of the activation border and drag the corner diagonally downward to reduce the size of the activation frame. You might need to make repeated adjustments to the size of the object frame and the activation frame to ensure that all adornments appear.

Finally, you might need to set the Size Mode property of the unbound object frame to Zoom. If the embedded spreadsheet is very large, the default Clip property may cause the adornments at the right and bottom edges of the activated workbook object to be clipped off.

IN THE REAL WORLD—OLAP AND PIVOTTABLES

Data warehouses and their smaller sibling, data marts, introduce a new database lexicon and an alternative approach to analyzing data. Traditional relational database structures comprise a two-dimensional set of columns and rows, analogous to a spreadsheet. Conventional aggregation techniques, typified by Jet crosstab queries, enable managers to review summary data. Front ends for data analysis usually provide multiple dropdown lists to choose attributes (tables and query criteria), such as products, employees, regions, and time periods. Excel PivotTables and PivotCharts are ideal for presenting two-dimensional crosstab query result sets.

The primary objective of data warehouses and marts is to provide a central source of decision-support information, available to all who need it, that lends itself to *unstructured analysis* by users. Unstructured analysis lets users, not database developers and administrators determine views of the data. One of the benefits of letting the user specify his or her own view of data is the ability to perform heuristic analysis. *Heuristic analysis* begins with an ad hoc question, the answer to which intuitively leads to another question, and so on. Online analytic processing (OLAP) almost universally involves interactively querying of data in a heuristic function. Developers and database administrators are very unlikely to be able to predefine queries that satisfy all requirements of all users, because the path of an analysis often evolves by serendipitous observation of interesting relationships between successive views of data. PivotTables currently are one of the best methods of enabling heuristic analysis.

OLAP introduces the concept of data analysis based on multidimensional data modeling (MDM) of a business process (from a data mart) or the operations of an entire enterprise (from a data warehouse). MDM revolves around numerical aggregations, such as dollar or unit sales, margin percentages, gross and net profits, and the like, the values of which represent the intersection of dimensions, such as product and time period. Unlike the two-dimensional crosstab or pivot table, MDM implies three or more data dimensions. Data models with five or six dimensions are common; the maximum number of dimensions usually is limited by the data store or the OLAP front-end toolset you choose but is likely to be 64 or more.

Creating data warehouses and marts, which involves the collection, cleansing, and storing of information in a central location, is well beyond the scope of this book. Microsoft SQL Server 7.0 and the Microsoft Data Engine (MSDE)—the embedded version of SQL Server that comes with Access 2000—include the Data Transformation Service (DTS) for relational and other tabular data. DTS automates much of the drudgery of creating the data store for a warehouse or mart. Microsoft OLAP Services for SQL Server is an OLAP data store that runs on Windows NT Server 4+. OLAP Services are included with SQL Server 7.0 but can be used with any client/server RDBMS that has an OLE DB data provider or an ODBC 3+ driver. MSDE doesn't include OLAP Services.

→ For more information on MSDE, **see** "Understanding the Role of MSDE," **p. 945**.

→ For a brief introduction to DTS, **see** "Downsizing Databases with the DTS Wizard," **p. 975**.

 → For additional information on using Excel 2000 for OLAP, **see** Chapter 27 of *Special Edition Using Microsoft Excel 2000*, which is included on the accompanying CD-ROM.

MEASURES AND DIMENSIONS

Measures are numerical values, such as unit and dollar sales, advertising and promotion expenditures, and populations. Measures often are called *metrics* or *facts*. The sources of internal measures commonly are online transaction processing (OLTP) databases for order entry and invoice processing. In this case, a line items table provides the values to aggregated into rollup tables. External measures, such as market research information, is called *syndicated data*. Syndicated data is available by subscription from a variety of market research firms and governmental agencies. Aggregated measures (rollups), regardless of the source, are stored in *fact tables* of data warehouses/marts or OLAP servers. If a relational database holds the facts table, an OLAP engine provides access to the measures.

Dimensions categorize measures; the most common dimension is a range of dates, usually called a (time) period. The next most popular dimensions are product classifications and geopolitical boundaries, which (with period) form the classic data cubes illustrated by Figure 20.42. Data cubes are not true cubes, because the sides of the cube are not necessarily of the same "length," that is, number of dimensions. A better term is data *hypercube*; a hypercube is an abstract mathematical object having three or more flat-sided dimensions with each dimension perpendicular to all other dimensions. Unless you're a mathematician, four- or more-sided hypercubes are difficult to visualize. Microsoft uses the term *data cube* for general representations of multidimensional data.

Dimensions, for the most part, are hierarchical; the time dimension hierarchy is year, quarter, month, and, for many businesses, week. Large retailers commonly analyze sales on a daily basis. For the recording industry, the product dimension hierarchy might be category, genre, artist, album, and media. A typical U.S. geopolitical dimension comprises country, region, state, Metropolitan Statistical Area (MSA), city, and ZIP code. Moving downward in the hierarchy of one or more dimensions, as in conventional decision-support applications, is called a *drill-down* operation.

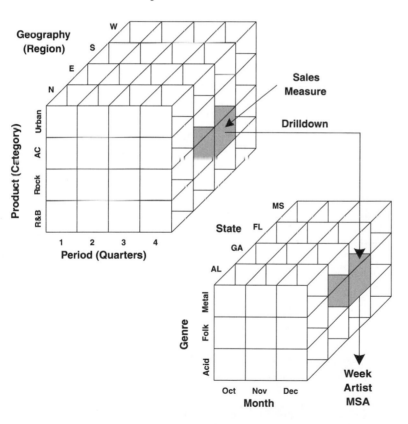

Figure 20.42
Three-dimensional data cubes for sales of a record company.

PART

V

CH

20

Note

The period and geography dimensions are consistent for a wide range of businesses. Minor inconsistencies exist between weeks, months, and quarters, so some firms define a quarter as 13 weeks; others as 3 months. The names of geopolitical dimensions vary between countries, but most countries have numerical or alphanumeric postal codes at the lowest level of the hierarchy. Product hierarchies vary widely, depending on type of business (retailer, distributor, manufacturer, or service provider) and class of goods or services sold.

So What's OLAP Have to Do with Access 2000?

The quick answer is "Not much now." Microsoft's PivotTable Service provides the connection between OLAP cubes running under Microsoft OLAP Services—or stored as local .cub files—and Excel 2000 PivotTables. You can embed an Excel worksheet containing an OLAP PivotTable in an Access form. When you activate the PivotTable object, you can manipulate the OLAP data in the same way as data from a Jet .mdb. Figure 20.43 shows an Excel PivotTable from the Sales cube of the demonstration FoodMart OLAP database that comes with Microsoft OLAP Services. The workbook is embedded in an unbound object frame and activated in Figure 20.43.

Figure 20.43
An Excel 2000 PivotTable from the FoodMart sample OLAP data source embedded in an Access form.

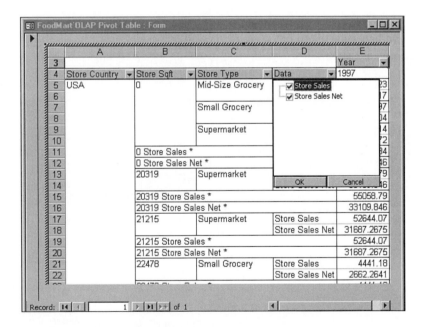

You can mix and match in an Access application Excel PivotTables populated from OLAP, SQL Server, and Jet databases, plus subforms populated by Jet crosstab queries. If you're an accomplished VBA programmer, you can use Automation to alter views of the PivotTables and write Multidimensional Expressions (MDX), an extension to SQL, to create local .cub files. A more cogent reason for learning OLAP fundamentals, however, is to become conversant with OLAP terminology—dimensions, measures, fact/metrics tables, and hierarchies. As you design crosstab queries and work with Excel PivotTables or PivotTable lists, keep the OLAP lexicon in mind. Hopefully, the next version of Access will provide an integral connection to OLAP data sources via OLE DB for OLAP. Adding new OLAP-centric features will make Access a viable front-end development tool for all data sources employed in the enterprise.

--rj

USING ACCESS WITH MICROSOFT WORD AND MAIL MERGE

In this chapter

Integrating Access 2000 with Word 2000   782

Using the Access Mail Merge Wizard   782

Creating and Previewing a New Form Letter   782

Using an Existing Main Merge Document with a New Data Source   786

Using Word 2000's Mail Merge Feature with Access Databases   789

Creating a New Mail Merge Data Source with Microsoft Query and an ODBC Data Source   789

Creating Form Letters from an Existing Query   797

Embedding or Linking Word Documents in Access Tables   798

Creating a Form to Display the Embedded Document   802

Troubleshooting   804

In the Real World—Microsoft Query and OLE DB   805

INTEGRATING ACCESS 2000 WITH WORD 2000

Members of the Microsoft Office 2000 software suite are specifically designed to simplify the construction of cooperative applications. *Cooperative applications* use two or more Windows productivity applications to perform a specified task. One of the principal uses for database applications is creating mailing lists for use with form letters. Thus Access 2000—a member of the Professional and Premium editions of Microsoft Office 2000—includes a Mail Merge Wizard that not only automates the process of creating Word 2000 Merge data files but also helps you create new form letters.

You also can use the reverse process and create form letters by using Word 2000's mail merge process. Creating form letters from Word 2000 accommodates users who don't have Access 2000 on their computers. Word 2000 uses 32-bit Microsoft Query (Msqry32.exe) and the 32-bit Open Database Connectivity (ODBC) application programming interface (API) version 3.51 to connect to Access 2000 and earlier .mdb files, as well as to a variety of other desktop database types.

As with Excel worksheets, you can embed or link Word documents in bound or unbound object frames and add a complete word processing system to your Access application. If you embed the Word document in the object frame, you can take advantage of OLE 2.1's in-place activation to make the operating environment of Access almost identical to that of Word. Word's menu supplements the Access menu, and Word's toolbars appear as docked or floating toolbars on your display. Word's document editing window, in Page view, appears within the confines of your object frame.

USING THE ACCESS MAIL MERGE WIZARD

Access 2000's Mail Merge Wizard can help you create a new main merge document or employ an existing main merge document from which to create form letters. The Mail Merge Wizard uses a table or a query as the data source for the merge data file. The sections that follow describe two methods of creating a form letter:

- Using the Mail Merge Wizard to create a new main merge document whose merge data source is an Access table
- Using an existing main merge document with a merge data source from an Access select query

CREATING AND PREVIEWING A NEW FORM LETTER

When you first try a new wizard, it's customary to create a new object rather than use the wizard to modify an existing object, such as a main merge document. The following steps use the Mail Merge Wizard to create a new main merge document from records in the Customers table of Northwind.mdb.

1. Open Northwind.mdb, if necessary, and select the Customers table in the Database window.

2. Click the arrow of the Office Links button of the toolbar and select Merge-It from the drop-down menu to launch the Microsoft Mail Merge Wizard. Its first and only dialog is shown in Figure 21.1.

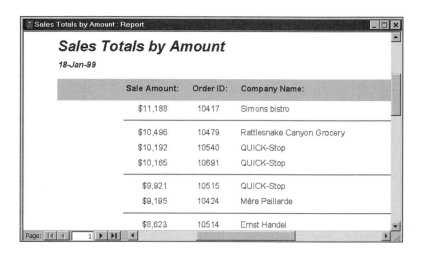

Figure 21.1
The sole dialog of the Microsoft Word Mail Merge Wizard.

3. Select the Create a New Document and Then Link the Data to It option to create a new main merge document using fields from the Customers table.

4. Click OK to launch Word 2000 if it isn't running, Word opens a new mail merge main document. (The Mail Merge Wizard uses dynamic data exchange (DDE) to communicate with Access 2000.)

5. Click the Insert Merge Field button to verify the fields from the Customers table in the drop-down list, as shown in Figure 21.2.

6. With the caret at the top of the document, choose Insert, Date and Time to display the Date and Time dialog; choose any date format you want and then click OK to add a date field to the main document.

Tip #182 from

¶ In Word 2000 click the Show/Hide button on Word's toolbar to display end-of-paragraph marks, space characters, tab characters, and other document symbols that are usually hidden. All figures of Word 2000 in this chapter were taken with the Show/Hide button in its down position.

PART
V

Cʜ
21

7. Add a blank line, click the Insert Merge Field button to display the drop-down list, and insert the CompanyName, Address, City, Region, PostalCode, ContactName, and ContactTotle fields from the Customers table to create the address section of the main document (see Figure 21.3).

Figure 21.2
Displaying the available merge fields in Word 2000's mail merge window.

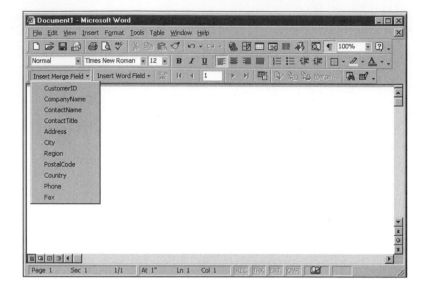

Figure 21.3
Adding the merge fields to the main merge document.

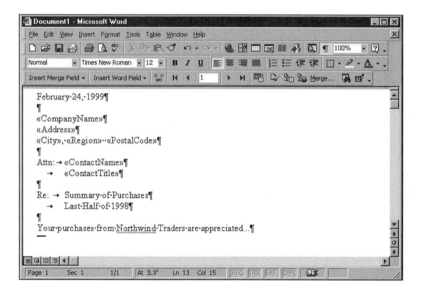

Note

Word doesn't permit spaces and other punctuation in merge data field names. The Mail Merge Wizard substitutes underscores (_) for spaces and other illegal characters in Access field names, when present.

 8. Click the View Merged Data button of the Mail Merge toolbar to preview the appearance of the first of your form letters.

Click the Find Record button of the toolbar, type **USA** in the Find What text box, and select Country from the In Field drop-down list. Click OK to find the first U.S. record.

9. The form letters go only to customers in the United States, so repeatedly click the Next Record button of the Mail Merge toolbar to find the first U.S. record. Alternatively, type **32** in the text box of the toolbar. The preview of the form letter for Great Lakes Food Market appears as shown in Figure 21.4.

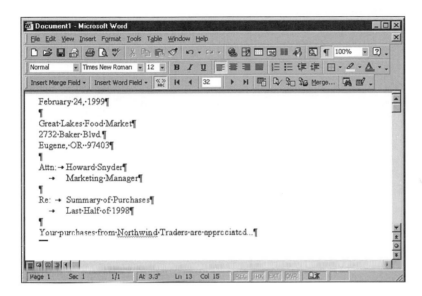

Figure 21.4
Previewing a form letter to a U.S. customer.

10. To send letters to U.S. customers, you need to create a query that returns only records whose Country column has the value "USA." Close Word and save your main merge document with an appropriate file name, such as **PurchaseSummary1998H2.doc**. This file is used in the next section, as well as later in the chapter when you open the Access data source from Word.

The Mail Merge Wizard uses DDE to communicate with Word, so you can't use Word 2000's query features to select and sort the merge data. If you attempt to do so, you break the DDE link between Word and Access. Thus you need to base your final mail merge document on an Access query if you want to select or sort your records.

PART
V

CH
21

USING AN EXISTING MAIN MERGE DOCUMENT WITH A NEW DATA SOURCE

After you create a standard main merge document, the most common practice is to use differing data sources to create form letters by addressee category. Take the following steps to use the main mail merge document you created in the preceding section, PurchaseSummary1997H2.doc, with a new data source based on a simple Access query:

1. Open a new query and add the Customers table.

2. Add the CompanyName, Address, City, Region, PostalCode, Country, ContactName, and ContactTitle, fields to the query.

3. Type **USA** as the criterion for the Country field and clear the Show check box to prevent Country from appearing in the query. Add an ascending sort to the PostalCode field. Your query design appears as shown in Figure 21.5.

Figure 21.5
The query design for a mailing list of U.S. customers.

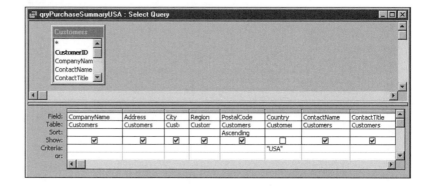

4. Click the Run button of the toolbar to verify the query result set (see Figure 21.6). Choose File, Save or Save As, and save the query with an appropriate name, such as **qryPurchaseSummaryUSA**.

Figure 21.6
The query result set for U.S.-based customers.

Company Name	Address	City	Region	Postal Code
The Cracker Box	55 Grizzly Peak Rd.	Butte	MT	59801
Split Rail Beer & Ale	P.O. Box 555	Lander	WY	82520
Save-a-lot Markets	187 Suffolk Ln.	Boise	ID	83720
Rattlesnake Canyon Grocery	2817 Milton Dr.	Albuquerque	NM	87110
Let's Stop N Shop	87 Polk St.	San Francisco	CA	94117
The Big Cheese	89 Jefferson Way	Portland	OR	97201
Lonesome Pine Restaurant	89 Chiaroscuro Rd.	Portland	OR	97219
Great Lakes Food Market	2732 Baker Blvd.	Eugene	OR	97403
Hungry Coyote Import Store	City Center Plaza	Elgin	OR	97827
Trail's Head Gourmet Provisioners	722 DaVinci Blvd.	Kirkland	WA	98034
White Clover Markets	305 - 14th Ave. S.	Seattle	WA	98128
Lazy K Kountry Store	12 Orchestra Terrace	Walla Walla	WA	99362
Old World Delicatessen	2743 Bering St.	Anchorage	AK	99508

Record: 1 of 13

Tip #183 from

RJ

> You must save the query before attempting to start the merge operation. If you don't save the query, you receive a "The source object for the for the Mail Merge Wizard must be a table or query" error message.

 5. With the query open, choose Tools, Office Links, Merge It with MS Word to launch the Mail Merge Wizard. With the Link Your Data to an Existing Microsoft Word Document option marked (the default), click OK to display the Select Microsoft Word Document dialog (see Figure 21.7).

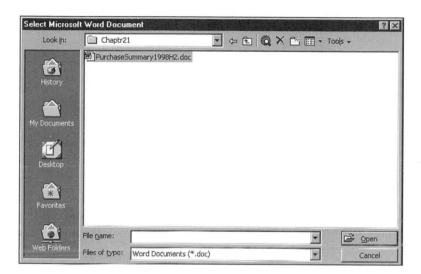

Figure 21.7
Selecting the main merge document.

6. Select your main merge document in the file list and click Open. After a few seconds for reading records, a message box, shown in Figure 21.8, appears when you change the data source for a merge document. Click Yes to change to the new data source.

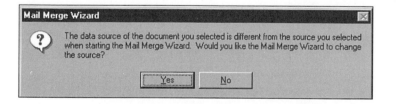

Figure 21.8
The message box that appears when you change the merge data source.

PART
V

CH
21

Tip #184 from

RJ

> If you attempt to connect to an open document, you receive a "File in Use" error message. Click Cancel, and then click OK when the "Command Failed" error message appears. Close the merge document, and try again.

7. Confirm that your query is the new merge data source by clicking the Insert Merge Field button and checking the field list. (The Country field shouldn't appear.)

Alternatively, you can click the Edit Data Source button on Word's Mail Merge toolbar to display the query in Access, as shown in Figure 21.9. (Click the Minimize button on Access's Query window and then click the Word document to return the focus to Word.)

Figure 21.9
Displaying the query result set from Word.

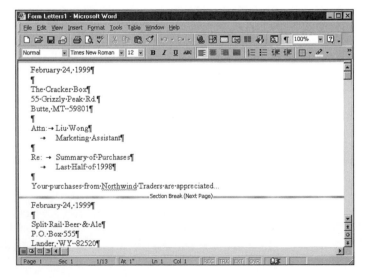

8. You can merge the main document and data source directly to the printer or create a series of form letters in a new document. The latter choice lets you inspect the letters before you print them. Click the Merge to New Document button to create the new form letter. The top of the first form letter appears as shown in Figure 21.10.

Figure 21.10
The final version of the form letter addressed to U.S. customers.

If you close Word at this point, make sure you save your changes to PurchaseSummary 1998H2.doc. The following sections use this file as the main merge document.

USING WORD 2000'S MAIL MERGE FEATURE WITH ACCESS DATABASES

In many cases, Access 2000 isn't available to Word users who need to create form letters from data contained in Access .mdb files. Office 2000 includes Microsoft Query and the necessary 32-bit ODBC drivers to connect to Access .mdb files, Excel spreadsheets, Microsoft SQL Server OLAP Services, SQL Server, Oracle, Foxpro, and text databases. Microsoft Query is modeled on Access's Query Design window, but Microsoft Query displays the query result set automatically in a separate pane below the design pane as you construct the query. Office 2000 applications launch and control Microsoft Query with DDE.

Note

> You need to have Microsoft Office 2000 installed on your PC to create the examples in this section. Access 2000 and Jet 4.0 require the 32-bit ODBC 4.0 drivers. Office 2000 includes the 32-bit ODBC driver for Access 2000 databases, Odbcjt32.dll.

Word 2000 includes the Mail Merge Helper, which is similar in concept to an Access wizard. The following three sections use the Mail Merge Helper to create a new Microsoft Query (MSQuery) data source and to use an existing MSQuery data source.

CREATING A NEW MAIL MERGE DATA SOURCE WITH MICROSOFT QUERY AND AN ODBC DATA SOURCE

Note

> ODBC and Microsoft Query must be installed on your computer system before you can use the procedures described in this and the following sections of this chapter. If ODBC and MSQuery aren't installed on your computer, rerun the Microsoft Office 2000 Setup program and add these items to your system configuration.

To use Microsoft Query (MSQuery) to create a merge data source from a Microsoft Access database, follow these steps:

1. Launch Word 2000, if necessary, and open the PurchaseSummary1997H2.doc main merge document you created earlier in this chapter in the section "Creating and Previewing a New Form Letter."

2. Click the Mail Merge Helper button of the mail merge toolbar to open the Mail Merge Helper dialog (see Figure 21.11). The entry in the Data label of the Data Source section is Northwind.mdb!Query qryPurchaseSummaryUSA. This syntax is used for specifying the topic of a DDE conversation when you use Access as a DDE server.

Figure 21.11
The Mail Merge Helper
dialog with an Access
DDE merge data
source specified.

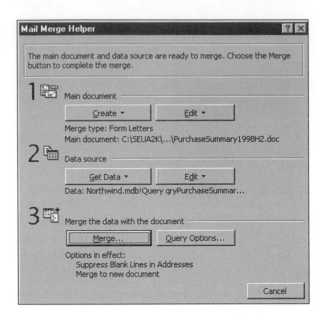

3. Click the Get Data button and select Create Data Source from the drop-down list to open the Create Data Source dialog. Word includes a set of default field names you can use to create merge data files (see Figure 21.12).

Figure 21.12
Word 2000's Create
Data Source dialog.

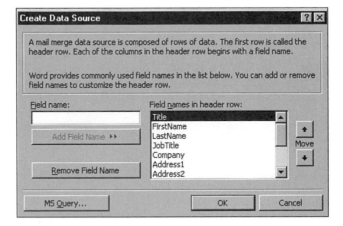

4. This example uses MSQuery to create the data source, so click the MS Query button to launch MSQuery. When MSQuery opens, the Choose Data Source dialog is active (see Figure 21.13).

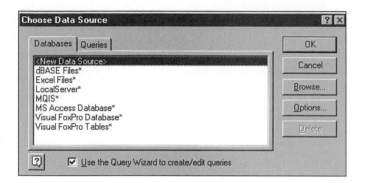

Figure 21.13
MSQuery's Choose
Data Source dialog.

5. Click the Databases tab to bring the Databases list to the front of the dialog (if necessary); select <New Data Source> in the Databases list and then click OK. MSQuery displays the Create New Data Source dialog (see Figure 21.14).

The Create New Data Source dialog contains four numbered controls: a text box, a drop-down list, a command button, and another drop-down list. When MSQuery first displays the Create New Data Source dialog, only the first text box is enabled. Each successive control is enabled as you complete each item. Figure 21.14 shows the Create New Data Source dialog after filling in all options for this data source. Each numbered control corresponds to an item of information that you must supply for MSQuery to create the data source: the data source's name, the driver for the data source, connection information for connecting to the data source, and an optional default table for the data source.

Figure 21.14
MSQuery's Create New
Data Source dialog.

PART

V

CH

21

6. In the first text box, type **PurchaseSummaryUSA** as the name of the new data source. As you type the data source name, MSQuery enables the drop-down list below it.

7. In the drop-down list (item 2 in the Create New Data Source dialog), select Microsoft Access Driver (*.mdb) as the driver for this data source.

8. Click the Connect button to display the ODBC Microsoft Access Setup dialog (see Figure 21.15). Click the Select button in the Database frame to display the Select Database dialog.

→ For detailed information on completing ODBC Data Sources, **see** "Linking Excel Worksheets," **p. 256**.

9. Maneuver to the folder containing Northwind.mdb (usually C:\Program Files\Microsoft Office\Office\Samples) and select Northwind.mdb (see Figure 21.15). Click OK to return to the ODBC Microsoft Access Setup dialog.

Figure 21.15
Choosing the connection for a new MSQuery data source.

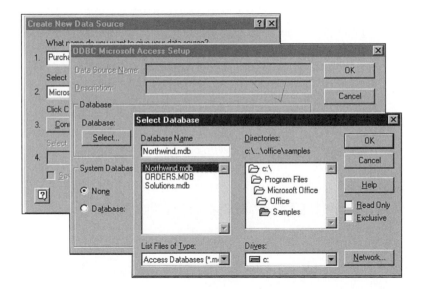

10. If you have secured Access or Northwind.mdb, click the Database option button in the System Database frame; then click the System Database button to open the System Database dialog. Select the System Database you're using and click OK to close the dialog. Click the Advanced button to open the Advanced dialog and then type your logon name and password in the text boxes. Click OK to close the Advanced dialog.

11. Click OK to close the ODBC Microsoft Access Setup dialog. The Create New Data Source dialog now displays the connected database's folder path and file name (or as much of it as will fit) next to the Connect button.

12. Optionally, you can select a table or query from the connected database as the default table for queries created from this data source. In the final drop-down list (item 4 in the Create New Data Source dialog), select Customers (refer to Figure 21.14).

13. Click OK to close the Create New Data Source dialog. MSQuery adds the newly created data source to the Databases list in the Choose Data Source dialog.

14. Select PurchaseSummaryUSA in the Databases list of the Choose Data Source dialog and click OK. MSQuery automatically starts its Query Wizard; the first dialog of the Query Wizard is shown in Figure 21.16.

    The Choose Columns dialog of the Query Wizard displays an expandable tree list of all tables and queries in the connected database, with the default table or query's branch selected and expanded for you as shown in Figure 21.16.

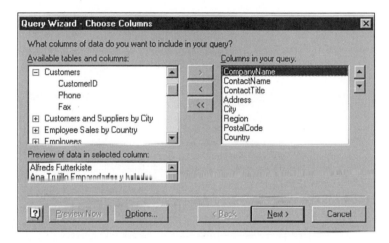

Figure 21.16
MSQuery's Query Wizard dialog in which you select the columns for the new query.

15. Select the CompanyName field in the Available Tables and Columns list; then click the > button to copy the CompanyName field to the Columns in Your Query list.

16. Repeat step 15 to add the ContactName, ContactTitle, Address, City, Region, PostalCode, and Country fields to the Columns in Your Query list (see Figure 21.16). The specific order of the columns is unimportant. Click Next to continue with the second Query Wizard dialog.

17. In the second step of the Query Wizard, you type criteria to restrict the data retrieved by MSQuery (see Figure 21.17). Select the Country field in the Column to Filter list, select **equals** in the first drop-down list in the Only Include Rows Where frame, and select **USA** in the second drop-down list (refer to Figure 21.17). Click Next.

PART

V

CH

21

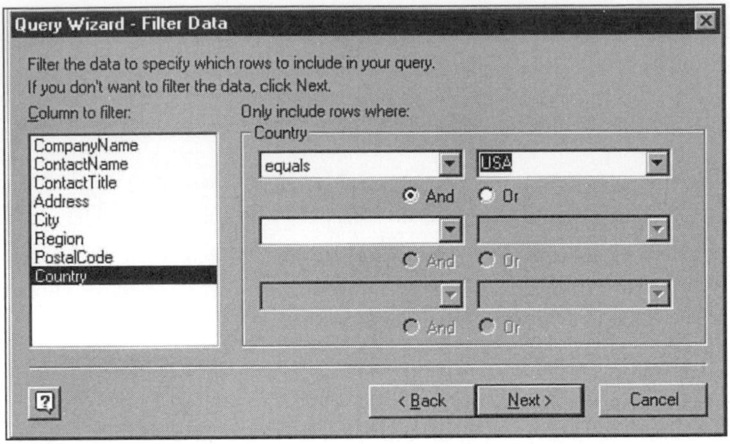

Figure 21.17
The Filter Data dialog
of MSQuery's Query
Wizard.

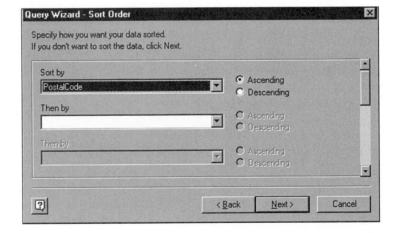

18. In the Query Wizard's Sort Order dialog, you select how you want to sort the retrieved data. Select **PostalCode** in the first drop-down list; MSQuery automatically selects the Ascending option (see Figure 21.18). Click Next.

Figure 21.18
The Sort Order dialog
of MSQuery's Query
Wizard.

19. Select the View Data or Edit Query in Microsoft Query option and then click Finish to complete the query (see Figure 21.19). Although you can immediately return data to Word or click the Save Query button to save your query, you should usually take a look at the finished query to make sure that it produces the results you desire.

The completed query is shown in Figure 21.20; notice that the MSQuery query design grid resembles the query design grid in Access. The only difference is that MSQuery shows the query's results in a table underneath the criteria rows. Use the scroll bars to view the data returned by the query. You can add or edit criteria in MSQuery much as you add or edit selection criteria in an Access query. MSQuery, however, uses single quotation marks (') for literal strings (as shown in Figure 21.20) instead of the double quotation marks (") used by Access.

Another difference between MSQuery and Access is that MSQuery does not have a Sort row in the query design grid. Instead, in MSQuery you sort rows by selecting a column in the query's result and then clicking one of the sort order buttons on the toolbar. Essentially, the process in MSQuery is the same as sorting a table's view in Access.

Figure 21.19
The final dialog of MSQuery's Query Wizard.

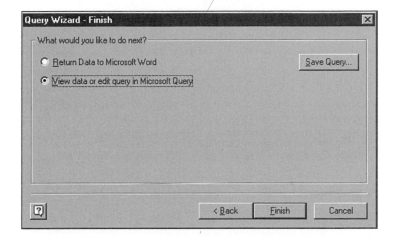

Figure 21.20
The completed query in MSQuery.

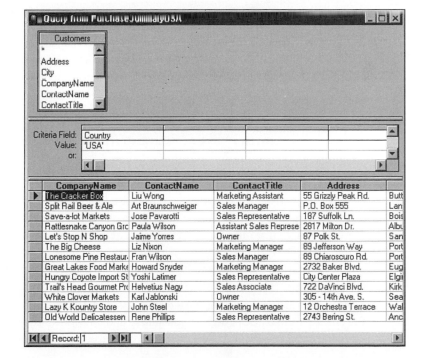

20. Choose Edit, Options to open the Options dialog, and clear the Qualify Table Names in SQL Statement check box, as shown in Figure 21.21 (top), then click OK to close the dialog.

Caution

If you don't clear the Qualify Table Names in SQL Statement check box, you're likely to encounter a "Could not merge the main document with the data source because the data records were empty or no data records matched your query options" error when you return to the Mail Merge Helper in step 23.

Figure 21.21
Clearing the Qualify Table Names in SQL Statement check box in the Options dialog (top), and the result of clearing the check box in the SQL dialog (bottom).

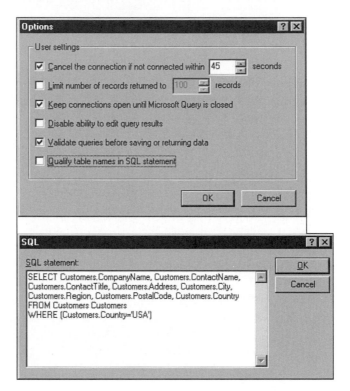

21. Click the SQL button to open the SQL dialog. Clearing the Qualify Table Names in SQL Statement check box doesn't remove the table name qualifiers (prefixes), such as Customers in Customers.CompanyName, but it does remove the reference to Northwind.mdb from the SQL FROM clause. After verifying that 'c:\Program Files\Microsoft Office\Office\Sample\Northwind'.Customers no longer appears in the SQL statement, as shown in Figure 21.21 (bottom), click OK to close the SQL dialog.

22. Choose File, Save to open the Save dialog. Assign a name, such as **PurchaseSummaryUSA.dqy**, to your query and click Save. By default, queries are saved in the \Application Data\Microsoft\Queries folder of your Windows directory.

You use the saved query in the section that follows, "Creating Form Letters from an Existing Query."

23. Choose File, Return Data to Microsoft Word to close MSQuery and return to the Mail Merge Helper. The entry in the Data label of the Data Source section is now C:\Program Files\Microsoft Office\Office\Samples\Northwind.mdb. Click the Merge button of Mail Merge Helper to open the Merge dialog.

24. Accept the default New Document selection in the Merge To drop-down list. Click the Check Errors button of the Merge dialog to display the Checking and Reporting Errors dialog. Click the Complete the Merge, Pausing to Report Each Error as It Occurs option (see Figure 21.22).

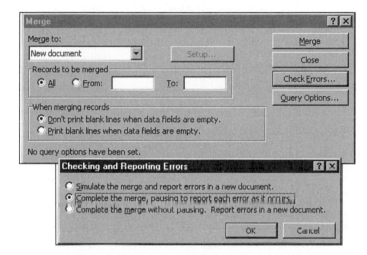

Figure 21.22
The Merge dialog and the Checking and Reporting Errors dialog.

25. Click OK to close the Checking and Reporting Errors dialog and click Merge to perform the merge. Word finishes merging the document and displays the first of the final form letters. After reviewing the form letters, close the form letters document; you don't need to save changes.

CREATING FORM LETTERS FROM AN EXISTING QUERY

After you create and save a query with MSQuery, you can use the saved query to create another set of form letters. MSQuery's saved queries are similar to Access queries saved as QueryDef objects in .mdb files. To use an existing .dqy file as the data source for a merge document, follow these steps:

PART

V

CH

21

Note

Versions of MSQuery prior to Office 97 saved queries in files with the .qry file extension. MSQuery in Office 97 and 2000 uses the .dqy file extension instead.

1. In Word 2000, click the Mail Merge Helper button to display the dialog.
2. Click the Get Data button and select Open Data Source from the drop-down list to display the Open Data Source dialog.
3. Choose the MS Query Files (*.dqy) item in the Files of Type drop-down list.
4. Select the PurchaseSummaryUSA.dqy file you saved in step 20 of the preceding section and click Open (see Figure 21.23). The message box shown in Figure 21.24 appears.

Figure 21.23
Choosing an existing MSQuery .dqy file in the Open Data Source dialog.

Figure 21.24
Making the .dqy file the permanent source of data for the main merge document.

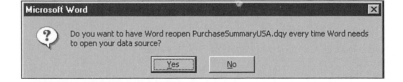

5. To make PurchaseSummary.dqy the permanent source of data for the PurchaseSummary1997H1.doc main merge document, click the Yes button of the message box to return to the Mail Merge Helper dialog. The path to and the name of your query file appear in the Data label of the Data Source section.

EMBEDDING OR LINKING WORD DOCUMENTS IN ACCESS TABLES

Many word processing documents are a collection of individual paragraphs, each of which may change depending on the purpose of the document. If the document is a contract, many of the paragraphs are likely to be *boilerplate*: standard paragraphs that are added based on the jurisdiction and purpose of the contract and relationship between the parties.

Similarly, books are collections of chapters; when an author is writing a book, each chapter may go through several editing stages. Keeping track of boilerplate files and maintaining collections of book chapter files in various editing stages can be a daunting project. Even if you establish a workable DOS file-naming convention, you can easily lose track of the relationship between the file name and the content of the file.

Applications that track documents and maintain revision records for documents fall into the category of *document management systems*. Document management systems differ from image management systems; the latter systems handle static bitmapped images (usually created by scanners) rather than dynamic document content (editable data). With its OLE 2.1 capability, Access 2000 is a logical candidate for the creation of document management applications.

You can create a simple document management system by designing a table with one or more fields of the OLE Object data type to contain embedded documents or links to individual document files. You need a minimum of two other fields: one to identify the source file name of the document and the other to provide a document description. You can use additional fields to indicate document ownership, track document status, hold key terms, and control who can modify the document. Figure 21.25 shows the design of a simple table that stores the manuscript of this edition in the form of individual chapters in an OLE Object field.

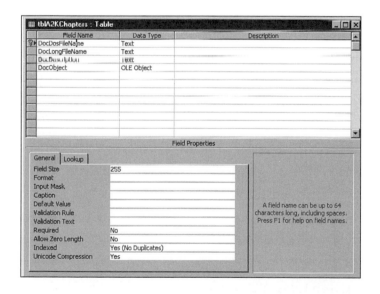

Figure 21.25
The design of the table for a simple document management system.

After you define the fields for your document table, you need to determine whether you want to embed the document's data in the table or link the documents to their source files. Make your choice based on the following criteria:

- Embedding the document lets you use in-place activation to review the document within Access. In-place activation is the less-intrusive process.

- Activating a linked document launches Word 2000 in its own window.

- Embedding the document provides an independent copy of the document that can serve as an archive. You can set the value of the Locked property of the object to Yes to allow the object to be activated but not altered.

- Linking the document lets you view changes to the document as they occur.

- Linking requires that the document remain in the same location. In most cases, moving the document to another drive or directory breaks the link.

- You can't save an embedded Word 2000 or Excel 2000 document to a file or print the embedded document using File menu choices in the in-place activated mode. The file menus of these applications don't replace the File menu of Access 2000 when the embedded objects are activated. However, you can open Word's window to make the Word File menu accessible.

Tip #187 from

R J

You can use Automation instructions in VBA modules to save an embedded Word 2000 document to a file or to print the document. The Object property of the object frame lets you manipulate embedded or linked objects with VBA code.

EMBEDDING OR LINKING A WORD 2000 DOCUMENT IN A TABLE

To embed or link a Word 2000 document in an OLE Object field of a table with a design similar to that shown in Figure 21.25, follow these steps:

1. Place the caret in the OLE Object field and then choose Insert, Object to display the Insert Object dialog (see Figure 21.26).

2. You can create an empty Word document by accepting the default, Create New, and then clicking OK. To link or embed an existing document, click the Create from File option; the Object Type list changes to the File text box. (You don't need to select Microsoft Word Document when you insert an object from a file.)

3. You can type the path and file name in the File text box or click the Browse button to display the Browse dialog (see Figure 21.27). Select the file you want to use in the File Name list and then click Open to close the Browse dialog and return to the Insert Object dialog.

4. The file you selected in the preceding step appears in the File text box. At this point, you can choose between linking and embedding the file. The example that follows uses embedded objects to demonstrate in-place activation (see Figure 21.28). If you want to link the file, mark the Link text box. Click OK.

5. Position the record selector of the table to a different record to save the embedded object or the link to the object's file in your table, together with its OLE presentation.

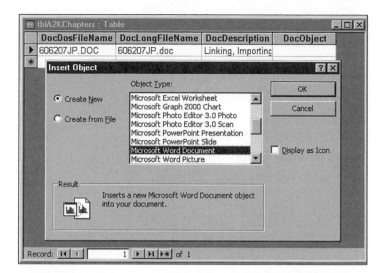

Figure 21.26
The Insert Object dialog.

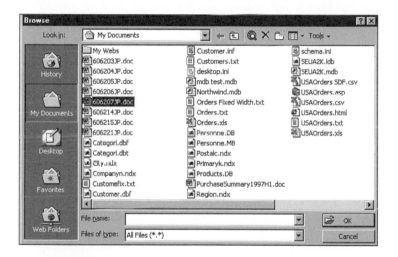

Figure 21.27
Selecting a source document file in the Browse dialog.

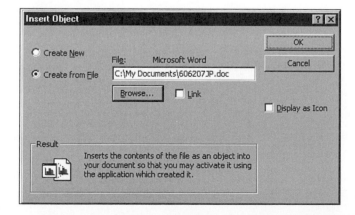

Figure 21.28
Embedding a Word 2000 document object from a file.

Repeat steps 1 to 5 for each document you want to add to the table. You can activate the document object in Word 2000's window by double-clicking the OLE Object cell. Viewing the documents you insert in the file lets you verify that their contents correspond to their description.

 If you don't find a Microsoft Word Document item in the list, see the "Missing OLE Server Registry Entries" topic of the "Troubleshooting" section near the end of this chapter.

CREATING A FORM TO DISPLAY THE EMBEDDED DOCUMENT

If your table contains only a few fields, you can use the AutoForm feature to create a simple form to display and edit your linked or embedded object. To create the document display form, follow these steps:

 1. With the table containing your Word objects open with the focus in Datasheet view, click the arrow of the New Object button of the toolbar and select AutoForm from the drop-down menu. The Form Wizard automatically creates a standard form.

 2. Click the Design View button of the toolbar and then relocate and resize the controls as necessary. Your bound object frame should occupy most of the display area. To view the entire document in its original format, set the Height property of the object frame to 11 inches and the Width property to 8.5 inches.

 3. Return to Form view to display the presentation of the document. Figure 21.29 shows the presentation of the initial version of the manuscript for this chapter of the book. The size of the bound object frame of Figure 21.29 is about 8.5×11 inches.

Figure 21.29
The presentation of a Word 2000 document in a bound object frame.

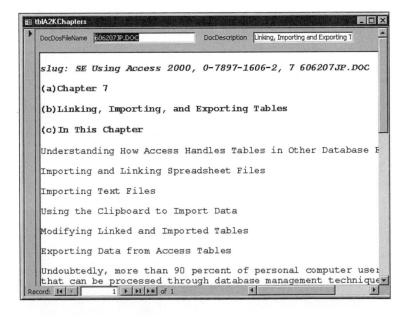

4. Double-click the surface of the object frame to activate the object. Activating the object launches Word 2000 if it isn't running. If you embedded the document, activation adds

Word's toolbars to the display as docked toolbars. Word's menu choices take over Access's Edit and View menus, and Word adds its Insert, Format, Tools, and Table menus to the menubar (see Figure 21.30).

You can move through the document with the Page Up and Page Down keys. All editing features of Word 2000 are available when the document object is activated, but you can only view the document in Page Layout view. You may use the scroll bar of the Access form to view parts of the page that aren't visible on your display. (Using 800-×-600-pixel or higher resolution solves the partial display problem.)

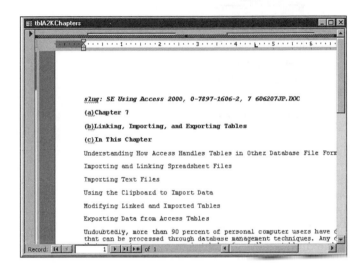

Figure 21.30
An embedded Word 2000 document activated in a bound object frame.

5. Click the surface of the form, outside the bound object frame area, to deactivate the object and return to Presentation view of the document.

6. To save the document to a file, to alter the page layout, or to print an embedded document, choose Edit, Document Object and select Open. Microsoft Word opens a separate window in which to edit the embedded document, and you can access the File menu of Word to save changes, as shown in Figure 21.31.

7. Choose File, Close and Return to *FormName* to close Word's window and return to Access.

PART
V
CH
21

Figure 21.31
Opening the embedded document in
Word a 2000 window.

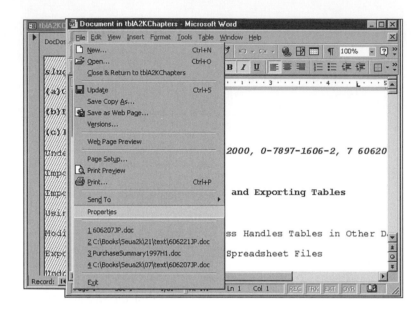

> ▶* You also can insert additional document objects directly into the form. To embed or link an
> object in Form view, position the record pointer on the blank (tentative append) record. An
> empty presentation appears in the bound object frame. Choose Insert, Object and follow
> steps 2 through 5 of the preceding section to embed or link additional document objects.

TROUBLESHOOTING

MISSING OLE SERVER REGISTRY ENTRIES

*The Microsoft Word Document entry doesn't appear in the Insert Object dialog's Object Type list, or
attempting to insert a Word document results in a message box stating that the registration database
entry is invalid or corrupted.*

The Registry entries for Word 2000 are missing or invalid. If the Word 2000 entry is missing, Word's Setup program probably did not complete its operation. (The last step of Setup adds entries to the Registry.) If the "corrupted" message appears, it is likely that you moved the Word files from the original directory in which Setup installed the files into a different directory. In either case, close Access, open Word, and choose Help, Detect and Repair to open the Detect and Repair dialog. With an active network connection to the installation server share or the Office 2000 distribution CD-ROM 1 in the drive, click Start to initiate the process.

IN THE REAL WORLD—MICROSOFT QUERY AND OLE DB

Microsoft Query arrived in the era of Access 1.0, and has changed only in minor respects over the years. Microsoft Query's layout clearly derives from the Access query design window. Microsoft Query is one of the few remaining Office-related tools that relies on DDE—instead of COM-based Automation—for interprocess communication. Access's Mail Merge Wizard is the other tool in which use of DDE appears to be cast in concrete. Continuing to employ DDE when "COM Everywhere" is Microsoft's rallying cry is another good example of not fixing an unbroken technology. This chapter introduced you to Microsoft Query, creating a tenuous connection to the following discussion of the product's new OLE DB feature.

Excel 2000 depends on Query 2000 (Q2K, Msqry32.exe) to connect to databases, and previous versions of Microsoft Query relied on ODBC drivers for database connections. Q2K now offers support for OLE DB for OLAP, but only when you open Q2K from within Excel 2000 by choosing Data, PivotTable or PivotChart Report or Data, Get External Data, New Database Query. Figure 21.32 shows the OLAP Cubes page of the Q2K's Choose Data Sources dialog. (Refer to Figure 21.13 for the appearance of the dialog when you open Q2K from Word or in standalone mode.

Figure 21.32
The OLAP Cube page of Microsoft Query 2000's Choose Data Sources dialog opened from Excel's PivotTable Wizard.

If you have a network connection to an installation of Microsoft OLAP Services for SQL Server, you can connect to the sample FoodMart OLAP database. Double-click the <New Data Source> item to open a Create New Data Source dialog similar to that for ODBC data sources. Type a name for your data source in text box 1, select the Microsoft OLE DB Provider for OLAP Services from list 2, click Connect, accept the default OLAP Server option. Next, type the server name in the Multi-Dimensional Connection dialog, and click Next to select the FoodMart database. Click Finish to return to the Create New Data Source dialog, select the Sales cube of FoodMart in list 3 (see Figure 21.33).

PART

V

CH

21

Figure 21.33
Specifying the name,
OLE DB for OLAP
provider, database,
and data cube in the
Create New Data
Source dialog.

Clicking OK returns you to the Choose Data Source dialog with your new OLAP data
source selected. Click OK, Next and Finish to open Excel with an empty PivotTable sheet.
Drag the fields from the PivotTable dialog to rows, columns, and data to create the hierarchical display of Store Country, Store Type, Store Sales, and Store Sales Net shown in
Figure 21.34. It's unfortunate that the PivotTable dialog isn't a resizable window to better
display dimension names as button captions, but tooltips overcome the truncated name
problem.

Figure 21.34
Designing the
PivotTable from the
data cube.

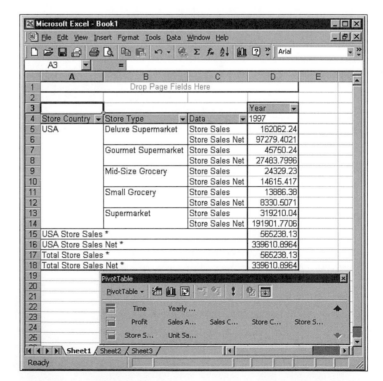

This "In the Real World" section isn't meant to be an exhaustive discussion of the subject of Q2K or OLAP tables; it's simply a shortcut to understanding the role of Q2K and to encourage your investigation of OLAP PivotTables. If you don't have OLAP Services installed, you can work with a local .cub file. Check the Microsoft Web site's OLAP pages at `http://www.microsoft.com/data/oledb/olap/` for downloadable .cub files to test. (The BobsVid.cub file included with the Microsoft Data Access SDK 2.0 doesn't work with the current OLE DB for OLAP provider version.)

--rj

USING ADVANCED ACCESS TECHNIQUES

22 Exploring Relational Database Design and Implementation   811

23 Working with Structured Query Language   851

24 Securing Multiuser Network Applications   885

25 Creating Access Data Projects   943

EXPLORING RELATIONAL DATABASE DESIGN AND IMPLEMENTATION

In this chapter

Reviewing Access 2000's New Database Design Features   812

Integrating Objects and Relational Databases   813

Understanding Database Systems   813

Data Modeling   821

Normalizing Data to the Relational Model   825

Using Access 2000's Table Analyzer Wizard   836

Generating a Data Dictionary with the Database Documenter   841

Using Access Indexes   844

Enforcing Database Integrity   844

Troubleshooting   849

In the Real World—Why Learn Relational Theory?   849

REVIEWING ACCESS 2000'S NEW DATABASE DESIGN FEATURES

You were introduced to a few of the elements of relational database design when you created the Personnel Actions table and joined it with the Employees table of the Northwind Traders database in Chapter 10, "Creating Multitable and Crosstab Queries." However, when you're presented with the challenge of designing a database from ground zero—especially a complex or potentially complex database—you need to understand the theory of relational database design and its terminology.

NEW 2000 Following are the new database structure and design features introduced by Access 2000's Jet 4.0 database engine:

- *Full support for Unicode.* Unicode, which stores all text characters in two data bytes, simplifies localizing (creating international versions) of Access databases and applications. An unfortunate side-effect of Unicode is a substantial increase in the size of text-heavy tables.

- *4KB pages replace 2KB pages.* The larger page size is required to maintain performance with the increased table size resulting from Unicode. 4KB pages increase the maximum database size from 1GB to 2.1GB.

- *Row-level locking for Recordsets.* Row locking reduces conflicts when multiple users UPDATE or INSERT records in the same data page. Row locking becomes more important as page size increases.

- *Lock escalation.* When an excessive number of row locks would be required for a large UPDATE or INSERT operation, Jet 4.0 attempts to place a temporary exclusive lock on the entire table.

- *Foreign keys without indexes.* Enforcing referential integrity in prior versions of Access required indexes on both primary and foreign keys. Foreign key indexes slow the addition of new records. Foreign key indexes are optional in Access 2000.

- *Ability to modify AutoNumber field properties.* You can set the SEED (starting value) and INCREMENT properties of AutoNumber (IDENTITY) fields with a Jet CREATE TABLE SQL statement. You can change the AutoNumber properties of existing tables with ALTER TABLE.

The Microsoft Data Engine (MSDE) adds a new dimension to database design and implementation in Access 2000. This chapter uses Jet 4.0 for its examples, but the database design techniques you learn are equally applicable to MSDE and SQL Server 7.0 databases. The principal difference between designing databases with Jet and MSDE is the user interface to the database engine. Jet uses the familiar Access database design model; MSDE and SQL Server 7.0 use the graphical MS Design Tools to create new databases and add database objects, such as tables, indexes, views, and stored procedures. MSDE is the primary subject of Chapter 25, "Creating Access Data Projects."

INTEGRATING OBJECTS AND RELATIONAL DATABASES

This chapter takes a step back and starts with the definition of data objects and how you identify them. Because Access is an object-enabled database development tool, the concepts of database design presented in this chapter have an object-oriented bent. The reason for this approach is two-fold:

- Jet 4.0 relational tables incorporate many of the features of client/server databases. Properties, such as validation rules and indexes, that prevent duplicate primary key entries, are combined in the table object. Details of relationships between tables and methods of enforcing referential integrity are stored in the database object.

- VBA treats the database itself and each of Access's database elements—tables, queries, forms, and reports—as programming objects.

After you've identified the data objects that are to be included in the tables of your database, you next design the tables to contain the data objects. You use a process called data *normalization* to create tables that conform to the relational database model. Normalization is the process of eliminating duplicate information in tables by extracting the duplicate data to new tables that contain records with unique data values. You then join the new tables by fields with common data values to create a relational database structure. Normalizing data is the subject of the "Normalizing Data to the Relational Model" section, later in this chapter.

The role of indexes in maintaining unique values in primary-key fields and organizing data tables was described briefly in preceding chapters. This chapter provides a brief explanation of how indexes are constructed and maintained by Access 2000 and the Jet 4.0 database engine. Properly designed indexes improve the performance of your applications without consuming excessive amounts of disk space or slowing the appending of new records to a crawl.

This chapter also deals with the rules that establish and maintain referential integrity—one of the most important considerations in designing a database. Referential integrity enforces uniqueness in primary keys and prevents the occurrence of orphaned records, such as records of invoices whose customer data records have been deleted.

UNDERSTANDING DATABASE SYSTEMS

Prior to this chapter, you've used the Northwind Traders demonstration database, created a few simple databases, and perhaps imported your own data in another database format into an Access 2000 table. No formal theories were presented to aid or hinder your understanding of the underlying design of the database examples. Now that you've gained some experience using Access, the more theoretical concepts of database design should be easier to understand.

This section takes a systems approach to database design, starting with a generalized set of objectives, outlining the steps necessary to accomplish the objectives, and then explaining the theory and practice behind each step.

THE OBJECTIVES OF DATABASE DESIGN

The strategy of database design is to accomplish the following objectives:

- Fulfill your needs or the needs of the organization for information in a timely, consistent, and economical manner.

- Eliminate or minimize the duplication of database content across the organization. In a large organization, eliminating duplication may require a distributed database. Distributed databases use multiple servers to store individual databases. The individual databases are linked to one another (to use Access terminology) through a local area network (LAN) or wide area network (WAN) so that they appear as a single database to the user.

- Provide rapid access to the specific elements of information in the database required by each user category. Operating speed is a function of the relational database management system (RDBMS) itself, the design of the applications you create, the capabilities of the server and client computers, and network characteristics.

- Accommodate database expansion to adapt to the needs of a growing organization, such as adding new products and processes, complying with governmental reporting requirements, and incorporating new transaction-processing and decision-support applications.

- Maintain the integrity of the database so that it contains only validated, auditable information. Most client/server databases, MSDE and SQL Server, provide built-in triggers to maintain database integrity and perform other operations. Triggers are sets of rules that are included in the database. If you violate a rule, the trigger sends an error message instead of executing the transaction. The Enforce Referential Integrity check box in Access's Relationships dialog, combined with field-level and table-level validation rules, creates the equivalent of a trigger.

- Prevent access to the database by unauthorized persons. Access provides a security system that requires users to enter a password to open a particular database.

- Permit access only to those elements of the database information that individual users or categories of users need in the course of their work. You can permit or deny users the right to view the data in specific tables of the database based on their username and password.

- Allow only authorized persons to add or edit information in the database. Permissions in Access are multilevel; you can selectively allow users to edit tables or alter their structure, as well as edit or create their own applications.

- Ease the creation of data entry, editing, display, and reporting applications that efficiently serve the needs of the users of the database. The design of the RDBMS's front-end features determines the ease with which new applications are created or existing ones can be modified. You have seen in the preceding chapters that Access is especially adept as a front-end application generator.

The first two objectives are independent of the database manager you choose. The RDBMS influences or determines the other objectives. Operating speed, data validation, data security, and application creation are limited by the capabilities built into the RDBMS and the computer environment under which it operates. If your database is shared on a network, you need to consider the security features of the network operating system and the client/server database system (if one is used) in the security strategy.

Note

Database replication and data warehouses present exceptions to the objective of minimizing data duplication. Access 2000 Briefcase replication lets mobile users carry on their laptop PCs a copy (replica) of selected database tables or parts of tables. When mobile users reconnect to the primary (design master) database, their changes update tables and they receive updates made by others. Data warehouses store copies of data collected from multiple databases in a non-relational structure. The structure of the data in the warehouse is optimized for online analytical processing (OLAP), which uses multidimensional techniques to determine time-based trends and cause-effect relationships between business activities, such as advertising and sales.

THE PROCESS OF DATABASE DESIGN

The process of designing a relational database system consists of 10 basic steps:

1. Identify the objects (data sources) that the database system is to represent.

2. Discover associations between the objects (when you have more than one object).

3. Determine the significant properties and behaviors of the objects.

4. Ascertain how the properties of the objects relate to one another.

5. Create a preliminary data dictionary to define the tables that form the foundation of the database.

6. Designate the relationships between database tables based on the associations between data objects contained in the tables, and incorporate this information in the data dictionary.

7. Establish the types of updates and transactions that create and modify the data in the tables, including any necessary data-integrity requirements.

8. Determine how to use indexes to speed up query operations without excessively slowing down the addition of data to tables or consuming excessive amounts of disk space.

9. Decide who can access and modify data in each table (data security), and alter the structure of the tables if necessary to ensure data security.

10. Document the design of the database as a whole; complete data dictionaries for the database as a whole and each table it contains; and write procedures for database maintenance, including file backup and restoration.

Each step in the design process depends on preceding steps. The sections in this chapter follow steps 1 through 8 in sequence. Database security is the subject of Chapter 24,

"Securing Multiuser Network Applications." A full discussion of database documentation is beyond the scope of this book, but this chapter explains how to use Access 2000's Documenter feature to create a data dictionary.

THE OBJECT-ORIENTED APPROACH TO DATABASE DESIGN

Databases contain information about objects that exist in the real world. These objects may be people, books in a library, paper invoices or sales orders, maps, money in bank accounts, or printed circuit boards. Such objects are *tangible*. Whatever the object, it must have a physical representation, even if it's only an image on a computer display that never finds its way to the printer, as in the mythical "paperless office." References to objects in this book, if not preceded by a word describing the type of object—such as "table object" or "OLE object"—indicate real-world, tangible objects.

Tangible objects possess *properties* and *behavior*. At first, this combination might appear to be applicable only to databases of persons, not books or bank balances. However, all database objects other than those in archival databases have both properties and behavior.

CONSIDERING STATIC AND DYNAMIC PROPERTIES OF OBJECTS

An object's properties determine the content of a database or table that contains object representations of the same type. Books are assigned subject codes, which are derived from the Dewey decimal system. Modern books have an identifying ISBN code, and most now have a Library of Congress catalog number. These numbers are properties of a book, as are the title, author, number of pages, and binding type. Such properties are *static*: They are the same whether the book is in the stacks of a library or checked out by a cardholder. Customer information for a bank account, such as the account number, name, and address, also is considered static, even though customers occasionally change addresses. Book circulation status and bank account balances are dynamic properties: They change from day to day or hour to hour.

DESCRIBING DATA ENTITIES AND THEIR ATTRIBUTES

A single object, including all its static properties, is called a *data entity*. Each individual data entity must be unique so that you can distinguish it from others. A bank's checking account customer is a data entity, for example, but money in the customer's account is not because the money is fungible and can't be (and doesn't need to be) uniquely identified. A customer might have more than one account, so a Social Security number or federal employer identification number doesn't suffice as a unique identifier. An account number must be assigned to ensure the uniqueness of each customer data entity.

Deposit slips and checks are objects that are represented in the database as other data entities that *relate* to the customer entity. Check numbers aren't unique enough to distinguish them as entities; many different customers might use a check numbered 1553. Combining the customer and check number doesn't suffice as a unique identifier because different banking firms might use the same customer number to identify different people. A bank identification number, customer number, and check number together can uniquely identify a debit entity. Each check contains this information printed in magnetic ink. The amount property of each debit (check) or credit (deposit) entity is used to adjust the balance in the customer's account by simple subtraction and addition, a process called a *transaction*.

You don't want to wait while an ATM (originally Automated Transaction Machine, now commonly called an Automatic Teller Machine) calculates your balance by processing every transaction since you opened your account. Therefore, a derived static property, the last statement balance, can be included in the customer data entity and updated once per month. Only last-statement-to-date transactions need to be processed to determine the current balance—a dynamic, *calculated* property. In Figure 22.1, lines connect static properties of bank account objects to the data entities derived from them. Properties of objects included in data entities, such as account number and customer name, are called *attributes*.

ACCOUNTING FOR THE BEHAVIOR OF OBJECTS WITH METHODS

The behaviors of related database objects determine the characteristics of transactions in which their data entities participate. Books in a library may be acquired, checked out, returned, and lost. Bank account behavior is very easy to describe: A customer opens the account; deposit transactions and interest accumulations (credits) increase the account balance; and checks, cash withdrawn from an ATM, and bank charges incurred (debits) reduce the balance. Crediting or debiting a bank account is an example of a transaction. Transactions occur in response to events, such as making a deposit or withdrawal at an ATM. Access implements transactions by using methods in response to events initiated by the user, such as opening a form or clicking a command button.

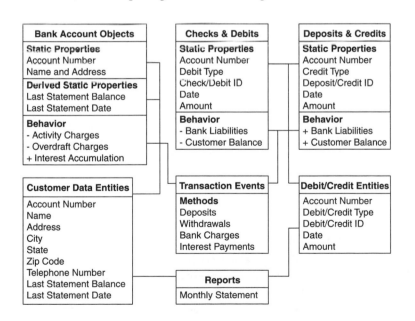

Figure 22.1
Relationships between objects, entities, events, and methods in a banking database.

In conventional relational databases, you can represent tangible objects and object properties as data entities, but not an object's real-world behavior. The OLE Object field data type, described in Chapter 19, "Adding Charts and Graphics to Forms and Reports," is an exception to this rule. The behavior of an OLE data object is determined by the methods available in the OLE server used to create the object or add the object to the OLE Object field. With conventional data entities, you emulate the behavior of tangible objects by applying the methods that you incorporate into your applications.

→ **See** "Adding a Bound Object Control to a Form or Report," **p. 734**.

Programs that you write using the RDBMS's native programming language(s) implement database methods. In the case of Access 2000, VBA functions and procedures implement the methods. Most users of Access 95 and earlier wrote Access macros to implement methods because they deemed writing macros to be simpler than writing programming code. If you write Access macros, you're programming; Access macro programming language is simpler than VBA, but has very limited capabilities.

Tip #190 from

Macro support in Access 2000 is intended only for backward compatibility; Microsoft and this book recommend that you use VBA for all new Access applications.

Access is unique among today's mainstream PC database managers because, by default, Access saves application objects (the queries, forms, reports, and VBA code that you create for the database) within the database file itself, not in separate SC, PRG, or EXE files as do other PC RDBMSs. Access data objects (tables) have self-contained properties and methods; most other PC RDBMSs require separate programs to validate data, display status text, and create indexes. Therefore, Access database files and the tables they contain conform to the object *paradigm*—a synonym for the word *model* that has become an object-oriented cliché.

Note

As observed in Chapter 24, it has become a generally accepted database design practice (GADDP) to use separate MDB files to contain application objects and data objects. Keeping your data object (tables) in a *Tables*.mdb file and linking the tables to your *AppObjs*.mdb file lets you update the application objects without affecting the existing data in the table objects.

→ **See** "Splitting Databases for File Sharing," **p. 893**.

COMBINING DIFFERENT ENTITIES IN A SINGLE TABLE

You can include representations of different types of objects in a single table as long as you can represent their properties and behavior in the same manner and yet distinguish between the different object types. For example, checks and debits are shown as a single data-object type in Figure 22.1, although one originates from a paper check and the other from an Electronic Funds Transfer debit. A Debit Type field can indicate the different sources. You can combine cash deposits and transfers from a savings account into a single data-entity type in a Credits table. You might want to combine both debits and credits in a single table, which you can do by using different codes for Debit Types and Credit Types.

To identify a debit or credit uniquely, you need to include fields for bank ID, customer number, debit/credit type, and transaction number. Although a check number can serve as the transaction number, the system must assign transaction numbers to other types of transactions, such as those conducted at ATMs. Access 2000 can use an AutoNumber field, called a Counter field in Access 2.0 and earlier, to add a unique transaction number (either incremented or random) to each data entity, including checks. The check number becomes a separate attribute.

DATABASE TERMINOLOGY

The real-world object is the basic source of information that is represented in a database as an entity. The following definition list begins with an entity, breaks it down into its component parts, and then establishes its position in the hierarchy of databases and tables.

- *Entity.* A unique representation of a single real-world object that is created by using the values of its attributes in computer-readable form. To ensure uniqueness, one or more of an entity's attributes must have values unlike the corresponding values of any other entity of the same class. The most common name for an entity is a table *record* or a query *row*. Entities are also called *data entities*, *data objects*, *data instances*, or *instances*.

- *Attribute.* A significant property of a real-world object. Every attribute carries a value that assists in identifying the entity of which it is a part and in distinguishing the entity from other members of the same entity class. Attributes are contained in table fields or query columns. An attribute also is called a *cell* or *data cell*, terms that describe the intersection of a row and a column (or a field and a record).

- *Attribute data type.* Basic attribute data types consist of all numeric (integer, floating-point, and so forth) and string (text or alphanumeric) data types without embedded spaces or separating punctuation. The string data type can contain letters, numbers, and special characters (such as those used in languages other than English). An attribute with a basic attribute data type is indivisible and called an *atomic type*.

  Text data types with spaces or other separating punctuation characters are called *composite attribute data types*. You can divide most composite types into basic data types by parsing. Parsing means to separate a composite attribute into basic attributes. For example, you can parse "Smith, Dr. John D., Jr." to Last Name (Smith), Title (Dr.), First Name (John), Middle Initial (D.), and Suffix (Jr.) basic attribute types. Special field types, such as Memo and OLE, are composite attribute data types that cannot be parsed to basic data types by conventional methods. You cannot create Access indexes that include Hyperlink, Memo, or OLE Object attribute data types.

- *Attribute domain.* The allowable range of values for an attribute of a given attribute data type. The attribute data type determines the domain unless the domain is limited by a process that is external to the data in the table. As an example of attribute domain limitation, the domain of an employee age attribute that has an integer data type might be limited by a data validation method to any integer greater than 13 and less than 90. Access validation rules, stored in tables, maintain domain integrity, limiting data entry to limits set by the data validation expression.

- *Attribute value.* The smallest indivisible unit of data in an entity. Attribute values are limited to those within the attribute domain. *Cell value* and *data value* are synonyms for attribute value.

- *Identifier.* An attribute or combination of attributes required to identify a specific entity (and no others) uniquely. Identifiers are called *primary-key fields* in Access and are used to create the primary index of the entities. When an entity's attribute values are duplicated in other entities' corresponding attributes, you need to combine various attributes to ensure a unique identifier for the entity. When more than one attribute is used as an identifier, the key fields are called a *composite* or *compound primary key*.

- *Table.* The collection (set) of all data entities of a single data entity type, also called an *entity class* or *entity type*.

- *Database.* The collection (set) of tables that store related entity classes.

Much of the formal terminology used to describe data objects in relational databases is quite technical and rather abstract. You need to understand the meaning of these terms, however, when you create the data models that form the basis of your database's design.

TYPES OF TABLES AND KEYS IN RELATIONAL DATABASES

Specific to relational databases are certain types of tables and keys that enable relationships between tables. Understanding these tables and keys is essential to comprehending relational databases and the rules of data normalization, which are discussed in the section "Normalizing Data to the Relational Model" later in this chapter. The following list defines the various relational keys and tables:

- *Base table.* In a relational database, a base table is the table that incorporates one or more columns of an object's properties and contains the primary key that uniquely identifies that object as a data entity. Base tables are often called *primary tables* because of the requirement for a primary key.

> **Note**
>
> Microsoft often uses the term *base table* to refer to a table in the native Jet MDB database structure. This book uses the term *base table* in accordance with the preceding definition.

- *Relation table.* A table that is used to provide linkages between other tables and isn't a base table (because it doesn't incorporate properties of an object or have a primary key field) is called a *relation table*. Key fields in relation tables each must be foreign keys related to a primary key in a base table.

Technically, a true relation table is composed wholly of foreign keys and contains no independent data entities. The Order Details table of the Northwind Traders database is an example of a relation table that contains data values that aren't foreign keys (the UnitPrice and Quantity fields, for example). Its OrderID field is related to the field of the same name in the Orders table. Likewise, the ProductID field is related to the ProductID field of the Products table. Although the Order Details table has a composite key, it isn't a true primary key; its purpose is to prevent duplication of a product entry in a specific order.

- *Primary key.* A primary key consists of a set of values that uniquely specifies a row of a base table, which in Access is the primary table. For any primary-key value, one and only one row in the table matches this value. You can base the primary key on a single field if each data cell's value is unique at all times.

- *Candidate keys.* Any column or group of columns that meets the requirements for a primary key is a candidate to become the primary key for the table. Name and Social Security number are candidate keys for identifying a person in the United States; however, the Social Security number is the more appropriate choice because two people can have the same name but not the same valid Social Security number.

- *Composite keys.* If you need data from more than one column of the table to meet the uniqueness requirement of a primary key, the key is said to be a composite or concatenated key.

- *Foreign keys.* A foreign key is a column whose values correspond to those contained in a primary key, or the far-left portion of a composite key, in another related table. A foreign key can consist of one column or group of columns (a composite foreign key). If the length of a foreign key is less than the corresponding primary key, the key is called a *partial* or *truncated foreign key.*

Examples of the preceding keys and tables are in the discussion of normal forms in the section "Normalizing Data to the Relational Model" later in this chapter.

DATA MODELING

The first step in designing a database is to determine which objects to represent within the database and which of the objects' properties to include. This process is called *data modeling.* The purpose of a data model is to create a logical representation of the data structure that's used to create a database. Data modeling can encompass an entire organization, a division or department, or a single type of object. Models that deal with objects, rather than the tables that you later create from the objects, are called *conceptual data models.*

Figure 22.2 illustrates two different approaches (conceptual data models) to database design: the bottom-up approach to create an application database, and the top-down method to develop subject databases. These two approaches, discussed in the following sections, result in databases with quite different structures.

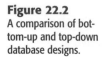

Figure 22.2
A comparison of bottom-up and top-down database designs.

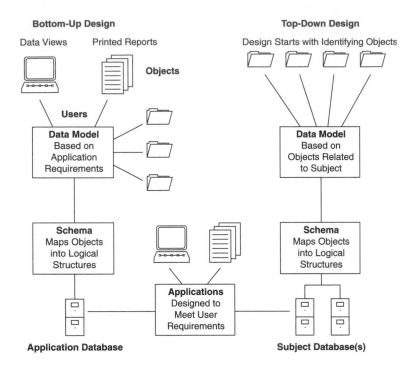

APPLICATION DATABASES

You can base data models on specific needs for data presented in a particular manner. For such a needs-based model, you can use the bottom-up approach and start with a view of the data on a display, a printed report, or both, as shown in the left-hand example in Figure 22.2. This approach results in an application database.

If you're creating a simple database for your own use or dealing with a single type of data object, the bottom-up approach might suffice because the presentation requirements and properties of the objects involved are usually well-defined. The problem with the bottom-up approach is that it often leads to multiple individual databases that might duplicate one another's information. Several persons or groups within an organization might have a requirement for an application database that includes, for example, a customer's table. When a new customer is added—or data for an existing customer is changed—in one application database, you need to update each of the other application databases. The updating process is time-consuming and subject to error.

SUBJECT DATABASES

A better approach is to base the design of the database on groups of objects that are related by subject matter. For a manufacturing firm, tables are usually grouped into databases devoted to a single department or function. The following lists some database examples:

- Sales database consisting of customer, sales order, sales quota, product discount, and invoice tables.

- Production database including product, price, parts, vendor, and cost accounting tables.

- Personnel database with employee, payroll, and benefits tables (large firms might include tables relating to health care providers and employment applicants).

- Accounting database incorporating general ledger and various journal tables.

Databases that consist of tables relating to a single class of subjects or functions are called *subject databases*. Even if you are creating the first database application for a small organization, starting with an overall plan for the organization's total information requirements in subject databases pays long-term dividends. If you decide or are assigned to create an invoicing application, for instance, you can establish sales, production, and personnel databases from the beginning, instead of splitting up a single invoice database later and rewriting all your applications to access tables within multiple databases.

Subject databases require top-down design, depicted in the right-hand diagram in Figure 22.2. In this case, the properties of the data objects, not the applications used with them, determine the design. Designing subject databases involves creating a diagram of the relevant objects and the associations between them and then creating models for each database involved. You distribute the model diagrams to users and then interview the users to determine their information needs based on the content of the model databases.

DIAGRAMMATIC DATA MODELS

Many methods exist of creating diagrams to represent data models. One of the more useful methods is the Entity-Relationship (E-R) diagram, developed by Peter Chen in 1976 (see Figure 22.3). You can use E-R diagrams to represent relationships between objects and to depict their behavior.

Data entities are enclosed within rectangles, data attributes within ovals, and relationships between entities within diamonds. Relationships between database objects, at the conceptual stage, can be defined by their behavior; therefore, E-R diagrams include at least one verb whose object, unless otherwise indicated, is to the right of the diamond relationship symbol. You add symbols to the diagram as the model's detail increases. One of the advantages of the E-R diagram is that you can use it to represent the conceptual design of very large systems with multiple databases in a relatively small amount of space.

Figure 22.3
An Entity-Relationship diagram of two data entities from Figure 22.1.

DATABASE SCHEMA

A graphic description of the layout of tables in the form of bars that contain their field names and show a simplified version of relationships between them can be employed to help users grasp the concept of the database. A diagram that shows the logical representation of data is called a *schema*. A schema, such as the one shown in Figure 22.4 for an ocean shipping line, is independent of the RDBMS used to implement the database.

Figure 22.4
The schema for the operations database of a shipping line.

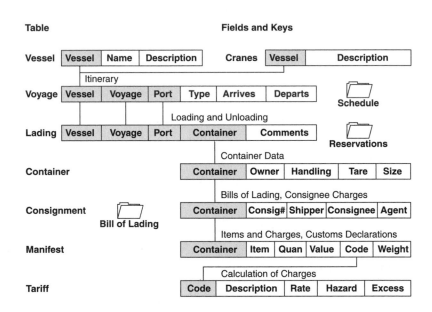

In Figure 22.4, the primary keys are shaded, and the relationships between the table keys are indicated by lines that connect the keys. Foreign keys are unshaded, except when they correspond to a component of a composite primary key. The descriptions shown between the bars are optional; they are useful in describing the relationships to users. You can expand a schema of this type to include the source documents involved, the reports to be generated, and the applications that pertain to all (or a portion) of the tables.

NORMALIZING DATA TO THE RELATIONAL MODEL

Up to this point, most of the subject matter in this chapter has been applicable to any type of database—hierarchical, relational, or even the new class of object database systems. However, because Access is a RDBMS, the balance of the chapter is devoted to relational databases. Access fully implements the relational model in its native database structure and you can link tables from other RDBMSs—including client/server tables—to Access databases. Thus, the discussion that follows is general in nature and applies to any database system with which Access is compatible or for which you have the appropriate OLE DB data provider or Open Database Connectivity (ODBC) driver.

The theory of relational database design is founded in a branch of mathematics called *set theory*, with a great deal of combinatorial analysis and some statistical methodology added. The set of rules and symbols by which relational databases are defined is called *relational algebra*. This chapter doesn't delve into the symbolic representation of relational algebra, nor does it require you to comprehend advanced mathematics. The chapter does, however, introduce you to many of the terms used in relational algebra for the sake of consistency with advanced texts, which you might want to consult on the subject of database design.

NORMALIZATION RULES

Normalization is a formalized procedure by which data attributes are grouped into tables and tables are grouped into databases. The purposes of normalization include the following:

- Eliminating duplicate information in tables.
- Accommodating future changes in the structure of tables.
- Minimizing the impact of database structural change on user applications that access the data.

Normalization is performed in steps; the first three and most common steps were described by Dr. E. F. Codd in his 1972 paper, "Further Normalization of the Data Base Relational Model." These steps are depicted in Figure 22.5. The following sections describe each of the five steps of the entire normalizing process.

FIRST NORMAL FORM

First normal form requires that tables be flat and contain no repeating groups. A flat table has only two dimensions—length (number of records or rows) and width (number of fields or columns)—and cannot contain data cells with more than one value. For a single cell to contain more than one data value, the representation of the cell's contents requires a third dimension, depth, to display the multiple data values. Flat tables and the flat-file databases referred to in Chapter 7, "Linking, Importing, and Exporting Tables," are similar in that both have two dimensions. Flat-file databases, however, consist of only one table and have no restrictions on the content of the data cells within the table.

Figure 22.5
A graphic representation of relational database normalization to the third normal form.

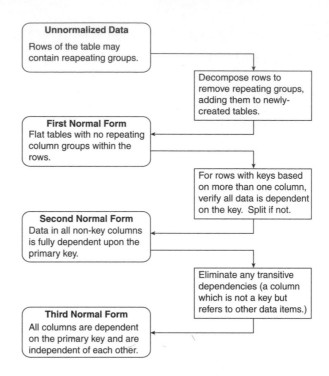

Access 2000's Table Analyzer Wizard does a good job of detecting duplicate information in tables created from flat files, but the files must be in first normal form (no repeating groups) for the analysis to succeed. The "Using Access 2000's Table Analyzer Wizard" section, later in this chapter, describes how to use the Table Analyzer Wizard to check for duplicate data and create a set of related tables to minimize or eliminate the duplication.

An example of unnormalized data for a shipping line appears in Figure 22.6. This presentation often is seen in the schedules published by transportation firms where the stops are displayed across the page. This example is representative of a schedule created by importing the worksheet file used to create the printed version of the schedule. In the examples of tables that follow, missing borders are the equivalent of an ellipsis; that is, a missing right border indicates that additional columns (fields) exist beyond the far-right column. A missing bottom border means that more rows (records) follow. (Those readers who are seasoned mariners might recognize the example as a mythical schedule for vessels of the former Pacific Far East Lines.)

Figure 22.6
A partial schedule of voyages for a shipping line.

Vessel	Name	Voyage	Embarks	From	Arrives	Port	Departs	Arrives	Port	Departs
528	Japan Bear	9203W	5/31/1998	SFO	6/6/1998	HNL	6/8/1998	7/15/1998	OSA	7/18/1998
603	Korea Bear	9203W	6/05/1998	OAK	6/19/1998	OSA	6/21/1998	6/25/1998	INC	6/28/1998
531	China Bear	9204W	6/20/1998	LAX	7/10/1998	PAP	7/11/1998	8/28/1998	SYD	9/2/1998
528	Japan Bear	9204W	8/20/1998	SFO	8/27/1998	HNL	8/29/1998	9/30/1998	OSA	10/2/1998

Note

The sample tables for the normalization process described in this and the following section are contained in PFEL.mdb, which is in the \SEUA2000\Chaptr22 folder of the accompanying CD-ROM.

Because the vessels stop at a number of ports, the Arrives, Port, and Departs columns are duplicated for each stop in the voyage. This type of data structure is allowed in COBOL, where the repeating group (Arrives, Port, and Departs) OCCURS any number of TIMES, but not in relational databases. The data in the preceding schedule isn't in first normal form because it contains repeating groups. The table must be decomposed (divided) into two tables, therefore, with the repeating groups (shown in shaded type in Figure 22.6) removed from the Schedule table and placed in two new tables, Ports and Vessel Voyages, as shown in Figure 22.7.

Vessel	Name	Voyage	Embarks	From
528	Japan Bear	9203W	5/31/1998	SFO
603	Korea Bear	9203W	6/05/1998	OAK
531	China Bear	9204W	6/20/1998	LAX
528	Japan Bear	9204W	8/20/1998	SFO

Arrives	Port	Departs
6/6/1998	HNL	6/8/1998
6/19/1998	OSA	6/21/1998
7/10/1998	PAP	7/11/1998
8/27/1998	HNL	8/29/1998
7/15/1998	OSA	7/18/1998
6/25/1998	INC	6/28/1998
8/28/1998	SYD	9/2/1998
9/30/1998	OSA	10/2/1998

Figure 22.7
The Ports and Vessel Voyages tables created from the Schedule table.

Now you need to provide for a link between the Ports and Vessel Voyages tables to retain the relationship between the data. This shipping line numbers voyages for each vessel with the year and which voyage this is for the year, as well as the general direction of travel (9204W is the fourth voyage of 1992, westbound). Thus, both Vessel and Voyage need to be used to relate the two tables. Neither Vessel nor Voyage is sufficient in itself because a vessel has multiple voyages during the year and the voyage numbers used here recur for other vessels. Because you must create a new Ports table to meet the requirements of the first normal form, you have the chance to order the columns in the order of their significance. Columns used to establish relationships are usually listed first, in the sequence in which they appear in the composite primary key, when more than one column is included in the key (see Figure 22.8).

Vessel	Voyage	Port	Arrives	Departs
528	9203W	HNL	6/6/1998	6/8/1998
603	9203W	OSA	6/19/1998	6/21/1998
531	9204W	PAP	7/10/1998	7/11/1998
528	9204W	HNL	8/27/1998	8/29/1998
528	9203W	OSA	7/15/1998	7/18/1998
603	9203W	INC	6/25/1998	6/28/1998
531	9204W	SYD	8/28/1998	9/2/1998
528	9204W	OSA	9/30/1998	10/2/1998

Figure 22.8
Linking fields are added to the Ports relation table.

Next, you establish the key fields for the Ports table that uniquely identify a record in the table. You need a primary key for the Ports table because other tables might be dependent on this table. Clearly, Vessel and Voyage must be included because these columns constitute the relationship to the Vessel Voyages table. You need to add the Port field to create a unique key (Vessel + Voyage can have duplicate values). Vessel + Voyage + Port creates a unique composite primary key because the combination takes into account stopping at a port twice—when returning eastbound, the voyage carries an "E" suffix.

Tip #191 from 	A spreadsheet application, such as Microsoft Excel 2000, can speed up the process of normalizing existing data, especially when the data contains repeating groups. Import the data into a worksheet, and then cut and paste the data in the repeating groups into a new worksheet. When the data for both of the tables is normalized, save the worksheets and then import the files to Access tables. This process is usually faster than creating make-table queries to generate normalized tables.

SECOND NORMAL FORM

Second normal form requires that data in all non-key columns be fully dependent on the primary key and each element (column) of the primary key when it's a composite primary key. *Fully dependent* means that the data value in each non-key column of a record is determined uniquely by the value of the primary key. If a composite primary key is required to establish the uniqueness of a record, the same rule applies to each value of the fields that make up the composite key of the record. Your table must be in first normal form before examining it for conformity to second normal form. Second normal form removes much of the data redundancy that's likely to occur in a first normal table.

Returning to the Vessel Voyages table, you can see that it requires a composite key, Vessel + Voyage, to create a unique key because the vessel number and vessel name recur. When you create such a key, however, you observe that Vessel and Name aren't dependent on the entire primary key because neither is determined by Voyage. You also find that the vessel name occurs for each of a vessel's voyages; for example, the Japan Bear appears twice. This lack of dependency violates the rules of the second normal form and requires Vessel Voyages to be split into two tables, Vessels and Voyages. One row is required in the Vessels table for each ship, and one row is required in the Voyages table for each voyage made by each ship (eastbound and westbound directions are considered separate voyages for database purposes). As was the case for Ports, a unique key is required to relate voyages to the vessel, so the vessel number column is added to the Voyages table, as shown in Figure 22.9.

Figure 22.9
The Vessels and Voyages tables created from the Vessel Voyages table.

Vessel	Vessel Name
528	Japan Bear
603	Korea Bear
531	China Bear

Vessel	Voyage	Embarks	From
528	9203W	5/31/1998	SFO
603	9203W	6/5/1998	OAK
531	9204W	6/20/1998	LAX
528	9204W	8/20/1998	SFO

THIRD NORMAL FORM

Third normal form requires that all non-key columns of a table be dependent on the table's primary key and independent of one another. Tables must conform to both first and second normal forms to qualify for third normal status.

Your Vessels and Voyages tables are now in third normal form because there are no repeating groups of columns, and the data in non-key columns is dependent on the primary key field. The non-key columns of Ports, Arrives, and Departs are dependent on the composite key (Vessel + Voyage + Port) and independent of one another. Ports, therefore, meets the requirements of first, second, and third normal forms. The departure date is independent of the arrival date because the difference between the two dates is based on the vessel's lading into and out of the port, the availability of berths and container cranes, and the weather.

To demonstrate normalization to the third normal form, suppose that you want to identify the officers of the vessel—master, chief engineer, and so on—in the database. Your first impulse might be to add their employee numbers, the primary key of an Employee table, to the Vessels table (see Figure 22.10).

Vessel	Vessel Name	Master	Chief	1st Mate
528	Japan Bear	01023	01155	01367
603	Korea Bear	00955	01203	00823
531	China Bear	00721	00912	01251

Figure 22.10
A table with a transitive dependency between vessels and crew members.

Such a table violates the third normal rule because none of the officers assigned to a vessel is dependent on the vessel itself. This type of dependency is called *transitive*. The master's, chief's, and first mate's maritime licenses allow them to act in their respective capacities on any vessel for which the license is valid. Any officer might be assigned to other vessels, as the need arises, or remain on board for only a portion of the voyage.

One method of removing the transitive dependency might be to add the employee numbers column to the Voyages table. This method doesn't provide a satisfactory solution, however, because the vessel could arrive at a port with one group of crew members and depart with another group. In addition, you need to specify the crew members who remain with the vessel while it is in port. A relation table, such as that shown for the Japan Bear in Figure 22.11, solves the problem. Duplicate values in the Port (departure port) and To (destination port) fields designate records for crew members responsible for the vessel while in port. The Crew table in Figure 22.11 qualifies as a relation table because all of its fields correspond to primary keys or parts of primary keys in the base tables—Vessels, Voyages, Ports, and Employees.

Vessel	Voyage	Port	To	Master	Chief	1st Mate
528	9203W	SFO	HNL	01023	01156	01367
528	9203W	HNL	HNL	01023	01156	01367
528	9203W	HNL	OSA	01023	01156	01367
528	9203W	OSA	OSA	01023	01156	01367
528	9203W	OSA	INC	01023	01156	01367

Figure 22.11
Removing transitive dependency with a relation table.

All your tables are now flat, contain no duplicate information other than that in the columns used for keys, and conform to the first through third normal forms.

FOURTH NORMAL FORM

Fourth normal form requires that independent data entities not be stored in the same table when many-to-many relationships exist between these entities. The table in Figure 22.11 violates fourth normal form because many-to-many relationships exist between the Vessel and the fields that identify crew members. The fourth normal form is discussed in the "Many-to-Many Relationships and Fourth Normal Form" section, later in this chapter, because it's the only normalization rule that is dependent on a specific type of relationship.

> **Note**
>
> Many database designers disregard the fourth and fifth normal forms; those designers consider these forms too esoteric or applicable only in specialized cases. Disregarding fourth normal form often results in poorly designed databases, but not necessarily malfunctioning ones.

FIFTH NORMAL FORM AND COMBINED ENTITIES

Fifth normal form requires that you be able to reconstruct exactly the original table from those tables into which it was decomposed. Fifth normal form requires that the tables comply with the rules for third normal form and, when many-to-many relationships are present, with the rule for fourth normal form.

The Voyages table appears to be quite similar to Ports. The From column is equivalent to Port, and Embarks is the same as Departs. Therefore, you can move the data in the Voyages table to the Ports table and delete the Voyages table. Figure 22.12 shows the new Ports table. The rows from the Voyages table don't have values in the Arrives column because they represent points of departure.

Figure 22.12
Records from the Voyages table appended to the Ports table.

Vessel	Voyage	Port	Arrives	Departs
528	9203W	HNL	6/6/1998	6/8/1998
603	9203W	OSA	6/19/1998	6/21/1998
531	9204W	PAP	7/10/1998	7/11/1998
528	9204W	HNL	8/27/1998	8/29/1998
528	9203W	OSA	7/15/1998	7/18/1998
603	9203W	INC	6/25/1998	6/28/1998
531	9204W	SYD	8/28/1998	9/2/1998
528	9204W	OSA	9/30/1998	10/2/1998
528	9203W	SFO		5/31/1998
603	9203W	OAK		6/5/1998
531	9204W	LAX		6/20/1998
528	9204W	SFO		8/20/1998

However, you cannot explicitly reconstruct the original table from the combined Voyages and Ports tables in all cases because you cannot distinguish an embarkation row from the other rows by a value in the table. A Null value in the Arrives field is a candidate to distinguish an embarkation, but Null values should be reserved for the "data not available" condition. You eliminate any ambiguity that using a Null value might cause—and bring the table into fifth normal form—by adding a single-character field, Type, with single-letter codes to define the type of call. In Figure 22.13, the codes E and S represent Embarkation and Scheduled call, respectively. Other codes might include M for Maintenance stop and R for Return voyage.

Vessel	Voyage	Port	Type	Arrives	Departs
528	9203W	HNL	S	6/6/1998	6/8/1998
603	9203W	OSA	S	6/19/1998	6/21/1998
531	9204W	PAP	S	7/10/1998	7/11/1998
528	9204W	HNL	S	8/27/1998	8/29/1998
528	9203W	OSA	S	7/15/1998	7/18/1998
603	9203W	INC	S	6/25/1998	6/28/1998
531	9204W	SYD	S	8/28/1998	9/2/1998
528	9204W	OSA	S	9/30/1998	10/2/1998
528	9203W	SFO	E		5/31/1998
603	9203W	OAK	E		6/5/1998
531	9204W	LAX	E		6/20/1998
528	9204W	SFO	E		8/20/1998

Figure 22.13
The Type field added to comply with fifth normal form.

Figure 22.14 demonstrates that you can reconstruct the content of the original Schedule table from the Vessels and Ports tables. Query1 creates the first five columns of the Schedule table by adding the criterion E for the Type field, which isn't shown. You can re-create the remaining columns of the Schedule table from Query2, which uses the criterion S for the Type field.

Query1 : Select Query

Vessel	Voyage	Vessel Name	Embarks	From
528	9203W	Japan Bear	5/31/1998	SFO
528	9204W	Japan Bear	8/20/1998	SFO
531	9204W	China Bear	6/20/1998	LAX
603	9203W	Korea Bear	6/5/1998	OAK

Record: 1 of 4

Query2 : Select Query

Vessel	Voyage	Vessel Name	Departs	Port	Arrives
528	9203W	Japan Bear	6/8/1998	HNL	6/6/1998
528	9203W	Japan Bear	7/18/1998	OSA	7/15/1998
528	9204W	Japan Bear	8/29/1998	HNL	8/27/1998
528	9204W	Japan Bear	10/2/1998	OSA	9/20/1998
531	9204W	China Bear	7/11/1998	PAP	7/10/1998
531	9204W	China Bear	9/2/1998	SYD	8/28/1998
603	9203W	Korea Bear	6/21/1998	OSA	6/19/1998
603	9203W	Korea Bear	6/28/1998	INC	6/25/1998

Record: 3 of 8

Figure 22.14
Datasheets of the two queries required to reconstruct the Schedule table.

TYPES OF RELATIONSHIPS

The subject of relationships between entities usually precedes discussions of normalization. Relationships come second in this book, however, because you can create valid relationships only between tables that have been structured in accordance with at least the first three normalization rules described in the preceding sections. This section describes the four basic types of relationships between tables and uses E-R diagrams to depict the relationships graphically.

ONE-TO-ONE RELATIONSHIPS

The simplest relationship between tables is a one-to-one relationship. In such a relationship, the tables have exact one-to-one row correspondence; no row in one table has more than one corresponding row in the other table. You can combine one-to-one-related tables into a single table consisting of all the tables' columns.

One-to-one relationships sometimes are used to divide very wide base tables into narrower ones. You might want to divide a wide table to reduce the time needed to view fields containing specific sets of data, such as the stock prices table in the example in Chapter 15, "Preparing Advanced Reports." Sometimes you must control access to the parts of tables that contain sensitive or confidential data. An example is an employee file: Everyone might have read-only access to the employees' names, but only members of the personnel department are authorized to view salary and other payroll information (see Figure 22.15).

Figure 22.15
Two tables with a one-to-one relationship.

Employee	Position	Last	First	MI		Employee	Salary
00668	Master	Johansson	Lars	F.		00668	6500.00
00721	Master	Karlsson	Bo	B.		00721	6250.00
00885	Chief	MacGregor	Paul	C.		00885	5100.00
00912	Chief	McDermott	John	R.		00912	5000.00
00955	Master	Olafson	Karl	T.		00955	6100.00
01023	Master	Kekkonen	Elno	K.		01023	6050.00
01156	Chief	McDougal	William	U.		01156	4900.00
01203	Chief	Kashihara	Matsuo			01203	4850.00

Tip #192 from

RJ

A better approach than restricting access to tables is to allow groups of users to see predefined query result sets (called `views` by MSDE and SQL Server) that expose only the columns needed by a particular group.

Figure 22.16 shows the E-R diagram for the Employees and Salaries tables. The number 1 added to each side of the relationship diamond indicates a one-to-one relationship. The participation of entities in relationships can be mandatory or optional. Optional relationships are symbolized by a circle drawn on the line connecting the optional entity with the relationship diamond. In the figure, the Paid-Salaries relationship is optional because some employees can be paid on an hourly basis and linked to a Wages table. Tables with mandatory one-to-one relationships are base tables. A table with an optional one-to-one relationship to a base table is a related table. Multiple tables with one-to-one relationships in which the corresponding records in the other tables are optional can reduce the database's disk space requirement.

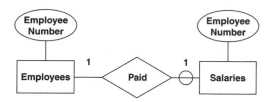

Figure 22.16
An E-R diagram for an optional one-to-one relationship.

ONE-TO-MANY RELATIONSHIPS

One-to-many relationships link a single row in one table with multiple rows in another table through a relationship between the primary key of the base table and the corresponding foreign key in the related table. Although the foreign key in the table containing the many relationships may be a component of a composite primary key in its own table, it's a foreign key for the purposes of the relationship. One-to-many relationships are by far the most common type of relationship.

The one-to-many relationship shown in Figure 22.17 links all records in the Ports table to one record in the Vessels table. The one-to-many relationship allows you to display all records in the Ports table for scheduled ports of call of the Japan Bear.

Vessel	Vessel Name		Vessel	Voyage	Port	Type	Arrives	Departs
528	Japan Bear		528	9203W	HNL	S	6/6/1998	6/8/1998
			528	9204W	HNL	S	8/27/1998	8/29/1998
			528	9203W	OSA	S	7/15/1998	7/18/1998
			528	9204W	OSA	S	9/30/1998	10/2/1998
			528	9203W	SFO	E		5/31/1998
			528	9204W	SFO	E		8/20/1998

Figure 22.17
A one-to-many relationship between the Vessels and Ports tables.

The E-R diagram in Figure 22.18 expresses this relationship; the degree of the Vessel entity relationships between the two tables is indicated by the "1" and "m" adjacent to their entities. Access's Relationships window uses the ∞ (infinity) symbol to represent the many side of relationships.

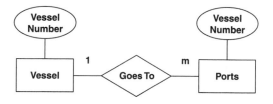

Figure 22.18
The E-R diagram for the one-to-many relationship of Figure 22.17.

MANY-TO-ONE RELATIONSHIPS

Many-to-one relationships are the converse of the one-to-many type. The many-to-one relationship allows you to display the vessel name for any record in the Ports table. If the roles of the participating entities are simply reversed to create the many-to-one relationship, the relationship is said to be *reflexive*; that is, the many-to-one relationship is the reflection of its one-to-many counterpart (see Figure 22.19). All many-to-one relationships in Access are reflexive; you can specify only a one-to-one or one-to-many relationship between the primary table and the related table by using the two option buttons in Access's Relationship dialog.

Figure 22.19
The Ports and Vessels tables in a reflexive many-to-one relationship.

Vessel	Voyage	Port	Type	Arrives	Departs
528	9203W	HNL	S	6/6/1998	6/8/1998
528	9204W	HNL	S	8/27/1998	8/29/1998
528	9203W	OSA	S	7/15/1998	7/18/1998
528	9204W	OSA	S	9/30/1998	10/2/1998
528	9203W	SFO	E		5/31/1998
528	9204W	SFO	E		8/20/1998

Vessel	Vessel Name
528	Japan Bear

If you select a record on the many side of the relationship, you can display the record corresponding to its foreign key on the one side. E-R diagrams for reflexive relationships are often drawn like the diagram in Figure 22.20. Reflexive relationships are indicated by the appropriate form of the verb placed outside the diamond that defines the relationship.

Figure 22.20
The E-R diagram for a reflexive many-to-one relationship.

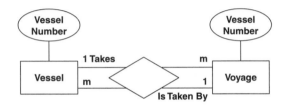

MANY-TO-MANY RELATIONSHIPS AND FOURTH NORMAL FORM

Many-to-many relationships cannot be expressed as simple relationships between two participating entities. You create many-to-many relationships by making a table that has many-to-one relationships with two base tables.

The Crews relation table, created in the "Third Normal Form" section of this chapter for assigning crew members to legs of the voyage, is shown again in Figure 22.21. The Crews table creates a many-to-many relationship between the Vessels table (based on the Vessel entity) and the Employees table (based on the employee number entities in the Master, Chief, and 1stMate fields).

Figure 22.21
The first version of the Crews relation table.

Vessel	Voyage	Port	To	Master	Chief	1st Mate
528	9203W	SFO	HNL	01023	01156	01367
528	9203W	HNL	HNL	01023	01156	01367
528	9203W	HNL	OSA	01023	01156	01367
528	9203W	OSA	OSA	01023	01156	01367
528	9203W	OSA	INC	01023	01156	01367

The table in Figure 22.21 has a many-to-one relationship with the Vessels table and a many-to-one relationship with the Employees table. This version of the Crews table creates a many-to-many relationship between the Vessels and Employees tables. The employees who crew the vessel are independent of one another; any qualified employee can, in theory, be assigned to fill a crew position on any leg of a voyage. The table in Figure 22.21 violates the fourth normal form because it contains independent entities.

Figure 22.22 shows the restructured Crews relation table that is needed to assign employees to legs of voyages. The table has one record for each employee for each leg of the voyage.

Employee	Vessel	Voyage	Port	To
01023	528	9203W	SFO	HNL
01156	528	9203W	SFO	HNL
01367	528	9203W	SFO	HNL
01023	528	9203W	HNL	HNL
01156	528	9203W	HNL	HNL
01367	528	9203W	HNL	HNL
01023	528	9203W	HNL	OSA
01156	528	9203W	HNL	OSA
01367	528	9203W	HNL	OSA
01023	528	9203W	OSA	OSA
01156	528	9203W	OSA	OSA
01367	528	9203W	OSA	OSA
01023	528	9203W	OSA	INC
01156	528	9203W	OSA	INC
01367	528	9203W	OSA	INC

Figure 22.22
The Crews table restructured to fourth normal form.

You can add new entities to this table, provided that the entities are wholly dependent on all the foreign key fields. An example of a dependent entity is payroll data that might include data attributes such as regular hours worked, overtime hours, and chargeable expenses incurred by each employee on each leg of a voyage. Such entities are called *weak* or *associative entities* because they rely on other base tables for their relevance. The Crews table is no longer considered strictly a relation table when you add associative entities because it no longer consists wholly of fields that constitute foreign keys.

The E-R diagram for the many-to-many relation table relating employees and the legs of a voyage to which the employees are assigned is shown in Figure 22.23. The circled Date connected to the Assigned Crew relationship expresses cardinality: One employee can be assigned to only one voyage on a given date. The cardinality of the relationship, therefore, is based on the departure and arrival dates for the leg. Automatically enforcing the condition that employees not be in more than one place at one time can be accomplished by creating a no-duplicates index consisting of all fields of the Crews table. Associative entities are shown in E-R diagrams as a relationship diamond within an entity rectangle. If you add payroll data to the Crews table, an associative entity is created. Assignment of an employee to a voyage is optional, as indicated by the circled lines; employees may have shore leave, be indisposed, or be assigned to shoreside duties.

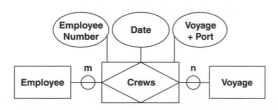

Figure 22.23
An E-R diagram for a many-to-many relationship with an associative entity.

Using graphic schema and E-R diagrams when you design an Access database helps ensure that the database meets your initial objectives. Schema also are useful in explaining the structure of your database to its users. E-R diagrams can uncover design errors, such as the failure to normalize tables at least to fourth normal form. Few experiences are more frustrating than having to restructure a large table because you realize its design wasn't fully normalized. Forethought, planning, and diagramming are the watchwords of success in database design.

USING ACCESS 2000'S TABLE ANALYZER WIZARD

Access 2000's Table Analyzer Wizard detects cells containing repeated data in table columns and proposes to create two new related tables to eliminate the repetition. This wizard uses Access 97's Lookup Wizard, described in Chapter 10, "Creating Multitable and Crosstab Queries," to create the relationship between the two new tables. After the wizard creates the new related tables, *NewName* and *Lookup*, your original table is renamed to *TableName*_OLD, and the Wizard creates a one-to-many INNER JOIN query named *TableName* to return a result set that duplicates the Datasheet view of the original table. Thus you need not change the references to *TableName* in your Access application objects.

→ **See** "Using Lookup Fields in Tables," **p. 365**.

The *Lookup* table must have a valid primary key field to provide unambiguous association of a single record in the *Lookup* table with a foreign key field in the *NewName* table. One of the problems associated with repetitious data is data entry errors, such as occasional misspelling of a company name or an address element in *Lookup*. The Table Analyzer Wizard detects and displays instances of minor mismatches in repeated cell values, such as a missing apostrophe, for correction. If such errors are not corrected, the *Lookup* table includes spurious, almost-duplicate entries that violate the rules of table normalization.

To demonstrate use of the TableAnalyzer Wizard to eliminate duplicate shipping address information in the Orders table of Northwind.mdb, follow these steps:

1. Open Northwind.mdb, if necessary, and launch the TableAnalyzer Wizard by choosing Tools, Analyze, Table.

2. Skip the two introductory dialogs by clicking the Next button twice to reach the Table Selection dialog shown in Figure 22.24.

3. Select the table with the duplicated data in the Tables list box (for this example, you select the Orders table). Next, clear the Show Introductory Pages check box to skip the two introductory dialogs whenever you use the Table Analyzer Wizard again. Click Next to continue.

4. If you let the Wizard decide, you can't change the primary key field of *Lookup*, so select the No, I Want To Decide option (see Figure 22.25). Click Next.

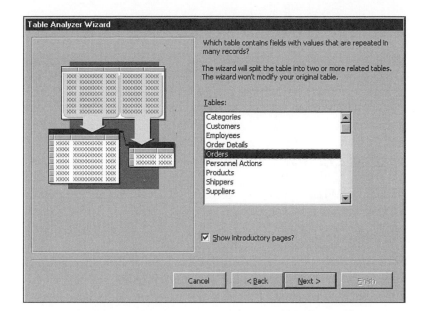

Figure 22.24
Selecting the table to analyze in the third TableAnalyzer Wizard dialog.

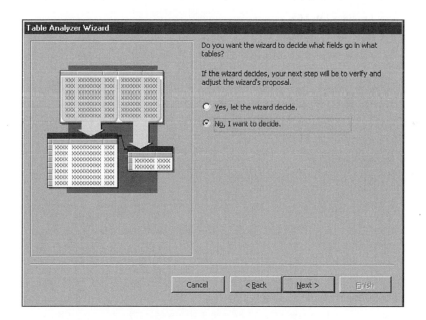

Figure 22.25
Selecting the option that lets you specify the table fields that contain duplicate data.

5. The Wizard displays a list of fields in the Orders table renamed to Table1. Click the Rename Table button (with the table and pencil icon) to open the Rename Table dialog, and type **SalesOrders** in the Table Name text box.

6. Click to select in the SalesOrders field list the first of the fields with duplicated information, ShipName; then press Shift and click the last of the fields to move, ShipCountry (see Figure 22.26).

Figure 22.26
Selecting the fields with duplicate data to move to a new table.

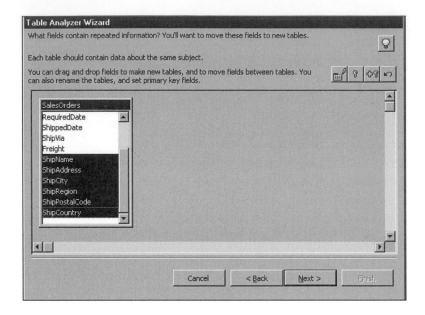

7. Holding the left mouse button down, drag the selected fields from the field list to an empty area to the right of the SalesOrder list. When you release the mouse button, the Wizard creates a new field list for proposed Table1 with a many-to-one relationship between SalesOrders and Table1. The relationship is based on a lookup field in SalesOrders and a Generated Unique ID (AutoNumber) field in Table1. An input box opens to rename Table1; type **ShipAddresses** in the Table Name text box (see Figure 22.27). Cclick OK to close the input box.

Figure 22.27
The renamed and modified tables proposed by the Wizard.

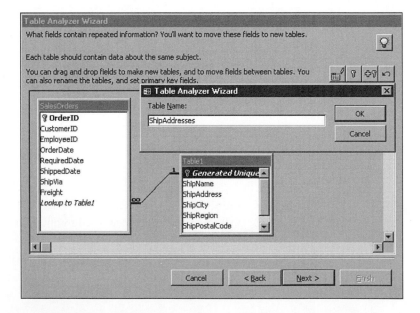

Tip #193 from

RJ

If you drag the duplicate data fields to create the new table, cancel the new table addition, and then attempt to change the name of the Orders table from Table1 to SalesOrders, you receive an "Invalid procedure call or argument" error message. To recover, click OK to close the message box, click Back and Next in the Wizard dialogs, then click the Rename Table button to enable the change from Table1 to **SalesOrders**. This is the first Table Analyzer Wizard problem that didn't get fixed in the retail release of Access 2000 (or Access 97).

8. CustomerID is a better choice than an AutoNumber field for the primary key field for ShipAddresses because there's currently only one correct ShipAddress per customer in the Orders table. Click and drag the CustomerID field from the SalesOrders field list to the ShipAddresses field list. With the CustomerID field selected in the ShipAddresses field list, click the Set Unique Key button (the one with the key icon only). The Generated Unique ID field disappears and the CustomerID field becomes the primary key for the proposed ShipAddresses table (see Figure 22.28). Click Next to continue.

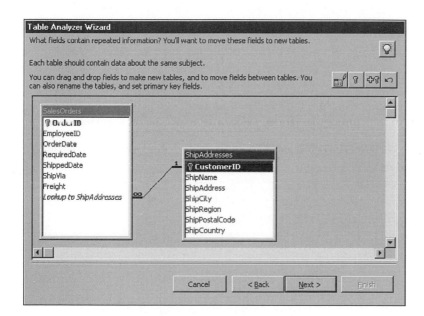

Figure 22.28
Specifying CustomerID as the primary key field for the ShipAddress table.

Tip #194 from

RJ

If you receive a "Method 'Selected' of object 'IFieldListWnd' failed" error message when attempting to set CustomerID as the primary key, click OK to dismiss the message box. Click to select the Generated Unique ID item in the ShipAddresses field list, click the CustomerID field, and then click the Set Unique Key button. This is the second Table Analyzer Wizard problem that didn't get fixed.

If the Wizard detects a misspelling of an entry in the lookup table, it opens a "Correcting typographical errors..." dialog. The Wizard bases the value in the Correction column on the frequency of exact duplication of records ("Alfreds Futterkiste" appears several times, and "Alfreds Futterkist," a deliberately induced error, appears only once in the ShipName column). Open the Correction list and select the correct record, if necessary (see Figure 22.29), for each error detected. The Wizard corrects the misspelled entry based on your list selection. Click Next to continue.

Tip #195 from

The Wizard corrects spelling errors only if you use a Generated Unique ID as the primary key of the newly generated table. If the the Wizard encounters a spelling error with a primary key you select, a spelling error throws a "The Microsoft Jet database engine cannot find the input table or query 'NORM_TT_*TableName*'" error. There is no workaround—other than always using a Generated Unique ID as the primary key—for this third Wizard problem that didn't get fixed. The entry for Centro Commercial Moctezuma appears in Figure 22.29 because there is only one record in the Orders table for this firm.

Figure 22.29
Correcting a misspelled entry in the ShipName field.

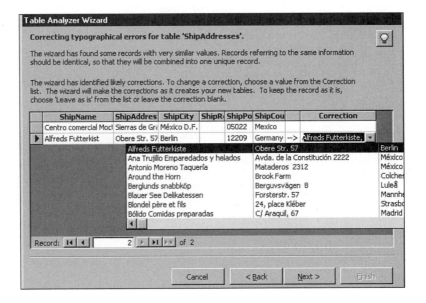

9. The wizard proposes to create a query, in this case named Orders, that substitutes for the original Orders table. Accept the Yes, Create the Query option. Clear the Display Help check box to prevent two Lookup Wizard Help screens from appearing when you complete the operation.

10. Click Finish to create the Orders query and display the temporary Orders query datasheet shown in Figure 22.30.

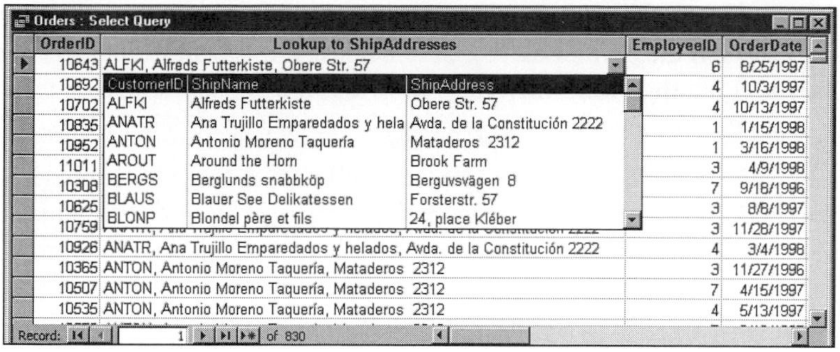

Figure 22.30
The temporary Orders query displaying the Lookup to ShipAddresses column.

11. The wizard has renamed the original Orders table to Orders_OLD. To return Northwind.mdb to its original state, open the Database window and delete the Orders query plus the SalesOrders and ShipAddress tables, and then rename the Orders_OLD table to Orders.

Tip #196 from

R J

Extracting the duplicate shipping address information from the Orders table to a new ShipAddress table is helpful to demonstrate use of the Table Analyzer Wizard. But this extraction isn't practical in the real world, where individual customers might have several shipping addresses. To make the ShipAddress table useful, you must add a field, such as ShipToID, to identify multiple shipping addresses for a single customer. Assign a value of 0 for the ShipToID field for the default shipping information created by the Wizard. Additional shipping addresses for a particular CustomerID are numbered 1, 2, 3, ... You need to redesign forms that specify shipping addresses to allow adding new ShipAddress records for customers. You must change the primary key to a composite primary key consisting of CustomerID + ShipToID, and you must use VBA code to create successive ShipToID values automatically for a particular CustomerID.

GENERATING A DATA DICTIONARY WITH THE DATABASE DOCUMENTER

After you've determined the individual data entities that make up the tables of your database and established the relationships between them, the next step is to prepare a preliminary written description of the database, called a *data dictionary*. Data dictionaries are indispensable to database systems; an undocumented database system is almost impossible to administer and maintain properly. Errors and omissions in database design often are uncovered when you prepare the preliminary data dictionary.

When you've completed and tested your database design, you prepare the final detailed version of the data dictionary. As you add new forms and reports to applications or modify existing forms and reports, you update the data dictionary to keep it current. Even if you're making a database for your personal use, a simplified version of a data dictionary pays many dividends on your time investment.

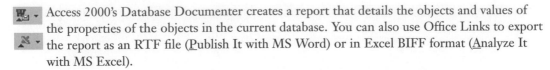 Access 2000's Database Documenter creates a report that details the objects and values of the properties of the objects in the current database. You can also use Office Links to export the report as an RTF file (Publish It with MS Word) or in Excel BIFF format (Analyze It with MS Excel).

In many cases, Documenter tells you more than you want to know about your database; the full report for all objects in Northwind.mdb, for example, requires about 400 printed pages. Most often, you only want to document your tables and, perhaps, your queries to create a complete data dictionary. The following steps show you how to create a data dictionary with Database Documenter:

1. Open the database you want to document, and then choose Tools, Analyze, Documenter. Documenter's Select Objects opening tabbed dialog appears with Tables selected, as shown in Figure 22.31 for Northwind.mdb.

Figure 22.31
Database Documenter's opening tabbed dialog.

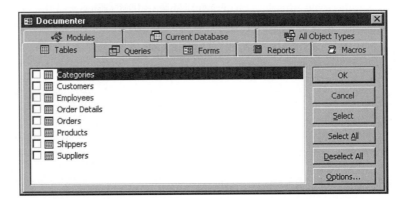

2. Click the tab for the type of object you want to document to display the list of objects. The All Object Types tab adds every object in the database to the list when you click Select All.

3. With the Tables page selected, click Options to display the Print Table Definition dialog. The most detailed set of information for tables and indexes is the default. If your Access database isn't secure, you can clear the Permissions by User and Group check box to eliminate reporting permissions data (see Figure 22.32). Click OK to return to the Documenter dialog.

4. Select the table(s) you want to document in the Tables list, and then click Select. (Clicking the check box for an item has the same effect.) Alternatively, if you want to document all tables of your database, click Select All. For this example, only the Orders and Order Details tables are documented.

5. Click the Queries tab to display the QueryDef objects in your database. Click the Options button to display the Print Query Definition dialog. Clear the Permissions by User and Group check box to eliminate security data from the report, and select the Nothing option for Fields and Indexes. Click OK to continue.

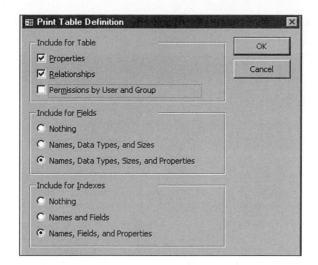

Figure 22.32
Setting options for documenting tables.

6. Click the Order Details Extended check box to add this query to the documentation, and then click OK to create the report, which is 13 pages long.

7. After a short period, the Object Definition print preview window appears (see Figure 22.33) with the Order Details table at the beginning of the list. Click the last page button to view the documentation for the Order Details Extended query.

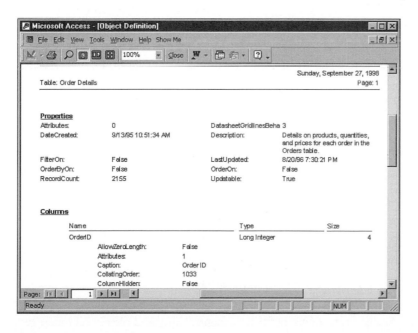

Figure 22.33
The first page of Database Documenter's report.

8. Click the Print button on the toolbar to print the report, or click the OfficeLinks button to create a doc_rptObjects.rtf or doc_rptObjects.xls file in your current folder.

9. Click the Close button on the toolbar to close the print preview window.

Documenting other objects in your database follows the same method outlined in the preceding steps. You can print data for the database itself by clicking the Current Database tab, or you can print data for selected forms, reports, macros, and modules.

Using Access Indexes

Access automatically creates an index on the primary key field. Adding other indexes to Access tables is a doubled-edged sword. You speed up the performance of queries because the index assists in the location of required records. Foreign key indexes speed access to related records; Access automatically adds an index on each foreign key when you establish relationships between tables. On the other hand, when you append a new record, Access must take the time to update each of the table's indexes. When you edit a field of a record that's included in one or more indexes, Access must update each of the indexes affected by the edit.

You can improve the performance of Access applications, especially with tables having large numbers of records or queries that join several tables, by observing these guidelines:

NEW 2000

- Minimize the number of indexes used with transaction-based tables, especially in networked multiuser applications that share tables. Access locks pages so that they aren't editable by other users when updating the data and indexes.

- Minimize the number of indexes in tables that are used regularly with INSERT and DELETE queries. The time required to update indexes is especially evident when making bulk changes to the data. Access 2000 lets you remove foreign key indexes to speed updates.

- For the best SELECT query performance, always use the key field of the primary table rather than the foreign key field of the related table in your queries.

- Add indexes to fields on which you set criteria. This is especially important for tables with more than 10,000 rows. If transaction-processing performance is more important than the speed of decision-support applications, add indexes only to those fields that occur most often in the criteria of your select queries.

Indexing becomes more important as the number of records in your tables increases. You might need to experiment to determine whether an index is effective in significantly increasing the speed of a query. If you find the index is warranted by improved query performance, check the speed of transaction processes with the new index before committing to its use.

Enforcing Database Integrity

The integrity of a database is composed of two elements: entity and referential integrity. Entity integrity requires that all primary keys must be unique within a table, and referential integrity dictates that all foreign keys must have corresponding values within a base table's primary key. Although the normalization process creates entity and referential integrity, either the RDBMS itself or your application must maintain that integrity during the data-entry process. Failure to maintain database integrity can result in erroneous data values and, ultimately, widespread corruption of the entire database.

ENSURING ENTITY INTEGRITY AND AUDITABILITY

Enforcing entity integrity within the table itself, the process used by Access, is more reliable than using application programming code to create unique primary key values. Access provides the following two built-in methods of ensuring entity integrity:

- *A key field that uses the AutoNumber data type* that creates unique values based on an automatically incremented long integer. Using incremental AutoNumber fields is the most common method for creating primary key fields. You can't create a duplicate primary key in this case because you cannot edit the values in fields of the AutoNumber data type. Don't use random AutoNumber fields to overcome index contention problems; random keys slow INSERT operations and make troubleshooting difficult.

- *An index on the primary key field* with the No Duplicates property. If you attempt to enter a duplicate value in the key field, Access displays an error message. Access automatically attempts to create a No Duplicates index on the field you designate as the primary key, as well as on AutoNumber fields.

Either of these methods ensures unique key fields, but an AutoNumber field is helpful in ensuring that documents such as sales orders, invoices, and checks are sequentially numbered. Sequential numbering is necessary for internal control and auditing purposes. AutoNumber (Incremental) fields normally begin with 1 as the first record in a table, but rarely does a real-world cash disbursement or invoice table start with check number 1 or invoice number 1. You can't create a table with a Long Integer Number field, enter the beginning number, and then change the field data type to AutoNumber. Access issues a warning message if you attempt this procedure. You can use an append query, however, to establish a specific beginning AutoNumber value.

Note

 NEW 2000

Alternatively, you can write a CREATE TABLE SQL statement and specify initial value and increment arguments of the INDENTITY(intSEED, intINCREMENT) modifier for one of the table's fields. It's much faster to use the cumbersome process described in this section than to write the very lengthy CREATE TABLE statement needed to create an tblInvoices table.

To create a starting AutoNumber field value of 123456 in the Invoice field of the Invoices table's first record, perform the following steps:

1. Open the Database window, select the Orders table, and press Ctrl+C to copy the table to the Clipboard.

2. Press Ctrl+V and type **tblInvoices** as the name of the table to create. Then select the Structure Only option, and click OK to create the new Invoices table with no records.

3. Open the tblInvoices table in Design view, click the select button of the Order ID field, and change the field data type from AutoNumber to Number (Long Integer).

4. Click the Datasheet View button on the toolbar, and click Yes to save your changes. Alternatively, choose File, Save. (Access 2000 doesn't allow two or more operations on AutoNumber fields in a single design operation.)

5. If you changed to Datasheet view, reopen the table in Design view, select the OrderID field, and press Insert to add a new field.

6. Type **InvoiceID** as the Field Name, and select AutoNumber (Increment) as the Data Type.

7. Click the Indexes button on the toolbar. Delete the Primary Key index on OrderID, which enables you to append a record that doesn't have a value for the key field (Null values aren't allowed in key fields). The tblInvoices table design appears, as shown in Figure 22.34. Close the Indexes window.

Figure 22.34
A table designed for adding an AutoNumber field with an arbitrary starting number.

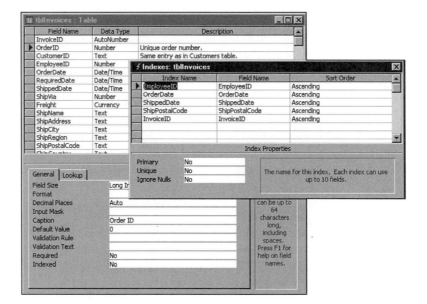

You also must set the value of the Required property of the CustomerID field to No and the Allow Zero Length property to Yes. Otherwise, the append query that follows won't execute.

8. Close the tblInvoices table and save your changes. Don't create a primary key field at this point.

9. Create a new temporary table named tblFirstInvoice with one field, named InvoiceID.

10. Set the InvoiceID field's Data Type property to Number and the Field Size property to Long Integer.

11. Change to Datasheet view; don't create a primary key field when asked; and enter a value in InvoiceID that's one less than the starting number you want (for this example, type **123455**).

12. Close the tblFirstInvoice table.

 13. Create a new query and add the tblFirstInvoice table. Click and drag the InvoiceID field symbol to the first column of the Query Design grid.

14. Choose Query, Append and select tblInvoices as the table to which to append the record. Click OK.

15. InvoiceID automatically appears as the Append To field (see Figure 22.35). Click the Run button on the toolbar, and click Yes in the "You are about to append 1 row(s)" message box to add the single record in tblFirstInvoice to the tblInvoices table.

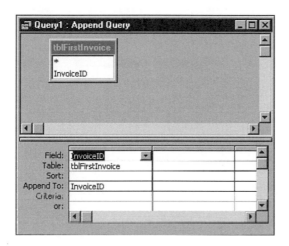

Figure 22.35
The append query to set the first value of an AutoNumber field.

16. Close Query1 without saving your changes.

The next record you append to tblInvoices is assigned the value 123456 in the InvoiceID (AutoNumber) field. To verify that this technique works properly for appended records, perform the following steps:

1. Create a new query, and add the Orders table. Click and drag the * symbol to the first column of the Query Design grid.

2. Choose Query, Append and select tblInvoices as the table to which to append the records from the Orders table. Click the Query to add the records from the Orders table.

3. Close Query1 and don't save the changes.

4. Open the tblInvoices table.

   Access has added numbers beginning with 123456 to the new Invoice field, corresponding to OrderID values of 10000 and higher, as shown in Figure 22.36.

Figure 22.36
The Invoice Data table with valid AutoNumber values starting with 123456.

InvoiceID	Order ID	Customer	Employee	Order Date	Required Date
123455	0				
123456	10248	Vins et alcools Chevalier	Buchanan, Stever	04-Jul-96	01-Aug-96
123457	10249	Toms Spezialitäten	Suyama, Michael	05-Jul-96	16-Aug-96
123458	10250	Hanari Carnes	Peacock, Margar	08-Jul-96	05-Aug-96
123459	10251	Victuailles en stock	Leverling, Janet	08-Jul-96	05-Aug-96
123460	10252	Suprêmes délices	Peacock, Margar	09-Jul-96	06-Aug-96
123461	10253	Hanari Carnes	Leverling, Janet	10-Jul-96	24-Jul-96
123462	10254	Chop-suey Chinese	Buchanan, Stever	11-Jul-96	08-Aug-96
123463	10255	Richter Supermarkt	Dodsworth, Anne	12-Jul-96	09-Aug-96
123464	10256	Wellington Importadora	Leverling, Janet	15-Jul-96	12-Aug-96
123465	10257	HILARIÓN-Abastos	Peacock, Margar	16-Jul-96	13-Aug-96
123466	10258	Ernst Handel	Davolio, Nancy	17-Jul-96	14-Aug-96
123467	10259	Centro comercial Moctezum	Peacock, Margar	18-Jul-96	15-Aug-96
123468	10260	Ottilies Käseladen	Peacock, Margar	19-Jul-96	16-Aug-96
123469	10261	Que Delícia	Peacock, Margar	19-Jul-96	16-Aug-96
123470	10262	Rattlesnake Canyon Grocery	Callahan, Laura	22-Jul-96	19-Aug-96
123471	10263	Ernst Handel	Dodsworth, Anne	23-Jul-96	20-Aug-96
123472	10264	Folk och fä HB	Suyama, Michael	24-Jul-96	21-Aug-96
123473	10265	Blondel père et fils	Fuller, Andrew	25-Jul-96	22-Aug-96
123474	10266	Wartian Herkku	Leverling, Janet	26-Jul-96	06-Sep-96
123475	10267	Frankenversand	Peacock, Margar	29-Jul-96	26-Aug-96
123476	10268	GROSELLA-Restaurante	Callahan, Laura	30-Jul-96	27-Aug-96

Record: |◄| ◄ | 1 | ► | ►| | ►* | of 831

If you receive an error message when you attempt to execute the query, see the "AutoNumber Starting Value Errors" topic of the "Troubleshooting" section near the end of the chapter.

Tip #197 from

R J

When adding an AutoNumber field to real-world data, delete the first blank record and then make the equivalent of the InvoiceID field the primary key field. Access automatically creates a no-duplicates index when you assign an AutoNumber field—or a field of any other data type—as a primary key field.

MAINTAINING REFERENTIAL INTEGRITY

Prior chapters have discussed the use of Access's database-level referential integrity enforcement capabilities. Maintaining referential integrity requires strict adherence to a single rule: *Each foreign key field in a related table must correspond to a primary key field in a base or primary table.* This rule requires that the following types of transactions be prevented:

- Adding a record on the many side of a one-to-many relationship without the existence of a corresponding record on the one side of the relationship.

- Deleting a record on the one side of a one-to-many relationship without first deleting all corresponding records on the many side of the relationship.

- Deleting or adding a record to a table in a one-to-one relationship with another table without deleting or adding a corresponding record in the related table.

- Changing the value of a primary key field of a base table on which records in a relation table depend.

- Changing the value of a foreign key field in a relation table to a value that doesn't exist in the primary key field of a base table.

A record in a relation table that has a foreign key with a value that doesn't correspond to the value of a primary key in a relation table is called an *orphan record*.

Whenever possible, use Access's built-in INNER JOIN, cascading updates, and cascading deletions features to maintain referential integrity at the database level. Don't rely on applications to test for referential integrity violations when adding records to relation tables or deleting records from base tables. Access gives you the opportunity to enforce referential integrity automatically between tables in a database by marking the Enforce Referential Integrity check box in the Relationships dialog. As noted in Chapter 11, "Modifying Data with Action Queries," you can specify cascade updates and deletes when you use Access's referential integrity enforcement capabilities. Access 2000 also enforces referential integrity in linked Access tables.

TROUBLESHOOTING

AUTONUMBER STARTING VALUE ERRORS

When I try to execute the append query that provides the starting value minus 1 to my table structure, I get an error message.

You have constraints on the fields of your destination table that don't allow Null values or empty strings in fields. Open your destination table in Design mode, and make sure the Required property of each field is set to No and that the Allow Zero Length property of each field of the Text data type is set to Yes. Also, make sure your destination table doesn't specify a primary key field.

IN THE REAL WORLD—WHY LEARN RELATIONAL THEORY?

Many books about Microsoft Access deal with relational database design theory in the first few chapters. A common approach is to have you create your own database, add a few tables having simple primary-foreign key relationships, then insert some records. The problem with this approach is two-fold:

- It's difficult enough for database beginners to comprehend Access's modus operandi without compounding the learning curve by performing unfamiliar operations out of context.

- Typing records identifying sales of various widgets or other uninteresting objects is an exercise in banality; few readers complete examples that involve the terminal boredom induced by long periods of repetitive data entry.

Understanding relational database design requires familiarity not only with the objects that make up the database, but with the use of these objects. Once you're comfortable with table and query basics, have a feeling for form and report design, and gained an introduction to

Web-based database applications, you're much better prepared to delve into the arcana of relational algebra, such as normalization.

After you've gained experience working with relational databases, their design appears intuitive and entirely logical. Thus it's somewhat surprising that Dr. Codd's relational database theory originated in 1970, well after the development of complex network and hierarchical architectures. Early relational databases suffered from performance problems; it wasn't until the late 1980s that RDBMSs became efficient enough to challenge the network and hierarchical databases running primarily on IBM mainframes. Ashton-Tate (later Borland, then Inprise) dBASE introduced relational databases to early PC owners. dBASE III+, which Aston-Tate released in 1984, added a runtime version that enabled folks without a dBASE III license to run dBASE III applications. dBASE delivered relational databases to the masses, and most 30-something (and over) programmers cut their relational design eye teeth with dBASE.

Increasing sales of PC-based RDBMSs spawned a multitude of booksmd]ranging from introductory-level tutorials to graduate-level texts—on relational database design theory and practice. One of the most interesting of the textbooks is Dr. Terry Halpin's *Conceptual Schema & Relational Database Design*, Second Edition (Prentice-Hall Australia, ISBN 0-13-355702-2, 1995), which the "In the Real World" section of the next chapter references in the context of Microsoft English Query, a natural-language query tool that's included with SQL Server 7.0. Dr. Halpin's Object-Role Modeling (ORM) language "simplifies the design process by using natural language, intuitive diagrams and examples, and by examining the informationn in terms of simple or elementary facts." Dr. Halpin contends ORM diagrams extend the capabilities of E-R diagrams, which are better suited for reverse-engineering, to "tasks of formulating, transforming or evolving a design."

Data marts and warehouses have begun to threaten the hegemony of the relational model with star and snowflake schema that define the dimensional hierarchy of multi-GB fact tables. The source of virtually all fact tables for data marts and warehouses are relational tables, so a firm grounding in relational databases is prerequisite to understanding online analytical processing (OLAP). If you're serious about getting the most out of Access 2000, consider purchasing a copy of Dr. Halpin's book or browse the bookstore shelves for titles on relational database design. Your investment will pay handsome dividends when you're able to create the optimum design to start, instead of attempting to restructure a badly-designed database after it's grown to 20 or 30 tables containing hundreds of thousands—or millions—of rows.

--rj

CHAPTER 23

WORKING WITH STRUCTURED QUERY LANGUAGE

In this chapter

Understanding the Role of SQL in Access 2000   852

Using Access to Learn SQL   853

Understanding SQL Grammar   854

Writing SELECT Queries in SQL   855

Using SQL Punctuation and Symbols   857

Using SQL Statements to Create Access Queries   858

Using the SQL Aggregate Functions   861

Creating Joins with SQL   863

Using UNION Queries   865

Implementing Subqueries   867

Writing Action and Crosstab Queries   868

Adding IN to Use Tables in Another Database   869

Comparing ANSI and Jet SQL   873

Using SQL Statements in Forms, Reports, and Macros   880

Troubleshooting   881

In the Real World—SQL As a Second Language   881

UNDERSTANDING THE ROLE OF SQL IN ACCESS 2000

This chapter describes Structured Query Language (SQL), the grammar of the language, and how Access translates queries you build in its Query Design view into Jet SQL statements. An SQL background helps you understand the query process and design more efficient queries. You need a basic knowledge of SQL to use the subquery and UNION query capabilities and for many of the applications you write in VBA. Simple examples of SQL are presented in other chapters in this book. These examples—usually figures that illustrate an SQL statement written by Access—demonstrate what occurs behind the scenes when you create a query or a graph.

Following are the new SQL reserved words introduced by Access 2000's Jet 4.0 database engine, ActiveX Data Objects (ADO) 2.1, and the ActiveX Data Extensions (ADOX) 2.1:

NEW 2000

- CREATE USER, ALTER USER, DROP USER, CREATE GROUP, ALTER GROUP, and DROP GROUP for managing users and groups.

- GRANT and REVOKE to add or remove user permissions for database objects.

- ALTER USER PASSWORD and ALTER DATABASE PASSWORD to change a password with user-level security or the password for database-level security, respectively.

- CREATE and DROP VIEW for adding and deleting SELECT QueryDef objects.

- CREATE and DROP PROCEDURE for adding and deleting QueryDef objects, including action queries.

- ON UPDATE CASCADE and ON DELETE CASCADE, the SQL equivalent of Access's cascading updates and deletions that you specify in the Relationships window.

- BEGIN and COMMIT TRANSACTION, the equivalent of VBA BeginTrans, CommitTrans, and RollbackTrans methods of the ADODB.Connection object.

- IDENTITY is a modifier that specifies an AutoNumber field in a CREATE TABLE statement. SET IDENTITY changes AutoNumber values, and SELECT @@ IDENTITY returns the value of the current record's AutoNumber field.

- WITH COMPRESSION is a modifier that specifies Unicode compression to minimize the files size of tables containing character fields.

- CONSTRAINT creates an index on the field name that precedes the expression. You can specify the index as the PRIMARYKEY or as a UNIQUE index. You also can establish a relationship between the field and the field of a foreign table with the REFERENCES modifier.

- CHECK creates an additional constraint that's similar to but more flexible than Access's table-level validation. CHECK's argument can compare values obtained from other tables by means of a SELECT statement.

- ALTER TABLE and COLUMN let you change a table field without adding a new column by copying the contents of the old column and then deleting it.

Note

The primary objective of the new extensions to Access 2000's Jet 4.0 SQL is to minimize the number of changes to SQL statements required to upsize conventional Access 2000 (Jet) applications to Access Data Projects (ADP), which connect to the Microsoft Data Engine (MSDE)—the embedded version of SQL Server 7.0—or SQL Server 7.0 running under Windows NT or 2000. All versions of SQL Server use Transact-SQL, Microsoft's SQL dialect. You must use ADO 2.1, ADOX 2.1, and the Microsoft Jet 4.0 OLE DB Provider to take advantage of these new Jet SQL reserved words. Chapter 18, "Designing Data Access Pages," introduces you to MSDE, and ADO is the subject of Chapter 27, "Understanding Universal Data Access, OLE DB, and ADO."

Tip #198 from

R J

SQL Server 7.0 Books Online provides very comprehensive information about SQL Server 7.0 and Transact-SQL. Unfortunately, SQL Server Books Online isn't included on the Office 2000 distribution CD-ROMs. To get SQL Server 7.0 Books Online, order an evaluation copy of SQL Server 7.0 on CD-ROM at http://www.microsoft.com/sql/. The Evaluation Edition of SQL Server 7.0 expires 120 days after installation, but Books Online doesn't expire.

USING ACCESS TO LEARN SQL

Structured Query Language, abbreviated *SQL* (usually pronounced "sequel" or "seekel," but more properly "ess-cue-ell"), is the common language of client/server database management. The principal advantage of SQL is that it's standardized—you can use a common set of SQL statements with all SQL-compliant database management systems. The first U.S. SQL standard was established in 1986 as ANSI X3.135-1986. The current version is ANSI X3.135-1992, usually known as SQL-92. ANSI is an acronym for the American National Standards Institute.

SQL is an application language for relational databases, not a system or programming language. SQL is a set-oriented language; thus ANSI SQL includes neither a provision for program flow control (branching and looping) nor keywords to create data-entry forms and print reports. Some implementations of SQL, such as Transact-SQL used by Microsoft SQL Server, add flow control statements (IF...ELSE and WHILE) to the language. Publishers of ANSI SQL-compliant RDBMSs are free to extend the language if the basic ANSI commands are supported.

Access is a useful learning tool for gaining fluency in SQL. This chapter shows you how to generate Access queries from SQL statements entered in the SQL dialog. If you use SQL with another RDBMS, such as Microsoft SQL Server, this chapter can help you make the transition from Jet SQL, Access's "flavor" of SQL, to Transact-SQL, the extended version of ANSI SQL used by Microsoft SQL Server.

Tip #199 from

R J

Learn SQL by osmosis. Each time you design a query in Access's Query Design view, open the SQL window and read the underlying SQL statement. The relationship between the SQL statement and graphic query design is quite evident for simple queries. As you advance to more complex queries with joins and aggregate functions, carefully compare the Jet SQL statement with the contents of the Query Design window's grid. Over time, you'll find that SQL lives up to its original name, SEQUEL—Structured English Query Language.

Many users of Access decision-support applications want to be able to define their own queries. When you open an Access 2000 database with the runtime version of Access, the Query Design window is hidden. Thus, you often must design forms that include control objects that users can manipulate to construct a Jet SQL statement that returns the desired query result set. You write VBA code to translate users' choices on the form into a Jet SQL statement; then create a VIEW or a QueryDef object (a persistent query definition whose name appears in the Database window) in the current database. SQL you create with VBA code is called *dynamic SQL*.

UNDERSTANDING SQL GRAMMAR

When you learn the grammar of a new language, it's helpful to categorize the vocabulary of the language by usage and then into the familiar parts of speech. SQL commands, therefore, first are divided into six usage categories:

- *Data Query Language (DQL)* consists of commands that obtain data from tables and determines how the results of the retrieval are presented. The SELECT command is the principal instruction in this category.

- *Data Manipulation Language (DML)* provides INSERT and DELETE commands, which add or delete entire rows, and the UPDATE command, which changes the values of data in specified columns within rows.

- *Transaction Processing Language (TPL)* includes BEGIN TRANS[ACTION], COMMIT [TRANSACTION¦WORK], and ROLLBACK [TRANSACTION¦WORK], which group multiple DML operations. If one DML operation of a transaction fails, the preceding DML operations are canceled (rolled back). Jet 4.0 SQL implements BEGIN TRANSACTION, COMMIT TRANSACTION, and ROLLBACK TRANSACTION.

- *Data Definition Language (DDL)* includes CREATE TABLE and CREATE VIEW instructions that define the structure of tables and views. DDL commands are used also to modify tables and to create and delete indexes. The keywords that implement data integrity are used with DDL statements. Jet SQL supports the CREATE TABLE, CREATE INDEX instructions.

- *Cursor Control Language (CCL)* can select a single row of a query result set for processing. Cursor control constructs, such as UPDATE WHERE CURRENT, are handled by ADO's cursor engine or the Jet database engine, so these commands aren't discussed in this chapter.

- *Data Control Language* (DCL) performs administrative functions that grant and revoke privileges to use the database, such as GRANT and REVOKE, a set of tables within the database, or specific SQL commands.

Keywords that make up the vocabulary of SQL are identified further in the following categories:

- *Commands*, such as SELECT, are verbs that cause an action to be performed.

- *Qualifiers*, such as WHERE, limit the range of values of the entities that constitute the query.

- *Clauses*, such as ORDER BY, modify the action of an instruction.

- *Operators*, such as =, <, or >, compare values and are used to create *joins* when JOIN syntax is not used. Jet SQL uses JOIN syntax by default, but lets you use operators to create joins.

- *Group aggregate functions*, such as MIN( ), return a single result for a set of values.

- Other *keywords* modify the action of a clause or manipulate cursors that are used to select specific rows of queries.

PART

VI

CH

23

> **Note**
>
> SQL keywords usually are capitalized, but the keywords aren't case sensitive. The uppercase convention is used in this book, and SQL keywords are set in the monospace type. You use *parameters*, such as *column_list*, to define or modify the action specified by keywords. Names of replaceable parameters are printed in lowercase italicized monospace type.

WRITING SELECT QUERIES IN SQL

When you create a SELECT query in Query Design mode, Access translates the query design into a Jet SQL SELECT statement. You can view the Jet SQL equivalent of your design at any point by choosing View, SQL View. Displaying and analyzing the SQL statements that correspond to queries you design or queries in the Northwind Traders sample database is useful when you are learning SQL.

The heart of SQL is the SELECT statement used to return a specified set of records from one or more tables. The following lines of syntax are used for an SQL SELECT statement that returns a *query table* (called a *result set*, usually a Recordset object of the dynaset type) of all or selected columns (fields) from all or qualifying rows (records) of a source table:

```
SELECT [ALL¦DISTINCT¦DISTINCTROW] [TOP n [PERCENT]] select_list
  FROM table_names
  [WHERE search_criteria]
  [ORDER BY column_criteria [ASC¦DESC]]
```

The following list shows the purpose of the elements in this basic select query statement:

- SELECT. The basic command that specifies a query. The *select_list* parameter determines the fields (columns) that are included in the result table of the query. When you design an Access graphical query, the *select_list* parameter is determined by the fields you add to the Fields row in the Query grid. Only those fields with the Show check box marked are included in the *select_list*. Multiple field names are separated by commas.

  The optional ALL, DISTINCT, and DISTINCTROW qualifiers determine how rows are handled. ALL specifies that all rows are to be included, subject to subsequent limitation. DISTINCT eliminates rows with duplicate data. As discussed in the section "Jet's DISTINCTROW and SQL's DISTINCT Keywords" later in the chapter, DISTINCTROW is a Jet SQL keyword, similar to DISTINCT, that eliminates duplicate rows but also enables you to modify the query result set.

  The optional TOP *n* [PERCENT] modifier limits the query result set to returning the first *n* rows or *n* percent of the result set prior to the limitation. TOP and PERCENT are Jet SQL, not ANSI SQL, keywords. You use the TOP modifier to speed display when you want to display only the most significant rows of a query result set.

- FROM *table_name*. Specifies the name or names of the table or tables that form the basis for the query. The *table_names* parameter is created in Access Query design view by the entries you make in the Add Table dialog. If fields from more than one table are included in the *select_list*, each table must be specified in the *table_names* parameter. Commas are used to separate the names of multiple tables.

- WHERE *search_criteria*. Determines which records from the select list are displayed. The *search_criteria* parameter is an expression with a text (string) operator, such as LIKE, for text fields or a numeric operator, such as >=, for fields with numeric values. The WHERE clause is optional; if you don't add a WHERE clause, all the rows that meet the SELECT criteria are returned.

- ORDER BY *column_criteria*. Specifies the sorting order of a Recordset object of the dynaset or snapshot type created by the query. A Recordset object of the snapshot type is a query result set that isn't updatable. Like the WHERE clause, ORDER BY is optional. You can specify an ascending or descending sort by the optional ASC or DESC keywords. If you don't specify a sort direction, ascending is the default.

The following lines show an example of a simple Jet SQL query statement:

```
SELECT CompanyName, CustomerID, PostalCode
  FROM Customers
  WHERE PostalCode LIKE '9*'
  ORDER BY CompanyName;
```

Jet SQL terminates statements by adding a semicolon immediately after the last character on the last line. If you don't type the semi-colon, Access's query parser adds it for you.

> **Note**
>
> Examples of SQL statements in this book are formatted to make the examples more readable. Access doesn't format its Jet SQL statements. When you enter or edit SQL statements in the SQL window, formatting these statements so that commands appear on individual lines makes the SQL statements more intelligible. Use Ctrl+Enter to insert *newline pairs* (the return and new line characters) before SQL keywords. Jet ignores spaces and newline pairs when it processes the SQL statement.

The preceding query results in a Jet `Recordset` object of three columns and as many rows as the number of records in the Customers table for companies located in ZIP codes with values that begin with the character 9, sorted alphabetically by the company name. You don't have to specify the table name with the field name in the `select_list` because this query uses only one table. When Access generates a Jet SQL statement, the table name always precedes the field name. Usually, Access processes queries you write in either ANSI SQL or Jet SQL syntax. This example differs from ANSI SQL only in the substitution of the Jet SQL * (asterisk) for ANSI SQL's % wild card.

USING SQL PUNCTUATION AND SYMBOLS

In addition to the comparison operators used for expressions, SQL uses commas, periods, semicolons, and colons as punctuation. The following list of symbols and punctuation is used in ANSI SQL and the Jet SQL dialect; differences between the two forms of SQL are noted where appropriate:

- Commas are used to separate members of lists of parameters, such as multiple field names, as in `Name, Address, City, ZIP`.

- Square brackets surrounding field names are required only when the field name includes spaces or other symbols—including punctuation—not allowed by ANSI SQL, as in `[Company Name]`. SQL Server 7.0 Transact-SQL doesn't support square brackets; substitute double quotation marks, as in `"Company Name"`.

- If fields of more than one table are involved in the query, a period is used to separate the table name from the field name, as in `Customers.[Company Name]`.

- ANSI SQL uses the single quote symbol (') to enclose literal string values. You can use the double quote (") or the single quote symbol to enclose literal values in Jet SQL statements. Using the single quote makes writing SQL statements in Access VBA easier.

- ANSI SQL use % and _ symbols as the wild cards for the `LIKE` statement, rather than the * (asterisk) and ? used by Jet SQL to specify zero or more characters and a single character, respectively. The Jet wild cards correspond to the wild cards used in specifying DOS group file names.

- Jet provides the # wild card for the LIKE statement to represent any single digit. Jet also requires the # symbol to enclose date/time values in expressions. This symbol isn't available in ANSI SQL.

- You can indicate the end of a Jet SQL statement by an optional semicolon (;).

- In Jet SQL, you can't use colons as prefixes to indicate user-declared variables you create in ANSI SQL. You cannot create variables with Jet SQL; user-declared variables in Access are limited to the Access VBA functions and procedures you write. You can, however, pass variable values as parameters to stored procedures of client/server RDBMSs. Using stored procedures requires employing an ADO ADODB.Command object or Access's SQL pass-through option when using Data Access Objects (DAO).

- ANSI SQL uses the ! (bang symbol or exclamation mark) as a not in operator for character lists used with LIKE. ANSI SQL uses != for not equal; Jet SQL uses <>.

As the preceding list demonstrates, relatively minor differences exist in the availability and use of punctuation and symbols between ANSI and Jet SQL.

Note

Indentation often is used in writing multiple-line SQL statements. Indented lines indicate continuation of a preceding line or a clause that is dependent on a keyword in a preceding line. The SQL parser ignores the indenting spaces, called *white space*.

USING SQL STATEMENTS TO CREATE ACCESS QUERIES

You can enter SQL statements in Query Design mode to create simple Access queries that are reflected in changes to the design of the Query grid. This method is another useful way to learn the syntax of SQL. If your entries contain errors in spelling or punctuation, Access displays a message box that describes the error and its approximate location in the statement. When you choose OK in the SQL dialog, Access translates your SQL statement into a graphical query design, when possible.

To create an Access select query with the SQL statement, follow these steps:

1. Open Northwind.mdb, if necessary, and then open a new query in Design view.

2. Close the Show Table dialog without adding a table name.

SQL 3. Click the SQL View button or choose <u>V</u>iew, S<u>Q</u>L View to open the Query1: Select Query SQL window.

4. Delete any text, such as SELECT;, that might appear in the SQL window.

5. Type the following SQL statement in the SQL window. Use Ctrl+Enter to create new lines. Your SQL statement appears as shown in Figure 23.1.

```
SELECT CompanyName, CustomerID, PostalCode
FROM Customers
WHERE PostalCode LIKE '9*'
ORDER BY CompanyName
```

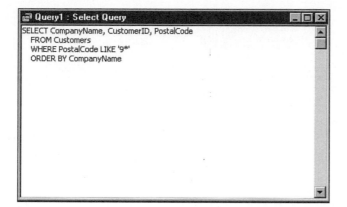

Figure 23.1
An SQL statement for a simple select query.

> **Note**
>
> By default, Access uses double quotes (") to identify string (text) values in SQL statements. As noted in the preceding section, the preferred SQL string identifier is the single quote (').

6. Choose <u>V</u>iew, <u>D</u>esign View. Access creates the equivalent of your SQL statement in a graphical query design (see Figure 23.2).

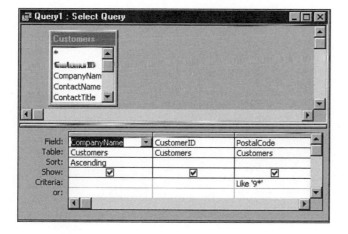

Figure 23.2
The query design created by Access from the SQL statement of Figure 23.1.

7. Click the Run Query button. The result of your query in Datasheet view appears as shown in Figure 23.3.

Figure 23.3
The query of Figures 23.1 and 23.2 in Datasheet view.

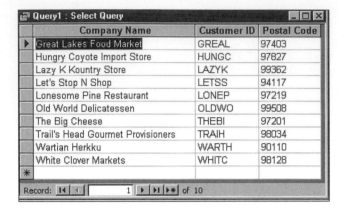

To change the sort field of the query, follow these steps:

1. Choose <u>V</u>iew, S<u>Q</u>L View to open the SQL window.

2. Change ORDER BY CompanyName to ORDER BY PostalCode and choose <u>V</u>iew, <u>D</u>esign View to open the Query Design window.

   The Query grid in Design mode displays Ascending in the PostalCode column rather than in the CompanyName column, indicating that the query result set is sorted by ZIP code.

3. Click the Run button to display the result set sorted in ZIP code sequence (see Figure 23.4).

4. Close, but don't save, the query.

Figure 23.4
The query of Figure 23.3 in ZIP code order.

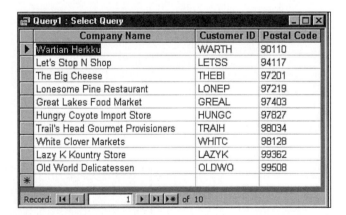

USING THE SQL AGGREGATE FUNCTIONS

If you want to use the aggregate functions to determine totals, averages, or statistical data for groups of records with a common attribute value, you add a GROUP BY clause to your SQL statement. You can further limit the result of the GROUP BY clause with the optional HAVING qualifier:

```
SELECT [ALL¦DISTINCT¦DISTINCTROW]
      aggregate_function(field_name) AS alias_name
    [, select_list]
  FROM table_names
 [WHERE search_criteria]
  GROUP BY group_criteria
    [HAVING aggregate_criteria]
 [ORDER BY column_criteria]
```

PART

VI

CH

23

The *select_list* includes the *aggregate_function* with a field_name as its argument. The field used as the argument of an aggregate function must have a numeric data type. The following list describes the additional required and optional SQL keywords and parameters to create a GROUP BY query:

- AS *alias_name*. Assigns a caption to the column. The caption is created in an Access query by the *alias:aggregate_function(field name)* entry in the Field row of the Query grid.

- GROUP BY *group_criteria*. Establishes the column on which the grouping is based. In this column, GROUP BY appears in the Totals row of the Query grid. The GROUP BY clause is required.

- HAVING *aggregate_criteria*. One or more criteria applied to the column that contains the *aggregate_function*. The *aggregate_criteria* of HAVING is applied after the grouping is completed. The HAVING clause is optional.

- WHERE *search_criteria*. Operates before the grouping occurs; at this point, no aggregate values exist to test against *aggregate_criteria*. Access substitutes HAVING for WHERE when you add criteria to a column with the *aggregate_function*. The WHERE clause is optional, but seldom is missing from an aggregate query.

> **Note**
>
> Not all client/server RDBMSs use the ANSI SQL AS *alias_name* construct. Microsoft SQL Server, Sybase System 10+, and IBM DB2, as examples, substitute a space for the AS keyword, as in SELECT *field_name alias_name*, ... (MSDE and SQL Server 7 accept either AS or a space). The ODBC driver for these databases uses special codes (called *escape syntax*) to change from Access/ANSI use of AS to the space separator. If you use ADO or Access's SQL pass-through feature with VBA and most client/server RDBMSs, you must use the space separator, not the AS keyword, for most client/server RDBMSs.

The following GROUP BY query is written in ANSI SQL, except for the # symbols that enclose date and time values:

```
SELECT ShipRegion, SUM(Freight) AS [Total Freight]
   FROM Orders
   WHERE ShipCountry='USA'
      AND OrderDate BETWEEN #01/1/1997# AND #12/31/1997#
   GROUP BY ShipRegion
   HAVING SUM(Freight)  > 50
   ORDER BY SUM(Freight) DESC
```

The query returns a result set that consists of two columns: Ship Region (states) and the totals of Freight for each Ship Region in the United States, for the years 1997. The result set is sorted in descending order.

To create an SQL GROUP BY query in Access, follow these steps:

1. Open a new query in Design view, close the Show Table dialog, and choose View, SQL View. Type the preceding GROUP BY sample code in the SQL window (see Figure 23.5).

2. Choose View, Design View. Your GROUP BY query design appears as shown in Figure 23.6.

Figure 23.5
An SQL statement that uses the SUM() aggregate function.

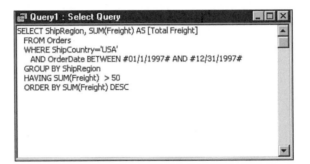

Figure 23.6
Access's graphical query design for the query shown in Figure 23.5.

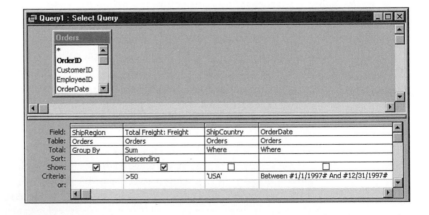

3. Click the Run Query button. The states with orders for 1997 having freight charges equal to $50 are shown ranked by total freight costs and are displayed in Datasheet view (see Figure 23.7).

4. Close, but don't save, your query.

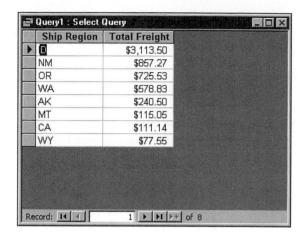

Figure 23.07
The aggregate query design of Figure 23.6 in Datasheet view.

CREATING JOINS WITH SQL

Joining two or more tables with Access's query designer uses the JOIN...ON structure that specifies the table to be joined and the relationship between the fields on which the JOIN is based:

```
SELECT [ALL¦DISTINCT¦DISTINCTROW]select_list
   FROM
   table_name {INNER¦LEFT¦RIGHT} JOIN join_table
      ON join_criteria
[table_name {INNER¦LEFT¦RIGHT} JOIN join_table
      ON join_criteria]
[WHERE search_criteria]
[ORDER BY column_criteria]
```

The elements of the JOIN statement are shown in the following list:

- *table_name* {INNER¦LEFT¦RIGHT} JOIN *join_table*. Specifics the name of the table that is joined with other tables listed in *table_names*. Each table participating in a join must be included before the JOIN clause. When you specify a self-join by including two copies of the field list for a single table, the second table is distinguished from the first by adding an underscore and a digit to alias the table name.

  One of the three types of joins, INNER, LEFT, or RIGHT must precede the JOIN statement. INNER specifies an equi-join; LEFT specifies a left outer join; RIGHT specifies a right outer join. The type of join is determined in Access's Query Design window by double-clicking the line connecting the joined fields in the table and clicking option button 1, 2, or 3 in the Join Properties dialog.

- ON *join_criteria*. Specifies the two fields to be joined and the relationship between the joined fields. One field is in *join_table* and the other is in a table in *table_names*. The *join_criteria* expression contains an equal sign (=) comparison operator and returns a True or False value. If the value of the expression is True, the record in the joined table is included in the query.

The number of JOIN statements you can add to a query usually is the total number of tables participating in the query minus one. You can create more than one JOIN between a pair of tables, but the result often is difficult to predict.

Access graphic queries create nested JOIN statements for multiple JOINs. As an example, Figure 23.8 illustrates a query design with successive JOINs between the Orders, Order Details, Products, and Categories tables of Nwind.mdb. The SQL syntax for the three nested JOINs appears in Figure 23.8. The SQL statement is formatted so that the ON clause for each JOIN statement is aligned vertically. The JOIN reserved word in Jet SQL creates the lines that connect the joined fields in Query Design view.

Figure 23.8
The Jet SQL implementa-
tion of three nested
equi-joins.

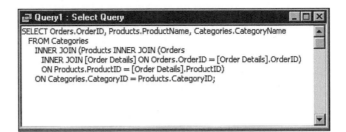

```
SELECT Orders.OrderID, Products.ProductName, Categories.CategoryName
   FROM Categories
      INNER JOIN (Products INNER JOIN (Orders
         INNER JOIN [Order Details] ON Orders.OrderID = [Order Details].OrderID)
         ON Products.ProductID = [Order Details].ProductID)
      ON Categories.CategoryID = Products.CategoryID;
```

You can create *equi-joins* in ANSI SQL with the WHERE clause, using the same expression to join the fields as that of the ON clause in the JOIN command. It's much simpler to write SQL statements using WHERE clauses to create relationships than to employ the JOIN syntax. The WHERE clause also is more flexible than the JOIN_... ON structure because you can use other operators such as BETWEEN_AND, LIKE, >, and <. These operators result in error messages when they are substituted for the equal sign (=) in the ON clause of the JOIN statement.

The following ANSI SQL-89 statement gives the same result as the Jet SQL statement in Figure 23.8:

```
SELECT Orders.OrderID, Products.ProductName,
      Categories.CategoryName
   FROM Orders, [Order Details], Products, Categories
   WHERE [Order Details].OrderID = Orders.OrderID
      AND Products.ProductID = [Order Details].ProductID
      AND Categories.CategoryID = Products.CategoryID;
```

You create multiple joins with WHERE clauses by separating each join expression with an AND operator. Figure 23.9 shows the Query Design view of the preceding SQL statement. JOIN syntax isn't used, so no join lines appear between the field lists in the upper pane. In this case, the Criteria row of the Query Design grid displays only the left element of the argument of each WHERE statement.

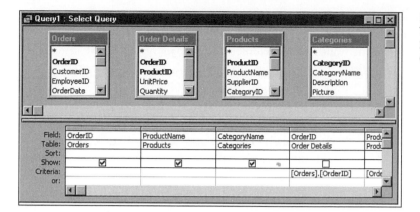

Figure 23.9
The equi-join of Figure 23.8 created by a WHERE clause.

USING UNION QUERIES

UNION queries let you combine the result set of two or more SELECT queries into a single result set. Northwind.mdb includes an example of a UNION query, which has the special symbol of two overlapping circles, in the Database window. You can create UNION queries only with SQL statements; if you add the UNION keyword to a query, the Query Design Mode button on the toolbar and the Query Design choice on the View menu are disabled. The general syntax of UNION queries is as follows:

```
SELECT select_statement
  UNION SELECT select_statement
    [GROUP BY group_criteria]
    [HAVING aggregate criteria]
 [UNION SELECT select_statement
    [GROUP BY group_criteria]
    [HAVING aggregate criteria]]
 [UNION. . .]
 [ORDER BY column_criteria]
```

The restrictions on statements that create UNION queries are the following:

- The number of fields in the *field_list* of each SELECT and UNION SELECT query must be the same. You receive an error message if the number of fields is not the same.

- The sequence of the field names in each *field_list* must correspond to similar entities. You don't receive an error message for dissimilar entities, but the result set is likely to be unfathomable. The field data types in a single column need not correspond; however, if the column of the result set contains both numeric and Jet Text data types, the data type of the column is set to Text.

- Only one ORDER BY clause is allowed, and it must follow the last UNION SELECT statement. You can add GROUP BY and HAVING clauses to each SELECT and UNION SELECT statement if needed.

Figure 23.10 shows the SQL statement to create a UNION query combining rows from the Customers and Suppliers tables. The syntax of the SQL statement illustrates the capability of UNION queries to include values from two different field data types, Text (CustomerID) and Long Integer (SupplierID), in the single, aliased ID column. The query result set appears in Figure 23.11 with the single record from the Suppliers table selected.

Tip #200 from

Use UNION queries to add (All) or other options when populating combo and list boxes. As an example, the following SQL statement adds (All) to the query result set for a combo box used to select orders from a particular country or all countries:

```
SELECT Country FROM Customers
   UNION SELECT '(All)' FROM Customers ORDER BY Country;
```

The parentheses around (All) causes it to sort at the beginning of the list; the ASCII value of "(" is 40 and "A" is 65. Automatic sorting of combo and list box items uses the ASCII value returned by the VBA Asc function.

→ For examples of use of a UNION query to add an (All) item to a combo box, **see** "Adding an Option to Select All Countries or Products," **p.1146**.

Figure 23.10
Creating a multiple-column UNION query with an SQL statement.

Figure 23.11
The result of the UNION query of Figure 23.10.

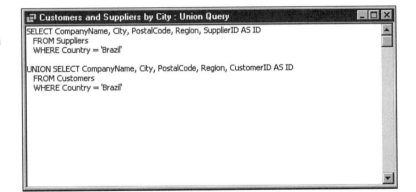

IMPLEMENTING SUBQUERIES

Early versions of Access used nested queries to emulate the subquery capability of ANSI SQL. (A *nested query* is a query executed against the result set of another query.) Access 2000 lets you write a SELECT query that uses another SELECT query to supply the criteria for the WHERE clause. Depending on the complexity of your query, using a subquery instead of nested queries often improves performance. The general syntax of subqueries is as follows:

```
SELECT field_list
   FROM table_list
   WHERE [table_name.]field_name
      IN (SELECT select_statement
[GROUP BY group_criteria]
   [HAVING aggregate_criteria]
[ORDER BY sort_criteria]);
```

PART

VI

CH

23

Figure 23.12 shows the SQL statement for a sample subquery that returns names and addresses of Northwind Traders customers who placed orders between January 1, 1997, and June 30, 1997. The SELECT subquery that begins after the IN predicate returns the CustomerID values from the Orders table against which the CustomerID values of the Customers table are compared.

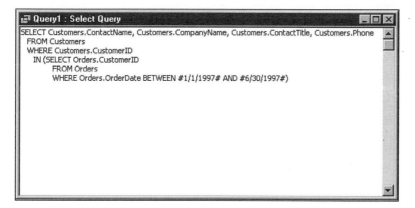

Figure 23.12
The SQL statement for a simple subquery.

Unlike UNION queries, you can create a subquery in Query Design mode. You type IN, followed by the SELECT statement as the criterion of the appropriate column, enclosing the SELECT statement within the parenthesis required by the IN predicate. Figure 23.13 shows the query design with part of the IN (SELECT statement in the Criteria row of the Customer ID column. Figure 23.14 shows the result set returned by the SQL statement of Figure 23.12.

Figure 23.13
Entering the SQL statement for a subquery in the Criteria row.

Contact Name	Company Name	Contact Title	Phone
Antonio Moreno	Antonio Moreno Taquería	Owner	(5) 555-3932
Thomas Hardy	Around the Horn	Sales Representative	(171) 555-7788
Christina Berglund	Berglunds snabbköp	Order Administrator	0921-12 34 65
Hanna Moos	Blauer See Delikatessen	Sales Representative	0621-08460
Frédérique Citeaux	Blondel père et fils	Marketing Manager	88.60.15.31
Laurence Lebihan	Bon app'	Owner	91.24.45.40
Elizabeth Lincoln	Bottom-Dollar Markets	Accounting Manager	(604) 555-4729
Victoria Ashworth	B's Beverages	Sales Representative	(171) 555-1212
Patricio Simpson	Cactus Comidas para llevar	Sales Agent	(1) 135-5555
Yang Wang	Chop-suey Chinese	Owner	0452-076545
Pedro Afonso	Comércio Mineiro	Sales Associate	(11) 555-7647
Elizabeth Brown	Consolidated Holdings	Sales Representative	(171) 555-2282
Ann Devon	Eastern Connection	Sales Agent	(171) 555-0297

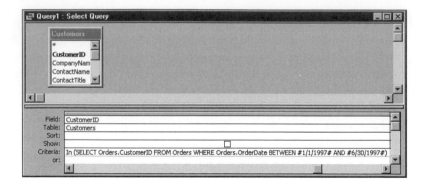

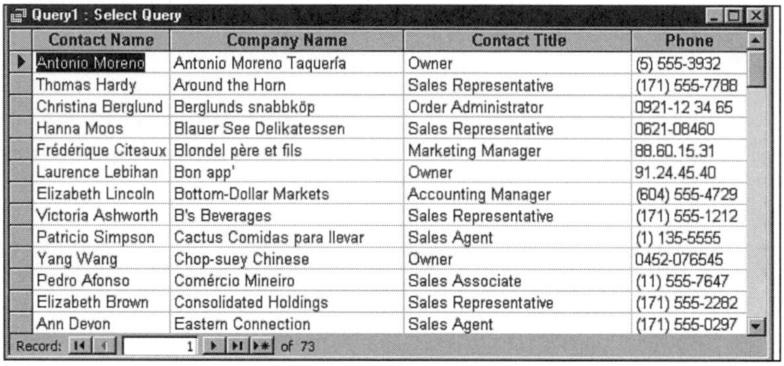

Figure 23.14
The query result set from the subquery of Figures 23.12 and 23.13.

WRITING ACTION AND CROSSTAB QUERIES

Data Manipulation Language (DML) commands are implemented by Access's action queries: append, delete, make-table, and update. Jet SQL reserved words that create crosstab queries—`TRANSFORM` and `PIVOT`—are included in this section because crosstab queries are related to DML queries. This sections shows the syntax for each type of Access action query.

Append queries use the following syntax:

```
INSERT INTO dest_table
   SELECT [ALL¦DISTINCT¦DISTINCTROW] select_list
   FROM source_table
  [WHERE append_criteria]
```

If you omit the `WHERE` clause, all the records of *`source_table`* are appended to *`dest_table`*.

Delete queries take the following form:

```
DELETE FROM table_name
  [WHERE delete_criteria]
```

If you omit the optional `WHERE` clause in a delete query, you delete all data in *`table_name`*.

Make-table queries use the following syntax:

```
SELECT [ALL¦DISTINCT¦DISTINCTROW] select_list
  INTO new_table
  FROM source_table
[WHERE append_criteria]
```

To copy the original table, substitute an asterisk (*) for `select_list` and omit the optional `WHERE` clause.

Update queries use the `SET` command to assign values to individual columns:

```
UPDATE table_name
  SET column_name = value [, column_name = value[, ...]]
[WHERE update_criteria]
```

PART

VI

CH

23

Separate multiple `column_name` entries and corresponding values by commas if you want to update the data in more than one field. Jet SQL supports the ANSI SQL `VALUES` keyword for adding records to tables the hard way (specifying the `VALUE` of each column of each record).

Crosstab queries use the Jet SQL keywords `TRANSFORM` and `PIVOT` to create various types of summary queries using the SQL aggregate functions. The following syntax applies to time-series crosstab queries:

```
TRANSFORM aggregate_function(field_name) [AS alias]
SELECT [ALL¦DISTINCT¦DISTINCTROW] select_list
  FROM table_name
  PIVOT Format(field_name),"format_type")
[IN (column_list)]
```

`TRANSFORM` defines a crosstab query, and `PIVOT` specifies the `GROUP BY` characteristics plus the fixed column names specified by the optional `IN` predicate. Crosstab queries, like queries with multiple or nested `JOIN`s, are better left to Access's Query Design window to create the query. You can edit the query as necessary after Access has written the initial SQL statement.

→ For more information on Jet crosstab queries, **see** "Creating Crosstab Queries" **p. 396**.

 If you encounter an Enter Parameter dialog when you attempt to run your SQL query, see the "Unexpected Enter Parameter Dialogs" element of the "Troubleshooting" section near the end of the chapter.

ADDING IN TO USE TABLES IN ANOTHER DATABASE

Access lets you open only one database at a time unless you write code to open another table with a VBA function or subprocedure. However, you can use Jet SQL's `IN` clause with a make-table, append, update, or delete query to create or modify tables in another database. Access provides the capability to make a table or append records to a table in another Access database through the Query Design window. You click the Another Database option in the Query Properties dialog for the make-table or append query and type the filename of the other database.

You must write an SQL query or edit a query created by Access to update data or delete records in tables contained in another database of any type or to perform any operation on a FoxPro, dBASE, or Paradox file that isn't attached to your database. The SQL query uses the IN clause to specify the external database or table file. The advantage of using the IN clause is simplicity—you don't have to attach the table before using it. The disadvantage of using the IN clause is that indexes associated with FoxPro, dBASE, and Paradox tables aren't updated when the content of the table is modified.

WORKING WITH ANOTHER ACCESS DATABASE

You can create a table in another Access database, delete all the records, and then append the records back to the table from which the records were deleted, using the IN clause to specify the name of the other database that contains the table. To try using the IN clause, open a new query or an existing query and follow these steps:

1. Choose File, New Database and create a new database named **Nwind.mdb** or whatever you like in your …\Office\Samples folder.

2. Reopen Northwind.mdb and choose View, SQL View to open the SQL window.

3. Delete the existing text and type the following line in the SQL window:

   ```
   SELECT * INTO Customers IN "Nwind.mdb" FROM Customers;
   ```

   SELECT_INTO creates a make-table query.

4. Click the Run Query button of the toolbar to make the new Customers table in your Nwind database. Click OK when the message box advises you of the number of records that are copied to the new Customers table created in OLE Objects. You can open Nwind.mdb to verify the existence of the new table.

5. Choose View, SQL View again, delete the existing text, and type the following line:

   ```
   DELETE * FROM Customers IN "Nwind.mdb"
   ```

   DELETE...FROM creates a delete query.

6. Click the Run Query button on the toolbar to delete the records in Nwind's Customers table. Click OK to confirm the deletion of the records.

Tip #201 from	You can't use the IN identifier with Jet DDL statements, such as DROP TABLE or CREATE TABLE.
RJ	

To append the records you deleted back into the Customers table of the Nwind database, follow these steps:

1. Choose File, Open Database and select your Nwind.mdb database, which contains the Customers table with no records.

2. Click the Query shortcut of the Database window, and then click the New button. Close the Show Table dialog without adding a table.

3. Choose <u>V</u>iew, S<u>Q</u>L View and type the following line in the SQL Text box:

```
INSERT INTO Customers SELECT * FROM Customers IN "Northwind.mdb"
```

INSERT INTO creates an append query. If your Nwind.mdb database is located elsewhere, add the path to Northwind.mdb to the preceding statement.

4. Click the Run Query button on the toolbar to add the records from Northwind.mdb's Customers table. Confirm the append by clicking OK in the message box.

Although you accomplish the same objectives by attaching a table from another database or copying tables to the Clipboard and pasting the table into another database, using an SQL query for this purpose is a more straightforward process.

USING THE IN CLAUSE WITH OTHER TYPES OF DATABASES

You can create or modify dBASE and Paradox tables by specifying in an IN statement the path to the file and the file type using the following special Jet SQL syntax reserved for foreign database file types:

```
IN "[drive:\]path" "database_type"
```

The path to the file is required even if the database is located in your \Access folder; you receive an error if you omit the path entry. You can use an empty string, "", to identify the current folder.

The database_type expression must be enclosed in quotation marks. It consists of one of the seven foreign file types supported by ISAM DLLs supplied with Access 2000, followed by a semicolon.

- dBASE III;
- dBASE IV;
- dBASE 5;
- Paradox 3.x;
- Paradox 4.x;
- Paradox 5.x;
- Paradox 7.0;

The semicolon after the file type name is required, but the database file type names are not case sensitive—dbase iii; is acceptable to Access.

Note

NEW 2000 Importing and exporting dBASE 7.0 and Paradox 8.0 files requires that you install the Borland Database Engine (BDE) 4+. BDE is available from Inprise Corp. (formerly Borland International). Details on the BDE are available at http://www.inprise.com. Access 2000 requires you to use the FoxPro ODBC driver (Vfpodbc.dll), included with Office 2000, for later versions of FoxPro files.

You can create a dBASE IV table from a query by using the following statement:

```
SELECT *
   INTO supplier
      IN "c:\dbase\samples" "dBASE IV;"
   FROM Suppliers;
```

You can append records to a dBASE IV file with the following statement:

```
INSERT INTO supplier
      IN "c:\dbase\samples" "dBASE IV;"
   SELECT *
      FROM Suppliers;
```

When deleting and updating records in foreign tables, use the syntax shown in the "Writing Action and Crosstab Queries" section, with the IN clause added.

CREATING TABLES WITH JET DDL

You can create new tables in your current database with Jet 4.0's DDL reserved words. Using SQL to create new tables is of primary interest to developers, not users, of Access applications because it's much easier to create new tables with the Access user interface than writing the equivalent DDL statements. For the sake of completeness, however, a brief description of Access 2000 SQL DDL statements follows:

- CREATE TABLE *table_name* (*field_name data_type* [(*field_size*)][, *field_name data_type*...]) creates a new table with the fields specified by a comma-separated list. Properties of fields are space delimited, so you need to enclose entries for *field names* with spaces in square brackets ([]). The *data_type* can be any valid Jet SQL field data type, such as TEXT(*field_size*) or INTEGER. (The default *field_size* argument value is 50 characters.)

> **Note**
>
>
> **NEW 2000**
> The *field_size* argument no longer is optional for TEXT fields. If you use the TEXT modifier without a *field_size* argument (in parenthesis), Jet interprets TEXT as the Memo field data type for conformance to Transact-SQL syntax. Jet SQL includes many new modifiers, such as CHARACTER VARYING, CHAR VARYING, VARCHAR, NATIONAL CHAR, NATIONAL CHAR VARYING, and others for localization and Unicode preferences.

- CONSTRAINT *index_name* {PRIMARYKEY¦UNIQUE¦REFERENCES *foreign_table* [(*foreign_field*)]} creates an index on the field name that precedes the expression. You can specify the index as the PRIMARYKEY or as a UNIQUE index. You also can establish a relationship between the field and the field of a foreign table with the REFERENCES *foreign_table* [*foreign_field*] entry. (The [*foreign_field*] item is required if the *foreign_field* is not a primary-key field.)

NEW 2000
- CHECK (*expression*) creates an additional constraint that's similar to but more flexible than Access's table-level validation. The *expression* argument can compare values obtained from other tables by means of a SELECT statement.

- CREATE [UNIQUE] INDEX *index_name* ON *table_name* (*field_name* [ASC¦DESC] [, *field_name* [ASC¦DESC], ...]) [WITH {PRIMARY¦DISALLOW NULL¦IGNORE NULL}] creates an index on one or more fields of a table. If you specify the WITH PRIMARY modifier, UNIQUE is assumed (and not required). DISALLOW NULL prevents addition of records with NULL values in the indexed field; IGNORE NULL doesn't index records with NULL field_name values.

- ALTER TABLE lets you add new fields (ADD COLUMN *field_name*...) or delete existing fields (DROP COLUMN field_name...).

NEW 2000

- ALTER COLUMN *table_name* (*field_name* *data_type* [*field_size*]) lets you change the properties of a single column.

- DROP INDEX *index_name* ON *table_name* deletes the index from a table specified by *table_name*.

- DROP TABLE *table_name* deletes a table from the database.

COMPARING ANSI AND JET SQL

Jet SQL doesn't include many of the approximately 200 keywords incorporated in the ANSI standard for SQL-92. Few, if any, commercial SQL-compliant RDBMSs for the PC implement much more than half of the standard SQL keywords. Most of the common SQL keywords missing from Jet's implementation are provided by the expressions you create with operators, built-in functions, or user-defined functions you write in Access VBA. The effect of many unsupported ANSI SQL keywords related to tables is achieved by making selections from Access's Database window or from menus.

SQL RESERVED WORDS IN ACCESS

Access doesn't support all the ANSI SQL keywords with identical reserved words in the Jet SQL language, but each update to Jet converges on the SQL-92 standard. In this chapter, *keywords* are defined as the commands and functions that make up the ANSI SQL language. Jet SQL commands and functions, however, are referred to here as *reserved words* to distinguish them from ANSI SQL.

The tables in the following two sections are intended to acquaint readers who are familiar with ANSI or similar implementations of SQL in other RDBMSs or database front-end applications with the Access implementation of Jet SQL. If you haven't used SQL, the tables demonstrate that SQL is a relatively sparse language, having far fewer keywords compared to programming languages like VBA, and that Jet SQL is even more sparse. Jet SQL has few reserved words to learn. You learned in Chapter 9, "Understanding Query Operators and Expressions," to use the Access operators and functions in expressions that Access substitutes for ANSI SQL keywords.

JET SQL RESERVED WORDS CORRESPONDING TO ANSI SQL KEYWORDS

Access supports the ANSI SQL keywords listed in Table 23.1 as identical reserved words in Jet SQL. Don't use these Jet SQL reserved words as the names of tables, fields, or variables. The reserved words in Table 23.1 appear in all capital letters in the Jet SQL statements Access creates for you when you design a query or when you add a graph to a form or report. Reserved words marked with an asterisk were introduced by Access 2000:

TABLE 23.1   RESERVED WORDS COMMON TO JET AND ANSI SQL

ADD	ALIAS	ALL
ALTER	ANY	AS
ASC	AVG	BEGIN*
BETWEEN	BY	CHECK*
COLUMN*	COMMIT*	CONSTRAINT
COUNT	CREATE	DELETE
DESC	DISALLOW*	DISTINCT
DROP*	EXISTS	FOREIGN
FROM	HAVING	IN
INDEX	INNER	INSERT
INTO	IS	JOIN
KEY	LEFT	LIKE
MAX	MIN	NOT
NULL	ON	OR
ORDER	OUTER	PARAMETERS
PRIMARY*	PROCEDURE	REFERENCES
RIGHT	ROLLBACK*	SELECT
SET	SOME*	TRANSACTION*
UNION	UNIQUE	UPDATE
VALUE	VALUES	VIEW
WHERE		

The keywords that relate to data types, CHAR[ACTER], FLOAT, INT[EGER], and REAL, aren't included in Table 23.1 because Jet SQL uses a different reserved word to specify these SQL data types (refer to Table 23.3 later in this chapter). The comparison operators (=, <, <=, >, and =>) are common to both ANSI SQL and Jet SQL. Access substitutes the <> operator for ANSI SQL's not-equal (!=) operator.

As in ANSI SQL, the IN reserved word in Jet SQL can be used as an operator to specify a list of values to match in a WHERE clause or a list created by a subquery. You also can use IN to identify a table in another database; this use is discussed earlier in the chapter in the section "Adding IN to Use Tables in Another Database."

ACCESS FUNCTIONS AND OPERATORS USED IN PLACE OF ANSI SQL KEYWORDS

Table 23.2 shows reserved words in Jet SQL that correspond to ANSI SQL keywords but are operators or functions used in Jet SQL expressions. Jet doesn't use ANSI SQL syntax for aggregate functions; you cannot use the SUM(DISTINCT *field_name*) syntax of ANSI SQL, for instance. Jet, therefore, distinguishes between its use of the Sum() aggregate function and the SQL implementation, SUM(). Expressions that use operators such as And and Or are enclosed in parentheses in Jet SQL statements; Jet SQL uses uppercase AND and OR (refer to the previous section) when criteria are added to more than one column.

TABLE 23.2 JET SQL RESERVED WORDS THAT SUBSTITUTE FOR ANSI SQL KEYWORDS

Jet SQL	ANSI SQL	Jet SQL	ANSI SQL
And	AND	Max()	MAX()
Avg()	AVG()	Min()	MIN()
Between	BETWEEN	Not	NOT
Count()	COUNT()	Null	NULL
Is	IS	Or	OR
In	IN	Sum()	SUM()
Like	LIKE		

The Jet IsNull() function that returns True (–1) or False (0), depending on whether IsNull()'s argument has a Null value, has no equivalent in ANSI SQL and isn't a substitute for IS NULL or IS NOT NULL qualifiers in WHERE clauses. Jet SQL does not support distinct aggregate function references, such as AVG(DISTINCT *field_name*); the default DISTINCTROW qualifier added to the SELECT statement by Jet serves this purpose.

JET SQL RESERVED WORDS, OPERATORS, AND FUNCTIONS NOT IN ANSI SQL

Jet SQL contains a number of reserved words that aren't ANSI SQL keywords (see Table 23.3). Most of these reserved words define Jet data types; some reserved words have equivalents in ANSI SQL, and others don't. You use Jet DDL reserved words to modify the properties of tables. VBA's SQL property DISTINCTROW is described in the following section. PIVOT and TRANSFORM are used in creating crosstab queries that are unique to Jet databases. (SQL Server 6.5's Transact-SQL added the ROLLUP and CUBE functions that provide aggregation capabilities similar to PIVOT and TRANSFORM.)

TABLE 23.3   JET SQL RESERVED WORDS NOT IN ANSI SQL

Jet SQL	ANSI SQL	Category	Purpose
BINARY	No equivalent	DDL	Not an official Jet field data type
BOOLEAN	No equivalent	DDL	Jet Yes/No field data type
BYTE	No equivalent	DDL	Byte field data type, 1 byte integer
CURRENCY	No equivalent	DDL	Jet Currency field data type
DATETIME	No equivalent	DDL	Jet Date/Time field data type
DISTINCTROW	No equivalent	DQL	Updatable Jet Recordset objects
DOUBLE	REAL	DDL	High-precision decimal numbers
LONG	INT[EGER]	DDL	Long Integer field data type
LONGBINARY	No equivalent	DDL	OLE Object field data type
LONGTEXT	VARCHAR	DDL	Memo field data type
OWNERACCESS	No equivalent	DQL	Run with owner's privileges parameters
PIVOT	No equivalent	DQL	Used in crosstab queries
SHORT	SMALLINT	DDL	Integer field data type, 2 bytes
SINGLE	No equivalent	DDL	Single-precision real number
TEXT(n)	CHAR[ACTER]	DDL	Text field data type
TRANSFORM	No equivalent	DQL	Creates crosstab query
? (LIKE wild card)	_ (wild card)	DQL	Single with LIKE character
* (LIKE wild card)	% (wild card)	DQL	Zero or more characters
# (LIKE wild card)	No equivalent	DQL	Single digit, 0–9
# (date specifier)	No equivalent	DQL	Encloses date/time values
<> (not equal)	!=	DQL	Jet uses ! as a separator

Jet provides four statistical aggregate functions that aren't incorporated in ANSI SQL. These functions are listed in Table 23.4.

TABLE 23.4 AGGREGATE SQL FUNCTIONS ADDED IN JET SQL

Jet Function	Category	Purpose
StdDev()	DQL	Standard deviation of a population sample
StdDevP()	DQL	Standard deviation of a population
Var()	DQL	Statistical variation of a population sample
VarP()	DQL	Statistical variation of a population

JET'S DISTINCTROW AND SQL'S DISTINCT KEYWORDS

Jet SQL's DISTINCTROW reserved word that follows the SQL SELECT keywords causes Jet to eliminate duplicated rows from the query's result. The effect of DISTINCTROW is especially dramatic in queries used to display records in tables that have indirect relationships. To create an example of a query that you can use to demonstrate the effect of Jet's DISTINCTROW SQL reserved word, follow these steps:

1. Open a new query in Northwind.mdb by clicking the Query shortcut in the Database window and then clicking the New button. Select Design View in the list box of the New Query window and then click OK to bypass the Query Wizards.

2. In the Show Table dialog, add the Customers, Orders, Order Details, Products, and Categories tables to the query, in sequence. Access automatically creates the required joins. Click Close to close the Show Table dialog.

3. Drag the CompanyName field from the Customers field list to the Field row of the first column of the Query Design grid. Select the Sort cell, open the drop-down list with F4, and choose Ascending Sort Order.

4. Drag the CategoryName field from the Categories field list to the Field row of the second column of the grid. Add an ascending sort to this field (see Figure 23.15).

5. Choose View, SQL View. The SQL statement that creates the query is shown in the SQL window in Figure 23.16.

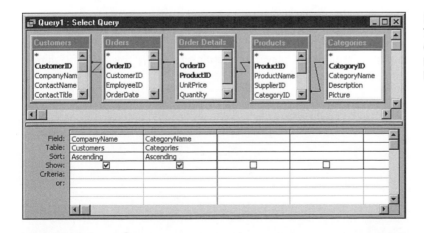

Figure 23.15
The design of a query to determine customers purchasing categories of products.

Figure 23.16
The SQL statement corresponding to the query design of Figure 23.15.

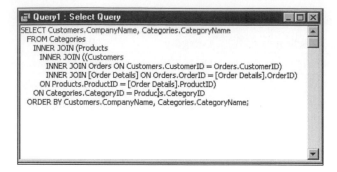

6. Click the Run Query button to execute the query. The number of rows (records) returned by the query—2,155 at the time of this writing—appears to the right of the navigation buttons at the bottom of the Query Datasheet window (see Figure 23.17). There are many duplicate rows in the query result set.

Figure 23.17
The query result set for the SQL statement of Figure 23.16.

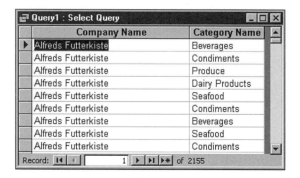

To demonstrate the effect of adding the DISTINCTROW reserved word to the SQL statement and to verify, in this case, that the effect of ANSI SQL's DISTINCT keyword and Jet SQL's DISTINCTROW reserved word is the same, follow these steps:

1. Choose View, SQL to edit the SQL statement.

2. Add the DISTINCTROW keyword to the SQL statement after the SELECT command.

3. Click the Run Query button. The new query result set has 598 rows with no duplicated rows (see Figure 23.18).

Figure 23.18
Eliminating duplicate rows with the Jet SQL *DISTINCTROW* modifier.

4. Choose <u>V</u>iew, <u>S</u>QL to edit the SQL statement again. Replace DISTINCTROW with DISTINCT.

5. Click the Run Query button again. You get the same result of 598 records that you obtain when you use the DISTINCTROW keyword.

6. Close, but do not save, the query.

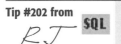

Tip #202 from

As an alternative to choosing <u>V</u>iew, SQL View from the Query menu, you can click the arrow adjacent to the View button of the toolbar and then select S<u>Q</u>L View from the drop-down menu. The number of mouse clicks is the same in either case.

A second option is to right-click the mouse button on a blank area of the upper pane of the Query Design window and choose S<u>Q</u>L View from the pop-up menu.

DISTINCTROW is a special Jet SQL reserved word and is unavailable in standard (ANSI) SQL; DISTINCTROW is related to, but not the same as, the DISTINCT keyword in ANSI SQL. Both words eliminate duplicate rows of data in query result tables, but they differ in execution. DISTINCT in ANSI SQL eliminates duplicate rows based only on the values of the data contained in the rows of the query, from left to right. You cannot update values from multiple-table queries that include the keyword DISTINCT.

DISTINCTROW eliminates duplicate rows based on the content of the underlying table, regardless of whether additional field(s) that distinguish records in the table are included. DIS-TINCTROW allows values in special kinds of multiple-table Recordset objects to be updated.

To distinguish between these two keywords, assume that you have a table with a Last_Name field and a First_Name field and only 10 records, each with the Last_Name value, Smith. Each record has a different First_Name value. You create a query that includes the Last_Name field, but not the First Name field. DISTINCTROW returns all 10 Smith records because the First Name values differ in the table. DISTINCT returns one record because the First_Name field that distinguishes the records in the table is absent in the query result table.

Versions before Access 97 included the default reserved word DISTINCTROW unless you purposely replaced it with the DISTINCT keyword by using the Query Properties dialog's Unique Values Only option. Access Query Properties dialog sets the value of the Unique Values (DISTINCT) and Unique Rows (DISTINCTROW) properties to No (see Figure 23.19). Set either of these query property values to Yes to automatically add the modifier to SELECT queries.

Figure 23.19
The Query Properties
dialog with default query
property values.

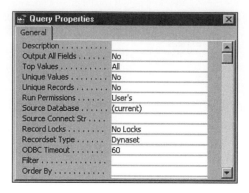

COMMON ANSI SQL KEYWORDS AND FEATURES NOT SUPPORTED BY JET SQL RESERVED WORDS

Most ANSI SQL keywords that aren't supported by Jet 4.0 are elements of SQL's Cursor Control Language. Transactions, which are implemented automatically for most operations by the Jet 4.0 database engine, can be explicitly declared only in Access VBA code. The record position buttons of Access queries and forms substitute for most Cursor Control Language statements in ANSI SQL that choose a particular row in a query. Table 23.5 lists these substitutes.

TABLE 23.5   COMMON ANSI SQL RESERVED WORDS NOT SUPPORTED IN JET SQL

Reserved Word	Category	Substitute
AUTHORIZATION	DCL	Privileges dialog
CLOSE	CCL	Document Control menu of query
CURRENT	CCL	Query Run mode, record position buttons
CURSOR	CCL	Query Run mode
DECLARE	CCL	Query Run mode (cursors are automatic)
FETCH	DQL	Text boxes on a form or report
: (variable)	DQL	VBA **Dim** statement prefix
!= (not equal)	DQL	VBA <> not-equal operator

USING SQL STATEMENTS IN FORMS, REPORTS, AND MACROS

If you create many forms and reports based on queries or that use queries, or if you use macros to run Select and Action queries, the query list in your Database window can become cluttered. You can use SQL queries you write or copy from the SQL dialog in place of the names of query objects and then delete the query from your database. You can use SQL statements for the following purposes:

- *Record Source property of forms and reports.* Substitute the SQL query text for the name of the query in the Record Source text box.

- *Row Source property in lists and drop-down combo lists on a form.* Using an SQL statement rather than a query object gives you greater control over the sequence of the columns in your list.

- *Value of the* SQL *property of a* QueryDef *object or the* strSource *argument of the* OpenRecordset *method in Access VBA code.* You use SQL statements extensively as property and argument values when programming applications with Access VBA, especially for SQL pass-through queries.

NEW 2000

- Source *property of an* ADODB.Recordset *object specified as the Record Source property of a form or report.* The capability to bind Access form and report objects to ADO Recordsets is a very important new feature of Access 2000.

- *Argument of the* RunSQL() *macro action.* Only SQL statements that create action queries can be used with the RunSQL() macro action. Using macros is strongly discouraged in Access 2000.

You can create and test your Jet SQL statement in Query Design mode and then copy the statement to the Clipboard. Paste the text into the text box for the property or into your VBA module. Then close the test query design without saving it.

TROUBLESHOOTING

UNEXPECTED ENTER PARAMETER DIALOGS

When I try to execute a query from my SQL statement, an Enter Parameter dialog appears.

You misspelled one of the table names in your *table_list*, one of the field names in your *field_list*, or both. If the Jet engine's query parser can't match a table name or a field name with those specified in the FROM clause, Jet assumes that the entry is a parameter and requests its value. Check the spelling of the database objects in your SQL statement. (If you misspell an SQL keyword, you usually receive a syntax error message box.)

IN THE REAL WORLD—SQL AS A SECOND LANGUAGE

It's tempting to let Access write all your SQL statements, thereby bypassing the need to learn two languages—SQL and VBA—to become a proficient Access developer. The reality is that you ultimately must master both SQL and VBA, because the two languages are inextricably intertwined in all non-trivial Access database front-ends. SQL is the *lingua franca* of all relational databases, just as VBA is the common programming language of Microsoft Office, Visual Basic, and many third-party applications, such as Visio.

PART

VI

CH

23

> **Note**
>
> **NEW 2000** SQL is the foundation for several new Microsoft query language extensions, including SHAPE syntax for generating hierarchical Recordsets and Multidimensional Expressions (MDX) for DataCubes and the PivotTable Service for online analytical processing (OLAP) with Microsoft OLAP Services. As more organizations adopt SQL Server 7.0, which includes OLAP Services (formerly Microsoft Decision Support Services), data warehouses will become commonplace in medium-sized enterprises, and smaller firms will set up data marts. It's a good bet that future versions of Access will add OLAP features.

If English is your native language, make SQL your second tongue and VBA your third. Proficiency in VBA makes learning VBScript, a subset of VBA, relatively easy. You need a working knowledge of VBScript to program Data Access Pages (DAP), the subject of Chapter 18, "Designing Data Access Pages."

MAKING CUSTOM QUERIES EASY FOR USERS

One of the most common applications for SQL aggregate queries created with VBA code is generating the WHERE clause constraints for SELECT query statements. You base the WHERE clause on user selections from one or more dropdown lists. To analyze orders, for example, users make selections in Product, Region, Employee, Start Date, and End Date dropdown lists. The simplified VBA code for the WHERE clause is:

```
strWhere = "WHERE Products.ProductID = " & cboProduct.Value & _
    " AND Customers.Region = '" & cboRegion.Value & _
    "' AND Employees.EmployeeID = '" & cboEmployee.Value & _
    "' AND Orders.OrderDate BETWEEN #" & cboStartDate.Value & _
    "# AND #" & cboEndDate.Value & "#"
```

You populate each list from the appropriate field(s) of a base table, and add an (All) item with a UNION query. When the user selects (All) you eliminate the corresponding WHERE clause constraint, as in:

```
strWhere = "WHERE "
If cboProduct.Value <> "(All)" Then
    strWhere = Products.ProductID = " & cboProduct.Value & _
End If
...
```

Chapter 29, "Programming Combo and List Boxes," shows you how to combine UNION queries with dropdown lists and VBA code to create forms for pre-designed, user-specified queries.

MICROSOFT ENGLISH QUERY

Microsoft English Query (MEQ) is an interesting alternative to the combo box approach for creating user-generated SQL SELECT statements. MEQ is a component of SQL Server 7.0 and is included with the almost-free Evaluation Edition described in the "Understanding the Role of SQL in Access 2000" section at the beginning of this chapter.

> **Note**
>
> MEQ began life as a component of SQL Server 6.5 Enterprise Edition. Although MEQ now is part of SQL Server 7.0, you can use MEQ with MSDE and, with some tweaking, Jet 4.0 databases.

MEQ accepts questions in natural English, such as "Who wrote the most books in 1998?" or "Which authors had the highest royalties in 1997?" A text parser analyzes the question and generates an SQL statement to query a particular database, in this case the venerable pubs sample database that comes with SQL Server 7.0 (but not with MSDE). The ability to type a question and see the resulting SQL statement makes MEQ a useful learning tool. You can read an overview of MEQ at `http://www.microsoft.com/sql/70/gen/eq.htm` and download a Web-related MEQ white paper from `http://www.microsoft.com/sql/70/whp-prs/eqp.htm`.

The Microsoft SQL Server Web site offers a demonstration of MEQ at `http://backof-fice.microsoft.com/showcase/livedemo/eqdemo/`. You type in a question for the Expedia database, in this case "What hotels near San Francisco have swimming pools?" When you click Search!, the text parser conforms your question to MEQ's grammar—"Which hotels near San Francisco have pools?" and generates the following SQL statement:

```
SELECT DISTINCT dbo.HotelProperty.HotelName AS "Hotel Name",
     dbo.HotelProperty.LocalPhoneNumber AS "LocalPhoneNumber",
     dbo.HotelProperty.StreetAddress1 AS "Street Address",
     dbo.HotelProperty.CityName AS "City",
     dbo.HotelProperty.StateRegionName AS "State or Region",
     pools.amenity AS "amenity",
     PointsOfInterest.HOTELID AS "CasinoID"
  FROM PointsOfInterest, pools, dbo.HotelProperty
 WHERE PointsOfInterest.WORD='San Francisco' AND
     PointsOfInterest.DISTANCE<3 AND
     pools.amenity IS NOT NULL AND
     PointsOfInterest.HOTELID=pools.hotelid and
     PointsOfInterest.HOTELID=dbo.HotelProperty.HotelID
```

MEQ sends the query to SQL Server via an ActiveX Data Objects (ADO) connection. Figure 23.20 shows the first of the 20 hotel records returned from the Expedia database by the preceding query.

Microsoft's Natural Language Processing (NLP) research group developed the text parser for MEQ as one of its natural language projects, which include speech recognition and other semantic tools. The natural language folks are responsible for much of the text parsing for questions posed to the Office Assistant. MEQ appears to be more effective than the Office Assistant, but that's damnation by faint praise. You can read about the activities of the NLP group at `http://research.microsoft.com/nlp/`.

MEQ relies on your ability to establish the semantics for your database with the MEQ authoring tool. MEQ semantics include entities—nouns that correspond to tables, such as HotelProperty—and relationships—verbs, adjectives, traits, and subsets—for table fields and joins. Trait phrasings—"hotels have pools"—and preposition phrasings—"hotels are in cities"—establish how the text parser interprets questions.

Figure 23.20
Microsoft's Microsoft English Query Demo page displaying a query result set from the Expedia database.

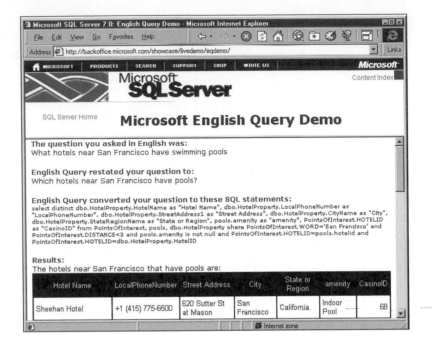

MEQ semantics are similar to those of Prof. Terry Halpin's Object Role Modeling (ORM) language that forms the underpinnings of Visio Corp.'s InfoModeler technology. InfoModeler has had several owners over the past few years and now is an element of Visio Enterprise. InfoModeler is one of the topics of the "Real World" section of Chapter 22, "Exploring Relational Database Design and Implementation." ORM is intended primarily for database design and reverse engineering, but ORM also is useful for learning the semantics of query design. You can learn more about InfoModeler and ORM at `http://www.visio.com/products/it-solutions/database/enterprise/index.html`. Halpin's book, *Conceptual Schema & Relational Database Design, Second Edition* (ISBN 0-13-355702-2, 1995) is a useful textbook to aid you in learning advanced query semantics. If you're interested in the structural linguistic theories of Prof. Noam Chomsky and his associates at the Massachusetts Institute of Technology, you'll undoubtedly enjoy working with MEQ and ORM.

--rj

CHAPTER 24

SECURING MULTIUSER NETWORK APPLICATIONS

In this chapter

Installing Access in a Networked Environment   886

Sharing Your Access Database Files with Other Users   887

Using Command-Line Options to Open a Shared Database   899

Maintaining Database Security   902

Understanding Database Object Ownership   914

Granting and Revoking Permissions for Database Objects   917

Sharing Databases on the Network   929

Accessing the Shared Workgroup and Data Files   935

Administering Databases and Applications   937

Troubleshooting   940

In the Real World—Shared-File versus Client/Server Back Ends   940

NETWORKING ACCESS 2000 APPLICATIONS

Access 2000 is likely to be the first networked Windows application many readers of this book use. Windows 9x's simple installation of low-cost and easy-to-administer Windows Networking should appeal to first-time network users. If you don't have a network now and you plan to create Access applications for other users to share, Windows 9x's or Windows NT workstation's built-in network operating system is a logical choice as a peer-to-peer "starter" network. A *peer-to-peer network* is a network in which any PC connected to the network is capable of sharing files in all—or designated—folders with any other PC connected to the network. PCs connected by peer-to-peer networks often are called members of a workgroup. Larger scale networks use dedicated file servers running under Windows NT 4.0, Windows 2000, or Netware. Access applications that share .mdb files on a peer-to-peer or file-server network are termed *multiuser applications*.

Microsoft designed Access specifically for multiuser operation in a networked, workgroup environment. For example, Microsoft has added a very sophisticated security system to Access designed for multiuser applications. If your network is already set up, you can choose to install your entire Access application on the network or share only the .mdb files containing tables and queries. Sharing data-only .mdb files is the most practical approach and is the subject of this chapter's "Splitting Databases for File Sharing" section.

If you don't have a network when you begin using Access, the process is simple to change your database files from single-user to shared status when you do install a network. This chapter explains how to set up and use Access in a variety of network environments, share database files, establish database security, and administer a multiuser database system.

Caution

Microsoft changes the Access file format in every major version. If you're upgrading to Access 2000 from a prior version and plan to share existing .mdb and workgroup system (MDA) files, don't convert any Access files to Access 2000 format unless all members of the workgroup have installed and are running Access 2000. Access 2.0 and earlier versions can't open Access 9x or Access 2000 .mdb or .mdw files. However, Access 2000 can link to data files created by earlier versions, so you don't need to upgrade data-only .mdb files.

NEW 2000 Access 2000 also can open Access 9x .mdb files, but you can't change design features of an Access 9x .mdb file unless you convert the file to the Access 2000 format. A new feature of Access 2000 is the ability to convert Access 2000 .mdb files to Access 97 format. This conversion is practical only for data files; data-type and Unicode limitations, plus new VBA features make Access 2000 to 97 client-side conversion a seldom-used feature.

→ **See** "Upgrading Access 2.0 Application .mdb Files to Access 2000," **p. 1188**.

INSTALLING ACCESS IN A NETWORKED ENVIRONMENT

You need an individual copy of the Access software for each workstation that uses Access or a license for each workstation that runs an Access application with the retail version of

Access 2000. For additional details, refer to the license information that Microsoft supplies with Office 2000.

Office 2000 Developer (formerly ODE—Office Developer Edition—now called MOD—Microsoft Office Developer) lets you distribute a runtime version of Access 2000. Runtime Access 2000 enables others to run applications you create but not to create or modify applications. Runtime Access enables multiple workstations to run your Access applications without an individual license for each workstation.

Tip #203 from

R J

No other member of Office 2000 has a runtime version; MOD is a good investment if many or all of the intended users of your application don't have Office 2000 Professional Edition.

Unlike 16-bit Access 1.1 and 2.0, which used a separate runtime executable file (MSARN??0.EXE), Access 2000 runtime uses the retail executable (Msaccess.exe) with a setting in the user's Registry that turns off the user's ability to use Msaccess.exe in Design mode. A runtime Access installation consumes a few megabytes less disk space than the retail version of Access because runtime Access does not include (and can't be used with) the Access help file and the Access wizards and builders.

SHARING YOUR ACCESS DATABASE FILES WITH OTHER USERS

While you're learning to use Access and designing your first Access applications, you use Access in single-user mode and maintain exclusive use of the database files you create. If your application is designed for use in a networked environment, however, you must set up a workgroup for the users who are sharing the database you created. The sections that follow describe how to create a folder for sharing files, modify Access applications for a multi-user environment, and set up a workgroup to provide security for shared .mdb files.

CREATING A FOLDER AND SYSTEM FILE FOR FILE SHARING

Sharing a database application requires that each user of the database share a common system file, derived from Access's System.mdw workgroup file, that contains information on the members of the workgroup, such as their logon names, passwords, and the groups of which they are members. Permissions for individual users to open and to modify objects are stored in the .mdb file. Permissions are discussed in the section "Maintaining Database Security" later in this chapter.

Tip #204 from

R J

If you intend to share your Access applications, make a backup copy of your original System.mdw file, preferably on diskette. Back up your System.mdw file each time you make a significant change. Use the backup copy to make a new System.mdw file in case your original System.mdw file becomes corrupted. Re-creating a System.mdw file that has many groups and users is a tedious process.

When you develop an application intended for shared use, it's common practice to create a new local folder to hold the application's .mdb file(s). You then use the Workgroup Administrator application (Wrkgadm.exe) to create a new system file specifically for the application and develop the application in its own folder. Access 2000's default extension for workgroup system files is .mdw. When the application is completed, you can copy the .mdb and .mdw files in this folder to the workgroup folder of the network or peer-to-peer server that's used to share them.

The location and name of the system file that Access 2000 uses when it's launched is specified by the SystemDB entry of the
`HKEY_LOCAL_MACHINE\SOFTWARE\Microsoft\Office\9.0\Access\Jet\4.0\Engines` hive of the Registry. The default Registry entry (key) for SystemDB is
`"C:\PROGRA~1\MICROS~2\OFFICE\SYSTEM.MDW"`, as shown in Figure 24.1; the path leads to the same folder that contains Msaccess.exe.

Caution

Unless you're familiar with editing Windows 9x's or Windows NT's Registry with the Registry Editor application (RegEdit.exe), don't edit Registry entries manually. An incorrect entry can cause Access or Windows to behave unexpectedly.

Figure 24.1
The Registry Editor displaying the Registry value for the SystemDB key that specifies the name and location of your Access 2000 system file.

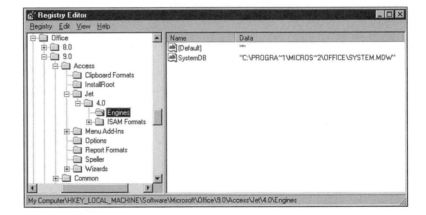

To establish a directory and a workgroup system file for the development of a sample shared database application, do the following:

1. Launch Explorer and add a new folder, called \Shared in this example, to the root folder of a local drive on your PC.

2. Open the \Shared folder and create a new subfolder, \Shared\Nwind.

3. Create a copy of Northwind.mdb (preferably a copy of the orginal version) in \Shared\Nwind, rename the file to Nwind.mdb, and then close Explorer. Alternatively, you can use Access's Compact feature to create a compacted copy of Northwind.mdb to Nwind.mdb in the \Shared\Nwind folder.

→ For a quick review of database compaction, **see** "Compacting and Repairing Databases," **p. 118**.

PART

IV

CH

24

4. Copy each of the sample Data Access Pages (DAP) from the …\Office\Samples folder to your \Shared\Nwind folder. The names of the files to copy are Analyze Sales.htm, Review Orders.htm, Review Products.htm, Sales.htm, and View Products.htm.

→ For details on adding themes to DAP, **see** "Using AutoPage to Create Columnar DAP," **p. 679**.

 5. Launch Workgroup Administrator (Wrkgadm.exe). Office 2000 Setup doesn't automatically add Workgroup Administrator to your Start menu. Wrkgadm.exe is located by default in your \Program Files\Microsoft Office\Office\1033 folder. Create a Desktop shortcut to Wrkgadm.exe if Workgroup Administrator does not appear in your Start, Programs, or Office menu. The opening dialog of Workgroup Administrator displays the name and location of the default system file, System.mdw (see Figure 24.2).

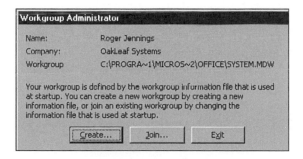

Figure 24.2
Workgroup Administrator's opening dialog.

6. Click the Create button to open the Workgroup Owner Information dialog in which you specify the Name, Organization, and optional Workgroup ID for the new workgroup system file (see Figure 24.3). Write down the Name, Organization, and Workgroup ID entries, which are case sensitive, and keep them in a safe place. If you must re-create the workgroup system file in the future, your entries must exactly match the original entries.

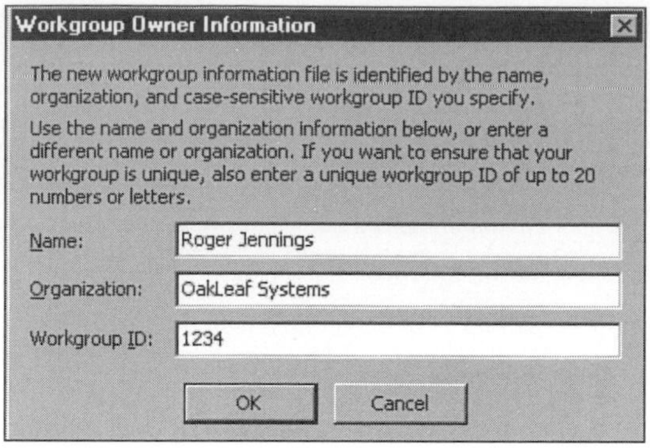

Figure 24.3
Specifying the Name, Organization, and optional Workgroup ID for a new workgroup system file.

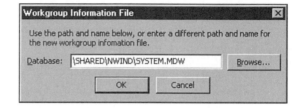

7. Click OK to display the Workgroup Information File dialog. Type the path and name of your workgroup folder, **\SHARED\NWIND\SYSTEM.MDW** in this case, in the Database text box (see Figure 24.4).

Figure 24.4
Entering the location and name of the shared workgroup file in the Workgroup Information File dialog.

8. Click OK to display the Confirm Workgroup Information dialog (see Figure 24.5). If the workgroup information is correct, click OK. A message appears to confirm that the new workgroup system file has been created (see Figure 24.6). Click OK to close the message box and return to the initial Workgroup Administrator dialog (see Figure 24.7).

Figure 24.5
Confirming the owner information for the new workgroup system file.

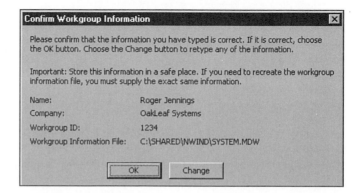

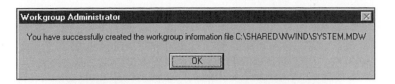

Figure 24.6
Access confirming that the new System.mdw workgroup system file is created.

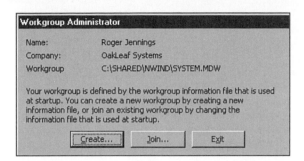

Figure 24.7
The Workgroup Administrator dialog, displaying the name and location of the new workgroup system file.

PART
IV
CH
24

9. Click Exit to close Workgroup Administrator. Access doesn't use the new workgroup system file until you close and relaunch Access.

10. Close Access, if it's open. Launch Access and open the \Shared\Nwind\Nwind.mdb database file with the new System.mdw system file active.

The dedicated System.mdw file contains information pertaining only to the database applications that you open when System.mdw is your active system file. You can develop an application using Access's default operating options and System.mdw and then change the options and create a new workgroup system file to provide for file sharing when you complete the application.

With the Workgroup Administrator, you can change the system database file that Access uses when launched. The procedure is described in the section "Choosing Workgroups with the Workgroup Administrator" later in this chapter.

Tip #207 from

Minimize the number of database objects you create when you develop applications to be shared. You must specifically grant or revoke permissions to groups or individual users for each object you create. Use SQL statements to replace query objects when possible (see Chapter 23, "Working with Structured Query Language"). Minimizing the number of objects also reduces the number of entries you must make when you establish database security restrictions (permissions) for your application.

PREPARING TO SHARE YOUR DATABASE FILES

To set up Access to share database files, you should verify the settings in the Advanced page of the Options properties sheet. You open the Advanced page by choosing Tools, Options and then clicking the Advanced tab (see Figure 24.8). The changes you make to Access options (called *preferences*) are stored for your account (Admin, the default) in the system database and apply to all databases you open thereafter using that system database.

Figure 24.8
The Advanced page of the Options properties sheet.

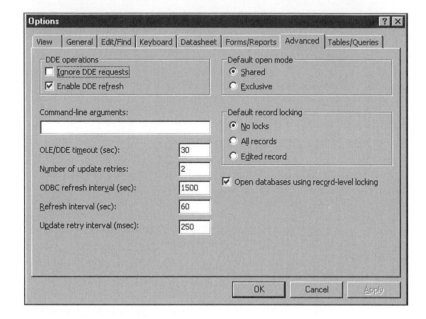

Following is a list in order of importance of the Advanced options that affect multiuser applications:

- *Default Open Mode* is set to Shared by default. Changing this setting to Exclusive so that only one user can open files improves performance. If you've changed the file open mode to Exclusive, you must return to the default Shared mode so that more than one user can open the file.

- *Default Record Locking* has three options designed to prevent more than one user from making simultaneous changes to the same record. No Locks, the default, causes a lock only when the edit occurs (*optimistic locking*). All Records locks the entire table when a user opens it for editing (*table locking*). Edited Records locks only the record(s) during the editing process (*pessimistic locking*).

NEW 2000
- *Open Databases Using Record-Level Locking* enables Access 2000's new row-at-a-time locking feature. Record-level locking makes INSERT and UPDATE operations on heavily trafficked databases less subject to contention problems than the page-level locking scheme of Access 97 and earlier. Record-level locking is the default.

- *Number of Update Retries* specifies the number of times Access attempts to update a locked record, at a rate determined by the value in the Update Retry Interval text box, before issuing a message box that the record is locked and cannot be updated.

- *Refresh Interval* determines how often the data displayed in a datasheet or form is rewritten automatically to reflect changes made by other members of the workgroup. *ODBC Refresh Interval* applies only to tables attached using the ODBC driver for tables linked from a foreign database, usually a client/server database.

Access 2000's default values are suitable for most multiuser applications. Unless you have a specific reason for making changes, accept the default values.

SPLITTING DATABASES FOR FILE SHARING

All Access developers agree that Access applications should be divided into two .mdb files: one containing only Access tables (also called *data objects*) and the other containing all other objects (called *application objects*). Splitting Access applications lets you link (attach) tables from the shared .mdb file to your application objects in a local .mdb file. Keeping the application objects on the user's computer minimizes network traffic and improves performance, especially on peer-to-peer networks. The major benefit of splitting Access applications, however, is the ability to easily update a user's application .mdb file without affecting current data stored in Jet tables.

> **Note**
>
> A secure version of Nwind.mdb and unsecure NwindData.mdb files you create in this chapter are located in the \Seua2k\Chaptr24 folder of the accompanying CD-ROM. If you don't intend to perform the examples in this chapter, copy the files to the C:\Shared\Nwind folder on your PC and connect to the System.mdw workgroup in this folder. Type **Access** as the logon ID and **2000** as the password to open your copy of the CD-ROM version of Nwind.mdb with Admins privileges. If you copy the files to a folder other than C:\Shared\Nwind, you must change the table links of Nwind.mdb and the database connections for the .htm files as described later in the chapter.

Microsoft recognized that most production database applications created with Access use the split design, so Access 2000 has a database utility to automate the process. Follow these steps to separate the tables from the application objects of the Nwind.mdb file using the Database Splitter Add-In:

1. Open Nwind.mdb in your \Shared\Nwind folder with \Shared\Nwind\System.mdw as your system database.

   Don't use your original copy of Northwind.mdb in …\Office\Samples for the examples in this chapter.

NEW 2000

2. With the Database window active, choose Tools, Database Utilities, Database Splitter to open the Database Splitter dialog, as shown in Figure 24.9. Prior versions of Access called the Database Splitter an add-in.

3. Verify that you have the copy of Nwind.mdb open, and then click the Split Database button to display the Database Splitter's Create Back-end Database dialog. The default file name is Nwind_be.mdb; "be" is an abbreviation for *back-end*.

Figure 24.9
The Database Splitter utility's opening dialog.

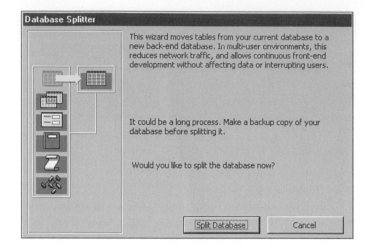

4. Type **NwindData.mdb** as the name of your back-end database file containing tables to link to application objects in Nwind.mdb (see Figure 24.10).

Figure 24.10
Selecting the directory and naming the back-end database file to contain the tables.

5. Click the Split button to create the back-end database. After a few seconds (depending on your computer's speed) of disk activity, you receive the message that the database is successfully split.

6. Click OK to close the Database Splitter dialog. The Tables page of your Database window appears, as shown in Figure 24.11. Arrows to the left of the table icons indicate linked files.

Figure 24.11
Newly created links to the tables moved to the back-end database.

7. To verify that the links to the tables are correct, choose Tools, Database Utilities, Linked Table Manager to display the Linked Table Manager's dialog, as shown in Figure 24.12. Like the Database Splitter, the Linked Table Manager formerly was classified as an add-in.

NEW 2000

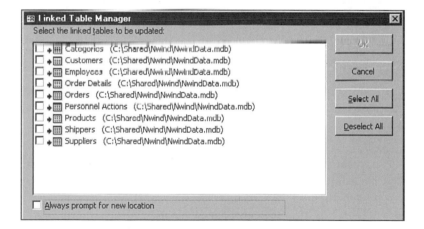

Figure 24.12
The Linked Table Manager utility, confirming the location and name of the back-end .mdb file containing the linked tables.

FIXING LINKS, DATA SOURCES, AND HYPERLINKS OF DAP

When you copy or move DAP, you must re-create the links to each page in the Database window. Otherwise, the links continue to point to the DAP in their original location; if you moved the DAP, the links are invalid because the original DAP are gone. This requirement applies to DAP you copy or move for any purpose, not just splitting databases. You also must change the data source for the DAP from the original database (Northwind.mdb) to the new back-end database (NwindData.mdb). Pages that have hyperlinks to other pages also need an update to the hyperlink URL.

UPDATING DATABASE WINDOW LINKS TO DAP

To change the location of the pointers to DAP in Nwind.mdb, do the following:

1. Click the Pages shortcut in the Database window, select the Analyze Sales page and press Delete, which opens the message box shown in Figure 24.13.

   If you haven't disabled the warning before deleting objects, you receive a message prior to that shown in Figure 24.13 requesting delete confirmation. You can turn off these warning messages by clearing the Confirm Document Deletions check box on the Edit/Find page of the Options dialog.

Figure 24.13
The message box that lets you select whether to delete both the link and the page or only the link.

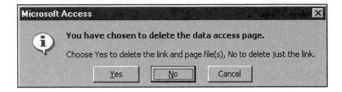

2. Click No to delete only the link. If you click Yes, you delete the .htm file from its original location.

3. Repeat step 2 for each page in the Pages list.

4. Click the Edit Web Page That Already Exists item to open the Locate Web Page dialog. Navigate to the \Shared\Nwind folder and select Analyze Sales.htm (see Figure 24.14). Click Open to open the page in Design view and re-create the page link to the file's new location. Change to Page view to verify the database connection, and then close the page.

> **Note**
>
> Links to the *PageName*_files folders for Cascading Stylesheet (CSS) files are relative, so changing the link to the .htm(l) page automatically takes care of linking templates to the pages.

5. Repeat step 4 for each of the remaining four pages.

CHANGING THE DATA SOURCE OF DAP

The data source of the DAP you copied and linked in the \Shared\Nwind folder is ...\Office\Samples\Northwind.mdb, so you must change the data source to \Shared\Nwind\NwindData.mdb. To change the data source for DAP, do the following:

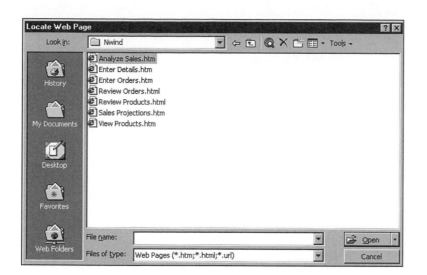

Figure 24.14
The Locate Web Page dialog for creating a page link in the Database window.

PART

IV

CH

24

1. Open each page in Design mode and click the toolbar's Field List button to open the Field List window.

2. Right-click the database name item at the top of the list (Northwind.mdb for this example), and choose Connection from the context menu to open the Data Link Properties sheet for the page.

3. Click the builder button to the right of the Database Name text box to open the Select Access Database dialog. Navigate to the shared folder (\Shared\Nwind), select the new back-end database (NwindData.mdb), and click OK to close the dialog and return to the Data Link Properties sheet (see Figure 24.15).

4. Click the Test Connection button to verify operability of the data source, and click OK when the Connection Succeeded message appears.

5. Repeat steps 1 through 4 for each of the DAP in your front-end .mdb file *except the Review Orders.htm and Sales.htm pages*.

6. The data source for the Review Orders.htm page is the Order Details Extended query in Nwind.mdb, which relies on links to the Order Details table in NwindData.mdb. Sales.htm depends on the Product Sales for 1997 query. Thus, you must select Nwind.mdb as the database for Review Orders.htm and Sales.htm when you repeat step 3.

Tip #208 from

R J

A better approach for DAP that depends on Jet queries against a shared database is to import the queries into the back-end database. Doing so creates a consistent data source for all DAP that connect to the database. Adding queries to shared back-end datbases isn't a generally-accepted practice; however, client/server back-end databases store views, stored procedures, and other application-related objects. Thus storing queries in Jet back-end databases is consistent with client/server architecture.

Figure 24.15
The Data Link Properties sheet for the updated connection to the new back-end database.

> **Note**
>
> Hopefully, future versions of the Database Splitter utility will handle the preceding chores for you automatically.

CHOOSING WORKGROUPS WITH THE WORKGROUP ADMINISTRATOR

If you have several workgroups that have overlapping user membership, you might want to place all the workgroup system databases in a single directory, such as \Shared, to make it easy for users to select a particular workgroup. (The workgroup system database doesn't have to be in the same directory as the shared .mdb file(s).) To use the Workgroup Administrator to change workgroups, follow these steps:

1. Launch Workgroup Administrator. Your current workgroup is identified by the .mdw file that appears in Workgroup Administrator's opening dialog.

2. Click the Join button to open the Workgroup Information File dialog. Your current workgroup system file appears in the Database text box (see Figure 24.16).

3. Type the well-formed path and name of the workgroup database file for the workgroup you want to join in the Database text box, or click the Browse button to display the Select Workgroup Information File dialog shown in Figure 24.17. In this case, choose the System.mdw in your \Program Files\Microsoft Office\Office folder to return to the normal Access configuration.

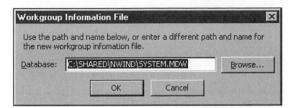

Figure 24.16
Your current workgroup displayed in the Workgroup Information File dialog.

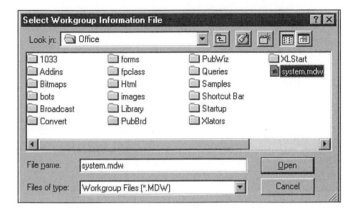

Figure 24.17
Selecting the workgroup database file for the new workgroup.

4. Select the drive and folder in which the System.mdw file for the new workgroup is located, and click Open to close the Select Workgroup Information File dialog. Your selection appears in the Workgroup Information File dialog.

5. Click OK to confirm your new workgroup selection; click OK when the message box confirms that you have joined the workgroup, and then click Exit of the Microsoft Workgroup Administrator's dialog to complete the process.

6. If Access is running, close it. Restart Access to use the new workgroup system file.

USING COMMAND-LINE OPTIONS TO OPEN A SHARED DATABASE

Access provides a number of options that you can use to customize how Access starts for each user. All users in a workgroup can share a common database, but you might want individual users to start Access with a different form. You can open a workgroup database automatically, execute a macro that opens a specific form, and supply a username or password when you start Access by entering options on the command line that you use to start Access for each workgroup member, as in the following example:

```
d:\msa_path\msaccess.exe [n:\mdb_path\mdb_name.mdb]
 [/User user_name ][/Pwd pass_word ][/X macro_name]
 [/Ro ][/Excl ] [{/Profile user_profile¦/Ini profile.ini}]
```

```
[/Repair] [/Nostartup]
[/Compact [target.mdb]] [/Convert target.mdb] [/Runtime]
[/Wrkgrp w:\mdw_path\system.mdw] [/Cmd cmd_value]
```

Spaces separate each of the optional command-line parameters. Table 24.1 describes the elements of the Access startup command-line options.

TABLE 24.1 COMMAND-LINE OPTIONS FOR LAUNCHING ACCESS

Command-Line Element	Function
d:\msa_path\msaccess.exe	Command to launch Access.
n:\mdb_path\mdb_name.mdb	Path and name of startup database file.
/User user_name	Start with user_name as username.
/Pwd pass_word	Start with pass_word as password.
/X macro_name	Run macro_name on startup.
/Ro	Open mdb_name for read-only use.
/Excl	Open mdb_name for exclusive use.
/Profile user_profile	Specify a user profile stored in the Registry named user_profile.
/Ini profile.ini	Open \Windows\profile.ini instead of using Registry entries.
/Repair	Repair the database, and then close Access.
/NoStartup	Don't display the Access startup dialog.
/Compact target.mdb	Compact into target.mdb or into the startup database if you omit target.mdb.
/Convert target.mdb	Converts a prior version .mdb file to an Access 2000 .mdb file with the name specified by target.mdb, which is required and cannot be the same name as mdb_name.
/Runtime	Starts Msaccess.exe in runtime mode for testing or to restrict users from entering Design mode.
/Wrkgrp system.mdw	Specifies a workgroup system file, system.mdw, on startup.
/Cmd cmd_value	Specifies a value to be returned by the VBA **Command** function.

Tip #209 from

Opening the local application .mdb with the /Excl parameter speeds operation of the application. The /Excl option applies to the local database, not the attached tables of the shared data .mdb file. Do not use the /Excl option if you want other users to be able to share the database. When you omit the /Excl option, shared or exclusive use of databases is determined by the Default Open Mode for Databases choice of the Multiuser Options, discussed in a previous section, "Preparing to Share Your Database Files."

Caution

Never use the /Ro option when opening a shared database. If you specify the /Ro option for one workstation, all workstations in the workgroup are restricted to read-only use of the database. Use the permissions features of Access, described in the "Maintaining Database Security" section of this chapter, to designate the users who can update the data in tables and those who cannot.

The sequence in which you enter the command-line options doesn't affect the options' operation; however, a convention is that the name of the file to open always immediately follows the command that launches the application. The /Cmd *cmd_value* entry must be the last command-line option.

1. Create a desktop shortcut to Msaccess.exe, and then right-click the shortcut and choose Rena<u>m</u>e from the context menu. Give the shortcut an appropriate name, in this case **Northwind Shared**.

2. Right-click the shortcut again and choose Prope<u>r</u>ties from the context menu. Click the Shortcut tab to display the Shortcut properties page.

3. After **"...\Msaccess.exe"**, add the path and name of your .mdb file, **/Nostartup**, and **/Wrkgrp C:\Shared\Nwind\System.mdw**. For this example, the full command line for the Windows 9x shortcut is "C:\Program Files\Microsoft Office\Office\Msaccess.exe" C:\Shared\Nwind\Nwind.mdb /Nostartup /Wrkgrp C:\Shared\Nwind\Nwind.mdb .

4. Optionally, type **C:\Shared\Nwind** in the Start In text box. If you specify in the Start In text box the folder holding the workgroup file, you don't need to add the path to the workgroup file to the command line; you must, however, include the full path in the *mdb name*.mdb parameter.

5. Select Maximized from the Run list to start Access maximized (see Figure 24.18).

Note

If you're using Windows 98 or Windows NT 4+, the name of the executable file must be enclosed within double quotes ("....exe") if the path or file (or both) contains spaces.

When you double-click the new shortcut, Access launches, uses the workgroup system database specified by the /Wrkgrp command-line parameter, and automatically opens the file specified on the command-line parameter. When you distribute your Access application .mdb to other users, include a copy of the shortcut.

Caution

Adding a user's password as an option to the startup command line violates one of the basic rules of database security: Do not disclose your password to any other person. The preceding example that uses a password as a command-line option does so only for the purpose of completely defining the options available. You should not use the /Pwd command-line option under any circumstances.

Figure 24.18
Entering command-line
parameters for an Access
shortcut in Windows 98.

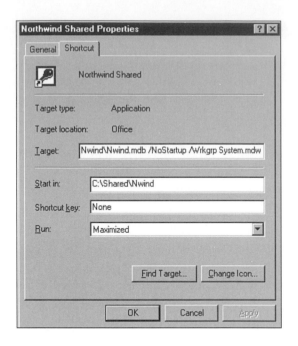

MAINTAINING DATABASE SECURITY

Database security prevents unauthorized persons from accidentally or intentionally viewing, modifying, deleting, or destroying information contained in a database. Database security is of primary concern in a multiuser environment, although you might want to use Access's security features to prevent others from viewing or modifying databases stored on your single-user computer. This section describes the multi-layered security features of networked Access databases and how you use these features to ensure a secure database system.

SPECIFYING THE PRINCIPLES OF DATABASE SECURITY ON A LAN

Ten basic principles of database security exist for databases installed on a LAN. Five of these principles are associated with the network operating system:

■ Each user of a network must be positively identified before the user can gain access to the network. Identification requires a unique username and secret password for each user. Users must not share their passwords with one another, and all passwords used should be changed every 60 to 90 days.

■ Each identified user of the network must be authorized to have access to specific elements of the network, such as server directories, printers, and other shared resources. Each user has a network account that incorporates the user's identification data and authorizations. The network file that contains this information is always encrypted and is accessible only by the network administrator(s).

- Actions of network users should be monitored to determine whether users are attempting to access elements of the network for which they don't have authorization. Users who repeatedly attempt to breach network security should be locked out of the network until appropriate administrative action can be taken.

- The network should be tamper-proof. Tamper-proofing includes installing security systems immune to hacking by ingenious programmers and testing routinely for the presence of viruses.

- Data stored on network servers must be protected against hardware failure and catastrophic destruction (fires, earthquakes, hurricanes, and so on) by adequate and timely backup. Backup systems enable you to reconstruct the data to its state at the time the last backup occurred.

The measures required to establish the first five principles are the responsibility of the network administrator for a server-based system. In a peer-to-peer network, network security measures are the responsibility of each person who shares his or her resources with others. The remaining five principles of database security are determined by the security capabilities of the database management system and the applications you create with it:

- The contents of tables in a database should be encrypted to prevent viewing the data with a file-reading or other snooping utility.

- Users must be further identified before they are allowed to open a database file. A secret password, different from a user's network access password, should be used. The database file that contains user identification and password data (database user accounts) must be encrypted. The encryption technique used should be sophisticated enough to prevent hackers from deciphering it. Only the database administrator(s) have access to this file.

Tip #210 from	Using a separate password for the database file is recommended especially for databases shared on peer-to-peer networks, which have simple security mechanisms. Using Windows NT's integrated security for access to client/server databases with your Windows NT domain account logon is an acceptable practice.

- Users must be assigned specific permission to use the database and the tables it contains. If users are to be restricted from viewing specific columns of a table, access to the table should be in the form of a query that includes only the fields the user s authorized to view. The RDBMS must provide for revoking specific permissions as the need arises.

- The data in tables should be auditable. Lack of auditability is an incentive to computer-based embezzling. Updates made by users to tables that contain financial data should be maintained in a log, preferably in another database, that identifies the user who made the entry and the date and time the update was made. Logs are useful in reconstructing database entries that occurred between the time the database was last backed up and the time data was restored from the backup copy.

■ Operations that update records in more than one table should be accomplished by transaction techniques that can be reversed (or *rolled back*) if updates to all the tables involved cannot be completed immediately.

Most network operating systems in use on PCs provide for the first five database security principles, but enforcement of password secrecy, monitoring of user transgressions, and virus surveillance often are ignored, especially in peer-to-peer networks. Access provides all five of the database security principles, but you must take specific actions to invoke and maintain these principles.

> **Note**
>
> One of the most frequent breaches of database security occurs when a temporary worker is hired to stand in for a user who is ill or on vacation. Instead of establishing a new network account, including a user name, password, and new user (or guest) account for the database, the employee's user names and passwords are divulged to the temporary worker for the sake of expediency. A temporary worker should be assigned his or her own identification for the network and database; remove the temporary worker's authorization when the regular employee returns to the job.

PASSWORD-PROTECTING A SINGLE DATABASE

Access 2000 offers password protection for individual database files. Setting a database password is the easiest way to partially secure a database while allowing others who don't know the password to use the copy of Access on your PC with other .mdb files. To activate the database password for a specific .mdb file, complete the following steps:

NEW 2000

1. You can't set a database password in shared access mode, so close the open database, and then choose File, Open Database to display the Open dialog. Select your .mdb file, click the arrow button to the right of the Open button, and choose Open Exclusive from the context menu to open the database in exclusive access mode (see Figure 24.19).

2. Choose Tools, Security, Set Database Password to display the Set Database Password dialog.

3. Type a password in the Password text box. Your entry is shown as a series of asterisks to prevent disclosing your password to others as you enter it. Passwords are case sensitive, so Uxmal is a different password from uxmal.

4. Type the password in the Verify text box to test your entry (see Figure 24.20). The verification test is not case sensitive. Click OK.

5. Close the database, and then reopen it. The Password Required dialog shown in Figure 24.21 opens.

6. Enter the password exactly as you typed it in step 3. Press Enter or click OK. If you enter the password correctly, Access continues the startup procedure. If you type an incorrect password, Access displays an error message and won't open the database.

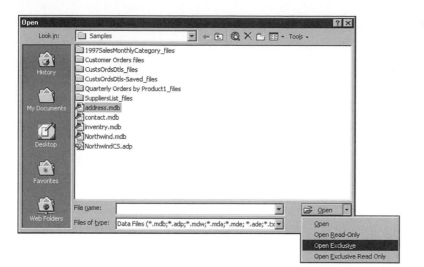

Figure 24.19
Opening an Access database in exclusive mode.

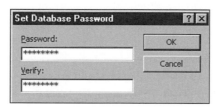

Figure 24.20
The Set Database Password dialog, establishing a password required to open a specific database.

Figure 24.21
Attempting to open a password-protected database.

To remove password protection from a database, open the database for exclusive access, and then choose Tools, Security, Unset Database Password. Type the password in the Password text box of the Unset Database Password dialog, and then click OK.

Caution

Don't use database password protection for databases that you intend to replicate using Access 2000's Briefcase Replication. Database password protection causes the replication process to fail.

MANAGING GROUPS AND USERS

Most client/server databases establish the following three groups of database users:

- *Administrators* (Admins) have the authority to view and update existing tables and add or delete tables and other database objects from the database. Members of the Admins group usually have permission to modify the applications contained in databases.

- *Regular members of workgroups* (Users) have permission to open the database and are granted permission to view and modify databases on a selective basis. Users ordinarily aren't granted permission to modify Access applications. In Access, Admins also are members of the Users group.

- *Occasional users of databases* (Guests) often are granted limited rights to use a database and the objects it contains but aren't assigned a user account. Guest privileges often are assigned to persons being trained in the use of a database application. Access 2000 doesn't define a Guests group.

When you install Access 2000, you're automatically made a member of the Admins and Users groups with the name Admin and have all permissions granted. You have an empty password and Personal Indentification code (PID), which means you don't need to enter a password to log onto the database(s) associated with the System.mdw database installed in the …\Office folder. When you're learning Access, you have little reason to establish database security. After you begin to create a useful database application, especially if it contains confidential information, you should implement basic security provisions, even on your own computer.

Note

NEW 2000 The term PID takes the place of the former Personal ID Number (PIN), which implies the use of numbers only. Using a combination of letters and numbers vastly increases the possible codes you can use and thus makes cracking a PID more difficult. The requirement for a combination of numbers and letters for user PIDs is new in Access 2000.

ESTABLISHING YOUR OWN ADMINS NAME, PASSWORD, AND PID

Access has two levels of security: application level and file level. The *application-level security system* requires each user of Access to enter a user name and a password to start Access.

File-level security is established by the network operating system, such as Windows NT Server, and grants users permissions for access to shared folders and/or individual files. Establishing single-user application-level security and preparing for multiuser security requires that you perform the following sequence of tasks:

1. Activate the logon procedure for Access. This action requires that you add a password for the Admin user. To remain Admin, you need not complete the remaining steps, but your only security is your password.

2. Create a new account for yourself as a member of the Admins group.

3. Log onto Access using your new Admins user account.

4. Remove the default Admin user account from the Admins group. The Admins group should include entries for active database administrators only. You can't remove the Admin user from the Users group.

Before you begin the following procedure, make a disk backup copy of the System.mdw file in use and any database files that you created or modified while using this System.mdw. If you forget the user name or password you assigned to yourself after deleting the Admin user, you can't log onto Access. In this case, you must restore the original version of the System.mdw file. Then you might not be able to open the database files with which the original version of the System.mdw file is associated unless you restore the backed-up versions. It's recommended that you modify the System.mdw file you created in the \Shared\Nwind folder as your system database for all the examples that follow in this chapter.

Caution

Don't use the Northwind.mdb database in your ...\Office\Samples folder for the examples that follow. You should preserve Northwind.mdb and the System.mdw file of your ...\Office\Access folder in the original state. Use the Nwind.mdb file created earlier in this chapter with the Database Splitter and use the System.mdw workgroup file located in the \Shared\Nwind directory.

Tip #211 from

You don't need to open a database to add or modify user accounts. All user account information is stored in System.mdw, which Access automatically opens when launched.

To activate the logon procedure for Access, complete the following steps:

1. A temporary password to the Admin user is necessary to activate Access's logon procedure. Choose Tools, Security, User and Group Accounts to open the User and Group Accounts properties sheet (see Figure 24.22). You are logged on as Admin, a member of the Admins and Users group, by default.

2. Click the Change Logon Password tab to display the Change Logon Password page.

Note

If you don't change the Admin user's password, you automatically are logged on as Admin with a blank password each time you start Access.

3. Press the Tab key to bypass the Old Password text box (this enters the equivalent of an empty password), and enter a difficult-to-guess password, such as **Xy8zW3ab**, in the New Password text box. Your entry is shown as a series of asterisks to prevent disclosing your password to others as you enter it. Passwords are case sensitive, so Xy8zW3ab is a different password from xy8zw3ab.

Figure 24.22
The default opening page, Users, of the User and Group Accounts properties sheet.

4. Type the password in the Verify text box to test your entry, as shown in Figure 24.23. The verification test is not case sensitive. Click OK to close the properties sheet.

Figure 24.23
The Change Logon Password page used to establish your new Admin password.

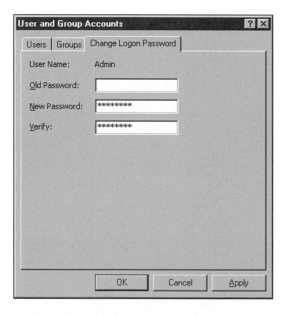

NEW 2000 5. Exit Access and launch it again, and then open the Nwind.mdb database. The Admin account is password-protected, so the Logon dialog appears. Prior versions of Access required you to log on to start Access after applying security features. Once you log onto a database, you can open, without a logon step, other databases for which your user name and password is valid.

6. Type **admin** in the Name text box, press Tab, and type the password exactly as you typed it in step 3 (see Figure 24.24). Press Enter or click OK. If you type the password correctly, Access continues the startup procedure.

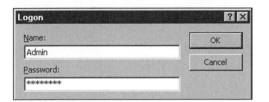

Figure 24.24
The Logon dialog that appears when you protect the Admin account with a password.

To add your new user account in the Admins group, do the following:

1. Choose Tools, Security, User and Group Accounts to display the User and Group Accounts properties sheet (refer to Figure 24.23). All members of the Admins group automatically are included (and must be included) in the Users group. Both Admins and Users appear in the Member Of list.

2. Click the New button to open the New User/Group dialog.

NEW 2000

3. Type the name you want to use to identify yourself to Access in the Name text box and enter a PID having four or more numbers and letters in the Personal ID text box (see Figure 24.25). The PID, with the Name entry, uniquely identifies your account. This precaution is necessary because two people might use the same logon name; the Name and PID values are combined to create a no-duplicates index on the Users table in your current system database file. Click OK to close the New User/Group dialog and return to the User and Group Accounts page.

4. *This is a critical step.* Select Admins in the Available Groups list and click the Add button to add the Admins group to your new user name (see Figure 24.26). If you fail to do this, you cannot later remove the Admin account from the Admins group. (Access requires that there be at least one member of the Admins group in each system database file.)

Note

When you log on with your new user name, you can't see the names of the last four databases you opened as Admin when you choose File, Open. Prior database selections are specific to each user.

5. You don't enter a password for the new user at this time because you still are logged onto Access as Admin. Click OK to close the User and Group Accounts properties sheet and then exit Access.

Figure 24.25

Adding a new account for the Admins group with the New User/Group dialog.

Figure 24.26

Adding the Admins group to your new user account.

6. Launch Access, type your new user name in the Logon dialog, and press Enter or click OK. Don't enter a password because you have an empty password at this point. User names aren't case sensitive; Access considers NewAdmin and newadmin to be the same user.

7. Choose Tools, Security, User and Group Accounts, select your new user name from the Name dropdown list, and click the Change Logon Password tab. Press Tab to bypass the Old Password text box and type the password you plan to use until it's time to change your password (to maintain system security). Passwords can be up to 14 characters long and can contain any character, except ASCII character 0, the Null character. Verify your password, and then press Enter or click OK to close the Password sheet.

8. Close and reopen Access and log on with your new user name and password. This step verifies that your new Admins user name and password are valid.

9. Choose Tools, Security, User and Group Accounts. Open the Users list of the User and Group Accounts page and select your new user name from the list. Verify that you are a member of the Admins and Users group.

10. Open the Users list again and select the Admin user. Select Admins in the Member Of list; then click Remove. Admin remains a member of the Users group, as shown in Figure 24.27. Click OK to close the properties sheet.

Figure 24.27
Removing the Admin user from the Admins group.

You use the same procedure to add other users as members of the default Admins or Users group or of new workgroups you create. You have not fully secured the open database because the Admin user still has full permissions for the objects in the database. Revoking the Admin user's permissions is discussed in the "Changing the Ownership of Database Objects" section later in the chapter.

Note

Write down and save your PID and the PID of every user you add to the workgroup for future reference. User names and PIDs aren't secure elements, so you can safely keep a list without compromising system security. This list should be accessible only to database administrators. You need a user's PID so that the user can be recognized as a member of another workgroup when the need arises. (See the "Granting Permissions for a Database in Another Workgroup" section near the end of this chapter.)

ESTABLISHING MEMBERS OF ACCESS GROUPS

Groups within Access's security system are not the same as workgroups. As discussed previously, a workgroup shares the same system database file that's located in a designated directory. The entries you made in the preceding steps were saved in the workgroup or system database file that was active when you launched Access. This section describes how to add new users to a group, a process similar to the one you used to add your new Admins account.

To add a new user to an existing group, you must be logged onto Access as a member of the Admins group and complete the following steps:

1. Choose Tools, Security, User and Group Accounts to open the User and Group Accounts dialog.

2. With the Users page active, click New. The New User/Group dialog appears. Type the new user's name and PID. Click OK to create the account and close the dialog. The Users dialog reappears. Make a note of the PID you used to add the new user. You must know the user's PID so that you can duplicate an entry for the new user in other workgroups.

3. The default group for all new users is Users. To add the user to the Admins group, select Admins in the Available Groups list and click the Add button to add Admins to the Member Of list (refer to Figure 24.26). All Access users must be members of the Users group. Click OK to return to Access's main window when your selections are complete.

4. Request the new user to log onto Access with the user name and change his or her password from the default empty value to a legitimate password.

   You can improve the level of security by typing the new user's password yourself, so that users cannot bypass the password step by leaving their password blank. To enter a password for a new user, close Access, log on as the new user, and enter the user's chosen password in the Change Logon Password page.

Before you add a significant number of users, decide whether you need additional groups and determine the permissions that should be assigned to each group other than Admins. These aspects of database security are discussed in the following sections.

Tip #212 from

> When requesting new users to enter their first password, emphasize the advantage of the use of longer passwords that combine upper- and lowercase characters and numbers because they improve system security. Users should not use their initials, names of spouses or children, birth dates, or nicknames; these are the entries that unauthorized users try first to gain access to the system.

ADDING A NEW GROUP

In most cases, Admins and Users are the only groups necessary for each workgroup you create. Members of a group usually share the same permissions to use database objects (which is the subject of the next section). Adding a new Access group isn't necessary, therefore, unless you have a category of users who are to have a different set of permissions than members of the Users group. Such a category could distinguish Users (who might be limited to viewing data) from members of a Data Entry group who have permission to update the data in tables.

To add a new group, perform the following steps:

1. Choose Tools, Security, User and Group Accounts. Then click the Groups tab. Currently defined groups appear in the Name dropdown list.

2. Click the New button to open the New User/Group dialog.

NEW 2000

3. Type the name of the group in the Name dialog and a four-digit Personal ID Number, as shown in Figure 24.28. Group names can be up to 20 characters long, must contain digits and letters, and can contain spaces, but punctuation symbols aren't allowed. You don't need to make a note of the PID in the case of groups because the PID is used only for indexing purposes.

Figure 24.28
Adding a new Data Entry group to the workgroup.

4. Press Enter or click OK. The Groups dialog reappears.

5. Click OK from the Groups dialog. You can delete the newly added group by clicking Delete.

After you add a new group, you must assign the default permissions that apply to all members of the group by using the procedure outlined in the "Granting and Revoking Permissions for Database Objects" section later in this chapter.

DELETING USERS AND GROUPS

Members of the Admins group have the authority to delete users from any group and to delete any group except Admins and Users. To delete a user or group, choose Tools, Security, User and Group Accounts, select the user or group to delete from the list box, and click Delete. You are asked to confirm the deletion. Admins and Users groups must each contain one user account; you cannot delete all users for either of these groups.

CLEARING FORGOTTEN PASSWORDS

If a user forgets his or her password and you are logged in to Access as a member of the Admins group, you can delete the user's password so that you or the user can enter a new password.

To clear a user's password, complete the following steps:

1. Choose Tools, Security, User and Group Accounts. Make sure the Users tab is active.

2. Open the Name list and select the user whose password you want to clear.

3. Click the Clear Password button (refer to Figure 24.27).

4. Make sure that the user whose password you cleared enters a new password, or log onto Access as the new user and enter a new password for the user.

As mentioned previously, entering the user's password as the database administrator is the only means of ensuring that the database security is enforced. There's no other means of ensuring that users assign themselves passwords. (Of course, perverse users can change their passwords to empty strings or "password" if they choose to do so.)

UNDERSTANDING DATABASE OBJECT OWNERSHIP

The user who creates an object becomes the owner of the object. (Access calls the owner of an object the object's *creator*.) Object owners have special status within the Access security system. The following two sections briefly describe owners' permissions and how to change the ownership of database objects.

Tip #213 from	A more detailed description of object ownership is contained in a "Microsoft Access for Windows 95" white paper that you can read at `http://www.microsoft.com/access-dev/articles/SECURE70.HTM`. The security model of Access 2000 differs only slightly from Access 95, but Access 2000's security implementation is more robust than prior versions.

OWNER PERMISSIONS FOR OBJECTS

The owner of an object has full (Administer) permissions for the object. No other user, including members of the Admins group, can alter the object owner's permissions for the object directly. For example, the Admin user is the owner of all the database objects in Northwind.mdb. Thus, anyone who uses the Admin user account has full permissions for all objects in Northwind.mdb. This is one of the reasons for assigning a password for the Admin account.

When a user other than the object's creator adds a new object to the database or to one of the existing objects in the database, this user becomes the owner of the object. For example, if user Margaret adds a control object to a form created by Larry, Margaret is the owner of the control object, not Larry. Mixed ownership of objects can lead to bizarre situations, such as the inability of the owner of a query to execute the query because the owner of the underlying tables has changed. (You can overcome this problem, however, by adding the WITH OWNERACCESS OPTION to the Jet SQL statement for the query or by changing the Run Permissions property of the query from User's to Owner's.)

When you create new database objects using the default Admin user ID, anyone else who has a retail copy of Access 2000 and uses the default Admin user ID also has full permissions for these objects. Thus, when you begin development of an application that you intend to share with others or that you want to prevent others from using or modifying, create a new account in the Admins group as described earlier in the chapter. Use your new Admins account when you create new applications.

CHANGING THE OWNERSHIP OF DATABASE OBJECTS

Following are the three methods of changing the ownership of existing Access database objects:

- Log on with the Admins account to which you want to assign ownership, create a new database file, and then choose <u>F</u>ile, <u>G</u>et External Data, <u>I</u>mport. Open the .mdb file containing the objects, and import all the objects into the new .mdb file. The user who creates the new .mdb file becomes the owner of the imported objects.

- Use the Change Owner page of the User and Group Permissions dialog.

- Use the Security Wizard to create a new secure database file, import the objects, and then encrypt the new database. Access 2000's new Security Wizard, the subject of the "Using the Security Wizard to Change Permissions" section later in the chapter, lets you change ownership of objects and assign permissions for objects in a series of dialogs.

To use the Change Owner feature that originated in Access 95, you must be a member of the Admins group for the database and follow these steps:

1. Open the database containing the objects whose ownership you want to change, C:\Shared\Nwind\Nwind.mdb for this example.

2. Choose Tools, Security, User and Group Permissions to open the User and Group Permissions dialog, and then click the Change Owner tab.

3. Choose the class of object you want to change in the Object Type dropdown list.

4. If you want to change the ownership of all the objects of the selected class, select the first item in the Object list, move to the bottom of the list, press the Shift key, and click the last item of the list.

5. Select the new owner's name from the New Owner dropdown list.

6. Click the Change Owner button to change the ownership of the selected items, from Admin to RogerJ in this example (see Figure 24.29).

Figure 24.29
Changing the ownership of all tables from Admin to a new owner.

Tip #214 from
RJ

Changing the ownership of tables in the application .mdb file only changes ownership of the links to the back-end tables in the data .mdb file. You also must change ownership of (and set appropriate permissions for) the data .mdb file.

7. Repeat steps 3 through 6 for each class of objects whose ownership you want to change.

The preceding process is the fastest way to remove permissions of the Admin user accrued from ownership of the original objects.

GRANTING AND REVOKING PERMISSIONS FOR DATABASE OBJECTS

The second layer of Access security is at the *database level*. Access lets the database administrator grant or revoke permissions to use specific database objects to all members of a group or to specific members of a group. Permissions grant authority for users to view or alter specific database objects. The permissions granted to the group are inherited by each member as he or she is added to the group. Thus, it's important that you establish the group permissions you want before adding users to a group.

Users who are members of more than one group, such as Admins and Users, inherit database object permissions from each group. You can grant additional permissions to individual members of a group, but you cannot revoke permissions that individual members inherit from the group. Permissions are stored within the database file as properties of individual database objects. Only members of the Admins group or users who have Administer permission can grant or revoke permissions for database objects.

Caution

Be sure to change the ownership of tables in the data .mdb file from the Admin account to your secure account in Admins. If you don't change ownership, any user of retail Access who uses the default Admin account can open the data .mdb file and make changes at will to the file. Your shared data .mdb file must use the same .mdw file as the application .mdb files to properly identify groups and users. The application .mdb file must grant all users at least Read Data and Update Data permissions for the linked table to permit users to refresh the links if you move the data .mdb file.

Table 24.2 lists the permissions offered by Access for database objects, ranked in ascending level of authority. Full permissions allow the user to use all the features of Access, including design functions. The description of the specific action allowed by a permission is listed in the Explicit Permissions column. Permissions at an authority level below Full Permissions require other permissions to operate; these required permissions are called implicit permissions.

TABLE 24.2 PERMISSIONS TO USE ACCESS DATABASE OBJECTS

Permission	Database Objects	Explicit Permissions	Implicit Permissions
Open/Run	Forms, reports, macros	Use or run objects	Read Data
Read Design	All	View objects	Execute for macros only
Modify Design	All	Alter, replace, or delete objects	Update Data and Execute

continues

PART

IV

CH

24

TABLE 24.2   CONTINUED

Permission	Database Objects	Explicit Permissions	Implicit Permissions
Administer	All database objects	All permissions	Not applicable
Read Data	Tables, queries, forms	View data in objects	Read Design
Update Data	Tables, queries, forms	Edit table data	Read Data
Insert Data	Tables, queries, forms	Append data in tables	Read Data
Delete Data	Tables, queries, forms	Delete data in tables	Read Data

If, for example, you allow a user to modify design, this user also must be able to modify data and execute objects. Therefore, Update Data and Open/Run permissions are implied by the Modify Design permission. This user, and any other users allowed to modify data, must be able to read data. All users having permission to read data must be able to read designs. When you establish permissions for a database object, Access adds the implicit permissions automatically.

The Admins and Users groups have full permissions for any new database objects you create. If you intend to share the database with other users, you probably don't want all members of the Users group to have permission to update database tables, and certainly you don't want members of the Users Group to be able to modify the design of your database objects. A more conservative set of permissions for the two groups follows:

- The Admins group has full permissions for all objects. Admins privileges should be assigned to as few individuals as possible. Make sure you have enough backup database administrators with Admins privileges to cover for the absence of the primary administrator. Members of the Admins group are also members of the Users group.

- The Users group has Open/Run and Read Data permissions. Update, Insert, and Delete Data permissions are granted for specific forms and reports. Users should never be granted Modify Design permission in databases.

You can add new groups with specific group permissions, such as Data Entry or Developers, to make assigning individual user permissions for database objects simpler. You can then remove all permissions from the Users Group.

> **Note**
>
> You can change the Run Permissions property of the query from User's to Owner's or add the WITH OWNERACCESS OPTION to Jet SQL statements to enable users without the required permissions to execute a query whose owner (the person who designed the query) has the required permissions for the underlying tables.

USING THE SECURITY WIZARD TO CHANGE PERMISSIONS

You can change the ownership of and permissions for all the objects in a database for which you have Administer permissions by importing all the database objects into a new database you create with a user ID other than Admin. Access 2.0 first made it easy to import all the database objects from one .mdb file into another .mdb file with its Import Database Add-In. Access 2000's greatly enhanced Security Wizard goes the Import Database Add-In one better by letting you choose the database objects to secure a copy of the database in a long series of steps. One of the primary benefits of the new Security Wizard is that you can add groups, users, and assign object permission in a series of linked dialogs.

PART

IV

CH

24

> **Caution**
>
> Don't use the Security Wizard with the Northwind.mdb database in your
> ...\Office\Samples directory. Use the Nwind.mdb and NwindData.mdb files created earlier
> in this chapter with the Database Splitter, and use the System.mdw file in your
> \Shared\Nwind directory.

NEW 2000

To test Access 2000's updated Security Wizard, follow these steps:

1. If you aren't logged onto Access, launch Access and log on with your new user ID that includes Admins group membership and open the database to secure, NwindData.mdb in this case.

2. Choose Tools, Security, User-Level Security Wizard to display the Security Wizard's opening dialog. Accept the default Modify My Current Workgroup Information File, unless you have a particular reason for creating a new .mdw file (see Figure 24.30). Click Next to open the second Wizard dialog.

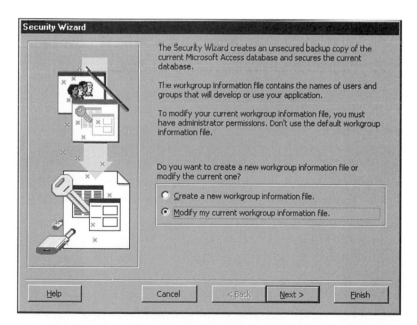

Figure 24.30
Choosing to modify the current .mdw file or create a new workgroup file.

3. By default, the Wizard secures all objects in the database. Click the appropriate tab that corresponds to the class of database objects that you don't want to make secure, and

then clear the check box for the individual object. If you want to secure all database objects, accept the Wizard's default. NwindData.mdb contains only tables (see Figure 24.31). Click Next to proceed to the third Wizard dialog.

Figure 24.31
Setting the types of objects to secure in the new database.

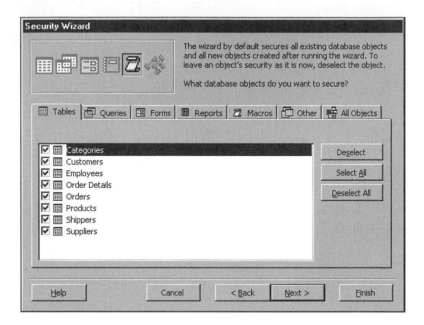

4. Secure Access 2000 databases offer you the option of providing a password for the Visual Basic Environment (VBE), also called the VBA Editor, if your database contains VBA code. NwindData.mdb doesn't (and won't ever) include code, so you safely can leave the password empty (see Figure 24.32). Click Next to open the fourth Wizard dialog.

5. Access 2000's Security Wizard has a collection of predefined groups with a specific set of access permissions appropriate to the group. Text within the Group Permissions frame describes the object permissions for each group. The Wizard adds the groups you specify in this dialog to the current .mdw file. Mark the check boxes of the groups to gain permissions for the tables of NwindData.mdb (see Figure 24.33). Click Next.

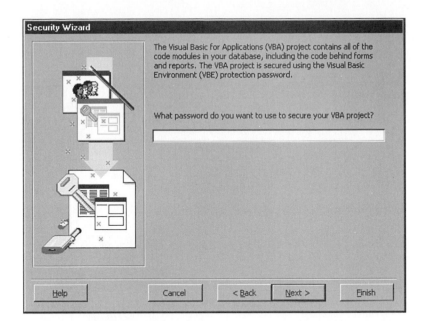

Figure 24.32
Specifying or omitting a password for the Visual Basic Environment.

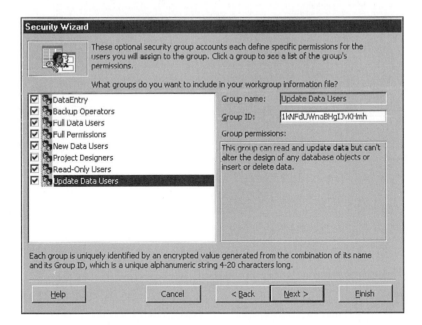

Figure 24.33
Specifying Wizard-added groups having permissions for selected objects.

**NEW
2000**

6. Traditionally, members of the Access Users group have full permissions for all objects. Select No, the Users Group Should Not Have Any Permissions, unless you have a very specific reason for doing otherwise (see Figure 24.34). Click Next to continue with the Security Wizard's task.

Figure 24.34
Removing from the Users group all permissions for objects in the secure database.

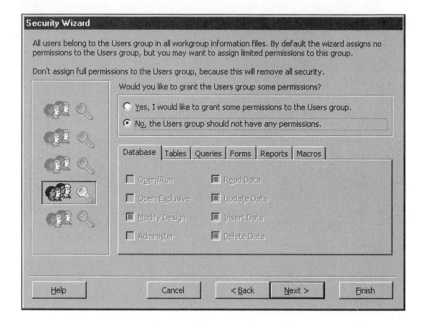

**NEW
2000**

7. Another new feature of the Access 2000 Security Wizard is the ability to add new users to your .mdw file during the securing process. Type the name of a new user in the User Name text box and provide a password, which appears in the clear in the Password text box (see Figure 24.35). Click the Add This User to the List button. You can add as many new users as you want at this point; click Next when you've finished adding users.

**NEW
2000**

8. You can assign or remove (except from Users) group memberships of all users in your workgroup file (see Figure 24.36). After making group assignments, click Next to open the last Wizard dialog.

Figure 24.35
Adding a new user to the current workgroup file.

Figure 24.36
Adding the new user added in Figure 24.35 to the Read-Only Users group.

9. The Wizard secures the current database, but creates a unsecured backup database copy in the process. The default name of the backup file is *DatabaseName*.bak (see Figure 24.37).

Figure 24.37
Specifying the path and file name for the unsecured backup copy of the new secure database file.

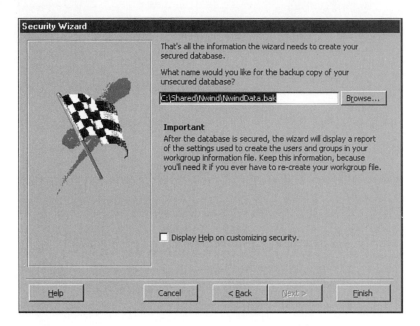

NEW 2000

10. Click Finish to put the Security Wizard to work. After a few seconds, the "One-step Security Wizard Report" shown in Figure 24.38 appears, indicating successful creation of the new secure database. Take the Wizard's advice to print a copy of the report and store it in a secure place for future reference. The report for the preceding steps is three pages. Close the report.

11. Closing the report opens a message box asking if you want to save a Report Snapshot (.snp) file that you can view with the Access Snapshot viewer. Click Yes to create and view NwindData.snp, which is identical to the report created in the preceding step.

12. Close the NwindData.snp window. The Wizard has added new users and assigned object permissions. You can confirm the Wizard's work in the User and Group Accounts and User and Group Permissions dialogs. Object permissions are the subject of the next section.

Note

Prior versions of the Security Wizard automatically encrypted the database. If you want the added security of database encryption, close the database, then choose Tools, Security, Encrypt/Decrypt Database, and specify the name of the encrypted file.

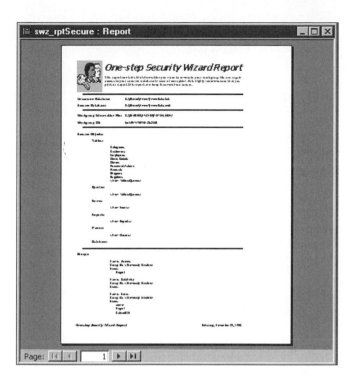

Figure 24.38
The Security Wizard's report indicating successful completion of the multi-step task.

The owner of all the objects in the new database is the user ID you used when you opened the source database. Only members of the Admins group have access of any kind to the newly secured database.

> **Note**
>
> This chapter uses the term *user ID* to identify users of Access. Internally, Access uses a *system ID* (*SID*) to identify users. The SID is a value that Access computes from the user ID, password, and PID. The SID is stored in the MSysUsers table of System.mdw as an encrypted binary value in a field of the Binary (varbinary) data type.

ALTERING GROUP PERMISSIONS MANUALLY

After you design your hierarchy of permissions and add initial user groups and users with the Security Wizard, you can change group permissions for each of the objects in your database. Only members of the Admins group can alter permissions for Groups or Users. The Permissions check boxes that are enabled depend on the type of object you choose. Open/Run, for example, is enabled only for database, form, report, and macro objects.

> **Note**
>
> When you first select the Admins group, none of the Admins group's permission check boxes are marked. Members of the Admins group inherit full object permissions from

continues

continued

> membership in the Users group. (By default, Users have full permissions for all objects.) If you revoke object permissions for the Users group, you add Administer permissions for the Admins group.

To change the permissions for a group, do the following:

1. Open the database for which group permissions are to be granted or revoked with the appropriate workgroup system database active.

2. Choose Tools, Security, User and Group Permissions to open the User and Group Permissions dialog .

3. Click the Groups option button to display the permissions for groups of users.

4. Open the Object Type dropdown list and select the type of database object whose permissions you want to change.

5. Select the specific object to which the new permissions will apply in the Object Name list. To select all objects, click the first item in the list, press the Shift key, and then click the last item in the list. Don't include <New ObjectType> in your multiple selection.

6. In the User/Group Name list, select the group whose permissions you want to revise, DataEntry for this example. No DataEntry permissions exist for tables because the Security Wizard removed all User group permissions.

7. Permissions currently granted to the group are shown by a check mark in the Permissions check boxes. Mark the Read Design, Read Data, Update Data, Insert Data, and Delete Data check boxes to allow the Data group to read, update, and add table data. If you have made multiple selections, you might need to click the check box twice to make a selection effective. Your Permissions page appears as shown in Figure 24.39.

8. Click the Apply button to make the new permissions effective for the selected database object(s).

9. Repeat steps 4 through 8 for each database object and object type whose DataEntry group permissions you want to change.

Tip #215 from

RJ

If you create macros that contain several individually named macros (to minimize the number of objects in the database), make sure each macro object contains named macros that correspond to a specific category of permissions. Named macros, for example, that invoke action queries to modify tables or add new records should be grouped in one macro object, and named macros that only display the contents of database objects should be located in a different macro object.

When you assign permissions to execute macro objects, you must assign Modify Data permission to those users who can execute macro objects that run action queries. Microsoft discourages the use of macros with Access 2000, and macros might not be supported in future version of Access.

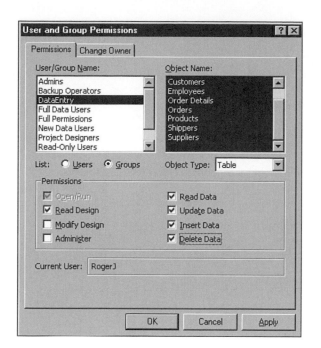

Figure 24.39
Revising permissions for all tables for the DataEntry group.

GRANTING ADDITIONAL PERMISSIONS TO SPECIFIC USERS

The process of granting additional permissions to a specific user is similar to the process used to alter group permissions. Permissions inherited by the user from the group to which the user is assigned are not shown in the Permissions dialog. To grant additional permissions to a specific user, complete the following steps:

1. Choose Tools, Security, User and Group Permissions. The Users option is the default for the User and Group Permissions dialog.

2. Select the user to whom additional permissions are to be granted in the User/Group Name list.

3. To assign permissions to a specific user so that the user can update data for an object, select the object using the Object Type and Object Name lists, and then click the Update Data, Insert Data, and Delete Data check boxes. Access automatically marks the implicit permissions, Read Design and Read Data, associated with the explicit permission, Update Data (see Figure 24.40). Click the Apply button after selecting each object whose permissions you want to change.

   Implicit permissions for individual users are displayed in the Permissions check boxes regardless of whether the implicit permissions also were inherited from group membership.

4. Repeat step 3 for each user who requires permissions for an object that aren't inherited from the user's group permissions. Click OK when you complete the permission changes for all users who require such changes.

Figure 24.40
The Permissions page for a new user with the new data permissions added.

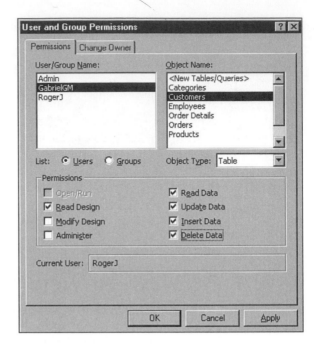

GRANTING PERMISSIONS FOR A DATABASE IN ANOTHER WORKGROUP

If your application requires that you attach a table in a secure database used by a different workgroup, the user needs to be a member of a group in the other workgroup and needs to be assigned appropriate permissions for the attached table. At this point, you need the list of PIDs for users, mentioned in the section "Establishing Your Own Admins Name, Password, and PID" earlier in this chapter.

To grant permission for a user to modify data in a table attached from another workgroup's database, perform the following steps:

1. Close Access; you must relaunch Access when you select another workgroup.

2. Launch the Workgroup Administrator application and specify the path to the workgroup database file of the workgroup that uses the database that contains the table to be attached.

3. Launch Access and open the database that contains the table to be attached.

4. Add an account for the user to the Users group with exactly the same user name and PID that was used to add the user account to his or her workgroup.

5. If you don't want this user to join the other workgroup, enter a password and don't disclose the password to the user.

6. Open the Permissions properties sheet, select the table to be attached, and assign the appropriate data permission for the table to the user.

You must use the same PID for the user in both workgroups because the account for the user is created from the user name and PID, and the accounts must be identical in both databases. You also must use the same PID number to reinstate the user's account if the workgroup system file becomes corrupted; you don't have a current backup, and Access can't repair it.

SHARING DATABASES ON THE NETWORK

After you've set up your user groups and modified the database object permissions for the groups as necessary, you can safely share the workgroup system database and your data .mdb file, and then distribute copies of your application .mdb file to the users. Before sharing the files, make sure to create a backup copy of each of the shared files and store the copies in a safe location. The following sections describe how to share files.

SHARING DATABASE FILES ON A WINDOWS 9X NETWORK

With a peer-to-peer Windows 9x network, you need only set up a network share of the folder in which you developed the application, \Shared\Nwind for the example in this chapter. The most common method of sharing folders with Windows 9x networking is to use share-level security. You must have access to the installation files for Windows 9x, either from the distribution CD-ROM or a network share, to complete the following procedure. To share a folder on your computer with share-level security under Windows 98, follow these steps:

1. Launch Control Panel and double-click the Network tool to open the Network properties sheet.

2. In the default Configuration page, select Client for Microsoft Networks, and click File and Print Sharing to open the File and Print Sharing dialog.

3. Mark the I Want to be Able to Give Others Access to My Files check box (see Figure 24.41), and click OK to close the dialog.

4. Click the Access Control tab and verify that the Share-Level Access Control option is selected (see Figure 24.42). Click OK to close the Network properties sheet, and then close Control Panel.

Figure 24.41
Setting up file sharing in Control Panel's Network properties sheet.

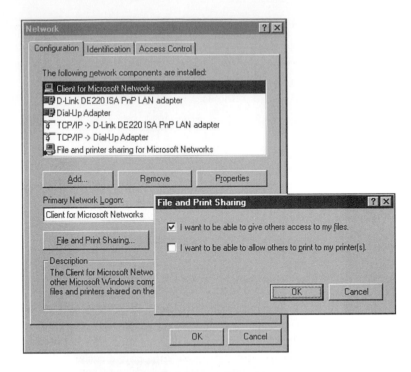

Figure 24.42
Setting share-level access control.

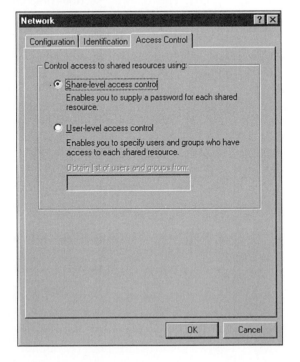

Tip #216 from

If you're connected to and have an account in a Windows NT Domain, you can use User-Level Access Control to specify domain users having access to your shares. If you previously have specified the User-Level Access Control option and change to Share-Level Access Control, all your current shares are removed. When you close Control Panel, you are requested to specify the location of the networking files required for file and print sharing, and then install the files. You must reboot Windows 9x for the new access control options to take effect.

5. Launch Explorer and select the folder to be shared, \Shared\Nwind for this example.

6. Choose File, Properties or right-click the folder icon and choose Sharing to open the *FileName* Properties sheet. Click the tab of the Sharing properties page.

7. Click the Shared As option button. The name of the folder appears as the default Share Name, NWIND in this example. Share names are limited to 12 characters and must not contain names, punctuation, or other special characters. Add an optional brief description of the share in the Comment text box.

8. To update data, users must have read-write access to the shared folder (often simply called a share). Other users need only read access to the folder. Click the Depends on Password option button in the Access Type frame.

9. Type the Read-Only Password and the Full Access Password in the two text boxes, as shown in Figure 24.43, confirm the two passwords, and then click OK to create the share.

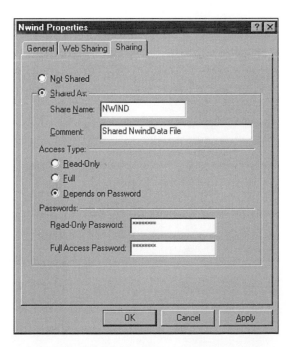

Figure 24.43
Creating a shared sub-folder with share-level access for a peer-to-peer Windows 9x network server.

In the examples presented in this chapter, both Nwind.mdb (the application database) and NwindData.mdb (the data .mdb file) are shared for read-write access, allowing users to launch Nwind.mdb from the server if they choose. Users should copy Nwind.mdb from the server share to their local computer and run the local copy to minimize network traffic. When connecting to the server share, users must enter the appropriate password for full or read-only access.

SHARING FILES WITH USER-LEVEL SECURITY

Specifying individual users with access to shares is a more secure alternative to simple share-based access control. You can specify users who are members of the Windows 9x workgroup to which you log on. If you're connected to a Windows NT network, you can grant share access to designated Windows NT groups or individual users. You must set up File Sharing for the Client for Microsoft Networks, as described in steps 2 and 3 of the preceding section, before sharing files with user-level security.

To set up user-level security under Windows 98, follow these steps:

1. Launch Control Panel and double-click the Network tool to open the Network properties sheet.

2. Click the Access Control tab and select the User-Level Access Control option. Type your workgroup name or the Windows NT domain name in the Obtain List of Users and Groups From text box (see Figure 24.44). Click OK to close the Network properties sheet, and then close Control Panel.

Figure 24.44
The Access Control page of the Network properties sheet for user-level access control.

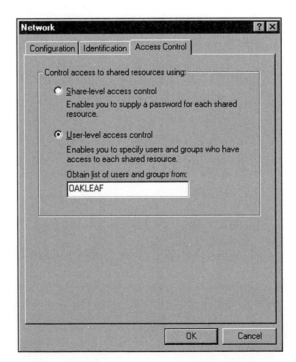

Note

As noted in the preceding section, if you previously specified the Share-Level Access Control option and change to User-Level Access Control, all your current shares are removed and you must reboot Windows 9x for the new Access Control option to take effect.

3. Launch Explorer and select the folder to be shared, \Shared\Nwind for this example.

4. Choose File, Properties or right-click the folder icon and choose Sharing to open the *ShareName* Properties sheet. Click the tab of the Sharing properties page. The Sharing page defaults to allowing everyone (The World) full rights for your share.

5. Click the Shared As option button. Add an optional brief description of the share in the Comment text box. Select The World and click Remove (see Figure 24.45).

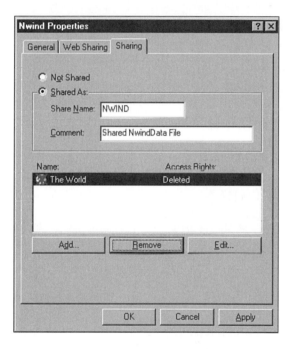

Figure 24.45
The Sharing properties page for user-level access control.

6. To specify groups or users having access to the share, click Add to open the Add Users dialog. Members of your workgroup appear in the lefthand list if you're using Windows 9x networking. If you're connected to a Windows NT Server domain, which is the case for this example, all the Windows NT groups and users appear in the list.

7. Select a group or user, and then click the Read Only, Full Access, or Custom button, as appropriate for your selection. Ordinarily, only you and Domain Admins should be granted Full Access to the share (see Figure 24.46).

Figure 24.46
Adding Windows NT Server groups for Read Only and Full access to the share.

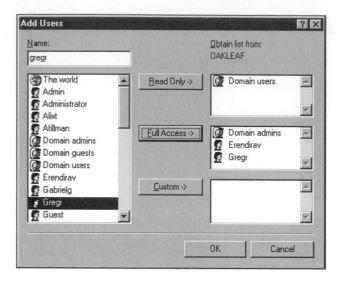

8. When you finish adding groups or users, click OK to close the Add Users dialog. The groups (and users, if any) you added for the share appear in the Sharing page. Click OK to close the *ShareName* Properties sheet.

The advantage to user-level access is that users don't need to enter a password when connecting to the share; the user ID and password used to log onto the network grants access to the share.

Tip #217 from

It's a relatively uncommon practice to share files from a Windows 9x peer-to-peer server when workgroup members are connected to a Windows NT server. Sharing the files from a Windows NT server that uses the Windows NT File System (NTFS), the subject of the next section, offers improved security.

SHARING DATABASE FILES FROM A NETWORK SERVER

The specific method of creating a server share on a dedicated network server depends on the network operating system (NOS) in use. Ordinarily, the network administrator creates the server share for you, and you need only move the files to be shared from your local folder to the shared server directory. If your NOS supports permissions for individual files, request full access rights to your workgroup database and data .mdb files. Windows NT Server supports permissions for individual files, if the files are located on an NTFS partition.

If you want users to be able to run the application .mdb from the server, grant read and execute access; otherwise, grant copy-only access so users can copy the application .mdb file to their local computer. Make sure, however, that you (the share owner) have full network permissions for all the shared files. Do not grant users more permissions for the shared files than they need.

ACCESSING THE SHARED WORKGROUP AND DATA FILES

Users access the server share by mapping the server share to a drive letter or by using Uniform Naming Convention (UNC). Using UNC eliminates the problem with users assigning different logical drive letters to server shares when mapping the share to their computer.

The network share you create, whether from your computer or from a network server, appears in the Network Neighborhood window for the selected server. In this example, Oakleaf0 is a Windows NT 4.0 Server (Primary Domain Controller), and Oakleaf1 is the workstation used to write this edition. The \Shared\Nwind directory of Oakleaf0 is shared as "NWIND," but appears as "Nwind" in the list of shares available from Oakleaf0 (see Figure 24.47). Double-clicking the Nwind share displays icons for the shared files. (Use of the term *directory*, rather than *folder*, is more common when referring to file servers.)

Figure 24.47
The \Shared\Nwind directory shared as NWIND on the Oakleaf0 server appears in Network Neighborhood as Nwind.

ATTACHING THE SHARED WORKGROUP SYSTEM FILE

Users of your application ordinarily use Workgroup Administrator to join the workgroup using the shared workgroup database file. You copy the shared data .mdb file and the System.mdw file to the server's shared directory. To access files using UNC (Uniform Naming Convention), you type ***ServerName**ShareName**FileName.ext***. If you're sharing files from your computer, *ServerName* is the name you assigned to your computer when you installed Windows 9x or Windows NT. Figure 24.48 shows how to specify a workgroup database file using UNC.

 Caution

Don't use a logical drive letter mapped from a share to specify the location of System.mdw. Users are likely to map shares to different logical drive letters.

Figure 24.48
Specifying the workgroup to join using UNC.

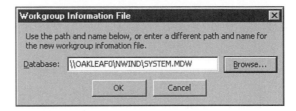

Workgroup Information File

Use the path and name below, or enter a different path and name for the new workgroup infomation file.

Database: \\OAKLEAF0\NWIND\SYSTEM.MDW   Browse...

OK   Cancel

If you receive a "'d:\path\filename.mdw' isn't a valid path" error, see the " Invalid Path Errors" topic in the "Troubleshooting" section near the end of this chapter.

Refreshing the Links to the Shared Data File

Before distributing your application .mdb file, you must change the links to point to the shared data .mdb file. This step is especially important if you have revoked the Design mode permissions for the Users group because the revocation prevents members of the Users group from refreshing the links. To refresh the links to point to the shared data .mdb file, follow these steps:

1. As a member of the Admins group, open the shared application .mdb file and choose Tools, Database Utilities, Linked Table Manager.

2. Click the Select All button, and then mark the Always Prompt for New Location check box. (If you don't mark this check box and the existing links are valid, you won't be able to refresh the links.)

3. Click OK to open the Select New Location of Categories dialog.

Tip #218 from

If a local copy of the linked file specified in the opening dialog of Linked File Manager exists and you don't mark the Always Prompt for New Location check box, the links are simply refreshed and the Select New Location of *TableName* dialog doesn't appear.

4. Open the Look In list and select Network Neighborhood, and then select the server and share to display the files in the share (see Figure 24.49). Select the data .mdb file and click Open.

5. The Linked File Manager automatically refreshes links for all the linked tables it finds in the selected data .mdb file. On completion of the refresh process, a message confirms that all linkages were refreshed and the Linked File Manager's dialog appears as shown in Figure 24.50. Click OK to close both the message box and the dialog.

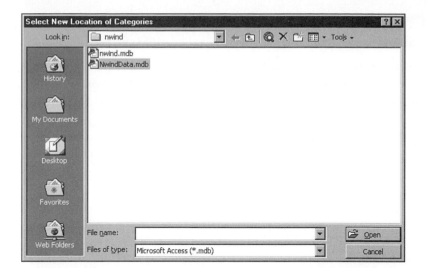

Figure 24.49
Selecting the shared data
.mdb file in the \Network
Neighborhood*Server-
Name\ShareName* folder.

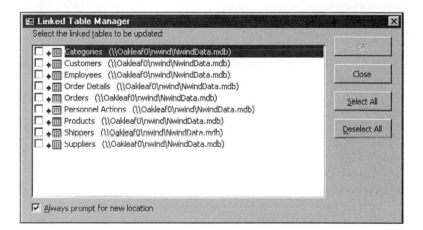

Figure 24.50
The Linked File Manager
confirms the links to the
data .mdb on the file
server.

After you refresh the links with the UNC location of the shared data .mdb file, you can distribute the application .mdb file to users.

ADMINISTERING DATABASES AND APPLICATIONS

Administering a multiuser database involves a number of duties besides adding and maintaining user accounts. The most important function of the database administrator is to ensure that periodic valid backup copies are made of database and system files. The database administrator's other responsibilities consist of routine database maintenance and periodic compacting and repairing databases. Compacting and repair operations are combined in Access 2000.

BACKING UP AND RESTORING DATABASES

The following maxims relate to maintaining backup copies of database files:

- The time interval between successive backups of databases is equal to the amount of data you are willing and able to re-enter in the event of a fixed disk failure. Except in unusual circumstances, such as little or no update activity, daily backup is the rule.

- Rotate backup copies. Make successive backups on different tapes or disk sets. One of the tapes or disks might have defects that could prevent you from restoring the backup. The backup device, such as a tape drive, can fail without warning you that the recorded data isn't valid.

- Test backup copies of databases periodically. You should test one different copy in the backup rotation sequence for restorability. If you rotate five daily backup tapes, for example, you should randomly choose one of the tapes, restore the database file from the tape, and open it with Access to ensure its validity every fifth day. Access tests each database object for integrity when you open the database file.

- Maintain off-site backups that you can use to restore data in case of a disaster, such as a fire or flood. The copy of the backup tape or disk that you test for restorability is a good candidate for an off-site backup copy.

You can back up database files on a network server by copying them to a workstation that has a fixed disk, but this technique doesn't provide backup security. The user of the workstation can erase or damage the backup copy if you don't create the off-site copy required for security against disasters.

Backing up data on network and peer-to-peer servers usually is accomplished with a tape drive device. These devices usually include an application that backs up all data on a network server or selected files on peer-to-peer servers at intervals and times you select. The simpler the backup operation, the more likely you are to have current backups. Regardless of how automated the backup procedure is, however, you must manually restore the test copy.

COMPACTING AND REPAIRING DATABASE FILES

NEW 2000 Compacting and repairing database files was discussed in Chapter 3, "Navigating Within Access." By default, Access compacts databases on closing, which is a new feature of Access 2000. It's possible, however, that an active networked data .mdb file, such as NwindData.mdb, is never closed under normal operating conditions. Thus, you should occasionally compact networked database files in which applications add and delete data to recover the disk space occupied by the deleted data. The procedure for compacting a database is similar to that described for encrypting and decrypting databases, the subject of the next section, except that you choose Tools, Database Utilities, Compact Database rather than Tools, Security, Encrypt/Decrypt Database.

→ **See** "Compacting and Repairing Databases," **p. 118**.

Tip #219 from

You can improve the operating speed of Access if you periodically defragment database files. Windows 9x's Disk Defragmenter utility tells you whether a disk drive has sufficient fragmentation to justify running the utility.

NEW 2000 If you receive a message that a database is corrupted or if the database behaves in an irregular manner, one or more of the objects it contains might be corrupt as the result of a hardware error. Databases can become corrupt as the result of a power failure when the computer is writing to the database file. Access 2000 combines the compaction and repair process in a single step. If Access can't repair the corruption, you must restore the latest backup copy. Test the backup copy with the existing *Workgroup*.mdw file; in some cases, you must restore the prior *Workgroup*.mdw file that contains the user account data for the database.

ENCRYPTING AND DECRYPTING DATABASE FILES

File-level security isn't complete until you encrypt the database. Encrypting the database prevents others from reading its contents with a text editing or disk utility application, such as is included with Symantec's Norton Utilities. Encryption of databases causes Access's operations on tables to slow perceptibly because of the time required to decrypt the data. Only members of the Admins group can encrypt or decrypt a database.

Note

If you're using a fixed disk data-compression utility, encrypting your database files reduces the percentage of compression to zero or a very small number. Encrypting files eliminates the groups of repeating characters that form the basis of most data-compression algorithms.

To encrypt or decrypt an Access database file, complete the following steps:

1. Make sure the disk drive of the computer on which the database is stored has enough free space to create a copy of the database you intend to encrypt or decrypt. Access makes a new copy of the file during the process.

2. All other workstations, including your own, must close the database file to be encrypted. You can't encrypt or decrypt a database file that's in use on any workstation.

3. Choose Tools, Security, Encrypt/Decrypt Database. The Encrypt/Decrypt Database dialog appears.

4. Select the name of the database file to be encrypted and click Save.

5. If the file already is encrypted, it is decrypted, and vice-versa. The title bar of the dialog that opens indicates whether the file is encrypted or decrypted in this operation. If you're interested only in whether the file has been encrypted, you can click Cancel now.

6. Type the name of the encrypted or decrypted file to create in the Encrypt FileName As dialog, and click Save. Normally, you type the same name as the original file; Access does not replace the original copy of the file if the process doesn't succeed.

Databases are compacted by Access when they are encrypted or decrypted.

Tip #220 from	You don't need to encrypt files while you're developing applications using files that aren't shared with others unless the files contain sensitive information. After the files are made shareable, a good security practice is to encrypt them, even if they don't contain confidential data.

TROUBLESHOOTING

INVALID PATH ERRORS

After changing the location of the workgroup database file, when you attempt to open a database, a "'d:\path\filename.mdw' isn't a valid path" message appears.

The drive letter, path, or file name entry isn't valid, or you can't connect to the server share specified by the UNC name, or, if mapped to a drive letter *n*:[*path*]. Use Explorer or Network Neighborhood to verify that your entry is correct and that your network connection to the server is working. In Explorer, choose <u>V</u>iew, <u>R</u>efresh to verify that the server connection currently is valid.

IN THE REAL WORLD—SHARED-FILE VERSUS CLIENT/SERVER BACK ENDS

Controversy over the future of conventional shared-file multiuser Jet applications borders on rampant among Access developers and Microsoft marketers. The shared-file, "Jet is alive and well" axis insists that Jet is a viable back-end for workgroup-size online transaction processing (OLTP) applications. The "Jet is dead" cabal, whose membership is dominated by SQL Server marketing honchos, consider the Microsoft Data Engine (MSDE) to be Microsoft's "strategic database" for Office applications and SQL Server 7.0 to be the natural back-end choice for everyone else. Hooking prospective purchasers of SQL Server 7.0 licenses by offering free samples of MSDE has a counterpart in other, less politically-correct marketing campaigns.

Shared-file proponents tend to favor traditional Data Access Objects (DAO), a mature technology now in version 3.6 but never likely to reach version 4.0. Members of the MSDE/SQL Server clan promote nascent OLE DB and ActiveX Data Objects (ADO) as where the action is for database connectivity. Clearly, there's a conservative versus radical slant to the politics of multiuser database connectivity, which gives rise to "ADP sucks," "DAO's dead," and similar unenlightening epithets in Access news groups.

The reality is that multiuser Jet does run out of steam in heavy-duty OLTP applications having many simultaneous users. The point at which concurrency and file corruption problems begin to appear in Jet back-end databases depends on a variety of factors. Each upgrade to Jet has improved multiuser reliability, but many developers still consider 20 to 50 simultaneous updating users to be the practical limit for Jet 4.0. The absolute maximum number of concurrent connections to any Jet database is 255. Thus Jet isn't a serious contender for an e-commerce orders database on a highly-trafficked Web site. The 1GB maximum table size and 32-index limit (including indexes created by relationships) makes Jet impractical for use in data marts and warehouses of medium or larger scope.

Jet offers the advantage of easy conversion from single-user, single-file mode to shared-file multiuser mode. The Database Splitter utility makes the transition almost automatic. Descriptions of the Jet security system range from Byzantine to Machiavellian, but Jet security is easier to fathom than SQL Server security. Access's User-Level Security Wizard takes most of the pain out of securing front-end and back-end .mdb files. You'd probably be surprised to learn how many production SQL Server databases have run unsecure for months or years with the default sa (system administrator) as the username and no password. If you seek multiuser simplicity in a small Windows 9x workgroup environment, shared-file Jet probably is your best bet.

MSDE is substantially more robust than Jet, especially for OLTP. MSDE is even simpler than Jet to administer; for example, you don't need to periodically compact SQL Server files as users edit and delete records. MSDE offers automated backup and restore operations and provides a transaction log that you can use to return restored tables to their exact state at the time of a crash. Although Microsoft "tunes" MSDE for fewer than 10 simultaneous users, initial tests indicate that MSDE running under Windows NT Server 4.0 can support many more clients. Windows NT 4.0 Workstation has a hard-coded limit of 10 inbound connections; the limit includes MSDE or file-sharing connections.

If you're starting an Access OLTP project from scratch, and you expect more than about 20 users to update database tables simultaneously, seriously consider moving to ADP. Although you can use the Access Upsizing Wizard to convert a conventional Access application to ADP, the upsizing process isn't bulletproof. You must rewrite Jet queries that contain Access-specific reserved words and functions missing from the Wizard's bag of tricks. You save time in the short and long run by conforming to SQL Server's Transact-SQL dialect when you design your queries.

Upsizing from MSDE to SQL Server 7.0 when your application reaches the point of no return with MSDE is a no-brainer, but it isn't cheap. You must be running Windows NT Server 4+, purchase an SQL Server 7.0 license, and buy a Client Access License (CAL) for each user. Microsoft Small Business Server (SBS) 4.5 is the most economical starting point for organizations that don't have Windows NT Server installed and need a package of SQL

Server 7.0, a messaging system (Exchange Server 5.5), and a high-performance intranet server (Internet Information Server 4.0). Be sure to buy the fastest Pentium III with the most memory (128MB minimum, 256MB preferred) and largest Ultrawide SCSI-3 fixed disk drive(s) that you can afford when you run all these servers on the same box. The SBS license requires that all server components must run on a single machine. Microsoft says "You may notice subtle differences from individual applications sold separately or Microsoft Back Office Server 4.5." If your server is short on RAM, you may notice some dramatic differences.

To mitigate the pain of SQL Server license costs, Microsoft gives you a free copy of SQL Server OLAP Services. Of course, the SQL Server folks hope you'll build data marts so large that they require their own dedicated server (and thus another SQL Server 7.0 license.)

--rj

CHAPTER 25

CREATING ACCESS DATA PROJECTS

In this chapter

Moving Access to the Client/Server Model   944

Understanding the Role of MSDE   945

Installing and Starting MSDE   947

Getting Acquainted with ADP   953

Using the Project Designer   956

Using the Upsizing Wizard to Create ADP   969

Downsizing Databases with the DTS Wizard   975

Connecting to Remote MSDE Databases   980

Establishing MSDE Security   983

Troubleshooting   986

In the Real World—ADP on Trial   987

MOVING ACCESS TO THE CLIENT/SERVER MODEL

NEW
2000
Access 2000's new Access Data Projects (ADP), also called Microsoft Access projects or Access client/server applications, let you connect to the Microsoft Data Engine (MSDE) on your PC or to networked SQL Server 6.5 and 7.0 databases without incurring the overhead of the Jet 4.0 database engine. MSDE is the embedded version of SQL Server 7.0 that runs under Windows 9x and Windows NT 4+. Following are the most important characteristics of ADP:

- Like Data Access Pages (DAP), ADP doesn't use .mdb files. ADP store database front-end forms, reports, and other application objects in a single .adp compound document file (docfile), not within a conventional Access .mdb file.

- The .adp file doesn't contain tables or queries; MSDE stores the tables and views. A *view* is a precompiled SQL SELECT query, equivalent to an Access select query saved as a QueryDef (query definition) object.

- MSDE stored procedures replace Access action queries. Like views, stored procedures are precompiled queries, but stored procedures aren't limited to SELECT queries. Stored procedures are especially efficient at performing INSERT, UPDATE, and DELETE operations.

- MSDE and SQL Server don't have the equivalent of Jet's lookup field or subdatasheet feature, so you lose these capabilities when migrating to a client/server back end.

- ADP dispense with Jet, Open Database Connectivity (ODBC), and Data Access Objects (DAO), substituting OLE DB data providers and ActiveX Data Objects (ADO) for database connectivity and data manipulation, respectively. OLE DB and ADO are the subjects of Chapter 27, "Understanding Universal Data Access, OLE DB, and ADO."

- Unlike DAP, you design ADP in Access's standard Form and Report views and use the standard toolbox to add native Access controls to the form.

You can "upsize" a conventional Access .mdb application to an Access project, a feature not implemented for DAP. You can also create in the ADP environment DAP bound to MSDE or SQL Server databases.

ADP are best suited to the following types of Access 2000 applications:

- Front ends to new or existing SQL Server 6.5 and 7.0 databases. Access 2000 includes a graphical designer for accessing existing SQL Server and MSDE databases or creating new databases.

- Applications that you expect to upsize to SQL Server 7.0 in the near future or even long term. Microsoft has made it easy to migrate ADP from MSDE on your PC to SQL Server running under Windows NT 4.0 or 2000. Using ADP, rather than Jet, assures a quick and seamless transition from MSDE to SQL Server.

- Projects that use two-way SQL Server 7.0 replication, rather than Access-to-SQL Server replication. SQL Server replication is more robust and flexible than the Access version. Replicating between MSDE and SQL Server 7.0 requires per-seat licensing of SQL Server.

Users of your Access project must have Access 2000 installed, unless you use Office 2000 Developer to create a runtime version of your ADP. If your Access project requires a local SQL Server database, users also must install MSDE. If the application connects to an SQL Server database, users must have the requisite client licenses for Windows NT or 2000 and SQL Server.

Tip #221 from	You can use a local Jet database with ADP client applications, but you must write VBA code to connect to the local database and manipulate its contents. You can use either DAO or ADO to make the connection to the .mdb, but using ADO is more efficient. If you use DAO to connect to the local .mdb file, clients must load both DAO and ADO, which consumes additional resources.

UNDERSTANDING THE ROLE OF MSDE

Microsoft's announcement in mid-1995 that Access 2000 would include an "alternate database" led to a flurry of "Jet is dead" pronouncements in the computer press. These stories gained credence when members of the SQL Server 7.0 team described their forthcoming product as "Microsoft's strategic database direction." The reality is that Jet obituaries are very premature. Jet plays a major role in more than 25 Microsoft products, and variants of the Jet database engine serve as the message store for Microsoft Exchange and the in-memory database of SQL Server 7.0. Jet is likely to be alive and well, at least through the first few years of the next century.

Regardless of Jet's survival in the twenty-first century, there's a definite trend toward the use of client/server back ends when database reliability is the primary objective. Web-based e-commerce requires client/server back ends for security and scalability. Thus ADP, MSDE, and SQL Server 7.0 will play an increasingly important role as even small firms migrate to Microsoft Small Business Server or BackOffice Server to host intranet and Internet applications.

SQL SERVER VERSIONS AND FEATURES

SQL Server 7.0 comes in Embedded (MSDE), Desktop, Standard, and Enterprise editions. MSDE and the Desktop version are intended to run under Windows 9x, Windows NT 4.0 Workstation (with Service Pack 4 or Service Pack 3 plus a mini-Service Pack applied), and Windows 2000 Workstation. You also can run MSDE under Windows NT 4.0 and 2000 Servers. The Standard and Enterprise editions run only under Windows NT 4.0 Server (with SP4 or SP3 and the mini-SP) and Windows 2000 Server. All versions of SQL Server share a common code base; thus data files are fully interchangeable between all versions.

The primary difference between MSDE and Desktop SQL Server 7.0 is that the embedded MSDE version doesn't include the Microsoft Management Console (MMC), SQL Server Enterprise Manager, and other graphic tools for creating and managing databases. MSDE installs osql, the command line replacement for isql, but there's no online help for the arcane syntax of osql. The basic database management tools you need for MSDE are provided by Access 2000.

Tip #222 from

Microsoft's SQL Server Web pages at `http://www.microsoft.com/sql/` offer detailed product and licensing information for SQL Server 7.0 (but not for MSDE).

Microsoft designed SQL Server 7.0 for ease of installation and minimum maintenance. Unlike prior versions, you don't need to create fixed-size .dat files (devices) to hold SQL Server objects. SQL Server 7.0 uses the FAT or NTFS file system to store all its objects. Files expand or contract automatically as tables grow or shrink, and you don't need to compact SQL Server databases to regain disk space after large-scale updates and deletions. SQL Server 7.0 databases are self-tuning, so you don't need to be an accomplished database administrator (DBA) to get maximum performance from MSDE. You do, however, need to know how to design *views*, SQL Server's version of Access SELECT queries, and write *stored procedures* in Transact-SQL, SQL Server's flavor of ANSI SQL, to optimize query execution.

Tip #223 from

Fortunately, the Access Upsizing Wizard (AUW) automatically creates most of the required views and stored procedures when you choose to upsize conventional Access applications to ADP. The "Using the Upsizing Wizard to Create ADP" section later in this chapter describes how to use this new feature.

MSDE BENEFITS

MSDE has many advantages over Jet databases for heavy-duty database applications. The following are the most important benefits of MSDE for Access 2000 users:

- MSDE uses a transaction log to maintain a record of changes to each database. In the event of database corruption, you restore the database from the last backup, and then apply the transaction log entries to return the restored database to its state just before the damage occurred.

- MSDE is a production-grade, client/server RDBMS, in the same category as the Windows NT versions of Oracle, Informix, and IBM DB2. You can share your MSDE file with other licensed Access users within the peer-to-peer server connection limits of Windows 9x and Windows NT Workstation. You also can run MSDE under Windows NT Server 4+.

- MSDE lets you validate SQL Server 7.0 applications on your client PC before committing the database(s) to a production server. You can also develop ADP on a laptop that's not connected to network—for instance, on the beach or at a ski lodge.

- MSDE takes advantage of a maximum of two processors under Windows NT 4.0 or 2000 when running on a multiprocessor PC. MSDE supports only a single processor under Windows 9x, because Windows 9x isn't a multiprocessing operating system.

- MSDE supports all the publish-subscribe scenarios of SQL Server 7.0 replication. Replication lets mobile (disconnected) users keep their local MSDE database synchronized with the server database and vice versa. SQL Server replication is beyond the scope of this book; SQL Server 7.0 Books Online provides detailed coverage of replication strategies.

Tip #224 from	The most economical way to obtain SQL Server 7.0 Books Online is to order the Evaluation Edition of SQL Server 7.0 on a US$9.95 CD-ROM from `http://www.microsoft.com/sql/70/trial.htm`. The Evaluation Edition expires in 120 days, but Books Online doesn't. You can't run MSDE and SQL Server 7.0 on the same machine, so copy the Books Online files from the \X86\Books folder of the CD-ROM to the \Mssql7\Books folder of your PC, and clear the Read-Only attribute of the copied files.

PART
VI
CH
25

- MSDE is an excellent learning tool to gain experience with client/server database design and operations without the expense of setting up a network and acquiring licenses for Windows NT or 2000 and SQL Server 7.0. Acclimating Office users and developers to SQL Server greatly increases the potential for Microsoft to sell additional licenses for the Standard and Enterprise editions of SQL Server 7.0.

Tip #225 from	MSDE has a 2GB database size limit, as does Jet 4.0. Microsoft says MSDE is "tuned for five or six individual users," but MSDE can support many more than six users and still deliver adequate or better performance.

INSTALLING AND STARTING MSDE

MSDE and the other SQL Server 7.0 versions have a common installation application that's not integrated with the Office 2000 setup program. MSDE is an optional Access 2000 feature, so lack of integration with Office setup isn't a critical omission. Installation of MSDE requires about 90MB of free disk space to start, plus space for the databases you add. You should have at least 32MB and preferably 64MB or more of RAM to run MSDE and Office 2000 simultaneously under Windows 9x. A minimum of 64MB is required to prevent excessive disk paging operations under Windows NT 4.0 or Windows 2000 Workstation.

To perform the manual installation of MSDE under Windows 9x or Windows NT, follow these steps:

1. Insert the Office 2000 distribution CD-ROM 1 in the drive and use Windows Explorer to navigate to the \Sql\X86\Setup folder.

Tip #226 from	If you're installing under Windows NT 4.0 with Service Pack 3 (SP3), you must run Hotfix.exe from your Office 2000 distribution diskettes. Hotfix.exe is a mini-service pack that adds a required fix for MSDE and SQL Server 7.0. You don't need to run Hotfix.exe if you've upgraded Windows NT 4.0 to SP4 or are installing MSDE under Windows 9x or Windows 2000.

2. Double-click Setupsql.exe to start the installation process.

3. If you're installing MSDE under Windows NT, a Select Install Method dialog opens, which lets you install MSDE on your PC or on a remote PC in your domain. Accept the local default, and click Next.

4. Click Next to bypass the Welcome dialog.

5. The User Information dialog requests that you type your name and company name. The defaults are the name and company entries you made when installing Office 2000. Click Next.

6. The Setup Type dialog lets you specify destination folders for MSDE program and data files. Accept the default C:\MSSQL7 folder (see Figure 25.1) unless you have a reason to do otherwise. The default settings install data and log files in a C:\Mssql7\Data folder. Click Next.

Figure 25.1
The Setup Type dialog for specifying the drive and folder in which to install MSDE.

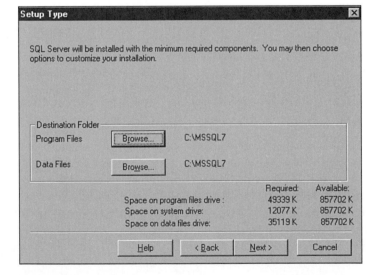

7. The Character Set/Sort Order/Unicode Collation dialog gives you several installation choices. Again, accept the default choices unless you are acquainted with the differences between character sets, sort orders, and Unicode collation settings (see Figure 25.2).

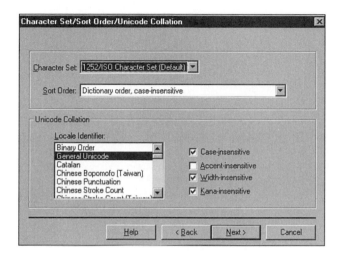

Figure 25.2
The setup dialog for character set, sort order, and Unicode collation properties.

8. The Network Libraries dialog enables TCP/IP Sockets connections to the database and lets you add the Novell NWLink IPX/SPX protocol, if you're running NetWare (see Figure 25.3). TCP/IP default port 1433 is the Internet Assigned Number Authority (IANA) port number for SQL Server. Click Next.

Note

Make sure that the Multi-Protocol check box is marked. Named Pipes, AppleTalk ADSP, and Banyan Vines options aren't enabled under Windows 9x. If you're installing under Windows NT, accept the default Named Pipe name, \\.\pipe\sql\query.

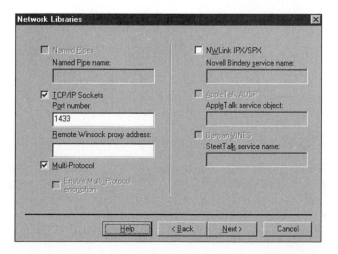

Figure 25.3
Specifying the network protocol(s) for your MSDE installation.

9. If you're installing under Windows NT, the Services Accounts dialog opens (see Figure 25.4). Accept the default Use the Same Account for Each Service, and Use a Domain User Account options. Type the account password in the Password text box. The Domain User Account should be an account with Administrator privileges.

Figure 25.4
The Services Accounts dialog, which appears only when you install MSDE under Windows NT or 2000.

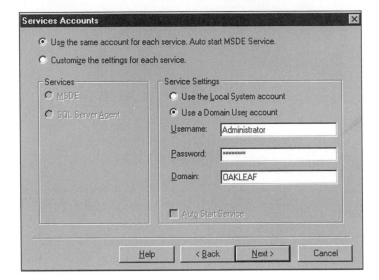

10. The Start Copying Files dialog informs you that installation starts when you click Next, so do so.

Copying and installing files takes about two or three minutes on a Pentium 200 PC with 64MB of RAM or greater.

11. At the end of the setup process, the Setup Complete dialog appears and requests you to reboot your PC, if you're running Windows 9x. Accept the default (reboot) option, if it appears, and click Finish to complete the installation.

The setup program adds an icon for SQL Server Service Manager's window to the notification area of the Windows 9x taskbar. (The SQL Server Service Manager's icon doesn't appear in the taskbar until you reboot Windows NT.) Setup also adds the following Start, Programs, Msde menu items:

■ *Client Network Utility*, opens the SQL Server Client Network Utility dialog to set up aliases and connection protocols to remote MSDE or SQL Server databases. Use of the SQL Server Client Network Utility is the subject of the "Connecting to Remote MSDE Databases" section near the end of the chapter.

■ *Import and Export Data* opens the Data Transformation Services (DTS) Wizard, one of the few SQL Server 7.0 tools included with MSDE. The Wizard makes it easy to import tables from and export tables to Jet .mdb files, but AUW makes the export process even simpler. Exporting data from SQL Server to a Jet 4.0 .mdb file is the subject of the "Downsizing Databases with the DTS Wizard" section later in the chapter.

- *Server Network Utility* opens the SQL Server Network Utility dialog. The General page lets you add or remove protocols after installation (NWLink IPX/SPX only on Windows 9x) and change the TCP/IP port number (see Figure 25.5). The Network Libraries page displays the location, file name, and version of the DLLs that support available network protocols (see Figure 25.6).

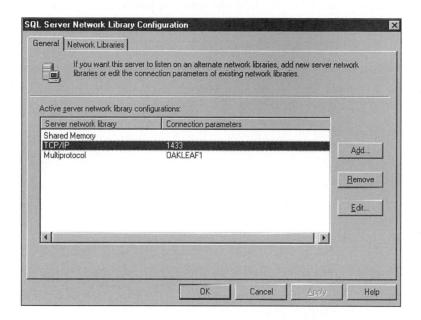

Figure 25.5
The General page of the SQL Server Network Utility dialog for making very limited changes to your MSDE installation.

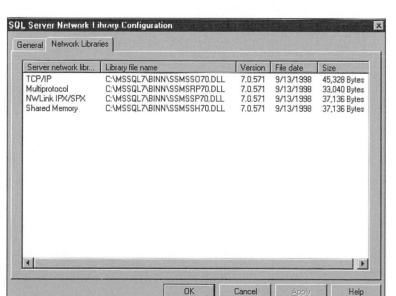

Figure 25.6
Server Network Utility's Network Libraries page displaying the supporting DLLs for available network protocols.

- *Service Manager* opens SQL Service Manager, which lets you start, pause, and stop MSDE. You must manually start MSDE under Windows 9x and Windows NT after setup completes. Marking the Auto-start Service When OS Starts check box causes Windows 9x, or Windows NT or 2000 Workstation or Server, to start MSDE during the boot process (see Figure 25.7, left). Make sure to auto-start MSDE unless you have compelling reasons not to do so. After you or the operating system start MSDE, the appearance of the server icon changes and the Pause and Stop buttons are enabled (see Figure 25.7, right).

Figure 25.7
SQL Service manager with MSDE stopped (left) and started (right).

	Tip #227 from
	You can also stop or start MSDE by right-clicking the icon in the taskbar tray and choosing MSSQLServer Start, Pause, or Stop from the context menu. The taskbar icon indicates the status of MSDE with a miniature version of the icons shown in Figure 25.7. If you open an Access project and MSDE is stopped, Access automatically attempts to start MSDE.

- *Uninstall MSDE* starts the uninstall process. Uninstalling MSDE doesn't delete any data (.mdf) or log (.mdl) files that you create.

	Tip #228 from
	SQL Service Manager under Windows 9x starts via a shortcut in Windows 9x's \Windows\Start Menu\Programs\Startup or Windows NT's \Winnt\Profiles\All Users\Start Menu\Programs\Startup folder. To uninstall MSDE, you must first delete the shortcut to Sqlmangr.exe in this folder, and then reboot your computer. (Ending the SQL Service Manager's task with Windows NT Task Manager doesn't work.) Under Windows NT, you also must stop the MSSQLServer and MSSQLServerOLAPService services with Control Panel's Services tool. You can't uninstall MSDE with SQL Service Manager or SQL Server running.

GETTING ACQUAINTED WITH ADP

Microsoft designed Access Data Projects as the entry point for building Access front-ends for client/server database back-ends. ADP also offer the opportunity for Access users and first-time developers to gain insight into the benefits and drawbacks of client/server computing. ADP aren't limited to use with MSDE or SQL Server; it's possible (but not easy) to use native OLE DB providers for mainstream client/server RDBMSs or, if your RDBMS doesn't yet have an OLE DB provider, an ODBC driver supplied by the database vendor. This chapter's content is limited to creating ADP that connect to MSDE.

ACCOMMODATING MSDE AND SQL SERVER 7.0 FEATURES

Each release of Access has demonstrated increasing compatibility with the then-current version of SQL Server. Following are some of the new Access 2000 features intended to increase conformance with new features of SQL Server 7.0:

- *Unicode support for localization.* Unicode defines a two-byte character set for all languages supported by Windows 9x, NT, and 2000. Using two bytes per character for all languages eliminates the need for double-byte character set (DBCS) installation for pictographic languages, such as Chinese and Korean. Access uses Unicode compression to minimize the increase in the size of databases having large, text-heavy tables.

- *Decimal data type.* Jet 4.0's new Decimal data type corresponds to the SQL Server decimal numeric data type that lets you set specific precision and scale values. The precision is the maximum number of digits in the number; scale is the maximum number of digits to the right of the decimal point. Jet 4.0's maximum precision or scale is 28, which is the default maximum precision for MSDE and SQL Server; MSDE and SQL Server support precision or scale up to 38, but you must start MSDE or SQL Server with the /p command line parameter to get the extra 10 digits.

- *ANSI SQL conformance.* Jet 4.0 offers two SQL syntax flavors—a new version more compliant with ANSI-92 and Transact-SQL, and a backward-compatible (legacy) version that supports prior versions of Access, Jet, and VBA. Unfortunately, the Access user interface (UI) supports only the legacy SQL syntax. You can only take advantage of ANSI-92 extensions to Jet SQL with OLE DB and ADO.

Along with the benefits of moving to MSDE or a client/server RDBMS environment come the following drawbacks:

- ADP doesn't support Access queries, so AUW converts SELECT queries to SQL views and action queries to stored procedures. SQL Server's Transact-SQL dialect doesn't support Access SQL's TRANSFORM and PIVOT keywords required to generate crosstab query result sets. If you plan to upsize applications that include crosstab queries, you must redesign the queries to accommodate Transact-SQL—doing so is not an easy process. The "Using the Upsizing Wizard to Create ADP" section later in this chapter lists details on limitations of AUW.

PART

VI

CH

25

Tip #229 from

To keep your crosstab queries in their present form, use AUW to migrate your tables to MSDE, as described in the previously mentioned section, but don't change your existing application .mdb to a project. The Wizard alters the links to your application .mdb to point to the MSDE tables, but your queries remain Access objects. You can partition the MSDE view to aggregate the data on the server and use the Access crosstab query to format the result.

- SQL Server doesn't support Access's Hyperlink pseudo field data type, but stores hyperlink text in Unicode text fields. You must set the Is Hyperlink property value of Access text and combo box controls to Yes to obtain standard Hyperlink field formatting.

- SQL Server also doesn't support Access's OLE object data type, but SQL Server does have an image data type in which you can store graphics and other multimedia data. You must export the graphics in OLE Object fields to files, then import the file data into SQL Server. It's usually a better practice to store graphics as files and add to the table a text field that holds the path to and the name of the file.

- AUW doesn't automatically update DAP database links from the Jet to the MSDE database. Each DAP in your project requires a manual change of the OLE DB data provider from Jet to SQL Server, as well as specifying the MSDE server and database names, login name, and password.

- You can't upsize a replicated or replicable Jet database. If your database uses replication, you must create a new version without the replication features, such as replication fields of tables. MSDE uses SQL Server, not Jet, replication.

Tip #230 from

The "Comparison of Microsoft Access and SQL Server SQL Syntax" help topic describes the differences between Jet SQL and Transact-SQL, and support for specific Jet SQL features by MSDE and AUW.

RUNNING THE NORTHWINDCS SAMPLE PROJECT

Access 2000 includes a sample project, NorthwindCS.adp, that emulates Northwind.mdb. NorthwindCS.adp uses a Transact-SQL script, NorthwindCS.SQL, to create a new MSDE database. Follow these steps to install the NorthwindCS MSDE database:

1. Open the NorthwindCS.adp project in the …\Office\Samples folder. If you haven't started MSDE, VBA code in the Startup module starts MSDE for you.

2. The first time you open the project, you receive the message shown in Figure 25.8. Click OK to run NorthwindCS.SQL on your local MSDE.

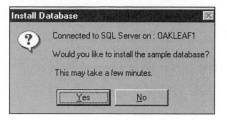

Figure 25.8
The message you receive when opening the NorthwindCS.adp sample database for the first time.

3. After a few seconds, you receive a "Created database on SQL Server" message. Click OK to close the message and open the Northwind Traders splash screen.

4. Mark the Don't Show This Screen Again check box and click Close to get rid of the splash screen. The Database window opens with the Tables page active, as illustrated in Figure 25.9.

Figure 25.9
The Tables page of the Database window for NorthwindCS.adp.

The Database window for Access Data Projects differs considerably from the conventional Access Database window with linked table connections. The most important alterations are as follows:

■ *Tables* stored in MSDE appear in the Tables page as though they are local tables. The right-pointing arrow symbol, which indicates a linked table of any type, including client/server tables, is missing. Opening a table in run mode displays a conventional Access datasheet; MSDE doesn't support lookup fields and subdatasheets.

■ *Views* use the Access select query symbol, but view definitions are stored in the MSDE database. Views differ significantly from Access `QueryDefs`; you can't apply a sort order to a view, nor can a view have parameters.

- *Database Diagrams* serve the same purpose as the Access Relationships window, but differ considerably in their visual presentation.

- *Stored Procedures* for executing parameterized and action queries are precompiled Transact-SQL statements (scripts). You click the Run button of the Database window's toolbar to execute stored procedures. Stored procedures offer a substantial performance improvement over direct execution of SQL statements.

The remaining Access application objects—forms, reports, pages, macros, and modules—are identical, with a few exceptions, to the corresponding objects of conventional Access applications that employ .mdb files for storage. The exceptions primarily are minor changes to form and report properties; as an example, you can set the Record Source property of a form or report to a stored procedure.

> **Note**
>
> The primary difference between the Access 97 and 2000 file structure is Access 2000's storage of all application objects (forms, reports, pages, macros, and modules) in a single compound document file, called a docfile. A conventional Access application saves its application object docfile within the application .mdb; an Access Data Project stores its docfile directly on disk as an .adp file.

USING THE PROJECT DESIGNER

ADP use a set of client/server graphical design tools called the "da Vinci toolset" during their development. Microsoft calls da Vinci *MS Design Tools*, but this book refers to the toolset as the *project designer*. Access's project design mode lets you alter the structure of tables, relationships, and views directly from the user interface. SQL Server and other client/server RDBMSs rely on SQL CREATE, ALTER, and DROP statements for design changes. The project designer executes the SQL statements for your design changes each time you exit design mode. The ability to alter the design of the equivalent to linked tables, unavailable in prior versions of Access, is an important new feature of Access 2000.

Executing SQL for database design operations lets you use the project designer with many client/server (also called SQL) databases, including SQL Server 6.5+ and Oracle 8.03+. Support for other client/server databases depends on the extent to which the RDBMS complies with ANSI SQL-92. The Visual Basic, Visual C++, Visual InterDev, and Visual J++ components of Visual Studio 6+ also use the da Vinci toolset for client/server database design. Thus the project designer brings Access 2000 into conformance with other Microsoft application design platforms, at least for client/server databases.

Tip #231 from

Access Data Projects are an excellent learning aid and prototyping tool for large-scale client/server database projects. You can quickly and easily create new MSDE databases, add tables, establish relationships, design views, and write stored procedures in the project designer. Creating data-enabled forms, reports, and HTML pages with Access 2000 is a much faster process than that of other design platforms. Once you've tested your proto-type MSDE database design, you deploy the .mdf and .ldf files directly to SQL Server 7+ running under Windows NT 4.0 or 2000 Server.

WORKING WITH MSDE TABLES

Tables displayed in run mode appear in conventional Access Datasheet view (see Figure 25.10). Date values appear in short date format, and money (Currency) fields default to the currency format you specify in the Currency page of Control Panel's Regional Settings tool. Windows 98 and Windows 2000 support the euro character (£); you need a "Europatch," available from http://www.microsoft.com/windows/euro.asp, to add the euro symbol to Windows 95 and Windows NT 4.0.

Tip #232 from

For year 2000 compliance, be sure to set your short date format to [m]m/[d]d/yyyy (or the date format convention appropriate to your locale) in the Date page of Control Panel's Regional Settings tool. The project designer's datasheet view uses the Windows short-date format; there's no provision in the project designer to alter the datasheet display format of any field data type.

PART

VI

CH

25

Table Design view, however, differs dramatically from that of tables linked through Jet. Figure 25.11 shows the Orders table in the project designer. SQL Server datatype names are in lowercase, a holdover from Microsoft SQL Server's origin as the PC version of Sybase SQL Server for UNIX. Table 25.1 lists the names and the correspondence of each project designer column to property values you set in Access's conventional Table Design view. SQL databases commonly substitute the term *column* for *field*; this book uses *field* for tables and *column* for query result sets and views. There are no significant changes to run or design mode menu choices and toolbars in the project designer.

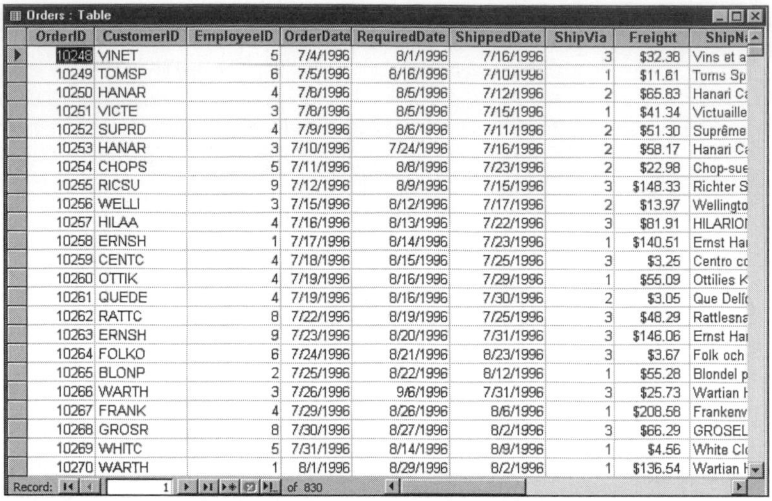

Orders : Table

OrderID	CustomerID	EmployeeID	OrderDate	RequiredDate	ShippedDate	ShipVia	Freight	ShipN
10248	VINET	5	7/4/1996	8/1/1996	7/16/1996	3	$32.38	Vins et a
10249	TOMSP	6	7/5/1996	8/16/1996	7/10/1996	1	$11.61	Toms Sp
10250	HANAR	4	7/8/1996	8/5/1996	7/12/1996	2	$65.83	Hanari Ca
10251	VICTE	3	7/8/1996	8/5/1996	7/15/1996	1	$41.34	Victuaille
10252	SUPRD	4	7/9/1996	8/6/1996	7/11/1996	2	$51.30	Suprême
10253	HANAR	3	7/10/1996	7/24/1996	7/16/1996	2	$58.17	Hanari Ca
10254	CHOPS	5	7/11/1996	8/8/1996	7/23/1996	2	$22.98	Chop-sue
10255	RICSU	9	7/12/1996	8/9/1996	7/15/1996	3	$148.33	Richter S
10256	WELLI	3	7/15/1996	8/12/1996	7/17/1996	2	$13.97	Wellingto
10257	HILAA	4	7/16/1996	8/13/1996	7/22/1996	3	$81.91	HILARIOI
10258	ERNSH	1	7/17/1996	8/14/1996	7/23/1996	1	$140.51	Ernst Hai
10259	CENTC	4	7/18/1996	8/15/1996	7/25/1996	3	$3.25	Centro cc
10260	OTTIK	4	7/19/1996	8/16/1996	7/29/1996	1	$55.09	Ottilies K
10261	QUEDE	4	7/19/1996	8/16/1996	7/30/1996	2	$3.05	Que Delí
10262	RATTC	8	7/22/1996	8/19/1996	7/25/1996	3	$48.29	Rattlesna
10263	ERNSH	9	7/23/1996	8/20/1996	7/31/1996	3	$146.06	Ernst Hai
10264	FOLKO	6	7/24/1996	8/21/1996	8/23/1996	3	$3.67	Folk och
10265	BLONP	2	7/25/1996	8/22/1996	8/12/1996	1	$55.28	Blondel p
10266	WARTH	3	7/26/1996	9/6/1996	7/31/1996	3	$25.73	Wartian H
10267	FRANK	4	7/29/1996	8/26/1996	8/6/1996	1	$208.58	Frankenv
10268	GROSR	8	7/30/1996	8/27/1996	8/2/1996	3	$66.29	GROSEL
10269	WHITC	5	7/31/1996	8/14/1996	8/9/1996	1	$4.56	White Cl
10270	WARTH	1	8/1/1996	8/29/1996	8/2/1996	1	$136.54	Wartian H

Record: 1 of 830

Figure 25.10
The Orders table in ADP Datasheet view with the Windows short date format set to m/d/yyyy.

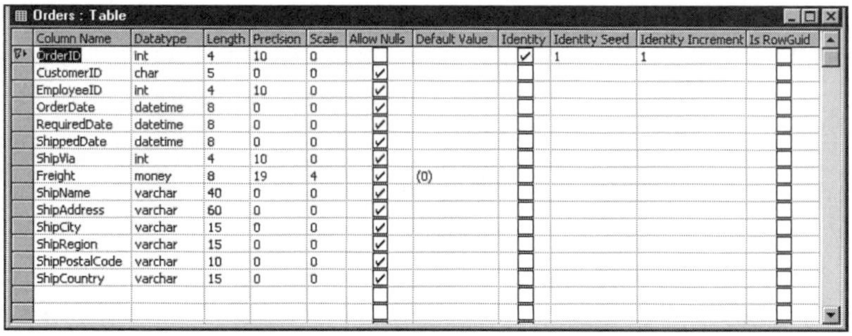

Orders : Table

Column Name	Datatype	Length	Precision	Scale	Allow Nulls	Default Value	Identity	Identity Seed	Identity Increment	Is RowGuid
OrderID	int	4	10	0			✓	1	1	
CustomerID	char	5	0	0	✓					
EmployeeID	int	4	10	0	✓					
OrderDate	datetime	8	0	0	✓					
RequiredDate	datetime	8	0	0	✓					
ShippedDate	datetime	8	0	0	✓					
ShipVia	int	4	10	0	✓					
Freight	money	8	19	4	✓	(0)				
ShipName	varchar	40	0	0	✓					
ShipAddress	varchar	60	0	0	✓					
ShipCity	varchar	15	0	0	✓					
ShipRegion	varchar	15	0	0	✓					
ShipPostalCode	varchar	10	0	0	✓					
ShipCountry	varchar	15	0	0	✓					

Figure 25.11
The Orders table in the project designer's Design view.

TABLE 25.1 A COMPARISON OF PROJECT DESIGNER COLUMNS AND ACCESS TABLE PROPERTIES

Column Name	Correspondence to Access/Jet Table Properties
Column Name	Same as Jet's Field Name, except spaces and punctuation (other than the underscore) aren't permitted in MSDE.
Datatype	Same as the combination of Jet's Data Type and Field Size, except datatypes use SQL Server terminology.
Length	Same as Jet's Field Size for text fields, except that `char` columns are fixed length.
Precision	Applicable primarily to `numeric` or `decimal` fields; specifies the total number of digits of the column (the `precision` property of `int`(eger) and `money` fields is fixed).
Scale	Applicable to `numeric` or `decimal` fields; specifies the number of digits to the right of the decimal point (the scale of `money` fields is fixed at 4).

Column Name	Correspondence to Access/Jet Table Properties
Allow Nulls	The inverse of Jet's Required property; a check mark (the default) allows null values in fields.
Default Value	Same as Jet's Default Value.
Identity	Equivalent to Jet's AutoNumber field data type with Increment as the New Values property; a check mark specifies that an int (same as Jet's Long Integer) field automatically creates a new value when appending a record.
Identity Seed	Specifies the starting value of a field with the identity property set.
Identity Increment	Specifies the increment between successive identity values (usually 1).
Is RowGuid	A check mark specifies that the row contains a globally unique identifier (GUID, pronounced "goo id") used primarily with timestamp fields for replication.

Note

The preceding table offers only a simplified comparison of MSDE/SQL Server and Access/Jet data types. For a full discussion of MSDE/SQL Server data types, refer to SQL Server 7.0's Books Online.

PART

VI

CH

25

The table Properties sheet for MSDE tables also differs greatly from Access's table properties sheet, which lets you change only the table's Description property and set Hidden, Replicable, and Row Level Tracking table attributes. In Table Design view, click the toolbar's Properties button to open the Properties sheet. The Properties sheet for MSDE tables has three pages—Table, Relationships, and Indexes/Keys. Figure 25.12 shows the Tables page of the Properties sheet for the Order Details table.

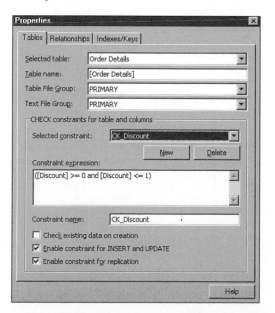

Figure 25.12
The Tables page of the Properties sheet for the Order Details table.

Following are brief descriptions of the elements of the Tables page:

- *Tables*. Although Tables is a drop-down list, you can only select the currently open table from the list.
- *Table Name*. ANSI SQL doesn't allow table names with spaces or punctuation (except underscores), so field names containing illegal characters must be enclosed between square brackets.

> **Note**
>
> Microsoft opened a Pandora's box by allowing Jet databases to include spaces and other non-alphanumeric symbols in database, table, and field names. The Northwind.mdb developers finally removed spaces from table names in Access 9x, but the space remains in the Order Details table. Access developers have complained long and loudly, but to no avail, about Microsoft's continuing use of spaces in Access object names.

- *Table File Group* and *Text File Group*. SQL Server 7.0 lets database administrators (DBAs) create multiple operating system files for a single table. DBAs also can assign SQL Server text fields, the equivalent to Jet's Memo data type, to their own file group. Users of MSDE aren't likely to need to create file groups.
- *Selected Constraint*. CHECK constraints are the SQL Server equivalent of Jet table-level Validation Rules. You can specify multiple check constraints; the Order Details table has three CHECK constraints—CK_Discount, CK_Quantity, and CK_UnitPrice—which you select from the drop-down list.
- *Constraint Expression*. The CHECK expression must evaluate to Boolean True or False. You add new constraints by clicking the New button and typing the expression and name in the text boxes.
- *Constraint properties*. You can test existing data for conformance to constraints, enable constraints for data addition and updates, and apply constraints to replicated data with the three check boxes at the bottom of the page.

EXPLORING MSDE VIEWS

Like tables, run mode for views uses conventional Access datasheets. Figure 25.13 shows the Order Details Extended view in run mode. The project designer doesn't support datasheet formatting options, so the Discount field is displayed as a decimal fraction rather than a percentage. Views don't offer a sort property (ORDER BY clause), so the Sort Ascending and Sort Descending buttons of the toolbar operate on the locally cached copy of the view's Recordset. Similarly, Filter by Form, Filter by Selection, and Find operate on the local Recordset.

Order Details Extended : View

OrderID	ProductID	ProductName	UnitPrice	Quantity	Discount	ExtendedPrice
10265	17	Alice Mutton	$31.20	30	0	$936.00
10279	17	Alice Mutton	$31.20	15	0.25	$351.00
10294	17	Alice Mutton	$31.20	15	0	$468.00
10302	17	Alice Mutton	$31.20	40	0	$1,248.00
10319	17	Alice Mutton	$31.20	8	0	$249.60
10338	17	Alice Mutton	$31.20	20	0	$624.00
10339	17	Alice Mutton	$31.20	70	0.05	$2,074.80
10346	17	Alice Mutton	$31.20	36	0.1	$1,010.88
10415	17	Alice Mutton	$31.20	2	0	$62.40
10430	17	Alice Mutton	$31.20	45	0.2	$1,123.20
10431	17	Alice Mutton	$31.20	50	0.25	$1,170.00
10444	17	Alice Mutton	$31.20	10	0	$312.00
10523	17	Alice Mutton	$39.00	25	0.1	$877.50
10530	17	Alice Mutton	$39.00	40	0	$1,560.00
10550	17	Alice Mutton	$39.00	8	0.1	$280.80
10564	17	Alice Mutton	$39.00	16	0.05	$592.80
10573	17	Alice Mutton	$39.00	18	0	$702.00
10607	17	Alice Mutton	$39.00	100	0	$3,900.00
10686	17	Alice Mutton	$39.00	30	0.2	$936.00

Record: 1 of 2155

Figure 25.13
The Order Details Extended view in run mode.

Note

VBA code and ADO let you apply a server-side filter to a table or view. Using server-side filters minimizes the amount of data sent to the client, which reduces network traffic and improves performance.

Changing to Design view opens the graphical view designer, the structure of which resembles the Access query designer (see Figure 25.14). Click the SQL button of the toolbar to display the SQL statement that creates the view. The upper diagram pane displays field lists for each table with a symbolic join. The key symbol indicates the primary key field(s) and the infinity symbol (∞) specifies the foreign key field. Primary key field(s) of the tables appear in bold type.

The view designer's toolbar adds the following five buttons:

- *Diagram* toggles the display of the diagram in the upper pane. You specify the type of join in a properties sheet.
- *Grid* toggles the display of the column information, which lets you alias columns, specify whether column data appears in the view, and add `WHERE` clause criteria.
- *SQL* toggles the lower text box that displays the Transact-SQL statement that generates the view.
- *Verify SQL Syntax* runs a grammar check on the SQL statement but doesn't execute the query to create the view.
- *Group By* substitutes `GROUP BY` for `WHERE` clauses in the grid. Group By properties let you add `ROLLUP` and `CUBE` statements for complex aggregation.

Figure 25.14
The Order Details
Extended view in run
mode.

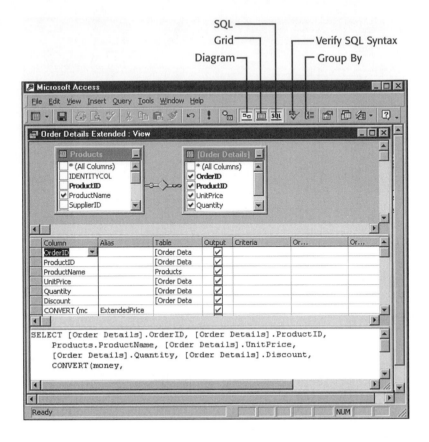

The SQL statement for the Order Details Extended view illustrates substitution of the SQL CONVERT function for VBA's **CCur** function to change the data type of the calculated column to money. The complete SQL statement for the view, less the CREATE VIEW statement to compile the query, is as follows:

```
SELECT [Order Details].OrderID, [Order Details].ProductID,
    Products.ProductName, [Order Details].UnitPrice,
    [Order Details].Quantity, [Order Details].Discount,
    CONVERT(money, [Order Details].UnitPrice *
        [Order Details].Quantity * (1 - [Order Details].Discount)
        / 100) * 100 AS ExtendedPrice
FROM Products INNER JOIN
    [Order Details] ON Products.ProductID = [Order Details].ProductID
```

To explore adding new tables and setting query properties, do the following:

1. Click the Show Tables button to open the Show Tables window, and then expand the Tables and Views nodes. Move the Products and Order Details tables to the right, and drag the Suppliers item to the left of Products to add an equi-join between the SupplierID fields (see Figure 25.15). Click the SupplierID check box of the Products table and the CompanyName check box of the Suppliers table to add the columns to the view.

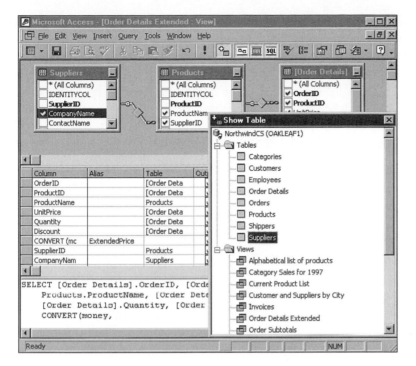

Figure 25.15
Adding the Products table to the Order Details Extended view.

2. Right-click the join line between the Order Details and Products and choose Properties to open the join Properties window (see Figure 25.16). You select the type of join from a drop-down list of the operators. Marking the All Rows from [Order Details] check box creates a RIGHT OUTER JOIN and squares the right side of the diamond join symbol. Marking both check boxes creates a FULL OUTER JOIN; the join symbol becomes a square. Scroll the SQL pane to read the JOIN changes to the view's SQL statement.

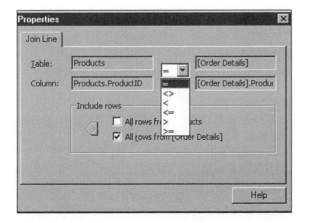

Figure 25.16
The Properties sheet for the join between the Products and Order Details tables.

3. Click the Group By button to add GROUP BY clauses to the columns. Like Access Totals queries, tabbing or selecting the Group By cell for each column lets you specify from a drop-down list Group By, Sum, Avg, Min, Max, Count, Expression, or Where.

4. Click the toolbar's Properties button with Group By on to open the view Properties sheet (see Figure 25.17). You can specify a TOP *n* [PERCENT] view by typing the expression in the Top text box, add the DISTINCT qualifier, encrypt the view, and specify CUBE, ROLLUP, or ALL extensions to the GROUP BY clause.

→ For a review of SELECT query qualifiers, **see** "Jet's DISTINCTROW and SQL's DISTINCT Keywords," **p. 877** and "Jet SQL Reserved Words, Operators, and Functions Not in ANSI SQL," **p. 875**.

Figure 25.17
The view Properties sheet for a view with an added GROUP BY clause.

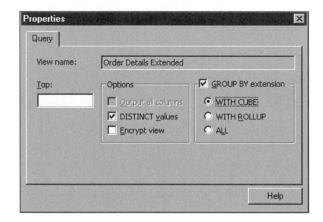

5. Click the toolbar's Verify SQL Syntax button to check the changes you made in the preceding steps. You receive a message box confirming the statement's validity. Deliberately introducing an error results in a message providing the approximate location of the mistake. Figure 25.18 illustrates the message that occurs if you delete the left bracket from the second instance of [Order Details] in the query.

Figure 25.18
An error message resulting from attempting to verify incorrect query syntax.

6. Close the view designer and don't save the changes you made. Modifications to the database are temporary until you close the designer and elect to save changes.

DIAGRAMMING TABLE RELATIONSHIPS

 Selecting the Database Diagrams shortcut and double-clicking the Relationships item opens the Relationships diagram, derived from Access's Relationships window. Click the arrow to the right of the Zoom Modes Dropdown button and select the percentage that displays all tables on your monitor (see Figure 25.19).

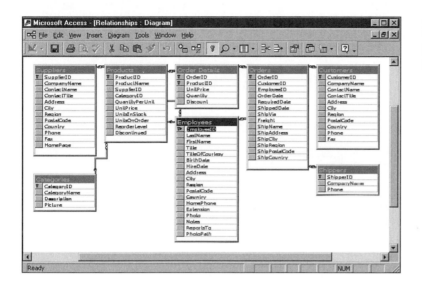

Figure 25.19
The Relationships diagram for the NorthwindCS database.

PART

VI

CH

25

You can do the following in the Relationships diagram:

- Modify the properties of any table in the database, including adding and deleting fields, or changing the properties of fields. Right-clicking the table header opens a versatile context menu with 15 choices. Choosing Column Properties expands the selected table window to display a reduced-size version of Table Design view (see Figure 25.20 and refer to Figure 25.11).

- Add or drop tables of the database. You can also start with a new MSDE database, and then add all the required tables, fields, and relationships in the Database Diagram window.

- View and alter relationships between tables by right-clicking the join line and choosing Properties.

 - Hide tables. Hiding a table also causes relationship symbols connecting the table to disappear.

- Print the diagram. If the size of the diagram exceeds the maximum paper size of your printer, you must cut and paste several sheets to obtain a complete diagram.

Figure 25.20
Selecting Column Properties from the Products table's context menu.

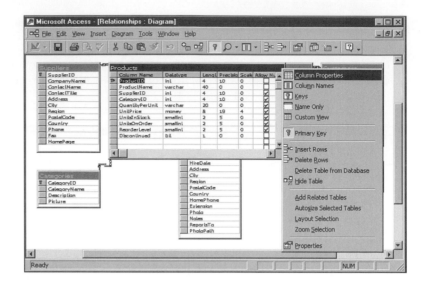

WRITING STORED PROCEDURES

 Clicking the Stored Procedures shortcut and one of the scripts of NorthwindCS.adp opens the stored procedure text editor with the procedure's SQL statement preceded by ALTER PROCEDURE (see Figure 25.21). ALTER PROCEDURE, like ALTER TABLE, is a new extension to SQL Server's Transact-SQL dialect. Colors highlight Transact-SQL reserved words, similar to color highlighting of VBA reserved words in the Office 2000 VBA Editor.

Figure 25.21
The Transact-SQL script for the Employee Sales by Country stored procedure.

Tip #233 from

If the SQL statement for the stored procedure you open appears as a single line of text, format the SQL statement into multiple lines with the Enter key, and add indentation for readability. The SQL parser disregards *white space*, which consists of carriage return, line feed, tab, and space characters. When you save your changes, the Stored Procedure retains the added formatting.

As noted in the "Running the NorthwindCS Sample Project" section earlier in the chapter, ADP requires you to write stored procedures for parameterized queries, typified by the Employee Sales by Country procedure. Transact-SQL doesn't support Jet's PARAMETERS reserved word; instead, you specify input parameters (@Beginning_Date and @Ending_Date), together with their data type(s), as input parameter variables. SQL Server identifies local (procedure-level) variables with a prepended @ character; global variables start with @@. In most parameterized procedures, the local parameter variables supply their values to a WHERE clause. When you execute the procedure, a standard Access Enter Parameter Value dialog appears for each parameter.

Clicking the Create a Stored Procedure in Designer shortcut opens a new Stored Procedure window with a marginally helpful procedure text skeleton (see Figure 25.22). You change StoredProcedure1 to the name for your new procedure, delete or alter the parameter declarations, type the query after AS, and specify or delete the RETURN value. Transact-SQL uses C-style comment identifiers (/*...*/); commenting disables the parameter templates and the SET NOCOUNT ON directive. You also can use — as an inline comment prefix, similar to the apostrophe (') in VBA.

PART

VI

CH

25

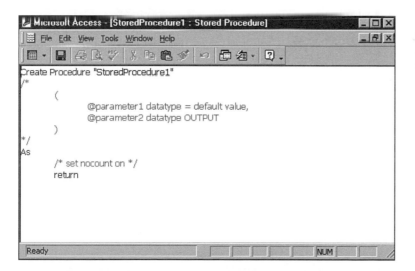

Figure 25.22
The skeleton template for a new Transact-SQL stored procedure.

ADDING TRIGGERS TO A TABLE

Triggers are stored procedures that execute automatically when INSERT, UPDATE, or DELETE operations occur on a table. The primary purpose of triggers is to maintain the database's referential integrity when you don't use SQL Server's declarative referential integrity (DRI) features. Unfortunately, SQL Server 7.0's DRI supports only cascading INSERT, not UPDATE or DELETE operations.

To edit or add a table trigger, follow these steps:

1. Right-click the table item in the Database window, and choose <u>T</u>riggers to open the Triggers for Table: *TableName* dialog.

2. Select the trigger you want to edit in the dropdown list and click Edit to open the *TriggerName*: Trigger window. Figure 25.23 shows the UPDATE trigger created in the following section by AUW from the \Shared\Nwind\Nwind.mdb application database. (Tables of the NorthwindCS database don't have triggers.)

Figure 25.23
The UPDATE trigger for the Customers table of the NwindSQL database.

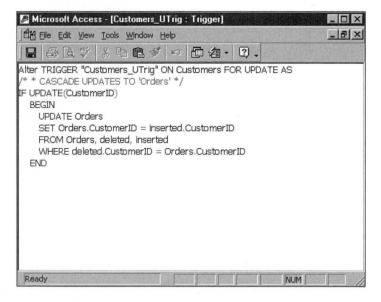

3. Close the trigger opened in the preceding step, and don't save changes, if any.

4. Repeat steps 1 and 2, but click New in the Triggers for Table: *TableName* dialog. Like stored procedures, adding a trigger opens a marginally useful skeleton of a trigger procedure (see Figure 25.24).

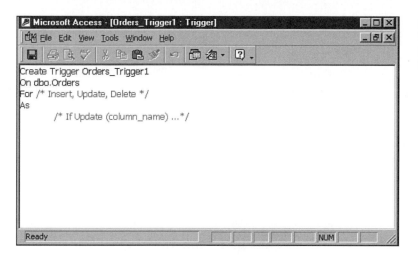

Figure 25.24
The CREATE TRIGGER skeleton offered by the table designer.

5. Close the trigger window without saving changes.

USING THE UPSIZING WIZARD TO CREATE ADP

Access 2000's version of the Upsizing Wizard adds the capability to generate a project from an existing Access application of either the single-database or split-database category. The most likely upsizing scenario is from a split database with the data .mdb file shared from a file server.

The Access 2000 version of AUW has several more limitations than prior versions when upsizing to MSDE or SQL Server and creating DAP. The four most important of these limitations are as follows:

- AUW won't upsize UNION, crosstab, or make-table queries; you must write your own UNION queries and make-table queries, if you need them, in Transact-SQL.

- AUW doesn't convert all Jet Validation Rule property values to SQL Server CHECK constraints, the ANSI SQL-92 replacement for Transact-SQL 6.x and earlier RULES.

- AUW doesn't convert fields of the Jet Hyperlink data type, because MSDE/SQL Server doesn't support this data type.

- AUW won't convert VBA expressions in Access SQL, such as CCur and IIf, to Transact-SQL CONVERT and block IF statements. You must write your own SQL Server view or stored procedure counterparts.

PART

VI

CH

25

RUNNING THE ACCESS UPSIZING WIZARD

Make sure MSDE is running by checking for the presence of a green arrow in the icon in the taskbar tray, and then follow these steps:

1. Open the secure C:\Shared\Nwind\Nwind.mdb database you created in Chapter 24, "Securing Multiuser Network Applications." You must use Workgroup Administrator to join the \Shared\Nwind\System.mdw workgroup file to open the secure database.

Note If you didn't create Nwind.mdb, NwindData.mdb, and the modified DAP files as described in Chapter 24, you can copy unsecured versions of these files from the \SEUA2K\Chaptr25 folder of the accompanying CD-ROM to a C:\Shared\Nwind folder on your PC.

2. Choose Tools, Database Utilities, Upsizing Wizard to launch the Wizard and open the first dialog (see Figure 25.25). You don't have an MSDE database at this point, so accept the default Create New Database option, and click Next to open the second Wizard dialog.

Figure 25.25
The Upsizing Wizard's opening dialog.

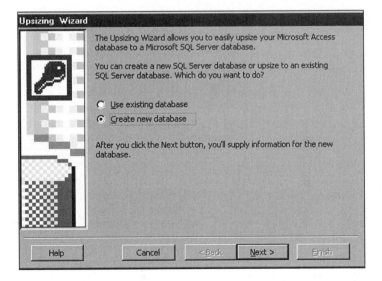

3. Type **(local)** or your computer's NetBIOS name (OAKLEAF1 for the examples in this chapter) in the What SQL Server... combo list, type **sa** (short for system administrator, the default administrative account for SQL server) in the Login ID text box, leave the Password text box empty, and accept the default NwindSQL as the database name in the bottom text box (see Figure 25.26). Click Next to connect to MSDE and open the third Wizard dialog.

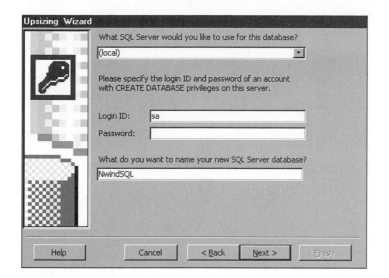

Figure 25.26
Specifying the server name, the MSDE login ID and password, and the name of the MSDE database to create.

Note

If you receive an error message that the Wizard can't log on to SQL Server and a login dialog appears, make sure MSDE is started, and then click OK to retry the connection.

4. Click the >> button to move all linked tables to the Export to SQL Server list (see Figure 25.27). Click Next.

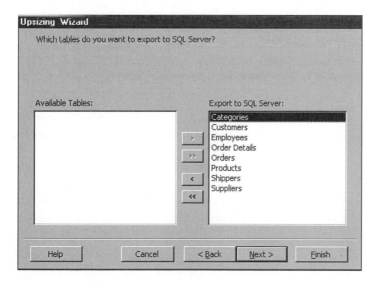

Figure 25.27
Selecting all tables of NwindData.mdb linked to Nwind.mdb for upsizing to MSDE.

5. The fifth Wizard dialog lets you choose whether to emulate attributes of your Jet database in the MSDE database. Accept the defaults for your first upsizing test (see Figure 25.28). Click Next to open the sixth dialog.

Figure 25.28
Accepting the Wizard's default values for MSDE database and table attributes.

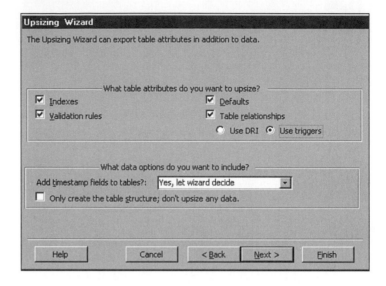

> **Upsizing Wizard**
>
> The Upsizing Wizard can export table attributes in addition to data.
>
> ── What table attributes do you want to upsize? ──
> ☑ Indexes   ☑ Defaults
> ☑ Validation rules   ☑ Table relationships
>   ○ Use DRI ● Use triggers
>
> ── What data options do you want to include? ──
> Add timestamp fields to tables?: [Yes, let wizard decide ▾]
> ☐ Only create the table structure; don't upsize any data.
>
> [Help]   [Cancel]   [< Back]   [Next >]   [Finish]

Tip #234 from

Specifying the default Use Triggers option lets you take full advantage of Access's referential integrity management features with cascading updates and deletions.

SQL Server uses `timestamp` fields to resolve conflicts between edits to the same record; unless otherwise specified, the edit with the latest `timestamp` value prevails.

Up to this point, the Access Upsizing Wizard (AUW) differs only in cosmetic details from prior AUW versions. The following step is new in Access 2000.

NEW 2000

6. The sixth Wizard dialog appears only if you initiate the upsizing process from the application .mdb file containing Access application objects, such as queries, forms, reports, pages, and VBA code modules. Select the Create a New Access Client/Server Application option to generate an Access Data Project from the original Nwind.mdb file. The default file name is *FileName*CS.adp. Accept the default file name, NwindCS.adp, for this example. Mark the Save Password and User ID check box to preserve permissions for the application objects, if the database is secure (see Figure 25.29).

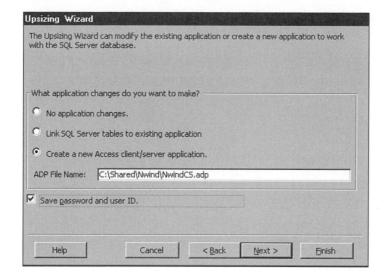

Figure 25.29
Specifying generation of an Access Data Project from the original .mdb file containing application objects.

7. Click Next to open the final Wizard dialog (see Figure 25.30).

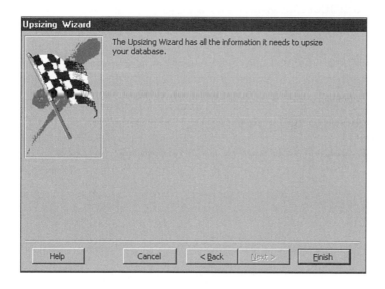

Figure 25.30
The final Upsizing Wizard dialog.

8. Click Finish to start the multi-step process of upsizing tables and queries to MSDE, then copying forms, reports, pages, and modules to Nwind.adp. A progress bar keeps you informed of the Wizard's activity (see Figure 25.31).

Figure 25.31
The progress dialog that appears during the upsizing and ADP generation process.

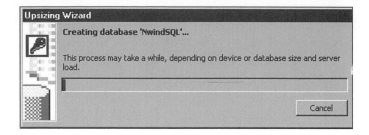

> **Note**
>
> When the Upsizing Wizard encounters a query that contains SQL statements that MSDE doesn't support, you receive an error message. If the unsupported SQL syntax is for DAP, Microsoft Internet Explorer appears in the message's title bar.

CHECKING THE WIZARD'S SUCCESSES AND FAILURES

When the Wizard finishes its work, the Upsizing Wizard Report opens in Print Preview mode (see Figure 25.32). The Report notifies you of problems the Wizard encountered with your application and the names of objects for which upsizing failed.

Figure 25.32
The Upsizing Report generated by the Wizard from Nwind.mdb.

To test the upsizing outcome, do the following:

1. Open each table in NwindCS to verify that structure and data migration to MSDE succeeded.

> **Note**
>
> In some cases, the Upsizing Report indicates failure to create a CHECK constraint, but inspection of MSDE table properties shows that the constraint was added.

2. Verify that the Wizard converted Access queries to either views or stored procedures. Due to the Wizard's limitations, some queries don't convert.

   Parts of queries that fail the conversion process appear with the prefix ut_qry#View when you click the Database window's Views shortcut or ut_qry# when viewing the list of Stored Procedures.

3. Check each form and report for operability. Forms and reports, as well as underlying VBA code, that depend on queries that failed to upsize also fail.

4. Test the operability of DAP. The Wizard stores DAP in your My Documents (Windows 9x) or \Winnt\Profiles\UserName\Personal (Windows NT) folder, unless you specified a different default database folder in the Options dialog.

> **Tip #235 from**
>
> *R J*
>
> Like forms and reports, DAP whose queries don't convert won't display data. If you want to share DAP, you must copy the DAP .htm files to your shared folder, delete the DAP shortcuts, and use the Edit Web Page That Already Exists shortcut to repoint the reference to the DAP in NwindCS.adp.

DOWNSIZING DATABASES WITH THE DTS WIZARD

Installing MSDE also installs SQL Server's DTS Wizard for converting Jet and other supported database types to SQL Server 7.0 databases. You might need to downsize an SQL Server 7.0 database to a Jet 4.0 .mdb file. If so, follow these steps:

1. Create a new Access database, NwindDS.mdb in the \Shared\Nwind folder, and then close Access.

2. Choose Start, Programs, Msde, Import and Export Data to open the first DTS Wizard dialog. Click Next.

3. In the Choose a Data Source dialog, accept in the Source list the default Microsoft OLE DB Provider for SQL Server item, accept (local) in the Server list, type **sa** in the Username text box, leave the Password text box empty, and select the NwindSQL database from the Database list (see Figure 25.33).

Figure 25.33
Specifying the server and database from which to downsize.

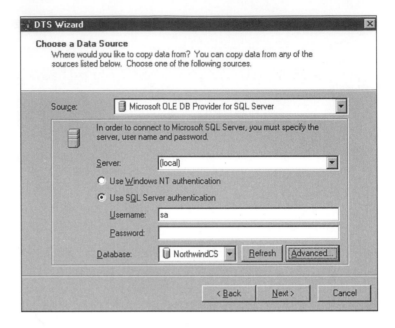

4. Click Next to open the Choose a Destination dialog. Select Microsoft Access as the data source type from the Destination list, click the Browse button of the File Name text box, navigate to the \Shared\Nwind folder, and double-click NwindDS.mdb.

5. Type **Admin** in the Username text box, and leave the Password text box empty if you're working from the unsecured version of System.mdw (see Figure 25.34). Otherwise, type an administrative login ID and password. Click Next.

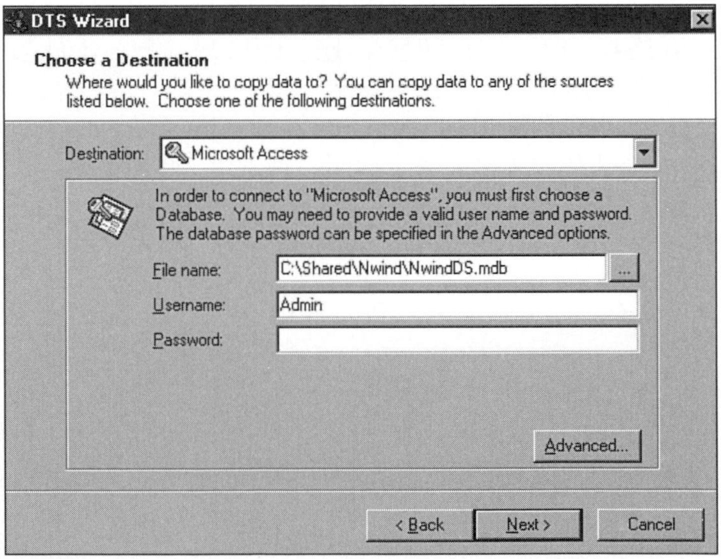

Figure 25.34
Specifying the Jet 4.0 destination database.

6. Accept the default Copy Table(s) from the Source Database option (see Figure 25.35), and click Next.

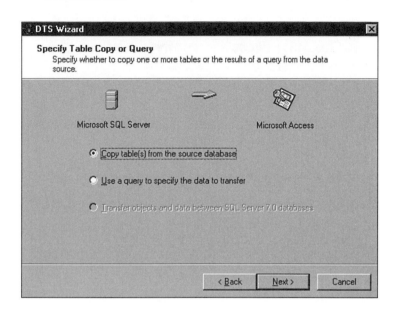

Figure 25.35
Directing the Wizard to copy the NwindSQL tables to NwindDS.mdb.

7. In the Select Source Tables dialog, click Select All to copy all tables from the source to the destination database (see Figure 25.36).

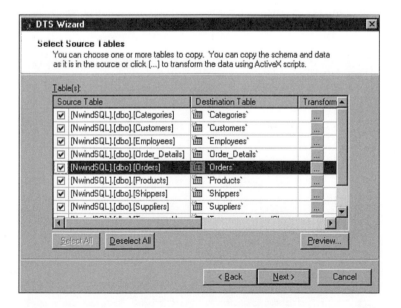

Figure 25.36
Selecting all tables for copying from the source to the destination database.

8. Select a table and click the Preview button to verify that the Wizard has the moxie to do its job. Pay particular attention to the Freight field of the Orders table (see Figure 25.37).

Figure 25.37
Previewing the Wizard's proposed data format for a downsized Orders table.

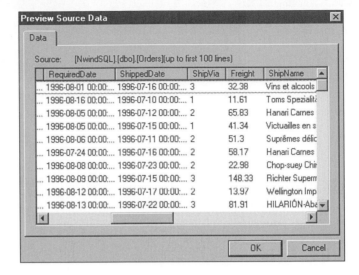

9. The Freight field appears in Preview without the currency symbol, so close the Preview dialog and click the Transform button for the Orders table to open the Column Mappings and Transformation dialog. Scroll to the Freight column and verify that the destination field data type is Currency (see Figure 25.38). Click Cancel to close the dialog, and click Next.

Figure 25.38
Verifying the source database data type for the Freight field of the Orders table.

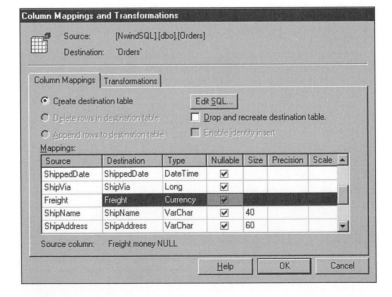

10. In the Save, Schedule and Replicate Package dialog, make sure the default Run Immediately check box is checked (see Figure 25.39). Click Next.

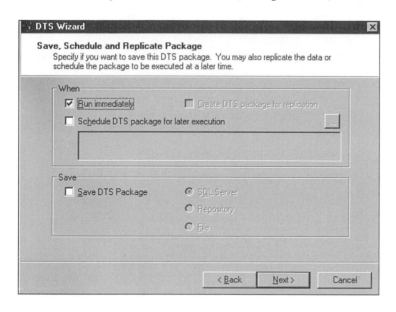

Figure 25.39
Scheduling the downsizing operation for immediate execution.

11. Review the Summary text in the Completing the DTS Wizard dialog by scrolling through the list of table names (see Figure 25.40), and then click Finish to start the downsizing operation.

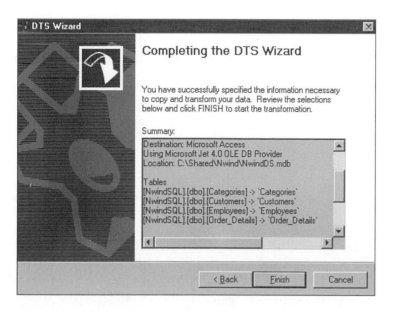

Figure 25.40
The DTS Wizard's almost final dialog.

12. The Wizard provides a report of the completion of each step in the downsizing process (see Figure 25.41).

Figure 25.41
The Wizard's downsizing progress report.

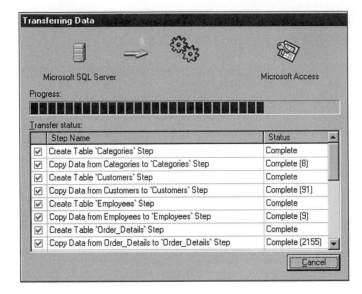

13. Click OK to dismiss the message box announcing completion of the Wizard's work, and then click Done to close the Transferring Data dialog.

14. Reopen NwindDS.mdb in Access and verify that all tables transferred intact and that the required number of records are present.

Unfortunately, the DTS Wizard doesn't migrate indexes and other database and table attributes to NwindDS.mdb. You can reverse the source and destination databases to upsize the tables (only) of Jet databases to MSDE or SQL Server 7.0, but table and database attributes also don't propagate in the reverse direction. Regardless of the deficiencies of the current version of AUW, upsizing with AUW is a more time-efficient approach than using DTS.

CONNECTING TO REMOTE MSDE DATABASES

If MSDE is running under Windows NT or 2000 (Workstation or Server) and your client PC runs Windows NT or 2000 Workstation, connecting to the remote MSDE database is simple. The Named Pipes protocol advertises the NetBIOS name of all Windows NT or 2000 PCs in your current domain that have MSDE or SQL Server installed. Thus you can select the MSDE or SQL Server to which to connect from the Servers drop-down lists of ADP connection dialogs. (If the server name doesn't appear, type it in the list's text box.) For Windows 9x clients or servers, you must specify the MSDE or SQL Server connection.

USING THE SQL SERVER CLIENT NETWORK UTILITY

MSDE running under Windows 9x and Windows 9x Access clients don't support the Named Pipes protocol, so you must establish server aliases with the SQL Server Client Network Utility. The following example sets up aliases to connect the OAKLEAF1 client, which runs Windows 98, to the following servers:

- OAKLEAF0 running SQL Server 7.0 Standard Edition under Windows NT 4.0 with Service Pack 4 (Northwind and NwindSQL databases).

- OAKLEAF3 running SQL Server 7.0 Enterprise Edition under Windows 2000, Beta 2 (Northwind database).

- OAKLEAF5 running MSDE under Windows 98 (NorthwindCS database).

To connect to one or more remote MSDE or SQL Server databases, do the following:

1. Choose Start, Programs, Msde, Client Network Utility to open the SQL Server Client Network Utility dialog with an empty Server Alias Configurations list with Named Pipes as the Default Network Library.

2. Open the Default Network Library and choose Multiprotocol or TCP/IP, depending on the libraries you selected when installing MSDE on the server.

3. Click Add to open the Add Network Library Configuration dialog and type as the Server Alias the computer name of the PC on which the remote MSDE or SQL Server database resides (see Figure 25.42).

   The Server Alias name automatically becomes the Computer Name; you can edit the Computer Name entry if you want different alias and computer names. Click OK to add the alias.

PART

VI

CH

25

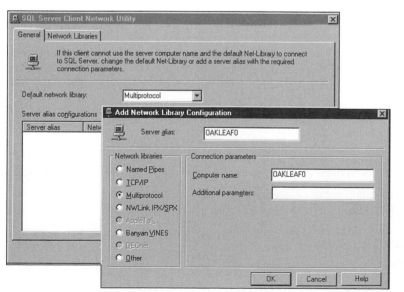

Figure 25.42
Specifying alias and computer names in the Add Network Library Configuration dialog.

4. Repeat step 3 for each installation of MSDE or SQL Server to which you want to connect. Figure 25.43 illustrates the addition of aliases for three PCs in the OAKLEAF domain.

Figure 25.43
Three aliases for servers in the OAKLEAF domain defined in the SQL Server Client Network Utility dialog.

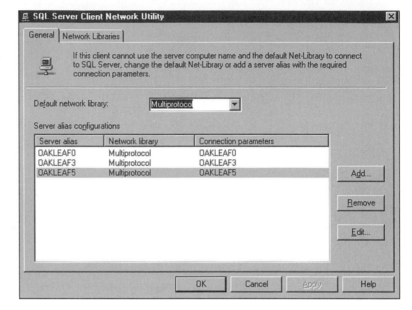

5. Click OK to save the server aliases and close the SQL Server Client Network Utility dialog.

TESTING AND USING REMOTE DATABASES

When you add an alias in the SQL Server Client Network Utility dialog, no tests for network connectivity, presence of MSDE or SQL Server, or status (stopped or started) occurs. If you have SQL Server 7.0 Enterprise Manager installed, you can verify the status of the server, but MSDE doesn't install the full set of SQL Server 7.0 management tools.

You can verify from ADP that a connection is valid and MSDE or SQL Server is present and running by doing the following:

1. Select the Pages shortcut and double-click Create Data Access Page in Design View.

2. Click the Field List button to open the Field List window with the Database tab active.

3. Right-click the database node, NorthwindCS (OAKLEAF1) for this example, and choose Connection to open the Data Link Properties sheet with the Connection tab active.

4. If the Select or Enter a Server Name drop-down list shows the servers you added, select the server to test. Otherwise, type the alias name in the text box.

5. Select the Use a Specific User Name and Password option, type **sa** in the User Name text box, and leave the Password text box empty.

6. Open the Select the Database on the Server list. After a second or two of network activity, the server populates the list with the names of available databases (see Figure 25.44). Select the database that you want to check.

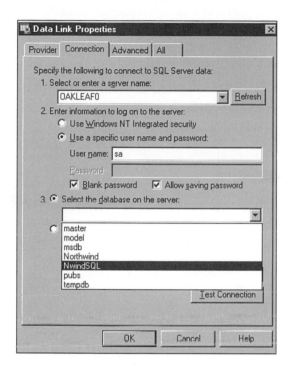

Figure 25.44
Available databases on an aliased remote SQL Server 7.0 installation.

PART

VI

CH

25

7. Click Test Connection to perform a final check on the connection to the remote database, then close the page without saving changes.

 If Access hangs or you receive an error message when attempting to connect to a remote MSDE or SQL Server database, see the "Remote Database Connection Errors" topic of the "Troubleshooting" section near the end of this chapter.

ESTABLISHING MSDE SECURITY

Integrated security is the best option for most Windows NT SQL Server installations. Integrated security lets you assign specific SQL Server privileges to Windows NT groups and users. When you run MSDE under Windows 9x, of course, the Integrated Security option isn't available.

By default, Access ADP log on to MSDE with the sa username and an empty password, the hallmarks of a totally unsecure server installation. Fortunately, ADP offer a simplified version of the security management features of SQL Server Enterprise manager. To establish database security for ordinary users of MSDE databases, do the following:

1. With an Access data project open, choose Tools, Security, Database Security to open the SQL Server Security dialog with the Server Logins tab active. By default, the only login is sa.

2. Click Add to open the SQL Server Login Properties - New Login dialog. Type the new common account name for ADP in the Name text box and a password in the Password text box. Open the Database list and select the default database for login (see Figure 22.45).

Figure 25.45
Adding a new MSDE user account for access to ADP.

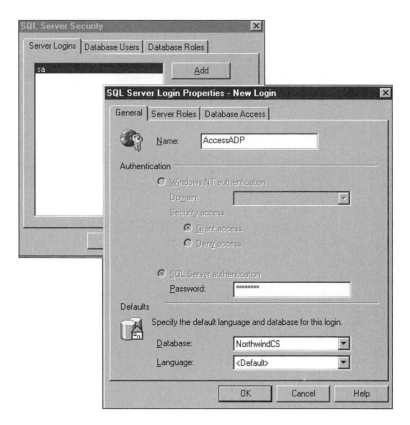

3. Click the Database Access tab and click the Permit check box for the MSDE ADP database(s) to which you want to grant the new username permissions. Accept the default public role for the selected database (see Figure 25.46).

Figure 25.46
Selecting the database(s) and roles for the new MSDE username.

4. With the public role selected, click Properties to open the Database Role Properties - public dialog, and click Permissions to open the Permissions dialog. By default, the public role has basic SELECT, INSERT, UPDATE, DELETE, EXECUTE, and declarative referential integrity (DRI) permissions, as available for each class of object (see Figure 25.47).

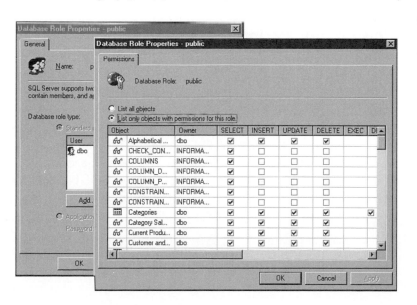

Figure 25.47
Default permissions for the public user of the NorthwindCS MSDE database.

5. Clear the check boxes for the permissions you don't want to grant the user, click OK three times, confirm the new account's password, and click OK to close the three dialogs. The new MSDE account appears in the Server Logins page of the SQL Security dialog. Click OK to close the dialog and return to Access.

To test the new account, follow the steps in the "Testing and Using Remote Databases" section earlier in the chapter. Substitute the new account name and password for sa and the empty password, and click Test Connection to verify your entries.

TROUBLESHOOTING

REMOTE DATABASE CONNECTION PROBLEMS

Access hangs or throws an error message when you attempt to connect to a remote MSDE or SQL Server database.

There are many causes for connection failures to remote databases, the most obvious being network problems. Verify that you can connect to the server PC and open server shares with Explorer. If you can connect to a server share but not the database, and your network runs NetBEUI and TCP/IP protocols, you probably have a TCP/IP problem. Use Control Panel's Network tool, disable the NetBEUI protocol, and verify the TCP/IP settings for your network interface card (NIC).

Another common cause of connection failures is incorrect spelling of the server name when you create the alias. The SQL Server Client Network Utility doesn't test for existence of the server when you define the server alias.

IN THE REAL WORLD—ADP ON TRIAL

The jury's out on ADP version 1.0 as a production database front end to MSDE back end databases. MSDE's lack of Enterprise Manager tools make ordinary database administration chores difficult or impossible. As an example, the Tools, Database Utilities, Drop SQL Database command simply disconnects ADP from the back-end database; the command doesn't delete the database. If you have an SQL Server 7.0 installation, you can use Enterprise Manager to administer MSDE, but only if it's running under Windows NT or 2000. You can't connect Enterprise Manager to MSDE under Windows 9x, because Windows 9x doesn't support the required Named Pipes protocol. Most MSDE users probably will migrate to SQL Server 7.0 when putting ADP into production, fulfilling Microsoft's objective in providing MSDE with Access 2000.

ADP DRAWBACKS

ADP offers no equivalent of locally stored Jet QueryDef objects; the server stores all queries as views or stored procedures. This approach is the opposite of that taken by Access's Database Splitter utility, which retains QueryDefs in the front-end .mdb file. It's logical to store queries that are common to many applications and users on the server, but application- or user-specific queries belong on the client side. As you increase the number of ADP queries, the database becomes bloated with views and stored procedures that clients execute only occasionally, if at all. Hopefully, the next version of ADP will provide a local QueryDef storage mechanism.

ADP requires ADO to connect to MSDE or SQL Server 7.0. ADO requires experienced DAO programmers to adopt an entirely new database object model. ADO, in turn, forces you to abandon ingrained Jet SQL habits in favor of ANSI SQL-92 syntax—wildcard changes from * and ? to % and _ and string identifiers moving from " to ' are the most obvious examples. The four DAO.Find... methods become a single ADODB.Find method with a one-field limit on the search criterion argument; workarounds for ADODB.Find limitations are inelegant, to be charitable.

Finally, the Access Upsizing Wizard is developmentally challenged when attempting to convert all but the most trivial Access applications from conventional .mdb files to ADP. Jet SQL TRANSFORM and PIVOT statements entice Access developers to make extensive use of crosstab queries as data sources for graphs and charts, as well as for summary forms and reports. SQL Server's Transact-SQL doesn't have TRANSFORM and PIVOT, so the Wizard blithely bypasses conversion of crosstabs. Apparently, the Microsoft Jet team wasn't able to convince SQL Server 7.0 product managers to add TRANSFORM and PIVOT to Transact-SQL. Adding these two non-ANSI reserved words to Transact-SQL, rather than the seldom-used ROLLUP and CUBE statements, would have been a boon to Access and SQL Server developers alike.

PART

VI

CH

25

Tip #236 from

R J

Check Microsoft's http://www.microsoft.com/accessdev/ site for a promised Ad-Hoc Query Tool that provides a graphic user interface similar to Enterprise Manager's Query Analyzer and ISQL/w. Microsoft says there's also an Action Query Wizard in the works to aid creation of stored procedures to replace Jet make-table, update, delete, and append queries.

SQL SERVER ADVANTAGES—ADP, MSDE, AND SQL SERVER 7.0

The verdict's in, however, for the SQL Server 7.0 trial—it's a *great* client/server RDBMS for the vast majority of database applications. SQL Server 7.0 won *InfoWorld* magazine's 1998 "Product of the Year Award" for database and server software, and *PC Week* magazine's "Best of Show Award" at Fall 1998 COMDEX. *Information Week* called SQL Server 7.0 "one of the 10 most important products of 1998." Links to SQL Server 7.0 reviews and awards are at `http://www.microsoft.com/sql/70/gen/reviews.htm`.

Most SQL Server 7.0 awards and reviews tout SQL Server OLAP Services as the product's primary new feature. There's no question that OLAP Services constitute an important new feature set, and OLAP topics play a role in many of the "In the Real World" sections of other chapters of this book. But OLAP Services currently are significant primarily in mid- and large-scale enterprises having masses of transaction and syndicated data to analyze. "OLAP for the masses" is an oxymoron, but inclusion of OLAP Services in SQL Server lets smaller firms test the benefits of OLAP without making a major software investment.

Where SQL Server 7.0 shines is in ease of installation, maintenance, and administration. You can run medium-sized SQL Server 7.0 installations without a trained DBA, and you'll probably find that SQL Server 7.0 databases require less maintenance attention than shared-file Jet back ends. Elimination of device (.dat) files is the primary contributor to reducing maintenance workload. SQL Server 7.0 also is largely self-configuring, eliminating the need to learn the arcane syntax of the `sp_configure` stored procedure required to modify the configuration of SQL Server 6.x and earlier.

Unlike Jet, SQL Server 7.0 databases are largely self-tuning and self-managing. (MSDE databases are entirely self-tuning and self-managing because no tuning or management tools are included with the embedded version.) Choosing the optimum set of indexes for server tables traditionally has been a hit-or-miss operation based on DBA intuition. SQL Server's Profiler and Index Tuning Wizard analyze table usage, and the Wizard recommends the fields to index. This is an especially important feature for databases having usage patterns that change significantly over time. You can learn more about SQL Server tuning features at `http://msdn.microsoft.com/developer/sqlserver/sql7perftune.htm`.

Whether SQL Server 7.0 benefits outweigh ADP drawbacks remains to be seen. You don't need to use ADP, however, to upsize your Access applications from shared-file back ends to MSDE or SQL Server 7.0. If you select the Link SQL Server Tables to Existing Application option, instead of creating an ADP, you gain most of the advantages of SQL Server 7.0 without the pain and suffering of rewriting complex Jet applications for ADP compliance. Query performance won't match that of views and stored procedures, but your crosstab queries execute without modification, and all Jet and VBA query functions remain intact. If MSDE provides the back end, create a simple Access project that connects to the database to handle table modifications and database security.

--rj

PROGRAMMING AND CONVERTING ACCESS APPLICATIONS

26 Writing Visual Basic for Applications Code 991

27 Understanding Universal Data Access, OLE DB, and ADO 1031

28 Responding to Events with VBA 6.0 1083

29 Programming Combo and List Boxes 1127

30 Working with ADO Recordsets, Forms, and Controls 1155

31 Migrating Access 9x Applications to Access 2000 1181

CHAPTER 26

WRITING VISUAL BASIC FOR APPLICATIONS CODE

In this chapter

Understanding the Role of VBA in Access   992

Introducing VBA 6.0   993

Where You Use VBA Code   993

Typographic and Naming Conventions Used for VBA   994

Modules, Functions, and Subprocedures   995

References to VBA and Access Modules   998

Data Types and Database Objects in VBA   1000

Symbolic Constants   1008

Controlling Program Flow   1010

Handling Runtime Errors   1016

Exploring the VBA Editor   1018

Examining the Utility Functions Module   1022

Printing to the Immediate Window with the Debug Object   1025

In the Real World—Macro Schizophrenia   1027

UNDERSTANDING THE ROLE OF VBA IN ACCESS

Historically, productivity applications, such as the members of Microsoft Office, have used *macros* (short for *macroinstructions*) to automate repetitive operations. Microsoft Word and Excel, for instance, let you capture a sequence of menu choices, mouse clicks, and keyboard operations. You save the captured sequence as a macro that you subsequently execute from a menu choice or a shortcut-key combination. The macros in recent versions of Word and Excel consist of Visual Basic for Applications (VBA) code, but you don't need to understand VBA programming to create and execute Word and Excel macros. Unfortunately, the keyboard and mouse actions you use with Access applications don't translate to a usuable macro. For better or worse, automation of Access applications requires programming.

Simple Access applications require you to write little or no VBA code. Most users of early versions of Access wrote Access macros, rather than various flavors of Access Basic to automate their applications. Starting with Access 95, however, Microsoft recommended that you use VBA code instead of macros, with the clear implication that macros might not be supported in future versions of Access. (Access 2000 does support macro operations, but the Microsoft documentation states that it does so primarily for backward compatibility.)

This chapter describes VBA, introduces you to VBA modules and procedures, shows you how to use the new VBA Editor to write and test VBA code, and helps you start writing user-defined functions. The chapter also includes examples of simple VBA programs.

NEW 2000 Following are the most important new VBA-related features of Access 2000, other members of Office 2000, and Visual Basic 6.0:

- *VBA Editor*, which replaces the dedicated Access code editor of prior versions, now is a common component that serves all Office 2000 members.

- `Decimal` data type improves the accuracy of operations on numbers with decimal fractions.

- *Array functions*—`Filter`, `Split`, and `Join`—provide array search, string-to-array, and array-to-string capabilities, respectively.

- *String functions*—`Replace`, `StrReverse`, and `InstrRev`—enhance VBA's character manipulation features.

- `Round` rounds numbers with decimal fractions to a specified number of decimal places.

- `MonthName` and `WeekDayName` return the localized name of the month and day, respectively, from a `Date` argument.

- `FileSystemObject` provides an object model for disk drives.

- `Assert`, when set to `False`, causes execution of code to halt and enter break mode.

- `Event` and `RaiseEvent` let you declare and fire events in class modules.

- `Friend` members of class modules have `Public` scope within an Access project (application), but aren't accessible from other projects.

- `Implements` lets class modules share property and method declarations.

- *AddressOf* supports callbacks in Windows API functions by providing the address of the calling VBA function or subprocedure.

- *Enum* lets you define custom enumerations for, as an example, sets of named constants that supply property values.

The items in the preceding list aren't of great significance to beginning VBA programmers. Advanced VBA coders, however, appreciate the incremental improvements to the language that occur with every upgrade.

INTRODUCING VBA 6.0

VBA is a real programming language, not a macro language. You can expect VBA to replace Access macros gradually—Microsoft recommends that you develop applications in Access by using VBA instead of macros. You create the preferred equivalent of macros with VBA functions and subprocedures. Although you can execute VBA subprocedures directly from an open code module, you more typically execute VBA subprocedures from user-initiated events, such as clicking a command button. (Chapter 28, "Responding to Events with VBA 6.0," explains how to use VBA subprocedures as event-handlers.) You execute VBA functions by calling them from calculated controls in forms and reports, from the Validation Rule property of a field or table, or from within a VBA subprocedure.

WHERE YOU USE VBA CODE

Short VBA procedures using the DoCmd object usually are sufficient to provide the methods needed by simple applications to run queries, display forms, and print reports. The built-in functions of Access allow you to perform complex calculations in queries. You might want or need to use Access VBA code for any of the following reasons:

- To create user-defined functions (UDFs) that substitute for complex expressions you use repeatedly to validate data, compute values for text boxes, and perform other duties. Creating a UDF that you refer to by a short name minimizes potential typing errors and allows you to document the way your expression works.

- To write expressions that include more complex decision structures than allowed by the standard **IIf** function (in an **If...Then...Else...End If** structure, for example), or to write expressions that need loops for repetitive operations.

- To perform transaction processing actions with the Jet 4.0 equivalents of SQL BEGIN TRANSACTION, COMMIT TRANSACTION, and ROLLBACK TRANSACTION statements.

- To manipulate ActiveX controls and other applications' objects with Automation code.

- To open more than one database in an application where attaching a table or using the SQL IN statement isn't sufficient for your application.

- To provide hard-copy documentation for your application. If you include actions in Access VBA code, you can print the Access VBA code to improve the documentation for your application.

■ To provide graceful error-handling if something goes wrong in your application. With Access VBA code, you can closely control how your application responds to errors such as missing forms, missing data, incorrect values entered by a user, and other problems. One of the shortcomings of Access macros is their inability to respond appropriately to execution errors.

TYPOGRAPHIC AND NAMING CONVENTIONS USED FOR VBA

This book uses a special set of typographic conventions for references to VBA keywords and object variable names in VBA examples:

■ Monospace type is used for all VBA code in the examples, as in `lngItemCounter`.

■ Bold monospace type is used for all VBA reserved words and type-declaration symbols, as in **Dim** and **%**. (Type-declaration symbols aren't used in this book; instead, your VBA code defines the data type of each variable prior to use.) Standard function names in VBA, as described in Chapter 9, "Understanding Query Operators and Expressions," also are set in bold type so that reserved words, standard function names, and reserved symbols stand out from variable and function names and values you assign to variables. Keywords incorporated by reference in Access, such as `DoCmd` (an Access-specific object) or `Recordset` (a data-specific object), are not set in bold.

■ Italic monospace type indicates a replaceable item, also called a *placeholder*, as in **Dim** *DataItem* **As String**. *DataItem* is replaced by a name that you supply.

■ Bold-italic monospace type indicates a replaceable reserved word, such as a data type, as in **Dim** *DataItem* **As** ***DataType***; ***DataType*** is replaced by a VBA reserved word corresponding to the desired VBA data type.

■ Names of variables that refer to Access objects, such as forms or reports, use a three-letter prefix derived from the object name, as in `frmFormName` and `rptReportName`.

Tip #237 from

Most of the three-letter prefixes used in this book correspond to those recommended by Microsoft or the "Leszynski Naming Conventions for Access," a white paper published by Stan Leszynski of Kwery Corporation. You can order copies of the standards in the form of help files or white papers at `http://www.kwery.com/`.

■ Names of other variables are preceded by a three-letter data type identifier, such as `varVariantVariable` and `intIntegerVariable`.

■ Optional elements are included within square brackets, as in `[OptionItem]`. Square brackets also enclose object names that contain spaces or special punctuation symbols.

■ Elements requiring you to choose from a set of alternatives are enclosed with French braces and separated by pipe symbols, as in **Do** {**While**¦**Until**} *Expression*...Loop.

■ An ellipsis (...) substitutes for code that isn't shown in syntax and code examples, as in **If...Then...Else...End If**.

MODULES, FUNCTIONS, AND SUBPROCEDURES

A *module* is a container for VBA code, just as a form is a container for control objects. Access 2000 provides the following four types of modules:

- *Access Modules.* You create an Access module to contain your VBA code the same way that you create any other new database object: Click the Module button in the Database window and then click the New button. Alternatively, you can click the New Object button on the toolbar and choose <u>M</u>odule from the drop-down menu. Figure 26.1 shows the IsLoaded() function of the Utility Functions module of Northwind.mdb. Access modules are also called *standard modules*.

- *Form Modules.* Form modules contain code in class modules to respond to events triggered by forms or controls on forms. Essentially, when you add code to a form object, you create a new class of object in the database. The event-handling procedures you create for the form are its new methods, hence the term *class module* for the code module associated with a particular form. You open a form module by clicking the Code button of the toolbar in Form Design view. Alternatively, choose <u>V</u>iew, <u>C</u>ode. Either of these methods opens a module that Access automatically names Form_*FormName*, where *FormName* is the name of the selected form. Forms in Access 2000 have a property—Has Module. If this property is set to Yes, then the form has an attached module; otherwise, it does not.

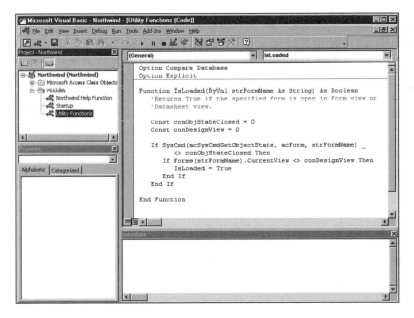

Figure 26.1
The VBA Editor displaying the IsLoaded() function of the Utility Functions module.

Another method of opening a form module is to click the ellipsis button for one of the event properties for a form or a control object on a form. Selecting Code Builder from the Choose Builder dialog displays the Form_*FormName* module with a procedure stub, **Private Sub** *ObjectName_EventName*()...**End Sub**, written for you. Access 2000 adds the VBA **Private** prefix by default. Figure 26.2 shows the VBA code for the CustomerID_AfterUpdate and part of the CustomerID_BeforeUpdate event-handling sub-procedures of Northwind.mdb's Orders form.

Figure 26.2
Typical event-handling subprocedures in a form class module.

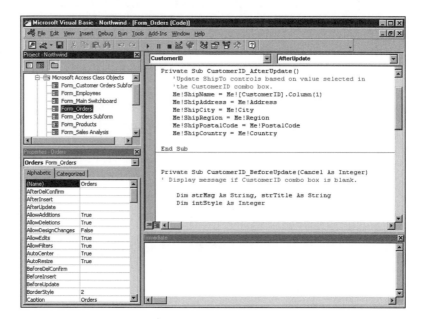

- *Report Modules.* Report modules contain code for responding to events triggered by reports, sections of reports, or group headers and footers. (Control objects on reports do not trigger events.) You open a report's class module the same way you open a form's class module. Report class modules are named Report_*ReportName* automatically. Like forms, whether an Access 2000 report has a class module depends on the setting of the Has Module property.

- *Class Modules.* A class module not associated with a form or report lets you define your own custom objects, together with their properties and methods. Writing unassociated class modules is beyond the scope of this book.

ELEMENTS OF MODULES

A module consists of a *Declarations section* and usually one or more *procedures* (interchangeably called *subprocedures*) or *functions*. As the name suggests, the Declarations section of a module is used to declare items (usually variables and constants, the subjects of following sections) used by the procedures and functions contained in the module. You can use a module without functions or procedures to declare **Public** variables and constants that can be used by any function or procedure in any module. Similarly, you use the **Public** prefix for functions and subprocedures to allow their use by code in any module. (**Public** replaces Access 2.0's **Global** keyword, but **Global** continues to work in Access 2000.)

Procedures are typically defined as subprograms referred to by name in another program. Referring to a procedure by name *calls* or *invokes* the procedure; the code in the procedure executes, and then the sequence of execution returns to the program that called the procedure. Another name for a procedure is *subroutine*. Procedures are defined by beginning (**Sub**) and end (**End Sub**) reserved words with a **Public**, **Private**, or **Static** prefix, as in the following example:

```
Private Sub ProcName
    [Start of procedure code]
    ...
    [End of procedure code]
End Sub
```

Tip #238 from

R J

You can refer to the procedure name to invoke the procedure, but VBA provides a keyword, **Call**, that explicitly invokes a procedure. Prefixing the procedure name with **Call** is good programming practice because this keyword identifies the name that follows as the name of a procedure rather than a variable.

Functions are a class of procedures that return values to their names, as explained in Chapter 9. C programmers would argue that procedures are a class of functions, called *void* functions, that do not return values. Regardless of how you view the difference between functions and subprocedures, keep the following points in mind:

- Access macros require that you write VBA functions (not subprocedures) to act in place of macro actions when using the RunCode macro action.

- The only way you can call a custom subprocedure in a VBA module is from a VBA function or another procedure. You can't directly execute a procedure in an Access module from any Access database object.

- Form and report class modules use subprocedures (not functions) to respond to events. Using form- and report-level subprocedures for event-handling code mimics Visual Basic's approach for events triggered by forms, controls on forms, and other objects.

- Function names in Access modules are global in scope with respect to Access modules unless they are declared **Private**. Thus, you cannot have duplicate **Public** function names in any Access module in your application. However, form and report class modules can have a function with the same name as a **Public** function in a standard module because form and report function and procedure names have form- or report-level scope. A function in a form module with the same name as a function in an Access module takes priority over the Access module version. Therefore, if you include the IsLoaded() function in a form module and call the IsLoaded() function from a procedure in the form module, the IsLoaded() function in the form module executes.

- To execute a VBA function in VBA code, you ordinarily use the function in an expression, such as

    ```
    intReturnValue = FunctionName([Arguments])
    ```

    when the function returns a value. You can ignore the return value by calling the function with subprocedure syntax.

Functions are created within a structure similar to procedures, as in the following example:

```
Private Function FuncName([Arguments])
    [Start of function code]
    ...
    [End of function code]
    FuncName = 123
End Function
```

In the preceding example, the FuncName = 123 statement returns the 123 to intReturnValue. Most functions return **True** or **False**, a numeric value, or a set of characters.

VBA introduces another class of procedure called property procedures that use the {**Property Let ¦ Property Get ¦ Property Set**}...**End Property** structure to create custom properties for Access objects, such as forms or controls. A discussion of property procedures is beyond the scope of this book.

REFERENCES TO VBA AND ACCESS MODULES

Access 2000 uses *references* to make objects available for use in modules. To view the default references, open a module in a new database, and then choose Tools, References to open the References dialog (see Figure 26.3). Current references, except to the currently open database, are indicated by a mark in the adjacent check box.

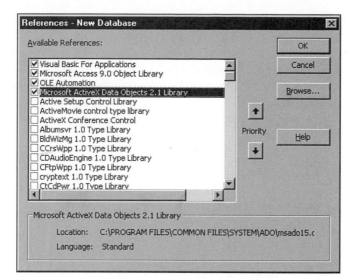

Figure 26.3
The four default object references for Access 2000.

NEW 2000 Microsoft ActiveX Data Objects 2.1 Library (ADO 2.1) is the default reference for new databases (or Access Data Projects) that you create with Access 2000. ADO 2.1 is the subject of the next chapter, "Understanding Universal Data Access, OLE DB, and ADO." If you open a database created with a prior version of Access, the Microsoft DAO 3.6 Library (DAO 3.6) is the default data object reference.

Referenced objects appear in the Project/Library drop-down list of the Object Browser. To view the Object Browser, open a module and press F2, click the Object Browser button on the toolbar, or choose View, Object Browser. <All Libraries> is the default selection in the Project/Library list. Figure 26.4 shows a few of the references to Form, Report, and Module objects in Northwind.mdb in the Classes list. Only objects that can act as VBA containers appear in the Classes list; tables, queries, and macros don't qualify.

PART
VII
CH
26

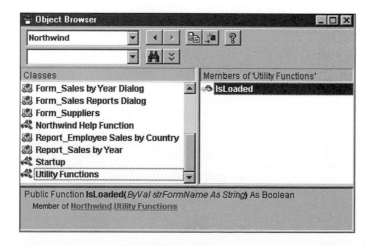

Figure 26.4
Object Browser displaying the calling syntax for the IsLoaded() function.

When you select a function or subprocedure name in a module, the function or subprocedure name and arguments, if any, appear in the window at the bottom of the Object Browser dialog. You can get help on Access, VBA, and other objects by clicking the help (?) button, which ignores user-defined functions and the event-handling subprocedures you write. The next chapter describes object classes and the use of the Object Browser in detail.

DATA TYPES AND DATABASE OBJECTS IN VBA

When you create VBA tables, all data types that you use to assign field data types and sizes (except for OLE and Memo field data types) have data type counterparts in VBA. With the exception of the **Variant** and **Currency** data types, VBA data types are represented in most other dialects of BASIC, such as Microsoft QuickBASIC and the QBasic interpreter supplied with MS-DOS 5 and later.

Traditional BASIC dialects use a punctuation symbol called the *type-declaration character*, such as **$** for the **String** data type, to designate the data type. The VBA data types, the type-declaration characters, the corresponding field data types, and the ranges of values are shown in the VBA Type, Symbol, Field Type, Minimum Value, and Maximum Value columns, respectively, of Table 26.1. The Field Types **Byte**, **Integer**, **Long Integer**, **Single**, and **Double** correspond to the Field Size property of the Number data type in tables, queries, forms, and reports. VBA adds the **Byte** and **Boolean** data types to support the 8-bit Byte and 16-bit Yes/No field data types.

TABLE 26.1 VBA AND CORRESPONDING FIELD DATA TYPES

VBA Type	Symbol	Field Type	Minimum Value	Maximum Value
Byte	None	Byte	0	255
Integer	%	Integer	–32,768	32,767
Boolean	None	Yes/No	**True**	**False**
Long	&	Long Integer, AutoNumber	–2,147,483,648	2,147,483,647
Single	!	Single	–3.402823E38 1.401298E–45	–1.401298E–5 3.402823E38
Double	#	Double	–1.7200069313486232E308 4.94065645841247E–324	4.9406564841247E–324 1.7200069313486232E308
Currency	@	Currency	–922,337,203,685, 477.5808	922,337,203,685, 477.5807
String	$	Text or Memo	0 characters	Approximately 2 billion characters
Date	None	Date/Time	January 1, 100	December 31, 9999
Variant	None	Any	January 1, 100 (date) Same as **Double** (numbers) Same as **String** (text)	December 31, 9999 (date) Same as **Double** (numbers) Same as **String** (text)

All data returned from fields of tables or queries is of the **Variant** data type by default. If you assign the field value to a conventional data type, such as **Integer**, the data type is said to be *coerced*.

You can dispense with the type-declaration character if you explicitly declare your variables with the **{Dim┊Private┊Public}...As *DataType*** statement, discussed later in this section. If you don't explicitly declare the variables' data type or use a symbol to define an implicit data type, VBA variables default to the **Variant** data type.

Using the **Variant** data type causes VBA code to execute more slowly than when you assign variables an explicit data type with the **{Dim┊Private┊Public}...As *DataType*** statement.

The # sign is also used to enclose values specified as dates, as in varNewYears = #1/1/2000#. In this case, bold type is not used for the enclosing # signs because these symbols are not intended for the purpose of the # reserved symbol that indicates the **Double** data type.

Database objects—such as databases, tables, and queries—and application objects (forms and reports), all of which you used in prior chapters, also have corresponding object data types in VBA. These object data types are defined by the object (also called *type* or *class*) library references. The most commonly used object data types of VBA and the object library that includes the objects are listed in Table 26.2.

TABLE 26.2   THE MOST COMMON DATABASE OBJECT DATA TYPES SUPPORTED BY VBA

Object Data	Library	Corresponding Database Object Type
Database	DAO 3.6	Databases opened by the Jet database engine when using DAO.
Connection	ADO 2.1	ADO replacement for DAO.Database object.
Form	Access 9.0	Forms, including subforms.
Report	Access 9.0	Reports, including subreports.
Control	Access 9.0	Controls on forms and reports.
QueryDef	DAO 3.6	Query definitions (SQL statement equivalents) when using DAO.
Command	ADO 2.1	ADO replacement for DAO.QueryDef object.
TableDef	DAO 3.6	Table definitions (structure, indexes, and other table properties).
DAO.Recordset	DAO 3.6	A virtual representation of a table or the resultset of a query created by DAO.
ADODB.Recordset	ADO 2.1	ADO replacement for the DAO.Recordset object.

> **Note**
>
> OLE DB is a new database connectivity architecture based on the Component Object Model (COM). OLE DB is the foundation of Microsoft's Universal Data Access initiative, which is described in the next chapter. ADO is an "Automation wrapper" over OLE DB, which makes OLE DB objects accessible to Access and all other applications that support Automation through VBA. `Recordset` is an object that's common to both DAO and ADO, so it's good programming practice to prefix `Recordset` with its source class identifier, as in `DAO.Recordset` or `ADODB.Recordset`.

Variables and Naming Conventions

Variables are named placeholders for values of a specified data type that change when your VBA code is executed. You give variables names, as you name fields, but the names of variables cannot include spaces or any other punctuation except the underscore character (_). The other restriction is that a variable cannot use a VBA keyword by itself as a name; keywords are called *reserved words* for this reason. The same rules apply to giving names to functions and procedures. Variable names in VBA typically use a combination of upper- and lowercase letters to make them more readable.

Implicit Variables

You can create variables by assigning a value to a variable name, as in the following example:

```
NewVar = 1234
```

A statement of this type *declares* a variable, which means to create a new variable with a name you choose. The statement in the example creates a new implicit variable, `NewVar`, of the **Variant** data type with a value of 1234. (Thus `NewVar` would be more appropriately named varNewVar.) When you don't specify a data type for an implicit variable by appending one of the type-declaration characters to the variable name, the **Variant** data type is assigned by default. The following statement creates a variable of the `Integer` data type:

```
NewVar% = 1234
```

Explicit Variables

It's a better programming practice to declare your variables and assign those variables a data type before you give variables a value. The most common method of declaring variables is by using the **Dim...As *Datatype*** structure, in which **As** specifies the data type. This method declares explicit variables. An example follows:

```
Dim intNewVar As Integer
```

If you do not add the **As Integer** keywords, `intNewVar` is assigned the **Variant** data type by default.

You can require that all variables be explicitly declared before their use by adding the statement `Option Explicit` in the Declarations section of a module. The advantage of using `Option Explicit` is that Access detects misspelled variable names and displays an error message when misspellings are encountered. If you don't use `Option Explicit` and you misspell a variable name, Access creates a new implicit variable with the misspelled name. The resulting errors in your code's operation can be difficult to diagnose. Access automatically adds an `Option Explicit` statement to the Declarations section of each module if you select the Require Variable Declaration option in the VBA Editor's Options dialog, which you open by choosing Tools, Options (see Figure 26.5).

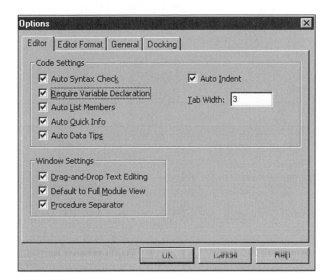

Figure 26.5
Setting the Require Variable Declaration option in the VBA Editor's Options dialog.

Scope and Duration of Variables

Variables have a property called *scope*, which determines when the variables appear and disappear in your VBA code. Variables appear the first time you declare them and then disappear and reappear on the basis of the scope you assign to them. When a variable appears, it is said to be *visible*—meaning that you can assign the variable a value, change its value, and use it in expressions. Otherwise, the variable is *invisible*; if you use a variable's name while it's invisible, you instead create a new variable with the same name.

The following lists the four scope levels in VBA:

- *Local (procedure-level) scope*. The variable is visible only during the time when the procedure in which the variable is declared is executed. Variables that you declare, with or without using `Dim...As` *Datatype* in a procedure or function, are local in scope.

- *Form-level and report-level scope*. The variable is visible only when the form or report in which it's declared is open. You declare form-level and report-level variables in the Declarations section of form and report modules with `Private...As` *Datatype*. (`Dim...As` *Datatype* also works.)

- *Module-level scope.* The variable is visible to all procedures and functions contained in the module in which the variable was declared. (Modules open when you open the database.) You declare variables with module scope in the Declarations section of the module with the same syntax as form- and report-level variables.

- *Global or public scope.* The variable is visible to all procedures and functions within all modules. You declare variables with global scope in the Declarations section of a module using **Public...As** *Datatype*.

The scope and visibility of variables declared in two different Access modules of the same database, both with two procedures, are illustrated by the diagram in Figure 26.6. In each procedure, variables declared with different scopes are used to assign values to variables declared within the procedure. Invalid assignment statements are shown crossed out in the figure. These assignment statements are invalid because the variable used to assign the value to the variable declared in the procedure isn't visible in the procedure.

Figure 26.6
Valid and invalid assignment statements for variables of different scopes.

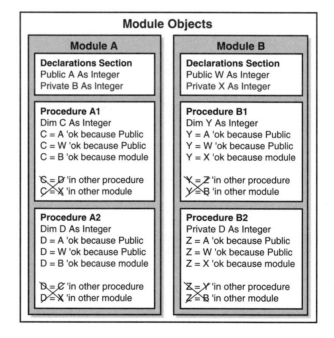

Variables also have a property called *duration*, or *lifetime*. The duration of a variable is your code's execution time between the first appearance of the variable (its declaration) and its disappearance. Each time a procedure or function is called, local variables declared with the **Dim...As** *Datatype* statement are set to default values with 0 for numeric data types and the empty string (" ") for string variables. The duration of these local variables is usually equal to the lifetime of the function or procedure—from the time the function or procedure is called until the **End Function** or **End Sub** statement is executed.

To preserve the values of local variables between occurrences (called *instances*) of a procedure or function, you substitute the reserved word **Static** for **Dim**. Static variables have a duration of your Access application, but their scope is determined by where you declare them. Static variables are useful when you want to count the number of occurrences of an event. You can make all variables in a function or procedure static variables by preceding **Function** or **Sub** with the **Static** keyword.

> Minimize the number of local variables that you declare **Static**. Local variables do not consume memory when they aren't visible. This characteristic of local variables is especially important in the case of arrays, discussed in the "VBA Arrays" section that follows shortly, because arrays are often very large.

USER-DEFINED DATA TYPES

You can create your own data type that consists of one or more Access data types. User-defined data types are discussed in this section pertaining to variables because you need to know what a variable is before you can declare a user-defined data type. You declare a user-defined data type between the **Type...End Type** keywords, as in the following example:

```
Type DupRec
    lngField1 As Long
    strField2 As String * 20
    sngField3 As Single
    dblField4 As Double
End Type
```

User-defined data types are particularly useful when you create a variable to hold the values of one or more records of a table that uses fields of different data types. The **String * 20** statement defines **Field2** of the user-defined data type as a fixed-length string of 20 characters, usually corresponding to the Size property of the Text field data type. **String** variables in user-defined data types traditionally have a fixed length, but VBA 6.0 lets you use variable-length strings. You must declare your user-defined data type (called a *record* or *structure* in other programming languages) in the Declarations section of a module.

You must explicitly declare variables to be of the user-defined type with the **Dim**, **Private**, **Public**, or **Static** keywords because no reserved symbol exists to declare a user-defined data type, as in **Dim** usrCurrentRec **As** tagDupRec. To assign a value to a field of a variable with a user-defined data type, you specify the name of the variable and the field name, separating the names with a period, as in usrCurrentRec.lngField1 = 2048.

VBA ARRAYS

Arrays are variables that consist of a collection of values, called *elements* of the array, of a single data type in a regularly ordered structure. Implicitly declared arrays are not allowed in VBA (or in Visual VBA). You declare an array with the **Dim** statement, adding the number of elements in parentheses to the variable name for the array, as in the following example:

```
Dim astrNewArray(20) As String
```

PART

VII

CH

26

This statement creates an array of 21 elements, each of which is a conventional, variable-length string variable. You create 21 elements because the first element of an array is the 0 (zero) element, unless you specify otherwise by adding the **To** modifier, as in the following example:

```
Dim astrNewArray(1 To 20) As String
```

The preceding statement creates an array with 20 elements.

You can create multidimensional arrays by adding more values separated by commas. The statement

```
Dim alngNewArray(9, 9, 9) As Long
```

creates a three-dimensional array of 10 elements per dimension. This array, when visible, occupies 4,000 bytes of memory (10×10×10×4 bytes/long integer).

You can create a *dynamic array* by declaring the array using **Dim** without specifying the number of elements and then using the **ReDim** reserved word to determine the number of elements the array contains. You can **ReDim** an array as many times as you want. Each time you do so, the values stored in the array are reinitialized to their default values, determined by the data type, unless you follow **ReDim** with the reserved word, **Preserve**. The following sample statements create a dynamic array:

```
Dim alngNewArray() As Long           'In Declarations sections
ReDim Preserve alngNewArray(9, 9, 9) 'In procedure, preserves prior values
ReDim alngNewArray(9, 9, 9)          'In procedure, reinitializes all
```

Dynamic arrays are useful when you don't know how many elements an array requires when you declare it. You can **ReDim** a dynamic array to zero elements when you no longer need the values it contains; this tactic allows you to recover the memory that the array consumes while it's visible. Alternatively, you can use the **Erase** reserved word followed by a dynamic array's name to remove all the array's elements from memory. (**Erase** used on an array with fixed dimensions merely reinitializes the array to its condition before you assigned any values to it.) Arrays declared with **Dim** may have up to 60 dimensions. You can only use the **ReDim** statement to alter the size of the last dimension in a multidimensional array.

Scope, duration rules, and keywords apply to arrays in the same way in which they apply to conventional variables. You can declare dynamic arrays with global and module-level scope by adding the **Public** or **Private** statement to the Declarations section of a module and then using the **ReDim** statement by itself in a procedure. If you declare an array with **Static**, rather than **Dim**, the array retains its values between instances of a procedure.

Tip #241 from

R J

Don't use the **Option Base** keywords to change the default initial element of arrays from 0 to 1. **Option Base** is included in VBA for compatibility with earlier BASIC dialects. Many arrays you create from VBA objects must begin with element 0. If you're concerned about the memory occupied by an unused zero element of an array, use the **Dim** *ArrayName*(1 **To** N) **As** *DataType* declaration. In most cases, you can disregard the zero element.

NAMED DATABASE OBJECTS AS VARIABLES IN VBA CODE

Properties of database objects you create with Access can be treated as variables and assigned values within VBA code. For example, you can assign a new value to the text box that contains the address information for a customer by name with the following statement:

```
Forms!Customers!Address = "123 Elm St."
```

The collection name `Forms` defines the type of object. The exclamation point (called the *bang* symbol by programmers) separates the name of the form and the name of the control object. The `!` symbol is analogous to the `\` path separator that you use when you're dealing with folder and file names. If the name of the form or the control object contains a space or other punctuation, you must enclose the name within square brackets, as in the following statement:

```
Forms!Customers![Contact Name] = "Joe Hill"
```

Alternatively, you can use the **Set** keyword to create your own named variable for the control object. This procedure is convenient when you need to refer to the control object several times. It's more convenient to type `txtContact` rather than the full "path" to the control object—in this case, a text box.

```
Dim txtContact As Control
Set txtContact = Forms!Customers![Contact Name]
txtContact.Value = "Joe Hill"
```

Tip #242 from	Specifying the `Value` property when assigning a value to a control isn't required because `Value` is the default property of controls and fields of `Recordsets`. It's good programming practice, however, to do so. Adding the `Value` property when manipulating `ADODB.Recordset` objects with VBA results in improved performance.
R J	

You can assign any database object to a variable name by declaring the variable as the object type and using the **Set** statement to assign the object to the variable. You do not create a copy of the object in memory when you assign it a variable name; the variable refers to the object in memory. Referring to an object in memory is often called *pointing* to an object; many languages have a pointer data type that holds the address of the location in memory where the variable is stored. VBA does not support pointers. The next chapter deals with creating variables that point to the Access 2000 database objects supplied by ADO 2.0.

OBJECT PROPERTIES AND THE With...End With STRUCTURE

VBA provides the **With...End With** structure that offers a shorthand method of setting the values of object properties, such as the dimensions and other characteristics of a form. The **With...End With** structure also lets you set the values of fields of a user-defined data type without repeating the variable name in each instance. To use the **With...End With** structure to set object property values, you must first declare and set an object variable, as in the following example:

```
Dim frmFormName As Form
```

```
Set frmFormName = Forms!FormName
With frmFormName
    .Top = 1000
    .Left = 1000
    .Width = 5000
    .Height = 4000
End With
```

When using the **With...End With** structure with user-defined data types, you don't use the **Set** statement. Names of properties or fields within the structure are preceded by periods.

SYMBOLIC CONSTANTS

Symbolic constants are named placeholders for values of a specified data type that do not change when your VBA code is executed. You precede the name of a symbolic constant with the keyword **Const**, as in **Const** sngPI **As Single** = 3.1416. You declare symbolic constants in the Declarations section of a module or within a function or procedure. Precede **Const** with the **Public** keyword if you want to create a global constant that's visible to all modules, as in **Public Const** gsngPI = 3.1416. Public constants can be declared only in the Declarations section of a VBA module.

You don't need to specify a data type for constants because VBA chooses the data type that stores the data most efficiently. VBA can make this choice because it knows the value of the data when it "compiles" your code.

> **Note**
>
> Office 2000's VBA is an interpreted language, so the term *compile* in a VBA context is a misnomer. When you "compile" the VBA source code that you write in a code-editing window, the VBA Editor creates a tokenized version of the code (called *pseudo-code*, or *p-code*) stored in a document or .mdb file. Only Visual Basic 6.0 compiles VBA 6.0 code to create an executable (.exe) file.

ACCESS SYSTEM-DEFINED CONSTANTS

VBA includes seven system-defined constants—**True, False**, Yes, No, On, Off, and **Null**—that are created by the VBA and Access type libraries when launched. Of these seven, you can use **True, False**, and **Null**, which are declared by the VBA library, in VBA code. The remaining four are declared by the Access type library and are valid for use with all database objects except modules. When the system-defined constants **True, False**, and **Null** are used in VBA code examples in this book, they appear in bold monospace type.

ACCESS INTRINSIC CONSTANTS

VBA provides a number of predeclared, intrinsic, symbolic constants that are primarily for use as arguments of DoCmd.*Action* statements. These statements let you execute standard database actions in VBA (such as opening forms, printing reports, applying sorts or filters, and so on). Access 2000 intrinsic constants carry the prefix ac, as in acExportMerge. You can display the list of Access intrinsic constants in the Object Browser by selecting Access in the Project/Library list and then selecting Globals in the Classes list.

When you select a constant in the Members Of list, its numeric value appears at the bottom of the Object Browser window (see Figure 26.7). A good programming practice is to use constant names rather than their numeric values when applicable. You may not use any of these intrinsic constants' names as names for constants or variables that you define.

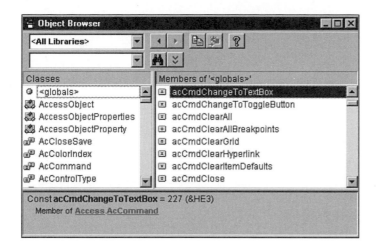

Figure 26.7
Displaying Access 2000 intrinsic constants in the Object Browser.

VBA NAMED AND OPTIONAL ARGUMENTS

Procedures often have one or more arguments that pass values from the calling statement to the called procedure. Traditionally, you must pass all the values required by the procedure in your calling statement. As an example, if a procedure accepts four arguments, *Arg1...Arg4*, your calling statement must provide values for *Arg1...Arg4*, as in the following example:

```
Sub CallingProc()
    ...
    Call CalledProc(100000, 200000, 300000, 400000)
    ...
End Sub

Sub CalledProc(Arg1 As Long, Arg2 As Long, Arg3 As Long, _
               Arg4 As Long)
    [Subprocedure code]
End Sub
```

Access 2000 lets you declare the arguments of the subprocedure to be **Optional**, eliminating the need to pass every parameter to the procedure. You use *named arguments* to pass values to specific arguments, as in the following example:

```
Sub CallingProc()
    ...
    Call CalledProc(Arg2:=200000, Arg3:=300000)
    ...
End Sub
```

PART

VII

CH

26

```
Sub CalledProc(Optional Arg1, Optional Arg2, Optional Arg3, _
               Optional Arg4)
    [Subprocedure code]
End Sub
```

The := operator specifies that the preceding element is the name of an argument; named arguments need not be entered in the order that the arguments appear in the called procedure. However, if you want to omit an argument or arguments, the corresponding argument name(s) of the called procedure must be preceded by the keyword **Optional**. Missing arguments return **Null** values to subprocedure code, but you can supply a default argument value in the subprocedure. If you omit the **As** *Datatype* modifier of an argument in the called procedure, the argument assumes the default **Variant** data type.

CONTROLLING PROGRAM FLOW

Useful procedures must be able to make decisions based on the values of variables and then take specified actions based on those decisions. Blocks of code, for example, might need to be repeated until a specified condition occurs. Statements used to make decisions and repeat blocks of code are the fundamental elements that control program flow in VBA and all other programming languages.

All programming languages require methods of executing different algorithms based on the results of one or more comparison operations. You can control the flow of any program in any programming language with just three types of statements: conditional execution (**If...Then...End If**), repetition (**Do While...Loop** and related structures), and termination (**End...**). The additional flow control statements in VBA and other programming languages make writing code more straightforward.

BRANCHING AND LABELS

If you have written DOS batch files or WordPerfect macros, you're probably acquainted with branching and labels. Both the DOS batch language and the WordPerfect macro language include the **GoTo** *Label* command. DOS defines any word that begins a line with a colon as a label; WordPerfect requires the use of the keyword LABEL and then the label name.

When BASIC was first developed, the only method of controlling program flow was through its GOTO *LineNumber* and GOSUB *LineNumber* statements. Every line in the program required a number that could be used as a substitute for a label. GOTO *LineNumber* caused the interpreter to skip to the designated line and continue executing the program from that point. GOSUB *LineNumber* caused the program to follow that same branch, but when the BASIC interpreter that executed the code encountered a RETURN statement, program execution jumped back to the line following the GOSUB statement and continued executing at that point.

SKIPPING BLOCKS OF CODE WITH GoTo

VBA's **GoTo** *Label* statement causes your code to branch to the location named *Label*: and continue from that point. Note the colon following *Label*:, which identifies the single word you assigned as a label. However, the colon isn't required after the label name following the **GoTo**. In fact, if you add the colon, you get a `Label not found` error message.

A label name must begin in the far-left column (1) of your code. This positioning often interferes with the orderly indenting of your code (explained in the next section), which is just one more reason, in addition to those following, for not using **GoTo**.

AVOIDING SPAGHETTI CODE BY NOT USING GoTo

The sequence of statements in code that uses multiple **GoTo** statements is very difficult to follow. It's almost impossible to understand the flow of a large program written in line-numbered BASIC because of the jumps here and there in the code. Programs with multiple **GoTo** statements are derisively said to contain "spaghetti code."

The **GoTo** statement is required for only one purpose in VBA: to handle errors with the **On Error GoTo** *Label* statement. Although VBA supports BASIC's `ON...GOTO` and `ON...GOSUB` statements, using those statements is not considered good programming practice. You can eliminate all **GoTo** statements in form and report modules by using Access's `Error` event and the DAO and ADO `Errors` collection. The `Error` event is described in the "Handling Runtime Errors" section later in this chapter, and the `Errors` collection is explained in the next chapter.

CONDITIONAL STATEMENTS

A conditional statement executes the statements between its occurrence and the terminating statement if the result of the relational operator is true. Statements that consist of or require more than one statement for completion are called *structured statements, control structures*, or just *structures*.

THE If...Then...End If STRUCTURE

The syntax of the primary conditional statement of procedural BASIC is as follows:

```
If blnCondition1 [= True] Then
    Statements to be executed if Condition1 is true
 [Else[If blnCondition2[ = True] Then]]
    Optional statements to be executed if blnCondition1
    is false [and blnCondition2 is true]
End If
```

The **= True** elements of the preceding conditional statement are optional and typically not included when you write actual code. **If** *blnCondition1* **Then** and **If** *blnCondition1* **= True Then** produce the same result when *blnCondition1* is **True**.

You can add a second condition with the **ElseIf** statement. The **ElseIf** condition must be true to execute the statements that are executed if bln*Condition1* is false. Note that no space is used between **Else** and **If**. An **If...End If** structure that incorporates the **ElseIf** statement is the simplified equivalent of the following:

```
If blnCondition1 Then
    Statements to be executed if Expression1 is true
Else
    If blnCondition2 Then
        Statements to be executed if Condition1% is
        false and blnCondition2 is true]
    End If
End If
```

A statement is executed based on the evaluation of the immediately preceding expression. Expressions that include **If...End If** or other flow-control structures within other **If...End If** structures are said to be *nested*, as in the preceding example. The number, or depth, of **If...End If** structures that can be nested within one another is unlimited.

Note that the code between the individual keywords that make up the flow-control structure is indented. Indentation makes code within structures easier to read. You usually use the Tab key to create indentation.

To evaluate whether a character is a letter and to determine its case, you can use the following code:

```
If Asc(strChar) > 63 And Asc(strChar) < 91 Then
    strCharType = "Uppercase Letter"
ElseIf Asc(strChar) > 96 And Asc(strChar) < 123 Then
    strCharType = "Lowercase Letter"
End If
```

You use the **If...End If** structure more often than any other flow control statement.

THE Select Case...End Select CONSTRUCT

When you must choose among many alternatives, **If...End If** structures can become very complex and deeply nested. The **Select Case...End Select** construct was added to procedural BASIC to overcome this complexity. In addition to testing whether an expression evaluates to true or false, **Select Case** can evaluate variables to determine whether those variables fall within specified ranges. The generalized syntax is in the following example:

```
Select Case VarName
    Case Expression1[, Expressions, ...]
        (Statements executed if the value of VarName
        = Expression1 or Expressions)
    [Case Expression2 To Expression3
        (Statements executed if the value of VarName
        is in the range of Expression2 to Expression3)]
    [Case Is RelationalExpression
        (Statements executed if the value of
        VarName = RelationalExpression)]
```

```
    [Case Else
        (Statements executed if none of the
        above cases is met)]
End Select
```

Select Case evaluates *VarName*, which can be a string, a numeric variable, or an expression. It then tests each **Case** expression in sequence. **Case** expressions can take one of the following four forms:

- A single value or list of values to which to compare the value of *VarName*. Successive members of the list are separated from their predecessors by commas.

- A range of values separated by the keyword **To**. The value of the first member of the range limits must be less than the value of the second. Each string is compared by the ASCII value of its first character.

- The keyword **Is** followed by a relational operator, such as <>, <, <=, =, >=, or >, and a variable or literal value.

- The keyword **Else**. Expressions following **Case Else** are executed if no prior **Case** condition is satisfied.

The **Case** statements are tested in sequence, and the code associated with the first matching **Case** condition is executed. If no match is found and the **Case Else** statement is present, the code following the statement is executed. Program execution then continues at the line of code following the **End Select** terminating statement.

If *VarName* is a numeric type, all expressions with which it's to be compared by **Case** are forced to the same data type.

The following example is of **Select Case** using a numeric variable, curSales:

```
Select Case curSales
    Case 10000 To 49999.99
        intClass = 1
    Case 50000 To 100000
        intClass = 2
    Case Is < 10000
        intClass = 0
    Case Else
        intClass = 3
End Select
```

Note that because curSales is of the **Currency** type, all the comparison literals also are treated as **Currency** values for the purpose of comparison.

A more complex example that evaluates a single character follows:

```
Select Case strChar
    Case "A" To "Z"
        strCharType = "Upper Case"
    Case "a" To "z'
        strCharType = "Lower Case"
    Case "0" To "9"
        strCharType = "Number"
```

```
    Case "!", "?", ".", ",", ";"
        strCharType = "Punctuation"
    Case ""
        strCharType = "Empty String"
    Case < 32
        strCharType = "Special Character"
    Case Else
        strCharType = "Unknown Character"
End Select
```

This example demonstrates that **Select Case**, when used with strings, evaluates the ASCII value of the first character of the string—either as the variable being tested or the expressions following **Case** statements. Thus, **Case < 32** is a valid test, although strChar is a string variable.

REPETITIVE OPERATIONS: LOOPING

In many instances, you must repeat an operation until a given condition is satisfied, whereupon the repetitions terminate. You might want to examine each character in a word, sentence, or document, or you might want to assign values to an array with many elements. Loops are used for these and many other purposes.

USING THE For...Next STATEMENT

VBA's **For...Next** statement allows you to repeat a block of code for a specified number of times, as shown in the following example:

```
For intCounter = intStartValue To intEndValue% [Step intIncrement]
    Statements to be executed
    [Conditional statement
    Exit For
    End of conditional statement]
Next [intCounter]
```

The block of statements between the **For** and **Next** keywords is executed (int*EndValue* - int*StartValue* + 1) / int*Increment* times. As an example, if int*StartValue* = 5, int*EndValue* = 10, and int*Increment* = 1, the execution of the statement block is repeated six times. You need not add the keyword **Step** in this case—the default increment is 1. Although **Integer** data types are shown, **Long** (integers) can be used. The use of real numbers (**Single** or **Double** data types) as values for counters and increments is possible but uncommon.

The dividend of the previous expression must always be a positive number if the execution of the internal statement block is to occur. If int*EndValue* is less than int*StartValue*, int*Increment* must be negative; otherwise, the **For...Next** statement is ignored by VBA.

The optional **Exit For** statement is provided so that you can prematurely terminate the loop using a surrounding **If...Then...End If** conditional statement. Changing the value of the counter variable within the loop itself to terminate its operation is discouraged as a dangerous programming practice. You might make a change that would cause an infinite loop.

USING For...Next LOOPS TO ASSIGN VALUES TO ARRAY ELEMENTS

One of the most common applications of the **For...Next** loop is to assign successive values to the elements of an array. If you have declared a 26-element array named Alphabet$(), the following example assigns the capital letters *A* through *Z* to its elements:

```
For intLetter = 1 To 26
    strAlphabet(intLetter) = Chr(intLetter + 63)
Next intLetter
```

The preceding example assigns 26 of the array's 27 elements if you used **Dim** Alphabet(26) **As String** rather than **Dim** Alphabet(1 **To** 26) **As String**. 63 is added to intLetter because the ASCII value of the letter *A* is 64, and the initial value of intLetter is 1.

A special case of the **For...Next** loop, **For Each** obj*Name* **In** col*Name*...**Next** obj*Name*, loop iterates each object (obj*Name*) in a collection (col*Name*).

→ For an example of the use of a For Each...Next loop, **see** "Customizing Applications with CommandBar Objects," **p. 1113**.

UNDERSTANDING THE Do While...Loop AND Do Until...Loop

A more general form of the loop structure is **Do While...Loop**, which uses the following syntax:

```
Do While blnCondition [= True]
    Statements to be executed
    [Conditional statement
    Exit Do
    End of conditional statement]
Loop
```

This loop structure executes the intervening statements only if bln*Condition* equals **True** (**Not False**, a value other than 0) and continues to do so until bln*Condition* becomes **False** (0) or the optional **Exit Do** statement is executed.

From the preceding syntax, the previous **For...Next** array assignment example can be duplicated by the following structure:

```
intLetter = 1
Do While intLetter <= 27
    strAlphabet(intLetter) = Chr(intLetter + 63)
    intLetter = intLetter + 1
Loop
```

Another example of a **Do** loop is the **Do Until...Loop** structure, which loops as long as the condition isn't satisfied, as in the following example:

```
Do Until {blnCondition <> True¦Not blnCondition}
    Statements to be executed
    [Conditional statement
    Exit Do
    End of conditional statement]
Loop
```

The **Not** `blnCondition` expression is more commonly used than `blnCondition` **<>** **True**, but either is acceptable.

VBA also supports the **While...Wend** loop, which is identical to the **Do While...Loop** structure, but you can't use the **Exit Do** statement within it. The **While...Wend** structure is provided for compatibility with earlier versions of BASIC and should be abandoned in favor of **Do {While¦Until}...Loop** in VBA.

MAKING SURE STATEMENTS IN A LOOP OCCUR AT LEAST ONCE

You might have observed that the statements within a **Do While...Loop** structure are never executed if `intCondition` is false when the structure is encountered in your application. You can also use a structure in which the conditional statement that causes loop termination is associated with the **Loop** statement. The syntax of this format is in the following example:

```
Do
    Statements to be executed
    [Conditional statement then
    Exit Do
    End of conditional statement]
Loop While intCondition [ = True]
```

A similar structure is available for **Do Until...Loop**:

```
Do
    Statements to be executed
    [Conditional statement
    Exit Do
    End of conditional statement]
Loop Until intCondition[ = False]
```

These structures ensure that the loop executes at least once *before* the condition is tested.

HANDLING RUNTIME ERRORS

No matter how thoroughly you test and debug your code, runtime errors appear eventually. Runtime errors are errors that occur when Access executes your code. Use the **On Error GoTo** instruction to control what happens in your application when a runtime error occurs. **On Error** isn't a very sophisticated instruction, but it's your first choice for error processing in Access modules. You can branch to a label or ignore the error. The general syntax of **On Error...** follows:

```
On Error GoTo LabelName
On Error Resume Next
On Error GoTo 0
```

On Error GoTo `LabelName` branches to the portion of your code with the label `LabelName:`. `LabelName` must be a label; it can't be the name of a procedure. The code following `LabelName`, however, can (and often does) include a procedure call to an error-handling procedure, such as `ErrorProc`, as in the following:

```
On Error GoTo ErrHandler
...
 [RepeatCode:
(Code using ErrProc to handle errors)]
...
GoTo SkipHandler
ErrHandler:
Call ErrorProc
[GoTo RepeatCode]
SkipHandler:
...
(Additional code)
```

In this example, the **On Error GoTo** instruction causes program flow to branch to the ErrHandler label that executes the error-handling procedure ErrorProc. Ordinarily, the error-handler code is located at the end of the procedure. If you have more than one error handler or if the error handler is in the middle of a group of instructions, you must bypass it if the preceding code is error-free. Use the **GoTo** SkipHandler statement that bypasses ErrHandler: instructions. To repeat the code that generated the error after ErrorProc has completed its job, add a label such as RepeatCode: at the beginning of the repeated code, and then branch to the code in the ErrHandler: code. Alternatively, you can add the keyword **Resume** at the end of your code to resume processing at the line that created the error.

On Error Resume Next disregards the error and continues processing the succeeding instructions.

After an **On Error GoTo** statement executes, it remains in effect for all succeeding errors until execution encounters another **On Error GoTo** instruction or you turn off error processing with the **On Error GoTo** 0 form of the statement.

If you don't trap errors with an **On Error GoTo** statement or if you've turned error trapping off with **On Error GoTo** 0, a dialog with the appropriate error message appears when a runtime error is encountered.

If you don't provide at least one error-handling routine in your VBA code for runtime Access applications you distribute with the Office Developer Edition, your application quits abruptly when the error occurs.

DETECTING THE TYPE OF ERROR WITH THE Err OBJECT

The Err object replaced the **Err** function of earlier versions of Access. The default property, Err.Number, returns an integer representing the code of the last error or returns 0 if no error occurs. This property ordinarily is used within a **Select Case** structure to determine the action to take in the error handler based on the type of error incurred. Use the Err.Description property, which replaces the **Error** function, to return the text name of the error number specified as its argument, as in the following example:

```
strErrorName = Err.Description
Select Case Err.Number
    Case 58 To 76
        Call FileError 'procedure for handling file errors
```

```
        Case 281 To 22000
            Call DDEError 'procedure for handling DDE errors
        Case 340 To 344
            Call ArrayError 'procedure for control array errors
    End Select
    Err.Clear
```

Tip #243 from

RJ

You can substitute the actual error-processing code for the `Call` instructions shown in the preceding example, but using individual procedures for error handling is the recommended approach. The `Err.Number` sets the error code to a specific integer. Use the `Err.Clear` method to reset the error code to 0 after your error handler has completed its operation, as shown in the preceding example.

The **Error** and **RaiseError** statements simulate an error so that you can test any error handlers you write. You can specify any of the valid integer error codes or create a user-defined error code by selecting an integer that's not included in the list. A user-defined error code returns `User-defined error` to `Error.Description`.

Using the Error Event in Form and Report Modules

Access includes an event, `Error`, that's triggered when an error occurs on a form or report. You can use an event-handling procedure in a form or report to process the error, or you can assign a generic error-handling function in an Access module to the `Error` event with an `=ErrorHandler()` entry to call the `ErrorHandler()` function.

When you invoke an error-handling function from the `Error` event, you must use the **Err** object to detect the error that occurred and take corrective action, as described in the preceding section.

Exploring the VBA Editor

You write VBA functions and procedures in the VBA Editor. To open the VBA Editor, click the Module shortcut of the Database window, and then double-click the name of the module you want to display. To open a new VBA module, click the New button; the VBA Editor window appears with default **Option**s set, as shown in Figure 26.8. The VBA Editor window incorporates a text editor, similar to Windows Notepad, in which you type your VBA code. VBA color-codes keywords and comments.

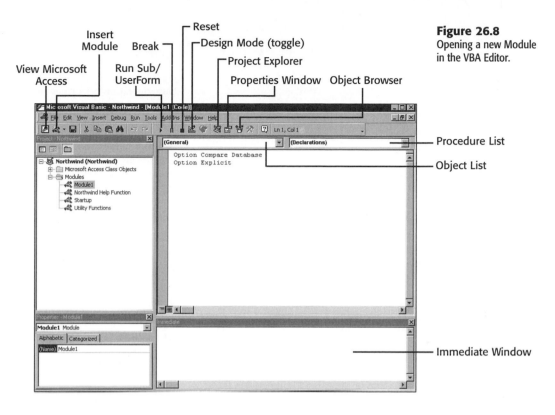

Figure 26.8
Opening a new Module
in the VBA Editor.

THE TOOLBAR OF THE MODULE WINDOW

Table 26.3 lists the purpose of each item in the toolbar of the Module window (refer to Figure 26.8) and the menu commands and key combinations that you can substitute for toolbar components. Buttons marked with an asterisk (*) in the Item column are new or changed with Access 2000.

TABLE 26.3   VBA-SPECIFIC ELEMENTS OF THE VBA EDITOR'S TOOLBAR AND
CODE EDITING WINDOW

Button	Item	Alternative Method	Purpose
	View Micro-Access*	<u>V</u>iew, <u>M</u>icrosoft Access or press Alt+F11	Displays the Access 2000 window.
	Insert Module	<u>I</u>nsert, Mod<u>u</u>le	Creates a new, empty module. Click the down arrow next to this button to create a new class module or to insert a new procedure or function.
	Find	<u>E</u>dit, <u>F</u>ind or press Ctrl+F	Similar to the Find feature used in Table or Form view; allows you to search for a specific word or phrase in a module.

continues

TABLE 26.3   CONTINUED

Button	Item	Alternative Method	Purpose
	Undo	Edit, Undo or press Ctrl+Z	Rescinds the last keyboard or mouse operation performed, if possible.
	Redo	Edit, Redo	Rescinds the last undo operation, if possible.
	Run Sub/* UserForm	Run, Run Sub/ User/Form or press F5	Starts the execution of the current procedure, or continues executing a procedure after its execution has been halted by a break condition. If the code editing window doesn't have the focus, this button is called Run Macro and opens the Macros dialog in which to select the macro to run, if any.
	Break*	Run, Break or press Ctrl+Break	Halts execution of a procedure.
	Reset	Run, Reset or press Shift+F5	Terminates execution of a VBA procedure and reinitializes all variables to their default values.
	Design Mode	Run, Design Mode	Toggles Design mode for UserForms.
	Project Explorer	View, Project Explorer or press Ctrl+R	Opens the Project Explorer window.
	Properties Window	View, Properties Window or press F4	Opens the Properties window for the object selected in the Projects Explorer.
	Object Browser	View, Object Browser or press Ctrl+F2	Opens the Object Browser dialog.
	Toolbox	View, Toolbox	Shows the Toolbox for adding controls to UserForms.
	Office Assistant	Help, Microsoft Access Help	Starts the Office Assistant for help.
N/A	Object List	None	Displays a list of objects in form or report modules. Only (General) appears for Access modules.
N/A	Procedure List	None	Displays a function or procedure in a module. Select the procedure or event name from the drop-down list. Procedures are listed in alphabetical order by name.

MODULE SHORTCUT KEYS

Additional shortcut keys and key combinations listed in Table 26.4 can help you as you write and edit VBA code. Only the most commonly used shortcut keys are listed in Table 26.4.

TABLE 26.4   PRIMARY KEY COMBINATIONS FOR ENTERING AND EDITING VBA CODE

Key Combination	Purpose
F3	Finds next occurrence of a search string.
Shift+F3	Finds previous occurrence of a search string.
F9	Sets or clears a breakpoint on the current line.
Ctrl+Shift+F9	Clears all breakpoints.
Tab	Indents a single line of code by four (default value) characters.
Tab with selected text	Indents multiple lines of selected code by four (default) characters.
Shift+Tab	Outdents a single line of code by four characters.
Shift+Tab with selected text	Outdents multiple lines of selected code by four characters.
Ctrl+Y	Deletes the line on which the caret is located.

You can change the default indentation of four characters per tab stop by choosing Tools, Options. Click the Module tab and then enter the desired number of characters in the Tab Width text box. This book uses a three-space tab.

THE VBA HELP SYSTEM

Microsoft provides an extensive, multilevel Help system to help you learn and use VBA. The majority of the help topics for VBA are supplied by a generic VBA help file that's applicable to all flavors of VBA. If you place the caret on a keyword or select a keyword and then press the F1 key, for example, a help window for the keyword appears (see Figure 26.9). If you click the "Example" hot spot under the name of the keyword, the window displays VBA sample code (see Figure 26.10).

PART

VII

CH

26

Figure 26.9
A Visual Basic Reference help window for the **Const** keyword.

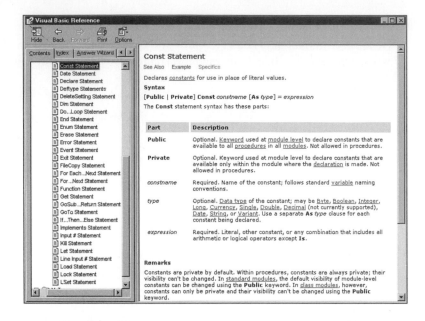

Figure 26.10
Sample code for using the **Const** keyword.

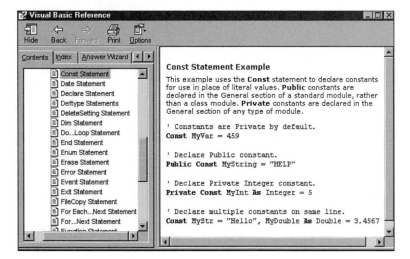

EXAMINING THE UTILITY FUNCTIONS MODULE

One recommended way to learn a new programming language is to examine simple examples of code and analyze the statements used in the example.

The sections that follow show how to open a module, display a function in the Module window, add a breakpoint to the code, and then use the Immediate window to execute the function.

ADDING A BREAKPOINT TO THE IsLoaded() FUNCTION

When you examine the execution of VBA code written by others, and when you debug your own application, breakpoints are very useful. This section explains how to add a breakpoint to the IsLoaded() function so that the Suppliers form stops executing when the Suppliers macro calls the IsLoaded() function and Access displays the code in the Module window.

To add a breakpoint to the IsLoaded() function, follow these steps:

1. If you have the VBA Editor open with Northwind as the current database, double-click Utility Functions in the Project Explorer. Otherwise, display the Database window, click the Modules shortcut, and double-click the Utility Functions module to open the VBA Editor with Utility Functions active.

2. Place the caret on the line that begins with If SysCmd(acSysCmdGetObjectState,...) and press F9.

   The breakpoint you create is indicated by changing the display of the line to reverse red and by the placement of a red dot in the margin indicator at the left of the window (see Figure 26.11, which has a line break added).

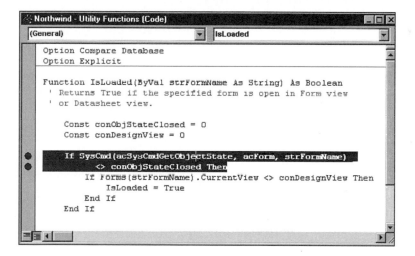

Figure 26.11
The IsLoaded() function with a breakpoint set.

3. Click the View Microsoft Access button and open the Suppliers form to execute the Form_Open procedure attached to the On Open event of the form. When the Suppliers form's Form_Open procedure calls the IsLoaded() function, the execution of IsLoaded() begins with the Const conObjStateClosed = 0 line and halts at the line with the breakpoint. When execution encounters a breakpoint, the module containing the breakpoint opens automatically. The line with the breakpoint turns yellow (see Figure 26.12).

Figure 26.12
The IsLoaded() function when the breakpoint is reached and the Utility Functions module opens in the VBA Editor.

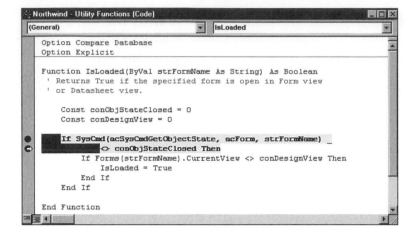

```
Northwind - Utility Functions (Code)                                    _ □ ×
(General)                              ▼   IsLoaded                      ▼
Option Compare Database
Option Explicit

Function IsLoaded(ByVal strFormName As String) As Boolean
  ' Returns True if the specified form is open in Form view
  ' or Datasheet view.

     Const conObjStateClosed = 0
     Const conDesignView = 0

     If SysCmd(acSysCmdGetObjectState, acForm, strFormName) _
              <> conObjStateClosed Then
          If Forms(strFormName).CurrentView <> conDesignView Then
               IsLoaded = True
          End If
     End If

  End Function
```

Tip #244 from

Datatips, which are similar in appearance to tooltips, display the name and value of variables in break mode. When you pass the mouse pointer over the SysCmd arguments, strFormName, or conDesignView, a datatip displays the value.

---

4. Press F5 or click the Run Sub/UserForm button to resume execution of the VBA code. Access displays the Suppliers form.

5. Close the Suppliers form to execute the Form_Close procedure that's attached to the form's On Close event. When the Suppliers form's Form_Close procedure calls the IsLoaded() function, execution occurs as described in step 3, and the IsLoaded() function again halts at the line with the breakpoint.

The element of the Forms collection to be tested is specified by strFormName. Access's SysCmd() function tests the Forms collection for the value of strFormName with the SysCmd(acSysCmdGetObjectState, acForm, strFormName) statement. If the specified form is open in either Form or Design view, SysCmd() returns **True**. The second test checks the value of the CurrentView property of the form to see if the form is open in Form view. If the result of the CurrentView comparison is **True**, the IsLoaded = **True** line executes and the IsLoaded() function returns **True** to the calling procedure, in this case the Suppliers form's Form_Open procedure. (When IsLoaded() is called as the form is opened, it actually returns **False**, because the form isn't yet loaded.) The IsLoaded() function is called again by the Suppliers form's Form_Close procedure, which is attached to the On Close event. At this time, because the Suppliers form is loaded, the IsLoaded() function does return **True**.

PRINTING TO THE IMMEDIATE WINDOW WITH THE Debug OBJECT

Previous chapters of this book introduced you to the VBA Editor's Immediate window and showed you how to obtain the values of variables with **?** *VarName* statements. When you want to view the values of several variables, you can use the **Debug** object to automate printing to the Immediate window. If you add the **Debug** object to a function that tests the names of each open form, you can create a list in the Immediate window of all the forms that are open.

→ For earlier examples of use of the Immediate window, **see** "Access Modules," **p. 73** and "Using the Immediate Window," **p. 329**.

To create a WhatsLoaded() function to list all open forms, follow these steps:

1. Load three or more forms by repeatedly opening the Database window, clicking the Form shortcut, and double-clicking a form icon. The Customers, Categories, Employees, and Main Switchboard forms are good choices because these forms load quickly.

2. In the Utility Functions module, type **Sub WhatsLoaded()** below the End Function line of the IsLoaded() function. The VBA interpreter adds the **End Sub** statement for you automatically.

3. Type the following code between the **Sub...** and **End Sub** lines:

```
Dim intCtr As Integer
For intCtr = 0 To Forms.Count - 1
    Debug.Print Forms(intCtr).FormName
Next intCtr
```

The **For Next** loop iterates the Forms collection. The **Debug.Print** statement prints the name of each open form in the Immediate window.

Note

The VBA Editor includes a powerful new feature called *statement autocompletion* to help you write VBA code. The interpreter monitors each line of code as you type it in. When you type variable declarations, use built-in Access and VBA functions, or use object methods and properties in your code, the interpreter displays a pop-up window to help you select appropriate values. Figure 26.13 shows the pop-up list window that appears after you type the **As** keyword in the first **Dim** statement of the code you enter in step 3. For procedures, functions, and methods, the pop-up help window lists all the arguments for the procedure, function, or method, so you don't have to remember all the possible arguments. You can turn this feature on and off by choosing Tools, Options and then selecting or clearing the Auto List Members check box on the Module tab of the Options dialog.

Figure 26.13
The pop-up list of data types displayed as you enter the **Dim** statement.

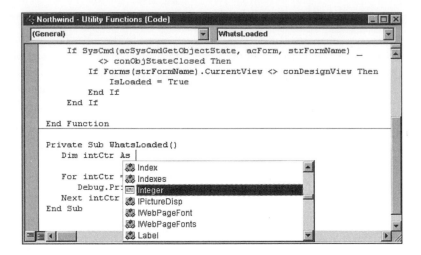

4. In the Immediate window, type **WhatsLoaded** and press Enter. (If the Immediate window isn't open, press Ctrl+G to open it.) The name of each form is added to the Immediate window by the **Debug.Print** statement (see Figure 26.14).

Figure 26.14
The **Debug** object used to print values of variables to the Immediate window.

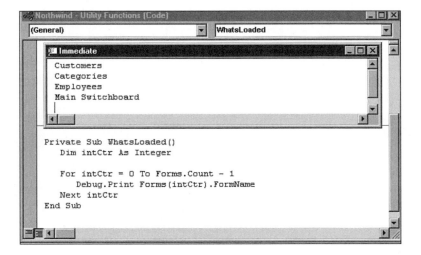

5. Close and don't save changes to the Utility Function module. Then close the other forms you opened for this example.

The **Debug.Print** statement is particularly useful for displaying the values of variables that change when you execute a loop. When you've completed the testing of your procedure, you delete the **Debug** statements.

USING TEXT COMPARISON OPTIONS

Tests of text data in fields of tables, query resultsets, and Recordset objects against **String** or **Variant** text data in modules depends on the value of the **Option** Compare... statement, which appears in the Declarations section of the Utility Functions module. To determine how text comparisons are made in the module, you can use any of the following statements:

- **Option** Compare Binary comparisons are case sensitive. Lowercase letters are not equivalent to uppercase letters. To determine the sort order of characters, Access uses the character value assigned by the Windows ANSI character set.

- **Option** Compare Text comparisons are not case sensitive. Lowercase letters are treated as the equivalent of uppercase letters. For most North American users, the sort order is the same as **Option** Compare Binary, ANSI. Unless you have a reason to specify a different comparison method, use **Option** Compare Text.

- **Option** Compare Database comparisons are case sensitive, and the sort order is that specified for the database.

Access adds **Option** Compare Database to the Declarations section when you create a new module, overriding the default. Binary and Database are keywords in VBA, but these words do not have the same meaning when used in the **Option** Compare... statement. For compatibility with changes in possible future releases of Access, you should not use Compare or Text as names of variables.

IN THE REAL WORLD—MACRO SCHIZOPHRENIA

Macros have been a common add-on to productivity applications since the early days of WordPerfect, Lotus 1-2-3, and other popular DOS word processing and spreadsheet applications. Each application took a different approach to automating repetitive operations, which resulted in a Tower of Macro Language Babel. WordPerfect 4.x and 5.x for DOS, in particular, had an arcane set of macro commands and peculiar program structure that frustrated thousands of erstwhile programmers.

About 10 years ago, Bill Gates decided that all Microsoft applications using macros would share a common macro language built on BASIC. BASIC is the acronym for Beginners All-Purpose Symbolic Instruction Code, an interpreted language developed at Dartmouth College. The intended application for BASIC was programming on terminal-based (usually Teletype) time-sharing computers. Gates' choice of BASIC for a macro language isn't surprising when you consider that Microsoft Corporation was built on the foundation of Gates' BASIC interpreter that ran in the 8KB of RAM common to the early predecessors of the PC, such as the Altair microcomputer. Gates reiterated his desire for a common macro language in an article that appeared in a late 1991 issue of the now-extinct *One-to-One with Microsoft* magazine.

Prior to Access 1.0, the only Microsoft application with a BASIC-like macro language was Word. WordBASIC, later Word Basic, was far more versatile, easy to understand, and useful than the competitors' pidgin-like languages. (It's not clear how or why BASIC became Basic, but it's likely to have been the result of trademark issues raised by lawyers.) Access 1.0 offered Embedded Basic (EB)—later to become Access Basic—as its programming language. Apparently Microsoft believed that Access Basic would be incomprehensible to average Access users, so Microsoft's product team tacked on a simplified macro language. Thus Access became saddled with two "macro" languages.

Visual Basic was the most popular Windows programming tool by the time Microsoft released Access 1.0. Visual Basic, Access, and Word each had their own Basic flavor. Microsoft touted Visual Basic as a programming language, while Access Basic and Word Basic retained the macro terminology. Excel was the next Microsoft application to gain Basic as a macro language, this time in the guise of Visual Basic, Applications Edition, a.k.a. Visual Basic for Applications. Microsoft's goal was to unify all three Visual Basic dialects under the VBA umbrella. Microsoft finally achieved Gates' objective with the release of Visual Basic 6.0 and Office 2000. There's a common aphorism that "after a few releases, Microsoft usually gets it right." But 10 years is a long time, even by Microsoft standards.

Note

Microsoft waffled over the years on the subject of licensing Embedded Basic (EB) variants to independent software vendors (ISVs). Early on, Microsoft announced an intention to license an EB version to ISVs, then changed course and withdrew the offer. The folks in Redmond changed their collective minds again in November 1996 and offered VBA licenses to ISVs. According to a presentation Bill Gates sent by satellite to March 1997 Developer Days attendees, Microsoft had then garnered 50 VBA licensees. Corel Systems, a staunch Microsoft competitor and the current owner of WordPerfect, announced in October 1998 that Corel WordPerfect Suite would adopt VBA.

Macro and *script* traditionally have been synonyms for code that automates operations in productivity applications, but Visual Basic, Scripting Edition, a.k.a. VBScript, ends that tradition. VBScript, a lightweight variant of VBA designed to compete with Netscape's JavaScript, appears primarily in Web-based applications. VBScript also can be used to automate repetitive operating system activities when run under the Windows Scripting Host (WSH). Access 2000 includes the HTML Source Editor, a.k.a. Microsoft Development Environment (MDE), described in Chapter 18, "Designing Data Access Pages," to aid in adding VBScript subprocedures to DAP. So Access 2000 now offers macro, script, and programming languages.

Calling VBA a macro language is undeserved damnation by faint praise. VBA is a true programming language and, because of its integration with Microsoft Office, is undoubtedly the most widely used of all programming languages—including COBOL and Java. VBA is easier to learn than Java and is an order of magnitude less difficult to master than C++ or COBOL. Although VBA doesn't qualify as a truly object-oriented programming language— it lacks inheritance and some other OO niceties—VBA is sufficiently object-enabled to handle virtually all common database-related programming chores. Unlike Java, VBA doesn't claim cross-platform capabilities, and it's capable of dealing only with COM-based objects. COM and the forthcoming COM+, however, provide adequate or better object management facilities for 32-bit Windows programmers. Microsoft's COM-based Millennium project (`http://www.research.microsoft.com/sn/Millennium/`) promises a "Self-Tuning, Self-Configuring, Distributed Systems" nirvana sometime after the turn of the century.

Once you gain experience with VBA in Access, you can leverage your programming skills in Visual Basic 6.0. A good foundation in VBA makes the transition to VBScript a snap. Even if you're an accomplished Access macro writer, use Access's Macro converter to automate the process of moving to VBA. Click Tools, Macros, and then choose Convert Macros to Visual Basic, Create Menu from Macro, Create Toolbar from Macro, or Create Shortcut Menu from Macro to bring your existing applications to current Access development standards.

--rj

PART

VII

CH

26

CHAPTER 27

UNDERSTANDING UNIVERSAL DATA ACCESS, OLE DB, AND ADO

In this chapter

Gaining a Perspective on Microsoft's New Data Access Components   1032

Interfacing with a Wide Range of Data Sources   1033

Creating `ADODB.Recordsets`   1038

Exploring Top-Level ADO Properties, Methods, and Events   1045

Working with the `ADODB.Connection` Object   1048

Using the `ADODB.Command` Object   1057

Understanding the `ADODB.Recordset` Object   1066

Troubleshooting   1080

In the Real World   Struggling with ADO   1081

GAINING A PERSPECTIVE ON MICROSOFT'S NEW DATA ACCESS COMPONENTS

Access 2000 represents the pivot point of Microsoft's strategy for data access. Under the umbrella of "*Universal Data Access*," Microsoft wants all Office users, not just Access developers, to abandon *Data Access Objects (DAO)*, *ODBCDirect*, and the *Open Database Connectivity (ODBC) Application Programming Interface (API)*. Microsoft proposes to substitute a completely new approach to data access based on a new collection of *Component Object Model (COM)* interfaces called *OLE DB*. To encourage Access users and developers to adopt OLE DB based programming, all traditional database technologies (referred to by Microsoft as *downlevel*, a synonym for "obsolete") are destined for maintenance mode. *Maintenance mode* is a technological purgatory in which Microsoft fixes only the worst bugs and upgrades occur infrequently, if ever. From 1999 on, OLE DB and its derivatives, ActiveX Data Objects (ADO) and ActiveX Data Object Extensions (ADOX), are Microsoft's mainstream data access technologies.

> **Note**
>
> **NEW 2000**
>
> When you upgrade an existing application from an earlier Access version to Access 2000, the new application uses DAO 3.6, which is backward compatible with versions 2.0 through 97. Upgraded client/server and other applications that use ODBC continue to use ODBC for data connectivity. All new applications you create in Access 2000 use ADO 2.1, ADOX 2.1, and OLE DB 2.0. New and upgraded applications that use Access (Jet) databases continue to use Jet 4.0. *Access Data Projects (ADP)* use ADO 2.1 and OLE DB to connect directly to the Microsoft Data Engine (MSDE) and SQL Server 6.5+, but don't use Jet.

Microsoft's primary goals for Universal Data Access are to

- Provide the capability to accommodate less common data types unsuited to SQL queries, such as spreadsheets, email messages, and file/directory systems
- Minimize the size and memory consumption of the dynamic link libraries (DLLs) required to support data access on Internet and intranet clients (PCs and hand-held "Internet appliances")
- Reduce development and support costs for the multiplicity of Windows-based data access architectures in common use today
- Extend the influence of COM in competition with other object models, primarily *Common Object Request Broker Architecture (CORBA)* and its derivatives

This chapter introduces the fundamentals of Universal Data Access and *Microsoft Data Access Components (MDAC)*. MDAC makes connecting to databases with OLE DB practical for Access users and developers. MDAC includes ADO and ADOX for conventional data handling, plus ADOMD for *multidimensional expressions* (MDX) to create and manipulate data cubes. All editions of Office 2000 install MDAC 2.1.

Note

Microsoft *SQL Server OLAP Services* (code-named *Plato* during its development) generates data cubes from online sources, such as transactional databases. Office 2000 installs Msadomd.dll and other supporting files for MDX and data cubes. Microsoft provides OLE DB for OLAP and the PivotTable Service to enable Excel 2000 PivotTables to manipulate data cubes. MDX and PivotTable services are beyond the scope of this book.

INTERFACING WITH A WIDE RANGE OF DATA SOURCES

Today's most popular methods of connecting with sources of data are the ODBC API, and DAO. Thirty-two-bit ODBC drivers now are available for virtually every client/server RDBMS; most popular *Indexed Sequential Access Method (ISAM)* databases (Jet, dBase, FoxPro, and Paradox); spreadsheets (Excel); and delimited text files. Microsoft Office traditionally has relied on ODBC drivers for most of its database connectivity features. Although other software publishers attempted to introduce ODBC alternatives, ODBC quickly became the de facto standard of the database industry. ODBC is a C/C++ API; making direct use of the ODBC API in Access applications requires a large number of VBA function prototype declarations (DECLAREs) and heavy-duty, low-level coding. Few, if any, Access developers access the ODBC API directly.

In 1994 Microsoft Access 2.0 introduced 16-bit DAO in conjunction with version 2.0 of the Jet database engine. Like ODBC, the Jet database engine is a C/C++ API. DAO provided what was then called an OLE Automation wrapper over the Jet API; up to that time OLE had been used primarily for creating and manipulating compound documents. DAO exposes a complex hierarchy of programmable data related objects with the DBEngine object at the top. Lower objects in the hierarchy, Workspaces, Databases, TableDefs, QueryDefs, and Recordsets, are object layers under DBEngine. Jet databases permit attaching other databases via ODBC, eliminating the need for low-level ODBC API programming. 32-bit Jet and DAO 3.0 appeared with the release of Access 95; Access 2000 introduces Jet 4.0 and DAO 3.6. Microsoft has sold tens of millions of Access licenses, making Jet the most widely used desktop database in the world and DAO the default database object model for Access users and for the majority of Access and Visual Basic programmers.

The DAO/Jet combination is a heavyweight. Dao360.dll, in your \Program Files\Common Files\Microsoft Shared\Dao folder, weighs in at 541KB. Msjet40.dll, in \Windows\System, tips the scales at 1,429KB. To eliminate the 2MB DAO/Jet footprint for Access client/server front ends, Microsoft introduced in Access 97 yet another object model, ODBCDirect. ODBCDirect lets client/server front ends communicate with back-end SQL RDBMSs without incurring the Jet overhead. ODBCDirect is a wrapper over *Remote Data Objects (RDO)*; RDO 2.0, part of Visual Basic 5.0 Professional Edition, wasn't licensed for use with Access 97. The proliferation of Microsoft data access object models caused choice crises among developers.

> **Note**
>
> Unfortunately, Access 2000 developers still must choose between using ADO 2.1 and DAO 3.6 because ADO hasn't gained full parity with the DAO feature set. When Microsoft releases the next version of Access, it's likely that ADO will offer a richer feature set than DAO offers. You also can expect interim releases of ADO updates and upgrades that will make ADO a more practical option for all Access programmers.

REDESIGNING FROM THE BOTTOM UP WITH OLE DB

To accommodate the widest variety of data sources, as well as to spread the gospel of COM, Microsoft's data architects came up with an entirely new approach to data connectivity—OLE DB. OLE DB consists of three basic elements:

- *Data providers* that abstract information contained in data sources into a tabular (row-column) format called a *rowset*. Microsoft currently offers native OLE DB data providers for Jet, SQL Server, and Oracle databases, plus ODBC data sources. Other Microsoft OLE DB providers include an OLE DB Simple Provider for delimited text files, the MSPersist provider for saving and opening Recordsets to files (called *persisted* Recordsets), and the MSDataShape provider for creating hierarchical data sets. The MSDataShape provider also plays an important role in ADP and when using VBA to manipulate the Recordset of Access forms. Office 2000 includes only Jet, SQL Server, MSPersist, and MSDataShape providers.

- *Data consumers* that display and/or manipulate rowsets, such as Access application objects or OLE DB service providers.

- *Data services* (usually called OLE DB *service providers*) that consume data from providers and, in turn, provide data to consumers. Examples of data services are SQL query processors and cursor engines, which can create scrollable rowsets from forward-only rowsets. A scrollable cursor lets you move the record pointer forward and backward in the Datasheet view of a Jet query.

> **Note**
>
> Version 2.0 of the OLE DB specification was current when this book was written. You get the latest information on OLE DB at www.microsoft.com/data/oledb/.

Figure 27.1 illustrates the relationship between OLE DB data providers, data consumers, and data services within Microsoft's Universal Data Access architecture. You should understand the relationships between these objects, because Microsoft commonly refers to them in ADO documentation, help files, and Knowledgebase articles. Database front ends written in C++ can connect directly to the OLE DB interfaces, which require function pointers and other low-level operations. High-level languages, such as VBA, use ADO as an intermediary to connect to OLE DB's COM interfaces. Msado15.dll, which implements ADO 2.1, has a memory footprint of about 327KB, about 60 percent of Dao360.dll's 547KB. ADO support files are in your \Program Files\System\Ado folder.

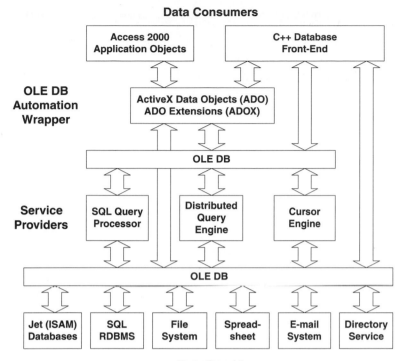

Figure 27.1
Microsoft's Universal
Data Access architecture
and typical OLE DB data
providers, services, and
consumers.

Note

ADO support file names have a 1.5 version number, as in Msado15.dll; the strange version-
ing of these files is required for backward compatibility with applications that used very
early versions of ADO.

MDAC 2.1 also supports Remote Data Services (RDS, formerly Advanced Database
Connector, or ADC). RDS handles lightweight ADOR.Recordsets for browser-based applications; RDS, which commonly is used for three-tier, Web-based applications, isn't covered
in this book.

MAPPING OLE DB INTERFACES TO ADO

You also need to know the names and relationship of OLE DB interfaces to ADO objects,
because Microsoft includes references to these interfaces in its technical and white papers
on OLE DB and ADO. Figure 27.2 illustrates the correspondence between OLE DB interfaces and the highest levels of the ADO hierarchy.

PART

VII

CH

27

Figure 27.2
Correspondence between
OLE DB interfaces and
ADO Automation objects.

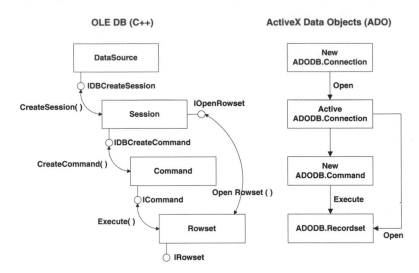

The OLE DB specification defines a set of interfaces to the following objects:

- *DataSource* objects provide a set of functions to identify a particular OLE DB data provider, such as the Jet or SQL Server provider, and determine whether the caller has the required *security permissions* for the provider. If the provider is found and authentication succeeds, a connection to the data source results.

- *Session* objects provide an environment for creating rowsets and isolating transactions, especially with *Microsoft Transaction Server (MTS)*, which now is part of Windows NT and 2000.

- *Command* objects include sets of functions to handle queries, usually (but not necessarily) in the form of SQL statements or names of *stored procedures*.

- *Rowset* objects can be created directly from Session objects or as the result of execution of Command objects. Rowset objects deliver data to the consumer through the IRowset interface.

ADO maps the four OLE DB objects to the following three top-level Automation objects that are familiar to Access programmers who've used ODBCDirect:

- `Connection` objects combine OLE DB's DataSource and Session objects to specify the OLE DB data provider, establish a connection to the data source and isolate transactions to a specific connection. The `Execute` method of the `ADODB.Connection` object can return a forward-only `ADODB.Recordset` object.

- `Command` objects are directly analogous to OLE DB's Command object. `ADODB.Command` objects accept an SQL statement, the name of a table, or the name of a stored procedure. `Command` objects are used primarily for executing SQL UPDATE, INSERT, DELETE, and SQL Data Definition Language (DDL) queries that don't return records. You also can create an `ADODB.Recordset` by executing an `ADODB.Command` object.

- *Recordset objects* correspond to OLE DB's Rowset objects and have properties and methods similar to Access 97's ODBCDirect `Recordset`. A `Recordset` is an in-memory image of a table or a query result set.

When you open a new Access 2000 database, Access automatically adds a reference to the Microsoft ActiveX Data Objects 2.1 Library for VBA programming. The `ADODB` prefix, the short name of the ADO type library, explicitly identifies ADO objects that share object names with DAO (`Recordset`) and DAO's ODBCDirect (`Connection` and `Recordset`). For clarity, all ADO code examples in this book use the `ADODB` prefix.

Tip #245 from	To make ADOX 2.1 accessible to VBA, you must add a reference to Microsoft ADO Ext. 2.1 for DDL and Security to your application. Unlike ADO 2.1, Access 2000 doesn't add the ADOX reference automatically to new database applications.

COMPARING ADO AND DAO OBJECTS

Figure 27.3 is a diagram that compares the ADO and DAO object hierarchies. The ADO object hierarchy, which can consist of nothing more than an `ADODB.Connection` object, is much simpler than the collection-based object hierarchy of DAO. To obtain a scrollable, updatable `Recordset` (dynaset) you must open an `ADODB.Recordset` object on an active `ADODB.Connection` object.

> **Note**
>
> Access VBA provides a DAO shortcut, `Set` *dbName* = CurrentDB(), to bypass the first two collection layers and open the current database, but `CurrentDB()` isn't available in VBA code for other members of Office 2000 or Visual Basic 6.0.
>
> Access VBA provides a similar ADO shortcut, `CurrentProject.Connection` that points to a default `ADODB.Connection` object with the Jet OLE DB Service Provider for the current database. Unlike `CurrentDB()`, which is optional, you *must* use `CurrentProject.Connection` as the `ADODB.Connection` to the currently open database. If you try to open a new `ADODB.Connection` to the current database, you receive a runtime error stating that the database is locked.

Unlike DAO objects, most of which are members of collections, you use the **New** reserved word with the **Set** instruction to create and the `Close` method or the **Set** *ObjectName* = **Nothing** statement to destroy instances of `ADODB.Connection`, `ADODB.Command`, and `ADODB.Recordset` objects independently of one another.

Figure 27.3
A comparison of ADO and DAO object hierarchies.

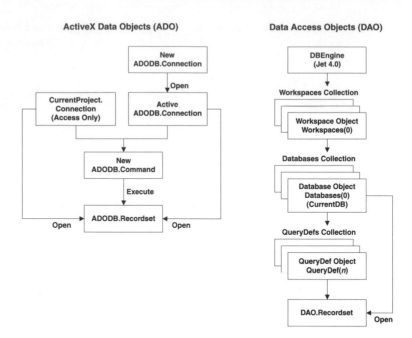

DAO supports a variety of Jet collections, such as Users and Groups, and Jet SQL *Data Definition Language (DDL)* operations that ADO 2.1 alone doesn't handle. ADOX 2.1 defines Jet-specific collections and objects that aren't included in ADO 2.1.

CREATING ADODB.Recordsets

The concept of database object independence is new to Access. The best way of demonstrating this feature is to compare DAO and ADO code to create a Recordset object from an SQL statement. DAO syntax requires successive instantiation of each object in the DAO hierarchy: DBEngine, Workspace, Database, and Recordset, as in the following example:

```
Dim wsName As DAO.Workspace
Dim dbName As DAO.Database
Dim rsName As DAO.Recordset

Set wsName = DBEngine.Workspaces(0)
Set dbName = wsName.OpenDatabase ("DatabaseName.mdb")
Set rsName = dbName.OpenRecordset ("SQL Statement")
```

As you descend through the hierarchy, you open new child objects with methods of the parent object.

The most common approach with ADO is to create one or more independent, reusable instances of each object in the Declarations section of a form or module:

```
Private cnnName As New ADODB.Connection
Private cmmName As New ADODB.Command
Private rstName As New ADODB.Recordset
```

Note

> This book uses cnn as the object type prefix for Connection, cmm for Command, and rst for Recordset. The cmm prefix is used because the cmd prefix traditionally identifies a command button control and the com prefix identifies the MSComm ActiveX control (Microsoft Comm Control 6.0).
>
> Although you're likely to find references to DAO.Recordset dynasets and snapshots in the Access documentation, these terms don't apply to ADODB.Recordset objects. See the CursorType property of the ADODB.Recordset object in the "Recordset Properties" section later in this chapter for the CursorType equivalents of dynasets and snapshots.

After the initial declarations, you set the properties of the new object instances and apply methods—Open for Connections and Recordsets, or Execute for Commands—to activate the object. Invoking the Open method of the ADODB.Recordset object, rather than the OpenRecordset method of the DAO.Database object, makes ADO objects independent. Object independence and *batch-optimistic*, for instance, let you close the ADODB.Recordset's ADODB.Connection object, make changes to the Recordset, and then re-open the Connection to send only the changes to the underlying tables. The examples that follow illustrate the independence of top-level ADO members.

DESIGNING A FORM BOUND TO AN ADODB.Recordset OBJECT

NEW 2000

Access 2000 forms have a new property, Recordset, that let you assign an ADODB.Recordset object as the RecordSource for one or more forms. The Recordset property of a form is an important addition, because you can assign the same Recordset to multiple forms. All forms connected to the Recordset synchronize to the same current record. Access developers have been requesting this feature since version 1.0, but Access 2000 forms bound in code to Recordset objects have the following limitations:

- Forms bound to an ADODB.Recordset object from an ADODB.Connection that uses an OLE DB data provider are read-only. This restriction applies to both the Jet and SQL Server data providers.

- Forms bound to an ADODB.Recordset object from an ADODB.Connection that uses MSDataShape as the connection provider and SQL Server as the OLE DB data provider are updatable if the underlying data source (table or query) is updatable.

- Forms in ADP must use ADO and an OLE DB provider to a client/server RDBMS. The only OLE DB client/server provider included with Office 2000 is for SQL Server/MSDE. Visual Studio 6.0 includes SQL Server and Oracle 8+ providers, but Access 2000 ADP connect only to MSDE or SQL Server. OLE DB providers for other client/server databases are available from third parties, such as Intersolv (http://www.intersolv.com/).

- Forms bound to a DAO.Recordset object are updatable if the data source is updatable. If you plan to use only Jet databases and need forms that let you update records, use DAO to create your Recordsets.

To create a simple project that uses VBA code to bind a read-only form to an ADODB.Recordset object, follow these steps:

1. Launch Access, if necessary, and open a new database named ADO_Test.mdb in your …\Office\Samples folder.

Add a new form in Design mode and save it as frmADO_Test.

2. Click the toolbar's Code button to open the VBA Editor and add the following code to the Declarations section of the frmADO_Test module:

```
Private strSQL As String
Private cnnNwind As New ADODB.Connection
Private rstNwind As New ADODB.Recordset
```

3. Add the following code to the Form_Load event handler:

```
Private Sub Form_Load()
    'Specify the OLE DB provider and open the connection
    With cnnNwind
        .Provider = "Microsoft.Jet.OLEDB.4.0"
        .Open CurrentProject.Path & "\Northwind.mdb", "Admin"
    End With

    strSQL = "SELECT * FROM Customers"
    With rstNwind
        Set .ActiveConnection = cnnNwind
        .CursorType = adOpenKeyset
        .LockType = adLockOptimistic
        .Open strSQL
    End With

    'Assign rstNwind as the Recordset for the form
    Set Me.Recordset = rstNwind

End Sub
```

> **Note**
>
> The preceding code includes several properties and one method (Open) that this chapter hasn't discussed. The objective of this and the following sections is to get you started with a quick demonstration of use of the Form.Recordset property. Properties and methods of the Connection and Recordset objects are the subject of the "Exploring Top-Level ADO Properties, Methods, and Events" section that follows shortly.

4. Return to Access and change to Form view to execute the preceding code and then open the Properties window. Your form appears as shown in Figure 27.4, with the first of 91 records selected by the navigation buttons. The form's Record Source property value is the SQL statement specified as the argument of the Recordset's Open method. Although the Recordset Type property value appears as Dynaset, which isn't a valid ADODB.Recordset type, the lack of an Add New Record navigation button demonstrates that the form is read-only.

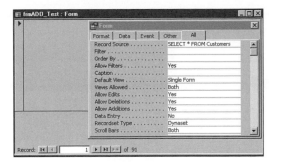

Figure 27.4
An empty form with its
Recordset property set
to an *ADODB.*
Recordset object
opened on the
Customers table.

 5. Change to Form Design mode. The Record Source property value is empty because the Form_Load code, which executes when you run the form, creates the data source object, rstNwind (see Figure 27.5). The source object for the form doesn't exist in Design mode.

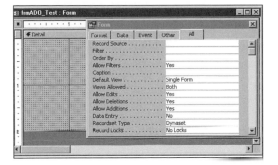

Figure 27.5
The form of Figure 27.4 in
Design mode with the
Record Source property
value empty.

Unfortunately, Access 2000 doesn't offer the equivalent of Visual Studio 6.0's Data View window or Visual Basic 6.0's Data Environment Designer, both of which provide Design-mode access to a predefined set of Connection and Command objects. To take advantage of the flexibility of binding forms and controls to Recordsets with VBA code, you must fore go most of Access's Design-mode conveniences, such as bound controls. The Data Environment Designer is included with the Microsoft Office 2000 Developer (MOD) edition.

PART
VII

CH
27

BINDING CONTROLS TO A RECORDSET WITH CODE

Adding the equivalent of bound controls to a form requires that you first add unbound controls and then bind the controls to the form's underlying Recordset with code. To create a simple data display form for the Customers table, do the following:

 1. Add seven unbound text boxes to the form. Name the text boxes **txtCustID**, **txtCompanyName**, **txtAddress**, **txtCity**, **txtRegion**, **txtPostalCode**, and **txtCountry**. Change the width of the text boxes to reflect approximately the number of characters in each of the Customer table's fields.

B 2. Change the label captions to **CustID**, **Name**, **Address**, **City**, **Region**, **Postal Code**, and **Country**, respectively. Apply the Bold attribute to the labels for readability (see Figure 27.6).

Figure 27.6
Text boxes to display the first seven fields of the Customers table.

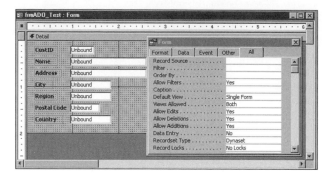

3. To bind the ControlSource property of each text box to the appropriate field of the Customers table, click the Code button and add the following lines of code immediately after the **Set Me**.Recordset = rstNwind line:

```
Me.txtCustID.ControlSource = "CustomerID"
Me.txtCompanyName.ControlSource = "CompanyName"
Me.txtAddress.ControlSource = "Address"
Me.txtCity.ControlSource = "City"
Me.txtRegion.ControlSource = "Region"
Me.txtPostalCode.ControlSource = "PostalCode"
Me.txtCountry.ControlSource = "Country"
```

4. Run the form in the default Single Form view and navigate the Recordset (see Figure 27.7).

Figure 27.7
The form of Figure 27.6 in Single Form view.

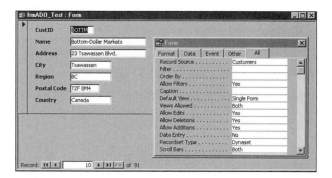

5. Change to Design mode and change the Default View property to Datasheet.

6. Run the form again. The seven fields of the text boxes provide data to the columns of the datasheet, and the label captions serve as column headers (see Figure 27.8).

CustID	Name	Address	City	Region	Postal Code	
ALFKI	Alfreds Futterkis	Obere Str. 57	Berlin		12209	C
ANATR	Ana Trujillo Emp	Avda. de la Con	México D.F.		05021	N
ANTON	Antonio Moreno	Mataderos 231	México D.F.		05023	N
AROUT	Around the Horr	120 Hanover Sq	London		WA1 1DP	L
BERGS	Berglunds snab	Berguvsvägen 8	Luleå		S-958 22	S
BLAUS	Blauer See Deli	Forsterstr. 57	Mannheim		68306	C
BLONP	Blondel père et	24, place Klébe	Strasbourg		67000	F
BOLID	Bólido Comidas	C/ Araquil, 67	Madrid		28023	S
BONAP	Bon app'	12, rue des Bou	Marseille		13008	F
BOTTM	Bottom-Dollar M	23 Tsawassen E	Tsawassen	BC	T2F 8M4	C
BSBEV	B's Beverages	Fauntleroy Circu	London		EC2 5NT	L
CACTU	Cactus Comidas	Cerrito 333	Buenos Aires		1010	A
CENTC	Centro comercia	Sierras de Gran	México D.F.		05022	N
CHOPS	Chop-suey Chin	Hauptstr. 29	Bern		3012	S
COMMI	Comércio Minei	Av. dos Lusíada	São Paulo	SP	05432-043	B

Record: 14 | 1 | ▶ | ▶I | ▶* | of 91

Figure 27.8
The form of Figure 27.6 in Datasheet view.

Tip #246 from

R J

To emulate a table Datasheet view with code, add to the form text boxes for every field of the table. To open a table-type `Recordset`, substitute the table name for the SQL statement as the argument of the rst*Name*.`Open` statement.

MAKING THE FORM UPDATABLE

You have two choices to make your form updatable—connect to MSDE/SQL Server or substitute DAO 3.6 for ADO 2.1. Using MSDE requires the fewest code changes, so for the first example you change the connection to the NorthwindCS MSDE database you generated in Chapter 25, "Creating Access Data Projects."

→ For more information about MSDE and the NorthwindCS SQL Server 7.0 database, **see** "Running the NorthwindCS Sample Project," **p. 954**.

CONNECTING TO THE NORTHWINDCS MSDE DATABASE

To substitute the MSDE version of the Northwind sample database for Northwind.mdb, do the following:

1. Start your local MSDE server if SQL Server isn't already running.

2. Make a copy of frmADO_Test as frmADO_MSDE, open frmADO_MSDE in Design mode, and open the VBA Editor for frmADO_MSDE.

3. Change the `.Provider = "Microsoft.Jet.OLEDB.4.0"` line to

   `.Provider = "MSDataShape"`

   The MSDataShape provider supplies a cursor that's fully compatible with Access forms and reports, and permits updating *Form*.`Recordset` objects.

4. Change the `.Open CurrentProject.Path & "\Northwind.mdb", "Admin"` line to

   `.Open "Data Provider=SQLOLEDB.1;Data Source=(local);" & _`
   `"UID=sa;PWD=;Database=NorthwindCS"`

   The preceding statement must be on a single line; the statement above is broken into two lines because of publishing limitations.

5. Add after the **Set Me**.`Recordset` = rstNwind line the following statement:

   Me.UniqueTable = "Customers"

> **Note**
>
> Even if your query returns data from a single table only, you should specify the table as unique. For result sets from queries with joins, it's most common to use the `UniqueTable` property value to specify the "most-many" table. As an example, if your query returns values from one-to-many joins between the Customers, Orders, and Order Details table, Order Details is the "most-many" table. Fields of the Order Details table contribute the uniqueness to the rows of the query result set.

 6. Run frmADO_MSDE in Datasheet view and verify that the form is updatable by temporarily editing any cell except primary-key values of the CustID (see Figure 27.9). You receive a constraint conflict error if you attempt to change a CustomerID value.

Figure 27.9
Datasheet view of an updatable form based on the MSDE Customers table.

> **Note**
>
> The Add New Record navigation button is enabled, but its status isn't indicative of form updatability. If you don't add the **Me.**UniqueTable value, the form isn't updatable.

SUBSTITUTING DAO 3.6 FOR ADO 2.1

The updatable alternative to MSDE is to use DAO, which requires major changes to the code of this and the preceding section. Listing 27.1 illustrates the code required to emulate the frmADO_Test form. DAO.Recordset objects are updatable (dynaset) by default, so you don't need to set properties of the Recordset object. You must add a reference to the Microsoft DAO 3.6 Object Library to your project to enable execution of the code of Listing 27.1.

LISTING 27.1   CODE TO BIND AN UPDATABLE FORM TO A DAO.Recordset OBJECT

```
Option Explicit
Option Compare Database

Private wsNwind As DAO.Workspace
Private dbNwind As DAO.Database
Private rstNwind As DAO.Recordset
```

```
Private Sub Form_Load()
    Dim strSQL As String
    strSQL = "SELECT * FROM Customers"

    'Open the current Workspace
    Set wsNwind = DBEngine.Workspaces(0)
    'Open the back-end Database
    Set dbNwind = wsNwind.OpenDatabase(CurrentProject.Path & "\Northwind.mdb")
    'Open the Recordset on the Database
    Set rstNwind = dbNwind.OpenRecordset(strSQL)

    'Assign rstNwind to the Recordset of the form
    Set Me.Recordset = rstNwind

    Me.txtCustID.ControlSource = "CustomerID"
    Me.txtCompanyName.ControlSource = "CompanyName"
    Me.txtAddress.ControlSource = "Address"
    Me.txtCity.ControlSource = "City"
    Me.txtRegion.ControlSource = "Region"
    Me.txtPostalCode.ControlSource = "PostalCode"
    Me.txtCountry.ControlSource = "Country"
End Sub
```

Note

The ADO_Test.mdb database in the SEUA2K\Chaptr27 folder of the accompanying CD-ROM contains the frmADO_Test, frmADO_MSDE, and frmDAO_Test forms described in the preceding two sections. Copy ADO_Test.mdb to your …\Office\Samples folder to enable the connection to Northwind.mdb. The frmADO_SHAPE form uses Microsoft's SHAPE syntax to create a hierarchical (SHAPEd) Recordset from the Customers, Orders, and Order Details tables of the NorthwindCS database.

EXPLORING TOP-LEVEL ADO PROPERTIES, METHODS, AND EVENTS

At this point in your ADO learning curve, a detailed list of properties, enumerations of constant values, methods, and events of ADO components might appear premature. Understanding the capabilities and benefits of ADO, however, requires familiarity with ADO's repertoire of properties, methods, and events. To get the most out of ADP, which doesn't support Jet 4.0 and DAO 3.6, and to program Data Access pages (DAP) you must have a working knowledge of ADO programming techniques.

DAO objects don't fire events; ADO objects do. Visual Basic 4.0 and RDO 1.0 added an event model for RDO's rdoEnvironment, rdoConnection, and rdoResultset objects. Visual Basic 5.0's RDO 2.0 increased the granularity of the data-related events, providing developers with much finer control over communication with SQL Server and other client/server RDBMSs. Access objects offer fine-grained events, but don't provide programmers with a lower-level event model for basic operations, such as connecting to the database and executing queries. Access 97's ODBCDirect offered an event model, but you couldn't bind ODBCDirect Recordsets to forms. ADO offers a complete event model, which is quite similar to that of RDO 2.0.

OBJECT BROWSER AND ADO

Object Browser is the most useful tool for becoming acquainted with the properties, methods, and events of ADODB objects. Object Browser also is the most convenient method for obtaining help with the syntax and usage of ADO objects, methods, and events.

To use Object Browser with ADODB, follow these steps:

1. Open in Design mode one of the forms you created in the preceding sections and then open the VBA Editor for its code.

2. Press F2 to open Object Browser.

3. Select ADODB in the library (upper) list.

4. Select one of the top-level components, such as Connection, in the Classes (left) pane.

5. Select a property, event, or method, such as Open, in the Members of '*ObjectName*' (right) pane. A short-form version of the syntax for the selected method or event appears in Object Browser's lower pane (see Figure 27.10).

Figure 27.10
Object browser displaying the syntax of the *ADODB.Connection. Open* method.

6. Click the Help button to open the help topic for the selected object, property, method, or event. Figure 27.11 shows the help topic for ADODB.Connection.Open.

ADO type libraries also include *enumerations* (lists) of numeric (usually **Long**) constant values with an ad prefix. These constant enumerations are specific to one or more properties. Figure 27.12 shows Object Browser displaying the members of the ConnectModeEnum enumeration for the Mode property of an ADODB.Connection object. The lower pane displays the **Long** value of the constant.

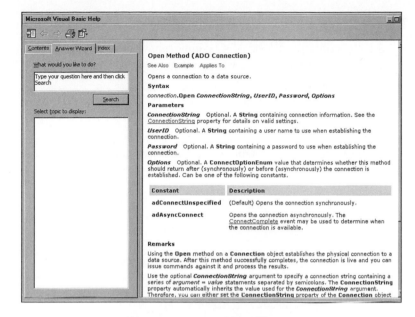

Figure 27.11
The help topic for the *ADODB.Connection.Open* method.

Figure 27.12
Object Browser displaying the ConnectModeEnum list of constants for the *ADODB.Connection* object's Mode property.

PART

VII

Cн

27

Tip #247 from

You can substitute the numeric value of enumerated constants for the constant name in VBA, but doing so isn't considered a good programming practice. Numeric values of the constants might change in subsequent ADO versions, causing unexpected results when upgrading applications to a new ADO release.

WORKING WITH THE ADODB.Connection OBJECT

The Connection object is the primary top-level ADO component. You must successfully open a Connection object to a data source before you can use associated Command or Recordset objects.

Connection PROPERTIES

Table 27.1 lists the names and descriptions of the properties of the ADODB.Connection object. In addition to the properties listed in Table 27.1, the Connection object has a collection of provider-specific properties that are beyond the scope of this book.

TABLE 27.1 PROPERTIES OF THE ADODB.Connection OBJECT

Property Name	Data Type and Purpose
Attributes	A **Long** read/write value that specifies use of retaining transactions by the sum of two constant values. The adXactCommitRetaining constant starts a new transaction when calling the CommitTrans method; adXactAbortRetaining starts a new transaction when calling the RollbackTrans method. The default value is 0, don't use retaining transactions.
CommandTimeout	A **Long** read/write value that determines the time in seconds before terminating an Execute call against an associated Command object. The default value is 30 seconds.
ConnectionString	A **String** read/write variable that supplies specific information required by a data or service provider to open a connection to the data source.
ConnectionTimeout	A **Long** read/write value that determines the number of seconds before terminating an unsuccessful Connection.Open method call. The default value is 15 seconds.
CursorLocation	A **Long** read/write value that determines whether the client-side (adUseClient) or the server-side (adUseServer) *cursor engine* is used. The default is adUseServer.
DefaultDatabase	A **String** read/write variable that specifies the name of the database to use if not specified in the ConnectionString. For SQL Server examples, the value often is pubs.
IsolationLevel	A **Long** read/write value that determines the behavior or transactions that interact with other simultaneous transactions (see Table 27.2).
Mode	A **Long** value that determines read and write permissions for the Connection (see Table 27.3).

Property Name	Data Type and Purpose
Provider	A **String** read/write value that specifies the name of the OLE DB data or service provider if not specified in the ConnectionString. The default value is MSDASQL, the Microsoft OLE DB Provider for ODBC. The most common providers used in the programming chapters of this book are Microsoft.Jet.OLEDB.4.0, more commonly known by its code name, "Jolt 4," and SQLOLEDB.
State	A **Long** read-only value that specifies whether the connection is open, closed, or in an intermediate state (see Table 27.4).
Version	A **String** read-only value that returns the ADO version number.

Note

Most property values identified in Table 27.1 as being read/write are writable only when the connection is in the closed state.

The ability to specify the *transaction isolation level* applies only when you use the BeginTrans...CommitTrans...RollbackTrans methods (see Table 27.5) to define a transaction on a Connection object. If multiple database users simultaneously execute transactions, your application should specify how it responds to other transactions in-process. Table 27.2 lists the options for the degree of your application's isolation from other simultaneous transactions.

TABLE 27.2   CONSTANT ENUMERATION FOR THE IsolationLevel PROPERTY

IsolationLevelEnum	Description
adXactCursorStability	Allows reading only committed changes in other transactions (default value).
adXactBrowse	Allows reading uncommitted changes in other transactions.
adXactChaos	The transaction won't overwrite changes made to transaction(s) at a higher isolation level.
adXactIsolated	All transactions are independent of (isolated from) other transactions.
adXactReadCommitted	Same as adXactCursorStability.
adXactReadUncommitted	Same as adXactBrowse.
adXactRepeatableRead	Prohibits reading changes in other transactions.
adXactSerializable	Same as adXactIsolated.
adXactUnspecified	The transaction level of the provider can't be determined.

PART

VII

CH

27

Note

Enumeration tables in this book list the default value first, followed by the remaining constants in alphabetical order.

Unless you have a specific reason to specify a particular ADODB.Connection.Mode value, the default adModeUnknown is adequate. The Jet OLE DB provider defaults to adModeShareDenyNone. Table 27.3 lists all the constants for the Mode property.

Tip #248 from

You often can improve performance of client/server decision-support applications by opening the connection as read only (adModeRead). Modifying the structure of a database with SQL's DDL usually requires exclusive access to the database (adModeShareExclusive).

TABLE 27.3   CONSTANT ENUMERATION FOR THE Mode PROPERTY

ConnectModeEnum	Description
adModeUnknown	No connection permissions have been set on the data source (default value).
adModeRead	Connect with read-only permission.
adModeReadWrite	Connect with read/write permissions.
adModeShareDenyNone	Don't deny other users read or write access.
adModeShareDenyRead	Deny others permission to open a read connection to the data source.
adModeShareDenyWrite	Deny others permission to open a write connection to the data source.
adModeShareExclusive	Open the data source for exclusive use.
adModeWrite	Connect with write-only permission.

Table 27.4 lists the constants that return the state of the Connection object. These constants also are applicable to the State property of the Command and Recordset objects.

Tip #249 from

It's common to open and close Connections as needed to reduce the connection load on the database. (Each open connection to a client/server database consumes a block of memory.) In many cases, you must test whether the Connection object is open or closed before applying the Close or Open method, respectively, or changing Connection property values.

TABLE 27.4   CONSTANT ENUMERATION FOR THE State PROPERTY

ObjectStateEnum	Description
adStateClosed	The Connection (or other object) is closed (default value).
adStateConnecting	A connection to the data source is in progress.
adStateExecuting	The Execute method of a Connection or Command object has been called.
adStateFetching	Rows are returning to a Recordset object.
adStateOpen	The Connection (or other object) is open (active).

Errors COLLECTION AND Error OBJECTS

Figure 27.13 illustrates the relationship between top-level ADO components and their collections. The dependent Errors collection is a property of the Connection object and, if errors are encountered with any operation on the connection, contains one or more Error objects. The Errors collection has one property, Count, which you test to determine whether an error has occurred after executing a method call on Connection objects as well as on Command and Recordset objects.

The Errors collection has two methods, Clear and Item. The Clear method deletes all current Error objects in the collection, resetting the value of Count to 0. The Item method, which is the default method of the Errors and other collections, returns an *object reference (pointer)* to an Error object. The syntax for explicit and default use of the Item method is

```
Set errName = cnnName.Errors.Index({strName¦intIndex})
Set errName = cnnName.Errors({strName¦intIndex})
```

The Error object has the seven read-only properties listed in Table 27.5. Error objects have no methods or events. The InfoMessage event of the Connection object, described in the "Connection Events" section later in this chapter, fires when an Error object is added to the Errors collection and supplies a pointer to the newly added Error object.

TABLE 27.5   PROPERTY NAMES AND DESCRIPTIONS OF THE Error OBJECT

Property Name	Description
Description	A **String** value containing a brief text description of the error.
HelpContext	A **Long** value specifying the error's context ID in a Windows Help file.
HelpFile	A **String** value specifying the full path to and name of the Windows Help file, usually for the data provider.
NativeError	A **Long** value specifying a provider-specific error code.
Number	A **Long** value specifying the index of the Error in the Errors collection.

PART

VII

CH

27

continues

TABLE 27.5 CONTINUED

Property Name	Description
Source	A **String** value containing the name of the object that generated the error, ADODB.*ObjectName* for ADO errors.
SQLState	A **String** value (SQLSTATE) containing a five-letter code specified by the ANSI/ISO SQL-92 standard, consisting of two characters specifying Condition, followed by three characters for Subcondition.

Figure 27.13
The *Connection, Command,* and *Recordset* objects with their associated collections.

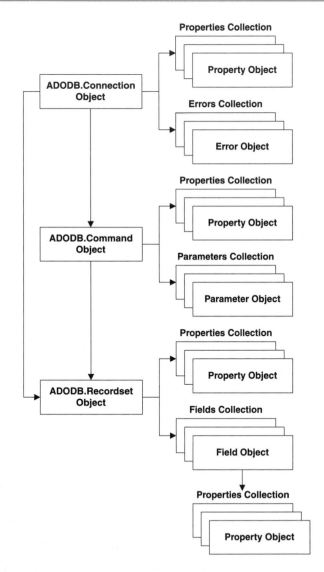

→ For the basics of error handling in VBA, **see** "Handling Run-time Errors," **p. 1016**.

Tip #250 from

Unfortunately, not all RDBMS vendors implement SQLSTATE in the same way. If you test the SQLState property value, make sure to follow the vendor-specific specifications for Condition and Subcondition values.

Listing 27.2 is an example of code to open a Connection (cnnNwind) and a Recordset (rstCusts) with conventional error handling; rstCusts supplies the Recordset property of the form. The "Non-existent" table name generates a "Syntax error in FROM clause" error in the Immediate window. The **Set** *ObjectName* = **Nothing** statements in the error handler recover the memory consumed by the objects.

LISTING 27.2   VBA CODE TO WRITE Error PROPERTIES TO THE IMMEDIATE WINDOW

```
Private Sub Form_Load
    Dim cnnNwind As New ADODB.Connection
    Dim rstCusts As New ADODB.Recordset

    On Error GoTo CatchErrors
    cnnNwind.Provider = "Microsoft.Jet.OLEDB.4.0"
    cnnNwind.Open CurrentProject.Path & "\Northwind.mdb", "Admin"
    With rstCusts
        Set .ActiveConnection = cnnNwind
        .CursorType = adOpenKeyset
        .LockType = adLockBatchOptimistic
        .Open "SELECT * FROM Non-existent"
    End With
    Set Me.Recordset = rstCusts
    Exit Sub

CatchErrors:
    Dim colErrors As Errors
    Dim errNwind As Error
    Set colErrors = cnnNwind.Errors
    For Each errNwind In colErrors
        Debug.Print "Description:  " & errNwind.Description
        Debug.Print "Native Error: " & errNwind.NativeError; ""
        Debug.Print "SQL State:    " & errNwind.SQLState
        Debug.Print vbCrLf
    Next errNwind
    Set colErrors = Nothing
    Set errNwind = Nothing
    Set rstCusts = Nothing
    Set cnnNwind = Nothing
    Exit Sub
End Sub
```

PART

VII

CH

27

Connection METHODS

Table 27.6 lists the methods of the ADODB.Connection object. Only the Execute, Open, and OpenSchema methods accept argument values. The OpenSchema method is of interest primarily for creating database diagrams, data transformation for data warehouses and marts, and online analytical processing (OLAP) applications.

TABLE 27.6   METHODS OF THE ADODB.Connection OBJECT

Method	Description
BeginTrans	Initiates a transaction; must be followed by CommitTrans and/or RollbackTrans.
Close	Closes the connection.
CommitTrans	Commits a transaction, making changes to the data source permanent. (Requires a prior call to the BeginTrans method.)
Execute	Returns a forward-only Recordset object from a SELECT SQL statement. Also used to execute statements that don't return Recordsets, such as INSERT, UPDATE, and DELETE queries or DDL statements.
Open	Opens a connection based on a connection string.
OpenSchema	Returns a Recordset object that provides information on the structure of the *data source*, called *metadata*.
RollbackTrans	Cancels a transaction, reversing any temporary changes made to the data source. (Requires a prior call to the BeginTrans method.)

The syntax of the Connection.Execute method to return a reference to a forward-only ADODB.Recordset object is

```
Set rstName = cnnName.Execute (strCommand, [lngRowsAffected[, lngOptions]])
```

Alternatively, you can use named arguments for all ADO methods. Named arguments, however, require considerably more typing than conventional comma-separated argument syntax. The named argument equivalent of the preceding **Set** statement is

```
Set rstName = cnnName.Execute (Command:=strCommand, _
    RowsAffected:=lngRowsAffected, Options:=lngOptions)
```

> **Note**
>
> This book prefixes argument names with a two- or three-character prefix denoting their data type, in accordance with "The Leszynski Naming Conventions for Microsoft Visual Basic" by Stan Leszynski. Use the argument name, without the lowercase prefix, to identify the named argument. You can purchase a copy of "LNC for Access," which includes Access-specific conventions, in white paper or Windows help file format at http://www.kwery.com/.

If strCommand doesn't return a Recordset, the syntax is

cnnName.Execute strCommand, [lngRowsAffected[, lngOptions]]

The value of strCommand can be an SQL statement, a table name, the name of a stored procedure, or an arbitrary text string acceptable to the data provider.

Tip #251 from

For best performance, specify a value for the lngOptions argument (see Table 27.7) so the provider doesn't need to interpret the statement to determine its type. The optional lngRowsAffected argument returns the number of rows affected by an INSERT, UPDATE, or DELETE query; these types of queries return a closed Recordset object. A SELECT query returns 0 to lngRowsAffected and an open, forward-only Recordset with 0 or more rows.

Note

Forward-only Recordset objects, created by what Microsoft calls a *firehose cursor*, provide the best performance and minimum network traffic in a client/server environment. However, forward-only Recordsets are limited to manipulation by VBA code. If you set the Recordset property of an ADO Data control to a forward-only Recordset, controls bound to the ADO Data control won't display field values.

TABLE 27.7   CONSTANT ENUMERATION FOR THE lngOptions ARGUMENT OF THE Execute METHOD

CommandTypeEnum	Description
adCmdUnknown	The type of command isn't specified (default). The data provider determines the syntax of the command.
adCmdFile	The command is the name of a file in a format appropriate to the object type.
adCmdStoredProc	The command is the name of a stored procedure.
adCmdTable	The command is a table name, generating an internal SELECT * FROM TableName query.
adCmdTableDirect	The command is a table name, retrieving rows directly from the table
adCmdText	The command is an SQL statement.

PART

VII

CH

27

The syntax of the Open method is

cnnName.Open [strConnect[, strUID[, strPwd]]]

Alternatively, you can assign the connection string values to the Connection object's Provider and ConnectionString properties. The following example is for a connection to Northwind.mdb:

With cnnNwind

```
        .Provider = "Microsoft.Jet.OLEDB.4.0"
        .ConnectionString = CurrentProject.Path & "\Northwind.mdb"
        .Open
End With
```

In this case, all the information required to open a connection to Northwind.mdb is provided as property values, so the Open method needs no argument values.

If you're creating a data dictionary or designing a generic query processor, the OpenSchema method is likely to be of interest to you. Otherwise, you might wish to skip the details of the OpenSchema method, which is included here for completeness. Schema information is called *metadata*, data that describes the structure of data.

Tip #252 from	ADOX 2.1 defines a Catalog object for Jet 4.0 databases that's more useful for Jet databases than the generic OpenSchema method, which is intended primarily for use with client/server RDBMs. The Catalog object includes Groups, Users, Tables, Views, and Procedures collections.

Connection EVENTS

Events are useful for trapping errors, eliminating the need to poll the values of properties, such as State, and performing asynchronous database operations. Microsoft modeled ADO's Connection events on a combination of the event models for RDO 2.0's rdoEngine, rdoEnvironment, and rdoConnection objects. (The ADODB.Connection object combines the functionality of these three RDO objects.) To expose the ADODB.Connection events to your application, you must use the **WithEvents** reserved word (without **New**) to declare the ADODB.Connection object in the General Declarations section of a class or form module and then use a **Set** statement with **New** to create an instance of the object, as shown in following example:

```
Private WithEvents cnnName As ADODB.Connection

Private Sub Form_Load
    Set cnnName = New ADODB.Connection
    ...
    Code using the Connection object
    ...
    cnnName.Close
End Sub
```

The preceding syntax is required for most Automation objects that *source* (expose) events. Event-handling subprocedures for Automation events often are called *event sinks*. Source and sink terminology derives from the early days of transistors; the source (emitter) supplies electrons and the sink (collector) accumulates electrons.

Table 27.8 lists the events that appear in the Procedures list of the code-editing window for the cnnName Connection object and gives a description of when the events fire.

TABLE 27.8   EVENTS FIRED BY THE ADODB.Connection OBJECT

Event Name	When Fired
BeginTransComplete	After the BeginTrans method executes
CommitTransComplete	After the CommitTrans method executes
ConnectComplete	After a Connection to the data source succeeds
Disconnect	After a Connection is closed
ExecuteComplete	On completion of the Connection.Execute or Command.Execute method call
InfoMessage	When an Error object is added to the ADODB.Connection.Errors collection
RollbackTransComplete	After the RollbackTrans method executes
WillConnect	On calling the Connection.Open method
WillExecute	On calling the Connection.Execute or Command.Execute method

Tip #253 from

Take full advantage of ADO events in your VBA data-handling code. Relatively few developers currently use event-handling code in ordinary database front ends. DAO, which offers no event model, dominates today's spectrum of Windows data access techniques. ADO's event model initially will be of primary interest to developers migrating from RDO to ADO. Developers of data warehousing and OLAP applications, which often involve very long-running queries, are most likely to use events in conjunction with asynchronous query operations.

USING THE ADODB.Command OBJECT

The Command object is analogous to RDO's rdoQuery object. The primary purpose of the Command object is to execute parameterized stored procedures, either in the form of the default *temporary prepared statements* or *persistent, precompiled SQL statements*. MSDE and SQL Server create temporary prepared statements exist only for the lifetime of the current client connection. Precompiled SQL statements are procedures stored in the database file; their more common name is *stored procedure*. When creating Recordsets from SQL statements, the more efficient approach is to bypass the Command object and use the Recordset.Open method.

Command PROPERTIES

The Command object has relatively few properties, many of which duplicate those of the Connection object. Table 27.9 lists the names and descriptions of the Command object's properties. Like the Connection object, the Command object has its own provider-specific Properties collection, described in the "Properties Collection of the Command Object" section later in this chapter.

TABLE 27.9   PROPERTIES OF THE Command OBJECT

Property Name	Description
ActiveConnection	A pointer to the Connection object associated with the Command. Use **Set** cmmName.ActiveConnection = cnnName for an existing open Connection. Alternatively, you can use a valid connection string to create a new connection without associating a named Connection object. The default value is **Null**.
CommandText	A **String** read/write value that specifies an SQL statement, table name, stored procedure name, or an arbitrary string acceptable to the provider for the ActiveConnection. The value of the CommandType property determines the format of the CommandText value. The default value is an empty string, " ".
CommandTimeout	A **Long** read/write value that determines the time in seconds before terminating a Command.Execute call. This value overrides the Connection.CommandTimeout setting. The default value is **30** seconds.
CommandType	A **Long** read/write value that specifies how the data provider inter-prets the value of the CommandText property. (CommandType is the equivalent of the optional lngCommandType argument of the Connection.Execute method, described earlier in the chapter (refer to Table 27.7). The default value is adCmdUnknown.
Name	A **String** read/write value specifying the name of the command, such as cmmNwind.
Prepared	A **Boolean** read/write value that determines whether the data source compiles the CommandText SQL statement as a *prepared statement* (a *temporary stored procedure*). The prepared statement exists only for the lifetime of the Command's ActiveConnection. Many client/server RDBMSs, including Microsoft SQL Server, support prepared statements. If the data source doesn't support prepared statements, setting Prepared to **True** results in a trappable error.
State	A **Long** read/write value specifying the status of the Command. Refer to Table 27.4 for ObjectStateEnum constant values.

Tip #254 from

R J

Always set the CommandType property to the appropriate adCmd... constant value. If you accept the default adCmdUnknown value, the data provider must test the value of CommandText to determine if it is the name of a stored procedure, a table, or an SQL statement before executing the query. If the targeted database contains a large number of objects, testing the CommandText value for each Command object you execute can signifi-cantly reduce performance.

Tip #255 from	The initial execution of a prepared statement often is slower than for a conventional SQL query because some data sources must compile, rather than interpret, the statement. Thus you should limit use of prepared statements to parameterized queries in which the query is executed multiple times with differing parameter values.

Parameters COLLECTION

To supply and accept parameter values, the Command object uses the Parameters collection, which is analogous to the rdoParameters collection of the rdoQuery object and similar to the DAO and ODBCDirect Parameters collections. ADODB.Parameters is independent of its parent, ADODB.Command, but you must associate the Parameters collection with a Command object before defining or using Parameter objects.

The Parameters collection has a single read-only **Long** property, Count, and the methods listed in Table 27.10. The syntax for the Count property is

lng*NumParms* = cmm*Name*.Parameters.Count

TABLE 27.10   METHOD NAMES, DESCRIPTIONS, AND CALLING SYNTAX FOR THE Parameters COLLECTION

Method Name	Description and VBA Calling Syntax
Append	Appends a Parameter object created by the cmm*Name*.CreateParameter method, described in the "Command Methods" section, to the collection. The calling syntax is Parameters.Append prm*Name*.
Delete	Deletes a Parameter object from the collection. The calling syntax is cmm*Name*.Parameters.Delete {str*Name*¦int*Index*}, where str*Name* is the name of the Parameter or int*Index* is the 0-based ordinal position (index) of the Parameter in the collection.
Item	Returns an object reference to a Parameter. The calling syntax is **Set** prm*Name* = cmm*Name*.Parameters.Index ({str*Name*¦int*Index*}).
Refresh	Retrieves the properties of the current set of parameters for the stored procedure or query specified as the value of the CommandText property. The calling syntax is cmm*Name*.Parameters.Refresh. If you don't specify your own members of the Parameters collection with the CreateParameter method, accessing any member of the Parameters collection automatically calls the Refresh method. If you apply the Refresh method to a data source that doesn't support stored procedures, prepared statements, or parameterized queries, the Parameters collection is empty (cmm*Name*.Parameters.Count = 0).

Tip #256 from	You gain a performance improvement for the initial execution of your stored procedure or query if you use the cmm*Name*.CreateParameter method to predefine the required Parameter objects. The Refresh method makes a round-trip to the server to retrieve the properties of each Parameter.

Parameter OBJECT

One Parameter object must exist in the Parameters collection for each parameter of the stored procedure, prepared statement, or parameterized query. Table 27.11 lists the property names and descriptions of the Parameter object. The syntax for getting and setting Parameter property values is

```
typPropValue = cmmName.Parameters({strName¦lngIndex}).PropertyName
cmmName.Parameters({strName¦lngIndex}).PropertyName = typPropValue
```

You don't need to use the Index property of the Parameters collection; Index is the default property of Parameters.

TABLE 27.11   PROPERTY NAMES AND DESCRIPTIONS FOR Parameter OBJECTS

Property Name	Description
Attributes	A **Long** read/write value representing the sum of the adParam... constants listed in Table 27.12.
Direction	A **Long** read/write value representing one of the adParam... constants listed in Table 27.13.
Name	A **String** read/write value containing the name of the Parameter object, such as prm*StartDate*. The name of the Parameter object need not (and usually does not) correspond to the name of the corresponding parameter variable of the stored procedure. After the Parameter is appended to the Parameters collection, the Name property value is read-only.
NumericScale	A **Byte** read/write value specifying the number of decimal places for numeric values.
Precision	A **Byte** read/write value specifying the total number of digits (including decimal digits) for numeric values.
Size	A **Long** read/write value specifying the maximum length of variable-length data types supplied as the Value property. You must set the Size property value before setting the Value property to variable-length data.
Type	A **Long** read/write value representing a valid OLE DB 2.0+ data type, the most common of which are listed in Table 27.14.
Value	The value of the parameter having a data type corresponding to the value of the Type property.

TABLE 27.12   CONSTANT VALUES FOR THE Attributes PROPERTY OF THE Parameter OBJECT

ParameterAttributesEnum	Description
adParamSigned	The Parameter accepts signed values (default).
adParamNullable	The Parameter accepts **Null** values.
adParamLong	The Parameter accepts long binary data.

TABLE 27.13   CONSTANT VALUES FOR THE Direction PROPERTY OF THE Parameter OBJECT

ParameterDirectionEnum	Description
adParamInput	Specifies an input parameter (default)
adParamOutput	Specifies an output parameter
adParamInputOutput	Specifies an input/output parameter
adParamReturnValue	Specifies the return value of a stored procedure

The Type property has the largest collection of constants of any ADO enumeration; you can review the entire list of data types by selecting the DataTypeEnum class in Object Browser. Most of the data types aren't available to VBA programmers, so Table 27.14 shows only the most commonly used DataTypeEnum constants. In most cases, you only need to choose among adChar (for **String** values), adInteger (for **Long** values), and adCurrency (for **Currency** values). You use the adDate data type to pass Date/Time parameter values to Jet databases, but not to most stored procedures. Stored procedures generally accept datetime parameter values as the adChar data type, with a format, such as mm/dd/yyyy, acceptable to the RDBMS.

TABLE 27.14   CONSTANT VALUES FOR THE Type PROPERTY OF THE Parameter AND Field OBJECTS

DataTypeEnum	Description of Data Type
adBinary	Binary value.
adBoolean	**Boolean** value.
adChar	**String** value.
adCurrency	**Currency** values are fixed-point numbers with four decimal digits stored in an 8-byte, signed integer, which is scaled (divided) by 10,000.
adDate	**Date** values are stored as a **Double** value, the integer part being the number of days since December 30, 1899, and the decimal part the fraction of a day.

PART

VII

CH

27

continues

TABLE 27.14   CONTINUED

DataTypeEnum	Description of Data Type
adDecimal	Exact numeric value with a specified precision and scale.
adDouble	**Double**-precision floating-point value.
adInteger	4-byte signed **Long** integer.
adLongVarBinary	Long binary value (Parameter objects only).
adLongVarChar	**String** value greater than 225 characters (Parameter objects only).
adNumeric	Exact numeric value with a specified precision and scale.
adSingle	**Single**-precision floating-point value.
adSmallInt	2-byte signed **Integer.**
adTinyInt	1-byte signed integer.
adVarBinary	Binary value (Parameter objects only).
adVarChar	**String** value (Parameter objects only).

Note

The values for the Type property in the preceding table are valid for the Type property of the Field object, discussed later in the chapter, except for those data types in which "Parameter objects only" appears in the Description of Data Type column. The members of DataTypeEnum are designed to accommodate the widest possible range of desktop and client/server RDBMSs, but the ad constant names are closely related to those for the field data types of Microsoft SQL Server 7.0 and MSDE, which support Unicode strings.

The Parameter object has a single method, AppendChunk, which you use to append long text (adLongText) or long binary (adLongVarChar) **Variant** data as a parameter value. The syntax of the AppendChunk method call is

```
cmmName.Parameters({strName¦lngIndex}) = varChunk
```

The adParamLong flag of the Parameter.Attributes property must be set in order to apply the AppendChunk method. If you call AppendChunk more than once on a single Parameter, the second and later calls append the current value of varChunk to the parameter value.

Command METHODS

Command objects have only two methods, CreateParameter and Execute. You must declare a ADODB.Parameter object, prmName, prior to executing CreateParameter. The syntax of the CreateParameter method call is

```
Set prmName = cmmName.CreateParameter [strName[, lngType[, _
   lngDirection[, lngSize[, varValue]]]]]
cmmName.Parameters.Append prmName
```

The arguments of CreateParameter are optional only if you subsequently set the required Parameter property values before executing the Command. For example, if you supply only the strName argument, you must set the remaining properties, as in the following example:

```
Set prmName = cmmName.CreateParameter strName
cmmName.Parameters.Append prmName
prmName.Type = adChar
prmName.Direction = adParamInput
prmName.Size = Len(varValue)
prmName.Value = varValue
```

The syntax of the Command.Execute method is similar to that for the Connection.Execute method except for the argument list. The following syntax is for Command objects that return Recordsets:

```
Set rstName = cmmName.Execute ([lngRowsAffected[, _
    avarParameters[, lngOptions]]])
```

For Commands that don't return rows, use this form:

```
cmmName.Execute [lngRowsAffected[, avarParameters[, lngOptions]]]
```

All the arguments of the Execute method are optional if you set the required Command property values before applying the Execute method. Listing 27.3 gives an example of the use of the Command.Execute method without arguments.

Tip #257 from

Presetting all property values of the Command object, rather than supplying argument values to the Execute method, makes your VBA code easier for others to comprehend.

Like the Connection.Execute method, the returned value of lngRowsAffected is 0 for SELECT and DDL queries and the number of rows modified by execution of INSERT, UPDATE, and DELETE queries. The avarParameters argument is an optional **Variant** array of parameter values. Using the Parameters collection is a better practice than using the avarParameters argument because output parameters don't return correct values to the array. For lngOptions constant values, refer to Table 27.7.

CODE TO PASS PARAMETER VALUES TO A STORED PROCEDURE

Most stored procedures that return Recordsets require input parameters to supply values to WHERE clause criteria to limit the number of rows returned. The code of Listing 27.3 executes a simple SQL Server 7.0/MSDE stored procedure with a Command object. The Sales by Year stored procedure of the NorthwindCS project has two datetime input parameters, @Beginning_Date and @Ending_Date, the values for which are supplied by strBegDate and strEndDate, respectively. The stored procedure, whose SQL statement follows, returns the ShippedDate and OrderID columns of the Orders table, the Subtotal column of the Order Subtotals view, and a calculated Year value. Rows return for values of the OrderDate field between the values of strBegDate and strEndDate.

```
ALTER PROCEDURE "Sales by Year"
  @Beginning_Date datetime,
```

```
@Ending_Date datetime
AS SELECT Orders.ShippedDate, Orders.OrderID,
    "Order Subtotals".Subtotal,
    DATENAME(yy,ShippedDate) AS Year
FROM Orders INNER JOIN "Order Subtotals"
    ON Orders.OrderID = "Order Subtotals".OrderID
WHERE Orders.ShippedDate Between @Beginning_Date And @Ending_Date
```

LISTING 27.3 CODE USING A Command OBJECT TO EXECUTE A PARAMETERIZED STORED PROCEDURE

```
Option Explicit
Option Compare Database

Private cnnOrders As New ADODB.Connection
Private cmmOrders As New ADODB.Command
Private prmBegDate As New ADODB.Parameter
Private prmEndDate As New ADODB.Parameter
Private rstOrders As New ADODB.Recordset

Private Sub Form_Load()
    Dim strBegDate As String
    Dim strEndDate As String
    Dim strFile As String

    strBegDate = "1/1/1997"
    strEndDate = "12/31/1997"
    strFile = CurrentProject.Path & "Orders.rst"

    'Specify the OLE DB provider and open the connection
    With cnnOrders
        .Provider = "SQLOLEDB.1"
        .Open "Data Source=(local);UID=sa;PWD=;Database=NorthwindCS"
    End With

    With cmmOrders
        'Create and append the BeginningDate parameter
        Set prmBegDate = .CreateParameter("BegDate", adChar, _
            adParamInput, Len(strBegDate), strBegDate)
        .Parameters.Append prmBegDate
        'Create and append the endingDate parameter
        Set prmEndDate = .CreateParameter("EndDate", adChar, _
            adParamInput, Len(strEndDate), strEndDate)
        .Parameters.Append prmEndDate

        Set .ActiveConnection = cnnOrders
        'Specify a stored procedure
        .CommandType = adCmdStoredProc
        'Brackets must surround stored procedure names with spaces
        .CommandText = "[Sales By Year]"
        'Receive the Recordset
        Set rstOrders = .Execute   'returns a "firehose" Recordset
    End With

    With rstOrders
        'Save (persist) the forward-only Recordset to a file
```

```
    On Error Resume Next
    'Delete the file, if it exists
    Kill strFile
    On Error GoTo 0
    .Save strFile
    .Close
    .Open strFile, "Provider=MSpersist", , , adCmdFile
End With

'Assign rstOrders to the Recordset of the form
Set Me.Recordset = rstOrders

Me.txtShippedDate.ControlSource = "ShippedDate"
Me.txtOrderID.ControlSource = "OrderID"
Me.txtSubtotal.ControlSource = "Subtotal"
Me.txtYear.ControlSource = "Year"
End Sub
```

Caution

When used in ADO code, you *must* enclose names of stored procedures and views having spaces with square brackets. Including spaces in database object names, especially in client/server environments, isn't a recommended practice. Microsoft developers insist on adding spaces in names of views and stored procedures, perhaps because SQL Server 7.0/MSDE supports this dubious feature. Use underscores to make object names more readable if necessary.

Note

NEW
2000

The code of Listing 27.3 uses a new ADO 2+ feature, persisted (saved) Recordsets. Stored procedures return forward-only ("firehose") Recordsets, which you can't assign to the Recordset property of a form. To create a Recordset with a cursor acceptable to Access forms, you must persist the Recordset as a file and then close and reopen the Recordset with the MSPersist OLE DB provider as the ActiveConnection property value. The "Recordset Methods" section, later in the chapter, provides the complete syntax for the Save and Open methods of the Recordset object.

Figure 27.14 shows the result of executing the code of Listing 27.3. The frmParams form that contains the code is included in the ADO_Test.mdb file described earlier in the chapter.

Ship Date	Order ID	Subtotal	Year
1/16/1997	10360	$1,313.82	1997
1/1/1997	10392	$1,440.00	1997
1/3/1997	10393	$2,556.95	1997
1/3/1997	10394	$442.00	1997
1/3/1997	10395	$2,122.92	1997
1/6/1997	10396	$1,903.80	1997
1/2/1997	10397	$716.72	1997
1/9/1997	10398	$2,505.60	1997
1/8/1997	10399	$1,765.60	1997
1/16/1997	10400	$3,063.00	1997
1/10/1998	10401	$3,868.60	1997
1/10/1997	10402	$2,713.50	1997
1/9/1997	10403	$855.02	1997
1/8/1997	10404	$1,591.25	1997
1/22/1997	10405	$400.00	1997

Record: I◄ ◄ 1 ► ►I ►* of 398

Figure 27.14
The Recordset created by executing the Sales by Year parameterized stored procedure.

UNDERSTANDING THE ADODB.Recordset OBJECT

Creating and viewing Recordsets is the ultimate objective of most Access database front ends. Opening an independent ADODB.Recordset object offers a myriad of cursor, locking, and other options. You must explicitly open a Recordset with a scrollable cursor if you want to use code to create the Recordset for assignment to the Form.Recordset property. Unlike Jet and ODBCDirect Recordsets, ADODB.Recordset objects expose a number of events that are especially useful for validating Recordset updates. Microsoft modeled ADODB.Recordset events on the event repertoire of the RDO 2.0 rdoResultset object.

Recordset PROPERTIES

Microsoft attempted to make ADODB.Recordset objects backward compatible with DAO.Recordset objects to minimize the amount of code you must change to migrate existing applications from DAO ADO. Unfortunately, the attempt at backward compatibility for code-intensive database applications didn't fully succeed. You must make substantial changes in DAO code to accommodate ADO's updated Recordset object. Thus most Access developers probably will choose ADO for new Access front-end applications and stick with DAO for existing projects.

Table 27.15 gives the names and descriptions of the standard property set of ADODB.Recordset objects. ADODB.Recordset objects have substantially fewer properties than DAO.Recordset objects have, and several added ADODB.Recordset objects don't have corresponding DAO.Recordset properties. The standard property set for ADODB.Recordset objects are those properties supported by the most common OLE DB data providers for relational databases.

TABLE 27.15   PROPERTY NAMES AND DESCRIPTIONS FOR ADODB.Recordset OBJECTS

Property Name	Description
AbsolutePage	A **Long** read/write value that sets or returns the number of the page in which the current record is located or one of the constant values of PositionEnum (see Table 27.16). You must set the PageSize property value before getting or setting the value of AbsolutePage. AbsolutePage is 1 based; if the current record is in the first page, AbsolutePage returns 1. Setting the value of AbsolutePage causes the current record to be set to the first record of the specified page.
AbsolutePosition	A **Long** read/write value (1 based) that sets or returns the position of the current record. The maximum value of AbsolutePosition is the value of the RecordCount property.
ActiveCommand	A **String** read/write value specifying the name of a previously opened Command object with which the Recordset is associated.
ActiveConnection	A **pointer** to a previously opened Connection object with which the Recordset is associated or a fully qualified ConnectionString value.

Property Name	Description
BOF	A **Boolean** read-only value that, when **True**, indicates that the record pointer is positioned before the first row of the Recordset and there is no current record.
Bookmark	A **Variant** read/write value that returns a reference to a specific record or uses a Bookmark value to set the record pointer to a specific record.
CacheSize	A **Long** read/write value that specifies the number of records stored in local (cache) memory. The minimum (default) value is 1. Increasing the value of CacheSize minimizes round trips to the server to obtain additional rows when scrolling through Recordsets.
CursorLocation	A **Long** read/write value that specifies the location of a scrollable cursor, subject to the availability of the specified CursorType on the client or server (see Table 27.17). The default is to use a cursor provided by the OLE DB data source.
CursorType	A **Long** read/write value that specifies the type of Recordset cursor (see Table 27.18). The default is a forward-only cursor.
DataMember	Returns a pointer to an associated Command object.
DataSource	Returns a pointer to an associated Connection object.
EditMode	A **Long** read-only value that returns the status of editing of the Recordset (see Table 27.19).
EOF	A **Boolean** read-only value that, when **True**, indicates that the record pointer is beyond the last row of the Recordset and there is no current record.
Filter	A **Variant** read/write value that can be a criteria string (a valid SQL WHERE clause without the WHERE reserved word), an array of Bookmark values specifying a particular set of records, or a constant value from FilterGroupEnum (see Table 27.20).
Index	A read/write **String** value that sets or returns the name of an existing index on the base table of the Recordset. The Recordset must be closed to set the Index value to the name of an index. The Index property is used primarily in conjunction with the Recordset.Seek method.
LockType	A **Long** read/write value that specifies the record-locking method employed when opening the Recordset (see Table 2.21). The default is read-only, corresponding to the read-only characteristic of a forward-only cursors.
MarshalOptions	A **Long** read/write value that specifies which set of records is returned to the server after client-side modification. The MarshallOptions property applies only to the lightweight ADOR.Recordset object, a member of RDS.
MaxRecords	A **Long** read/write value that specifies the maximum number of records to be returned by a SELECT query or stored procedure. The default value is 0, all records.

continues

TABLE 27.15   CONTINUED

Property Name	Description
PageCount	A **Long** read-only value that returns the number of pages in a Recordset. You must set the PageSize value to cause PageCount to return a meaningful value. If the Recordset doesn't support the PageCount property, the value is -1.
PageSize	A **Long** read/write value that sets or returns the number of records in a logical page. You use logical pages to break large Recordsets into easily manageable groups. PageSize isn't related to the size of table pages used for locking in Jet (2KB) or SQL Server (2KB in version 6.5 and earlier, 8KB in version 7.0) databases.
PersistFormat	A **Long** read/write value the sets or returns the format of Recordset files created by calling the Save method. The two constant values of PersistFormatEnum are adPersistADTG (the default format, Advanced Data TableGram or ADTG) and adPersistXML, which saves the Recordset as almost-readable XML.
RecordCount	A **Long** read-only value that returns the number of records in Recordsets with scrollable cursors if the Recordset supports approximate positioning or Bookmarks. (See the Recordset.Supports method later in this chapter.) If not, you must apply the MoveLast method to obtain an accurate RecordCount value, which retrieves and counts all records. If a forward-only Recordset has one or more records, RecordCount returns -1 (**True**). An empty Recordset of any type returns 0 (**False**).
Sort	A **String** read/write value, consisting of an SQL ORDER BY clause without the ORDER BY reserved words, that specifies the sort order of the Recordset.
Source	A **String** read/write value that may be an SQL statement, a table name, a stored procedure name, or the name of an associated Command object. If you supply the name of a Command object, the Source property returns the value of the Command.CommandText text property. Use the lng*Options* argument of the Open method to specify the type of the value supplied to the Source property.
State	A **Long** read/write value representing one of the constant values of ObjectStateEnum (refer to Table 27.4).
Status	A **Long** read-only value that indicates the status of batch operations or other multiple-record (bulk) operations on the Recordset (see Table 27.22).

The most obvious omission in the preceding table is the DAO.Recordset NoMatch property value used to test whether applying one of the DAO.Recordset.Find... methods or the DAO.Recordset.Seek method succeeds. The new ADODB.Recordset.Find method, listed in the "Recordset Methods" section later in this chapter, substitutes for DAO's FindFirst, FindNext, FindPrevious, and FindLast methods. The Find method uses the EOF property value for testing the existence of one or more records matching the Find criteria.

Another omission in the ADODB.Recordset object's preceding property list is the PercentPosition property. The workaround, however, is easy:

rst*Name*.AbsolutePostion = **Int**(int*PercentPosition* * rst*Name*.RecordCount / 100)

Tables 27.16 through 27.22 enumerate the valid constant values for the AbsolutePage, CursorLocation, CursorType, EditMode, Filter, LockType, and Status properties.

TABLE 27.16 CONSTANT VALUES FOR THE AbsolutePage PROPERTY

PositionEnum	Description
adPosUnknown	The data provider doesn't support pages, the Recordset is empty, or the data provider can't determine the page number.
adPosBOF	The record pointer is positioned at the beginning of the file. (The BOF property is **True**.)
adPosEOF	The record pointer is positioned at the end of the file. (The EOF property is **True**.)

TABLE 27.17 CONSTANT VALUES FOR THE CursorLocation PROPERTY

CursorLocationEnum	Description
adUseClient	Use cursor(s) provided by a cursor library located on the client. The ADOR.Recordset requires a client-side cursor.
adUseServer	Use cursor(s) supplied by the data source, usually (but not necessarily) located on a server (default value).

TABLE 27.18 CONSTANT VALUES FOR THE CursorType PROPERTY

CursorTypeEnum	Description
adOpenForwardOnly	Provides only unidirectional cursor movement and a read-only Recordset (default value).
adOpenDynamic	Provides a scrollable cursor that displays all changes, including new records, that other users make to the Recordset.
adOpenKeyset	Provides a scrollable cursor that hides only records added by other users; similar to a DAO.Recordset of the Dynaset type.
adOpenStatic	Provides a scrollable cursor over a static copy of the Recordset. Similar to a DAO.Recordset of the Snapshot type, but updatable.

PART

VII

CH

27

TABLE 27.19   CONSTANT VALUES FOR THE EditMode PROPERTY

EditModeEnum	Description
adEditNone	No editing operation is in progress (default value).
adEditAdd	A tentative append record has been added, but not saved to the database table(s).
adEditInProgress	Data in the current record has been modified, but not saved to the database table(s).

TABLE 27.20   CONSTANT VALUES FOR THE Filter PROPERTY

FilterGroupEnum	Description
adFilterNone	Removes an existing filter and exposes all records of the Recordset (equivalent to setting the Filter property to an empty string, the default value).
adFilterAffectedRecords	View only records affected by the last execution of the CancelBatch, Delete, Resync, or UpdateBatch method.
adFilterFetchedRecords	View only records in the current cache. The number of records is set by the CacheSize property.
adFilterPendingRecords	View only records that have been modified but not yet processed by the data source (for Batch Update mode only).

TABLE 27.21   CONSTANT VALUES FOR THE LockType PROPERTY

LockTypeEnum	Description
adLockReadOnly	Specifies read-only access (default value).
adLockBatchOptimistic	Use Batch Update mode instead of the default Immediate Update mode.
adLockOptimistic	Use *optimistic locking* (lock the record or page only during the update process).
adLockPessimistic	Use *pessimistic locking* (lock the record or page during editing and the updated process).

TABLE 27.22   CONSTANT VALUES FOR THE Status PROPERTY (APPLIES TO BATCH OR BULK Recordset OPERATIONS ONLY)

RecordStatusEnum	Description of Record Status
adRecOK	Updated successfully.
adRecNew	Added successfully.
adRecModified	Modified successfully.

RecordStatusEnum	Description of Record Status
adRecDeleted	Deleted successfully.
adRecUnmodified	Not modified.
adRecInvalid	Not saved; the Bookmark property is invalid.
adRecMultipleChanges	Not saved; saving would affect other records.
adRecPendingChanges	Not saved; the record refers to a pending insert operation).
adRecCanceled	Not saved; the operation was canceled.
adRecCantRelease	Not saved; existing record locks prevented saving.
adRecConcurrencyViolation	Not saved; an optimistic concurrency locking problem occurred.
adRecIntegrityViolation	Not saved; the operation would violate integrity constraints.
adRecMaxChangesExceeded	Not saved; an excessive number of pending changes exist.
adRecObjectOpen	Not saved; a conflict with an open storage object occurred.
adRecOutOfMemory	Not saved; the machine is out of memory.
adRecPermissionDenied	Not saved; the user doesn't have required permissions.
adRecSchemaViolation	Not saved; the record structure doesn't match the database schema.
adRecDBDeleted	Not saved or deleted; the record was previously deleted.

Fields COLLECTION AND Field OBJECTS

Like DAO's Fields collection, ADO's dependent Fields collection is a property of the Recordset object, making the columns of the Recordset accessible to VBA code and bound controls. Like the Parameters collection described earlier in the chapter, the Fields collection has one property, Count, but only two methods, Item and Refresh. You can't append new Field objects to the Fields collection, unless you're creating a persisted Recordset from scratch or you use ADOX's ALTER TABLE DDL command to add a new field.

All but one (Value) of the property values of Field objects are read-only, because the values of the Field properties are derived from the database schema. The Value property is read-only in forward-only Recordsets and Recordsets opened with read-only locking. Table 27.23 gives the names and descriptions of the properties of the Field object.

PART

VII

Cн

27

TABLE 27.23   PROPERTY NAMES AND DESCRIPTIONS OF THE Field OBJECT

ActualSize	A **Long** read-only value representing the length of the Field's value by character count.
Attributes	A **Long** read-only value that represents the sum of the constants (flags) included in FieldAttributeEnum (see Table 27.24).

continues

TABLE 27.23 CONTINUED

DefinedSize	A **Long** read-only value specifying the maximum length of the Field's value by character count. For example, a Jet text or SQL Server varchar field may have a maximum (defined) size of 25 characters but the length of the data in the specified field of the current record.
Name	A **String** read-only value that returns the field (column) name.
NumericScale	A **Byte** read-only value specifying the number of decimal places for numeric values.
OriginalValue	A **Variant** read-only value that represents the Value property of the field before applying the Update method to the Recordset. (The CancelUpdate method uses OriginalValue to replace a changed Value property.)
Precision	A **Byte** read-only value specifying the total number of digits (including decimal digits) for numeric values.
Type	A **Long** read-only value specifying the data type of the field. Refer to Table 2.16 for Type constant values.
UnderlyingValue	A **Variant** read-only value representing the current value of the field in the database table(s). You can compare the values of OriginalValue and UnderlyingValue to determine whether a persistent change has been made to the database, perhaps by another user.
Value	A **Variant** read/write value of a subtype appropriate to the value of the Type property for the field. If the Recordset isn't updatable, the Value property is read-only.

Tip #258 from

Value is the default property of the Field object, but a good programming practice is to set and return field values by explicit use of the Value property name in VBA code. In most cases, using varName = rstName.Fields(n).Value instead of varName = rstName.Fields(n) results in a slight performance improvement.

TABLE 27.24 CONSTANT VALUES AND DESCRIPTIONS FOR THE Attributes PROPERTY OF THE Field OBJECT

FieldAttributeEnum	Description
adFldMayDefer	The field is deferred, meaning that Values are retrieved from the data source only when explicitly requested.
adFldUpdatable	The field is read/write (updatable).
adFldUnknownUpdatable	The data provider can't determine whether the field is updatable. Your only recourse is to attempt an update and trap the error that occurs if the field isn't updatable.

FieldAttributeEnum	Description
adFldFixed	The field contains fixed-length data with the length determined by the data type or field specification.
adFldIsNullable	The field accepts **Null** values.
adFldMayBeNull	The field can return **Null** values.
adFldLong	The field has a long binary data type, which permits the use of the AppendChunk and GetChunk methods.
adFldRowID	The field is a row identifier (typically an identity, AutoIncrement, or GUID data type).
adFldRowVersion	The field contains a timestamp or similar value for determining the time of the last update.
adFldCacheDeferred	The provider caches field values. Multiple reads are made on the cached value, not the database table.

The Field object has two methods, AppendChunk and GetChunk, which are applicable only to fields of various long binary data types, indicated by an adFldLong flag in the Attributes property of the field. The AppendChunk method is discussed in the "Parameter Object" section earlier in this chapter. The syntax for the AppendChunk method call, which writes **Variant** data to a long binary field (fld*Name*), is

fld*Name*.AppendChunk var*Data*

> **Note**
>
> ADO 2.1 doesn't support the Access OLE Object field data type, which adds a proprietary object wrapper around the data (such as a bitmap) to identify the OLE server that created the object (for bitmaps, usually Windows Paint).

The GetChunk method enables you to read long binary data in blocks of the size you specify. Following is the syntax for the GetChunk method:

var*Name* = fld*Name*.GetChunk(lng*Size*)

> **Tip #259 from**
>
>
>
> A common practice is to place AppendChunk and GetChunk method calls within Do Until...Loop structures to break up the long binary value into chunks of manageable size. In the case of the GetChunk method, if you set the value of lng*Size* to less than the value of the field's ActualSize property, the first GetChunk call retrieves lng*Size* bytes. Successive GetChunk calls retrieve lng*Size* bytes beginning at the next byte after the end of the preceding call. If the remaining number of bytes is less than lng*Size*, only the remaining bytes appear in var*Name*. After you retrieve the field's bytes, or if the field is empty, GetChunk returns **Null**.

> **Note**
>
> Changing the position of the record pointer of the field's `Recordset` resets `GetChunk`'s byte pointer. Accessing a different `Recordset` and moving its record pointer doesn't affect the other `Recordset`'s `GetChunk` record pointer.

Recordset METHODS

`ADODB.Recordset` methods are an amalgam of the `DAO.Recordset` and `rdoResultset` methods. Table 27.25 gives the names, descriptions, and calling syntax for `Recordset` methods. OLE DB data providers aren't required to support all the methods of the `Recordset` object. If you don't know which methods the data provider supports, you must use the `Supports` method with the appropriate constant from `CursorOptionEnum`, listed in Table 27.28, to test for support of methods that are provider dependent. Provider-dependent methods are indicated by an asterisk after the method name in Table 27.25.

TABLE 27.25 NAMES AND DESCRIPTIONS OF METHODS OF THE `Recordset` OBJECT

Method Name	Description and Calling Syntax
AddNew	Adds a new record to an updatable `Recordset`. The calling syntax is `rstName.AddNew [{varField¦avarFields}, {varValue¦avarValues}]`, where `varField` is a single field name, `avarFields` is an array of field names, `varValue` is single value, and `avarValues` is an array of values for the columns defined by the members of `avarFields`. Calling the `Update` method adds the new record to the database table(s). If you add a new records to a `Recordset` having a primary-key field that is not the first field of the `Recordset`, you must supply the name and value of the primary-key field in the `AddNew` statement.
Cancel	Cancels execution of an asynchronous query and terminates creation of multiple `Recordsets` from stored procedures or compound SQL statements. The calling syntax is `rstName.Cancel`.
CancelBatch	Cancels a pending batch update operation on a `Recordset` whose `LockEdits` property value is `adBatchOptimistic`. The calling syntax is `rstName.CancelBatch [lngAffectRecords]`. The optional `lngAffectRecords` argument is one of the constants of `AffectEnum` (see Table 27.26).
CancelUpdate	Cancels a pending change to the table(s) underlying the `Recordset` before applying the `Update` method. The calling syntax is `rstName.CancelUpdate`.
Clone	Creates a duplicate `Recordset` object with an independent record pointer. The calling syntax is **Set** `rstDupe = rstName.Clone()`.
Close	Closes a `Recordset` object, allowing reuse of the `Recordset` variable by setting new `Recordset` property values and applying the `Open` method. The calling syntax is `rstName.Close`.
Delete	Deletes the current record immediately from the `Recordset` and the underlying tables, unless the `LockEdits` property value of the `Recordset` is set to `adLockBatchOptimistic`. The calling syntax is `rstName.Delete`.

Method Name	Description and Calling Syntax
Find	Searches for a record based on criteria you supply. The calling syntax is rst*Name*.Find str*Criteria*[, lng*SkipRecords*, lng*SearchDirection*[, lng*Start*]], where str*Criteria* is a valid SQL WHERE clause without the WHERE keyword, the optional lng*SkipRecords* value is the number of records to skip before applying Find, lng*SearchDirection* specifies the search direction (adSearchForward, the default, or adSearchBackward), and the optional var*Start* value specifies the Bookmark value of the record at which to start the search or one of the members of BookmarkEnum (see Table 27.27). If Find succeeds, the EOF property returns **True**; otherwise, EOF returns **False**.
GetRows	Returns a two-dimensional (row, column) **Variant** array of records. The calling syntax is avar*Name* = rst*Name*.GetRows(lng*Rows*[, var*Start*[, {str*FieldName*|lng*FieldIndex*|avar*FieldNames*|avar*FieldIndexes*}]]), where lng*Rows* is the number of rows to return, var*Start* specifies a Bookmark value of the record at which to start the search or one of the members of BookmarkEnum (see Table 27.27), and the third optional argument is the name or index of a single column, or a **Variant** array of column names or indexes. If you don't specify a value of the third argument, GetRows returns all columns of the Recordset.
GetString	By default, returns a tab-separated **String** value for a specified number of records, with records separated by return codes. The calling syntax is str*Clip* = rst*Name*.GetString (lng*Rows*[, str*ColumnDelimiter*[, str*RowDelimiter*, [str*NullExpr*]]]), where lng*Rows* is the number of rows to return, str*ColumnDelimiter* is an optional column-separation character (vbTab is the default), str*RowDelimiter* is an optional row-separation character (vbCR is the default), and str*NullExpr* is an optional value to substitute when encountering **Null** values (an empty string, " ", is the default value).
Move	Moves the record pointer from the current record. The calling syntax is rst*Name*.Move lng*NumRecords*[, var*Start*], where lng*NumRecords* is the number of records by which to move the record pointer and the optional var*Start* value specifies the Bookmark of the record at which to start the search or one of the members of BookmarkEnum (see Table 27.27).
MoveFirst	Moves the record pointer to the first record. The calling syntax is rst*Name*.MoveFirst.
MoveLast	Moves the record pointer to the last record. The calling syntax is rst*Name*.MoveLast.
MoveNext	Moves the record pointer to the next record. The calling syntax is rst*Name*.MoveNext. The MoveNext method is the only Move... method that you can apply to a forward-only Recordset.
MovePrevious	Moves the record pointer to the previous record. The calling syntax is rst*Name*.MovePrevious.

continues

TABLE 27.25 CONTINUED

Method Name	Description and Calling Syntax
NextRecordset	Returns additional Recordset objects generated by a compound SQL statement, such as SELECT * FROM Orders; SELECT * FROM Customers, or a stored procedure that returns multiple Recordsets. The calling syntax is rst*Next* = rst*Name*.NextRecordset[(lng*RecordsAffected*)], where lng*RecordsAffected* is an optional return value that specifies the number of records in rst*Next*. If no additional Recordset exists, rst*Next* is set to **Nothing**.
Open	Opens a Recordset on an active Command or Connection object. The calling syntax is rst*Name*.Open [var*Source*[, var*ActiveConnection*[, lng*CursorType*[, lng*LockType*[, lng*Options*]]]]]. The Open arguments are optional if you set the equivalent Recordset property values, which is the practice recommended in this book. For valid values, refer to the Source, ActiveConnection, CursorType, and LockType properties in Table 27.15 and to the CommandTypeEnum values listed in Table 27.7 for the lng*Options* property.
Requery	Refreshes the content of the Recordset from the underlying table(s), the equivalent of calling Close then Open. Requery is a very resource-intensive operation. The calling syntax is rst*Name*.Requery.
Resync	Refreshes a specified subset of the Recordset from the underlying table(s). The calling syntax is rst*Name*.Resync [lng*AffectRecords*], where lng*AffectRecords* is one of the members of AffectEnum (see Table 27.26). If you select adAffectCurrent or adAffectGroup as the value of lng*AffectRecords*, you reduce the required resources in comparison with adAffectAll (the default).
Save	Creates a file containing a persistent copy of the Recordset. The calling syntax is rst*Name*.Save str*FileName*, where str*FileName* is the path to and the name of the file. You open a Recordset from a file with a rst*Name*.Open str*FileName*, Options:=adCmdFile statement. This book uses .rst as the extension for persistent Recordsets.
Seek	Performs a high-speed search on the field whose index name is specified as the value of the Recordset.Index property. The calling syntax is rst*Name*.Seek avar*KeyValues*[, lng*Option*], where avar*KeyValues* is a **Variant** array of search values for each field of the index. The optional lngOption argument is one of the members of the SeekEnum (see Table 27.29) constant enumeration; the default value is adSeekFirstEQ (find the first equal value). You can't specify adUseClient as the CursorLocation property value when applying the Seek method; Seek requires a server-side (adUseServer) cursor.

Method Name	Description and Calling Syntax
Supports	Returns **True** if the Recordset's data provider supports a specified cursor-dependent method; otherwise, Supports returns **False**. The calling syntax is bln*Supported* = rst*Name*.Supports(lng*CursorOptions*). Table 2.30 lists the names and descriptions of the CursorOptionsEnum values.
Update	Applies the result of modifications to the Recordset to the underlying table(s) of the data source. For batch operations, Update applies the modifications only to the local (cached) Recordset. The calling syntax is rst*Name*.Update.
UpdateBatch	Applies the result of all modifications made to a batch-type Recordset (LockType property set to adBatchOptimistic and CursorType property set to adOpenKeyset or adOpenStatic) to the underlying table(s) of the data source. The calling syntax is rst*Name*.UpdateBatch [lng*AffectRecords*], where lng*AffectRecords* is a member of AffectEnum (see Table 27.26).

The "Code to Pass Parameter Values to a Stored Procedure" section, earlier in the chapter, illustrates use of the Save and Open methods with persisted Recordsets.

Tip #260 from

RJ

The Edit method of DAO.Recordset objects is missing from Table 27.25. To change the value of one or more fields of the current record of an ADODB.Recordset object, simply execute rst*Name*.Fields(*n*).Value = var*Value* for each field whose value you want to change and then execute rst*Name*.Update. ADODB.Recordset objects don't support the Edit method.

Tip #261 from

RJ

To improve the performance of Recordset objects opened on Connection objects, set the required property values of the Recordset object and then use a named argument to specify the int*Options* value of the Open method, as in rst*Name*.Open Options:=adCmdText. This syntax is easier to read and less prone to error than the alternative, rst*Name*.Open , , , , adCmdText.

PART

VII

CH

27

TABLE 27.26 NAMES AND DESCRIPTIONS OF CONSTANTS FOR THE lngAffectRecords ARGUMENT

AffectEnum	Description
adAffectAll	Include all records in the Recordset object, including any records hidden by the Filter property value (the default).
adAffectCurrent	Include only the current record.
adAffectGroup	Include only those records that meet the current Filter criteria.

TABLE 27.27   NAMES AND DESCRIPTIONS OF BOOKMARK CONSTANTS FOR THE varStart ARGUMENT

BookmarkEnum	Description
adBookmarkCurrent	Start at the current record (the default value).
adBookmarkFirst	Start at the first record.
adBookmarkLast	Start at the last record.

TABLE 27.28   NAMES AND DESCRIPTIONS OF CONSTANTS FOR THE Supports METHOD

CursorOptionEnum	Permits
adAddNew	Calling the AddNew method.
adApproxPosition	Setting and getting AbsolutePosition and AbsolutePage property values.
adBookmark	Setting and getting the Bookmark property value.
adDelete	Calling the Delete method.
adHoldRecords	Retrieving additional records or changing the retrieval record pointer position without committing pending changes.
adMovePrevious	Calling the GetRows, Move, MoveFirst, and MovePrevious methods (indicates a bidirectional scrollable cursor).
adResync	Calling the Resync method.
adUpdate	Calling the Update method.
adUpdateBatch	Calling the UpdateBatch and CancelBatch methods.

Table 27.29 lists the SeekEnum constants for the optional lngSeekOptions argument of the Seek method. Unfortunately, the syntax for the ADODB.Recordset.Seek method isn't even close to backward-compatible with the DAO.Recordset.Seek method.

TABLE 27.29   NAMES AND DESCRIPTIONS OF CONSTANTS FOR THE Seek METHOD'S lngSeekOptions ARGUMENT

SeekEnum	Finds
adSeekFirstEQ	The first equal value (the default value).
adSeekAfterEQ	The first equal value or the next record after where a match would have occurred (logical equivalent of >=).
adSeekAfter	The first record after where a equal match would have occurred (logical equivalent of >).
adSeekBeforeEQ	The first equal value or the previous record before where a match would have occurred (logical equivalent of <=).

SeekEnum	Finds
adSeekBefore	The first record previous to where a equal match would have occurred (logical equivalent of <).
adSeekLastEQ	The last record having an equal value.

Tip #262 from

Use the Find method for searches unless you are working with a table having an extremely large number of records. Find takes advantage of index(es), if present, but Find's search algorithm isn't quite as efficient as Seek's. You'll probably encounter the threshold for considering substituting Seek for Find in the range of 100,000 to 1,000,000 records. Tests on the Beckwith.mdb Jet and Beckwith SQL Server Students table (50,000) rows show imperceptible performance differences between Seek and Find operations.

DISCONNECTED RecordsetS

If you set the value of the Recordset's LockEdits property to adBatchOptimistic and the CursorType property to adKeyset or adStatic, you create a batch-type Recordset that you can disconnect from the data source. You can then edit the Recordset offline, reopen the Connection object, and send the updates to the data source over the new connection. A Recordset without an active connection is called a *disconnected* Recordset. The advantage of a disconnected Recordset is that you eliminate the need for an active server connection during extended editing sessions.

Following is an example of VBA pseudocode that creates and operates on a disconnected Recordset and then uses the UpdateBatch method to persist the changes in the data source:

```
Set rstName = New ADODB.Recordset
With rstName
    .ActiveConnection = cnnName
    .CursorType = adStatic
    .LockEdits = adBatchOptimistic
    .Open "SELECT * FROM TableName WHERE Criteria", Options:=adCmdText
    Set .ActiveConnection = Nothing 'Disconnect the Recordset
    'Close the Connection, if desired
    'Modify the field values of multiple records here
    .Update   'Update the locally-cached Recordset
'Reopen the connection, if closed
    Set .ActiveConnection = cnnName
    .UpdateBatch   'Send all changes to the data source
End With
rstName.Close
```

PART

VII

CH

27

If calling the UpdateBatch method causes conflicts with other users' modifications to the underlying table(s), you receive a trappable error and the Errors collection contains Error object(s) that identify the conflict(s). Unlike transactions, which require all attempted modifications to succeed or all to be rolled back, Recordset batch modifications that don't cause conflicts are made permanent in the data source.

Recordset EVENTS

Recordset events are new to users of DAO. Table 27.30 names the Recordset events and gives the condition under which the event fires.

TABLE 27.30   NAMES AND OCCURRENCE OF Recordset EVENTS

Event Name	When Fired
EndOfRecordset	When the record pointer attempts to move beyond the last record.
FieldChangeComplete	After a change to the value of a field.
MoveComplete	After execution of the Move or Move... methods.
RecordChangeComplete	After an edit to a single record.
RecordsetChangeComplete	After cached changes are applied to the underlying tables.
WillChangeField	Before a change to a field value.
WillChangeRecord	Before an edit to a single record.
WillChangeRecordset	Before cached changes are applied to the underlying tables.
WillMove	After execution of the Move or Move... methods.

TROUBLESHOOTING

CURSOR TYPES FOR THE Form.Recordset PROPERTY

I receive a "The object you entered is not a valid Recordset property" message when I assign my ADODB.Recordset *to the* Recordset *property of a form.*

The Recordset you created has a ForwardOnly or Dynamic cursor, or has a server-side cursor. Binding a form to a Recordset you create with code requires CursorLocation = adUseClient; the CursorType property must be set to adOpenKeyset or adOpenStatic; and the LockType can't be adLockReadOnly. The standard code for opening an updatable Recordset is

```
With rstName
    Set .ActiveConnection = cnnName
    .CursorLocation = adUseClient
    .CursorType = adOpenStatic 'or adOpenKeyset
    .LockType = adLockOptimistic
    .Open strSQL
End With
```

MSDATASHAPE AND SQLOLEDB PROVIDERS

I've opened a Recordset *against an MSDE table with a client-side Keyset cursor that has a tentative append record in Datasheet view of my form, but I can't edit any cells.*

You must specify MSDataShape as the `Provider` property of the `ADODB.Connection` and then include `Data Provider=SQLOLEDB[.1]` in the `ConnectionString`. (The .1 version number is optional.) The typical code for opening on a local copy of MSDE a connection that lets you generate an updatable `Recordset` for a form is:

```
With cnnName
    .Provider = "MSDataShape"
    .Open "Data Provider=SQLOLEDB.1;Data Source=(local);" & _
       "UID=sa;PWD=;Database=DBName"
End With
```

SPACES IN ADO OBJECT NAMES

When I attempt to open a `Command` *object on the stored procedures of NorthwindCS, I receive a "Syntax error or access violation" message.*

SQL Server 7.0 (unfortunately) supports spaces in object names, such as views and stored procedures. However, SQL Server wants these names enclosed within double quotes. Sending double quotes in an object name string is a pain in VBA, but surrounding the object name with square brackets also solves the problem. For example, `cnnName.CommandText = "Sales By Year"` fails but `cnnName.CommandText = "[Sales By Year]"` works.

IN THE REAL WORLD—STRUGGLING WITH ADO

"Everything has to be somewhere" is a popular corollary of the Law of Conservation of Matter, so just about everything you need to know about ADO is concentrated in this chapter. The problem with this "laundry list" approach to describing a new set of data-related objects is that readers are likely to doze off in mid-chapter. If you've gotten this far (and have at least scanned the intervening code and tables), you probably surmised that ADO is more than just a replacement for DAO—it's an entirely new approach to database connectivity.

WHY LEARN ADO?

The quick answer is for Web-based database applications. Microsoft designed OLE DB and ADO expressly for HTML- and XML-based applications, such as DAP—the subject of Chapter 18, "Designing Data Access Pages." You can use VBScript or JScript (Microsoft's variant of JavaScript) to open and manipulate ADO `Connection`, `Command`, and `Recordset` objects on Web pages. With DAO, you're stuck with conventional Access applications that require users to have a copy of Office 2000 or you to have the Microsoft Office 2000 Developer Edition (MOD) so you can supply run-time versions of your Access 2000 applications.

Tip #263 from

Many Access developers have expressed dismay that users must have Office 2000 client licenses and Internet Explorer 5+ installed to take full advantage of DAP and the Office Web Components (OWC). Microsoft's command of the PC productivity suite market is such that it's only a matter of time before almost every sizable organization installs an Office 2000 Standard Edition or better. Fortunately. DAP clients don't need the Office 2000 Professional Edition. MDAC 2.1 is *distributable*, meaning that the license to use the technology is free to all Windows developers and users. It's a sure bet that all future MDAC upgrades also will be freely distributable.

Another incentive for becoming ADO-proficient is migrating from Jet 4.0 to DAP. When SQL Server marketing honchos say that SQL Server is Microsoft's "strategic database direction," believe them. Jet isn't dead, but the handwriting's on the wall; ultimately SQL Server will replace Jet in all but the most trivial database applications. You can expect SQL Server 7.0, OLE DB, and ADO to receive the bulk of Microsoft's future development effort after Windows 2000 hits retailers shelves. In the meantime, expect SQL Server 7.0 (including MSDE) to dominate the "sweet spot" of the client/server RDBMS market—small- to mid-size firms—plus division-level and Web site RDBMS installations of the Fortune 1000.

The ultimate answer to "Why learn ADO?", however, is "Microsoft wants YOU to use ADO." Like the proverbial one-ton gorilla, Microsoft usually gets what it wants.

WHERE'S ADOX?

This chapter pays lip-service to ADOX, but doesn't delve into the nitty-gritty details of Jet SQL extensions for DDL and security. Microsoft's purpose in adding ADOX is an attempt to establish parity between DAO and ADO, primarily for developers using Jet 4.0 databases with the members of Visual Studio 6.0. Visual Basic 6.0 developers, especially, need the ADOX security extensions to manage Jet database permissions with VBA code.

Unless you write commercial Access applications that use VBA to build their own databases, it's a far better strategy to take advantage of Access 2000's table design and graphical relationships features to create tables, and the User-Level Security Wizard to manage user and group permissions for Access front- and back-end objects.

WHAT'S THE UPSHOT?

Version 2.1 of ADO and ADOX don't have the maturity of DAO 3.6. In particular, missing features—such as non-updatable form `Recordsets` and limitations of the `Find` method—perplex users migrating from DAO to ADO. The ADO limitations aren't fatal, and probably will be overcome in subsequent MDAC upgrades. ADO 2.1 wasn't released to manufacturing (RTMed) when this book was written in early 1999, but Microsoft asked ADO beta testers in early February to prepare for an MDAC 2.5 beta program to begin in the second quarter of 1999. Expect frequent and significant upgrades to OLE DB, ADO, and other MDAC components; but infrequent, bug-fix-only updates to DAO. Jet might not be dead, but DAO has at least one foot in the grave.

--rj

CHAPTER 28

RESPONDING TO EVENTS WITH VBA 6.0

In this chapter

Introducing Event-Driven Programming   1084

Understanding the Role of Class Modules   1084

Examining Project Class Module Members in the Object Browser and Project Explorer   1089

Adding Event-Handling Code with the Command Button Wizard   1092

Using Functions to Respond to Events   1096

Understanding Access 2000's Event Repertoire   1098

Working with Access 2000's DoCmd Methods   1105

Customizing Applications with CommandBar Objects   1113

Specifying a Custom CommandBar and Setting Other Startup Properties   1117

Referring to Access Objects with VBA   1118

Troubleshooting   1123

In the Real World—Dealing with Event-Driven Programming   1124

INTRODUCING EVENT-DRIVEN PROGRAMMING

All Windows applications are *event-driven*, which means that an event, such as a mouse click on a command button or a change in the position of a record pointer, executes individual blocks of application programming code. Thus, the majority of the VBA code you write consists of event-handling subprocedures—also called *event procedures* or *event handlers*—that are contained within [{**Public**|**Private**}] **Sub** {Form|Report}_[*ObjectName_*]*EventName* ... **End Sub** structures of *class modules*. Class module is the VBA term that replaces Access 2.0's and Access 95's use of *code-behind-forms* (CBF) to describe Access Basic or Access-specific VBA code embedded within a Form or Report container. In the preceding chapter, you took advantage of the Form_Load event to execute VBA code to open and manipulate Recordset objects. This chapter describes how to write Access VBA event-handling code in Form and Report class modules to automate your Access 2000 applications.

Early versions of Access emphasized the use of Access macros to respond to events. Microsoft promoted Access macros as a simplified programming language for users with little or no programming experience. The repertoire of approximately 40 Access macro actions proved adequate to automate relatively simple applications. One of the major drawbacks of Access macros is the inability to handle errors gracefully. Thus, virtually all Access developers have abandoned macros in favor of programming. Now that all the principal members of Microsoft Office offer VBA and use the same VBA Editor, Access macros are on their way to oblivion. There's no guarantee that future versions of Access will continue to support Access macros.

UNDERSTANDING THE ROLE OF CLASS MODULES

Class modules are containers for VBA code that relate to a particular class of objects. Access 2000 defines two classes (collections)—Forms and Reports—that contain VBA code for a particular instance of the class: a Form or Report object, respectively. In object-oriented programming terms, class modules encapsulate VBA code within a Form or Report object. Code encapsulation lets you create reusable objects. For example, when you copy a form from one Access database to another, the copy you make includes the code in the form's class module.

Access's Form and Report class modules differ from *conventional* modules in that a Form or Report object is integral to the code and contributes the object's properties (appearance). Conventional modules, such as Northwind.mdb's Utility Functions, appear in the Modules page of the Database window. Your event-handling code creates a custom set of methods (behavior) that are applicable to the object. When you open a form or report, you create the *default instance* of the corresponding Form or Report object. The default instance of the object appears in the Forms or Reports page of the Database window. VBA 6.0 also lets you create additional temporary, nondefault instances of Forms and Report objects with the **New** reserved word. You need not add an explicit reference to the associated form or report in your code, although in certain expressions you use the **Me** self-reference to specify the current instance of the Form or Report object.

Note

NEW 2000 Prior versions of Access called the window that displays class module code the *Class Module* window. Access 2000 has adopted the VBA Integrated Design Environment (IDE), which uses the term *Editor* window.

→ For help navigating through this window, **see** "Exploring the VBA Editor," **p. 1018**.

THE MAIN SWITCHBOARD CLASS MODULE

The Northwind Traders Main Switchboard form is a good starting point for gaining an understanding of class modules and simple event-handling code. The Main Switchboard form contains two event-handling subprocedures: one each for the Display Database Window and Exit Microsoft Access command buttons, plus a single OpenForm function that services the Categories, Suppliers, Products, Orders, and Print Sales Reports command buttons. Figure 28.1 illustrates the relationships between the command buttons and the function or subprocedure that executes when you click the button.

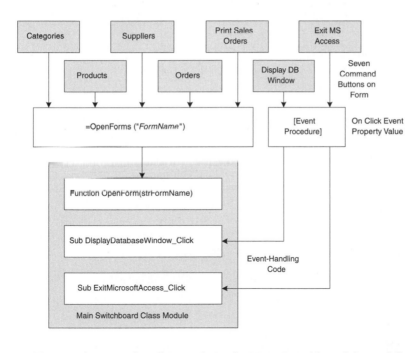

Figure 28.1
Relationships between command buttons and event-handling code in the Main Switchboard form.

To view the event-handling code in the Main Switchboard form, follow these steps:

1. Open the Main Switchboard form in Design view.

2. Click the Code button of the toolbar to open the Editor window, Form_Main Switchboard, for the Main Switchboard form. By default, the Editor window opens with the Declarations section at the top of the window.

3. Open the left drop-down list, which Microsoft calls the Object box, to display a list of the control objects of the form, plus the Form object (see Figure 28.2).

Figure 28.2
Selecting a form control object in the Object list of the Editor window.

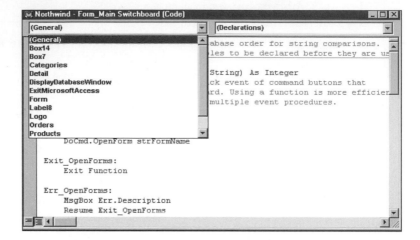

4. Select one of the control buttons, such as DisplayDatabaseWindow, from the Object list to display the subprocedure—**Sub** Form_DisplayDatabaseWindow_Click—for the On Click event of the Display Database Window command button (see Figure 28.3).

Figure 28.3
VBA code for the DisplayDatabaseWindow_Click event that opens the Database window with the Categories form selected.

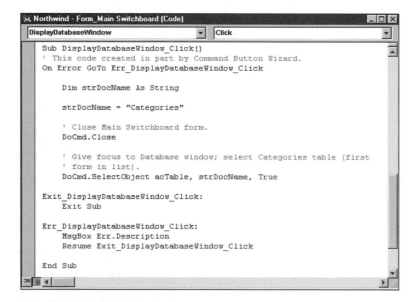

Undocking and closing unused components of the VBA Editor makes it easier to view and write code in the Editor window, especially at lower monitor resolutions. To undock the individual VBA Editor windows, choose Tools, Options, click the Docking tab, and clear all the check boxes.

5. Open the right drop-down list, which Microsoft calls the Procedure box, to display a list of events applicable to the selection in the Object box. The Click event appears in bold type because the DisplayDatabaseWindows_Click event subprocedure contains VBA code. When you select an event, such as DblClick, without an existing subprocedure, Access creates a *subprocedure stub*. A subprocedure stub in a class module consists only of the **Private Sub** [*ObjectName_*]*EventName*...**End Sub** entries (see Figure 28.4).

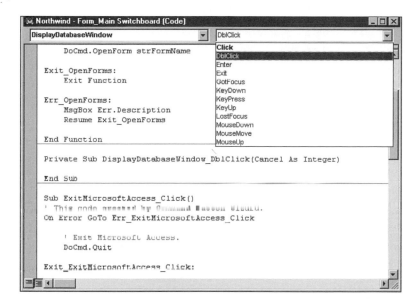

Figure 28.4
A VBA subprocedure stub created by Access for the DblClick event.

All VBA procedures have **Public** scope unless you specify otherwise; procedures that you declare with **Sub** or **Public Sub** are visible to all other class modules and conventional code modules. When you create a procedure stub in a class module, Access adds the **Private** modifier. **Private** subprocedures and functions have slightly less overhead than **Public** subprocedures and function and improve performance in large Access applications. The function and subprocedures of the Form_Main Switchboard class module are declared without the default **Private** modifier.

→ For more information on VBA scope and visibility, **see** "Scope and Duration of Variables," **p. 1003**.

PART

VII

CH

28

EVENT-HANDLING CODE IN THE MAIN SWITCHBOARD FORM

Listing 28.1 shows all the code contained in the Form_Main Switchboard class module. Each of the procedures includes standard error-handling code consisting of **On Error GoTo** _Err_Lable_...**Resume** _Exit_Label_...**Exit {Function¦Sub}** statements. Adding error handling to every procedure you write is a generally accepted VBA programming practice.

→ For details on use of the **On Error** command, **see** "Handling Runtime Errors," **p. 1016**.

LISTING 28.1   EVENT-HANDLING CODE OF THE FORM_MAIN SWITCHBOARD CLASS MODULE

```
Option Compare Database  'Use database order for string comparisons.
Option Explicit 'Requires variables to be declared before they are used.

Function OpenForms(strFormName As String) As Integer
'This function is used in the Click event of command buttons that
'open forms on the Main Switchboard. Using a function is more efficient
'than repeating the same code in multiple event procedures.
On Error GoTo Err_OpenForms

    'Open specified form.
    DoCmd.OpenForm strFormName

Exit_OpenForms:
    Exit Function

Err_OpenForms:
    MsgBox Err.Description
    Resume Exit_OpenForms
End Function

Sub ExitMicrosoftAccess_Click()
'This code created by Command Button Wizard.
On Error GoTo Err_ExitMicrosoftAccess_Click

    'Exit Microsoft Access.
    DoCmd.Quit

Exit_ExitMicrosoftAccess_Click:
    Exit Sub

Err_ExitMicrosoftAccess_Click:
    MsgBox Err.Description
    Resume Exit_ExitMicrosoftAccess_Click
End Sub

Sub DisplayDatabaseWindow_Click()
'This code created in part by Command Button Wizard.
On Error GoTo Err_DisplayDatabaseWindow_Click

    Dim strDocName As String
    strDocName = "Categories"

    'Close Main Switchboard form.
    DoCmd.Close
```

```
        'Give focus to Database window; select Categories table (first
        'form in list).
        DoCmd.SelectObject acTable, strDocName, True

    Exit_DisplayDatabaseWindow_Click:
        Exit Sub

    Err_DisplayDatabaseWindow_Click:
        MsgBox Err.Description
        Resume Exit_DisplayDatabaseWindow_Click
    End Sub
```

Tip #266 from

R J

The Default to Full Module view and Procedure Separator settings of the Editor page of the Options properties sheet make reading VBA code easier. By default, all the procedures in the class module appear after the Declarations section of the class module in the alphabetical order of the procedure name, separated by a horizontal gray line. With Full Module view specified, you can use the scroll bars to view all the procedures within a module.

Access 2000's DoCmd object, which replaces the DoCmd statement of Access 2.0 and earlier versions, is the key to manipulating Access application objects with Access VBA. The DoCmd statement of Access 2.0 used the DoCmd *ActionName[Argument(s)]* syntax, in which *ActionName* was one of approximately 40 predefined macro actions. Application-specific reserved words, such as DoCmd, preclude a common version of VBA for all members of Office plus Visual Basic; thus, DoCmd is now an Access-specific object, not a reserved word. The macro actions of Access 2.0 and earlier are now called *methods of the DoCmd object*. When you convert an Access 2.0 or earlier database to Access 2000, DoCmd.*MethodName* statements automatically replace DoCmd *ActionName* statements.

EXAMINING PROJECT CLASS MODULE MEMBERS IN THE OBJECT BROWSER AND PROJECT EXPLORER

Each Form and Report object in the current database that has a class module appears in the Classes list when you select the project name of the current database in the Project/Library (upper) drop-down list of the Object Browser (see Figure 28.5). By default, the project name for an Access database is the file name of the database without a file extension; thus, the project name for Northwind.mdb is Northwind. The default <globals> object displays in the righthand Members Of '<globals>' list all the procedures in conventional Access modules. These procedures also appear in Members Of '*ModuleName*' entries for each module in the project.

PART

VII

CH

28

Tip #267 from

R J

To launch the Object Browser, open a form in Design view, click the Code button of the toolbar to display the class module for the form, and then choose View, Object Browser or press F2.

Figure 28.5
Object Browser display-
ing objects in the
Northwind project
(Northwind.mdb).

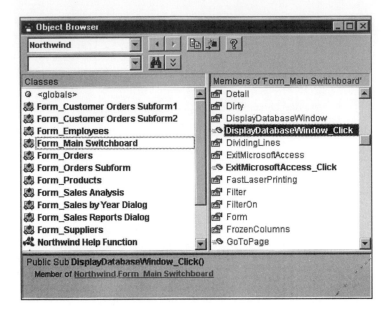

When you select a Form or Report object, items representing properties of the Form or
Report object and each of the control objects added to the Form or Report object appear in
the Members Of '*ObjectName*' list. Each procedure also appears (in bold type) in the list.
Figure 28.5 shows list items for the DisplayDatabaseWindow_Click and
ExitMicrosoftAccess_Click event handlers. If you double-click a procedure item, the
Editor window displays the procedure's code.

> **Note**
>
> VBA 6.0 lets you define your own classes and write custom class modules. Custom class
> modules give you the opportunity to define a set of properties and methods for the object
> class you create. Custom class modules appear in Object Browser's Classes list, and the
> properties and methods you define appear in the Members Of '*ObjectName*' list.

**NEW
2000**
The Project Explorer window displays all Form and Report Microsoft Access Class Objects,
plus modules that contain global code accessible to all class modules (see Figure 28.6).
Double-clicking a list item opens its Editor window. You can change the project name by
selecting the Project node, opening the Properties window for the project, and changing
the Name property value (see Figure 28.7). You also can rename a module in its Properties
window. Independent (also called standalone) Class Objects have an Instancing property;
Form and Report Class Objects don't have properties.

Figure 28.6
Project Explorer's window for the Northwind(.mdb) project.

Figure 28.7
Opening the project Properties window to change the name of a project or module.

ADDING EVENT-HANDLING CODE WITH THE COMMAND BUTTON WIZARD

Event-handling subprocedures represent the most common approach to handling events that are generated by control objects and Recordset objects bound to forms and reports. Command buttons are the most common control object to initiate user-generated events. The easiest way to create a simple VBA event-handling subprocedure is to add a command button to a form with the Command Button Wizard. The Command Button Wizard writes most or all of the code for the most commonly used Click event handlers.

To add a command button and its associated event-handling code for opening the Categories form, follow these steps:

1. Open Northwind.mdb, if necessary, and open a new form in Design view.

2. Click the Toolbox button of the toolbar, if necessary, to display the Toolbox.

3. Make sure the Control Wizard toggle button is depressed, and then click the Command Button tool and add a small button on the form. The first dialog of the Command Button Wizard appears.

4. Select Form Operations in the Categories list and Open Form in the Actions list (see Figure 28.8). Selecting Form Operations displays a sample button with a small form icon. Click Next to continue.

Figure 28.8
Selecting the category and action for the command button in the first Command Button Wizard dialog.

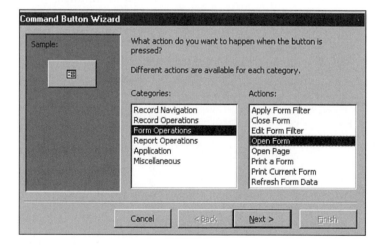

5. Select Customers (or another form) in the What Form Would You Like the Command Button to Open? list (see Figure 28.9), and click Next to continue.

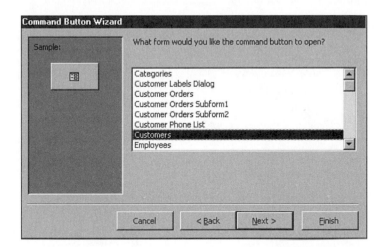

Figure 28.9
Selecting the name of the form to open.

6. If the form to open is bound to a table or query, you can allow the form to display all records or add a filter to display only a single record based on the value of a field in your new form. For this example, accept the Open the Form and Show All the Records option (see Figure 28.10), and click Next to continue.

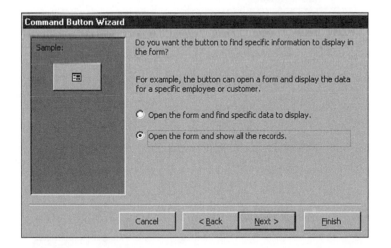

Figure 28.10
Selecting whether to apply a record filter or allow the opening form to display all records.

7. You can select from a variety of bitmapped icons for the button by marking the Show All Pictures check box. Alternatively, select the Text option button and type a caption for the command button in the text box (see Figure 28.11). Click Next to continue.

Figure 28.11
Adding a text caption to the command button.

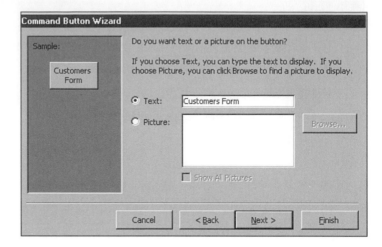

8. Type a meaningful name for the command button, such as **cmdOpenCustomers**, in the text box (see Figure 28.12). The cmd prefix is the naming convention for command buttons. Click Finish to add the event-handling code to the class module for the new form and close the last Command Button Wizard dialog.

Figure 28.12
Specifying the name of the command button.

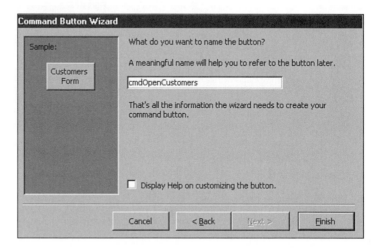

9. Click the Code button of the toolbar to display the class module for your new form. Figure 28.13 shows the subprocedure added to the module by the Control Wizard. Click the View Microsoft Access button to return to your new form in Design view.

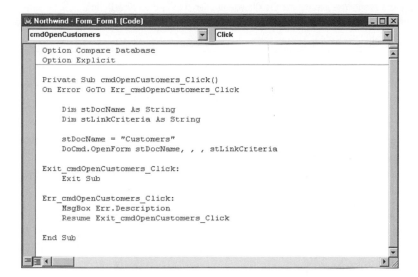

Figure 28.13
The event-handling sub-procedure for the Open Customers command button.

```
Option Compare Database
Option Explicit

Private Sub cmdOpenCustomers_Click()
On Error GoTo Err_cmdOpenCustomers_Click

    Dim stDocName As String
    Dim stLinkCriteria As String

    stDocName = "Customers"
    DoCmd.OpenForm stDocName, , , stLinkCriteria

Exit_cmdOpenCustomers_Click:
    Exit Sub

Err_cmdOpenCustomers_Click:
    MsgBox Err.Description
    Resume Exit_cmdOpenCustomers_Click

End Sub
```

The event-handling subprocedure you created in the preceding steps is bound to the On Click event of the cmdOpenCustomers button. Select the command button, click the Properties button of the toolbar to display the properties sheet for the button, and click the Event tab. The [Event Procedure] entry for the On Click event specifies the cmdOpenCustomers_Click event handler. When you open the drop-down list for the On Click event, [Event Procedure] and the names of all the macros, if any, in your database appear (see Figure 28.14).

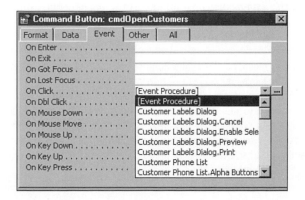

Figure 28.14
Selecting between a sub-procedure and existing Access macros to handle an event.

PART

VII

CH

28

> **Note**
>
> **NEW 2000** You can create a simple event-handling subprocedure stub for any event of an existing control by clicking the builder button for the event and then double-clicking the Code Builder item in the Choose Builder list. In this case, it's up to you to fill in the code to handle the event. You can bypass the Choose Builder step and go directly to the Editor window by marking the Always Use Event Procedures check box in the Forms/Reports page of the Options dialog.

USING FUNCTIONS TO RESPOND TO EVENTS

You can create your own Main Switchboard form by adding additional command buttons to the form for opening other forms. It's much more efficient, however, to use a single procedure to perform a set of identical tasks in which only the name of the form changes. Minimizing the amount of code in a form speeds opening of the form and minimizes the size of your database file.

Access lets you call a function and pass one or more parameter (argument) values to the function in response to events. A function (not a subprocedure) is required, despite the fact that Access disregards the return value, if any, of the function. Control Wizards won't write the function code for you, nor will the Code Builder create a function stub. You must write the function yourself before calling it from an event. The OpenForms function in preceding Listing 28.1 is an example of using a function as an event handler.

You can easily change code written by the Command Button Wizard to a general-purpose function that opens any form whose name you pass as an argument. Figure 28.15 shows a simple modification of the cmdOpenCustomers_Click subprocedure (refer to Figure 28.13), substituting a user-defined function for the event handler. When you substitute **Function** for **Sub** in the first line, the VBA interpreter automatically changes **Exit Sub** to **Exit Function** and **End Sub** to **End Function**. You change the name of the function, add the strFormName parameter, pass the strFormName parameter to the OpenForm action, and eliminate code that's not needed for the function.

Tip #268 from

R J

If you don't change the name of the subprocedure or pass the caret (insertion point) through the line containing the **Function** reserved word when converting from a subprocedure to a function, you receive a compile error. The VBA interpreter holds the existing subprocedure name in memory until the line is reinterpreted. Thus, creating a function of the same name results in a duplicate procedure name in the same class module if you simply press the Enter key when making the change. Duplicate procedure names aren't permitted within in the same module, nor are duplicate names of **Public** procedures permitted within the same project.

⚡ *If you encounter compilation errors after changing the type or name of a function or procedure, see the "Calling Procedures and Functions in Class Modules" topic of the "Troubleshooting" section near the end of this chapter.*

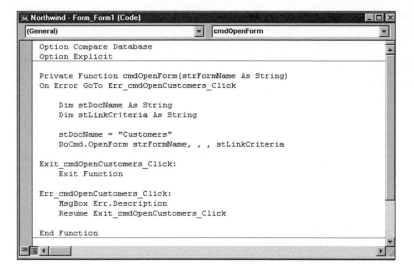

Figure 28.15
A simple modification of the subprocedure in Figure 28.13 for creating an event-handling function.

The simple changes to the subprocedure code shown in Figure 28.15 violate several good VBA programming practices. Argument variables should be assigned an explicit data type, and error-handling code should reflect the name of the function. Figure 28.16 shows the final version of the cmdOpenForm function.

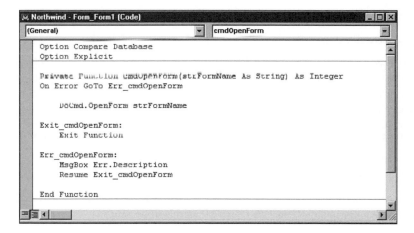

Figure 28.16
Cleaning up the code of the cmdOpenForm function.

The syntax to enter in the event text box for executing a function is as follows:

```
=FunctionName([Argument1[, Argument2[, ...]]])
```

PART

VII

CH

28

The arguments are optional, but unless you pass an argument value, such as a form name, there's no advantage to using a function call as an event handler. Arguments must be passed as literal values, such as "FormName" or a numeric value. Figure 28.17 shows the entry you type in the On Click text box to open the Categories form, **=cmdOpenForm("Categories")**. To create buttons to open other forms, copy the command button to the Clipboard, paste the copy to your form, and change the Categories caption to the name of the form you want to open.

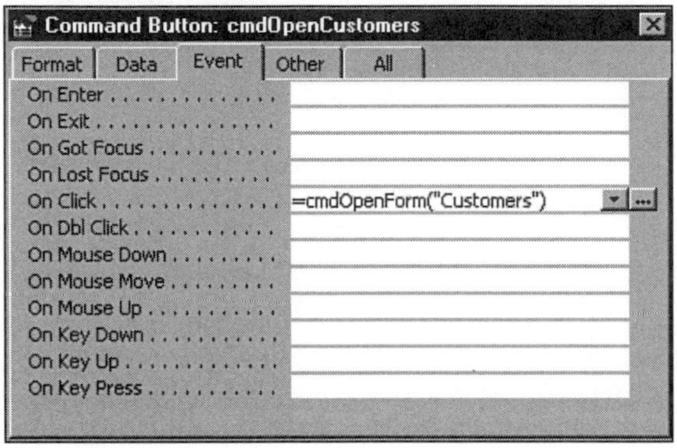

Figure 28.17
Specifying the function name and literal argument value for an event handler.

UNDERSTANDING ACCESS 2000'S EVENT REPERTOIRE

When you interact with an object by using the keyboard or the mouse, you can change the object's state. The object's state is stored with the other data about the object. Access makes some of the changes in the object's state available as opportunities to interrupt normal processing. These special changes in an object's state are called *events*. An event is a change in the state of an object at which you can interrupt normal processing and define a response.

The best way to understand events is to categorize each by the type of action that causes the event to occur. There are 11 categories:

- *Mouse events* are triggered when you click form objects.
- *Keyboard events* are triggered by forms and form controls when you type or send keystrokes with the SendKeys action while the Form object has the focus.
- *Window events* are triggered by opening or closing forms or reports.
- *Focus events* are triggered when a form or form control gains or loses the focus or when a form or report becomes active or inactive.
- *Data events* are triggered by forms and form controls when you change data in controls or records, or by forms when the focus moves from one record to another.
- *Filter events* are triggered by forms when you apply or remove filters.

- *Print events* are triggered by reports and report sections when you print or preview a report.
- *Error events* are triggered by a form or report that has the focus when an error occurs.
- *Timing events* are triggered by forms when a specified time interval passes.

NEW 2000 🔑
- *Class module events* fire when you open or close an instance of a class. You can use the new **With Events** qualifier and the **RaiseEvent** command to define custom events.
- *Reference events* fire when you add or remove a reference to an object or type library in the new **References** collection.

Table 28.1 groups Access 2000's events according to their source.

TABLE 28.1 EVENTS GROUPED BY CAUSE

Category	Source	Events
Mouse events	The user creating mouse actions	Click DblClick MouseDown MouseUp MouseMove
Keyboard events	The user typing on the keyboard or **SendKeys** sending keystrokes	KeyDown KeyUp KeyPress
Window events	Opening, closing, or resizing a window	Open Load Unload Close Resize
Focus events	An object losing or gaining the focus, or a form or report becoming active or inactive	Enter GotFocus Exit LostFocus Activate Deactivate
Data events	Making changes to a control's data, displaying records in a form, or moving the focus from one record to another in a form	Current BeforeInsert AfterInsert Delete BeforeDelConfirm AfterDelConfirm BeforeUpdate AfterUpdate Change Updated Dirty NotInList

continues

PART

VII

CH

28

TABLE 28.1   CONTINUED

Category	Source	Events
Filter events	Opening or closing a filter window, or applying or removing a filter	Filter ApplyFilter
Print events	Selecting or arranging data for printing	Format Print Retreat NoData Page
Error event	Generating an error	Error
Timing event	A specified period of time expiring	Timer
Class module events	Opening a new instance of a class module or terminating an instance of a class module	Initialize Terminate
Reference event	Adding or removing a reference to an object or type library	ItemAdded ItemRemoved

Note

NEW 2000

Access 2000 adds the `Dirty` event (and `Dirty` property) of bound forms. The `Dirty` property fires and the `Dirty` property is set to **True** when you change underlying data by typing in a bound text box or combo box, or change a page by clicking a Tab control. The `Dirty` event doesn't fire if you change a value with code, nor does it fire for any action on an unbound form.

Each event that an object triggers has a corresponding event property listed in a separate category of the object's property sheet. Table 28.2 lists the events for each object. ''Control objects are listed first, followed by `Form` and `Report` objects (according to their order in the Toolbox).

TABLE 28.2   EVENTS CLASSIFIED BY OBJECT TYPE

Object	Mouse	Keyboard	Window	Focus	Data and Filter	Print	Error and Timing
Label	Click DblClick MouseDown MouseUp MouseMove						
Text Box	Click DblClick MouseDown MouseUp MouseMove	KeyDown KeyUp KeyPress AfterUpdate	Enter Exit BeforeUpdate	GotFocus LostFocus	Change		
Option Group	Click DblClick MouseDown MouseUp MouseMove	Enter Exit	BeforeUpdate AfterUpdate				
Toggle Button	Click DblClick MouseDown MouseUp MouseMove	KeyDown KeyUp KeyPress AfterUpdate	Enter Exit BeforeUpdate	GotFocus LostFocus			
Option Button	Click DblClick MouseDown MouseUp MouseMove	KeyDown KeyUp KeyPress AfterUpdate	Enter Exit BeforeUpdate	GotFocus LostFocus			

continues

PART
VII

CH
28

TABLE 28.2 CONTINUED

Object	Mouse	Keyboard	Window	Focus	Data and Filter	Print	Error and Timing
Check Box	Click DblClick MouseDown MouseUp MouseMove	KeyDown KeyUp KeyPress AfterUpdate	Enter Exit BeforeUpdate	GotFocus LostFocus			
Combo Box	Click DblClick MouseDown MouseUp MouseMove	KeyDown KeyUp KeyPress AfterUpdate	Enter Exit BeforeUpdate	GotFocus LostFocus	Change NotInList		
List Box	Click DblClick MouseDown MouseUp MouseMove	KeyDown KeyUp KeyPress AfterUpdate	Enter Exit BeforeUpdate	GotFocus LostFocus			
Command Button	Click DblClick MouseDown MouseUp MouseMove	KeyDown KeyUp KeyPress	Enter Exit	GotFocus LostFocus			
Image	(None)						
Object Frame	Click DblClick MouseDown MouseUp MouseMove	Enter Exit	GotFocus LostFocus	Updated			

Object	Mouse	Keyboard	Window	Focus	Data and Filter	Print	Error and Timing
Bound Object Frame	Click DblClick MouseDown MouseUp MouseMove	KeyDown KeyUp KeyPress AfterUpdate	Enter Exit BeforeUpdate	GotFocus LostFocus	Updated		
Subform/ Subreport	Enter Exit						
Page Break							
Line Rect- angle	Click DblClick MouseDown MouseUp MouseMove						
Tab Control	Click DblClick MouseDown MouseUp MouseMove	KeyDown KeyUp KeyPress	Enter Exit	GotFocus LostFocus	Change		
Form Sections	Click DblClick MouseDown MouseUp MouseMove						

continues

TABLE 28.2   CONTINUED

Object	Mouse	Keyboard	Window	Focus	Data and Filter	Print	Error and Timing
Form	Click	KeyDown	Open	GotFocus	Filter		Error
	DblClick	KeyUp	Load	LostFocus	ApplyFilter		Timer
	MouseDown	KeyPress	Unload	BeforeUpdate	Dirty		
	MouseUp	Close	AfterUpdate				
	MouseMove	Resize	BeforeInsert				
	Activate	AfterInsert					
	Deactivate	BeforeDelConfirm					
	Current	AfterDelConfirm					
	Delete						
Report Page Header/ Footer	Format Print						
Group Header/ Footer	Format Print Retreat						
Report Detail Section	Format Print Retreat						
Report	Open Close Activate Deactivate	NoData					

Usually the corresponding event property is the event name preceded by the word *On*; for example, the `Click` event triggered by a command button becomes the On Click property in the button's property sheet. Figure 28.18 shows the Event page of the property sheet for a text box displaying the 15 events that the text box control can trigger. Notice that all event properties—except the Before Update and After Update data event properties—follow the pattern of preceding the event name with `On`.

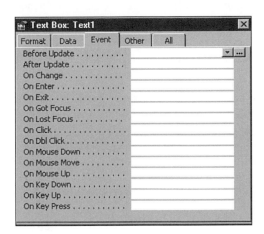

Figure 28.18
The event names that are applicable to a text box control.

WORKING WITH ACCESS 2000'S DoCmd METHODS

Some of the `DoCmd` methods duplicate menu commands, such as <u>P</u>rint, <u>C</u>lose, and Apply <u>F</u>ilter/Sort. Other methods substitute for mouse actions. For example, you can use the `SelectObject` method to select a database object in the same way that you select an open window by clicking it or select a database object in the Database window by clicking the object's name. Other `DoCmd` methods provide capabilities that aren't available through menu commands, such as `Beep`, which emits a beep sound, or `MsgBox`, which displays a custom message.

 NEW 2000 Table 28.3 lists available `DoCmd` methods grouped by task. Access 2.0 provided 47 macro actions; Access 95 added two new `DoCmd` methods: `Save` and `SetMenuItem`. Access 2000 replaces the `DoMenuItem` action or method with the `RunCommand` method, which lets you execute any native menu choice or standard toolbar button. The `AddMenu` item in the Method column of Table 28.3 is an Access 95 and earlier macro action; it's not a method of the `DoCmd` object and cannot be executed from Access VBA code.

PART

VII

CH

28

TABLE 28.3   *DoCmd* METHODS GROUPED BY TASK

Category	Task	Method
Manipulating	Copy or rename a database object	CopyObject, Rename
	Delete a database object	DeleteObject
	Open a table, query, form, report, or module	OpenTable, OpenQuery, OpenForm, OpenReport, OpenModule
NEW 2000	Open one of the new Access objects	OpenDataAccessPage, OpenDiagram, OpenStoredProcedure, OpenView
	Close a database object	Close
	Save a database object	Save
NEW 2000	Print the current database object	PrintOut,
	Select a database window object	SelectObject
	Copy or rename an object	CopyObject, Rename
	Update data or update the screen	RepaintObject, Requery, ShowAllRecords
	Set the value of a field, control, or property	SetValue
	Print the active object	
Executing	Carry out a menu command	RunCommand
	Run a query	OpenQuery, RunSQL
	Run a macro or a VBA procedure	RunMacro, RunCode
	Run another Windows or DOS application	RunApp
	Stop execution of a macro	StopMacro, StopAllMacros
	Stop execution of Access	Quit
	Stop execution following an event	CancelEvent
Working with data in forms and reports	Select or sort records	ApplyFilter
	Find a record	FindRecord, FindNext
	Move to a particular location	GoToControl, GoToRecord, GoToPage

Category	Task	Method
Importing and exporting data	Output data from a table, query, form, report, or module in .xls, .rtf, or .txt formats	`OutputAs`
	Include in an email message data from a table, query, form, report, or module in .xls, .rtf, or .txt format	`SendObject`
	Transfer data between Access and other data formats	`TransferDatabase, TransferSpreadsheet, TransferText`
Miscellaneous	Create a custom menubar	`AddMenu, SetMenuItem`
	Sound a beep	`Beep`
	Display or hide a toolbar	`ShowToolbar`
	Send keystrokes to Access or a Windows application	`SendKeys`
	Display an hourglass	`Hourglass`
	Display or hide system information	`Echo, SetWarnings`
	Display custom messages	`MsgBox`

Note

Methods applicable to macros—such as `RunMacro`, `RunCode`, `StopMacro`, and `StopAllMacros`—are obsolete in Access 2000; these `DoCmd` methods are included for backward compatibility only.

ARGUMENTS OF DoCmd METHODS

Most `DoCmd` methods require additional information as arguments to specify how the method works. For example, when you use the `OpenForm` method, you must specify the name of the form to open as the `strFormName` argument. Also, to specify whether you want to display the Form, Design, Print Preview, or Datasheet view, you must use the `intView` argument. To specify whether you want to allow editing or adding new records, you must use the `intDataMode` argument. Finally, to specify whether you want the form to be hidden, behave like a dialog, or be in normal mode, you must use the `intWindowMode` argument. You specify the values of arguments of the **Integer** data type by substituting Access intrinsic constants, which use the ac prefix, as in

```
DoCmd.OpenForm strFormName, acNormal, strFilterName, strCriterion, acEdit,
acDialog, strOpenArg
```

PART

VII

CH

28

The `acNormal`, `acEdit`, and `acDialog` argument values are Access intrinsic constant values for the `intView`, `intDataMode`, and `intWindowMode` arguments, respectively. You can also specify the numeric value of the constant, but there's no guarantee that the numeric values of Access constants will remain the same in future versions of Access. Thus, using the names of Access intrinsic constants is better programming practice than supplying numeric values for method arguments. Access 2000's online help for `DoCmd` methods lists the Access constants that are applicable to each argument of the method.

Table 28.4 is an alphabetical list of `DoCmd` methods, together with the descriptive names of the argument(s) applicable to each method. Methods marked with an asterisk (*) are not recommended for new Access applications, but are included for backward compatibility with existing macros.

TABLE 28.4 DoCmd METHODS, ARGUMENT NAMES, AND PURPOSE

Method	Argument Name	Purpose
AddMenu*	Menu Name Menu Macro Name Status Bar Text	Adds a drop-down menu choice to a custom menubar or adds a custom shortcut menu choice. Replaced by programmable CommandBars in Access 2000.
ApplyFilter	Filter Name Where Condition	Filters the data available to a form or report using a filter, query, or SQL WHERE clause.
Beep	No arguments	Produces a beep tone for use in warnings or alerts.
CancelEvent	No arguments	Cancels the normal processing that follows the event. This action is useful if a user enters invalid data in a record; then the macro can cancel the update of the database. See Help on CancelEvent for a list of applicable events.
Close	Object Type	Closes the active (default) window or a specified Object Name window.
CopyObject	Destination Database New Name	Duplicates the specified database object in another database or the original by using a different name.
Delete Object	Object Type Object Name	Deletes the specified object. Leaves the arguments blank to delete the object selected in the Database window.

Method	Argument Name	Purpose
DoMenuItem	N/A	Replaced by RunCommand.
Echo	Echo On Status Bar Text	Turns screen refresh on or off during code execution. Hides results until they are complete and speeds code operation.
FindNext	No arguments	Finds the next record specified by the FindRecord or the Find method.
FindRecord	Find What Match Case Direction Search As Formatted Search In Find First	Finds the next record after the current record that meets the specified criteria. Searches through a Table, Form, or Recordset object.
GoToControl	Control Name	Moves the focus to the specified field or control in the current record of the open form, form datasheet, table datasheet, or query datasheet. To move the focus to a subform's control, use the GoToControl method twice, first to move to the subform control and then to move to the control on the subform.
GoToPage	Page Number Right Down by Tab	Selects the first field in the tab order on the designated page in a multipage form.
GoToRecord	Object Type Object Name Record Offset	Displays the specified record in an open table, form, or query datasheet.
Hourglass	Hourglass On	Displays an hourglass in place of the mouse pointer during execution. Use this action while running long procedures.
Maximize	No arguments	Maximizes the active window.
Minimize	No arguments	Minimizes the active window to an icon within the Access window.
MoveSize	Right Down Width Height	Moves or changes the size of the active window.

PART

VII

CH

28

continues

TABLE 28.4 CONTINUED

Category	Task	Method
MsgBox*	Message Beep Type Title	Displays a warning or informational message box and waits for the user to click the OK button. Replaced by VBA **MsgBox** command.
OpenDataAccessPage	Page Name Page View	Opens the specified Data Access Page in browse mode (default) or Design view.
OpenDiagram	Diagram Name	Opens the specified data diagram of a project.
OpenForm	Form Name View Filter Name Where Condition Data Mode Window Mode	Opens or activates a form in one of its views. You can restrict the form to data-matching criteria, different modes of editing, and whether the form acts as a modal or popup dialog.
OpenModule	Module Name Procedure Name	Opens the specified module and displays the specified procedure.
OpenQuery	Query Name View Data Mode	Opens a select or crosstab query or runs an action query.
OpenReport	Report Name View Filter Name Where Condition	Opens a report in the view that you specify and filters the records before printing.
OpenStoredProcedure	Procedure Name View Mode Data Mode	Opens a stored procedure in normal (default), Design, or Preview mode (projects).
OpenTable	Table Name View Data Mode	Opens or activates a table in the view that you specify. You can specify the data-entry or edit mode for tables in Datasheet view.
OpenView	View Name View Mode	Opens a view in normal (default) Design, or Preview mode (projects).
OutputTo	Object Type Object Name Output Format Output File Autostart	Copies the data in the specified object to a Microsoft Excel (.xls) or rich-text format (.rtf) or to a DOS text (.txt) file. Autostart = Yes starts the application with

Method	Argument Name	Purpose
		the association to the extension.
Print	Print Range Page From Page To Print Quality Copies Collate Copies	Prints the active datasheet, report, or form.
PrintOut	Same as Print	Used in VBA, because **Print** is a VBA reserved word.
Quit	Options	Closes Access, saving altered objects according to the command that you specify.
Rename	New Name	Renames the object selected in the Database window.
RepaintObject	Object Type Object Name	Forces pending recalculations and screen updates for the controls of the specified database object or the active database object if you leave the arguments blank. Does not show new, changed, or deleted records from the object's underlying source.
Requery	Control Name	Updates the data in the specified control by repeating the control's query if the control is based on a query or by displaying new, changed, or deleted records if the control is based on a table. Leave the argument blank to requery the source of the active object.
Restore	No arguments	Restores a maximized or minimized window to its previous window.
RunApp*	Command Line	Runs a Windows- or an MS-DOS–based application. Access 2000 uses the VBA Shell function to run other applications.
RunCode*	Function Name	Runs a user-defined function written in VBA. Replaced by direct execution of code.
RunCommand	Menu Bar Menu Name Command Subcommand	Runs any command on a built-in Access 2000 menubar or toolbar if the bar is appropriate for the view when the macro carries out the command.

continues

TABLE 28.4   CONTINUED

Method	Argument Name	Purpose
RunMacro*	Macro Name Repeat Count Repeat Expression	Runs the specified macro. Enter the macro name's full syntax to run an individual macro in a macro group. Use the Repeat Count and Repeat Expression arguments to specify how many times to run the macro. Replace macros with VBA procedures in Access 2000 applications.
RunSQL*	SQL Statement	Runs an action query as specified by the SQL statement. (To run a select query, use the OpenQuery action instead.) Replaced by the Execute method of a QueryDef object.
Save	Object Type Object Name	Saves the specified database object. Leave the arguments blank to save the active window.
SelectObject	Object Type Object Name In Database Window	Selects a specified database object.
SendKeys	Keystrokes Wait	Sends keystrokes to any active Windows application.
SendObject	Object Type Object Name Output Format To Cc Bcc Subject Message Text Edit Message	Sends the specified datasheet, form, report, or module in an electronic mail message. You can't send a macro. This action requires that you have a MAPI-compliant electronic mail application on your computer.
SetMenuItem	Menu Index Menu Item Menu Sub Item Flag	Sets the state of a menu item on a custom menu to check a command or make it unavailable (grayed, or disabled).
SetValue*	Item Expression	Sets the value of a field, control, or property on a form, form datasheet, or report. Replaced by VBA code to set values.
SetWarnings	Warnings On	Turns default warning messages on or off. Does not suppress error messages or system dialogs that require you to input text or select an option.

Method	Argument Name	Purpose
ShowAllRecords	No arguments	Removes any filters and requeries the active object.
StopAllMacros*	No arguments	Stops all macros that are currently running. VBA code replaces macros in Access 2000.
StopMacro*	No arguments	Stops the current macro. VBA code replaces macros in Access 2000.
TransferDatabase	Transfer Type Database Type Database Name Object Type Source Destination Structure Only	Imports data from another database, exports data to another database, or links a table in another database to the current database. The other database can be an Access or SQL database.
Transfer Spreadsheet	Transfer Type Spreadsheet Type Table Name File Name Has Field Names Range	Imports data from a spreadsheet file or exports Access data to a spreadsheet file.
TransferText	Transfer Type Specification Name Table Name File Name Has Field Names	Imports data from a text file or exports Access data to a text file.

The OutputTo, TransferDatabase, TransferSpreadsheet, and TransferText methods deserve special attention by application developers. These bulk transfer methods greatly simplify the data interchange between Access and other Office 2000 applications, such as Excel and Word. The more complex DoCmd methods, together with Access 2000's flexible report generation capabilities, are often the deciding factor when choosing between Visual Basic 6+ or Access 2000 for developing database front ends. Visual Basic doesn't offer equivalents of the bulk transfer Access methods.

CUSTOMIZING APPLICATIONS WITH CommandBar OBJECTS

Office 2000 applications use CommandBar objects to create menubars, popup menus, toolbar buttons, and toolbar combo boxes. To gain VBA programming access to CommandBar objects, your database must include a reference to the Microsoft Office 9.0 Object Library, Mso9.dll (see Figure 28.19). Mso9.dll includes other objects that are common to Office 2000, such as the Balloon object of the Office Assistant object and the DocumentProperty object for files. Figure 28.20 shows the Microsoft Office Objects help topic that displays the collections and objects exposed by Mso9.dll. The top-level collections and objects—CommandBars, Assistant, FileSearch, and DocumentProperties—are members of Access 2000's Application object.

Figure 28.19
Creating a reference to the Microsoft Office 9.0 Object Library.

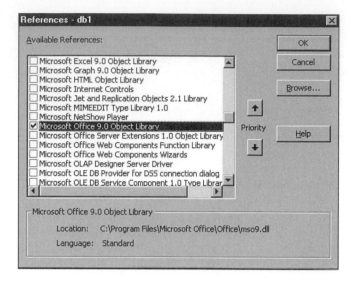

Figure 28.20
The hierarchy of Office 2000 collections and objects from the the Microsoft Office Objects help topic.

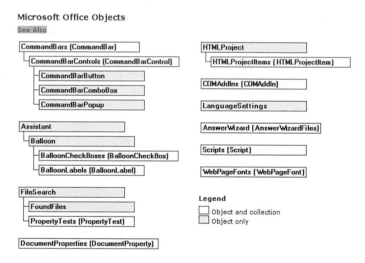

 With a reference to Mso9.dll, Office 2000 object classes appear in the Object Browser's window when you select the Office library (see Figure 28.21). Selecting a class or member of the class and then clicking the Object Browser's Help (?) button displays the Microsoft Office Visual Basic help topic for the selection. Using Object Browser's Help button is the easiest way to obtain the VBA syntax for programming specific Office objects.

The Immediate window is useful for gaining familiarity with programming Office objects. Figure 28.22 shows how to obtain property values of the CommandBars collection, CommandBar objects, and the Control objects of CommandBars. The Access 2000 version of Northwind.mdb has 141 CommandBars, up 37 from the 104 in Access 97. Unlike most other Access collections that begin with an index value of 0, the first member of Office collections has an index value of 1. The Application. preface in the first statement of Figure 28.22 is optional; the Application object is assumed when referring to top-level Access objects. To view the members of the Access Application class, open the Access library in Object Browser and select Application in the Classes list.

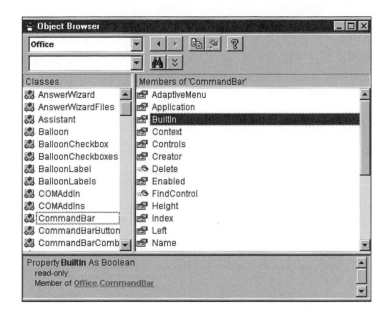

Figure 28.21
A few of the Office object classes and members displayed in Object Browser.

Note

If you've hidden unused windows in the Editor, press Ctrl+G to open the Immediate (formerly the Debug) window.

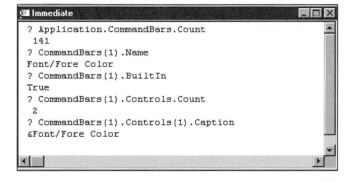

Figure 28.22
Using the Immediate window to obtain property values of CommandBars and their Control objects.

The following simple VBA subprocedure, added to a temporary new module, Module1, iterates the CommandBars collection and prints the Name and Visible property values of each CommandBar in the Immediate window:

```
Sub PrintCommandBars()
   Dim msoBar As CommandBar
   For Each msoBar In CommandBars
      Debug.Print msoBar.Name, msoBar.Visible
   Next msoBar
End Sub
```

Northwind.mdb has a custom command bar that adds the Show Me entry to Access's main menubar. When you run the preceding subprocedure from the Immediate window, the NorthwindCustomMenuBar appears in about the middle of the list with its Visible property True. Figure 28.23 shows some of the property values of NorthwindCustomMenuBar. The Show Me menu choice is the fifteenth member of the Controls collection of the menu bar, with a Caption property value of "Show Me". The OnAction property value, "=ShowHelpAPI()", uses the ShowHelpAPI function of the Northwind Help Module to open the help file for the Northwind Traders sample database. To display the ShowHelpAPI function, open a module, choose Edit, Find, and then search for "ShowHelp" with the Current Database option selected.

You can change the properties of existing command buttons with VBA code. As an example, typing the following code in the Immediate window immediately changes the Show Me menu choice to Show You:

```
CommandBars("NorthwindCustomMenuBar").Controls(15).Caption = "Show &You"
```

You add a new CommandBar object by applying the Add method to the CommandBars collection, setting the properties of the new CommandBar object, and adding members to the CommandBar object's Controls collection. A full exposition of VBA programming of custom CommandBar objects is beyond the scope of this book. Most of the developer-level books for Access 2000 listed in the "Bibliography" section of the Introduction to this book cover custom CommandBar programming in detail.

Figure 28.23
Property values of the NorthwindCustom MenuBar and its added Control object, Show Me.

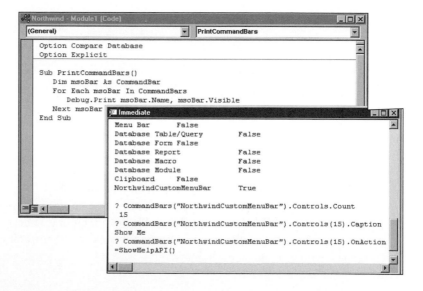

SPECIFYING A CUSTOM CommandBar AND SETTING OTHER STARTUP PROPERTIES

The Startup dialog lets you assign an application title to the database, specify a form to open when the application starts, and specify the name of a custom CommandBar as Access's main menubar. To set Startup properties, follow these steps:

1. Make the Database window active and choose Tools, Startup to open the Startup dialog. Click the Advanced button to expand the dialog.

2. Type a name for your application in the Application Title text box; the application name replaces Access's default title bar caption. If you have a special icon file (*Filename*.ico), you can specify the icon file in the Application Icon text box.

3. If you've created a custom CommandBar for your application, select the CommandBar in the drop-down Menu Bar list.

4. Open the Display Form/Page list and select the form that you want to appear when you open the database (see Figure 28.24). You can elect to hide the Database window and the status bar by clearing the Display Database Window and Display Status Bar check boxes.

5. The remaining check boxes let you limit use of your application's menubars, shortcut menus, and toolbars. You can also restrict viewing of VBA code when an error occurs and disable Access's special key combinations.

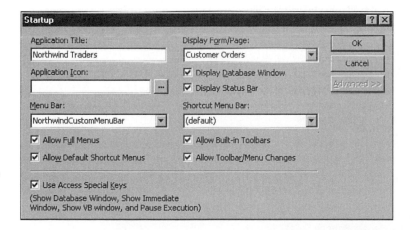

Figure 28.24
Setting the Application Title, Menu Bar, and Display Form properties in the Startup dialog.

Tip #269 from

RJ

Don't clear any of the Startup dialog's check boxes until you're ready to release your application to users. Limiting Access's built-in menu, toolbar, and code-viewing feature set is likely to impede your development activities.

6. Click OK to assign the changes you made and close the Startup dialog.

REFERRING TO ACCESS OBJECTS WITH VBA

One of the reasons for using the term *Access VBA* in this book is that Access defines its own set of objects and uses specialized VBA syntax to refer to many Access objects. Although Form objects are common to most Office 2000 members as well as Visual Basic, a subform (a form embedded in a form) is unique to Access. You find Report objects and subreports only in Access. The syntax for referring to a subform or subreport and for referring to controls contained in a subform or subreport is unique to Access. Even if you're an experienced Visual Basic programmer, you must become acquainted with the new syntax to write VBA code and refer to objects that are unique to Access.

REFERRING TO OPEN FORMS OR REPORTS AND THEIR PROPERTIES

You can refer to a form or report only if it's open. Access uses the Forms and Reports collections to keep track of which forms and reports are open. The Forms collection is the set of open forms, and the Reports collection is the set of open reports. Because Access lets you use the same name for a form and a report, you must distinguish between the two by specifying the collection. The syntax for the reference is the collection name followed by the *exclamation point operator* (!), more commonly called the *bang operator*, and the name of the form or report:

```
Forms![FormName]
Reports![ReportName]
```

Use the bang operator (!) to separate the collection name from the name of an object in the collection. You need to use the square brackets ([...]) to enclose object names that include spaces or other punctuation that's illegal in VBA statements.

A Form or Report object has properties that define its characteristics. The general syntax for referring to a property is the object name followed by the dot operator and the name of the property:

```
Forms![FormName].PropertyName
Reports![ReportName].PropertyName
```

Use the dot (.) operator to separate the object's name from the name of one of its properties. For example, Forms!frmProducts.RecordSource refers to the RecordSource property of the open frmProducts form. You can get or set the value of the RecordSource property with the following two VBA statements:

```
strSource = Forms!frmProducts.RecordSource
Forms!frmProducts.RecordSource = strSource
```

To get or set the value of a form property in the form's own class module, you use the **Me** self-identifier, as in:

```
strSource = Me.RecordSource
Me.RecordSource = strSource
```

The **Me** self-reference is valid only for the instance of the form open in Form view. Thus, you can't use the two preceding statements in the Immediate window unless you create a breakpoint in your code, open the form in Form view, and then execute the procedure that contains the breakpoint. Figure 28.25 shows the Immediate window opened by a breakpoint and set at the first active line of code of the `ReviewProducts_Click` subprocedure of Northwind.mdb's Suppliers form. In breakpoint mode, typing **? Me.RecordSource** returns Suppliers—the name of the table to which the Suppliers form is bound.

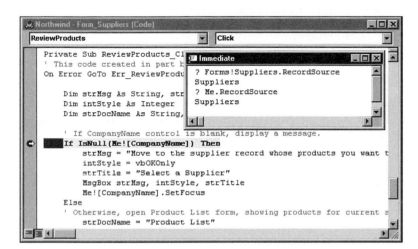

Figure 28.25
The Immediate window opened by reaching a breakpoint during VBA code execution.

→ For detailed instructions on using breakpoints, **see** "Adding a Breakpoint to the `IsLoaded` Function," **p. 1023**.

A form's property sheet lists the form properties that you can set in Design view. Forms also have properties that you can't set in Design view and that do not appear in the property sheet, such as the default `Form` property. The `Form` property refers to the collection of controls on a form. Similarly, a report's default `Report` property refers to the collection of controls in a report.

REFERRING TO CONTROLS AND THEIR PROPERTIES

The following is the general syntax for referring to a control on a form or report:

```
Forms![FormName].Form![ControlName]
```

```
Reports![ReportName].Report![ControlName]
```

As before, the bang operator separates the collection name from the object name. The `Form` property is the default property that Access assumes for a form; therefore, you need not include the `Form` property explicitly in the reference. The following expression is the full identifier syntax for a form control:

```
Forms![FormName]![ControlName]
```

PART

VII

CH

28

Similarly, the following is the full identifier syntax for a report control:

`Reports![ReportName]![ControlName]`

For example, `Forms!frmProducts!ProductName` refers to the `ProductName` control on the open `frmProducts` form.

The syntax for referring to a control's property includes the reference to the control, followed by the dot operator, and then followed by the property name:

`Forms![FormName]![ControlName].[PropertyName]`

`Reports![ReportName]![ControlName].[PropertyName]`

For example, `Forms!frmProducts!ProductName.Visible` refers to the `ProductName` control's `Visible` property.

A control also has a default property. The default property of a text box is the `Text` property. To refer to the value in the `ProductName` text box control in the last example, you could use any of the following equivalent references:

`Forms!frmProducts.Form!ProductName.Text`

`Forms!frmProducts!ProductName.Text`

`Forms!frmProducts.Form!ProductName`

`Forms!frmProducts!ProductName`

Notice that the last two expressions refer both to the control's text value and to the control itself.

When you refer to a control on the active form or report, you can use a shorter version of the reference and refer to the control as follows:

`[ControlName]`

Likewise, you can refer to the control property as follows:

`[ControlName].PropertyName`

Normally, you can use either the short or full syntax to refer to a control on the active form or report. However, in some cases you must use the short syntax. For example, the `GoToControl` action's `ControlName` argument requires the short syntax. You can explicitly refer to a control on the form of the class module with `Me!ControlName` statements. When you refer to a control on a form or report that's not the active object, you usually must use the full identifier syntax.

REFERRING TO CONTROLS ON A SUBFORM OR THE MAIN FORM

The key to understanding the syntax for referring to a control on a subform is to realize that the subform is a form that's bound to a subform control on the main form. The subform control has the usual attribute properties that control its display behavior, such as size and visibility, as well as linking properties that relate the records in the subform to records in the form, including the `SourceObject`, `LinkChildFields`, and `LinkMasterFields` properties. In addition, the subform control has the `Form` property. A subform control's `Form` property refers to the controls contained on the subform.

The following is the syntax for referring to the subform control:

```
Forms![FormName]![SubformControlName]
```

The syntax for referring to a control on a subform bound to a subform control is as follows:

```
Forms![FormName]![SubformControlName]![ControlName]
```

When the form is active, the following short syntax refers to a control on a subform of the active form:

```
[SubformControlName]![ControlName]
```

The `Form` property of the subform, required in Access 95 and earlier when referring to controls on a subform, now is the subform control's default property, so you don't need to include it in the reference. Normally, you use the subform's name as the name of the subform control. For example, if sbfSuppliers is the name of a form bound to a subform control also named sbfSuppliers on the frmProducts form, the following is the full syntax for referring to the `SupplierName` control on the subform:

```
Forms!frmProducts!sbfSuppliers[.Form]!SupplierName
```

The short syntax is as follows:

```
sbfSuppliers[.Form]!SupplierName
```

When the focus is in a subform's control, you can refer to a control on the main form by using the control's `Parent` property. The `Parent` property refers to the collection of controls on the main form. In the previous example, to refer to the `ProductName` control on the main form from VBA code in the class module of a subform, use the following syntax:

```
Parent!ProductName
```

All the preceding syntax examples in this section apply to reports and subreports; just change `Forms` to `Reports` and `Form` to `Report`.

> **Note**
>
> The `ShowSales_Click` subprocedure of the ShowSales form in the Developer Solutions database (Solutions.mdb) provides examples of VBA code that uses references to properties of a subform.

USING ALTERNATIVE COLLECTION SYNTAX

An alternative to the *CollectionName*!*ObjectName* syntax is to specify *CollectionName* and supply *ObjectName* as an argument value:

```
Forms("frmProducts")!sbfSuppliers!SupplierName
```

The advantage of the argument method is that you can substitute a **String** variable for the literal argument value:

```
Forms(strFormName)!sbfSuppliers!SupplierName
```

You also can pass a 0-based **Long** value to specify the ordinal (position) of the object in the collection:

```
Forms(2)!sbfSuppliers!SupplierName
```

Passing the ordinal value, however, isn't a safe programming practice because the ordinal position of objects in a collection change as you add or delete members.

RESPONDING TO DATA EVENTS TRIGGERED BY FORMS AND CONTROLS

Recordsets underlying forms and reports trigger data events when you move the record pointer or change the value in one or more cells of the Recordset. The most common use of data events is to validate updates to the Recordset; you add validation code to the event-handling subprocedure for the BeforeUpdate event. The use of code, instead of setting field-level or table-level ValidationRule property values, is that VBA provides a much more flexible method of ensuring data consistency. Validation rules you write in VBA commonly are called *business rules*. Business rules often are quite complex and require access to multiple lookup tables—some of which might be located in other databases.

→ **See** "Validating Data Entry," **p. 194**.

Listing 28.3 shows an example of a set of validation rules for postal codes in the Suppliers table of Northwind.mdb, the Recordset of which is bound to the Suppliers form. The BeforeUpdate event, which triggers before a change is made to the Recordset, includes a predefined Cancel argument. If you set Cancel = **True** in your event-handling code, the proposed update to the Recordset does not occur.

LISTING 28.3   A VBA VALIDATION SUBPROCEDURE FOR INTERNATIONAL POSTAL CODES

```
Private Sub Form_BeforeUpdate(Cancel As Integer)
' If number of digits entered in PostalCode text box is
' incorrect for value in Country text box, display message
' and undo PostalCode value.

    Select Case Me!Country
        Case IsNull(Me![Country])
            Exit Sub
        Case "France", "Italy", "Spain"
            If Len(Me![PostalCode]) <> 5 Then
                MsgBox "Postal Code must be 5 characters", 0, _
                    "Postal Code Error"
                Cancel = True
                Me![PostalCode].SetFocus
            End If
```

```
        Case "Australia", "Singapore"
            If Len(Me![PostalCode]) <> 4 Then
                MsgBox "Postal Code must be 4 characters", 0, _
                    "Postal Code Error"
                Cancel = True
                Me![PostalCode].SetFocus
            End If
        Case "Canada"
            If Not Me![PostalCode] Like _
                "[A-Z][0-9][A-Z] [0-9][A-Z][0-9]" Then
                MsgBox "Postal Code not valid. " & _
                    "Example of Canadian code: H1J 1C3", _
                    0, "Postal Code Error"
                Cancel = True
                Me![PostalCode].SetFocus
            End If
    End Select
End Sub
```

The VBA code examples in this chapter cover only the basics of using VBA 6.0 for responding to events triggered by forms, controls, and Recordsets bound to forms or reports. A full course in VBA programming exceeds both the scope and the publishing limitations of this book. Many of the examples in this chapter are drawn from the sample databases supplied with Access 2000. You can adapt many of the techniques illustrated in the event-handling subprocedures of the sample databases to custom applications you create. To become an expert in VBA programming requires study, experimentation, and perseverance. Periodicals, books, and Web sites, such as those listed in the "Other Sources of Information for Access" section of the introduction to this book, are likely to satisfy the studious reader. There's no substitute, however, for experimentation. Writing and testing code is the only sure way to become proficient in VBA programming.

TROUBLESHOOTING

CALLING PROCEDURES AND FUNCTIONS IN CLASS MODULES

After adding test code to a form class module, you encounter a "Compile Error - Sub or Function not defined" error message when running the code from the Immediate window.

To execute from the Immediate window subprocedures or functions in class modules, you must preface the name of the subprocedure or function with the name of the class module. For example, if you add the PrintCommandBars function to the Main Switchboard form's class module, and type **PrintCommandBars** in the Immediate window, you get the error message. You must preface the command with the class module name, as in **[Form_Main Switchboard].PrintCommandBars.** (Add the square brackets only if the form name contains a space.) You also must add the class name prefix when calling with code subprocedures or functions from another class module or conventional module. You don't need to add the form name prefix to call public functions in conventional modules.

MISSING OBJECTS IN COLLECTIONS

"Object not found in this collection" errors occur with explicit object names or values passed as argument values.

You misspelled the object name or failed to assign a value to an argument variable. To check the names of objects, especially those with long or convoluted names, type **?** *CollectionName***(0)** in the Immediate window to return the name of the first collection. If you don't obtain the expected name, replace **0** with increasing values.

IN THE REAL WORLD—DEALING WITH EVENT-DRIVEN PROGRAMMING

Beginning programmers and Web page designers often find that understanding Windows' event-driven programming model to be quite difficult. The same problem befalls many programmers experienced in conventional procedural languages, such as assembly, COBOL, Pascal, and xBase. With a very few exceptions, VBA code in an Access application or script in a DHTML page executes only in response to a predefined event. (The primary exceptions are variable and Windows function prototype declarations that precede VBA subprocedure and function code in modules.)

Early versions of Access and Visual Basic offered a relatively sparse event model, and DAO doesn't fire events in any version. Each upgrade to Access and Visual Basic added to the platform's events, a process described in press releases as "increasing event granularity." The OLE Controls of Access 2.0 and Visual Basic 4.0 were in-process Automation servers with event sources. Forms and other containers for OLE Controls came to be known as event sinks. The source-sink nomenclature derives from the early days of transistors—emitters serve as a source of electrons and collectors act as electron sinks. Field effect transistors gained electron drains, and other devices had electron traps. Familiarity with plumbing fixtures, along with solid-state physics and thermodynamics, was *de rigeur* to a basic understanding of semiconductor theory.

The first Office data object model that offered events was Access 97's ODBCDirect, an object wrapper over Visual Basic 4.0 Enterprise Edition's Remote Data Object (RDO) 1.0. The ability to intercept data-related events, such as when making a connection or starting and ending query execution, offer the ability to handle connection errors and asynchronous data operations. An *asynchronous data operation* is one in which control returns to your program after query execution starts. When the query completes, the corresponding event lets you write code to process the resulting Recordset. Your application isn't in a state of suspended animation while waiting for a "query from hell" to complete.

Access 2000 continues to support ODBCDirect, now based on Visual Basic 5.0's improved RDO 2.0, which bypasses Jet 4.0 to provide better client/server performance than DAO 3.6. OLE DB and ADO, however, provide a much richer (more granular) event model, as demonstrated by the event-related sections of the preceding chapter. ("Rich event model" also is a common term in today's press releases). For optimum front-end VBA programming flexibility, you can't beat ADO's event model. If the past history of Access and VBA upgrades prevails, you can expect future versions of OLE DB and ADO to give VBA programmers even more precise control over data access operations.

--rj

CHAPTER 29

PROGRAMMING COMBO AND LIST BOXES

In this chapter

Streamlining Decision Support Front Ends   1128

Constraining Query Choices with Combo Boxes   1128

Designing the Decision-Support Query   1129

Creating the Form and Adding a List Box   1130

Converting Your Combo Box Form to an Access Data Project   1138

Conforming Row Source SQL Statements to Transact-SQL Syntax   1140

Drilling Down from a List Box Selection   1142

Adding New Features to List and Combo Boxes   1145

Iterating List Box Items and Selecting an Item   1145

Dealing with Jet-Specific Functions in Migrating to ADP   1150

Troubleshooting   1152

In the Real World—Access Combo and List Boxes   1153

STREAMLINING DECISION SUPPORT FRONT ENDS

Decision-support applications deliver information used by management to analyze business trends. Data warehouses and data marts, today's hottest database technology topics, form the back end for decision-support applications in larger organizations. Microsoft Decision Support Services (MSDSS), more commonly known by its code-name Plato, is a component of SQL Server 7.0. MSDSS supports online analytical processing (OLAP), a technique primarily intended for extracting time-based trends and other relationships from massive amounts of data. OLAP is beyond the scope of this book, but the data selection and display techniques you learn in this chapter are applicable to larger-scale OLAP activities.

The source data for the tables that make up a data warehouse or mart is a condensed version (called a *roll-up*) of the content of production databases used by online transaction processing (OLTP) applications. Roll-ups use SQL aggregate queries to sum values, typically orders and sales. It's also common practice to average gross margins, days-to-ship, and the like. Creating roll-ups of production data for decision support, usually on a server not running OLTP databases, maximizes the performance of both activities. If managers need to analyze the detail data behind the aggregate information provided by the decision-support application, *drill-down* techniques provide limited access to the underlying OLTP records. The critical feature of decision-support applications is accuracy of data retrieval and presentation; execution speed is the next most important criterion.

Tip #270 from

R J

> Decision-support applications involve read-only access to data, so you aren't limited to datasheet or form/subform views of queries. Access list boxes offer faster performance and easier multi-record navigation than subforms, which are intended primarily for data entry. Combo boxes are the ideal control for letting users make ad hoc choices of the information they want to see.

This chapter shows you how to combine combo boxes and list boxes with VBA code to create an interactive form for a simple decision-support application having a drill-down feature.

CONSTRAINING QUERY CHOICES WITH COMBO BOXES

Users of decision-support applications, especially managers, aren't likely to be able or want to use Access's graphical Query Design window. Instead, most users prefer to pick criteria (SELECT query WHERE clause elements) from one or more lists of available options. One primary advantage of offering users a set of choices to construct a query is the ability to prevent execution of ad hoc queries that return an excessive number of rows. Accidentally returning thousands of rows or—even worse—a Cartesian product of a million rows or more can bring a multiuser application or the entire network to its knees. Network and database administrators call such events *queries from hell*.

Tip #271 from

Combo boxes are the better choice for generating WHERE clause criteria because they occupy less room on forms than list boxes. Also, you can navigate quickly to a combo box item by typing the first few characters of the item in the combo box's text box element.

The following sections describe how to create a form with two combo boxes that displays a list of orders from a specified country that include a particular product.

DESIGNING THE DECISION-SUPPORT QUERY

Query designs is one of the most important elements of decision-support applications. One primary objective of decision-support systems is fast response time. To return selected information quickly, the query design should be as simple as possible. Include in the query only those fields needed to display necessary information, plus the foreign key fields to be selected in the combo boxes.

Follow these steps to create the minimal query for the information to be returned from the combo box selections:

1. Open the Northwind sample database or create a working copy of Northwind.mdb by compacting it to another file, such as Nwind.mdb. (Using a working copy prevents inadvertent damage to Northwind.mdb.)

→ For a refresher in compacting a database to a new file, **see** "Compacting and Repairing Databases," **p. 118**.

2. Create a new query in Design view and add the Customers, Orders, and Order Details tables.

3. Drag the CompanyName and Country fields of the Customers table, the OrderID and ShippedDate fields of the Orders table, and the ProductID of the Order Details table to the Query Design grid (see Figure 29.1).

4. Click the Datasheet button of the toolbar to test your query, and then close and save your query as **qryCombo1**.

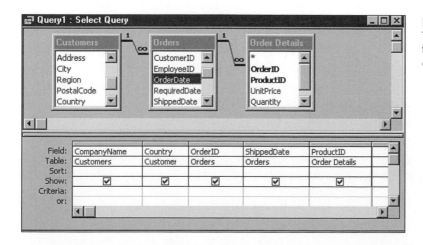

Figure 29.1
The Query Design view of the initial combo box query.

CREATING THE FORM AND ADDING A LIST BOX

An Access list box is the most efficient control for displaying the read-only query result sets of decision-support applications. List boxes consume fewer computer resources than subforms, are easier for users to navigate, and have the properties and events needed to give your application drill-down capabilities. *Drill-down* is the process of providing users with more detailed information about a specific item in the list. Later, the section "Drilling Down from a List Box Selection" shows you how to add drill-down capabilities to the form you create here.

→ For list and combo box basics, **see** "Using List Boxes and Combo Boxes," **p. xxx**. [Ch 13]

To create an unbound form with a list box, follow these steps:

1. Create a new unbound form in Design view. (Don't specify a Record Source for the form.) Adjust the size of the form to about 4.5 by 2 inches.

2. Choose <u>E</u>dit, Fo<u>r</u>m, and then click the Properties button for the form. Click the Format tab and set Scroll Bars to Neither, Record Selectors to No, and Navigation Buttons to No. Type **Order Query with Criteria from Combo Boxes** as the value of the Caption property.

3. With the Control Wizards button pressed, add a list box from the Toolbox to the form. Adding the list box opens the first dialog of the List Box Wizard.

4. Select the List Box Wizard's I Want the List Box to Look Up the Values in a Table or Query option, and click Next.

5. Select the Queries option in the View frame, select qryCombo1 (created in the preceding section) from the list, and click Next.

6. Select the CompanyName field in the Available Fields list and click the > button to add the field to the Selected Fields list. Repeat the process for the OrderID and ShippedDate fields, and then click Next.

> **Note**
>
> You don't display the Country or Product ID in the list box because these fields are specified by combo box selection.

7. Adjust the widths of the columns to suit the list headers and data. Click Next.

8. Select OrderID as the column to uniquely identify the row. Click Next.

9. Type **Orders by Country and Product** as the caption for the list box's label, and click Finish to add the list box to the form.

10. Move the label to the top of the list box and click the toolbar's Bold button to make the label's caption more visible.

11. Select the list box, and change the Name property value of the combo box to **lstOrders**. Select Yes as the value of the Column Heads property (see Figure 29.2).

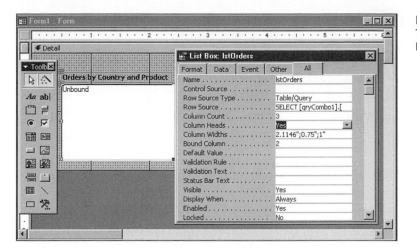

Figure 29.2
The list box in Form
Design view.

 12. Click the Form View button to check the layout of the list box. Choose <u>W</u>indows, Si<u>z</u>e
to Fit Form to set the dimensions of the form window. Your form appears as shown in
Figure 29.3.

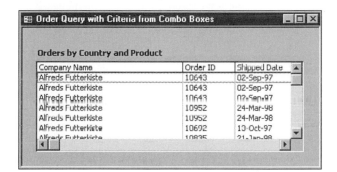

Figure 29.3
The list box in Form view
displaying the first few
rows of the query result
set of qryCombo1.

13. Choose <u>F</u>ile, <u>S</u>ave, and name your form **frmCombo1**.

ADDING THE QUERY COMBO BOXES TO THE FORM

You need one combo box to select the country and another to select the product.
Northwind.mdb doesn't have a Countries table, so the data source for the country combo
box is the Country field of the Customers table. The data source for the product combo box
is the Products table.

→ For detailed combo box instructions, **see** "Using the Combo Box Wizard," **p. 503**.

To add the two combo boxes to the form, follow these steps:

1. Add from the Toolbox a combo box to the upper left of the form; the first dialog of the
Combo Box Wizard opens.

2. Select the I Want the Combo Box to Look Up the Values in a Table or Query and click Next.

3. With the Tables option selected, pick Customers from the list and click Next.

4. Select Country in the Available Fields list and click the > button to move Country to the Selected Fields list. Click Next.

5. Adjust the width of the Country column and click Next.

6. Accept Country as the caption for the label and click Finish to add the combo box to the form.

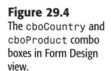

7. Adjust the position and size of the label, and then click the Bold button.

8. Click the Data tab of the Properties window and verify that the value of the Limit to List property is Yes.

9. Click the Other tab of the Properties window and type **cboCountry** as the value of the Name property.

10. Repeat steps 1 and 2.

11. With the Tables option selected, pick Products from the list and click Next.

12. Select ProductID in the Available Fields list and click the > button to move ProductID to the Selected Fields list. Do the same for ProductName, and then click Next.

13. Adjust the width of the ProductName column to accommodate long product names, and click Next.

14. Type **Product** as the caption for the label, and click Finish to add the combo box to the form.

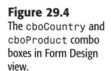

15. Adjust the position and size of the label, and then click the Bold button.

16. Click the Data tab of the Properties window, and set the value of the Limit to List property to Yes.

17. Click the Other tab of the Properties window, and type **cboProduct** as the value of the Name property (see Figure 29.4).

Figure 29.4
The cboCountry and cboProduct combo boxes in Form Design view.

18. Click the Form View button and test both combo boxes (see Figure 29.5).

Note

Figure 29.5 is a double exposure created from two display captures. You can't open both combo boxes simultaneously.

19. Choose File, Save to save the changes to frmCombo1.

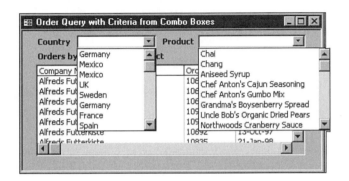

Figure 29.5
The two combo boxes open in Form view.

The Country combo box in Figure 29.5 has an obvious defect: multiple instances of country names that aren't in alphabetical order. These problems arise from the SQL statement that the Combo Box Wizard creates as the value of the combo box's Row Source property:

```
SELECT [Customers].[CustomerID], [Customers].[Country]
    FROM [Customers];
```

The Combo Box Wizard automatically includes the primary key field of the table (CustomerID) as the bound column, so you must remove the [Customers].[CustomerID] column from the SQL statement and modify cboCountry's properties to accommodate this change. Adding an ORDER BY Country clause provides the sort sequence. ANSI SQL's DISTINCT or Access SQL's DISTINCTROW qualifier solves the duplication problem.

→ For the differences between the two SELECT qualifiers, **see** "Jet's DISTINCTROW and SQL's DISTINCT Keywords," **p. 877**.

To make the required changes to the Country combo box, do the following:

NEW 2000

1. Select the cboCountry combo box, and click the Properties button. Access 2000 lets you change most of the properties of combo boxes in run mode.

2. Click the Data tab, and then edit the value of the Row Source property to the following:

```
SELECT DISTINCT Country FROM Customers ORDER BY Country;
```

You don't need to include the square brackets around table and field names because neither includes spaces or other SQL-illegal characters. The table name prefix for field names isn't needed because only the query includes just one table.

Make sure the Row/Source Type property value remains set to Table/Query after you make the change.

3. Click the Format tab and change the value of the Column Count property from 2 to 1.

4. Remove the first 0"; element of the Column Widths property value (see Figure 29.6).

5. Click the Form View button and test your modified combo box. As shown in Figure 29.7, the duplicates are removed and the country names are in alphabetical order.

Figure 29.6
Reducing the Column Count property from 2 to 1 and eliminating the hidden column for the original query's CustomerID column.

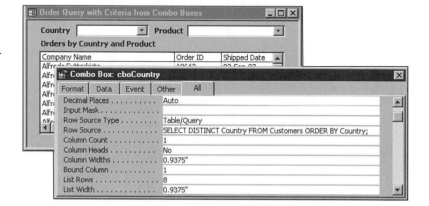

Figure 29.7
The alphabetized Country combo box with duplicates removed.

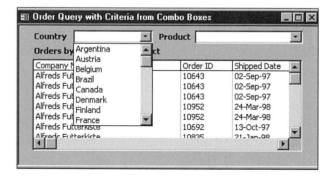

It's easier for users to choose a product if the contents of the Product combo box are alphabetized by doing the following:

1. Select the cboProduct combo box, and open its Properties window.

2. Click the Data tab, and add **ORDER BY ProductName** to the end of the SQL statement in the Row Source text box.

3. Verify that cboProduct displays the product names in alphabetical order.

ADDING CODE TO CREATE THE QUERY'S SQL STATEMENT

Selections you make in the combo boxes return the values required for the WHERE clause criteria of the query that serves as the Row Source property of the lstOrders list box. Selecting an item in the combo list returns the value of the bound column to the combo box's Value property. The Row Source property value of the lstOrders list box created by the List Box Wizard is as follows:

```
SELECT [qryCombo1].[CompanyName],
    [qryCombo1].[OrderID], [qryCombo1].[ShippedDate]
  FROM [qryCombo1];
```

A model SQL statement that simplifies the query syntax, uses the combo box values, and sorts the rows in reverse date order (newest orders first) is this:

```
SELECT CompanyName, OrderID, ShippedDate
  FROM qryCombo1
  WHERE Country = cboCountry.Value AND
    ProductID = cboProduct.Value
  ORDER by ShippedDate DESC;
```

To write the VBA code to create the SELECT query based on combo box values and add instructions for the user, follow these steps:

1. Choose View, Tab Order to open the Tab Order dialog. Click the Auto Order button to set a cboCountry, cboProduct, lstOrders sequence. Click OK to close the dialog.

2. Select the list box label and change the value of its Name property to **lblList**.

3. Click the Code button to display the class module for the frmCombo1 form in the VBA Editor and add the following code for the SQL statement to the Declarations section, immediately below **Option** Explicit:

```
Private Const strSQL1 = "SELECT CompanyName, OrderID, ShippedDate " & _
    "FROM qryCombo1 WHERE Country = '"
Private Const strSQL2 = "' AND ProductID = "
Private Const strSQL3 = " ORDER by ShippedDate DESC;"
Private strSQL As String
```

Tip #272 from

RJ

The single quotation marks (') are required to set off **String** values within SQL statements. Numeric values don't require quotation marks.

---

4. Add the following code for messages to the Declarations section:

```
Private Const strMsg1 = "Select a product from the list"
Private Const strMsg2 = "Select a country from the list"
```

5. Type **Private Sub FillList** to create a subprocedure stub to fill the list box.

6. Add the following code to the FillList stub to create the SQL statement for the list box's RowSource property, refresh the list box by applying the Requery method, and change the caption of the list box label to display the WHERE clause criteria:

```
strSQL = strSQL1 & Me!cboCountry.Value & _
    strSQL2 & Me!cboProduct.Value & strSQL3
Me!lstOrders.RowSource = strSQL
Me!lstOrders.Requery
Me!lblList.Caption = "Orders from " & _
Me!cboCountry.Value & " for " & _
Me!cboProduct.Column(1)
If Me!lstOrders.ListCount = 0 Then
Me!lblList.Caption = "No " & Me!lblList.Caption
End If
```

Note

A combo box or list box's Column(n) property returns the value of the specified column. The first column (n = 0) of cboProduct is ProductID; the second (n = 1) is ProductName.

7. Select cboCountry from the Object list and select AfterUpdate from the Procedure list to create the **Private Sub** cboCountry_AfterUpdate() event-handler stub.

8. Add the following code to the AfterUpdate() stub to alter the caption of the list box label:

```
If Me!cboProduct.Value > 0 Then
    Call FillList
Else
    Me!lblList.Caption = strMsg1
End If
```

9. Repeat steps 7 and 8 for the cboProduct combo box, but change the code for step 8 as follows:

```
If Me!cboCountry.Value <> "" Then
    Call FillList
Else
    Me!lblList.Caption = strMsg2
End If
```

10. Select Form from the Object list and Activate from the Procedure list to create a Form_Activate event-handling stub.

11. Add to Form_Activate the following code to generate the list from persisted country and product selections:

```
If Me!cboCountry.Value <> "" And Me!cboProduct.Value > 0 Then
    Call FillList
Else
    Me!lblList.Caption = strMsg2
End If
```

12. Return to Form Design view, select the lstOrders list box, click the Data tab of the Properties window, and delete the default Row Source value so that the full result set of qryCombo1 doesn't appear when you open the form.

13. Click the Form View button to run the code. If you previously selected country and product criteria, the form displays the query result set.

Listing 29.1 contains all code added in the preceding steps. If error messages arise when compiling your code or displaying the form, compare it with this listing.

LISTING 29.1   VBA CODE FOR THE `frmCombo1` **CLASS MODULE AS IT APPEARS IN THE EDITING WINDOW**

```
Option Compare Database
Option Explicit

Const strSQL1 = "SELECT CompanyName, OrderID, ShippedDate " & _
    "FROM qryCombo1 WHERE Country = '"
Const strSQL2 = "' AND ProductID = "
Const strSQL3 = " ORDER by ShippedDate DESC;"
Private strSQL As String

Const strMsg1 = "Select a product from the list"
Const strMsg2 = "Select a country from the list"

Private Sub cboCountry_AfterUpdate()
    If Me!cboProduct.Value > 0 Then
        Call FillList
    Else
        Me!lblList.Caption = strMsg2
    End If
End Sub

Private Sub cboProduct_AfterUpdate()
    If Me!cboCountry.Value <> "" Then
        Call FillList
    Else
        Me!lblList.Caption = strMsg1
    End If
End Sub

Private Sub FillList()
    strSQL = strSQL1 & Me!cboCountry.Value & _
        strSQL2 & Me!cboProduct.Value & strSQL3
    Me!lstOrders.RowSource = strSQL
    Me!lstOrders.Requery
    Me!lblList.Caption = "Orders from " & _
        Me!cboCountry.Value & " for " & _
        Me!cboProduct.Column(1)
    If Me!lstOrders.ListCount = 0 Then
        Me!lblList.Caption = "No " & Me!lblList.Caption
    End If
End Sub

Private Sub Form_Activate()
    If Me!cboCountry.Value <> "" And Me!cboProduct.Value > 0 Then
        Call FillList
    Else
        Me!lblList.Caption = strMsg2
    End If
End Sub
```

Save your form, and then test your work by selecting values from the Country and Product combo boxes to display the query result set (see Figure 29.8). You can type a few letters in the Country or Product list boxes, and then press Enter to figure the AfterUpdate event for the closest matching item.

Figure 29.8
Displaying the result of a query for U.S. orders for ikura (Japanese salted salmon eggs, a common sushi ingredient).

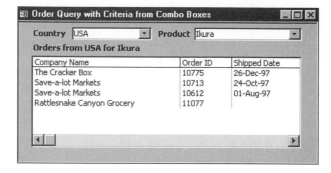

 If you encounter errors when you test your form, see the "Run-Time Error '2465'" and "Spurious Paramater Messages" topics of the "Troubleshooting" section near the end of this chapter.

 The completed frmCombo1 form is included in VBACombo.mdb, located in the \Seua2k\Chaptr29 folder of the accompanying CD-ROM. VBACombo.mdb has tables linked from
...\Office\Samples\Northwind.mdb.

CONVERTING YOUR COMBO BOX FORM TO AN ACCESS DATA PROJECT

The Access Upsizing Wizard (AUW) does a fair job of converting entire Access 2000 applications to Access Data Projects (ADP). In some cases, the AUW can't upsize a form to an operable version in ADP. The frmCombo1 form you created in the preceding sections provides a good example of the problems you encounter when upsizing forms to ADP.

Tip #273 from

It's often a better approach to upsize your front-end application incrementally, migrating individual forms and reports by importing the objects from the original .mdb file to the new .adp file. This approach lets you test each form with MSDE or SQL Server 7.0, and conform Access SQL to Transact-SQL statements to make the form operable.

→ For an explanation of the frailties of the AUW, **see** "Using the Upsizing Wizard to Create ADP," **p. 969**.

Note

The NorthwindCS MSDE database from NorthwindCS.mdb and NorthwindCS.sql must be installed to execute the code in the following example. The "Running the NorthwindCS Sample Project" section of Chapter 25, "Creating Access Data Projects," provides instructions for installing NorthwindCS.

IMPORTING AND TESTING THE COMBO BOX FORM

To import to an .adp file and test `frmCombo1` against MSDE, do the following:

1. Start MSDE with SQL Service Manager, if MSDE isn't running.

2. Choose File, New, and double-click Project (Existing Database) to open the File New Database dialog.

3. Type **OrdersByProductAndCountry.adp** as the File Name, and click Create to close the dialog and open the Data Link Properties sheet.

4. Type **(local)** for the Server Name, **sa** as the User Name, accept the Blank Password option, and select NorthwindCS from the drop-down list. Click the Test Connection button to check the Data Link properties you specified (see Figure 29.9).

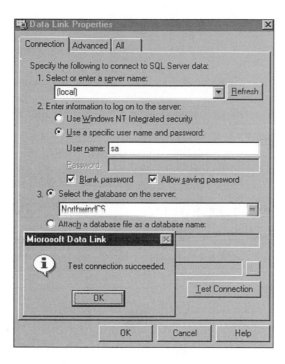

Figure 29.9
The Data Link Properties sheet for the connection to the NorthwindCS MSDE database.

5. Click OK twice to return to the Database window for the new project.

6. Choose File, Get External Data, Import to open the Import Objects dialog. Click the Forms tab, select frmCombo1 in the list, and click OK to import the form to the project.

7. Run the form. The Country combo box works, but no records appear in the Orders list box, despite the fact that selections generate the correct label caption text.

CONFORMING ROW SOURCE SQL STATEMENTS TO TRANSACT-SQL SYNTAX

Most of the problems you encounter when upsizing forms with combo boxes whose Row Source property values contain SQL statements derive from Access queries that use Jet-specific syntax. The conventional approach to upsizing Jet SELECT QueryDef objects is to convert them to views. SQL Server views don't support ORDER BY statements, which the combo boxes need to alphabetize their drop-down lists. Thus you can't use an MSDE view to load the combo boxes.

The Jet SQL statement for the Row Source of cboProduct is as follows:

```
SELECT [Products].[ProductID], [Products].[ProductName]
   FROM [Products]
   ORDER BY ProductName.
```

Transact-SQL executes the preceding statement, but the combo box has problems with the Recordset that MSDE delivers.

A typical Jet SQL statement generated by the FillList subprocedure for the Row Source property of lstOrders is this:

```
SELECT CompanyName, OrderID, ShippedDate
   FROM qryCombo1
   WHERE Country = 'USA' AND ProductID = 39
   ORDER by ShippedDate DESC;
```

The qryCombo1 QueryDef is missing, but MSDE doesn't throw a "Can't find 'qryCombo1'" error in this case; instead, the query fails silently. The fix is to substitute qryCombo1's SQL statement for the preceding SELECT and FROM clauses, as in the following:

```
SELECT Customers.CompanyName, Customers.Country,
      Orders.OrderID, Orders.ShippedDate, [Order Details].ProductID
   FROM (Customers
      INNER JOIN Orders ON
         Customers.CustomerID = Orders.CustomerID)
      INNER JOIN [Order Details] ON
         Orders.OrderID = [Order Details].OrderID;
```

Do the following to make frmCombo1 run with MSDE:

1. In design or run mode, select cboProducts, open its Properties window, and remove the square brackets from the text of the Record Source property. Brackets aren't required for table and field names that don't have spaces or other illegal ANSI SQL object naming characters.

2. Open the .mdb file in which you created frmCombo1 in another instance of Access, open qryCombo1 in Query SQL view, select the SQL statement, and copy it to the Clipboard. Close this instance of Access.

3. In your project, change to Design mode, if necessary, and click the Code button to open the VBA Editor.

4. Select the strSQL1 constant text beginning with SELECT and ending with qryCombo1, then replace the selected text by pasting the copied SQL statement, and then remove the unneeded Customers.Country field identifier from the SELECT clause. Also remove the semicolon statement terminator, if you included it in the Clipboard copy.

5. Make the strSQL1 constant value more readable by splitting the string, as follows:

```
Private Const strSQL1 = "SELECT Customers.CompanyName, " & _
    "Orders.OrderID, Orders.ShippedDate, " & _
    "[Order Details].ProductID FROM (Customers " & _
    "INNER JOIN Orders ON Customers.CustomerID = Orders.CustomerID) " & _
    "INNER JOIN [Order Details] ON Orders.OrderID = " & _
    "[Order Details].OrderID WHERE Country = '"
```

6. Run frmCombo1, verifying that cboProduct and lstOrders now behave properly, and then change its name to frmComboMSDE.

You can check the lstOrders SQL statement by selecting its Row Source property, and then pressing Shift+F2 to display the entire statement in the Zoom dialog (see Figure 29.10).

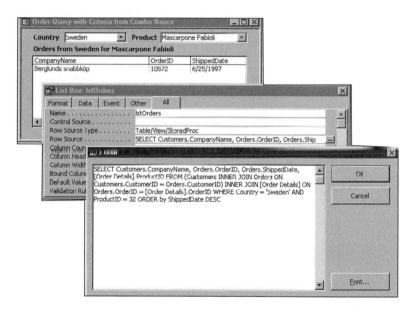

Figure 29.10
Displaying the persisted Row Source property value of the lstOrders list box in the Zoom dialog.

DRILLING DOWN FROM A LIST BOX SELECTION

The most common use of a drill-down form that displays a list of orders is to present the line items of a particular order. It's relatively easy to add and program a line items list box, based on the Order Details table, to the form you created in the preceding sections. An additional use of a line items list box is to verify that the cboProduct combo box correctly performs its assigned role.

> **Note**
>
>
>
> The following sections add features to the frmComboMSDE form imported from OrdersByProductAndCountry.adp. If you're interested only in the .mdb version, you can use the original frmCombo1. Both versions are included in the VBACombo.mdb file in the \SEUA2K\Chaptr29 folder of the accompanying CD-ROM. You must change the server name from OAKLEAF1 to the computer name of your PC to run OrdersByProductAndCountry.adp.

CREATING THE DRILL-DOWN QUERY AND ADDING THE LIST BOX

Create the query and add the list box with the following steps:

1. In your .mdb file, create a new query and add the Order Details and Products tables.

2. Drag the Product Name field of the Products table and the OrderID, UnitPrice, Quantity, and Discount fields of the Order Details table to the Query Design grid. Move the OrderID field to the first column of the query. OrderID doesn't appear in the line items list box; it's required to link to the OrderID column of lstOrders.

3. Add a calculated field defined by typing the following expression in the sixth column of the Field row:

   ```
   Extended: CCur(Format([Order Details].[UnitPrice]*
   [Quantity]*(1-[Discount]),"$#,###.00"))
   ```

   Figure 29.11 illustrates the design of the query.

Figure 29.11
The design of the query for the drill-down list box.

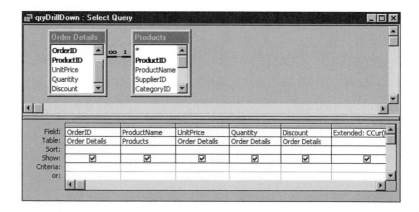

4. Run the query to verify your design, and then close it, saving it as **qryDrillDown**.

5. Increase the height of frmCombo1 to about 3 inches to accommodate an additional list box.

6. Add a list box with the same width as lstOrders and a height of about 3/4 inch to the bottom of the form.

7. Select the Table or Query option in the first Wizard dialog and click Next.

8. Select Queries and qryDrillDown, and then click Next.

9. Click the >> button to add all query columns to the Selected Fields list, and then select the OrderID field and click < to remove it. Click Next.

10. Adjust the widths of the columns to fit the size of the data in the fields. Click Next.

11. Accept the default ProductName column for the default value of the list box. Click Next.

12. Replace the default caption of the label for the combo box with **Line Items**. Click Finish.

13. Move the label to a spot above the new list box, and click the Bold button.

14. Select the new list box, click the Format tab of the Properties window, and change the value of the Column Heads property to Yes.

15. Click the Form View button to check your design (see Figure 29.12).

PART

VII

CH

29

Figure 29.12
The list box for the drill-down query in Form view, displaying the first few rows of the entire Order Details table.

PROGRAMMING THE DRILL-DOWN LIST BOX

The List Box Wizard supplies the following SQL statement as the Row Source property of the new list box:

```
SELECT [qryDrillDown].[ProductName],
    [qryDrillDown].[UnitPrice], [qryDrillDown].[Quantity],
    [qryDrillDown].[Discount], [qryDrillDown].[Extended]
  FROM [qryDrillDown];
```

The simplified SQL statement used to populate the Line Items list box from an order selected in the lstOrders list box is as follows:

```
SELECT ProductName, UnitPrice, Quantity, Discount, Extended
  FROM qryDrillDown
  WHERE OrderID = lstOrders.Value;
```

The following steps complete the modification of the list box and add VBA code to execute the preceding query:

1. Return to Form Design view, select the drill-down list box, click the Other tab of the Properties window, and change the value of the Name property to **lstLineItems**.

2. Select the label for lstLineItems and change the value of its Name property to **lblLineItems**.

3. Click the Code button and add the following string constants to the Declarations section of the frmCombo1 class module:

```
Private Const strSQL4 = "SELECT ProductName, UnitPrice, Quantity, " & _
    "Discount, Extended FROM qryDrillDown WHERE OrderID = "

Private Const strMsg3 = "Double-click an order to display line items"
Private Const strMsg4 = "Line items for order "
Private Const strMsg5 = "Line items"
```

4. Select lstOrders from the Object list and DblClick from the Procedures list to add a lstOrders_DblClick subprocedure stub.

5. Add the following code to the lstOrders_DblClick stub to set the value of the RowSource property of the list box and requery the control:

```
If Me!lstOrders.Value <> "" Then
    With Me!lstLineItems
        strSQL = strSQL4 & Me!lstOrders.Value & ";"
        .RowSource = strSQL
        .Requery

    End With
    Me!lblLineItems.Caption = strMsg4 & Me!lstOrders.Value
End If
```

6. Add the following line to the end of the cboCountry_AfterUpdate and cboProduct_AfterUpdate event handlers to clear the list box when setting new query criteria and change the label caption:

```
With Me!lstLineItems
    .RowSource = ""
    .Requery

End With
Me!lblLineItems.Caption = strMsg5
```

7. Add the following line above the **End If** line of the FillList subprocedure to change the Line Item list box label's caption:

   Me!lblLineItems.Caption = strMsg3

8. Return to Acccess and open the form in Form view. Double-click one of the order items to populate lstLineItems (see Figure 29.13).

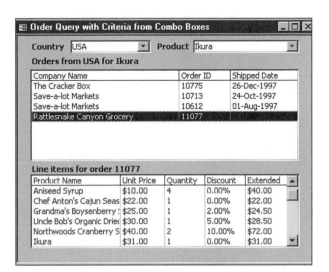

Figure 29.13
The Line Items list box displaying rows from the Order Details table.

ADDING NEW FEATURES TO LIST AND COMBO BOXES

List and combo boxes offer various properties and methods that are accessible only through VBA code. The next two sections describe programming techniques that take advantage of additional list and combo box features.

ITERATING LIST BOX ITEMS AND SELECTING AN ITEM

Access list boxes share many common properties with the native ListBox control of Visual Basic 5.0 and earlier. The ListCount property returns the number of items in the list, the ItemData or Column property returns a value from the list, and the Selected property sets or returns whether the row is selected. This example emphasizes a product in the Line Items list box by automatically selecting the row corresponding to the cboProduct selection. The Column property is more versatile than the ItemData property; ItemData is restricted to values in the bound column.

Follow these steps to add the code required to automatically select a product in the lstLineItems list box:

1. Add this statement to the Declarations section of the frmComboMSDE (or frmCombo1) class module:

   Private intCtr **As Integer**

2. Add these lines immediately above the **End If** statement of the `lstOrders_DblClick` event handler:

```
With Me!lstLineItems
    For intCtr = 0 To.ListCount - 1
        If.Column(0, intCtr) = Me!cboProduct.Column(1) Then
.Selected(intCtr) = True
            Exit For
        End If
    Next intCtr
End With
```

The optional second argument of the `Column` property specifies the row. The **If...Then** statement determines a match between the text values of the ProductName columns of `lstLineItems` and `cboProduct`.

 3. Open the form in Form view. Double-click one of the order items to fill `lstLineItems` and select the specified product (see Figure 29.14).

Figure 29.14
The Line Items list box displaying the selected row from the Order Details table.

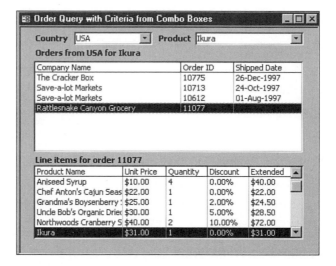

Company Name	Order ID	Shipped Date
The Cracker Box	10775	26-Dec-1997
Save-a-lot Markets	10713	24-Oct-1997
Save-a-lot Markets	10612	01-Aug-1997
Rattlesnake Canyon Grocery	11077	

Line items for order 11077

Product Name	Unit Price	Quantity	Discount	Extended
Aniseed Syrup	$10.00	4	0.00%	$40.00
Chef Anton's Cajun Seas	$22.00	1	0.00%	$22.00
Grandma's Boysenberry :	$25.00	1	2.00%	$24.50
Uncle Bob's Organic Drie	$30.00	1	5.00%	$28.50
Northwoods Cranberry S	$40.00	2	10.00%	$72.00
Ikura	$31.00	1	0.00%	$31.00

Tip #275 from

You can use code similar to what's in this example to emulate a SELECT query against the content of any list box or combo box. Selecting a list box item ensures that the item is visible in the text box, regardless of its location in the list.

ADDING AN OPTION TO SELECT ALL COUNTRIES OR PRODUCTS

It's often useful to give users the option to pick all items represented by combo box selections. In this chapter's example, selecting all countries or all products (but not both) represents an enhancement to the application. How you add an "(All)" choice to `cboCountry` and `cboProduct` and write the code for the appropriate SELECT query to fill `lstOrders` isn't obvious, at best.

A UNION query is the most straightforward way to add custom rows to a combo or list box populated by an SQL statement. You specify your own values for each column returned by the SELECT query to which the UNION clause applies. The UNION query to populate cboCountry is as follows:

```
SELECT Country FROM Customers
    UNION SELECT '(All)' FROM Customers ORDER BY Country;
```

You don't need the DISTINCT modifier of the original SELECT statement because UNION queries don't return duplicate rows. The '(All)' custom item is surrounded with parentheses because (sorts before numerals and letters, making (All) the first item in the list. The Customers table has no (All) record, but all UNION queries require a FROM *TableName* clause.

➡ For UNION query syntax, **see** "Using UNION Queries," **p. 865**.

Similarly, the UNION query to fill cboProduct is as follows:

```
SELECT ProductID, ProductName FROM Products
    UNION SELECT 0, '(All)' FROM Products ORDER BY ProductName;
```

Here you must supply a numeric value—in this case 0—for the first column of the query (ProductID) and the '(All)' string value for the second column (ProductName). UNION queries require that both SELECT statements return the same number of columns, and all rows of each column must be of the same field data type. ProductID is an AutoNumber field, which starts with 1 unless you make the effort to begin autonumbering with a higher value.

➡ For a field data type refresher, **see** "Choosing Field Data Types, Sizes, and Formats," **p. 140**.

In addition to adding the (All) item to the combo boxes, you must alter your SELECT queries to populate lstOrders when you select (All). In the all countries case, the Jet SELECT query is as follows:

```
SELECT CompanyName, OrderID, ShippedDate
    FROM qryCombo1
    WHERE ProductID = cboProduct.Value
    ORDER by ShippedDate DESC;
```

This is the Transact-SQL-compliant version:

```
SELECT Customers.CompanyName, Customers.Country,
    Orders.OrderID, Orders.ShippedDate, [Order Details].ProductID
    FROM (Customers
       INNER JOIN Orders ON
          Customers.CustomerID = Orders.CustomerID)
       INNER JOIN [Order Details] ON
          Orders.OrderID = [Order Details].OrderID
    WHERE ProductID = cboProduct.Value
    ORDER by ShippedDate DESC;
```

For the all-products situation, the Jet query is the following:

```
SELECT CompanyName, OrderID, ShippedDate
    FROM qryCombo1
    WHERE Country = cboCountry.Value
    ORDER by ShippedDate DESC;
```

The Transact-SQL–compliant version is similar to the preceding statement; only the WHERE clause criterion changes.

The preceding changes require you to add logic to detect when you select (All) and change the assembly of the SQL statement to suit. The following steps add the (All) selection to both combo boxes:

1. Return to Form Design mode, select cboCountry, and change its Row Source property value to the following:

```
SELECT Country FROM Customers UNION SELECT '(All)'
FROM Customers ORDER BY Country;
```

2. Select cboProduct and change its Row Source property value to the following:

```
SELECT ProductID, ProductName FROM Products
UNION SELECT 0, '(All)' FROM Products;
```

3. Open the frmComboMSDE (or frmCombo1) class module.

4. Add a line to the Declarations section to provide the SQL statements for the UNION queries for the RowSource properties of the combo boxes. Then add the revised SELECT statement to populate lstOrders:

```
Private Const strSQL5 = "SELECT Customers.CompanyName, " & _
    "Orders.OrderID, Orders.ShippedDate, " & _
    "[Order Details].ProductID FROM (Customers " & _
    "INNER JOIN Orders ON Customers.CustomerID = Orders.CustomerID) " & _
    "INNER JOIN [Order Details] ON Orders.OrderID = " & _
    "[Order Details].OrderID "
Private Const strSQL6 = "WHERE Country = '"
Private Const strSQL7 = "WHERE ProductID = "

Private Const strMsg6 = "You can't select (All) countries and products"
```

5. Select Form from the Object list and Load from the Procedures list to create the Form_Load event handler.

6. Change the code for the cboCountry_AfterUpdate event handler above the line **With Me!lstOrders** as follows to indicate that you can't execute a query that returns all orders:

```
If Me!cboProduct.Value > 0 Then
    Me!lblList.Caption = strMsg1
    Call FillList
Else
    If Me!cboCountry.Value = "(All)" Then
        MsgBox strMsg6
    Else
        Me!lblList.Caption = strMsg2
    End If
End If
```

7. Change the code for the cboProduct_AfterUpdate event handler above the line **With Me!lstOrders** to the following:

```
If Me!cboCountry.Value <> "" Then
    If Me!cboCountry.Value = "(All)" And _
        Me!cboProduct.Value = 0 Then
        MsgBox strMsg6
    Else
        Me!lblList.Caption = strMsg1
        Call FillList
    End If
Else
    Me!lblList.Caption = strMsg2
    Call FillList
End If
```

8. Change the code for the **FillList** subprocedure above the **Me!lstOrders.RowSource =** strSQL line as follows:

```
If Me!cboProduct.Value = 0 Then
    strSQL = strSQL5 & strSQL6 & Me!cboCountry.Value & _
        "'" & strSQL3
ElseIf Me!cboCountry.Value = "(All)" Then
    strSQL = strSQL5 & strSQL7 & Me!cboProduct.Value & _
        strSQL3
Else
    strSQL = strSQL1 & Me!cboCountry.Value & _
        strSQL2 & Me!cboProduct.Value & strSQL3
End If
```

9. Return to Access, close the form, and reopen it in Form view. Select (All) in cboCountry and a product in cboProduct. Click lstOrders to verify your additions (see Figure 29.15).

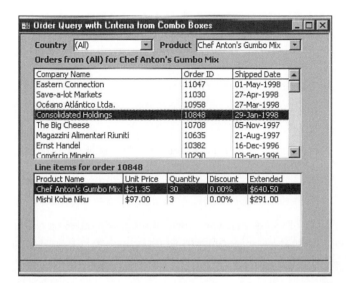

Figure 29.15
Displaying orders from all countries for Chef Anton's Gumbo Mix.

DEALING WITH JET-SPECIFIC FUNCTIONS IN MIGRATING TO ADP

Jet-specific functions such as **CCur** and **Format**, like PIVOT and TRANSFORM, don't have exact counterparts in Transact-SQL. The Jet SQL statement for the lstLineItems list box uses both CCur and Format in the calculated Extended column. The changes made to frmComboMSDE in the two preceding section are compatible with Transact-SQL. To test frmComboMSDE in your OrdersByProductAndCountry.adp project, do the following:

1. Close the .mdb file and open OrdersByProductAndCountry.adp.

> **Note**
>
> If you receive an error with 'qryDrillDown' in the message when opening the form, open the form's properties sheet, select the Line Items list, and delete the offending Row Source property text.

2. Choose File, Get External Data, Import, and import frmComboMSDE to the project.

3. Open frmComboMSDE and test various combinations of country and product, including (All), to verify that lstOrders fills correctly.

4. Double-click an item in the Orders list. There are no items in the Line Items list because MSDE can't execute the Jet query.

The offending Row Source syntax that causes the Line Items query to fail is this:

```
SELECT ProductName, UnitPrice, Quantity, Discount, Extended
   FROM qryDrillDown WHERE OrderID = 11077;
```

The first problem is that qryDrillDown is missing from your .asp file. Thus you must start the fix by importing the SQL from qryDrilldown:

```
SELECT [Order Details].OrderID, Products.ProductName,
    [Order Details].UnitPrice, [Order Details].Quantity,
    [Order Details].Discount,
     CCur(Format([Order Details].[UnitPrice]*
   [Quantity]*(1-[Discount])),"$#,###.00")) AS Extended
   FROM Products INNER JOIN [Order Details]
     ON Products.ProductID = [Order Details].ProductID;
```

Substituting the Jet SQL statement for the SELECT and FROM clauses of the original Row Source property value doesn't work because Transact-SQL doesn't have CCur and Format functions. You must use Transact-SQL's CONVERT statement to handle the currency conversion.

Fortunately, the Order Details Extended view in NorthwindCS.adp offers an example of the CONVERT function syntax required to display columns whose values require explicit currency formatting (see Figure 29.16).

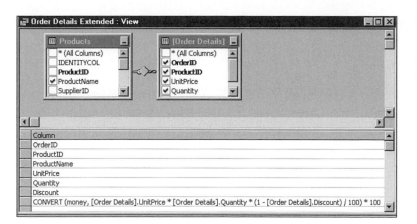

Figure 29.16
Design view of the Order Details Extended view of the NorthwindCS database.

Specifying the SQL Server money data type is equivalent to the CCur and Format operations. The required CONVERT function is as follows:

```
CONVERT (money, [Order Details].UnitPrice *
[Order Details].Quantity *
(1 - [Order Details].Discount) / 100) * 100
```

The typical Transact-SQL statement for the Row Source property of lstLineItems becomes the following:

```
SELECT Products.ProductName, [Order Details].UnitPrice,
   [Order Details].Quantity, [Order Details].Discount,
   CONVERT (money, [Order Details].UnitPrice *
      [Order Details].Quantity *
      (1 - [Order Details].Discount) / 100) * 100 AS Extended
   FROM Products INNER JOIN [Order Details]
      ON Products.ProductID = [Order Details].ProductID
   WHERE OrderID = 11077
```

To fix the Row Source property of lstLineItems, do this:

1. Change to Design mode and delete the string value assigned to the strSQL4 constant.

2. Replace the the value of the strSQL4 constant with the following:
   ```
   Private Const strSQL4 = "SELECT Products.ProductName, " & _
      "[Order Details].UnitPrice, " & _
      "[Order Details].Quantity, [Order Details].Discount, " & _
      "CONVERT (money, [Order Details].UnitPrice * " & _
         "[Order Details].Quantity * " & _
         "(1 - [Order Details].Discount) / 100) * 100 AS Extended " & _
      "FROM Products INNER JOIN [Order Details] " & _
         "ON Products.ProductID = [Order Details].ProductID " & _
      "WHERE [Order Details].OrderID = "
   ```

3. Retest the form by double-clicking an item in the Orders list. The Extended values are formatted properly, but the Discount values appear as decimal fractions.

4. If you want to display discount as a percentage, substitute the following for the [Order Details].Discount field identifier:

```
CONVERT(varchar, [Order Details].Discount * 100)
   + '%' AS Discount
```

SQL users the + symbol, not the ampersand (&), for string concatenation.

Figure 29.17 shows the effects of the preceding changes on the Line Items list.

Figure 29.17
The ADP version of the Line Items list with Transact-SQL formatting applied.

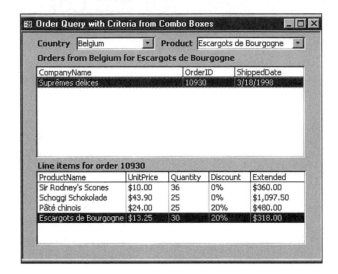

> **Note**
>
> Modifications made to the query for the Record Source property value of lstLineItems aren't compatible with Jet SQL. Thus, the versions of frmComboMSDE in the VBACombo.mdb and OrdersByProductAndCountry.adp sample files are incompatible at this point.

TROUBLESHOOTING

RUN-TIME ERROR '2465'

I receive a "Run-Time Error '2465'" message in Form view.

The most likely cause of this error is failure to change the default Name property value of a combo box or list box to cboCountry, cboProduct, or lblList. Alternatively, you might have misspelled one of the names. Select the Other page of the Properties sheet and select each object to make sure the Name property value is correct.

SPURIOUS PARAMATER MESSAGES

A "Parameter" message appears in Form view.

One field name in your SQL statement doesn't correspond to a field name of qryCombo1. Double-check your values of the strSQL1, strSQL2, and strSQL3 constants against the field names included in qryCombo1.

IN THE REAL WORLD—ACCESS COMBO AND LIST BOXES

Access's bound combo and list boxes offer many advantages over corresponding native controls available to Visual Basic programmers. Automatic multi-field capability in both combo and list boxes, and formatted columns in Access list boxes are just two of the advantages of the Access version. When you migrate to ADP, another advantage of Access combo and list boxes becomes evident—they populate from Transact-SQL statements sent to the server and don't require views.

The downside of sending SQL statements to MSDE or SQL Server is that performance suffers because SQL Server optimizes and compiles the query before execution. Compare the time required to first populate the Line Items list box using a connection to MSDE's NorthwindCS database on your PC to that for Jet's Northwind; Jet is considerably faster. (The performance difference is accentuated on a slower PC or one having 32M or less RAM.) After you run the query once, however, the performance difference is minimal because SQL Server stores the compiled version in memory. When you re-execute the query, SQL Server 7.0 checks to see if it's in memory; if so, it executes the copy without recompilation.

Stored procedures optimize combo and list box performance by eliminating the initial optimization and compilation step. If your query is complex—and especially if it requires multiple joins between large tables—substitute a parameterized stored procedure to return the Recordset that populates list and combo boxes. Stored procedures return read-only Recordsets that have forward-only (Microsoft calls them *firehose*) cursors.

Access multi-column list boxes still have a few warts that need attention in future versions. For instance, you can't specify the alignment of individual columns; numeric values (including currency) and dates should right-align. A long-standing complaint of Access developers is the lack of the simple syntax for adding items to VBA combo boxes—the AddItem method. The callback method of programmatically adding items to Access combo and list boxes is gruesome, and writing code to generate a value list is almost as bad. Developers also complain about the 2K limit on the length of the SQL statement used as the RowSource property of combo and list boxes, as well as the RecordSource property of forms.

Several independent software vendors provide ActiveX control versions of combo and list boxes that have quite flexible formatting capabilities and simplified approaches to population. The Development Exchange's Product Search page at http://www.devx.com/free/products/pgsearch.asp offers a comprehensive list of ActiveX control suppliers and their products.

Regardless of their shortcomings, Access's native combo and list boxes are effective tools for both decision support and online transaction processing front-ends. Consider replacing all read-only subforms with multicolumn list boxes, even if doing so requires some extra VBA code. Your customers—the users of your application—will appreciate their speedy response and space-saving format. You also gain the respect of DBAs when you substitute stored procedures for ad hoc queries against production databases.

--rj

CHAPTER 30

WORKING WITH ADO RECORDSETS, FORMS, AND CONTROLS

In this chapter

Navigating Recordsets with VBA   1156

Using the Find Method and Bookmarks   1162

Modifying Rows of Recordsets   1164

Populating a Combo Box from a Recordset   1165

Altering the Sequence of Combo Box Lists   1169

Filling List Boxes from Recordset Objects   1171

Formatting Value List Combo Box Columns   1174

Porting frmComboVBA to an Access Data Project   1178

Troubleshooting   1178

In the Real World—Adapting to ADO   1179

NAVIGATING RECORDSETS WITH VBA

Recordsets are the foundation for all Access data-related operations. The VCR-style navigation buttons of datasheets and bound forms manipulate the record pointer of the underlying `Recordset`. The following sections show how you emulate Access's navigation buttons with Visual Basic for Applications (VBA) code and use loops to automate processing of an entire `Recordset`.

This chapter's examples and sample code use ActiveX Data Objects (ADO) 2.1 `ADODB.Recordsets` exclusively. As noted in Chapter 27, "Understanding Universal Data Access, OLE DB, and ADO," the foundation for Access's future is ADO. ADO is Microsoft's chosen data model for Internet and intranet applications, the Microsoft Data Engine (MSDE), and SQL Server 7.0. New databases you create with Access 2000 use ADO 2.1 by default. Access Data Projects (ADP) and Data Access Pages (DAP) require you to use ADO 2.1+. Unlike Data Access Objects (DAO), a technology that is intimately tied to the Jet database engine, OLE DB makes ADO independent of the `Recordset`'s underlying data source. Thus Microsoft can—and undoubtedly will—upgrade ADO independently of future upgrades to Access. It's highly unlikely that Microsoft will upgrade DAO beyond the version 3.6 that's included with Access 2000.

GENERATING THE TEMPORARY Recordset

You often use temporary `Recordsets` for specific purposes, such as populating a list or combo box. When the `Recordset` operation completes, you close it, releasing its connection to the underlying database. When you close a `Recordset` object, you can reopen the object for another set of `Recordset` operations. Alternatively, you can **Set** the `Recordset` to **Nothing** to free its memory resources, but you can't reopen the object. It's a common practice to create temporary `Recordsets` when opening a form that contains the unbound controls that rely on `Recordsets` for their data.

Perform the following steps to a create a new database that opens temporary `Recordsets` with VBA:

1. Create a working copy of Northwind.mdb by compacting it to another file, such as Nwind.mdb, if you haven't done so already. (Using a working copy prevents permanent changes to Northwind.mdb when you update `Recordset` objects later in this chapter.)

2. Open a new database named **ADO_VBA.mdb** in the same folder as Nwind.mdb.

3. Create a new unbound form in Design view. (Don't specify a Record Source for the form.)

4. Click the Code button to display the form's class module in the VBA Editor; then add the following code to the Declarations section to create three form-level variables immediately below **Option Explicit**:

```
Private cnnNwind As New ADODB.Connection
Private rstTemp As New ADODB.Recordset
Private strSQL As String
```

5. Select Form in the Object list to create the `Form_Load` event-handling stub.

6. Add this code to the `Form_Load` event handler to create an updatable `Recordset` based on the Record Source property value that loaded the `cboProducts` combo box in the preceding chapter:

```
With cnnNwind
    .Provider = "Microsoft.Jet.OLEDB.4.0"
    .ConnectionString = CurrentProject.Path & "\Nwind.mdb"
    .Open
End With
strSQL = "SELECT ProductID, ProductName FROM Products " & _
    "ORDER BY ProductName"
With rstTemp
    Set .ActiveConnection = cnnNwind
    .CursorType = adOpenKeyset
    .LockType = adlockOptimistic
    .Source = strSQL
    .Open
End With
Stop
```

→ **See** "Adding the Query Combo Boxes to the Form," **p. 1131** for information on creating these controls in a form.

→ For the basics of ADO `Connection` and `Recordset` code, **see** "Working with the `ADODB.Connection` Object," **p. 1048** or "Understanding the `ADODB.Recordset` Object," **p. 1066**.

The **Stop** statement is temporary; without the **Stop** statement, the variable values go out of scope when **End Sub** executes.

7. Click the Form view button to execute the code you added to the `Form_Load` stub. The VBA Editor window opens with a yellow arrow in the left margin pointing to the breakpoint generated by the **Stop** statement (see Figure 30.1).

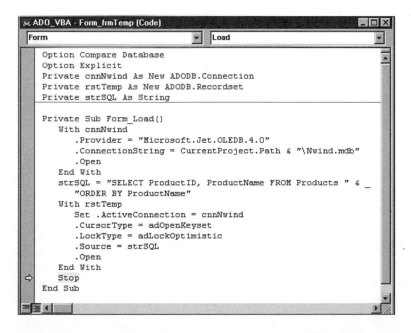

Figure 30.1
Creating a code break-point with the *Stop* statement.

8. Press Ctrl+G to open the Immediate window, if necessary, and type **?** **rstTemp.RecordCount** to verify that your code returned rows. At this point, any value other than 0 indicates rows returned. You also can test other Recordset property values, such as Fields.Count and CursorType. The default Recordset CursorType is forward only; setting the CursorType property value to adOpenKeyset, adOpenStatic, or adOpenDynamic creates an updatable Recordset (see Figure 30.2).

Figure 30.2
Testing properties of the
rstTemp Recordset
object.

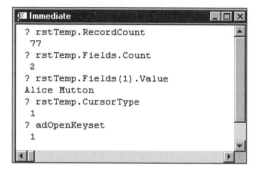

```
Immediate                              _ □ X
? rstTemp.RecordCount
 77
? rstTemp.Fields.Count
 2
? rstTemp.Fields(1).Value
Alice Mutton
? rstTemp.CursorType
 1
? adOpenKeyset
 1
```

Note

NEW 2000

Unlike DAO.Recordset objects, you obtain a valid RecordCount property with keyset (adOpenKeyset) and static (adOpenStatic) cursors. Dynamic (adOpenDynamic) and forward-only (adOpenForwardOnly) cursors return -1 (**True**) if the Recordset contains one or more records.

APPLYING Move... METHODS

The five Move... methods—Move, MoveFirst, MoveLast, MoveNext, and MovePrevious—are the basic positional commands for the record pointer of ADO and DAO Recordsets. Only Move takes an argument—the number of rows to move relative to the current row, as in Move 10.

Note

The only Move... method you can apply to a forward-only Recordset is MoveNext. Forward-only Recordsets (where CursorType equals adOpenForwardOnly) are the fastest and least resource intensive of all Recordset types.

To try the Move... methods in the Immediate window, do the following:

1. Clear the prior statements from the Immediate window and type **rstTemp.MoveLast**.

2. Type **? rstTemp.Fields(1).Value** to verify that MoveLast returned the record pointer to the last record, Zaanse koeken.

> **Note**
>
> The default property of the `Field` object is `Value`, so you don't need to append **.Value** in the Immediate window examples. As mentioned in Chapter 27, however, explicit use of the `Value` property is a good programming practice and boosts performance slightly.

3. Type rstTemp.MoveFirst, rstTemp.Move 10 and then ? rsTemp.Fields(1).Value to test the `Move` method.

    If you attempt to move by an increment greater than the number of remaining rows, you don't receive an error message. If you try to read the record, however, you receive a runtime error.

Tip #276 from

> Invoking the `MoveLast` method on a large, updatable `Recordset` requires Jet to retrieve references to all rows of the `Recordset`. Such an operation causes a large burst of traffic when operating in a networked, multiuser environment. Avoid using the `MoveLast` method unless it's absolutely necessary.

Using the EOF and BOF Properties in Loops

The `EOF` (end of file) and `BOF` (beginning of file) `Recordset` properties have their roots in dBASE and other file-oriented RDBMSs. The `EOF` property returns **True** when you attempt to move beyond the last row of the `Recordset`; an example is applying a `Move 100` instruction to a `Recordset` with 77 rows. Similarly, `BOF` returns **True** if you try a `Move -100` operation on the `Recordset` (see Figure 30.3). `EOF` and `BOF` both return **True** for an empty `Recordset` (RowCount = 0).

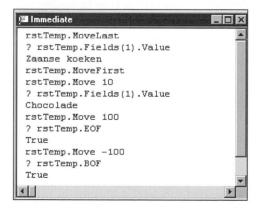

```
rstTemp.MoveLast
? rstTemp.Fields(1).Value
Zaanse koeken
rstTemp.MoveFirst
rstTemp.Move 10
? rstTemp.Fields(1).Value
Chocolade
rstTemp.Move 100
? rstTemp.EOF
True
rstTemp.Move -100
? rstTemp.BOF
True
```

Figure 30.3
Using the *Move* method to test *EOF* and *BOF* property values.

The most common use of the EOF and BOF property values is traversing an entire Recordset within loop structures, such as the following:

```
rsName.MoveFirst
Do Until rsName.EOF
    'Recordset operation code
    rsName.MoveNext
Loop
```

or

```
rsName.MoveLast
Do While Not rsName.BOF
    'Recordset operation code
    rsName.MovePrevious
Loop
```

To test a loop with the Debug.Print method, do the following:

1. Press F5 to exit the event handler, return to the VBA Editor, and then add the following code before the **Stop** statement:

```
Do Until rstTemp.EOF
    Debug.Print rstTemp.Fields(0), rstTemp.Fields(1)
    rstTemp.MoveNext
Loop
```

2. Return to the form and then click the View button twice to rerun the Form_Load event handler.

3. Press Ctrl+G to display the last few rows of the Recordset in the Immediate window (see Figure 30.4).

Figure 30.4
The Immediate window displaying the last few rows of a *Recordset* iterated by a loop structure.

Tip #277 from

R J

When ADO opens a Recordset, the record pointer automatically is positioned at the first row. It's a good programming practice, however, to always add the MoveFirst method before traversing the entire Recordset.

PART

VII

CH

30

Tip #278 from

Add the `MoveNext` method immediately after you create the loop structure. If you accidentally omit `MoveNext`, your procedure enters an endless (infinite) loop, and you must press Ctrl+Break to regain control of the application. In a very tight loop (little or no loop code), Ctrl+Break often doesn't work. In this case, you must use Task Manager to terminate Access; you lose the code and any form design changes you haven't saved.

USING THE `AbsolutePosition` PROPERTY

The `AbsolutePosition` property of a `Recordset` is similar to, but not identical to, the record count (`RECNO()`) function and `GOTO` command of xBase. `AbsolutePosition` returns a zero-based **Long** integer indicating the current position of the record pointer. You can set the value of `AbsolutePostion` to move the record pointer to a specific position in the `Recordset`. These operations are reliable only for a `Recordset` with a static cursor. (You can't use `AbsolutePosition` with a dynamic or forward-only cursor.) In a multiuser environment, however, users might delete or add rows to dynamic-type `Recordsets`, so repeated execution of `rstName.AbsolutePosition = 50` might not return the same row. To make sure that you return to a specific record, use the `Bookmark` property (one of the subjects of the next section). Figure 30.5 shows typical Immediate window operations using `AbsolutePosition`.

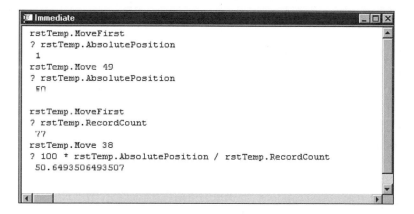

Figure 30.5
Examples of the use of the `Absolute Position` property of the `Recordset` object.

Tip #279 from

**NEW
2000**

ADO doesn't support the `DAO.Recordset.PercentPosition` property. You can return the equivalent of the `PercentPosition` property with a `sngPercent = ` **CSng**(100 * `rstName.AbsolutionPostion/rstName.RecordCount`) statement. Similarly, you can set `rstName.AbsolutePosition = ` **CLng**(100 * `sngPercent/rstName.RecordCount`), as illustrated in Figure 30.5. **CLng** rounds values with a decimal fraction of exactly .5 to the nearest even integer.

USING THE Find METHOD AND Bookmarks

 NEW 2000 ADO's single Find method replaces the four Find... methods—FindFirst, FindLast, FindNext, and FindPrevious—of DAO.Recordsets. Find executes a query on the Recordset and positions the record pointer at the designated row, if such a row exists. The syntax of the Find method is

```
rstName.Find strCriteria[, lngSkipRecords[, lngSearchDirection[, lngStart]]]
```

where strCriteria is a valid SQL WHERE clause without the WHERE keyword, the optional lngSkipRecords value is the number of records to skip before applying Find, lngSearchDirection specifies the search direction (adSearchForward, the default, or adSearchBackward), and the optional lngStart value specifies the Bookmark value of the record at which to start the search or one of the members of BookmarkEnum.

> **Note**
>
> **NEW 2000** OLE DB, and thus ADO, limits the WHERE clause criterion for the Find method to a single expression containing a field name, comparison operator (<, <=, =, >=, >, <> or Like), and value. The DAO.Recordset.Find... methods accept any valid WHERE clause, including the AND or OR operators, and permit more than one column name. The inability of the ADODB.Recordset.Find method to use compound criteria is a serious deficiency; you must write very inelegant workarounds to find record(s) matching multifield or other compound criteria.

If Find fails with adSearchForward, the EOF property returns **True**; otherwise, EOF returns **False**. With adSearchBackward, the BOF property returns **True** on failure; otherwise, BOF returns **False**. In these two cases, EOF and BOF, respectively, provide the logical equivalent of the bidirectional DAO.Recordset.NoMatch property.

→ For the full syntax of the Find method, **see** "Recordset Methods," **p. 1074**.

To find all of the records (starting at the first record) whose ProductNames begin with Queso (see Figure 30.6), you apply the Find method to find the first matching record as follows:

```
rstTemp.Find "ProductName Like 'Queso*'"
```

If the first Find operation succeeds, you must move forward one record from the current record to find successive matches, as in

```
rstTemp.Find "ProductName Like 'Queso*'", 1
```

Similarly, to perform a successive backward search, the syntax is

```
rstTemp.Find "ProductName Like 'Queso*'", 1, adSearchBackward
```

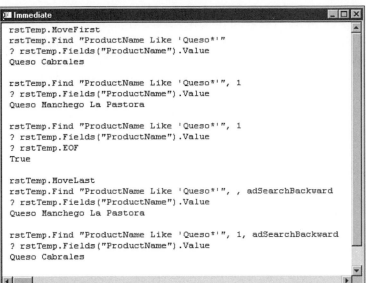

Figure 30.6
Finding all rows beginning with Queso.

NEW Like DAO, ADO uses the Bookmark property to identify a specific row in a Recordset. An
2000 ADO Bookmark is a binary value, which you access with a **Variant** variable, not the **String**s
used to store DAO.Bookmark values. To mark a row to which you want to return later, use a
varName = rstName.Bookmark instruction. To reposition the record pointer to the row, execute rstName.Bookmark = varName (see Figure 30.7). If you Bookmark a row in a Recordset
and someone else deletes the row, you receive a runtime error.

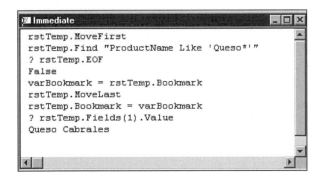

Figure 30.7
Using a *Bookmark* variable to mark and return
to a specific row in a
Recordset.

> **Note**
>
> **NEW** Some Recordsets, such as those created over linked Paradox tables without a primary
> **2000** key, don't support the Bookmark property. The following expression tests whether a
> Recordset supports Bookmarks:
>
> blnBookmarkable = rstName.Supports(adBookmark)
>
> The preceding expressison replaces the Bookmarkable property of DAO.Recordsets.

→ For the enumeration of Supports constants, **see** Table 27.28, **p. 1078**.

MODIFYING ROWS OF Recordsets

You can perform CRUD (Create, Read, Update, and Delete) operations on most dynamic Recordsets with VBA code. To test whether a Recordset is updatable (editable), check the return value of the rstName.Supports(adUpdate) expression, which replaces DAO.Recordset's Updatable property. You can't edit forward-only Recordsets, and most dynamic queries with INNER or OUTER JOINs aren't editable.

EDITING AND ADDING ROWS

NEW 2000 Unlike DAO.Recordset objects, which are updatable by default, ADODB.Recordsets default to read-only locking. To make an ADODB.Recordset updatable, you must set the LockEdits property of the Recordset to adLockOptimistic (the most common choice), adLockPessimistic, or adLockBatchOptimistic. Before performing the tests for updatability, do the following:

1. Add a .LockType = adLockOptimistic statement after the .CursorType = adOpenKeyset statement in the Form_Load event handler.

2. Press F5 to exit the Form_Load event handler, and return to Access.

3. Save your form as **frmTemp** for use in the examples of the next section.

4. Click the View button twice to reopen the form and re-execute the Form_Load event handler with the added code.

→ For an enumeration of LockType constants, **see** Table 27.21, **p. 1070**.

To edit (update) the current row, simply set the new value of each field you want to change. ADODB.Recordets don't require or support the DAO.Recordsets Edit method. The changes don't become permanent until you apply the Update method. Following is the generalized syntax for an update operation on fields other than an AutoNumber or identity primary key (usually Field(0)) of the current row:

```
rsName.Fields(1) = "New String Value"
rsName.Fields(2) = New Numeric Value
...
rsName.Fields(n) = "New String Value"
rsName.Update
```

You add rsName.AddNew before the field value assignment statements to insert a new row into the Recordset. Fields to which you don't assign values are supplied with default values if specified; otherwise, fields contain **Null** values. If the primary key field uses the AutoNumber data type or has the MSDE identity property, don't attempt to assign a value to the field. Figure 30.8 shows examples of update and AddNew operations on rstTemp in the Immediate window.

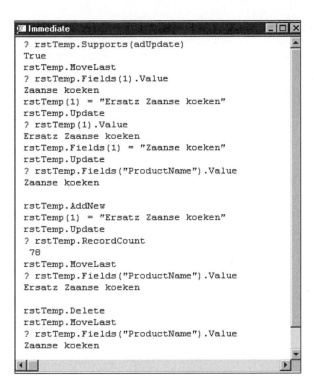

Figure 30.8
Experimenting with the
Update, AddNew, and
Delete methods in the
Immediate window.

DELETING ROWS

Deleting the current row is simple—just invoke the `Delete` method. Applying the `Update` method isn't required. You receive no warning that you're about to irrevocably remove a record from the underlying table. (The deleted row doesn't disappear from the underlying table until you move the record pointer.) The last three statements in Figure 30.8 illustrate deleting the Ersatz Zaanse koeken row and confirming that the row is gone (forever). The last row of the table becomes Zaanse koeken.

POPULATING A COMBO BOX FROM A `Recordset`

Combo boxes, list boxes, and other bound controls maintain a connection to their underlying Jet tables. Combo boxes create their connection when you open the combo list. List boxes create a connection when you open the form. Neither connection closes until you close the form. Connections to tables create permanent user read locks; updating a table creates a temporary write lock during the update process.

A Jet database has a maximum of 255 concurrent user locks. You seldom, if ever, run out of locks in a single-user environment, but it's quite easy to hit the Jet lock limit with a widely deployed multiuser application that uses combo and list boxes. For example, 50 simultaneous users of the decision-support application described in Chapter 29, "Programming Combo and List Boxes," would generate 200 read locks because two combo boxes and two list boxes are on the form. As the application gains more users, Jet might run out of read locks. In such a case, some users of the application encounter a runtime error when attempting to open a combo box.

You can minimize the number of user read locks by populating combo boxes from a temporary, forward-only Recordset object, which you close immediately after filling the combo list. Replacing the RowSource query of the combo box with a list of items, called a *value list*, reduces the number of read locks by half. The following sections describe the changes required to the combo boxes and code of the Order Query with Criteria from Combo Boxes form (frmCombo1) to populate the two combo boxes (cboCountry and cboProduct) with a temporary Recordset.

Tip #280 from

Client/server databases, such as SQL Server, can support a very large number of connections and locks, but connections and locks consume a significant amount of server memory. Minimizing connections and locks is an important element of client/server front-end design.

CREATING frmCombo2 AND ALTERING THE COMBO BOX DESIGN

The examples in this chapter enhance the sample application you created in Chapter 29. To create a copy of frmCombo1 and modify the design of its two combo boxes, follow these steps:

1. Choose File, Get External Data, Import and import frmComboMSDE from the .mdb file (not the .adp file) you used for the examples of Chapter 29.

Note

If you didn't create Chapter 29's frmComboMSDE, you can import it from the \Seua2K\Chaptr29\VBACombo.mdb database on the accompanying CD-ROM. Running frmComboMSDE at this point creates an error because ADO_VBA doesn't contain the required tables.

---

2. Rename frmComboMSDE to **frmComboVBA**.
3. To test frmComboVBA before making changes, choose File, Get External Data, Link Tables and then link the Customers, Order Details, Orders, and Products tables. You must import qryDrilldown from your Chapter 29 database to make the Line Items list operable at this point.

4. Open frmComboVBA in Run or Design mode, select the cboCountry combo box, and click the Properties button.

5. Change the Row Source Type property value to Value List and set Limit to List to Yes.

6. Delete the entire SELECT query of the Row Source property text box (see Figure 30.9).

7. Select cboProduct and repeat steps 5 and 6.

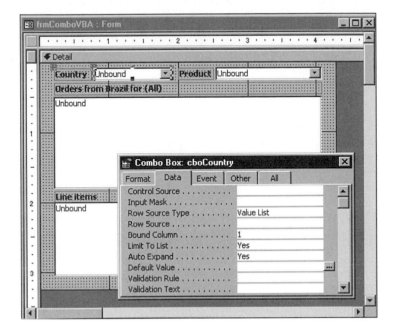

Figure 30.9
Changing the Row Source
Type and Row Source
property values of the
cboProduct combo
box.

PART

VII

CH

30

8. Open frmTemp in Design mode and then click the Code button to open the VBA Editor. Delete the Stop statement in the Form_Load event handler and copy the entire Form_Load event handler to the Clipboard.

9. Return to Access and open the VBA Editor for the frmComboVBA class module. Paste the Form_Load code immediately after the Declarations section.

10. Add the following two lines to the Declarations section of the frmComboVBA class module:

```
Private strList As String
Private cnnNwind As New ADODB.Connection
Private rstTemp As New ADODB.Recordset
```

11. Return to Access and click View twice to reopen the form and test the added code.

POPULATING THE COMBO BOXES WITH CODE

Value lists use the semicolon (;) as a record separator, similar to the format of comma-separated values in .csv files. You populate single-column value lists, such as cboCountry's, with single rows in a Row1Value;Row2Value;Row3Value;...Row*i*Value sequence, where *i* is the row count. Multicolumn value lists such as cboProduct's require a row-column sequence— Row1Col1Value;...Row1Col*j*Value;Row2Col1Value;...Row2Col*j*Value;...Row*i*Col*j*Value— where *i* is the row count and *j* is the column count. Thus value list code requires that you create a semicolon-separated string in the appropriate format from the values of field(s) of the Recordset.

> **Note**
>
> Combo and list boxes that use value lists are limited to a maximum of 2,047 characters, 255 **Long** integers, or 511 **Integers** in the list. Thus value lists should be used only for relatively small combo or list boxes.

> **Tip #281 from**
>
>
>
> To gain optimum performance, use forward-only cursors and read-only locking for populating combo and list boxes. Using forward-only is especially advantageous when connecting to client/server databases.

The SQL UNION query statements for creating the two Recordsets are identical to those used by Chapter 29's frmCombo1 to supply the RowSource property of the combo boxes.

The following steps add the code to the Form_Load event handler to open a temporary Recordset and populate the two combo boxes:

1. Change the .CursorType = adOpenKeyset line to .CursorType = adOpenForwardOnly.
2. Delete the .LockType = adLockOptimistic line. By definition, forward-only cursors are read-only.
3. Change the strSQL = ... line to
   ```
   strSQL = "SELECT Country FROM Customers " & _
       "UNION SELECT '(All)' FROM Customers ORDER BY Country"
   ```
   The preceding SQL statement is identical to that of the original Row Source of the Country combo box.
4. Add the following code to populate the Country combo box immediately before the **End Sub** statement:
   ```
   strList = ""
   Do Until rstTemp.EOF
       strList = strList & rstTemp.Fields(0).Value & ";"
       rstTemp.MoveNext
   Loop
   Me!cboCountry.RowSource = strList
   ```

5. Add the following code to populate the Product combo box immediately after the preceding code:

```
strSQL = "SELECT ProductID, ProductName FROM Products " & _
    "UNION SELECT 0, '(All)' FROM Products ORDER BY ProductName"
With rstTemp
    .Close
    .Source = strSQL
    .Open
End With
strList = ""
Do Until rstTemp.EOF
    strList = strList & rstTemp.Fields(0).Value & ";" & _
        rstTemp.Fields(1) & ";"
    rstTemp.MoveNext
Loop
Me!cboProduct.RowSource = strList
```

`ADODB.Recordsets` retain property values, whether opened or closed, until you execute a `Set rstName = Nothing` statement. You must apply the `Close` method to the `Recordset` to change any of its property values.

6. Add the following code at the beginning of the `FillList` subprocedure to prevent errors due to `Null` value lists when opening the form for the first time:

```
If IsNull(Me!cboCountry) Or IsNull(Me!cboProduct) Then
    Exit Sub
End If
```

7. Test the code by returning to Access, clicking the View button twice to execute the new code in `Form_Load`, and selecting a combination of Product and Country values from the combo boxes.

8. Save your changes to frmComboVBA.

ALTERING THE SEQUENCE OF COMBO BOX LISTS

The `UNION` query that creates the two `Recordsets` adds the (All) item at the beginning of the list. `UNION` queries are slower than conventional `SELECT` queries, so adding the (All) item by modifying the value list improves performance. Also, you can discourage users from running (All) queries by putting (All) at the end of the list. If USA is the most common country selection, you can move USA to the top of the list. To modify your value list code to make these changes, do the following:

1. Return to Design view and open the VBA Editor if necessary.

2. Add these two lines, which remove the `UNION` element of the query, to the Declarations section of the class module:

```
Private Const strSQL8 = "SELECT DISTINCT Country FROM Customers " & _
    "ORDER BY Country"
Private Const strSQL9 = "SELECT ProductID, ProductName FROM Products"
```

The `DISTINCT` reserved word is required in the country SQL statement to remove duplicate rows; `UNION` queries automatically remove duplicate rows.

3. Change the two `.Source = strSQL` statements to `.Source = strSQL8` and `.Source = strSQL9`, respectively.

4. Change the first `strList = ""` statement to
   ```
   strList = "USA;"
   ```

5. Add this line after the first **Loop** statement:
   ```
   strList = strList & "(All);"
   ```

6. Add this line immediately before the **Me!cboProduct.RowSource = strList** statement:
   ```
   strList = strList & "0;(All);"
   ```

7. To prevent USA from appearing twice in the `cboCountry` list, wrap the `strList = strList & rsfTemp.Fields(0) & ";"` line with an **If...Then** statement:
   ```
   If rstTemp.Fields(0) <> "USA" Then
       strList = strList & rsfTemp.Fields(0) & ";"
   End If
   ```

   Listing 30.1 includes all the code of the `Form_Load` event handler.

8. Press Ctrl+S to save your code, return to Access, and click the View button twice to test your modified combo boxes (see Figure 30.10).

> **LISTING 30.1   CODE TO POPULATE THE _cboCountry_ AND _cboProduct_ COMBO BOXES FROM A TEMPORARY _ADODB.Recordset_**

```
Private Sub Form_Load()
    With cnnNwind
        .Provider = "Microsoft.Jet.OLEDB.4.0"
        .ConnectionString = CurrentProject.Path & "\Nwind.mdb"
        .Open
    End With
    With rstTemp
        Set .ActiveConnection = cnnNwind
        .CursorType = adOpenForwardOnly
        .Source = strSQL8
        .Open
    End With
    strList = "USA;"
    Do Until rstTemp.EOF
        If rstTemp.Fields(0).Value <> "USA" Then
            strList = strList & rstTemp.Fields(0).Value & ";"
        End If
        rstTemp.MoveNext
    Loop
    strList = strList & "(All);"
    Me!cboCountry.RowSource = strList
    strSQL = "SELECT ProductID, ProductName FROM Products " & _
        "UNION SELECT 0, '(All)' FROM Products ORDER BY ProductName"
    With rstTemp
        .Close
        .Source = strSQL9
        .Open
    End With
```

```
    strList = ""
    Do Until rstTemp.EOF
        strList = strList & rstTemp.Fields(0).Value & ";" & _
            rstTemp.Fields(1) & ";"
        rstTemp.MoveNext
    Loop
    strList = strList & "0;(All);"
    Me!cboProduct.RowSource = strList
End Sub
```

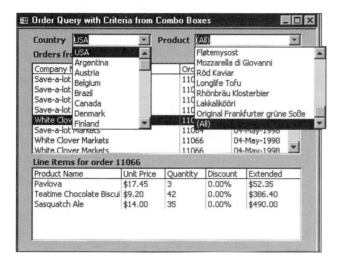

Figure 30.10
Revisions to the list
sequences of the
cboCountry and
cboProduct combo
boxes made possible by
using a value list (double-
exposure screen capture).

FILLING LIST BOXES FROM Recordset OBJECTS

You can use techniques similar to those for combo boxes to populate list boxes. List boxes
that include many fields, have column headings, or both require additional code. You must
test for queries that return no records and value lists with lengths greater than 2,047 characters. If your list box includes column headings, you must add the headings to the value list
before appending rows from the Recordset. One benefit of using a Recordset is that you
can detect RecordCount = 0 and display a message box that the query returned no records.

You use the rst*Name*.Fields(*n*).Name property value, where *n* equals 0 to one less than the
rst*Name*.Fields.Count value, to supply the value list elements for the column names.
Although you could manually assign the list of field names to the beginning of the value list
string, using the Name property of the Field object is a good programming practice because
it makes your code more generic.

The following steps convert the 1stOrders list box to the value list type for queries that return fewer than 2,048 characters:

1. Change the Row Source Type property value of the 1stOrders list box from Table/Query to Value List.

2. Delete all the code after the last **End If** statement of the FillList subprocedure.

3. Replace the deleted code with the following:

```
strList = ""
With rstTemp
    If .State = adStateOpen Then
        .Close
    End If
    .Source = strSQL
    .Open
    If .RecordCount Then
        For intCtr = 0 To .Fields.Count - 2
            strList = strList & .Fields(intCtr).Name & ";"
        Next intCtr
        Do Until .EOF
            For intCtr = 0 To .Fields.Count - 2
                strList = strList & .Fields(intCtr).Value & ";"
            Next intCtr
            .MoveNext
        Loop
        .Close
        If Len(strList) > 2047 Then
            Me!lblList.Caption = "List too long for Value List"
            Exit Sub
        Else
            Me!1stOrders.RowSource = strList
        End If
        Me!lblList.Caption = "Orders from " & _
            Me!cboCountry.Value & " for " & _
            Me!cboProduct.Column(1)
        Me!lblLineItems.Caption = strMsg4
    Else
        Me!lblLineItems.Caption = "No orders from " & _
            Me!cboCountry.Value & " for " & _
            Me!cboProduct.Column(1)
    End If
End With
```

Tip #282 from

Testing the State property of the Recordset prior to attempting to close it is a good programming practice. If you attempt to apply the Close method to a closed Recordset, you receive a runtime error.

---

4. Save your changes and test frmComboVBA to verify that the column headers are added and that 1stOrders displays the correct information.

As an aid to troubleshooting your modifications to FillList, Listing 30.2 includes all the subprocedure's code.

LISTING 30.2   CODE TO FILL THE *lstOrders* LIST BOX FROM A TEMPORARY *Recordset*

```
Private Sub FillList()
    If Me!cboProduct.Value = 0 Then
        strSQL = strSQL5 & strSQL6 & Me!cboCountry.Value & _
            "'" & strSQL3
    ElseIf Me!cboCountry.Value = "(All)" Then
        strSQL = strSQL5 & strSQL7 & Me!cboProduct.Value & _
            strSQL3
    Else
        strSQL = strSQL1 & Me!cboCountry.Value & _
            strSQL2 & Me!cboProduct.Value & strSQL3
    End If
    strList = ""
    With rstTemp
        If .State = adStateOpen Then
            .Close
        End If
        .Source = strSQL
        .Open
        If .RecordCount Then
            For intCtr = 0 To .Fields.Count - 1
                strList = strList & .Fields(intCtr).Name & ";"
            Next intCtr
            Do Until .EOF
                For intCtr = 0 To .Fields.Count - 1
                    strList = strList & .Fields(intCtr).Value & ";"
                Next intCtr
                .MoveNext
            Loop
            If Len(strList) > 2047 Then
                Me!lblList.Caption = "List too long for Value List"
                .Close
                Exit Sub
            Else
                Me!lstOrders.RowSource = strList
            End If
            Me!lblList.Caption = "Orders from " & _
                Me!cboCountry.Value & " for " & _
                Me!cboProduct.Column(1)
            Me!lblLineItems.Caption = strMsg4
        Else
            Me!lblLineItems.Caption = "No orders from " & _
                Me!cboCountry.Value & " for " & _
                Me!cboProduct.Column(1)
        End If
        .Close
    End With
End Sub
```

FORMATTING VALUE LIST COMBO BOX COLUMNS

To eliminate all long-term read locks from execution of frmComboVBA, you also must convert the lstLineItems list box to use a Recordset-based value list. When you create a value list from a Recordset with currency and percentage formatting, the format attributes are lost. You use the Type property of the Field object to detect fields of the Currency data type. There's no Percentage field data type, so you must explicitly identify field(s) that require percentage formatting.

Follow these steps to make the modifications to the lstLineItems list box:

1. Change the Row Source Type property value of the lstOrders list box from Table/Query to Value List.

2. Delete these lines from the lstOrders_DblClick event handler:

```
With Me!lstLineItems
    .RowSource = strSQL
    .Requery
End With
```

   Leave the strSQL = strSQL4 & Me!lstOrders.Value line intact.

3. Replace the deleted lines with the following code, which is quite similar to that added to the FillList subprocedure:

```
strList = ""
With rstTemp
    If .State = adStateOpen Then
        .Close
    End If
    .Source = strSQL
    .Open
    If .RecordCount Then
        For intCtr = 0 To .Fields.Count - 1
            strList = strList & .Fields(intCtr).Name & ";"
        Next intCtr
        Do Until .EOF
            For intCtr = 0 To .Fields.Count - 1
                strList = strList & .Fields(intCtr) & ";"
            Next intCtr
            .MoveNext
        Loop
        If Len(strList) > 2047 Then
            Me!lblLineItems.Caption = "List too long for Value List"
            .Close
            Exit Sub
        Else
            Me!lstLineItems.RowSource = strList
        End If
    End If
    .Close
End With
```

4. Indent the remaining existing code and then add an **End If** statement before the **End Sub** line.

5. Unless you connected to the same .mdb file in which you created Chapter 29's qryDrilldown query, the strSQL4 value fails when used as the Source property of your Recordset. Change the value of strSQL4 to

```
Private Const strSQL4 = "SELECT Products.ProductName, " & _
    "[Order Details].UnitPrice, " & _
    "[Order Details].Quantity, [Order Details].Discount, " & _
    "[Order Details].UnitPrice * " & _
        "[Order Details].Quantity * " & _
        "(1 - [Order Details].Discount) AS Extended " & _
    "FROM Products INNER JOIN [Order Details] " & _
        "ON Products.ProductID = [Order Details].ProductID " & _
    "WHERE [Order Details].OrderID = "
```

The preceding SQL statement also is valid for use with MSDE in an Access Data Project (ADP).

6. Save your changes and open frmComboVBA. Make a combo box selection and double-click an item in lstOrders to execute your added code. The items in lstLineItems have lost their formatting (see Figure 30.11).

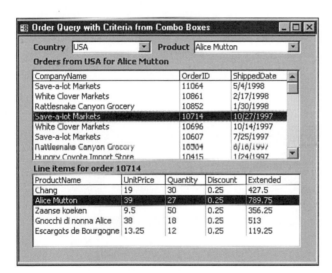

Figure 30.11
Loss of formatting of items in the lstLineItems list box as a result of substituting a value list for a query.

7. Add this line below the **Private Sub** line:

```
Dim strItem As String
```

8. To format the fields in the lstLineItems list box, replace the code within the **For** intCtr = 0 **To** .Fields.Count - 1...**Next** intCtr loop with

```
If IsNull(strItem) Then
    strItem = ""
Else
    strItem = .Fields(intCtr).Value
    If .Fields(intCtr).Type = adCurrency Or intCtr = 4 Then
        strItem = Format(strItem, "$####.00")
```

```
        ElseIf intCtr = 3 Then
            strItem = Format(strItem, "#0.0%")
        End If
    End If
    strList = strList & strItem & ";"
```

> **Note**
>
> If you add the comma thousands separator to the currency formatting string
> ("$#,###.00"), the value list fails because its parser interprets commas as semi-colons.
> Hopefully, this problem will be fixed in a future version of Access.

9. To alias the line item column headings, change the first line of the value of strSQL4 to

```
Private Const strSQL4 = "SELECT ProductName AS Product, " & _
    "UnitPrice AS [Unit Price], Quantity, Discount, " & _
    "Extended FROM qryDrillDown WHERE OrderID = "
```

You also can improve the readability of the orders list by changing the first two lines of
the strSQL1 assignment to

```
Private Const strSQL1 = "SELECT Customers.CompanyName AS Customer, " & _
    "Orders.OrderID AS [Order #], Orders.ShippedDate AS [Date Shipped] " & _
```

Make the same change to strSQL5.

10. Save your changes and reopen frmComboVBA. Make a combo box selection and double-
click an item in lstOrders to execute your new code. The items in lstLineItems have
regained their formatting (see Figure 30.12).

Figure 30.12
Formatting applied with
the *Format$* function to
the items in the
lstLineItems list box.

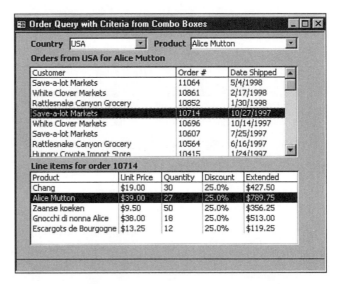

If you experience a runtime error in step 8, check your code against Listing 30.4. The
listing shows all the code of the modified lstOrders_DblClick event handler to aid
troubleshooting.

LISTING 30.4   CODE TO POPULATE THE lstLineItems LIST BOX FROM A TEMPORARY Recordset AND FORMAT THE ELEMENTS OF THE VALUE LIST

```
Private Sub lstOrders_DblClick(Cancel As Integer)
    Dim strItem As String
    If Me!lstOrders.Value <> "" Then
        strSQL = strSQL4 & Me!lstOrders.Value
        strList = ""
        With rstTemp
            If .State = adStateOpen Then
                .Close
            End If
            .Source = strSQL
            .Open
            If .RecordCount Then
                For intCtr = 0 To .Fields.Count - 1
                    strList = strList & .Fields(intCtr).Name & ";"
                Next intCtr
                Do Until .EOF
                    For intCtr = 0 To .Fields.Count - 1
                        If IsNull(strItem) Then
                            strItem = ""
                        Else
                            strItem = .Fields(intCtr).Value
                            If .Fields(intCtr).Type = adCurrency _
                                Or intCtr = 4 Then
                                strItem = Format(strItem, "$####.00")
                            ElseIf intCtr = 3 Then
                                strItem = Format(strItem, "#0.0%")
                            End If
                        End If
                        strList = strList & strItem & ";"
                    Next intCtr
                    .MoveNext
                Loop
                If Len(strList) > 2047 Then
                    Me!lblLineItems.Caption = "List too long for Value List"
                    .Close
                    Exit Sub
                Else
                    Me!lstLineItems.RowSource = strList
                End If
            End If
            .Close
        End With
        lblLineItems.Caption = strMsg4 & Me!lstOrders.Value
    End If
    With Me!lstLineItems
        For intCtr = 0 To .ListCount - 1
            If .Column(0, intCtr) = Me!cboProduct.Column(1) Then
                .Selected(intCtr) = True
                Exit For
            End If
        Next intCtr
    End With
End Sub
```

PORTING FRMCOMBOVBA TO AN ACCESS DATA PROJECT

The SQL statements that fill the combo and list boxes of frmComboVBA no longer include Jet-specific syntax, such as **CCur** or **Format**. Formatting the Row Source property of value lists also eliminates the need to use the Transact-SQL CONVERT function for formatting when connecting to MSDE. Thus it's easy to alter the Connection properties to port frmComboVBA to MSDE or SQL Server 6.5+, taking advantage of ADP's CurrentProject.Connection property.

1. Open a new project (Existing Database) named **OrdersByProductAndCountryVBA.adp** in the folder in which you created ADO_VBA.mdb.

2. In the Data Link Properties sheet, type **(local)** as the Server Name, **sa** as the User Name, and select NorthwindCS as the Database.

3. Click Test Connection and click OK to create the default connection.

4. Choose File, GetExternalData, Import; select ADO_VBA.mdb; and import frmComboVBA.

5. Test frmComboVBA with the existing connection using the Jet OLE DB provider.

6. In the VBA Editor, delete the **With** cnnNwind...**End With** statements in the Form_Load event handler.

7. Change the **Set** .ActiveConnection = cnnNwind line to

   Set .ActiveConnection = CurrentProject.Connection

8. Start MSDE, if necessary, with SQL Service Manager.

 9. Return to Access and click the View button twice to rerun the Form_Load event handler to test the new connection to the NorthwindCS MSDE database.

Tip #283 from	The SQL statements for filling the Orders and Line Items list boxes are excellent candidates for conversion to SQL Server parameterized stored procedures. Stored procedures are likely to improve the performance of frmComboVBA significantly.

TROUBLESHOOTING

MAKING ADODB.RecordsetS UPDATABLE

I've opened a Connection *and* Recordset, *but the* Recordset *is read-only. I can't edit, add, or delete records.*

The most likely culprit is either forgetting to specify a read-write CursorType property value (adKeyset, adDynamic, adStatic) or not setting the LockType property value to adLockOptimistic or adLockPessimistic. Unlike DAO.Recordset objects, which default to a Recordset of the dynaset type, ADODB.Recordsets default to a forward-only (firehose) cursor with read-only locking.

I fixed the CursorType *or* LockType *problem, but my* Recordset *still isn't updatable.*

The underlying query isn't updatable. Import your SQL statement into Access's SQL Query window to create a temporary query. Run the query and check whether the tentative append record appears and whether you can edit the values of fields that you want to alter with your form. If the query has INNER JOINs and runs against MSDE or SQL Server, make sure that you've specified the correct name for the *UniqueTable* property.

IN THE REAL WORLD—ADAPTING TO ADO

Many Access (and Visual Basic) developers with a long-term investment in memorizing the DAO hierarchy are loathe to adopt ADO and its flattened object model. One of the tenets of business process reengineering—which has finally received some of the bad press it deserves—is empowering cubical dwellers and assembly-line workers by flattening corporate organization charts. The underlying theory is that empowered employees are happier and more productive, which results in improvements to the bottom line of income statements.

Unfortunately, ADO doesn't empower DAO programmers, because ADO/ADOX 2.1 doesn't yet have feature parity with DAO 3.x, nor is the performance of ADO 2.1 substantially better than DAO 3.6. Problems with the ADODB.Find method are just one of the issues raised by DAO proponents as a reason for avoiding migration to the Lotusland of Universal Data Access. Few Access and Visual Basic programmers have indicated that ADO 2.x, at least so far, has made them happier, more productive, or improved the bottom line of their employers or their own businesses.

If your work involves Web-based operations, and you use Microsoft programming tools, you *must* become fluent in ADO-speak. You can't use DAO with HTML-compatible scripting languages, such as VBScript or JavaScript/JScript. (You can use DAO with Visual Basic 6.0's Internet Applications and Web Classes, if you insist, but that's the subject of another book.) As more large commercial Web sites adopt Microsoft's Active Server Pages (ASP) technology, scripted data access and HTML presentation generated by .asp files is becoming far more common than conventional VBA-based applications. For an example of a high-powered site running ASP, check out the recently reinvigorated *TV Guide* site. The C-band satellite program guide at http://listings.tvguide.com/listings/framebase.asp quickly delivers about 200 rows of programming data from a syndicated database into an attractively-formatted table.

ADO provides the back-end Connections and Recordsets for XML-based technologies, such as Data Access Pages. XML and ADO are the foundation of Microsoft's new e-commerce initiatives announced in San Francisco during March, 1999. When this book was written BizTalk—Microsoft's XML-based e-commerce framework—was projectorware. You can bet that BizTalk, purported to be based on "industry standards," will depend on ADO for database connectivity (whenever the retail version arrives). ADO doesn't yet have the status of an "industry standard," but it's well on its way. Access developers who don't learn new ADO tricks are destined for the dog house of the database life cycle - maintaining legacy DAO applications.

--rj

CHAPTER 31

MIGRATING ACCESS 9X APPLICATIONS TO ACCESS 2000

In this chapter

Understanding the .mdb File Upgrade Process   1182

Converting Unsecured Files from Access 9x to Access 2000   1182

Upgrading on First Opening the File in Access 2000   1182

Upgrading After Opening the File in Access 2000   1185

Converting Secured Access 9x Files   1186

Upgrading in a Mixed Access 9x and 2000 Environment   1187

Upgrading the Back-End Database and Workgroup File   1187

Upgrading Access 2.0 Application .mdb Files to Access 2000   1188

Converting from Win16 to Win32 Function Calls   1189

Accommodating the 32-Index Limit on Tables   1191

Converting 16-Bit OLE Controls to 32-Bit ActiveX Controls   1191

Troubleshooting   1191

In the Real World—The Upgrade Blues   1191

UNDERSTANDING THE .MDB FILE UPGRADE PROCESS

Each version of Access—1.0, 1.1, 2.0, 95, 97, and 2000—has a different database file structure at the binary (byte) level. The differences between 16-bit .mdb files created with versions 1.0 and 1.1 were relatively minor; thus you could use the Compact feature of Access to convert version 1.0 .mdbs to version 1.1, or vice versa. The file formats of later versions of Jet databases are sufficiently different to require, with the exception of Access 2000, one-way conversion during the upgrade process.

NEW 2000 Access 2000 lets you convert data .mdbs from Access 2000 (Jet 4.0) to Access 97 (Jet 3.5x) format. You also can convert Access 2000 application .mdbs that don't contain objects—such as Data Access Pages (DAP)—or references—to ActiveX Data Objects (ADO and ADOX) or Data Access Objects (DAO) 3.6—that are missing in Access 97.

NEW 2000 Access 2000 now saves ordinary forms, reports, and modules in compound document files (DocFiles), which are stored within application .mdb files. This change is needed to support Access Data Projects (ADP), which save application objects in .adp DocFiles, not in conventional .mdb files.

> **Caution**
>
> Don't convert shared data (back-end) .mdb files or workgroup .mdw files to Access 2000 (Jet 4.0) format until all users who connect to these files have upgraded their application .mdb (front-end) files to Access 2000. Prior versions of Access can't link to Jet 4.0 tables; you receive an "Unrecognized data format" error message if you attempt to link an Access 9x front end to Jet 4.0 .mdb or .mdw files.

CONVERTING UNSECURED FILES FROM ACCESS 9X TO ACCESS 2000

The definition of an unsecured Access 9x file is an .mdb file containing data objects, application objects, or both that you or others created with Access's default Admin account, with or without Access 97's database-level password protection. In this case, the Admin account has Administrator privileges and is the owner of all objects in the .mdb file(s).

> **Note**
>
> This section does not apply to .mdb files you create as the Admin user with password protection for the Admin account. If the Admin user has a password , the .mdb file is secure.

UPGRADING ON FIRST OPENING THE FILE IN ACCESS 2000

Conversion of unsecured Access 9x .mdb files to Access 2000 format is straightforward. If you're opening the Access 9x .mdb file for the first time in Access 2000, do the following:

1. Close the Access 9x .mdb file if it is open. You must have exclusive access to the file for conversion to proceed.

2. Compact the file in Access 9x. Compacting the file immediately before conversion often speeds the conversion process and ensures against problems during conversion.

3. Open the Access 9x .mdb file in Access 2000, which opens the Convert/Open Database dialog (see Figure 31.1). If you have database-level password protection in effect, you must type the password to open the .mdb file.

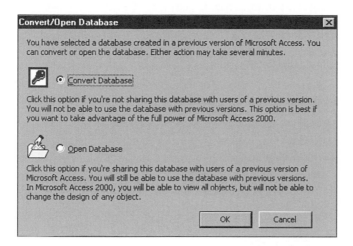

Figure 31.1
The dialog that appears the first time you open an Access 9x .mdb file in Access 2000.

4. Accept the default Convert Database option and click OK to open the Convert Database Into dialog.

5. Replace the default db1.mdb with a new file name for the converted file (see Figure 31.2). Unlike the compact/repair process, you can't use the original file name and overwrite the Access 9x file with the Access 2000 version.

Figure 31.2
Specifying the name for the upgraded .mdb file.

Tip #284 from

Keep a backup copy of your Access 9x .mdb files after conversion in a different folder or on removable media. You might find it necessary to restore your backup in the event you discover unexpected changes in your application caused by conversion artifacts. After you move the Access 9x file(s) to a new location, you can rename the converted file(s) to the original name(s).

6. Click Save to close the dialog and perform the conversion. After a few seconds—or minutes, if the file is large—your newly converted file appears in the Database window (see Figure 31.3).

Figure 31.3
The newly converted Access 2000 version of the file in the Database window.

Note

You don't need to convert the existing default workgroup file, System.mdw, which Access 97 installs in your \Windows\System or \Winnt\System32 folder. Access 2000's default System.mdw file is located in your \Program Files\Microsoft Office\Office folder. If your application is secure, however, you must first compact the Access 97 workgroup file in Access 2000, and then use Workgroup Administrator to join the workgroup defined by your Access 97 System.mdw.

You can't open or convert Access 97 .mde files in Access 2000. When you attempt to open an .mde file, the terse message shown in Figure 31.4 appears. This restriction makes it impossible to run many current demonstration versions of commercial Access 97 applications under Access 2000. If you don't have Access 97 installed, you must wait for the upgraded version from the publisher.

Figure 31.4
The message you receive when attempting to open or convert an Access 97 .mde file.

UPGRADING AFTER OPENING THE FILE IN ACCESS 2000

When you elect to open an unsecured Access 9x file in Access 2000, you can't change the design of any Access object. If you've previously opened an Access 9x file in Access 2000 and selected the Open Database option in the Convert/Open Database dialog, the Convert/Open Database dialog doesn't appear on successive open operations. You receive the message shown in Figure 31.5 the first time you open an Access 9x database.

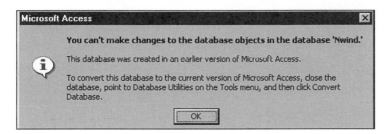

Figure 31.5
The message you receive the first time you open an Access 9x .mdb file in Access 2000.

When you click OK, Access 2000 sets a flag in the database to indicate that you've acknowledged the message shown in Figure 31.4. After this point, opening the Access 9x database no longer displays the Open/Convert Database dialog.

You can't save changes to the design of any object in an Access 9x database opened in Access 2000; you receive the message shown in Figure 31.5 when you open an object in Design mode. The New button of the Database window's toolbar is disabled, and no Create... shortcuts appear in the Database window list for any object class.

Note

You can open Access 9x objects in Design mode, and even make changes to the design. However, you can't save (persist) the design changes.

If you want to take advantage of new Access 2000 features or make changes to the design of existing objects, do the following to convert a previously opened database to Access 2000 (Jet 4.0) format:

1. Compact the file to be converted in Access 9x.
2. Launch Access 2000 without opening a current database.

3. Choose Tools, Database Utilities, Convert Database, To Current Access Version to open the Database to Convert From dialog.

4. Navigate to and select the Access 9x database to convert (see Figure 31.6).

Figure 31.6
Opening an Access 9x database for conversion to Access 2000.

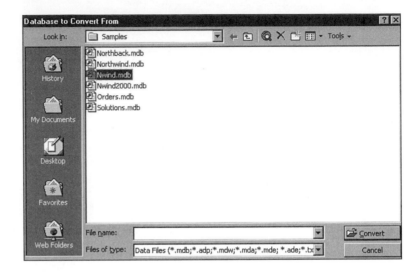

5. Click Convert to open the Convert Database Into dialog.

6. Replace the default db1.mdb with a new file name for the converted file (refer to Figure 31.2).

7 Click Save to close the dialog and save the file in Access 2000 format.

CONVERTING SECURE ACCESS 9X FILES

Converting secure Access 2000 files is a complex process that requires advance planning. Multiuser networked applications are the most common environment for secure Access files. In this case, the issue is upgrading the shared data file(s) in back-end .mdbs, which contain only tables and, in some cases, queries. Converting client PCs with Access 9x front ends isn't a concern, because the front-end .mdbs connect transparently to Access 9x and Access 2000 back-end databases.

To upgrade either the front-end or back-end .mdb file(s), you must open the files exclusively under an account that has Modify Design or Administer permission for all objects in the .mdb file. Alternatively, you must be the owner (creator) of all of the database's objects. All users must close their front-end applications for you to obtain exclusive-open access to the back-end .mdb file.

VBA code in secured forms and modules becomes unsecured when converting to Access 2000 because the change to the VBA Integrated Design Environment results in a different storage mechanism for your code. After you convert secured front-end .mdbs containing any VBA code, you must use the VBA IDE to password protect the code.

UPGRADING IN A MIXED ACCESS 9X AND 2000 ENVIRONMENT

If you have many database users or several shared databases in operation, it's unlikely that you can upgrade all database users at one time without incurring excessive downtime. In this case, you must perform the following sequence of operations:

NEW 2000

1. Launch Access 2000 without opening a database and compact the shared workgroup file, usually System.mdw. You *must* compact (*not* convert) the workgroup file to make it fully compatible with Access 2000 clients. Compacting the workgroup file in Access 2000 doesn't change its version.

2. Thoroughly test the Access 2000 version of the application .mdb with the existing Access 97 data .mdb file(s) and the compacted Access 97 System.mdw file.

3. Convert and distribute upgraded versions of the application (client) .mdb file to its users.

PART

VII

CH

31

UPGRADING THE BACK-END DATABASE AND WORKGROUP FILE

After you've upgraded all of your client .mdbs, you complete the upgrade process as follows:

1. Compact with a new name the shared data .mdb file so that you can covert the file to a new version with the same name as the old version.

2. Upgrade the data .mdb file to Jet 4.0.

   Don't delete the original .mdb file. You might need to revert to the original files in case you encounter conversion problems.

3. Create a local copy of the existing shared workgroup file and join the local workgroup so you can compact the original workgroup file.

4. Compact with a new name the shared workgroup file and then convert it to Jet 4.0 with the original name.

   Don't delete the original .mdw file. You might need it as conversion insurance.

5. After testing the new configuration, request each user to open Workgroup Administrator and rejoin the workgroup with the new workgroup file.

UPGRADING ACCESS 2.0 APPLICATION .MDB FILES TO ACCESS 2000

Many Access 2.0 applications have remained in use because of delays in upgrading all client PCs in an organization—especially laptops—to 32-bit Windows 9x. The following list describes the principal problems you encounter when upgrading 16-bit Access 2.0 application .MDB files to Access 2000 format:

- `DoMenuItem` actions that refer to menu choices that have changed in Access 2000 produce an unexpected result. Access 2000 replaces `DoMenuItem` action with the `RunCommand` action in macros and Access VBA code.

- `SendKeys` operations that execute Access 2000 menu choices and make selections in dialogs are likely to fail because of changes in the Access 2000 menu structure and the design of Access 2000 dialogs.

- Variable names that conflict with the names of VBA 6.0 reserved words result in failure of Access 2000 to compile modules and to execute procedures containing the conflicting variables.

- Access Basic statements that use the dot (.) operator to refer to a field of a `Recordset` object or a member of a collection fail. Use the VBA bang (!) operator, as in `Orders!OrderID` or `Forms!Orders`.

The opening and compiling process, which enables Access 2.0 and 9x applications, makes Access Basic modules of Access 2.0 or Access VBA of Access 9x compatible with VBA 6.0. Fortunately, the opening and compiling process occurs only once.

Tip #286 from

If you make changes to an Access 2.0 or 9x application, the enabling process reoccurs when you first open the application. Make sure you compile all modules in your earlier-version file before opening it in Access 2000.

If your application .mdb contains code that VBA 6.0 can't handle, you must change the code manually. As an example, Access 2.0's NWIND.mdb sample database contains a sub-procedure, `ShowEvents`, in the Utility Functions module that the Access 2000 VBA interpreter won't compile. Each line that contains the `Events` variable name is colored red. You can't save corrections to Access Basic code in Access 2000, so you must make any required changes to the unconverted .mdb file in the appropriate version of Access. In the case of the `ShowEvents` subprocedure, you change the variable name from `Event` to `strEvent` in three locations. You must then recompile the code changes in the original version of Access and try to open the .mdb file again in Access 2000.

 If you receive a "Can't find project or library" error message when you attempt to open or convert an Access 9x file, see the "Missing Project or Library" topic of the "Troubleshooting" section at the end of this chapter.

Tip #287 from

Access 2000 doesn't include an equivalent to Access 97's DAO 2.5/3.5 Compatibility Library, which permits compiling code with the remnants of Access 2.0's VBA code conventions that are incompatible with DAO 3.5+. If your Access 2.0 code won't compile in Access 2000, you can save a considerable amount of time and aggravation by updating the code to DAO 3.5x standards in Access 97, then converting the Access 97 version to Access 2000.

CONVERTING FROM WIN16 TO WIN32 FUNCTION CALLS

If your Access 2.0 application makes use of calls to the Windows Application Programming Interface (API), you must convert the function declarations from the 16-bit (Win16) to the 32-bit (Win32) version. You cannot call 16-bit functions from 32-bit code, and vice-versa. You receive a "Calls to 16-bit DLLs won't work under Windows 95 or Windows NT" message when the VBA interpreter encounters a 16-bit Windows API declaration.

Win32 API functions with arguments of the **String** data type come in two types: ANSI (suffix A) and Unicode (suffix W, for wide). Access 2000 uses the ANSI versions. Most Windows API function arguments that were of the **Integer** data type in the Win16 version must be declared as **Long** in the Win32 version. Examples include all Win32 handles, such as hWnd and hDC, and values of **Integer** fields in structures. To avoid the need to change all function calls to Win32 API functions in your Access VBA code, you alias the function calls, as shown in the following example:

```
Declare Function OriginalName Lib "lib32" _
Alias "OriginalName[A]" ([ArgumentList]) As Datatype
```

OriginalName is the name of the Win16 function in your Access VBA function calls. Win32 libraries, for the most part, have a 32 suffix, as in Kernel32.exe and GDI32.exe. In the majority of cases, you need only include the A suffix in the **Alias** name if **As String** appears in ArgumentList. For most Win32 functions, Datatype is **Long**.

The Win API Viewer, which is included with the Microsoft Office 2000 Developer (MOD) and Visual Basic 6.0, lets you copy **Declare** statements for Win32 function calls to the Clipboard and then paste them into the Declarations section of your modules. If you don't have the MOD or Visual Basic 6.0, you must either have the Win32 Software Development Kit (SDK) or guess the correct Win32 API function name and data types and then try to compile and execute your code.

CONVERTING AND ADDING REFERENCES TO LIBRARIES AND ADD-INS

In addition to converting your application .mdb file to Access 2000, you also must convert any Access 2.0 custom libraries and add-ins used by your application to 32-bit versions. Converting your own libraries and add-ins follows the same process as converting .mdb files. If you use third-party libraries, you are likely to need updated Access 2000 versions; the source code of many third-party libraries is password protected.

PART

VII

CH

31

Note

If you are using only a few functions in a library, such as the WIZLIB.MDA library included with Access 2.0, consider creating a new library or incorporating the function code in your Access 2000 application. Doing so eliminates dealing with problems converting library functions you don't need. Copy the required function(s) to the Clipboard and paste the code into an Access 2000 module. (You can run prior versions of Access and Access 2000 simultaneously.)

Access 2.0 and earlier use the [Libraries] section of MSACC??0.INI to attach libraries to any application opened in Access. Access 2000 uses references to 32-bit libraries in place of entries in MSACC??0.INI. To add a reference to a library, such as Access 2000's Utility.mda, follow these steps:

1. Open a module and choose Tools, References to open the References dialog.
2. Click the Browse button to open the Add Reference dialog.
3. Select Add-ins (*.mda) in the Files of Type drop-down list.
4. Maneuver to the folder that contains your library, select the library file, and click the OK button to add the reference at the bottom of the Available References list.
5. When you close and reopen the References dialog, the new reference appears as the last active reference.

Access 2000 library references are stored in your .mdb file; thus you must create a reference to a library in each .mdb file that uses the library. Unlike [Libraries] entries in MSACC??0.INI, the full path to the library is hard-coded. You may need to alter the reference for users who don't install your application in the folder specified by the reference in your .mdb file. Access 2000 lets you modify references with VBA; all members of Office 2000 expose a References collection.

Hard-coded reference paths are a compelling reason to move existing library code to your Access application .mdb if you use only a few library functions. If your library code does not contain visible objects, other than message boxes and modal dialogs, an alternative is to convert the library to an in-process Visual Basic 32-bit ActiveX DLL that you manage with Automation code.

Tip #288 from

R J

Access 2000, unlike Access 2.0 and earlier, allows duplicate function names in libraries. If you have duplicate function names in libraries, your application calls the function in the library with the highest priority in the Available References list of the References dialog.

Access 2.0 used the [Menu Add-Ins] section of MSACC20.INI to specify the function name of the entry point for an add-in and the [Libraries] section to attach the .MDA file that contains the add-in. These entries are replaced by the Registry entries in Access 2000. If your Access 2000 application uses add-ins, a record in the USysRegInfo table of the add-in is required to make it visible to the Add-In Manager.

ACCOMMODATING THE 32-INDEX LIMIT ON TABLES

Access 2000 imposes a limit of 32 indexes per table. Each relationship between tables creates an index on the two tables that participate in the relationship, a feature introduced in Access 95. If you have a very complex database with many relationships between tables, you may exceed the 32-index per table limit.

Although your Access 2.0 table may have less than 32 indexes, when you convert the table to Access 2000, the additional indexes for relationships may exceed the limit of 32. In this case, you either cannot convert the database or, if the database converts, you lose indexes. Your only option in this situation is to reduce the number of indexes on your table in your prior version of Access and then try the conversion process again.

CONVERTING 16-BIT OLE CONTROLS TO 32-BIT ACTIVEX CONTROLS

If your Access 2.0 application uses 16-bit OLE Controls and you have the 32-bit ActiveX version of the original control, Access 2000 automatically updates the control to the 32-bit ActiveX version. The ActiveX control must be registered for the conversion to work. If you don't have a 32-bit ActiveX version of the control, an empty control container appears on your form.

TROUBLESHOOTING

MISSING LIBRARY OR PROJECT MESSAGE

You receive a "The expression EventName you entered as the event property setting produced the following error: Can't find project or library" message when attempting to open or convert an Access 97 application .mdb.

The most common cause of this error message results from use of Access 97's Microsoft DAO 2.5/3.5 Compatibility Library, which permits compiling code with the remnants of Access 2.0's VBA code conventions that are incompatible with DAO 3.5+. You must update the code to DAO 3.5x standards in Access 97, then convert the Access 97 version to Access 2000. To do so, substitute a reference to the Microsoft DAO 3.51 Object Library for the Microsoft DAO 2.5/3.5 Compatibility Library. Correct the unsupported syntax by repeatedly compiling the code until all modules compile and the application runs properly. Then convert the .mdb file to Access 2000 format.

IN THE REAL WORLD—THE UPGRADE BLUES

There's Chicago Blues, Delta Blues, Bay Area Blues, Texas Blues, and probably another five or ten genres, sub-genres, or derivatives, not counting R&B. There's no question, however, that the most pervasive, low-down variant is the Access Upgrade Blues:

"I got the Access upgrade blues
Can't get my app to compile
Been workin' on it a week
Looks like it's gonna take a while."

> **Note**
>
> If you're unfamiliar with (San Francisco) Bay Area Blues and its roots in Texas Blues, check out "The Southeast Texas-East Bay Music Connection" at
> `http://www.oakmusic.com/Juneteenth/Texas-EastBay.htm`.

Every upgrade to Access (except the 1.0 to 1.1 transition) undoubtedly increased the market for mood-altering substances—both legal and illegal—among Access developers. Migrating from Access 97 to Access 2000 isn't a piece of cake. The larger and more complex your Access application, the more taxing the process. Access Basic detritus from Version 2.0 or earlier plagues the conversion of mature Access applications. (Many developers didn't upgrade Access 2.0 applications to Access 95 because of performance issues). Thus the more history behind your code, the greater the chance that it breaks when upgrading. Microsoft gains an immediate economic return on its investment in the transition to a common VBA 6.0 code base and editor for all Office applications; Access developers must settle for the deferred gratification of long-term standardization benefits.

The obvious temptation is not to upgrade the application to Access 2000. This approach is viable only for applications you distribute as self-contained runtime versions generated by the Office 97 Developer Edition's Setup Wizard. Runtime versions install roughly 50 MB of Access 97, Jet 3.51, DAO 3.51, and other obsolete dependency files on Office 2000 users' PCs. The Access 97 runtime baggage probably won't be a problem for today's desktop PCs, but road warriors' laptops usually have much less available disk space than desktops.

If you avoid temptation and bite the upgrade bullet, take the opportunity to optimize your VBA code. Make sure that the first line in every module is **Option** Explicit, substitute variable declarations for explicit references to objects used more than once in your code, and minimize the use of the **Variant** data type. Search for all instances of **CreateObject**, which results in late binding, and replace the call with an object variable declaration, such as **Private** objName **As** *ObjectName*, for a class member to force early binding. When you complete the optimization process, your Access 2000 application *might* execute as quickly as its 16-bit Access 2.0 predecessor.

Once you've converted your application to Jet 4.0 and DAO 3.6, and then gone through an exhaustive testing process, your next decision is whether to move from DAO to ADO and ADOX 2.1. Take a hint from Microsoft—Access 2000 automatically uses DAO 3.6 for upgraded apps and ADO/ADOX for new ones. Universal Data Access (UDA), OLE DB, and ADO may be the "wave of the future" for database compatibility, but surfing the current ADO/ADOX version demonstrates no significant performance improvement or other benefits that justify the time and effort required for conversion. ADO/ADOX 2.1 don't offer full parity with DAO 3.6, and many workarounds for missing DAO features are inelegant, at best.

Don't let the preceding admonition discourage you from adopting ADO/ADOX for new Access projects. DAO 3.6 is likely to be Microsoft's last iteration of this venerable object model. From 1999 forward, Microsoft will direct virtually all of its data connectivity investment to improving and expanding the capabilities of OLE DB and ADO. You can expect upgrades to ADO on a much more frequent basis than new Office or Visual Studio versions; the beta version of an ADO upgrade was in the works when this book was written.

Web-based applications require OLE DB and ADO to support scripting, DHTML, and XML; and Access Data Projects don't accommodate DAO. If you employ object-oriented programming methodology, your classes must use ADO to assure object compatibility across all Access application types. Take the time to learn OLE DB fundamentals and gain expertise in ADO/ADOX. The ADO/ADOX learning curve isn't as steep as you might think. Your investment will pay handsome dividends as future versions of Access and other Microsoft database development platforms move to a Web-centric model that conforms to Microsoft's Distributed interNet Architecture (DNA) vision.

--rj

PART

VII

CH

31

PART VIII

APPENDIX

Appendix A   Glossary   1197

GLOSSARY

accelerator key   A key combination that provides access to a menu choice, macro, or other function of the application in lieu of a mouse click, usually by combining Alt+*key*. An accelerator key is identified on menus by an underlined character. It is sometimes (incorrectly) called a *shortcut key*, but shortcut keys usually consist of Ctrl+*key* combinations.

Access Data Project   See *ADP*.

Access Developer's Toolkit   See *ADT* and *ODE*.

Access SQL   Former name of Jet SQL, a dialect of ANSI SQL. See *Jet SQL*.

activation   An OLE 2+ term meaning to place an object in a running state, which includes binding the object, or to invoke a method of the object. See also *binding*.

active   In Windows, the currently running application or the window to which user input is directed; the window with the focus. See also *focus*.

Active Server Pages   See *ASP*.

ActiveX   A Microsoft trademark for a collection of technologies based on the Common Object Model (COM) and Distributed Common Object Model (DCOM). See *COM* and *DCOM*.

ActiveX components   A replacement term for OLE Automation miniservers and in-process servers, also called *Automation servers*. See *Automation*.

ActiveX controls   Insertable objects supplied in the form of OCX files that, in addition to offering a collection of properties and methods, also fire events. ActiveX controls are lightweight versions of earlier OLE controls that also use the .ocx file extension.

ActiveX Data Objects   See *ADO*.

ActiveX Data Object Extensions   See *ADOX*.

ActiveX documents   Files that can be inserted into the Microsoft Binder, such as files created by Microsoft Excel 7+ and Word 7+, as well as displayed in their native format in Internet Explorer 3+. ActiveX documents originally were called *Document Objects* or *DocObjects*.

ActiveX scripting   Another name for Visual Basic, Scripting Edition (VBScript), a simplified version of VBA designed for client- and server-side automation of Web pages.

ActiveX server framework   ActiveX scripting for creating server-side Internet and intranet applications. Unlike ActiveX scripting, the ActiveX Server Framework allows file and other low-level operations.

ADC   An abbreviation for *Advanced Data Control*, the predecessor to Remote Data Service. See *RDS*.

add-in   Wizards and other programming aids, usually in the form of Access libraries, that help Access programmers create and deploy applications. You use Access's Add-In Manager to install Microsoft and third-party add-ins. COM add-ins are a new class of add-in objects introduced in Office 2000. See also *COM* and *builder*.

address   The numerical value, usually in hexadecimal format, of a particular location in your computer's random-access memory (RAM).

ADO   An abbreviation for *ActiveX Data Objects*, which are similar in concept to the Data Access Object (DAO) and Remote Data Object (RDO). ADO uses Microsoft's new OLE Database (OLE DB) technology to access data from various data sources, including text files and mainframe databases. ADO 2.1 is the preferred database connectivity method for Access 2000. See *OLE DB*.

ADO MD   An abbreviation for *ADO Multidimensional (Expressions)*, the Automation library that provides access to `CubeDef` and `Cellset` objects created with the PivotTable Service or Microsoft SQL Server OLAP Services (formerly Microsoft Decision Support Services, MSDSS). See *Cellset*, *CubeDef*, *MDX*, *OLAP*, and *PivotTable Service*.

ADODB   An abbreviation and object library name for ADO 2.0. `ADODB` is used as an object prefix to specify the source of ADO data object, as in `ADODB.Recordset`.

ADOX   An abbreviation for ActiveX Data Object Extensions, a set of extensions to ADO 2.1+ that support Jet 4.0's new SQL Data Definition Language reserved words, such as `CREATE GROUP` and `ALTER USER`. See *data definition*.

ADP   An abbreviation for *Access Data Project*, an alternative to conventional Access client/server applications, which store application objects (forms and reports) in .mdb files. ADP requires an ADO 2.1 connection to one of the four versions of SQL Server 7.0 (Microsoft Data Engine or MSDE, Desktop, Standard, or Enterprise editions). ADP stores application objects in OLE docfiles having an .adp extension. See *ADO*, *docfiles*, and *MSDE*.

ADT   An abbreviation for the *Access Developer's Toolkit* for Access 2.0 and Access 95 that allowed distribution of files needed to run (but not design) Access 2.0 and Access 95 applications. For Access 97 and 2000, the ADT is replaced by the Office Developer's Edition (ODE), which provides all ADT features plus developer products for other Office applications. See *ODE*.

ADTG   An abbreviation for *Advanced Data TableGram*, a Microsoft-proprietary MIME format used by RDS to marshal Recordsets between client and server via the HTTP protocol. See *HTTP*, *MIME*, and *RDS*.

Advanced Data TableGram   See *ADTG*.

aggregate functions   The ANSI SQL functions AVG(), SUM(), MIN(), MAX(), and COUNT(), and Access SQL functions StDev(), Var(), First(), and Last(). Aggregate functions calculate summary values from a group of values in a specified column and are usually associated with GROUP BY and HAVING clauses. See also *domain aggregate functions*.

aggregate object   An OLE 2.0 term that refers to an object class containing one or more member objects of another class.

alias   A temporary name assigned to a table in a self-join or to a column of a query, or to rename a table, implemented by the AS reserved word in ANSI SQL. You can use AS to rename any field or table with Jet SQL; SQL Server's Transact-SQL substitutes a space for AS. **Alias** is also an embedded keyword option for the VBA **Declare** statement. The **Alias** keyword is used to register prototypes of DLL functions so that the function can be called from programs by another name. Aliasing the ANSI versions of 32-bit Windows API functions to function names without the A suffix is common when converting Access 97 and earlier applications to Access 2000, which uses Unicode for text data.

ANSI   An acronym for the *American National Standards Institute*. ANSI in the Windows context refers to the ANSI character set that Microsoft decided to use for Windows (rather than the IBM PC character set that includes special characters such as those used for line drawing, called the *OEM character set*). The most common character set is *ASCII (American Standard Code for Information Interchange)*, which for English alphabetic and numeric characters is the same as ANSI. Windows 9x and Windows NT include ANSI (suffix A) and Unicode (suffix W) versions of Windows API functions. See *ASCII* and *Unicode*.

API   An abbreviation for *Application Program Interface*. Generically, a method by which a program can obtain access to or modify the operating system. In 32-bit Windows, the 1,000 or so functions provided by Windows 9x and Windows NT DLLs that allow applications to open and close windows, read the keyboard, interpret mouse movements, and so on. Programmers call these functions *hooks* to Windows. VBA provides access to these functions with the Declare statement. See also *DLL*.

application   The software product that results from the creation of a program, often used as a synonym for the programming (source) code that creates it. In this book, Microsoft Word, Microsoft Excel, WordPerfect for Windows, and Lotus 1-2-3 are called *mainstream Windows productivity applications*. Applications are distinguished by the environment for which they are designed (such as Windows, DOS, Macintosh, and UNIX) and their purpose. Windows applications carry the DOS executable file extension, .exe. This book uses the terms *application* and *project* interchangeably.

argument   A piece of data supplied to a function that the function uses or acts on to perform its task. Arguments are enclosed in parentheses. Additional arguments, if any, are separated by commas. Arguments passed to procedures usually are called *parameters*.

array   An ordered sequence of values (elements) stored within a single named variable, accessed by referring to the variable name with the number of the element (index or subscript) in parentheses, as in `strValue = strArray(3)`. VBA arrays may have more than one dimension, in which case access to the value includes indexes for each dimension, as in `strValue = strArray(3,3)`.

ASCII   An acronym for the *American Standard Code for Information Interchange*. A set of standard numerical values for printable, control, and special characters used by PCs and most other computers. Other commonly used codes for character sets are ANSI (used by Windows 3.1+), Unicode (used by Windows 9x and Windows NT), and EBCDIC (Extended Binary-Coded Decimal Interchange Code, used by IBM for mainframe computers). See *Unicode*.

ASP   An acronym for *Active Server Pages*, Microsoft's server-side technology for dynamically creating standard HTML (Internet) Web pages. Conventional ASP uses VBScript or ECMAScript to manipulate ASP objects. Access 2000 lets you export forms in ASP format for Web deployment. See *ECMAScript* and *WebClasses*.

assign   To give a value to a named variable.

asynchronous   A process that can occur at any time, regardless of the status of the operating system or running applications.

attached table   A table that's not stored in the currently open Jet database (native or base table), but which you can manipulate as though the table were a native table. In Jet 3+ terminology, an attached table is a linked table. See *linked table*.

authentication   The process of verifying a user's login ID and password.

Automation   An ActiveX and OLE 2+ term that refers to a means of manipulating another application's objects.

Automation client   An ActiveX- or OLE 2–compliant Windows application with an application programming (macro) language, such as VBA, that can reference and manipulate objects exposed by (OLE) Automation servers.

Automation server   Technically, any COM- or OLE 2–compliant Windows application that supports Automation operations by exposing a set of objects for manipulation by Automation client applications. This book restricts the term *Automation server* to applications that expose application objects, but aren't ActiveX full servers. The members of Office 2000 are examples of full automation servers.

AutoNumber   A Jet 3+ replacement for the Counter field data type of Jet 2.0, Access 1.x, and Access 2.0. AutoNumber fields may be of the Increment or Random type. Fields of the Increment AutoNumber field data type usually are used to create primary keys in cases where a unique primary key can't be created from data in the table.

background In multitasking computer operations, the application or procedure that's not visible onscreen and that doesn't receive user-generated input. In Windows, a minimized application that doesn't have the focus is in the background.

base date A date used as a reference from which other date values are calculated. In the case of VBA and SQL Server, the base date is January 1, 1900.

base tables The permanent tables from which a query is created, usually acting as the one side of a one-to-many relationship. Jet also uses the term *base table* to refer to a table in the current database in contrast to a linked (attached) table. See *linked table*.

batch A group of statements or database operations processed as an entity. Execution of DOS batch files, such as AUTOEXEC.BAT, and SQL statements are examples of batch processes.

batch update A process in which multiple update operations on a `Recordset` are conducted on a locally cached copy of the `Recordset`. When all updates are completed, calling the `UpdateBatch` method attempts to make permanent (persist) all changes to the underlying tables in a single operation.

binary file A file whose content doesn't consist of lines of text. Executable (.exe), dynamic link library (.dll), and most database files are stored in binary format.

binary string A string consisting of binary, not text, data that contains bytes outside the range of ANSI or ASCII values for printable characters. Access 2000 requires that you store binary strings as arrays of the Byte data type to avoid problems with Unicode/ANSI conversion.

binding The process of connecting one object to another through interfaces. In Access 2000, local object binding is accomplished by COM interfaces and remote object binding by DCOM interfaces. See *COM*, *DCOM*, and *data binding*.

bitwise A process that evaluates each bit of a combination, such as a byte or word, rather than process the combination as a single element. Logical operations and masks use bitwise procedures.

Boolean A type of arithmetic in which all digits are bits—that is, the numbers may have only two states: on (true or 1) or off (false or 0). Widely used in set theory and computer programming, Boolean, named after the mathematician George Boole, also is used to describe a VBA data type that may have only two states: true or false. In VBA, true is represented by &HFF (all bits of an 8-bit byte set to 1) and false by &H0 (all bits set to 0). **Boolean** is a VBA data type.

bound See *binding*.

break To cause an interruption in program operation. Ctrl+C, the standard DOS break key combination, seldom halts operation of a Windows application. Windows applications generally use the Esc key to cause an operation to terminate before completion.

breakpoint   A designated statement that causes program execution to halt after executing the statement preceding it. To toggle breakpoints on or off, press F9 on the line of code before which you want execution to halt.

Briefcase replication   A feature of Jet 3+ running under Windows 9x or Windows NT 4.0 that permits the creation of Jet replication sets stored in Briefcase folders, which can be updated by mobile users. Subsequently, the briefcase replicates are used to update the design-master replica to synchronize the design-master replica with the contents of the briefcase replicas. ADO 2.0 doesn't support Jet replication. See *design-master replica*.

buffer   An area in memory of a designated size (number of bytes or characters) reserved, typically, to hold a portion of a file or the value of a variable. When string variables are passed as arguments of DLL functions, you must create a buffer of sufficient size to hold the returned string. This is accomplished by creating a fixed-length string variable of the necessary size, using the String function, before calling the DLL function.

builder   A component that provides assistance in defining new objects, writing SQL statements, or creating expressions. Buttons with an ellipsis symbol commonly open builders.

built-in functions   Functions that are included in a computer language and don't need to be created by the programmer as user-defined functions.

business rules   A set of rules for entering data in a database that are specific to an enterprise's method of conducting its operations. Business rules are in addition to rules for maintaining the domain and referential integrity of tables in a database. Business rules most commonly are implemented in a three-tier client/server database environment. See *three tier*.

cache   A block of memory reserved for temporary storage. Caches usually store data from disk files in memory to speed access to the data. By default, Windows 9x and NT cache all disk read and write operations.

caption   The title that appears in a window's title bar. Access calls the text of a label, check box, frame, and command or option button control object the Caption *property*.

caret   The term used by Windows to indicate the cursor used when editing a text field, usually shaped as an I-beam. The caret, also called the *insertion point*, can be positioned independently of the mouse pointer.

Cartesian product   Named for René Descartes, a French mathematician. Used in JOIN operations to describe all possible combinations of rows and columns from each table in a database. The number of rows in a Cartesian product is equal to the number of rows in table 1 times that in table 2 times that in table 3, and so on. Cartesian rows that don't satisfy the JOIN condition are disregarded.

cascading deletion   A trigger that deletes data from one table based on a deletion from another table to maintain referential integrity. Declarative referential integrity (DRI) is another means of implementing cascading deletions. Triggers or DRI usually are used to delete detail data (such as invoice items) when the master record (invoice) is deleted. Jet 2+

provides cascading deletion as an optional component of its referential integrity features. See *referential integrity*.

case sensitivity   A term that defines whether an interpreter, compiler, or database manager treats lowercase and uppercase letters as the same character. Most are not case sensitive. C is an exception; it is case sensitive, and all its keywords are lowercase. Many interpreters, including VBA, reformat keywords to its standard—a combination of uppercase and lowercase letters. VBA doesn't distinguish between uppercase and lowercase letters used as names for variables.

Cellset   The multidimensional equivalent of an ADO `Recordset`. See *ADO MD*, *CubeDef*, *OLAP*, and *PivotTable Service*.

chaptered `Recordset`   See *hierarchical `Recordset`*

child   In Windows, usually a shortened form of *MDI child window*. Also used in computer programming in general to describe an object that's related to but lower in hierarchical level than a parent object.

chunk   A part of a RIFF or standard MIDI file that's assigned to a particular function and may be treated as a single element by an application. VBA uses the term *chunk* to refer to a part of any file that you read or write with the `GetChunk` and `AppendChunk` methods. See *RIFF*.

class identifier   See *CLSID*.

clause   The portion of a SQL statement beginning with a keyword that names a basic operation to be performed.

client   The device or application that receives data from or manipulates a server device or application. The data may be in the form of a file received from a network file server, an object from an ActiveX component or Automation server, or values from a DDE server assigned to client variables. See *Automation client*.

client tier   A logical entity that represents a networked computer where an Access application interacts with a client/server database or a browser displays a Web page from a remote data source. See also *middle tier* and *data source tier*.

CLSID   An identification tag that's associated with an Automation object created by a specific server. CLSID values appear in the Registry and must be unique for each ActiveX component or Automation server and for each type of object that the server can create. See *Registry*.

clustered index   An index in which the physical record order and index order of a table are the same.

code   Short for *source code*, the text you enter in your program to create an application. Code consists of instructions and their parameters, functions and their arguments, objects and their events, properties and methods, constants, variable declarations and assignments, and expressions and comments.

code template   Self-contained groups of modules and resources that perform a group of standard functions and that may be incorporated within other applications requiring these functions, usually with little or no modification.

coercion   The process of forcing a change from one data type to another, such as `Integer` to `String`.

collection   A group of objects of the same class that are contained within another object. Collections are named as the plural of their object class—for example, the Parameters collection is a group of `Parameter` objects contained in a `Command` object.

COM   An acronym for *Component Object Model*, the name of Microsoft's design strategy to implement ActiveX and OLE 2+. Distributed COM (DCOM) allows networked and cross-platform implementation of ActiveX and Automation. See *DCOM*.

COM+   Microsoft's answer to a future competitive threat from Enterprise JavaBeans. Microsoft's goals for COM+ include absorbing MTS, making COM components easier to deploy and manage, improving system performance, and increasing server scalability from hundreds to thousands of clients. COM+ adds event services, load balancing, asynchronous queuing services with MSMQ, and an in-memory database for the MTS catalog. See *COM*, *DCOM*, *MSMQ*, and *MTS*.

command   A synonym for *instruction*, specifies an action to be taken by the computer.

comment   Explanatory material within source code not designed to be interpreted or compiled into the final application. In VBA, comments are usually preceded by an apostrophe (`'`) but can also be created by preceding them with the `Rem` keyword.

common dialog   A standardized dialog, provided by Windows 9x and Windows NT, that may be created by a Windows API function call to functions contained in Cmdlg32.dll and its successors. Common dialogs include File Open, File Save, Print and Printer Setup, ColorPalette, Font, and Search and Replace.

comparison operators   See *operator*.

compile   To create an executable or object (machine-language) file from source (readable) code. In Access, *compile* means to create pseudocode (tokenized code), not native code, from the VBA source code you write in the code-editing window.

Component Object Model   See *COM*.

composite key or index   A key or index based on the values in two or more columns. See also *index* and *key or key field*.

composite menu   A menu that includes menu choices from an Automation server application that uses in-place (in-situ) activation (editing). Creating a composite menu also is called *grafting a menu*. ActiveX documents graft their menus to those of Internet Explorer 3+.

compound   In computer programming, a set of instructions or statements that requires more than one keyword or group of related keywords to complete. `Select Case...Case...End Select` is an example of a compound statement in VBA.

compound document   A document that contains OLE objects created by an application other than the application that originally created or is managing the document. OLE 2+ (not ActiveX) creates compound documents.

concatenation   Combining two expressions, usually strings, to form a longer expression. The concatenation operator is **&** in SQL and VBA, although VBA also permits the + symbol to be used to concatenate strings.

concurrency   The condition when more than one user has access to a specific set of records or files at the same time. Also used to describe the capability of a database management system to handle simultaneous queries against a single set of tables.

container   An object or application that can create or manipulate compound documents or host ActiveX controls.

conversation   In DDE operations, the collection of Windows messages passed between two different applications—the client and server—during an interprocess communication.

CORBA   An acronym for *Common Object Request Broker Architecture*, the primary competitor to Microsoft's COM- and DCOM-based technologies. See *COM* and *DCOM*.

correlated subquery   A subquery that can't be evaluated independently. Subqueries depend on an outer query for their result. See also *subquery* and *nested query*.

counter   A special field data type of Access 1.x and 2.0, and Jet 2.0 tables that numbers each new record consecutively; called an *AutoNumber field* in Jet 3+. See *AutoNumber*.

CubeDef   An ADO MD object that provides the metadata for multidimensional data, such as that provided by Microsoft SQL Server OLAP or PivotTable Services. See *ADO MD*, *Cellset OLAP*, and *PivotTable Service*.

current database   The database opened in Access by choosing Open Database from the File menu (or the equivalent) that contains the objects of an Access application.

current record   The record in a Recordset object whose values you modify. The current record supplies values of the current record's data cells to control objects that are bound to the table's fields. The current record is specified by a record pointer.

current statement   The statement or instruction being executed at a particular instance in time. In debugging or stepwise operation of interpreted development environments such as Access, the current statement is the next statement that will be executed by the interpreter when program operation is resumed.

custom control   The former name for a control object not native to the application. Visual Basic 3.0 and Visual C++ 3.0 used 16-bit Visual Basic Extension custom controls (VBXs). Visual Basic 4.0 supported 16-bit VBXs and OCXs, plus 32-bit OCXs. Access 2000 supports only 32-bit OCXs. See *ActiveX controls* and *OLE Control*.

Data Access Object   The original container for all database objects in Access, often abbreviated *DAO*. The top member of the Jet DAO hierarchy is the DBEngine object, which contains Workspace, User, and Group objects in collections. Database objects are contained in Workspace objects. ADO 2.1 is the preferred alternative to DAO 3.6 in Access 2000, although DAO 3.51 and earlier are supported for backward compatibility. See also *ADO*.

Data Access Pages   See *DAP*.

data binding   Connecting two or more data-related objects, usually a data consumer to a data provider, to pass a Recordset or other data object between objects. Access 2000 has the capability to bind a variety of OLE DB data providers to OLE DB data consumers via ADO. See *data consumer* and *data provider*.

data consumer   An OLE DB term for an object that presents and/or manipulates data. All Access 2000 data-bound controls are OLE DB data consumers.

data definition   The process of describing databases and database objects such as tables, indexes, views, procedures, rules, default values, triggers, and other characteristics. SQL's Data Definition Language (DDL) defines the components of SQL-compliant databases.

data dictionary   The result of the data definition process. Also used to describe a set of database system tables that contain the data definitions of database objects, often called *metadata*.

data element   The value contained in a data cell, also called a *data item* or simply an *element*. A piece of data that describes a single property of a data entity, such as a person's first name, last name, Social Security number, age, sex, or hair color. In this case, the person is the data entity.

data entity   A distinguishable set of objects that is the subject of a data table and usually has at least one unique data element. A data entity might be a person (unique Social Security number), an invoice (unique invoice number), or a vehicle (unique vehicle ID number, because license plates aren't necessarily unique across state lines).

data integrity   The maintenance of rules that prevent inadvertent or intentional modifications to the content of a database that would be deleterious to its accuracy or reliability. See *domain integrity* and *referential integrity*.

data provider   An OLE DB term for an object that connects to a database or other source of persistent data and supplies data to a data consumer. The SQLOLEDB OLE DB data provider for SQL Server is an example of a native OLE DB provider. MSDASQL, the OLE DB data provider for ODBC, is a nonnative (indirect) data provider.

data shaping   The process of creating a hierarchical (also called *chaptered*) Recordset object using SHAPE syntax. See *hierarchical Recordset* and *SHAPE statements*.

data sharing   The feature that allows more than one user to access information stored in a database from the same or a different application.

data source   A database or other form of persistent (file) data storage. Data source commonly is used to describe an ODBC data source name (DSN). In Access 2000, a data source is a named OLE DB data provider or service provider.

data source tier   A logical entity that represents a server running a client/server RDBMS, such as SQL Server, also called the *data services*. See also *client tier*, *middle tier*, and *three-tier*.

data type   The description of how the computer is to interpret a particular item of data. Data types are generally divided into two families: strings that usually have text or readable content, and numeric data. The types of numeric data supported vary with the compiler or interpreter. Most programming languages support a user-defined record or structure data type that can contain multiple data types within it. Field data types, which define the data types of database tables, are distinguished from Access table data types in this book.

database   A set of related data tables and other database objects, such as a data dictionary, that are organized as a group.

database administrator   The individual(s) responsible for the administrative functions of client/server databases. The database administrator (DBA) has privileges (permissions) for all commands that may be executed by the RDBMS and is ordinarily responsible for maintaining system security, including access by users to the RDBMS itself and performing backup and restoration functions.

database device   A file in which databases and related information, such as transaction logs, are stored. Database devices usually have physical names (such as a filename) and a logical name (the parameter of the USE statement). In SQL Server 6.5 and earlier, database devices use the .dat file extension. SQL Server 7.0 dispenses with database devices and stores databases and logs in conventional operating system files.

database object   A component of a database. Database objects include tables, views, indexes, stored procedures, columns, rules, triggers, database diagrams, and defaults.

database owner   The user who originally created a database. The database owner has control over all the objects in the database but may delegate control to other users. Access calls the database owner the *creator*. The database owner is identified by the prefix dbo in SQL Server.

date function   A function that provides date and time information or manipulates date and time values.

DCOM   An acronym for *Distributed Common Object Model*. Allows communication and manipulation of objects over a network connection. Windows NT 4.0 is the first Microsoft operating system to support DCOM (formerly called NetworkOLE). See *COM*.

DDE   An abbreviation for *dynamic data exchange*. DDE is a method that Windows and OS/2 use to transfer data between different applications. Automation implemented by ActiveX components provides a more robust method for communication between applications or components of applications.

deadlock   A condition that occurs when two users with a lock on one data item attempt to lock the other's data item. Most RDBMSs detect this condition, prevent its occurrence, and advise both users of the potential deadlock situation.

debug   The act of removing errors in the source code for an application.

declaration   A statement that creates a user-defined data type, names a variable, creates a symbolic constant, or registers the prototypes of functions incorporated within dynamic link libraries.

declaration section   A section of a VBA module reserved for statements containing declarations.

declare   In text and not as a keyword, to create a user-defined data holder for a variable or constant. As a VBA keyword, to register a function contained in a dynamic link library in the declarations section of a module.

default   A value assigned or an option chosen when no value is specified by the user or assigned by a program statement.

default database   The logical name of the database assigned to a user when he or she logs in to the database application.

demand lock   Precludes more shared locks from being set on a data resource. Successive requests for shared locks must wait for the demand lock to be cleared.

dependent   A condition in which master data in a table (such as invoices) is associated with detail data in a subsidiary table (invoice items). In this case, invoice items are dependent on invoices.

design-master replica   The member of a Jet replica set that allows changes in the design of objects, such as tables. The design-master replica usually (but not necessarily) is the .mdb file that is updated by briefcase replicas of the file. See *Briefcase replication*.

Design mode   One of two modes of operation of Access 2000, also called *design time* or *design view*. Design mode lets you create and modify database objects and write VBA code. The other mode is Run mode, also called *runtime* (when the application is executing).

destination document   A term used by OLE 1.0 to refer to a compound document.

detail data   Data in a subsidiary table that depends on data in a master table to have meaning or intrinsic value. If a user deletes the master invoice records, the subsidiary table's detail data for items included in the invoice lose their reference in the database—they become *orphan data*.

detail table   A table that depends on a master table. Detail tables usually have a many-to-one relationship with the master table. See also *detail data*.

device   A computer system component that can send or receive data, such as a keyboard, display, printer, disk drive, or modem. Windows uses device drivers to connect applications to devices.

DHTML   An abbreviation for *Dynamic HTML,* a proprietary flavor of HTML that permits client-side scripting to modify the appearance and/or content of a Web page without requiring repeated round trips to the Web server. Microsoft and Netscape implement DHTML differently, so DHTML is suitable only for intranets.

dialog   A pop-up modal child window, also called a *dialog box,* that requests information from the user. Dialogs include message boxes, input boxes, and user-defined dialogs for applications, such as choosing files to open.

DIB   An acronym for *Device-Independent Bitmap,* a Windows-specific bitmap format designed to display graphic information. DIB files take the extension .dib and use a format similar to .bmp.

difference   In data tables, data elements that are contained in one table but not in another.

directory list   An element of a file-selection dialog that selectively lists the subfolders of the designated folder of a specified logical drive.

distributed database   A database, usually of the client/server type, that's located on more than one database server, often at widely separated locations. Synchronization of data contained in distributed databases is most commonly accomplished by the two-phase commit or replication methods. See *replication* and *two-phase commit.*

Distributed Transaction Coordinator   See *DTC.*

DLL   An abbreviation for *dynamic link library,* a file containing a collection of Windows functions designed to perform a specific class of operations. Most DLLs carry the .dll extension, but some Windows DLLs, such as Gdi32.exe, use the .exe extension. Functions within DLLs are called (*invoked*) by applications, as necessary, to perform the desired operation.

docfile   The file format for creating persistent OLE objects, now called ActiveX documents. Docfiles usually have the extension .ole. Fully OLE 2–compliant applications create docfiles with specific extensions, such as .doc (Word) and .xls (Excel). Access 2000 stores ADP forms, reports, and modules on disk as docfiles. OLE 2.1 requires that docfiles include file property values derived from the File menu's Properties command. See also *ActiveX documents* and *ADP.*

document   A programming object that contains information originating with the user of the application, rather than being created by the application itself. Document data usually is stored in disk files. Access tables, forms, and reports are documents, as are Excel or Lotus 1-2-3 worksheets. DAO has a Documents collection that exposes Access forms, reports, and other application-specific objects to VBA code. In Windows 9x and Windows NT 4.0, a document is a file with an association to an application that can display or manipulate the file. See *DAO.*

domain aggregate functions   A set of functions, identical to the SQL aggregate functions, that you can apply to a specified domain, rather than to one or more Table objects. Access supports domain aggregate functions; DAO and ADO do not. See also *aggregate functions.*

domain integrity   The process of assuring that values added to fields of a table comply with a set of rules for reasonableness and other constraints. For example, domain integrity is violated if you enter a ship date value that's earlier than an order date. Jet maintains domain integrity by field-level and table-level validation rules. See *business rules*.

DTC   An abbreviation for Microsoft's *Distributed Transaction Coordinator*, a feature of SQL Server required to support distributed transactions and Microsoft Transaction Server (MTS). See *distributed database* and *MTS*.

dynamic data exchange   See *DDE*.

dynamic link library   See *DLL*.

dynaset   A set of rows and columns in your computer's memory that represent the values in an attached table, a table with a filter applied, or a query result set. You can update the values of the fields of the underlying table(s) by changing the values of the data cells of an updatable dynaset object. In Jet 2+, Dynaset is a type of Recordset object. See also *Recordset*.

ECMAScript   The official name for Netscape's JavaScript, now that standardization of JavaScript is under the aegis of the European Computer Manufacturers Association (ECMA).

embedded object   A source document stored as an OLE object in a compound or container document.

empty   A condition of a VBA variable that has been declared but hasn't been assigned a value. Empty is not the same as the Null value, nor is it equal to the empty or zero-length string (" ").

enabled   The ability of a control object to respond to user actions such as a mouse click, expressed as the True or False value of the Enabled property of the control.

environment   A combination of the computer hardware, operating system, and user interface. A complete statement of an environment follows: a 166MHz Pentium computer with a VGA display and two-button mouse, using the Windows 9x operating system.

environmental variable   A DOS term for variables that are declared by PATH and SET statements, usually made in an AUTOEXEC.BAT file and stored in a reserved memory location by DOS. In Windows 9x and Windows NT, required environmental variables are stored in the Registry, although Windows 9x accepts environmental variables in the AUTOEXEC.BAT file for backward compatibility with 16-bit Windows applications. The environmental variables may be used by applications to adjust their operation for compatibility with user-specific hardware elements or folder structures.

equi-join   A JOIN in which the values in the columns being joined are compared for equality and all columns in both tables are displayed. An equi-join causes two identical columns (both joined columns) to appear in the result.

error trapping   A procedure by which errors generated during the execution of an application are rerouted to a designated group of code lines (called an *error handler*) that performs a predefined operation, such as ignoring the error. If errors aren't trapped in VBA, the standard modal message dialog with the text message for the error that occurred appears.

event   The occurrence of an action taken by the user and recognized by one of the object's event properties, such as VBA's `Click` and `DblClick` event handlers for most controls. Events are usually related to mouse movements and keyboard actions; however, events also can be generated by code with the `Timer` control object and during manipulation of database objects. ADO `Connection`, `Command`, and `Recordset` objects trigger many data-related events.

event driven   The property of an operating system or environment, such as Windows, that implies the existence of an idle loop. When an event occurs, the idle loop is exited and event-handler code, specific to the event, is executed. After the event handler completes its operation, execution returns to the idle loop, awaiting the next event.

exclusive lock   A lock that prevents others from locking data items until the exclusive lock is cleared. Exclusive locks are placed on data items by update operations, such as SQL's `INSERT`, `UPDATE`, and `DELETE`. Jet and SQL Server 6.5 use page locking. SQL Server 6.5 provides row locking for `INSERT` operations, and SQL Server 7.0 provides both `INSERT` and `UPDATE` row locking.

executable   Code, usually in the form of a disk file, that can be run by the operating system in use to perform a particular set of functions. Executable files in Windows carry the extension .exe and may obtain assistance from dynamic link libraries (DLLs) in performing their tasks.

exponent   The second element of a number expressed in scientific notation, the power of 10 by which the first element, the *mantissa*, is multiplied to obtain the actual number. For `+1.23E3`, the exponent is `3`, so you multiply `1.23` by `1,000` (10 to the third power) to obtain the result `1,230`.

expression   A combination of variable names, values, functions, and operators that return a result, usually assigned to a variable name. `Result = 1 + 1` is an expression that returns `2` to the variable named `Result`. `DiffVar = LargeVar-SmallVar` returns the difference between the two variables to `DiffVar`. Functions may be used in expressions, and the expression may return the value determined by the function to the same variable as that of the argument. `strVar = Mid$(strVar, 2, 3)` replaces the value of `strVar` with three of its characters, starting at the second character.

facts table   The table of a multidimensional database, also called a *measures table*, that stores numeric data (metrics). The facts table is related to the dimension tables. See *ADO MD, metrics, PivotTable Service, star schema*, and *snowflake schema*.

FAT   An acronym for *file allocation table*, the disk file system used by MS-DOS, Windows 9x, and (optionally) Windows NT. Windows NT is compatible with the 16-bit FAT system but not the optional 32-bit FAT (FAT32) for Windows 9x that Microsoft announced in mid-1996. See *HPFS* and *NTFS*.

field   Synonym for a column that contains attribute values. Also, a single item of information in a record or row.

fifth normal form   The rule for relational databases requiring that a table that has been divided into multiple tables must be capable of being reconstructed to its exact original structure by one or more JOIN statements.

file   The logical equivalent of a table. In dBASE, for instance, each table is a single .dbf file.

first normal form   The rule for relational databases that dictates that tables must be flat. Flat tables can contain only one data value set per row. Members of the data value set, called *data cells*, are contained in one column of the row and must have only one value.

flag   A variable, usually **Boolean** (True/False), that's used to determine the status of a particular condition within an application. The term *set* is often used to indicate turning a flag from False to True, and *reset* for the reverse.

flow control   In general usage, conditional expressions that control the execution sequence of instructions or statements in the source code of an application. **If...Then...End If** is a flow-control statement.

focus   The currently selected application, or one of its windows, to which all user-generated input (keyboard and mouse operations) is directed. The object with the focus is said to be the *active object*. The title bar of a window with the focus is colored blue for the default Windows color scheme.

font   A typeface in a single size, usually expressed in points, of a single style or having a common set of attributes. *Font* often is misused to indicate a typeface family or style.

foreground   In multitasking operations, the application or procedure that's visible onscreen and to which user-generated input is directed. In Windows, the application that has the focus is in the foreground.

foreign key   A column or combination of columns whose value must match a primary key in another table when joined with it. Foreign keys need not be unique for each record or row. See also *primary key*.

form   An Access Form object contains the control objects that appear on its surface and the code associated with the events, methods, and properties applicable to the form and its control objects.

form level   Variables that are declared in the Declarations section of an Access form. These variables are said to have *form-level scope* and aren't visible to procedures outside the Form object in which the variables are declared, unless declared with the **Public** reserved word.

fourth normal form   The rule for relational databases that requires that only related data entities be included in a single table and that tables may not contain data related to more than one data entity when many-to-one relationships exist among the entities.

frame   In Windows, a rectangle, usually with a single-pixel-wide border, that encloses a group of objects, usually of the dialog class. Option buttons commonly are enclosed in frames so that only one option button of the group can be selected.

front end   When used with database management systems, an application, a window, or a set of windows by which the user may access and view database records, as well as add to or edit them.

full server   An OLE 2–compliant executable application that can provide embeddable or linked documents for insertion into OLE 2+ container documents. Excel 2000, Word 2000, and WordPad are examples of OLE 2.1 full-server applications. Access 2000 is not a full server, because you can't embed or link an Access .mdb file in an OLE 2.1 container application.

function   A subprogram called from within an expression in which a value is computed and returned to the program that called it through its name. Functions are classified as internal to the application language when their names are keywords. You can create your own user-defined functions in VBA by adding code between **Function** *FunctionName*...**End Function** statements.

global   Pertaining to the program as a whole. Global variables and constants are accessible to, and global variables may be modified by, code at the form, module, and procedure level. VBA uses the reserved word **Public** to create or refer to global variables.

globally-unique identifier   See *GUID*.

global module   A code module (container) in which all global variables and constants are declared and in which the prototypes of any external functions contained in DLLs are declared. Use of a global module in Access applications is common, but is not required if you don't need to share access to variables, procedures, and functions from multiple forms.

group   In reports, one or more records that are collected into a single category, usually for the purpose of totaling. Database security systems use the term *group* to identify a collection of database users with common permissions. See also *permissions*.

GUID   An acronym for globally-unique identifier, pronounced "goo-id." GUIDs consist of 32 hexadecimal characters surrounded by French braces, as in {00000535-0000-0010-8000-00AA006D2EA4}, which the operating system creates from a combination of numeric values, including PC-specific values. COM makes extensive use of GUIDs to identify objects, interfaces, and other COM elements. Jet 4.0 and SQL Server 7.0 have a new GUID data type, the primary use of which is to uniquely identify rows in a table for replication purposes.

handle   An unsigned `Long` integer assigned by Windows 9x and Windows NT to uniquely identify an instance (occurrence) of a module (application, `hModule`), task (`hTask`), window (`hWnd`), or device context (`hDC`) of a graphic object. Handles in 32-bit Windows applications, including applications for Windows 9x and Windows NT, are 32-bit unsigned long integers (`dw`, or double words). Also used to identify the sizing elements of control objects in Design mode. See also *sizing handle*.

header file   A file type used by C and C++ programs to assign data types and names to variables and to declare prototypes of the functions used in the application. C header files usually carry the extension .h.

hierarchical menu   A menu with multiple levels, consisting of a main menu bar that leads to one or more levels of submenus from which choices of actions are made. Almost all Windows applications use hierarchical menu structures.

hierarchical `Recordset`   A `Recordset` that contains detail records in the form of a `Variant` array. Hierarchical `Recordset`s are more efficient than conventional `Recordset`s for display-ing one-to-many query result sets, because cells of the one side aren't repeated. Only Visual Basic 6.0's new Hierarchical FlexGrid control is capable of displaying hierarchical `Recordset`s.

host   Any computer on a network running an Internet Protocol (IP). See *IP* and *IP address*.

hotlink   A DDE (dynamic data exchange) operation in which a change in the source of the DDE data (the server) is immediately reflected in the object of the destination application (the client) that has requested it.

HTML   An abbreviation for *Hypertext Markup Language*, a variant of SGML (Standardized General Markup Language), a page-description language for creating files that can be formatted and displayed by World Wide Web browsers.

HTTP   An abbreviation for *Hypertext Transport Protocol*, the transport protocol used by the World Wide Web and private intranets.

identifier   A synonym for *name* or *symbol*, usually applied to variable and constant names.

idle   In Windows, the condition or state in which Windows and the application have processed all pending messages in the queue from user- or hardware-initiated events and are waiting for the next event to occur. The idle state is entered in VBA when the inter-preter reaches the `End Sub` statement of the outermost nesting level of procedures for a form or control object.

Immediate window   A modeless dialog in which you may enter VBA expressions and view results without writing code in a code-editing window. You also can direct information to be displayed in the Immediate window with the `Debug` object.

index   For arrays, the position of the particular element with respect to others, usually beginning with `0` as the first element. In the context of database files or tables, *index* refers to a lookup table, usually in the form of a file or component of a file, that relates the value of a field in the indexed file to its record or page number and location in the page (if pages are used).

infinite loop   A `Do While...Loop`, `For...Next`, or similar program flow-control structure in which the condition to exit the loop and continue with succeeding statements is never fulfilled. In `For...Next` loops, infinite looping occurs when the loop counter is set to a value less than that assigned to the `To` embedded keyword within the structure.

initialize   In programming, setting all variables to their default values and resetting the point of execution to the first executable line of code. Initialization is accomplished automatically in VBA when you start an application.

inner query   Synonym for *subquery*. See *subquery*.

in-place activation   The ability to activate an object (launch another application) and have the container application take on the capabilities of the other application. The primary feature of in-place activation (also called *in-situ activation*) is that the other application's menu choices merge with or replace the container application's menu choices in the active window.

in-process   A term applied to Automation servers, also called *ActiveX DLLs*, that operate within the same process space (memory allocation) of the Automation client. In-process servers commonly are called *InProc servers*. See *out-of-process*.

insertion point   The position of the cursor within a block of text. When the cursor is in a text field, it is called the *caret* in Windows.

instance   The temporary existence of a loaded application or one or more of its windows.

instantiate   The process of creating an instance of an object in memory.

integer   A whole number. In most programming languages, an integer is a data type that occupies two bytes (16 bits). Integers may have signs (as in the VBA `Integer` data type), taking on values from –32,768 to +32,767, or be unsigned. In the latter case, integers can represent numbers up to 65,535.

interface   A connection between two dissimilar COM objects or Automation clients and servers. Another common phrase is *user interface*, meaning the "connection" between the display/keyboard combination and users. Adapter cards constitute the interface between the PC data bus and peripheral devices such as displays, modems, CD-ROMs, and the like. Drivers act as a software interface between Windows and the adapter cards. A *bridge* is an interface between two dissimilar networks. Use of *interface* as a verb is jargon.

intersection   The group of data elements included in both tables that participate in a `JOIN` operation.

intranet   A private network that uses Internet protocols and common Internet applications (such as Web browsers) to emulate the public Internet. Intranets on LANs and high-speed WANs provide increased privacy and improved performance compared with today's Internet.

invocation path The route through which an object or routine is invoked. If the routine is deeply nested, the path may be quite circuitous.

invoke To cause execution of a block of code, particularly a procedure or subprocedure. Also indicates application of a method to an object.

IP An abbreviation for *Internet Protocol*, the basic network transmission protocol of the Internet.

IP address The 32-bit hexadecimal address of a host, gateway, or router on an IP network. For convenience, IP addresses are specified as the decimal value of the four address bytes, separated by periods, as in 124.33.15.1. Addresses are classified as types A, B, and C, depending on the subnet mask applied. See *subnet mask*.

IPX/SPX Abbreviation for *Internetwork Packet Exchange/Sequenced Packet Exchange*, the transport protocol of Novell NetWare, supported by Windows NT's NWLink service.

item The name given to each element contained in a list or the list component of a combo box.

JDBC An abbreviation for *Java Database Connector*, despite the insistence of Sun Microsystems that JDBC "doesn't stand for anything." JDBC is Java's purportedly platform-agnostic version of ODBC, which it closely resembles.

Jet Microsoft's name for the database engine native to Access and Visual Basic. The name *Jet* came from the acronym for *Joint Engine Technology*, the predecessor of Jet 3.6 used by Access and Jet 3.51 used by Visual Basic 6.0.

Jet SQL The dialect of ANSI SQL used by the Data Access Object and by all versions of Microsoft Access. For the most part, Access SQL complies with ANSI SQL-92. Jet SQL offers additional features, such as the capability to include user-defined functions within queries.

join A basic operation, initiated by the SQL JOIN statement, that links the rows or records of two or more tables by one or more columns in each table. See also *equi-join* and *inner join*.

jump In programming, execution of code in a sequence that's not the same as the sequence in which the code appears in the source code. In most cases, a jump skips over a number of lines of code, the result of evaluation of a conditional expression. In some cases, a jump causes another subroutine to be executed.

key or key field A field that identifies a record by its value. Tables are usually indexed on key fields. For a field to be a key field, each data item in the field must possess a unique value. See also *primary key* and *foreign key*.

key value A value of a key field included in an index.

keyword A word that has specific meaning to the interpreter or compiler in use and causes predefined events to occur when encountered in source code. Keywords and reserved words are not exactly the same. You can use keywords as variable, procedure, or function names, but you can't use reserved words as variable or constant names. Using keywords for this purpose, however, isn't a good programming practice.

label In VBA programming, a name given to a target line in the source code at which execution results on the prior execution of a `GoTo LabelName` instruction. A label also is an Access control object that displays, but can't update, text values.

LAN An acronym for *local area network*, a system comprising multiple computers that are physically interconnected through network adapter cards and cabling. LANs allow one computer to share specified resources, such as disk drives, printers, and modems, with other computers on the LAN.

launch To start a Windows application.

leaf level The lowest level of an index. Indexes derive the names of their elements from the objects found on trees, such as trunks, limbs, and leaves.

library A collection of functions, compiled as a group and accessible to applications by calling the function name and any required arguments. DLLs are one type of library; those used by compilers to provide built-in functions are another type.

library database An Access database that's automatically attached to Access when you launch it. Access library databases usually have the extension .mda; compiled libraries, which hide the orignal source code, use the extension .mde. Attachment of library databases to Access is controlled by Registry entries. Visual Basic doesn't have an equivalent of Access libraries.

linked object A source document in a compound document that's included by reference to a file containing the object's data; in this case, the source document is not embedded in the compound document.

linked table A table that's not stored in the currently open Access database (native or base table), but which you can manipulate as though it were a native table. Linked tables were called *attached tables* in Access 1.x and 2.0, and Jet 2.0.

livelock A request for an exclusive lock on a data item that's repeatedly denied because of shared locks imposed by other users.

local The scope of a variable declared within a procedure, rather than at the form, module, or global level. Local variables are visible (defined) only within the procedure in which they were declared. VBA uses the prefix `Private` to define functions, subprocedures, and variable of local scope.

local area network See *LAN*.

lock   A restriction of access to a table, portion of a table, or data item imposed to maintain data integrity of a database. Locks may be *shared*, in which case more than one user can access the locked element(s), or *exclusive*, where the user with the exclusive lock prevents other users from creating simultaneous shared or exclusive locks on the element(s). Jet classifies locks as *optimisic* (a lock applied only when physically changing table data) and *pessimisitic* (a lock applied for the duration of the user's editing operation.) Access 2000 uses *page locks* (4KB of the .mdb file), which may lock several adjacent records; prior versions of Access used 2KB pages. Some RDBMSs provide *row locks* that lock only a single record. SQL Server 6.5 uses row locking for INSERT operations and page locking for UPDATE and DELETE operations. SQL Server 7.0 offers row locking for all three operations.

logical   A synonym for Boolean, a data type that may have true or false values only. Logical is also used to define a class of operators whose result is only True or False. VBA includes a Boolean data type.

loop   A compound program flow-control structure that causes statements contained between the instructions that designate the beginning and end of the structure to be repeatedly executed until a given condition is satisfied. When the condition is satisfied, program execution continues at the source code line after the loop termination statement.

LRPC   An acronym for *lightweight remote procedure call* used for OLE 2+ and some ActiveX operations between OLE clients and OLE full servers on a single computer. LRPC requires both applications involved in the procedure call to be resident on the same computer. See *remote procedure call (RPC)*.

machine language   Program code in the form of instructions that have meaning to and can be acted on by the computer hardware and operating system. Object files compiled from source code are in machine language, as are executable files that consist of object files linked with library files.

mantissa   The first element of a number expressed in scientific notation that's multiplied by the power of 10 given in the exponent to obtain the actual number. For +1.23E3, the exponent is 3, so you multiply the mantissa, 1.23, by 1,000 (10 to the third power) to obtain the result: 1,230.

MAPI   An acronym for the Windows *Messaging API* created by Microsoft for use with Microsoft Mail, which implements Simple MAPI. Microsoft Exchange Server implements MAPI 1+ (also called *Extended MAPI*).

marshal   To package and send interface method parameters across thread or process boundaries. In database applications, marshaling is most commonly applied to moving Recordsets between a server and a client.

master database   A database that controls user access to other databases, usually in a client/server system.

master table A table containing data on which detail data in another table depends. Master tables have a primary key that's matched to a foreign key in a detail table and often have a one-to-many relationship with detail tables. Master tables sometimes are called *base tables*.

MDE An acronym for *Microsoft Data Engine*, a special version of the Desktop edition of Microsoft SQL Server 7.0 that is included with Access 2000. MSDE and ADP primarily are intended to accommodate replication between SQL Server 7.0 databases running on Windows NT Server 4+ and mobile or disconnected users of Access 2000. See *ADP*.

MDX An acronym for *Multidimensional Expressions*, an SQL-like language for creating and manipulating multidimensional data (cubes) created by Microsoft SQL Server OLAP Services. See *ADO MD*, *Cellset*, *CubeDef*, *OLAP*, and *PivotTable Service*.

memo An Jet field data type that can store text with a length of up to about 64,000 bytes. (The length of the Text field data type is limited to 255 bytes.)

metadata Data that describes the structure, organization, and/or location of data. Metadata commonly is called "data about data."

metafile A type of graphics file, used by Windows and other applications, that stores the objects displayed in the form of mathematical descriptions of lines and surfaces. Windows metafiles, which use the extension .wmf, are a special form of metafiles. Windows 9x and Windows NT 4.0 also support enhanced metafiles (.emf).

method One characteristic of an object and a classification of keywords in VBA. Methods are the procedures that apply to an Access object. Methods that apply to a class of objects are inherited by other objects of the same class and may be modified to suit the requirements of the object by a characteristic of an object.

metrics Numeric data, also called *measures*, contained within a facts table of a multidimensional database. See *facts table*.

Microsoft Data Engine See *MSDE*.

Microsoft Transaction Server See *MTS*.

middle tier A logical entity that connects a data source tier to a client tier and implements business rules or performs other data-related services. See also *business rule*, *client tier*, *data source tier*, and *three-tier*.

MIME An acronym for *multipurpose Internet mail extensions*, an Internet standard that lets binary data be published and read on the Internet or intranets. The header of a file containing binary data exposes the MIME type of the data. Recordsets transported by RDS use a special MIME data type called the Advanced Data TableGram protocol (ADTG).

miniserver An applet with OLE server capabilities and having an .exe file extension that you can't run as a standalone application.

mirroring See *disk mirroring*.

MISF   An abbreviation for *Microsoft Internet Security Framework*, a set of high-level security services that rely on CryptoAPI 2.0 functions to provide certificate- and password-based authentication. MISF also incorporates secure channel communication by using Secure Sockets Layer (SSL) 2.0 and 3.0 plus Personal Communications Technology (PCT), Secure Electronic Transactions (SET) for credit-card purchases, and the Microsoft Certificate Server for issuing authentication certificates.

mission critical   A cliché used in software and hardware advertising to describe the need to use the promoted product if you want to create a reliable database system.

modal   A dialog that must be closed before users can take further action within the application.

modeless   A window or dialog that users can close or minimize without taking any other action; the opposite of *modal*.

module   A block of code, consisting of one or more procedures, for which the source code is stored in a single location (a `Form` or `Module` object in Access). In a compiled language, a code module is compiled to a single object file.

module level   Variables and constants that are declared in the `Declarations` section of a VBA module. These variables have module-level scope and are visible (defined) to all procedures contained within the module, unless declared `Public`, in which case the variables are visible to all procedures.

moniker   A handle (pointer) to the source of a compound document object.

MSMQ   An acronym for *Microsoft Message Queue Server*, a middle-tier component (similar to Microsoft Transaction Server) that uses messaging techniques to permit execution of transactions over unreliable network connections. See *middle tier*.

MTS   An acronym for *Microsoft Transaction Server*, a component-based transaction monitor (TM) and object request broker (ORB) for developing, deploying, and managing the middle tier of component-based applications. Access 2000 applications can connect to MTS objects using VBA code. See also *middle tier*, *ORB*, *three-tier*, and *TPM*.

Multidimensional Expressions   See *MDX*.

multiprocessing   The capability of a computer with two or more CPUs to allocate tasks (threads) to a specific CPU. Symmetrical multitasking (SMP), implemented in Windows NT, distributes tasks among CPUs by means of a load-sharing methodology. Applications must be multithreaded to take advantage of SMP.

multitasking   The ability of a computer with a single CPU to simulate the processing of more than one task at a time. Multitasking is effective when one or more of the applications spends most of its time in an idle state waiting for a user-initiated event, such as a keystroke or mouse click.

multithreaded   An application that contains more than one thread of execution; a task or set of tasks that executes semi-independently of other task(s). The Jet 3.51 database engine is multithreaded (three threads); VBA is capable of creating multithreaded DLLs. See *thread*.

multiuser   Concurrent use of a single computer by more than one user, usually through the use of remote terminals. UNIX is inherently a multiuser operating system. Jet uses the term *multiuser* to refer to database applications that share a common .mdb file on a network file server.

named pipes   A method of interprocess communication, originally developed for OS/2, that provides a secure channel for network communication.

natural join   A SQL JOIN operation in which the values of the columns engaged in the join are compared, with all columns of each table in the join that don't duplicate other columns being included in the result. Same as an equi-join except that the joined columns aren't duplicated in the result. See *equi-join*.

NBF   An abbreviation for *NetBEUI Frame*, the transport packet structure used by NetBEUI.

nested   An expression applied to procedures that call other procedures within an application. The called procedures are said to be "nested" within the calling procedure. When many calls to subprocedures and sub-subprocedures are made, the last one in the sequence is said to be "deeply nested."

nested object   An OLE 2+ compound document incorporated in another OLE 2+ compound document. You can nest OLE 2+ documents as deeply as you like. OLE 1.0 doesn't supported nested objects.

nested query   A SQL SELECT statement that contains subqueries. See *subquery*.

NetBEUI   An abbreviation for *NetBIOS Extended User Interface*, the transport protocol of Microsoft Networking. NetBEUI isn't a routable network, so its popularity is declining compared with TCP/IP.

NetBIOS   An abbreviation for *Network Basic Input/Output System*, the original network API for MS-DOS and the foundation for NetBEUI.

newline pair   A combination of a carriage return, the Enter key (CR or Chr(13)), and line feed (LF or Chr(10)) used to terminate a line of text onscreen or within a text file. Other characters or combinations may be substituted for the CR/LF pair to indicate the type of newline character (soft, hard, deletable, and so on). The VBA newline constant is VbCrLf.

NFS   An abbreviation for *Network File Server*, a file format and set of drivers, created by Sun Microsystems Incorporated, that allows DOS/Windows and UNIX applications to share a single server disk drive running under UNIX.

nonclustered index   An index that stores key values and pointers to data based on these values. In this case, the leaf level points to data pages rather than to the data itself, as is the case for a clustered index. Equivalent to SET INDEX TO *field_name* in xBase.

normal forms   A set of five rules, the first three originally defined by Dr. E.F. Cobb, that are used to design relational databases. Five normal forms are generally accepted in the creation of relational databases. See *first normal form*, *second normal form*, *third normal form*, *fourth normal form*, and *fifth normal form*.

normalization   Creation of a database according to the five generally accepted rules of normal forms. See also *normal forms*.

not-equal join   A JOIN statement that specifies that the columns engaged in the join don't equal one another. In Access, you must specify a not-equal join by using the SQL WHERE *field1* <> *field2* clause.

NT   An abbreviation for *New Technology* used by Windows NT.

NTFS   An abbreviation for *New Technology File System*, Windows NT's replacement for the DOS file allocation table (FAT) and OS/2's high-performance file system (HPFS). NTFS offers many advantages over other file systems, including improved security and the capability to reconstruct files in the event of hardware failures. Windows 3.1+ and Windows 9x can access files stored on NTFS volumes via a network connection but can't open NTFS files directly.

null   A variable of no value or of unknown value. The default values—**0** for numeric variables and an empty string (**" "**) for string variables—aren't the same as the **Null** value. The NULL value in SQL statements specifies a data cell with no value assigned to the cell.

object   In programming, elements that combine data (properties) and behavior (methods) in a single container of code called an *object*. Objects inherit their properties and methods from the classes above them in the hierarchy and can modify the properties and methods to suit their own purposes. The code container may be part of the language itself, or you can define your own objects in source code.

object code   Code in machine-readable form that your computer's CPU and operating system can execute. Object code is usually linked with libraries to create an executable file.

object library   A file with the extension .olb that contains information on the objects, properties, and methods exposed by an .exe or .dll file of the same filename that supports Automation. See also *type library*.

object permissions   Permissions granted by the database administrator for others to view and modify the values of database objects, including data in tables.

object request broker   See *ORB*.

ODBC   An abbreviation for the Microsoft *Open Database Connectivity* API, a set of functions that provide access to client/server RDBMSs, desktop database files, text files, and Excel worksheet files through ODBC drivers. ODBC most commonly is used to connect to client/server databases, such as Microsoft SQL Server, Sybase, Informix, and Oracle. Microsoft intends for OLE DB to replace ODBC and probably won't provide significant enhancements for ODBC.

ODBCDirect   A feature of the Jet 3.5+ database engine that lets you use ODBC to access client/server databases without needing to load all of Jet 3.6. ODBCDirect conserves client resources if you need to connect only to SQL Server or another client/server RDBMS. ADO 2.1 provides features equivalent to ODBCDirect.

ODE   An acronym for *Office 2000 Developer Edition*, which includes a royalty-free license to distribute Msaccess.exe for run-time use, the run-time version of Microsoft Chart, additional ActiveX controls, and other distributable components of Access 2000. The ODE also includes the Setup Wizard you use to create images of the distribution disks for your application. Other developer-oriented features of the ODE are printed manuals, the Replication Manager, and the Microsoft Help Compiler.

offset   The number of bytes from a reference point, usually the beginning of a file, to the particular byte of interest. The first byte in a file, when offset is used to specify location, is always 0.

OLAP   An acronym for *online analytical processing*, a technology that operates on nonrelational, multidimensional databases (data cubes). Microsoft SQL Server OLAP Services, a component of SQL Server 7.0, enables the creation, manipulation, and distribution of multidimensional data. See *ADO MD*, *PivotTable Service*, and *star schema*.

OLE Automation   An extension of OLE 2+ that provides the framework (interfaces) for applications and libraries to expose programmable objects that can be manipulated by client applications. Applications that expose programmable objects are called Automation servers or ActiveX components. See *automation* and *programmable object*.

OLE Control   An in-process OLE Automation server with the extension .ocx that exposes a single object, plus the properties, methods, and events of the object. OLE Controls have been superceded by 32-bit ActiveX controls. *See ActiveX controls*.

OLE DB   A new Microsoft framework for providing a uniform interface to data from various sources, including text files and mainframe databases. OLE DB is intended to replace ODBC as a means of database access, but includes an ODBC provider that takes the place of the ODBC driver manager. ADO is an Automation wrapper for OLE DB. See also *ADO* and *ODBC*.

OLE DLL   A synonym for an in-process OLE Automation server implemented as a Windows DLL. See *in-process*.

online analytical processing   See *OLAP*.

OLTP   An abbreviation for online transaction processing. OLTP most commonly refers to large-scale database applications that update multiple tables, such as order entry and reservation systems, which use transaction processing to assure data integrity. See *transaction*.

operand   One variable or constant on which an operator acts. In 1 + 2 = 3, 1 and 2 are operands, + and = are the operators. See *operator*.

operator   A keyword or reserved symbol that, in its unary form, acts on a single variable, or otherwise acts on two variables, to give a result. Operators may be of the conventional mathematics type such as + (add), – (subtract), / (divide), and * (multiply), as well as logical, such as **And** or **Not**. The unary minus (-), when applied to a single variable in a statement such as intVar = -intVar, inverts the sign of intVar from - to + or from + to -.

optimistic locking   A method of locking a record or page of a table that makes the assumption that the probability of other users locking the same record or page is low. With optimistic locking, the record or page is locked only when the data is updated, not during the editing process (LockType property set to adLockOptimistic).

ORB   An acronym for *object request broker*, a server-based application that provides a means for client applications to locate and instantiate middle-tier objects in three-tier applications. See *middle tier*, *MTS*, and *three tier*.

outer join   A SQL JOIN operation in which all rows of the joined tables are returned, whether or not a match is made between columns. SQL database managers that don't support the OUTER JOIN reserved words use the *= (LEFT JOIN) operator to specify that all the rows in the preceding table return and the =* (RIGHT JOIN) to return all the rows in the succeeding table.

outer query   A synonym for the primary query in a statement that includes a subquery. See also *subquery*.

out-of-process   An (OLE) Automation server in the form of an executable (.exe) file that operates in its own process space (memory allocation) and uses lightweight remote procedure calls (LRPCs) to communicate with the Automation client. The term *OutOfProc* often is used as shorthand for *out-of-process*.

page   In tables of client/server RDBMSs, such as Microsoft SQL Server 7.0 and Access 2000 databases, a 4K block that contains records of tables. Client/server and Access databases lock pages, whereas DOS desktop databases usually lock individual records. Most RDBMSs require page locking when variable-length records are used in tables.

parameter   The equivalent of an argument, but associated with the procedure that receives the value of an argument from the calling function. The terms *parameter* and *argument*, however, are often used interchangeably. An ADO Parameter object provides or returns a value to or from a query or a stored procedure.

parse   The process of determining whether a particular expression is contained within another expression. Parsing breaks program statements into keywords, operators, operands, arguments, and parameters for subsequent processing of each by the computer. Parsing string variables involves searching for the occurrence of a particular character or set of characters in the string and then taking a specified set of actions when found or not found.

permissions   Authority given by the system administrator, database administrator, or database owner to perform operations on a network or on data objects in a database.

persistent (graphics)   A Windows graphic image that survives movement, resizing, or overwriting of the window in which it appears. Persistent images are stored in global memory blocks and aren't released until the window containing them is destroyed.

persistent (objects)   An object that's stored in the form of a file or an element of a file, rather than only in memory. Jet `Table` and `QueryDef` objects are persistent because they're stored in .mdb files. `Recordset` objects, on the other hand, usually are stored in memory. Such objects are called *temporal* or *impersistent objects*. ADO 2.0 lets you persist `Recordset` objects as files.

pessimistic locking   A method of locking a record or page of a table that makes the assumption that the probability of other users locking the same record or page is high. With pessimistic locking, the record or page is locked during the editing and updating process (`LockType` property set to `adLockPessimistic`).

PivotTable Service   A Microsoft-trademarked desktop OLAP implementation that used ADO MD to operate on persistent (file-based) multidimensional data cubes created by a subset of Microsoft SQL Server OLAP Services. See *ADO MD*, *Cellset*, *CubeDef*, and *OLAP*.

point   In typography, the unit of measurement of the vertical dimension of a font, about 1/72 of an inch. The point is also a unit of measurement in Windows, where it represents exactly 1/72 of a logical inch, or 20 twips. Unless otherwise specified, all distance measurements in VBA are in twips.

pointer   A data type that comprises a number representing a memory location. Near pointers are constrained to the 64K default local data segment. Far pointers can access any location in the computer's memory. Pointers are used extensively in C-language applications to access elements of arrays, strings, structures, and the like. VBA has only one pointer data type—to a zero-terminated string when the **ByVal...As String** keywords are applied to a VBA string passed to an external function contained in a dynamic link library.

poke   In DDE terminology, the transmission of an unrequested data item to a DDE server by the DDE client. In BASIC language terminology, placing a byte of data in a specific memory location. VBA doesn't support the BASIC `POKE` keyword and uses the `DDEPoke` method for DDE operations.

PPP   An abbreviation for *Point-to-Point Protocol*, the most common Internet protocol for connection to TCP/IP networks via conventional and ISDN modems.

PPTP   An abbreviation for *Point-to-Point Tunneling Protocol*, a Microsoft-sponsored protocol included with Windows NT 4.0 that uses encryption to assure privacy of communication over the Internet. See *VPN*.

precedence   The sequence of execution of operators in statements that contain more than one operator.

primary key   The column or columns whose individual or combined values (in the case of a composite primary key) uniquely identify a row in a table.

primary verb   The default verb for activating an OLE 2+ object. `Edit` is the default verb for most OLE objects, except multimedia objects, whose default verb is usually `Play`.

print zone   The area of a sheet of paper on which a printer can create an image. For most laser printers and standard dot-matrix printers, this area is 8 inches wide. The vertical dimension is unlimited for dot-matrix printers and usually is 13.5 inches for a laser printer with legal-size paper capabilities.

procedure   A self-contained collection of source code statements, executable as an entity. All VBA procedures begin with the reserved word `Sub` or `Function` (which may be preceded by the `Public`, `Private`, `Static`, or `Property` reserved words) and terminate with `End Sub` or `End Function`.

program   All code required to create an application, consisting basically of declarations, statements, and—in Windows—resource definition and help files.

programmable object   An object exposed by an Automation server with a set of properties and methods applicable to the object. The application programming language of an Automation client application can manipulate the exposed object.

projection   A projection identifies the desired subset of the columns contained in a table. You create a projection with a query that defines the fields of the table you want to display but without criteria that limit the records that are displayed.

property   One of two principal characteristics of objects (the other is methods). Properties define the manifestation of the object—for example, its appearance. Properties may be defined for an object or for the class of objects to which the particular object belongs, in which case they are said to be *inherited*.

protocol   A description of the method by which networked computers communicate. Windows NT and Windows 9x allow the simultaneous use of multiple network protocols, including TCP/IP, NetBEUI, and IPX/SPX.

protocol stack   Network protocol software that implements a specific protocol, such as TCP/IP.

proxy   An object that supplies parameter marshaling and communication methods required by a client to instantiate an Automation component running in another execution environment, such as on a server. The proxy is located on the client PC and communicates with a corresponding stub on the server. See *three-tier*.

pseudo-object   Objects contained within other OLE 2+ objects, such as the cells of a spreadsheet object.

qualification   A search condition that data values must meet to be included in the result of the search.

qualified   To precede the name of a database object with the name of the database and the object's owner, or to precede the name of a file with its drive designator and the path to the directory in which the file is stored. The terms *well-qualified path* and *well-formed path* to a file appear often in documentation.

query   A request to retrieve data from a database with the SQL SELECT instruction or to manipulate data in the database, called an *action query* by Access.

QueryDef   A persistent Jet object that stores the Jet SQL statements that define a query. QueryDef objects are optimized, when applicable, by the Jet database engine's query optimizer and stored in a special optimized format.

RDBMS   An abbreviation for *relational database management system*. An RDBMS is an application that can create, organize, and edit databases; display data through user-selected views; and print formatted reports. Most RDBMSs include at least a macro or macro language, and most provide a system programming language. Access, dBASE, Paradox, and FoxPro are desktop RDBMSs.

RDS   An acronym for *Remote Data Service*, a purportedly lightweight version of ADO 2.0 that provides transport for Recordset objects via DCOM or HTTP over intrancts.

record   A synonym for a user-defined data type, called a *structure* in C and C++. Also used in database applications to define a single element of a relational database file that contains each field defined for the file. Records don't need to contain data to exist, but Jet doesn't append a record without a value in at least one field. A record is the logical equivalent of the row of a table.

Recordset   A temporary local image of a table or a query result set stored in the PC's memory or virtual memory. Recordset objects are the primary means for manipulating data with VBA.

reference   In VBA, the incorporation of pointers to specific sets of programmable objects exposed by Automation servers and manipulated by VBA code in the Automation client. You create a VBA reference to a set of objects exposed by an Automation component in the References dialog that's accessible by choosing References from the Tools menu when a module is the active Access object. After you declare a reference to the set of objects, the VBA interpreter checks the syntax of your code against the syntax specified for the referenced object. You also can use predefined intrinsic constants for the referenced objects in your VBA code.

referential integrity   Rules governing the relationships between primary keys and foreign keys of tables within a relational database that determine data consistency. Referential integrity requires the values of every foreign key in every table be matched by the value of a primary key in another table. Access 2+ includes features for maintaining referential integrity, such as cascading updates and cascading deletions.

refresh   To redisplay records in Access's datasheet views or in a form or report so as to reflect changes others in a multiuser environment have made to the records.

Registry   A database that contains information required for the operation of Windows 9x and Windows NT, plus applications installed under Windows 9x and Windows NT. The Windows Registry takes the place of Windows 3.1+'s REG.DAT, WIN.INI, and SYSTEM.INI files, plus *PROFILE*.INI files installed by Windows 3.1 applications. The Registry also includes user information, such as user IDs, encrypted passwords, and permissions. Windows 9x and Windows NT include Regedit.exe for editing the Registry. ActiveX Components and OLE 2+ servers add entries to the Registry to specify the location of their .exe files. Automation servers add Registry entries for each object they expose. The Windows NT and Windows 9x Registries vary in structure and thus are incompatible.

relation   Synonym for a table or a data table in an RDBMS.

relational database   See *RDBMS*.

relational operators   Operators such as >, <, <>, and = that compare the values of two operands and return True or False depending on the values compared. They are sometimes called *comparative operators*.

Remote Automation Object   An out-of-process Automation server, usually called an RAO, that resides on a server and is accessible to RAO-compliant applications that connect to the server with DCOM. Most RAOs now are hosted within Microsoft Transaction Server. See also *DCOM and MTS*.

Remote Data Object (RDO)   A substitute for the Jet 3.6 Data Access Object that provides a more direct connection to the ODBC API. Jet 3.6 offers ODBCDirect as an alternative to RDO. ADO 2.1 provides features equivalent to Visual Basic 5.0 Enterprise Edition's RDO 2.0. See also *ODBCDirect*.

Remote Data Service   See *RDS*.

remote procedure call (RPC)   An interprocess communication method that allows an application to run specific parts of the application on more than one computer in a distributed computing environment.

replication   The process of duplicating database objects (usually tables) in more than one location, including a method of periodically rationalizing (synchronizing) updates to the objects. Unlike Jet 3.0, version 3.5 supports partial replication. Database replication is an alternative to the two-phase commit process. Microsoft SQL Server 6.5+ supports replication of databases across multiple Windows NT servers. See *Briefcase replication* and *two-phase commit*.

reserved word   A word that's reserved for specific use by the programming language. You can't assign a reserved word as the name of a constant, variable, function, or subprocedure. Although the terms *reserved word* and *keyword* often are used interchangeably, they don't describe an identical set of words. VBA reserved words are set in bold monospace type in this book. See *keyword*.

restriction   A query statement that defines a subset of the rows of a table based on the value of one or more of its columns.

RGB   A method of specifying colors by using numbers to specify the individual intensities of its red, green, and blue components, the colors created by the three "guns" of the cathode-ray tube (CRT) of a color display.

rollback   In transaction processing, the cancellation of a proposed transaction that modifies one or more tables and undoes changes, if any, made by the transaction before a COMMIT or COMMIT TRANSACTION SQL statement.

routine   A synonym for *procedure*.

row   A set of related columns that describe a specific data entity. A synonym for *record*.

row aggregation functions   See *aggregate functions*.

rowset   An OLE DB term for a set of rows returned by a fetch with a block cursor. ADO creates Recordsets from rowsets.

rule   A specification that determines the data type and data value that can be entered in a column of a table. Rules are classified as validation rules and business rules. See *business rules*.

Run mode   The mode when Access 2000 is executing your project. Run mode is called *runtime* by Microsoft; however, the term *runtime* normally is used with errors that occur when running the executable version of an application.

running state   The state of an OLE 2+ object in which the application that created the object is launched and has control of the object.

scalable   The property of a multiprocessing computer that defines the extent to which addition of more processors increases aggregate computing capability. Windows NT 4.0 Server is generally considered to be scalable to four Intel processors. Microsoft claims that Windows NT 4.0 Enterprise Edition is scalable to substantially more processors.

scope   In programming, the extent of visibility (definition) of a variable. VBA has global (**Public**, visible to all objects and procedures in the application), form/report (visible to all objects and procedures within a single form or report), module (visible to all procedures in a single module file), and local (**Private**, visible only within the procedure in which declared) scope. The scope of a variable depends on where it's declared. See also *form level*, *global*, *local*, and *module level*.

screen object   A VBA object and object class defined as the entire usable area of the video display unit. All visible form and control objects are members of subclasses of the Screen object.

second normal form   The rule for relational databases requiring that columns that aren't key fields each be related to the key field—that is, a row may not contain values in data cells that don't pertain to the value of the key field. In an invoice item table, for instance, the columns of each row must pertain solely to the value of the invoice number key field.

seek   To locate a specific byte, record, or chunk within a disk file. The Seek method of Access VBA can be used only with DAO Recordset objects of the Table type and requires that the table be indexed. ADO 2.1 adds a Seek method; previous versions of ADO didn't offer Seek.

select list   The list of column names, separated by commas, that specify the columns to be included in the result of a SELECT statement.

selection   In Windows, one or more objects that have been chosen by clicking the object or otherwise assigning the focus to the object. When used with text, it means the high-lighted text that appears in a text box or window. See also *restriction*.

self-join   A SQL JOIN operation used to compare values within the columns of one table. Self-joins join a table with itself, requiring that the table be assigned two different names, one of which must be an alias.

separator   A reserved symbol used to distinguish one item from another, as exemplified by the use of the exclamation point (!, bang character) in Access to separate the name of an object class from a specific object of the class, and an object contained within a specified object. The period separator (., dot) separates the names of objects and their methods or properties.

sequential access file   A file in which one record follows another in the sequence applicable to the application. Text files, for the most part, are sequential.

service provider   An OLE DB term for an object that is both a data consumer and a data provider to another data consumer. OLE DB service providers include query engines and other intermediaries, such as the Remote Provider for enabling ADO 2.0 data sources to use Remote Data Service. See *RDS*.

session   In DAO, an instance of the Jet 3.6 database engine for a single user represented by the Workspace object. You can establish multiple sessions that become members of the Workspaces collection. With ADO, a Connection object represents a session. In RDBMS terminology, the period between the time that a user opens a connection to a database and the time that the connection to the database is closed.

SHAPE statements   An SQL-like language for defining parent-child relationships within hierarchical Recordsets. See *hierarchical Recordsets*.

shared application memory   Memory that's allocated between processes involved in an LRPC call. See also *LRPC*.

shared lock   A lock created by read-only operations that doesn't allow the user who cre-ates the shared lock to modify the data. Other users can place shared locks on data so they can read it, but none can apply an exclusive lock on the data while any shared locks are in effect.

shortcut key   A Ctrl+*key* combination that provides access to a menu choice, macro, or other function of the application in lieu of selection with the mouse. See *accelerator key*.

SID   An acronym for *security ID*, a numeric value that identifies a logged-in user who has been authenticated by Windows NT or a user group. Access uses SIDs to authenticate users of secured databases.

single-stepping   A debugging process by which the source code is executed one line at a time to allow you to inspect the value of variables, find infinite loops, or remove other types of bugs.

sizing handle   The small black rectangles on the perimeter of control objects that appear on the surface of the form or report in Design mode when the object is selected. You drag the handles of the rectangles to shrink or enlarge the size of control objects.

SMB   An abbreviation for *Server Message Block*, a networking protocol used by NetBEUI to implement Microsoft Networking.

snowflake schema   An alternative to the star schema for multidimensional data. Snowflake schema store dimension definitions in a set of hierarchical tables, rather than the star schema's individual tables. See *ADO MD*, *facts table*, *PivotTable Service*, and *star schema*.

source code   The readable form of code that you create in a high-level language. Source code is converted to machine-language object code by a compiler or interpreter.

source document   A term used by OLE 1.0 to refer to a compound object in a container document.

SQL   An acronym, pronounced as *sequel* or *seekel*, for *Structured Query Language*, a language developed by IBM Corporation for processing data contained in mainframe computer databases. (*Sequel* is the name of a language, similar to SQL, developed by IBM but no longer in use.) SQL has now been institutionalized by the creation of an ANSI standard for the language.

SQL aggregate functions   See *aggregate functions*.

star schema   The most common schema (database design) for multidimensional data. Multiple base tables storing dimension definitions form the points of a star. The body of the star is the dependent facts table. See *ADO MD*, *facts table*, *PivotTable Service*, and *snowflake schema*.

statement   A syntactically acceptable (to the interpreter or compiler of the chosen language) combination of instructions or keywords and symbols, constants, and variables that must appear on a single line or use the line-continuation pair (a space followed by an underscore) to use multiple lines.

static   When referring to a variable, a variable that retains its last value until another is assigned, even though the procedure in which it is defined has completed execution. All global variables are static. Variables declared as **Static** are similar to global variables, but their visibility is limited to their declared scope. The term is also used to distinguish between statically linked (conventional) executable files and those that use DLLs.

stored procedure   A set of SQL statements (and with those RDBMSs that support them, flow-control statements) that are stored under a procedure name so that the statements can be executed as a group by the database server. Some RDBMSs, such as Microsoft SQL Server, precompile stored procedures so that they execute more rapidly.

string   A data type used to contain textual material, such as alphabetic characters and punctuation symbols. Numbers can be included in or constitute the value of string variables, but can't be manipulated by mathematical operators.

stripe set   See *disk striping* and *fault tolerance*.

structure   Two or more keywords used together to create an instruction, which is usually conditional in nature. In C and C++ programming, a user-defined data type. See also *compound*.

Structured Query Language   See *SQL*.

stub   Shortened form of *proxy stub*. See *proxy*.

stub   A procedure or user-defined function that, in VBA, consists only of `Sub` *SubName*...`End Sub` or `Function` *FnName*...`End Function` lines with no intervening code. Access automatically creates stubs for subprocedures for event-handling code stored in `Form` and `Report` objects. Stubs block out the procedures required by the application that can be called by the main program. The intervening code statements are filled in during the programming process.

subform   A form contained within another form. Access supports subforms, but Visual Basic doesn't.

subnet mask   A local bit mask (set of flags) that specifies which bits of the IP address specify a particular IP network or a host within a subnetwork. An IP address of 128.66.12.1 with a subnet mask of 255.255.255.0 specifies host 1 on subnet 128.66.12.0. The subnet mask determines the maximum number of hosts on a subnetwork.

subprocedure   A procedure called by a procedure other than the main procedure (WinMain in Windows). In Access, all procedures except functions are subprocedures because Msaccess.exe contains the WinMain function.

subquery   A SQL `SELECT` statement that's included (nested) within another `SELECT`, `INSERT`, `UPDATE`, or `DELETE` statement or nested within another subquery.

subreport   A report contained within another report.

syntax   The set of rules governing the expression of a language, often called *grammar*. As with English, Spanish, Esperanto, or Swahili, programming languages each have their own syntax. Some languages allow much more latitude (irregular forms) in their syntax. VBA has a relatively rigid syntax, whereas C provides more flexibility at the expense of complexity.

system administrator　The individual(s) responsible for the administrative functions for all applications on a LAN or users of a UNIX cluster or network, usually including supervision of all databases on servers attached to the LAN. If the system administrator's (SA's) responsibility is limited to databases, the term *database administrator* (DBA) is ordinarily assigned.

system colors　The 20 standard colors used by Windows for elements of its predefined objects such as backgrounds, scroll bars, borders, and title bars. You can change the system colors from the defaults through the Control Panel's Color and Desktop tools.

system databases　Databases that control access to databases on a server or across a LAN. Microsoft SQL Server 6.5 has three system databases: the master database, which controls user databases; tempdb, which holds temporary tables; and model, which is used as the skeleton to create new user databases. SQL Server 7.0 doesn't have a model database. Any database that's not a user database is a system database.

system function　Functions that return data about the database rather than from the content of the database.

system object　An object defined by Access rather than by the user. Examples of system objects are the Screen and Debug objects.

system table　A data dictionary table that maintains information on users of the database manager and each database under the control by the system. Jet system tables carry the prefix MSys.

T-1　The most common moderate-speed telecommunication connection between LANs to create a WAN. Dedicated T-1 lines provide 1.544Mbps of bandwidth. T-1 lines also are the most common method of connecting servers to the Internet.

tab order　The order in which the focus is assigned to multiple control objects within a form or dialog with successive pressing of the Tab key.

table　A database object consisting of a group of rows (records) divided into columns (fields) that contain data or Null values. A table is treated as a database device or object.

TCP/IP　An abbreviation for *Transport Control Protocol/Internet Protocol*, the networking protocol of the Internet, UNIX networks, and the preferred protocol for Windows NT networks. TCP/IP is a routable network that supports subnetworks. See *IP*.

text box　A Windows object designed to receive printable characters typed from the keyboard. Access provides two basic types: single-line and multiline. Entries in single-line text boxes are terminated by pressing Enter. Multiline text boxes accept more than one line of text, either by a self-contained word-wrap feature (if a horizontal scroll bar is not present) or by pressing Ctrl+Enter.

text file　A disk file containing characters with values ordinarily ranging from Chr(1) through Chr(127) in which lines of text are separated from one another with newline pairs (Chr(13) & Chr(10)).

theta join   A SQL JOIN operation that uses comparison or relational operators in the JOIN statement. See also *operator*.

third normal form   The rule for relational databases that imposes the requirement that a column that's not a key column can't depend on another column that's not a key column. The third normal form is generally considered the most important because it's the first in the series that isn't intuitive.

thread   A part of a process, such as an executing application, that can run as an object or an entity.

three-tier   The architecture of a database application, usually involving a client/server RDBSM, where the front-end application is separated from the back-end RDBMS by a middle-tier application. In Access applications, the middle tier usually is implemented as an Automation component, which implements the database connection, enforces business rules, and handles transfer of data to and from databases of the RDBMS. See *business rules* and *process server*.

time stamp   The date and time data attributes applied to a disk file when created or edited. SQL Server and the ODBC API support the time-stamp field, which resolves concurrency issues when updating tables.

timer   An native Access form property that's invisible in Run mode and used to trigger a Timer event at preselected intervals.

title bar   The heading area of a window, usually blue, in which the title of the window appears, usually in bright white (reverse).

TM   An abbreviation for *transaction monitor*, an application that manages database transactions, usually between more than one database, to assure data consistency during INSERT and UPDATE operations. See also *MTS*.

toggle   A property of an object, such as a check box, that alternates its state when repeatedly clicked or activated by a shortcut key combination.

topic   In DDE conversations, the name of the file or other identifying title of a collection of data. When used with help files, the name of the subject matter of a single help screen display.

transaction   A group of processing steps that are treated as a single activity to perform a desired result. A transaction might entail all the steps necessary to modify the values in or add records to each table involved when a new invoice is created. RDBMSs that can process transactions usually include the capability to cancel the transaction by a rollback instruction or to cause it to become a permanent part of the tables with the COMMIT or COMMIT TRANSACTION statement. See *rollback*.

transaction monitor   A synonym for transaction manager. See *TM*.

TRANSACT-SQL   A superset of ANSI SQL used by Microsoft SQL Server. TRANS-ACT-SQL includes flow-control instructions and the capability to define and use stored procedures that include conditional execution and looping.

trigger   A stored procedure that occurs when a user executes an instruction that may affect the referential integrity of a database. Triggers usually occur before the execution of INSERT, DELETE, or UPDATE statements so that the effect of the statement on referential integrity can be examined by a stored procedure before execution. See also *stored procedure*.

twip   The smallest unit of measurement in Windows and the default unit of measurement of VBA. The twip is 1/20 of a point, or 1/1440 of a logical inch.

two-phase commit   A process applicable to updates to multiple (distributed) databases that prevents a transaction from completing until all the distributed databases acknowledge that the transaction can be completed. The replication process has supplanted two-phase commit in most of today's distributed client/server RDBMSs. See *replication*.

type   See *data type*.

type library   A file with the extension .tlb that provides information about the types of objects exposed by an ActiveX component or Automation server. See *object library*.

unary   See *operator*.

UNC   An abbreviation for *Uniform Naming Convention*, the method of identifying the location of files on a remote server. UNC names begin with \\. Windows 9x and Windows NT support UNC; 32-bit Windows applications must support UNC to qualify for application of Microsoft's "Designed for Windows 9x" logo. All Microsoft Office 95 applications support UNC.

Unicode   A replacement for the 7- or 8-bit ASCII and ANSI representations of characters with a 16-bit model that allows a wider variety of characters to be used. Windows 9x and Windows NT support Unicode. Access 95 automatically converts Unicode to ANSI and vice versa.

uniform data transfer (UDT)   The interprocess communication (IPC) method used by OLE 2+. OLE 1.0 uses DDE for IPC.

unique index   An index in which no two key fields or combinations of key fields on which the index is created may have the same value.

Universal Data Access   Microsoft's all-encompassing database strategy based on COM, DCOM, OLE DB, ADO, MTS, Internet Information Server, ASP, and other proprietary Windows technologies. See *ADO, ASP, COM, DCOM, MTS,* and *OLE DB*.

UNIX   Registered trademark of Novell Incorporated (formerly of AT&T) for its multi-user operating system, now administered by the Open Systems Foundation (OSF). Extensions and modifications of UNIX include DEC Ultrix, SCO UNIX, IBM AIX, and similar products.

update A permanent change to data values in one or more data tables. An update occurs when the INSERT, DELETE, UPDATE, or TRUNCATE TABLE SQL commands are executed.

user defined A data type, also called a *record*, that's specified in your VBA source code by a **Type...End Type** declaration statement in the Declarations section of a module. The elements of the user-defined record type can be any data type valid for the language and may include other user-defined types.

user-defined transaction A group of instructions combined under a single name and executed as a block when the name is invoked in a statement executed by the user.

validation The process of determining whether an update to a value in a table's data cell is within a preestablished range or is a member of a set of allowable values. Validation rules establish the range or set of allowable values. Access 2+ supports validation rules at the field and table levels.

variable The name given to a symbol that represents or substitutes for a number (numeric), letter, or combination of letters (string).

VBA An abbreviation for *Visual Basic for Applications*, the official name of which is Visual Basic, Applications Edition. VBA is Microsoft's common application programming (macro) language for members of Microsoft Office and Visual Basic. Each application has its own "flavor" of VBA as a result of automatically created references to the application's object hierarchy in VBA code.

VDT An abbreviation for *Visual Data Tools*, which comprises the Query Designer and Database Designer. VDT (commonly called the *da Vinci* toolset) lets you create views, modify data structures, and add tables to Microsoft SQL Server databases. Access Data Projects use a subset of the VDTs to create new tables, modify table structure, and add data to tables.

view The method by which the data is presented for review by users, usually onscreen. Views can be created from subsets of columns from one or more tables by implementing the SQL CREATE VIEW instruction.

Visual Basic for Applications See *VBA*.

Visual Data Tools See *VDT*.

VPN An abbreviation for *Virtual Private Network*, a means of establishing secure communication channels on the Internet with various forms of encryption. See *PPTP*.

WAN An acronym for *wide area network*, a system for connecting multiple computers in different geographical locations through the use of the switched telephone network or leased data lines, by optical or other long-distance cabling or by infrared, radio, or satellite links.

wild card A character that substitutes for and allows a match by any character or set of characters in its place. The DOS ? and * wild cards are similarly used in Windows applications.

Win32   An API for creating 32-bit applications that run under Windows 9x and Windows NT. Applications written to the Win32 API are purported to provide substantially improved performance when run under Windows 9x and Windows NT.

Winsock   An acronym for *Windows Sockets*, a networking API for implementing Windows applications that use TCP/IP, such as FTP and Telnet.

workstation   A client computer on a LAN or WAN that's used to run applications and is connected to a server from which it obtains data shared with other computers. It's possible, but not common, for some network servers to be used as both a server and a workstation (Windows NT permits this). The term is also used to describe a high-priced PC that uses a proprietary microprocessor and proprietary architecture to create what some call an "open system."

WOSA   An acronym for the *Windows Open Services Architecture* that's the foundation for such APIs as ODBC, MAPI, and TAPI. Microsoft also develops special vertical-market WOSA APIs for the banking, financial, and other industries.

xBase   Any language interpreter or compiler or a database manager built on the dBASE III+ model and incorporating all dBASE III+ commands and functions. Microsoft's Visual FoxPro and Computer Associates' Clipper are xBase dialects.

XML   An abbreviation for *eXtensible Markup Language*, a derivative of SGML (Standardized General Markup Language), that permits definition of custom markup tags. XML is especially useful for displaying and manipulating data when using the Internet HTTP protocol.

Yes/No field   A field of a table whose allowable values are Yes (True) or No (False). Yes/No fields were called *logical* or *Boolean fields* by Access 95 and earlier.

INDEX

Symbols

> placeholders, 148

– (minus sign), 322

; (semicolon)
recordsets, 1168
SQL statements, 858

[] (brackets)
collection names, 1118
SQL statements, 857
validation rules, 197

\ path separator, 1007

_ (underscore), SQL statements, 857

! (exclamation point)
as bang operator, 1118
as identifier operator, 325
named database objects, 1007
separating table and field, 328
SQL statements, 858

" (double quotes)
comma-delimited text files, 273
SQL statements, 859

 # (pound sign)
as placeholder, 147
date values, 1001
date/time literals, 328
Hyperlink data type, 611
SQL statements, 858

$ (dollar sign), as placeholders, 147

% (percent symbol)
as placeholders, 147
format expressions, 348

& (ampersand), 325
accelerator keys, 498
as placeholders, 148
concatenating different data types, 332
concatenation operator, 195

' (single quote), SQL statements, 857

* (asterisk)
as placeholders, 148
SQL statements, 857
wildcards, Like operator, 327

, (comma) placeholders, 147

. (dot operator), 325
as placeholders, 147
object names, 1118
SQL statements, 857

/ placeholders, 148

/*...*/ (comment identifiers), 967

/p command line parameter, 953

0 placeholder, 147

16-bit .MDB files, upgrading, 1182

3D column charts, 728

: (colon)
as placeholders, 148
GoTo statement, 1011
SQL statement, 858

:= operator, 1010

< placeholders, 148, 188

= (equal sign), 322
assignment vs comparison, 323
calculated text boxes, 494
JOIN statement, 863

? (question mark)
as wildcard, Like operator, 327
SQL statements, 857

@ placeholders, 148

A

A2KOLTP.mdb, 476

AbsolutePage property, 1066
constant enumeration, 1069

AbsolutePosition property, 1066
recordsets, 1161

accelerator keys, specifying, 498

access
authorization, 814
decision-support applications, 1128
one-to-one relationships, 832

Access 2.0, converting to 2000, 1188-1189
custom libraries, 1189-1190
indexes, 1191
OLE Controls, 1191

Access 2000
Access 2.0 conversion, 1188-1189
indexes, 1191
libraries, 1189-1190
OLE Controls, 1191
Access 9x conversion
back-end databases, 1187
secure files, 1186-1187
shared environments, 1187

unsecured files,
1182-1186
workgroup file, 1187
action queries, 410
customizing, 46-47
events, 1098-1105
installing, 42-46
Internet compatibility, 599
migration, 1192-1193
new features
Database window, 37-38
forms, 38-39
four-digit year, 36-37
HTML help, 41
Intellimenu, 40
Name AutoCorrect, 39
online collaboration, 41
reports, 38-39
single-document interface,
40
upgrading to, 51
version compatibility, 35

Access 97, Access 2000 conversion, 52
back-end databases, 1187
networking, 1187
secure files, 1186-1187
unsecured files, 1182-1186
workgroup file, 1187

Access Data Projects. *See* **ADP**

Access forms. *See* **Access PivotTable Wizard**

Access HTML Template Tags, 637-638

Access modules, 995

Access PivotTable Wizard, 746
PivotTable forms, creating,
747-754

Access Upsizing Wizard. *See* **AUW**

accessing shared workgroups, 935
refreshing links, 936-937
system file, 935-936
UNC (Uniform Naming
Convention), 935-936

action queries, 311, 410
alternatives to, 428
append queries, 416-418

browse-mode updating, 428
deleting records, 418-421
DML, 868-869
form-based updating, 429
make-table, 411
converting select query,
413-414
designing/testing select
query, 411-412
relationships, 414-415
tblShipAddresses table, 416
updates with SQL, 429-430
updates with SQL Server
stored procedures, 430

Activated mode, object frames, 769

Active Server Pages (ASPs), 606, 649

active-matrix LCDs, form design, 475

ActiveCommand property, 1066

ActiveConnection property, 1058, 1066

ActiveX controls, 605
Chart Web Control, 728
OWC, 22

ActiveX Data Objects (ADO), 660

ActualSize property, 1071

acute, HTML character, 634

Add Network Library Configuration dialog box, 981

Add New Record navigation button, updatable forms, 1044

Add Reference dialog box, 1190

Add Subdatasheet dialog box, 376

Add-In Manager, 132

add-in wizards, mde files, 123

add-ins, 132, 532
importing databases with
images, 243
Report Snapshot, 588

AddItem method, 1153

addition, 323

AddMenu method, 1108

AddNew method, 1074

addresses, Hyperlink data type, 611

Administer permission, 918

administering multiuser databases, 937
backups, 938
compacting, 938-939
encryption, 939-940
repairing, 938-939

Administrators (Admins), setting up, 906-912

ADO (ActiveX Data Objects), 602, 660, 1032, 1156
2.1 Library for VBA, 1037
compared to DAO,
1037-1038
DAO comparison, 1179
DAP, 658
default references, 999
events, 1045
learning, 1081
mapping OLE DB to,
1035-1037
MSDE views, 961
Object Browser, 1046-1047
object independence, 1039
Recordset object, creating,
1038
recordsets
AbsolutePosition property,
1161
BOF (beginning of file)
properties, 1159-1161
Bookmark property, 1163
combo boxes, 1165-1177
deleting, 1165
editing, 1164-1165
EOF (End of file) proper-
ties, 1159-1161
Find method, 1162-1163
Move... methods,
1158-1159
stored procedures, names,
1065
top-level properties,
1045-1047
upgrading Access, 52, 290

ADODB
Command object
methods, 1062-1063
Parameter object,
1060-1062
Parameters collection,
1059
properties, 1057-1058
stored procedures, passing
parameters to,
1063-1065
Connection object
Errors collection,
1051-1053
events, 1056-1057
methods, 1054-1056
properties, 1048-1051
Recordset object
bound controls, 1041-1043
bound forms, 1039-1041
disconnected, 1079
events, 1080
Fields collection,
1071-1073
methods, 1074-1079
properties, 1066-1071
updatable forms,
1043-1045
recordsets, creating, 1038
adornments, defined, 752
ADOX, 1032, 1082
ADP (Access Data Projects),
129, 944-945, 1138
accommodating MSDE and
SQL Server, 953-954
crosstab queries, 407
disadvantages, 987
Jet databases
conversion, 1151-1152
function comparisons,
1150-1151
MSDE, 26
security, 983-986
tables, 957-960
views, 960-964
NorthwindCS database,
954-956
objects, 26
Project Designer, 956
query combo boxes
converting, 1138
importing from, 1139

relationship diagramming,
965-966
stored procedures, 966-968
tools, 26
triggers, 968-969
Unicode, 953
Upsizing Wizard, 969-974
Upsizing Report, 974-975
.adp files, 944
Advanced button, Import
Text Wizard, 271
Advanced Filter/Sort opera-
tion, 219-221
Advanced options, 104-105
Advanced settings, 47
AfterUpdate event, 1136,
1138
aggregate functions,
387-388, 855, 861-863
aggregate queries
Chart Web Control, 729
optimizing, 407
aliases, 305
PivotTable list queries, 692
Align to Grid command,
adding to Toolbox, 485
ALIGN=RIGHT attribute,
632
aligning
Combo Box control text,
512
controls, 554-556
groups of, 461
ALL qualifier, 856
Allow Additions property,
tentative append records,
470
Allow Deletions property,
form design, 469
Allow Zero Length property,
139
Alphabetical Contact Listing
report, 72
alphabetical grouping, 573
Alt+Backspace key, 188
Alt+F1 key, 97
Alt+F2 key, 97
Alt+F4 key, 97

Alt+Shift+F2 key, 97
ALTER PROCEDURE
statement, 31
stored procedures, 966
ALTER TABLE statement,
DDL, 873
AM/PM placeholders, 148
ampersand (&), 325
accelerator keys, 498
Analyze command (Tools
menu), 842
Analyze Sales Data Access
page, 24
Analyze Sales page, 669-671
And condition, filter by
form, 215-216
AND operator, multiple
joins, 864
ANSI
character table, Chr function, 327
finding characters, 211
translating characters, 275
ANSI SQL
compared to Jet
DISTINCT and
DISTINCTROW,
877-880
functions and operators,
875-877
reserved words, 873-875
equi-joins, 864
punctuation, 857
subqueries, 867
unsupported in Jet, 880
VALUES keyword, 869
ANSI X3.135-1986, 853
Answer Wizard, 41, 112
APIs (Application
Programming Interfaces),
Win16 converting to
Win32, 1189
Append command (Query
menu), 847
Append dialog box, 417
Append method, 1059
append queries, 416-418
SQL, 868

AppendChunk method, 1062, 1073

appending records
dBASE IV, 872
IN clause, 870
records, 194
text data to tables, 277

application databases, data modeling, 821-822

Application object
CommandBars, 1115

application objects, 130, 818
ADP, 956
VBA, 1001

application-level security, 906

applications
cooperative, 782
creating from template files, 57-62
decision-support, 297, 1128. *See also* decision-support applications
design, 56
elements of, 130
front-end, 129
multiuser applications, 886
creating folders, 887-891
shared servers, running from, 934

Apply Filter/Sort button, Form view, 469

ApplyFilter method, 1108

area charts, 720

argument variables, 330
assigning data type, 1097

arguments
DoCmd methods, 1107-1113
name prefixes, 1054
named, 1010
referencing controls, 1121
VBA, 1009

arithmetic expressions, 195

arithmetic operators, 322-323

arranging selections, combo boxes, 1169-1171

Array functions, 992

arrays, 1005-1006
dynamic, 1006
multidimensional, 1006

arrow keys, 188

AS keyword, 861, 1002

Asc function, 335, 573

aspect ratio, 738
zooming, 739

ASPs (Active Server Pages), 21, 606, 649
exporting queries to, 651-653
ODBC data source, 650-651
session timeouts, 652
versus DAP, 654-655

assignment operators, 323-324

Assistant Capabilities group, 117

associated labels, 459
editing contents, 463
selecting controls, 460

asterisk (*)
Like operator, 327
SQL statements, 857

asynchronous data operations, 1124

attaching. *See* linking

Attachment Manager. *See* Linked Table Manager

attribute data types, 819

attributes, 816-819
ALIGN=RIGHT, 632
attribute domain, 819
identifiers, 820
identity, 28
primary-key fields , 820
values, 820

Attributes property, 1048, 1060, 1071
constant enumerations, 1061, 1072

auditability, 903

authorization, 814, 902

Array functions, 992

Auto-Compact on Close (Jet 4.0), 35

auto-start, MSDTC, 51

autocompletion, 1025

Autocompletion ToolTip, 330

AutoCorrect, 176

AutoDialer form, 68

AutoFilter (Excel), filtering PivotTable data, 759

AutoFormat, 448
background bitmaps, 452
customizing, 449-451
form default values, 447
naming, 450
PivotTable reports, 763
reports, 545

Automation, Graph9, 717

Automation objects, 1036

AutoNumber
New Values property, 140
pasting records, 279
troubleshooting, gap in field values, 182

AutoNumber fields, 63, 141, 812
changing data types, 179
entity integrity, 845-847
replacing SSN, 157
troubleshooting, 849

AutoPage
columnar DAP, 679-681
design, 682-685
Record Navigation control, 681-682
properties, 685-687

Autostart, IE 5, 628

AUW (Access Upsizing Wizard), 1138
ADP, 954
combo box form/ADP conversions, 1138
combo box/ADP conversions, 1138
disadvantages, 987

Available Database Tables list, 730

Avery mailing labels, 562

Avg function, 387

B

Back Color property, 451

back-end databases, Access 9x to 2000 conversion, 1187

backgrounds
bitmaps, 452-455
colors, 451-452

Backspace key, 188

backups, shared databases, 938

backward compatibility, 35
macros, 818

.bak files, 244

banding, 535

bang operator (!), 1118
form controls, referencing, 1119
identifiers, 328
named database objects, 1007
SQL statements, 858

base tables, 820

BASIC, 1027

batch-optimistic, 1039

BDE (Borland Database Engine), 233

Beep method, 1108

BeforeUpdate event, 1122

BEGIN TRANSACTION statement, 430

BeginTrans method, 1054

BeginTransComplete event, 1057

Between operator, 326

binary tree searching, Knuth, Donald E., 229

binding
Chart control to PivotTable list, 698
controls to
ADODB.Recordset object, 1041-1043
drop-down lists, 503

forms to
ADODB.Recordset object, 1039-1041
Option Group control, 499

Birth Date field, 149

bitmaps
aspect ratio, 739
backgrounds, 452-455

blues music, 1192

.bmp format, 740

BODY tag, 662

BOF (beginning of file) properties, 1067
recordsets, 1159-1161

boilerplates, 798

Bookmark button, hyperlinks, 616

Bookmark property, 1067
recordsets, 1163

bookmarks (MS Word), linking to, 614-617

Books Online, SQL Server 7, 853, 947

Boolean data type, 141

Boolean operators, 324

Border Style property, controls, 463

borders
AutoFormat, 449
colors/styles, 455
controls, 462-463
report tables as HTML, 642
style values, 456

bottom-up data modeling, 821

bound controls, 480
Bound Object Frame tool, 736
events, 1103
HTML, 658
Hyperlink controls, 658
Object control, 483
Object Frame, 710, 734
embedded Word 2000 documents, 803
employee photo, 735-738
photos, 735

reports, 588
scaling graphic objects, 737-740
reports, 536
linking subreports, 581-584
text boxes, 493-494
Page Field list, 687

brackets []
SQL statements, 857
validation rules, 197

branching statements, 1010

breakpoints
adding to IsLoaded function, 1023-1024
Stop statement, 1157

browse updating, 384

browse-mode editing, 406

browse-mode updating, 428

Builders, 484

bulk transfer methods, 1113

business rules, 186, 1122

buttons
command, 1092
Form Design toolbar, 445
recordset navigation, VBA, 1156
standard toolbar in Form Run mode, 468
toggle, 91

C

C++, OLE DB, 1034

cab files, 23

CacheSize property, 1067

calculated controls, 481
reports, 551
calculated fields, 553-555
record source, 552-553

calculated fields
queries, creating with expressions, 347-348
Report Wizard, editing controls, 549
reports, Report Wizard, 549

calculated text boxes, 493-495

calculated values, linking reports, 584

calculations
aggregate functions, 387-388
based on all records, 388-391
based on records, 389
based on selected records, 391-393

Call keyword, 997

Call statement, error processing, 1018

callback method, 1153

calling subprocedures, 997

calls, Win16 to Win32 conversions, 1189

Calls form, 69

"Can't evaluate expression" message, 349

"Can't find project or library" error, 1191

Cancel method, 1074

CancelBatch method, 1074

CancelEvent method, 1108

CancelUpdate method, 1074

candidate fields, 159

candidate keys, 821

Caption property, 139, 493
field data types, 245
Tab control, 518

Caption sections
DAP grouped pages, 701
Review Orders page, 668

carriage return (CR) character, 327

Cascade Delete Related Records check box, 172

Cascade Update Related Fields check box, 172

Cascading Style Sheets (CSS), 660

cascading updates/deletes, 172
deletions, 72
   relationships, 425-426
   testing, 425
relationships, 425-426
testing, 426-427

case sensitive passwords, 904

Case statement, 1013

Catalog report, exporting to HTML, 641

CategoryName filter, 673

CBF (code-behind-forms), 1084

CBool function, 338

Cbyte function, 338

CCL (Cursor Control Language), 855

CCur function, 338

CD Key (installing Access), 42

CDate function, 338

CDbl function, 338

.cdx files, 233

character sets
finding, 211
Unicode, 143

characters
placeholders, 146
special for HTML, 634

Chart control, 22

Chart Objects list, 728

Chart Type dialog box, 721

Chart Web Control, 728
designing queries, 729-730

Chart Wizard
PivotTable lists, 691
time-series summary query, 711
unlinked graphs, 712-717

charts, 710
area, 720
office, single-column series, 730-733
percentage distribution, 721
properties, 733-734
stacked column, 721
troubleshooting, axis reversed, 743
visualizing data, 744

Check Box control, 482
events, 1102
reports, 588

CHECK constraint
DDL, 872
MSDE tables, 960
Upsizing Report, 975

Checking and Reporting Errors dialog box, 797

child windows, 40

.chm files, 41, 107

Choose Columns dialog box, 793

Choose Data Source dialog box, 791

Choose My Own Primary Key option, 253

Chr function, string literals, 327

CInt function, 338

circular relationships, 356

circumflex, HTML character, 634

Class Module window, 1085

Class modules, 56, 77, 995-996, 1084
calling, troubleshooting, 1123
events, 1099-1100
Northwind database, Main Switchboard, 1085-1087
viewing with Object Browser, 1089-1091

classes
family name, 328
Object Library, 1114

Classes list, 1089

clauses (SQL), 855
FROM, 856
GROUP BY, 861
IN, external databases, 869
ORDER BY, 856
   UNION queries, 865
WHERE, 856
   query combo boxes, 1136

Clear method, 1051

Click event handlers, Command Button Wizard, 1092

Click events, Display-DatabaseWindow, 1086

Client Network Utility, 950, 981-982

Client Server Visual Design Tools, 26

client/server RDBMSs, 232, 944-945
ADP Project Designer, 956
front-end applications, 129

clients
Internet, 602
file sharing, comparisons, 940-942

Clipboard
copying controls, 495
to other forms, 501-502
copying Help window text, 110
copying queries to, 309
copying tables, 180
deleting controls, 462
exporting data, 283-284
importing data with, 277-278
pasting new records, 278-281
replacing by pasting records, 282
Paste Errors table, 281
text controls, 463

clipboard operations, 190-191

Clippit, 114

CLng function, 338

Clone method, 1074

Close method, 1054, 1074, 1108
recordsets, 1172

Cmd command, 900

cmdOpenForm function, 1097

cmm prefix, 1039

code characters, grouping report data, 572

code editor, 56
functions, 1096

Code window, 79

code-behind-forms (CBF), 1084

coding
drill-down list boxes, 1143-1145
query combo boxes, 1135-1138

collaborating online, 41

collections
Errors, 1051-1053
Fields, 1071-1073
Recordset object, 1071-1073
Forms, 1118
iterating through with For Each...Next statement, 1015
missing objects, troubleshooting, 1124
Parameter, 1059
Reports, 1118

colon (:)
GoTo statement, 1011
SQL statements, 858

Color Builder, 456-457

color depth, aspect ratio, 739

colors
controls, 462-463
dithering, 456
form objects, 451
background, 451-455
Color Builder, 456-457
foreground/borders, 455

Column Count property, 1134

column headings, fixed, crosstab queries, 402

Column property, 1136
list boxes, 1145

Column Spacing property, 564

Column Widths property, 1134

Column Widths text box, 509

columnar AutoPage, 684

columns, 132
changing width, 226
freezing, 207
thawing, 209

header names, queries, 305-307
mail merge data sources, 793
newspaper, 565
queries, filtering for Web pages, 634
viewing, query design, 316

Columns page, 563

COM (Component Object Model), 601, 605
Add-Ins, 532
OLE DB, 1002

combinatorial hashing, 229

Combo Box control, 482, 502-503
Combo Box Wizard, 503-507
events, 1102
finding records, 512-515
populating with Query Builder, 507-509
static values, 509-512

Combo Box Wizard, 503-507, 1131-1133
Find Specific Records function, 512

combo boxes, 1128, 1153-1154
changing, 1133-1134
optimization, 1153
properties, 1145
queries, 1128-1129
adding to forms, 1131-1134
ADP (Access Data Projects) conversion, 1138
designing, 1129
importing form, 1139
Row Source SQL statements, 1140-1141
SQL statement, 1135
VBA code, 1135-1138
recordsets, 1165-1167
arranging selections, 1169-1171
populating, 1168-1169
porting forms, 1178
value lists, 1174-1177

combo lists, 148

comma-delimited text files
importing, 266
with text-identifier characters, 274-275
without text-identifier characters, 273-274

command bars, 86, 93

Command Button control,
482
events, 1102

Command Button Wizard,
event-handling code,
1092-1095

command buttons, 1092
naming conventions, 1094
properties, changing with
VBA, 1116

Command object, 1036
methods, 1062-1063
Parameter object,
1060-1062
Parameters collection, 1059
properties, 1057-1058
stored procedures, passing
parameters to, 1063-1065
troubleshooting, spaces in
names, 1081

CommandBar object,
1113-1116
startup properties, 1117

commands
ALTER PROCEDURE, 31
Cmd, 900
Compact, 900
Convert, 900
Data menu
Filter, AutoFilter, 759
Filter, Show All, 759
Refresh Data, 755, 758
Excl, 900
Ini, 900
macro, 900
NoStartup, 900
Profile, 900
Pwd, 900
Query menu, Append, 847
Repair, 900
Ro, 900-901, 928
Runtime, 900

SQL, usage categories, 854
starting sharing options,
899-901
Tools menu
Analyze, 842
Database Utilities, 938
References, 1190
User, 900
VBA Module window tool-
bar, 1019
Wrkgrp, 900

CommandText property,
1058

CommandTimeout property,
1048, 1058

CommandType property,
1058

commas (,), SQL statements,
857

comment identifiers, 967

comments, HTML tem-
plates, 637

committing changes, 473

CommitTrans method, 1054

CommitTransComplete
event, 1057

Compact command, 900

Compact Database Into dialog box, 119

compacting databases,
118-120, 938-939
Access 9x to 2000 conver-
sion, 1183

comparison operators, 195,
323-324
ANSI SQL vs Jet SQL, 874
Find method, 1162

compiling VBA, 1008

composite attribute data
types, 819

composite keys, 821

composite primary key, 137

composite sorts, 209

compression
.jpg, 741
Unicode, 144

concatenating, 357

different data types, 332
operators for, 325
strings, 195

conceptual data models, 821

Conditional Formatting, 39

conditional statements, 1011
If...Then, 1011-1012
Select Case, 1012-1014

Confirm options, 103

Confirm Workgroup
Information dialog box,
890

ConnectComplete event,
1057

Connection object, 1036
Errors collection,
1051-1053
events, 1056-1057
methods, 1054-1056
Open method, 1046
properties, 1048-1051

Connection property, 1178

connections
disconnected Recordsets,
1079
remote databases, trou-
bleshooting, 986

ConnectionString property,
1048, 1055

ConnectionTimeout prop-
erty, 1048

ConnectModeEnum list,
1047

Const keyword, 1008

constant enumerations
AbsolutePage property,
1069
Attributes property, 1061,
1072
CursorLocation property,
1069
CursorType property, 1069
EditMode property, 1070
Execute method, 1055
Filter property, 1070
IsolationLevel property,
1049
lngAffectRecords argument,
1077

lngSeeOptions argument, 1078
LockType property, 1070
Mode property, 1050
State property, 1051
Status property, 1070
Supports method, 1078
Type property, 1061
varStart argument, 1078

constants, 339
  intrinsic, 1008-1009
  symbolic, 339, 1008
  system defined, 1008

CONSTRAINT statement, DDL, 872

constraints
  conflicts, updatable forms, 1044
  database diagrams, 30
  MSDE tables, 960

Contact ID field, 71

Contact Management application
  forms, 67-72
  Main Switchboard form, 66-67
  reports, 72-73
  table objects, 62-66

Contacts folder (Outlook)
  linking to, 262
  importing, 258
  Access tables to, 258-262

ContactTypes table, 64

contention, browse-mode editing, 428

Contents page (Help window), 109-110

context menus, 96

context-sensitive help, 107-108

continuous forms, designing, 527-528

Continuous Forms view, 496

control flow. *See* flow control

Control grouping, 39

Control Panel, Launch, 932

Control Source property, 497, 553

Control Wizard, 482, 484, 532
  list boxes, 1130
  Option Group, 497
  Personnel Actions table, 521-523

Control-menu box, 88

controls, 434
  3D effect, 455
  adding to reports, 588
  adding to Tab pages, 520
  adding with Toolbox, 487
  aligning groups of, 461
  aligning to grid, 459-460
  arranging, 441
  associated labels, 459
  binding to
    ADODB.Recordset object, 1041-1043
  borders, 455
  bound object frame, 734
    employee photo, 735-738
    photos, 735
    reports, 588
    scaling graphic objects, 737-740
  calculated, reports, 551-555
  categories of, 480
  color/border styles, 462-463
  Combo box, 502-503
    Combo Box Wizard, 503-507
    populating with Query Builder, 507-509
    static values, 509-512
  converting types, 520
  copying, troubleshooting, 530
  copying with Clipboard, 495, 501-502
  DAP, 682
  data events, 1122-1123
  deleting with Clipboard commands, 462
  editing, 457-458
  event handling, Command Button Wizard, 1092

events, 1100
Expand, 664
fine adjustment, 461
Fore Color property, 455
foreground color, 455
form design, 480
Format Painter, 463-464
grouping, 434
hyperlinks, 621-622
Image, 741-743
Label
    adding to form headers, 490-491
    formatting text, 491-492
List Box, 502-503, 1145
Movie, 659
moving multiple, 460-461
MSHFlexGrid, 374
native, 480
Office Chart, 695-698
OWC, 22
Personnel Actions form, 465
PivotTable list, IE 5, 689-690
PivotTables, altering properties in IE 5, 690-691
properties, referencing, 1119-1120
Properties window, 157
rectangles, 588
referencing by arguments, 1121
reports, 535
    aligning, 554-556
    formatting, 556-557
    line spacing, 557-558
    Report Wizard, 546-551
reverse video, 463
selecting multiple, 460-461
sizing, multiple controls, 492
sizing single control, 458-459
subforms, referencing, 1120-1121
Tab, 516
    adding pages, 516
    deleting pages, 518
    page order, 517
    placing other controls, 520
    properties, 518-520

Tab Order property, 473

Tab Stop property, 474

text
changing content, 463
Formatting toolbar, 446

Text Box, formatting text, 491-492

toolbox, 442

unbound object frames, reports, 588

ControlSource property, 1042

conventional (vanilla) HTML, 599

Convert command, 900

Convert Database Into dialog box, 1183, 1186

Convert Database utility, 1186

Convert From dialog box, 1186

CONVERT function, 962, 1150-1151

Convert/Open Database dialog box, 1183

converting
Access 2.0 to 2000, 1188-1189
ADP, query combo boxes, 1138
compile errors, troubleshooting, 123
data types, 338-339
databases to 2000 format, 120-121
databases to 97 format, 121
files, 886
function calls, Win16 to Win32, 1189
Jet 3.5x to Jet 4.0, 1182
Jet databases, ADP, 1151-1152

cooperative applications, 782

copying
controls, troubleshooting, 530
filtered datasheets, 227
sorted datasheets, 227
tables, 180-181

CopyObject method, 1108

copyrights, 647

corrupted databases, 120
repairing, 939

Count function, 387

Create New Data Source dialog box, 650, 791

Create New Data Source Wizard, 239

CREATE TABLE statement, 845
DDL, 872

CREATE TRIGGER statement, 969

CreateParameter method, 1062

Criteria expression, 303

criterion expressions, parameter queries, 395

cropping, 738

crosstab queries, 294, 311, 396
ADP, 954
Chart Wizard, 714
DML queries, compared, 868
fixed column headings, 402-403
graphs, 723-725
monthly product sales query, 400-402
optimizing, 407
PivotTables, 775
PivotTables, compared, 746
quarterly product sales query, 396-400
subreports, 576
time-series, 869

Crosstab Query Wizard, 396-402

CRUD (Create, Read, Update, and Delete), 1164

CSng function, 339

CSS (cascading style sheets), 21, 660
DAP, 666
upgrading Access, 53

CStr function, 339

.csv files, 273

Ctrl++ key, 191

Ctrl+C key, 190

Ctrl+End key, 188

Ctrl+Enter key, 191

Ctrl+F4 key, 97

Ctrl+F6 key, 97

Ctrl+Home key, 188

Ctrl+Insert key, 190

Ctrl+Shift+> key, 189

Ctrl+Shift+< key, 189

Ctrl+spacebar key, 189

Ctrl+V key, 190

Ctrl+X key, 191

Ctrl+Z key, 188, 191

Ctrl+" key, 191

Ctrl+< key, 188

Ctrl+- key, 191

Ctrl+' key, 191

Ctrl+; key, 191

.cub files, 778

Cube page, 805

Currency data type, 141, 390
default field value, 165

currency formatting, PivotTable lists, 695

Current Database Only group, 104

current record, 68

Cursor Control Language (CCL), 855

CursorLocation property, 1048, 1067
constant enumeration, 1069

cursors
firehose, 1055
Recordset object, troubleshooting, 1080

CursorType property, 1067, 1178
constant enumeration, 1069

custom display formats, 146-149

Custom installation, 42

custom libraries, Access 2.0 to 2000 conversions, 1189-1190

Custom Setup, 42

Customer Labels report, 563

customers, matching with orders received, 358

Customers table, filtering by form, 215

Customers.asp, 654

Customize dialog box, 486
  toolbars, 93

customizing
  Access 2000, 46-47
  Datasheet view, 225-227
  PivotTables, 754
    filtering, 759
    formatting, 754-757
    slicing data, 757-759
  report styles with AutoFormat, 545
  reports, sections, 585-587
  toolbars, 93-96, 484-486
  VBA Editor, shortcut keys, 1021

CustOrdsDtls.htm form, 702

CVar function, 339

CVErr function, 339

D

d placeholders, 148

da Vinci Tool, 28-29, 31

DAO (Data Access Objects), 1033
  ADO comparison, 1179
  ADODB.Recordset object, 1066
  compared to ADO, 1037-1038
  Recordset object, creating, 1038
  recordsets
    AbsolutePosition property, 1161
    BOF (beginning of file) properties, 1159-1161

Bookmark property, 1163
combo boxes, 1165-1177
deleting, 1165
editing, 1164-1165
EOF (End of file) properties, 1159-1161
Find method, 1162-1163
Move... methods, 1158-1159
  updatable forms, 1044

DAO.Recordset object, binding updatable forms, 1044

Dao360.dll, 1033

DAP (Data Access Pages), 21-25, 129, 599, 631, 649, 658-659, 889
  adding images, 742
  ADO top-level properties, 1045
  Analyze Sales page, 669-671
  AutoPage
    columnar DAP, 679-681
    design, 682-685
    Record Navigation control, 681-682, 685-687
  compared to ASPs, 649
  controls, 682
  copying, 889, 895-896
  filenames, 680
  grouped pages
    related table fields, 701-703
    three-level hierarchical structure, 699-702
  HTML Source Editor, 33-34, 668-669
  JavaScript, 33
  OLE Object fields, 704
  OWC, 22
  Page Field list, adding PivotTables, 687-689
  page links, 679
  Page Wizard, 674-679
  PivotTable list control in IE 5, 689-690
  PivotTable lists
    formatting, 693-695
    Office charts, 695-698
    queries, 692-693

  PivotTables, altering properties in IE 5, 690-691
  read-write pages, 673-674
  Review Orders page, 667-668
  Review Products page, 663-666
  Sales page, 671-672
  sources, changing, 896-898
  themes, 676
  troubleshooting
    lost data sources, 704
    lost style, 704
  updating links, 896
  upgrading, 52
  versus ASPs, 654-655

Data Access Pages. *See* DAP

data access. *See* Universal Data Access

Data Binding, 660
  DAP, 658

data blocks, 194

data consumers, 1034

Data Control Language (DCL), 855

data cubes, 777

Data Definition Language (DDL), 854

data dictionaries, 133
  Database Documenter, 841-842, 844

data entities. *See* entities

data entry, 82
  datasheet entry, 204
  Datasheet view, 199
  forms, 67-72
    appearance, 463
  heads-down, 203-204
  Input Mask property, 139
  keyboard operations, 186
    clipboard operations, 190-191
    editing keys, 188-189
    experimental copies, 187
  Keyboard options, 104
  order of fields, 473-474
  setting options, 192
  test data, 186

validating, 194-195
  field-level rules, 195-197
  table-level rules, 197-199
  testing, 201-202

Data events, 1098-1099, 1122-1123

data extraction, 82

data hypercube, 777

data instances. *See* **entities**

Data Link Properties sheet, 897

Data Links, 27

Data Manipulation Language (DML), 854

data marts, 711, 775

Data menu commands
  Filter, AutoFilter, 759
  Filter, Show All, 759
  Refresh Data, 755, 758

data modeling, 821-822
  application databases, 822
  conceptual data models, 821
  diagrammatic data models, 823
  schema, 824
  subject databases, 823

data normalization, 813

data objects. *See* **objects**

data organization, 82

data presentation, 82

data providers, 1034
  Recordset object methods, 1074

Data Query Language (DQL), 854

data services, 1034

data sheets, printing, 560

Data Source control, 22

data sources, 650
  bound controls, 480
  bound reports, 536
  DAP
    changing, 896-898
    Page Field lists, 687
    troubleshooting, 704
  interfacing, 1033

mail merge, MSQuery, 789-797
mail merge documents, 786-789
MSQuery, mail merge, 789-797
transaction-processing forms, 435
unlinked subreports, 584
Visual FoxPro tables, 238

Data Transformation Service (DTS), 776

Data Transformation Services (DTS) Wizard, 950

Data Type property, 138

data types
  arrays, 1005-1006
  attribute data types, 819
  changing, 178-179
  choosing, 140-141
  composite attribute data types, 819
  conversion functions, 338-339
  creating default values, 340
  da Vinci editor, 30
  decimal, 35
  Decimal, Precision property, 139
  Double, Variants, 333
  Format property, 144-145
  formatting, 144-145
  Hyperlink, 611
  Jet SQL vs ANSI SQL, 875
  matching fields, 161
  Null value, 146
  Number, subtypes, 142-143
  OLE Object field, 818
  parameter queries, 394
  relationships, 167
    changing relationships, 179
  Short Date format, 37
  subtypes, 141
  symbolic constants, 1008
  Text, fixed-width, 143-144
  type-declaration character, 1000
  Variant, 331-333, 1001
  VBA, 1000-1001
    user-defined, 1005

data visualization, 744

data warehouses, 711, 775

data-bound PivotTables. *See* **Access PivotTable Wizard**

data-type checking, turning off, 331

Database Creations, Inc., 592

database diagrams, 27
  ADP, 956

database directory, default, 103

Database Documenter, 841-844

database level security, 917-918

Database object, 56
  VBA, 1001

Database Splitter, 893-894, 941

Database to Compact From dialog box, 119

Database Utilities command (Tools menu), 118, 938

Database window, 37-38, 86
  data-entry forms, 67
  displaying join structure, 355
  Table objects, 62
  toolbar, 37

Database Wizard, 57-61

databases, 820
  creating new, 133-135
  DAP. *See* DAP
  data modeling, 821-822
    application databases, 822
    conceptual data models, 821
    diagrammatic data models, 823
    schema, 824
    subject databases, 823
  definition of, 129
  designing
    basic steps, 815-816
    strategy, 814-815
  elements of, 128-130
  files. *See* files

identifying file formats,
234-235
integrity, 844
  entity integrity, 844-848
  referential integrity, 844,
    848-849
Jet 4.0 database engine, 812
MSDE, 812
object paradigm, 818
objects
  attributes, 816-817
  concept of, 816
  methods, 817-818
  properties, 816
relational
  normalization, 813
  theory, 849-850
replication, 815
security, 902
  groups, 906
  passwords, 904-905
  principles of, 902-904
splitting, 893-895
subject, 823
tables
  combining entities,
    818-819
  flat tables, 825
DataCubes, 22
DataMember property, 1067
datasheet entry, 204
**datasheet updating, versus
form-based updating, 429**
Datasheet view, 35, 82, 496
  binding controls, with code,
    1043
  compared to heads-down
    data entry, 203-204
  creating tables, 164
  customizing, 225-227
  default options, 105-106
  linked Paradox files, 238
  primary keys, original sort
    order, 209
  Quick Sort, 208
  Run mode, 85
  subdatasheets, 136
  Table Datasheet toolbar, 89

datasheets
  exporting to HTML,
    628-631
  formatting, 226
  removing gridlines, 225
DataSource objects, 1036
DataSource property, 1067
Date data type
  changing data types, 179
  conversion functions,
    338-339
  custom format, 149
Date Delimiter, 272
date functions, 333-335
**Date/Time control, copying
  with Clipboard, 495**
Date/Time data type
  formatting, 144
  grouping report data, 574
date/time literals, 328
Date/Time text box, 495
DateAdd function, 333
DateDiff function, 333
DatePart function, 333
dates
  calculated text boxes, 494
  four-digit year, 36-37
  four-digit year format, 385
  grouping report data, 574
  Personnel Action table,
    design, 158
  specifying range, 327
  Y2K expressions, 349
DateSerial function, 334
DateValue function, 334
Day function, 334
.db files, 233
DBAs, naming objects, 183
dBASE, 233
  accessing with IN clause,
    871-872
  field data type conversion,
    244
  Linked Table Manager, 245
  sdf files, 274
DBEngine object, 1033
.dbf files, 233
  identifying, 234

DblClick event, 1087
.dbt files, 233
  identifying, 234
**DCL (Data Control
  Language), 855**
**DCOM (Distributed COM),
  601, 605**
**DDE (Dynamic Data
  Exchange)**
  hyperlinks, 621
  mail merge data sources,
    789
  Mail Merge Wizard, 783
  Operations options, 104
**DDL (Data Definition
  Language), 854**
  ADO, 1038
  creating tables, 872-873
Debug object, 1025-1026
**Debug window. *See*
  Immediate window**
debugging
  breakpoints, 1023-1024
  Debug object, 1025-1026
  runtime errors, 1016-1017
    Err object, 1017-1018
    Error event, 1018
  text comparison options,
    1027
decimal data type, 35, 992
  ADP, 953
  Precision property, 139
**Decimal Places property,
  139**
Decimal Symbol, 273
**decimals, Scale property,
  139**
**decision-support applica-
  tions, 297, 435, 1128**
  queries
    combo boxes, 1128-1129,
      1131-1134
    list boxes, 1130-1131
Declarations section, 997
  user-defined data types,
    1005
**declarative referential
  integrity (DRI), 968**
declaring variables, 1002

Default Cell Effect options, 105

Default Colors group, 105

Default Gridlines Showing options, 105

default instances, 1084

default options, 98-100
Datasheet view, 105-106
system, 100
advanced, 104-105
edit/find, 103
general, 101-102
keyboard, 104
view, 100

Default to Full Module view, 1089

Default Value property, 139

Default Value text box, 165

default values
creating with expressions, 340
fields, 165-166

Default View, property values, 496

Default View property, 1042

Default Web Site (IIS), 609

DefaultDatabase property, 1048

DefinedSize property, 1072

defragmenting databases, 939

Delete Data permission, 918

Delete key, 188

Delete method, 1059, 1074
recordsets, 1165

delete queries, SQL, 868

Delete_Object method, 1108

deleting
controls
Report Wizard, 546
with Clipboard commands, 462
duplicated data, 411
groups, 914
header/footer sections, 444
passwords, 914

records, 194
with action queries, 418-421
report sections, 585-587
Tab control pages, 518
tables, 156
toolbars, 486

delimited text files
data providers, 1034
delimiting characters, 273
comma-delimited, 273-275
tab-delimited, 275
import specifications, 271
importing, 266

delimiter characters, import- ing delimited text files, 268

dependency, transitive, 829

descending sort
DAP with Record Navigation control, 682
query design, 316

Description property, 135, 138
Err object, 1017

Design View, 84
adding lookup fields, 366
altering tables, 176
DAP, 25
embedded documents, 802
opening tables in, 156
Toolbox, 481

Designer (DAP), 658
AutoPage, 683
columnar design, 685
grouped pages, 699
HTML, 666
properties window, 686

designing databases, 56
action queries, 417
ADP Project Designer, 956
basic steps, 815-816
colored backgrounds, 451
continuous forms, 527-528
DAP, AutoPage, 682-685
embedded/linked Word documents, 800
expressions, 350
forms
audience, 475
client monitor resolution, 475

Combo Box controls, 509
consistency and simplicity, 475-477
Form Design window, 442-444
Personnel Actions table, 487-488
Tab control, 516
objects
attributes, 816-818
concept of, 816
properties, 816
Personnel Actions table, 158-159
assigning information fields, 159-160
queries, 315-317
Chart Web Control, 729-730
query combo boxes, 1129
reports, 591
control layout, 546
Report Wizard, 536
separating objects from data, 130
strategy, 814-815
table design versus database design, 182
tables, combining entities, 818-819
testing, 186
update queries, 422
visualization of data, 710
visualizing data, 743
Web pages, graphics files, 639

desktop database develop- ment applications, 232
importing tables, 233

desktop PCs, form design, 475

Desktop version (MSDE), 945

Detail section
expanding, 490
form properties, 457

development, test data, 186

Development Exchange Web site, 1153

DevX, 655

DHTML (Dynamic HTML), 33-34, 606, 659
  Behaviors, 660
  DAP, 658
  DOM, 661-663
  supporting technologies, 659-660

Diagram button, 961

diagrammatic databases, data modeling, 823

dialog boxes
  Add Network Library Configuration, 981
  Add Reference, 1190
  Add Subdatasheet, 376
  Append, 417
  AutoFormat, 450
  Chart Type, 721
  Checking and Reporting Errors, 797
  Choose Columns, 793
  Choose Data Source, 791
  Command Button Wizard, 1092
  Compact Database Into, 119
  Confirm Workgroup Information, 890
  Convert Database Into, 1183, 1106
  Convert From, 1186
  Convert/Open Database, 1183
  Create New Data Source, 650, 791
  Create New Data Source Wizard, 239
  Customize, 486
    toolbars, 93
  Database to Compact From, 119
  Edit Hyperlink, 598, 613
  Edit Relationships, 169, 414
  Edit Switchboard Item, 76
  Edit Switchboard Page, 76
  Encrypt FileName As, 939
  Enter Parameter, 869
  Enter Parameter Value, 393-394

  Export Query, 636
  File New Database, 134
  Find, 212
  Format Cells, 755
  Format Data Series, 726
  Insert Object, 767, 801
  Insert Picture, 61, 453, 742
  Join Properties, 379
  Join Type, 169
  Link, 236
  Link Tables, 242
  Locate Web Page, 897
  Logon, 909
  Mail Merge Helper, 790
  Make Table, 312
  Network Libraries, 949
  New, 134
  New Data Acces Page, 730
  New Form, 488, 747
  New Report, 536
    subreports, 577
  New Table, 152
  New Toolbar, 486
  ODBC Data Source Administrator, 650
  Options, 99
  Page Setup, 308
    margins, 559
    paper layout, 561
  Password Required, 904
  Paste Link, 773
  Paste Table As, 181, 366
  PivotTable Field, 755
  PivotTable Options, 750
  Print Query Definition, 842-843
  Print Table Definition, 842
  Printer Setup, 534
  References, 1190
  Relationship, 834
  Rename Table, 837
  Replace, 213
  Row Height, 226
  Save Import/Export Specification, 645
  Select Data Source, 239
  Select Directory Containing Free Tables, 241
  Select Source Tables, 977
  Select Unique Record Identifier, 242

  Select Workgroup Information File, 898-899
  Services Accounts, 950
  Set Database Password, 904-905
  Setup Type, 47, 948
  Show Table, 299
  Sorting and Grouping, 570, 574
    Keep Together property, 562
  Subreport Field Linker, 582
  Summary Options, 540
  Suppliers Import Specification, 643
  Switchboard Manager, 121
  System Database, 792
  Unhide Columns, 225
  User and Group Permissions, 915, 927
  User Information, 47
  Workgroup Administrator, 891
  Workgroup Owner Information, 889

.dib format, 741

dictionaries, Database Documenter, 841-842, 844

Digital Nervous System, 600-602

Dim statement, 1001
  declaring arrays, 1005

dimension axis, changing, 762

dimensions, defined, 750

Direction property, 1060

Dirty event, 1100

Disconnect event, 1057

disconnected Recordsets, 1079

Disk Defragmenter utility, 939

disk space
  installation, 42
  insufficient memory, 743

Display When (Format) property, 530

DisplayDatabaseWindow_ Click event, 1086

displaying
  custom formats, 146-149
  freezing fields, 207
  Number subtypes, 142
  Object Browser, 1089
  toolbars, 93
DISTINCT qualifier, 856
  ANSI SQL compared to Jet
    SQL, 877-880
**DISTINCTROW qualifier,
856**
  ANSI SQL compared to Jet
    SQL, 877-880
**Distributed interNet
Applications Architecture,
601**
dithering, 456
division, 323
**DML (Data Manipulation
Language), 854**
  action queries, 868-869
**Do Until...Loop statement,
1015**
  AppendChunck and
    GetChunck methods,
    1073
**Do While...Loop statement,
1015-1016**
**DocFiles (document files),
1182**
docked command bars, 95
docking, toolbars, 94, 484
Docking page, 33
DoCmd object, 1089
  methods, 1105-1107
    arguments, 1107-1113
  VBA code, 993
**document Control-menu
box, 88**
**document files (DocFiles),
1182**
document imaging, 566
**document management sys-
tems, 799**
**Document Object Model
(DOM), 659**
document parent object, 662

**Document Type Definition
(DTD), 598**
document windows
  maximized, 87-88
  minimized, 88-89
**Documenter (Database),
841-842, 844**
**DocumentProperty object,
CommandBar objects,
1113**
documents
  embedded, displaying in
    forms, 802
  mail merge, 783
**dollar sign ($), placeholders,
147**
**DOM (Document Object
Model), 659**
  ECMAScript, 663
  HTML, 661-663
  Java, 663
domain integrity
  test data, 186
  testing Personnel Actions
    table, 199
  update queries, 422
  validation rules, punch-card
    verification, 204
**domains, attribute domains,
819**
**DoMenuItem method, 1109,
1188**
dot operator (.), 325, 1118
Double data type
  changing data types, 178
  Variants, 333
**double quotes ("), SQL
statements, 859**
down arrow key, 189
downsizing, 975-980
**DQL (Data Query
Language), 854**
.dqy files, 797
drag-and-drop
  fields for queries, 300
  toolbars, 484
**dragging and dropping,
reports as subreports, 582**

**DRI (declarative referential
integrity), 968**
drill-down operations, 777
**drill-down techniques,
1128-1130**
  list boxes, 1142
    coding, 1143-1145
    queries, 1142-1143
drivers, Visual FoxPro, 240
**DROP INDEX statement,
DDL, 873**
**DROP TABLE statement,
DDL, 873**
drop-down lists, 148, 502
  adding to lookup fields,
    366-370
**DSNs (data source names),
650**
**DTDs (Document Type
Definition), 598**
**DTS (Data Transformation
Service), 776**
DTS Wizard, 950, 975-980
duplicated fields
  Table Analyzer Wizard,
    Invalid procedure call
    message, 839
duplicated data
  deleting, 411
  make-table query fields,
    416
  removing with append
    queries, 417
**duplicated query result sets,
eliminating, 362**
duplicated records
  deleting with DISTINCT-
    ROW statement, 879
  exporting with clipboard,
    284
  preventing, with key fields,
    172
duration, 1004
dynamic arrays, 1006
dynamic controls, 434
**dynamic data exchange
(DDE), hyperlinks, 621**
**Dynamic HTML
(DHTML), 606**

dynamic properties, 816-817

dynamic SQL, 854

dynamic Web pages, 628, 648-649
ASPs, 649
exporting queries to, 651-653
ODBC data source, 650-651

E

E+ placeholders, 148

E- placeholders, 147

E-R (Entity-Relationship) diagrams, 823
many-to-many relationships, 835
many-to-one relationships, 834
one-to-many relationships, 833
reflexive relationships, 834

Echo method, 1109

ECMAScript, 606, 663

ect Role Modeling (ORM) language, 884

EDI (electronic document interchange), 566

Edit Hyperlink dialog box, 598, 613

Edit Relationships dialog box, 169, 414

Edit Switchboard Item dialog box, 76

Edit/Find settings, 47, 103

editing, 82
controls, 457-458
data with keyboard operations, 186
clipboard operations, 190-191
editing keys, 188-189
experimental copies, 187
hyperlinks, 613-614
Registry, 888

EditMode property, 1067
constant enumeration, 1070

editor (VBA), 32, 1018
Help system, 1021-1022
integrating with Access, 32
Module window, toolbar, 1019-1020
shortcut keys, 1021

Editor window, 1085
selecting form controls, 1086
undocking components, 1087

ElementName window, 683

elements of arrays, 1005

ElseIf statement, 1012

email, sending reports in Snapshot format, 589

embedding
displaying in forms, 802-804
Word documents, 798-802

EmplOrdersByCountry.htm page, 698

employee remuneration data, 158

employees, security, 904

Employees table, 156

empty strings, 1004

Empty Variant data type, 333

Enabled property, bound object frames, 737

Encrypt FileName As dialog box, 939

encryption, 903, 939-940

End If statement, 1146

End key, 188

End Select statement, 1012-1014

End Sub keyword, 997

End Type keywords, 1005

End With statement, 1007

End-User License Agreement (EULA), 43

EndOfRecordset event, 1080

Enforce Referential Integrity check box, 170, 415, 425

enforcing, 170

Enter key, 189

Enter Parameter Value dialog box, 393-394, 869

Enter/View Contacts button, 68

Enter/View Other Information button, 72

Enterprise Manager, remote databases, testing, 982

entities, 159, 819. *See also* objects
attributes, 816-818
combining in tables, 818-819
entity integrity, 844-848
referential integrity, 844, 848-849
tables, 820

entity classes. *See* tables

Entity-Relationship (E-R) diagram, 823
many-to-many relationships, 835
many-to-one relationships, 834
one-to-many relationships, 833
reflexive relationships, 834

enumerations, ADO type libraries, 1046

EOF (End of file) properties, 1067
recordsets, 1159-1161

equal sign (=), 322
assignment, 323
calculated text boxes, 494
JOIN statement, 863

equi-joins, 356
ANSI SQL, 864
Jet SQL, 864
single-column, 357-359

Erase keyword, 1006

Err object, 1017-1018

Error events, 1018, 1099-1100

error messages, validation rules, 203

Error object, properties, 1051

Error statement, 1018

error-handling, 1088
VBA code, 994

errors
Can't find project or library, 1191
paths, 940
Run-Time Error '2465', 1152
Spurious Paramater, 1153

Errors collection, Connection object, 1051-1053

Esc key, 188-189

escape characters, 150

eTEK International, 593

euro character, 957

event handling, 1084
coding with Command Button Wizard, 1092-1095
Main Switchboard form, 1085
Northwind database, Main Switchboard, 1088-1089
responding with functions, 1096-1098

event procedures, 1084

Event properties, 78

event sinks, 1056, 1124

event-driven programming, 1084, 1124

events
Access 2000, 1098-1105
ADO, 1045
AfterUpdate, 1136, 1138
BeforeUpdate, 1122
BeginTransComplete, 1057
CommitTransComplete, 1057
ConnectComplete, 1057
Connection object, 1056-1057
data, 1122-1123
Dirty, 1100
Disconnect, 1057

DoCmd methods, 1105-1107
arguments, 1107-1113
Error, 1018
ExecuteComplete, 1057
forms, 997
Form_Load event handler, temporary recordsets, 1157
InfoMessage, 1057
record finding combo boxes, 514
Recordset object, 1080
report class modules, 997
WillConnect, 1057
WillExecute, 1057

Excel
importing worksheets, 248-256
linking worksheets, 256-258
MSQuery, 805
normalization, 828
OLE Server
embedding worksheets, 767-770
extracting values from objects, 771-772
linking cell ranges, 772-774
pasting ranges, 278
PivotTables, 746, 754
Access PivotTable Wizard, 746
crosstab queries, compared, 746
filtering, 759
formatting, 754-757
forms, creating, 747-754
queries, creating, 747
slicing data, 757-759
snapshots of query results, saving, 751

Excel PivotCharts, creating from PivotTables, 764-766

Excel PivotTables. See PivotTables

ExcelOLE.mdb database, 774

Exchange Public Folder, linking, 263

Exchange/Outlook Wizard, 258
linking with, 262-264

Excl command, 900

exclamation point (!)
as bang operator, 1118
named database objects, 1007
SQL statements, 858

executable (.exe) files, 1008

Execute method, 1054, 1063
constant enumeration, 1055

ExecuteComplete event, 1057

Exit Do statement, 1015

Exit For statement, 1014

Expand control, 22, 664

explicit variables, 1002-1003

exponentiation operator, 323

Export Query dialog box, 636

exporting, 232-233
as HTML files, 628
as text files, 284-286
dBASE, Paradox, 871
file formats, 286
queries, to ASPs, 651-653
with clipboard, 283-284

Expression Builder, 484
query criteria, 345-346
table-level validation rules, 197-199

expressions, 82, 320-321
constants, 339
Control Source property, 553
creating, 340
creating default values, 340
default field values, 166
failure to execute, 349
functions, 328-329
data-type conversion, 338-339
date and time, 333-335
Immediate window, 329-331
text manipulation, 335-338
Variant data type, 331-333

grouping report data, 572
identifiers, 328
literals, 327-328
operators, 322
arithmetic, 322-323
assignment, 323-324
comparisons, 323-324
concatenation, 325
identifier, 325-326
logical, 324-325
query criteria, 341-344
calculating field values,
347-348
Expression Builder,
345-346
real world applications,
350-351
selected record calculations,
391
sorting report data, 574
SQL, punctuation, 857-858
statement contents, 321
update queries, 349
validating data, 340-341

Extensible Markup
Language (XML), 660

Extensible Query Language
(XQL), 661

Extensible Style Language
(XSL), 661

extensions
.adp, 944
.chm, 107
.chm, 41
.cub, 778
graphics, 740
.hlp, 107
.htc, 660
.htm/.html, 628
.mde, 123
.nfo, 109
.ocx, 483
.sdf, 274
.snp, 588
SQL, 853

external databases
accessing with IN clause,
869-871
dBASE, Paradox,
871-872
creating queries from,
403-405

queries, troubleshooting,
405

extracting data, append
queries, 416

extranets, 21, 600

F

F1 key, 97
context-sensitive help, 107
F2 key, 188
F8 key, 189
F11 key, 97
F12 key, 97
fact tables, 776
defined, 749
family name, 328
Fawcette Technical
Publishing's DevX Web
site, 655
field data types
converting on import,
244-245
Excel worksheets, 248
importing worksheets, 254
Field Delimiter, 272
Field Name property, 138
Field object
Name property, 1171
Type property, 1174
Field Properties pane, 157
Field Size property, 138, 141
fixed-width Text fields, 143
numeric data type, 142
FieldChangeComplete
event, 1080
fields, 132
aggregate functions, 861
aliasing, 307
AutoNumber field, 63
troubleshooting, 849
bound text boxes, 493-494
calculated
controls, 553-555
creating with expressions,
347-348
Report Wizard, 549
text boxes, 494-495

candidate, 159
DAP, 681
grouped pages, 701-703
data entry
order of, 473-474
setting options, 192
data types, 140-141
changing, 178-179
document management sys-
tems, 799
duplicate, Table Analyzer
Wizard, 839
editing, 176
editing keys, 188
shortcut keys, 191
entity integrity, 845-847
filtering, composite criteria,
221
Format property, 556-557
formats, 140-141
forms
rearranging, 437
removing from tab order,
474
freezing, 207
function keys, 97-98
grouping report data, 572
grouping reports, 537
grouping/sorting report
data, 571
hiding in datasheets, 225
Hyperlink data type, 611
importing with clipboard,
replacing records, 282
joins, 355
lookup, 64, 365-366
foreign key dropdown lists,
366-370
making all accessible, 386
mapping to Outlook fields,
261
naming, 138, 183
navigating, 189
Null value, 146
Order Amount, 388
outer joins, 378
Personnel Actions table,
159-160
properties, 161
primary keys, 172
indexes, 844
properties, 137-140
queries

subdatasheets, 377
troubleshooting, 315
rearranging sequence,
    176-178
referential integrity,
    848-849
reordering for sorting,
    208-209
replacing values, 212-213
selecting for Query Design
    queries, 299-302
self-joins, 380
setting default values,
    165-166
sizes, 140-141
sorting, single, 208
Table Design window, 157
Text, fixed-width, 143-144
unequal, theta joins, 382
unhiding, *225*
validation rules, 195-197
VBA data types, 1000
Fields collection, 1071-1073
**fifth normal forms (normal-
    ization), 830-831**
file data sources, 650
file formats
    exporting data, 286
    identifying, 234-235
    Jet 4.0, 35
    saving queries, 307
**File New Database dialog
    box, 134**
file-level security, 906
filelist.xml, 678
Filename.ico, 1117
filenames, DAP, 680
files, 132
    converting, 886
    data dictionaries, 133
    document management sys-
        tems, 799
    libraries, 132
    master database, 132
    mdb upgrades, 1182
    sharing, 887
        *client/server comparisons,
            940-942*
        creating folders, 887-891
        DAP. See DAP
        Options properties sheet,

891-893
servers, 934-935
*splitting databases,
    893-895*
*starting command options,
    899-901*
workgroups, 898-899
supplemental, 233
System.mdw, 887
unsecured. *See* unsecured
    files
Fill/Back Color button, 451
FillList subprocedure, 1149
**Filter by Selection button,
    Form view, 469**
Filter Design window, 219
Filter events, 1098, 1100
**Filter property, 77, 136,
    1067**
    constant enumeration, 1070
**Filter, AutoFilter command
    (Data menu), 759**
**Filter, Show All command
    (Data menu), 759**
filtering, 206, 212. *See also*
    sorting
    advanced, 218-219
    by form, 215-218
    by selection, 213-215
    composite criteria, 221-222
    compound criteria, 219-221
    copying filtered datasheets,
        227
    PivotTable data, 759
    PivotTable lists, 670
    Record Navigation control,
        681-682
    removing, 223
    saving as queries, 223-224
    Table Datasheet toolbar, 90
financial functions, 329
Find button, Form view, 469
Find dialog box, 212
Find Last Name box, 512
Find method, 1075
    recordsets, 1162-1163
Find options, 103
finding

matching records, 209-212
    records, with Combo Box
        control, 512-515
FindNext method, 1109
FindRecord method, 1109
firehose cursors, 1055
firehoses, 1153
**first normal forms (normal-
    ization), 825-828**
First function, 387
**fixed column headings,
    crosstab queries, 402-403**
fixed-length fields, 143
fixed-point numbers, 143
**fixed-value lookup lists,
    370-372**
**fixed-width Text fields,
    143-144**
    import specifications, 272
    importing, 266, 276
flat tables, 825
flat-file managers, 82
floating toolbars, 95
floating-point numbers, 143
flow control, 1010
    conditional statements,
        1011
        If...Then, 1011-1012
        Select Case, 1012-1014
    GoTo statement, 1011
    looping, 1014
    SQL, 853
Focus events, 1098-1099
folders
    file sharing, creating,
        887-891
    Outlook, exporting to, 258
fonts
    AutoFormat, 449
    datasheet display, 225
    Datasheet Formatting tool-
        bar, 92
    report data, grouping, 571
    text controls, formatting,
        491
    toolbars, 94
**Footer section, form proper-
    ties, 458**

footers
blank forms, 488-490
printing forms, 529-530
report sections, 585

For Each...Next statement, 1015

For...Next statement, 1014-1015

Fore Color property, 455

foreground colors, 455

foreign keys, 821
cascading deletions/updates, 424
drop-down lists, adding to lookup fields, 366-370
indexes, 812
referential integrity, 848-849
relational tables, 821
subdatasheets, 375

forgotten passwords, erasing, 914

Form class modules, 1084

Form Design mode, Report Design toolbar, 544

Form Design toolbar, 443

Form Design view, 442-444
aligning controls to grid, 459
combo boxes, 1132
Formatting toolbar, 446-447
list boxes, 1131
toolbar buttons, 444-446
unlinked graphs, 717

Form Detail bar, 444

Form Footer, 443-444
sizing, 458

Form Header, 444, 457
sizing, 458

form letters, 782-785
from existing queries, 797-798

form modules, 995

Form property, displaying in Design view, 1119

Form Sections control, events, 1103

Form Selector button, 443

Form view, 85
combo boxes, 1133
editing, 434
extracting values from objects, 771
toolbar buttons, 468-469

Form Wizard, 436-441
Tab Order, 473
transaction-processing forms, 436-441

form-based updating, 429

Format Cells dialog box, 755

Format Data Series dialog box, 726

Format function, calculated fields, 348

Format Painter, 463-464
Table Datasheet toolbar, 90

Format property, 138, 556-557
Currency, 390
data types, 144-145
Number subtypes, 142

FormatCurrency function, 337

FormatDateTime function, 337

FormatNumber function, 338

FormatPercent function, 338

formats (Access), converting, 120-121

formatting
AutoFormats, 448
controls, 554-557
line spacing, 557-558
custom, 146-149
customizing, PivotTables, 754-757
data, Query Field Properties window, 384-386
data types, 144-145
escape characters (\), 150
fields, 140-141
graphs, 719

input masks, 151
Label/Text Box control text, 491-492
PivotTable lists, 693-695
PivotTable reports, 763-764
rowsets, 1034
Web pages, creating unformatted, 631

Formatting toolbar, 443
Form Design window, 446-447
Format Painter button, 463
Line/Border Color button, 462
Line/Border Width button, 462
object colors, 451
background, 451-455
Color Builder, 456-457
foreground/borders, 455
reports, 544
Table Datasheet view, 91-92

forms, 67-72, 434
ADP, importing, 1139
aligning controls to grid, 459-460
appearance, Database Wizard, 60
arranging controls, 111
AutoDialer, 68
AutoFormat, 448-449
customizing, 449-451
binding to ADODB.Recordset object, 1039-1041
blank with header/footer, 488-490
bound object frame control, 734
employee photo, 735-738
photos, 735
scaling graphic objects, 737-740
bound text boxes, 493-494
calculated text boxes, 494-495
Calls, 69
column visibility, 466
combo boxes
adding, 1131-1134
ADP conversions, 1138

compared to reports, 534-535

continuous, 527-528

controls
  adding with Toolbox, 487
  aligning groups of, 461
  Clipboard commands, 462
  Format Painter, 463-464
  hyperlinks, 621-622

copying controls, Clipboard, 501-502

data entry, 82
  order of fields, 473-474

data events, 1122-1123

default values, 447-448

Default View, property values, 496

Design view, 77-79

designing
  audience, 475
  client monitor resolution, 475
  consistency and simplicity, 475-477
  tools, 483

editing controls, 457-458

embedding worksheets, 767-770

Error event, 1018

event handling, responding with functions, 1096

events, 1104

extracting values from OLE objects, 771-772

fields, removing from tab order, 474

footers, printing, 529-530

Form Design window, 442-444
  Formatting toolbar, 446-447
  toolbar buttons, 444-446

frmPersonnelActionEntry, 521

headers
  adding labels, 490-491
  printing, 529-530
  sizing, 458

lightweight, 621

linking, Subform/Subreport Wizard, 524

list boxes, creating, 1130

Main Switchboard, 66-67

.mdb files, 128

naming, 441

new features, 38-39

normalization
  fifth normal form, 830-831
  first normal form, 825-828
  fourth normal form, 830
  second normal form, 828
  third normal form, 829-830

object colors, 451
  background, 451-455
  Color Builder, 456-457
  foreground/borders, 455

Option Group control, adding with Wizard, 497-501

Personnel Actions
  properties, 465-466
  subform properties, 466-467

Picture Alignment property, 454

Picture property, 453

Picture Size Mode property, 454

Picture Tiling property, 455

Picture Type property, 454

PivotTables, creating, 747-754

porting, combo boxes, 1178

printing, 560

properties
  displaying in Design view, 1119
  VBA, 1118-1119

record-navigation buttons, 469

Recordset property, 1039

referencing controls, 1120

selecting multiple controls, 460-461

SQL queries, 880-881

standardized, 451

styles, 440

subforms, 66

switchboard, 66

Switchboard Manager, 75-77

synchronizing, 69

Tab control, 516
  adding pages, 516
  deleting pages, 518
  page order, 517
  placing other controls, 520
  properties, 518-520

transaction-processing, 435
  data sources, 435
  Form view toolbar buttons, 468-469
  Form Wizard, 436-441
  Personnel Actions form, 469-473

transparent backgrounds, 452

unbound graphs, 723

updatable, 1043
  NorthwindCS MSDE database, 1043-1044
  substituting DAO with ADO, 1044-1045

viewing embedded documents, 802-804

Forms collection, 1118

formulas
  importing worksheets, 248
  pasting Excel ranges, 278

Form_Load event handler
  ADODB.Recordset object, 1040
  temporary recordsets, 1157

four-digit year dates, 36-37

four-digit year formatting, 145

fourth normal forms (normalization), 830

FoxPro. *See* **Visual FoxPro**

frames, 434

freezing fields, 207
  thawing, 209

Friend members, 992

frmADO_Test form, 1044

frmPersonnelActionEntry form
  deleting Tab pages, 518
  final formatting, 523
  Find Last Name box, 512
  main form, 521

subforms, 523
Tab control, 516, 519

frmPersonnelActions form, 489
arranging controls, 464
background color, 451
text boxes, 493

frmPersonnelActionsEntry form, Combo Box controls, 503

frmPhotoForm form, Image control, 742

FROM clause, 856

front-end applications, 129

front ends, OLE DB, 1034

FrontPage 2000, 603
opening ASPs, 649

frozen values, 248

FULL OUTER JOIN, MSDE views, 963

function calls, Win16 to Win32 conversions, 1189

function keys
global, 97
table objects, 97-98

functions, 82-84, 320, 328-329, 997. *See also* **sub-procedures**
aggregate, 387-388, 861-863
ANSI SQL compared to Jct SQL, 875-877
arguments, 1009
Asc, 573
Autocompletion ToolTip, 330
calling, troubleshooting, 1123
Chr, string literals, 327
cmdOpenForm, 1097
CONVERT, 962, 1150-1151
data-type conversion, 338-339
date and time, 333-335
Format, calculated fields, 348
Immediate window, 329-331

InStr, validating data, 341
IsLoaded, 74, 995
adding breakpoints, 1023-1024
calling syntax, 999
VBA code, 998
IsNull, 875
Jet databases, 1150-1151
MonthName, 333
MsgBox, 340
Now, 328
OpenForm, 1085
report data, grouping by range, 573-574
responding to events, 1096-1098
ShowHelpAPI, 1116
Sum, 389, 862
ANSI versus Jet, 875
SysCmd, 1024
text manipulation, 335-338
Variant data type, 331-333
WeekdayName, 333

G

GADDP (generally accepted database design practice), 818

General field properties, 138

General settings, 46, 101-102

general-purpose functions, 329

generally accepted database design practices (GADDPs), 818

GetChunk method, 1073

GetRows method, 1075

GetString method, 1075

.gif format, 741

given name, 328

global constants, 1008

global function keys, 97

Global keyword, 997

global variables, SQL Server, 967

globals object, 1089

GoTo SkipHandler statement, 1017

GoTo statement, 1010-1011

GoToControl method, 1109

GoToPage method, 1109

GoToRecord method, 1109

grafted menus, 717

graininess, 739

granting permissions, 917-918

Graph9, 710
Chart Objects list, 728
graph queries, 710-712
modifying graphs, 717-725
PivotCharts, 764

graphic queries, JOIN statement, 864

graphics
file formats, 740
Image control, 741-743
importing, 243
visulizing data, 743

graphics formats, 434
background bitmaps, 452

graphs
from crosstab queries, 723-725
linking to records, 725-728
modifying with Graph9, 717-722
multiline, 730
queries, 710-712
unlinked, 712-717
visualizing data, 744

graphs. *See* **charts**

Grid button, 961

gridlines, removing from datasheets, 225

grids, 157
aligning control groups, 461
aligning controls, 459-460
dot spacing, 460
function keys, 97-98

group aggregate functions, 855

Group By button, 961

GROUP BY clause, 861
    MSDE views, 964
    queries, 862
group sections (reports), 535
grouping, report data, 570-571
    by alphabetic code characters, 572
    by date and time, 574
    by numeric value, 571-572
    by range, 573-574
    creating with Report Wizard, 536-543
    with subgroups, 573
Grouping Options button, 538
groups, 38, 906
    Admins (Administrators), 906
        setting up, 906-912
    creating, 913-914
    deleting, 914
    Keep Together property, 561
    memberships, 912-913
    passwords, erasing, 914
    users, adding, 912
groups/totals reports, 535
guests, 906

H

h placeholders, 148
hardware, security, 903
hashing algorithms, 229
HAVING qualifier, 861
HEAD tag, 662
Header section, 233
    adding labels to, 490-491
    blank forms, 488-490
    Database Wizard, 60
    fixed, crosstab queries, 402
    fixed-width text files, 276
    form properties, 457
    importing, field data types, 244
    linking Excel worksheets, 257
    .mdb files, 234

    printing forms, 529-530
    queries, changing names, 305-307
    report sections, 585
    Review Orders page, 668
heads-down data entry, 203-204
Height property
    line spacing, 557
    SectionUnbound object, 695
help
    context-sensitive, 107-108
    Help button, 107
    Help menu, 108-109
        Show the Office Assistant, 115
    help pages, 682
    Help window, 109-112
        Answer Wizard, 112
        Contents page, 109-110
        copying text from, 110
        hyperlinks, 110
        Index, 112-113
        options, 113
        repositioning, 110
        tutorials, 110
    HTML, 124
    Object Browser, 1000
    Office Assistant, 114-118
    VBA Editor, 331, 1021-1022
heuristic analysis, 775
hidden system tables, 135
hierarchical displays, related tables, 406
History subform, 527-528
.hlp files, 107
Home key, 188
Home Page Hyperlink field, 612
horizontal bar graphs, Sales DAP, 672
horizontal ruler, Form Design window, 443
horizontal scrolling, Web pages, 635
Hotfix.exe, 948

Hour function, 334
Hourglass method, 1109
.htc files, 660
.htm files, filenames, 680
HTML (Hypertext Markup Language), 598
    ASPs, advantages, 655
    creating queries, 634-636
    creating unformated pages, 631-634
    DOM, 661-663
    exporting query datasheets to, 628-631
    exporting reports to, 639-642
    exporting tables to, 628-631
    help, 41, 124
    IDC, 648
    importing, troubleshooting, 654
    importing data from HTML tables, 643-648
    space character, 651
    special characters, 634
    specification download, 599
    tags, 630
    viewing source in IE 5, 637
HTML Source Editor, 33-34, 668-669, 1028
<HTML> tag, 662
HTML templates, 637-638
    exporting query datasheets to, 638-640
HTTP (Hypertext Transmission Protocol), 649
http:// prefix, 617
Hue/Saturation area, 456
human resources, Personnel Actions table, 159
hypercubes, 777
Hyperlink data type, 141, 611
hyperlinks, 598, 606-611
    controls, 621-622
    editing/inserting, 613-614
    Help window, 110
    linking to Web pages, 617-618

linking Word bookmarks, 614-617
opening Access objects, 619-620
protocols supported, 622
ScreenTips, 618-619
testing, 611-612
URL prefixes supported, 622

I

IDC (Internet Database Connector), 648
identifier operators, 325-326
identifiers, 328, 820
identity attribute, 28
IDs (identifications), 902
PID, 906
SID, 925
.idx files, 233
IE (Internet Explorer)
Internet client, 602
PivotTable list control, 689-690
PivotTables, altering properties, 690-691
IE 4+, ScreenTips, 598
IE 5
Autostart option, 628
DAP, 22-25, 658
HTML templates, 637
hyperlinks, 612
opening ASPs, 649
PivotTable lists, filtering, 670
viewing source, 637
IEFT RFC, 659
If...Then statement, 1011-1012, 1146
IIS (Internet Information Server), 604
Default Web Site, 609
virtual directories, 607-611
Image control, 48, 712, 741-743
images, 710
importing, 243-244
Picture property, 518

Immediate window, 32, 320
CommandBar objects, 1114
functions, 329-331
printing property values to, 1115
printing to, 1025
recordsets, Move... method, 1158-1159
implicit variables, 1002
Import Errors table, 254, 271
Import Spreadsheet Wizard, 250
Import Text Wizard, 266-271
advanced options, 271-273
importing, 232-233
appending text to tables, 277
clipboard, 277-278
pasting new records, 278-281
replacing by pasting records, 282
combo box ADP form, 1139
converting field data types, 244-245
dbs with images, 243-244
fixed-width text files, troubleshooting, 288
HTML table data, 643-648
troubleshooting, 654
ISAM tables, 235-238
Outlook folders, 258-262
spreadsheet files, 248-256
spreadsheets, troubleshooting, 288
text files, 264-265
delimited, 273-275
fixed-width, 276
Import Text Wizard, 266-273
troubleshooting
field properties, 156
passwords, 287
versus linking, 246-247
IN clause, external databases, 869-871
dBASE, Paradox, 871-872
In operator, 196, 326

in-place activation (OLE objects), 800
in-situ editing, 466
incremental AutoNumber fields, entity integrity, 845-847
indented lines, 858
indenting statements (VBA), 1012
Index page (Help window), 112-113
Index property, 1067
Index Server, 604
Indexed property, 140
indexes, 174-175, 813, 844
Access 2.0 to 2000 conversions, 1191
foreign keys, 812
imported worksheets, 252
Knuth, Donald E., 229
limit, 1191
null values, troubleshooting, 287
query optimization, 206
result set sort order, 358
single-column equi-joins, 357
single-field, 174
sorting records, 206
troubleshooting, extras added, 182
Indexes window, 137
infinity symbol, 355
InfoMessage event, 1057
InfoModeler, 884
inherited properties, overriding, 528
Ini command, 900
INNER JOIN reserved word, 365
inner joins, 356
Input Mask property, 139
Input Mask Wizard, 151
input masks
adding new records, 193
placeholders, 150-151
updating queries, 384

Insert Data permission, 918

INSERT INTO statement, apppend queries, 871

Insert Object dialog box, 767, 801

Insert Picture dialog box, 61, 453, 742

INSERT statement, 430

inserting hyperlinks, 613-614

installations
network, 886-887

installing
Access 2000, 42-46
MSDE, 47-51, 947-952
PWS, 604

instances. *See* entities

Instancing property, Project Explorer, 1090

InStr function, 335
validating data, 341

intDataMode argument, 1107

integer division, 323

integrated security, 983

integrity, 814, 844
entity integrity, 844-848
referential integrity, 813, 844, 848-849

Intellimenus, 40, 94

interfaces, OLE DB, mapping to ADO, 1035-1037

international (extended) characters, Find What text box, 211

International style, 451

Internet, 598-599. *See also* Web pages; Web sites
ASPs, 21
clients, 602
copyrights, 647
DAP, 705
Data Access Pages, 21
Digital Nervous System, 600-602

distribution of Windows add-ons, 51
hyperlinks, 606
editing/inserting, 613-614
linking to Web pages, 617-618
linking Word bookmarks, 614-617
opening Access objects, 619-620
ScreenTips, 618-619
testing, 611-612
Microsoft technologies, 605-606
MSN, 624
query design, 316
server-side components, 604-605
standards, 659
upgrading Access, 53
URLs, 622

Internet Database Connector (IDC), 648

Internet Information Server (IIS) 4.0, 604

Internet Services API, 605

Internet-compliant content, 628

Internet-compliant technologies, 599

Intranet-only technologies, 600

intranets, 598
DAP, 705
navigating with hyperlinks, 606-611
troubleshooting connections, 623

intrinsic constants, 339, 1008-1009
DoCmd methods, arguments, 1108

intView argument, 1107

intWindowMode argument, 1107

inventory reports, 536

invoice-entry database, 131

invoking subprocedures, 997

Is Hyperlink property, 954

Is keyword, Select Case statement, 1013

Is operator, 326

ISAM tables, linking/importing, 235-238

ISAPI, 605

IsLoaded function, 74, 995
adding breakpoints, 1023-1024
calling syntax, 999
VBA code, 998

IsNull function, 875

IsolationLevel property, 1048
constant enumeration, 1049

isql, 946

italic type, 146

Item method, 1051, 1059

ItemData property, list boxes, 1145

J

Java, DOM, 663

JavaScript, 33

Jet database engine, 812
ADODB.Recordset object, 1039
ADP, 945
ADP conversions, 1151-1152
Auto-Compact on Close, 35
cascading deletions/updates, 424
conforming with MSDE, 35-36
converting, Jet 3.5x to Jet 4.0, 1182
crosstab queries, 868
optimizing, 407
DAO, 1033
DDL, creating tables, 872-873
downsizing to, 975
equi-joins, 864
Expression Service, Nz function, 339
functions, 1150-1151

Hyperlink data type, 611
indexes, 813
linking Excel worksheets, 256
MSDE advantages over, 946
MSDE comparisons, 941
native OLE DB data provider, 650
OLE DB, DAP, 666
row-level locking, 36
SQL
  punctuation, 857
  VALUES keyword, 869
SQL extensions, 853
table properties, 958

Jet SQL
ANSI words unsupported, 880
compared to ANSI
  DISTINCT and DISTINCTROW, 877-880
  functions and operators, 875-877
  reserved words, 873-875

Join Properties dialog box, 169, 379

JOIN statement, 863

Join Type button, 169

joins, 131, 354
displaying structure, 355
equi-joins, 356
MSDE views, 963
multicolumn equi-joins, selecting unique values, 362-365
multitable queries, 355-357
outer, 356, 378-380
queries, indirect relationships, 360
query criteria, VBA expressions, 343
resultset sort order, 358-360
self, 356, 380-381
single-column equi-joins, 357-359
SQL statements, 863-865
theta, 356
  not-equal with criteria, 382-383

types of, 354

.jpg format, 741

JScript, 606

Justified and Vertical Alignment options, 39

K

Keep Together property, 561-562, 587

key fields
entity integrity, 845
primary keys, 172
referential integrity, 848-849

Keyboard events, 1098-1099

keyboard object selection, 38

keyboard operations, data entry, 186
clipboard operations, 190-191
editing keys, 188-189
experimental copies, 187
options, 104

keyboard shortcuts. *See* shortcut keys

keys
Alt+Backspace, 188
Backspace, 188
candidate , 821
clipboard operations, 190
composite , 821
Ctrl+End, 188
Ctrl+Home, 188
Ctrl+Shift+>, 189
Ctrl+Shift+<, 189
Ctrl+spacebar, 189
Ctrl+Z, 188
Ctrl+<, 188
Delete, 188
down arrow, 189
End, 188
Enter, 189
Esc, 188-189
F2, 188
F8, 189
foreign , 821
Home, 188

primary , 821
relational databases, 820-821
Shift+F8, 189
Shift+spacebar, 189
Shift+>, 189
Shift+<, 189
shortcut, 191
Tab, 189
up arrow, 189

keys, editing, 188-189

keyset (adOpenKeyset) cursor, 1158

keywords (SQL), 855
AS, 861, 1002
Call, 997
Const, 1008
constants, 339
Dim, 1001
End Sub, 997
End Type, 1005
End With, 1007
Erase, 1006
Exit Do, 1015
For, 1015
Global, 997
Help index, 113
Is, Select Case statement, 1013
Loop, 1015-1016
Next, 1014-1015
Option Base, 1006
Optional, 1010
Public, 997
ReDim, 1006
Resume, 1017
Set, named database objects, 1007
Step, 1014
Sub, 997
To, 1006
Type, 1005
Until, 1015
VALUE, 869
VBA Help system, 1021
Wend, 1016
While, 1015-1016
With, 1007

Knuth, Donald E.
indexes, 229
sorting, 228

L

Label control, 482
  adding to form headers, 490-491
  alignment, 554
  events, 1101
  formatting text, 491-492
  Monthly Sales by Category report, 580
"Label not found" error message, 1011
labels, 434
  associated, 459
    selecting controls, 460
  borders, 462
  Form Wizard, 441
  naming, 441
labels (macro), 1010
  syntax, 1011
landscape-printing orientation, unbound reports, 585
LANs (Local Area Networks)
  database designs, 814
  query design, 316
laptops, form design, 475
Large Icons check box, 94
Last function, 387
Launch Control Panel, 932
Layout Wizard, 688
layouts (reports), 535
leading zeros, 273
left outer joins, 378
Len function, 335
length of flat tables, 825
Leszynski Naming Conventions for Access, 994
Let Access Add Primary Key option, 253
libraries, 132
  Access 2.0 to 2000 conversions, 1189-1190
  troubleshooting, 1191
lifetime, 1004
lightweight forms, 621

Like operator, 326
  query criteria, 343
Line control, 483
Line Items list box, 1146
line spacing, 557-558
line-feed (LF) character, 327
line-item sources, 711
Line/Border Color button, 462
Line/Border Width button, 462
Link Child Fields property, 136, 584
Link dialog box, 236
Link Master Fields property, 136, 584
Link Master Fields value, 375
Link Spreadsheet Wizard, 256
Link Tables dialog box, 242
Linked File Manager utility, 936-937
linked graphs, 712, 725
Linked Table Manager, 895
Linked Table Manager add-in, 245-246
linking, 84, 232
  cell ranges (Excel), 772-774
  DAP, 679
  dbs with images, 243
  forms, Subform/Subreport Wizard, 524
  ISAM tables, 235-238
  Outlook folders with Exchange/Outlook Wizard, 262-264
  reports, troubleshooting, 591
  spreadsheet files, 256-258
  subreports to bound reports, 581-584
  tables, with Linked Table Manager, 245-246
  versus importing, 246-247
  Visual FoxPro tables, 238-242
  Word documents, 798-802

links
  DAP, updating, 896
  one-to-many relationships, 833
  shared workgroups, refreshing, 936-937
List Box control, 482, 502-503
  events, 1102
List Box wizard, 1130
list boxes, 1153-1154
  drilling down, 1142
    coding, 1143-1145
    queries, 1142-1143
  Line Items, 1146
  optimization, 1153
  properties, 1145-1146
  queries, 1130-1131
  recordsets, 1165-1167
    populating, 1171-1173
    value lists, 1174-1177
  selecting all, 1146-1149
list suffixes, 669
List Width property, unambiguous selections, 373
ListBox control, 1145
ListCount property, list boxes, 1145
listings
  binding updatable forms, 1044
  cboCountry/cboProduct Combo Boxes, populating, 1170-1171
  Command object, parameterized stored procedure, 1064
  event handling, Main Switchboard form, 1088-1089
  Fill the lstOrders List Box, 1173
  Populate the lstLineItems list box, 1177
  validation subprocedure, 1122
  VBA Code for the frmCombo1 Class Module, 1137
  writing Error properties to Immediate window, 1053

literals, 327-328

lngAffectRecords argument, 1077

Locate Web Page dialog box, 897

LockEdits property, record-sets, 1164

locking records, 812
  sharing files, 892

LockType property, 1067
  constant enumeration, 1070

logical data types, conversion functions, 338-339

logical operators, 195, 324-325

Logon dialog box, 909

Long Integer data type
  changing data types, 178
  formatting, 144
  paID field, 161

Long property, 1059

look and feel, form design, 475

lookup fields, 64, 365-366
  compared to subdatasheets, 373
  foreign key dropdown lists, 366-370
  reports, 549

lookup lists, fixed-value, 370-372

Lookup tables, creating, 836

Lookup wizard, 836
  fixed-value lookup lists, 370-372

Loop keyword, 1015-1016

looping statements, 1014

Loopup Wizard, adding dropdown lists, 366-370

M

m placeholders, 148

macro command, 900

macros, 83, 992, 1027
  Access vs VBA, 20
  backward compatibility, 818

.mdb files, 129
  SQL queries, 880-881

mail clients, Outlook, 262

mail merge
  Access databases, 789
  data sources, MSQuery, 789-797
  form letters, from existing queries, 797-798
  newline pairs, 273
  tab-delimited text files, 275

Mail Merge Helper, 789

Mail Merge Wizard, 782
  data sources, 786-789
  form letters, 782-785

mailing labels, 535
  multicolumn reports, 562-565

mailing lists
  Criteria expression, 303
  selecting records for, 302

mailing reports, 588-589

main forms, fitting subforms, 467

Main Switchboard
  class modules, 1085-1087
  event-handling code, 1088-1089
  Forms Design view, 77

Main Switchboard form (Contact Management application), 66-67
  event handling, responding with functions, 1096

mainframe computers, rollups, 711

maintenance mode, 1032

Make Table dialog box, 312

make-table queries, 311-313, 411
  compared to append queries, 417
  converting select query, 413-414
  designing/testing, 411-412
  parameters, 313-314
  relationships, 414-415
  SQL, 868
  tblShipAddresses table, 416

many-to-many relationships, 167, 834-836
  single-column equi-joins, 357

many-to-one relationships, 64, 167, 833-834

margins, 308, 558-561
  changing general options, 101
  General options, 102

MarshalOptions property, 1067

master database file, 132

mathematic functions, 329

mathematics, set theory, 825

Max function, 387

Maximize method, 1109

maximized windows, 87-88

MaxRecords property, 1067

.mb files, 233

.mda files, 56, 132, 234
  backwards compatibility, 35
  contents of, 128-130
  file upgrades, 1182
  objects, 818

MDAC (Microsoft Data Access Components), 1032
  Office 2000, 1082

.mde files, 123, 132

MDI applications, 87

MDM (multidimensional data modeling), 776

MDX (multidimensional expressions), 1032

.mdx files, 233

Me self-reference, 1119
  class modules, 1084

measures, 776
  defined, 749

Medium Date display, converting to four-digit format, 385

members (workgroup), 886
  Object Browser, 1089

memberships, groups, 912-913

Memo data type, 140
    changing data types, 179

memo fields
    importing images, 243
    indexing, 599
    query design, 317

memo files
    images, 243
    troubleshooting, 287

memory requirements, MSDE, 947

Menu Animations drop-down list, 94

menu negotiation, 717, 737

menubars. *See also* toolbars
    CommandBar, startup properties, 1117
    table view, 86

menus
    Form Design window, 444-446
    versus switchboards, 67

MEQ, 882-884

merge data files, creating, 283

Merge It with MS Word option, 309

META tag, 662

metadata, 1056

methods
    AddItem, 1153
    AddMenu, 1108
    AddNew, 1074
    Append, 1059
    AppendChunk, 1062, 1073
    ApplyFilter, 1108
    Beep, 1108
    BeginTrans, 1054
    callback, 1153
    Cancel, 1074
    CancelBatch, 1074
    CancelEvent, 1108
    CancelUpdate, 1074
    Clear, 1051
    Clone, 1074
    Close, 1054, 1074, 1108
        recordsets, 1172

Command object, 1062-1063
CommitTrans, 1054
Connection object, 1054-1056
Connection.Open, 1046
CopyObject, 1108
CreateParameter, 1062
Delete, 1074
    recordsets, 1165
Delete_Object, 1108
DoCmd, 1105-1107
    arguments, 1107-1113
DoCmd object, 1089
DoMenuItem, 1109
Echo, 1109
Execute, 1054, 1063
    constant enumeration, 1055
Find, 1075
    recordsets, 1162-1163
FindNext, 1109
FindRecord, 1109
GetChunk, 1073
GetRows, 1075
GetString, 1075
GoToControl, 1109
GoToPage, 1109
GoToRecord, 1109
Hourglass, 1109
Item, 1051, 1059
Maximize, 1109
Minimize, 1109
Move, 1075
    recorsets, 1158-1159
MoveFirst, 1075
MoveLast, 1075
MoveNext, 1075
MovePrevious, 1075
MoveSize, 1109
MsgBox, 1110
NextRecordset, 1076
Open, 1054, 1076
OpenDataAccessPage, 1110
OpenDiagram, 1110
OpenForm, 1110
    arguments, 1107
OpenModule, 1110
OpenQuery, 1110
OpenReport, 1110
OpenSchema, 1054, 1056
OpenStoredProcedure, 1110

OpenTable, 1110
OpenView, 1110
OutputTo, 1110
Parameters collection, 1059
Print, 1111
PrintOut, 1111
Quit, 1111
Recordset object, 1074-1079
    creating, 1039
Refresh, 1059
Rename, 1111
RepaintObject, 1111
Requery, 1076, 1111, 1136
Restore, 1111
Resync, 1076
RollbackTrans, 1054
RunApp, 1111
RunCode, 1111
RunCommand, 1111
RunMacro, 1112
RunSQL, 1112
Save, 1076, 1112
Seek, 1076
SelectObject, 1112
SendKeys, 1112
SendObject, 1112
SetMenuItem, 1112
SetValue, 1112
SetWarnings, 1112
ShowAllRecords, 1113
StopAllMacros, 1113
StopMacro, 1113
Supports, 1077
    constant enumerations, 1078
TransferDatabase, 1113
TransferSpreadsheet, 1113
TransferText, 1113
Update, 1077, 1079
UpdateBatch, 1077

metrics, 776

Microsoft, Internet, history of, 624

Microsoft Data Access Components (MDAC), 1032

Microsoft Data Engine (MSDE), 812

Microsoft Decision Support Services (MSDSS), 1128

Microsoft Development Environment (MDE), 1028

Microsoft English Query (MEQ), 882-884

Microsoft Management Console (MMC), 607

Microsoft Office Developer (MOD), 887

Microsoft Query, 789

migration, problems, 1192-1193

Millenium+ accounting application, 593

Millennium project, 1029

Min function, 387

Minimize method, 1109

minimized windows, 88-89

miniservers, 710

minus sign (–), 322

Minute function, 334

MMC (Microsoft Management Console), 607

MOD (Microsoft Office Developer), 887

Mod operation, 323

Mode property, 1048
    constant enumeration, 1050

modes, 82

Modify Design permission, 917

Module objects, 56

modules, 56, 73-74, 83, 995-996
    Declarations section, 997
    elements of, 997-998
    global constants, 1008
    mdb files, 129
    runtime errors, On Error statement, 1016

modulus, 323

monitoring users, 903

monospace type, 146

Month function, 334

monthly product sales crosstab query, 400-402

Monthly Sales by Category report, 578-581

Monthly Sales query, parameter queries, 393-394
    data types, 394-395

monthly sales reports, 576

MonthName function, 333-334

More Controls tool, 483

mouse
    context-sensitive help, 107
    events, 1098-1099
    selecting multiple controls, 460
    sizing controls, 458

Move method, 1075
    EOF/BOF properties, 1159
    recordsets, 1158-1159

MoveComplete event, 1080

MoveFirst method, 1075

MoveLast method, 1075

MoveNext method, 1075

MovePrevious method, 1075

MoveSize method, 1109

Movie control, 659

Movie tool, 39, 434

moving controls, 457-458

MSDataShape provider
    ADODB.Recordset object, 1039
    updatable forms, 1043

MSDE (Microsoft Data Engine), 25-26, 812, 945
    ADP, 944, 953-954
    benefits of, 946-947
    conforming with Jet, 35-36
    connecting to remote
        SQL Server Client Network Utility, 981-982
        testing remote databases, 982-983
    DAO alternative, 1044
    installing, 47-51, 947-952
    integrity, 814
    Jet comparisons, 941
    memory requirements, 947
    Properties sheet, 959

security, 983-986
SQL Server, 945-946
    upgrading to, 941-942
starting, 50
tables, 957-960
updatable forms, 1043
versions, 945
views, 832, 960-964

MSDSS (Microsoft Decision Support Services), 1128

MSDTC auto-start, 51

MsgBox function, 340

MsgBox method, 1110

MSHFlexGrid control, 374

Msjet40.dll, 1033

MSN (Microsoft Network), 624

Mso9.dll, 1113

Msqry32.exe, 782

MSQuery object
    mail merge data source, 789-797
    OLE DB, 805
    sorting rows, 795

MTS (Microsoft Transaction Server), Session objects, 1036

multicolumn equi joins, selecting unique values, 362-365

multicolumn reports, 535
    printing as mailing labels, 562-565

multidimensional arrays, 1006

multidimensional data modeling (MDM), 776

multidimensional expressions (MDX), 1032

multiline graphs, 730

multiline text boxes, 493

multimedia, 710

multiple-field sorting, 208

multiplication, 323

multiprocessors, MSDE, 947

MultiRow property, Tab control, 518

multitable queries, optimizing, 406-407

multiuser applications, 886
creating folders, 887-891

multiuser databases. *See also* networking
administering, 937
backups, 938
compacting, 938-939
encryption, 939-940
repairing, 938-939

multiuser environments, importing tables, 235

multiuser security, 906

N

n placeholders, 148

Name AutoCorrect, 39, 176, 434

Name property, 1058, 1060, 1072
Field object, 1171

named arguments, 1009
Connection object methods, 1054

named constants, 339

named database objects, 1007

Named Protocol, 49

naming conventions
Admins group, 909-910
AutoFormats, 450
collections, bang operator (!), 1118
command buttons, 1094
dot operator (.), 1118
fields, 183
spaces, 159
forms, 441
grouping reports, 542
htm files, 680
labels, 441
SQL reserved words, 874
tables, 183
variables, 1002
VBA, 994

native controls, 480

Natural Language Processing (NLP), 883

navigating switchboards, 67

navigation buttons (recorsets), VBA construction, 1156

Navigation sections, Review Orders page, 668

.ndx files, 233

nested If statements, 1012

nested queries, 390
performance, 730
subqueries, 867

NetMeeting
Internet client, 602
online collaboration, 42

NetShow Services, 605

NetWare, installing MSDE, 49

Network Libraries dialog box, 949

Network properties sheet
Access Control page, 932

networking, 886
Access 9x to 2000 conversion, 1187
backups, 938
compacting databases, 938-939
encryption databases, 939-940
installing Access, 886-887
ownership, 914-915
changing, 915-917
permissions, 915
peer-to-peer, 886
repairing databases, 938-939
security, 902
groups, 906
passwords, 904-905
principles of, 902-904
user-level, 932-934
sharing files
client/server comparisons, 940-942
servers, 934-935

troubleshooting, paths, 940
Windows 9x, 929, 931-932
workgroups
accessing, 935
refreshing links, 936-937
system file, 935-936
UNC, 935-936

networks, query design, 316

New Data Access Page dialog box, 730

New dialog box, 134

new features
Database window, 37-38
forms, 38-39
four-digit year, 36-37
HTML help, 41
Intellimenu, 40
Name AutoCorrect, 39
online collaboration, 41
reports, 38-39
single-document interface, 40

New Form dialog box, 488, 747

New keyword, ADO objects, 1037

New object shortcuts, 86

New Record button, 472

New Report dialog box, 536
subreports, 577

New reserved word, class modules, 1084

New Table dialog box, 152

New Toolbar dialog box, 486

New Values property, 140

newline characters, 327

newline pairs
delimited text files, 273
exporting data as text files, 285
exporting queries, 310
SQL, 857

newspaper columns, 565

Next keyword, 1014-1015

NextRecordset method, 1076

.nfo files, 109

NLP, 883

no entry, 146

NoMatch property, 1068

nonlinked graphs, 712

normalization, 813, 825-826
  fifth normal form, 830-831
  first normal form, 825-828
  fourth normal form, 830
  relationships, 831-832
    many-to-many, 834-836
    many-to-one, 833-834
    one-to-many, 833
    one-to-one, 832-833
  second normal form, 828
  third normal form, 829-830

North American Customers query, 651

Northwind database, 57, 151
  adding tables, 156-157
  Combo Box controls, 503
  CommandBar objects, 1114
  complex queries, 303-305
  Customer Labels report, 563
  DAP, Review Products page, 666
  date formats, 146
  deleting records with action queries, 419
  displaying objects in Object Browser, 1090
  editing/inserting hyperlinks, 613-614
  experimental copy, 187
  external access, 870
  frozen columns, 207
  grouping reports, 536
  Home Page Hyperlink field, 612
  hyperlinks
    opening Access objects, 619-620
    screentips, 618-619
  joins, 355
  linking to Web pages, 617-618
  linking Word bookmarks, 614-617
  mail merge documents, 783

Main Switchboard
  class modules, 1085-1087
  event-handling code, 1088-1089
  MSDE version, 1043
  Personnel Actions table
    adding records, 199
    creating, 160-165
    designing, 158-160
  printing queries as reports, 307-309
  query column header names, 305-307
  Query Design window, 298
  Relationships window, 355
  Simple Query Wizard, 294
  single-column equi-joins, 358
  Switchboard form, 122
  Table Wizard, 151-156
  testing hyperlinks, 611-612
  transaction-processing forms, 436
  VBA
    adding breakpoints, 1023
    functions, 329

NorthwindCS database
  ADP, 954-956
  Relationships diagram, 965

NorthwindCS.adp project, 27-31

NoStartup command, 900

not equal (!=, <>), 858

notebooks, form design, 475

Now function, 328, 334

Null values, 146, 831
  default field values, 165
  missing arguments, 1010
  troublshooting, 287

Null Variant data type, 333

Number data type, 140
  converting data types, 179
  default field value, 165
  formatting, 144
  subtypes, 142-143

Number of Columns property, 563

numeric data type
  aggregate functions, 861
  changing data types, 178
  conversion functions, 338-339
  extracting values from objects, 772
  Field Size property, 138
  grouping reports, 538

numeric formatting, PivotTable lists, 695

numeric literals, 327

numeric operands, 322

NumericScale property, 1060, 1072

NuvoMedia's Rocket eBook, 124

NwindSQL database, triggers, 968

Nwindtem.htm template, 637

Nz function, 339

O

OAKLEAF clients, 981

Object box, 1086

Object Browser, 32
  ADODB, 1046-1047
  class modules, 1089-1091
  displaying intrinsic constants, 1008
  Object library, 1114
  viewing, 999

Object Definition print preview window, 843

Object fields, document management tables, 799

Object Frame control, events, 1102

object frames
  adornments, troubleshooting, 775
  embedding workbooks, troubleshooting, 775
  Size Mode property, 738

Object Grouping, 38

Object Library,
CommandBar objects,
1113

object references, 1051

objects, 813
  ADP, 26
  application, 130
  application objects, 818
  attributes, 816-819
  Command
    methods, 1062-1063
    Parameter object,
      1060-1062
    Parameters collection,
      1059
    properties, 1057-1058
    stored procedure parame-
      ters, 1063-1065
  CommandBar, 1113-1116
  concept of, 816
  Connection
    Errors collection, 1051
    events, 1056-1057
    methods, 1054-1056
    properties, 1048
  controls, events, 1100
  data modeling, 821-822
    application databases, 822
    conceptual data models,
      821
    diagrammatic databases,
      823
    schema, 824
    subject databases, 823
  Database, 56
  DBEngine, 1033
  Debug, 1025-1026
  default instances, 1084
  DoCmd, 1089
  entities, 819
    combining in tables,
      818-819
  Err, 1017-1018
  Error, Connection object,
    1051
  events, 1098
  Field, 1071-1073
    Name property, 1171
    Type property, 1174
  Formatting toolbar, 446
  forms, default values, 447
  given name, 328

independence, 1038
iterating through with For
  Each statement, 1015
mail merge documents, 782
MDB files, 818
.mdb files, contents of, 128
Module, 56
Name AutoCorrect, 39
named database objects,
  1007
Object Browser, 1090
object paradigm, 818
OLE
  editing, 736
  extracting values, 771-772
  troubleshooting, 743
OLE DB interfaces, 1036
opening with hyperlinks,
  619-620
ownership, 914-915
  changing, 915-925
  permissions, 915
Parameter, 1060-1062
permissions
  changing, 918-926
  granting, 927-929
persistent, 223
pointing to, 1007
primary tables, 172
properties, 816
  setting with With state-
    ment, 1007
Query, 56
QueryDef, filters, 223
Recordset, 303
  disconnected, 1079
  events, 1080
  Fields collection,
    1071-1073
  methods, 1074-1079
  properties, 1066-1071
  SELECT queries, 857
  updating queries, 383
referencing, 998-1000
shortcuts, 37
state, 1098
Table, Contact
  Management application,
  62-66
VBA, 1000-1001

Objects bar, 37, 86

OCW (Office Chart
  Wizard), 728
  office chart properties,
    733-734
  office charts, single-column
    series, 730-733
  queries, 729

.ocx files, 483

ODBC (Open Database
  Connectivity), 1033
  ASPs, 650-651
  linking Excel worksheets,
    256
  linking Visual FoxPro
    tables, 238-242
  mail merge data sources,
    789-797

ODBC Data Source
  Administrator dialog box,
  650

ODBCDirect, 1033

Office 2000
  DAP, 1082
  installing, 44
  installing PWS, 604
  Internet enhancements,
    598-599
  new features
    HTML help, 41
    Intellimenu, 40
    online collaboration, 41
    single-document interface,
      40
  upgrading, 52

Office Assistant, 114-118
  CommandBar objects, 1113
  hiding, 114
  make-table action queries,
    312
  turning off, 109

Office Chart control,
  PivotTable lists, 695-698

Office Chart Wizard
  (OCW), 728
  office chart properties,
    733-734
  office charts, single-column
    series, 730-733
  queries, 729
  single-column series,
    730-733

Office Clipboard, 277

Office Developer, 887

Office library, 1114

Office Professional, 20

Office Server Extensions (OSE), 600, 604

Office Web Components (OWC), 599, 603, 658

OLAP (online analytical processing), 22, 1128
 Cube page, 805
 dimensions, defined, 750
 measures and facts, defined, 749
 PivotTables, 746, 775

OLE (Object Linking and Embedding)
 bound object frame control, 734
 editing objects, 736
 sound clips, 740
 unbound controls, 481

OLE Automation wrappers, 1033

OLE Controls, Access 2.0 to 2000 conversions, 1191

OLE DB, 660, 1002, 1032, 1034-1035
 DAP, Review Products page, 666
 mapping interfaces to ADO, 1035-1037
 MSDE, 26
 MSQuery, 805
 upgrading Access, 53
 versus ODBC, 238

OLE miniservers, 710

OLE Object data type, 141
 ADP, 954

OLE Object fields, 818
 bound object frames, reports, 588
 DAP, 704
 document management tables, 799
 query design, 317
 troubleshooting
  opening, 743

OLE Servers, Excel
 embedding worksheets, 767-770
 extracting values from objects, 771-772
 linking cell ranges, 772-774

OLTP (online transaction processing), 1128
 drill-down techniques, 1128
 form design, 475-476
 row-level locking, 36

On Error GoTo instruction, 1016

OnAction property, showing in Immediate window, 1116

one-to-many forms, 435

one-to-many relationships, 167, 355, 833
 equi-joins, 356
 lookup fields, 365
 make-table queries, 415
 Personnel Actions table, 470, 487
 transaction-processing forms, 437
 updating queries, 384

one-to-one relationships, 166, 832-833

online analytical processing (OLAP), 1128

online collaboration, 41

online transaction processing (OLTP), 1128

Open method, 1054, 1076

Open Mode, shared, 892

Open permission, 917

OpenDataAccessPage method, 1110

OpenDiagram method, 1110

OpenForm function, 1085

OpenForm method, 1110
 arguments, 1107

opening files, Access 9x to 2000 conversion, 1182-1185

OpenModule method, 1110

OpenQuery method, 1110

OpenReport method, 1110

OpenSchema method, 1054, 1056

OpenStoredProcedure method, 1110

OpenTable method, 1110

OpenView method, 1110

operating modes, 84
 table view, 86

operator syntax, 195

operators, 195, 320-322
 &, 195
 :=, 1010
 ANSI SQL compared to Jet SQL, 875-877
 arithmetic, 322-323
 assignment, 323-324
 Between, 326
 Boolean, 324
 categories of, 322
 comparison, 323-324
  Find method, 1162
 concatenation, 325
 identifier, 325-326
 In, 196, 326
 Is, 326
 Like, 326
 logical, 324-325
 SQL, 855

optimistic locking, sharing files, 892

optimizing, 844, 1153
 multitable queries, 406-407
 query design, 315-317

Option Base keywords, 1006

Option Button control, 482
 reports, 588

Option Compare statements, 1027

Option Explicit statement, 1003

Option Group control, 482, 497-501
 binding, 499
 events, 1101

Option Group Wizard, 497-501

Option Value property, 497

Optional keyword, 1010

options
Help window, 113
selection rectangle, 461
Snap to Grid, 459

Options dialog box, 99

Options page, Office Assistant, 116

Options properties sheet, file sharing, 891-893

Or condition, filtering by form, 215

Order Amount field, 388

ORDER BY clause, 856, 1140
sorting, 228
UNION queries, 865

Order By property, 136

Order Date input mask, updating queries, 386

Order Details Extended view, 28, 961

Order Details table, 667

order entry, DAP, 674

Orders datasheet, 227

Orders table, Order Amount field, 388

OriginalValue property, 1072

ORM, 884

orphan records, 171, 849

OSE (Office Server Extensions), 600, 604

osql, 946

outer joins, 356, 378-380

Outlook
as default mail client, 262
importing from, 258-262
linking tables, 262
linking with Exchange/Outlook Wizard, 262-264
reports in Snapshot format, 588
viewing Snapshot reports, 589

Output Field Properties window, 383

OutputTo method, 1110

overhead, 181

overiding, field properties, 528-529

OWC (Office Web Components), 22, 599
distinguishing from Excel PivotTables, 669
Graph control, PivotTable lists, 671

ownership, 914-915
changing, 915-925
permissions, 915

P

Page Break control, 483

Page Design toolbar, Office Chart control, 695

Page Design view
chart properties, 733
HTML Source Editor, 33

Page Field list, adding PivotTables (OWC), 687-689

Page Footer, 529
deleting, 578

Page Header, 529
control layout, 547
deleting, 578, 586
line spacing, 557

Page Order list, 517

Page Setup dialog box, 308
margins, 559
paper layout, 561

Page view
PivotTable control properties, 690
Run mode, 85

Page Wizard, 674-679

PageCount property, 1068

pages, databases, 812

PageSize property, 1068

paginating reports, 543

Paint, 735

paper layout, 561

paperless offices, 566

paradigm object, 818

Paradox, 233
accessing with IN clause, 871-872
field data type conversion, 244
identifying file formats, 235
importing, containing images, 243
Linked Table Manager, 245

Parameter object, Command object, 1060-1062

Parameter queries, 311, 393-394
data types, 394-395
IDC, 648
Web pages, 635

parameters, 313-314
Excel, 900
stored procedures, 1063-1065
VBA functions, 1096

Parameters collection, Command object, 1059

Parameters dialog box, printing reports, 566

Parent property, referencing controls, 1121

parent windows, 40

parsing, 819

passing arguments, 1098

passive-matrix LCDs, form design, 475

passthrough queries, crosstab queries, 408

Password Required dialog box, 904

passwords, 814, 903
Admins group, 907-908, 911
creating, 904
setting, 904-905
troubleshooting, 287
unsetting, 905
workgroups, 900

Paste Append, 279

Paste Errors table, 281

Paste Link dialog box, 773

Paste Table As dialog box, 181, 366

paths
relative links, 630
troubleshooting, 940

PC-8 characters, 275

.pcx files, 243, 741

peer-to-peer networking, 886
Windows 9x, 929, 931-932

pencil symbol, 471

percent symbol (%), format expressions, 348

percentage distribution charts, 721

PercentPosition property, 1069
recordsets, 1161

performance
external database queries, 404
form colors, 457
nested queries, 730
optimization, 844
prepared statements, 1059
searching fields, 212

period (.), SQL statements, 857

permissions, 814, 903
Administer, 918
changing, 924-926
manually, 925
Security wizard, 918-925
Database Documenter, 842
Delete Data, 918
granting, 917-918
addtional, 927-928
workgroups, 928-929
Insert Data, 918
Modify Design, 917
MSDE security, 986
Open, 917
owner, 914-915
Read Data, 918
Read Design, 917
revoking, 917-918
Run, 917
Update Data, 918

Permissions property, 918

persistent database objects, 223

PersistFormat property, 1068

Personal Indentification code (PID), 906

Personal Web Server (PWS), 604

Personnel Actions form, 435
bound object frame control, scaling graphic objects, 737-740
employee photos, 735-738
Form Wizard, 436-441
properties, 465-466
subform properties, 466-467
transaction processing, 469
appending records, 470-472
committing/rolling back, 473
editing data, 472

Personnel Actions table, 366, 442
adding controls with Toolbox, 487
adding fixed-list lookup list, 370
adding records, 199-200
Caption property, 493
Control Wizards, 521-523
creating, 160-165
default field values, 165
designing, 158-159
assigning information to fields, 159-160
index, 173
joins, 169
Label control, formatting text, 491
main form query, 487
Option Value property, 497
primary key, 173
primary tables, 172
rearranging fields, 176
relationship, 167
self-joins, 380
testing validation rules, 201-202

transaction-processing forms, 435
validating data with expressions, 340

pessimistic locking, 892

PFEL.mdb, 827

Phone Dialer, 69

photos, bound object frame control, 735

pick lists, 502

Picture Alignment property, 454

Picture property, 453
Tab control, 518

Picture Size Mode property, 454

Picture Tiling property, 455

Picture Type property, 454

PID (Personal Indentification code), 906
Admins group, 909, 912

PIN. *See* **PID**

pinstripes, 743

PIVOT statement, crosstab queries, 869

PivotCharts, creating from PivotTables, 764-766

pivoting, 762

PivotTable control, 22

PivotTable Field dialog box, 755

PivotTable Options dialog box, 750

PivotTable Property Toolbox, 690

PivotTables, 746
Access PivotTable Wizard, 746
adding with Page Field list, 687-689
altering properties in IE 5, 690-691
collapsing/expanding display, 760-762
crosstab queries, compared, 746
DAP, Analyze Sales page, 669-671

data cubes, 806
dimension axis, changing, 762
filtering, 759
formatting, 754-757
formatting reports, 763-764
forms, creating, 747-754
list control in IE 5, 689-690
lists
formatting, 693-695
Office Chart control, 695-698
queries, 692-693
OLAP, 775
OLAP Cube page, 805
PivotCharts from, 764-766
queries, creating, 747
Sales page, 671
slicing data, 757-759
snapshots of query results, saving, 751

pixels, 738
control borders, 462

placeholders, 146
input masks, 150-151

Plato, 1033, 1128

pointing to objects, 1007

points, 102

pop-up Help window, 108

pop-up menus, 96

populating
combo box recordsets, 1168-1169
list boxes, 1171-1173

porting forms, combo boxes, 1178

postal codes, importing HTML tables, 644

pound sign (#)
date values, 1001
date/time literals, 328
Hyperlink data type, 611
SQL statements, 858

Precision property, 139, 1060, 1072

predefined form styles, 440

predefined report styles, 541

prefixes
named arguments, 1054
naming conventions, 183
object types, 1039

Prepared property, 1058

prepared statements
Parameter object, 1060
performance, 1059

Presentation mode, 769

Preserve keyword, 1006

Primary Key property, 137-138

primary keys, 821
appending records, troubleshooting, 427
cascading deletions/updates, 424
cascading updates, testing, 426
composite, 137
database diagrams, 30
entity integrity, 845
equi-joins, 356
identity attribute, 28
imported worksheets, 253
importing HTML tables, 646
importing text files, 269
indexes, 844
linking FoxPro tables, 242
MSDE views, 961
new tables, 153
optimizing queries, 406
Order By property, 136
pasting numerous records, 281
Personnel Actions table, 472
referential integrity, 848-849
relationships, 172-174
resultset sort order, 358
second normal form, 828
sorting records, 206
Table Analyzer Wizard, correcting spelling errors, 840
tables with appended records, 418
validation rules, testing, 201

primary tables, 172, 820

Print events, 1099-1100

Print method, 1111

Print Preview, 72, 308
Run mode, 85
toolbar, 545

Print Query Definition dialog box, 842-843

Print Table Definition dialog box, 842

printable characters, 327

Printer Setup dialog box, 534

printers, 566

printing, 84
conventional reports, 558-561
crosstab queries, 403
embedded documents, 800
form footers, 529-530
form headers, 529-530
multicolumn reports, as mailing labels, 562-565
queries, Database Documenter, 842-843
queries as reports, 307-309
Relationships window, 354
report sections, 587
reports, 534
control alignment, 554
troubleshooting, 565-566

PrintOut method, 1111

private intranets, 598

Private scope, 1087

procedures. *See* **subprocedures**

Products on Hand by Category report, 552

ProductsAndSuppliersBy Category page, 679

Profile command, 900

Project Designer, 956

Project Explorer, class modules, 1089-1091

Project/Library list, displaying intrinsic constants, 1008

projects, viewing class modules, 1089-1091

properties, 816-817
AbsolutePage, 1066
constant enumeration, 1069
AbsolutePosition, 1066
recordsets, 1161
ActiveCommand, 1066
ActiveConnection, 1058, 1066
ActualSize, 1071
ADO, 1045-1047
Allow Additions, tentative append records, 470
Attributes, 1048, 1060, 1071
constant enumeration, 1061, 1072
AutoNumber field, 812
Back Color, 451
BOF, 1067
Bookmark, 1067
recordsets, 1163
border styles, 456
CacheSize, 1067
Caption, 493
field data types, 245
Tab control, 518
Column, 1136
list boxes, 1145
Column Count, 1134
Column Spacing, 564
Column Widths, 1134
combo boxes, 1145
Command object, 1057-1058
CommandBar object, startup, 1117
CommandText, 1058
CommandTimeout, 1048, 1058
CommandType, 1058
Connection, 1178
Connection object, 1048-1051
Errors collection, 1051
ConnectionString, 1048, 1055

ConnectionTimeout, 1048
Control Source, 497, 553
controls, referencing, 1119-1120
ControlSource, 1042
CursorLocation, 1048, 1067
constant enumeration, 1069
CursorType, 1067, 1178
constant enumeration, 1069
Data Link Properties sheet, 897
data modeling, 821-822
application databases, 822
conceptual data models, 821
diagrammatic databases, 823
schema, 824
subject databases, 823
DataMember, 1067
DataSource, 1067
Default View, 496
DefaultDatabase, 1048
DefinedSize, 1072
Description, Err object, 1017
Direction, 1060
Display When (Format), 530
EditMode, 1067
constant enumeration, 1070
EOF, 1067
Error object, 1051
Event, 78
Field Size, 143
fields, 137-140
overriding, 528-529
file sharing, 891-893
Filter, 77, 1067
constant enumeration, 1070
Fore Color, 455
Form, displaying in Design view, 1119
Format, 144-145, 556-557
forms
background bitmaps, 452
VBA, 1118-1119
Height, line spacing, 557

Index, 1067
Instancing, Project Explorer, 1090
Is Hyperlink, 954
IsolationLevel, 1048
constant enumeration, 1049
ItemData, list boxes, 1145
Keep Together, 561-562, 587
Link Child Fields, 584
Link Master Fields, 584
list boxes, 1145-1146
ListCount, list boxes, 1145
LockEdits, recorsets, 1164
LockType, 1067
constant enumeration, 1070
Long, 1059
MarshalOptions, 1067
MaxRecords, 1067
Mode, 1048
constant enumeration, 1050
MultiRow, Tab control, 518
Name, 1058, 1060, 1072
Field object, 1171
Network properties sheet, Access Control page, 932
NoMatch, 1068
Null value, 146
Number of Columns, 563
NumericScale, 1060, 1072
Object Browser, 1090
office charts, 733-734
Option Value, 497
OriginalValue, 1072
PageCount, 1068
PageSize, 1068
Parent, referencing controls, 1121
PercentPosition, 1069
recordsets, 1161
Permissions, 918
PersistFormat, 1068
Personnel Actions form, 465-466
subforms, 466-467
Picture, 453
Tab control, 518
Picture Alignment, 454
Picture Size Mode, 454

Picture Tiling, 455
Picture Type, 454
PivotTable control, 690
Precision, 1060, 1072
Prepared, 1058
Primary Key, 137
Provider, 1049
query updates, 383
Record Navigation control, 685-687
Record Source, 552, 1041
RecordCount, 1068, 1158
Recordset, 1039
    testing, 1158
Recordset object, 1066-1071
recordsets
    AbsolutePosition, 1161
    BOF (beginning of file), 1159-1161
    EOF (End of file), 1159-1161
RecordSource, 1153
Row Source, 1135, 1151
    Combo Box controls, 507
Row Spacing, 564
RowSource, 1136, 1153
Selected, list boxes, 1145
setting with With statement, 1007
Sharing properties page, 933
ShowDelButton, 686
Size, 1060
Size Mode, 738
Sort, 1068
Source, 1068
State, 1049, 1058, 1068
    constant enumeration, 1051
    recordsets, 1172
Status, 1068
    constant enumeration, 1070
Style, Tab control, 518
Tab control, 518-520
Tab Order, 473
Tab Stop, 474
TabFixedHeight, Tab control, 519
tables, 135-140
Text, referencing, 1120

Type, 1060, 1072
    constant enumeration, 1061
    Field object, 1174
UnderlyingValue, 1072
UniqueTable, 1044
Updatable, recordsets, 1164
User and Group Accounts properties sheet, 907
ValdationRule, 1122
Value, 1060, 1072, 1135
    assigning with VBA, 1007
Version, 1049

Properties sheet, MSDE tables, 959

Properties window, 39
    controls, 457
    Form Design view, 77
    Tab control, 519

property procedures, 998

property sheets, Options dialog, 100

protecting hardware, 903

protocols
    MSDE, 951
    URLs, 622

Provider property, 1049

Proxy Server, 604

Public keyword, 997

Public scope, 1087

publishing, 84

punched-card verification, 204

punctuation, SQL statements, 857

PurchaseSummary1997H1. doc, 786

pushers, 20

Pwd command, 900

PWS, 604

.px files, 233

Q

.qry files, 797
qry1997SalesMonthlyBy Category query, 723, 725
qryChartWizard query, 713

qryDrillDown error, 1150
qryPersonnelActions, 489
qryPivotTable query, 767
qualifiers (SQL), 855
    HAVING, 861
Quarterly Orders by Product page, 680
quarterly product sales crosstab query, 396-400
queries, 294
    Action, 311, 410
    action
        alternatives, 428
        deleting records, 418-421
        DML, 868-869
    ADP, 953
    append, 416-418
    as table properties, 373
    AutoNumber field, 847
    categories of, 354
    CCur conversion function, 338
    Chart Web Control, 729-730
    charts, 710
    Combo Box controls, 507
    combo boxes, 1128-1129
        adding to forms, 1131-1134
        ADP (Access Data Projects) conversion, 1138
        designing, 1129
        importing form, 1139
        Row Source SQL statements, 1140-1141
        SQL statement, 1135
        VBA code, 1135-1138
    copying to Clipboard, 309
    creating Web pages from, 634-636
    criteria, 305
    Crosstab, 294, 311, 396
    crosstab
        fixed column headings, 402-403
        graphs from, 723
        monthly product sales query, 400-402
        quarterly product sales query, 396-400
    DAP with AutoPage, 679

Database Documenter, printing, 842-843
designing, 315-317
DISTINCTROW keyword, 877
drill down, list boxes, 1142-1143
exporting datasheets to HTML, 628-631
expressions, 341-344
    calculating field values, 347-348
    Expression Builder, 345-346
    failure to execute, 349
external databases, IN clause, 870
form letters, 797-798
formatting data, 384-386
from external databases, 403-405
graphs, 710-712
linking tables, 82
list boxes, 1130-1131
mail merge documents, data sources, 786
main form, 487
make-table, 311-313
    parameters, 313-314
    relationships, 414-415
    tblShipAddresses table, 416
.mdb files, 128
merging with MS Word, 309-310
multicolumn equi-joins, 362-365
multitable, 355-357
    optimizing, 406-407
nested, performance, 730
one-to-many relationships, lookup fields, 365
Parameter, 311, 393-394
parameter, data types, 394-395
PivotTable lists, 692-693
Quarterly Orders by Product, 681
Query Design window, 298-299
    column header names, 305-307
    complex, 303-305

printing as reports, 307-309
selecting fields, 299-302
selecting records, 302-304
record-selection criteria, Expression Builder, 345
records, linking graphs to, 725-728
reports, record source, 552
resultsets, sort order, 358
saving filters as, 223-224
Select, 311, 1146-1147
SELECT statement, 855-857
selecting records with VBA functions, 341
self-joins, 380
Simple Query Wizard, 294-298
SQL, 852
    custom queries, 882
SQL aggregate functions, 387
SQL statements, 858-860
    subqueries, 867-868
subdatasheets, 376-378
subreports, 576
summary, 296
tables with indirect relationships, 360-362
time-series summary, 711
TopNPercent, 587
troubleshooting
    linked tables are not updatable, 405
    missing objects, 405
    required fields, 315
    updating summary queries, 315
types of, 311
UNION, 354, 865-866, 1147
    combo boxes, 1169-1171
updatable forms, 1044
update, 421-424
    VBA expressions, 349
updating tables, 383-384
    formatting data, 384-386
viewing SQL, 855
Query Builder, 484
populating Combo Box control, 507-509

Query Design view, 298-299, 854, 1129
column header names, 305-307
complex queries, 303-305
crosstab queries, 400
displaying hidden tables, 361
filters, saving, 224
Personnel Actions table, 488
printing queries as reports, 307-309
SELECT queries, 855
selecting fields, 299-302
selecting records, 302-304
SQL statements, entering, 858
subqueries, 867
Query Field Properties window, 384-386
Query menu command, Append, 847
Query objects, 56
query optimization, 206
query resultsets, 303
QueryDef object
filters, 223
SQL queries, 881
question mark (?)
Like operator, 327
SQL statements, 857
Quick Sort, 208
Quit method, 1111
quotation marks (" "), comma-delimited text files, 273

R

radio buttons. *See* Option Button control
RaiseError statement, 1018
Rating static-value combo box, 511
RDBMSs (Relational Database Management Systems), 130-132, 825
compared to spreadsheets, 130
design, 814

keys, 820-821
methods, 818
normalization, 813,
  825-826
  fifth normal form,
    830-831
  first normal form,
    825-828
  fourth normal form, 830
  many-to-many relation-
    ships, 834-836
  many-to-one relationships,
    833-834
  one-to-many relationships,
    833
  one-to-one relationships,
    832-833
  second normal form, 828
  third normal form,
    829-830
replication, 815
rollups, 711
set theory, 825
SQL, 853
supplemental files, 233
tables, 820-821
theory, 849-850

RDO (Remote Data
  Objects), 1033

rdoQuery object. *See*
  Command object

RDS, 1035

Read Data permission, 918

Read Design permission,
  917

read-only access
  decision-support applica-
    tions, 1128
  one-to-one relationships,
    832

read-write DAP, 673-674

Record Navigation control,
  22, 658
  filtering/sorting, 681-682
  properties, 685-687
  read-write DAP, 673
  Review Products page, 663

record pointers, 86

Record Source property,
  552, 1041
  SQL queries, 881

record sources, calculated
  controls, 552-553

record-level locking, 35

record-navigation buttons,
  forms, 469

RecordChangeComplete
  event, 1080

RecordCount property,
  1068, 1158

records, 132
  adding, 193
  adding to Actions table,
    199-200
  append queries, 416-418
    troubleshooting, 427
  appending
    IN clause, 870
    Personnel Actions table,
      470-472
  calculations
    aggregate functions,
      387-388
    based on all records,
      388-391
    based on selected records,
      391-393
  cascading deletions, 72
    relationships, 425-426
    testing, 425
  cascading updates
    relationships, 425-426
    testing, 426-427
  committing changes, 473
  deleting with action queries,
    418-421
  duplicated, key fields, 172
  editing, 194
  editing existing, 472
  editing with subdatasheets,
    34
  equi-joins, 356
  filtering, 206, 212
    advanced form, 218-219
    by form, 215-218
    by selection, 213-215
    composite criteria,
      221-222

  compound criteria,
    219-221
  saving as queries, 223-224
  troubleshooting, 228
  finding matches, 209-212
  finding with Combo Box
    control, 512-515
  groups, 194
  importing with clipboard,
    278-281
  indirectly related, querying,
    361
  line-item, 711
  linking graphs to, 725-728
  locking, sharing files, 892
  navigating, 189
  orphan, 171
  orphan records, 849
  outer joins, 378
  pencil symbol, 471
  queries, selecting with VBA
    functions, 341
  relationships, 167
  replacing by pasting, 282
  rolling back changes, 473
  SELECT queries, 855
  selecting for Query Design
    queries, 302-304
  self-joins, 380
  sorting, ascending, 206, 208
  subdatasheets, 136, 204
  tentative append, 63, 470
  update queries, 421-424
  updating, file sharing, 892

Recordset object, 303
  binding controls,
    1041-1043
  creating, 1038
  disconnected, 1079
  DISTINCTROW state-
    ment, 879
  events, 1080
  Fields collection,
    1071-1073
  methods, 1074-1079
  OLE DB, 1037
  properties, 1066-1071
  SELECT queries, 857
  troubleshooting
    cursor types, 1080
    data providers, 1080
  updating queries, 383

Recordset property, 1039
testing, 1158

RecordsetChangeComplete event, 1080

recordsets
AbsolutePosition property, 1161
ADO, DAO comparison, 1179
BOF (beginning of file) properties, 1159-1161
Bookmark property, 1163
combo boxes, 1165-1167
arranging selections, 1169-1171
populating, 1168-1169
porting forms, 1178
value lists, 1174-1177
CRUD (Create, Read, Update, and Delete), 1164
data events, 1122-1123
deleting, rows, 1165
editing, 1164-1165
EOF (End of file) properties, 1159-1161
Find method, 1162-1163
firehoses, 1153
indirect relationship queries, 362
linking data to embedded worksheet cells, 772
list boxes, populating, 1171-1173
Move... methods, 1158-1159
row locking, 812
stored procedures, 1063, 1065
temporary, 1156-1158
updatable, troubleshooting, 1178-1179
VBA navigation buttons, 1156
virtual tables, 82

RecordSource property, 1153

Rectangle control, 483

rectangles, reports, 588

ReDim statement, 1006

Reference events, 1099-1100

References command (Tools menu), 1190

References dialog box, 1190

referencing, 998-1000

referential integrity, 65, 813
action queries, 410
cascading deletions/updates, 425
cutting records, 194
deleting records, 421
enforcing, 170-171
cascading updates/deletes, 172
field-level validation rules, 196
make-table queries, 414
relationships, 169
triggers, 968
updating queries, 384
upsizing, 972
validation rules, testing, 201

reflexive relationships, 833-834

Refresh Data command (Data menu), 755, 758

Refresh Data menu choice, disabled, troubleshooting, 774

Refresh method, 1059

refreshing, file sharing, 893

Registry
Control Wizards, 532
editing, 888
four-digit year formatting, 145
Word 2000 entries, troubleshooting, 804

relational algebra, 825

relational databases. *See* **RDBMSs**

relational tables, 820-821

Relationship dialog box, 834

relationships, 64, 129, 131, 166-171, 831-832
cascading deletions/updates, 425-426
changing, 179-180

circular, 356
defining, Personnel Actions table, 487
diagramming, 965-966
displaying, 356
enforcing referential integrity, 171
cascading updates/deletions, 172
indexes, 174-175
indirect, queries, 360-362
lookup fields, 365
make-table queries, 414-415
many-to-many, 834-836
many-to-one, 833-834
new tables, troubleshooting, 427
one-to-many, 355, 833
one-to-one, 832-833
outer joins, 378
primary keys, 172-174
referential integrity, 65
reflexive, 833-834
updating queries, 384

Relationships window, 167-168, 833
printing, 354
_1, _2 suffixes on tables, 370

relative links, path prefixes, 630

relative paths, 607

remote databases
MSDE
SQL Server Client Network Utility, 981-982
testing/using, 982-983
troubleshooting connections, 986

Rename method, 1111

Rename Table dialog box, 837

RepaintObject method, 1111

Repair command, 900

repairing databases, 120, 938-939

repetitive stress injury (RSI), 186

Replace dialog box, 213

replacing
records, 194
values, 212-213

replication, 815
ADP, 954
MSDE, 947

Report class modules, 1084

Report Design mode, toolbar, 544

Report Footers, deleting, 586

report modules, 996
Error event, 1018

Report Snapshots, 39, 588
Relationships diagrams, 354

Report View, print margins, 558

Report Wizard
aligning/formatting controls, 554-556
calculated controls, 551
calculated fields, 553-555
record source, 552-553
deleting/relocating/editing controls, 546-551
formatting controls, 556-557
line spacing, 557-558
grouping reports, 536-543
by numeric values, 571
grouping/sorting data, 570
mailing lists, 562

Report Wizards, 534

reports, 72-73
adding controls, 588
adding images, 742
aligning/formatting controls, 554-556
AutoFormat, 545
bound, linking subreports, 581-584
bound object frame control, 734
employee photo, 735-738
photos, 735
scaling graphic objects, 737-740

calculated controls, 551
calculated fields, 553-555
record source, 552-553
categories of, 535
compared to forms, 534-535
controls, referencing, 1120
creating, 570
customizing, sections, 585-587
DAP Page Wizard, 674
data presentation, 82
designing, 591
exporting to HTML, 639, 641-642
formatting controls, 556-557
line spacing, 557-558
functions, 350
grouping data, 570-571
by alphabetic code characters, 572
by data and time, 574
by numeric value, 571-572
by range, 573-574
with subgroups, 573
imported text files, 271
linking, troubleshooting, 591
mailing in Snapshot format, 588-589
.mdb files, 128
Monthly Sales by Category report, 578-581
multicolumn, printing, 562-565
new features, 38-39
Page Footer, 529
Page Headers, 529
pagination, 543
PivotTables
formatting, 763-764
PivotCharts from, 765
printing, 558-561
troubleshooting, 565-566
printing queries as, 307-309
query design, 317
reducing length, 587
Report Wizard, editing controls, 546-551
Security wizard, 924

Snapshots, troubleshooting, 591
sorting data, 570-571, 574-575
SQL queries, 880-881
subreports, 576-577
unbound, 584-585
unbound graphs, 723
viewing in Snapshot format, 589-590
windows, 543-545

Reports collection, 1118

Requery method, 1076, 1111, 1136

Required property, 139

reserved words
ANSI SQL compared to Jet SQL, 873-875
INNER JOIN, 365
SQL, 852
WithEvents, 1056

resizing, DAP controls, 683

resolution, form design, 475

Restore method, 1111

restricting access, one-to-one relationships, 832

result sets
duplicates, eliminating, 362
multicolumn equi-joins, 363
query design, 315
SELECT queries, 855
sort order, 358, 360
UNION queries, 865

Resume keyword, 1017

Resync method, 1076

reverse video, 190, 463

reversed transactions, 904

Review Oders page, 667-668

Review Products page, 663-666

revoking persmissions, 917-918

RIGHT OUTER JOIN, MSDE views, 963

right outer joins, 378

Ro command, 900-901, 928

Rocket eBook, 124

RollbackTrans method, 1054

RollbackTransComplete event, 1057

rolled back transactions, 904

rolling back changes, 473

rollups, 711, 1128

Round rounds, 992

Row Height dialog box, 226

Row Source property, 370, 1135, 1151
  Combo Box controls, 507
  combo boxes, upsizing to Transact SQL, 1140-1141
  crosstab queries, 723
  Find Record combo box, 515

Row Spacing property, 564

rows, 132
  changing height, 226
  locking, 812
    action queries, 410
  recordsets
    deleting, 1165
    editing, 1164-1165

Rowset objects, 1036

rowsets, 1034

RowSource property, 1136, 1153

rpt1997MonthlyCategory Sales report, 581

rpt1997MonthlyCategory Sales subreport, 583-584

RSI (repetitive stress injury), 186

Run mode, 84, 301
  Default View, property values, 496. See also Form view

Run permission, 917

Run-Time Error '2465' messages, 1152

RunApp method, 1111

RunCode macro action, 997

RunCode method, 1111

RunCommand method, 1111

RunMacro method, 1112

RunSQL method, 1112
  SQL queries, 881

Runtime Access 2000, 887

Runtime command, 900

runtime errors, 1016-1017
  Err object, 1017-1018
  Error event, 1018

S

s placeholders, 148

Sales page, 671-672

Save Import/Export Specification dialog box, 645

Save method, 1076, 1112

saving
  embedded documents, 800
  filters as queries, 223-224
  snapshots of PivotTable query results, 751

sbfPATest subform, 527

sbfPersonnelActions subform, arranging controls, 465

Scale property, 139

scaling graphics, 737-740

schema information, 824, 1056

scope, 1003-1005
  static variables, 1005

screen resolution, toolbar icons, 94

ScreenTips, 94, 598, 618-619
  toolbar buttons, 486

scripts, 1028

scrollable cursors, 1034

.sdf files, 274

SDI applications, 87

SDI emulation, 40

search and replace, 206

Search Only Current Field option, 470

searching
  hyperlinks, 611
  indexes, 174

Second function, 334

second normal forms (normalization), 828

sections (reports), 535
  adding to reports, 585

SectionUnbound object, Height property, 695

secure files, Access 9x to 2000 conversion, 1186-1187

security, 84, 814, 902
  application-level, 906
  Database Documenter, 842
  database level, 917-918
  file-level, 906
  groups, 906
    adding users, 912
    Admins (Administrators), 906-912
    creating, 913-914
    deleting, 914
    erasing passwords, 914
    memberships, 912-913
  MSDE, 983-986
  multiuser, 906
  one-to-one relationships, 832
  ownership, changing, 918-925
  passwords, 904-905
  permssions
    changing, 918-926
    granting, 927-929
  principles of, 902-904
  user-level, 932-934

Security wizard, 915
  permissions, changing, 918-925

Seek method, 1076

Select Case statements, 1012-1014

Select Data Source dialog box, 239

Select Directory Containing Free Tables dialog box, 241

Select Objects tool, 482

Select queries, 311, 429, 855-857, 1146-1147
converting to make-table queries, 413-414
converting to update queries, 423
creating with SQL statements, 858
dynamic Web pages, 648
making for make-table queries, 411-412
MSDE views, 964
subdatasheets, 376
subqueries, 867
UNION queries, 865

Select Source Tables dialog box, 977

Select Unique Record Identifier dialog box, 242

Select Workgroup Information File dialog box, 898-899

Selected property, list boxes, 1145

selected text, filtering, 213

selecting
controls, 457-458
records, 194
rectangular data blocks, 190

selecting all, list boxes, 1146-1149

selection criterion, parameters, 313

selection rectangle, 461

selections, combo boxes, arranging, 1169-1171

SelectObject method, 1112

self joins, 356, 380-381

semicolon (;)
recordsets, 1168
SQL statements, 858

SendKeys, 1188

SendKeys method, 1112

SendObject method, 1112

SEQUEL, 854

server aliases, Client Network Utility, 981

Server Network Utility, 951

server round-trip, 649

server-side components, 604-605

servers
desktop database-development applications, 233
sharing files, 934-935, 940-942
workgroups, sharing, 935

service providers, 1034

services, 601
foreign , 821

Services Accounts dialog box, 950

Session objects, 1036

session timeouts, 652

SET command, SQL update queries, 869

Set Database Password dialog box, 904-905

Set instruction, ADO objects, 1037

Set keyword, named database objects, 1007

Set statement, named arguments, 1054

set theory, 825

SetMenuItem method, 1112

Setup Type dialog box, 47, 948

Setupsql.exe, 948

SetValue method, 1112

SetWarnings method, 1112

SGML, 598

shapes, 588

sharing files, 887
backups, 938
client/server comparisons, 940-942
creating folders, 887-891
DAP. See DAP
Options properties sheet, 891-893
servers, 934-935
splitting databases, 893-895

starting command options, 899-901
workgroups, 898-899
accessing, 935
refreshing links, 936-937
system file, 935-936
UNC, 935-936

Sharing properties page, 933

Shift+Delete, 191

Shift+Enter, 191

Shift+F1 key, 97
context-sensitive help, 108

Shift+F12 key, 97

Shift+F8 key, 189

Shift+spacebar key, 189

Shift+> key, 189

Shift+< key, 189

ShipCountry dimension, 762

Shipping Address table, make-table queries, 412

Short Date format, 37, 146

Short Date mask, updating queries, 386

shortcut keys, 191. See also function keys
Clipboard commands, controls, 462
VBA modules, 1021

shortcut menus, 96

shortcuts, objects, 37

shorthand codes, 434

Show Database Window button, 156

Show Direct Relationships button, 356

Show Me menu, 93, 1116

Show ScreenTips on Toolbars check box, 94

Show Table dialog box, 299
Relationships window, 168

Show the Office Assistant, 115

ShowAllRecords method, 1113

ShowDelButton property, 686

ShowHelpAPI function, 1116

ShowSales form, 1121

SID (system ID), 925

Simple Provider, 1034

Simple Query Wizard, 294-298

Single Form view, 496

single quote ('), SQL statements, 857

single-column equi-joins, 357-359

single-column reports, 535

single-document interface, 40

single-field indexes, 174

single-line bound text boxes, 493

single-line text boxes, 493

Site Server, 604

sites
Development Exchange, 1153
Southeast Texas-East Bay Music Connection, 1192

Size Mode property, 738

Size property, 1060

sizing
controls, 459, 555
Label control, 491
multiple controls, 492

Slate Web site, 655

slicing PivotTable data, 757-759

snaking column style, 564

Snap to Grid, 459

Snapshot Viewer, 39
mailing reports, 588-589
PivotTable query results, saving, 751
troubleshooting, 591
viewing reports, 589-590

snooping utilities, security, 903

.snp files, 588

Social Security numbers
input masks, 150
replaced by AutoNumber field, 157

Sort Ascending button, 209
Form view, 469

Sort Ascending toolbar, Help window, 112

Sort Descending button, Form view, 469

sort fields, SQL statements, 860

Sort property, 1068

sorting, 206-207. *See also* filtering
advanced, 218-219
copying sorted datasheets, 227
Knuth, Donald E., 228
MSDE views, 960
MSQuery, 795
multifield, 219-221
multiple fields, 208-209
original order, 209
query design, 315
Query Design queries, 302-304
Record Navigation control, 681-682
report data, 570-571, 574-575
resultset order, 358, 360
single fields, 208
Table Datasheet toolbar, 90
thawing fields, 209

Sorting and Grouping dialog box, 570, 574
Keep Together property, 562

Sorting and Searching (Donald E. Knuth), 228

sound clips, 740

Source property, 1068
SQL queries, 881

sources. *See* data sources

Southeast Texas-East Bay Music Connection Web site, 1192

space character, HTML, 651

spacing
exporting data to Word, 284
field names, 159
merge data field names, 784
report controls, 554-558

spaghetti code, 1011

Special Effects button, 455

specifications, 659

splat character (*), 327

Spreadsheet control, 22

spreadsheets
compared to RDBMSs, 130
importing, 248-256
troubleshooting, 288
linking, 256-258
normalization, 828

Spurious Paramater messages, 1153

SQL (Structured Query language), 852-853
Access support, 953
aggregate functions, 387-388, 861-863
compatibility, operators, 327
CONVERT function, 962
custom queries, 882
extensions, 853
forms, 880-881
joins, 863-865
keywords, AS, 861
macros, 880-881
newline pairs, 857
object separator, 328
punctuation, 857-858
queries, creating, 858-860
Query Builder, populating Combo Box controls, 507
query combo boxes, 1135
Transact-SQL upsizing, 1140-1141
Recordset object, creating, 1038
reports, 880-881
reserved words, 852
SELECT statement, 855-857
stored procedure, 1063
subqueries, 867-868

syntax, 854
table name qualifiers, 224
unexpected Enter
  Parameter dialog, 881
UNION queries, 865-866
updating, 429-430
viewing statements, 855
views, 944
white space, 858, 967
wild cards, 857

SQL button, 961

SQL Server
ADP, 953-954
advantages, 988
Books Online, 947
Client Network Utility,
  981-982
downsizing to Jet, 975
integrity, 814
MSDE, 945-946
OLAP Services, 1033
triggers, 968
updating with stored procedures, 430
upgrading from MSDE,
  941-942
views, 832

SQL Server 7
Books Online, 853
compared to MSDE, 25
conforming with Jet, 35-36
Microsoft English Query
  (MEQ), 882

SQL-92, 853

square brackets ([...])
collection names, 1118
validation rules, 197

stacked column charts, 721

standard modules, 995

standardized forms, 451

star character (*), 327

**starting workgroups, com-
mand options, 899-901**

Startup mode, 84
CommandBar settings,
  1117

**State property, 1049, 1058,
1068**
constant enumeration, 1051
recordsets, 1172

**statement autocompletion,
1025**

statements. *See also* **SQL**
BEGIN TRANSACTION,
  430
Call, error processing, 1018
Case, 1013
Case Else, 1013
conditional, 1011
  If...Then, 1011-1012
  Select Case, 1012-1014
contents of, 321
CREATE TABLE , 845
Do Until...Loop, 1015
Do While...Loop,
  1015-1016
ElseIf, 1012
End If, 1146
End Select, 1012-1014
Error, 1018
Exit Do, 1015
Exit For, 1014
For...Next, 1014-1015
If...Then, 1146
INSERT, 430
INSERT INTO, append
  queries, 871
JOIN, 863
looping, 1014
On Error GoTo, 1016
Option Compare, 1027
Option Explicit, 1003
ORDER BY, 1140
queries, creating, 858-860
RaiseError, 1018
SELECT, 429, 855-857
  UNION queries, 865
SQL, query combo boxes,
  1135
Stop, 1157
TRANSACTION, 430
While...Wend, 1016

**static (adOpenStatic) cursor,
1158**

static controls, 434

Static keyword, 1005
arrarys, 1006

static labels, 490

static properties, 816-817

static variables, 1005

static Web pages, 628
exporting reports to, 640

Status bar, 86

Status property, 1068
constant enumeration, 1070

StDev function, 387

StDevP function, 387

Step keyword, 1014

Stop statement, 1157

**StopAllMacros method,
1113**

StopMacro method, 1113

stored procedures, 26
ADP, 956, 966-968
Command object, 1057
  *passing parameter values,
  1063-1065*
Command object proper-
  ties, 1061
Command objects, 1036
MSDE, 946
passing variables, 858
triggers, 968-969
updating, 430

Straight Edge theme, 676

StrComp function, 336

stretching images, 739

**String data type, conversion
functions, 338-339**

string functions, 335, 992

string variables, 1004

strings
concatenating, 195, 325
Input Mask property, 139
Null value, 146

structured statements, 1011

structures. *See* **user-defined
data types**

**Style property, Tab control,
518**

styles
AutoFormat, reports, 545
AutoFormats, 448
borders, 455
forms, 440
reports, 541
storing, 546

Sub keyword, 997

subaddresses, Hyperlink data type, 611

Subdatasheet Expanded property, 136

Subdatasheet Height property, 136

Subdatasheet Name property, 136

subdatasheets, 56, 136, 204
  adding to queries, 376-378
  adding to tables, 374-375
  browse-mode editing, 406
  compared to lookup fields, 373
  optimizing, 406
  related records, viewing/editing, 34
  subforms, 434

Subform control, 483

subform editing, 527

Subform/Subreport Wizard, 523-527

subforms, 66, 434
  column visibility, 466
  fitting in main forms, 467
  in-situ, 39
  properties, 466-467
  referencing controls, 1120

subgroups, grouping report data, 573

subject databases, 823
  data modeling, 823

subprocedures, 997
  arguments, 1009
  calling, troubleshooting, 1123
  event handling, Command Button Wizard, 1092
  FillList, 1149
  function parameters, 1096
  instances, 1005
  naming, 1096
  property, 998
  security, 84

Subreport Field Linker dialog box, 582

subreports, 535, 576-577
  linking to bound report, 581-584
  unlinked, 584-585

subroutine. *See* subprocedures

subscription scheme, 51

subtraction, 323

subtypes, 141
  Number, 142-143

suits, 743

Sum function, 387-389, 862
  ANSI vs Jet, 875

summary calculations, SQL aggregate functions, 387

Summary Options button, 540

Summary Options dialog box, 540

summary queries
  converting to parameter query, 393
  crosstab, 396
  Simple Query Wizard, 296
  updating, troubleshooting, 315

supplemental files, 233

Suppliers Import Specification dialog box, 643

Suppliers.html, 629

Supports method, 1077
  constant enumerations, 1078

Switchboard forms, 66
  adding to existing dbs, 121-123
  control-based hyperlinks, 621
  data-entry forms, 67
  Design view, 77

Switchboard Manager, 75-77

Switchboard Manager dialog box, 121

symbolic constants, 339, 1008
  intrinsic, 1008-1009
  system defined, 1008

symbols, SQL statements, 857

synchronizing forms, 69

syndicated data, 776

SysCmd function, 1024

system data sources, 650

System Database dialog box, 792

system defaults, 100
  advanced, 104-105
  edit/find, 103
  general, 101-102
  keyboard, 104
  view, 100

System ID (SID), 132, 925

system tables, 234

system-defined constants, 1008

System.mdw, 132, 887

T

Tab Control, 483, 516
  adding pages, 516
  deleting pages, 518
  events, 1103
  page order, 517
  placing other controls, 520
  properties, 518-520

Tab key, 189

tab order, removing fields from, 474

Tab Order property, 473

Tab Stop property, 474

tab-delimited text files, 275

TabFixedHeight property, Tab control, 519

Table Analyzer Wizard, 826, 836-838, 840-841
  duplicate fields, Invalid procedure call message, 839
  Method 'Selected' of object failed message, 839
  typographical errors, correcting, 840

Table Datasheet view
Clipboard operations, 190
customizing, 225
filtering, 206
sorting, 206
toolbars, 89-91
Formatting, 91-92

Table Design view
ADP, 957
field properties, 137
grid, 157

table locking, 892

Table objects, Contact Management application, 62-66

table of contents, Help window, 109

Table Properties window, 135, 137

TABLE tag, 662

Table Wizard, 151-156

tables, 132, 820. *See also* **records; reports; queries**
action queries, 410
adding records, 193
adding to existing databases, 156-157
designing, 158-160
adding to MSDE views, 962
ADP, 955
append queries, 416-418
appending data to, 417
appending text data, 277
auditability, 903
bound reports, linking subreports, 581
browse-mode editing, 428
committing changes, 473
components, 86
converting to tab-delimited format, 309
copy and paste, 180-181
creating in Datasheet view, 164
creating with Jet DDL, 872-873
current record, 68
DAP grouped pages, 701-703

DAP with AutoPage, 679
data entry, test data, 186
dBASE IV, 872
deleting, 156, 181
deleting duplicated data, 411
displaying embedded documents, 802
displaying in Query Design window, 361
document management systems, 799
duplicated records, preventing, key fields, 172
editing records, 194
editing related records with subdatasheets, 34
entities, combining, 818-819
equi-joins, 356
exporting to HTML, 628-631
exporting to Outlook Contacts folder, 258-262
fields
altering, 176
data types, 178-179
default values, setting, 165-166
formatting, 140-141
making all accessible, 386
Null value, 146
rearranging sequence, 176-178
filtering, 206, 212
advanced, 218-219
by form, 215-218
by selection, 213-215
composite criteria, 221-222
compound criteria, 219-221
saving as queries, 223-224
filters, removing, 223
fixed-value lookup lists, 370-372
flat tables, 825
formatting, overriding, 384
freezing fields, 207
hierarchical display, 406
HTML, file sizes, 634
importing, 233

indexes. *See* indexes
ISAM, linking/importing, 235-238
Jet properties, 958
joins, 131, 354
multitable queries, 355-357
SQL statements, 863-865
linking, 82
relinking with Linked Table Manager, 245-246
linking versus importing, 246-247
Lookup, creating, 836
lookup fields, 365-366
foreign key drop-down lists, 366-370
reports, 549
make-table action queries, 313
make-table queries, 411
converting select query, 413-414
designing/testing, 411-412
designing/testing select query, 412
relationships, 414-415
tblShipAddresses table, 416
matching records, 209-212
.mdb files, 128, 818
MSDE, 957-960
multicolumn equi-joins, 362
name qualifiers, SQL, 224
naming, 183
spaces, 159
normalization, 813
object paradigm, 818
opening objects with hyperlinks, 619-620
optimizing performance, 844
outer joins, 378
overhead, 181
Personnel Actions table
adding records, 199-200
creating, 160-165
properties, 135-140
overriding, 528-529
queries, as table properties, 373

records, linking graphs to, 725-728

Recordset object, 303

relational databases, 820-821

relationships, 64, 166-171
changing, 179-180
diagramming, 965-966
enforcing referential integrity, 171-172
indexes, 174-175
primary keys, 172-174
troubleshooting, 427

rolling back changes, 473

rollups, 711

self-joins, 380

sorting, 206-207
thawing columns, 209

subdatasheets, 374-378

Table Analyzer wizard. *See* Table Analyzer wizard

Table Wizard, 151-156

updating multiple records, 421-424

updating with queries, 383-384
formatting data, 384-386

upsizing, 972

validation rules, 197-199

VBA, 1000

viewing, 85

Visual FoxPro, linking with ODBC, 238-242

Word documents, 798-802

Tables page, 960

tabular reports, 535

tags, 630
Access HTML Template, 638
DOM, 662
TD, 632
TR, 632

tamper-proofing, 903

tblShipAddresses table, 416
make-table queries, 416
relationships, 414
update queries, 421

TD tag, 632, 662

telephone numbers, input masks, 150

templates
creating applications from, 57-62
creating new databases, 133
HTML, 637-638
exporting query datasheets to, 638-640

temporary employees, security, 904

temporary recordsets, 1156-1158

tentative append record, 63, 193, 470
updating tables, 383

test tables, cascading deletions/updates, 425

testing forms, 473

text, 327
colored backgrounds, 451
concatenating, 325
formatting, 491-492
line spacing, 557

Text Box control, 434, 482, 493
alignment, 554
binding to Recordset object, 1041
bound controls, 480
bound, 493-494
calculated, 494-495
events, 1101
Form Wizard, 441
formatting text, 491-492
function keys, 97-98
Monthly Sales by Category report, 580
reassigning values with VBA, 1007
shortcut keys, 191

text comparison options, 1027

text controls
changing content, 463
Formatting toolbar, 446

Text data type, 140
fixed-width, 143-144
input mask placeholders, 150
parameter queries, 394

Text Export Wizard, 285

Text fields, changing data types, 179

text files
appending to tables, 277
exporting data as, 284-286
importing, 264-265
delimited, 273-275
fixed-width, 276
Import Text Wizard, 266-273
troubleshooting, 288
viewing, 274

text manipulation functions, 335-338

Text property, referencing, 1120

text-coding schemes, grouping reports, 539

text-formatting commands, Datasheet Formatting toolbar, 91

text-identifier characters, 273-275

thawing fields, 209

themes, 21
DAP, 676

theta joins, 356
not-equal with criteria, 382-383

thin-client computing, 625

third normal forms (normalization), 829-830

.tif files, 741

time
calculated text boxes, 494
grouping report data, 574

time data type, conversion functions, 338-339

Time Delimiter, 272

time functions, 333-335

time-series crosstab queries, SQL, 869

time-series graphs, 710

time-series summary queries, 711

Time/Date control, copying with Clipboard, 501

TimeSerial function, 334
TimeValue function, 335
Timing events, 1099-1100
TITLE tag, 662
To modifier, 1006
Toggle Button control, 482
  events, 1101
toggle buttons, 91
toggling, 188
  selecting controls, 459
toolbars
  adding/deleting buttons,
    485
  anchoring, 484
  Customize dialog, 486
  customizing, 93-96,
    484-486
  Database window, 37, 86
  deleting, 486
  displaying, 93
  docking, 94, 484
  Form Design window,
    443-444
  Formatting, 446-447
  PivotTable lists, 693
  Print Preview mode, 545
  Report Design mode, 544
  repositioning, 95
  resetting to default, 486
  Table Datasheet view,
    89-91
    Formatting, 91-92
  VBA Module window,
    1019-1020
Toolbox, 442, 480-483
  adding controls, 487
  adding controls to reports,
    588
  Bound Object Frame, 736
  docking, 484
  Label control, 490
  PivotTable control, 690
  unbound object frames, 767
tools
  ADP, 26
  Color Builder, 456-457
Tools menu commands
  Analyze, 842
  Database Utilities, 938
  References, 1190

ToolTips, 94
top-down data modeling,
  821
top-level ADO, 1039
TopN queries, 587
TopNPercent queries, 587
Total row, aggregate functions, 388
TPL (Transaction
  Processing Language), 854
TR tags, 632, 662
Transact-SQL. *See also* SQL
  comment identifiers, 967
  Jet function comparisons,
    1150-1151
  MSDE, 946
  Row Source SQL upsizing,
    1140-1141
  stored procedures, 966
  string concatentation, 325
transaction isolation level,
  Connection object properties, 1049
transaction logs, MSDE, 946
transaction processing, 435
  VBA code, 993
TRANSACTION state-
  ments, 430
transaction-processing
  forms, 435
  data sources, 435
  Form view toolbar buttons,
    468-469
  Form Wizard, 436-441
  Personnel Actions form,
    469
    appending records,
      470-472
    committing/rolling back,
      473
    editing data, 472
  visual layout, 452
transactions, 817
  Connection object, proper-
    ties, 1049
  reversed, 904
TransferDatabase method,
  1113

TransferSpreadsheet
  method, 1113
TransferText method, 1113
TRANSFORM statement,
  crosstab queries, 869
transitive dependency, 829
Transparent button, forms,
  452
transparent controls, 462
triggers, 27, 31, 814
  ADP, 968-969
trigonometric functions, 329
troubleshooting, 1153
  appending records, 427
  AutoNumber, gaps in field
    values, 182
  AutoNumber field, 849
  calling procedures/func-
    tions, 1123
  charts, axis reversed, 743
  collections, missing objects,
    1124
  Command object, spaces in
    names, 1081
  constraint conflict errors,
    1044
  converting, compile errors,
    123
  copying controls, error
    messages, 530
  corrupted databases, 120
  DAP
    lost data sources, 704
    lost style, 704
  embedding workbooks in
    object frames, 775
  expression queries, four-
    digit dates, 349
  filtering, records not found,
    228
  HTML table import, 654
  importing
    fixed-width text files, 288
    spreadsheets, 288
  incorrect password, 287
  indexes, extras added, 182
  intranet connections, 623
  libraries, 1191
  link expression errors, 591
  memo files, 287

null index value, 287
object frames, unappearing adornments, 775
OLE
opening, 743
Word Document entry, 804
paths, 940
printing reports
blank pages, 565
Parameters dialog, 566
PWS, installing, 604
queries
linked tables are not updatable, 405
missing objects, 405
required fields, 315
updating summary queries, 315
query expressions, failure to execute, 349
Recordset object, data providers, 1080
Recordset object, cursor types, 1080
recordsets, updating, 1178-1179
Refresh Data menu choice, disabled, 774
relationships, new tables, 427
remote databases, 986
reports, Snapshots, 591
Run-Time Error '2465', 1152
SQL queries, unexpected Enter Parameter dialog, 881
updgrading, 1192-1193
validation rules
error messages from validation enforcement, 203
field property paste failures, 202
multiple record selection paste failures, 202
truncation, 178
turning off data-type checking, 331
tutorials, Help window, 110
twips, margins, 102

Type keyword, 1005
Type property, 1060, 1072
constant enumeration, 1061
Field object, 1174
type styles, Database Wizard, 60
type-declaration character, 1000
Typical Themes, 676

U

UDA, MSDE, 26
UDFs, 993
unbound combo boxes, record selection, 514
unbound controls, 481
Unbound Header section, Analyze Sales page, 669
unbound labels, 490
Unbound Object control, 482
unbound object frames
embedding Excel worksheets, 767
reports, 588
unbound reports, 535, 584-585
unbound text boxes, 493
UNC (Uniform Naming Convention), 935
UnderlyingValue property, 1072
underscore (_)
spaces in merge data field names, 784
SQL statements, 857
Unhide Columns dialog box, 225
Unicode, 35, 143
ADP, 953
Substitution Font, 46
support, 812
Uniform Naming Convention (UNC), 935
uninstalling MSDE, 952

UNION queries, 354, 865-866, 1147
combo boxes, arranging selections, 1169-1171
Unique Records property, 363
updating queries, 383
Unique Values Only test, 427
Unique Values property, updating tables, 383
UniqueTable property, 1044
Universal Data Access, 1032
UNIX, .html files, 628
unlinked graphs, 712-717
unlinked subreports, 584-585
unnormalized data, 826
unprintable characters, 327
unsecured files, Access 9x to 2000 conversion, 1182, 1184-1186
unsetting passwords, 905
unstructured analysis, 775
Until keyword, 1015
up arrow key, 189
updatable
forms, 1043
NorthwindCS MSDE database, 1043-1044
substituting DAO with ADO, 1044-1045
recordsets, troubleshooting, 1178-1179
Updatable property, recordsets, 1164
updatable tables, 193
Update Data permission, 918
Update method, 1077
update queries, 421-424
expressions, 349
SQL, 869
UpdateBatch method, 1077-1079

updating
browse-mode, 428
DAP links, 896
form-based, 429
records, file sharing, 892
SQL, 429-430
SQL Server stored proce-
dures, 430
with queries, 383-384
formatting data, 384-386

upgrading, 52
DAP, 52
data access components,
1032
file conversions, 886
linking features, 288
mdb files, 1182
problems, 1192-1193

**upsizing, Row Source SQL
statements, Transact-SQL,
1140-1141**

Upsizing Report, 974-975

**Upsizing Wizard, 31, 351,
969-974**
Upsizing Report, 974-975

**URLs (Uniform Resource
Locators), 622**
characters allowed, 608
http:// prefix, 617
Hyperlink data type, 611
linking to local files, 614
links to intranet pages, 617
prefixes supported, 622
relative paths, 607

**USAOrders.xls spreadsheet,
255**

**Use Four-Digit Year
Formatting options, 36**

**User and Group Accounts
properties sheet, 907**

**User and Group
Permissions dialog box,
915, 927**

User command, 900

User Information dialog, 47

user interface, forms, 434

**user-defined data types,
1005**

**user-defined error codes,
1018**

**user-defined functions
(UDFs), 993**

user-level security, 932-934

**User-Level Security wizard,
941**

usernames, 814
workgroups, 900

users, 906
adding to groups, 912
monitoring, 903
MSDE security, 984
permissions, 903
granting/revoking, 917

utilities
compacting, 118-120
Convert Database, 1186
converting to 2000 format,
120-121
converting to 97 format,
121
Database Splitter, 893-894,
941
Disk Defragmenter, 939
Linked File Manager,
936-937
Linked Table Manager, 895

**Utility Functions module,
329**
breakpoints, 1023-1024
Immediate window, Debug
object, 1025-1026
text comparison options,
1027

V

Val function, 336

validating data
data entry, 194-195
field-level rules, 195-197
table-level rules, 197-199
expressions, 340-341
functions, 320
overriding properties, 529

**Validation Rule property,
136, 139, 186**
referential integrity, 171

validation rules
[] (brackets), 197
comparison operators, 324

testing, 201-202
troubleshooting
*error messages from vali-
dation enforcement, 203*
*field property paste fail-
ures, 202*
*multiple record selection
paste failures, 202*

**Validation Text property,
136, 139**

**ValidationRule property,
1122**

**value lists, combo boxes,
1174-1177**

**Value property, 1060, 1072,
1135**
assigning with VBA, 1007

Value text box, 553

values
attribute, 820
combo lists, 1168
NULL, 831

VALUES keyword, 869

Var function, 387

variables
data types, 1001
declaring, 1002
duration, 1003-1005
explicit, 1002-1003
implicit, 1002
named database objects,
1007
naming conventions, 1002
Public, 997
scope, 1003-1005
SQL, user-declared, 858
SQL Server, 967
testing with Select Case,
1012
user-defined data types,
1005
viewing values in
Immediate window, 1025

Variant data type, 1001
functions, 331-333
index instructions, 173
subtypes, 332

VarP function, 387

varStart argument, 1078

VBA (Visual Basic for Applications), 992-993
ADO 2.1 Library, 1037
AppendChunk method, 1062
argument list, 330
argument variables, 1097
arguments, 1009
arrays, 1005-1006
Asc function, 573
Autocompletion ToolTip, 330
binding controls, 1041-1043
binding forms, ADODB.Recordset, 1040
breakpoints, 1023-1024
class modules, 1084
    Object Browser, 1089-1091
code, indenting, 1012
code editor, 56, 79
collections, troubleshooting, 1124
Command object, properties, 1058
CommandBar objects, 1113-1116
compiling, 1008
Connection object
    events, 1057
    methods, 1054
    properties, 1048
constants, 339
    intrinsic, 1008-1009
    system defined, 1008
control properties, 1119-1120
controls
    referencing, 1120-1121
    referencing by arguments, 1121
CreateParameter method, 1062
DAO, compared to ADO, 1037
data handling, ADO events, 1057
data types, 1000-1001
database objects, 1001
Debug object, 1025-1026
disconnected Recordsets, 1079

dynamic SQL, 854
Editor, 1018
    Help system, 1021-1022
editor, integrating with Access, 32
Editor
    Module window toolbar, 1019-1020
    shortcut keys, 1021
    statement autocompletion, 1025
Error object, properties, 1051
event handling
    Main Switchboard, 1085-1087
    responding with functions, 1096-1098
event-driven programming, 1084, 1124
events, record finding combo boxes, 514
Execute method, 1063
explicit variables, 1002-1003
expressions, 195
    creating, 340
    creating default values, 340
    query criteria, 341-348
    real world applications, 350-351
    update queries, 349
    validating data, 340-341
flow control, 1010
    conditional statements, 1011
    Do While...Loop, 1015-1016
    For...Next, 1014-1015
    GoTo statement, 1011
    If...Then statements, 1011-1012
    looping, 1014
    Select Case statements, 1012-1014
forms, properties, 1118-1119
Form_Load event handler, ADODB.Recordset object, 1040

functions, 328-329, 997
    code editor, 1096
    data-type conversion, 338-339
    date and time, 333-335
    Immediate window, 329-331
    text manipulation, 335-338
    Variant data type, 331-333
Graph9, 717
help files, 331
IDE, 20
identifiers, 328
implicit variables, 1002
Item method, 1051
listings
    binding updatable forms, 1044
    Command object, parameterized stored procedure, 1064
    writing Error properties to Immediate window, 1053
literals, 327-328
mdb files, 129
mde files, 123
Me self-identifier, 1119
modules, 73-74, 83, 995-996
    elements of, 997-998
MSDE views, 961
named database objects, 1007
naming conventions, 994
Null value, 146
Object Browser, ADODB, 1046
objects, 1000-1001
operators, 322
    arithmetic, 322-323
    assignment, 323-324
    comparisons, 323-324
    concatenation, 325
    identifier, 325-326
    logical, 324-325
Option Compare statements, 1027
Parameter object, properties, 1060

Parameter property, setting values, 1060
Parameters collection, methods, 1059
query combo boxes, 1135-1138
Recordset object
    methods, 1074
    properties, 1066
recordset navigation buttons, 1156
referencing, 998-1000
runtime errors, 1016-1017
    Err object, 1017-1018
    Error event, 1018
spaghetti code, 1011
SQL, 852
subprocedures
    naming, 1096
    troubleshooting, 1123
substituting numeric values, 1047
symbolic constants, 1008
temporary recordsets, 1156-1158
text comparison options, 1027
user-defined data types, 1005
validation functions, 320
Value property, 1072
variables
    duration, 1003-1005
    naming conventions, 1002
    scope, 1003-1005
    where to use, 993-994
With statement, 1007
WithEvents keyword, 1056
VBA Editor, 992
VBScript, 606, 1028
verification, 204
Verify SQL Syntax button, 961
Version property, 1049
vertical ruler, Form Design window, 443
video collection table, 152
view options, 46, 100
viewers, DAP, 22

viewing
    filtered records, 212
    linked graphs, 725
    maximized windows, 87
    Object Browser, 999, 1089
    PivotTables, collapsing/expanding, 760-762
    query design, 316
    records in subdatasheets, 34
    relationships, 356
    reports in Snapshot format, 589-590
    system tables, 234
    tables, 85-86
    text files, 274
views, 26, 83, 832
    ADP, 955
    Default View, properties, 496
    Form Design, 77-79
        combo boxes, 1132
        list boxes, 1131
    Form view, combo boxes, 1133
    freezing fields, 207
    MSDE, 960-964
    Query Design, 1129
views (SQL), 944
virtual directories, 607
Virtual Directory Wizard, 607-610
virtual tables, 82
viruses, tamper-proofing, 903
Visual FoxPro, 233
    Linked Table Manager, 245
    linking tables with ODBC, 238-242
visualizing data, 743
void functions, 997

W

W3C Recommendation, 659
WANs (Wide Area Networks)
    database designs, 814
    query design, 316

Web pages
    ASPs
        exporting queries to, 651-653
        ODBC data source, 650-651
    Chart Web Control, 728
    creating from queries, 634-636
    creating unformatted, 631-634
    DAP, 25
    design, graphics files, 639
    dynamic, 628, 648-649
    exporting query datasheets to, 628-631
    exporting reports to, 639, 641-642
    exporting tables to, 628-631
    horizontal scrolling, 635
    HTML templates, 637-638
        exporting query datasheets to, 638-640
    interactivity, 625
    linking to, 617-618
    static, 628
Web sites
    COM, 605
    DHTML, 606
    Digital Nervous System, 601
    Fawcette Technical Publishing's DevX, 655
    FrontPage 2000, 603
    HTML specification, 599
    IIS 4.0, 604
    InforModeler, 884
    MEQ, 883
    NetMeeting, 602
    NetShow, 605
    OLE DB, 1034
    ORM, 884
    Proxy Server, 604
    Scripting Technologies page, 606
    Site Server, 605
    Slate, 655
    Snapview, 588
    virtual directories (IIS), 607
    Windows DNA white paper, 601
    Windows Media, 603

Web-based decision support, 628

Weekday function, 335

WeekdayName function, 333, 335

Wend keyword, 1016

What's This? button, 107

WHERE clause, 856
equi-joins, 864
multiple joins, 864
query combo boxes, 1136

While keyword, 1015-1016

While...Wend statement, 1016

white space, 858
SQL statements, 967

widowed records, 561-562

width, flat tables, 825

Width property, columns, 563

wildcards
Like operator, 327
SQL statements, 857

WillChangeField event, 1080

WillChangeRecord event, 1080

WillChangeRecordset event, 1080

WillConnect event, 1057

WillExecute event, 1057

WillMove event, 1080

Win16 function calls, Win32 conversions, 1189

Window events, 1098-1099

windows
maximized, 87-88
minimized to icons, 88-89
Object Definition print preview, 843
Relationships, 833
reports, 543-545

Windows 9x
peer-to-peer networking, 929, 931-932
user-level security, 932-934

Windows Media, Internet client, 603

Windows NT
.htm files, 628
server-side components, 604

Windows Paint, 735

Windows Scripting Host (WSH), 1028

WinHelp32, 124

With statement, 1007

WithEvents reserved word, 1056

wizards, 56, 531-532
Access PivotTable, PivotTable forms, 747-754
Answer, 41, 112
Chart, unlinked graphs, 712-717
Combo Box, 503-507, 1131-1133
Command Button, event-handling code, 1092-1095
Control, 484
Control, list boxes, 1130
Create New Data Source, 239
Crosstab Query, 396-402
Database, 57-61
DTS, 975-980
Exchange/Outlook, 258
linking with, 262-264
Form, 436-441
Import Spreadsheet, 250
Import Text, 266-271
advanced options, 271-273
Input Mask, 151
Layout, 688
List Box, 1130
Lookup, 836
adding dropdown lists, 366-370
fixed-value lookup lists, 370-372
Mail Merge, 782
data sources, 786-789
form letters, 782-785
.mde files, 123
OCW, 728
Option Group, 497-501

Page, 674-679
Security, 915
permissions, 918-925
Simple Query, 294-298
Subform/Subreport, 523-527
Table, 151-156
Table Analyzer, 826, 836-838, 841
typographical errors corrected, 840
Text Export, 285
Upsizing, 31, 351, 969-974
Upsizing Report, 974-975
User-Level Security, 941
Virtual Directory, 607-610

Word 2000
bookmarks, linking to, 614-617
delimited text files, 275
embedded documents, displaying, 802-804
embedding/linking to tables, 798-802
exporting filtered datasheets to, 227
exporting sorted datasheets to, 227
exporting to with clipboard, 784
integrating, 782
mail merge
data sources, 786-789
databases, 789
form letters, 782-785
merging queries to, 309-310

Word Basic, 1028

WordPerfect
delimited text files, 275
secondary merge files, 273

workbooks, embedding, troubleshooting, 775

workflow systems, document processing, 566

Workgroup Administrator, sharing workgroups, 898

Workgroup Administrator (Wrkgadm.exe), 888-891

Workgroup Administrator dialog box, 891

workgroup files, 132
Access 9x to 2000 conversion, 1187
form default values, 447

Workgroup Owner Information dialog box, 889

workgroups
Access 2000 conversions, Access 9x, 1187
members, 886
permissions, granting, 928-929
shared
accessing, 935
refreshing links, 936-937
system file, 935-936
UNC (Uniform Naming Convention), 935-936
sharing, 898-899
starting command options, 899-901
System.mdw, 887

worksheets
adding PivotCharts, 764
embedding in forms, 767-770
extracting values from objects, 771-772
importing, 248-256
linking, 256-258
linking cell ranges, 772-774

World Wide Web. *See* **WWW**

Wrkgadm (Workgroup Administrator), 889-891

Wrkgadm.exe (Workgroup Administrator application), 888

Wrkgrp command, 900

Wrong data type message, 349

WWW (World Wide Web), 598
navigating with hyperlinks, 606-611
sites
Development Exchange, 1153
Southeast Texas-East Bay Music Connection, 1192

X - Y - Z

xBase files, linking/importing with images, 243

.xlc files, 247

.xls files, importing, 249

XML (eXtensible Markup Language), 21, 598, 660
upgrading Access, 53

XQL (eXtensible Query Language), 661

XSL (eXtensible Style Language), 661

y placeholders, 148

Y2K
four-digit date queries reverting to two-digit, 349
four-digit year formatting, 145
four-figit year format, 385
short date format, 957

Year function, 335

Yes! I Can Run My Business small-business accounting application, 592

Yes/No data type, formatting, 144

zero-length strings (""), 139

zip codes, sorting records, 208

zooming images, 739

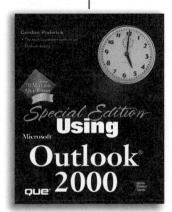

Other Related Titles

Roger Jennings Database Developer's Guide with Visual Basic 6
Roger Jennings
ISBN: 0-672-31063-5
$59.99 US /
$89.95 CAN

Platinum Edition Using Windows 98
Ron Person, et al.
ISBN: 0-7897-1489-2
$49.99 US / $74.95 CAN

F. Scott Barker's Microsoft Access 2000 Power Programming
F. Scott Barker
ISBN: 0-672-31506-8
$49.99 US / $74. 95 CAN

Alison Balter's Mastering Microsoft Access 2000 Development
Alison Balter
ISBN: 0-67-31484-3
$49.99 US / $74.95 CAN

Microsoft Access 2000 Development Unleashed
Stephen Forte
ISBN: 0-672-31291-3
$39.99 US / $59.95 CAN

Paul Sheriff Teaches Visual Basic 6
Paul Sheriff
ISBN: 0-7897-1898-7
$24.99 US / $37.95 CAN

Waite Group's Visual Basic Source Code Library
Brian Shea
ISBN: 0-672-31387-1
$34.99 US / $52.95 CAN

Database Access with Visual Basic
Jeffrey P. McManus
ISBN: 1-56276-567-1
$39.99 US / $59.95 CAN

Platinum Edition Using Access 2000
Roger Jennings
ISBN: 0-78698-?????-?
No price available yet

Using Microsoft SQL Server 7
Brad McGehee
ISBN: 0-7897-1628-3
$29.99 US /
$44.95 CAN

Sams Teach Yourself Microsoft SQL Server 7.0 in 21 Days
Richard Waymire and Rick Sawtell
ISBN: 0-672-31290-5
$39.99 US /
$59.95 CAN

que®
www.quecorp.com

All prices are subject to change.

cial Edition Using Microsoft Access 2000

ger Jennings

you for purchasing *Special Edition Using Microsoft Access 2000* by Roger Jennings, the most comprehensive book
h new and experienced Microsoft Access users. Please help us improve the next edition of *Special Edition Using
oft Access 2000* to best fit your needs by taking a few minutes to answer these questions and then returning the
to us.

n tear out this form and mail it to the address on the back.

---

es your job involve training other users to use Microsoft Access or Microsoft Office software or supporting other users in
help desk setting?
   Yes   ❑   No

d you purchase Access as part of Microsoft Office or as a standalone product?
   Standalone (please skip to question 4)
   Part of Office 2000 (please answer question 3)

hich version of Microsoft Office 2000 do you own?
   Small Business Edition   ❑   Premium Edition   ❑   Not Sure
   Professional   ❑   Developer Edition

o you have Microsoft Access for personal use, business application use, or to develop professional applications for clients?
check all that apply.)
   Personal   ❑   Business   ❑   Application Development

id you buy this book for personal use or daily reference on the job?
   Personal   ❑   Professional   ❑   Both

here did you buy this book?
   Bookstore   ❑   Direct from Publisher   ❑   Warehouse Club   ❑   Internet Site
   Computer Store   ❑   Office Club   ❑   Department Store   ❑   Consumer Electronics Store
   Mail Order   ❑   Other _____

What operating system do you have on the computer(s) on which you use Access 2000?
   Windows 95   ❑   Windows 98   ❑   Windows NT 4   ❑   Windows 2000   ❑   Not Sure

What other *Que Special Edition Using* books about Microsoft Office 2000 applications have you bought or do you plan to
uy?

pecial Edition Using Microsoft Office 2000   *Special Edition Using Microsoft Excel 2000*
   Bought   ❑   Plan to buy   ❑   Bought   ❑   Plan to buy

pecial Edition Using Microsoft Word 2000   *Special Edition Using Microsoft FrontPage 2000*
   Bought   ❑   Plan to buy   ❑   Bought   ❑   Plan to buy

pecial Edition Using Microsoft Outlook 2000   *Special Edition Using Microsoft Publisher 2000*
   Bought   ❑   Plan to buy   ❑   Bought   ❑   Plan to buy

pecial Edition Using Microsoft PowerPoint 2000
   Bought   ❑   Plan to buy

lease rate the following factors in making your decision to buy this book:
   = Very Important   2 = Somewhat Important   3 = Not Important

)ue brand name reputation	1 2 3	*Special Edition Using* brand name reputation	1 2 3
Author reputation	1 2 3	Price of book	1 2 3
Length of book	1 2 3	Description of book on cover	1 2 3
Thorough comparison of coverage versus other books	1 2 3	Contents of CD-ROM with book	1 2 3
Store clerk recommendation	1 2 3	Recommendation of coworker, colleague, or friend	1 2 3
Other	1 2 3		

lease rate the quality of the *Signature Tips* in this book:
❑   Excellent   ❑   Good   ❑   Fair   ❑   Poor

10. Please check the appropriate box for each application to indicate how often you use the Office 2000 applications and ^ level of user you consider yourself with each:

I use this program...   *I consider my user level for this pro*

	Over 4 Hours Daily	1-3 Hours Daily	A few Minutes Daily	Less Than Once a Week	Never	Beginner	Intermediate	Ex
Word	❏	❏	❏	❏	❏	❏	❏	❏
Excel	❏	❏	❏	❏	❏	❏	❏	❏
PowerPoint	❏	❏	❏	❏	❏	❏	❏	❏
Publisher	❏	❏	❏	❏	❏	❏	❏	❏
Access	❏	❏	❏	❏	❏	❏	❏	❏
FrontPage	❏	❏	❏	❏	❏	❏	❏	❏
Outlook	❏	❏	❏	❏	❏	❏	❏	❏
PhotoDraw	❏	❏	❏	❏	❏	❏	❏	❏

11. Please evaluate the amount and the level of coverage in this book for each Access topic:

	Amount of coverage			*Level of coverage*		
	Not Enough	The Right Amount	Too Much	Too Low	The Right Level	Too Adva
Tables/Fields	❏	❏	❏	❏	❏	❏
Forms	❏	❏	❏	❏	❏	❏
Reports	❏	❏	❏	❏	❏	❏
Queries	❏	❏	❏	❏	❏	❏
Data Integrity	❏	❏	❏	❏	❏	❏
Relational Design	❏	❏	❏	❏	❏	❏
Data Access Pages	❏	❏	❏	❏	❏	❏
Access Data Projects	❏	❏	❏	❏	❏	❏
Decision Support	❏	❏	❏	❏	❏	❏
Internet/Intranets	❏	❏	❏	❏	❏	❏
Integration with other applications	❏	❏	❏	❏	❏	❏

12. Please write any additional comments about this book, either positive or negative, here.

13. Please write today's date here. _____

FOLD HERE AND TAPE TO

CD-ROM INSTALLATION

WINDOWS 95 INSTALLATION INSTRUCTIONS

1. Insert the CD-ROM disc into your CD-ROM drive.
2. From the Windows 95 desktop, double-click the My Computer icon.
3. Double-click the icon representing your CD-ROM drive.
4. Double-click the icon titled START.EXE to run the CD-ROM interface.

Note

If Windows 95 is installed on your computer and you have the AutoPlay feature enabled, the START.EXE program starts automatically whenever you insert the disc into your CD-ROM drive.

WINDOWS NT INSTALLATION INSTRUCTIONS

1. Insert the CD-ROM disc into your CD-ROM drive.
2. From File Manager or Program Manager, choose Run from the File menu.
3. Type <drive>\START.EXE and press Enter, where <drive> corresponds to the drive letter of your CD-ROM. For example, if your CD-ROM is drive D:, type D:\START.EXE and press Enter. This will run the CD-ROM interface.